THE GREAT WAR

VOLUME I

This Volume Combines Volume 1 & Volume 2
of an Original 13 Volume Set.

Reprinted 1999 from the 1914 & 1915 editions
TRIDENT PRESS INTERNATIONAL
Copyright 1999

ISBN 1-582790-25-6 Standard Edition

Printed in Croatia

Vice-Admiral Sir John Rushworth Jellicoe, K.C.B. K.C.V.O.
Commander-in-Chief, Home Fleets.

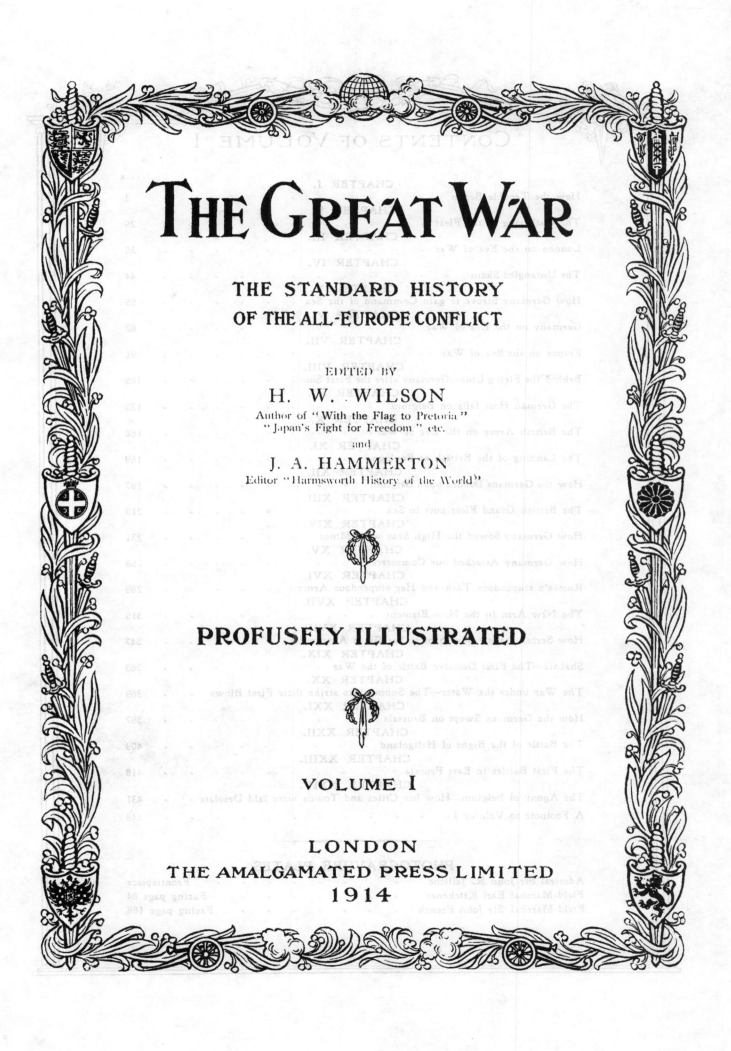

THE GREAT WAR

THE STANDARD HISTORY
OF THE ALL-EUROPE CONFLICT

EDITED BY

H. W. WILSON

Author of "With the Flag to Pretoria"
"Japan's Fight for Freedom" etc.

and

J. A. HAMMERTON

Editor "Harmsworth History of the World"

PROFUSELY ILLUSTRATED

VOLUME I

LONDON
THE AMALGAMATED PRESS LIMITED
1914

CONTENTS OF VOLUME I

PHOTOGRAVURE PLATES

PART 1 OF
THE GREAT WAR,
the Standard History of
the All-Europe Conflict,
including eye - witnesses'
stories of striking
incidents throughout the
field of operations.

2099
La N 5 216
complete

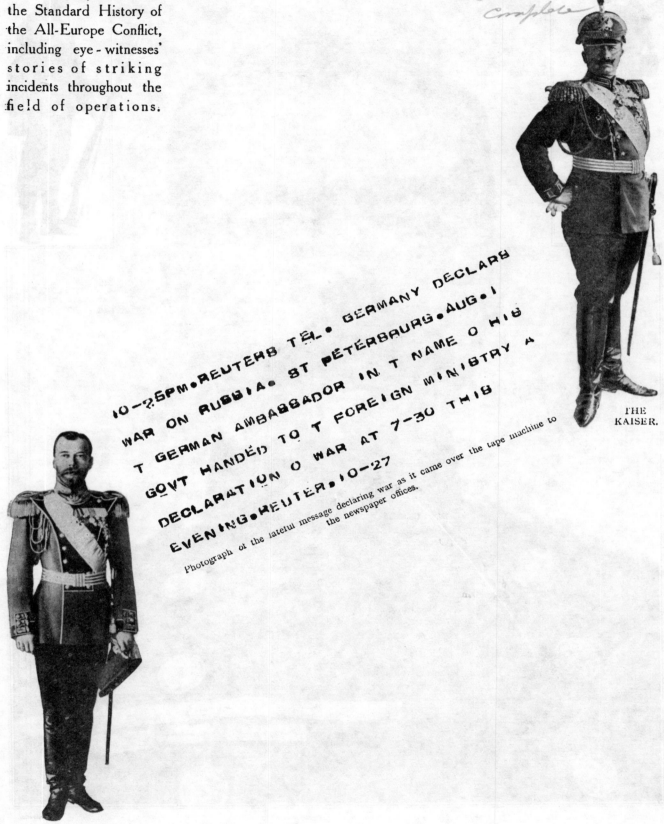

THE KAISER.

THE TSAR.

10-2.5PM•REUTERS TEL• GERMANY DECLARS WAR ON RUSSIA• ST PETERBAURG•AUG•1 T GERMAN AMBASSADOR IN T NAME O HIS GOVT HANDED TO T FOREIGN MINISTRY A DECLARATION O WAR AT 7-30 THIS EVENING•REUTER•10-27

Photograph of the fateful message declaring war as it came over the tape machine to the newspaper offices.

[Bassano.

THE MAN WHO GETS THINGS DONE.

Earl Kitchener, whose appointment as War Minister was greeted with satisfaction throughout the Empire.

BRITISH TERRITORIALS GUARDING THE RAILWAY AT ROCHESTER.

THE GREAT WAR

The Standard History of the All-Europe Conflict.

Edited by H. W. WILSON,
Author of "With the Flag to Pretoria," etc.

CHAPTER I.—HOW THE TROUBLE BEGAN.

War Springs from a Schoolboy's Crime—Britain's Home Troubles Encourage Germany—A Surprise for the Kaiser—Red Ruin in Six Weeks—A Changed Europe—Dark Days for Germany—The Tragedy of the Archduke Francis Ferdinand—Why Servia hates Austria—A Dramatic Dinner—A Revolting Double Murder—Austria's Excuse for Fighting—The All-Europe Conflict Begins.

THE greatest war of modern times, and perhaps in the whole history of the human race, was begun by Germany using the crime of a schoolboy in Bosnia as her excuse. On Sunday, June 28th, 1914, a student named Prinzep shot and killed the Archduke Francis Ferdinand, heir to the thrones of Austria-Hungary, and his wife, the Duchess of Hohenberg, in the streets of Serajevo.

The Austro-Hungarian Government and its supporter and adviser, the German Government, determined to take advantage of the crime to make a great step forward in Europe. Austria had for many years regarded the steadily growing power of Servia with uneasiness. This peasant state, with the prestige of her recent victories against Turkey and Bulgaria, and with her greatly increased territories, was becoming too strong. Now, when she had not yet had time to recover from her last wars, was the time to curb her.

The situation in Europe seemed to encourage the German peoples in this adventure. England, it was thought, could do nothing, for she had her hands full with her Home Rule troubles; with the threats of civil war in Ireland. Russia was in the midst of the reorganisation of her army, and could never again be better defied than then. As for France, Germany believed herself quite competent to deal with her, and sought for an opportunity of doing so.

Then, on the pretence of righteous indignation at the murder of the Archduke, Austria-Hungary put forward a series of demands which Servia could not possibly have met without the virtual destruction of her independence. Two days only were given for reply, and when Servia, granting all legitimate demands, asked for arbitration over some impossible clauses, a declaration of war quickly followed.

Russia, the friend and patron of Servia, attempted to mediate in favour of the little kingdom. Then Ger-

A GROUP OF TYPICAL YOUNG OFFICERS ON A BRITISH WARSHIP.

many intervened and confronted Russia as the ally and defender of Austria. When negotiations between Germany and Russia became critical, Germany demanded of France what course of action she would take if war broke out between Germany and Russia. Declarations of war between Austria and Germany on the one side and Russia on the other followed. Without waiting to declare war, Germany proceeded to attack France, pouring her armies through the neutral territory of Luxemburg and Belgium.

It soon became clear that Germany and Austria had made initial miscalculations. It had been assumed that England would do nothing owing to her internal troubles, and that Belgium would be powerless to attempt more than a nominal resistance. In England, however, the first sign of serious trouble brought about an immediate and complete union of the nation. Internal differences were sunk. In Ireland the seemingly impossible took place, Ulstermen and

H.M.S. Orion, super-Dreadnought, which created a world-wide revolution in naval construction. She carries ten 13.5-in. guns, which, every two minutes, can discharge 5½ tons of steel and lyddite, the range being twenty-one miles. She has also sixteen 4-in. guns. It is said that no other type of warship could survive for six minutes within five miles of her. She is of 22,500 tons displacement, and her 27,000 h.p. engines drive her at twenty-one knots.

THE BIG GUNS OF THE GERMAN WARSHIP SCHARNHORST.

Nationalists becoming brothers in arms ; in Parliament, party differences vanished, and the Government called the leaders of the Opposition into its inner councils ; controversies were postponed ; Great Britain presented a united front. When Germany proceeded to violate Belgian neutrality, not only did the Belgians offer a wholly unexpected and very successful defence against almost overwhelming odds, but England — bound by Treaty to respect and protect Belgian independence—declared war against Germany.

Thus the German peoples plunged humanity into the Great War. Less than six weeks after the firing of the pistol shots at Serajevo every nation in Europe was at war, or ready for war. Even little Montenegro boldly hurled her defiance against the authorities at Vienna. Eight nations were fighting, and eighteen million men under arms The very talk of war, before the first shell came tearing through the air, spread ruin over the whole of Europe, as even the Black Death had never spread in the Middle Ages. Millionaires found themselves bankrupt. Stock Exchanges had to close. Even the London Stock Exchange was forced temporarily to suspend operations, a measure never taken before, and our Government had, for the first time in British history, to suspend the right to demand payment of debts. The cost of many staple foods doubled almost in a day. Events followed one another so suddenly that many thousands of holiday-makers, who had gone for a few weeks to the Continent, found themselves hemmed in suddenly among hostile peoples, unable to obtain money, turned out of hotels, and often enough refused food or lodgings. Hundreds of them were forced to remain long after the war was in progress—many in the greatest distress. Paris, the brightest city in Europe, became almost at a

GERMAN NAVAL OFFICERS AT MESS.

breath a city of darkness and quiet, with no traffic, with cafés closed at eight at night, with many shops shut, and military rule omnipotent. The Londoner who had taken his family for their annual holiday to Felixstowe or Harwich found himself ordered to leave the town, as the authorities might blow up the houses at any moment to leave a clear sweep for the guns, ready to greet approaching foes. Innumerable business houses, yesterday flourishing, found their trade gone, their markets closed, and their men in the fighting line.

The whole life of Europe was revolutionised at a bound, and the whole future of the world changed. The great war of 1914 may be short and sharp, or long drawn out. It may be rapidly concluded by a series of sweeping victories, or victory may incline now to one side, now to the other. But however it ends—and Britain is confident that it can have but one end—Europe will never be the same again. Nations will be revolutionised. Rulers may go, kingdoms may disappear, and small nations may draw closer together. The great German Empire, the outcome of the genius of Bismarck and Moltke, may possibly split up once more into its old components. Humanity will pay a great price—how great we now scarce dare contemplate. Much that our civilisation has laboriously built up and carefully guarded may perish. One result will, however, almost certainly follow. The great military machine, erected by the relentless ambition of one man, which has so long threatened the peace of Europe, will be broken.

WAR FEVER IN GERMANY. THE POPULACE CHEERING THE KAISER ON THE OUTBREAK OF HOSTILITIES.

Thus were the pistol shots of a student used by Germany to submit to the bloody arbitrament of war the three great issues which for the past twenty years have distracted Europe — the struggle between German and Russian, between Teuton and Slav; the passionate French indignation at the treatment of Alsace-Lorraine, the provinces torn from France in 1870 by the Prussian military despotism; and the German desire to wrest from Great Britain the command of the sea.

Two great rivals stood out in the early stages of the negotiations—Germany, dreaming of a vast Teutonic State, stretching from the Belgian coast to Salonika ; and Russia, the leader and protector of Slavonic nations.

Let us return to the memorable day at Serajevo. The Archduke Francis Ferdinand, nephew of the venerable Austrian Emperor, and heir to the thrones of Austria and Hungary, had resolved to visit the Bosnian capital This pretty little town is one of the most interesting in Europe. Less than forty years ago it was a Turkish fort with a few huts around, and it still has some 20,000 Mohammedan inhabitants. Men call it the " Damascus of the North." Alongside of the Mohammedan quarter are seen modern Germanised streets, beer-halls and cafés, shops full of costly wares, splendid public buildings, and a fine railway station. Austria made Serajevo her headquarters when Bosnia and Herzegovina were placed under her protection in 1878, as her share of the spoil after the Russo-Turkish War. She increased her hold there when she annexed the two states in 1909. Austria brought Serajevo prosperity, but not contentment. The inhabitants resented being taken over by Austria. They were Slavs. They wanted to join the people of their own race, Servia, the peasant kingdom, and Servia wanted them. Their resentment, despite all Austria's efforts, grew year by year.

Francis Ferdinand knew of Bosnia's discontent. He had visions of his own. He would win over these people by a mixture of severity and kindness. Some of his friends believed that he dreamed of making his crown a triple and not a double one. The Austrian Emperor already rules over two

IN THE FIRST FEW DAYS OF THE WAR THE BANK RATE WENT UP TO TEN PER CENT.! HERE A MAN IS SEEN SIGNALLING A RISE TO FOUR PER CENT.

separate states, differing in speech, race, and ways—Austria and Hungary. Men would have it that Francis Ferdinand dreamed of a third people, the Southern Slavs, forming a nationality under the crown of Vienna. What is more probably true is that his ambition inclined towards a steady advance of the Austrian flag to the East, bringing it in time to the Mediterranean at Salonica. In order to carry out this campaign it was necessary, or at least desirable, that Bosnia should be placated. So he visited Serajevo, to promote his campaign for winning over these peoples.

SHOPS BEARING GERMAN AND AUSTRIAN NAMES FARED BADLY IN PARIS, MANY BEING WRECKED. THE ABOVE ARE THE PREMISES OF AN AUSTRIAN JEWELLER.

He was a man well calculated to accomplish a great task in statecraft. Francis Ferdinand was one of the most striking and forceful characters among the heirs to European thrones. In 1889, the death of the Crown Prince Rudolph made him suddenly and unexpectedly heir to the old Emperor. Rudolph died under circumstances of mystery which have not even yet been fully cleared up. He was found dead in his bed in a hunting-lodge he was accustomed to visit in circumstances which made it not very clear whether his end had come from suicide or from murder. Rudolph, a man of brilliancy and of great accomplishments, had ruined his future through his own evil life. Francis Ferdinand was a prince of another type—a man of strong convictions, principles, and will power. Up to now he had passed a somewhat aimless life. From the hour that he became heir to the throne he applied himself seriously to great affairs.

A year after his change of station he showed his independence and shocked the traditions of the Austrian Imperial House—the most rigid, punctilious, and exclusive in the world—by morganatically marrying Countess

Sophie Choteck, a member of a noble Bohemian family. He had to make a declaration that neither his wife nor children could ever possess any title to the Austrian throne. Instead, however, of keeping his morganatic wife in the background, he associated her with himself in all his work. She was made a princess, and given the title of Duchess of Hohenberg, and

was his constant companion. Too powerful to be slighted, too clever to let herself be ignored, she earned widespread respect and admiration. There is no reason to doubt that had her husband reached the throne, precedent would have been modified, and she would have taken the rank and courtesy titles of Empress of Austria and Queen of Hungary. The King of England and the German Emperor were prepared to

THE FINANCIAL CRISIS DUE TO THE WAR. THE TOP PHOTOGRAPH SHOWS A RUN ON A PARIS SAVINGS BANK. THE BOTTOM ONE REPRESENTS A SCENE OUTSIDE THE BANK OF ENGLAND, LONDON.

recognise her. And it was as a preliminary to such recognition that she was invited to England with her husband on a visit to our King and Queen a few weeks before her end. Francis Ferdinand and his wife planned great schemes for their land. They were ambitious for its power, authority, and prosperity. So it was that when the Archduke went to Servia his wife accompanied him.

The Imperial pair arrived at Serajevo on the Sunday morning, and, after inspecting the troops, drove in a motor towards the Town Hall, where the civil authorities were waiting to receive them. As they drove along Appel Quay a bomb was hurled at them by a young printer, Cabrinovitch by name, twenty years old. The Archduke, it is said, warded off the bomb with his arm. An aide-de-camp, seated in a motor-car behind, was wounded in the neck by fragments of the bomb, as it exploded, and several passers-by received injuries. The Royal pair were not hurt. When their motor-car reached the Town Hall, and the mayor, ignorant of the attempt, set out to make the address of welcome, Francis Ferdinand turned on him brusquely. "What is the good of your speeches? I come to Serajevo on a visit, and I get bombs thrown at me. It is outrageous!"

The procession drove back in due course from the Town Hall, and then a second attempt was made. Gavrilo Prinzep, a Bosnian High School student, hurled another bomb. This bomb did not explode. Quickly the lad fired three shots from a

THE KAISER CONSULTS A WAR MAP WITH A MEMBER OF HIS MILITARY STAFF.

THE KAISER'S AMBITION IS TO SEE THIS FLAG DOMINATING THE WORLD.

GERMAN INFANTRY ON THE MARCH. THEY ARE VERY HEAVILY LADEN, AND IT IS GENERALLY EXPECTED THAT THIS FACT WILL SERIOUSLY INTERFERE WITH THEIR MOBILITY.

Browning automatic pistol. The first bullet struck Francis Ferdinand in the throat. His wife threw herself in front of him, seeking to cover his body with her own, and embraced him tenderly. A second bullet entered her body. Yet a third bullet went home. Francis Ferdinand, as they were driven rapidly off to the governor's palace, opened his eyes to make one last request to his wife. "Sophie, live for our children!" But the Duchess of Hohenberg was herself mortally stricken, and both died almost immediately.

YORKSHIRE LIGHT INFANTRY GUARDING A RAILWAY AT DUBLIN.

Cabrinovitch and Prinzep were both secured. Both were of Slav nationality. They denied having accomplices. They even denied, at first, that they knew one another. But examination brought daily more and more evidence that this was no isolated outrage, but part of a great plot. The day on which the attempt

LONDON TERRITORIALS, PREPARED TO MEET THE KAISER'S FORCES.

BRITISH ARTILLERY ON MANŒUVRES.

was made, the anniversary of a famous battle, was significant. The town was found to be full of conspirators. If Prinzep had failed, another opportunity would have been found on the same day to commit the murder. As detail after detail became known, a great flame of hatred of the Servian people, as Slavs, was kindled throughout Austria. And in the passion so excited the masters of statecraft in Berlin and Vienna saw their opportunity. It was not difficult to start a war. The people of Austria, at least, were in the temper for it; but that the Emperors of Germany and Austria never guessed how far and how rapidly the war-fever would spread is certain.

SECTION 2 OF CHAPTER I.

WHY did men of Serb race plot to murder the heir to the Austrian throne? What gave rise to the old enmity between the two countries?

The struggle between Austria and Servia is really the struggle between two great races—the Teutons and the Slavs. The Slavs, led by Russia, have, during the past half century, found themselves. They are knit together by ties of religion, sympathy, and blood. To the average man in St. Petersburg—be he peasant, soldier, or noble—the story that Austria was striving to crush the Slav people of Servia came with as potent appeal as we would feel were we to learn that Canada or Australia were threatened by some foreign Power with annihilation. German unity and ambitions have grown steadily in recent years, but mixed with great confidence there has always been some apprehension of Germany's eastern neighbour, Russia, with its immense population and vast resources. Germany, with Russia on one side and France on the other, has always recognised and prepared against the danger of being crushed by these two, as a nut is crushed between the sides of a pair of crackers. Each advance of Germanic peoples has been regarded by the Russians with suspicion. Each advance of the Slavs in Europe has been regarded by the Teutons with feelings almost approaching alarm.

The German nations and Russia found their constant bone of contention in the Balkan Peninsula. All were obliged to recognise that in time Turkey, corrupt and effete, must be driven back to the gates of Constantinople. Who was to have her lands? Russia's ambition was to see a group of strong and independent Slav states covering the peninsula. Austria, with Germany behind her, wanted to assert a formal protectorate over some of the states, or to annex as much territory as she could get. Year by year the struggle, now open, now concealed, went on. It caused war after war. It incited endless intrigues, plots, and murders. Time after time it brought all Europe to the verge of a struggle, such as is now on us.

Servia, near neighbour of the Austrian Empire, has naturally been coveted and contested ground. The tale of how the Servian peasants, two hundred years ago, rose against the almost omnipotent Turk and, after long years of fighting, won their partial independence, is one of the romances of the Near East. Sturdy, simple, industrious, and amazingly brave, the Servian people have from the first revealed many admirable qualities. The globe-trotters who judged them from the artificial gaieties of Belgrade, with up to recently its vice and its flaunting extravagance, made a great mistake. The real Servian, the man who has won war after war, is the peasant, the farmer, the countryman, who, among his mountains, living honestly and working hard, has helped to build up a great people.

Servia was and is ambitious. If Austria dreamed of occupying the Balkan Peninsula far down to the Black Sea, Servia dreamed first of complete independence from Turkey, cutting off

Photo,
Bourne & Shepherd
India.

THE MAN THE KAISER FEARS.
EARL KITCHENER, THE NEW WAR MINISTER.

the nominal suzerainty that long remained, and then of becoming the centre of a great Slavonic dominion. It was to link up with itself Bosnia and Herzegovina, Slavonia and Dalmatia, Montenegro and Sanjak of Novi Bazar. A new empire was to arise in the south-east of Europe. This little race of pig-keepers—the main industry of Servia—surrounded by powerful neighbours, aimed high, and knew no fear.

The Austrian nation was not ignorant of Servia's dream. " If the divided Serbs should ever come together," they said, " they would impose invisible barriers on the spread of Germanism in the Balkan Peninsula." Accordingly, when forty years ago Servia, under Prince Milan, was making ready for war against Turkey, Austria was planning in the council chamber to thwart her. The story of the wars, that ended in the Russo-Turkish War of 1878, need not be repeated here. In the end, after some defeats, Servia found herself an independent kingdom, and Prince Milan became King. In the hour of triumph, however, came the bitterest check. Austria had secretly arranged with Russia, Servia's great neighbour in the north, that, as the price of Austrian neutrality, the Turkish provinces of Bosnia and Herzegovina should not be handed over to Servia. When the Powers of Europe came together in Berlin, the two provinces were placed under Austrian protection.

THE DEADLY BROADSIDE. H.M.S. MONARCH FIRING HER 13·5 GUNS.

Belgrade, now the capital of Servia, became the battleground of Russian and Austrian diplomacy. King Milan was popular with his army and with the country. Unfortunately for him he thought, after the war of 1878, it would be better for the interests of Servia to be friendly with Austria than to co-operate with Russia. His people did not share his delusion. His relations with his wife, Queen Nathalie, were very unhappy, and ended in his divorcing her. Nathalie was strongly sympathetic to Russia, and her woes were paraded throughout Europe. Revolutions broke out, trouble of every kind developed, and the end was that Milan, to the general surprise of his friends, abandoned his crown, abdicating in favour of his son Alexander, and retired to Paris. One of the conditions he made when he abdicated was that the Regents placed over his son should never allow the boy's mother to see him.

Here was a lad in his thirteenth year, abandoned by both his parents, placed under the care of a group of Regents, and given the worst possible training that could be imagined to prepare him for his great office. He found himself the centre of intrigues, even as a boy. His Regents did their best to keep their promise to his father and isolate him from his mother. Alexander apparently retained some affection for both his parents. Gradually he grew impatient of being under the rule of tutors, and one night, when only sixteen, he invited the Regents and their ministers to a dinner in the palace, nominally in their honour. He got up during the dinner and announced to them that for the next few hours they must consider themselves his prisoners. The army, he said, was just then proclaiming him of full age and reigning King, and from that moment he would assume full Royal powers.

The nation supported Alexander in his act. Nations never love Regents. Thus it was that this boy of sixteen took over control of one of the most turbulent and difficult of states. His mother came back, his father returned, and was appointed commander-in-chief of the army. It was intended in due course to marry Alexander to a German princess. But Alexander had plans of his own. He had met and become familiar with a young and pretty widow, Madame Draga Maschin, who lived in modest fashion in Belgrade. Madame Draga had many admirers, and scandal made very free with her name. Let it be said, in justice to her, that some of the best men in Servia declare to this day their firm belief that scandal was false. Until she yielded to the King, say they, she lived a respectable life. Draga attracted attention in different quarters. Queen Nathalie who, despite her quarrels with her husband, was of a very sympathetic nature, noticed her, became her patron, completed her education, and made her one of her Court ladies.

Alexander was thrown much in company with Draga, and was charmed with her. His admiration soon turned to violent love. Queen Nathalie at first liked to see her son and the beautiful Court lady together. She had no

SPRING-CLEANING A BRITISH WARSHIP. THIS PICTURE GIVES AN EXCELLENT IDEA OF THE SIZE OF THE FUNNELS AND MASTS.

H.M. DESTROYER BANSHEE IN A ROUGH SEA. THE BEST PHOTO OF ITS KIND EVER TAKEN.

suspicion of the real relations that rapidly sprang up between the two, and when by chance she discovered a letter from Draga showing that she had a love intrigue with the King, she at once dismissed her. In time Draga became the mistress of the King.

To cut a long story short, while Milan was seeking to arrange his son's marriage with a German princess, and had gone to Carlsbad to complete some of the negotiations, Alexander suddenly issued a proclamation announcing that he was about to marry Draga. There was a tremendous scandal. Every ancient scandal about her was revived. Old love-letters of hers to other men were, it was said, hawked about secretly in the streets of Belgrade. Draga as the King's mistress was one thing; as his wife quite another! The country was disappointed, for it had looked to add to the prestige and power of Servia by the alliance of the King with one of the greater ruling houses of Europe. The King's Ministers opposed the marriage. He dismissed them all. One Court group sought to promote a plot to dethrone Alexander and reinstate his father in his place. The plot came to nothing.

The Emperor of Russia saved the situation for Alexander for the moment by agreeing to become the principal witness at the wedding. But Draga was to find her throne a very thorny one. Everyone was against her. King Milan died soon afterwards—his friends said of a broken heart at the conduct of his son—at Vienna. The politicians were furious against Alexander because he suspended the constitution and pursued the chiefs of the Radical party, which opposed him, with relentless persecution. Nothing that Draga did was right. It was believed, and not without reason, that she intended to pass off a child of her sister as her own, in order to have an heir to the throne. The Army was offended—not alone because it felt the slight to its dignity in Draga being made Queen; it was hurt by the promotion of her brothers to high places in the Army, and by favouritism shown to the Queen's old friends.

Had Alexander and Draga and the Servians been left alone, some compromise in a very unhappy situation might have been arrived at. But, unfortunately, two Powers were working underground, and using the situation in their own interest. Alexander had been at the start somewhat in favour of Austria, and there is little doubt but that the Russian Government worked hard at that time to secure the end of his reign, and the succession of a Russian Grand Duke in his place. The action of the Emperor of Russia in becoming a witness at his marriage won the young King over to the Russian side, and thus it was that Austrian gold and Austrian influence were used for his undoing. Again things changed. Now Russia was secretly opposing him. The politicians who worked around Belgrade were not supposed to be hampered by too many scruples. A systematic and relentless campaign against Alexander and Draga was carried on.

Finally, a party of officers came together and determined to make an end to the situation. Better, they said, for the King and Queen to die, if necessary, than for the nation to perish. There were eighty-six military conspirators, and they took solemn

THE GREAT WAR LORDS.
The Kaiser compares notes with Admiral Von Tirpitz (facing camera).

oath to kill any comrade who turned traitor to their cause. At their head was Colonel Maschin, brother-in-law to the Queen by her first husband, who regarded her with special hate. Some of the conspirators had been offended by the haughtiness of the Queen's brothers ; some had been dismissed from high office because they had openly expressed disapproval of the King's marriage. Others—there is no reason to deny—were actuated by a real sense of

THE TSAR OF RUSSIA,
whom the Kaiser expected to find a powerful adversary.

patriotic anger at what they considered the degradation of the King's office.

They went to work very carefully. Nothing was left to chance, for they well knew that failure would mean death or flight for all. It was arranged that reliable troops should surround the palace ; an aide-de-camp had been suborned to open the outer door ; the keys of the gate were to be secured by a trick ; the officers would rush in, catch the King and Queen asleep, and quickly do their dreadful business.

The King and Queen were staying in the Konak, the old Turkish palace. One evening in June, 1902, they had a small party to dinner, and afterwards sat listening to the music of a military band playing outside. The evening was somewhat close, and when they retired to their room the Queen amused herself some time by examining a great box of new clothes that had just arrived from Paris. They went to bed ; and about two in the morning were awakened by

KING OF THE BELGIANS,
whom the Kaiser did NOT regard as powerful, but who gave him a painful surprise.

[H. Walter Barnett.

THE RIGHT HON. SIR EDWARD GREY.

All parties are agreed that Britain's Foreign Secretary acted splendidly in a great crisis, and did everything possible to avert war.

the loud explosion of a dynamite cartridge, blowing in the outer door of the palace. They tried to turn on the electric light, but it would not turn, and the whole palace was suddenly plunged into darkness. They looked outside their window. They could see a line of troops there, and the sound of rifle fire told that fighting was going on. In the passages of the palace were to be heard shouts, cries, oaths, sharp commands, an occasional pistol shot, and the heavy footsteps of men rushing from room to room. The steps came nearer. Alexander and Draga hastily hid themselves in a small alcove which opened out of the bed-room by a secret iron door, papered to look like the wall.

What had happened? The conspirators, according to their programme, soon after midnight marched their troops around the palace. The soldiers had been told that they were engaged in a confidential task, and that they were to obey Colonel Maschin, in the King's name. They were to take no notice of anything that happened. A police commissioner, seeing the troops moving in the direction of the palace, telephoned to the Prefect of Police, who was at home. The Prefect, thinking the matter of no importance, told the commissioner not to worry him, but to inform the Central Police Station. The commissioner rang up the police-station. The officer in charge had gone out to enjoy himself with some friends. The clerk who took the message did not know what to do, and so did nothing. Otherwise everything might have ended very differently.

A group of officers approached one of the gates of the palace. A young lieutenant had drugged or intoxicated the captain in charge, and taken his key from him. As the officers rushed through the easily-opened gate some of the guard tried to resist them. A sergeant was shot, and an aide-de-camp to the King, Petrovich by name, was wounded in the arm.

Now the officers were at the entrance door of the palace itself. According to their plans, the officer guarding this door, who was in sympathy with them, should open it at an agreed signal. The signal was given time after time, with no result. The guardian of the door had drunk himself to unconsciousness. There

was no time to lose. The King's friends might at any moment come up in force. A dynamite cartridge was hastily attached to the door, and it was blown in. The explosion was heard throughout the city, and brought crowds of people hurrying towards the palace. It not only burst the door open, but shattered the electric light connection, casting the palace into darkness. As the drunken guardian of the door, awakened by the explosion, staggered to his feet, one of his angry friends shot him through the head.

Some gendarmes tried to interfere. They were overpowered by the outer line of troops. The conspirators rushed to the King's bed-room, but could not find him or the Queen. They beat the walls, in vain searching for a secret entrance, while the cowering pair hid, afraid to stir, on the other side of the partition. They sent for candles, and began a man hunt through the dark rooms, searching from cellar to attics. Petrovich was brought in, bound and wounded. They beat him with their swords, and demanded that he should betray his master's hiding-place. He coolly misdirected them, trying to send them to the New Palace. Maschin suspected his trick, and he paid for it later with his life.

Again the conspirators returned to the bed-room. One officer started firing through the walls. A bullet struck Draga, and she uttered an irrepressible moan. Now they had them! On a promise to spare their lives the door was opened. The King had only time to slip on a pair of trousers and a red shirt, and the Queen had on little more than a petticoat, a pair of stays, and one silk stocking. Draga was crouching in the corner, overcome by terror.

What followed is not quite clear. According to one account, Colonel Maschin presented a document to the King, saying that he promised to abdicate or to banish Draga, and demanded his signature. The King replied by firing at Maschin, whereupon the officers shot him.

Draga was more slowly finished, screaming with terror while the officers riddled her with bullets. According to another account, the King stepped forth, and demanded what the officers wanted of him, reminding

[Elliott & Fry.

THE RIGHT HON. WINSTON CHURCHILL,
First Lord of the Admiralty.
When war was declared, our Navy was ready for anything.

A BRITISH MINE-LAYER. THE MINES ARE CARRIED ALONG RAILS AND LOWERED OVER THE STERN OF THE VESSEL.

THE HAZARD OF WAR. THIS HOUSE—AT SOUTHSEA—WAS ACCIDENTALLY HIT BY A SHOT FIRED FROM A BRITISH WARSHIP. THE MISSILE STRUCK THE WATER AND RICOCHETTED.

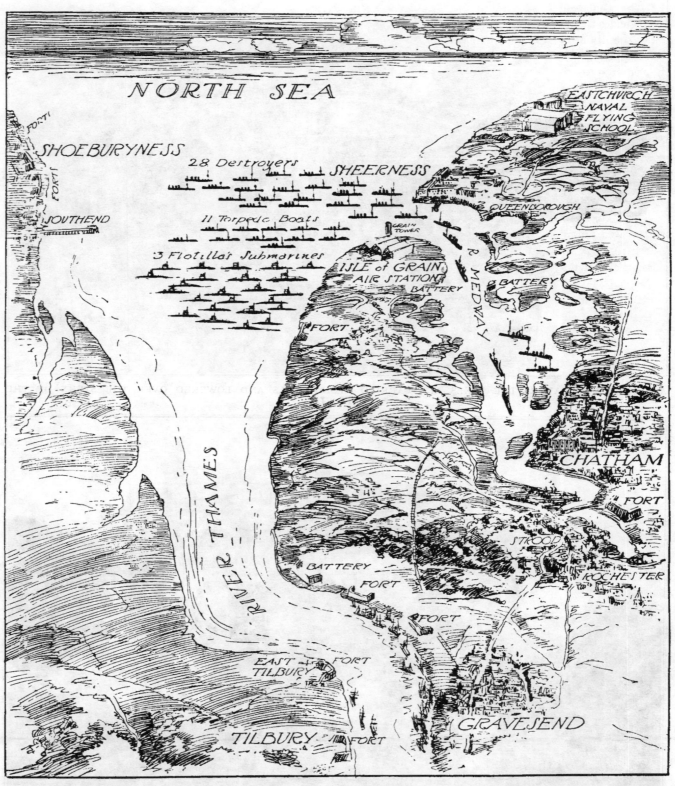

THE ESTUARY OF THE THAMES IS VERY WELL GUARDED, AS THIS MAP SHOWS, AND ANY ENEMY VENTURING
INTO IT WOULD MEET WITH A HOT RECEPTION.

them of their oath of fidelity. One lieutenant shot at him, and the others followed, murdering both.

The scene that followed was, even according to the accounts of the regicides themselves, revolting. " If the drama was accomplished under conditions which are very regrettable and perhaps shameful, that happened against the intention of the actors," they say. " When they entered the palace the conspirators did not intend to inflict so horrible a death on the victims, but once the sword is drawn and fighting begins no one can see how it will end."

The officers fired shot after shot at the prostrate bodies. They gashed at the pair ; they smashed in their features ; the still warm body of the Queen had all kinds of. nameless outrages inflicted on it. They had to fling the bodies out of the window into the courtyard below. The King, not yet dead, despite thirty-six wounds, clung with one hand to the ledge. An officer cut his fingers off. The Queen's body was hacked almost to pieces. Then the two mutilated corpses were allowed to lie in the courtyard for hours until the Russian Minister saw them there, some hours later, and persuaded the triumphant group to have them removed.

While one group thus murdered the King and Queen, others, under the plans devised by Maschin, went to the homes of the chief supporters of the King—the Premier, the Queen's two brothers, some high officers, and the like— and shot them down. The burial of the King and Queen took place amid every circumstance that could demonstrate contempt and

[*Speaight*

VICE-ADMIRAL
SIR JOHN R. JELLICOE,
Controller of the Navy, on whom victory at sea now depends. He has had a decoration conferred upon him by Kaiser William. He is a survivor of the disaster to H.M.S. Victoria.

loathing. Maschin would not even let the corpses be buried together.

The story of the crime sent a thrill of horror through Europe. The Powers withdrew their Ministers as a sign of protest, and for some years to come Servia was granted no diplomatic intercourse by the great nations of Europe.

Servia had to have a nominal ruler, and so the regicides summoned a prince of another Servian Royal house—Prince Peter— who had been living a very Bohemian life in exile in Paris.

Heath

H.S.H. PRINCE LOUIS OF BATTENBERG.
After becoming a naturalised British subject, he entered the British Navy in 1868, and rose to positions of command.

Peter was crowned, and for some time Europe ignored him. He was well described as " the type of decayed military man whom one sees at Continental gaming resorts, with shifty eyes, deep lines, and apologetic manners, but vestiges of smartness, and a certain suavity of manner." His courage no one denied. He had proved it by taking the throne. He had demonstrated it earlier by fighting for France against Germany, and by leading a small body of insurgents in Bosnia. But penurious exile and shady adventures, the life of the Bohemian in Paris, do not make the best preparations for kingship. Placed in power by the Army, the Army had its way under him. His son, the Crown Prince George, proved too riotous and outrageous even for the not very rigid Servians, and some adventures of an exceedingly risky type ended in his relinquishing his right to the throne. Many of his friends believe, however, that when the moment comes he will come to the front again. How far King Peter has been

Speaight.]

REAR-ADMIRAL DAVID BEATTY.
He served in the Soudan and China, and has proved himself a very capable officer.

A ZEPPELIN AIRSHIP OVER BERLIN. GERMANY EXPECTS GREAT THINGS OF HER AIR-CRAFT.

a mere figurehead, how far he has participated in recent Servian developments few can say. Immediately before the present crisis he announced his temporary retirement because of ill health, his son, the Crown Prince Alexander, being given authority to carry on affairs in his absence. The retirement may be permanent.

Servia has not allowed her Royal scandals, her internal troubles to abate her ambitions or to check her progress. Her ambition to join up Bosnia and Herzegovina with herself has never faltered. This ambition has been fostered by the discontent of Austria's two Serb provinces — a discontent which nothing that the Austrian Government can do allays.

What are the reasons for this discontent? Austria is able to show that she has accomplished a vast amount of material good in these parts. When they were taken over they were in the most wretched and backward condition. "The country was a veritable *tohu bohu* of corruption, cruelty, and crime," wrote one eminent Near Eastern authority some years ago. "Violence and inhumanity above were met by cunning and treachery

below. Life and property were proverbially insecure : murder was encouraged by impunity, robbery systematised by law, and oppression tempered only by assassination and rebellion. The *kmet*, or serf, was compelled to pay the value of half the produce of his land in gold, as estimated by his master, long before the harvest. The rights of property were frequently transgressed in regard to Mohammedans ; they were never respected in case of the Christians. The agricultural instruments were the same as those employed in the days of the Trojan War."

Austria brought in law, order, industry. Cities were rebuilt ; fresh trades were started ; coal mines were worked ; the old serfs were encouraged by advances of money to purchase the land they cultivated ; schools were opened. "For the material prosperity of the land, they have almost wrought miracles," their friends boasted.

A GERMAN 11-IN. GUN USED AT LIEGE.

A BRITISH AEROPLANE WITH A QUICK-FIRING GUN.

GERMAN RESERVISTS, ARRESTED IN ENGLAND WHEN ABOUT TO EMBARK FOR THE FATHERLAND, BEING
MARCHED AWAY AS PRISONERS OF WAR.

AUSTRIAN RESERVISTS ON THE WAY TO JOIN THEIR REGIMENT.

But there are deeper causes in making a country contented than material prosperity. Many years after Austria-Hungary assumed the direction of these two states the people petitioned the Hague Conference, declaring "the Austrian domination is a thousand times more insupportable than that of the Turks." Their chief complaint was over religion. The Austrian authorities, they said, treat the Greek Orthodox Church and the Mohammedans with great injustice.

"There is no guarantee for personal liberty," wrote Madame Novikoff. "The administration is carried on in absolute defiance of modern conceptions of justice. The police make domiciliary visits without any judicial warrant at any hour of the day or night, and never hesitate to shoot the unfortunate peasants who object to the infliction of the worst outrage upon their wives and daughters. Espionage is erected into a Govermental system. Bogus conspiracies are artificially got up in order to get rid of any one whom the Government dislikes. Natives of the country are forbidden to go from one arrondissement to another without police authorisation. In towns a state of siege is proclaimed, and the ill-treatment of the citizens in the streets is quite a normal thing.

"The severest punishments are meted out to any who correspond with Servians in Servia or Montenegro. The provinces are overrun with Jesuits and Jews, and the Austro-Hungarian Government does not hesitate to

VIVE LA FRANCE! FRENCH SOLDIERS READY TO ENTRAIN AT A PARIS RAILWAY STATION.

1 and 2—Queen Draga and King Alexander of Servia, assassinated by Servian officers, June, 1903.

3—Archduke Ferdinand, Austria's heir, assassinated with his morganatic wife at Sarajevo, in Bosnia, June, 1914.

4—King Peter of Servia, proclaimed June 15th, 1903.

5—Francis Joseph, the Austrian Kaiser, whose wife, the Empress Elizabeth, was assassinated at Geneva in 1898. The Emperor's brother Maximilian, and his only son Rudolph, died violent deaths. His brother Ludwig became insane.

employ even more disreputable means to demoralise the character and ruin the physique of the unfortunate population committed to their care. The whole administration of Bosnia and Herzegovina is in the hands, not of the natives of the country, but of foreigners. According to the last official statistics, there were 1,841 functionaries in Bosnia and Herzegovina; of these only 189, little more than 10 per cent., were Orthodox Servians, 106 were Mussulmans; of the others, 1,546 were foreigners. This locust horde of functionaries are as corrupt as they are inefficient."

The Bosnians begged the appointment of a European commission to inquire into the justice of their accusations. Austria's reply was to change the status of Bosnia and Herzegovina. These provinces had hitherto been only under her protection and administration. She formally annexed them, and left Europe to do its worst.

Servia was furiously angry. For a time there seemed every probability of war, and the situation was eased over with great difficulty. Russia would not help openly, although Russian sympathy and money were behind Servia. From the day of annexation Belgrade became the centre of

UNITED WE STAND! The Ulster (top photo) and Nationalist Volunteers have fraternised (doubtless to the astonishment of the Kaiser) to meet the common enemy.

an open Pan-Slav, anti-Austrian campaign. Some of the highest Servian officials openly supported the movement; practically everyone sympathised with it.

Servia strengthened her armies. She was supremely confident of herself. "These people are some of the finest fighters in Europe," said one international military critic, when discussing their ambitions with me some years ago. "When Austria tackles them she will experience some surprises." Servia showed her strength when the great war came against Turkey two years ago. Then she turned against her old ally, Bulgaria, and astonished Europe by inflicting a signal defeat on her. She emerged from these two wars with vastly increased territories and with new prestige.

Austria surveyed the new situation with uneasiness. This Servia was becoming too strong and too troublesome. Her agitators were ever at work throughout Bosnia. She would not let the Pan-Slav movement die. There was always the possibility that she would obtain the assistance of the Tsar, and present a still more dangerous front.

ENTHUSIASTIC RECRUITS, ANXIOUS TO SERVE THEIR COUNTRY, DRILLING IN HYDE PARK, LONDON.

One of the striking revelations of this war is the fact that, although in times of peace it is difficult to keep up the strength of our military forces, immediately a crisis arises tens of thousands of our young men flock to the Standard.

[*Central Press.*

FRENCH SAPPERS LAYING MINES AT BELFORT, WHICH IS ONE OF THE MOST STRONGLY FORTIFIED TOWNS ON THE GERMAN FRONTIER.

Some disaster was bound to come. So it was that when Prinzep horrified Europe by the brutal assassination of Francis Ferdinand and his wife, and it was possible to show that this crime had been promoted by Pan-Slavs at Belgrade, Vienna seized the opportunity to act.

Servia held an open blade at the heart of Austria. The blade should be wrenched from her hand. And so the Great War began. At

WATCHING THE MOUTH OF THE TYNE.

PART OF THE BRITISH FLEET IN MOUNT'S BAY, CORNWALL.

first, an unsuspecting world imagined that it was merely the opening of another of those Balkan wars to which we have recently become accustomed. It soon became evident, however, that Russia and Germany would be concerned in any war between Austria and Servia, and even France was soon shown to be in such a position that she, too, would be drawn into the vortex.

But what of Britain? On her attitude hung much—very much; and the moment it was made known precisely what Britain would do should there be any violation of gallant little Belgium, all the Courts of Europe awoke to the fact that the world was on the brink of the biggest war it had ever seen. Britain had made her position quite clear. To a German invasion of Belgium she would never consent. It was to be war—war between the most powerful nations in Europe.

CHAPTER II.—THE GATHERING OF THE FLEET.

A Day to Remember—The King at Spithead—Forty Miles of Ships—When Ignorance was Bliss—A Layman's Impressions—Commanders at Twenty-two—Muster of Aeroplanes—Warnings and Misgivings—Sunday Night at Whitehall—All Leave Stopped—Forth to War—Admiral Jellicoe : the Man Who Knows—Mr. Churchill and Prince Louis of Battenberg.

SATURDAY, July 18th, 1914, will ever remain as one of the abiding dates in the story of the events which were now to follow so fast one upon another. On that day, in accordance with a long announced arrangement, the King paid an informal visit to his Fleet assembled at Spithead. From a statistical standpoint, records a naval writer describing the scene, " the gathering of ships was the greatest ever known. Though Spithead had been overflowed for the first time in the history of the Navy, and though some 260 of the vessels mobilised in this test of the British Reserves had been necessarily dispatched for want of room to other anchorages, no fewer than 232 ships and submarines, manned by over 70,000 men, were gathered to greet the Sea King, besides some thirty aeroplanes and waterplanes and two airships. In the lines, which ran for forty miles, there were twenty-four vessels of Dreadnought type, from the first of the class to the Iron Duke and Marlborough, frowning monsters, thirteen of which mounted the new 13·5 in. gun, thirty-five older battleships, twenty armoured cruisers, thirty-five protected cruisers, seventy-eight destroyers, among them most notable the lean black hulls of the new L class, sixteen submarines, seven mine-layers, six auxiliaries, and eleven minor craft."

[Cribb.

IN BATTLE ARRAY. SOME OF BRITAIN'S DREADNOUGHTS. INSET: A FEW OF THE TEETH WHICH OUR JACK TARS ARE LONGING TO USE.

D

SOME OF THE TARGETS USED BY THE NAVY, BADLY BATTERED AFTER A COURSE OF PRACTICE.

How many of the visitors from London to Portsmouth that morning realised the significance of the great spectacle? If any of them were thinking about politics at all, it was the problem of Ulster which stood uppermost in their minds. And the announcement of the King's delayed arrival promulgated at midday contributed to this view. There were rumours of a fresh and last attempt to bring Sir Edward Carson and Mr. Redmond to an understanding. But of the abyss yawning directly in the path of European diplomacy not a word. So far as the general public was concerned, nothing was further from their minds than that before seventeen days were out this great engine of war—which they contemplated with confidence, but without boastfulness—would be at the grim business for which it was called into being.

A guest in one of the ships of the Second Battle Squadron on that and the succeeding day has left his impressions of that memorable scene. He writes as a layman, without any pretence at special knowledge. But since they recall the very last appearance in time of peace of the glorious British Navy at the summit of its preparation, they are given here. Spithead, this observer found, "the same as ever—windy and grey, choppy seas and scudding clouds, and then sunshine and a calm and blue skies, all within the same half-hour. To me the wind and the greyness fitted best with the endless lines of black ships. As one passed down the avenues made by these numberless fortresses there came the feeling of being in a vast town of iron castles, each standing alone and independent of the other. But they were not silent castles by any means. One saw the cluster of life in all of them, heard the sound of bugles, had one's eyes turned constantly this way and that by the ceaseless coming and going of picket-boats, so commonplace a business of the sea, and yet so fascinating. My first impression of a battleship is always 'How small it looks!' That is a deception due to the harmony and

ANOTHER TYPE OF TARGET, RIGGED UP AS A TORPEDO-BOAT.

completeness of all its details. And it is a deception quickly corrected when, from a picket-boat, one sees the seamen like ants upon the decks of some great leviathan. And the fancy is dispelled even more effectively when one goes aboard one of these huge ships of the line, and finds oneself wandering over seemingly illimitable expanses of deck.

"They seem so vast and so complex to be run by such young men. For youth is the next overpowering impression on such a day. At least, it was so to me. In the ship where I was, of nine hundred souls I saw not a man who looked over twenty-five, except the flag-captain and the rear-admiral, and neither the rear-admiral nor the flag-captain looked over forty. One found oneself talking with apparent lads of twenty-two, who, one discovered presently, were commanders, and had seen every corner of the globe. And the youthfulness of aspect was reflected in the gaiety of spirits, genuine and remarkable when, looking back, one remembers that many there, for all their apparent outward carelessness, must have had some intuition that behind this pageant there lurked a shadow of what was to be. I hasten over the other things which were striking in that display, among them the muster of aeroplanes. The sound of these new engines is more than the sight; it comes as a revelation of unexpected

H.M.S. HERO, WHICH WAS USED AS A TARGET FOR OUR MODERN HEAVY GUNS.

noise. And there is another revelation—how much surer and safer it looks, this flying over water and high above the ships, than one's imagination of it. What else abides in the mind? The night cut into a thousand glistening pathways by the searchlights from the ships; and the early morning, with its Portsmouth steamers 'crammed and jammed and packed' with liberty men; and the singing in the ward-room on Saturday night, the sound of which still remains in my ears, and is like a knife in my heart; and Divine service on the quarterdeck on Sunday morning, so touching in its simplicity and sincerity."

THE BATTERED EDINBURGH AS SHE APPEARED IMMEDIATELY AFTER BEING USED AS A TARGET.

Thus the final week-end of pageant and preparation passed. On Monday morning, July 20th, the King led his Fleet to sea, and the following days were spent in tactical exercises in the Channel. Towards the end of the week the First and Second Fleets put into Portland, preparatory to dispersing to their home ports for the purpose

E

of giving the usual midsummer leave. This was Friday, July 24th. So far as the outside world was aware, there was not a speck in the sky.

But the two men at Whitehall mainly responsible for the preparation of the Fleet knew a little different. The First Lord of the Admiralty, Mr. Winston Churchill, and the First Sea Lord, Prince Louis of Battenberg, must already have had their warnings and misgivings. It was not until Saturday morning that the general public learnt of the Austrian note to Servia. During the ensuing thirty-six hours events marched quickly. They are dealt with elsewhere in this history. It is sufficient to say here that Sunday night found my Lords of the Admiralty at their posts at Whitehall; Mr. Churchill had had to come up by car from the Norfolk coast, where his family was established for the summer. By midnight the Fleets at Portland were informed that there could be no leave at present, and no dispersal. Ships which had already sailed for their home ports were brought back by wireless.

A SUPER-DREADNOUGHT STARTS HER CAREER.
Here the huge vessel is seen half-way down the slipways when being launched.

There followed many hours of preparation and activity. On Wednesday morning, July 29th, with their crews dressing ships and cheering, and their bands playing, the ships, which had been the pride of the peaceful gathering at Spithead only ten days before, steamed forth to war. They passed into the fog of war—they, and the gallant crews who manned them. And those who could not hear, but only trusted, sought with all their hearts Divine protection for those at sea.

The youth of the leaders of this mighty force was generally remarked, and held to be a feature of good omen. The man on whose shoulders was to fall the brunt of naval operations, Admiral Sir John Rushworth Jellicoe, was not yet fifty-five. Forty-two out of these fifty-five years had been spent in the profession to the

PLACING A 15-TON ARMOUR PLATE INTO THE BELT OF A BRITISH BATTLESHIP.
The building of a modern battleship involves the payment for labour of £1,500,000, spread over two years, about 8,000 men being constantly employed.

GUNS OF H.M.S. LORD NELSON "OUT" FOR BATTLE-PRACTICE.
It costs the British nation something like £ 50 every time one of these great guns is fired.

highest post of which he was now appointed—Commander-in-Chief of the Home Fleets. The actual hoisting of his flag in the Iron Duke had some of the elements of the dramatic. Originally intended—before a ripple had come to disturb the surface of international calm—to succeed Sir George Callaghan at the end of the year, the outbreak of war accelerated the appointment. On Wednesday, August 5th, the announcement was made that he had assumed supreme command, with the acting rank of admiral, and that Rear-Admiral Charles E. Madden had been appointed to be his Chief of the Staff. Within a few hours both had taken up their appointments.

The record of their Service careers up to that moment can be swiftly given. A captain at thirty-eight, a rear-admiral ten years later, the new Commander-in-Chief was a lieutenant in H.M.S. Agincourt during the Egyptian War, 1882. For his services he received the Egyptian medal. In 1893 he was in the Victoria, and survived the great disaster when she was rammed and went down. That was only the beginning of service in many parts of the world. Through it all he carried his coolness and his skill, climbing the ladder by merit and merit only, and gaining for himself a reputation that was considered equal to the occasion which had arisen. Three years his junior Rear-Admiral Madden likewise received his baptism of fire in the Egyptian War of 1882. In 1907 he was captain of H.M.S. Dreadnought, and Chief of the Staff of the Home Fleets. Thenceforward constantly employed both at Whitehall and afloat, Admiral Madden and his brother-in-law—he and Sir John married daughters of Sir Charles Cayzer, the famous shipowner—were often placed by the voice of prophecy in the positions where the great crisis found them.

Under Admiral Jellicoe's supreme command, and in charge of divisions of this great fleet, were gathered a little knot of men all in the prime of life, and all of them worthy of the trust placed in them by the officers and men under their commands. Rear-Admiral Sir Lewis Bayly, vice-admiral commanding the First Battle Squadron, not yet fifty-seven, began his Service career in 1870, and in 1875 was fighting against pirates up the River Congo. He was a shipmate of Sir John Jellicoe in the old Agincourt, and went through the Egyptian War of 1882. He received the £80 prize for torpedo-lieutenant in 1884. In 1907 he was appointed commodore in charge of destroyers of the Home Fleet, and from 1908 to 1911 he was in charge of

A REVOLUTION IN WARFARE.

Since the last great war many astonishing changes have occurred in the methods of conducting operations. Motor-'buses for carrying troops and gas-tubes for filling airships were, of course, unheard of during the Franco-Prussian War.

the Royal War College. Rugged in look and in character, and with the habit of making himself obeyed, "Luigi" Bayly had as his second-in-command Rear-Admiral Evan-Thomas, fifty-two years of age. The two men entrusted with the

destinies of the Second Battle Squadron were Sir George Warrender, who first saw fighting with the Naval Brigade in the Zulu War in 1879, and Sir Robert Arbuthnot, regarded as one of the keenest officers in the Service, and one who never expected from others what he could not do himself. Added to these, as rear-admiral commanding the First Battle Cruiser

A REVOLUTION IN WARFARE.

The water-filter was an aid to health undreamt of on the battle-fields of a generation or two ago, and the telephone (lower photograph) was, of course, also unknown in those days.

Squadron, Sir David Beatty was already known to the public as the man who had become a captain at twenty-nine, and reached flag rank before he was forty.

The state of war between England and Germany, beginning at eleven p.m. on Tuesday night, August 4th, is described elsewhere. The mobilisation was effected behind a curtain of secrecy rigidly respected by the Press. The three men mainly responsible for the final preparations have been mentioned already, but no history of Naval events would be complete without a more detailed reference to all three. Mr. Winston Churchill, the clever son of gifted parents, was described by Mr. Balfour as made of sterner stuff than Lord Randolph Churchill, whose audacity in politics and brilliance in debate the son inherited. For nearly three years this young Minister, still at the outbreak of hostilities under forty, had flung himself into Naval matters. A man who makes neither mistakes nor enemies makes nothing in this world. At least Mr. Winston Churchill brought into the Service a spirit of thoroughness and invincible youth. Those who most resented that a young layman should tackle subjects to which they had given their whole Service lives admitted—grudgingly perhaps—that this man from outside had got a grip of things. There was a quiet confidence in the efficiency of his administration now to be put to the supreme test. To his lieutenant, Prince Louis of Battenberg, the First Sea Lord, was also accorded the trust and confidence of the commissioned ranks of the Service. Recognised as perhaps one of the most brilliant tacticians in the British Navy, liked for his simple and unassuming manner, his profession and the public regarded him as a worthy successor of Lord Fisher and Sir Arthur K. Wilson, who from their retirement were to watch the weapon which they had forged being put to the test. But at that solemn moment it was generally felt that fleets are not only perfected in Whitehall, and the sympathies of very many went out to Sir George Callaghan, the fine old seaman, silent and strong and self-contained, who for nearly three years had commanded the Home Fleets. "The men would follow him anywhere," was the verdict on him of one of his captains.

To the new Commander-in-Chief, Sir John Jellicoe, on the outbreak of the war, his Majesty the King, expressing what was unuttered in the hearts of all his subjects, sent the following message :

F

" At this grave moment in our national history I send to you, and through you to the officers and men of the Fleets of which you have assumed command, the assurance of my confidence that under your direction they will revive and renew the old glories of the Royal Navy, and prove once again the sure shield of Britain and of her Empire in the hour of trial. GEORGE R.I."

The admiral's reply gave in simple words the spirit of the Fleet :

" On behalf of the officers and men of Home Fleets, beg to tender our loyal and dutiful thanks to your Majesty for the gracious message, which will inspire all with determination to uphold the glorious traditions of the past.

" COMMANDER-IN-CHIEF, HOME FLEETS.'

CHAPTER III.—LONDON ON THE EVE OF WAR.

GERMAN OBSERVATION LADDERS.

The old, old cry of " Wolf ! "—Stock Exchange Sensations — The Criminal at Work—-All Eyes on the Government — Germany's Hopes of Civil War in Ireland— The Fateful Fourth of August.

ALTHOUGH the text of Austria's ultimatum to Servia was in Sir Edward Grey's hands on the morning of Friday, July 24th, and in every newspaper office the same evening ; although the urgency of the crisis to Europe and Great Britain was insisted upon by every leading English paper from the following morning onwards, yet it was almost a full week before the public awoke to the fact that a European war was actually upon us. It was the cry of " Wolf ! " once too often. Everyone had heard so much about the coming Armageddon which never came, that they had begun to believe that it never would come. A few who had made some study of international politics or were possessed of some inside information as to German extraordinary preparations read in the first line of the Austrian ultimatum that the day had dawned. The man in the street saw nothing True, he learnt of financial panics in foreign capitals. They were no new thing. They had happened intermittently any time during the last three years. And when the pace abroad became so strong that Continental bourses closed their doors, he hugged himself in the proud thought that our own stock exchanges were never likely to follow so baneful an example. Even seven failures in one day over here caused no general excitement.

On Friday, July 31st, this condition of general confidence received a three-fold shock. The Bank rate was raised from 4 per cent. to 8 per cent., the highest figure recorded since 1873. Before noon next day it had gone up to 10 per cent. The second shock concerned the London Stock Exchange. At ten o'clock on the Friday morning a notice was posted on the door of the House to the effect that the committee, acting upon representations from leading members, had decided upon closing until further notice. There followed within a few hours a conference of the leading bankers with the Government, the result of which was officially intimated as follows :

UHLANS CHECKED BY BARBED-WIRE ENTANGLEMENT NEAR LIEGE.
INSET: GENERAL LEMAN, THE HEROIC DEFENDER.

"Interviews have taken place to-day between the Prime Minister, the Chancellor of the Exchequer, and representatives of the Bank of England and the leading joint-stock banks in regard to the financial situation. It is understood to have been decided that the situation is not at present such as to justify any emergency action in regard to the supply of legal tender currency, but in the event of further developments taking place necessitating Government action, the Treasury will be prepared to take such action immediately."

Panic is not a fair word to describe the effect of these drastic measures on the vast numbers who understood little of their actual technical bearing. There was none. But there was acute anxiety. Men and women dimly understood that securities would be for a time unsaleable, that money would be scarce, and that the prices of the necessities of life might consequently rise. They had wider visions of dearth of customers and lack of employment. For the first time that week they ceased to ask: "What has Servia to do with us?" They no longer shrugged their shoulders at the mention of Armageddon, but turned feverishly to the newspapers in the attempt to elicit from conflicting messages from foreign capitals whether the issue was to be peace or war. Part of the inner history of that tortuous diplomacy has already been divulged. It will be dealt with here in its proper order. But the public, during that final time of confusion before the sword cut every knot, were confronted with a tangled skein. Each day ran a similar course. The earlier editions brought news of renewed hopes of peace, of

IN GOOD HANDS.
One of the first Belgian victims of the war in hospital.

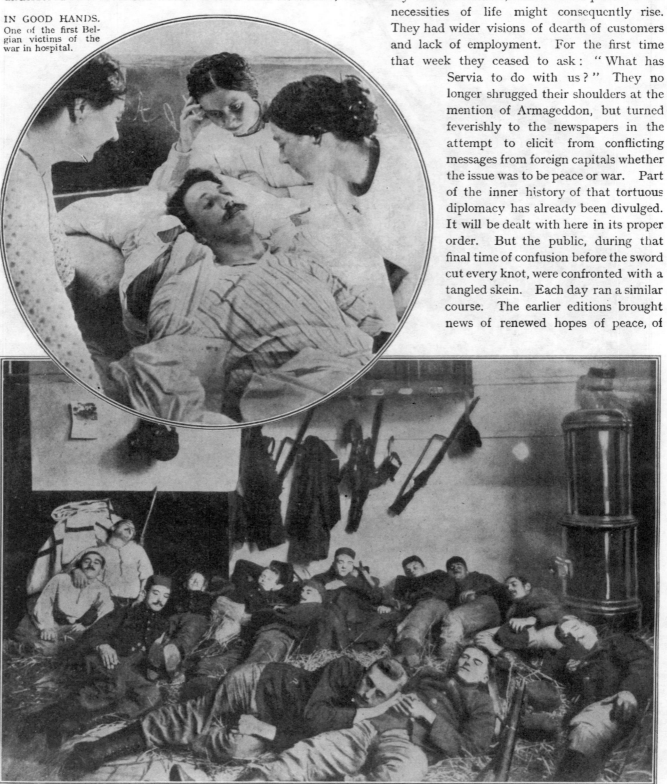

BELGIAN SOLDIERS ENJOYING A WELL-EARNED REST AFTER TAKING PART IN THE BRILLIANT
DEFENCE OF LIEGE.

SOLDIERS GUARDING FOREIGNERS' SHOPS IN PARIS.
Several establishments bearing German and Austrian names were wrecked.

BROTHERS-IN-ARMS.
King George and the President of France.

resumed conversations between Vienna and St. Petersburg, of personal efforts towards the desired end made by statesmen and potentates. In the evening there came a few cold words about ultimatums and mobilisation Men felt as a simple litigant has often felt in conflict with a sharp attorney who promises an easy compromise and flings in his writ all in the same half-hour. The plain man began to see that there was some sharp attorney at the back of all this confusion of hopes and fears. The conviction grew until it became overpowering. And so it was that there ascended to Heaven a general sigh of relief on Sunday morning when the British public awoke to find Germany at war with Russia and invading France, and knew the criminal at work.

That Sunday, August 2nd, is never likely to be forgotten by any Londoner. Week-day daily papers made an unusual Sabbath appearance, and in such centres as Charing Cross and Piccadilly Circus were literally torn from the hands of shouting newsvendors. Men's minds turned to recollections of pictures by Meissonier—Uhlans riding slowly through the border woods of France, terrified peasantry, a French sentry gazing eastward. But the earliest telegrams told them that the opening locale of the war of 1870 was not to be repeated. By midday the British metropolis was aware that the neutrality of Luxemburg had been violated by the German troops. The Cabinet, which had been sitting since early morning, were made acquainted with the news, and with a piece of information still more vital—namely, that there were German designs upon the neutrality of Belgium. For the next few hours the whole attention of London, and of the whole British Empire, was turned upon Mr. Asquith and his

Government. Bank Holiday found its usual crowds at Hampstead, in Epping Forest, at Kew and Richmond ; but everywhere one heard the words " Germany," " France," " Belgium," and such snatches of conversation, " There is no alliance ! " " We are not bound ! " " We cannot keep out ! "   In truth everyone was waiting for the announcement in Parliament that afternoon, expected from the Prime Minister, actually made by Sir Edward Grey. But when it was generally known through London that if Germany violated Belgian neutrality, or transferred the French war to the sea, she must be prepared to fight Great Britain, men recognised that there could no longer be hesitation. All individual questions as to ways and means disappeared before the question of national honour.

The debate of August 3rd, when Sir Edward Grey made his momentous announcement as to Germany's intended attack on Belgium, was also rendered memorable by a declaration of Irish loyalty on the part of Mr. Redmond. Only nine days before, on the very Sunday when Austria had shown her hand towards Servia, a collision between Nationalist gun-runners and the Dublin police had resulted in bloodshed. Coming as it did at the end of the abortive Buckingham Palace conference between the Ulster and Nationalist leaders, the foreign ill-wishers of Great Britain regarded this catastrophe as the outbreak of the long-promised civil war. Without a doubt Germany was counting on such a development. In her eyes, Great Britain, on the brink of armed conflict within her own islands, was a negligible quantity. Mr. Redmond's speech gave Berlin her answer. His words

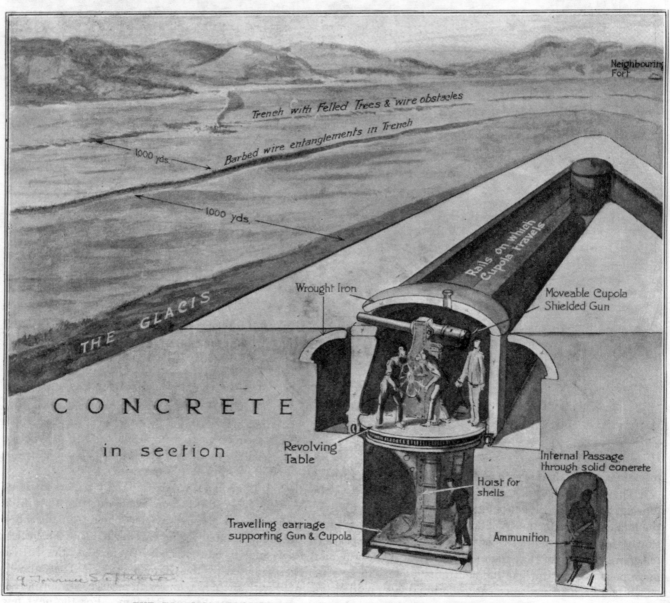

THE FORTIFICATIONS WHICH CONFOUNDED THE GERMANS AT LIEGE.
The fort seen in the foreground is so solidly built as to be almost indestructible. To storm such a fort, with barbed-wire entanglements barring the invaders' progress, was well-nigh a hopeless task.

AFTER LIEGE, NAMUR.
Namur is believed to be even more formidable than Liege. Notice the fortifications on the crest of the hill. The Belgians, always suspicious of Germany's intentions, have left nothing at all to chance.

did something more. They marked the close of the long quarrel between Ireland and the English people. In words that will be remembered while the British race endures, he declared :

" I say that the coasts of Ireland will be defended from foreign invasion by her armed sons, and for this purpose armed Nationalist Catholics in the South will be only too glad to join arms with the armed Protestant Ulstermen in the North. Is it too much to hope that out of this situation there may spring a result which will be good, not merely for the Empire, but good for the future welfare and integrity of the Irish nation ? . . . If the dire necessity is forced upon this country, we offer to the Government of the day that they may take their troops away, and that if it is allowed to us, in comradeship with our brethren in the North, we will ourselves defend the coasts of our country."

It was a trumpet call of patriotism, to which Sir Edward Carson responded. But it came too late to warn the jealous Power across the North Sea.

Meanwhile, the public learnt with satisfaction the further steps taken by Government to deal with the dangers of a financial or commercial crisis. On the same day as Sir Edward Grey's statement, the Chancellor of the Exchequer introduced a Postponement of Payments Bill—in other words, the machinery for a general moratorium, should such a measure be found necessary. Within a few days the Lord Chief Justice had drawn up special directions with respect to practice in relation to the moratorium. What the public gathered was that, if need be, honest debts, in view of the hardship of extraordinary times, would not be pressed until the war was over. Public confidence was also restored by the decision of Government to undertake the State insurance of merchant vessels so as to secure the carriage of food to these islands. The extension of the August Monday Bank Holiday until Thursday night and the issue of one pound and ten shilling notes helped to restore normal conditions. On Friday, August 7th, the Chancellor of the Exchequer was able to announce to the House of Commons that the arrangements made by the Government for the re-opening of the banks had proved perfectly satisfactory throughout the country. The "Times" summarised his chief points — namely, that the Bank of England had received that day gold amounting to over five and a half millions; that there was no sign of hoarding anywhere; that trade was everywhere resuming normal conditions; and that the Bank Rate, which had already earlier in the week been reduced from 10 to 6 per cent., would be further reduced next day to 5 per cent. There remained a further step taken by the Government, announced in the papers of August 13th — to guarantee the Bank of England from any loss it might incur in discounting any bills of exchange accepted by them prior to August 4th, 1914.

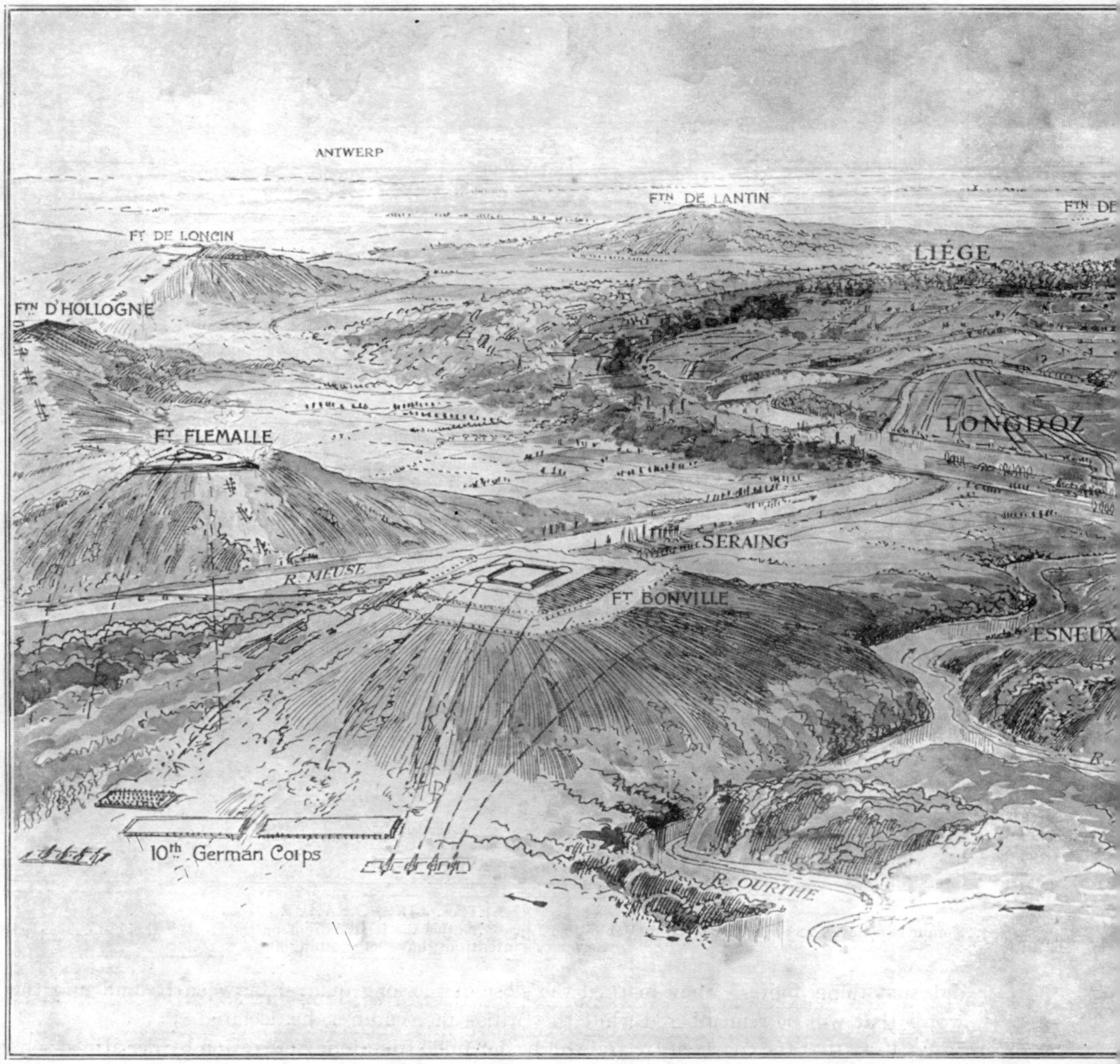

THE SCENE OF THE FI

A bird's-eye view of Liege and the surrounding district, showing the positions of the forts, and t

The effect on trading and employment of all these remedial measures speedily made themselves felt by the general public. It would be untrue to say that, during the earlier days of apprehension, there was no panic buying of large stores of provisions, no selfish inflation of prices on the part of retailers. But the general good sense of the community soon corrected any tendency in the former direction, while the prompt action of the Government in fixing the maximum prices of commodities put a term to the enterprise of the few avaricious shopkeepers.

But the touch of evil times had already made itself felt. On July 27th there was a disquieting collapse on the Stock Exchange. Consols fell to the lowest figure ever recorded in their present form of $2\frac{1}{2}$ per cent. A leading newspaper indicated how representative securities had fared during the slump of those pre-war days:

	Now.	Closing Wednesday.	Fall.	Fall per cent.
Consols	$72\frac{1}{4}$	$75\frac{1}{2}$	$3\frac{1}{4}$	$4\frac{1}{4}$
South-Eastern Defd.	37	$43\frac{3}{4}$	$6\frac{3}{4}$	$15\frac{1}{2}$
Canadian Pacific ..	$178\frac{1}{4}$	$190\frac{1}{2}$	$12\frac{1}{4}$	$6\frac{1}{2}$
Shell Oil	$4\frac{1}{8}$	$4\frac{19}{32}$	$\frac{15}{32}$	10
Malacca Rubber ..	$2\frac{3}{4}$	$3\frac{5}{16}$	$\frac{9}{16}$	17
De Beers	$14\frac{7}{8}$	$15\frac{15}{16}$	$1\frac{1}{16}$	$6\frac{1}{2}$
Russo-Asiatic ..	$6\frac{1}{16}$	7[illegible]	1[illegible]	23

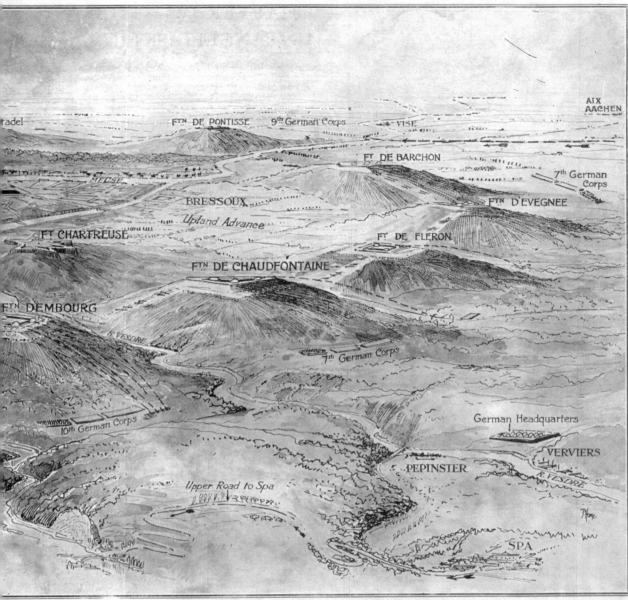

AIX
AACHEN
FᵀᴺDE PONTISSE 9ᵗʰ German Corps VISE
Fᵀ DE BARCHON
7ᵗʰ German Corps
BRESSOUX Fᵀᴺ D'EVEGNEE
Upland Advance
FᵗCHARTREUSE FᵀDE FLERON
FᵀᴺDE CHAUDFONTAINE
FᵀᴺDEMBOURG
R.VESDRE
7ᵗʰ German Corps
German Headquarters
VERVIERS
10ᵗʰ German Corps R.VESDRE
PEPINSTER
Upper Road to Spa
SPA

IT OF MODERN TIMES
acles in the form of rivers, hills, and wooded country, and the disposition of the invading force.

The action of the Government in guaranteeing the underwriting of ships against war risks came not a minute too soon. Although the risk of capture by hostile cruisers, directly war should be declared, may have been a vain imagination, it was an imagination which brought to a standstill the whole carrying trade of the country. Owners were afraid to send their ships to sea uncovered, while underwriters were quite unable to accept further war risks with the danger of war being declared at any moment. Added to this, there was no quotation for securities, with the result that brokers and business men had not command over capital. Credit had vanished.

Such was the effect of the financial crisis which harassed London during those last days of feverish diplomacy, and it was due to the financial solidity of the nation, no less than to its levelheadedness and the promptness of Government measures, that the declaration of war, instead of precipitating worse conditions, cleared the atmosphere.

It was on August 4th that the dreaded announcement was made in the following proclamation :

"A STATE OF WAR.

" His Majesty's Government informed the German Government on August 4th, 1914, that unless a satisfactory reply to the request of his Majesty's Government for an assurance that Germany would respect the neutrality of Belgium was received by midnight of that day, his Majesty's Government would feel bound to take all steps in their power to uphold that neutrality, and the observance of a treaty to which Germany was as much a party as Great Britain.

" The result of this communication having been that his Majesty's Ambassador at Berlin had to ask for his passports, his Majesty's Government have accordingly notified the German Government that a state of war exists between the two countries as from 11 p.m. to-day."

That fateful fourth of August will be remembered throughout the world as one of the most eventful days of modern times. Whatever differences of opinion the nation had shown as to whether Britain should take part in the conflict, once the gauntlet had been thrown down those differences disappeared.

WILL GERMANY'S AIR FLEET HAVE A DECIDING INFLUENCE ON THE WAR?
While it is clear that the Germans have not very great faith in their Navy, they are unspeakably proud of their fleet of airships, which often cruise over their cities to arouse enthusiasm among the populace.

CHAPTER IV.—THE UNTANGLED SKEIN.

Peace At No Price—Sir Edward Grey's Warning—Private Information About German Intrigue—The Perfidy of the German Government—Britain Takes the Plunge.

THE story of that momentous week's diplomacy is like a nightmare. Now that the full truth has been presented to the world, it discloses an attitude of cynicism hard to be credited. On July 23rd, while the German War Lord was ostentatiously enjoying himself on his annual northern cruise, Austria took the opportunity of presenting to Servia a host of demands which formed a very drastic ultimatum, requiring submission within forty-eight hours, with the alternative of war. Servia was required to condemn "the propaganda directed against Austria," and take proceedings against all accessories to the plot against the Archduke Franz Ferdinand who were in Servia. Austrian delegates were to supervise the proceedings, and Servia was also to arrest certain Servian officials whose guilt was alleged. These exorbitant conditions made it quite obvious that no concessions on Servia's side would be accepted.

Nevertheless, a virtual acceptance followed. Acting on the advice of Russia, Servia acceded to all that was required of her, making only two

A GROUP OF TYPICAL MEN OF THE GERMAN NAVY.
They are conscripts, and do not get so long a training as British tars, so it is questionable whether they are so efficient as our men.

reservations of the most reasonable character. These reservations were enough for "the wolf drinking higher up the stream." Austria at once declared herself dissatisfied, and though the actual declaration of war was delayed for a few hours, a state of war practically existed between the two countries from Saturday evening, July 25th.

That was the beginning of efforts on the part of Great Britain, as sincere as they were indefatigable, to localise the conflict. Sir Edward Grey repeated his solemn warnings in every chancellery of Europe. The very

THE GERMAN DREADNOUGHT GOEBEN, WHICH DISTINGUISHED ITSELF BY RUNNING AWAY FROM THE BRITISH
SHIPS IN THE MEDITERRANEAN AND SEEKING THE PROTECTION OF TURKEY.

Photos]   *[Russell & Sons.*

REAR-ADMIRAL THE HON.
R. F. BOYLE.

day that he was apprised of the violent tone of Austria's note to Servia — the actual day it was presented—he warned the Austrian Ambassador in London that if as many as four Great Powers of Europe were engaged in war, it would involve the expenditure of such a vast sum of money and such interference with trade, that a complete collapse of European credit and industry would follow. The reply of Russia to this warning was quite conciliatory. The Russian Foreign Minister assured the British Minister that Russia had no aggressive intentions, and would take no action unless forced. Austria's action, M. Sazonoff added, in reality aimed at overthrowing Russia's influence in the Balkans.

Thus the position stood on the afternoon of Monday, July 27th, when Sir Edward Grey made his first announcement to the House. He was able to state that his suggestion of a joint conference, composed of the ambassadors of Germany, France, Italy, and himself, with a view to mediation between Austria and Russia, had been accepted by all except Germany, which Power had expressed its concurrence with the plan in principle, but opposed the details on the ground that there was a prospect of direct conversations between Austria and Russia. That German statement was true outwardly. In substance it reeked of insincerity. On that Monday afternoon the Russian Ambassador warned Austria that Russia would not give way, and expressed his hope that some arrangement might be arrived at before Servia was invaded.

Austria's reply came on Tuesday. It took the shape of a formal declaration of war upon Servia.

That Tuesday, July 28th, was a very vital day. Here in England people believed Germany's professions that her one desire was for peace. They might have believed otherwise had they known what was going on behind the scenes in the various European capitals. Russia still declared her willingness to open conversations with Austria. But in Paris at the same moment the German Ambassador was refusing to give to Russia's ally any assurance that Servian independence would be respected. The next step, taken on the same day, was the refusal of the Austrian Government to delay warlike proceedings.

And what about the German Government through these twenty-four hours? It informed Sir Edward Grey that it had made representations at Vienna in favour of mediation by the four Powers. But its attitude was always this: Its representations could only be in the nature of advice; there could be no attempt to interfere with Austria's discretion as a sovereign state. The sincerity of these assertions may be gauged by a further fact. All through this time Germany declared that she had had no previous knowledge of the contents of the Austrian note to Servia. Here is the statement on this point made by Sir M. de Bunsen (British Ambassador to Vienna) to Sir Edward Grey on July 30th:

" . . . . Although I am not able to verify it, I have private information that the German

COMMODORE R. Y. TYRWHITT.

REAR-ADMIRAL H. L. TOTTENHAM.

VICE-ADMIRAL SIR JOHN JELLICOE'S FLAGSHIP, IRON DUKE, BEING COALED AT SEA. INSET: VICE-ADMIRAL JELLICOE.

Drawn specially for "The Great War" by Chas. Pears.]   *[Photo by Russell & Sons.*

Ambassador knew the text of the Austrian ultimatum to Servia before it was despatched and telegraphed it to the German Emperor. I know from the German Ambassador himself that he endorses every line of it."

Fair words from Germany, and all the while her ally, to whose actions she was privy, was pressing forward to war. Naturally the Russian Foreign Minister complained that conversations were useless in the face of such facts. Nor was it unreasonable that Russia should declare that her forces would be mobilised the day that Austria crossed the Servian frontier. From that time forward a change came over the scene. Whether it was owing to the fact that the Austrian Ambassador in Berlin declared that Russia was not in a position to make war, or to the fact that she herself had been preparing for many months, this much is certain, the attitude of Germany suddenly stiffened. From the mist of words and assurances with which the German Chancellor enveloped our ambassador in Berlin, this one point emerges—that Germany meant to regard the partial mobilisation of Russia as a ground for war. It was useless for Russia to protest that this partial mobilisation was merely a precaution. It was useless for the Tsar himself to offer to give his word that no use would be made of any of his forces. It was equally useless that Germany knew, as subsequent facts have proved, that her own state of mobilisation was very much further advanced than that of Russia. Every day the public read statements that

LIKE LOCUSTS.
This café in Mouland, having escaped the fire which consumed the rest of the town, was cleared of everything of value
by the devastating Germans.

conversations between Vienna and St. Petersburg had been renewed. The public heard of suggestions for a compromise emanating from Berlin. They all meant nothing. Just as Servia was presented with conditions which it was never intended that she should accept, so Europe was treated to a variety of temporising pretexts which had no object at all save to give Germany the longest possible time in which to make her preparations, while lulling the suspicions of other States to rest.

On Friday, July 31st, she was quite ready, and she launched her ultimatum to St. Petersburg. It is significant that only on that day was the Russian general mobilisation ordered. By six o'clock on Saturday evening war between the two Empires began, and by Sunday morning Germany was invading France.

At this point Great Britain passed from the position of general peacemaker to that of a principal. As Sir Edward Grey stated in the House of Commons a few hours later, the question whether Austria or Russia should dominate the southern Slav races was no concern of England. As he also told the House, we were bound by no secret alliance to France, and we were absolutely free to choose our course with regard to the crisis which had overtaken her. But there were two cardinal points in the situation which had arisen which intimately concerned Great Britain. The first essential feature of our diplomacy was that France should not be brought into such a condition in Europe that she became a species of vassal State to Germany.

That position was understood in Berlin, and from it there arose one of the most extraordinary diplomatic incidents that ever took place even in the house of Bismarck. Writing to Sir Edward Grey on July 29th—the day on which Germany's attitude to Russia had so suddenly stiffened—the British Ambassador at Berlin stated that he had been made the recipient of a most remarkable offer from the Chancellor, Dr. Bethmann-Hollweg.

"He said that, should Austria be attacked by Russia, a European conflagration might, he feared, become inevitable, owing to Germany's obligations as Austria's ally, in spite of his continued efforts to maintain peace. He then proceeded to make the following strong bid for British neutrality. He said that it

THE RAVAGES OF WAR.
Having burned and sacked the town of Mouland, the last of the German soldiers leave to turn more snug homes into smoking ruins.

was clear, so far as he was able to judge the main principle which governed British policy, that Great Britain would never stand by and allow France to be crushed in any conflict there might be. That, however, was not the object at which Germany aimed. Provided that neutrality of Great Britain were certain, every assurance would be given to the British Government that the Imperial Government aimed at no territorial acquisitions

While the forts of Liege were still held by the Belgians, the town itself was occupied by Germans, who looted the place. Some of the officers are here seen enjoying the commandeered provisions.

at the expense of France should they prove victorious in any war that might ensue.

"I questioned his Excellency about the French Colonies, and he said that he was unable to give a similar undertaking in that respect."

The British Government was thus asked to stand coldly by while its friend, France, was attacked and crushed, and the little State of Belgium, whose neutrality it had guaranteed, was invaded. Sir Edward Grey might have been expected to reply to this "infamous proposal," as Mr. Asquith called it, with an instant rupture of diplomatic relations. But, instead, he continued "conversations," which brought no honour to the British Government. It is true that he telegraphed on July 30th:

ANGELS OF MERCY.
British Red Cross nurses leaving London for the front. The value of the work of these unselfish ladies cannot be overestimated.

HER MAJESTY QUEEN ALEXANDRA,
Whose keen interest in the work of the nurses has deeply touched the nation.

"His Majesty's Government cannot for a moment entertain the Chancellor's proposal that they should bind themselves to neutrality on such terms.

"What he asks us in effect is to engage to stand by while French colonies are taken and France is beaten, so long as Germany does not take French territory as distinct from the colonies.

"From the material point of view such a proposal is unacceptable, for France, without further territory in Europe being taken from her, could be so crushed as to lose her position as a Great Power and become subordinate to German policy.

"Altogether apart from that, it would be a disgrace for us to make this bargain with Germany at the expense of France—a disgrace from which the good name of this country would never recover."

But after this declaration the English Foreign Minister made another fruitless effort next day to satisfy Germany by abandoning the Triple Entente. On the morning of July 31st he informed the German Ambassador that if Germany could get any reasonable proposal put forward which made it clear that Germany and Austria were striving to preserve European peace, and that if Russia and France were unreasonable in rejecting it, he would support it at St. Petersburg and Paris, and go the length of saying that, if Russia and France would not accept it, his Majesty's Government would have nothing more to do with the consequences. Otherwise, he told the German Ambassador that if France became involved, Great Britain would be drawn in.

8

PROVISIONING A WARSHIP.

This drawing gives a splendid idea of the hugeness of the task of keeping a big warship in fighting trim. It represents the food for the officers and men only. The food for the guns is, of course, another very big item

The practical application of Sir Edward Grey's telegram of July 31st was made clear in his speech to the House of Commons on the afternoon of August 3rd. He laid it down, and he stated that he had given France on the previous day the written assurance, that if the German Fleet came into the Channel or through the North Sea to assail her, our Fleet would protect her to the uttermost.

On the same afternoon, in the same place, Sir Edward Grey enunciated once again the other dominant principle of British foreign policy—that England can never look with indifference on the seizure by a great Continental Power of any portion of Belgium or Holland. More than a hundred years ago it was declared by Napoleon, who knew a little about political geography, that Antwerp was a pistol levelled at the head of London.

On July 31st Sir Edward Grey inquired by telegraph both at Paris and Berlin whether the two Governments would engage to respect the neutrality of Belgium. From France there came the assurance that the Government was resolved to respect Belgium's neutrality, unless compelled to act otherwise by reason of its violation at the hands of another Power. From Germany there was the answer that the Secretary of State, Von Jagow, could not reply to the British request until he had consulted the Emperor and Chancellor. He doubted, however, whether the German Government could give any answer without revealing its plan of campaign. He furthermore alleged the commission of hostile acts by Belgium.

It was German diplomacy at its worst. While Herr von Jagow was declaring his inability to reply, he very well knew what his Government was preparing behind the scenes.

And it was not long before his Majesty's Government likewise received full information. On August 4th Sir Edward Grey was informed that the German Government had proposed that Belgium should grant its armies free passage through Belgian territory. The kindly offer was accompanied by the usual Prussian threat that this small State would be crushed out of existence if it refused to comply. In short, it was an ultimatum presented at seven o'clock on Sunday evening, August 2nd, to expire within twelve hours. Directly the British Government received this definite information a telegram was sent early in the morning to the British Ambassador in Berlin requesting an assurance that the neutrality of Belgium would be respected by Germany. An immediate reply was requested. To this the German Foreign Secretary repeated "most positively the formal assurance" that, even in the case of armed conflict with Belgium, Germany would, under no circumstances whatever, annex Belgian territory.

THE GREAT WAR LORD.
One wonders if he is now "sorry he spoke."

The Prime Minister told the story of these negotiations in the House on Tuesday, August 4th, and he stated that the Government could not regard the German reply as in any sense a satisfactory communication. He added: "We have, in reply to it, repeated the request we made last week to the German Government that they should give us the same assurance in regard

A SLIGHT ON DAME NATURE

The upper photograph is a view of one of the prettiest spots in Belgium, namely, Dinant. Notice the forts at the top of the rock. It is surely a sin to turn such a lovely place into a battlefield. The lower picture shows the citadel at Huy. Inset: Belgian soldiers, one of whom is wearing a handkerchief under his cap to protect himself from the heat.

to Belgian neutrality as was given by France; and we have asked that the reply to that request and a satisfactory answer to the telegram of this morning should be given before midnight."

By eleven p.m. that evening England and Germany were at war.

And what excuse did Germany give for this attack upon a small and friendly country which had done her no wrong, and whose integrity she, no less than Britain, had pledged herself by treaty to respect and defend? The Kaiser's Government pretended that authentic news had been received that France meant to attack Germany through this neutral territory. The pretence and the lie are refuted from the German Chancellor's own lips. He spoke in the Reichstag on August 4th. This is what he said:

" Gentlemen, we are now in a state of necessity, and necessity knows no law! Our troops have occupied Luxemburg, and perhaps "—as a matter of fact, the speaker knew that Belgium had been invaded that morning—

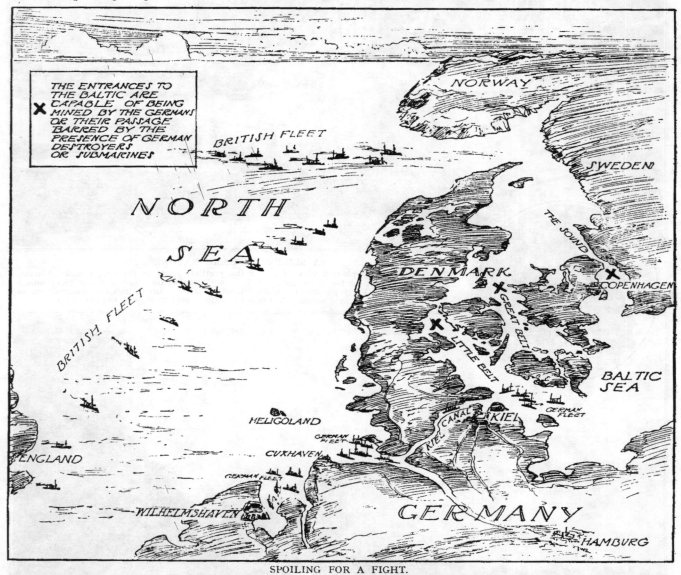

SPOILING FOR A FIGHT.
Immediately war was declared the British fleets stole quietly out into the North Sea, eager to try conclusions with the enemy. The German fleet, however, had planned to postpone the great sea fight.

" are already on Belgian soil. Gentlemen, that is contrary to the dictates of international law. It is true that the French Government has declared at Brussels that France is willing to respect the neutrality of Belgium as long as her opponent respects it. We knew, however, that France stood ready for the invasion. France could wait, but we could not wait. A French movement upon our flank upon the lower Rhine might have been disastrous. So we were compelled to override the just protest of the Luxemburg and Belgian Governments. The wrong— I speak openly—that we are committing we will endeavour to make good as soon as our military goal has been reached. Anybody who is threatened, as we are threatened, and is fighting for his highest possessions can have only one thought—how he is to hack his way through."

A TRAGEDY OF THE WAR.

German Lancers entering Mouland, Belgium. Four peasants fired on the invaders from the farmhouse seen on the right, and were promptly taken by the troops and shot.

CHAPTER V.—HOW GERMANY STROVE TO GAIN COMMAND OF THE SEA.

The Irony of Fate—Kaiser Wilhelm's Great Ambition—How He Revolutioned The Navy—His Navy a Mushroom Growth— Recent Increases of Rival Fleets.

IT is one of the ironies of Fate that the great European war should have been forced upon us just at the time when preparations were under way to celebrate the hundredth anniversary of the conclusion of our last great conflict at sea. From the middle of 1812 to the end of 1814 we were fighting the United States, and we fought them not because of any basic difference of policy, but because, in defence of what they

THE (MIS)MANAGING DIRECTOR OF THE ARMY OF AGGRESSION.
H.I.M. the Kaiser takes his favourite place at the head of his troops.

regarded as their national rights, they stood between us and the steps which we were compelled to take if we were to throw the whole weight of our naval strength into the fight against the Napoleonisation of Europe. Since 1814 the British Empire has engaged in many wars, but never until this year have we found ourselves in conflict with a nation whose avowed policy was to challenge our right to the title of Mistress of the Seas. For over a century, from Trafalgar down to the Teutonic challenge to the rest of civilised Europe, we maintained the command of the sea by the weight of our prestige and by the strength and efficiency of our Navy. In that period we spent upon our Fleet a total of approximately 1,500 millions sterling. We built squadrons upon squadrons of ships which fulfilled their highest mission—the preservation of peace—by never firing a shot in anger. They came new from the builder's yard, they served their appointed time in our commissioned fleets, and they ultimately faded out of the public gaze into the hands of the shipbreaker; but every British warship which, during the last hundred years, has completed her effective life without meeting an enemy, has been a monument to the success of British policy and the influence of British naval power. Lord Rosebery has said that the heaviest expenditure on armaments is cheaper than the smallest European war. Lord Charles Beresford has put the same epigram into different form by declaring that " battleships are cheaper than battles." But the meaning of both is the same. The British Navy was doing its best and most effective work when it was preserving the maritime peace of the world.

Now we have come to the time when the British Navy has no longer been able to preserve peace. For a hundred years we have commanded the sea in equity, claiming no advantages for ourselves because we had the power to sweep any rivals off the seas, but striving always to preserve the principle that the seas were free high-ways. In times of peace we have never used our sea power for the purposes of aggression or suppression, and every nation has enjoyed equal trading rights with ourselves. We have maintained a supreme Navy because we depend for our food, for the raw materials which keep our manufacturing industries at work, and for the cohesion of our world-spread Empire upon the absolute freedom of the seas.

For the greater part of the nineteenth century the British Navy was regarded as a peace machine. We believed that as long as we kept our Fleet at a reasonable standard of strength,

GERMAN INFANTRY IN ACTION.
The Germans thoroughly understand the art of making and using trenches.   Inset : A clever device for cutting trenches very quickly.

BELGIAN INFANTRY FIRING UPON UHLANS FROM BEHIND A BARRICADE IN A VILLAGE NEAR THE HISTORIC FIELD OF WATERLOO. INSET: BELGIANS GUARDING THE CITY OF BRUSSELS.

no foreign Power would dare to attack it or to challenge the supremacy which we had used so beneficently. But from the time when the Emperor William II. succeeded to the throne of the German Empire, British sea-power has been regarded from a different point of view. All the nations of the world were willing to accept British naval supremacy as an established, and even as a desirable fact ; but the monarch who is now the German Emperor cherished from the beginning of his reign the ambition that Germany might be able to supplant us as the Mistress of the Seas. He told his subjects that the future of Germany lay upon the water (" Unsere Zukunft liegt auf dem Wasser ") ; he declared to them that " the trident of Neptune must be in our fist " ; and when we were in the midst of the dark days of the South African War he deplored in public that the comparative weakness of the German Navy did not enable that country to take advantage of British preoccupation, and " to further our flourishing commerce and our interests oversea."

When William II. became German Emperor in 1888 his Navy did not occupy a position of any great importance among the fleets of the world. It included a dozen armoured ships of over 5,000 tons, but not one whose displacement ran into five figures : while at the same date the British Fleet comprised fifty-six armoured ships of more than 5,000 tons, fourteen of them being of more than 10,000. Before the Kaiser had been on the throne a year, however, a Bill providing for the expansion of the Navy was forced through the Reichstag.

The first important measure of German naval expansion was an Act, dated April 10th, 1898, which provided for the construction and maintenance of a fleet of the following dimensions : 19 battleships, 4 armoured coast-defence ships, 12 large cruisers, and 30 small cruisers. The possession of such a fleet as this would have greatly strengthened Germany's position at sea, but could have been in no sense a menace to us ; and the Act was therefore passed without attracting much attention in this country. Unfortunately, however, it did not remain for long the measure of Germany's naval ambitions. During the first days of the South African War the Kaiser made an extraordinary speech. " We are in bitter need of a strong German Navy," he said. " If the increases demanded during the first years of my reign had not been continuously refused, in spite of my continued entreaties and warnings, how differently should we now be able to further our flourishing commerce and our interests oversea ! " The argument did not fail to take effect On June 14th, 1900, the Reichstag adopted a new Navy Act, by which the fleet provided for two years before was almost doubled. It enacted that the German Fleet should consist of 38 battleships, 14 large cruisers, and 38 small cruisers, the last of these ships to be laid down in 1917 and completed in 1920.

The Navy Act, of course, did not make the Navy, but it gave a clear indication of the energy with which Germany was determined to push home her bid for naval power. A memorandum attached to the Navy Act of 1900 gave the principles upon which German naval development was to be governed. " To protect Germany's sea trade and colonies in existing circumstances there is only one means—Germany must have a battle fleet so strong that even for the strongest sea Power a war against it would involve such dangers as to imperil its position in the world. For this purpose," the memorandum went on, " it is not absolutely necessary that the German battle fleet should be as strong as that of the greatest naval Power; for such a Power will not, as a rule, be in a position to concentrate all its fighting forces against us. But even if it should succeed in meeting us with considerable superiority of strength, the defeat of a strong German fleet would so substantially weaken the enemy that, in spite of the victory he might have obtained, his own position in the world would no longer be secured by an adequate fleet." Since 1900 the German Navy Act has been three times amended and increased.

The rate of construction was accelerated in 1908, probably as the result of the influence of the Dreadnought,

WILL THEY RIVAL THE FAMOUS C.I.V.'S OF THE TIME OF THE BOER WAR?
The Citizen Army of Territorials marching along the Strand, London. Most of the men are eager to cross the Channel to get into the thick of the fight.

the epoch-making battleship laid down for the British Navy in October, 1905. This vessel differed so radically from all battleships of earlier design that, although the latter would naturally retain a proportion of their usefulness for some years to come, the rate of their decline into obsolescence was greatly quickened. Even more significant than the building of the Dreadnought, however, was the fact that at the end of 1905 there was a change of Government in this country, and Mr. Balfour was succeeded as Prime Minister by Sir Henry Campbell-Bannerman. There is not the slightest reason to think that the new Premier was not as keen a believer in the necessity for the maintenance of a supreme British Navy as any of his contemporaries, but it is quite as certain that he almost stood alone in his sincere and childlike belief in the innocence of German naval policy, and the desire of that nation to come to an amicable understanding with ourselves regarding the relative strengths of our fleets. The old Government, before going out of office, had prepared a " Statement of Admiralty Policy," in which it was declared that our position and the policy of foreign Powers necessitated the minimum output of four armoured ships of the largest type annually. The new Government, whose honesty in the matter has never been called into question, believed that such a programme might be regarded as provocative by foreign Powers, and especially by Germany,

[Drawn specially for "The Great War" by Chas. Pears.

GUARDING THE NATION'S FOOD SHIPS.

Every night the Thames estuary bears the above striking appearance. The river is swept constantly with searchlights from British destroyers, and it would go hard with any enemy who attempted to interfere with our freedom of the port.

so in their first year (1906-7) they laid down only three ships instead of four. The change had no effect upon Germany, who laid down the three ships for which provision had been made in the Navy Act and its amendments. In 1907 came the Second Peace Conference at the Hague, to which the British representative went with full authority to discuss an agreement for the reduction of armaments and the limitation of expenditure if other nations were that way disposed ; and to add another proof of his unquestioned sincerity, Sir H. Campbell - Bannerman gave us a programme for that year of three battleships,

COLOURED TROOPS FOR THE ALLIES.
Algerian sharpshooters crossing France en route to the German frontier. They are keen fighters and, despite German allegations to the contrary, are far from "savage" in their methods.

but declared that the third would only be laid down in the event of no agreement being arrived at by the Conference. The great majority of people never expected that any agreement would be arrived at—and they were right. We had to build our third ship.

But the British Government were not yet entirely convinced of the futility of their efforts, and they determined to show by actual, concrete example that they were prepared to go almost to any lengths to prove their sincerity in the cause they had at heart. During the first two years of their administration they had laid down only the same number of battleships as Germany—six ; and in 1908 they took the grave risk of reducing our programme

WHERE INNOCENCE IS BLISS.
German troops unloading baggage and ammunition. To the juvenile spectators war is merely an amusing entertainment.

(already cut down from the declared necessary minimum of four) to two ships only. What was the result ? It may have been only an unhappy conicidence, reflecting no suggestion of malice upon the German Government, but in the year when our Dreadnought programme was reduced from three ships to two the German programme was advanced from three ships to four.

After many years of fruitless effort, during which the Government had come near to placing our naval position in jeopardy, it was at last realised that Germany was determined to brook no outside interference in her naval policy. We had met her in conference ; we had promised to reduce our building programmes if she would follow our example; we had even gone so far as to reduce our programmes twice in the hope that the example would be followed. With what result? Mr. Asquith told the House of Commons in March, 1909, that the British Government had frequently endeavoured to ascertain whether any proposal for a mutual reduction of armaments would be accepted by the German Government.

"But," he went on, "we have been assured more than once, and in the most formal manner, that their naval expenditure is governed solely by reference to their own needs, and that their programme does not depend upon ours. . . . . If that is so, it is perfectly clear that there is no room for a mutual arrangement for reduction. I regret it very much, but I do not complain. . . . It is no business of ours to offer either criticism or advice, but to accept the facts as they state them, and we must adapt our programme to our national requirements."

After this, therefore, we reconciled

BELGIANS IN ARMOURED MOTOR-CARS, ONE OF WHICH CARRIES A MITRAILLEUSE GUN. THEY ARE POSTED ON ONE OF THE MAIN ROADS. INSET: A WOUNDED GERMAN IN A COTTAGE AT HAELEN.

BELGIAN TROOPS NEARING THE SCENE OF BATTLE. THEY PAY LITTLE ATTENTION TO SMARTNESS IN DRESS, BUT ARE NONE THE WORSE FOR THAT WHEN IT COMES TO FIGHTING.

ourselves to the facts, and set about making up some of the leeway we had lost in a vain attempt to bring about a better state of affairs. In 1909–10 we laid down eight Dreadnoughts to Germany's four; but in the following year we came down to a proportion of only five to four, which was repeated in 1911–12. Early in 1912 yet another law was passed, increasing the German Navy by three battleships and two small cruisers. The additional shipbuilding thus provided for was not considerable; but far more remarkable were the provisions made for the increase in the instantly-ready striking strength of the German Navy.

WHERE SOME OF THE HOTTEST FIGHTING OCCURRED
Dinant, Belgium, as seen from the fort. Here the Germans suffered a heavy defeat. The river is the Meuse.

Before the new law the fleet authorised to be kept in full commission in the waters of Northern Europe consisted of 17 battleships, 4 battle cruisers, 12 small cruisers, and 66 destroyers. Under the new law the force was raised to 25 battleships, 8 battle cruisers, 18 small cruisers, and 99 destroyers. Quoting the words of Mr. Churchill, the effect of the amendment was to place nearly four-fifths of the entire German Navy in permanent full commission.

When Mr. Churchill told us that our Navy had to be ready at its "average moment" to meet an enemy at his "selected moment," he was simply hinting at the fundamentals of Germany's naval ambitions. At her "selected moment," Germany could have the whole of the High Sea Fleet ready; while we might have a fair proportion of our ships in dockyard hands, or in distant seas.

Unfortunately for Germany, although the moment for war was of her own choosing, it found the High Sea Fleet incomplete, and the British Navy absolutely ready. When Germany threw the glove in the face of England, the British Fleet was in such a condition of preparedness for war as it had probably never enjoyed.

CHAPTER VI.—GERMANY ON THE EVE OF WAR.
By An Eye-Witness.

Beating the War Drums—Riots in Berlin—The Part the Crown Prince Played—Ambassadors Insulted—Run on Banks—Kaiser's Memorable Speech—Ultimatum to Russia—Militarism Let Loose—A Frantic Spy Hunt—Voting £265,000,000.

L ONG before the shadow of war had fallen upon the German Empire, the leading German newspapers, including even the pacifist Press, set to work to arouse the "furor Teutonicus" on which Germany has always relied to tide the civil population over the food and money crisis which accompanied the early days of the war. Day after day the "Berliner Tageblatt" beat the war-drum, and declared that war with Russia would be almost a holy war. The result was that when Austria presented her ultimatum to Servia, and when, one day later, a flood of special editions of the "Tageblatt" and "Lokalanzeiger" poured over the German capital the news that Austria had pronounced the

Servian reply to her ultimatum inadequate, Germans throughout the Empire were already prepared to burst into a wild war enthusiasm, an orgy of war-mafficking such as took by surprise many worthy folk who had talked for years of the civilisation of Germany and the effects of German education.

Throughout the night of Saturday, July 25th, huge crowds, led in some cases by amateur buglers, paraded the Linden. held open-air demonstrations outside the Reichstag and in front of the Austrian Embassy. Servian flags were burnt in the street, Servian residents mobbed and insulted, and several cafés, frequented chiefly by Russians, were partially demolished. Attempts to wreck the Servian Legation in Charlottenburg were frustrated

HOW THE WAR AFFECTS CIVIL LIFE.

In the top photograph are shown peasants reaping, while in the same field Belgian soldiers are digging trenches. In the circle is shown a carriage stopped by Brussels Town Guards, who have required the ladies to produce their passports. The third picture is a snapshot of an ambulance cavalcade, composed of all sorts of tradesmen's carts. The leading van belonged to a firm of dyers before being commandeered by the Belgian Government.

by large bodies of mounted police—who, however, displayed a gentleness in their treatment of the rioters which must have amazed those who believed that the police of Berlin were mainly intended to keep order.

The demonstration of Saturday was no mere exhibition of sympathy with Austria ; it was a violent outburst of that intense hatred of Russia which for years has been characteristic of Germany. The Press, which, under the guise of lofty sentiments, had stirred up the war fever, was obliged next day to issue a police warning that demonstrations would now be suppressed— not, indeed, because of any official objection to the war fever or its violent exhibition, but because some sixty thousand Socialists had been summoned by the party leaders to attend counter-demonstrations throughout Berlin and its neighbourhood

Demonstrations against war were to be repressed with all the accustomed vigour of the armed police, and there was considerable fear that the zeal of the police president's army corps, when once released, might be cooled upon the persons of war demonstrators as well as of Socialists. Frankly, it must be admitted that the Socialists' demonstration was a failure. The war fever in Berlin had reached a temperature at which sanity and even, as was to be seen later, an official cold douche were equally

A FLIGHT FOR LIFE.

This extraordinary scene was the outcome of a swift and terrible German attack on Tirlemont. The town was shelled, and the inhabitants made such haste to get away that they left nearly all their belongings behind. The upper picture shows how the Germans treated the village of Mouland. The women were given half an hour in which to remove such of their belongings as had not been burnt, but the empty cart seems to suggest the burning had been thorough.

GERMANS ON THE MARCH.
The covers worn over their helmets are to hide the metal facings, which are too easily seen in the sun.

ineffective. Berlin was fighting mad whilst London was still discussing the Ulster crisis.

On Tuesday and Wednesday of the week of fate, whilst the Kaiser was in council at Potsdam, the war fever seemed to foreign observers to cool down a little; but night was made hideous with the incessant repetition of Haydn's beautiful tune to the Austrian National Anthem, to which is also set that astonishingly blatant German war-song, "Deutschland, Deutschland, ueber alles." Scarcely a street escaped the half-hourly visitations of bands made up largely of old men and young students—those, that is to say, who could do the shouting, but were in no danger of having to face cold steel.

It was an extraordinary exhibition, so utterly unlike the proverbial stern calm attributed to the "nation in arms," that one began to wonder whether this fevered excitement was not the product rather of alcohol than of enthusiasm. Long before the actual crisis had arisen, dispassionate observers realised that the part of the population reached by the popular German Press was just as hysterical as that of any other Continental capital. It must be remembered, however, that whilst the official and semi-official Press was still preaching peace, still declaring that Germany would not dream of moving a man or a gun so long as her own safety enabled her to withhold her hand, a number of people in Berlin, and in other great cities of Germany, were fully aware that the fighting flag had already been unfurled.

As early as July 6th and 7th—two or three days, that is to say, after the burial of the Archduke Franz Ferdinand at Artstetten — German officers attached to Colonial contingents, or on political service in Africa, had received a sudden notification that they might immediately take a holiday in Europe. The explanations given, as a South-West African official himself informed the writer, were of

THE CHURCH OF HAELEN.
Spire, tower, and roof were badly damaged by German guns

H

the flimsiest. At Swakopmund, the extraordinary excuse was offered that the officials were overworked ; that it had been a hot season ; that there was a heavy period of civil organisation coming ; that, in short, all officers of the active or reserve forces could leave immediately in order to catch a steamer which would take them home.

Telegrams notifying their return were received by their families, and many of their relatives, comparing notes with Colonial friends on leave in Germany, shook their heads and refused from that hour to believe the talk of peace.

In other cases reserve officers at home received hints—unofficially, it is true, but nevertheless from people most unlikely to be ill-informed—that they would do well to spend their holidays within the German frontiers. In short, for many reasons, a considerable proportion of the population of Berlin which was in touch with Army circles had made up its mind that the great fight was coming a full fortnight before the mobilisation orders were issued.

To some extent, also, the feeling of an impending crisis was accentuated by the Crown Prince's violent commentaries on bellicose books and pamphlets. Anglophobe and Russophobe writers received messages of high approval from the prince, who was certainly amongst those who neither expected nor desired anything save a violent outcome of the Servian crisis. It is not, therefore, surprising that the mob, unchecked by those who were supposed to maintain order in Berlin, spurred on by newspapers professing all manner of righteousness, and led— as the writer himself saw — in many cases by uniformed officials, broke out into an orgy of violent excitement such as has rarely or never before disgraced a civilised city.

The insults heaped upon the French, Russian, and English Ambassadors were the direct outcome of a State-aided, police-encouraged lawlessness. Independent and unprejudiced

"STAND BACK!"
John Bull helps little Belgium to bar the progress of the German invader.

witnesses asserted, for instance, that when ladies from the Russian Embassy left to take their train to the frontier, the mob began throwing stones at them and shouting the filthiest words at the women, whilst the police maintained for a long time an attitude of strictly passive disapproval. The whole fury of the populace was directed in the early days against Russia; the attack on the British Embassy was the result largely of bitter popular disappointment, consequent upon the steady flow of misleading information supplied throughout the crisis by the German authorities.

It is significant that the same angry crowd which several times attempted to mob the Russian Embassy divided their cheers almost impartially on more than one occasion between Austrian and British Embassies; whilst the French Embassy, in its exposed position on the Linden, was left almost entirely unnoticed.

If the purpose of the Government in assisting the Press to arouse the "furor Teutonicus" was to carry the public over the first days of panic, some such assistance was certainly badly needed. For many years the German financial authorities had organised down to the last pfennig the financial measures which would be necessary on the outbreak of a great European war.

They had calculated what the "panic demand for gold" would be, and taken their measures to meet it. It appears, however, that they had not calculated upon the sudden disappearance of small change, and the hoarding of silver, and even nickel, by shopkeepers. The writer took the trouble on Wednesday, July 29th, to experiment in various parts of Berlin with a series of banknotes of the value of ten shillings each. There was, of course, no difficulty

[Alfieri.

BELGIANS BURN THEIR OWN HOUSES.

In order to clear the ground in front of the fortifications near Antwerp, the Belgians had to raze many of their houses to the ground. The top photograph shows a soldier throwing paraffin over a cottage. In the oval picture a bucket of paraffin is being handed up for the destruction of the interior. The bottom picture shows the work almost completed.

in changing them in banks and railway stations; but small shopkeepers, bakers, dairymen, petty grocers and little tradesmen invariably gave the reply that they had no small change; in many cases they even refused half-sovereigns in gold, and some of them readily admitted that they were hoarding small change.

Of the few people outside the small special circle who knew definitely from the outset what was the character of the Austrian demands upon Servia, there was one man who had received some time before the middle of July an intimation that a collision between Germany and Russia might be expected. That man was Director Guttmann, of the Dresdner Bank. At a time when the German Foreign Office was assuring all and sundry that Germany was quite unacquainted with the character of the Austrian demands, the Crown Prince had already warned his friend, Director Guttmann, that the optimism displayed by the Berlin Stock Exchange was unwarranted, and might prove disastrous.

The Crown Prince himself is believed to have sent a warning to friends not to believe semi-official statements published by the " Frankfurter Zeitung " from Vienna, to the effect that the Austrian note to Servia would not take the form of an ultimatum. As a result of this warning, the Bourse to some extent discounted the crisis when it came, but the crash followed inevitably when the exchanges of Vienna, Budapest and elsewhere began to throw large masses of industrial securities on the German market.

A run on small savings banks by country depositors began as early as Saturday, July 25th, and the writer saw a letter written on that day by a farmer near Thorn, on the Russian frontier, in which he declared that it was even then impossible to obtain gold for large notes except at an absurd discount. This was doubtless due to the action of speculators who attempted to renew the coup brought off in 1911, when German £5 notes were bought for gold in the country districts at 10 to 20 per cent. discount.

THE DOGS OF WAR.

Our canine friends are playing a big part in the war. Motor-cyclist scouts use them to carry messages, and for seeking out the wounded they also prove useful. They even draw quick-firing guns.

On Tuesday, July 28th, there were large withdrawals of gold by German depositors; the great German banks warned managers of their branch establishments to pay gold reluctantly; in Charlottenburg and elsewhere in Western Berlin the banks refused to pay more than 10 per cent. of any call in gold, and then not more than £50 to any one person. The Imperial Bank lost two millions in withdrawals between Thursday, July 23rd, and Monday the 27th, while Monday and Tuesday saw an enormous rush on all municipal savings banks.

Long lines of women, chiefly domestic servants and factory hands, formed queues outside the main offices of the municipal savings bank. Throughout Tuesday the banks paid demands in full, but on Wednesday morning

A STRIKING ACHIEVEMENT.

With astounding secrecy a large British army was transported across the English Channel in the middle of August, 1914. The public knew nothing of it till it was officially announced that the force had been landed in France "without a single casualty." When it is remembered what has to be carried with an army—guns, horses, pontoons, etc.—it will be realised how remarkable was the feat.

The two top photographs show our men leaving the ship and being welcomed by French ladies. At the bottom (left hand) is a group of French and British soldiers fraternising, while on the right are our men preparing to take away the pontoons. The centre picture shows how horses are landed.

HOW OUR TRANSPORTS W
A French airship passing over a British destroyer and two submarines. From the dirigible, submerged

...rines would be easily discernible. With this protection the British transports were safe from molestation.

they put into force the clause allowing them to demand a month's notice before withdrawals, and on Thursday morning the offices were guarded by police armed with sabres and revolvers.

An attempt was made to continue dealing in some securities on the Bourse on a cash basis, but business was practically at a standstill three days before war was declared.

The fall in the value of securities on the Berlin Exchange, which was calculated between Tuesday and Wednesday at over one hundred millions, brought instant ruin to scores of people who a few days before had accounted themselves wealthy men. One of the best-known bankers in Thuringia, August Saal, shot himself in

his bank at Weimar on Wednesday night, leaving a note to state that he was faced by utter ruin. In Potsdam, Eugen Bieber, a well-known private banker, killed his wife and then took cyanide of potassium on Thursday morning. He left a statement to the effect that he had lost £13,000 in two days, and that the rest of his fortune was about to vanish.

A great Hanoverian bank, the Norddeutsche Handelsbank, with head offices at Geestemünde, closed on Wednesday night, July 29th, bringing ruin to hundreds of commercial and agricultural depositors

Paper money was now being refused throughout the provinces, and the early trains on Thursday brought a number of people from the country to Berlin in search of gold. By Thursday evening several private banks in Berlin had in turn suspended payment.

THE WONDERFUL ENTHUSIASM OF BRITAIN'S YOUNG MEN.
These three photographs tell a stirring tale. Hundreds of motor-cyclists mustered on Wimbledon Common, London, to offer their services to the Government. The Central London Recruiting Depot (bottom picture) was besieged by men eager to join the Army. The middle photograph shows recruits drilling in Hyde Park.

Simultaneously with this terrible crisis in the money market, there was a rush to obtain stores of provisions, with the result that prices advanced by 25 and 50 per cent. At Saarbrück, in the western war area, and at other places on the eastern and western frontiers, extraordinary scenes took place outside the shops of provision dealers. In several towns rioting broke out, the mob literally storming the stalls of flour merchants and dealers in tinned foods. Many tradesmen closed their doors, on the ground that their stock was exhausted, but before police protection could be obtained, the doors were burst in and the crowd seized what it could, throwing paper money on to the counter for payment, demanding no change, and only anxious to obtain a stock of provisions at any price.

Berlin was probably the last city to be affected by the food panic. Prices had advanced considerably on Thursday, July 30th, but the rush took place chiefly in Charlottenburg, for a reason which may be here explained.

Through Charlottenburg passes the great avenue, Kaiserdamm and Bismarck-Strasse, which forms the continuation of the military road

IN THE FIRST LINE OF DEFENCE.
Prince Albert, who has gone to his post in H.M.S. Collingwood.

A GOOD EXAMPLE.
H.R.H. The Prince of Wales sets a good example. He long ago learned how to handle a rifle, and, when war broke out, promptly joined the Grenadiers and went on active service.

OUR POPULAR PRINCE
is followed by a cheering crowd as he leaves Buckingham Palace for a walk.

from the camp at Döberitz. Along this road residents in Charlottenburg were accustomed to watch the passage of troops in the early morning; both on Wednesday and Thursday they had noticed that while apparently not more troops than usual were entering the city, all that came wore the new green-grey field uniform, and there was an unusual proportion of artillery.

Such news spreads quickly, and when it became known that a number of small tradesmen and professional men, who were also officers of the reserve, had closed their places of business without notice, the panic became widespread.

Before Thursday night the police had already summarily closed a number of small stores which were charging large prices for provisions of various kinds, and on Friday morning it was impossible to get paper money taken at any except big stores and establishments. The writer even failed to persuade a baker to take a 20-mark note (£1) in payment of a household bill for July.

In the meantime the Kaiser was preparing to stage as near a repetition as might be of the historic events preceding the victories of 1870. He had broken off his summer cruise only when Austria, in accordance unquestionably with the arrangements agreed upon with Germany, had rejected Servia's concessions. He arrived at Kiel on Monday morning, July 27th, and here the authorities permitted, if they did not actually encourage, a demonstration on the quays and jetties of the War Harbour.

Many people expected him to return immediately to Berlin, and big crowds surrounded the palace all day, but the Kaiser was faithful to the 1870 precedent. His special train, greeted all along the line by thousands, circled Berlin, and arrived soon after midday at the Royal Station of Wildpark, outside Potsdam. The Kaiserin had returned early in the day from her summer palace at Wilhelmshöhe, near Cassel, the scene of the famous "reconciliation" between the Kaiser and King Edward in 1907.

To keep up the fiction that Germany was not prepared for the war, and that nobody was more surprised than the Kaiser, a statement was issued from Potsdam to the effect that practically the whole of the palace staff—housekeepers, servants, cooks, lackeys, and scullions—had to be recalled by telegram late on Sunday night from their summer holidays as far north as Copenhagen, and south from the Austrian Tyrol. The gravity of the hour was reflected by the little group of people who met the Kaiser on his arrival at Wildpark.

Brown from his cruise, but with hollow eyes, and with a frown furrowing his forehead, the Kaiser stepped from his saloon. He handed the Kaiserin a bouquet of flowers, then turned at once to the Chancellor and Foreign Secretary. For nearly half an hour he talked to the two men, on whom nominally at least still rested the fate

"NO ROAD THIS WAY!"
How the Germans barricaded a railway arch near Liege. Note the sentries on guard above.

RUSSIA.
THE TSAR REVIEWS HIS TROOPS IN ST. PETERSBURG BEFORE DEPARTURE FOR THE WAR.

BELGIUM.
THE CIVIC GUARDS OF BRUSSELS THROW UP TRENCHES IN THE OUTSKIRTS OF THE CITY.

BRITAIN.
SWANSEA WOMEN WHOSE HUSBANDS AND SONS ARE ON ACTIVE SERVICE WAITING TO REGISTER FOR ARMY PAY.

THE BRITISH EXPEDITIONARY FORCE IN BOULOGNE.

of Europe. Gradually, as he talked, the frown relaxed ; then he turned to the naval and military officers, the heads of his War Cabinets, the representatives of the Admiralty and the General Staff, and the generals of his own headquarters staff, who stood in a group waiting with such patience as they could command, until the political conversations were at an end.

It was a scene significant of the events which were to follow. There were scarcely more than three hundred people outside the station when the Royal car whirled the War Lord to the New Palace, which he was only to leave again clothed in the grey-green uniform in which he later travelled to the front.

Throughout Tuesday and Wednesday, whilst the panic following the war fever swept through the country and affected his capital, the Kaiser remained in council at Potsdam. A curious incident of these days was the smuggling into Berlin of the Crown Prince by a little local station—it was feared that a colossal demonstration on the arrival of the " Black Prince " might evoke from him some untimely explosion such as would unmask the German intentions.

Accordingly the prince travelled from Zoppot before daybreak to the outer platform at Charlottenburg. Here a closed car awaited him and took him to Potsdam, where he had a long conference with the Kaiser. On Wednesday the Kaiser held a conference which began at 5.30 p.m., and lasted until the early hours of Thursday morning. Apparently there were actually two conferences, in one of which the Kaiser received the plans for the immediate

COLOURS FOR IRISH NATIONALIST VOLUNTEERS.
Mr. John Redmond, M.P., having declared that Irish Volunteers, both Nationalist and Ulster, could be relied upon to defend Ireland against any invader, presents colours to the Maryborough Corps of Nationalists.

future arranged by Admiral von Tirpitz and the chief of the Admiralty staff ; the other, according to information obtained later, appears to have been a final discussion with the Chancellor and the Foreign Secretary, and will no doubt have been mainly concerned with the carefully made plans for maintaining the appearance of pacific intentions to the last moment.

The White Book, published by the German Foreign Office on the following Tuesday, August 4th, gave details of the communications which at this time were passing between the Kaiser and Tsar. There must apparently have been a contest of opinion at this historic conference of Wednesday, July 29th, for while a number of communiqués issued from Potsdam during the evening referred to the pacific character of Russian assurances, the "Lokalanzeiger" was empowered, clearly by the military authorities,

GERMANS UNDER ARREST AT SWANSEA DOCKS.

AN UNEXPECTED SEASIDE ATTRACTION. Recruits drilling on the sands in South Wales.

GENTLEMEN RANKERS. The London Artists Corps drilling in a churchyard.

to declare that these assurances were in grave contrast to Russian military preparations.

It was believed in Berlin that the General Staff had demanded and all but secured the Kaiser's signature to the order for mobilisation soon after midnight on Wednesday, July 29th, and colour is lent to this view by an extraordinary incident on Thursday afternoon. Shortly after two the "Lokalanzeiger" scattered broadcast over the city special editions, distributed gratis, announcing that a general mobilisation had been declared.

Long before that announcement could be contradicted, the news had spread like wild-fire through the city. It had even been telegraphed by the Russian Ambassador to St. Petersburg, and in all quarters, officers and men were hurrying to their appointed quarters. The explanation given by the "Lokalanzeiger" was so absurd that it may be worth while to quote it.

The paper asserted that a junior member of the staff, left in charge whilst the managing editor, news editor, and others were at luncheon, had heard a rumour that mobilisation was ordered, and big with a sense of his own importance had hurriedly sent out the special edition ready prepared. It is more probable that the unfortunate junior member of the staff had actually nothing whatever

PRIVATE SELF-SACRIFICE.
Lord Tredegar's yacht Liberty, lent for use as a hospital ship.

to do with the blunder, and that the "rumour" took the form of a telephone message to the chief editor from the General Staff, which was openly discontented at the necessity imposed upon it of calling in the reserves without the official proclamation of mobilisation.

Thus Thursday passed in anxiety, uncertainty and

NEW USE FOR A BIG SHOP.
A famous trading establishment in Brussels which became a hospital during the earliest days of the war.

panic. On Friday morning people were beginning to believe that Russia had once more " climbed down." Even officers stoutly maintained up to noon that there would be no war, and a number of English people who had arranged to leave Berlin by the Flushing and Hook of Holland trains at one o'clock went so far as

THE RED CROSS OVER A ROYAL PALACE.
King Albert set a good example by handing over his Brussels palace for the benefit of the wounded.

to cancel their plans. Those who were better informed or better advised had good reason to congratulate themselves.

Ten minutes after the train had left the station a bugle was sounded somewhere along the military road, and before two a storm of special papers burst over the city, containing the news in curt official language that the Kaiser, in conformity with paragraph 68 of the Imperial Constitution, had decreed a state of war throughout all Germany except Bavaria, and that his Majesty would return at once to Berlin. " As in 1870."

If the population in Berlin, long taught in every school to regard the history of 1870 as a kind of German

RED RUIN.
A wrecked Belgian house being guarded against looters.

TO HAMPER THE GERMANS
The Belgians destroyed their own railway, from Landen to St. Croud, to delay the advance of the invaders.

THE EFFECT OF A GERMAN SHELL ON A HOUSE IN HAELEN, BELGIUM.

gospel, had failed hitherto to trace in the Emperor's conduct of affairs his faithful adherence to the great precedent, it made no such mistake now. Throwing all business to the winds, the population flocked to the city, and tightly packed crowds, such as Berlin had never seen before, thronged every available inch of room from the Brandenburg Gate to the Royal palace.

The sound of the well-known bugle on the Royal car awoke a tornado of cheers, which swept from the entry of the city through the park to the palace. Again and again the Royal car was held up by the crowd, pressing round to cheer. By three o'clock the Kaiser had entered his palace, and for the first time since he left Berlin to welcome the British Squadron at Kiel. the Imperial Standard floated again over the ancient roof.

It had been expected that the proclamation of the state of war would be followed immediately by the order for general mobilisation, but the Kaiser and his advisers proposed to play a crafty game to the end.

By 4.30 p.m. the civil government of Germany had disappeared. All public offices banks, stations. and the palaces of the princes were doubly and trebly guarded by sentries with fixed bayonets The police, now appearing everywhere with revolvers worn outside their coats, interfered right and left to close shops offending against the orders controlling the price of provisions, and commanding the acceptance of paper money, which had been issued by the general commanding in the Mark (or district) of Brandenburg

Berlin as a self-governing community had disappeared from the map; she was now no more than a portion of the " Mark Command." From this moment, every German who had attended a government school knew what was expected of him. The order of events was laid down in advance, and some 6,000 Berliners, fully aware of the next stage in the great drama, flocked to the palace, there to await the speech that was coming. About a quarter past six the Kaiser, with all his family, appeared on the great bronze balcony, from which forty-four years previously his grandfather had addressed the tiny population of Berlin on the outbreak of the war with France.

It was some minutes before the wild storm of cheering could be sufficiently quelled to enable the Kaiser to be heard. Finally his naval son, Prince Adalbert, stepped to the railings of the balcony and held up both hands. Then there was a sudden hush, and in a voice that rang out over the enormous crowd the Kaiser said:

A VALUABLE ARM OF THE FRENCH FORCE.
The mounted infantry, when awheel, can move quickly on the roads, and are also well able to get through wooded or otherwise difficult country by folding up their machines and carrying them on their backs.

" This is a dark day and a dark hour The crisis which is forced upon us is of no diplomat's making, but the result of an envy which for years has pursued Germany. The sword is being forced into my hand. If, at this last hour, the efforts I am making fail to bring our opponents to their senses, I trust that, with God's help, we shall so wield the sword that when all is over we may sheathe it again with honour. This war will demand of us enormous sacrifice in life and money, but we shall show to God. Go to church and, our foes what it means to provoke Germany. And now I commend you all kneeling there, pray Heaven to help our gallant army."

Gradually the crowd began to disperse from the palace, and about an hour later there issued from the postern gate facing the Spree a motor closed and with the blinds drawn. It hurried by side streets through the town to the park, and then turning up through the famous Avenue of Victory crossed to the quiet Bellevue Palace, the favourite Berlin residence of the Kaiserin. In the car were Prince Oscar, the Kaiser's fourth soldier-son, and his fiancée, Countess Anna Bassewitz. Almost unnoticed by the immense crowds the Royal family gathered in a quiet room overlooking the English garden at the side of the palace, and here took place the first of those " war-nuptials " which were the most prominent feature of the churches of Berlin throughout Saturday.

The twenty-four hours which followed will never be forgotten by those who spent them in the Kaiser's capital. All night long crowds, no longer jubilant but silent, and exceedingly anxious, waited in suspense outside the public offices and the Royal palace. At any hour the order for mobilisation might be expected, but as hour by hour passed, and still the fateful announcement did not appear, a curious sense of disappointment came over the city. At midnight it was known that Germany had presented to Russia an ultimatum which it was supposed must expire in the early hours of Saturday.

On Saturday morning it was learned that the ultimatum expired at eleven o'clock, Berlin time, and now once more a crowd, no longer cheering but with blanched faces and eyes heavy and drawn from the all-night watch, began to gather round the palace. A tremor ran through the whole city; the atmosphere was no longer charged with war fever or excitement There was an ultimatum, everybody knew, to France as well as to Russia, and so

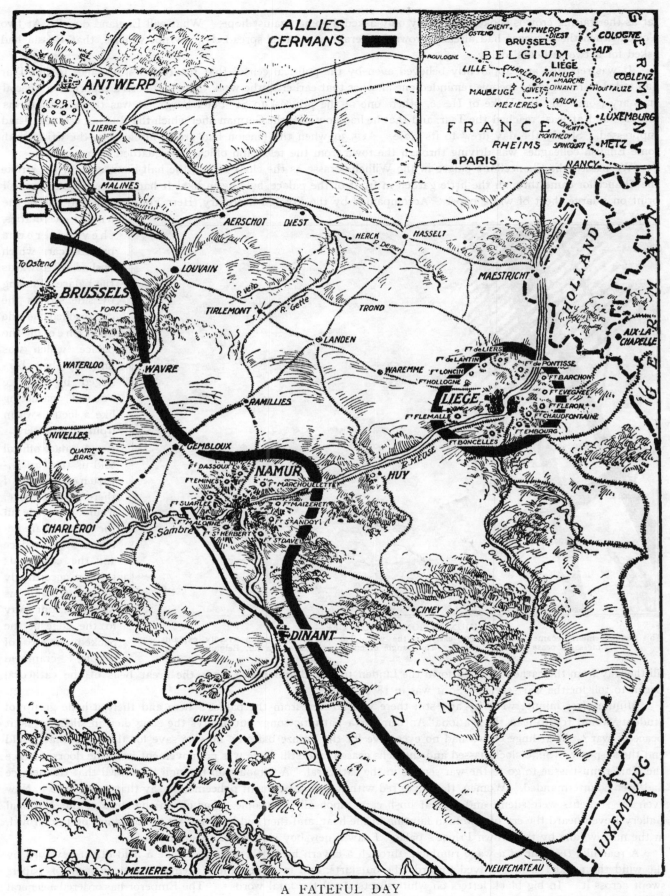

A FATEFUL DAY

This map shows, roughly, how the German and Allied Armies were placed the day before Namur so unexpectedly fell. The nearest point of the French frontier is one day's march south of Namur.

far as the waiting crowds spoke at all, they only asked, hoping against hope, " What will England do ? "   At two o'clock, when the suspense had already grown intolerable a rumour spread. I know not whence, that Russia had asked for a twelve hours' delay.

It was reported and apparently believed even by the political censor that the Kaiser's messages to the Tsar had failed to reach him : people reminded one another that earlier in the week there had been a report of a special emissary (some said the Duke of Hesse, others one of the princes) to St. Petersburg.   It was thought that this message had at least reached the Tsar, and that he had now seen the German offer which the Russian war party had suppressed.   Slowly the day drew to its close.   At 5.30, when the tension had grown intolerable, the writer with some English colleagues was driving through the town from the telegraph office, now guarded by reservists.

We passed the Chancellor's palace in the Wilhelmstrasse as the clock struck the half-hour, and on the stroke the Chancellor came through the little garden in front of the palace, holding in his left hand three or four lines of print on a large sheet of white paper.   Accompanied by the Foreign Secretary, Herr Von Jagow, and one of the

under-secretaries, they entered a private car, which dashed off towards the palace. Passing by side streets the car reached the side entrance of the palace, which was immediately be-sieged by a huge crowd, gathering like a locust-swarm from all quarters.

A palace official told us that an an-nouncement, if there were one, would be made in the great square be-tween the palace and the cathedral ; thither accordingly we drove, and as we made our way to the edge of the packed mass of people, crammed

"COMMUNICATION IS CUT OFF——
This announcement became common very early in the war. The above photograph vividly explains why messages cease to come through. This tangle of cut wires is near Namur, Belgium.

all the way from the cathedral steps down the Linden to the Brandenburg Gate, the great bells of the cathedral began to toll for the war service.   So it was in 1870.

Minute after minute went by and still there was no sign from the palace ; here and there a little group of students would try to lead the National Anthem, or a patriotic song, but always the song died in silence. Is it peace or war ? That huge crowd had no eyes save for the bronze balcony, no ears save for the word that would end the suspense. Six o'clock passed and the bells ceased, and still there was no movement from the doors whence the Kaiser must issue to go to the war service in the cathedral.   A rumour ran through the crowd that the service had been countermanded. Women, their eyes red with weeping, besought policemen to say that it was true.   Now even the students were silent, and a great hush came upon all the people. Far off on the steps of the National Gallery I even heard the cry of a woman fainting in the heat, and then suddenly out on the outskirts of the crowd, in the narrow lane by the Crown Prince's palace, I saw a newsboy wave a white sheet.

A roar like the roar of a wave rumbling through a cavern broke the silence.   Like a field of corn swayed by the wind the packed crowd swayed towards the outskirts, and in an instant it seemed the snowstorm of papers swept across it.   In big black letters on white sheets stood the fatal words : " The Emperor has ordered a general mobilisation of all the armed forces of the Empire."   The die was cast.

If the original outbreak of war frenzy a week before had been striking, the sudden quiet which came over Berlin for twenty-four hours after the issue of the mobilisation order was no less remarkable. It was sufficiently comprehensible, h o w e v e r, simply because the city now had time to think. It is true that on Sunday and Monday gold and silver change appeared to have vanished from circulation, and it is true also that there was no cessation of the extraordinary spy - hunting mania, whereof some account follows below, but on the whole Germany seemed on the first day of mobilisation to have recovered its wits.

The Kaiser, still playing the 1870 drama, caused it

WAR IN THE AIR.
A naval Zeppelin. In this class of aircraft Germany easily holds the lead.

to be announced that patriotic demonstrations in front of the palace could no longer be permitted as he urgently required complete rest. A cordon of military and police was accordingly drawn all round the palace, the public being completely excluded from the precincts. This, too, was in accordance with 1870 precedent. The most striking incident of the Sunday was the great open-air service on the Königsplatz. Round the Bismarck statue thirty thousand men and women, reservists and their kinfolk, assembled, as it were on the battlefield. At half-past eleven high above the immense crowd appeared the black cassock and white bands of the preacher, whilst behind him the sun shone in noontide blaze on the gilded roof of the Reichstag buildings. A military band led the chorale, " Let us now pray unto the God of Justice."

Thereafter one of the Court chaplains, Dr. Döhring, delivered a stirring address on a text taken from the Revelation of St. John, chap. ii. verse 10 : " Be thou faithful unto death, and I will give thee a crown of life." Then followed the moment of intensest pathos in this historic week. Lifting his hand where he stood on the dais at the foot of the statue of the Iron Chancellor, Dr. Döhring began to recite the Lord's Prayer, a n d sentence by sentence that

H.M. SEAPLANE 126.
This machine, which carries a quick-firing gun, and is much more mobile than an airship, is one of many of the kind keeping watch on the East Coast.

huge congregation repeated the prayer after him. Women burst into tears, and strong men hid their faces ; then once more the military band gave the signal, and from thirteen thousand voices rose the famous chorale, the Niederlaendische Dankgebet, the hymn which a hundred years before had proclaimed to the world the end of Napoleon's reign of terror on the battlefield of Waterloo.

In silence, as befitted this wonderful service, the congregation broke up and streamed east and west, north and south, back to their homes. They were compelled to go for the most part on foot, because trams, underground railways, motor-'buses, and taxi-cabs were overcrowded by reservists hurrying to their appointed quarters.

It was curious to note that whereas all through the week theatres, cafés, and dancing-halls had been almost empty, now, when the tension was over, all places of amusement appeared to fill again. The " city that knows no night " went about its customary Sunday pleasures as though the imperial commander had issued the order " Carry on."

Passing the principal cafés of the Friedrichstrasse at about two o'clock on Sunday morning I found them as full as at any time in the height of Berlin's most fashionable season. The bands were playing ragtime music, and people were dancing as though the whole terrible week of panic had been but a nightmare an evil dream from which the city had awakened. If in the hour of fate " Business as usual " was the motto of London, " Pleasure as usual " was assuredly the motto of Berlin.

Elsewhere very different scenes were being enacted. Immediately after the proclamation of a state of siege on Friday the leading newspapers had published, doubtless on the suggestion of the military authorities, the craziest incitements to violence against foreigners. It was the duty of all good citizens, the papers declared, not only to keep their eyes open for people who might be supposed to have evil intentions against railway bridges, stations, post offices, and the like, but instantly to unmask the spies and hand them over for summary justice to the military authorities.

WIRING A MINE.
British sailors putting the finishing touches to a mine just before submerging.

The result was a craze for spy-hunting which would almost have been humorous had its results not been so infamous. At the corner of the Brandenburg Gate a German officer who rashly appeared in a worn uniform instead of the new field-grey was surrounded by a mob, which tore the coat from his shoulders, battered him, and then handed him over to the police When he had established his identity he was calmly informed that it was better the people should make a few mistakes than that one spy should escape detection

At no time within the last ten years, at any rate, had Prussian officialdom, particularly such part of it as could claim any kind of military or police authority, been distinguished by its moderation When civil government was suspended, the military bloodhounds that had so long strained against the leash were let loose indeed. In some instances, reported to the writer not by foreigners, but by German friends, ladies who came into collision with Prussian officers on the side-walks or in the crowd received swinging buffets from their country's uniformed defenders ; old men who failed to get out of the way of these heroes sufficiently quickly were knocked down, whilst every petty official felt himself at last master of all civilians in Berlin, and made no effort to disguise his contempt for everyone out of uniform.

The extraordinary spy-mania which ran through the country on the heels of the crazy newspaper proclamation

Bassano

Field Marshal Earl Kitchener
Secretary of State for War.

Poor country-folk in the neighbourhood of Brussels fleeing from their burning villages along the high road to the capital.   Inset : Kaiser with busby of the "Death's Head" Dragoons.

THE GHASTLY SYMBOL OF A CHRISTIAN EMPEROR AND SOME EXAMPLES OF HIS HANDIWORK.
The happy, prosperous village of Mouland, in Belgium, after the German barbarians had done with it.

K

THE UNAVAILING BARRICADES OF BELGIUM'S CAPITAL.
Owing to the prudent decision of the Belgian Government not to defend the city against the invaders, the numerous hastily thrown-up barricades had all to be removed before the Germans entered Brussels on August 20th, 1914.

referred to before, produced probably its mildest effect in Berlin. Many hours before there was even talk of war with England, American newspaper correspondents on their way to Russia were held up at small German stations, thrown into prison-cells with common criminals, and kept there for days, despite the protests of the American Embassy.

The energies of the population, no longer occupied in cheering the Kaiser, or trying to kiss the hands of generals leaving the public offices, were diverted to the game of spy-hunting. The entire country completely lost its head, and the possession of a well-cut coat, a well-filled pocket-book, and particularly of a motor-car, was sufficient to ensure for almost any foreigner prompt arrest and usually maltreatment.

The spy-hunt will remain one of the blackest chapters in the history of the German Empire, and it should **The duplicity of the Kaiser** not be forgotten that it began and was officially advocated at a time when the Kaiser was still talking of eleventh-hour efforts for peace. So far as the food panic was concerned, it appeared to have considerably decreased as soon as the civil government was replaced by military control. Maximum prices were established on Friday, and people were reminded of a fact that they had apparently overlooked—namely, that all the great cities had taken measures as early as Wednesday to secure large reserves of flour.

At the time of the outbreak of war Berlin had within its boundaries a sufficient supply of rye and wheat meal to carry the civil population over a period of about fourteen days. In addition, arrangements had been made for bringing supplies to the city by canal, as it was recognised that the transportation of foodstuffs over the railways would be impossible, at any rate for several weeks. Acting on the advice of Professor Ballod, some cities —including, it was understood, Dresden, Leipzig, and Frankfurt—had already stored a large reserve of flour and foodstuffs.

The most immediate need, before war had actually broken out, was rather for means of transportation than

WAR-WEARY BELGIANS RESTING BY THEIR GUNS AT NAMUR BEFORE THE FINAL BOMBARDMENT.

A BITTER DAY FOR BRUSSELS

Silent crowd of Belgians watching the march of the conquerors through their undefended capital.   Inset: The Palace of Justice at Brussels.

The rumbling ammunition waggons in the spectacular procession of the Teutonic War Lord passing down the Boulevard Botanique.

Flaunting the Kaiser's strength of arms before the humbled subjects of King Albert.

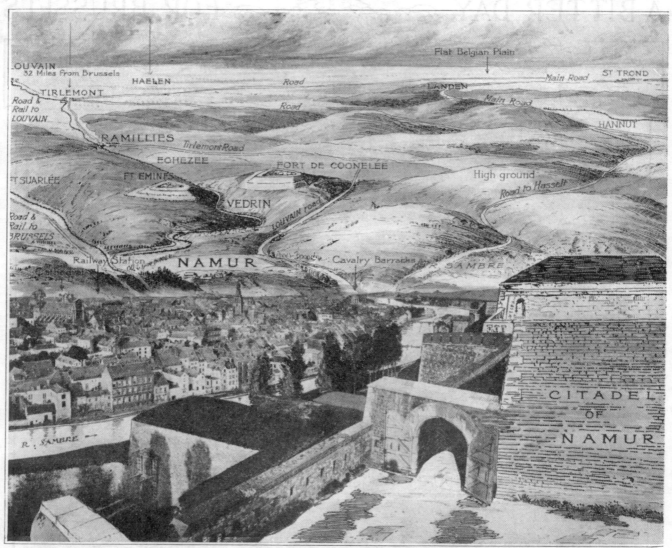

BIRD'S-EYE VIEW OF THE LAND BETWEEN THE FORTIFIED TOWNS OF LIEGE AND NAMUR—
When Vise had been sacked and burnt and Liege taken, the Belgians hotly contested the advance of the enemy at Tongres, Hasselt,
St. Trond, Landen, Haelen, Diest, and Tirlemont.

for actual produce. The big dairies found their horses commandeered, so that in many cases they were unable to supply milk through large areas ; in some parts of the city milk was virtually unobtainable throughout Saturday, there having been apparently no organisation in existence to provide, so far as concerned this and similar matters, for the emergency needs of the civil population.

There was one other feature of the commencement of mobilisation which must have forcibly struck all who witnessed it. Although the mobilisation was nominally proclaimed on Saturday evening, it was actually in force practically throughout Germany to the full extent on Friday evening. Trains were everywhere com-

Mobilisation a fact before proclamation mandeered by the military authorities, luggage vans were hastily cleared wherever they happened to be ; luggage was simply piled by the side of the railways, for the most part without any attempt to get it under cover, or to make it possible for owners to identify it later. It was just at the end of the German holiday season, which began with the commencement of the school holidays on July 3rd.

There was a wild rush of people from the holiday resorts in the mountains and by the sea, and large numbers of holiday-makers with their families were caught on Friday by the sudden seizure of the railways for military purposes. It is true that they might have taken warning, but it must be remembered that civilians in Germany had no experience of any such disorganisation of traffic as now took place, and it seems improbable that many of those whose luggage was thus summarily ejected can ever have recovered their property. Possibly this seizure of the railways before the public announcement was necessary, but at least it was significant of the complete disregard of the civilian and his needs which inspired military Germany from the hour when the crisis became acute.

—AROUND WHICH THE SEVEREST FIGHTING TOOK PLACE DURING THE OPENING WEEKS OF THE WAR.
After the occupation of Louvain and Brussels, the German forces executed a great turning movement towards Namur, whose ancient citadel looks down on the Meuse and Sambre, some 600 feet below, and captured the town on August 24th, 1914.

There were two more dramatic scenes which a few English residents in Berlin were able to watch before England, too, declined any longer to submit to the German menace. On Tuesday morning, August 4th, while the question of peace or war with England still hung for a moment in the balance, the Kaiser held a solemn opening session of the Reichstag in the White Hall of the Imperial Palace, that same hall where, little more than a year before, he had welcomed the King of England and the Tsar of Russia to the marriage of his daughter. Now, as then, a group of pages in the silver livery of the Kings of Prussia took away the few chairs in the great hall, and threw open behind the dais the windows, through which the noon sun poured into the magnificent chamber. Then, by twos and threes, came the black-coated members of the Imperial Parliament, never so insignificant or so impotent as in this hour of fate.

The fateful figure in grey-green To the left of the throne stood in double row the members of the Federal Council, ablaze with their decorations and military insignia; opposite them, under the marble gallery, where the Kaiserin sat with her daughter, the Duchess of Brunswick, on one side and the Crown Princess on the other, stood the generals comprising the Kaiser's headquarters staff. When the room had thus filled, with the uniforms diversified here and there by the sombre black of a few Reichstag members (many of whom were themselves wearing the uniform of lieutenants of the reserve), a little procession formed near the doors of the private chapel and came slowly down the white staircase.

The Chancellor, in his major's uniform, walked between the Foreign Secretary and the Secretary to the Treasury; behind them came the rest of the Imperial Secretaries; and last of all, alone and unattended, fully ten steps behind his adjutants, strode a short, lean figure in the grey-green uniform of field service, with the Prussian pickel-haube instead of his eagle-helmet. A low, half-suppressed cheer was raised by the members of the Reichstag as the Kaiser strode through the hall and took his stand under the black and red canopy, over which stood the blazon of the Black Eagle.

With a low obeisance, the Chancellor handed to the Kaiser the formal official text of the Royal address. It was a repetition of what Kaiser and Chancellor had already said, a claim that German policy was upright, and a denunciation of the envy, hatred, and malice which for years had pursued German progress and prosperity.

THE FLIGHT TO AND FROM BRUSSELS.

Before its occupation by the Germans the roads to and from Brussels were filled with refugees on foot and in all kinds of vehicles, carrying the few household articles they hurriedly gathered on leaving their homes. The great railway stations at Brussels were besieged by immense crowds anxious to get to Ostend and Antwerp.

The Kaiser read the speech in short, staccato explosions; his voice was choked with anger, or appeared so. Then, throwing aside the sheet of paper, he came down to the first step of the dais, and made his appeal for German unity in the face of the coming danger. "I have no knowledge any longer of party or creed, I know only Germans, and in token thereof I ask all of you to give me your hands."

One by one the leaders of all the parties, except the Socialists, stepped forward to grasp the outstretched hand of the War Lord. Then the Kaiser turned on his heel, and whilst a triple cheer rang out in the Council chamber, he walked with bowed head towards the stairway.

An hour later the members of the Reichstag assembled again in their own gilded chamber on the Koenigsplatz. With the barest of preliminaries the session was opened, and the Chancellor rose to demand the most colossal war credit ever asked of any nation in the world's history. Two hundred and sixty-five millions of pounds was the sum Germany required for the beginning of her war, and the Reichstag, Socialists included, voted it without a dissenting vote. Germans were already on Belgian soil, the world was in arms against the Empire, and Germany must hack her way through! Such were the ringing words wherewith the philosopher-Chancellor hurled German defiance in the face of England and of the world.

Before five o'clock on Tuesday afternoon there was no longer any question that Germany had torn up all treaties, all her most solemn undertakings, and was prepared to defy the armies of this generation and the judgment of all the generations that are to come.

BELGIAN INFANTRY FIGHTING A RETIRING ACTION IN THE WITHDRAWAL FROM LOUVAIN.

"RIDER AND HORSE—FRIEND, FOE, IN ONE RED BURIAL BLENT!"
Lord Byron's famous line from his verses on Waterloo is illustrated in ghastly reality by this photograph of an actual scene from one of Belgium's many stricken fields.

CHAPTER VII.—FRANCE ON THE EVE OF WAR.
By an Eye-Witness.

Gathering of the War Clouds—Menace of Germany's Increased Army—Three Years' Service Bill Introduced—Political Plot Against the President—Inner History of the Caillaux Trial—Germany's Declaration of War—How France Received It—Mobilisation of the Army—German Shops Raided—Paris, a City of Silence—War Minister's Confidence.

AWAITED constantly for forty-four years, yet entirely unexpected when it came at last—so it was that the greatest of all the great struggles of her history began for France.

The political volcano of Europe had rumbled and threatened so often without any eruption taking place that Frenchmen, although as individuals they follow international affairs with a closer interest than any nation, had begun to believe that the danger existed rather in imagination than in fact. The crisis of 1908, when Austria converted into annexation her occupation of Bosnia and Herzegovina, had caused a moment of acute tension, but Russia gave way before the menacing attitude of allied Austria and Germany, and Europe's peace had remained unbroken.

Germany's bold bid for a share in Morocco in 1911, and especially the drastic step of sending the cruiser Panther **Rumblings before** to seize the port of Agadir, sent another thrill of apprehension through France **the storm** and through all Europe. The wars in the Balkans that began in the autumn of 1912 involved international questions so delicate that it seemed impossible for the Great Powers not to be drawn into the struggle.

Yet when the Balkans had at last returned to a state of precarious peace, not a shot had been exchanged by the soldiers of the six great countries of Europe. The sabre had often been rattled; it had never been drawn.

Nevertheless, the Government of France had been lulled to no false security. Often as danger-points had been passed, frequently though the peace of Europe had been preserved when it seemed almost inevitably lost, the more enlightened of French statesmen kept their eyes closely fixed on the barely veiled preparations which

BARRICADES IN THE STREETS OF BRUSSELS.

the ambitious eastern neighbour of their country was ceaselessly making with the aim of attempting to seize by force the position of world-preponderance which she was unable to attain by peaceful means.

The enormous increase in the German forces announced in April of 1913, which was to bring the peace strength of the German Army up to the unprecedented figure of 866,000 men, demanded an instant reply from France, if the margin of military strength between herself and her rival were not to be allowed to broaden beyond all possibility of adjustment. However much it might be urged in Germany that the menace of the ever-growing military strength of Russia was the reason for the constant increase of the German Army, France realised that it was herself that these vast armaments chiefly threatened. For she knew that if the day of war came, the slowness with which the mobilisation of her Russian ally must necessarily be carried out would expose her, for a month at any rate, to the full weight of the German military power. During that month every effort would be made to crush France, in time to hurry the victorious German armies back across the whole width of the Empire to meet the slowly gathering hosts of Russia.

BELGIAN COLUMN ON THE MARCH TO THE VICTORIOUS BATTLE OF HAELEN.
The progress of the troops was screened by artillery fire from the wooded country in the background. On their arrival at Haelen they succeeded in effecting a decided check to the invaders.

It was the perception of this danger that brought into being the famous " Three Years' Service Bill," which, after dividing France into two bitterly opposed camps for eighteen months, was recognised at last, when the storm burst, as the salvation of the nation.

It was in March, 1913, that the Briand Ministry introduced a Bill for increasing the term of service with the colours from two to three years. In Germany, where a population of 64,000,000 had always provided a margin of men over and above the requirements of recruiting, it had been easy to enlarge the Army by merely calling to service with the colours a number of recruits who would otherwise have been allowed to pass the category of men capable of service but untrained, known as the " Ersatz Reserve."

France had no such superfluity to draw upon. Her population of 40,000,000 has remained practically stationary for some years past. How was she to reply to the increase which Germany had resolved upon for her own Army?

There was only one solution, but it was a desperate one. Each individual Frenchman must be called upon to make the sacrifice of another

SANDBAG BARRICADE IN A BRUSSELS STREET.

THE COURAGEOUS CIVIL GUARD OF BRUSSELS NOT RECOGNISED AS SOLDIERS.
Before entering Brussels the Germans intimated that they could not "recognise" the Civil Guard as soldiers. Despite their protests, the men were marched to the Town Hall and had there to deliver up their weapons. Many wept at not being allowed to fight the invaders.

whole year of his life for the defence of his country. The least reflection is enough to bring home to anyone how tremendous an effort this change in her military service meant for France. It implied the almost incalculable loss to the industry of the nation of an extra year of the life of every one of her able-bodied sons, and that year must be surrendered at the very time when the men concerned were at the zenith of health and energy and ambition.

On the threshold of manhood the career of every sound Frenchman would be interrupted in order that he might spend three years in the unproductive tasks and amid the narrowing surroundings of the barrack and the camp. However well a French youth

THE WAR OFFICE, BRUSSELS,
at the outbreak of the war.

might have spent the apprenticeship of his later boyhood, he stood a great chance of losing all that he had learnt during the long three years that he would be obliged to devote to dull garrison routine, before he could start in earnest on his life's work.

It is small wonder that this gigantic tax on the very life's blood of the nation's industry aroused the bitterest opposition among the working classes who would be called upon to contribute most dearly to it. Many schemes for half measures—such as service for thirty months—were proposed by the more moderate antagonists of the Three Years' Bill, but all were rejected by the Army Commission and the Chamber.

L

The Socialist party organised a powerful agitation against the Bill, and urged, instead, the adoption of the favourite scheme of its eloquent leader, Jean Jaures, who advocated a " national militia " system, based on six months' preliminary service with the colours, followed by eight periods of eleven to twenty-one days' field training between the ages of twenty-one and thirty-four.   In this idea of the " armed nation," the Socialists saw, indeed, a first step towards the realisation of an assured condition of world-peace.

A national militia, they argued, could never be used for purposes of aggression ; while, on the other hand, no Foreign State could hope to attack with any chance of success a whole people in arms, organised and led by officers of its own choosing.   But these schemes, though agreeable in theory, were futile in presence of the

Socialistic theories disappear in war

national danger which threatened France, and the chiefs of the French Army, which is already one of the most democratic in the world, had little trouble in convincing everyone but M. Jaures and his obstinate followers in the Chamber of Deputies that the splendid Army of Germany, the most severely disciplined and highly trained in all the history of war, could not be faced with a host of semi-trained militiamen, however patriotic their spirit and democratic their principles.

The Briand Ministry fell from office on another vexed question—that of proportional representation in elections for the Chamber of Deputies—but the Barthou Cabinet, which succeeded it, carried on the struggle for the Three Years' Bill, and in July it became law, and was promulgated.   The Socialists organised mass demonstrations against it, and the staccato jeer of " Hou, Hou ! les trois ans ! " became for a time a familiar shout in the streets of Paris —or even, when the Socialist demonstrators met the counter-manifestations of patriotic societies, a political battle-cry.

There were indeed serious outbreaks of mutiny against the new period of service in some of the garrisons on the eastern frontier, and particularly at Rodez (Aveyron), where the colonel of a battalion was attacked by his men, and only prevented them from breaking out of barracks to march to a midnight demonstration against Three

A WOUNDED BARBARIAN IN THE HUMANE HANDS OF A CHIVALROUS FOE.

After a skirmish with the local gendarmerie outside Ostend on August 25th, a number of wounded Uhlans were brought into the town. They were treated with humane solicitude by captors far too chivalrous to rival the ruthless example of the Kaiser's vengeful cavalrymen.

Years' Service by standing in the gateway with a loaded rifle and threatening to shoot the first man who tried to pass.

The investigations and courts-martial which followed proved that these outbreaks had been organised by the General Confederation of Labour, the great Syndicalist organisation of France. The Government took in hand at once the task of abolishing the secret means which the Syndicalists had used in their attempts to corrupt the allegiance of the French soldier, the chief of them being a system for the distribution of pocket-money bribes called the "sou de soldat." The secretary of the federation was imprisoned.

Amid all this travail, however, Three Years' Service in France was born. In spite of the loud protests of the politicians, in spite of the secret plotting of the Anarchists, the great mass of the French nation resigned itself patiently to the heavy burden. None the less, they realised two things—one, that they had played their last card, and that if the Germans availed themselves of their fifty per cent. advantage of population to add yet another increase to their Army, France would be left without any reply to make; and the other, that the sacrifices they had now consented to make in labour, in time, and in loss of wealth resulting from reduced

BRAGGART UHLANS SHOW THEMSELVES COWARDS AT HEART.
Belgian peasants report that the scouting parties of Uhlans who first reached their villages were extremely suspicious of evil play. Having demanded refreshments, they refused to drink from the glasses offered them until some of the villagers supped the drink, and thus proved it had not been poisoned. And these are the creatures who ravished Belgian women and children.

output, were so heavy that war itself could add but little to them except the fact of actual bloodshed.

In the autumn of 1913 the last Frenchman to do Two Years' Service left the colours, and two drafts, the recruits of twenty-one years and at the same time the class aged twenty, who would otherwise not have come up for service till the following year, were added to the Army. France's reply to the increased armaments of Germany was made.

Meanwhile, what cause of quarrel was in sight ? The most cautious statesman might have answered in the early summer of 1914 that there was none. The old idea of a "war of revenge" had died in France with the

France had ceased to dream revenge

generation that remembered 1870. Paul Déroulede, the tall, gaunt, fiery, picturesque orator and poet, was the last of the preachers of undying hatred for the German. He died in February, 1914. Paris gave him a national funeral, and in doing so was burying, not only a man who had gained the personal affection of his countrymen, but also the idea with which he had been identified. France still remembered the "Terrible Year" with sorrow, but she had ceased to find bitterness in its recollection. Indeed, her sorrow was assuaged by a feeling of assurance that the intrigues and the fecklessness, the arrogance and the treachery, that had done so much to bring about her downfall in 1870 were simply impossible in the new France of to-day.

Copyright drawing by R. Caton Woodville.]   *[From material supplied first-hand by J. W. Parker and A. Muirhead.*

SCENE FROM THE BATTLE OF HAELEN, WHERE THE BELGIANS DEFEATED THE INVADERS.

The battle of Haelen, between Liege and Brussels, was fought on August 12th and 13th, 1914, and the Germans, who attacked in the traditional close formation, were decimated by the fire from the Belgian mitrailleuses. "Men and horses fell like flies," till they were ordered to retire, and the battle ended, according to the Belgian official report, "all to the advantage of the Belgian forces." The guns were drawn by dogs specially trained for the work, that lie down quietly during the action. The Belgian artillery were supported by cavalry who in small detachments charged the enemy across the fields.

Strong in this belief, Frenchmen bore with an easy temper the annoyances that arose from time to time out of the racial incompatibility between themselves and their German neighbours. There was the affair of Saverne, when Alsatian townsmen were dragooned and slashed by brutal and ill-mannered German officers; there was the arrest and sentence of Hausi, the artist and author who had made the griefs of the people of Alsace-Lorraine and their ever-active sympathies for France his special theme; there was, too, the extravagant campaign carried on in Germany against the French Foreign Legion. Lecturers were sent about the

German fictions about France

country, pamphlets were circulated, and even otherwise responsible newspapers published articles describing the fantastic methods which the French military authorities were accused of employing to obtain recruits for the Legion.

Young Germans were alleged to be drugged in railway stations, and smuggled across the frontier to the nearest recruiting station, while the life of the legionary in Africa was represented as a nightmare of hardships and ill-usage.

AERIAL MILITARY PHOTOGRAPHY.
Example of plan of a distant hostile place obtained by the German invention illustrated in the lower left-hand corner.

As a matter of fact, one of the most frequent reasons given by Germans who presented themselves to be received into the Foreign Legion was the brutal treatment they received from the officers and "unter-offiziere" of the regiments in which they had been called to serve their time in the German Army.

Yet such irritations passed over the surface of French life, and left it untroubled. The volatile Frenchman of an earlier generation, quick to resentment, reacting readily to an emotional appeal, even though it were based on no material foundation, seemed to have passed away. Modern France is cool and self-confident, practical rather than sentimental, determined rather than enthusiastic. Nothing is more certain than the fact that if France had not been deliberately attacked by Germany, the two countries need never again

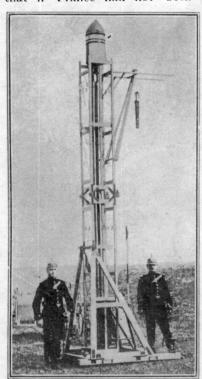

THE CAMERA IN A PARACHUTE.
By means of this apparatus a folded parachute is shot up to a great height, and when it unfolds, the camera it carries automatically photographs the fortress, town, or other place about which information is wanted.

have fought. Bismarck used to say, after 1870, that if France had really no intention of molesting his country, and if Germans could be assured of her peaceful intentions, the sword would never again be drawn between France and Germany. Time, and the cynical ambition of Bismarck's successors, have given the lie to that statement. On the other hand, the whole story of French diplomacy during the critical days immediately before Germany's declaration on August 3rd, 1914, of war on France is one, first of incredulity that war was likely, and secondly, of desperate efforts to preserve the peace.

"Until Thursday," said M. Abel Ferry, Under-Secretary of State for Foreign Affairs, to the writer on Saturday, August 1st, the day that Germany declared war on Russia, "we believed that Austria and Germany were bluffing. In a memorandum on the situation which I prepared for the use of the President of the Republic I judged the possibility that the two German Powers intended to provoke war as the least probable explanation of their attitude, and described such an issue of the crisis as very unlikely. Even now," went on this member of the French Cabinet, "we can hold Russia back; we can make her accept anything if thereby the peace of Europe may be assured. But for that," he added, "the word must come from England. If England announces firmly that she will support France and Russia, Germany will draw back."

Wrong though M. Ferry was in his supposition that the absence of a public declaration of England's attitude was encouraging Germany to play a desperate game of bluff—for the White Paper published by the British Government shows clearly how, as early as July 29th, Sir Edward Grey had clearly warned Germany that an attack by her on France would mean war with England, too—yet this avowal of his, while peace and war were yet in the balance, is enough proof of the overwhelming wish for peace that was

H.M.S. Highflyer.

One of the minor incidents in the War, but of historic interest, in so far as it involved the first serious naval loss to Germany, was that in which H.M.S. Highflyer figured so gallantly off the West Coast of Africa on August 27th, 1914. It had long been known that at the outbreak of a war between Germany and England, it was the intention of the Germans to equip the best of their transatlantic liners as "commerce destroyers"

and send these cruising throughout the seven seas to the terror of British shipping. But the only one of these ocean greyhounds that succeeded in putting to sea when hostilities were declared, was the Kaiser Wilhelm der Grosse. She was in the very act of securing a prize in the British steamer Galician, off the coast of Africa, when H.M.S. Highflyer hove in sight, and, engaging the German, speedily sent the Kaiser Wilhelm der

sse to the bottom of the sea. On the news being telegraphed to the
miralty, the message, "Bravo, Highflyer!" was sent back by wireless,
heer the plucky little British man-o'-war, which had so promptly
troyed the would-be destroyer. Our illustration has been specially
wn for "The Great War" by Mr. C. M. Padday, from sketches made
oard the Highflyer before she left England for southern waters.

The Kaiser Wilhelm der Grosse.

THE BRITISH MEDITERRANEAN FLEET ASSEMBLED AT MALTA BEFORE THE WAR.
Some of these warships co-operated with the French Fleet under Admiral Boué de Lapeyrere in the successful blockade of the Austrian Navy in the Adriatic.

the chief characteristic of the French Cabinet up to the very outbreak of the war.

The France upon which the hurricane of August, 1914, was to burst was, then, a nation which from a military point of view had done everything possible to prepare herself; for the charges brought in the Senate by M. Humbert in July, to the effect that the Army's reserve of boots was old and inadequate, and that the frontier forts lacked munitions and wireless equipment, although they appeared at the time to be admitted by the War Minister, M. Messimy, who had recently returned to office, seem now, in the light of facts, to have had little foundation, and were possibly cunningly intended to prepare the way for an increased demand for Army credits. In the diplomatic department of the national life the prevailing sentiment was a supreme desire to go on living at peace. What were the circumstances of the French people in their own home? They were strangely complicated, and are none the less interesting because the cobweb of confusion in which the life of the nation had involved itself was blown away by the first breath of war, and left France simplified, purified, united in a most sudden and astonishing way, to meet the political earthquake that was to shake the foundations of Europe.

The new spirit in old France

It was a brilliant and fascinating scene on which one looked at Longchamps racecourse, the afternoon of the Grand Prix, the climax of the Paris season, and the day (June 28th, 1914) when the first cloud that foretold the coming storm rose above the horizon in the form of the assassination of the Archduke Franz Ferdinand of Austria. There, in the sun-flooded paddock under the shade of the thick chestnut-trees, was crowded the cosmopolitan society of Paris. There were people of every civilised race of the whole world, all drawn to Paris by the common desire to spend money in the most glittering city of Europe. Americans elbowed Russians; there were rajahs from Central India, and cattle-breeders from the plains of Argentine.

In the midst of this wide-gathered throng, and yet distinct from it, were the Parisians themselves, who were again divided for social purposes into two classes—the old and conservative families of rank and tradition, and the great unorganised throng whose only common quality was the habit of unbounded extravagance.

Ministers and mannequins stood side by side. The dresses which the great *couturiers* had sent for display to the Grand Prix that afternoon were some of the most fantastic which that not easily startled show-ring of fashion had ever seen. One particularly, in which

HISTORIC PICTURE OF THE KAISER'S YACHT.
This photograph of the Imperial yacht, the Hohenzollern, was taken in Norway on July 27th, 1914, when the Kaiser was hurriedly setting out for Germany the day before the outbreak of war between Austria-Hungary and Servia.

the upper part of the body was covered with little more than black gauze, attracted great attention. It would be the keynote of dresses for Deauville and Dinard next month, people told each other. No one suspected that there would be no Dinard season this year, and that, six weeks later, the very *couturiers* themselves would be wielding bayonets instead of scissors and pins.

Up above, at the front of the Presidential stand, sat M. Poincaré, the President of the French Republic, and his wife. It is seldom possible to judge M. Poincaré's feelings from his face. Its pale, drawn cheeks, with their short, greyish beard and their small, alert dark eyes, give always the impression of a mask that is worn of choice. The whole bearing of the President—nervously correct, studiously non-committal—is only a result of the rigid self-control and concentration in which the vitality of the man finds its chief expression.

But the impression which it conveys to an onlooker is that M. Poincaré is constantly upon his guard. And, indeed, until the Great War

FRENCH TROOPS PULLING DOWN GERMAN FRONTIER MARK.

This frontier post, bearing the Black Eagle of Germany and the words "Deutsches Reich"—German Empire—stood at the head of the Col de la Schlucht in the Vosges, across which the French advanced about August 7th, 1914.

came to compress the conflicting currents of French life into one coherent stream by the mighty pressure of overwhelming danger to the national existence, there were reasons enough why M. Poincaré should walk circumspectly.

On that June day a most relentless and active political plot was in existence to drive him from the office of President of the Republic. The Radical-Socialist party were his bitterest enemies. M. Clemenceau, the ex-Premier, and one of the most vigorous intellects in France, had never forgiven him for triumphing at the Presidential election over his own candidate, M. Pams. Almost daily M. Poincaré was attacked in the leading column of "L'Homme Libre" by that mordant pamphleteering pen of which its editor, M. Clemenceau, is so skilled a master. M. Poincaré's private and political career had been an honourable one, but that did not protect him from the most unscrupulous attempts on the part of his political opponents to discredit his family, and to undermine the growing influence which he was acquiring in the country, and which had even brought upon him the accusation of aiming at the creation of a personal régime.

FRENCH VILLAGERS' NIGHT WATCH FOR SPIES.

After all the able-bodied men left for the battlefield, the French villages were guarded, night and day, by the curé and the old peasants, who stopped every stranger in order to examine his papers.

REINFORCEMENTS OF FRENCH INFANTRY MARCHING TO SUPPORT THE RIGHT WING OF THE ALLIES.

And in addition to these, the subterranean workings that were undermining the life of France on the eve of war, there was the famous trial of Mme. Caillaux, which was a focus of intrigue. Her husband, Joseph Caillaux, was a financier who had been Premier at the time of the last Franco-German crisis in 1911, when the German pretensions to Morocco were bought off by the cession of a part of the French Congo. In the negotiations between the two countries at that time, it was M. Caillaux who, as Premier, had gone behind the back of his Foreign Minister, De Selves, to make secretly to Germany more conciliatory offers than the French Cabinet had approved. Since then M. Caillaux had been continuously more prominent than any man in France.

As Finance Minister he had made himself responsible for the hotly-debated project of introducing an income
Political intrigue in France
tax. His opponents laid at his door charge after charge of political corruption and abuse of his ministerial position ; but pugnacity was the essence of the man's nature, and he met every attack with defiance. His shrill voice had the power of holding the crowd ; he was expert in appeals to self-interest, and he made full use of all the influence which a temperament of boundless ambition and intense energy gave him over the great multitude of his more easy-going countrymen.

In the last months of 1913 and the early months of the following year, a vigorous newspaper campaign against M. Caillaux was carried on in the " Figaro," one of the leading newspapers of Paris, by its editor, M. Gaston Calmette. On March 16th this campaign was brought to a sudden and tragic end. Mme. Caillaux, the wife of the Minister, went down to the offices of the " Figaro," waited an hour for M. Calmette to come in, and then, directly she was admitted to his room, fired five shots from an automatic pistol into his body.

M. Calmette died the same night. The wife of the Minister was arrested, and M. Caillaux himself resigned his seat in the Cabinet. From then until the trial, which began on July 20th, and only ended on July 28th, France was divided into two bitterly opposed parties, for and against Caillaux, for the dominant personality of the man caused him instantly to be identified with his wife's crime.

There were riots on the boulevards of Paris, and the Press attacked or defended the Minister with tedious reiteration week after week. Yet when, after a trial that was the most sensational and the most disorderly ever seen in France, the jury brought in the astounding verdict of acquittal in favour of Mme. Caillaux, the war-cloud was already looming so heavily over France that all the bitter passions which would in normal times have broken loose on that sultry night to fill Paris with rioting and tumult seemed suddenly petty and insignificant.

The humiliation which politics had inflicted on French justice was overlooked in the presence of the gigantic danger, whose imminence had just begun to dawn upon men's minds.

It was therefore by no means a settled and internally peaceful France upon which the Great War broke in

France disciplined by her danger

August, 1914. The magnificent unanimity and whole-heartedness with which every rank and class, every creed and party of Frenchmen, threw themselves into the cause of the defence of their country was rather brought about by the great flood of patriotic enthusiasm that broke from every heart in France, and swept away all the enmities and jealousies that had seemed a few days before so deep-rooted and so bitter.

In a night, in an hour, all divisions passed utterly away, and France rose up, reluctantly, but determined and knit into unshakable union, to meet the German challenge of her right to live.

No one who was present at that sitting of the Chamber of Deputies on August 4th, to which Germany's declaration of war was read, can well forget the unprecedented sight of every member of that usually so divided house now applauding with one voice, now silent as one man, disciplined by the national danger. From the blue-blooded Conservatives and Royalists on the Right to the most advanced Socialists on the Extreme Left, all the shades and cliques and groups and blocs of that intricately subdivided house had disappeared. The deputies of France were Frenchmen and nothing more.

And no less surprising was the self-controlled temper of the public. The frantic demonstrations of popular hysteria with which the war of 1870 had begun showed no sign of reproducing themselves. It was not that they were repressed or prevented ; the mood of the people was simply too sober and determined to permit them. For a few nights in succession a crowd of young larrikins did indeed march up and down the boulevards, singing the " Marseillaise " ; but the ordinary Parisian passer-by looked on with no more than toleration.

On the night of August 3rd, the evening on which the German Ambassador handed to M. Viviani, the Foreign Minister, the declaration of war on France, there was indeed a sudden demonstration against German and Austrian shops and cafés—their windows were broken, and, in some cases, the goods in their show-cases were stolen by the crowd. But these incidents, for which apaches from the outer boulevards were chiefly responsible, were at once stopped by the police. Measures of a rigour that almost seemed unnecessary were indeed taken. All restaurants and cafés were compelled to close at 8 p.m. ; the terrasses—the little rows of tables set out upon the pavement at which the Parisian has always loved to sit in summer—were suppressed ; the loitering even of a single person in the streets was actively prevented ; and the drinking of absinthe, which was almost the national beverage of France, was forbidden even in private houses.

Paris quickly fell into a condition of unnatural calm, only comparable to a London Sunday. As the mobilisation, which began

AN INCIDENT OF THE FRENCH ADVANCE INTO BELGIUM.
This picturesque scene shows one of the French dragoons, who were the heralds of the first French advance, delivering his passport to an alert Belgian picket.

TROOP OF FRENCH LANCERS PASSING THROUGH A BELGIAN VILLAGE ON THE LOOK-OUT FOR RAIDING UHLANS.

on August 2nd, continued to draw more and more men away from their employment in the capital, shops began to close, works shut down, commercial houses suspended business. Trade fell, indeed, at first into even greater stagnation than the lack of hands made necessary, for the Government proclaimed a moratorium which permitted banks to refuse to pay out more than five per cent. of any sum greater than £10 which they held to the credit of their customers when the decree was issued, and this permission was interpreted by most banking houses as a command.

The Frenchman's old-established passion for hoarding coin received, of course, a great stimulus from the anxieties of the moment, and for some days it was exceedingly difficult to change the hundred-franc note which forms so large a part of the circulation of France. Waiters in the cafés would give a fifty-franc note for forty-five francs in silver, and retail business of every kind was almost brought to a standstill until the Bank of France issued notes of five and twenty francs, which immediately restored a normal state of affairs, for the solvency of the State had never for a moment been doubted.

Every foreigner in Paris was required to register himself with the police, and Germans and Austrians who did not leave the country were taken down under guard to the West of France, where they were assigned strictly supervised districts in which to live, and where work was found for those who had not means to pay for their support.

Calm efficiency of French War Office

Meanwhile, the mobilisation of the Army went on with the regularity of well-tested machinery. The disorder which the widespread changes of staff naturally caused in other departments of State had no counterpart at the Ministry of War, intensely busy though it instantly became. On the railways throughout France civilian traffic almost entirely ceased, while day and night, at half-hour intervals, train after train, heavily laden with troops and war material, thundered towards the eastern frontier.

The secrecy that was maintained from the first by the military authorities had never been known in any earlier war. Not only were no Press correspondents allowed to accompany the Army, but newspapers were forbidden, under penalty of suppression, to publish any but officially issued news about the war, and the soldiers themselves were prevented from communicating in any way with their friends

GENERAL JOFFRE.
The French Commander-in-Chief of the Allied Armies. Born in 1852, his extraordinary military genius led him steadily to the supreme command.

THE FIRST GERMAN SOLDIERS TO ENTER FRANCE—BATCH OF PRISONERS ARRIVING AT ROANNE.

at home. Parents saw their sons leave for the front, but they had no means of knowing whither they went or how they fared.

Yet France remained entirely patient under her great ordeal, realising to the full that she must now fight for her very life. " We know," said the War Minister, M. Messimy, to the writer, " that this is a struggle out of which we shall come either victorious or dead—and we intend to be victorious."

CHAPTER VIII.—BEHIND THE FIRING LINE.

Germany After the First Shot.　　By an Eye-Witness.

How Germany Mobilised—Effect of War on Commerce—Empty Holiday Resorts—The German Officer in his True Colours—Wholesale Arrests of " Spies "—Story of the Phantom Gold—An English Family's Adventurous Escape—British Consul Insulted—Scandalous Treatment of a Consular Party—German Bitterness Against All Things English—The Problem of Feeding Germany—Cessation of Mob Law—Menace of the Russian Advance—Summoning of the Landsturm—Dislocation of Employment—Newspapers Censored—The Socialist Movement—" Paris Within a Month ! "—Amusements Restricted.

GENERAL PAU.

The intrepid leader of the French forces operating in Alsace. A veteran of 1870, he lost his arm in that great combat.

WITHIN a few hours of the order for general mobilisation the whole German Empire underwent an extraordinary change. At every railway station there suddenly sprang up not camps of tents, but long lines of pitch-pine sheds, every board ready cut so that it could be dropped into its place. When the first detachments of reserves appeared, according to the time-table in the hands of every sergeant, at their appointed station they found shelter from sun and rain, and long tables whereon the Red Cross organisation had prepared water, lemonade, and even sausages.

So exact were all the arrangements in all these respects, at any rate throughout Prussia, that on the receipt of the order for mobilisation even ice was ready to cool the drinking water. From every village throughout the huge Empire little knots of men began to trudge to the stations, whence they would be transported to their regimental headquarters. Although nominally all were not required for eight, or even ten days, on the fifth day of mobilisation (Thursday, August 6th) the country was deserted. As the writer passed in the Ambassador's train across

Copyright drawing by R. Caton Woodville.

[*From a sketch on the spot by Louis Weirter*]

BRINGING UP THE GUNS: BRITISH ARTILLERY GETTING INTO POSITION AT THE BATTLE OF MONS.

Eye-witnesses of the opening stages of the German attack upon Mons, which began on Saturday, August 22nd, and lasted some thirty-six hours, relate that the British artillery seemed to be better served than that of the enemy, and the batteries posted in the wooded hills to the south of the town inflicted heavy loss s on the Germans. According to the "Times" Paris correspondent, they added that "the British were apparently doing more than holding their own." As Lord Kitchener said in his telegram of congratulation to Sir John French, "we are all proud of them." General Joffre conveyed his congratulations and sincere thanks for the protection so successfully given by our army to the French flank.

that huge level plain which reaches from the Silesian forests to the Teutobürg hills, the open country appeared as if suddenly it had been swept of all inhabitants. In the golden cornfields stood waggons, half laden ; here and there a ladder leaned against a half-finished rick ; even the women had disappeared, and the only sign of life over mile after mile of the great plain was a silent figure, standing rifle in hand, by a bridge or level crossing.

For years people had talked about and discussed the German mobilisation ; vague legends had been published of partial mobilisation in 1911, and again in 1912, and earlier during the **Completeness of German mobilisation** Moroccan crisis ; but never before in the history of Germany—or, indeed, in any other country—had there been any experience of this sudden stopping of work of a busy nation, this sudden draining of town and country of every man of military age.

It is difficult to impress on English readers this wonderful change. Already, on Saturday, August 8th, a number of factories had closed through want of men. Vast transport organisations had suddenly ceased work for want of horses and lorries. By Tuesday the work of desolation—there is no other word to describe it—was fully accomplished. Industrial life in Germany was cut short at the blare of a trumpet. This, indeed, was the most impressive feature of German mobilisation, particularly to those who escaped by the slow-moving train from

BRITAIN'S HEROIC SONS IN A FRENCH VILLAGE ON THE WAY TO THE BATTLE HILL OF MONS.
Our gallant soldiers, soon to be famous for their long, steady stand on August 23rd, against six attacks by superior German forces, are here seen adorned with flowers brought by grateful French women while resting on their march to the fighting-line.

the howling mobs, which for over a week had made sleep in the cities impossible, into the silent places of the great sandy Mark, once described in bitter sarcasm as " the sandbox of the Holy Roman Empire."

Many a time as I approached Hanover towards evening had I watched the holiday crowds pouring out of the city to the great beer restaurants amongst the trees near the city. Now, as then, the gardens, with their scrubbed deal tables and their long lines of chairs, were awave with little flags and pennons ; now, as then, amongst the large and more popular restaurants one saw here and there the smaller, less gorgeous hostelry over whose rustic gate stood the ancient sign of German hospitality : " We will not break the ancient rule ; you may cook your own coffee and bring your own stool."

But now all these gay summer resorts were empty. The guests, the waiters, and the **The debris of shattered holidays** innkeepers themselves were gone. Presently we came to a little river alongside whose banks the railway runs. About every hundred yards stood a sentry, often an old man armed with a shot-gun, and without a uniform. Anchored to the bank, a mile or two from the nearest station, lay a little fleet of pleasure boats, the cushions piled together about the stern, a tarpaulin roughly thrown over the engine, and the owners (for the most part, doubtless officers) called away in the middle of their summer cruise to join their regiment in the reserve.

Now and again, approaching the local station, I could see a pile of luggage—desolate holiday trunks, folding perambulators, a bundle of spades, and little coloured flags wherewith the Germans delight to deck their sand

THE MOUNTED VANDALS OF THE KAISER: GERMAN CAVALRY CAMP BY THE BELGIAN FRONTIER.
Some of the men are seen wearing the pickel-haube with its canvas cover, and others the soft undress cap. The helmets are stuck on sword and rifle by the horse lines, while the lances are fixed ready by the chargers' flanks.

redoubts by the seaside. When the mobilisation order came, trains were seized and luggage thrown out. Doubtless there was in this, as in many other matters, a little too much zeal. Not all the wild confusion into which the civil population was thrown was by any means necessary.

It is significant, for example, that twenty-four hours before the order for mobilisation was given international trains approaching the German frontier were held up, and passengers compelled in some cases to walk to the nearest frontier station. But it must be remembered that in all her recent history Germany has never had an opportunity to practise the mobilisation of her whole Army, and the wonder is, perhaps, that it worked as smoothly as it did. From the moment when war became inevitable, Germany—or, at least, Prussia—carried out to the letter the rule devised by her General Staff—" take care of the civilian only when you have taken care of everything connected with the forces."

The outbreak of war was the signal, as has already been pointed out, for the complete abdication of the civil power. The hour for which the German military caste had waited was come at last; every lieutenant felt himself instantly relieved of all necessity any longer to regard the ordinary rules of civil life. Officers, who claim also to be gentlemen, threw off any pretence of consideration, of regard for the claims of friendship, and even of common courtesy.

Germany throws off the mask of civilisation

It is probable that, to some extent, the extraordinary state of affairs in German towns and cities which would follow the outbreak of war had been foreseen by the authorities. The pinch of unemployment would come not in the first week, but after a fortnight, or longer, and if the civilian population were to sit down, as the German system required, to wait doggedly with tightened belts and in silence, save for such scraps of news as the German General Staff might feel disposed to publish, it was necessary that disorder, thinly veiled as patriotic enthusiasm, should not be too sternly repressed at the outset.

Hence there was no attempt to punish the ringleaders of the wild mob which tried to sack the British Embassy. For over a fortnight there was even no attempt to check the extraordinary mania over South Germany for hunting phantom gold, supposed to be in transport from France to Russia. Actually, the sudden arrest of Englishmen and even Englishwomen throughout Germany on a charge of espionage began, and perhaps reached its climax, before the English ultimatum to Germany had expired.

It must be remembered that the population of German cities had been fed for weeks on the craziest lies. Ulster, they learnt, was in a state of rebellion; English troops had refused to obey orders (and it must not be forgotten that to the German military mind there was and is no distinction between unwillingness to shoot unarmed citizens and refusal to march against an armed enemy). Suddenly, at seven o'clock on Tuesday evening, August 4th, this fabric of lies was shattered when the " Berliner Tageblatt " scattered through the city flaring placards, " Great Britain breaks off diplomatic relations."

The shock was admittedly, for one moment, paralysing. That which the greater part of the population had believed impossible from reasons of British domestic policy, and improbable because of their sublime faith in British selfishness, had happened. The childish chatter about the unity of the Germanic race, which no sane observer of Prussian manners in the last decade could ever have seriously believed, was probably less responsible for the outrageous treatment of English-speaking people throughout Germany than the sudden angry realisation of the fact that the Press and Foreign Office had alike utterly misled public opinion regarding the actual unpreparedness of England for any war ; and the bitter word " Betrayed," which was on thousands of lips in Berlin on the night of August 4th, was directed as much against German diplomacy as against supposed English treachery.

On the heels of every armed host since the world began there have followed a number of ruffians,

GERMANY'S WAR CHEST.

It has been popularly believed that Germany's store of gold, partly derived from the war indemnity wrested from France in 1871, was kept under close guard in the fortress at Spandau, especially for this great conflict.

GERMAN TROOPS HALTING ON THE WAY TO BRUSSELS.
Stopping for the midday ration of bread and ham, served out to them from the field transport.

AT THE OPENING OF THE GERMAN INVASION—A BRIEF REST AFTER THE FIGHT AT VISE.
Some of the 100,000 German soldiers who first broke into Belgium and, after attacking Vise on August 3rd, marched on to Liege.

THE TSAR EXHIBITING AN IKON OR SACRED PICTURE TO HIS KNEELING SOLDIERS.

fishing in troubled waters. Every leader of a popular cause, resorting to armed force, may and must reckon that in his wake will follow not only fighting men, but also a large crowd of half-savage harpies—not ready to fight, but only too delighted to bully. Of the crowds which attacked the embassies, legations, and consulates throughout Germany on the outbreak of war, no small proportion were excited youths, students drunk with their own alcoholic enthusiasm, the riff-raff of the poorer quarters of the cities, eager to seize this opportunity of unbridled licence.

For several days after the outbreak of war, the police-stations, not only of Berlin but of almost all other big German cities, particularly in the industrial districts, were packed with strange crowds of gentlemen arrested as spies, huddled together with the lowest classes of the population. In the waiting-room of the little police-station in Mittelstrasse, where the writer was confined for a while with several English and American prisoners, were also gangs of under-aged ruffians, bearing marks of

THE TSAR.
With his Commander-in-Chief, the Grand Duke Nicholas.

RUSSIAN RESERVISTS HASTENING TO JOIN THE COLOURS IN ST. PETERSBURG.

SERVIAN ARTILLERY WITH OXEN TEAMS, PASSING THROUGH NISH, ON THEIR WAY TO THE DRINA.

EVIDENCES OF THE RUIN WROUGHT IN BELGRADE BY THE AUSTRIAN BOMBARDMENT.

FRENCH GUNS HANDLED EFFECTIVELY BY THE SERVIANS.

A very important instrument in the crushing victory that the Servian Forces won against the Austro-Hungarian troops on the Drina, August 20-26th, was the artillery supplied by French manufacturers to Servia.

HIGHLANDERS MARCHING
THROUGH BOULOGNE TO THE
FRONT.

the vice which was probably more characteristic of Berlin in the days before the war than of any other great city in Europe.

One such was stripped whilst we were under detention, and the police took from him a pistol, an eight-inch dagger, and a life-preserver. Pickpockets naturally felt this was indeed their harvest, and for once the ruthless police of Berlin were in no position to control the situation, for the authorities had of their own act permitted the mob to get out of hand. It

The Berlin mob gets out of hand

will, perhaps, never be known how many people in Berlin were injured for life, not by the sabres of the police, nor by rifle and revolver of sentry or guard, but by the knife, which at all times has played an extraordinary part in the criminal history of Berlin.

If it be remembered that in times of peace scarcely any motor-cyclist in Germany has ridden at night without a revolver in his pocket; if it be remembered that the great forests, which stretch from Berlin north and south and east and west, have harboured for years desperate gangs of ruffians, it will easily be seen that the suspension for a few hours only of the strong hand of the civil government may easily have been the cause of the unfortunate amount of lawlessness for which harmless civilians may often have been held responsible.

Outside the cities, particularly through South Germany, a yet more dangerous licence was per-

mitted One of the German papers—I think it was the "Lokalanzeiger" —published on Sunday, August 2nd, an amazing story from Nuremberg, to the effect that a huge quantity of gold, stated variously at twenty, forty, eighty, and even a hundred and sixty thousand pounds, had been in transport before the war from France to Russia.

When the war broke out, so the story ran, this gold had been hurriedly transferred to motor-cars, wherein it was to find its perilous way across Germany. From time to time further stories of this phantom gold appeared. Now it had been transferred to cars carrying the Red Cross flag; now they were American cars, with the gold guardians disguised as harmless tourists; and finally the crazy Press announced that countryfolk through Thuringia and Franconia would do well to look out for motor-cars containing middle-aged ladies. These, they said, were the gold-carriers in disguise.

There followed upon this the craziest gold-hunt throughout all Southern Germany. Villagers armed with sticks, shot-guns, and anything that came handiest, took to making unprovoked attacks upon motor-cars of all kinds.

FRENCH SOLDIER ON GUARD AT BRITISH CAMP NEAR BOULOGNE.
An interesting picture taken during the silent movement of the British Expeditionary Force to French soil, just before the advance to the Belgian frontier.

Amongst the victims were an Austrian officer, an Austrian countess, a lady of title in South Germany, and doubtless a number of other people of less prominence. For nearly a fortnight the authorities seem to have taken no step to put an end to this extraordinary folly. Finally, the General Staff was obliged to issue a notice inquiring whether the inhabitants of South German cities really any longer believed the idiotic story, and warning them that attacks on motor-cars for the future would be severely discouraged.

It was left, however, for the pacifist organ, the "Berliner Tageblatt," to complain querulously that it did not altogether approve of the discouragement of national enthusiasm. It complained in particular that, whilst it was doubtless right to avoid undue harshness in the treatment of English-speaking peoples, for fear they might prove to be Americans, it was perhaps unwise to check mob violence against foreigners, lest perchance it should discourage the seeking out of spies. If the cloak of humbug wherewith Germany—or, at least, the Prussian Press—has for so many years disguised its true sentiments needed any further rending asunder, its attitude in the fortnight preceding the war, and its sentiments after the outbreak, would have sufficed.

If it fared ill with anybody who could by any chance be suspected of being a foreigner (for to the German mind every foreigner was an ex-officio spy) in the cities, the fate of those who tried to travel across Germany after the outbreak of war was no less unpleasant. One by one unhappy **The encouragement of mob law** Englishmen, caught, often with their wives, in Germany by the outbreak of war, struggled through to England, and brought stories of hardship and maltreatment such as have been unexampled since the days when freebooters rode through Germany, carrying torture, murder, and robbery to every homestead. A British Consul, travelling with his son and wife to the Danish frontier, was held up, and whilst his wife was kept in durance in one prison, he and his son were thrown into a cell with a wisp of straw to lie on, without sanitation and almost in darkness. Here he was kept for several days before a crazy officialdom consented to his release.

THE UNIVERSAL KHAKI.
A Grenadier Guard on duty at Buckingham Palace. The fine trappings of peace were everywhere subordinated to the halftones of war.

Travellers coming from the German health resorts of Nauheim, Homburg, Wiesbaden, and other centres along the Rhine were arrested again and again, subjected to the most barbarous indignities, and, in many cases, finally detained as being of military age.

Two explanations of the savagery with which a number of English people were treated in Germany upon the outbreak of war have been given at various times. It is alleged that in many cases persons arrested in the Rhineland were confronted by sergeants or other non-

ONLOOKERS AT THE RECRUITING ON THE HORSE GUARDS PARADE.
Recruiting receives a considerable stimulus by the infection of example as well as by news from the front. Many of those who go to look on at other men responding to the national call are themselves fired to the same response.

AN INCIDENT IN THE HARD-FOUGHT RETREAT FROM BELGIUM: BRITISH TROOPS ON THE RIVER BANK PREPARED TO RESIST THE GERMAN ADVANCE.

Yard by yard the Anglo-French troops (as the French Minister of War courteously called the allied forces) vigorously and sternly resisted the overwhelming German forward movement, and scenes similar to this with burning buildings and broken bridges were to be seen on the Sambre and other rivers of the Belgian-French borderland.

commissioned officers accustomed themselves throughout their military career to scenes of brutality, and quite unable to realise that the stripping of ladies in the open road to seek for bombs or secret documents was in any way unusual.

Had the ill-treatment ceased with these insults, the explanation might have been accepted, because the same excuse has been repeatedly offered to account for the brutality of many of the German police, who are for the most part retired Army men. But not even Germans could swallow such childish explanations of the assault with sticks and stones upon the British Embassy, as were offered on the following day. It was asserted that members of the Embassy staff, or some of the servants, had thrown small coins amongst the crowd, and that this infuriated the mob.

THE TRAMP OF WAR IN THE MIDST OF PEACEFUL ENGLAND.
An Army Transport convoy passing along a Buckinghamshire lane. Above, a battalion of the London Scottish marching through Hyde Park after parade. In circle, horses commandeered by the London Scottish.

The absurdity of this statement is shown by the fact that three minutes before the assault the Wilhelmstrasse, in which the Embassy is situated, was almost clear of people. When the news of the rupture of diplomatic relations circulated along the Linden a crowd of students and other people, including, as a matter of fact, a number of political detectives, gathered instantly, and the assault was committed within three minutes of the receipt of the news. Later, the Berlin papers "assumed" that the coins had been thrown by Englishmen residing in the adjoining Hotel Adlon—a suggestion which was even more childishly silly.

Another explanation offered for the maltreatment of foreigners by people in authority was that to a great extent the authorities in question were such as had not come fully under the salutary influence of German civilian education. There is, perhaps, some justice in this plea, though it must be remembered that capable critics of

German education have long maintained that at best its influence on the moral character of the nation was virtually nil. How foreigners were actually treated, even such as could by no possibility be mistaken for other than harmless travellers, may be illustrated from the two first-hand accounts which follow :

Mr. George Bonar said : " On July 1st I left my wife, with two little boys, aged nine and seven, and a nurse, at Ems, and went to Norway for a fortnight's fishing. When war was declared I could not get back to them in time. The hotel people advised my wife not to run away, but to wait till the mobilisation was over and the railways free again. On August 3rd things got so bad that she decided to leave. With the children and nurse she left Ems by the 4 p.m. train, which she was assured would take her through to Brussels.

" At Herbesthal, the last town in Germany, they were peremptorily ordered to get out, as there was no longer a connection with Belgium. The only thing for them to do was to walk over the frontier to the nearest Belgian town, which was Wilkenraad. It was a miserable night, and rain fell heavily. At Wilkenraad hundreds of people of all nationalities were walking about the streets in the pouring rain unable to get accommodation. A woman took pity on the plight of my children, and put them up for the night. My wife had no money, but gave her some jewellery.

Miseries of harmless travellers

" It was thought that if they could get to Verviers they would be able to reach Ostend. A cart was obtained, and a hood was put over it to protect them from the rain. The party was composed of my wife and two children, the nurse, three American ladies, and a Scottish gentleman named Mackenzie, aged seventy-eight. On the road from the German town of Eupen they met the first German troops marching to Belgium. They were stopped, and the waggon was commandeered. The whole party walked to the little village of Baelen-Dolhain, where a Belgian Custom-house officer, M. Michel Blaise, gave them shelter.

" On August 4th the three Americans and two young men from the Chilean Legation in Berlin, realising the impossibility of making their way through Belgium, decided to return to Germany. My wife could not move, because, owing to exposure, the elder boy had developed a severe attack of bronchitis ; and Mr. Mackenzie was too old and lame to undertake a long walk. On August 9th firing was heard in the village. My wife took fright, and with the little boy who was ill, the other, and the nurse, went down into the cellar.

" Mr. Mackenzie and M. Blaise accompanied them. As they ran downstairs my wife noticed that a similar

THE BRITISH MARINES LANDED FOR THE PROTECTION OF OSTEND.
The German advance to the south having resulted in the evacuation of Belgium by the allied forces, much popular nervousness was felt on both sides of the "Narrow Seas" at the prospect of a German occupation of Ostend, only 66 miles from the English shore. The landing of a considerable force of Royal Marines, who are here seen marching into the town from the wharves, completely dissipated that nervousness.

ROYAL MARINE OUTPOST AT OSTEND.
A party temporarily entrenched by the roadside in readiness
for raiding Uhlans.

ROYAL MARINES MARCHING
INTO OSTEND.

THE CALM, UNRUFFLED GUARDIANS OF BELGIUM'S PLEASURE CITY.
Flying bodies of Uhlans were reported in almost every part of Western Belgium not
occupied in force by the German army. To check these raids the Royal Marines
were distributed in parties outside Ostend.

house on one side of them was ablaze. Almost immediately after they had reached the cellar they heard firing through all the windows overhead. After some time the doors and windows were broken in, and they were horrified to find that the soldiers were setting fire to the house. With one of the boys in her arms, and followed by the other, my wife ran into the street in front of the troops who were facing the house.

" ' Are we to be shot ? ' she cried, speaking in German ; and, for answer, she was ordered to stand on one side. She was followed by M. and Mme. Blaise. The moment M. Blaise appeared he was shot down and killed. Three bullets entered his body. Mr. Mackenzie was then seen coming along the passage. My wife ran up to the officer in charge of the troops, who was on horseback, and clutching him by the leg, cried : ' For God's sake don't shoot that man !   He is a Britisher merely taking refuge here ! '   ' Das macht nicht aus ' (' That does not matter ') the officer replied.   He gave the order to shoot, and Mr. Mackenzie fell with a bullet in his breast.   One shot killed him.   My wife is perfectly certain the officer heard what she said.

"The ground floor of the house was by this time burning fiercely.   My children were standing in the street in pyjamas and with bare feet, and my wife asked permission

EFFECTS OF THE TERRIFIC BOMBARDMENT OF LIEGE.
The ruins of a fort subjected to the fire of German 11 in. siege-guns.

HEROIC DEFENDERS OF BELGIUM IN THE HISTORIC TRENCHES OF LIEGE.

The above is one of the earliest authentic war pictures received in England.   It was taken in one of the actual trenches before Liege, where the gallant Belgian infantry for three days repelled attack after attack from the Germans, until General Leman was compelled to evacuate the town.

to go into the house to rescue some clothes for them.   At first the officer refused ; but at last he consented, and allowed two soldiers to go with her.   Three times my wife entered the burning house and reached the first floor, and threw down clothing to the soldiers.   Her hair, eyelids, and eyebrows were singed, and my children are now wearing scorched clothing.   My wife afterwards searched Mr. Mackenzie's body, and took about five pounds and his watch, which she gave to a poor Belgian woman who had lost both home and husband.   She retained his rings, which she brought home to give to his relatives. Finally, after a series of adventures, she reached Cologne, and was escorted by a Dutch gentleman to England."

WITHIN A TRENCH NEAR LIEGE.
Belgians in one of the trenches thrown up in the woods a few miles from Liege, waiting the next of the series of German attacks.

THE GERMAN MASTERS OF LIEGE AMONG THE RUIN AND DESOLATION THEY HAD CAUSED.

When the persistent German attacks had, utterly regardless of the cost in lives, succeeded in silencing one or more of the forts of Liege, and made a gap in the defences connecting them, the capture of the town became inevitable. Here German infantry are seen among the ruins of burnt-out houses in the Place de l'Universite.

The following is a detailed account of the insults and indignities offered by the Germans to the British Consul at Dantzic, Mr. Francis E. Drummond-Hay, and his wife and children, and the party who were accompanying him.

Authenticated accounts by members of his party show that not only the men, but also women and children of the Consular party, were subjected to treatment of a character that in many respects cannot be narrated in the public Press.

For some time before England and Germany were at war the wildest excitement prevailed in Dantzic. As far back as July 30th the Consul's telegrams were stopped or tampered with, and his telephonic connection cut off. (Great Britain declared war on Germany on August 4th.)

Mr. Drummond-Hay, Member of the Victorian Order, has had a long and distinguished official record, and for some time has been his Majesty's Consul for West and East Prussia and Posen, resident at Dantzic.

His first intimation that war had broken out was on the morning of August 5th, when a police officer visited the Consulate.

He was told he was under arrest, and must leave as soon as possible. The officials further intimated that even his life was in danger.

He was then conveyed to his private residence, six miles out of Dantzic, and told that he and his family had an hour to pack and clear out.

Mrs. Drummond-Hay, with her eldest son—a boy of sixteen who had just arrived from Cheltenham on his holidays

DESTRUCTION IN THE TOWN OF LIEGE.

Victorious German soldiers in the ruins of a house, in one of the principal squares, which was completely burnt out.

—a younger son of eight, and Miss Stagg, the governess, had previously received a visit from the officials, and were in great distress, being unable to telephone to the Consul at his office in town.

On the arrival of the Consul at his private residence the police gave them an hour to pack their handbags.

Maltreating a British consul The party then left the house in a motor escorted by police and soldiers en route for the station. At every street corner rifles were levelled at them, and they were hooted at and insulted.

Arriving at the station, they were joined by the French Vice-Consul and a party of ten British refugees. Here they were molested by soldiers, who demanded passes, and after being taken by the police to a waiting-room were put into a waiting train.

They were told this would take them to Stettin, but that if they looked out of the carriage windows or left the train they would be shot. Instead of six hours the journey to Stettin occupied twenty-two hours.

The crowds on the platform were angry and menacing; insulting phrases were written on the carriages, and all food was refused.

When Stettin was reached the party were again told they were under arrest and that they would be locked

THE CHIEF OF THE VALIANT BELGIAN NATION RIDING AT THE HEAD OF HIS TROOPS.
From the first King Albert aroused the enthusiastic admiration, not only of his own subjects, but of all the nations friendly to the Triple Alliance, by his self-sacrificing and fearless efforts both on the field and in the control of his people's destinies.

up in the town. After managing to secure a sandwich the Consul and his party were bundled into another train for a further nineteen hours' run to Hamburg.

On this train they were again submitted to the greatest indignities. They were searched, insulted at night time, and unable to sleep.

A drunken sergeant with a levelled revolver entered their carriage, and the behaviour of all the soldiers and officials on the train caused the greatest distress, particularly to the ladies.

At Hamburg the travellers were for the first time courteously received by a German officer, who behaved as a gentleman. After a hurried wash the refugees were put into another train to convey them to the Dutch frontier.

There the worst of their trouble began. After an examination of luggage the police refused to accept their passes, and they were told they would have to remain.

The ladies, they were informed, were free, but the men must stay. For seven hours the Consul and his companions were kept at the station, a man standing over them with a loaded rifle.

BELGIAN ARTILLERY FALLING BACK ON LOUVAIN FROM TIRLEMONT, ON AUGUST 19TH, 1914.
In the distance can be seen the columns of smoke arising from the burning town.

LOUVAIN, THE "OXFORD OF BELGIUM," WANTONLY DESTROYED BY THE GERMAN VANDALS ON AUGUST 25TH, 1914.

According to the official report, a German corps, on August 25, after receiving a check, withdrew in disorder into the town of Louvain. A German guard at the entrance to the town fired on their routed fellow-countrymen, mistaking them for Belgians. In spite of all denials from the authorities the Germans, in order to cover their mistake, pretended that it was the inhabitants who had fired on them, whereas the inhabitants, including the police, had been disarmed more than a week before. Without inquiry, and without listening to any protests, the German commander-in-chief announced that the town would be immediately destroyed. Soldiers furnished with bombs set fire to all parts of the town, and the splendid church of St. Pierre, the University buildings, the library, and the scientific establishment were delivered to the flames. A town of 45,000 inhabitants. the intellectual metropolis of the Low Countries since the 15th century, Louvain is now no more than a heap of ashes.

After a time the ladies, after having been searched in a most indelicate fashion, were separated from their friends and sent off to a hotel, while the men were marched off to prison and thrown into cells

There they were searched, and the Consul and three others placed in a cell. The apartment measured twelve feet by five feet, and contained straw, a blanket, and a jar of water.

There the party were locked in and left the whole of one night and the following day, the cells being destitute of every sanitary arrangement.

At 9.30 on the following morning they were let out for half an hour and paraded with criminals before being re-conducted to their cell.

The guard who brought food was armed with a revolver, had with him a police dog, and he was followed by a rifleman. In fact, as members of the party say, they were like " rats in a trap."

Prussia in her true colours　　On the following morning the ladies, who were completely broken down with anguish and suspense, were allowed to see their relatives. Mr. Drummond-Hay pleaded that his young son should not be longer kept a prisoner, and he was allowed to go out and join his mother.

At ten o'clock on the following night the Consul was told that he and his family and staff could leave. They reached Flushing after a further long and tedious journey ten days after their departure from Dantzic.

Behind the firing-line Prussia threw off the thin veneer of civilisation which for forty years has disguised her true character, and showed herself in her true colours—as a land but little removed from barbaism.

Yet these were strange contrasts, and it shall be admitted that where the civil government of Germany still retained, or succeeded in recovering some vestige of control, the civil officials did try, however faintheartedly, to stem this extraordinary flood of militarist outrage. During the day which followed the outbreak of war between Britain and Germany the Emperor's court marshal sent a special message to the English chaplain in Berlin, the Rev. H. N. Williams, informing him that he would do all in his power to assist the chaplain to keep open the English Church of St. George in the gardens of the Monbijou Palace, that he would arrange that there should be

THE DEFENCES OF A MAIN ARTERY OF ANTWERP.

In view of the German advance, the Belgian Government was moved from Brussels to Antwerp on August 17th, 1914, and on the same day the Town Guard was mobilised. The greatest Belgian fortress, and so long as its sea communications could be preserved, Antwerp was regarded as impregnable. In this photograph a guard is seen behind a rampart of sandbags piled on the banks of the Willebroeck Canal.

BELGIAN LANCERS BIVOUACKED IN A WOOD.
The Belgian cavalry had taken advantage of every natural feature of the country to check German raids and harry their outposts, while all the time gradually falling back upon their last great stronghold of Antwerp, into which, from the first, it was intended the whole Belgian Army should withdraw, in order to sally forth at the critical moment later to assist the Anglo-French forces.

no difficulty in English residents attending service at their church as usual, and that he would be glad to learn of any arrangements for relieving distress among English residents.

Similarly, in some of the western cities, Englishmen returning stated that the officials treated them, at least with reserve, and often with decided courtesy. It was only when they came into contact with some rampant lieutenant, overwhelmed with a sudden sense of his own relief from the bonds of civil restraint, or with some half-crazy police-sergeant, ignorant, for the most part, of the very look of a passport, that maltreatment ensued. It is abundantly evident, from this and many similar instances, that what happened in Germany was the breakdown of the whole system of civil government, even where it was merely intended that it should be reinforced or controlled in its broadest outlines by the military governors. The Prussian military system and the German civil code came into conflict, and the victory of rampant militarism was assured from the outset.

The sudden revolt against, or, as is more probable, the general fear of anything that might look foreign produced some results which, under other circumstances, would have been truly ludicrous. Most of the German cities had gradually become flooded with an international nomenclature of shops, and cafés, even streets. On the outbreak of war there was a hasty change, and whilst in London a Gambrinus still placidly continued its business, the cafés of Berlin hastily deleted even names that might suggest a foreign origin.

Curious results of Germanic fervour

Sign painters had a busy fortnight changing the name of the Hotel Bristol, the Englischer Hof, the Café Piccadilly, the Prince of Wales's tailoring establishment, the London Bar, the Queen's Restaurant, the Palais de Danse, and a host of other establishments. The Café Piccadilly, the largest establishment of its kind in the world, was converted into the Hoch Deutschland Kaffee Haus, the Queen's Restaurant became the Speise Haus, 1870, and the restaurants suddenly indulged in an orgy of newly-invented German names for foreign dishes.

Greengages, for example, known for forty years and more to German gourmets as Reine claude, suddenly became raenekloden or, as in Cologne, renge lodden. The word sauce was banned, and its place taken by the curious Germanised equivalent " sosse." " Russian eggs," a favourite Berlin dainty, suddenly disappeared from the bill of fare, and were replaced by a mysterious dish called " sauceeggs." Elsewhere the enthusiastic patriotism of young ladies' schools produced equally curious results. In a girls' high school in the Rhineland a deputation

GERMAN LOOTERS RETURNING TO CAMP.
Remorseless in its prosecution of every phase of war by the sternest and most savage measures the German army spared the inhabitants in nothing. Here a party is seen returning from looting a Belgian farmstead.

of Rhenish damsels waited upon the head teacher at the beginning of the day's work and informed her that it was not to be expected that patriotic German girls should consent any longer to learn the tongues of alien enemies.

French and English, they declared, must forthwith disappear from the curriculum, and it was only when the mistress pointed out that up to the present they could still learn " American " that the young ladies consented to resume their study of the language of Shakespeare.

The tumult and excitement which ran riot through Germany in the first week of the war cooled rapidly, as had been expected, when mobilisation was complete. German thoroughness was not likely long to leave the question of the harvest, the problem of provision for the civil population, and of maintaining the large numbers of women and the lesser numbers of men thrown out of work, to the well-intentioned efforts of amateur organisations. Little by little the military control closed its grip upon the whole country.

Mob law ceased on August 15th, when the steady growth of the Russian pressure in the east, combined with Austrian defeats by the Servians, made it necessary for the Germanic allies to call up the Landsturm. Now market-place, theatre, bar, and avenue were cleared of the crowds who had done so much fighting with their lips. The summoning of the Landsturm came, to some extent, as a surprise, for even the day before many people appeared to have thought that this last call on the population of the nation in arms could be avoided. What it meant to the country can be shown by a single instance. The tram system of Berlin, probably in peace time the most effective as it is the cheapest passenger transport system in any European city, employed about nine thousand men as drivers and conductors.

Germany's last call on her people

Three thousand of these were called away by the first mobilisation order, but when the order summoning the Landsturm was promulgated the company found itself with about a thousand men to continue its work. These were employed at once as drivers, whilst the conductors were replaced by women, in many cases the wives of men sent to the front. They were paid at an average rate of about fourpence an hour. Similarly, the companies controlling the taxi-cabs, so far as they had not simply withdrawn their cabs altogether, obtained permission to employ a number of women who held licences as drivers.

In place of petrol, which was virtually unobtainable, owing to the commandeering of all supplies for the Army, they took to using benzol, which itself became very scarce, and even alcohol. Very soon there was an outcry about this employment of the wives of men already sent to the front. It was pointed out by newspaper after newspaper that these women were already insured so far as possible, against actual starvation, by the Government.

On the other hand, there were, not hundreds, but many thousands, of young women, largely unmarried girls, who had

THE WORLD WIDE MENACE OF THE SPY.
A German spy found on one of the docks at Montreal escorted to the Military Prison. The Canadian authorities had carefully guarded all important points against spies and the enemy's agents.

Specially painted by R. G. Mathews for "The Great War"]   *[from sketches supplied by a correspondent in Antwerp.*

THE ZEPPELIN BOMBARDMENT OF ANTWERP ON AUGUST 24TH IN DEFIANCE OF THE HAGUE CONVENTION.

On the night of August 24th, 1914, a Zeppelin airship sailed over Antwerp and dropped shrapnel bombs, killing ten persons, including four women, injuring a number of others, and causing much damage to the Royal Palace and other buildings. An attempt was made to repeat the raid on the following night. These raids aroused much indignation both in Europe and America, as they were in direct contravention of the provisions of the Fourth Hague Convention, which Germany signed.

P

VICE-ADMIRAL BEATTY.
In Command of First Battle Cruiser Squadron.

COMMANDER GOODENOUGH.
H.M. Light Cruiser Southampton.

COMMANDER KEYES.
Commodore of the Submarine Service.

H.M.S. Lion, Flagship of Admiral Beatty, with the Battle Cruiser Squadron.

WATCHING AND WAITING

The North Sea was only kept clea
for British and neutral shipping by th
ceaseless patrol of the British Fleet. A
different times the grouping of th
naval forces would be re-adjusted to som
extent (as after the successful trans
portation of the Expeditionary Force), an
the German scouting vessels, out to gai
information of these movements, woul
have come more or less into contact wit
British sentinels. The desultory fightin
that would result fairly frequently wa
probably what was referred to in th
official report as "a certain liveliness in
the North Sea." The German patrol

REAR-ADMIRAL MOORE.
Third Sea Lord.

REAR-ADMIRAL CHRISTIAN.
Mentioned in official account of the action on
August 28th, 1914.

COMMANDER TYRWHITT.
of the Arethusa.

THE ENEMY'S APPROACH

uld, of course, run no risk of an
gagement, but would make for safety
the first intimation of forces supporting
e sentinel craft. It is no part of a
ut's business to get caught. It had
en often said by the enemy that they
uld be able to take advantage of fog to
d our ships or our shores. There was a
ze off Heligoland on August 28th, but
vas the German fleet that was raided,
t as a few years ago when a British
iiser squadron visited Kiel it found its
station whilst the German vessels sent
to greet it waited outside for the fog
to lift.

H.M. Destroyer Laertes of the First Fleet, damaged in the action on August 28th, 1914.

Specially painted for "The Great War" by C. M. Padday.]

THE SPIRIT OF OUR OLD NAVY YET LIVES—THE "DRAKE TOUCH" IN THE NORTH SEA.

The cruisers and destroyers making up the outer guard of the German Fleet safely ensconced behind Heligoland appeared to have supposed that the indiscriminate laying of mines must deter the British Fleet from any considerable operations in the North Sea. Accordingly, their scouts and patrols showed some activity, referred to in an earlier official statement as "a certain liveliness." But their security was false. Based upon information obtained by submarines, the First Light Cruiser and the First Battle Cruiser Squadrons on August 28th, 1914, engaged the German vessels in the Bight of Heligoland in an "operation of some consequence," as it was styled in the official report. This cutting-out action, strongly reminiscent of the tactics delighted in by Drake, was brilliantly successful. Led by the Arethusa, a new oil-fuelled light cruiser, with an attendant fleet of destroyers and submarines, and aided at a concerted moment by the Battle Cruiser Squadron, the British ships sank three German cruisers and two destroyers and damaged many others, without the loss of a British ship of any kind, and with light casualties. Portraits of the commanding officers engaged in this most skilfully handled operation appear on the preceding page.

been thrown on to the streets by the ruthless dismissals carried out by the large stores, wholesale houses, and factories.

So far as the factories were concerned the dismissals were to a great extent unavoidable, since the men trained to control the machinery, overseers, foremen, clerks and managers, were alike now bearing arms. But it would appear that the huge stores, which had gradually become the foremost feature of the shopping world of German cities, acted immediately after the outbreak of war upon principles which were hard to reconcile with the patriotic announcements pasted in their windows. At the end of August, when the legal notices of dismissal took effect, many hundreds of young girls, who had at all times found it difficult to make ends meet, were thrown upon the street.

German brutality begins at home

Charitable organisations did their best to deal with the situation. Cheap kitchens sprang up in all quarters of the town, and the most famous of these organisations, the " Lina Morgenstein," issued an appeal for premises where their relief kitchens could be established. Satisfying meals began to be provided at incredible prices ; young girls thrown out of work could obtain a full meal for prices as low as a penny-halfpenny and as high as fourpence. Side by side with this army of girls there was another, even more pitiable class, for whom it was difficult to make any satisfactory arrangement. This was the great class of lodging - house keepers, proprietors of pensions, and still more of women who had subsisted by letting rooms to factory girls and foreigners.

FRENCH CAVALRY TO AID THE BELGIANS AT NAMUR.
Before the fall of Namur rendered Franco-Belgian operations in that district useless, French cavalry reinforcements were pushed forward to support and cover Belgian infantry round Namur. One of the many devices adopted against the ubiquitous raiding Uhlans was the blocking of roads by obstructions such as that which Belgian soldiers are seen removing. Inset : A Belgian soldier writing on the field to his family.

The city of Berlin, in particular, began suddenly to realise to what extent it had depended for its very existence upon Russians, Americans, Austrians, Swedes, and other foreigners. Whole classes of its female population, with scores of tradesmen, found themselves faced, not only by ruin, but by actual lack of food to appease their hunger, and the Government was compelled— earlier, probably, than had been supposed—to step in to save these people from sheer starvation. Very soon, too, it became clear to Germany what had been effected by the silent, unsensational work of the British Fleet. In all directions the military governors had to announce that great restrictions must be placed upon the use of electricity, coal, gas, and so forth. Largely with this object an order was issued suspending inter-urban traffic after midnight.

Effects of British sea command

It is true that the dancing-halls of the city, which had given Berlin its peculiar cachet, were allowed to keep open their doors in many instances, but they were forbidden to employ orchestras playing ragtime tunes, they were compelled to reduce their lighting plant, and a sharp control was even exercised upon the supply of alcoholic beverages. To all intents and purposes the stopping of tram and train service after midnight put an end to the night life of Berlin. The business of the civil population, as the military government conceived it, was not to keep things going, but to discontinue almost all forms of relaxation involving expenditure. Electric light advertisements, illuminated sky signs, and even the excessive illumination of shop-windows was either forbidden or greatly restricted.

GERMAN CAVALRY RAIDERS CROSSING THE MEUSE IN CANVAS BOATS.
Parties crossed the river in canvas boats bound together with lances, while the men used other lances as oars.   The horses were made to swim across.

Nor did the newspapers escape the heavy hand of the military authorities.   The reckless flooding of the streets with free-editions announcing great German victories was summarily stopped ; and just as at the outset the Government had seized the opportunity to favour those individuals who had for years subserved their purposes, so now they took the same line against such papers as had in peace times dared to criticise Army or bureaucracy. The publication of military news was restricted to the bare statements issued by the General Staff, and the authorities saw to it that these announcements reached the reptile Press sooner than papers which had been numbered amongst the critics of the Government system.

But they were careful, as in all else, to maintain the cloak of righteousness.   At first, for example, the sale of Socialist papers was forbidden on bookstalls and in the street ;   but even this restriction was removed as soon as

Berlin's cloak of righteousness

the iron had eaten into the Socialist soul, and the international theorists upon whom a few foreign observers had set their hopes had in turn taken up that patriotic attitude which competent critics had always expected of them.   It may none the less be true that there was amongst considerable sections of the community a conviction that the war had been thrust upon them, not by dire necessity, but by the ungoverned ambitions of the militarist caste.

But the temper of the mob, inflamed, as has been seen, by the deliberate action of the authorities, was such that even the expression of the mildest criticism was like to prove dangerous to life and limb.   The most strenuous advocates of the general strike, and even that arch-enthusiast, Rosa Luxemburg, were left unmolested by the authorities, who, grinning in their sleeves, commended such unpatriotic personages to the gentle attentions of the mob.

To revert for a moment to the effect of the war upon German commercial life, it should be remembered that, to a very large extent, even in peace time, the trade and commerce of German towns had depended upon the requirements of members of the armed forces.   There was work enough, of course, in Essen and Dusseldorf, in the tinned meat factories in the neighbourhood of Berlin and in the Rhineland, in the huge establishments manufacturing war stores of every kind, but elsewhere there was a sudden cessation of demand

Many tradesmen, especially in small garrison towns, had subsisted upon the patronage of Army men of the active or retired services. These found their trade suddenly vanish, and indeed it became clear that the repeated warnings of people watching the progress of Germany against the growth of luxury and extravagance in all classes were justified more by the sudden cessation of this demand for luxuries than by any apparent weakening of the stamina of the nation in its hour of need. Of the many thousands of men, and more especially of women, who found themselves suddenly without employment and without means of subsistence, a large proportion had been employed in the production of articles unknown, or almost unknown, to the nation which fought the war of 1870 ; and it may well be that the growth of luxury recoiled sooner upon the heads of those who had ministered to it than upon those who had indulged therein.

In Germany, no less than elsewhere, there was not only an overlapping of charity, but also at the outset, a remarkably unintelligent employment of voluntary assistance. This was most noticeable on the whole in the case of the Post Office. Whilst there were crowds of women clamouring for any employment of any kind that would give them a

IN THE OLD ALSATIAN LAND AGAIN.
When the French outposts entered their old lost province of Alsace, the first thing they saw was a vision of two children gathering wood, heedless of war and its horrors.

roof to cover them and bread to eat, the German Post Office began to employ as volunteers the sons of good families (even noblemen's children are said to have been amongst them) to fill the places of postmen, letter-sorters, and other officials sent to the front.

Protest after protest began to appear in the popular Press, but some weeks passed before the Government took it in hand to remedy a shortcoming, which in well organised Germany was, to say the least of it, less to be expected than elsewhere. The measures taken for getting in the harvest were, on the other hand, both prompt and so far as could be judged, effective. So soon as the mobilisation was completed, the Government announced that a large number of free tickets would be issued to suitable persons of either sex willing to be transported where the need for harvest hands was greatest. In particular, these free tickets were issued to people desiring to return from the cities to homes in the country, where the harvest was still in progress.

It was calculated that in such cases the cost of maintenance was reduced from nearly three pounds to about fifteen shillings a month—that

EXILES FOR THE TERM OF THE WAR.
German prisoners at a French railway station. It is said that the German private accepted his captivity with calmness and equanimity, but that officers proved unable to adjust themselves to their situation.

HAPPILY ENCAMPED AMIDST THE RUINS THEY HAVE MADE.
German infantry resting in the yard of a Belgian farmhouse destroyed in the fighting.

is, of course, the cost to the State in the way of consumption of food, light, and the other necessities of existence whereof Germany soon found herself obliged to be extremely economical. Wherever schools could be used in the early days without long transport by rail, the schoolboys were virtually compelled to assist in the work of the harvest ; and even later, when the potato crop was being gathered, they were

Boys forced to the harvest employed to gather the bundles of dried potato halm, and, later, to sort the tubers themselves. Towards the end of August, when communication by train once more began to be more or less possible, large numbers of people left Berlin and other cities for the open country, carrying with them, for the most part, no more than a blanket wherewith to modify the unaccustomed bed of straw in a barn, which was all that they were offered. The average payment for their services was about ninepence a day.

Other official measures to control the sudden dislocation of employment were, for example, the announcement that an eight hours' day would be made the maximum in all trades not concerned immediately with the provisioning of the Army. As has already been pointed out in a previous chapter, one of the earliest signs of the money stringency was the disappearance of small change.

In some parts of Germany, particularly, it would appear, in the mining districts of Silesia, it became necessary for the municipalities to issue local notes for small change. The authorities of Gleiwitz, the well-known mining town, for example, issued local paper notes of the value of one shilling, having currency only within the town and its immediate district.

Much self-congratulation was expressed by the German Press over the fact that Germany, alone of the great nations, found it unnecessary to resort officially to a moratorium. There is, however, an explanation of this fact which seems to have been unduly overlooked. The German civil code provides for a kind of private moratorium between debtor and creditor in the event of war. It is true that the provision is not automatic, and that in each

TRANSPORTS OF THE INVADING GERMAN ARMY IN BELGIUM.
Forage waggons passing through Mouland, a village on the Belgian frontier of Holland north of Visé, and one of the first to be burnt by the
invading army from Aix la Chapelle.

separate case it is necessary for the debtor to apply for a postponement of payment through the courts, but arrangements were made whereby such applications should be heard swiftly and relief granted instantly. The result, of course, was that whilst the Empire did not publicly resort to a moratorium, the actual use of this system of officially recognised and controlled private moratoria was very extensive, and served the same purpose. It would almost appear as if here, too, Germany had rather successfully thrown a veil over the actual facts of her situation.

In any case, the German claim that the special measures resorted to by other countries were, for her, quite unnecessary is scarcely justified by the facts. The virtual cessation of foreign business necessarily hit the country very hard, but the collapse of her industrial and commercial activities with the consequent growth of unemployment, was not so immediately apparent as it would have been had she not sent one-tenth of her total population into the firing line. German economists **Victory for Germany speedily or never** had always reckoned that the real pinch would not come until eight or ten weeks after the outbreak of war, and it was because she realised this that Germany, so far as one could judge from published statements, had always largely depended on sudden overwhelming strategy and tactics rather than upon a long war, fought to the last man and the last gun.

Victory must come, her economists appeared to believe, either speedily or never, and this was the real clue to that curious parrot cry of her newspapers, " Paris within a month." A long war, Germany well knew, would be decided behind the firing-line.

Not until the war had been in progress for nearly a fortnight was it possible to see how changed was this German people from the hardy folk that had fought forty years previously. Little by little her population had been drawn to the great urban centres, her people had grown accustomed, if not to luxury, at least to conveniences.

FRENCH CAVALRY MOVING TO CO-OPERATE WITH BELGIAN FORCES AT NAMUR.
This forward movement had to be abandoned after the unexpected fall of Namur had rendered impossible the outflanking operations through the Ardennes, of which it was hoped to have been the pivot.

Their palates had been spoiled for hard fare by delicacies. Their tastes had grown less stern and their requirements greater.

It may have come, therefore, somewhat as a shock to those who still preached that the Germany of 1914 was the Germany of 1870 grown richer and better prepared to find that edicts had to be issued, one after another,

No " ragtime " or comedy in Berlin

restricting the amusements of the people in war time. Between August 15th and the end of the month one finds such announcements successively. Cafés and dancing halls were only allowed to present such music as suited the circumstances in which the nation found itself. Ragtime was not to be tolerated, songs must be either grave or patriotic, theatres were to present only pieces of a warlike or patriotic nature, musical comedy was virtually taboo, and the tingel-tangel, the café chantant, and the cabaret were recommended to close their doors.

The Saturday and Sunday dances beloved of German maidservants were suppressed, and the nation was warned that in this grave crisis of its history gravity must be enforced where it was not voluntarily practised.

It is true, however, that these were largely measures necessitated by the change in the character of the urban population.

It will have been noticed that the crack regiments sent to the western front were drawn very largely from the east and from the south. Here dwelt in peace time the dour yeomen who forced a scanty livelihood from ungenerous soil under unfavourable conditions.

The German General Staff was under no illusion as to the quarters whence it drew the best troops, for the men who had turned the sandy deserts of Eastern Prussia into a garden were the men who might be expected to turn defeat into victory on the field.

Hence the policy of transferring many of the eastern regiments to the fighting-line in the west was not entirely dictated by the desire to avoid any possible reluctance to lay waste, if necessary, a country which was their own homeland, or to fire upon frontier folk who for years had been their neighbours.

THE FRENCH SOLDIER'S DINNER.
With cauldrons of soup and loaves tucked under their arms the frugal meal is complete.

THE FLOWER OF THE FRENCH ARMY AT NAMUR.
A squadron of French Lancers quartered at an inn near Namur. They were to have taken part in the general offensive designed against the German line of communications through the Ardennes.

CHAPTER IX.—THE GERMAN HOST FALLS ON BELGIUM.

" Only a Scrap of Paper ! "—Luxemburg's Neutrality Brushed Aside—Kaiser's Mistaken Idea of Belgian Weakness—King Albert's Supreme Appeal to Great Britain—Sir Edward Goschen's Negotiations at Berlin—British Ultimatum—Belgium's Neutrality Must be Respected—British Ambassador's Remarkable Conversation with Imperial Chancellor—War !—German Army Moves on Liege—Awful Punishment from the Forts—Assault after Assault—The Town Falls—A City of Death—The Forts Crumble One by One—General Leman a Prisoner

"ONLY a scrap of paper ! " said the German Imperial Chancellor, amazed and indignant, to the British Ambassador in Berlin. A treaty ! A promise ! A pledged word !

Surely a very little thing to go to war for ! " Only a scrap of paper ! " But the scrap of paper meant Britain's word given to a weaker nation. And we choose to keep faith and to honour our bond.

* * *

DISMOUNTED FRENCH CAVALRY FIGHTING A REAR-GUARD ACTION.
One of the hundreds of small contests in the long, fiercely pressed strategic retirement of the allied forces through Northern France.

Germany, aiming at the heart of France, had the choice of two lines of attack, once war was declared. The first was barred by a succession of fortresses. The second was protected by a barrier of a more intangible kind—the pledged word and the honour of the nation. The rulers of Germany resolved to let honour go, to break their pledge, and to move forward by the second path.

The central idea of the German plan of campaign against France has always been surprise, speed, and overwhelming force. The entire forces of the Empire were to be mobilised at once, and immense masses of soldiers hurried in the direction of Paris, before France had time to complete her plans or assemble her troops. To this end every effort had long been directed. Everything had been kept ready year by year along the frontiers of Alsace-Lorraine and Luxemburg, from the little stocks of emergency rations renewed each week the holsters of every cavalryman, to stores of provisions in the towns, the hay waiting in the mangers, and chloroform and lint in the hospitals. Sufficient carts and horses or motor-waggons were always available.

Along the line of frontier there were hospital stores and bedding to deal with 160,000 sick and wounded men within six weeks of the outbreak of war. Nothing was left to chance. Endless lines of detraining platforms at the frontier stations, sufficient in number and length for Army units, were prepared. Germany was ready.

The direct line of attack lies along the border of Alsace and Lorraine, from Longwy, near the Grand Duchy of Luxemburg, to Belfort, on the edge of Switzerland. Along this whole line France has built a series of strong linked forts and other defences between Belfort, Epinal, Toul, and Verdun. These four great fortresses, with their supporting chains of forts and long lines of entrenchments, present a formidable front. It would be madness to expect to capture them by storm, even with the most recklessly brave attack. They would require

INDIAN TROOPS FOR EUROPE.
Great satisfaction was aroused by the announcement that it was decided to bring over divisions of Indian troops to reinforce British troops in the field.

weeks and possibly months of formal investment. They presented an obstacle which even the German Imperial will had to admit might be fatal. They might be taken in time, after great slaughter and at great price, as Port Arthur was taken by the Japanese. But the delay would enable France to make herself ready.

The other choice before Germany was to attack France through neighbouring states—the Grand Duchy of Luxemburg and the Kingdom of Belgium. Germany, however, had pledged and repeated her word in solemn treaties to leave the neutrality of these two states inviolate.

The Grand Duchy of Luxemburg is a survival from mediæval Europe—a little state planted down between France, Germany, and Belgium, less than a thousand square miles in area, with a population of a little over a quarter of a million people. In other words, it has an area of something less than the county of Northampton, and a population considerably less than that of the borough of Bradford. It has long been one of the most placid, peaceful, and prosperous corners of Europe.

Its ruler, the Grand Duchess Marie Louise Adelheid, governed her little Duchy in constitutional fashion through her Upper House and representative Parliament. All the formalities of a

OFFICERS AND MEN OF SIKH REGIMENT.
The burning desire displayed by all sections of the Indian Army to serve in Great Britain's hour of need sufficiently dispelled certain absurd German hopes.

great Court were maintained. The people had long been very prosperous. Education was abundantly provided for in excellent schools. There were Courts of Law, local tribunals, and a High Court of Justice. What Luxemburg lacked was a defensive force. Its old-times fortifications had been dismantled, and its Army consisted of a small troop of Royal Guards, who, in addition to their military duties, performed auxiliary work as postmen.

Luxemburg was for many centuries the very heart of the fighting ground of Europe. Campaign after campaign swept over its borders. In 1867 it all but caused a war between France and Prussia. The Powers of Europe extended to the little state their protection in that year. In a treaty drawn up at that time, to which

Great Britain, France, and Prussia gave their adherence, the Grand Duchy of Luxemburg was declared neutral territory, and Europe pledged itself to maintain its neutrality.

With Belgium there was a similar obstacle. Here, too, we have a little country that was for untold centuries a land of strife. It was nicknamed the "cock-pit of Europe," and with good reason. Here the struggles of many nations, the struggles of religions, and the struggles of race seemed to centre themselves. Here Catholic Spain and Protestant Holland met. Here the first Churchill won his dukedom. Here Napoleon met his Waterloo. Soon after the close of the Napoleonic wars the Powers of Europe determined to bring peace to Belgium. The neutrality and independence of the land were defined in a treaty drawn up in 1831, and finally ratified in 1839, to which England, France, and Prussia were parties. No Power was to invade Belgium, no Power was to attack her, no Power was to move its troops through Belgian territory. This pledge was subsequently repeated and confirmed on more than one occasion.

The "cock-pit of Europe" in peace

Under this European pledge of peace, Belgium flourished amazingly. Fresh industries sprang up, and great manufacturing and merchant towns, such as Antwerp and Liege, attained prosperity. Antwerp became one of the greatest ports in the world. Scores of thriving centres of population came into being. Brussels grew to be a little Paris, and its delights and glories, its art treasures, and its pleasant life, drew visitors from everywhere. There was Louvain, the Oxford of the low countries, a centre of culture ; and Malines, of lace fame, a combination of quaintness and modernism. Ostend grew to be the most fashionable watering-place in Northern Europe.

AMERICAN VOLUNTEERS FOR THE FRENCH ARMY ON THEIR WAY TO ENLIST IN PARIS.
American private sympathies are almost entirely with the forces of the Triple Alliance, and in Paris American residents are translating their sympathies into practice, as in the case of the party seen above on their way to enlist.

The Belgian people, under the protection of the great Powers, almost forgot in time the generations of cruel suffering that they had endured. Here and there you would find in the country homes relics of the bad, old days —assignats left by Napoleon's soldiery, old pistols used as a defence in former days against military marauders. They were now nothing but historic curiosities.

The people, the Walloons and the Flemings, kindly, industrious, and prudent, rejoiced in their settled life. Their farms were enlarged, their herds flourished, their store-houses were filled, their children grew up without fear. No longer had they to tell tales of parents shot or daughters ravished by invading soldiery. Their lovely country—the Ardennes, the valley of the Meuse, the Belgian Luxemburg, the   **Kaiser underestimates Belgian grit** long sea coast—became one of the pleasure spots of the world.

Only the pledged word of Germany, as has been said, stood between her and the easy road by which to attack France. The Kaiser and his advisers resolved to break their troth and to invade the two neutral states. No one imagined that the Belgians could offer serious resistance to Germany if her armies attempted to march through Belgium. Less than an eighth the size of Germany, with a weak Army, with insufficient troops to guard properly her three great fortified cities of Antwerp, Liege, and Namur, the very idea of Belgium withstanding the German will seemed ludicrous, not alone to German military men, but also to the majority of the serious students of European politics. Moreover, a steady process of Germanising Belgium had been for some time in progress. In Antwerp commercial affairs were largely in German hands. German influence predominated in finance, in the export trade, and in manufactures. German chauvinists dreamed of the time when Belgium would fall like a ripe apple into the lap of their Empire. Some of them had even published maps of Europe with Belgium coloured red like Greater Germany. "We will sweep Belgium on one side like *that*," the Kaiser is reported to have said on one occasion to a friend when discussing Belgium, sweeping his arm characteristically as he did so.

Some days before the outbreak of war, Sir Edward Grey communicated with both the French and German Governments, asking if they were prepared to respect Belgium's neutrality. France promptly replied that she was ; the German Foreign Minister declared that he rather doubted whether he could answer at all, as any reply that might be given would disclose part of the German campaign in the event of war.

During the week ending August 2nd, the Germans moved a considerable force, about 600,000 men, in the direction of the French and Luxemburg frontiers. They were resolved to strike hard, to strike quickly, and to strike with resistless force. In the early hours of Sunday morning, August 2nd, strong forces of German soldiers entered Luxemburg. One force arrived by train, another moved along the roadways by motors, and the troops seized the railways, the bridges, the telegraph stations, the telephones, and all means of communication. Every man had his place, and every man moved to his place with automatic precision.

All the details of this military occupation had been planned in

OVERWORKED RED CROSS MEN.
For the non-combatants attached to the Expeditionary Force in France, like the R.A.M.C. men seen resting in the photograph, there was an immense amount of work and not a little risk since the Germans took to marking out Red Cross men especially.

advance. They were all supervised and directed by young men who had acted as clerks and assistants in business houses and in factories in the Duchy, and who now put on their uniforms as officers in the German Army. These young men quickly indicated all citizens liable to German military service, such as expatriated Alsatians, and all who had prominently shown anti-German sentiment. These were arrested.

The first German party was commanded by a major. As it marched up the Boulevard de la Liberté in the city of Luxemburg, and crossed the Adolphe Bridge, it was met by a Cabinet Minister, M. Myschen, who had arrived in a motor, and had turned his car lengthways across the road to bar the way. M. Myschen held a copy of the treaty

ENGLISH NURSES AT HAVRE.
Attached to the British Expeditionary Force even the nurses ran some risks if they are near the fighting-line. It was stated that no fewer than twelve French Red Cross nurses were shot by the Germans.

guaranteeing Luxemburg's independence in his hand, and showed it to the German officer, who replied that he knew the treaty, but that it was his business to execute his orders, which he would do. The young Grand Duchess herself then drove up in a motor, which was also placed across the bridge beside that of the Minister. She demanded that the neutrality of the Luxemburg should be respected. The major gruffly bade her go home.

That same afternoon the German Minister presented a telegram from the German Imperial Chancellor to the Luxemburg Minister of State, saying that the military measures taken by the Germans there did not constitute

HOW ONE BRITISH GUNNER FOUGHT   AGAINST SEVERAL GERMAN BATTERIES.

Few stories of heroism are finer than that told by Mr. Hamilton Fyfe of a Royal Field Artillery gunner. His battery had so galled the Germans that they concentrated on it the fire of several batteries, until, one by one, the guns were silenced, and all but one of the gunners slain. He went on serving his gun as best he could, steadily and calmly, and would have gone on till he, too, dropped, had he not been ordered to leave his gun.

a hostile act—they were simply measures to protect the working of the railways connected with the German system against a possible attack by French troops.

The people of the Luxemburg, who have never loved the Germans, were now to know what German military occupation meant. Within a few hours the whole Grand Duchy was in the occupation of the German armies. Outposts were placed at every frontier, and the Duchy itself was turned into a base for further advances. Military headquarters were established, and the fields, the houses, and the woods were overrun with soldiery.

"Soon afterwards the work of military destruction began," wrote Dr. Dillon, in the "Daily Telegraph," " villages and farmhouses being demolished, and thickets cut down for strategic purposes. Terror reigns throughout Luxemburg since then. A farmer with provisions, being stopped and his waggons seized, grumbled. He was arrested, taken before a court-martial, and has not been heard of since. From Luxemburg to Rodange the fields are devastated, houses razed to the ground, trenches dug, and whoever casts a glance at these is arrested as a spy. In a word, the population of the Grand Duchy is learning the meaning of the words ' reign of terror.' "

On the following day, Monday, August 3rd, the German Minister presented an ultimatum to Belgium, asking from her an attitude of friendly neutrality and permission for German troops to pass through Belgian territory, and promising in return to maintain the independence of the kingdom of Belgium and its possessions. If Belgium refused, Germany declared, she would be treated as an enemy. Twelve hours were given for a reply, the twelve hours expiring at seven o'clock on Tuesday morning.

The King of the Belgians turned to England. King Albert telegraphed to King George, " I make a supreme appeal to the diplomatic intervention of your Majesty's Government to safeguard the integrity of Belgium."

MEMBERS OF THE FRENCH STAFF IN THE FIELD.

England promptly intimated to Germany that she would fulfil her treaty obligations, and help Belgium, if necessary, by force of arms.

The full story of the negotiations that followed between England and Germany was told in a remarkable official report written by Sir Edward Goschen, our former Ambassador at Berlin, and published by the British Government later in the month. On Tuesday morning, when, following the refusal of King Albert to yield to the German demands, German troops crossed the frontier, Sir Edward Goschen called upon the German Secretary of State, Herr von Jagow, and inquired whether the Imperial Government would refrain from violating Belgian neutrality. Herr von Jagow at once replied that he was sorry to say that his answer must be " No." German troops had already crossed the frontier. The Imperial Government had been obliged to take this step because they had to advance into France by the quickest and easiest way, so as to be able to get well ahead with their operations, and endeavour to strike some decisive blow as early as possible.

It was a matter of life and death for them, for if they had gone by the more southern route they could not have hoped, in view of the paucity of roads and the strength of the fortresses, to have got through without formidable opposition, entailing great loss of time. This loss of time would have given time to the Russians to bring up their troops to the German frontier. " Rapidity of action was **British Ultimatum presented in Berlin** the great German asset, while that of Russia was an inexhaustible supply of troops."

Our Ambassador pointed out the gravity of the situation thus created, and asked whether there was not still time to draw back and avoid possible deplorable consequences. The answer was that it was impossible.

That same afternoon, acting on further instructions from Downing Street, Sir Edward Goschen again went to the German Imperial Foreign Office—this time to present a British ultimatum. He informed the Secretary of State that unless the German Government could give assurances by twelve o'clock that night that they would proceed no further with their violation of the Belgian frontier and stop their advance, he had been instructed to demand his passports, and to announce that the British Government would have to take all steps in their power to uphold the neutrality of Belgium and the observances of a treaty to which Germany was as much a party as ourselves. This meant war.

Again came a refusal. The safety of the German Empire, Herr von Jagow said, made it absolutely necessary that the German troops should advance through Belgium. The British Ambassador asked if, in view of the terrible consequences which would necessarily ensue, it would not be possible, even at the last moment, that this answer should be reconsidered. Again came a negative. The British Ambassador then replied that in the case of a refusal he would have to demand his passports.

Sir Edward Goschen resolved to leave no step unturned, asked for an interview with the German Imperial Chancellor, Dr. von Bethmann-Hollweg. The interview was a very painful one. The Chancellor began a long harangue. Just for a scrap of paper, Great Britain was going to make war on a kindred nation, who desired nothing better than to be friends with her. What Great Britain had done was unthinkable ; it was like striking a man from behind who was fighting for his life between two assailants. He held Great Britain responsible for all the terrible things that might happen.

Our Ambassador replied that it was a matter of life and death to Great Britain that she should keep her solemn engagement to do her utmost to defend Belgium's neutrality, if attacked. Otherwise, what confidence could anyone have in engagements given by Great Britain in the future ?

" But at what price will that compact have been kept? Has the British Government thought of that?" the Chancellor asked. "I hinted to his Excellency," said Sir Edward Goschen, "as plainly as I could, that fear of consequences could hardly be regarded as an excuse for breaking solemn engagements. But his Excellency was so excited, so evidently overcome by the news of our action, and so little disposed to hear reason, that I refrained from adding fuel to the flame by further argument."

This conversation took place early in the evening. About half-past nine, Herr von Zimmerman, Under-Secretary of State, came to see our Ambassador, who told him that the British Government expected an answer to a definite question by twelve o'clock that night, and in default of a satisfactory answer they would be forced to take such steps as their engagements required. Herr Zimmerman said that was, in fact, a declaration of war, as the Imperial Government could not possibly give the assurance required, either that night or any other night. And

a declaration of war it was.

Britain keeps her pledge—war declared

During that same day, and for some days before, Germany had been acting. Early on Tuesday morning, German troops, who were waiting in a large number of motor-cars—rumour placed them at 3,000 cars—received word to make a dash forward to secure the bridges and seize the railways of Belgium, and hurl their forces through the country in the direction of France. They did not anticipate any serious resistance. The men were assured by their officers that the Belgians would receive them in friendly fashion.

But the Belgians knew what was coming, and were too quick for the invaders. Before the German motor-cars could move ahead, the bridges across the Meuse in the south of Belgium had been blown up, and every

MEMBERS OF THE BRITISH EXPEDITIONARY FORCE HAPPY ON THEIR WAY TO THE FRONT.
Everywhere on its journeys in France the British Expeditionary Force aroused the keenest interest and enthusiasm. Glimpses such as those given above of the men thoroughly at home in a foreign though friendly land, cooking meals when they could get them, and cheerfully supporting travel hardships, endeared our soldiers to the French.

R

village and every fort prepared to resist.   At the first threat of war the entire Belgian people had become as one. All minor differences were forgotten.   Social Democrats and Conservatives joined hands ; workmen and employers obliterated their quarrels.   From capitalists to common labourers the nation was united.   The women outdid the men in the great burst of national enthusiasm and resolution.

RUIN IN THE PRINCIPAL SQUARE OF LOUVAIN.
Showing the gutted cathedral, and also the Hotel de Ville, which was spared.

A SCENE OF DESOLATION NEAR LOUVAIN RAILWAY STATION.
Over a thousand houses in the city were utterly destroyed.

The fortified city of Liege stood directly in the line of the German troops.   It was necessary for them to buy or to capture it.   Liege is the Birmingham of Belgium, one of the most notable and charming cities in the country, splendidly and beautifully placed, with a great history behind it.

It is the capital of the Walloon country, and has long been noted for the sturdy independence of its people. It is an important industrial centre, a community of gunsmiths—there being no fewer than 40,000 gunsmiths in the city and suburbs.   In addition to manufacturing cheap rifles for a large part of the world, it has a cannon factory for the casting of big guns, and had supplied much of the artillery for the Belgian Army.   In the suburb of Seraign, five miles away, the great Cockerill ironworks, which rank among the largest in the world, are placed.   They were founded eighty-three years ago by an Englishman, but have been for many years solely under Belgian control.   Zinc foundries, engine factories, locomotive, cycle, and motor works, and a flax-spinning factory, are among Liege's industries.

For hundreds of years the beauty of the city, the activity,

GENERAL VIEW OF LOUVAIN, THE SCENE OF THE MOST SENSELESS CRIME OF THE WAR.
This photograph, the first to reach London, was taken from Mont Cæsar, and presents a vivid picture of the barbaric destruction wrought in the centre of Belgian intellectual culture by the Germans with bomb and fire on August 25th, 1914.

BOMBARDMENT OF DEFENCELESS MALINES.
On both August 28th and August 30th, 1914, without apparent reason, a German force bombarded the beautiful old town of Malines, although it was undefended and empty of inhabitants. Terrible damage was done, and not even the cathedral spared.

the intelligence, and the enterprise of its people have been the theme of many writers. The fine public buildings, the churches, the handsome Academy of Fine Arts, and the university, are placed in a wonderfully picturesque situation.

Next to Antwerp, Liege was the greatest fortified place in Belgium. It was surrounded by a series of detached forts, constructed about a quarter of a century ago under General Brialmont, a famous Belgian engineer. There were twelve of these detached forts, each from three and a half to five and a half miles from the city, in a circumference measuring thirty-one miles. Each of these forts was an independent unit.

On the right bank of the Meuse were the forts of Barchon, Evegnée, Fléron, Chaudfontaine, Embourg, and Boncalles. The two chief of these covered the main line of railway from Cologne. On the left bank of the river the forts were Pontine, Liers, Lantin, Loncine Hollogne, and Flémalle. Six of these forts were large and six small. The larger forts were considered by many impregnable. Each consisted of a triangular mass of concrete with, sunk in it, revolving and disappearing steel turrets. Their armament consisted of two 6 in. howitzers, four 5 in.

DAMAGE AND DESTRUCTION OF PRIVATE HOUSES.
Vivid pictures of the fell work of German shells.

GERMAN SACRILEGE—WRECKING HISTORIC CHURCHES.
Churches in other places, as well as the 15th century church at Malines, were bombarded with deliberation and without military necessity of any kind.

quick-firing guns, and three outer quick-firing guns in disappearing turrets. The forts were well equipped with machine-guns and with searchlights, protected with armour, and surrounded by moats. The small forts had two guns fewer than the larger ones.

Military experts were by no means unanimous in their views concerning the value of the forts of Liege. Many, including, it is said, the Kaiser himself, thought that owing to the careless way in which they were generally looked after and the absence of an adequate force of troops, or of sufficient ammunition, they were negligible. There was some excuse for thinking so, as it was notorious that the forts had been for a long time guarded with great laxity. What the Germans evidently did not know was that, some months before war was declared, a brave and active military commander, General Leman, had taken charge, had secured troops, and had placed the twelve forts in strong position.

" The Walloons," said one German writer, the notable Baedeker, " are an active, intelligent, and enterprising race. '*Cives Leodicenses sunt ingeniosi, sagaces et ad quidvis audendum prompti,*' is the opinion expressed by Guicciardini with regard to the Liegeois. Indefatigable industry and a partiality for severe labour are among their strongest characteristics, but they have frequently manifested a fierce and implacable spirit of hostility towards those who have attempted to infringe their privileges."

Germany was to find that the men of Liege were still true to their ancient reputation. They had often faced internal fighting in the centuries that had passed. Time after time they had fought against invaders. Charles the Bold of Burgundy

GERMAN SUPPLIES ON THEIR WAY THROUGH BELGIUM TO FRANCE.

captured the town in 1468, razed its walls, and slew thousands of the inhabitants. Between then and the beginning of the last century it was taken and re-taken by different nations at least ten times, and after almost every capture there was a general slaughter of the people. Now the Liegeois were to undergo the same experience once more, and were to show that they had not lost their old courage and powers of endurance.

On the first news of the outbreak of war everyone responded enthusiastically to the call to arms. The people

GERMAN MACHINE-GUN COMPANY IN A BELGIAN WOOD.
German machine-guns were smartly handled and with terrible effect. The type of weapon seen here can be fired without being mounted on tripods.

assisted the Government in every possible way to prepare for the attack of the Germans. They gave up their motor-cars, their food, their cattle and their horses, willingly and gladly. " They were one and all filled with the determination to defend the country," writes a professor at the local university. The people in Liege were extremely patriotic, and there was not the slightest sign of flinching. A number of troops were poured in, according to report nearly 20,000 men, and the city made ready to meet all emergencies. On the morning of Monday, August 3rd, M. Kleyer, the burgomaster, was informed that the situation was very serious, and that strong German forces were mustered on the frontier. At seven o'clock on Tuesday morning the forts sounded the alarm, announcing that war had been declared. The German army had entered Belgium, and troops were already seen in the outer suburbs.

THE COMMISSARIAT WAGGONS, THE SINEWS OF THE ARMY, MASSED IN THE PLACE D'ANVERS.
A distinct feature of the German occupation of Brussels, for the purpose of overawing the Belgians, was the detached and almost casual interest displayed by the spectators and inhabitants.

THE GERMAN ARMY'S SPECTACULAR OCCUPATION OF BRUSSELS.
Companies of infantry and artillery standing at ease in the Grand Place while several troops of Lancers march through on their triumphal progress.

THE OFFENSIVE MAINTAINED BY THE BELGIAN ARMY IN THE NORTH.
After the fall of Liege and Namur, and the concentration of the main army in and about Antwerp, scattered companies and regiments continuously arrived from all parts of Belgium, and served as reinforcements to maintain the offensive by harrying the Germans. Here a battery is seen taking up an advanced position some miles from Antwerp.

General Leman, the military commander of the city, a man whose fame was soon to ring through Europe, was an officer in the Belgian Engineer Corps, and was formerly professor and examiner in mathematics in the military school, where he had risen to the post of Director of Studies. He had hitherto been regarded as a bookman rather than as a good soldier in the field. He was famous as a mathematician, and had written mathematical treatises known throughout the world. A man of the desk and the study, a theorist, a schoolmaster, he might have been considered the least fitted to deal with a rough-and- **Huge German army rolls down to Liege** tumble invasion, and to face the first onrush of the enthusiastic and overwhelming forces of Germany. He was to prove, however, that the student soldier can make a masterly leader in action.

On Tuesday morning the German army moved out in the direction of Liege. Spectators say that the advance was a magnificent sight. The army rolled slowly down to the River Meuse, bringing with it innumerable machine-guns and motor-waggons. The troops were in their green-grey uniform. Aeroplanes soared in the sky reconnoitring overhead. It was noted that the uniforms were new in every detail. The troops

BELGIAN SAPPERS PREPARE THE WAY FOR "CAPTAIN FLOOD."
Sea and river flood, ever powerful allies in the history of Flanders, were turned to brilliant advantage by Belgian engineers against a German movement to cut off communications between Antwerp and Ostend on September 5th, 1914. German troops between Malines and Termonde were flooded out by opening the dykes of the Scheldt, and large captures of men and artillery were made by the Belgian forces. In the photograph above sappers are seen removing obstructions to the flow of the waters.

appeared as if they were carrying out a triumphâl march. As an English girl said about that time, " They looked like soldiers on the stage."

The first objective of the army was the frontier town of Visé, a Belgian Custom-house station, a little place of 3,600 people, the centre at that time of a prosperous, agricultural community. Visé, with its noted parish church, its pilgrim resort of the Loretto chapel on the hill, its good hotels, and its quaint town hall, was well known to many as a holiday resort. The Germans expected to occupy the town without resistance.

The German cavalry were met by Belgian cavalry, whom they drove back. A great mass of German infantry quickly followed, and a little band of four hundred Belgians did their best to oppose the Germans from the other side of the river. The Belgians blew up the two central arches of the railway bridge,

The terror of the Hun in the town of Vise and prepared to defend Visé itself. In this they were supported by many of the people. The peasants and the farmers, even the women, helped them by every means in their power. After three hours' fighting the Belgian forces were driven back in the direction of Liege.

Then the Germans took a terrible revenge. They had determined beforehand, by striking terror at the beginning, to crush any resistance on the part of the community at large. The policy

BELGIAN LANCER WITH UHLAN'S HORSE AND TROPHIES.

of terrorism was relentlessly carried out. The burgomaster of Visé was put against the wall and shot. Many other persons—not soldiers in uniform—men or women found with arms in their hands, or suspected of bearing arms, were immediately put to death. Visé itself was burned to the ground.

The Germans later attempted to justify this policy. " The only means of preventing surprise attacks from

THIRD BELGIAN INFANTRY OF THE LINE ENTERING LIEGE FOR ITS DEFENCE.

After the bombardment and incessant assault upon the forts of Liege had proceeded for three days, General Leman, influenced by the civil authorities, offered to permit the Germans to occupy the town to save it from bombardment. This offer having been rejected, without the surrender of the forts, the bombardment began, and on August 6th, 1914, the gallant defenders of the town found it necessary to retire, leaving the way open for the German entry, which was hailed in Berlin, prematurely, as a great German triumph.

the civil population," said an official message on August 22nd, " has been to interfere with relentless severity, and to create examples which by their frightfulness would be a warning to the whole country." Visé was certainly a terrible warning. The Germans on their arrival found it a town of plenty. In a few hours it was a ruin, many of its former prosperous people killed, others driven forth with nothing but what they stood up in ; children crying for their parents, and mothers searching for their little ones. Orphans and fatherless moved on towards the Dutch frontier, to throw themselves on the mercy of the pitiful and sympathetic people there.

The fighting at the mill bridge at Visé was specially severe. " The German infantry were in deep masses," wrote Mr. J. M. N. Jeffries, the special correspondent of the " Daily Mail," who witnessed the early fighting, " flanked by batteries of field guns and quick-firing guns. The 12th Belgian line regiment took up their position behind the walls of the houses along the Meuse. The fusillade lasted **The German tornado breaks on Vise** half an hour. The Germans then brought up guns in front of Luxhe and Hallembaye, while the German sappers constructed a bridge of boats. The men at Fort Barchon let them build the bridge, but once it was finished they destroyed the pontoons with some shells. During the fight at Visé a Belgian sergeant, stepping out from the ranks, knelt down amid a hail of bullets to take aim at a group of German staff officers, bringing down three. The German losses were eighty, and the Belgians twelve killed and wounded."

The Belgians, retiring on Liege, destroyed everything before them—bridges, tunnels, railways, rolling stock. Village after village was fired in order that it might not give shelter to the invaders. Thus the village of Boncelles was dressed with tar, which was poured on

TROPHIES OF VICTORY.
German cavalry equipment captured in the battle of Haelen, August 13th, 1914, by the victorious Belgians

all the woodwork. The soldiers then set fire to the church, the presbytery, and two large villas. When the Belgians came to a tunnel they pulled up the rails for some distance inside, and then ran an engine in. The driver jumped off the locomotive just before it entered. The engine was derailed when it reached the point where the rails had been torn up, thus blocking the line. Other engines were run in against it, making the whole **Hatred and hostility for the invaders** entrance one confused and tangled mass of wreckage. In places, the roads were ruined, explosives being planted underneath,

ABANDONED BY THE FLEEING GERMANS.
In order to lighten their load when in flight from the Belgians after the battle of Haelen, German soldiers threw away haversacks, rifles, coats, and numberless other articles, which were gathered up for use by the Belgians.

connected by electric wires, and detonated as the German troops advanced. Traps were set everywhere. At each corner a sharpshooter waited, ready to die provided he had killed some of the enemy first.

The Germans had expected a friendly population ; they were staggered at the indications of hatred and of settled hostility that met them at every turn. They retorted by burning houses, shooting people, and by showing a systematic savagery, in accordance with orders from their headquarters.

But the loss of a few score or of a few hundred men could do little to check the German army, estimated at 160,000, which followed the advance guard. As the Germans attempted to cross the river they came under the fire of the guns from the forts, guns directed in the early stages by aeroplanes. The Germans attempted to make pontoon bridges. The bridges were scarcely completed before well-directed shots demolished them. The gunners in the forts had every range taken, and could place the shells with automatic regularity on any spot desired within range.

But even the destruction of the bridges could not hold the Germans back. They crossed the Meuse in small boats, in rafts, in any way that they could. They sent their war aeroplanes and a Zeppelin airship to reconnoitre over Liege. The Zeppelin was struck by the fire from a fort, and fell. One German airman, it is said, who flew over Liege was attacked by a Belgian war aeroplane, which charged at a height of over 1,500 feet

GERMAN PRISONERS IN A CONVENT AT BRUGES.

GERMANS ARRESTED IN LONDON IMMEDIATELY AFTER DECLARATION OF WAR UNDER GUARD AT "OLYMPIA."

GERMAN PRISONERS IN THE CAMBERLEY COMPOUND.
Some were naval prisoners brought to England after the Heligoland engagement.
Barbed wire entanglements, charged with electric currents, made escape hopeless.

and cut it in half. The airman was reported to have escaped with his life.

On Tuesday night the German soldiers, impatient at the delay, crept past the forts in towards the town As they were moving quietly across the open space a great search-light suddenly played on them, covering them with a blaze of light, and the guns of the forts opened a tremendous fusillade. The Germans, dazzled by the light, not knowing where to go, unable to resist, moved almost blindly about in the shambles of death. There was nowhere to hide, no escape from the pitiless, unceasing hail of shrapnel. It is said that not a single man of this bold party

CHEERFUL SPIRIT — **OF THE FRENCH SOLDIER.**
Infantrymen on the march snatch- gay adventure.   Both rest and food were
ing rest and a meal by the inevitably haphazard during the long and
roadside, in all the spirit of perilous retreat from Belgium to the Marne.

returned to the German lines. The few not killed were taken prisoners.

On Wednesday, August 5th, the Germans opened a violent attack against the Barchon fort. The ever-growing cannonading gradually extended to the forts of Fleron, Embourg, and Boncalles. The artillery practice was very good, but the shells used were far too light to have much effect on the steel cupolas and concrete-supported sides of the forts. During the afternoon the German infantry advanced and attempted to storm the forts. They came on in close order, endeavouring by sheer weight of numbers to carry all before them. But rush and dash and daring are of very little use against men armed with modern guns behind the walls of a well-equipped fort. The Belgian heavy guns and howitzers seemed to fill the heavens with bursting shell.

As the German troops got closer, machine-guns played on them. Still they pushed on. They made for the wide openings between the forts—openings in which were entrenchments held by Belgian infantry. At the critical moment, when the German soldiers, or those left of them, paused and reeled under the awful punishment they were receiving from the guns, the Belgian infantry, at the word of command, leaped out, bayonet in hand, and gave them a taste of cold steel. The German line broke, and was thrown back a considerable distance in great confusion.

German request for armistice refused

It was estimated that as a result of the first two days' fighting no fewer than 25,000 Germans were killed or wounded. That is a figure impossible to verify. Certain it is that the death roll was heavy, and the real loss may have reached 8,000. The German commander at the front requested an armistice for twenty-four hours to bury the dead and attend to the wounded. The Belgian general, suspecting, with good reason, that such delay was mainly intended to give the enemy time to bring up heavier guns and more troops, refused the request. The fighting around Liege was too grim, too vital, to permit of delicate courtesies.

On Friday, August 17th, at about two a.m., an extraordinary incident occurred that revealed the reckless daring and want of chivalry of the German army. A little party of German cavalrymen—two officers and six soldiers—made a desperate effort to kill General Leman. They rode into the city dressed as Englishmen, and exchanged greetings in English with people. Arrived at headquarters, they stated that they were British officers who had come to the rescue of Liege, and they desired to see the general. Something in their manner made one aide-de-camp—Major Marchand—suspicious, and he hastily closed the door leading into the general's private apartments, and raised the alarm. A bullet at short range stopped him. Members of the

SUPPLYING THE NEEDS OF BELGIUM'S ALLIES.
By a special proclamation the Belgian Government required the inhabitants to meet all needs of the allied armies.   French dragoons are here seen dragging a heavy forage waggon to their temporary headquarters.

general's staff and some gendarmes present rushed on the Germans. The latter, hastily firing a volley, attempted to escape, but were pursued, and all shot down, after their coup had come within a hair's breadth of success.

Additional masses of German troops arrived on Thursday, crossing the Meuse by a pontoon bridge, which they had placed in position near Maestricht, close to the Dutch border, out of reach of the guns of the forts. They were now able to bring up heavier siege-guns. Zeppelins and aeroplanes drove back the Belgian aircraft, and began to drop high explosives on the steel cupolas of the forts.

The Germans attempted assault after assault. They were absolutely reckless of life, and were willing to pay a very high price for immediate success. In some of their advances they repeated the tactics of the Third Japanese Army when storming Liaoyang, and used the bodies of their own comrades fallen in front **Awful barricade of** of them as ramparts behind which to pause before making further advance. Tales told **dead and wounded** by the defenders show the gruesomeness of the advances, and the courage displayed. Here is the story of a Belgian officer who shared in the defence :

FRENCH SENEGALESE TROOPS.
The Germans had the impudence to protest against the use of these troops, who proved far less bloodthirsty than the inhuman hordes of Kaiser.

" Some of us late arrivals only managed to get to our post when the German attack began. It was night-time. We replied very sharply with our guns. Until the dawn came we had no very distinct idea what our practice was. Then we noticed heaps of slain Germans in a semicircle at the foot of our fort. The German guns must have been very much less successful, because they rarely hit us that night. They did better

FRANCE'S COLONIAL WARRIORS WITH THE ALLIES
The Zouaves, here illustrated, rank among the finest soldiers in the world. They are chiefly Frenchmen of the most adventurous nature, and serve in the African Colonies.

at daybreak. We did better still. As line after line of the German infantry advanced we simply mowed them down. It was terribly easy, monsieur, and I turned to a brother officer of mine more than once and said ' Voila ! They are coming on again in a dense, close formation ! They must be mad ! ' They made no attempt at deploying, but came on, line after line, almost shoulder to shoulder, until, as we shot them down, the fallen were heaped on top of the other in an awful barricade of dead and wounded men, that threatened to mask our guns and cause us trouble. I thought of the French saying, " *C'est magnifique, mais ce n'est pas la guerre !* ' No, it was slaughter—just slaughter !

" So high became the barricade of the dead and wounded that we did not know whether to fire through it or to go out and clear openings with our hands. We should have liked to extricate some of the wounded from the dead, but we dared not. A stiff wind carried away the smoke of the guns quickly, and we could see some of the wounded men trying to release themselves from their terrible position. I will confess that I crossed myself ; I could have wished that the smoke had remained ! But —would you believe it ?—this **Liege Civil Guard lays** veritable wall of dead and dying enabled those wonderful Germans to creep closer, and **down its arms** actually to charge up the glacis. They got no further than half way, for our machine-guns and rifles swept them back. Of course, we had our losses, but they were slight compared with the carnage inflicted on our enemies."

The citizens of Liege had no desire to see their beautiful streets reduced to ruins. So far as can be judged from the information available, they urged General Leman to endeavour to induce the Germans to leave the city untouched The Belgians demanded a conference, and a German parlementaire met the general and the civil authorities. The German demand was simple—the instant surrender of the forts and the town. General Leman, probably influenced by the civil authorities, offered to permit the Germans to occupy the town to save it from bombardment As for the forts, they were perfectly intact, and he intended to hold them to the end.

"It must be all or nothing," replied the German representative, "otherwise the town will be bombarded."

Germans enter the town of Liege.
At eight o'clock that night the bombardment started. Later in the night—it was said at the time in obedience to orders from Brussels—the Belgian troops occupying the town, apart from the forts, retired, and their place was taken by German troops, who came in and occupied the city.

The machinery of the great fort Fleron is said to have been put out of order by the German fire, and this may have given the Germans a safe path in. "After some three or four days," says Professor Paul Hamelius, of the University of Liege, "rumours began to get about that the Germans were approaching, and about Thursday evening the Belgian soldiers retired to the forts, and the Germans took possession of the town. They appeared to enter the place by arrangement, for the civil authorities just previous to the entry of the German troops called

HAPPY AND CONFIDENT IN THEIR ABILITY TO SERVE THEIR COUNTRY.
A battalion of the Honourable Artillery Company, one of the smartest London corps, marching through the City.

together the Civil Guard and ordered them to lay down their arms. Everyone else who had arms was ordered to give them up, and there was, therefore, no resistance of any kind made when the German troops came in."

The evacuation of the citadel, which controls the town apart from the forts, was completed at about three o'clock on Friday morning. Two hours later the Germans entered and occupied the citadel and the provincial government offices. General von Emmich, the commander of the 10th German Army Corps, with the title of the Commander of the Army of the Meuse, received the burgomaster and reassured him about the treatment of the people. "Let the city go on in the usual way," he said. "Open **Premature "triumph" in Berlin** the shops, do your daily work, and you have nothing to fear." It seems as though the local authorities, anxious to spare their beautiful city from bombardment and destruction, endeavoured to induce General Leman to cease fighting and to make terms with the enemy. The general, while consenting, for reasons which are not yet known, to the withdrawal of the Belgian field forces, which retreated in order and rejoined the main body of the Belgian Army behind, himself retired to one of the forts and continued his heroic resistance.

The news of the surrender of the town was hailed throughout Germany as a great triumph. "Liege has fallen !" The word went out from the Kaiser's palace. He sent an aide-de-camp to the waiting crowds to proclaim

[From the painting by John St. Helier Lander.

BRIGADIER-GENERAL SIR PHILIP CHETWODE, BART., D.S.O.

Sir Philip Chetwode commanded the 5th Cavalry Brigade, which was, according to Sir John French's despatch of September 7th, 1914, posted at Binche, on the extreme British right, at the beginning of the combined operations. On August 28th the Brigade fought a brilliant action with the German cavalry, in the course of which the 12th Lancers and Royal Scots Greys routed the enemy and speared large numbers in flight.

THE GLORIOUS CHARGE OF THE NINTH LANCERS

A magnificent feat of the Ninth Lancers, recalling the famous Balaclava charge, was accomplished during the retreat of the Allied left from Le Cateau on 25th August, 1914. A German battery of eleven guns, posted in a wood, and disguised with quantities of forage, had caused havoc in the British ranks.

DURING THE GREAT RETREAT FROM MONS TO CAMBRAI.

All attempts at silencing the guns having proved ineffectual, the Ninth Lancers rode straight at them, across the open, through a hail of shells from other German batteries, and cut down all the gunners and put every gun out of action. The whole of the Allied Forces rang with praise of the charge.

BRITISH INFANTRY'S GREAT BAYONET CHARGE THROUGH ENVELOPING GERMAN FORCES.

There was a great feat of arms at Solesmes, east of Cambrai, on August 26th. A number of British infantry regiments held an exposed position. They were expecting support all day, but this support was delayed, the enemy crept round, and the British force, to avoid being encircled, charged the gradually closing German ring with the bayonet. The men went at it, yelling and shouting, and they got through where there was a gap of no more than eight hundred yards between the enveloping German forces. On this gap the German artillery was pouring out shells with its unfailing regularity.

the triumph. Policemen on bicycles dashed down the Unter den Linden, shouting the tidings around. All Berlin rejoiced—but rejoiced somewhat prematurely. Only the city had gone. The forts, with the possible exception of one, still held out—the forts which with their powerful artillery swept the river, paralysed the railway, and dominated the main roads.

General Leman retired to one of the forts, and the city came under German rule. For a few days the municipality was allowed to carry on its work; then a German military governor assumed control. If the people imagined that they were to save themselves from any misery by their surrender, they were quickly to learn their error. One of the first acts of the Germans **Liege forts continue their heroic resistance** was to seize seventeen leading inhabitants, including the Bishop of Liege, as hostages for the good behaviour of the people. "Our soldiers have been fired upon by civilians," the governor told them. "If this occurs again, you will be held responsible. We will strike a blow at the beginning against such doings that will be heard everywhere."

Most of the hostages were released a few hours later. The Germans elaborated protective measures. On Saturday, August 8th, machine-guns were placed in every commanding position. Barricades were thrown up and trenches dug. More and more troops poured in, and were quartered on the inhabitants. Houses were turned

AT HOME WITH THEIR ALLIES: MEN OF THE BRITISH EXPEDITIONARY FORCE IN ROUEN.
The photograph shows a company of British infantry travelling on the transported chassis of a London motor-omnibus.

into hospitals for the wounded from the fighting outside. The goods of the people were taken freely as required. All day long the thunder of the guns against the forts and the whistle of the shells might be heard

A Dutch journalist who remained in the city gave a picture of life at the time:

"War," he says, "flings aside all the common estimates of human life. What was barbarous yesterday passes without comment to-day. Take, as an example, the Restaurant du Phare, where I sit writing. It is half a café, half a hospital. Around me are German officers eating and drinking. At the other end of the room, behind a thin veil of palms, lie the wounded—I see them as I look up from my paper. Yet no one takes any notice of this terrible combination. Only the people outside show any interest, as they gather to study the list of the wounded which is displayed there. True, it is a small list, but a restaurant where café life goes on as usual is no place for wounded. There is a far longer list on the other side of the road on the shop windows of the Bon Marché, which is full of wounded."

The one military punishment—death

Here and there the people, driven to desperation, tried to defend themselves or to protect their goods. The punishment was immediate and overwhelming—death for all civilian men on the spot where resistance had begun, and the burning of houses. In a very short time Liege became a city of death. Men and women, even children, would be shot down at the mere whim of drunken soldiers. One night the people around the Place de l'Université, on one side of the river, and the Quai de Pecheurs on the opposite bank, were awakened by the sound of firing and by flames and smoke licking up their houses. As they rushed into the street the soldiers stopped them, shooting one after another.   Within a very short time the inhabitants, or those left of them, scarcely dare look up when a stranger passed, lest their glance should be thought a crime worthy of the one military punishment—death. "The smell of powder and of decaying bodies was truly awful," wrote one young Englishman who penetrated the city in disguise. "The spirit of death seemed to be everywhere."

The surrender of the city did not lessen the stubbornness of the defence of the forts. But they were now at a great disadvantage. Communication with the north had ceased. General Leman probably anticipated early relief from the French armies, for he was too good a soldier not to know that isolated forts, however strong, unsupported by a field army, are doomed.

The Germans brought up their heavy siege train. They were now to bring into operation the great howitzers which they had manufactured after the Japanese War, as the result of what their military attachés had seen

Immense howitzers batter Liege forts

Japanese howitzers accomplish. The work of these howitzers was watched with profound interest. Many generals, even in the German Army, disbelieved in them ; France scoffed at them But German expert opinion had given them its approval. "Our howitzers can quickly reduce any position, however strongly fortified, to such a condition that it can be successfully stormed," the German Staff maintained. The howitzers were of almost incredible size. German newspapers claim that 17 in. howitzers had been secretly manufactured by Krupps, and were now used. Actually the calibre (i.e., diameter of shell thrown) seems to have been 11 in. Throwing a high explosive shell, operated safely at such a distance that the artillerymen could be well protected from the fire of the forts, the howitzers could at their leisure hurl missiles which must smash even the mighty defences of Liege.

Picture the scene. The forts, probably not too well provided now with ammunition or food, automatically raised their cupolas and fired at anything in sight. Men could no longer line the earthworks, for bursting shells covered them. Zeppelins dropped down explosives from above ; the shells rained death incessantly. The acrid smoke of the high explosives penetrated the forts, a smoke that stupefies, numbs, and sometimes renders men half unconscious. An hour under such a rain of missiles must have been a purgatory. The heroes of Liege held on day after day, listening every moment for sounds of the relieving army which never arrived.

In the first descriptions sent out officially in Germany of the capture of Liege, nothing was said about the forts still holding out. "Liege is completely in German hands. The enemy's losses were heavy," said a German official message on August 9th. Nine days afterwards another official message was sent out declaring, "The secret of Liege may now be revealed. The enemy were not aware that heavy artillery was to be used in the attack upon them, and believed themselves secure inside their forts ; but the weakest of the guns of our heavy artillery compelled every fort against which they directed their fire to surrender after a short bombardment. Within a short time our artillery reduced those forts to ruins."

KILLED WHILE SUCCOURING HIS ENEMY.
A private, in the great battle of Mons, which was fought on August 30th and 31st, 1914, offered water to a wounded German, and was shot at the same instant.

THE BARBARIANS IN BRUSSELS.
At the head of the promenading column, here seen passing the cathedral church of Ste. Gudule, were four gendarmes, twenty yards in advance of the German soldiers, and their duty was to shout to the inhabitants to close their windows.

This report was promptly denied by the French Legation in London, which declared that the forts were still holding out. Certain it is that the defence of Liege checked the German advance for a fortnight.

The end came at last. Fort after fort was battered and broken by the dominating German fire. In one fort the defenders blew everything up when they could hold out no longer, rather than surrender. At Chaudfontaine a shell penetrated the magazine and blew the place to atoms. General Leman was everywhere; apparently there were underground passages by which communication could be maintained between the forts.

Fort Loncin was the last to stand out. Here Leman and a small group of survivors made a final stand. Three out of four of the garrison had been killed or incapacitated; the general himself could scarcely move, his legs having been partly crushed by a fall of masonry; most of the guns were out of action. The general made all ready for the end, burning papers, destroying everything of military value, preparing to blow up the place at the last moment.

Fort after fort battered and broken

Then came a tremendous, concerted bombardment from the entire strength of the German howitzers. The watching German officers could see steel cupolas split and concrete walls crumble under the fire. A strong infantry force had moved up, ready to storm the fort. The fire paused; the infantry leaped in. As they advanced a magazine exploded, killing some of them. There was no more fighting. Those of the garrison left were helpless.

A German officer related the fate of General Leman himself. After a German shell had exploded the magazine in one of the forts, German soldiers entered on the work. They came on the body of the general, with blackened face, lying amid the ruins. "Respect the general! He is dead!" said his adjutant, who stood guarding the prostrate figure. General Leman was not dead. Later on he recovered consciousness. When he offered his sword to the German general, the latter refused to accept. "Military honour has not been violated by your sword," he said. "Keep it." General Leman had remained unmoved up to now. But at this tears sprang to his eyes.

He and the brave defenders of Liege had done their work well. At the outset it had been thought impossible that they could hold out for more than a day. Had the Allies been ready to take advantage of the opportunity thus afforded them, the outcome of the first part of the war might have been very different.

The President of the French Republic bestowed the Legion of Honour on the city of Liege, on account of its heroic defence against the Germans. This is an honour only bestowed previously on one other city.

A NOVEL SIGHT FOR BRUSSELS: GERMAN CAVALRY HALTED IN THE CHAUSSEE DE LOUVAIN.
The above photograph of the spectacular German promenade through Brussels, and those given on the preceding and following pages, are the finest records of this historic event. They give a peculiarly vivid impression of the swaggering strangers within the gates of Brussels.

CHAPTER X.
THE BRITISH ARMY ON THE EVE OF WAR.

Great Britain With the Army of a Third-Class Power—Germany's Constant Preparations Arouse No Alarm—Advantages and Disadvantages of a Voluntary System—Strength of the Army on the Eve of War—The Territorial System—Lord Haldane's War Office Reforms—Ready for War in All Directions—The British Expeditionary Force—Colonial Forces.

NOTWITHSTANDING the terrible lesson of the South African conflict, and the innumerable reports of committees and commissions advising reform, the outbreak of war with Germany found Great Britain still " attempting to maintain the largest Empire the world has ever seen with military armaments and reserves that would be insufficient for a third-class military Power."

For this defect all parties and the nation itself were responsible. Preparation for war is the task of years. It involves immense sacrifices and vast expenditure. Abroad every able-bodied man had long been required to give up a substantial part of his life to the defence of his country. In Germany, the citizen serves for two years in the infantry, for three in the cavalry and artillery ; in France for three years, whatever the arm. In Great Britain the nation had displayed an invincible opposition to serving for even three months.

The attitude of a section of the public was thus set forth in a pamphlet published shortly before the war .

" To most young men of active mind and body it is pleasant enough to command and to do the brain work of soldiering. It is another story to do the drudgery and the obedience. It is no great deprivation for a man who comes from a position of some means to have to spend a year or two in learning the game of fighting It is a far more onerous burden to the workman to lose months or years of his best working life in wasted effort and uneconomic

THE FLOWER OF THE GERMAN ARMY IN THE BRUSSELS PARADE.

The Kaiser's crack troops were sent to impress the people of Brussels. In this splendid photograph (from a private source in Brussels) a group of Hussar officers is seen in the Chaussée de Louvain studying Belgian papers and enjoying a brief rest before their rush through Belgium to attempt that crushing blow at France which was the keynote of German strategical theory for the first phase of the war.

exercise, producing nothing, earning nothing at the very time of life when young men ought to be making their position and measuring their ability.''

Every word in this statement is true.   But what the writer forgot, and what this war is proving, is that without security, without freedom, without national independence, everything else is of little moment.   What shall it profit a working man to have '' made his position,'' or '' measured his ability,'' if his doom is to live as the helot of a German conqueror, and to see his earnings taken from him or his womenkind put up against a wall and shot by an alien soldiery ?   What if he gains the whole world and loses his soul ?

On the very eve of war the British Army was reduced.   For a generation the British military system had been an anachronism. It was based upon voluntary service, which means the willingness of a certain number of patriotic and public-spirited men to bear the onerous duty of fighting and dying for the

BORDEAUX, WAR COUNCIL HEADQUARTERS.

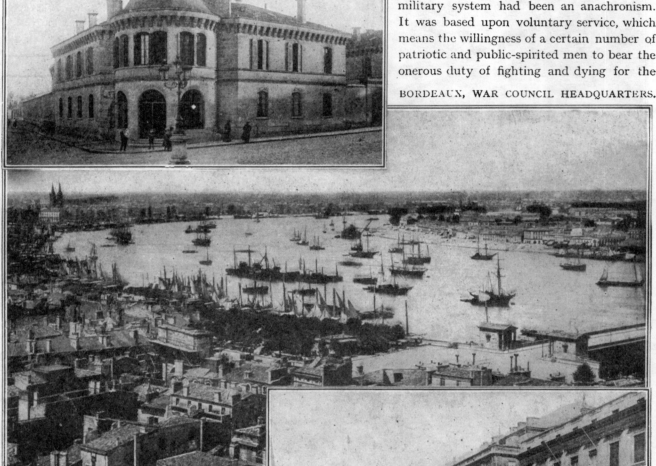

BORDEAUX, TEMPORARY SEAT OF THE FRENCH GOVERNMENT.

Owing to the possibility of the investment of Paris, and the absolute necessity of preserving complete freedom of action for the national administration, the French Government, with the Chamber of Deputies and the foreign Embassies, removed to Bordeaux on September 3rd, 1914.

THE PREFECTURE, PRESIDENT POINCARE'S BORDEAUX RESIDENCE.

nation.   This system survived, not because the British people were altogether negligent or faint-hearted by nature, but because their chief attention was riveted upon party quarrels, and because they lived in an island, and had come to believe that they were secure against attack so long as their Navy could keep the sea.   Moreover, a large part of their Army was required for work in tropical countries.   For such duty compulsory service troops are not suited.

In a remarkable article which he contributed to the '' Daily Mail,'' the great American writer, Admiral Mahan, pointed out in 1910 that the sense of security produced by the '' water-walled bulwark '' begets an optimistic attitude towards external dangers. Continuance of peace induces a practical disbelief in the possibility of war, and practical disbelief results in inaction. For a century the British race had lived secure and had seen wars or the menace of wars sweep over Europe and the world, leaving the British Isles untouched and unscathed, till it had come to imagine that it was protected by some special dispensation of Providence. The iron temper, the extraordinary capacity for organisation which Germany had displayed, the constant growth of the German armaments, aroused no real alarm.

Thus the British forces on land were weak in number. There was a regular Army composed of admirable soldiers, enlisted for seven or eight years with the colours (i.e. in the active ranks) and five or four years in the reserve, the total term of liability being twelve years. These troops, by their condition of service, could be employed in any quarter

GERMAN GUN-DRILL AT TSINGTAU.

THE TOWN AND HARBOUR OF TSINGTAU.
Japan declared war on Germany on August 23rd, 1914, and immediately commenced operations to reduce the strongly fortified port of Tsingtau (or Kiao-chau), " leased " by Germany from China.

TSINGTAU POLICE AT THE GERMAN PORT.

of the globe. The advantage of voluntary service for a long term of years is that greater professional ability is obtained, and that, as all who join do so willingly, there are likely to be fewer shirkers. The superiority over a compulsory service army due to this cause has been calculated by good military authorities at thirty per cent. That is to say, a voluntary service army of 100,000 men should be equal to a compulsory service army of 130,000 men.

As against these advantages there are signal defects. A long-service voluntarily recruited force is very costly. It will be small in numbers and will have no large reserve. It is apt to become a class apart from the population. The officers, because they have not constantly to strain all their faculties in teaching a continual succession of short-service men, are liable to deteriorate, though it must be said that the British officer in this war has proved his

ONE OF THE SHARP SERVIAN THORNS IN THE AUSTRIAN SIDE.
A sharpshooter in his rifle-pit in the public gardens of Belgrade, overlooking the Danube, and commanding Semlin, on the Austrian frontier.

magnificent quality. The supply of recruits depends upon the state of trade, falling when trade is good and rising when trade is bad.

Extreme severity of training is likely to deter men from joining. " Our desires with regard to the training of the men," said Sir Evelyn Wood before the South African War Commission, " are strictly limited by what the recruiting officer tells us is the character of the training which would be agreeable to the population which we hope will come into the Army." Again, where the system of service is voluntary, the men enlisted will represent only one class of the population. Where it is compulsory, all classes are in the ranks. Lastly, there is always difficulty in obtaining sufficient officers where service is voluntary. Where it is compulsory, officers can be obtained from those who would have to serve as privates, if they did not enter the commissioned ranks.

The strength of the British regular Army in Great Britain and the Colonies was 156,110 officers and men in 1914, on the eve of war, 12,000 short of the establishment (or nominal strength). There were, in addition, 78,400 British troops serving in India. The regular Reserve, all trained men, numbered 146,000,

NEUTRAL SOLDIERS' THIRST FOR NEWS.
Dutch soldiers eagerly perusing the special newspaper issued in Holland for soldiers and sailors

THE MIGHTY RUSSIAN AVALANCHE SURELY AND STEADILY ON THE MOVE.
An outstanding feature in the public mind during the early phases of the war was a supreme confidence in the steady advance of the allied Russian forces in Austro-German territories.

and the Special Reserve, consisting of partially trained men, numbered 63,000. All these were liable to foreign service. From this host of men, however, important deductions had to be made. About 30,000 of the regular Army were under twenty and unfit for foreign service. Another 10,000 must be subtracted for men of military age in hospital or incapable of taking the field. Before the Army embarked for foreign service, these men had to be eliminated and replaced by reservists. At the same time, all the units—regiments, squadrons, and batteries—required further complements of reservists to bring them up to war strength ; and these reservists, joining from civil life, needed some days or weeks of training before they could support the trials and privations which fall upon the soldier in war. It was not that the spirit was lacking. But only constant practice can harden the soldier's feet to the work of accomplishing long marches and enable him to carry his burden of 90 lb. weight.

In the German Army the reservists in the first line army corps are fewer in number ; weakly men are replaced immediately from the reserves in time of peace, and the reservists themselves are constantly called up for training. The defects which hampered the British Army were not found in Germany to the same extent, a fact which covers with the greater glory the splendid performance of the British regulars in Belgium and France.

GUARDS ON A NEUTRAL FRONTIER.
Swiss and German outposts facing each other on the frontier near Basle.

In the second line behind the regular Army was the Territorial force. This was organised and established by Lord Haldane, then Mr. Haldane, in an Act passed in 1907. Its organisation, however, was accompanied by a grievous reduction in the regular Army, the active ranks of which were diminished by about 20,000 men, and the reserves by at least 20,000 men. At the same time the old Volunteers were swept away. The Territorial force was, therefore, not a new creation. It simply replaced an older and a larger force.

Originally, Lord Haldane aimed at an armed nation with an armed force of 900,000 men. He coupled with his scheme a plan for compul-

COLONIALS TRAINING FOR 2ND KING EDWARD'S HORSE.
A splendid cavalry regiment formed in London of Colonials with war experience. They are here seen at the White City.

from men employed in industry and in business, a longer and more arduous training was impracticable.

The Territorial Force on the eve of war was about 63,000 men short of its proper strength. That is to say, it numbered about 250,000 men instead of 313,000, and of those in the ranks nearly 17,000 were in 1913 under eighteen years of age. Yet its existence was a sign that patriotism was still strong in the heart of many of the younger men. For those who enlisted and served in it did so with the knowledge that its training was perfunctory and its armament out of date. Bismarck's great saying, "If we are obliged to stake the blood of our people against our enemies in

THE PRINCE OF WALES MARCHING AT THE HEAD OF HIS BATTALION OF THE GRENADIER GUARDS.
The Prince, as a lieutenant of the Guards, puts his men through a course of drill at the Wellington Barracks after the march.

sory military training in schools, which he hurriedly abandoned in the face of opposition.

Finally, his Territorial force was established with a nominal strength of 313,000 officers and men. It differed from the old Volunteers in that it was organised in brigades and divisions, which were composed of all arms (i.e. of infantry, cavalry, or

2ND KING EDWARD'S HORSE DRILLING AT THE WHITE CITY.
This fine regiment was organised by Major Norton Griffiths.

the field, then we are bound to provide them with the best weapons of offence and defence that money can procure," was not applied by either of the British parties. The Territorial guns were old-fashioned, and the rifles in many of the units not of the latest pattern.

Alarmed at the weakness and want of training of the Territorial Force, and at the insufficiency

yeomanry, artillery, and engineers). This organisation was a real gain from the military standpoint. But the force lacked training. All that the men serving in it underwent was fifteen days in camp each year and a certain number of drills. As it was recruited voluntarily, of the regular Army, for many years before the war Earl Roberts, that glorious soldier who had restored victory to the British colours in South Africa, had called upon the nation to accept some form of compulsory service for home defence. So far back as 1905 he declared that " There is no option but to introduce universal training for home defence." Year after year he repeated his disregarded warnings from manifold platforms, with a persistence which was heroic.

But his efforts were in vain. When he pointed to General von Bernhardi's notorious work, " Germany and the Next War," which proclaims the necessity of attacking and humbling Great Britain, he was accused of libelling the Germans. He was actually denounced by the politicians for " an infamous attempt to try and stampede the country into conscription," for inaugurating a " devil's dance," and for offering provocation to Germany.

Thus the British nation, firmly convinced that a strong Navy would protect it from every peril, neither armed

nor prepared on land. Under the shadow of the German menace, which grew blacker with each year, as the German military estimates increased, as the strength of the German Army was constantly raised, as the number of German Dreadnoughts and destroyers available rose, it married or was given in marriage, and continued peaceably eating and drinking, working, and quarrelling over partisan issues, until the actual shock of war fell upon it, and in a moment revealed the errors of its false prophets.

It woke from its slumber and repented of its

"WRITING HOME "—THE FIRST THOUGHT.

BRITISH NURSES FOR THE ALLIED FRONT.
A contingent arriving at Dieppe.

WOUNDED IN A BRUSSELS HOSPITAL.

fault. But not in a moment, in a month, or a year could the mischief be undone. Thousands of recruits might come forward, but there were none to drill them, and neither uniforms nor arms. There were no barracks in which to lodge the men. Worst of all, there was no supply of trained officers to command the new levies.

Under Lord Haldane's scheme an Expeditionary Force of 160,000 men, nearly all regulars, was constituted for employment abroad in case of need. The best feature of Lord Haldane's reforms was that all the arrangements for the rapid mobilisation and embarkation of this force were worked out by the War Office and the Committee of Imperial Defence, which was another creation of Lord Haldane. The War Office, indeed, notwithstanding its inadequate resources, displayed a surprising efficiency, and had all its plans prepared when the upheaval came. Every measure which would be requisite in a great war had been considered and studied beforehand. Thus, on the outbreak of war a series of Acts of Parliament could be speedily passed to meet the emergency and protect the nation's existence, and time was not wasted in futile discussion.

But the bitter fact remained that no large army could be instantly placed on the Continent. The British nation had not realised the swiftness of modern war or the enormous masses of men employed in it. Up to the very last it believed that preparations for war could begin after war had broken out, and that effort at the last moment could repair the consequences of years of apathy and inaction. For that belief, for the mistakes of years, the nation was doomed to pay dearly indeed, and its gallant sons and soldiers in the field to suffer unceasingly in the terrific fighting of the first month of the war on land, in the long and arduous retreats, in the battles where another army corps might have turned the scale, had that army corps not been wanting at the front.

At its full strength the Expeditionary Force was about equal to three of the army corps in which the armies of Europe are organised. It consisted of one division of cavalry, composed of four brigades with 6,550 men and

Strength of British Expeditionary Force twenty-four guns, and six infantry divisions. Each infantry division was composed of three brigades, and mustered 18,000 officers and men, with eighteen 4·5 in. howitzers (short guns firing a heavy shell at a high angle) ; four heavy 60-pounder guns ; fifty-four field guns, firing an 18 lb. shell ; and twenty-four machine-guns.

Besides these units, two siege artillery brigades were organised to assist the Expeditionary Force if required. The first took into the field sixteen 6 in. howitzers, firing 100 or 122 lb. shells. The second was equipped with eight howitzers of yet heavier type, the details of which cannot be disclosed.

In artillery the British army corps was distinctly inferior to the German, which took into the field one hundred and twenty-six field guns, eighteen 4·5 in. howitzers, sixteen 6 in. howitzers, and eight heavy 8·3 in. mortars.

Of the other States of the British Empire, India, besides the British garrison of 78,400 British troops, had her splendid native army, with a strength of 164,000 officers and men, and reserves amounting to 35,700 men. In addition to these were 20,000 Imperial Service troops maintained by the native States, which in this crisis displayed noble loyalty, and 42,000 European and Eurasian volunteers.

The Commonwealth of Australia had in 1911 imposed a system of compulsory military training upon its manhood, though the period was exceedingly short, amounting only to sixteen days, or slightly in excess of the training required of the British Territorial Force. There was a nominal total of about 170,000 men at the end of 1913 who had received some training in arms, and for whom officers could be supplied from the Australian contingents which had served so gallantly in the South African War. The **Military power of the Dominions** Australian is by physique and habit of life a good soldier, inured to fatigue, and usually a fine horseman, intelligent, energetic, and full of initiative. In the Dominion of New Zealand a Defence Act passed in 1909 provided for the training in arms of every able-bodied New Zealander. A Territorial Force of about 30,000 men existed, and it was composed perhaps of the most admirable material in the world. In South Africa all citizens were rendered liable to compulsory service by a Defence Act passed in 1912. The South African Army was in process of organisation when the war broke out. Here, again, the material was excellent, as a very large part of the population, British or Boer, had taken part in the war of 1899-1902, and the Boers were a people with great military traditions, and soldiers who had obtained great experience in the field.

In Canada there existed a permanent trained force of 3,500 officers and men, with an active militia of 73,900 officers and men, the ranks of which could be filled in the case of necessity by compulsion. The organisation of this force, however, had made little progress before the war.

THE CEASELESS VIGIL IN THE NORTH SEA: A DESTROYER'S SEARCHLIGHT DISCOVERING A TRAWLER.

Field-Marshal Sir John D.P. French K.C.M.G. G.C.B.
Commander-in-Chief, British Forces in the Field.

VIEW OF THE PORT OF
BOULOGNE

CHAPTER XI.

WHERE THE BRITISH TROOPS
LANDED

THE LANDING OF THE BRITISH AT BOULOGNE.

By George C. Curnock, Special Correspondent of the " Daily Mail."

Secrecy of the Transport Movements—Guard of French Submarines—Service of Interpreters—Coming of French and British Staff
Officers—Argyle and Sutherland Highlanders Land—Preparing Camps and Hospitals—Boulogne Beflagged—" Are We
Downhearted ? "—Exchange of Favours—Admiration for Men and Guns—Royal Flying Corps—Leaving Boulogne for the
Front—King George's Message to the Men—Lord Kitchener's Admonition—Boulogne Deserted and Isolated.

BOULOGNE was early made a base for the reception and despatch to the front of the British Expeditionary Force. In many respects it was well fitted for that purpose. Lying well behind the old tidal dock and out of sight of the Quai Chanzy, where the cross-Channel boats land their passengers from Folkestone, is the Loubet Dock (Basin Loubet), with a frontage on three sides equipped with electric cranes and railway sidings.

Here it was possible for five transports to berth at one time and discharge, not only troops, but all the vast impedimenta of a modern army—its guns, transport waggons, horses, ambulances, stores, and motor-vans.

Great secrecy was maintained regarding the despatch of the Expeditionary Force. The whole of the first portion had been landed in Boulogne before the British public was even aware that it had left the shores of England. The regiments comprising it were ordered to leave their depots without knowing where they were going. They entered railway trains, the drivers of which were

THE ARRIVAL OF GENERAL FRENCH AND THE BRITISH EXPEDITIONARY FORCE AT BOULOGNE.
A few days after the declaration of war the British Expeditionary Force began to reach French soil. Boulogne became for the time a khaki
camp, where British troops were mustered before being drafted north to the Franco-Belgian frontier. The whole Expeditionary Force was
landed "with the greatest precision and without a single casualty," to quote an official communiqué.

U

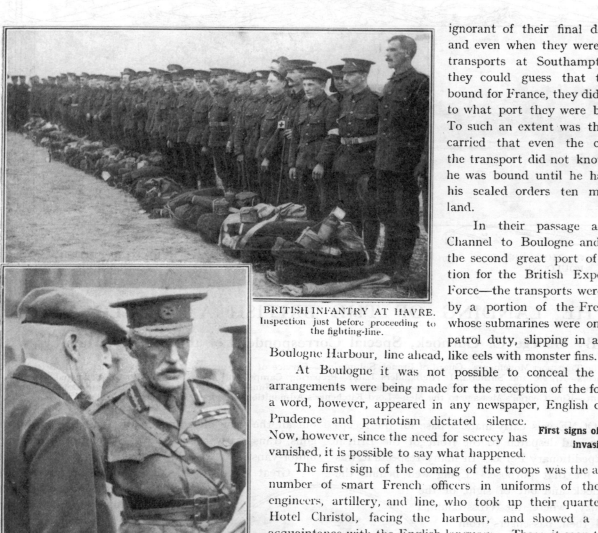

BRITISH INFANTRY AT HAVRE.
Inspection just before proceeding to the fighting-line.

BRITISH CAVALRY ENTRAINING AT BOULOGNE.
Some of the British force entrained on the quay for the front without resting in the French port. Inset picture shows Sir Horace Smith-Dorrien at Folkestone before crossing the Channel, where he was so soon to win a glorious name for military genius.

ignorant of their final destination, and even when they were placed in transports at Southampton, while they could guess that they were bound for France, they did not know to what port they were being sent. To such an extent was this secrecy carried that even the captain of the transport did not know whither he was bound until he had opened his sealed orders ten miles from land.

In their passage across the Channel to Boulogne and Havre—the second great port of debarkation for the British Expeditionary Force—the transports were guarded by a portion of the French Fleet, whose submarines were on constant patrol duty, slipping in and out of Boulogne Harbour, line ahead, like eels with monster fins.

At Boulogne it was not possible to conceal the fact that arrangements were being made for the reception of the force. Not a word, however, appeared in any newspaper, English or French. Prudence and patriotism dictated silence. Now, however, since the need for secrecy has vanished, it is possible to say what happened.

First signs of welcome invasion

The first sign of the coming of the troops was the arrival of a number of smart French officers in uniforms of the cavalry, engineers, artillery, and line, who took up their quarters at the Hotel Christol, facing the harbour, and showed a surprising acquaintance with the English language. These, it soon transpired, were staff interpreters detailed for duty with the British troops.

As showing the ramifications of the French military service, which takes in men of all classes and professions wherever they may be, in France or abroad, it may be stated that one of these interpreters was a Birkenhead and Liverpool cotton merchant, another was the French master of a famous West Country public school, another was a member of a French shipping firm who had spent several years at its branch in Newcastle.

A fourth was a barrister who has made frequent appearances in the British High Court, a fifth was a French count, well known in English society, a sixth had hunted every season in England with the Pytchley for years past, a seventh was a man of leisure who knew London as well as Paris, and an eighth was a former Embassy attaché. To such men as these, and many more, subsequently

BRITISH CAVALRY IMMEDIATELY AFTER DISEMBARKING AT BOULOGNE.
There were three great camps in which the British Expeditionary Force gathered while they were massing at Boulogne before advancing to the front. It is an interesting fact that the same three camps were used by Napoleon for the French army he prepared when projecting the invasion of England.

fell the duty of aiding the landing and despatch of the British troops, and afterwards of accompanying them in the field, where not a few have already fallen fighting by the side of their English and Scottish brothers-in-arms.

The second notable sign of the coming of the troops was the sudden appearance of British staff officers at the same hotel, and a motor-car driven by an English private, which made many hurried visits to the famous old Chateau Tour de l'Ordre, in the Haute Ville (upper town) of Boulogne, where Colonel Daru, the governor, had his headquarters.

Preparing for the British army

These were followed by more cars of French ownership, in which staff officers of both armies scoured the country round. The third sign of the coming of the troops from England was a sudden order given to the merchants of Boulogne to clear their goods from the sheds lining the Basin Loubet—an order obeyed with alacrity, seeing that the goods had not paid duty. Then the first transport came, bringing vast stores of camp equipment and just a bare handful of troops. Only a handful, but, to the joy of the people of Boulogne and the English residents, they were men of a splendid Scottish regiment—the Argyll and Sutherland Highlanders. The Boulonnais will long remember the " A. and S." men. They were the first to come and the last to go. For two weeks they were quartered in the old barracks behind the post office. None knew that they had landed until they came swinging along the road past the tidal dock and the Central railway station, over the bridge and lock gates opened by Napoleon III., and round the little square to the barracks, khaki-clad, but kilted for all that, with knees bare and pipes skirling, while the crowd lined the road and

BRITISH ARTILLERY PASSING ALONG ONE OF THE STREETS OF BOULOGNE.

FRENCH SOLDIERS WATCHING THE ARRIVAL OF THE BRITISH.
Boulogne to a man—and woman—gave the British Expeditionary Force a warm welcome, and no welcome was more cordial than that of the French soldiers, who expressed an admiration for their new comrades-in-arms that soon became mutual.

cheered, running from the quays and shops to see the British come at last. What soldiers they were, these Highlanders! How strong and sturdy they looked, every man with his face sun-burned by much marching in Scotland, every one smiling and happy, looking to left and right with wonder at the brown-smocked fishermen and the fish-wives of the quays, and the dancing waters of the harbour then crowded with trawlers.

For a day or two Boulogne saw no more—or, at least, only small details who came, as these did, with the first stores and camp material. The military authorities were not idle. During these waiting days they prepared five camping grounds for the troops on the hills around Boulogne.

To those who knew the military history of the place the selection of these camps was a matter of great interest. There was the Marlborough Camp on the Calais Road, almost under the shadow of the column erected to the memory of the first Napoleon, the St. Martin Camp, in two sections, on the road to St. Omer, and the St. Leonard Camp, also in two sections, on the road to Pont de Briques.

LANDING OF THE BRITISH EXPEDITIONARY FORCE AT BOULOGNE IN AUGUST, 1914.
The first British troops to land were a contingent of Scottish Highlanders, and their arrival evoked a welcome of rapturous enthusiasm from both the civil and military population of the French port, where memories of "the Auld Alliance" between Scotland and France still linger and bring the Scotsman even more closely to the hearts of the French people than the Englishman.

Each of these spots was selected by Napoleon for the troops which he gathered together at Boulogne in the first decade of the last century, while down below, in the harbour of Boulogne itself, lay the hundreds of light-armed vessels in which he proposed to transport them for the invasion of England. French Territorial troops, the middle-aged men of the fields and towns, were employed to clear the ground for these camps, and for a day the fields, ripe for harvest, were strangely occupied by soldiers in blue coats and red trousers, each man swinging a scythe or raking together the crops with the skill of men well used to such labour. As they worked, the children of the neighbouring villages merrily gleaned after them, understanding little of the omen of the man with the scythe reaping this harvest of war.

There followed more men in blue and red, digging trenches, laying water-pipes and erecting stand-pipes for **The great camps at Boulogne** the soldiers ; then the Highlanders pitching tents, until the bare fields were ordered lines of canvas ; and standing there, with a fair blue sky overhead and the clean Channel breeze sweeping up and over the hill, one might well think for a brief moment that war was a lovely and delightful thing, since it brought men from the towns and overcrowded cities to such sweet air and so glorious an outlook.

Near the Marlborough Camp, in the grounds of an old convent, a base hospital for the British was prepared, at first with only a few beds, but afterwards with many At this date, in the first two weeks of the war, it was apparently thought that Boulogne would become a permanent base, through which troops could be poured, and to which the sick and wounded might return. How quickly that idea was abandoned, those who watched the arrival and departure of the troops realised. It vanished when the German hordes burst through Mons and Charleroi into France, disappearing with many another fair plan and joyous hope like snow in summer-time. Thus was all made ready for the arrival of the troops—methodically and in good order, without rush or excitement, and in accordance with a fixed plan and pre-arranged time-table.

Boulogne was already well accustomed to the sight of khaki, though the bulk of the troops had not yet arrived, when the mayor of the city, M. Felix Adam, issued a poster of which the following is a translation :

" ARRIVAL OF THE BRITISH TROOPS.
" Appeal to the Inhabitants.

" My dear Citizens,—This very day arrive in our town the valiant British troops, who come to co-operate with our brave soldiers to repel the abominable aggression of Germany. So before the invasion of the barbarians all Europe rose against the like race (*la race germaine*) who menaced the peace of the world and the security of other people.

" Boulogne, which is one of the homes of the Entente Cordiale, will give to the sons of the United Kingdom an enthusiastic and brotherly welcome. The citizens are requested on this occasion to decorate the fronts of their houses with the colours of the two countries.

" *At the Hotel de Ville, August 10th, 1914.*

" Le Maire de Boulogne, Felix Adam.

" *Vise.* Le Gouveneur de la Place, Daru."

Obedient to this summons the whole town of Boulogne burst into a display of bunting. All French houses in the main streets have brackets ready fixed for the reception of a flagstaff, and from these hung the colours of Great Britain, France, and Belgium, whose plucky defiance to the barbarian German had already

ON THE TRAIL OF THE INVADERS.
Belgian bugler sounding the advance at Melle, a village near Ghent, where the Germans, pushed back from Termonde, had camped on the night of September 8th, afterwards destroying the place.

BELGIAN CAVALRY AT REST CONCEALING THEMSELVES FROM THE DANGER IN THE SKY.
A detachment of Belgian lancers halt at midday in the shadow of a wood. Advantage is taken of any natural cover that will shield them from German aeroplane scouts, and artificial protections are also erected, such as screens of wheatsheaves, supported by lances, under which the Belgians can conceal themselves both from the bomb-dropping air scouts of the enemy and the fierce rays of the sun.

BELGIAN COLUMN RESTING IN THE NOONDAY SUN.

BELGIAN STAFF OFFICERS DISCUSSING PLANS.

awakened enthusiasm for that brave little nation. At this time the whole of the Hotel Christol was taken for the British transport staff under Colonel Asser, and the whole town was alive with troops of the two nationalities. Boulogne was nearing the height of the war fever. Most of the shops and hotels were still open. Some of the summer visitors remained, and in the country near were many English residents, still enjoying the peace and beauty of their villas and country places, confident that the coming of the British troops meant security from the alarms of war.

In this week, too, Boulogne bade farewell to the second battalion of the 8th Infantry, a regiment composed of stout-hearted Boulonnais, so soon to shed their blood on the fields of Belgium. Then those who were waiting for the arrival of the British saw the real meaning of the war for the people

A COMPANY OF BELGIAN LANCERS WHOSE DARING HARASSED THE GERMAN ADVANCE.
The French and British soldiers, brave though they showed themselves to be at every turn, hardly surpassed the extraordinary daring and gallantry of the plucky Belgians, who bore the first thrust of German aggression and were beaten back only by overwhelming odds.

BELGIAN BIVOUAC ON THE OUTSKIRTS OF MALINES.
Malines was only less badly treated than Louvain by the enemy.
Lying midway between Brussels and Antwerp, it came between the
hammer of German aggression and the anvil of Belgian resistance.
Shot and shell reduced a large portion of the city to ruins,
and then the Germans spent their insensate brute fury upon the
helpless civil population.

of France. They saw the wives and sisters
of the men in the ranks kissing them farewell
with tears of pride and sorrow in their
eyes. They saw a woman of the people walk
in and out of the ranks and solemnly give
her right hand and a kiss to the cheek of
a hundred men—heartrending benediction—
and then run quickly away. They saw the
colonel march down the ranks, with a word
and a jest for "mes enfants" ("my children"), showing that fine camaraderie which
is typical of the relations between French
officers and men.

While yet the French troops were leaving
for the front in Belgium, the British troops
came at last in their thousands to Boulogne, an
invasion which began in great force
on August 13th, and continued for
ten days. The Basin Loubet was
the scene of the debarkation.
Into this commercial harbour
swung ships of two to five thousand
tons burden, piloted by tugs,
and berthed with great ease
along the quays. Many of them
bore names which showed that
they had been taken from Transatlantic service. All were crowded
with troops, and their decks
cumbered with waggons.

As soon as the ships were
moored, the broad gangways were
run out, the electric cranes began
to swing, and out of each poured

**BELGIAN OUTPOSTS BEHIND
CUT CORN.**
This picture reminds us of the undaunted
bravery of the soldiers of Belgium, who were
resourceful to a degree in withstanding the
flood of German army corps that laid waste
their fields and cities.

HASTENING TO DEFEND THEIR COUNTRY—BELGIAN CAVALRY FOR THE FRONT.
When war's alarums called up the Belgian soldiers the response was immediate, and mobilisation
rapid. These cavalrymen are carrying their kitbags on their way to entrain for the point of
attack on the eastern frontier.

BRITISH NURSES AT THE KING'S PALACE IN BRUSSELS.
British women had appeared in Brussels on their mission of mercy before the British army was able to reach the firing-line. The Belgian soldiers were greatly interested in them.

its splendid living freight and its equally magnificent equipment of war. Among the first of the troops to be landed were the Middlesex regiment. Competent observers said they had never seen a finer line regiment on the march. Every man was of the best fighting age, from twenty-five to thirty-five, all seasoned and hard as nails. The great bulk of the men were reservists, and a fair sprinkling of them had South African ribbons. As

they passed the barracks behind the post office, where the early comers of the Argyll and Sutherland Highlanders were clustered behind tall iron railings, the lads from Scotland hurled at them the old football cry —to-day a British slogan of war on many a battlefield : " Are we downhearted ? " And back from the ranks as they passed came the

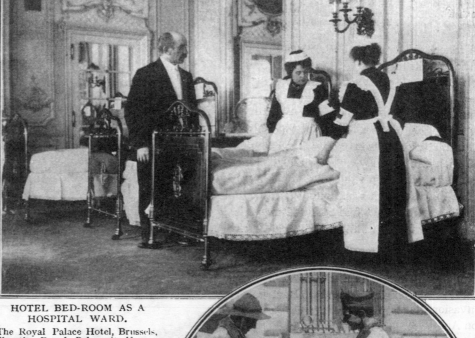

HOTEL BED-ROOM AS A HOSPITAL WARD.
The Royal Palace Hotel, Brussels, like the Royal Palace itself, was transformed into a hospital for the wounded.

answer with a thunderous roar: " No-o-o-o-o-o ! " By the following day this call and its answer was heard along the Rue Faidherbe and up the steep Grande Rue. The townspeople caught it and shouted it to the men of

Setting out with laughter to the front

Worcester and the Oxford and Bucks, and the latter added their own cry: "Shall we win ? " To which they gave their long-drawn answer: " Y-e-e-e-s-s ! "

It was a scene to fill with laughter and tears every true British heart Watch them as they pass with their brown, jolly faces, and shirts wide open at the throat, shouting, and showing as they shouted the working of great throat muscles and dazzling rows of white teeth. Were ever men so fit for the terrors and ardours of war !

BELGIAN BOY SCOUTS ACTED AS DESPATCH-BEARERS FOR THE WAR OFFICE.

EXPELLING THE CIVIL RESIDENTS OF LOUVAIN FROM THEIR HOMES.

Germany's inexpiable crime of Louvain on August 25th, 1914, remains her eternal shame. The university with its world-famed library, many beautiful churches, and great parts of the residential and business sections of the city were given over to bomb and flame. Before the fire of destruction was let loose upon the condemned city the people were herded out by the merciless invaders. The brutal and cowardly Uhlans are here seen driving before them the priests, old men, women, and children.

Hour after hour they passed. See the Highland Light Infantry marching with saucy step and a rolling swing to the maddening skirl of the pipes. Hear the Connaught Rangers singing " It's a long, long way to Tipperary—it's a long way to go," while the officers ride between, full of pride in their men, quietly smiling as they ride, and raising hands in salute to their brother French officers on the pavements.

No wonder that the " France Du Nord " said in its issue of August 15th : " The gallant bearing of the men, their gaiety, fine looks, muscular appearance, as well as their splendid conduct, are of happy augury."

" Never have I seen such splendid men ! " Little wonder either that a Frenchwoman, standing on the steps of an hotel in Boulogne and watching the men march by in their thousands, so full of youth and life, placed her hand to her throat in a gesture of dismay, and gasped, " Ah, it makes me sick at heart to see so many fine men marching to war. They are so full of life. Never have I seen such splendid men ! Oh, but they are brave to go laughing, when so many will never return."

The infantry were the first to come. In addition to the troops already mentioned, the Royal Scots, Gordons, and Royal Irish passed through Boulogne, with other regiments which came on the midnight tide, and went scurrying away to the front before Boulogne was awake For ten days the camps on the hills fulfilled their purpose in giving the men a good night's rest under canvas, and a hot meal before they started for the scene of the fighting. Boulogne flocked to these camps, making much of the soldiers, and giving them little favours, cigarettes, cakes. In return for these the soldiers gave them their shoulder-pins, the letters distinguishing each regiment, and half the girls and women of Boulogne were soon wearing them as brooches. Others went to the camps to admire the work and equipment of the British troops among them French professional soldiers, who said they had never seen such arrangements for the care and comfort of troops on active service " Your men," said one officer, " ought to fight well on that meat and jam ! "

Very soon the character of the troops landing in Boulogne began to change. The infantry stream slackened and a tide of artillery set in. To the pleasure of seeing firm and well-knit men marching through the streets of a city—which has seen the soldiers of a thousand years—on foot, was added that of seeing battery after battery of the Royal Field Artillery, the Royal Horse Artillery, and the Royal Garrison Artillery.

Here again the pick and flower of the British Army was on view in the full panoply of war. By the time these arrived the German invader had encompassed Liege, and had fought his way across the bloody fields of Belgium to Brussels. Now indeed, those who watched the guns of the artillery pass felt that these compact weapons of war were here in the streets of

WAR-WORN BELGIANS REST IN THE SHADE OF A CALVARY.
No war picture could be more impressive than this simple photographic view of a tired group of Belgian cavalrymen snatching a brief rest outside a church at Ziel, near Ghent, where the elaborate sculptured image of the Crucifixion is a reminder that the barbaric Teuton has crucified Christ again on the blood-drenched fields of Belgium.

WAITING FOR THE GERMAN ENEMY AT HAMME, BETWEEN ANTWERP AND GHENT.
Belgian infantry, behind hastily-constructed defence works, are ready for Germans who may seek to cross the river, the bridge of which has been destroyed to impede their advance. The photograph was taken from a hayloft.

Boulogne for the defence of France, and to aid her against a powerful and unscrupulous enemy. Sentiment gave place to wonder and admiration.

The guns, so beautifully kept ; the horses so well chosen, young, powerful beasts for the light field artillery, massive shire horses for the 60-pounders ; the men, riding like centaurs, man and beast one—they hardly knew which to admire the more. Only those who have seen a picked battery of the Royal Horse Artillery riding to war can realise that perfect accord of man, horse, and gun which made the march of the guns through Boulogne the most moving spectacle of this amazing week.

Those of the artillery who were given a rest day in Boulogne spent it at the St. Leonard Camp on the national road to Pont de Briques   Here they were within sight of the chateau which Napoleon chose for his headquarters, varying it with an occasional stay at the Tour de l'Ordre in the great old walled town on the hill.   To the artillery succeeded other branches of the service—the cavalry represented by dragoons, hussars, and Scots Greys,

The moving panorama of the British army whose stay in Boulogne was shorter than that of any branch—the Army Service Corps, who came and went every day, the Royal Army Medical Corps, who on some days outnumbered all others and came with endless ambulance waggons and a vast number of men, and the pontoon section of the Engineers, with their ungainly boats and huge oars sticking therefrom, rattling through the streets and along the road to Pont de Briques.

Almost last of all came a corps which was unlike anything Boulogne had seen before, a hundred men marching through the Rue Victor Hugo without arms, each clad in knee breeches, putties, and well-shaped jackets, each with a jaunty cap on the side of his head, and the words " Royal Flying Corps " proudly inscribed in a semicircle on his shoulder. It was curious to note the difference in physiognomy between these keen-eyed, aquiline-featured men and the square-jawed country lads who preceded them driving Royal Medical Corps waggons.

It was still stranger to see the transport section of the Royal Flying Corps, a miscellaneous collection of motor-waggons impressed hastily into the service, some of them bearing the names of well-known furnishing houses of London, others with the advertisement of " the best advertiser in the world," a London omnibus and a London taxi-cab, the smart car of the parks, and the roughly equipped chassis of a machine intended to beat records at Brooklands, and now carrying spare parts of an aeroplane. So much Boulogne saw of the Flying Corps on land. It had seen a good deal more in the air a few days earlier, when no fewer than thirty-six Army aeroplanes flew the Channel in the early morning, and went circling off like homing pigeons to the British base at Amiens, later to give a good account of themselves on the long road through France.

The departure of the British troops by train from Boulogne to the front was the signal for fresh outbursts of

A SHAMEFUL WAR OF SACRILEGE.
The church of Melle, near Ghent, one of the many that were deliberately wrecked by the Germans' fire and shell, in pursuance of their policy of terrorism.

enthusiasm on the part of the Boulonnais, a warm-hearted people much akin to those of the sea-coast on the other side of the Channel. Many of the troops went away from the railway sidings on the quay in full view of the town. Here the fisher-girls gathered, and stood for hours laughing and chatting with the British soldiers, trying to say " good-bye " in English, trying to join in the chorus of English songs, and appreciate the humour of English music-halls.

At another siding might be seen thirty British soldiers hauling guns upon flat trucks with long ropes, working with a will at anything which would bring them a march

nearer the Germans, or persuading artillery horses to enter the troop trains which filled every railway line. The last comers did not wait long before they went into action. By the time the last of the Expeditionary Force had landed, the British were trying in vain to hold up the German advance on the Belgium frontier. Men came to Boulogne one day, and within twenty-four hours they were lying in trenches at Cambrai. Within a week some of them were back again, with bandaged arms and heads. The whole landing was an episode in the beginning of this great war worthy of note for its calmness and order.

Reporting its safe despatch, Lord Kitchener announced to the world that :

ONE OF THE MANY BELGIAN SANCTUARIES DEFILED BY GERMANS.
" Strange the offerings that you press on the God of Righteousness ! "

" The Expeditionary Force as detailed for foreign service has been safely landed on French soil. The embarkation, transportation, and disembarkation of men and stores were alike carried through with the greatest precision and without a single casualty."

Each man before he left England received a twofold message. The first came from the King, and was read by commanding officers to the regiments before they left Southampton. It ran as follows :

" You are leaving home to fight for the safety and honour of my Empire. Belgium, which country we are pledged to defend, has been attacked, and France is about to be invaded by the same powerful foe. I have

LOYAL INDIA

"Among the many incidents that have marked the unanimous uprising of the population of my Empire in defence of its unity and integrity, nothing has moved me more than the passionate devotion to my Throne expressed both by my Indian subjects and by the Feudatory Princes and the Ruling Chiefs of India, and their prodigal offers of their lives and their resources in the cause of the realm. Their one-voiced demand to be foremost in the conflict has touched my heart, and has inspired to the highest issues the love and devotion which, as I well know, have ever linked my Indian subjects and myself."

King George's Message to the Princes and People of India, September 10th, 1914.

The King-Emperor as Colonel-in-Chief of King George's Own Lancers (Indian Army).

The magnificent rally of the Princes and people of India and their enthusiastic insistence that they should have a share in the defence of the Empire against German aggression is perhaps the most glorious chapter in the history of Britain's great Crown Colony. It was a revelation to the enemy and caused a chill in Berlin. The grateful acceptance of India's offers did more to raise the people of India to the height of the Imperial ideal than a century of just administration.

The Maharajah of Mysore, who contributed fifty lakhs of rupees, equal to £333,333, towards the cost of the war.

Speaking at Glasgow on September 10th, Earl Curzon said he wo These men, he said, were taking part in our battles because the power; it stood for justice, uprightness, and

Sir Pertab Singh, who, although seventy years of age, "refused to be denied his right to fight for the King-Emperor." He went to the field of war along with his nephew—the sixteen-year-old Maharajah of Jodhpur.

The camel corps commanded by the Maharajah of Bikaner, an Indian prince who was one of the most enthusiastic supporters of Indian participation in the war.

About two-thirds of the Indian Army is formed on the "class company" system, two or three races and castes in their separate companies forming one regiment. In the remaining third, all the troops in one regiment are of the same race. The photograph shows the Imperial Cadet Corps, most of whom were in the Indian Expeditionary Force.

Types of Indian—

...es of the Bengal Lancers fluttering down the streets of Berlin."
...ere members stood to them for something much more than
...above photograph shows the Bengal Lancers.

The Maharajah of Patiala, whose family have been staunch friends of the British, was selected to accompany the Indian forces.

The Gurkhas are the smallest of the Indian troops, and the minimum height accepted is five feet. But none are braver in attack or more skilled in hand-to-hand fighting.

The Maharajah of Bikaner, who volunteered for active service and accompanied the Indian Expeditionary Force to Europe. He placed a camel corps at the service of the Government.

-Native Cavalry.

The men of the Indian Army may be divided into two main categories—Mohammedans and Hindus. Five languages are spoken, but "Urdu," the language of the camp, is the official language of the Army, and is understood by all. The photograph shows members of the Imperial Cadet Corps, with Lord Hardinge, Viceroy of India, seated in the centre.

THE LIFE-LONG HUNGER FOR "LA REVANCHE" INSPIRES THE FRENCH CAVALRY TO SUPREME ENDEAVOUR WHEN LET LOOSE UPON THE GERMAN ENEMY.

The theory that the value of cavalry had departed under modern conditions of warfare received its deathblow at the opening stages of the war. Time after time cavalry charges proved the decisive factors of attack, and for reconnoitring prior to an advance the services of the cavalry arm were invaluable. Good horsemanship, dash and efficiency in swordsmanship are the qualities that make cavalry attack effective. This drawing shows French cavalry charging Uhlans in a country lane where the restricted field of action jams up the contending companies in a hot mêlée.

implicit confidence in you, my soldiers. Duty is your watchword, and I know your duty will be nobly done. I shall follow your every movement with deepest interest, and mark with eager satisfaction your daily progress. Indeed, your welfare will never be absent from my thoughts.

"I pray God to bless you and guard you, and bring you back victorious.

"GEORGE R. AND I.

"August 9th, 1914."

They also received and were bidden to carry with them in their pay-books the following wise instructions from Lord Kitchener:

"You are ordered abroad as a soldier of the King to help our French comrades against the invasion of a common enemy. You have to perform a task which will need your courage, your energy, your patience. Remember that the honour of the British Empire depends on your individual conduct. It will be your duty not only to set an example of discipline and perfect steadiness under fire, but also to maintain the most friendly relations with those whom you are helping in this struggle.

"The operations in which you are engaged will for the most part take place in a friendly country, and you can do your country no better service than

ON THE GERMAN LINE OF COMMUNICATIONS.
German commissariat waggons passing through the ruined village of Visé with munitions for the main German army in Belgium.

by showing yourselves in France and Belgium in the true character of a British soldier. Be invariably courteous, considerate, and kind. Never do anything likely to injure or destroy property, and always look upon looting as a disgraceful act. You are sure to meet with a welcome, and to be trusted. Your conduct must justify that welcome and that trust. Your duty cannot be done unless your health is sound, so be constantly on your guard against any excesses.

A SMILING VILLAGE ON AUGUST 1st—A RUIN ON AUGUST 4th.
The little Belgian village of Visé was one of the first places to suffer from Germany's aggression. Situated near the frontier, it was enveloped on August 3rd, 1914. Some German detachments crossed the frontier in motors, followed by large bodies of cavalry. A stubborn defence was put up. When the invaders entered the town, not only did they set fire to it, but they shot down non-combatants without mercy.

"In this new experience you may find temptations, both in wine and women. You must entirely resist both temptations, and while treating all women with perfect courtesy you should avoid any intimacy.

"Do your duty bravely. Fear God. Honour the King.   KITCHENER, FIELD-MARSHAL."

When the last transport had discharged its freight and the last troop train had gone to the front, the whole of the transport and medical corps gathered at Boulogne for the arrival of the troops collected up their belongings and left the town. By this time the great German advance had begun, and the Pas de Calais was threatened

THIRSTY GERMAN SOLDIERS AT VISE.

by the invader. Even the base hospital had to go, taking itself to Amiens, and then to Rouen and Havre.

Boulogne, filled with the ancient memories of great bygone fights and sieges, was deserted of all save the Territorial troops, local levies raised among the men who were past the age of active service but could be called upon to fight in the last line of defence. Colonel Daru, the governor of the place, a holder of an ancient and honourable post, looking upon his seven-hundred-year-old fortifications and his 1870 guns, felt the loneliness and isolation of the chateau in the high town, and moved to the Hotel Christol, now vacated by its British staff. Here he remained for ten days more, though the town had been declared " ville ouverte "—open and defence-less—hating to go, but impelled by the uselessness of remaining. Then the Territorial troops went, and the Engineers of the garrison, with their only modern howitzer, to Paris.

Two more days passed, and word came that the railway line to Paris via Amiens was cut by the blowing up of the bridge at Pic-quigny. Trains no longer came direct to Boulogne from the capital. The stream of refugees slackened. The

boats of the South-Eastern service to England were running half-full. Rumours of a German advance upon the port were in the air. A British destroyer—Gipsy—came into the harbour with instructions ; and out of Boulogne steamed, mournfully hooting, a score or more of great steam trawlers. Finally, the governor, who had seen the beginning of the greatness of Boulogne as a seaport in the war, who had welcomed General French with ceremonial courtesy on his way to the front, who had attended in state the passing of the body of General Grierson from France to England, went also. A steamer of the Newhaven-Dieppe service entered the harbour, and quietly, without a word of farewell, the governor and his staff departed for Havre.

Before the first week of September had passed Boulogne was almost cut off from the interior of France, connected with England by a single daily boat, emptied even of its sailing craft. It lay open and defenceless and silent to the world, while still the flags hung out in honour of the coming of the British fluttered from a thousand houses.

GERMAN TELEGRAPH CORPS AT WORK.

GERMANS FILLING THEIR LEATHER WATER-SACKS.
During the earlier stages of the war in Belgium the weather was extremely hot, and the combatants suffered greatly from thirst. The water pail was carried round the ranks twice daily, as seen in the top picture, when possible, but usually only once. Water-sacks were replenished whenever the opportunity offered; but the invaders suffered greatly from thirst.

CHAPTER XII.

HOW THE GERMANS DASHED UPON BELGIUM.

Belgium the Innocent Victim—French Scheme of Defence—Necessity for an Undivided Army—Factor of Time—The Power of a Re-organised Russia—Destructive Capacity of German Siege Guns—Mobility of Motor-cars for Military Transport—King Albert's Intrepid Defiance of Germany—Indiscriminate German Cruelty in Belgium—Belgium Aflame with Patriotic Zeal—Reliance on French and British—Beginning of the German Invasion—Summary Treatment of Civilians—German Violation of the Laws of Civilised Warfare—Damning Proof from the German Side—Evidences of Murder and Outrage—Delay Before Liege—Work of the German Cavalry—A Peasantry Driven by Cruelty to Reprisal—Various Outpost Skirmishes—Belgian Victory of Haelen—German Advance in Force—Defeat of Belgium's Field Army at Tirlemont and Louvain.

THE story of the ruin of Belgium in the early days of the Great War will go down to history as one of the greatest tragedies in ancient or modern times. Here was a little nation forced, through no fault or desire of its own, into the forefront of the conflict. Its small army had to endure the assault of one of the greatest military Powers in the world. Its people—kindly, simple, home-loving, and patriotic—found, in spite of their utmost endeavours, their beautiful and historic cities laid to waste, their homes made desolate, thousands of their manhood destroyed, and the entire fabric of their organised life shattered.

They had to suffer to the last extreme the systematic and cold-blooded cruelty of a powerful and relentless soldiery. The miseries heaped up on them recall in degree and in enormity the abominations inflicted on the Netherlands when Spain endeavoured to secure her dominion there. For a parallel to many of the outrages we must go back to the days of the Thirty Years' War, or to the time when the Tartar hosts forced their way westwards through Central Asian plains.

Why Belgium was left to the "Huns" Why did not the Allies make greater efforts to prevent this calamity? This is the question that has been asked, not alone by many Belgians themselves, but by multitudes of their friends and admirers in England and elsewhere. Why did not the armies of France hurry across the frontier, hold the line of the Meuse, and keep the German invaders back?

The reason is that the ablest military brains of France were convinced that any attempt to make the frontier line of Belgium the main line of defence would have involved not only the immediate but the permanent ruin of Belgium and the destruction of France also. The aim of Germany at the beginning of the war was to strike at Paris, the heart of France, as quickly as possible, and to break down French resistance before Russia could lend her ally effective support. The purpose of France was to parry the German blow and to make a counter-move into German territory.

Two generations of French staff commanders, since the war of 1870, had sought to fathom how Germany would strike, and how her blow could best be met. French military strategy was dominated by two ideas, both handed down from the Franco-Prussian War. The first was political, the necessity to reconquer Alsace and Lorraine,

BELGIAN TRIGGERS READY FOR INVADING
TEUTONS.
The Belgian infantry excelled in sharpshooting from
hastily-improvised cover, as the Germans found out to
their cost.   These photographs were taken during the
fighting on the retreat to Antwerp.

French General Staff determined that in this
war they would keep their armies together, at
whatever sacrifice of territory or of men.

It is necessary to understand this central
idea of French military strategy to follow
with any comprehension the movements in
the armies in the early days of the war.
When on Sunday, August 2nd, the Germans,
by their cleverly-planned coup, seized the
Grand Duchy of Luxemburg, they secured

the lost provinces.   This led France to mass
her armies on the eastern frontiers from
Belfort to Longwy.   The second reason was
military.   In 1870 France suffered defeat
after defeat because her armies became
separated and could be attacked in detail
by overwhelming German forces.   Bazaine's
army, caught in Metz, was driven to yield.
MacMahon's weak army, isolated and hemmed in at
Sedan, after a heroic resistance, capitulated.   The

a pivotal point from which they could advance in
various directions.   Moving almost directly westwards
they could strike at Longwy.   Moving more northwards,
through Belgian Luxemburg, they could, when once
they had captured Liege, secure the road to Northern
France.   Moving further south they could strike
at France along the line of the great fortresses.

It was necessary that
France, if she attempted to
protect all the principal
French and Belgian territory
from attack, should cover the

BELGIAN CAVALRY RESTING AFTER THEIR BRILLIANT VICTORY AT HAELEN.
On August 12th and 13th, 1914, the Belgians successfully resisted a German attempt to turn their flank at Haelen, and inflicted considerable loss
upon the enemy.   After the battle the Belgians erected shelters of wheat-sheaves to protect them from the oppressive sun and aerial scouts.

UHLANS MAKING USE OF A CAPTURED BELGIAN DOG-CART.
Dogs are commonly employed as draught animals in the everyday life of Belgium, and one of their principal uses is to pull the carts of small tradesmen. They are also put to service by the Belgian Army, being especially useful in hauling the light but deadly machine-guns.

enormous front from Belfort to Namur, and from Namur along the banks of the Meuse to Liege. Had this line been held, the German invasion of Belgium would have been impossible. But in attempting to hold it the French armies would probably have been split into two separate parts, either of which could have been shattered by the Germans at their leisure.

The French plan of keeping the French armies undivided involved enormous sacrifices. It meant, in the first place, that Belgium must be overwhelmed by the German invaders. It meant, further, that if the Germans chose

Importance of an undivided army
to push their armies up to the coast they could penetrate into the rich manufacturing and mining districts of Northern France and ravage them as they willed. It is impossible to believe that the French generals did not realise this, and did not submit to it solely as a bitter and inevitable necessity. Otherwise, after the outbreak of war, there was ample time for the French to pour their armies into Southern Belgium, to reinforce the whole line of Belgian troops towards Liege and to drive back the Uhlans from Brussels and Central Belgium.

Every day that France could hold the armies of Germany back, and keep her own main forces undivided, was a day nearer victory, for France was not fighting this war alone. Great Britain held the seas against Germany, and the British Expeditionary Force was on its way to aid France on land. To the east, Russia was

REGIMENT OF BELGIAN INFANTRY MARCHING INTO ACTION.
To British eyes, accustomed to short khaki coats, breeches, and putties, the uniform of Belgian infantrymen—which resembles the French—seems heavy and cumbersome. Overcoats, buttoned back at the knees to allow free passage for the legs, are generally worn by Belgian private soldiers, but not by their officers.

GERMAN TROOPS OCCUPYING THE CITY OF LIEGE WHILE THE FORTS STILL THUNDERED DEFIANCE OF THE INVADERS' ADVANCE.

The attack on Liege was begun on August 4th, 1914, and a vigorous defence was maintained by the intrepid General Leman. On August 9th the Germans penetrated between the forts and entered the city. The picture represents the Place du Marché, in the centre of the city, where the Germans are seen commandeering much-needed bread. Dogs are used for street transport in Belgium, and are here seen drawing food supplies for the invaders. The forts of Liege fell one by one under assault by the heavy German siege-guns, and on August 24th Major Namech blew up Fort Chaudfontaine to prevent it from falling into the hands of the Germans. General Leman was made prisoner only while unconscious from the fumes from bursting shells and when overwhelmed in the debris of his ruined fort.

moving against Germany, somewhat slowly, but in such
numbers and so well prepared
that it seemed as though her
advance must be irresistible.

Russia could hurl at least
two million men against Germany and Austria. These two
millions could be constantly
reinforced by fresh hosts, more
than making good any losses in
the field. The Russia that
Germany had now to face to the
east was no longer the Russia of
the days preceding the Japanese
War, a great nation living
mainly on its own military
reputation. Russia had learnt
her lesson in the defeats and the

BELGIAN ARTILLERY RETIRING BEFORE THE INVADING ARMY.
When the full flood of invasion was let loose on gallant little Belgium she had to draw back her forces
to avoid annihilation. This photograph was taken in Ghent, and shows Belgian artillery who
had retreated from Termonde resting in the Place d'Armes.

humiliations of 1904-5. She had revised her methods, reconstituted her military personnel, re-equipped her men,
and now she presented to the world the largest army, one of the best equipped, and one of the most efficient
military machines in the world.

Russia had taken seriously to heart the lessons of the Japanese War. For some time following the Peace
of Washington very careful investigations were made to discover the reasons for the hitherto unsuspected fighting
weakness that had been revealed. The Russian armies had done much better in the closing days of the fighting
in Manchuria than the world at large realised. They had held up their foes for some
months, and had planted themselves in a position that was nearly impregnable. They
closed the war with a maximum of military strength on the front line of fighting. But
the Russians were, nevertheless, deeply humiliated. Memories of the Yalu, Liaoyang, of the Shaho, of Port
Arthur, and of Mukden, could not be obliterated. Russia had been disgraced in her own eyes.

**A re-created Russian
Army**

It was this that led Russia to re-create her Army. Great generals were sent into shameful retirement; Army
contractors who were discovered to have used the hours of national peril for their own gain were punished with

merciless severity. The Russian
preparations since 1910 had
been directed, with scarce a
show of concealment, to one
purpose—the defence of the
Empire against Austrian and
German attacks. A French
Military Commission which
visited Russia three years ago
was amazed to find how far her
preparations had been pushed
forward.

In the early days of August,
1914, when the French General
Staff were laying down their
final scheme of defence, they
knew that the Russian mo-
bilisation had already begun,
and that within a few weeks
the Russian armies would be
attempting to cross the Vistula, thus forcing Germany to

AN INCIDENT IN LOUVAIN ON THE EVE OF ITS DESTRUCTION.
Two of these riders are Belgian civilians, who have captured riderless horses, and are carrying the
arms and equipment of men killed in battle. Their risk was great, because, if captured by the
German enemy, civilians carrying arms were shot without compunction or formality.

transfer her forces to resist the threatened eastern invasion. Then would come France's hour of great opportunity.

And so the French plan of campaign was devised. Strong armies were to attempt the invasion of Alsace and Lorraine, where they expected to meet the main forces of Germany. Here, too, they believed that they would be advancing among a friendly population, anxious to throw off the German yoke. While the main French forces advanced in Lorraine, smaller forces would hold the Germans back to the north. Some army corps would be pushed up to help the Belgians. Infantry would advance to Namur, the military key of the Upper Meuse. Cavalry would sweep along through the Ardennes and through Central Belgium, driving back the German cavalry. The lines of communication behind would be held in force by Territorials—the regiments of men from thirty years old upwards.

It was not expected that Liege could stand out for long. Most authorities did not anticipate that it would resist the full German attack beyond two or three days at the most. Thus the centre of Belgium might be exposed **The French plan of** to invasion. But Namur and the mountainous region to the south of the Meuse should be **campaign** capable of stubborn resistance. Behind them, even if the Germans came in unexpected force to the north, the prepared French defences from Lille to Mézieres should keep them in check for a sufficient time to enable Russia to show her power.

In their calculations the French commanders did not give sufficient value to two factors. They underestimated the enormous destructive capacity of the newest siege artillery, more particularly of the great howitzers which Germany was known to have in reserve. Still more important, they did not make allowances for the revolution in mobility caused by the adoption of the motor-car for military transport. Germany had prepared to use the motor-car to the full for the transportation of guns, of ammunition, of supplies, and of men. The front line of her armies now consisted of two arms—cavalry and armoured motor-cars carrying guns. For her infantry, thousands of motor-trolleys were waiting, capable of carrying the men as far in one day as they could walk in six days, and bringing them to their destination fresh, with energies unexhausted, and with strength unimpaired.

Following the attacks on Liege, described in a previous chapter, the German Emperor made another effort to win the Belgians to his side. He approached King Albert, through Queen Wilhelmina of Holland, and promised, in recognition of Belgian valour, to guarantee the most considerate treatment of the Belgian population, and every respect for the integrity of Belgian territory, if Belgium would abandon her resistance and allow the German troops a right of way in their attack upon France.

A BATTERY OF MODERN FRENCH ARTILLERY.
The extreme mobility of the light French field guns enabled them to be used with wonderful effect. The famous 75 millimeter especially harassed the German advance through northern France, and played havoc with the enemy during their retreat from the Battle of the Marne. The ease of movement of this gun was described by a spectator as being like "leaping from one height to another."

COMPANY OF GERMAN AIR SCOUTS RECEIVING TELEPHONE INSTRUCTIONS FROM THE BASE.

The air scout service, like the armoured motor-car, constituted a new arm of war. Good work was done by air scouts on both sides of the firing-line, but gradually the superior resource and higher initiative of the British air scout established an individual ascendancy over the German air scout. In his despatch of September 11th, 1914, Sir John French wrote regarding the British Flying Corps; "Something in the direction of the mastery of the air has already been established."

King Albert replied with an absolute negative. "Great Britain, France, and Russia," he said, "have promised formally to support us in the struggle upon which we are engaged. French armies are hastening to our appeal and are already on our soil. If they are powerless to preserve us from a disaster, honour would not allow us to draw back. What Belgium has so well begun, France and Great Britain, with her help, will succeed in terminating. They will chase the routed enemy towards Germany, and our honour will not only be safe, but our name for ever glorious."

The scene in Belgium in these early days of the war was full of interest. The people were fired with passionate enthusiasm and with hatred for the foe. To the traditional dislike and fear of Germany had been added fresh bitterness caused by the stories of merciless cruelty and severity pouring in from a hundred villages to the south. Neither age nor sex, neither calling nor cloth, protected anyone from the iron hand of the invading soldiery. The tales that came from Visé, from Port-sur-Suille, from the Ardennes, and from elsewhere, told of murder and pillage, in which priests and babes in arms, old men and young mothers, were alike victims. These horrors fired every peasant's heart and steeled his arm. Throughout the villages of the rich plains of Central Belgium every roadway was barricaded with farmers' carts, or with piles of stones and heaps of brushwood, and behind each barricade peasants waited with their weapons.

Steeled to resistance by atrocities

ONE OF THE NEW FACTORS IN WARFARE: HOW THE BELGIAN ARMOURED CAR BECAME THE TERROR OF THE UHLANS.

New factors in warfare were the armoured motor-car, the Zeppelin, and the aeroplane. All are capable of good service to the armies employing them, when they are manned by courage and guided with skill. The Belgians made good use of the armoured car, as the tale of German casualties could tell. At Diest a crew of Belgians in an armoured car chased a party of thirty-one Uhlans, and the mitrailleuse accounted for twenty-eight of them. Two were made prisoners, and only one escaped. The daring Belgian officers who manned these cars were afterwards decorated by King Albert.

At the head of the nation was King Albert, simple, brave, and kindly, who placed himself in the foremost ranks of the workers for defence. King Albert was seen everywhere, inspiring, stimulating, and hastening the preparations. He laid aside all the trappings of state. He moved among his troops without escort and without pomp, living often enough as they lived, glad of the occasional opportunity to show himself in the trenches when there was fighting to be done. King Albert proved himself a man, every inch of him.

Thus the Belgian nation stood ready, inspired and inflamed with patriotic zeal, its people willing to sacrifice everything for their country. As the regiments set out for the south, priests marched by their side, holding up the cross, and urging them to fight to the end for the sake of the faith. Brave little Belgian soldiers! Alas! Belgium was to learn, as the world at large was to learn in a very few days, that superb courage, supreme self-sacrifice, tremendous enthusiasm, count for almost nothing against drill, discipline, numbers, and military efficiency. The nation that would resist a great Power has to marshal all its forces, not in the days of war, when the foe is hammering at the gates, but in the days of peace, when all seems well.

The Belgian military forces were not formidable. There was a field army with a nominal war strength of 100,000 men, and a garrison army of 80,000 men.

GREY DAWN ON THE BATTLEFIELD.
Full of the mystery and strange appeal of the rising morn on the unknown fortunes of another day of battle, this fine photograph was taken on the outskirts of a wood in France, where a British cavalry regiment had bivouacked for the night during the ever-memorable retreat from the Belgian frontier.

Both of these were in the course of re-organisation under a law passed in 1913. But the Belgians had never, in recent years, taken their military preparations with sufficient seriousness. They had not dreamt of attempting by themselves to resist the hosts of Germany. There had been a tendency to rely for defence on treaty rights rather than fighting power. There came spasms of enthusiasm, when enormous sums were voted for defence purposes, but too often the schemes were never carried through.

Fortress guns were bought at heavy outlay, but their delivery was purposely delayed by Messrs. Krupp, and the fortresses were not built to receive them. The defences of Liege and Namur were not modernised, and were for long left under the care of a few soldiers. Military training was too short. Until 1910 the Army had been recruited partly by voluntary enlistment and partly by a system of conscription, which allowed most men who did not wish to serve to avoid service. The period of training for infantry, engineers, and garrison artillery was not more than fifteen months, and was obviously inadequate. In January, 1910, a law had been passed introducing many reforms. The peace Army at that time was less than one-third of its nominal strength. The new scheme of reform read admirably on paper, but it had not yet been carried out. For example, one section of the reserve was to be the Civil Guard class, numbering nearly 50,000 men, with a large reserve who were to be employed in times of war on lines of communication and in garrisoning fortresses. The military preparedness of the Civil Guard may be judged from the fact that the authorities began issuing Mauser rifles to them, and instructing them in the use of them, after the outbreak of the war.

The Belgians relied mainly on the assistance of the French and of the British. All they hoped to do was to check the invaders until their Allies came up. A few days after the outbreak of the war official news was published that French infantry were already to the east of Liege. On August 14th it was announced in Paris that the French troops which had entered Belgium by Charleroi had joined up with the Belgians; three French officers had been attached to the Belgian headquarters, and two Belgian officers represented the Belgian Army with the French troops. At the same time it was announced in Brussels that the transportation of French troops into Belgian territory was, on that same date, August 14th, entirely complete.

France and Belgium join forces The French infantry, reported at the beginning to the west of Liege, disappeared; at all events, no more was heard of them. The French army took up a strong line between Dinant and Namur, and further occupied a position between Nivelles and Gembloux, and in the neighbourhood of Wavre. Why, it may be asked, did they not do more?

It is hard to answer the question. Even allowing for the fact that the French, for strategic reasons, did not mean to push in considerable force into Central Belgium, the weakness of their movements to the north, in the early days of the war, remained a mystery. They allowed the Germans to strike at the moment chosen by themselves, and to divide them from the Belgians, thus permitting the former to concentrate their main strength on the Belgian forces. They arrived too late to save Namur. They were clearly inadequate in numbers. A miscalculation was made by the French General Staff. Perhaps the true cause of the failure to defend Belgium was the non-arrival of the British Expeditionary Force. It reached the front five and a half days later than the appointed date.

THE FRENCH FLEET GUARDED THE CHANNEL DURING TRANSPORT OF THE BRITISH EXPEDITIONARY FORCE.
This photograph was taken on board a cross-Channel steamer on Sunday, August 9th, 1914, five days after the declaration of war, when the passenger boat was passing through the French fleet, one of whose ships is seen in the distance. At that time the British Expeditionary Force was being transported to France under a guard of the French fleet, whose submarines were on constant patrol duty.

BELGIAN ARTILLERY IMMEDIATELY AFTER
MOBILISATION.
The physique of the average Belgian is excellent, and it only needed the spur of a just cause to make him a most formidable foe in the defence of his country.

FRESH FRUIT FOR WEARY FIGHTING MEN.
This kindly Belgian peasant has a pail filled with pears, and he was photographed distributing the fruit to tired soldiers returning from the fight at Melle.

It was not the intention of the Belgians to attempt to hold Belgian Luxemburg southwards and eastwards of of the River Meuse. Their southern defences mainly rested upon Liège to the east, Namur to the west, and Dinant to the south, the defences of the Meuse being further helped by a fortified position at Huy. The main Belgian field army, including the force that retired from Liège, was concentrated around the beautiful old university city of Louvain, extending thence in a south-eastward direction to the French at Gembloux. The intention was to defend the line of the River Meuse as long as possible, and then, if necessary, to retire upon the fortresses of Namur and Antwerp.

The people of the Ardennes and of Belgian Luxemburg were not prepared to allow the enemy to invade them without resistance. They had prepared for the most troublesome of all campaigns for a regular army to meet—a peasant war. Every rustic had his weapon, and every man was anxious to use **Belgium becomes a nation in arms** it. Not only in the Ardennes, but away up towards the Dutch frontier, the feeling of the people was everywhere the same. They hated the Germans. They knew them ; they knew their pride, their arrogance, their intense materialism. They wanted no more of them.

In the southern countryside, at the moment when war broke out, besides parties of infantry and armed gendarmerie, there were other forces of every kind. There were armies of cyclist scouts, who moved in troops, surrounding, isolating, and destroying small parties of Uhlans. There were the Civil Guards, counting in their ranks many young men of good family, who by serving in this way escaped the burden of fighting in the ranks of the Army as privates. And there were the plain, ununiformed people.

The countryside was made ready. Tracts of roadways were undermined, to be blown up as German soldiers went over them ; barricades were piled up. The people meant to make their foe pay dearly for every yard.

War between Germany and Belgium was not opened until the morning of Monday, August 3rd. According to the evidence of people living in various frontier villages, the German troops crossed into Belgium as early as

PONT DES ARCHES AT LIEGE BLOWN UP BY BELGIANS.

BELGIANS BLOWING UP A BRIDGE AT TERMONDE.

TERMONDE RAILWAY BRIDGE AFTER ITS DESTRUCTION

THE DESTROYED BRIDGE OVER THE RIVER ESCAUT
AT WETTEREN, BETWEEN ALOST AND GHENT.

The brave Belgians did not hesitate to destroy millions of pounds' worth of bridges, railways, and tunnels in their determined efforts to impede the advance of the ruthless invaders of their country. Ten days after the war opened it was estimated that the buildings, bridges, etc., destroyed in this way represented a total value of forty million pounds sterling.

Sunday, August 2nd. They came only in small parties, as advance scouts, rather than to make any vigorous attack; they were very polite, and had many excuses for intrusion. Sometimes the excuse was that they wanted their horses shod; at other times they had missed their way; or, again, they required some information and had come to ask it.

On August 3rd they arrived in increasing numbers. They asked for accommodation in convents and in schools. "They asked nicely," wrote one resident of a frontier village, "but gave the impression that if refused they would take more." Then on the 4th disguise was thrown off, and the troops poured in in force. The first fight between the Germans and the Belgians at Visé, where the Belgians destroyed a bridge on the road to Liège and the Germans rushed and sacked the little town, showed the methods and the intentions of the invaders.

The German soldiers entered Belgium with the idea that they would be allowed to pass through the country with little or no resistance. They were amazed when they found themselves the objects of universal hatred. They quickly adapted themselves to the new situation. It has been a cardinal policy of the German militarists that in no circumstances must the civil population be allowed to join in hostilities. In the Franco-Prussian War the Prussian generals were relentlessly cruel in carrying out this rule. The franc-tireurs, the French volunteers, were refused recognition as soldiers. Any of them caught were at once shot, and any village harbouring them was destroyed, and a proportion of its male inhabitants put to death. Any civilian who interfered with the lines of communication was shot, and the neighbouring villages fined or destroyed. The Germans now showed that they meant to enforce the same regulations in the new war, but to enforce them even more ruthlessly, and with a systematic brutality and a thoroughness hitherto unknown in civilised warfare

The conduct of the Germans outraged humanity. War is, at its best, hideous, brutal, and cruel. Hardness, severity, and relentlessness are admittedly among its essentials. The general who shows weakness, who hesitates to sacrifice his own men, has mistaken his vocation. But in war conducted between civilised nations it has been customary to soften some of the worst brutalities. Just as the decent boxer does not hit below the belt, so civilised nations have agreed that there are certain things they will not do. They will not make war by spreading disease among their enemies, by killing their wounded, by shooting soldiers once made prisoners, by punishing non-combatants. Women, children, and the aged are left out of the fight. Apart from definite provisions made by the civilised powers for the conduct of war, there are unwritten understandings which, it was imagined, were enforced by the common conscience of humanity.

When reports came from the front that the German armies were violating these conditions, the world at large hesitated to accept the accusation. It is easy to bring charges of atrocities. Necessary severity can be made to look like unspeakable cruelty. But soon the reports that poured in from every point along the line of war were so detailed and so completely substantiated that they could not be disbelieved. Germany was not going to conduct this war according to rules, even according to the common rules of humanity. She meant to conduct it in its harshest, its most forbidding, and its most terrifying form.

At Visé the Belgians tasted the German quality. The capture of this town has been described in an earlier chapter. The people openly helped the troops to resist; they were fighting for their Fatherland. There was no concealment about it, no firing from hidden places by men who afterwards intended to escape as innocent peasants. The people saw their homes attacked and took up arms to defend them.

Some few years ago, when, in a popular play in London, "An Englishman's Home," the final tragedy was the military execution of an ordinary English householder because he had taken part in a fight against the invaders, many people considered the incident overdrawn. The man's act, they argued, was natural and patriotic; it was absurd to think that if the Germans succeeded they would shoot him in cold blood for what he had done. What seemed ridiculously exaggerated in a London play was carried out on a wholesale scale at Visé. Every house was burnt and everything destroyed. Many of the men were shot as soon as the Germans got possession of the town—shot in cold blood when they had been secured and disarmed, and those who were not shot were made prisoners, and have since been put to work on the roads or in constructing defences for the enemy. The women and children were treated in such fashion that fourteen of them died within a few days of reaching Dutch territory.

As the Germans advanced in Belgium they systematically made the southern country a desert. The evidence, not of a Belgian, but of a German war correspondent, Herr Heinrich Binder, of the "Berliner Tageblatt," on this subject is conclusive. He made an official tour in company with the foreign military attachés through those parts of

DINANT BEFORE GERMAN VANDALISM DESTROYED IT.

DINANT, WITH ITS CITADEL, WRECKED CHURCH, AND BROKEN BRIDGE, AFTER THE GERMANS HAD PASSED.

THE SCENE OF HAVOC FROM THE BROKEN BRIDGE.

ANOTHER BROKEN BRIDGE OVER THE MEUSE AT DINANT.

Dinant is one of the many Belgian towns whose churches, houses and bridges were shattered into heaps of pitiful ruins by the brute fury of the Kaiser's legions while they were "hacking their way" through into France.

THE MAIN GATEWAY OF TERMONDE IN RUINS.
This gateway was destroyed by Belgian soldiers so that it should not
interfere with their artillery fire when replying to the German attack.

Belgium in the occupation of the German army.

"I inspected the villages of Battice and Hervé," he wrote. "They have been razed to the ground. Of about five hundred houses at Hervé only nineteen remain. Corpses are lying all over the place; everywhere there is the smell of burning. The church is a broken heap of ruins. Some houses have been spared because shots were not fired from them. They bear notices such as 'Don't shoot,' 'Well disposed,' or 'Spare us; we are innocent.' The same picture reproduced itself all the way to Liège. Not by any means has everything been demolished indiscriminately; between whole rows of houses which have been blown up one may see houses which have been carefully left alone, with pretty gardens and groups of playing children.

SURROUNDED BY DESOLATION A STATUE STANDS UNHARMED.
The Germans arrived at Termonde and proceeded to bombard it on September 5th, 1914. It was entered and plundered on the same evening.
The photograph shows the harvest of desolation reaped by the bombardment, and a statue which their bursting shells left unharmed.

"Every forty yards the high road has been torn up and barricades have been built. The odour of corruption arises from the cellars of the ruined houses, and is often so strong that we cannot remain. Since the German soldiers have been in the country the work of reconstruction is going on. Landwehr men may be seen sitting with Belgian families at the doors of village houses as if peace had been won. In all villages the inhabitants instinctively put up their hands or saluted as we passed. White

TERMONDE DELIBERATELY DESTROYED BY THE GERMANS.
Before the German entry Termonde was a town of some 1,400 houses. The German troops went systematically through street after street firing each building separately, spraying the lower floors with an inflammable liquid and then setting fire to them. Three buildings of importance and about one hundred others were spared. The remainder were hopelessly wrecked as seen here.

flags, cloths, and handkerchiefs float over every house. The land is as though dead."

The German authorities laid down the same regulation they had enforced in the Franco-Prussian War—that any civilian caught firing against the troops would be instantly shot, and any place from which firing came would be destroyed They further declared that each community would be punished as a whole for any attacks made on troops or lines of communication there. From a military

BELGIAN INFANTRY AMONG THE SHATTERED RUINS OF TERMONDE.
The terrible ruthlessness of the Germans' military machine enabled them to revel in Teutonic " higher civilisation " in hapless Belgium, but no sooner had they passed to another debauch of destruction than Belgian soldiers were on their heels, worrying their transport and cutting off small parties. The inset picture shows a Belgian look-out on an old fortress overlooking Alost.

point of view, justification cannot be claimed for these rules. In 1870 they were condemned by the German authorities, Geffcken and Bluntschli, as indefensibly harsh. Their cruelty was aggravated by the manner in which the Germans carried them out. Throughout Southern Belgium whole communities were punished for mere suspicion of crime ; villages were burnt and their inhabitants murdered to hide the blunders of individual officers.

When the Germans took possession of a village or a town they usually seized the burgomaster, the curé, the schoolmaster, the doctor, and other prominent citizens, and held them as hostages for the good behaviour of the people. It was not enough for the villagers to remain neutral ; there must be

THE ALERT BELGIAN SOLDIERY PASSING THROUGH TERMONDE AFTER THE GERMAN EVACUATION.

ALL THAT REMAINED OF HIS DAUGHTERS!
This resident of Melle returned to his burned home. His daughters were murdered by Germans before the house was fired, and he is holding up a charred foot of one of them found among the ashes.

no attack by the Belgian troops on the German troops. In many cases, although the terrified inhabitants did nothing, the hostages were shot because Belgian cavalry advanced and fired on the Germans. Every refinement of mental torture that could be devised was inflicted on the people. Hostages were left hour after hour expecting death at any moment; in some cases the Germans said they would only shoot half of them, and left the victims themselves to pick out which half should be shot.

This was not all. Little groups of soldiers, away from the control of superior officers, got out of hand; they plundered, they outraged, they murdered at their will. It was clear that the word had gone forward to strike terror into the hearts of the country-side. It was as though a horde of barbarians had descended upon the land, and many people who could not escape preferred death rather than to fall into their hands. "The Belgian railway porter," wrote one correspondent,

BELGIAN WOMEN REMOVING SOME OF THEIR GOODS TO PLACES OF SAFETY.

"who told me calmly that he had a stick of dynamite in his house, and that he would blow up the building, with his wife, himself, and children, rather than permit the invaders to enter, was probably indulging in no exaggeration."

The simple and graphic diary of a young English girl, Miss Lydia Evans, who was at a convent school at Fouron, near Visé, when the Germans entered, gives some interesting sidelights on the attitude of the troops. Miss Evans at first

had no reason to complain of the appearance and manners of the Prussian soldiers. "They were exceedingly polite," she wrote on August 3rd, when German troops invaded the convent. "They are magnificent. The meanest soldier is perfectly equipped, everything perfectly new, and splendid horses. They are like theatre soldiers, they are so perfect. There were awfully nice and talked a lot." But very soon the soldiers showed their rougher side. Here are some extracts from the entries during the days that followed:

SOME OF THE HAPLESS VICTIMS OF GERMAN BARBARISM IN BELGIUM.

"August 6th.—A curate near here has been shot. The Germans are very nice if you give them what they want, but if they are refused the pistol comes out. Old Mother Thérèse was at the door when a soldier asked her for a kettle. She refused, and he nearly shot her.

"August 7th.—A most fearful noise was heard about two o'clock. They say that it was a fort blown up. A German aeroplane passed yesterday. The soldiers are camping in the woods. There are seven wounded here. Nearly all the others are taken to Aix-la-Chapelle.

"August 8th.—Went to mass in the

PROOF POSITIVE OF THE DELIBERATE DESTRUCTION OF BELGIAN HOMES BY THE PITILESS INVADERS.
Photographs showing German inscriptions on houses in Termonde to be spared. That on the left reads "Spare this—good people" (Germans), and on the right, "The house behind to be spared—only defenceless women" (a German convent).

village. A man told us that the Germans had burnt two big farms at Warsage (the next village). Two women and two men arrived from Liège. They said that the people had been living in caves for the last two days and nights. These poor people saw awful sights in coming across the fields, which were covered with dead. We have heard that Berneau is burnt, and the women and children hung. The Germans are furious at having lost such a number of men before seeing the French. A soldier passed last night, and Maria lifted up a corner of the curtain. In a minute he had out his revolver and threatened to shoot her. Some of the soldiers opposite the convent were drunk.

"August 9th.—An aeroplane passed right over us, and seemed to drop something white. The soldiers are going about in bands, destroying and laying waste every house and garden. They pass with bottles of wine and their pockets bulging out with things they have stolen. They set a house on fire just near the convent. There are 40,000 soldiers between here and Niouland.

German pillage and drunkenness

"August 10th.—There was a terrific crash at the door. Four German officers who had come in a motor pointed their revolvers and asked for wine. They looked as if they had been drinking. We had a fearful fright after dinner. An officer followed by a soldier came to ask us where the curé was, and threatened to shoot us because we could not tell him. Miss MacMahon had to lead him to the rector's house, with a revolver pointed at her back all the way. The houses on either side are burning. The nuns asked the German officers if they would spare the convent. They laughed, and said they would make it a cemetery for their dead. They took away the wounded, and as soon as they had gone the nuns woke us up, and we started out, following all the back roads."

Here are two other cases investigated by a Belgian official committee of inquiry, which reported as follows:

"During the night of August 10th German cavalry entered Velm in great numbers. The

AMBULANCE WAITING FOR WOUNDED.
This photograph was taken near Boncelles, just west from Liège, during the heroic defence of the forts.

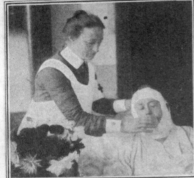

IN A DUTCH RED CROSS HOSPITAL.

FRIEND AND FOE UNDER THE WING OF THE RED CROSS.
The Hotel Flandria, Ghent, the biggest of Belgium's hotels, was used as a Red Cross hospital for Belgian, British, and German wounded.

PRIESTS UNDER THE RED CROSS MINISTER TO THE VICTIMS OF BATTLE.
Red Cross bearers and priests at Hofstade, between Brussels and Ghent. Many of them were deliberately shot by the Germans.

A BELGIAN REGIMENT RETIRING TO ANTWERP AFTER HARRYING THE INVADERS.
After offering a resistance to the German invaders so courageous and stubborn that it won the admiration of the world, the Belgian army retired to Antwerp, one of the strongest fortresses in Europe. There it recuperated and prepared to meet any German attack, or to take the offensive as soon as opportunity offered. This picture shows an infantry regiment falling back on Antwerp after the hard fighting around Ghent.

inhabitants were asleep. The Germans, without provocation, fired on M. Deglimme-Gevers' house, broke into it, destroyed furniture, looted money, burnt barns, hay and corn stacks, farm implements, six oxen, and the contents of the farmyard. They carried off his wife, half naked, to a place two miles away. She was then let go and was fired upon as she fled, without being hit. Her husband was carried away in another direction and fired

Official proof of German butchery upon. He is dying. The same troops sacked and burned the house of a railway watchman.

"Farmer Jef Dierick, of Neerhespen, bears witness to the following acts of cruelty committed by German cavalry at Orsmael and Neerhespen on August 10th, 11th, and 12th:

"An old man of the latter village had his arm sliced in three longitudinal cuts; he was then hanged, head downwards, and burned alive. Young girls have been raped, and little children outraged at Orsmael, where several inhabitants suffered mutilations too horrible to describe. A Belgian soldier belonging to a battalion of cyclist carbineers, who had been wounded and made prisoner, was hanged, whilst another, who was tending his comrade, was bound to a telegraph pole on the St. Trond road and shot.

"The town of Aerschot was entered by the Germans on Wednesday, August 19th, without any resistance whatever having been made. As the German troops marched through, the inhabitants closed their doors and windows and sat within in order that there might be no suspicion that they were planning an attack. The German soldiers broke into their houses, ordered the people to leave, and as they went into the street seized the first six male inhabitants and shot them under the eyes of their wives and children. Next day the Germans returned again, once more, ordered the people to leave their houses, marched them in a body to a place two hundred yards from the town, and there shot the burgomaster (mayor), his fifteen-year-old son, and eleven prominent citizens. They then burnt the place.

BELGIAN GUNS, MADE BY KRUPP, ON THEIR WAY TO BE TURNED AGAINST THE GERMANS.
Artillery duels were a prominent feature of the early stages of the war, and what success the Germans won was due in great measure to the power and number of their guns.   Most of the Belgian guns were of Krupp manufacture, and they were turned against the country of their origin with deadly effect at Liège, and again at the Battle of Haelen on August 13th, 1914.   This illustration depicts a detachment of Belgian artillery preparing to go into action at Ziel, near Ghent.

" At Linsmeau some Belgian infantry and two gendarmes attacked German cavalry occupying the village, drove them out, and killed their officer.   The people of the village took no part in the fighting.   Nevertheless, a strong force of German cavalry rode out on August 10th, retook possession of the place, arrested all the people, destroyed two farms and six outlying houses, took eleven of the inhabitants, placed them in a ditch, and smashed in their skulls with their rifles."

" The authorities enraged the public against Germany by assiduously circulating false reports," declared the German authorities later, when attempting to justify their action.   " They were under the impression that with the aid of the French they would be able to drive the Germans out of Belgium in two days."   The Germans further claimed that the Belgian peasantry were guilty of numerous outrages against wounded German troops.   There may have been offences in individual cases.   When people find **German excuses for admitted outrages** their homes burnt, their children murdered, and themselves ruined, they are apt, human nature being what it is, to revenge themselves as best they can.   But certain it is that many of the worst German outrages were committed against people who had committed no offence, who had not even offered open or secret resistance.

Thirteen army corps, the pick of Germany's forces, totalling at least 650,000 men, with 2,200 field guns and heavy guns, and a very full equipment of machine-guns, were waiting to advance into Belgium.   Their progress was delayed for some days by the resistance of Liège, the guns of the forts there controlling the three main roads, the railway and the River Meuse.   While one portion of the army was besieging Liège, two cavalry divisions, numbering over 10,000 men, crossed the Meuse close to the Dutch frontier and advanced through the country.

It was not, of course, the intention of the German General Staff to employ the whole of the thirteen corps

THE CLEVER REPAIR BY GERMAN ENGINEERS OF A RAILWAY BRIDGE AT TONGRES.
This bridge was blown up by the retreating Belgians to embarrass the advance of the Germans, whose engineers made a temporary repair by using piers of timber. It must be admitted that the invaders excelled in such work.

against the little Belgian Army. To do this would have been like using a steam-hammer to crack a filbert. The total field force that King Albert could bring against the Germans did not exceed 100,000 men, and was probably

very considerably less. There is no need to reckon in this force the Civil Guards and similar bodies, which had little more than a paper existence. The Civil Guards, as a matter of fact, were disarmed in nearly every case before the Germans arrived.

The German cavalry screen succeeded in driving the Belgian forces back to the line represented by the towns of Diest, Haelen, Tirlemont, and Jodoigne. It isolated Liège, and formed an impenetrable barrier, completely concealing the movements of the German armies and the preparations in progress to their rear. This was so much the case that, on the day before they struck the blow which shattered the Belgian field army, it was considered doubtful, both in the Belgian headquarters and in London, if they had yet succeeded in moving any considerable force

ONE OF BELGIUM'S CORPS OF CLEVER CYCLIST—
The extreme mobility of cyclists made them very valuable for reconnoitring and sharpshooting. Antwerp, after the evacuation of Brussels,

HOLDING UP THE MOTOR TRAFFIC.
This simple barrier across the main road in a Belgian village prevented the passage of hostile or unauthorised motor-cars.

BARRICADE IN A BRUSSELS SUBURB.
Transport vehicles drawn across the road by Civil Guards, in order to hold up traffic for inspection before allowing it to pass.

BELGIUM'S EXCELLENT FIELD ARTILLERY BOLDLY REPLIES TO THE CHALLENGE OF THE INVADERS.
A photograph taken when the guns were firing upon the Germans. Each gun has its caisson or ammunition waggon alongside, and the soldier running between the two guns is carrying a message received by field telephone.

across the Meuse. "The situation of the Allies on the Meuse remains favourable," wrote one of the best-informed of the British military critics on August 18th. "So far as we know, the Germans are not north of the Meuse in force. . . . . There is no sign or word of a German advance." The critic in writing this was only expressing the general sentiment among those on the side of the Allies in the best position to know.

The German cavalry, pushing through the villages and keeping in touch with the Belgian outposts, behaved with barbarous cruelty. In one place they shot seven of the inhabitants, one for having run away, the others for no reason at all. If villagers looked at them in a way they did not like, they would, if they were in a good humour, inflict merely contemptuous punishments on them, such as compelling them to hold up their hands for half an hour, to roll in the dust, to kneel and beg pardon, and the like. If they happened to be in a bad humour, the

—SOLDIERS LEAVING ANTWERP ON SCOUTING DUTY.
held over 2,000 of these intrepid cycling soldiers, who waited "at the ready," eager to take the offensive against the enemy.

FEEDING THE BELGIAN FIELD GUNS.
A nearer view of one of the guns shown at top of the page. The empty shells lying behind have spent their charges upon the ranks of the advancing enemy.

EMPTY HOUSES BUT FULL TRENCHES.
All the residents of this Belgian village had fled, and its only occupants were soldiers who threw up earthwork entrenchments like this and there calmly awaited the enemy.

bodies of the Belgians afterwards recovered by their friends showed, some of them, such evidences of horrible torture as cannot be described in print.

On Sunday, August 9th, the famous " Death's Head " Hussars, a " crack " cavalry regiment, passed through the ruins of Visé and penetrated as far as Tongres. They lowered the Belgian flag hanging from the town hall, commandeered the municipal money chests, and seized ten thousand francs at the post office. Uhlans (Prussian lancers) raided Hasselt, and there secured no less than two million francs (£80,000) belonging to the National Bank of Belgium. This was an act of sheer robbery forbidden by the laws of war.

Murder followed by robbery

The scenes all along the line where the two armies were in touch were full of interest and excitement. The Belgians, worn and grim, fought behind hedges and roadside barricades, in shallow trenches, and behind the walls of village houses. The Germans, as they advanced, drove out the villagers and destroyed all before them. The Belgian authorities by this time had given instructions that civilians were in no circumstances to take part in the fighting, but were to leave the war to the soldiers. The story of the German atrocities had, however, already convinced most people that this was the only course. At a multitude of points little parties of Uhlans would come

BELGIAN HEAVY ARTILLERY READY TO GO INTO ACTION.
The distant range of field artillery is 6,000 yards; of heavy artillery 10,000 yards. The effective range of the former is 4,000 yards; of the latter 5,000 yards. Heavy artillery can seldom avoid firing over the heads of its own troops. When the front ranks of the opposing forces are so close together that gun fire might injure friend as well as foe, fire is directed upon objects behind the enemy's skirmishers, or upon the supposed positions of his reserves. This photograph shows Belgian heavy artillery being drawn up to the firing-line.

into contact with little parties of Belgian infantry or cavalry; there would be a charge, a volley, a struggle. Now an ambush would be laid, and some Uhlans would dash carelessly to death. Now the Germans in turn would conceal their cavalry or their machine-guns, and the Belgians would move forward unconsciously to destruction.

A skirmish of some moment occurred at Tirlemont on Tuesday and Wednesday, August 11th and 12th. Two thousand German cavalry advanced in the direction of that town, and were attacked by a regiment of Belgian lancers. The latter were driven back by the superior German machine-gun fire. On the Wednesday morning the Germans attempted to take the offensive. They were met by the steady fire of a body of Belgian infantry, and were forced back for some distance. About the same time a regiment of German dragoons attempted to surprise the Belgian troops at Aineffe. After a three hours' fight, they were driven off, leaving one hundred and fifty-three dead on the field, and one hundred and two prisoners in the hands of the Belgians.

Successes of Belgian skirmishers

Another outpost affair took place near Eghezee, when a body of three hundred and fifty Uhlans, with sixty cyclist scouts, were surprised at a village while sitting quietly in the cafés enjoying themselves. Their horses were grazing in the fields and the men were wholly unprepared. Their own cyclists rode in to give the alarm. The

THE GLORY OF RHEIMS FOR SEVEN HUNDRED YEARS.

The bombardment of Rheims on September 19th, 1914, did great and irreparable damage to its magnificent cathedral, one of the sublime architectural glories of Christendom, and a great masterpiece of thirteeneth-century Gothic. At the time of this act of vandalism beds of straw in the cathedral were occupied by German wounded under the care of French Red Cross nurses.

BB

Nowhere out of France was there the equal of Rheims Cathedral as it stood before German shells crashed into the historic fabric. Nowhere in France itself was there a building more venerated by tradition, history, and the shades of the departed great. Rheims Cathedral was a beautiful example of thirteenth-century Gothic, and one hundred and fifty years of long labour were spent on its erection before its lofty towers finally rose above the completed structure. Within its walls Joan of Arc the consecration of Charles VII.—the successors of Clovis were anointed here with the sacred phial supposed to have been sent from Heaven for his baptism. association of history and legend—the supreme beauty of one of the world's gems of architecture—was no protection when Germany had decreed des

r guns thundered from their entrenchments on the north the masses of
hat carried fire and demolition in their path. The act of wanton
sm took place on September 19th and 20th, 1914, and these days will be
nes in the calendar of Christendom. The fabric was seriously injured and the
vere shot from many of the statues that adorned the magnificent west front.

The belfry collapsed and the bells melted in the heat. The nave suffered more
than any other part. At the time of the bombardment one hundred and thirty
German wounded, tended by French Red Cross nurses, lay in the Cathedral, which had
been turned into a hospital; and although the French did their best to save them,
the blackened corpses of thirteen lay among the cinders when the fire had spent itself

BRITISH TORPEDO CRAFT DISPLAY EXCEPTIONAL SEAWORTHINESS DURING A TERRIFIC STORM IN THE NORTH SEA.

The monotony of waiting for a foe, which preferred the inglorious seclusion of its own ports to battle in the open, was relieved for a section of the British Fleet by a heavy gale during the early part of September. For twenty-four hours the smaller craft were buffeted about, with hatches battened down, and sailors standing at their posts lashed to the rails. On one destroyer a surgeon, rendering first-aid to a disabled man, was nearly carried overboard. He managed to grip the rail as his body struck the water, and his fingers were cut to the bone before he was rescued. Sometimes vessels had their sterns out of the water, and their propellers racing madly, but they rode out the weather none the worse, exhibiting exceptional seaworthiness.

OUTWORKS OF A BELGIAN FORT REPLYING TO THE MIGHTY GERMAN SIEGE-GUNS.
The German attack reduced the forts at Liège to a heap of ruins by using siege-guns, cumbrous masses of steel, each weighing not less than forty tons. The placing of one of these siege-guns in position is about equal to erecting a large machinery plant. Liège was protected by cupola forts, which are covered in. This photograph shows an uncovered temporary fort answering the attack of German siege-guns.

Uhlans in a sudden panic rushed off, leaving horses, rifles, machine-guns and everything behind them. The Belgians succeeded in killing about forty of the men as they ran.

An action of some importance occurred on August 12th and 13th at Haelen. A force of German cavalry and artillery, accompanied by a small body of infantry, numbering probably 10,000 in all, attempted to move around Tirlemont to outflank the Belgian army. They found themselves opposed by a Belgian division of cavalry and a mixed brigade, numbering between 7,000 and 10,000.

Towards eleven o'clock on August 12th the Germans were seen on the Steevoorn-Haelen road. The Belgian artil-

COILS OF IRON WIRE TO PROTECT GERMAN TRENCHES.
A German trench at Melle, near Ghent, protected by tons of wire, brought from Hamburg for the purpose. Shells landing among the coils of wire have a narrowed field of destruction, and, as the wire is more apt to be twisted and bent than it is to break, the coils can be used frequently.

lery, which was well placed, opened fire on them, and a fierce fight followed which lasted until early evening. The Belgian guns wrought great destruction. The Germans tried to ride through the enemy by sheer dash and daring. At one point their cavalry dashed at a series of formidable Belgian barricades, only to be picked off and driven back by the infantry fire. Then there came a fierce charge, when the German cavalry and the Belgian cavalry rode right into one another, and a hand-to-hand conflict ensued.

The country was very unfavourable to the Germans, its broken nature making cavalry advances difficult. The invaders, even according to the account of their

BRUSSELS' BRAVE BURGOMASTER.
When the German general in command of Brussels placarded the walls of the city with a notice requesting the inhabitants to remove all Belgian flags, M. Max, the burgomaster, protested against this command, but his posters were everywhere covered up with blank paper.

enemies, showed extreme courage. At one point the German cavalry even attempted to charge a line of Belgian machine-guns, and pushed forward, despite immense slaughter, until sheer butchery forced it back.

The Germans revealed in this fight the qualities which were to carry them far in the days that immediately followed. "They may not have shown much pluck before," said one Belgian major at the end of the day, "but they have certainly shown it to-day." But this was a case where the rush tactics of the Germans were in vain. They had finally to retire with a loss of about a thousand men. The conduct of the Belgian troops during this fight aroused very high praise.

High courage on both sides

The battle of Haelen was one of those fights where the individual soldier had a chance to distinguish himself, and the Belgians told many tales of the bravery of their own men afterwards. There was, for example, one farrier-sergeant by name Rousseau, of the Chasseurs à Cheval, who, with a little band of eight men, charged a whole company of Uhlans and routed them, bringing a dozen horses back as trophies. One lieutenant, asked to send reinforcements, summoned the town fire brigade of Diest, and collected up what soldiers he could find along the road. He and his little band rushed to the point where they were wanted, stormed a Prussian battery and drove it back, the lieutenant himself seizing a soldier's rifle and shooting dead the Prussian officer in command. The day ended in a Belgian victory.

By this time the Belgians were becoming exceedingly confident. At first they had almost despaired of their prospects in the war. Now they thought they had proved in fight after fight

that they could hold their own, even against the Germans. Had they been better acquainted with the methods of the German General Staff they would have known that the settled policy of the German Army was to play with the enemy during the time of preparations for a great move as a cat plays with a mouse. The German plan, as admitted by such writers as General von Bernhardi, is to offer a relatively weak front during a period of concentration, to send out a dense screen of cavalry to keep in touch with the enemy, to make a show of weakness, to discover the strength of the foe and their dispositions, and then, when the right moment comes, to attack "like a thunderbolt from the clouds."

The Germans at the beginning did not condescend to make elaborate preparations against the Belgians. Doubtless, they hoped and expected that forces such as that sent against Haelen would be

TRENCHES FROM WHICH BELGIAN FIRE MOWED DOWN GERMAN COLUMNS.
The inset picture shows a company of Belgian infantry in a trench near Alost waiting to give the German advance guard a warm reception. In the lower picture a Belgian field trench is being used as cover, and the officer on the ladder is watching for the advance of the enemy.

GROUP OF BELGIAN CAVALRY INCLUDING GENERAL LEMAN, THE BRILLIANT DEFENDER OF LIEGE.
General Leman's name will go down in history on that glorious roll of fame which contains the names of men who courted death by "facing fearful odds." He was taken prisoner only after his forts had been demolished and he himself lay unconscious from the fumes of exploded shells.

FACSIMILE OF LETTER FROM GENERAL LEMAN.
Shortly before the war a friend of General Leman received this letter from him. It was torn up, but when the world was ringing with the name of Belgium's great hero the lady recovered the "scraps of paper." It has a human interest in view of the modesty that shows through its few lines. The translation is as follows:
"Camp de Beverloo,
"June 7th, 1914.
"My dear Madam,—The camp does not cause me to forget you, believe me. Still, I am so pressed that I have not an instant to give to my children and my friends. The King comes on the 11th to assist at a manœuvre that I shall do my best to command. I shall have about 25,000 men. On the 12th we leave camp. I believe that about the 20th or a little sooner I ought to come to Brussels for service, after which we count upon having you at Liège, my dear madam. Besides, I shall write you in time. Be good enough to accept with my homage the cordial assurance of my deep friendship. G. LEMAN."

sufficient in themselves to sweep away any opposition. When they found their mistake they reverted to their regular tactics, paused, gathered strength, and then struck.

The Belgians, after the first fortnight of war, came somewhat to despise the foe. The Germans were ill-equipped, short of food, lacking enthusiasm, and driven unwillingly to fight, said the Belgians. "I go out to capture the Germans," said one Belgian hero, "not with a gun but with a buttered roll; I hold the roll out; the Uhlans when they see it are so hungry that they rush up and surrender themselves in order to get food." Doubtless, some of the Uhlans and hussars, hastily pushed through the country, did march on short commons. But Belgium was only too soon to discover that the army behind was well provided.

On Saturday, August 15th, the Germans moved forward to strike their real blow. The forts of Liège were no longer able to offer a serious resistance. The little town of Huy, with its important bridge over the Meuse, eastward of Namur, **Germans move in strength** which had been taken after a fierce struggle, opened up an important thoroughfare. The German armies were now able to move in strength into the heart of Belgium. Behind the cavalry screen four army corps moved forward. Their aircraft swept northwards, and from this moment little more was heard of the Belgian aeroplanes, which up to this stage had been doing useful work. One German army moved in great strength westwards towards Dinant. Its doings will be dealt with later. Another moved up behind the northern cavalry screen.

On August 16th the Germans attacked in force the position to the south-east of Wavre, where the Belgian and French armies met. They came in crescent formation, their aim being to turn the right flank of the Belgian army. The Belgian headquarters reported that the attempt had been vigorously repulsed, but the repulse was not permanent.

GERMANS IN THE HEART OF ANTWERP——AS PRISONERS.
The Antwerp populace looked on with feelings of gladness mingled with sorrow as this large draft of German prisoners was marched through their city en route for safe keeping in England. Gladness—that so many of the modern Huns were rendered innocuous for the duration of the war; and sorrow from the recollection of Louvain, Malines, and Termonde, wrecked by the henchmen of the Imperial treaty-breaker.

On Monday the Germans advanced all along the line from Wavre to the Dutch frontier at great speed and with irresistible force. On Tuesday they opened an overwhelming artillery fire on Tirlemont. Their infantry and cavalry were sometimes as many as ten to one against their enemy. The German aeroplanes acted as scouts; they located the Belgian forces, signalled the exact position to their own guns, and enabled them to aim the shrapnel with overwhelming effect.

When the Belgian lines had been shaken sufficiently by shrapnel fire the German cavalry poured in, stabbing, shooting, and sabring. They swept through the ranks out into the villages behind. The people there were in their homes or working in the fields, confident in the power of their own soldiers to protect them. Suddenly the German cavalry swooped on them, and neither age nor sex was spared. As the people who escaped

The irresistible German advance

rushed madly across the fields and along the hedges the German guns opened out on them. It was battle practice against old men, women, and children. War had come in earnest now. Those fortunate enough to escape found two trains waiting about five miles from the town. They rushed on them, and were carried to Brussels, where their tale of pillage, death, and woe caused consternation.

"Never," one correspondent in Brussels wrote, "have I seen such a picture of war as a peasant woman and five children who stood bewildered in the Place de la Gare here, all of them crying as if their hearts would break. It was a terrible story the woman had to tell. 'They shot my husband before my eyes,' she said, 'and trampled two of my children to death. I am the mother of nine, and I have only five with me; the others are lost.'"

On Wednesday, August 19th, the Belgian field army made a stand at Louvain itself. The Belgians had chosen their position well, and it was expected that they would offer a stubborn resistance. After some fighting, however,

BRITISH MANHOOD POURING INTO FRANCE TO SPEED VICTORY AND PEACE.
As the transports carrying British troops swung into French ports the waiting crowds hailed the arrivals with welcoming cheers, which were echoed back from the ships with interest and enthusiasm, accompanied by the inspiring cry, " Are we downhearted ? " and answered again by a great resounding chorus of " No ! "

the Belgian forces suddenly retired. They had been beaten all along the line by the force of the German onset. The Germans were showing the qualities which were to carry them so far later in the war. The recklessness in advancing, the wholesale sacrifice of life, the powerful artillery fire concentrated on central points, the innumerable machine-guns dealing death on the enemy whenever they dared advance, and the aeroplanes, helped them to victory. Among the many descriptions of individual fights one fragment, by Mr. Raymond Coulson, stands out :

"The Belgian lancers, six hundred, were out scouting. As they were trotting down a long road they suddenly sighted the enemy and began to charge. On the left, they came unexpectedly on a large, deep hole that threw a considerable part of their line into disorder. Then, entirely without warning, there burst over on the front the sharp, terrible roar of the mitrailleuses. The cavalry were running into a nest of little Maxim guns the Germans had brought up on horses.

The road to Brussels won

"They rode until their saddles were emptied. We saw them in a small hollow. Two minutes later a number of riderless horses scattering widely over the countryside told us what they were meeting. Yet in the face of that stream of lead they actually dismounted and tried, with carbines, to worry the Maxims. At the same time they found themselves exposed to infantry fire from the woods. They came back at a gallop, a small scattered remnant of the host. At the same moment German guns began to open up around the semicircle of horizon.

"Shells burst like puffballs on green fields, searching our wide front. The thunder of big guns, the rhythmic beat of pom-poms, the roar of mitrailleuses, and the rattle of rifle fire came suddenly from ahead all the way from right to left. Around the skyline village after village went up in a pillar of black smoke."

The German advance was irresistible. The Belgian troops in attempting to stay it lost very heavily. Three regiments were almost annihilated. In the end the Belgian field army was for the time broken, and withdrew in the direction of the forts of Antwerp to find protection there. Brussels, the capital, was left open to the foe

ADMIRAL SIR JOHN RUSHWORTH JELLICOE, K.C.B., K.C.V.O., COMMANDER-IN-CHIEF OF THE HOME FLEETS.

Sir John Jellicoe's appointment to the supreme command of the British Home Fleets was acclaimed by the nation as a wise choice, in full confidence of his high ability for the task of guarding our coasts from the hostile Navy. His brilliant record has scarcely a parallel. From his examination as sub-lieutenant, when he came ahead of all his fellows by over one hundred marks, he had an unbroken career. As a writer said in a London paper at the opening of the war: "It would almost seem as though the man to whom the chief command of the British Navy has been entrusted had been specially saved by Providence for the accomplishment of some great task." He had a great share in fashioning the naval weapon of which he is in control. Swift in judgment, inflexible in will, he spared neither himself nor others when work was to be done.

BRITISH FIRST BATTLE-
CRUISER SQUADRON

CHAPTER XIII.

PUTTING TO SEA,
LED BY H.M.S. LION.

THE BRITISH GRAND FLEET PUTS TO SEA.

Exceptional Readiness of British Fleet—The Silent Movement to the Point of Danger—The Components of the Rival Fleets—
Italian Support Lost to Germany—The Position in the Mediterranean—British Naval Bases—The Russian Squadrons—
British Inability to Operate in the Baltic—The Attitude of Secrecy—Foreign Ships Added to British Strength—The Two
Schools of Naval Policy—Power of the 13·5 in. Gun—Ships under Construction in Germany and England at the Declaration
of War—The Suicidal Policy of the "Little Navy" Party—The Strong Policy of Mr. Churchill—Mobilisation—War.

IN so far as her naval ambitions were concerned, Germany staked everything upon being able to strike us at an unguarded moment. It will be readily apparent that, though in normal circumstances we have about one hundred and fifty ships of all classes in full commission in home waters, there must almost invariably be a large number of vessels which, for some reason or another, are not instantly ready for war. Some would be in dockyard hands undergoing refit, possibly with half their guns dismounted, some would be giving well-earned leave to their crews, and the others might be scattered between twenty or thirty ports round the British coasts.

This is the state of things upon which Germany had reckoned, and she may also, in her utter ignorance of the spirit of the British people, have relied upon the divisions which might have been caused in our ranks by the Irish question. But, in any case, her plans went completely adrift.

Six months before the war became even a possibility, the British Admiralty decided that every available British warship in home waters should in July be placed on a war footing. In normal conditions the Home Fleet consists of the First Fleet, which is always fully manned and ready for war; the Second Fleet, which has half its men on board in peace, and can be prepared for war in twenty-four hours by drawing the remainder of its crews from the depots and training establishments; **Britannia awake** and the Third Fleet, which can only be made ready for war by calling up a portion of the naval reserves.

On March 17th, 1914, Mr. Churchill, the First Lord of the Admiralty, announced that every ship in the Home Fleet would be placed on a war footing between July 15th and July 25th, and that "the whole of the Royal Fleet Reserve"—some 30,000 strong—would be called out for eleven days. There is said to be a "little cherub that sits up aloft to keep watch o'er the lot of poor Jack," and at this juncture, at all events, he did his work exceedingly well. Before the time had come for the reservists to be discharged it had already become clear **Preparing for possibilities** that a serious war-cloud was gathering. Although the ships which had been specially commissioned were paid off in the usual way, all were warned that there was a possibility of a general mobilisation being ordered at any moment, and that, if such mobilisation were necessary, they would be required to report themselves in just the same fashion at the same ports, and to join the same ships, as had been the case a fortnight before.

The result was that when the German attitude towards Belgium made it impossible for Great Britain to remain a passive onlooker, the British Fleet was in a condition of readiness for war such as it could not possibly have enjoyed for more than four weeks out of any average year. The whole of the Fleet that is ordinarily kept in full commission was concentrated at Portland under its commander-in-chief, and on July 29th this force of one hundred and fifty ships—battleships, cruisers, and destroyers—steamed out to take up its position in readiness for war, in stirring array, with bands playing and crews cheering. After that date no information of the

THE BRITISH GRAND FLEET PUTTING TO SEA — THE MODERN ARMADA THAT RULES THE WAVES.

The leader in this impressive procession is the Iron Duke, the super-Dreadnought of 25,000 tons, which Admiral Jellicoe made his flagship. Behind her follows her sister ship, the Marlborough, and then others of the twenty-five Dreadnoughts and super-Dreadnoughts which the gallant admiral led to the North Sea. The hydroplane had been made a wing of the naval arm shortly before war began.

THE FIRST LIGHT CRUISER SQUADRON OF THE BRITISH HOME FLEET.
The photograph shows the squadron putting to sea. The Arethusa was the first of the squadron to win distinction. By his brilliant part in the daring naval escapade in Heligoland Bight, on August 27th, 1914, Commodore Tyrwhitt made his name ring through the Empire.

whereabouts of any British warship appeared in the newspapers. The British Navy, trained for ten years to expect an attack from Germany, moved silently away to take up the stations that had been allotted to it.

The reserves, that on July 25th had been discharged to their private concerns ashore, were again warned that at any moment their services might be required. In less than a week, on August 2nd, when it had become evident that Germany was determined to defy practically the whole of Europe, they were recalled to the flag.

The position was remarkable from two points of view. In the first place, Germany had made war upon us **Britain's strongest moment** not at our weakest, but at our strongest moment. Having received good notice of the probability of war, and, further, having assembled all its forces for a " test mobilisation," the British Navy was in an ideal condition to begin hostilities.

In the second place, it had become more or less an axiom in our national history that never in any circumstances would the British Navy be able to assume the initiative. It was assumed that the enemy must be ready before Great Britain. Critics who studied our naval and military dispositions regarded it as a practical certainty that we should be taken unawares. But they always hoped that, after a year or two of uphill fighting, our superior staying power might enable us to retrieve initial disaster. Now, however, thanks to an extraordinary stroke of fortune, the Admiralty had the situation well in hand when the war began. Every ship capable of effective service was ready for sea, with not more than half a dozen **An extraordinary stroke of fortune** exceptions, because the dockyards had for many weeks been working at full pressure to prepare the Fleet for the great test mobilisation at Spithead. A large number of reservists had only just completed their annual training with the Fleet, and so were more efficient than they would have been at any other time of the year.

The fighting forces of Great Britain and Germany in the North Sea at this time were commanded by Admiral Sir George Callaghan (replaced in August by Admiral Sir John Jellicoe) and Admiral von Ingenohl respectively. The principal ships in the main squadrons of the two Navies are shown in the table on page 222.

These were the main fighting squadrons of the fleets in the North Sea, according to the lists issued by the two Admiralties before the outbreak of war. The main squadrons were supported by a large number of less

FLEET OF BRITISH DREADNOUGHTS PUTTING OUT TO SEA.
The building of the Dreadnought in 1906 opened a new era in naval construction. The Dreadnought was the biggest battleship ever built up to that time, with a normal displacement of 17,900 tons, and carrying ten 12 in. guns and twenty-four 12-pounders. When war opened, the British Home Fleet included twenty-two ships of the Dreadnought type, and three super-Dreadnoughts.

ONE OF THE EIGHTY-FIVE DESTROYERS IN THE BRITISH HOME FLEET AT THE OPENING OF WAR.
The destroyers of the K class numbered twenty at the date of the declaration of war, and the photograph shows one of them riding a heavy sea. These destroyers are of 920 tons displacement, 24,500 horse-power, and a designed speed of thirty-two knots. They carry four torpedo tubes.

BRITISH.		GERMAN.	
Flagship of Home Fleet.		**Flagship of High Sea Fleet.**	
Iron Duke		Friedrich der Grosse	
(super-Dreadnought type)—10 guns.		(Dreadnought type)—10 guns.	
First Battle Squadron.		**First Battle Squadron.**	
Dreadnought type—10 guns.		**Dreadnought type—12 guns.**	
Marlborough.	Hercules.	Nassau.	Helgoland.
Collingwood.	Vanguard.	Westfalen.	Thuringen.
St. Vincent.	Neptune.	Rheinland.	Ostfriesland.
Colossus.	Superb.	Posen.	Oldenburg.
Second Battle Squadron.		**Second Battle Squadron.**	
Super-Dreadnought type—10 guns.		**Pre-Dreadnought type—4 guns.**	
Conqueror	Monarch.	Deutschland.	Schleswig-Holstein
		Hannover.	Lothringen.
Dreadnought type—10 guns		Pommern.	Hessen.
King George V.	Audacious.	Schlesien.	Preussen.
Centurion.	Orion.		
Ajax.	Thunderer.		
Third Battle Squadron.		**Third Battle Squadron.**	
Pre-Dreadnought type—8 guns.		**Dreadnought type—10 guns.**	
King Edward VII.	Dominion.	Kaiser.	
Africa.	Hibernia	König Albert	
Britannia.	Hindustan.	Kaiserin.	
Commonwealth.	Zealandia.	Prinzregent Luitpold.	
Fourth Battle Squadron.		**Fourth Battle Squadron.**	
Dreadnought type.			
Dreadnought—10 guns.			
Bellerophon—10 guns.		NONE.	
Temeraire—10 guns.			
Pre-Dreadnought type.			
Agamemnon—14 guns.			
Battle Cruisers.		**Battle Cruisers.**	
Dreadnought type—8 guns.		**Dreadnought type.**	
Lion.	Queen Mary.	Von der Tann—8 guns.	
Princess Royal.	New Zealand.	Seydlitz—10 guns.	
		Moltke—10 guns.	

The number of guns given refers to big guns. In the super-Dreadnought type the guns are of 13·5 in. calibre.

powerful craft and smaller vessels. With the British Grand Fleet, as it was named, were eight armoured cruisers, eight light cruisers, five depot ships and old cruisers, eighty-five destroyers, and six mine-sweepers (vessels specially fitted for the difficult and dangerous business of removing the enemy's mines and clearing a safe passage through mined waters for the fleet).

With the German High Sea Fleet were eight light cruisers and seventy-seven destroyers. In addition to these ships many other vessels were mobilised by each side and attached to each fleet.

The British Navy, moreover, was free to concentrate all its attention upon the task of paralysing or destroying the German naval forces. Italy, the third partner in the Triple Alliance (or combination of Germany, Austria, and Italy), refused to support her former allies in a conflict in which all her sympathies were with Great Britain and France. She had not been consulted before the German Government provoked war. The German Foreign Office appears to have assumed that she could be bullied or coerced into aiding Germany. That calculation proved pitiably at fault.

The loss of the support of the Italian Navy was a grave blow to Germany and Austria. Italy had a powerful fleet in the Mediterranean, which might well have turned

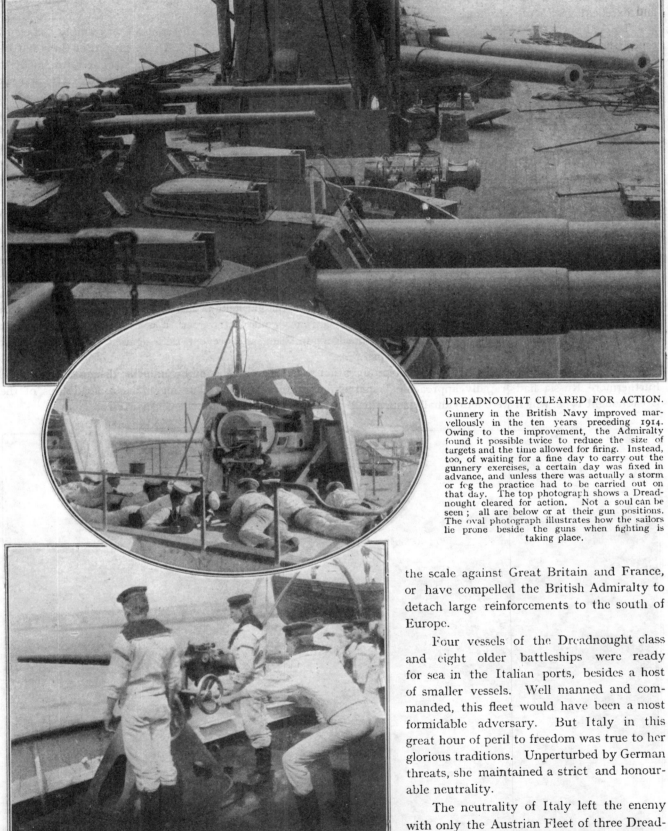

DREADNOUGHT CLEARED FOR ACTION.
Gunnery in the British Navy improved marvellously in the ten years preceding 1914. Owing to the improvement, the Admiralty found it possible twice to reduce the size of targets and the time allowed for firing. Instead, too, of waiting for a fine day to carry out the gunnery exercises, a certain day was fixed in advance, and unless there was actually a storm or fog the practice had to be carried out on that day. The top photograph shows a Dreadnought cleared for action. Not a soul can be seen; all are below or at their gun positions. The oval photograph illustrates how the sailors lie prone beside the guns when fighting is taking place.

A LIGHT QUICK-FIRING GUN AT WORK.
Battleships, of course, depend upon their heavy guns—their 12 in. or 13·5 in. weapons —but they also carry small-bore armament. This picture shows a 3-pounder quick-firing gun in action, with its crew at their appointed duties.

the scale against Great Britain and France, or have compelled the British Admiralty to detach large reinforcements to the south of Europe.

Four vessels of the Dreadnought class and eight older battleships were ready for sea in the Italian ports, besides a host of smaller vessels. Well manned and commanded, this fleet would have been a most formidable adversary. But Italy in this great hour of peril to freedom was true to her glorious traditions. Unperturbed by German threats, she maintained a strict and honourable neutrality.

The neutrality of Italy left the enemy with only the Austrian Fleet of three Dreadnoughts, three Lord Nelsons, and a number of older ships, which had the support of a small but powerful German squadron, in the

Mediterranean. The German ships were the fast battle-cruiser Goeben and the light cruiser Breslau, both new and excellent vessels of their kind.

To deal with the Austrians and the Germans, the French navy in the Mediterranean was amply sufficient, especially as it could command the assistance of the British Mediterranean Fleet. This consisted of three battle-cruisers—Inflexible, Indefatigable, and Indomitable—powerful ships, but inferior in speed, size, and armament to the Goeben, four older armoured cruisers, four light cruisers, sixteen destroyers, sixteen torpedo boats, and six submarines.

The French and British fleets had at their disposal a magnificent series of naval bases, which were admirably
**The position in the
Mediterranean** placed. At the entrance to the Mediterranean was the great British fortress of Gibraltar, with docks for Dreadnoughts and a repairing yard.   Nor far from the entrance to the Adriatic, in which sea the Austrian Fleet has its headquarters, was the British base of Malta, and the immense French harbour of Bizerta, with a dock capable of containing any one of the allied Dreadnoughts.

A factor which unquestionably affected the German Navy and hampered it in its struggle with the British Fleet was the existence of a Russian squadron in the Baltic. This squadron was not, indeed, powerful. It consisted of four fair battleships of pre-Dreadnought type, with six armoured cruisers, and about one hundred torpedo craft, destroyers, and submarines. It could not venture to risk battle against the German Fleet. But if the German Fleet attempted to match its whole force against the British Navy, and was destroyed, then the Russian Navy would command the Baltic, and could cover the landing of Russian forces at vulnerable points on the German coast, and incalculably assist the work of the main Russian field armies. The existence of the Russian Fleet thus compelled the German admirals to play a cautious game. Moreover, a certain number of German destroyers and submarines were required to watch the Russian Fleet, and prevent raids against the German coast line, thus weakening the German Navy in the North Sea.

The effect of the Russian Navy on the naval operation was, then, serious, and cannot be dismissed from view. Furthermore Russia had, rapidly approaching completion in August, 1914, four magnificent battleships of the Dreadnought type, which were individually superior to anything ready for sea in the German Fleet.

THE "LION" THAT GROWLED TO GOOD PURPOSE IN HELIGOLAND BIGHT.
The British battle-cruiser Lion earned distinction by its exploit in Heligoland Bight on the evening of August 27th, 1914, when five German ships of war were sent to the bottom. This photograph was taken at sea from the bows of the sister battle-cruiser, the Queen Mary.

THE GATE OF THE MEDITERRANEAN TO WHICH BRITAIN HOLDS THE KEY.

"Gib," as Gibraltar is familiarly known, stands at the gateway of the Mediterranean, which cannot be entered if Britain forbids. It is a coaling station of prime importance for the Fleets of Great Britain and her Allies. The photograph was taken soon after war began. The boom across the harbour is closed, and the four ships at anchor are—reading from the left—H.M.S. Sutlej, H.M.S. Albion, H.M.S. Indomitable, and the French cruiser Amiral Charner, which were on guard to prevent the Goeben and Breslau from joining the German main fleet, but these fled eastward and sought safety by an inglorious sale to Turkey.

The British Fleet could not enter the Baltic for many reasons—the first that the entrances through the Sound and Great Belt were in Danish hands, and were mined, while the Kiel Canal gave the German Navy a free passage; the second that a fleet operating in the Baltic would be liable to have its colliers, oil ships, and supply ships attacked by German cruisers and torpedo craft operating from the numerous German naval bases; the third that the British Navy was not sufficiently strong to place in both the Baltic and North Sea forces superior to the German High Sea Fleet. Had the strength of the British Navy been divided into two detachments, each weaker than the German Fleet, one or other would have been attacked, when a defeat was always possible.

As Admiral Mahan pointed out, the sound British policy was to hold the North Sea in force, and leave the Baltic until such time as the strength of the British Navy had grown with the completion of new ships.

The secrecy and celerity with which the British Admiralty made its preparations for war were remarkable, and must have come as a great shock to those who had been taught to regard the Navy as effete and its administration as chaotic. Newspapers were asked not to mention the name of any British warship, or the movement of any of our forces, unless the information were conveyed to them officially for publication.

Activity amid silence

Officers and men were reminded by the Admiralty that the efficiency of its preparations depended largely upon their discretion in avoiding all reference in their conversation and letters to matters connected with the Navy or the dockyards. A strict censorship over all correspondence was put in operation, with the result that the Fleet carried into the period of war its traditional quality of silence.

In the last week of July all the national dockyards and the private shipbuilding establishments began to work with redoubled haste upon ships nearing completion, so that they might be added to the Fleet at sea

H.M.S. MONARCH, ONE OF OUR SUPER-DREADNOUGHTS.

This great battleship is seen passing down the Tyne. She was completed in April, 1912, one of the four super-Dreadnoughts of the Orion class, which were fitted with ten 13·5 in. guns, sixteen 4 in. guns, four 3-pounders, and three torpedo tubes. She developed a speed of 21·88 knots on her trial voyages.

with the least possible delay. Further, on the day following the declaration of war the Admiralty announced that they had taken over four ships which were building in this country for foreign Powers. The Turkish battleships Sultan Osman I. and Reshadieh, the former carrying fourteen, and the latter ten heavy guns, were brought under the British flag, and renamed Agincourt and Erin respectively, while two large and fast destroyers which had been built for Chili were also appropriated, and entered the British Navy as the Faulkner and Broke.

The Agincourt is a vessel of 27,500 tons, and 23 knots. She had a strange career. In the first instance, she was built for the Brazilian Government. When nearing completion she was sold to obtain money in the financial crisis, which, in 1913, compelled the Brazilian Government remorselessly to cut down its expenditure. Purchased by Turkey, she was rapidly pressed forward that she might be employed against the Greek Fleet in the war with Greece which Enver Pasha and the "Young Turks" meditated. She was a vessel of notable qualities, the largest Dreadnought completed for sea for any European navy. She carried no fewer than fourteen 12 in. guns, placed in pairs in separate turrets, and twenty 6 in. guns. No previous vessel had mounted more than thirteen heavy guns, and the most recent British Dreadnoughts to be completed mount only ten, though these are of larger size (13.5 in.) than those carried in the armoured turrets of the Agincourt.

Britain's newest battleships

There have always been two schools of thought in the British Navy. The first desires that we should have

numerous guns of moderate power mounted in the battle-ship, so that the enemy may be attacked by a veritable hail of projectiles. The second would sacrifice number of guns to the power of the individual shell, and aims at destroying the enemy's ship by a few crushing blows from giant shells.

The Agincourt, with her numerous battery of 12 in. guns, corresponds to the ideas of the first school, as the ships of the new Queen Elizabeth class, still incomplete, each mounting eight 15 in. guns, reflect the opinions of the second. Only the actual test of battle can decide which school is right. It is some-thing that in the Agin-court the British Navy has a vessel which seems to have been designed to

BUILT FOR TURKEY—COMMANDEERED BY BRITAIN.
At the outbreak of war, two Dreadnoughts for Turkey were being built, and on the point of completion, in British shipyards. They were to be called the Sultan Osman I. and the Reshadieh. The British Government placed an embargo upon them and, now known as H.M.S. Agincourt and H.M.S. Erin, they are shown here. Turkey was cruelly disappointed, for all through the summer of 1913 collections had been made in Constantinople to pay for the Dreadnoughts; but, by way of consolation, Turkey purchased the German warships Goeben and Breslau after the war broke out.

illustrate the ideas of those who believe in a multitude of guns. The Erin closely resembles the latest British super-Dreadnoughts, and is well qualified to act with them. She is a ship of 23,000 tons, and 21 knots. Her battery consists of ten enormous 13.5 in. guns, mounted in pairs, in steel-plated towers or turrets. These big guns discharge a shell weighing about 1,400 lb., and containing a bursting charge of lyddite—one of the deadliest high explosives known to man. They can be loaded and fired twice a minute, though in actual practice it is found that about one round a minute is all that is possible if good shooting is to be made, as the gun-layers must wait to see the fall of each shell before firing the next round, and must allow the smoke and heat tremor caused by the discharge of such monster weapons to disperse.

The last word in gun power

One large armoured cruiser, the Salamis, was building in Germany before the war for Greece. She was laid down in July, 1912, and is believed to have been very rapidly pushed forward, especially after the date, early

The German cruiser Moltke, the sister ship of the coward Goeben, was completed in October, 1911. A vessel of 23,000 tons displacement, she was fitted to carry ten 11 in. guns, twelve 6 in. guns, twelve 24-pounders, and four 20 in. torpedo tubes. Her speed of 28·4 knots made her the fastest cruiser in the world.

The German 4,350-ton cruiser Köln which, with its sister ship the Mainz, was sunk in Heligoland Bight on August 28th, 1914.

The pre-Dreadnought Deutschland, considered unsatisfactory through being overgunned, the secondary guns firing projectiles too heavy for man-handling.

The Dreadnought Thüringen, one of the Helgoland type, a class completed in 1911 and 1912, having a displacement of 21,000 tons, a speed of about 22 knots, and carrying twelve 12 in., fourteen 6 in. guns, fourteen 24-pounders, and six 20 in. torpedo tubes.

The German destroyer G194, one of eight 654-tons boats, which have a speed of 31½ knots and carry two 24-pounder guns and four 18 in. torpedo tubes.

The Submarine U9, with which the Germans claimed to have torpedoed and sunk the three British cruisers Aboukir, Hogue, and Cressy, on September 22nd, 1914.

SOME TYPES OF GERMANY'S BATTLESHIPS AND SMALL CRAFT.

PANORAMIC VIEW OF THE GERMAN BATTLE FLEET AT ANCHOR IN KIEL HARBOUR, BELIEVED—
Kiel is the chief naval base of the Baltic, and vast sums have been expended to transform it into what the Germans consider the most elaborately equipped naval station in the world. The Krupp and Howaldt companies have extensive shipbuilding yards at Kiel, and there.

in 1914, when the German Government resolved to make war on Russia and France. That she would be taken over by the German Navy was regarded as certain, though there was some doubt when she would be ready for sea. It was considered possible that by great and special exertions she might be complete in the autumn of 1914, and the British Navy was ready for her presence in the German line in the great battle to come. A ship of about 19,000 tons and 23 knots, she was designed to mount eight 14 in. guns and twelve 6 in. weapons.

The ships nearing completion for Germany at the outbreak of war were the battleships Markgraf, Grosser Kurfürst, and König, all of 25,500 tons and mounting ten 12 in. guns, which could be changed for more powerful weapons. In addition to these was the battle-cruiser Derfflinger, of about 28,000 tons, armed with eight 12 in. guns, some smaller weapons, and with a speed of nearly 30 knots. For the British Navy the super-Dreadnoughts Benbow and

GUN OF A SUBMARINE PROTECTED FROM WATER.
The newest German submarines at the opening of the war were armed with a disappearing gun protected from water. The upper picture shows the gun entirely concealed ; in the lower it is being raised.

EMDEN——A VALUABLE GERMAN HARBOUR IN TERRITORY FORMERLY DUTCH.
Emden, one of Germany's most valuable harbours, is two miles from the mouth of the Ems, from which it takes its name. A canal connects Emden with Wilhelmshaven. A German cruiser which did considerable damage to British shipping in the Bay of Bengal was named after this town.

—BY PRUSSIAN WAR LORDS TO BE THE BEST EQUIPPED NAVAL STATION IN THE WORLD.
too, are situated the great Imperial yards. The Kiel Canal, also known as the Kaiser-Wilhelm Canal, was completed for the passage of Dreadnoughts just prior to the present war, and now permits the biggest German vessels to sail through from the North Sea to the Baltic.

GUN OF GERMAN SUBMARINE READY FOR ACTION.
The trapdoor immediately behind the base of the submarine gun opens upwards, and the gun is slowly raised on a pillar, when it is ready for service.

Emperor of India, mounting ten 13·5 in. guns apiece, with sixteen 6 in. guns in addition, were in hand, and should have been delivered in the spring of 1914.

The huge battle-cruiser Tiger, of 27,500 tons and 30 knots, mounting eight 13·5 in. and twelve 6 in. guns, ought to have been delivered in May, 1914. Unfortunately, all these three ships had been greatly delayed, and not one of them was ready when Admiral Jellicoe steamed off to take up his battle position.

The nation paid dearly at a critical moment for the mischievous activity of the " Little Navy " party —nicknamed the " Suicide Club " in the House of Commons. The efforts of these misguided men had prevented the voting of sufficient credits, and had hampered the efforts of the British Admiralty at every turn. To this same party was due the weakness in small, fast cruisers which prevented the British Fleet from wiping out German commerce-destroyers in the first few weeks of war.

WILHELMSHAVEN—ONE OF GERMANY'S GREATEST NAVAL BASES.
Some of Germany's finest battleships in the war-dock of Wilhelmshaven, under the shelter of the forts. Bought by Prussia in 1853, soft, swampy ground, without any natural advantage save situation, the site of Wilhelmshaven has been turned into a fortress of the first rank.

The nation owed a great debt to Mr. Churchill, who had resisted to the best of his power the enemies of a strong British Navy. In the teeth of their opposition he had secured a vote of £51,550,000 for 1914-15, the largest on record, and he had done his utmost to accelerate construction in the shipyards and to make good the arrears which had accumulated. But for his exertions it might have gone very badly with British arms at sea.

Again, when war became certain, Mr. Churchill showed magnificent energy and insight. It was, we believe, on his initiative that the purchase of foreign ships was made by a stroke of the pen. There were certainly members of the Cabinet who cavilled at his bold measures, because they imagined that Germany would at the last moment draw back, or that the British Navy was sufficiently strong. But in the end Mr. Churchill had his way and overcame all antagonism.

The two Chilian destroyers bought were vessels built for ocean work of a remarkable type. They displaced 1,800 tons, so that they were virtually small

THE GERMAN " HIGH SEA " FLEET, WHICH PROMPTLY SHUT ITSELF UP IN HARBOUR AT THE OUTBREAK OF WAR.
The strength of the German High Sea Fleet at the declaration of war is indicated in the table on page 222. The creator of the German Navy was the Kaiser himself, ably assisted by the enthusiastic Von Tirpitz, his Secretary of State for the German Imperial Navy, and Von Kœster, the president of the German Navy League. The great challenge to British naval predominance was the German Navy Law of 1900, which virtually doubled Germany's naval establishment, and provided for an automatic naval expansion. The upper portrait is of Admiral von Kœster, and the lower is that of Admiral von Tirpitz.

cruisers ; they steamed 32 knots, and they mounted a powerful battery of six 30-pounder guns and two machine-guns

As against these two destroyers taken over by Great Britain, the German Admiralty was said to have seized a number of destroyers and submarines building in Germany for various foreign Powers, and two fast, small cruisers of 4,500 tons which the Russian Government had ordered from a Dantzic firm of shipbuilders.

On August 2nd it became known in London that Germany had on the previous day begun the mobilisation of her Army—actually that mobilisation had been quietly proceeding throughout the last week in July. Mr. Winston Churchill acted with admirable energy and decision. The order to mobilise the Fleet Reserve was issued forthwith, and forty-eight hours later every British ship of any fighting value was at sea.

MINES EXPLODED

CHAPTER XIV.

BY COUNTER-MINING.

HOW GERMANY SOWED THE HIGH SEAS WITH MINES.

Calculating Brutality on Sea as Well as on Land—History of the Submarine Mine—British Objections to Mines—" Observation " Mines—" Electric Contact " Mines—Justification of Mines in Territorial Waters—Use of Mines in Russo-Japanese War— Danger of Drifting Mines—British Opposition to " Automatic " Mines—The Hague Conference Restrictions regarding Mine-laying—Mine Sweeping—Use of Trawlers by British Navy—The Merited Fate of a German Mine-layer—The Tragedy of the Amphion—Splendid Discipline of British Seamen.

THE irresistible avalanche of men which Germany poured into Belgium in the early days of the war incurred, by inhumanities in the field, the aversion of the whole civilised world. Advancing through a country whose neutrality Germany had pledged herself to respect, they carried on a campaign of pillage and wanton sacrifice, both of life and property, which will be remembered and recorded against them as long as history lasts.

But the calculating brutality of the German campaign on land was surpassed by the cruelty of Germany's methods of conducting war at sea. For many years Germany had cherished the idea of opening war on Britain by launching a surprise destroyer attack upon the British battle squadrons. Happily, this design was frustrated. The clumsiness of German diplomatic methods and the evident belief of German statesmen that Great Britain was so effete as to be ready to betray her friends for the sake of keeping peace, gave the British Government ample warning of the approach of a crisis : and when the climax arrived and the Government, in honour bound, and with the unanimous approval of the country, held to the maxim that " an Englishman's word is his bond," the British Fleet was found in all respects

A GERMAN CONTACT MINE.
Contact mines are anchored with cables of sufficient length to let them float under the surface at any desired depth, while a longer cable connects two mines. When a ship strikes the connecting cable, the two mines are thus brought into contact with the hull on both sides. The projections at the top are the contact horns, or " whiskers," and when these are driven in by striking the ship's bottom the detonating charge goes off and the explosion follows.

ready for the emergency. Germany had staked heavily upon being able to take her adversary by surprise. For all practical purposes her failure to do so set the seal securely and definitely upon any hopes she may have entertained of wresting the command of the sea from British hands. But this initial miscarriage of her plans, though it was fatal to her maritime ambitions, caused Germany to resort to an even more detestable form of naval warfare—if, indeed, that term can properly be used. Having failed in her object of taking the British Fleet off its guard and engineering a torpedo attack upon our big ships, while peace yet remained nominally unbroken—and, what is more, having realised for several days before war was declared that her cherished schemes in this direction were inevitably doomed to failure by the readiness of the British Navy—she threw herself back upon the barbaric policy of scattering explosive mines broadcast upon the open waters of the North Sea. Such an act of itself would be sufficient to put Germany beyond the pale of civilisation ; and the discredit of the act was enhanced by the fact that this mine-scattering business began while a state of peace still existed between the two countries.

The submarine mine, in one form or another, goes back a long way in naval history. When the Spanish were besieging Antwerp in 1585, the defenders constructed a number of " explosion vessels " filled with powder, which they allowed to drift down the river among the enemy's ships, and fitted with a clockwork mechanism, which ensured the explosion of the charge after a certain interval. The efficacy of these weapons naturally depended upon the skill shown in timing the clockwork in relation to the rate of drift ; but the Spaniards lost severely through their agency. Towards the end of the eighteenth century, a good deal of scientific attention began to be given to the mine—to give it its modern name—and the famous American inventor Bushnell manufactured a number of drifting " explosive machines," which inflicted a certain amount of damage upon our ships during the War of American Independence

Earliest uses of sea mines

In more recent times the mine has naturally become a more dangerous implement of war. It was used—but with little success—by the Russians in the Crimean War, to protect their coasts and harbours from the approach of British and French ships ; but several vessels were sunk by mines in the American Civil War. Germany used them extensively for the defence of her harbours in the Franco-Prussian War, and they certainly served their purpose then : for, although the French Navy was infinitely superior to the German, it dared not carry out any offensive operations on the German coast.

Great Britain has never looked with favour upon the mine. It is repugnant to British instincts, inasmuch as it strikes below the belt, and gives the vessel attacked no opportunity of fighting for its own safety. The use of the mine for harbour defence has always been regarded as legitimate, however, and until 1904 all the more important British naval and mercantile ports were defended by a field of " observation mines." These weapons fall into two classes, of which the first can only be fired by an observer on shore. The mines are anchored to the bottom in the approaches to the harbour, and contact with passing ships will not explode them. The observer has a chart of the minefield, and is able to follow the exact course of any vessel entering the harbour ; and if she is a ship whose presence is undesirable, he has only to press a button completing the electrical circuit to a particular mine, and the vessel which at that moment is passing over it is destroyed.

The other type of harbour-defence mine is known

PHYSICAL SKETCH MAP OF WILHELMSHAVEN AND DISTRICT.
Wilhelmshaven is about 50 miles south of Heligoland, and within its shelter Germany's " High Sea " Fleet rested in inglorious security during the earlier months of the war. The East Frisian Islands form a screen behind which German ships were able to glide about and dart out from any of the many channels into the North Sea to sow their dastard mines in the path of neutral shipping.

WORKING A GUN ON A GERMAN BATTLESHIP.
These German gunners are working a 6 in. gun, which is the standard secondary gun of the German fleet. The biggest naval guns are 15 in., but at the opening of war none of the ships of either side designed for 15 in. guns were completed. The heaviest guns ready for sea were the 13·5 in. of the British ships of the Iron Duke class, the biggest German guns being the 12 in. of the Kaiser class of battleship.

THE FIRST MINE-LAYER SUNK IN THE WAR.
At noon on August 5th the British Third Torpedo Flotilla sank the German vessel Königin Luise, a passenger steamer of 2,163 tons gross and 20 knots speed, which, fitted as a mine-layer, had been dropping its deadly cargo in the North Sea.

as the "electric-contact" type. Such weapons are not fired independently by an observer ashore, but they are quite innocuous until the shore battery, with which they are connected by cable, is switched on. When that has been done, a ship, on striking the mine, causes the circuit-closer in its interior to complete the electric circuit and so explode the gun-cotton. As a general rule mines of this description carry only about eighty pounds of explosive; but those of the observation type may contain any weight from five hundred to one thousand five hundred pounds. In both cases the mine is anchored to the bottom by means of a block of iron or concrete, and the mine floats on the end of a cable about nine feet or so beneath the surface of the water.

It has always been assumed that a nation is justified in laying mine-fields in its own territorial waters—that is in the entrance to its harbours and within three miles of its coast-line—since the object in view in such cases is simply that of self-defence. The war between Russia and Japan in 1904–5, however, brought into prominence quite a different type of mine and a new form of naval warfare. The Russians then used mines which, after a very short time, ceased to be under any sort of control at all. They belonged to what is known as the "mechanical contact" or "electro-mechanical contact" type, which, having once been placed in position, would remain in a "live" condition almost indefinitely, ready to explode at any moment when a ship should come into contact with them. They were sown by the Russians in open waters through which it was assumed the Japanese would have to approach in any naval assault upon Port Arthur. The Japanese laid similar mines—though never in the open

Mines in territorial waters

DD

sea—in the channels through which the Russian fleet would have to pass in any attempt to break the Japanese blockade

The first step in this direction was taken by the Russians, who, after the successful raid by Japanese torpedo craft upon the ships in Port Arthur on the night of February 7th, 1904, sent out the specially-designed mine-layer Yenesei to scatter mines round the approaches to the harbour, with the object of preventing any further Japanese attack. Three hundred mines, each containing five hundred and fifty pounds of explosive, were successfully placed in position. But just when the three hundred and first mine had been dropped over the side, one of those previously laid broke away from its anchor and rose to the surface. The Yenesei moved ahead in

A lesson from the Russo-Japanese War order to avoid this weapon, and in doing so struck another. There was an immediate and terrific explosion, and the vessel, her bows torn away, went to the bottom in a very few minutes, carrying the greater part of her crew with her.

Some two months later the Japanese sent in a flotilla of mine-layers, screened by torpedo-craft, to lay mine-fields in Russian territorial waters, in the neighbourhood of Port Arthur; and when the work had been successfully accomplished the mine-layers steamed away while the other craft remained behind to tempt the Russian fleet out of its harbour. The ruse was completely successful. A Russian fleet of three battleships and four cruisers

MINE SWEEPER

CABLE FOR HAULING KITE

SWEEPING WIRE ATTACHED TO TRAWLER & LET OUT TO ANY DISTA

TWO BRITISH MINE-SWEEPERS AT THE DANGEROUS WORK OF CLEARING THE SEA OF THE GERMAN—
Nothing is more dangerous than the work of mine-sweeping, the men engaged incurring tremendous risk of disaster to their ships and of swift death to themselves. The British Navy employs trawlers and their crews for this hazardous work. The vessels are mostly ships of 150 tons, and they work in pairs, with a strong steel hawser stretched between them, this being weighted with two heavy "kites," or sinkers, as

came out as soon as steam could be raised and went in pursuit of the Japanese decoy squadron, which was driven off without mishap. The commander of the Russian fleet, Admiral Makaroff, who flew his flag in the battleship Petropavlovsk, was properly regarded as the most able officer in the whole of the Russian Navy, and, seeing that the Japanese vessels were, to all appearances, simply trying to lure him into the neighbourhood of a superior force, he turned his fleet about after chasing them to a safe distance and made to return to his port.

Soon after his retreat had begun, and when the Russian squadron was close to Port Arthur, it was thrown into a state of confusion by a huge column of water which rose into the air on the starboard (or right hand) side of the flagship. There ensued a terrific explosion; and **Russian victims of Japanese mines** before this had died away another column rose on the other side of the doomed flagship.

The Petropavlovsk had run in between two mines which were connected by a cable, and so had brought first one and then the other into contact with her sides. It is believed that the force of the explosion of the mines detonated the magazines, for a series of minor explosions followed the bursting of the mines, and within two minutes a battleship of 11,000 tons went to the bottom, carrying with her the most distinguished officer in the whole of the Russian Navy and close upon seven hundred other officers and men ; only about forty were saved.

Many other ships were sunk during the war through coming into contact with submarine mines. On May 15th, 1904, the Japanese battleship Hatsuse, while cruising ten miles off the coast, struck two of these weapons and went quickly to the bottom with enormous loss of life, and on the very same day the battleship Yashima, also Japanese, struck a mine and was so badly damaged that she had to be run ashore to prevent her from sinking. Other battleships were damaged by mines during the course of the war, and several smaller vessels were sunk ; but the incidents mentioned will serve to explain the importance with which **Value of mines to small Powers** the mine came to be regarded as a result of the war in the Far East. It was realised that a Power of quite minor importance from a naval point of view might, with the assistance of the mine, be able not only to defy the forces of a superior naval Power, but also, to threaten the battleships of the stronger nation with destruction without risking a single important unit.

This view was confirmed and modified by the aftermath of the orgy of mine-laying which marked the Russo-Japanese War. There is no evidence to show that Japan scattered drifting mines indiscriminately in the open

—MINES, COLLISION WITH WHICH WILL SEND THE LARGEST BATTLESHIP TO SWIFT DESTRUCTION. Seen in the picture. As the hawser is dragged along it comes into contact with the ropes holding the mines to their anchors and pulls these along so that the mines explode by contact with each other, or they are harmlessly exploded by fire from light guns if they come to the surface. The principal mine-sweepers of the British Navy are the Seaflower, the Seamew, the Spider, the Sparrow, and the Driver.

sea, though the Russian Navy is believed to have so acted. The mines which were laid were, however, for the most part sown and anchored in those waters which were regarded as most likely to be visited by the enemy's ships ; but there was one factor for which no allowance was made. As already pointed out, the mines were anchored to the bottom by means of a cable attached to a heavy weight, and no doubt both sides expected that after the war was over they would be able to send mine-sweeping flotillas to the mined areas and remove **Dangers of drifted mines** such of the weapons as might remain. Yet events proved only too conclusively that a mine once anchored was not necessarily permanently anchored.

Winds and storms, currents, and the ebb and flow of tides worked together to chafe and wear away the cables joining the mines to their anchors, with the result that large numbers of these " floating volcanoes " began to drift about into all sorts of places where, even if the war had continued, the chances would have been all against their coming into contact with a hostile ship. Nevertheless, their power for destruction was in no way diminished. Many innocent neutral merchant vessels were sent to the bottom or seriously damaged through striking drifting

ONE OF GERMANY'S 240-TON SUBMARINES BUILT IN 1906.

Germany held secret her submarine strength and the details of her newest additions to her submarine fleet, so that when war opened information on the subject was lacking.   The six submarines, U2 to U7, all about 240 tons displacement, were believed to be over-engined and to suffer from excessive vibration.   The size of submarines steadily increased after these were built, and at the time war was declared Great Britain had eight submarines of 1,200 tons displacement.

mines in districts far remote from any possible scene of war ; and for several years after peace was concluded trading ships on the Chinese coast continued to meet disaster through this agency.   It was officially estimated by the Chinese Government that at least eight hundred Chinese lost their lives after the war through their ships coming into contact with mines which had been laid during the war and which had broken away from their moorings and drifted south.

The general result of the experience of the Russo-Japanese War was to instil into most civilised nations a determined opposition to the use of submarine mines of the contact type in any shape or form.   The right of every

TWO BRITISH MINE-LAYERS AT WORK DROPPING THEIR DEADLY ENGINES OF DESTRUCTION.

The British Admiralty converted seven old second-class cruisers into mine-layers. All were ships of the Apollo class, dating from 1891, and being of 3,400 to 3,600 tons.   The mines are carried on each side of the upper deck, and when being sown they are run along to platforms cut into the stern and dropped overboard to make dangerous the path of attacking enemy ships.   To the credit of Great Britain, it must be recorded that she did her best to abolish the evil of mine-laying, and was only forced to contemplate this system of warfare when Germany had already adopted and developed it to the menace of the British Navy.

CANADA'S SPLENDID RALLY TO THE FLAG

GROUP OF CANADIAN OFFICERS, WITH COLONEL SAM HUGHES SEATED IN THE CENTRE.

THE 48TH HIGHLANDERS (CANADIAN) LEAVING TORONTO BEFORE EMBARKING FOR EUROPE.

" Our self-governing Dominions demonstrated, with a spontaneousness and unanimity unparalleled in history, their determination to affirm their brotherhood with us, and to make our cause their own. From Canada, Australia, New Zealand, South Africa, and from Newfoundland the children of the Empire assert, not as an obligation, but as a privilege, their right and their willingness to contribute money, material, and, what is better than all, the strength and sinews, the fortunes, and lives of their best manhood."—Mr. Asquith at Guildhall, Sept. 4th, 1914.

CANADIAN ROYAL GRENADIERS
at Valcartier Camp, Quebec, marching off to rifle practice.

CANADIAN INFANTRY DRAWN UP FOR INSPEC
Valcartier Camp was the gathering ground of the Canadian F

CANADIAN HIGHLANDERS DETRAINING
at Valcartier Camp, where the units of the Canadian contingent assembled before sailing.

CANADIAN
The hardy life of these men made them fighting material wi

CANADIAN ARTILLERY HAULING A 4.7 IN. GUN INTO POSITION.
Canada started with the intention of providing a contingent of 22,000 men for war service, but the response to the call for volunteers—

DUKE OF CONNAUGHT AT VALCARTIER CAMP.
and held 20,000 men before they sailed for the field of war.

CANADIAN CAVALRY DETACHMENT
exercising at Montreal prior to their departure.

ONTIERSMEN.
e world, every man of them worth three German conscripts.

ONTARIO ROYAL ARTILLERY ON PARADE.
For brawn and muscle, intelligence and judgment, these men are unexcelled.

THE CANADIAN 9TH ARTILLERY LEAVING THE FORT AT TORONTO.
—was so generous from every Province of the Dominion between Halifax and Vancouver that the number was far exceeded.

BRITISH MINE-SWEEPERS AT THEIR HAZARDOUS WORK CLEARING THE SEAS OF MINES LAID BY GERMANS.

The exact method of "mine-sweeping" is explained with graphic clearness on pages 234 and 235. The value of the hydroplane for helping in this work has been triumphantly established. As the airman flies over the water he can see with remarkable clearness objects below the surface of the water, and in ordinary weather conditions he can detect the presence of mines without difficulty.

nation to defend its own harbours with mines was universally admitted, and it was just as unanimously granted that a nation acting on the offensive was justified in placing mines off the coasts of its enemy anywhere within the territorial three-mile limit. At the same time, the war of 1904-5 had proved in a ghastly manner the damage which might be inflicted by mines upon innocent merchant ships which not only had no concern in the war, but which might not enter the mine-sown waters until some years after the war was ended.

As a natural result of the war between Russia and Japan, however, all the Powers began to cultivate the submarine mine as a weapon of war. In 1905 Germany laid down two ships specially designed for laying mines on the high seas. These were the Albatross and Nautilus, both of which were fitted to carry four hundred mines It was not until some time after this that the British Admiralty fell into line, and then seven old second-class cruisers were taken in hand and converted into mine-layers. This was the course followed by the majority of foreign Powers; and although it was generally recognised and admitted that the laying of mines was, to say the least of it, an unsportsman like method of carrying on war, those who were opposed to its use were forced to admit that the mine was a destructive agent of enormous power ; and, when one or two Powers insisted upon retaining it, it was impossible for the others altogether to ignore it.

Nevertheless, the British Government continued to use every effort to restrict the employment of mines in war, and even to prohibit their use altogether. They were particularly anxious to abolish the " automatic " mine—that is, the mine which explodes instantly upon being touched by a passing vessel ; and in the instructions which were issued to Sir Edward Fry, the British representative at the Second Peace Conference at The Hague in 1907, there occurs the following :

" 15. His Majesty's Government would view with satisfaction the abandonment of the employment of automatic mines in naval warfare altogether. Failing the acceptance of such total prohibition, they earnestly hope that the employment of these engines of war will only be sanctioned under the strictest limitations."

The German delegate had evidently received very different instructions, and he opposed every attempt to restrict the use of mines, declaring that rules on the subject were unnecessary, and that "conscience, good-sense, and the sentiment of duties imposed by the principles of humanity will be the surest guides for the conduct of seamen, and will constitute the most efficacious guarantee against abuse." The meaning of this is quite clear—Germany wanted a free hand in the use of mines ; and, what is more, she got what she wanted

First of all, however, let us recall what the German delegate—Baron Marschall von Bieberstein—had to say at The Hague on the subject of the German officer's gentlemanliness and humanity. " The officers of the German Navy—I say it with a high voice "—declared the baron, ' will always fulfil in the strictest manner the duties which flow from the unwritten law of humanity and civilisation " ; and, later on : " As to the sentiments of humanity and civilisation, I cannot admit that any Government or country is in these superior to that which I have the honour to represent." In the light of subsequent events, both afloat and ashore, one can only conclude that the baron was possessed of a perverted sense of humour.

THE LAERTES—ONE OF THE VICTORS IN HELIGOLAND BIGHT.
In the action off Heligoland Bight on August 28th, 1914, the superior gun power and strength of the British destroyers were conclusively demonstrated. The Liberty, Laurel, and Laertes, which were in the thick of the fighting, have each a displacement of 945 tons, a speed of 29 knots, three 4 in. guns, and a crew of 135.

SPEED OF TRAIN—48 MILES PER HOUR

WATER LINE

SPEED OF TORPEDO—48 MILES PER HOUR

THE MODERN TORPEDO AT FULL SPEED EQUALS THE

DIAGRAMMATIC PICTURE ILLUSTRATING THE DISCHARGE AND SPEED OF A MODERN—
The science of destruction finds its highest—or its lowest—expression in the deadly torpedoes, by whose agency the 12-in. armour-plate of a super-Dreadnought may be shattered. The torpedo is discharged from its tube under the water-line of a battleship, from a destroyer or from a submarine, and, going to its fell work, it traverses the water at the speed of the " Flying Scotsman." The engine inside the torpedo is

We can now see what the Conference actually did to " restrict " the use of mines. The first two articles of Convention 8 read as follows :

" Article 1.—It is forbidden :

" 1. To lay unanchored automatic contact mines, unless they be so constructed as to become harmless one hour at most after the person who laid them has ceased to control them :

" 2. To lay automatic contact mines which do not become harmless as soon as they have broken loose from their moorings ;

" 3. (This related to torpedoes.)

" Article 2. The laying of automatic contact mines off the coast and ports of the enemy with the sole object of intercepting merchant shipping is forbidden.

It will be noticed, first of all, that there was no restriction placed upon the localities in which mines might be laid. All that was decided was that they should not be put down with the " sole object " of interfering with merchant ships, which amounts to no restriction at all, as it would be quite impossible to prove what the " sole object " was of the Power which laid the mines. It permitted the laying of mines if the object mainly was to destroy merchantmen, and provided there was some chance, however remote, of destroying warships.

Article 1 did indeed amount to a restriction upon the indiscriminate use of mines, and endeavoured to ensure that if they failed in their first object of destroying hostile warships they should whether anchored or drifting,

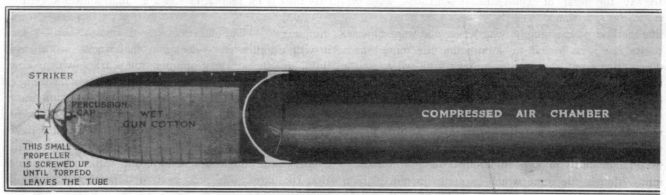

STRIKER

PERCUSSION
CAP

WET
GUN COTTON

COMPRESSED AIR CHAMBER

THIS SMALL
PROPELLER
IS SCREWED UP
UNTIL TORPEDO
LEAVES THE TUBE

THE WONDERFUL MECHANISM THAT GIVES THE TORPEDO ITS DIRECTION—

—TORPEDO WHICH TRAVELS THROUGH THE WATER AT THE RATE OF AN EXPRESS TRAIN.
driven by compressed air, which causes two propellers to revolve in opposite directions.   A gyroscopic device keeps it in the desired path and at the desired depth.   A pin on the " warhead " of the torpedo receives the first impact of the blow when the torpedo hits its mark, and when this is driven in it ignites the fulminate of mercury, which in turn explodes the gun-cotton with which the torpedo is charged.

present the least possible menace to innocent merchant ships.   Whatever good might have been done by this article, however, was quite nullified by Article 6 of the same Convention, which runs as follows : " The Contracting Powers which do not at present own perfected mines of the description contemplated in the present Convention, and which, consequently, could not at present carry out the rules laid down in Articles 1 and 3 (the latter providing only that " every possible precaution must be taken for the security of peaceful shipping "), undertake to convert the *matériel* of their mines as soon as possible, so as to bring it into conformity with the foregoing requirements."

The use of the phrase " as soon as possible " practically gave the contracting Powers *carte blanche* to decide whether they would abide by the Convention or not.   Those that did not want to do so could always plead that they had been quite unable to construct " perfected mines of the description contemplated."

In short, instead of restricting the use of mines, the second Peace Conference resulted in practice in the removal of all restraint upon their employment.   It was not specifically laid down that they should be used only in territorial waters—that is, within three miles of the coast-line of the belligerent Powers—nor was the employment of drifting mines forbidden.   A nation which chooses to lay down anchored mines so designed as to break away from their moorings within half an hour, thenceforward to drift about the seas to the danger alike of foe and friend and innocent neutrals, is well within the letter of the law as represented by The Hague Convention.

The spirit of the latter is entirely in the direction of protecting innocent ships and restricting the use of mines ;

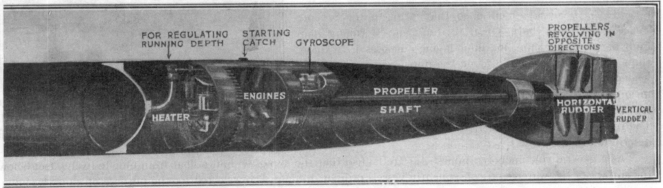

—AND DESTRUCTIVE POWER AS A WEAPON OF NAVAL WARFARE.

but an unscrupulous nation would obviously not concern itself very much about the spirit of things, even if it condescended to abide by the letter of the law. Even here we should not have been unprepared for the course which Germany adopted, for her representative at the Conference was careful to point out that although nobody would have recourse to mine-laying without " urgent military reasons," " military acts are not ruled exclusively by the stipulations of international law."

The automatic contact mine sown in the sea is, as a rule, considerably smaller than the observation mine used for harbour defence. The charge varies from 76 lb. in the smallest to about 200 lb. in the largest and latest, though there is good reason to believe that Germany may have used much more formidable machines.

These are sometimes known as " offensive " mines, because they can be used for the attack of fleets and for laying off the mouth of an enemy's harbour with the object of destroying his ships if they endeavour to come out. They may be either cylindrical or conical in shape, the former being favoured in both the British and German Navies. They are usually fitted with a couple of electric batteries, which become active half an

THE MEN WHO WERE NOT DOWNHEARTED.
British soldiers in France with their shoulders to the wheels of a baggage waggon in difficulties. The lower picture shows a company of the British Expeditionary Force leaving a French military base by rail for the field of fire.

hour or so after the mine is dropped, and are so constructed that on the mine being struck by anything passing it a pendulum is set in motion, which completes the circuit and detonates the explosive charge. In other types explosion is caused by the fracture of a thin glass tube containing a chlorate of potash mixture : but the former is the type most generally favoured, and in both cases the principle is the same.

We have already mentioned that, prior to the Second Peace Conference, both Great Britain and Germany had built or fitted out ships for mine-laying purposes. In these ships the mines are stowed along the upper and lower decks, whence they can be run to the specially-constructed stern by means of rails and dropped into position. As soon as it was realised that mine-laying would form an important feature in naval warfare, a method was devised whereby the menace of the mine might in part be removed. The result was the introduction of a class of ship known as a " mine-sweeper," which is itself almost a full description of the vessels.

As a general rule anchored mine-fields are laid so that the explosive mines float from nine to twelve feet below the surface of the water, and consequently vessels of light draught were selected for the purpose of mine-sweeping. Germany fitted out a number of old torpedo-boats for the purpose but in the British Navy, on the advice of, and

A REGIMENT OF STURDY HIGHLANDERS MARCHING THROUGH A QUIET FRENCH VILLAGE.

BRITISH CAVALRY PASSING THROUGH A MAIN THOROUGHFARE IN ROUEN.

LIGHT-HEARTED BRITISH INFANTRY MARCHING OUT TO ENGAGE THE GERMANS.

By day and by night, the ancient quiet of sleepy old towns and villages in Northern France was disturbed by the steady tramp of armed men and the jangle of cavalry—reinforcements to assist the British army in its task of helping to beat back the German invader. True to his promise, Lord Kitchener was steadily increasing the British force, and the unavoidable wastage of war was soon more than made good.

GERMAN SOLDIERS AT REST.
"Music hath charms to soothe the savage breast" and if the proverb is true, it is to be assumed that this company of German soldiers enjoying some stolen Belgian cigars to the accompaniment of a melodion, was not guilty of the atrocities by which Germany advertised her culture.

after experiments had been carried out by Lord Charles Beresford when he commanded the Channel Fleet, ordinary steam fishing-trawlers were adapted for the new work.

The most important thing in mine-sweeping is to discover the mine-field. Only too often its existence is not known until some unfortunate ship has come to grief in it ; but sometimes a mine breaks loose and is seen before it has done any damage ; sometimes a mine is carelessly laid and floats idly, but still anchored, on the surface ; while the seaplane has added another factor of security, inasmuch as an observer up aloft can, on a fine day, and when the sea is not too greatly disturbed, see some considerable distance below the surface and, perhaps, detect a mine-field in time to warn a following fleet of its existence.

When the mines have been located the sweepers get to work—and dangerous work it is. They steam in pairs, a strong steel hawser being stretched between them. To this hawser two heavy "kites" or sinkers are attached, so as to keep it well to the bottom ; and the trawlers then proceed slowly to "sweep" the mined area. As the hawser is drawn along the bottom, it comes into contact with the wire ropes that connect the mines with their anchors, and drags them along. In this way many mines are exploded by coming into contact with each other, and if any are brought to the surface intact they are generally destroyed by light guns being fired at them.

SPADE WORK BEING PERFORMED BY GERMAN SOLDIERS.
The German invaders were skilled in making entrenchments, and this set the French and British Allies many hard and costly tasks in dislodging them, and beating them back to new entrenchments, from which they had again to be dislodged.

BERLIN REJOICING OVER "VICTORY."

The "victory" announced by megaphone to this crowd assembled outside the Royal Palace in Berlin had existence only in the vivid and perverted imagination of the famous "lie bureau" which, by fabricated news, did its best to keep up the spirits of the German populace. It will be noticed that the crowd included a large proportion of young men. The lower picture shows one of Berlin's "penny dinners" which were served daily, and were inaugurated when the pinch of war began to be acutely felt by the people.

The British Admiralty began to purchase a number of trawlers in 1909-10, and shortly afterwards a branch of the Royal Naval Reserve, known as the Trawler Section, was brought into existence, consisting of a number of skippers and men of the fishing fleets who volunteered to be trained for the risky work of mine-sweeping. At the same time arrangements were made with a number of owners whereby large numbers of their trawlers would be taken over by the Admiralty in case of war; and indeed, before the Great War was a fortnight old, over a hundred of these vessels had been placed in commission with the Royal Navy, while about two hundred and fifty skippers had offered their services to the Admiralty. Many of them, alas! were destined to lose their lives in carrying out the work for which they had so nobly volunteered—a work of infinite value, not only to the Navy, but also to the British and neutral merchant ships whose constant crossing and recrossing from Norway, Sweden and Denmark to our East Coast ports did so much to keep down the level of food prices in the early days of the war.

The widespread use which Germany made of the submarine mine is directly traceable to the breakdown of her too cunning diplomacy and the consequent derangement of the war plans which had been perfected for use against Great Britain. It is now established that when Germany realised, as she did a week before the war, that the British Navy was prepared

Breakdown of German diplomacy

local defence of its own harbours. It will not lay them in front of the enemy's harbours because the object it has in view is not to shut the enemy inside, but at all costs to get him out and to force him into action. Neither will it lay mines on the high seas, for its own ships are there, and not those of the enemy.

The weaker nation, however, will not only scatter mines along its own coasts to prevent the approach of the stronger enemy; it will also, provided it is sufficiently unscrupulous, use its best endeavours to distribute them broadcast on the seas, knowing that its

ITALIAN AND FRENCH—
Although a member of the Triple Alliance with Germany and Austria, Italy was not consulted when the Austrian ultimatum was sent to Servia, and, therefore, proclaimed her neutrality when the conflagration

GENERAL JOFFRE WANTS TO FIND OUT.
General Joffre's eyes are nearly concealed by his eyebrows, but very little escapes them. No detail in the organisation of his armies is too small to be beneath his notice, and he is here seen questioning a French lieutenant regarding the equipment and condition of his men.

—SOLDIERS FRATERNISING.
first burst upon Europe. Italy has many French sympathies, and this photograph depicts a group of the famous Italian Bersaglieri fraternising with French Alpine Chasseurs on the Franco-Italian frontier.

for any eventuality, she decided upon an indiscriminate use of the mine, and began to place these engines of destruction, before war was declared, in positions where they might be expected to sink British ships —whether warships or merchantmen did not matter much to Germany. If our warships were sent to the bottom our naval superiority would be affected. If merchantmen came to grief, the resulting panic among shipowners would—or so Germany thought—hasten the day when we should be starved into submission.

The submarine mine is essentially the weapon of the weaker Power, a fact which may explain the attitude which Great Britain and Germany respectively adopted towards its use at the Second Hague Conference. The stronger Power, save in very special circumstances, has no use for mines other than for the

own ships are safe from them (since they cannot get to sea at all), and trusting that here and there one of the enemy's vessels may be sent to the bottom.

Our naval authorities knew before the declaration of war was made that active preparations were going forward in Germany with a view to the wholesale scattering of mines in the North Sea, and, in consequence of this knowledge, arrangements were immediately made for a systematic search of those waters for any ship which might be engaged in the work. On the morning of August 5th—war had begun the previous night at 11 p.m. —there steamed through the Straits of Dover, in search of German mine-layers, the British Third Destroyer Flotilla, commanded by Captain Cecil H. Fox in the light cruiser Amphion, and consisting of eighteen of the latest destroyers completed for the British Fleet.

BORN FIGHTERS FROM ALGERIA EAGERLY ASSIST THE ALLIES.
Commonly called Turcos, these soldiers are mainly pure-blooded Arabs, Mohammedans to whom death in battle is a passport to Paradise.

The Amphion was a comparatively small ship of 3,440 tons, laid down at Pembroke Dockyard in March, 1911, and completed in 1913 at a cost of £272,670. Her designed speed was 25 knots, and her armament consisted of ten 4 in. guns and two torpedo-tubes. The destroyers, known as the " L " class, were all built to the same design, the earliest of them having been laid down in June, 1912. They displaced 965 tons, and carried three 4 in.

A COMPANY OF TURCOS EXAMINING SPOILS OF WAR.
Although Turcos carry equipment weighing over 80 lb., they are not afraid to supplement it with any military trifles that take their fancy.

guns and two double torpedo-tubes, while turbine machinery, driven by furnaces burning oil fuel exclusively, gave them a speed of 29 knots. Captain Fox, the head of this flotilla of mosquito craft, was only forty-one years old at this time, and had already had a great deal of experience in destroyer work.

While the Third Flotilla was proceeding on its lynx-eyed search for possible German mine-layers, it fell in with a fishing trawler

FROM THE HOT SANDS OF AFRICA TO THE SODDEN TRENCHES ALONG THE RIVER AISNE.
The Turcos seen here, leaving Amiens for the firing-line, exhibited especial daring at the Battle of Mons on August 24th, 1914.

which reported having seen in a certain place off the East Coast a suspicious-looking vessel " throwing things overboard." Needless to say, everyone knew instinctively what those " things " were. This was at about ten o'clock in the morning, and the flotilla immediately set off in the direction which the skipper of the trawler had indicated.

Before very long they sighted a small, fast liner belonging to the German Hamburg-Amerika Company, which, her work having apparently been completed, was making at full speed towards the German coast. She had, in fact, laid a line of submarine mines off the coast of Suffolk, extending to a point about **On the trail of** sixty miles out to sea ; but this of course, was not known at the time. The character of **a German mine-layer** the ship was never in doubt. As the flotilla drew near a shot was fired as a signal for her to heave to ; but, instead of doing so, she put on extra steam, in the vain hope of escaping from ships which had a superiority in speed of nearly fifty per cent.

Seeing that it was the intention of the ship to get away if she could, Captain Fox detached four destroyers in pursuit—the Lance, Laurel, Lark, and Linnet. It took them some little time to come up with their quarry, but

THE TSAR INSPECTING RUSSIAN AVIATORS BEFORE THEY LEFT FOR THE FRONT.

At the outbreak of war, Russia was reputed to possess 500 aeroplanes, and the Russian aviators were credited with being very courageous and adaptable in the management of them. This photograph shows the Tsar bidding farewell to officers of his Flying Corps before their departure for the front. The second on the right is the instructor, a Frenchman, distinguishable by his uniform.

when they did so there was no question as to the issue. The destroyers surrounded the unhappy ship, and the action —if such it can be called—began about midday. It was very quickly over. According to the accounts of eye-witnesses, only four shots were fired at the doomed German ship. The first carried away the bridge from which she was navigated. The second seems to have gone wide ; but the third and fourth were sent clean into her stern, with such effect that they ripped it completely away, opening the interior of the ship to the sea.

Within six minutes from the firing of the first shot the German ship heaved her bows in **A triumph of** the air and went to the bottom. She proved to have been the Königin Luise, a vessel of **naval marksmanship** 2,163 tons and 20 knots—an apparently innocent passenger ship which had obviously been taken in hand long before the war began and converted into a mine-layer. She carried a crew of about 130, of whom about fifty were saved by the boats of the British destroyers. The majority of the men who were picked up were grateful for the humane action of the British, but the captain of the Königin Luise was almost mad with fury at the loss of his ship, and, as his vessel began to settle down, threatened to shoot any member of his crew who showed signs of surrendering to the rescuing ships. He himself had to be taken by force.

THE PATH OF THE COSSACK THROUGH WAR-SMITTEN GALICIA.

This scene shows a troop of Cossacks passing through a Galician village, with the national school in the background. The Cossack is the finest mounted soldier in the world. He is trained to horsemanship from boyhood, and it is no uncommon thing for him to ride below his horse if it serves his purpose to deceive the enemy into supposing that the animal is riderless.

After the prisoners, of whom many were wounded, had been distributed among the ships of the flotilla—the majority being taken on board the Amphion—Captain Fox proceeded with the plan of search which had up to now been so successful The position in which the Königin Luise had been sunk and the approximate area in which her mines had been laid were communicated to the proper authorities, so that the mine-sweepers could be set to work without delay, and for the remainder of the day the Third Flotilla carried out a systematic search of the southern area of the North Sea in the hope of being able to find more of the enemy's ships and send them to the bottom.

The day was uneventful ; the only incident of note occurring when the Amphion, sighting the smoke of a big **The tragedy of the Amphion** ship on the horizon. gave chase, and, on coming up with the suspected vessel, discovered her to be one of the usual North Sea passenger boats conveying Prince Lichnowsky, the late German Ambassador, across from Harwich to the Hook of Holland, en route for Germany. The vessel was warned to avoid the mine-field towards which she was steering.

The work of the flotilla continued carefully throughout the night, the Amphion leading and the destroyers being spread out fanwise over a wide area. In the early morning, after the ships had for some time been on a southerly course, they again approached the area in which the Königen Luise had been sunk, and a detour was made to avoid the danger zone. What followed is best described in the official statement issued on August 19th.

" This was successfully done until 6.30 a.m. (August 6th), when the Amphion struck a mine. A sheet of flame instantly enveloped the bridge, which rendered the captain insensible, and he fell on to the fore-and-aft bridge. As soon as he recovered consciousness he ran to the engine room to stop the engines, which were still going at revolutions for twenty knots.   As all the fore part was on fire, it proved impossible to reach the bridge or to flood the fore magazine.   The ship's back appeared to be broken, and she was already settling down by the bows.   All efforts were therefore directed towards placing the wounded in safety in case of explosion, and towards getting her in tow by the stern.   By the time the destroyers closed in. it was clearly time to abandon the ship.   The men fell in for this purpose with the same composure that had marked their behaviour throughout. All was done without hurry or confusion, and twenty minutes after the mine was struck the men, officers, and captain left the ship.

THE TRAIL OF WAR IN A SCENE OF PEACE.
Scenes such as this were common in the districts where War's Red Reaper had wielded his scythe. The photograph was taken near the Marne, and it shows a German soldier lying dead in a field of stubble.

"AMPHION" SURVIVORS, RESCUED FROM THE SEA, REACHING ENGLAND AND SAFETY.

On August 6th, 1914, two days after war opened, the British light cruiser Amphion, after sinking a German mine-layer, fell a victim to floating mines which the mine-layer had strewn in the path of neutral commerce. Of the crew 148 were killed by the explosion or by drowning, and 143 were saved by the Amphion's attending fleet of destroyers. The survivors were landed on the Harwich coast in the plight seen in the picture— hatless, shoeless, and clad only in shirts and trousers. Captain Fox, who commanded the Amphion, was given command of the new flotilla leader Faulknor, one of the two vessels under construction for the Chilian Navy, and taken over by the British Government.

" Three minutes after the captain left his ship another explosion occurred which enveloped and blew up the whole fore part of the vessel. The effects showed that she must have struck a second mine, which exploded the fore magazine. The Amphion was actually sunk in the same way as the battleship Petropavlovsk in the Russo-Japanese War. She struck a cable upon which mines were strung, and the momentum of the ship though considerably checked by the explosion of the first mine and the stoppage of the engines, was sufficient to carry her against the second mine. Débris falling from a great height struck the rescue boats and destroyers, and one of the Amphion's shells burst on the deck of one of the latter, killing two of the men and a German prisoner rescued from the cruiser.

" The after part now began to settle quickly, till its foremost part was on the bottom, and the whole after part tilted up at an angle of forty-five degrees. In another quarter of an hour this, too, had disappeared. Captain Fox speaks in high terms of the behaviour of officers and men throughout. Every order was promptly obeyed without confusion or perturbation."

In this brief official statement describing the first British loss of the war—a loss, too, brought about in the most dispiriting and nerve-wrecking of all possible circumstances—the British nation learned again what it already knew in its heart, that the courage, the coolness, and the discipline of the British seaman had not deteriorated from the glorious standard of the past. These men of the Amphion were inspired by none of the enthusiasm and the excitement of battle. Their ship was shattered under them by an unseen enemy—an enemy they could not fight, against which they had no protection.

A severe test of British seamen

Yet, after the first shock of the explosion which wrecked the fore part of the ship, everything was carried out as if at manœuvres. The force of the explosion tore the funnels from their bases, and the guns and mountings from their emplacements, and threw them high into the air. The majority of those who lost their lives were mercifully killed outright by the first explosion, and as this occurred right in the bows of the ship, where the men's berths were, the petty officers and men inevitably suffered severely. One hundred and forty-eight of the latter were killed or drowned, together with about twenty German prisoners rescued from the Königin Luise.

The only officer to lose his life was Staff-Paymaster Joseph T. Gedge. A large number of men were injured more or less severely, the majority suffering from burns and scalds caused by the shattering of the boilers and the ignition of the oil fuel which the ship carried in her double bottoms.

General view of the great shipbuilding yards of Blohm and Voss, in Hamburg, which give employment to about 10,000 men.

The turbine machine shop at the engineering yard of Blohm and Voss, Hamburg, who built the Goeben and the Moltke, the world's swiftest battle-cruisers, at the outbreak of hostilities. The famous Vulcan yards are also in Hamburg.

Glimpse of the Imperial Works in Kiel, with the Prinz Heinrich under construction. The upper inset picture shows one of the 150-ton floating cranes used in the Imperial shipyards at Kiel, and the lower inset picture a turbine for a German destroyer, made in the same works.

GERMANY'S WAR PREPARATIONS AT HAMBURG AND KIEL.

The behaviour of the destroyers was not the least heroic part of this unfortunate occurrence. The fact that the Amphion had struck a mine in the area previously passed over by the Königin Luise was proof enough that the whole flotilla was in the midst, or at any rate on the edge, of an invisible mine-field. Yet they all closed in round the doomed ship, lying as close in as they dared, and lowering their boats to pick up the survivors, while all the time the powder and shells in the Amphion's magazine were exploding and turning the wrecked ship into a veritable volcano. It was indeed marvellous that only three men— **The great risk to** one of them a German prisoner—should have been killed by the shower of missiles **the rescuing ships** that were thrown over a wide area round the sinking ship.

The loss of the Amphion—the first warship to be sunk in the war—came not unnaturally as a shock to the people of this country. The material loss, however, was slight the ship being one of but little fighting power; and it was instantly realised that, bound as we were to prove ultimately successful at sea, the desired end— the annihilation of the enemy's fleet—could not be attained without some sacrifice on our part. There was further consolation in the fact that the Amphion was not sunk in action, but by means of mines sown indiscriminately and illegally on the high seas.

THE BRITISH DESTROYER LARK CONVOYING A PASSENGER STEAMER ACROSS THE CHANNEL.
The destroyer Lark, along with her sister destroyers Lance, Laurel, and Linnet, all acting under Captain Fox on the ill-fated Amphion, chased and sunk the German mine-layer Königin Luise on August 6th, 1914, and helped to save the survivors of the Amphion's crew when the German floating mines had done their deadly work.

As the First Lord of the Admiralty declared in the House of Commons two days after the disaster: " The indiscriminate use of mines, not in connection with military harbours or strategic positions—the indiscriminate scattering of contact mines about the seas, which may destroy not merely enemy vessels or warships, but peaceful merchantmen passing under neutral flags, and possibly carrying supplies to neutral countries—this use of mines is new in warfare, and it deserves to be considered attentively, not only by us who are, of course, engaged in the war, and who may naturally be prone to hasty judgment in such matters, but also by the nations of the civilised world. The Admiralty are not at all alarmed or disconcerted by such incidents. We **Indiscriminate** have expected a certain number, and we continue to expect a certain number of such incidents, **use of sea mines** and our arrangements provide for reducing such occurrences to the minimum possible."

The later experience of the war was to show that, in spite of the great and unceasing efforts made by our Navy to clear the seas of these wildly-scattered mines, Mr. Churchill's expectation that we should lose more ships by their agency was destined to be realised. But the spirit in which the Navy was prepared to face these unseen and shamefully-prepared dangers was nobly exemplified by a brief announcement which the Admiralty issued on the very day following the destruction of the Amphion. It was to the effect that Captain Fox would take command of the new flotilla leader Faulknor, on the completion of that ship, and resume the command of the Third Destroyer Flotilla. The Faulknor was one of two vessels (the other being the Broke) which had been completing in this country for the Chilian Navy, and which the British Admiralty had taken over on the outbreak of war.

The key sketch shows only a very small section of the battle, but may be taken as typical of the whole. For the sake of clearness the enemy's positions are more visible than would actually be the case. The havoc of shells in the foreground has had to be omitted. The firing-line is irregular—its formation depending on the nature of the ground. Thus, to prevent the enemy from advancing sheltered by the "dead ground" afforded by the fold of the land on the right front, part of the line occupies the small hill on the right of the drawing.

The far-flung battle-line of the world's greatest armed struggle showed war upon a more stupendous scale than ever before. The great "Battle of the Rivers" in Northern France engaged in deadly conflict twenty times the number of combatants that decided the fate of Europe at Waterloo. The modern battle is warfare reduced to a specialised science, which has reached as high a stage of perfection as—or higher than—any of the sciences of peace. The great engines of death, the range of modern artillery, and the destructive power of high explosives have robbed war of its picturesque side. The dash of cavalry and the spear-to-breast charges

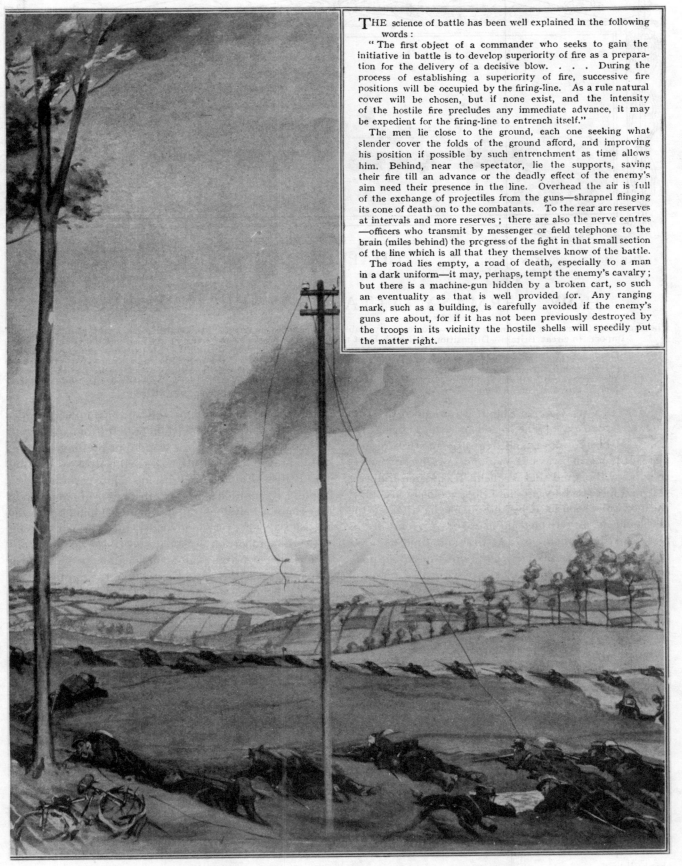

THE science of battle has been well explained in the following words :

"The first object of a commander who seeks to gain the initiative in battle is to develop superiority of fire as a preparation for the delivery of a decisive blow. . . . During the process of establishing a superiority of fire, successive fire positions will be occupied by the firing-line. As a rule natural cover will be chosen, but if none exist, and the intensity of the hostile fire precludes any immediate advance, it may be expedient for the firing-line to entrench itself."

The men lie close to the ground, each one seeking what slender cover the folds of the ground afford, and improving his position if possible by such entrenchment as time allows him. Behind, near the spectator, lie the supports, saving their fire till an advance or the deadly effect of the enemy's aim need their presence in the line. Overhead the air is full of the exchange of projectiles from the guns—shrapnel flinging its cone of death on to the combatants. To the rear are reserves at intervals and more reserves ; there are also the nerve centres —officers who transmit by messenger or field telephone to the brain (miles behind) the progress of the fight in that small section of the line which is all that they themselves know of the battle.

The road lies empty, a road of death, especially to a man in a dark uniform—it may, perhaps, tempt the enemy's cavalry ; but there is a machine-gun hidden by a broken cart, so such an eventuality as that is well provided for. Any ranging mark, such as a building, is carefully avoided if the enemy's guns are about, for if it has not been previously destroyed by the troops in its vicinity the hostile shells will speedily put the matter right.

of infantry are still incidents in a great battle, but subordinate incidents. The main part of a battle consists of a long succession of artillery and rifle duels, where it is the objective of each side to conceal its positions, to protect its combatants, to find the range of the opposing lines, and to deal out death by an accurate and overwhelming fire of heavy guns, machine-guns, and rifles, so that the enemy is compelled to evacuate his position, or is so weakened that he is no longer able to resist effectively the charge of cavalry or the cold steel of an infantry attack.

The significance of this picture is explained by the diagram above.

HOW GERMANY ATTACKED OUR COMMERCE.

The Growth of Germany's Mercantile Marine—Fostered by Subsidy—Economic Value of the British Navy—Importance of Food Imports to Great Britain—Disposition of British Fleet at Outbreak of War—The Navies of our Dominions—German Naval Disposition and Coaling Stations—Policy of Arming Merchant Vessels—Britain's Grip Upon Germany's Ocean Communications—How Wireless Telegraphy Helped in Naval War—Fear for Food Famine in First Days of War—Treatment of Hostile Ships—Disturbance in Insurance Market—British Government Relieves the Situation—Operations of the German Dresden against Allied Shipping—Adventures and Fate of the Kaiser Wilhelm der Grosse and the Bethania—The Value of Speed in Naval Raids—The Allies' Command of the Sea.

WHEN the German Empire was founded the total tonnage of the merchant ships flying the black, white, and red flag of the German mercantile marine was 982,355, and in eighteen years—that is, by the time that Wilhelm II. became Emperor—it had increased by no more than 300,000 tons. But the new ruler soon let it be known that he regarded the development of the mercantile marine as one of his most cherished ambitions. At the same time, he never failed to emphasise the fact that a great merchant navy could have no permanent existence without a powerful war fleet to protect it and to assist in its expansion.

The development of German merchant shipping was considerably aided by the payment of subsidies, which enabled the companies in receipt of them to carry goods at low rates and so take trade from their competitors. The loss, if any, was made up by the Imperial Government. At the same time, great encouragement was given by various artificial means to the expansion of the shipbuilding industry. The effect of these measures is plainly visible in the great

THE GERMAN 3,600-TON CRUISER DRESDEN,
which is the sister ship of the Emden, and which sunk the British merchantmen Hyades and City of Winchester in South American waters soon after war began.

strides which have been made. In 1870 the German mercantile marine stood fifth in order of tonnage among the merchant navies of the world, but by the beginning of the present century it was second, surpassed only by the British Empire, and it has since continued to improve its position. In 1870 there were approximately seven and a half tons of merchant shipping under the British flag for every one under the German, but by 1912 the proportion was only a little over four tons to one in our favour, the actual figures being: British Empire, 13,846,365 tons; Germany, 3,153,724 tons.

Nevertheless, the British mercantile marine remained by far the greatest and the most important, but with every ton added to it the maritime risks of the Empire were increased. The task of our ships was to carry our trade between these islands and countries oversea, and to bring to the teeming millions of our country those supplies of food and raw material which we are unable to produce for ourselves. Every additional ship was a hostage to fortune—a further indication of the ever-increasing dependence of Great Britain upon

General view of Krupp's Germania shipbuilding works at Kiel. The vicious Krupp interests dominated the Kaiser and German Imperial policy, being indeed the chief primary cause of the war.

General view of the fitting and finishing shop in a large German armament manufactory. The biggest German naval gun is 15 in. diameter and throws a projectile of 1,675 lb. weight. The inset picture shows an armour plate being bent under a 10,000-ton hydraulic press.

An iron foundry in the Germania shipbuilding works of the great Krupp firm at Kiel. The other private yard at Kiel is owned by the firm of Howaldt, but the Imperial yard employs as many men—about ten thousand—as the two private yards combined.

THE MAKING OF GERMANY'S SHIPS AND GUNS AT KIEL.

WHERE SOME OF GERMANY'S FINEST BATTLESHIPS WERE BUILT.

The entrance to the Imperial shipbuilding yards at Kiel, which before the war employed about 10,000 men. The hanging bridge is a wonderful piece of engineering, the towers being 200 feet high and 400 feet apart, while the "ferry" is suspended by steel cables and operated by electricity. The waterway is always open for the largest ships to pass, and the ferry traffic is possible at all times except during the actual minutes that a ship is entering. Kiel, a fortified town of about 150,000, is one of the best havens in Europe, and is Germany's chief war port. It is the headquarters of the German Navy, with a naval academy and a university.

the command of the sea. Owing to the success with which the British Navy kept the trade routes open during the Great War it is doubtful whether even now we realise the complete dependence of our country upon its maritime trade. This could only be adequately brought home to us by the defeat of the Navy.

The bulk of the workmen in this country are dependent for their weekly wage upon the importation of raw material and the export of the manufactured article, and the failure of the Navy to keep open the trade routes would mean a wholesale closing down of factories and workshops, and particularly of those great firms in the North which rely upon the regular delivery of the raw materials of the cotton, wool, and other textile industries imported to the annual value of £150,000,000.

The question of food is not less important than the question of work and wages. Year by year we are becoming less and less able to feed ourselves. Thousands of acres of land have passed out of cultivation, and thou-

THE BIRTHPLACE OF BRITAIN'S GUNS.
The main gate of Woolwich Arsenal, where, in times of great pressure, 20,000 men work day and night manufacturing artillery.

sands of workers have left the land for the manufacturing centres, and by so doing have increased the dependence of the country upon the command of the sea.

The latest available figures show that we import food to the annual value of £280,000,000 a year. This means that every day of the year food to the value of £780,000 is landed in our ports. It means that if our Navy were unable to protect the ocean highways along which hundreds of British merchantmen are daily ploughing their way we should starve. How long we could exist if these supplies were cut off has been variously estimated. It might be as long as three months if we had our harvest in hand. It might be as short as three weeks if the catastrophe overtook us at a less favourable moment. In any case, the stoppage of our sea-borne trade would inevitably mean disaster—universal unemployment followed by universal starvation.

Nations which have contemplated war with Great Britain have reckoned not a little upon the damage which they would be able to inflict upon us by interfering with our merchant shipping, and they did so with fairly good reason. They argued from the experience of the wars of the French Revolution, when the price of wheat rose to treble the peace figure. During the twenty years from 1793 to 1812 we lost no fewer than 10,871 merchant ships, an average of 543 a year. As our merchant shipping is far greater now than it was then, and as we are dependent to an infinitely greater extent upon the security of our merchant shipping, both for food and for trade, it was freely assumed, both by British thinkers and by our enemies, that the attack of British commerce offered the surest means of bringing this country to its knees.

THE FAMOUS "GOLD SHIP"—THE KRONPRINZESSIN CECILIE.
On July 28th, 1914, this great 19,500-ton North German Lloyd liner left New York for Germany carrying gold to the value of £2,000,000 for the Bank of England, and when nearing Europe she received a wireless message from Germany advising her to avoid the English Channel and try to reach her home port via the North of Scotland, but she was afraid of capture and steamed back to America, where she entered Bar Harbour, Maine, on the morning of August 5th, and had to remain inactive during the war. Attempts to sell her along with other German ships to American owners have failed on account of the opposition of the anti-German allies.

There is not the slightest doubt that any serious interference with our merchant shipping would have been followed by disaster at home.

It was not alone upon the actual work of their cruisers at sea that our prospective enemies depended. They also assumed that on the mere approach of war British shipowners would be appalled at the prospect of their vessels being sunk or captured by the warships of the enemy, and would lay their vessels up in harbour rather than expose them to this risk. Infinite reliance was placed upon the assumed " nervousness " of British shipping. It was the very general belief in this country

The safeguarding of British trade

that even in the most favourable circumstances the opening weeks of a war with a strong naval Power would see the cost of food advance to almost prohibitive prices, which might, or might not, be reduced as time went on by the increasing success of the British Navy in running down the enemy's commerce destroyers. That this protective work might be begun with the least possible delay, squadrons of British cruisers were maintained throughout the nineteenth century in various parts of the world, so as to be immediately available in the event of war to safeguard British trade passing through the areas which it was their duty to patrol.

In the ten years immediately preceding the outbreak of war these squadrons had, unfortunately, been grievously reduced. The rapid increase in the strength of the German Navy in the North Sea led the British Admiralty to weaken greatly the force of the British Navy

THE TREMENDOUS FORCE OF A SEA-MINE EXPLOSION.
A graphic representation of the effect caused by exploding a submarine mine. The fate of a great ship that has the ill-fortune to strike one of these mines can be understood from the gigantic upheaval caused by the explosion as seen above. At first, our Government refrained from sowing the sea with mines, and announced on August 23rd, 1914, that no mines had up to that time been laid, but on October 3rd it was officially stated that mines had been laid in a specified area in the southern part of the North Sea, chiefly to protect the approaches to the Thames.

GG

in distant seas, in order that the ships and men thus released might be used to strengthen our fleet in home waters.

On the eve of the outbreak of war our principal naval forces on foreign stations outside Europe were composed as follows :

In the East Indies. one old battleship and two light cruisers.

In the Far East, one old battleship, two armoured cruisers, two light cruisers and eight destroyers.

At the Cape of Good Hope, three light cruisers, all slow and obsolete.

On the Pacific Coast of America, two ancient sloops.

On the South-East Coast of America, one light cruiser.

On the West Coast of Africa, one gunboat.

On the Atlantic Coast of North America, four armoured cruisers and one light cruiser.

Besides these ships, the naval forces of Australia, New Zealand, and Canada were placed at the disposal of the Admiralty immediately on the outbreak of war. Of these the Australian Fleet was by far the most important. It included the battle-cruiser Australia, the flagship, and two other modern sea-going vessels in the light cruisers Sydney and Melbourne, these three ships being all capable of steaming twenty - five knots. There were two older cruisers, a few coast defence craft, three destroyers, and two submarines. Canada had never attempted to carry out a definite naval policy, and the only warships she was able to hand over to the Imperial Government were two old ships which she had bought a few years before with the object of training her own personnel and establishing a Canadian Navy. As soon as war was declared she purchased a couple of submarines that were building at San Francisco for the

Chilian Navy, and so added two useful units to the defence of the Pacific Coast.

New Zealand was only able to hand over three ancient cruisers to the Admiralty, but we must not forget that this patriotic Dominion had already presented the Empire with a ship equal in power to the Australia. This vessel, the New Zealand, was to have been stationed as flagship in the Far East, but, at the request of the Admiralty, New Zealand permitted her to be kept in European waters, where she figures in the battle order of the Grand Fleet.

Altogether there were about twenty British ships of the cruising classes on foreign stations immediately before the outbreak of war, and only six of these were capable of high speed. There were many eminent naval authorities who looked back to the last great naval wars, when we had been compelled to keep nearly five hundred cruising ships in commission, and predicted that the Admiralty was following a policy which would lead to disaster, and that hostile cruisers would be able to inflict immense loss on our commerce at the outset.

So far as could be discovered from the disposition of her warships, Germany did not place any great reliance upon commerce destroying as a means of bringing about the downfall of this country. Indeed, General von Bernhardi, in his much-discussed book, " Germany and the Next War," said that although the war against British commerce must be boldly and energetically prosecuted, and should start unexpectedly, he nevertheless saw that Germany would have an almost impossible task before her, and that " no very valuable results can be expected from a war against England's trade."

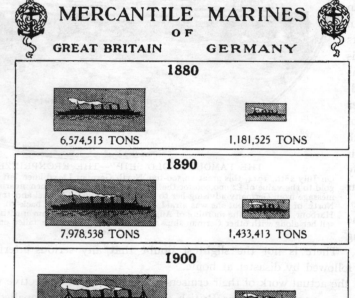

MERCANTILE MARINES
OF
GREAT BRITAIN   GERMANY

1880
6,574,513 TONS   1,181,525 TONS

1890
7,978,538 TONS   1,433,413 TONS

1900
9,304,108 TONS   1,941,645 TONS

1910
11,555,663 TONS   2,903,570 TONS

1912
11,894,791 TONS   3,153,724 TONS

The parallelograms in this chart are drawn to scale, and they illustrate the growth and comparative importance of the British and German mercantile fleets since the year 1880. The British tonnage does not include colonial shipping, which would add about two million tons to the 1912 figures if included. They help to expose the fallacy of the German contention that Germany's merchant fleets required a protecting navy equal in number and power to the British Navy.

LUDERITZ BAY, COALING STATION OF GERMAN SOUTH-WEST AFRICA, CONTAINS COPPER MINES AND DIAMOND FIELDS.

GERMAN COLONIAL SOLDIER ASTRIDE A ZEBRA AT DAR-ES-SALAAM, COALING-STATION OF GERMAN EAST AFRICA.

APIA, THE CAPITAL OF GERMAN SAMOA.   A STREET IN LOME, THE PORT OF TOGOLAND.

TSING-TAU, PORT OF KIAO-CHAU, WHICH GERMANY SEIZED FROM CHINA, AND JAPAN BLOCKADED ON AUGUST 24, 1914.

Any nation that aspires to maritime power must possess, at various strategic points, stations where her vessels can obtain the coal or oil which enables them to keep the sea. After the outbreak of war Germany was gradually relieved of her coaling-stations. The first to go was the Port of Lome, in Togoland, containing a valuable wireless-telegraphy station, captured on August 8th, 1914. Togoland completely surrendered on August 26th. Apia, in German Samoa, interesting as the burial-place of R. L. Stevenson, the novelist, was surrendered to a New Zealand force on August 30th. Germany's oldest colonial possession was acquired in 1884. Altogether her dependencies, before the war, totalled 1,027,820 square miles, their white population numbering 24,389, and their native population 12,041,603.

The most powerful squadron which Germany kept on a foreign station in time of peace was that in the Far East, which consisted of two armoured and three light cruisers, and a number of gunboats. In the Indian Ocean was one fast cruiser. There were also a couple of old ships in the South Pacific, and four fast vessels in the Atlantic. The British forces immediately available for the attack on these German ships were greatly superior in numbers, though in fast ships Germany outstripped us. We had an enormous advantage, however, in the continuous line of British ports and coaling stations which extends round the globe, while Germany could boast no more than five bases outside the North Sea. These were Kiao-Chau in the Far East, Samoa in the Pacific, Dar-es-Salaam in East Africa, Lüderitz Bay in South-West Africa, and Lome in Togoland, on the West Coast of Africa.

The value of coaling stations
In her plans for the attack of British commerce Germany had to allow for the ease with which these few coaling stations could be masked or captured by squadrons of British cruisers. We shall see later how she overcame this difficulty.

Besides the regular cruisers of her fighting Navy, Germany had made preparations for fitting out a large number of merchant ships with guns and naval crews, and commissioning them on the outbreak of war for commerce destruction. This it was legitimate for her to do, although the same difficulties of coaling and replenishing

BERLIN CELEBRATES SEDAN DAY.
September 2nd is "Sedan Day," the blackest day in the French calendar, and the anniversary of the crowning disaster of the Franco-German War. The German armies tried hard to achieve a greater Sedan on September 2nd, 1914, but no such fortune attended their arms, and they had to content themselves by celebrating the first Von Moltke's great triumph by pulling in procession through the streets of Berlin guns captured from France and Russia during the opening weeks of the greater war.

stores which faced her regular cruisers would apply also to these armed merchantmen. But she also laid plans in another direction, which can best be described in the words that Mr. Churchill used in the House of Commons in March, 1913. "It was made clear at the Second Hague Conference and at the London Conference," he said, "that certain of the Great Powers had reserved to themselves the right to convert merchant steamers into cruisers, not merely in national harbours, but if necessary on the high seas. There is now good reason to believe that a considerable number of foreign merchant steamers may be rapidly converted into armed ships by the mounting of guns.

The arming of merchant ships

"The sea-borne trade of the world follows well-marked routes, upon nearly all of which the tonnage of the British mercantile marine largely predominates. Our food-carrying liners and vessels carrying raw material following these trade routes would in certain contingencies meet foreign vessels armed and equipped in the manner described. If the British ships had no armament they would be at the mercy of any foreign liners carrying one effective gun and a few rounds of ammunition."

Mr. Churchill went on to say that it would be obviously absurd to meet this menace by building cruisers in numbers equal to those of the armed merchantmen, and described a scheme by which a number of British food-

From the painting by John St. Helier Lander.

GENERAL SIR HORACE LOCKWOOD SMITH-DORRIEN G.C.B., D.S.O.

One of our ablest military leaders, Sir Horace Smith-Dorrien more than justified his appointment to high command in the British Expeditionary Force. He enhanced a reputation already high by his masterly conduct of the retreat of his army corps from Mons during the memorable week ending August 29th, 1914. In his historic dispatch of September 7th, Sir John French expressed his high appreciation of General Smith-Dorrien's services to his country in these words : " I cannot close the brief account of this glorious stand of the British troops without putting on record my deep appreciation of the valuable services rendered by General Sir Horace Smith-Dorrien. I say without hesitation that the saving of the left wing of the army under my command on the morning of the 26th August could never have been accomplished unless a commander of rare and unusual coolness, intrepidity, and determination had been present to personally conduct the operation."

HH

THE cost of war is great, not only in money, but in what to a nation is more than money—her glorious manhood.

When a country enters war with a high purpose and with her conscience clean she can face the loss with fortitude and reckon the result well worth the cost. Mr. Asquith, in his great speech at Edinburgh, on September 18th, 1914, expressed the opinion of the Army, the Navy, the nation, and the Empire when, speaking of those who had fallen in the cause, he said: "We shall not mourn them too much. One crowded hour of glorious life is worth an age without a name."

THE figures in this picture, sketched by our artist, who was a spectator of the scene at Waterloo Station, London, are expressive of the spirit that wins great battles, and "wins through" to victory. A contingent of British infantry was entraining for the field of war, and at the same moment a trainload of British wounded drew up at the opposite platform.

The camaraderie of arms and enthusiasm for the work in hand inspired the men as they greeted each other. The sight of those who carried home the wounds of battle was the touch of nature that aroused all the kinship of a common cause, and cheer after cheer was sent across the thronging platform, to be sent back again in feebler tones, but with as high an enthusiasm.

IT was announced officially on August 30th that reinforcements amounting to double the loss suffered to that date had joined the British Expeditionary Force, and this appeared to be the policy upon which the Army authorities acted in the matter of making good the gaps in the ranks during the early stages of the war before it was possible to augment considerably the strength of the fighting arm. The artist has tried to convey that idea into his work.

The ineradicable British habit of enjoying the sporting side of everything—even of war—invested the discomforts of trench work and the hardships of the camp with an interest that overcame all obstacles and disconcerted the attacking foe.

THE DARING HORSEMANSHIP OF THE DREADED COSSACKS.

As fighters on horseback, the Cossacks have always had a personal ascendency over all other cavalry, and in the Great War of the Nations they maintained that ascendency. This scene shows them standing in stirrups crossed over the saddles and swimming their horses across a river. The Cossacks hold their land by a military service tenure, and are liable to duty for life. Service begins at the age of nineteen and lasts for twenty-four years in three distinct periods. First, there is three years' training in their home settlements, followed by twelve years in regimental headquarters. The second is a "home" furlough period, when the man keeps his horse and equipment ready for service, with a short term of training annually. Then there is a four-year period, when the Cossack is required only to keep his arms and equipment ready for service, with one training term of three weeks. Finally, for five years he is in the Reserves, and is only called upon for war service.

carrying ships using the trade routes most likely to be threatened would be armed, " for purposes of self-defence," with two 4·7 in. guns mounted in the stern. By the time that war came, about forty ships had been armed in this way. Their equipment would not have been the slightest use to them in the event of their being attacked by a regular cruiser, or even by a merchant cruiser commissioned in the ordinary way, but it was believed that it would be sufficient to repel the attack of any vessel commissioned in the manner which the First Lord of the Admiralty had described.

Mr. Churchill was hotly attacked by the friends of Germany in England, who pretended to doubt whether a ship not properly commissioned and not under the control of its Government was, in international law, entitled to fire a gun, even in self-defence. In the early stages of the war the United States Government issued a proclamation to the effect that, as these vessels were virtually warships, they would not be allowed to use American ports. Subsequently, however, the embargo was removed, on condition that the

BELGIAN SOLDIERS LYING IN WAIT FOR GERMAN PATROLS BEHIND HASTILY-CONSTRUCTED STREET DEFENCES.

BELGIAN ARTILLERY IN ACTION
at Audogom, ten miles north of Alost.

HAVOC CAUSED BY THE GERMAN SIEGE ARTILLERY ON THE OUTER FORTIFICATIONS OF NAMUR.
After the heroic defence of Liège, and its successful arrest of the German advance for three weeks, it was anticipated that a similar defence would be offered by the Belgian fortress of Namur, but the heavy German siege-guns made havoc of it, and it fell on August 24th, 1914. This photograph was taken in one of the trenches of Namur, and illustrates the awful destruction wrought by the German artillery.

guns were of not more than 6 in. calibre, that they were mounted aft, and that the crew of the ship was not increased in consequence of their being mounted.

The most effective defence of British shipping, and the most deadly attack on that of our enemy, however, was provided by the Grand Fleet at home. A glance at a map will show that the British Isles lie like an enormous breakwater across the seaward communications of Germany. Excepting vessels engaged in the Baltic trade and in local coastwise traffic, every ship desiring to enter a German port has to pass near the shores of the British Isles.

The first measure which the British Navy took when war became inevitable was to move to its war stations. Although no one knew at the time where the fleets had gone, everyone knew what was the task

they had set out to perform. They had gone to set a final seal upon the naval communications of Germany by holding in force the English Channel and what is known as the "north-about" route into the North Sea—the route that leads round the coast of Scotland to the German seaboard. The effect of this, when war broke out, was that no German ship, whether war vessel or trader, could enter or leave the North Sea without running the gauntlet of the British Navy. A few vessels may

have succeeded in getting through by hugging the coast of Norway, and hiding during the day in the numerous fjords by which those shores are so picturesquely scarred; but for all practical purposes the grip of the British Fleet upon the oceanic communications of Germany was complete. By this disposition of our forces the maritime trade of Germany was brought to a standstill. Such vessels as were actually at sea had to choose between seeking the shelter of a neutral port and being captured by British cruisers. Those already in neutral ports were, wherever possible, warned by wireless to remain there; and those in German ports were unable to get out. By this same disposition our enemies were prevented from making any considerable addition to the forces available for the attack on British trade. One or two vessels, among them the Kaiser Wilhelm der Grosse, were certainly added to the cruiser squadron in the Atlantic, but in all probability these got out of the North Sea before war was declared, and before our own ships had any power to stop them. As for the merchant cruisers and armed merchantmen, upon which Germany was relying to no small extent, there is good reason to believe that many of these carried their guns and mountings permanently on board, and that ammunition was shipped from transports either at sea or, what is more likely, in neutral harbours.

Britain's grip on German sea routes

Wireless telegraphy was one of the new factors in the war against commerce, and was expected to play an important part in both the attack and the defence of commerce. After the first few days of war there was practically no German commerce left at sea for our ships to attack, and their energies were therefore

TYPES OF KRUPP GUNS IN USE BY THE GERMAN ARMY.
The mules are carrying portions of a 12-pounder Krupp mountain gun, one of them carrying the gun itself, and the second the mounting, while a third and a fourth mule, not seen in the picture, carry the shield and the ammunition respectively. The centre picture shows a Krupp 12-pounder anti-aircraft gun in position for firing, and the gun in the lowest photograph is an 11 in. Krupp howitzer with its motor-tractor.

TROPHIES OF WAR CAPTURED BY BOTH SIDES.

At the top is a view of the main street in Cologne, where guns captured from the French are on exhibition; in the centre we have a glimpse of the barracks at Liege, in the hands of the Germans, with guns captured from the Belgians; and the third picture shows the Place Royale, in Nancy, where thirty guns taken from the Germans in Alsace are displayed.

concentrated upon hunting down the vessels which Germany had sent to sea for the destruction of our own merchantmen. With the assistance of wireless, merchantmen so equipped would be able to communicate at once to the nearest British warship the whereabouts of any hostile ship that might be encountered. We found later on that, whenever a German cruiser fell in with a defenceless British merchant ship, her first action was to threaten the ship with instant destruction if any single letter was signalled by its wireless operator. In those vessels which German cruisers stopped and boarded, but did not destroy, the wireless apparatus was invariably rendered useless, so that the whereabouts of the hostile ship could not be communicated.

We were also to find that, although in certain circumstances wireless telegraphy was a considerable assistance to our ships in their work, the Germans were frequently able, by tapping and decoding our messages, to secure information enabling them both to waylay our merchant ships and to elude our cruisers. In order to prevent the leakage of news near home, the whole of the wireless service was taken over by the Government before the outbreak of war, and all privately-owned stations were ordered to be dismantled. Concurrently with the declaration of hostilities, an order was issued prohibiting the employment of wireless by all ships (with, of course, the exception of warships) in home waters. But the Germans were able to obtain much information through neutral wireless stations in the United States, in South America, and in the Dutch East Indies.

In spite of the excellent reasons we had for believing in the ability of the British Navy **Fears for our** to keep the trade routes clear and so to maintain an uninterrupted supply of food from **food supply** oversea, the first few days of war led to something very much like a panic both in shipping circles, where reliance on the power of the Navy should have been highest, and among the general public. Perhaps the real reason for this state of affairs lay not so much in distrust of the Fleet as in ignorance of its strength and organisation.

There was a wild rush for food supplies. Those who gave way to alarm honestly believed that provisions would, in a very short time, be forced up to famine prices. They proceeded to spend as much as they could afford upon the purchase of stocks sufficient to last them for months. Even the big stores were cleared out of their supplies of tinned milk and preserved meats, and in outlying districts flour became almost unprocurable.

Ministers appealed to the people to take things calmly, assuring them that there was no cause for alarm; then the panic was allayed, and prices began to settle down again. The alarmists, including several British newspapers, which published horrifying **The British Isles athwart Germany's path**

articles before the war as to the risk of famine, were surprised to discover that food ships were arriving at our ports almost as regularly as if war did not exist. Within a week or two the cost of food had sunk almost to its normal level. Those who had rushed in with huge orders for potted meats and comestibles found their larders loaded with all sorts of provisions which in the ordinary course they could not eat, and which had been bought at inflated prices. Meanwhile, in the markets and the shops, the usual articles of food—bread, vegetables, provisions, fresh meat—were being sold in undiminished quantities and at very little above normal prices.

The reasons for this were that the British Navy was keeping our trade routes comparatively clear of hostile ships, and that many cargoes of food bound for Germany were diverted to the United Kingdom. Thus, by this one stroke, the position of our enemies was rendered still less favourable, while our own people reaped the benefit. In this fashion was the influence of British sea power doubly demonstrated. It is true that Germany did not depend upon food supplies from oversea to anything like the same extent as Britain; but our enemies were yet to discover that the stoppage of ocean trade was a vital factor in the progress of the war.

BRUSSELS IN THE GRIP OF THE INVADING GERMAN.
In the upper picture German soldiers are seen quartered in the Palais de Justice, one of the modern architectural glories of Europe; and in the lower picture, taken from the Hotel de Ville, they are seen in the Grande Place crowding round the army kitchens for their midday meal.

The warfare against commerce began immediately on the declaration of hostilities. Scores of German ships then lying in British harbours were seized by the Customs authorities, and the same fate naturally befell the British ships in German ports. The Declaration of London, which was subsequently adopted, with certain modifications, by the allied Powers as their code of conduct throughout the naval war, lays down that " when a merchant ship belonging to one of the belligerent Powers is at the commencement of hostilities in an enemy port, it is desirable that it should be allowed to depart freely, either immediately, or after a reasonable number of days of grace, and to proceed, after being furnished with a pass, direct to its port of destination, or to any other port indicated to it."

On the day of the declaration of war, the King issued a proclamation stating that, provided our ships were treated equally well in the enemy's ports, German merchantmen would be allowed to leave at any time up to midnight on August 14th—ten days after the declaration. At the same time the Government reserved the right to seize all ships of over 5,000 tons, or having a speed of fourteen knots or above ; the obvious reason being that such vessels were capable of being converted into effective commerce raiders after they returned to a German port.

Great hauls of German merchantmen

At sea, the attack upon merchant shipping was prosecuted with vigour, and in this respect we held an enormous advantage over our enemies because of the number of cruisers we had available for such work, and the fact that all ships making for Germany from any country but Sweden, Norway, or Holland, had to make their way past our squadrons in the Channel and the North Sea. Many German ships were captured as they came up the Channel, and others in the attempt to reach their home ports by running round the North of Scotland. Nor was it only in home waters that this war upon German commerce was waged ; for when Great Britain went to war the Empire went to war, and at every British port throughout the world where there was a German ship, that ship was detained.

WITH THE KAISER'S HOSTS IN BELGIUM.
A German outpost, in the lower photograph, is waiting not far from the suburbs of Brussels for an expected Belgian attack ; and in the upper, some infantry of the German Ninth Army, commanded by General von Boehn, are on the march.

Our cruisers, advised at once by cable and wireless of the outbreak of war, were instantly on the lookout for German ships at sea ; but, unfortunately, the success of their activities was largely curtailed by Germany's initiative in forcing war upon us. On August 1st, and possibly even before then, urgent cables were sent from Germany to all the neutral ports used to any great extent by German vessels, ordering that such ships as were there should remain in port, and that all German vessels within wireless range should be advised immediately to return.

By this means the British Navy was robbed of the opportunity of capturing such large ships as the Grosser Kurfürst and the Friedrich der Grosse, of the Norddeutscher Lloyd line, which had just left New York and promptly returned there ; while further evidence of Germany's determination to drag this country into the war is provided by the fact that orders were sent at the end of July to many German ships in British ports oversea that they were to make for the nearest neutral port with all possible speed, the object being to prevent their detention by the British authorities.

Even before war was declared, therefore, we had gone far towards driving German commerce off the seas. German liners, food-carrying ships, and tramps, either drew their fires and prepared for an indefinite sojourn in

THE FLOWING TIDE OF RECRUITING.
Upper Picture : A section of the Old Public Schools and University Men's Force at their first parade in Manchester. Five thousand recruits for this force were obtained within ten days. Lower Picture : Recruits for the Seaforth Highlanders, raised by the exertions and financial support of a few prominent Scots in London, leaving the London Scottish headquarters, Buckingham Gate, London, en route for Bedford and war service.

a neutral harbour, or else scurried back in response to the wireless advice to the nearest non-British port. The pressure of British sea-power thus made itself felt before a state of war existed. New York and Boston became crowded with German shipping afraid to venture to sea because of the probability of war and the certainty of British naval predominance.

Just prior to Great Britain's declaration of war, a great deal of interest was aroused by the doings of the Kronprinzessin Cecilie, a 23½-knot 19,500-ton liner belonging to the Norddeutscher Lloyd. This vessel left New York on July 28th, with £2,000,000 in gold, bound for Plymouth, Cherbourg, and Bremen, the gold being consigned to London and Paris. She had almost reached the British Isles when she was informed by wireless of the probable declaration of war between Great Britain and Germany, and she seems at first to have endeavoured to proceed straight to Bremen round the North of Scotland.

Thinking better of this manœuvre, she turned tail and fled at full speed back to America, where she arrived only just in time ; for while a state of war existed from midnight on August 4th, the ship arrived at Bar Harbour, off the coast of Maine, at half-past six on the following morning, after an exciting run. Disguised by painting

The escape of the " Gold Ship " her funnels a different colour, and spreading canvas over her bow and stern, she made for the nearest point at which she could claim the protection of the United States, and she subsequently crept along the American coast to the most convenient harbour.

The safe arrival of the ship was not altogether unwelcome in this country, because the delivery of the cargo of gold had been insured principally in the London market, which would have become responsible for payment of the loss if the cargo had been captured. As the gold was consigned to London and Paris, and as there could have been no question of liability to Germany, an enemy Power, such anxiety as was felt in insurance circles in this country was hardly justified. One of the most interesting features in the full-speed run of the Kronprinzessin Cecilie back to America was that a number of American bankers, who happened to be among the passengers, offered to buy the vessel and place her under the American flag. It is to the credit of the German captain that.he refused the offer and preferred to take his chance.

Our own merchant shipping at the beginning of the war gave way to a state of temporary panic hardly less complete than that of our enemies. By a stroke of good fortune there happened to be a strike in progress among the engineers of a large section of our merchant shipping, with the result that many vessels which might at the outbreak of war have been in German ports were actually laid up at home, and so were saved to us. Many owners, who had been frightened by " scare " articles, cancelled the sailings of their ships ; but the panic manifested itself most strongly in the insurance market.

The great bulk of British shipping—about four-fifths—was covered by a mutual system of insurance, which provided an indemnity for war risks incurred by ships actually at sea at the outbreak of war, up to the time they reached the nearest British or neutral port. Although this met the interests of the shipowners well enough, it is **Effect of exorbitant insurance rates** obvious that it involved a grave danger to the country, inasmuch as it offered a direct inducement to ships to make for the nearest port at the outbreak of war, and to remain there until its close. The insurance rates for covering actual war risks leaped up to an absolutely prohibitive figure, as much as seventy-three guineas per cent. being asked in some cases. The result of this was to close down several routes altogether for a brief period, since voyages could only have been undertaken at serious financial loss.

The first move back to normal conditions was brought about by the scheme of State Insurance for shipping which Mr. Lloyd George announced in the House of Commons on the day of the declaration of war. He pointed

out that what was wanted was a scheme to encourage shipping to keep the seas, in order that the supply of food and raw material might be maintained and our trade kept going in war as in peace. It was therefore arranged that, as regards the insurance of the ships themselves, the Government was to fix the premium and to receive eighty per cent. of it, and to assume the responsibility for eighty per cent. of the risk, the remainder being covered by the insurance companies and combinations. The Government also opened an office for the State insurance of cargoes, reserving the right to vary the premiums from a maximum of five guineas to a

IN A STRANGE LAND, BUT CERTAINLY NOT DOWNHEARTED.

British soldiers are comfortable in the midst of discomfort. An alfresco meal, with coal-heaps for background, stone cobbles for tables sans linen, sans plates, sans almost everything, was all in the day's work to our soldiers in France. The upper photograph shows such a rough-and-ready meal; the lower one, Royal Marine Light Infantry landing at a Continental seaport.

BRITISH AIRSHIP OVER LEICESTER SQUARE, SEPTEMBER 22ND, 1914.
On September 10th, 1914, the Commissioner of Police of the Metropolis advised the public that a British airship would sail over London, and warned inhabitants not to be alarmed at its presence, or fire at it in the mistaken belief that it was hostile. On September 22nd a naval airship sailed round the City of London and the West End, passing over the Admiralty, the War Office, and Buckingham Palace. This drawing, by an eye-witness, represents it as it appeared from Leicester Square.

minimum of one guinea per cent. These arrangements had a vastly reassuring effect on the mercantile community. The terms offered were exceptionally favourable, and indicated the confidence of the Government in the ability of the British Navy to control the trade routes, and to keep them clear of hostile ships. Liners, cargo boats, and tramps began to resume their normal sailings.

Their progress was at first watched with a natural anxiety, because we had received no intimation, either of the hostile forces available for attacking them, or of the plans laid by the Admiralty for checking the schemes of the enemy. Enormously to the surprise of those who had croaked so loudly of risks, it was found that the great majority of our ships not only completed their voyages in safety, but that they crossed thousands of miles of ocean without seeing even a sign of war.

One or two fell in with the enemy, and in South American waters two British ships, the Hyades and the City of Winchester, were sunk soon after the outbreak of hostilities by the German light cruiser Dresden, which was lying in wait on the trade routes north of Pernambuco. In the South Atlantic the British Fleet was represented before the war only by the light cruiser Glasgow, and although she was larger, more powerfully armed, and slightly faster than the German vessel, the task of finding and rounding-up the enemy in such an enormous

BRITISH GIRLS PRESENTING CIGARETTES TO FRENCH SOLDIERS IN PARIS.

A British girl hands cigarettes to French Cuirassiers as they pass through Paris on the way to the front. France possesses twelve regiments of cuirassiers, having steel cuirasses with a brass plate. Germany has an equal number, the cuirass being of white metal. These cuirasses weigh from 13½ to 16 lb. British Life Guards and Royal Horse Guards wear, in peace time, steel cuirasses which cost £3 6s. each. Russia's four regiments of cuirassiers wear cuirasses made of iron and copper, weighing 30 lb.

expanse of ocean was naturally one of infinite difficulty. The crews were taken off the British merchantman before they were sunk ; and the loss was somewhat mitigated by the fact that the Hyades, although a British ship, had been chartered by a German firm in Buenos Aires to take a cargo of maize to Germany by Rotterdam.

In the North Atlantic one or two exciting incidents occurred during the early days of the war, but owing to the great superiority of the British and French forces in those waters, things quickly began to resume their normal condition. When war was declared, the Cunard liner Lusitania was lying at New York, and it was reported that the German cruisers Karlsruhe and Strassburg were keeping a discreet eye on the route to Fishguard, in the hope of being able to account for this vessel, which, besides being one of the largest and fastest boats in the British mercantile fleet, was also held at the disposal of the Admiralty for conversion, if need be, into a merchant cruiser.

The British commander-in-chief on the North Atlantic station therefore suggested that the Lusitania should cross under convoy, guarded by one of the cruisers under his command ; but there was no cruiser there which had anything like the speed of the Cunarder, whose skipper therefore declined the offer, and determined to trust to his pace. The Lusitania left New York on midnight on August 5th, and, with lights out, proceeded on a course different from that ordinarily followed by Transatlantic shipping. **The Lusitania's fortunate escape** Nevertheless, she was seen and chased by the German cruiser Dresden, which at that time had not proceeded south ; but, thanks to her speed, she was able to get safely away. In this she was largely favoured by fortune, for hardly had she successfully shaken off her pursuer, than one of the turbines broke down, and she had to complete the voyage at a speed of under twenty knots.

She arrived safely in British waters ; but what was intended at the outset to be the quickest run across the Atlantic yet made proved to be the slowest the Lusitania had ever recorded. It was distinctly fortunate that the breakdown in the engine department did not occur while the German cruiser was in sight, for either the Dresden, the Strassburg, or the Karlsruhe could easily have overtaken the great liner at the reduced speed she was forced to adopt.

A similar adventure befell the French liner Lorraine. She also was at New York at the outbreak of war, ready to return to France with four hundred and fifty reservists for the French Army on board. In view of the known presence of German cruisers in the Atlantic, the captain called his officers and crew together and asked them whether they should risk the run across. The reply was an enthusiastic affirmative, and the vessel left New York twelve hours after the Lusitania. Her speed was considerably less than that of the British liner, and things looked unpleasant for her when, on the very evening of her departure, she sighted the Dresden.

There seems little doubt, however, that the German cruiser had consumed too much fuel in her fruitless chase of the Lusitania to be able to pursue the French ship for long, and the Lorraine got safely away. Shortly after escaping this danger the wireless operator on the liner intercepted messages passing between the other German cruisers, from which it was obvious that they were keeping a sharp look-out for her. Here again, however, fortune stepped in. A fog descended on the Atlantic, and with its assistance the Lorraine was enabled to get beyond the possibility of capture, and reached Havre in safety.

The experiences of these vessels, although they came through unscathed, were sufficient to add to the disinclination of shipowners to send their vessels to sea. It goes without saying that there are comparatively few merchant ships with a speed equal even to the twenty-one knots of the Lorraine, and none could reasonably hope for the providential fog which came to the assistance of that ship. The general effect, **A fog that saved a French ship** therefore, might have been serious; but confidence was quickly restored by an announcement made by the Admiralty on August 6th—only two days after the war had begun—to the effect that the whereabouts of all the German cruisers in the Atlantic was known, and that the necessary steps had been taken to deal with them.

In point of fact, immediately on the outbreak of war, the Admiralty had greatly increased our cruiser strength in the North Atlantic, and the French forces of the same character had also been considerably strengthened. As Germany was known to have no more than five cruisers in the whole of the Atlantic Ocean—Austria having none—while twenty-four British cruisers were scouring that ocean, it was

A KIND-HEARTED FRENCH TROOPER ASSISTS HOMELESS PEASANTS.
The plight of many thousands of peaceful French and Belgian peasants, driven from their humble cottages and farms through fear of German brutality, was pitiable in the extreme. This photograph shows a French cavalryman handing a money gift to some ruined peasants who have abandoned their home, and fled with their two small children, rather than face the unknown terrors of a visit from German soldiers.

seen that the risks to shipping were almost negligible. The result was a rapid drop in insurance rates and a corresponding increase in the volume of merchant shipping.

During the early days of the war we heard, as a matter of fact, very little of the doings of German commerce destroyers, and the first which came into prominence was the Kaiser Wilhelm der Grosse. There was no news of her until she was rounded up and sunk by a British cruiser, but subsequent revelations showed that she had quite an adventurous career before she was sent to the bottom. In normal circumstances she was a vessel belonging to the Norddeutscher Lloyd running between Bremen and New York. Built in 1897, she was six hundred and twenty-six feet long, and displaced 14,349 tons, while her designed **Escapades of the Kaiser Wilhelm der Grosse** speed was twenty-two and a half knots. She was, moreover, one of those vessels which Germany had arranged to take over in the event of war, and to fit out as a commerce destroyer.

She was lying at New York at the outbreak of war, preparing to make her ordinary passage across the Atlantic; but as soon as she received the news all her passengers and ordinary cargo were put ashore, and, filling up with coal and stores, she slipped away out of sight. Exactly what her proceedings were will probably never be known. It was practically impossible for her to get into a German port, because as soon as war was declared a cordon of British warships was drawn across the approaches to the German harbours. The next exploit in which she figured

SALUTING THE FLAG OF A FAMOUS FRENCH REGIMENT.

The flag of the Chasseurs-à-pied is decorated with a Roman Eagle, a sergeant of the regiment having captured an Austrian Eagle at the Battle of Solferino on June 24th, 1859. There are thirty battalions of the Chasseurs-à-pied, light infantry, corresponding to the Rifle Corps of the British Army, and their uniform consists of dark-blue tunics and iron-grey trousers.

was the capture of an English fishing vessel, the Tubal Cain, off Iceland. This happened much too soon after her departure from New York to permit of the possibility of her having embarked her armament and ammunition at a German port. Either she carried these accessories on board, or else she shipped them in a neutral port or from a vessel which she met at sea. It is at least certain that she did not return to Germany for them.

In point of fact, there is no reason to doubt that the Kaiser Wilhelm der Grosse had carried her war instructions on board ever since she was first put into service. She had evidently been ordered in certain **Harassing British African trade** circumstances to attack British trade on the South African route; for within a few days she was cruising to the south of the Canary Islands. Here she had a merry but a brief existence, though her career was marked throughout by a courtesy which was sadly lacking among the Germans ashore.

On August 14th, the Union Castle liner Galician, homeward bound from the Cape, was approaching the Canaries when she received a wireless message from the British cruiser Carnarvon asking her to state her exact

A LULL IN THE FIGHT AT SOISSONS IN THE GREAT BATTLE OF THE RIVERS.

Soissons, on the River Aisne, saw much of the fiercest fighting during the course of the great battle. Shells from the opposing armies screamed through and over the town, and hand-to-hand conflicts took place in the trenches near by. This picture shows an African Chausseur, two Turcos, and three British soldiers photographed in front of a building that suffered severely from artillery fire.

position. As the captain of the liner had been warned of the possibility of finding hostile ships in his track, he was probably far from displeased to know that a British warship was somewhere in the neighbourhood—at any rate, within wireless call. Everything went well until, shortly after noon on the following day, a large vessel was seen coming up astern. Anxious eyes watched her, but not until the pursuing ship had almost come up with the Galician was it possible to recognise her as the Kaiser Wilhelm der Grosse.

Immediately the wireless operator in the liner began to send out the " S.O.S." message, hoping that the Carnarvon would still be within reach ; but hardly had the first letter been clicked out when the German cruiser interrupted with a peremptory : " Send one letter more and I sink you." The Galician was ordered to heave to,

German Navy men who were gentlemen and a boat's crew from the Kaiser Wilhelm went aboard. Their first action was to destroy the wireless gear, and then the passengers and crew were drawn up on deck for examination. Two of them turned out to be soldiers returning to England, and these were made prisoners, and instructed to pack their belongings and prepare to return with the Germans.

To everyone else the boarding party were studiously polite, and rather apologetic for the work they had to do. They requisitioned a quantity of quinine, for which they paid, but they refused to accept a gift of cigars and cigarettes which was pressed upon them, because, as they said, " We should not like it to be said that we robbed the ship." Their examination complete, the Germans went back to the Kaiser Wilhelm with their prisoners, and instructions were given for the Galician to follow closely. This she did all night, the ships steaming in a southerly direction with shrouded lights half through the night, the object of the German vessel being to get well off the main trade route. Soon after midnight the cruiser signalled : " Provision all your boats for five days. You will have to abandon your ship."

What this meant everyone knew. They were to be set adrift and left to be picked up by a passing vessel, or to find their way to the nearest coast, while the German cruiser sent the Galician to the bottom. There was no help for it, however, and the work was begun with a will ; but within half an hour there came another signal from the Kaiser Wilhelm. " No more orders. You are released. Good-bye ! "

THE RIFT OF DAWN IN THE TRENCHES ON THE BATTLE-LINE.
This impressive picture was taken in one of the trenches in France when a sentry stood guard over his fellows who were sleeping after a stiff and exhausting fight on the day before. On this occasion they had been allowed to sleep undisturbed through the night, instead of having the frequent experience of having to rouse themselves and spring to their rifles to make or repel an attack.

GERMAN "COMMERCE DESTROYER" DESTROYED.

"Bravo, Highflyer!"—In these two words, sent by wireless, the British Admiralty conveyed their congratulations to the British light cruiser Highflyer after the successful attack on the Kaiser Wilhelm der Grosse on August 27th, 1914, off the West Coast of Africa. The photograph shows the German ship, a Norddeutscher Lloyd liner of 14,349 tons, which was converted into a "commerce destroyer" as soon as war was declared, after the Highflyer's guns had finished her career and she was about to disappear for ever beneath the Atlantic waves.

The people on board the Galician, it is hardly necessary to say, were vastly relieved by this sudden change in their prospects, even though at first they could make neither head nor tail of it. The cruiser went off at full speed, and was soon out of sight, while the Galician went about, and resumed her voyage to Teneriffe.

Arriving there two days later she learned that the wireless message which the Kaiser Wilhelm had interrupted with a threat to sink her had just gone far enough to indicate to two of our cruisers in the vicinity that a British ship was in danger somewhere to the south. They had, therefore, set off in that direction, endeavouring to get in touch with the Galician by means of wireless. That ship, of course, did not receive the messages, but they were picked up by the German, who must have come to the conclusion that the British ships were getting too near to be comfortable, and much too near to allow of the people being taken off the Galician prior to that ship being sunk.

FLOATING DOCK AT TSING-TAU.

Germany expended vast sums on the equipment of Kiao-Chau, her colony in China, of which Tsing-Tau is the port, which Japan began to blockade on August 24th, 1914.

Other escapades of the Wilhelm der Grosse Another British ship, the Arlanza, was also stopped and released by the Kaiser Wilhelm der Grosse, but there were two which did not come so well out of the meeting. On August 16th the New Zealand Shipping Company's steamer Kaipara, from Monte Video, was approaching the Canaries cautiously, having, like the Galician, been warned of possible enemies, when, in the early morning, the Kaiser Wilhelm der Grosse was sighted in chase. As before, an attempt was made to use the wireless apparatus, but again came the threat from the German ship: "If you use your wireless, I will use my guns."

The warning was effective, and the captors proceeded about their business without the least delay. A boat put off, and the Kaipara was boarded. Her wireless was smashed, explosives were placed in the hold, and the crew ordered to take their belongings, get into the boats, and go aboard the Kaiser Wilhelm. When the last man had got aboard the cruiser opened fire. Fifty-three shots were sent into the Kaipara, and at half-past twelve she sank. The captured crew were treated with the utmost courtesy. One of the officers, when he had a chance later on of telling of his experiences, said: " We were provided with some of the saloon berths, and the Germans were most polite to us. It was evident that they did not altogether relish their task. The commander remarked that it was a painful proceeding for him to have to sink our vessel, as it appeared to be wanton destruction of valuable property." However, this did not prevent him from carrying out **Sinking of the Kaipara and Nyanga** his orders to the best of his ability, for within a few hours of the sinking of the Kaipara another British ship, the Nyanga, was rounded up and treated in exactly the same fashion. Having accomplished this, the Kaiser Wilhelm der Grosse went into Rio del Oro Bay, in Spanish territory, on the West African coast,

where she coaled from a German tramp steamer, the Duala, which had been disguised to represent as closely as possible a Union Castle liner. She then proceeded to sea and cruised about for a week, without, however, doing any further damage, the reason being partly, no doubt, that her exploits had scared British shipping off the route. On August 27th she had again to put into Rio del Oro

SOME INTERESTING UNITS OF THE GERMAN NAVY.
The German gunboat Panther, seen in the top picture, was the ship sent out by the Kaiser to Agadir during the historic dispute about Morocco in July, 1911, and it was erroneously reported sunk in the Mediterranean on August 2nd, 1914. In the middle picture we see the German Dreadnought Helgoland, completed in 1911, a battleship of 21,000 tons displacement and twelve 12 in. guns, and below is the small cruiser Bremen, a 23-knot boat of 3,250 tons, completed in 1904, which proved of some little use to Germany in the early stage of the war in chasing and harassing British merchantmen.

to coal, being met this time by the colliers Magdeburg, Bethania, and Arucas; and it was here that she came to the end of her adventurous career. What happened can best be described in the words of Chief-Officer Wilde, of the Kaipara, who was still a prisoner on board.

" I think it was on the Wednesday, about half-past twelve, while the Kaiser Wilhelm was coaling, that we heard the boatswain piping, and the men rushed up on deck with pistols and bayonets. A petty officer, who spoke English, remarked to me, ' You'll be all right by-and-by I think it's a British cruiser.' Nothing happened, and coaling was resumed shortly afterwards, the impression being that there had been a false alarm. At two-thirty, however, the captain-lieutenant came to us and said: Gentlemen, you will please go to the collier at once A British cruiser is going to open fire.' We got what clothes we could and jumped aboard the collier Arucas.

The end of a great liner

" Orders were also given to a large number of officers and men of the Kaiser Wilhelm to board the colliers.

THROWING OVERBOARD ALL INFLAMMABLE LUXURIES WHEN A BATTLESHIP IS CLEARED FOR ACTION.

When battleship decks are cleared for action their cabins must be denuded of unnecessary woodwork, lest a hostile shell burst near and start a dangerous fire. From one of the big ships that, early in August, began the blockade of the German North Sea coast, fully one thousand pounds' worth of handsome furniture, including two pianos and an organ, was flung overboard into the North Sea. The officers' quarters principally suffered. To use the phrase of a sailor who assisted at the sacrifice, " It was like throwing a gentleman's drawing-room into the sea."

They did so, and as they jumped from the Kaiser Wilhelm many of them threw their arms into the sea. Suddenly the British cruiser, which proved to be the Highflyer, opened fire, and the Kaiser Wilhelm replied. The Arucas was still made fast to the Kaiser Wilhelm, and the shells whizzed over our heads. The first shot gave us a bit of a shock, but we soon got accustomed to it, and our men conducted themselves with great coolness.

"I took charge of the wheel of the collier for a time, and gradually we moved away from the doomed vessel, which never had a chance against the cruiser, owing to the short range of her guns. We could see the shells from the Kaiser Wilhelm dropping short. One of the Highflyer's first shots disabled the German's port quarter gun and took part of the bridge away. I think the Arucas was about eleven miles away when the Kaiser Wilhelm went down, so that we did not see her sink. Before we had got under way, and while the shells were passing over our heads, some amusement was caused in the Arucas by one of our number impersonating a bookie and asking for bets on the result of the shooting. The Bethania, on board which were a number of the Kaiser Wilhelm's crew, was hit amidships by one of the shells from the Highflyer. The Arucas made for Las Palmas, where we joined the Inanda and sailed for London the same day."

THE MAGDEBURG, A SMALL GERMAN CRUISER
of 4,550 tons, ran ashore at the entrance to the Gulf of Finland on August 27th, 1914, and was blown up by her captain.

The Kaiser Wilhelm was a much heavier vessel than the Highflyer, displacing over 14,000 tons as against the British cruiser's 5,600 ; but the latter was armed with eleven 6 in. guns as against the German vessel's ten 4·1 in., and had a further advantage in having been built specially for war purposes and in catching the Kaiser Wilhelm at a moment when she was unprepared. Indeed, had the ships met at sea the Highflyer would, in all probability, have failed to account for the German liner, since the latter was appreciably faster and could have shown a clean pair of heels. As it was, however, the Highflyer had rendered excellent service. She had suffered practically no damage herself, and lost only one man killed and five slightly wounded ; while she had sent to the bottom the only hostile vessel believed to be at large on that particular trade route.

The Admiralty sent a congratulatory message to Captain H. T. Buller, of the Highflyer, in which they paid a tribute to the considerate manner in which the men of the lost ship had carried out their work.

THE GERMANIA,
yacht owned by head of the Krupp concern, had come before the war to the Solent and was detained at Southampton by order of the British Prize Court.

THE KOENIGSBERG, 3,400-TON GERMAN CRUISER
that attacked and sunk the small British cruiser Pegasus when the latter was at anchor refitting in the harbour of Zanzibar, on September 20th, 1914.

The message ran : "Bravo. You have rendered a service, not only to Britain, but to the peaceful commerce of the world. The German officers and crew appear to have carried out their duties with humanity and restraint, and are therefore worthy of all seamanlike consideration." Prisoners of war would have been perfectly certain of receiving this consideration from British seamen. One of the most

Lowering a boarding boat. The crew are armed with cutlass and pistol. They board suspicious craft and examine papers, holds, and so on.

It takes a matter of two minutes for the boat, which is in charge of a lieutenant-commander, to be lowered and manned.

The boat remains alongside while the officer and part of the crew search the suspected craft.

Finding everything on the foreign trawler satisfactory, the boarding boat returns. These boats include interpreters in their crew.

Morning service on a man-of-war is attended daily by officers and men. The prayers are printed on large cards. Inset: Keeping the sailors fit. They run round the deck, an officer leading the way, every morning after prayers.

WITH A BRITISH CRUISER IN THE NORTH SEA IN WAR TIME.

striking effects of the sinking of the Kaiser Wilhelm der Grosse was an immediate drop of twenty-five per cent. in the insurance rates for ships trading to and from South African and South American ports

An interesting sequel to this action occurred about a fortnight later, when the British warship Vindictive, patrolling the Western Atlantic, took into Kingston, Jamaica, as a prize of war, the Hamburg-Amerika liner Bethania, one of the ships from which the Kaiser Wilhelm had been coaling when she was surprised by the Highflyer. Most of the four hundred men on board proved to have been those who had left the armed ship on the approach of the cruiser (the British soldiers on board the former were, by the way, retaken), and from them it was learned that the Bethania had left Barry on July 10th, arriving at Genoa on the 25th. She left a few days later " for the west coast of South America "; but if that was in reality her intended destination she received wireless orders to modify her programme, and became a floating coal-depot for German commerce marauders.

In laying their plans for a war with Great Britain our enemies had to give

AUSTRIAN SIEGE-GUNS FOR BELGIAN FORTS.
The importance of the thorough conquest of Belgium, from the German point of view, was evidenced by their call upon Austria for assistance when the latter country was being so sorely pressed by the Russians in Galicia. The great siege-gun seen here in its several sections—its motor-tractor (on the right), its gun carriage with recoil apparatus (in the centre waggon), and the gun itself (on the left)—is a formidable engine of war, which is fortunately not easily mobile, and is therefore almost impossible for use in field work. The upper picture shows the gun without its mounting, and a number of Austrian officers.

much careful consideration to the situation in which they were placed by their lack of coaling stations, and, as we have already seen, an attempt to overcome the difficulty was made by scattering depot ships all over the world. These vessels, which included many luxurious liners belonging to the great German shipping firms, were converted, some of them, into colliers. Some of them also carried stores of food, ammunition, and other things necessary for preserving the fighting efficiency of the German cruisers.

Every ship was given a settled programme, which was not to be deviated from except under pressure of superior force. Definite arrangements were made whereby a certain cruiser would be met at a certain place on a certain date by a ship carrying stores; and when the store-ships had exhausted their supplies they could return to a neutral port to replenish them, provided always that they were able to elude the British and French ships on the look-out for them. In the early stages of the war this plan was carried out with considerable success, although from the beginning it was clearly only a matter of time before the over-whelming superiority of the Franco-British naval forces would wear down and wipe

THE AUSTRIAN BATTLESHIP ZRINYI
of 14,500 tons, completed in 1911. The British and French naval strength in the Mediterranean prevented the Austrian Fleet from taking any aggressive part in the early stage of the war.

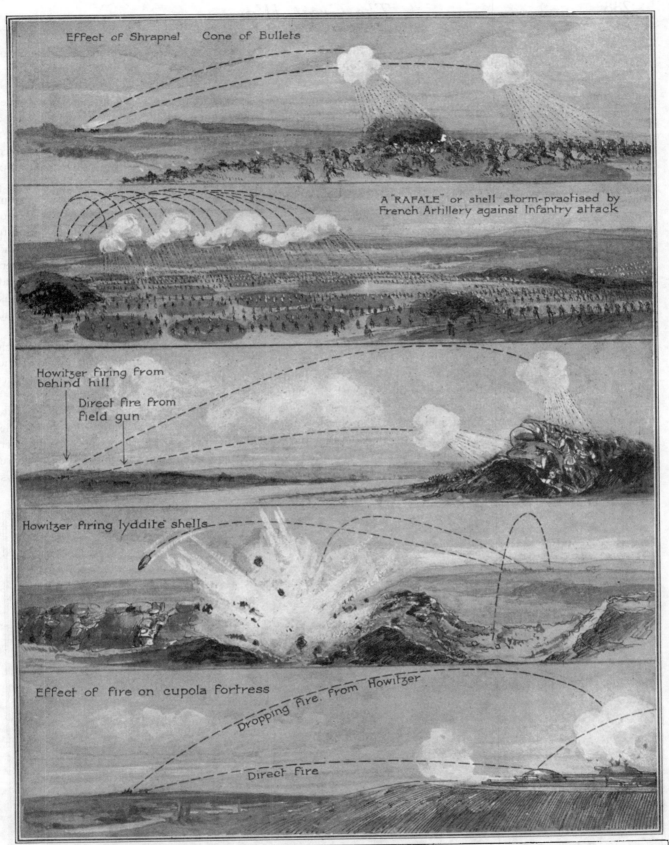

Effect of Shrapnel   Cone of Bullets

A "RAFALE" or shell storm-practised by French Artillery against Infantry attack

Howitzer firing from behind hill

Direct fire from field gun

Howitzer firing lyddite shells

Effect of fire on cupola fortress

Dropping fire from Howitzer

Direct fire

THE VARIOUS KINDS OF GUN-FIRE EMPLOYED IN MODERN ARTILLERY PRACTICE.

First diagram : Shrapnel-fire on advancing infantry. The shells are timed to explode, when once the range is found, at a certain distance ; it is unnecessary for them to hit an object. Second diagram : Shell-storm practised by French artillery. Fired at a high angle, the shells burst in mid-air over the advancing troops. Third diagram : A comparison between the effects of howitzer and field-gun fire on men in trenches. The howitzer fires at a high angle from behind a covering hill and drops its shell into the trenches ; the field gun, in the open, fires direct, and its shell bursts in front of the sandbags, and is therefore practically harm-

less. Fourth diagram : Howitzers firing against entrenchments high-explosive shells which burst only on contact. When a lyddite shell does hit its object the result is a terrific explosion. Great cavities are made in the ground, and for hundreds of yards round the actual point of contact the tremendous shock is felt. Fifth diagram : Howitzer and field-gun fire on a cupola fortress. Howitzers are the only effective weapons against such fortresses ; howitzer shells drop on to the iron covering of the cupola and reduce it to scrap iron. The field gun fires direct, and if it strikes the cupola the projectile simply delivers a glancing blow and rebounds.

out every German ship on the seas	The fate of the Kaiser Wilhelm der Grosse and the Bethania are instances of what was to be expected, not all at once, but ultimately.

A similar position arose on one occasion early in the war in the Western Atlantic	On August 7th the armoured cruiser Suffolk discovered the German light cruiser Karlsruhe coaling at sea from the Norddeutscher Lloyd liner Kronprinz Wilhelm.	Unfortunately, the German ship had ample warning of the Suffolk's approach, and, having a greater superiority in speed (she was designed for twenty-eight knots as against the British ship's twenty-three), was able to slip away.	The Suffolk at once sent a wireless message to the Berwick and the Bristol, which joined her in the chase.	The Berwick, however, was no faster than the Suffolk, but the Bristol, a twenty-five knot ship, began to draw ahead of them.

The Karlsruhe was considerably faster than the Bristol, but as the latter got further and further away from
Escape by reason of higher speed
her consorts the German ship began to hang back, as though prepared to engage the Bristol in single combat.	Night was beginning to fall, and the sea was rough, making accurate shooting almost impossible.	Nevertheless, these two cruisers fought for half an hour, and although the Bristol was not hit once she claimed to have put several shells into the German.	Then, however, the Suffolk and Berwick came rapidly up, and the Karlsruhe again put on speed and ran.	The Bristol fired at the retreating ship with her forward 6 in. gun as long as she was within range, and when the Karlsruhe took refuge later in the neutral port of San Juan, Porto Rico, it was stated that her stern was riddled with shell, and that she had one of her after guns smashed, and eight men injured.

This was only one of the many incidents during the war which brought home the disadvantages under which our ships laboured through their inability to outreach German ships in speed.	It is certain that the whole of the German ships operating on the high seas would have been hunted down and sunk much more quickly than was actually the case if we had advanced step by step with Germany as she increased the speed of her cruisers.

Other German ships carrying supplies for the commerce raiders were captured or sunk in various places; but, apart from armed merchantmen, not a single German cruiser outside European waters was accounted for during the first seven weeks of the war.	Nevertheless, the damage they did was infinitesimal, and by the middle of September only twelve British ships had been sunk at sea.	On the other hand, German commercial shipping was everywhere held up.	Only in very few cases was it necessary for a British warship to sink a vessel, as there was nearly always a British port close handy into which the ship could be sent as a prize, a facility Germany did not enjoy.

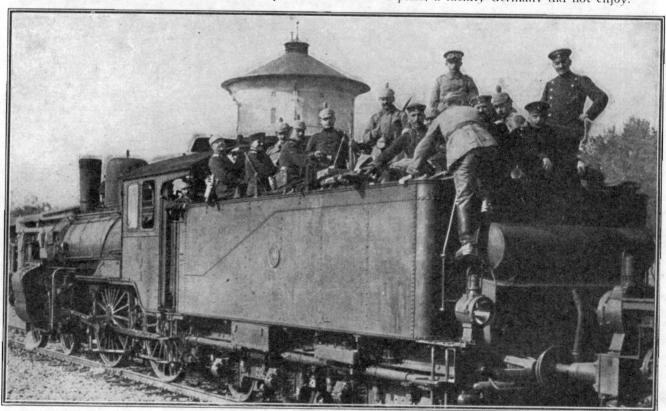

FROM BERLIN FOR THE EASTERN FRONTIER.
The Russian raid into East Prussia in August, 1914, caused the Kaiser's war lords to dispatch large bodies of troops eastwards in haste. The trains were crowded, and soldiers packed like sardines had to ride even in the engine-tenders and on top of the coal supply.

CHAPTER XVI.

RUSSIA'S STUPENDOUS TASK AND HER STUPENDOUS ARMY.

German High Policy—Origin of the Triple Alliance—The Dual Alliance—The German Problem of the War on Two Fronts— Kuropatkin's Work for Russia—Vast Extent of Russia's Dominions and the Difficulty of Attacking Her—The Country and Fortresses of East Prussia—The Military Value of German and Austrian Railways—Russia's Power of Defence and Attack—Germany's Naval Supremacy in the Baltic—System of Russian Conscription—Russia's Fighting Strength—Quality of the Russian Soldier—Russia's Military Leaders—The Tsar's Pledge to Poland.

THE German Empire, proclaimed in the old palace of the French Kings at Versailles in January, 1871, inherited the tradition of Prussian diplomacy, and a cardinal point in that tradition was friendship with Russia. To his dying day the aged Emperor William I. clung to this ideal, and as he lay on his death-bed almost his last word to his son and successor was a recommendation to "cultivate the friendship of the Tsar."

But even before Kaiser William I. passed away on March 9th, 1888, German policy had taken a new departure. The old Emperor had long ceased to be entirely master in his own house, and the direction of affairs was largely controlled by the arbitrary will of Prince Bismarck. At the Congress of Berlin, in 1878, the German Chancellor had sided with Lord Salisbury in opposing Russia's claim to parcel out the Balkan lands at her own good pleasure after the war with Turkey. Bismarck at the time protested that he was the best of friends to the Tsar, and that he was acting as " an honest broker " in effecting a compromise between the rival ambitions of Austria and Russia in the Balkan Peninsula in the interest of a lasting peace. But it was the beginning of a gradual drifting apart of the two neighbours who had so long been

M. SERGIUS SAZONOFF,
the Russian Foreign Minister, who played a great part in determining the policy of Russia during the last days of July, 1914. A dignified speaker, after the manner of Lord Lansdowne, he was formerly secretary to the Russian Embassy in London.

friends, and often allies. Within a twelvemonth of the Berlin Congress a treaty of alliance was signed between Germany and Austria. It was not published till nine years later, but, long before its publication, it was a secret known to half the world. The alliance was represented as a league of peace intended to prevent any disturbance of the existing state of affairs, either on the Danube or the Rhine, by Russian ambitions in the Balkan lands or the French longing for a reconquest of Alsace-Lorraine. Italy joined the league in 1886, and it thus became the Triple Alliance.

The treaty with Austria had no sooner been signed than Germany began quietly and unobtrusively to fortify her eastern frontier and develop her railway system in Pomerania, East Prussia, and the province of Posen. Russia replied by a gradual change in the peace stations of her Army, so as to keep the greater part of it permanently in garrisons and fortresses between Moscow and the Austro-German border. At the same time the relations between St. Petersburg and Paris became more and more friendly, and an *entente* developed into an alliance between France and Russia.

Long before this new treaty had been actually signed German statesmen and soldiers had recognised the practical certainty

RUSSIANS RIDE TO BATTLE WITH MUSIC AND SONG.
Many of the Russian regiments have vocal and instrumental orchestras that accompany the troops to battle in place of the regimental bands. The singers are specially trained, and with cymbals, bells, and other hand instruments accompany the martial and national songs they sing while marching along. The effect of this is most inspiring, and raises the ardour of the soldiers to a pitch that the music of an ordinary regimental band could not do.

that, in case of war with France on the Rhine, Russia would take the field as her ally. In German military literature of the last twenty-five years the problem of " the war on two fronts " is a frequent topic of debate. Germany realised that she must be ready to meet both a French advance towards the Rhine and a Russian march across the Vistula, in the event of her being involved in war with either of her neighbours. The accepted German theory of defence against this double attack was that the mobilisation and concentration of the Russian armies would lag behind that of the French ; that this would enable the main force of the German armies to be flung against France, with a fair prospect that a decisive battle would be fought on that side before the Russian pressure on the eastern frontier could become serious, and that the defence of this frontier might at the outset be safely entrusted to a small part of the German first-line troops, backed by Landwehr forces, and supported by the main mass of the Austrian Army.

The alliance with Italy was relied upon to remove all anxiety as to a hostile movement on the Italian frontiers of Austria, and to divert from the main front of operations in the west a portion of the French Army, which would be required to meet an Italian attack on the line of the Alps and along the Riviera.

In Russia there is less open discussion of military possibilities than in other countries. But we know something of the anticipations of the Russian Staff as to conflict with Germany and Austria from a remarkable document summarised by General Kuropatkin in his work, " The Russian Army and the Japanese War," published in 1909.

Kuropatkin's work for Russia

Kuropatkin was appointed Minister of War at St. Petersburg in 1898, and held that post until February, 1904, when he left Europe to take command of the Russian armies in the Far East against the Japanese. His first act as Minister of War was to arrange for the drawing up of an elaborate report on the condition of the Russian Army, and the defence of the various frontiers of the Empire, as well as on the opportunities existing in these regions for a counter-attack.

Among the passages from this report embodied in his book there is a very full summary of his views as to the possibilities of military action on the Austro-German frontiers. These are of special interest now that

Russia has had to put forth her strength in this very direction.

Here in Great Britain it has been the fashion to speak as if an attack on this eastern frontier of the Central European Powers would be a comparatively easy matter for the huge armies of the Tsar. The "Russian steam-roller" has become a favourite phrase of the journalists, a popular suggestion of a huge moving mass crushing down every obstacle to its advance.

But Kuropatkin, in his official report from the War Ministry, dated 1900, frankly recognises that the obstacles on this western frontier of Russia are of the most serious character, and speaks of the failure of a Russian advance upon it as quite possible. He had no illusions as to the difficulties of the task that would be imposed upon an army operating in this direction.

To understand the conditions of the military problem, and to follow with intelligent interest the record of the campaign in Eastern Europe, one must have some clear ideas about the forces that Russia could place in the field, and the character of the region in which they had to operate.

THE WONDERFUL HORSE OF THE WONDERFUL COSSACK.
More than half the reputation of the Cossack should be credited to his horse, a small animal, short of limb and neck, but a wonderful stayer, thriving on poor food, docile, intelligent, indifferent to weather and ignorant of the luxury of a stable. On forced marches he can carry three men, one on each stirrup and one in the saddle, as seen in the picture.

Everyone knows that Russia is beyond all comparison the most extensive State in Europe, but few realise the enormous size of her territory. When a traveller from England on his way to Moscow reaches the frontier station at Wirballen he feels he is nearing his journey's end, for at last he is on Russian ground. But he is still actually nearer his starting point on the Continent at Ostend than he is to Moscow, and when he reaches that city he is still only half way across European Russia. Once only in the whole course of history has a western conqueror marched into the heart of Russia and seized the Holy City of Moscow. That was when Napoleon dated his bulletin of victory from the Kremlin in 1812, and his success, such as it was, proved his ruin.

Great extent of Russian territory

Her vast extent, and the ease with which wide tracts of country can be laid waste before an advancing enemy by the mere firing of wooden villages and barns, still make Russia secure against any far-reaching scheme of foreign invasion. Only her coasts and her frontier provinces are open to attack

The Russian land frontier towards Austria and Germany is 1,500 miles long. The greater part of this extended line is the frontier of Russian Poland. The province projects westward from the main mass of the Russian territory like a huge bastion wedged in between German lands on the north and west and Austrian

OFFICERS IN THE RUSSIAN ARMY AT RELIGIOUS SERVICE IN A PUBLIC SQUARE BEFORE GOING TO WAR.
The soul of Russia was stirred to its depths by the attempts to bring the southern Slavs under the heel of the Germanic Empires, and every man in the Russian armies entered the campaign fired by religious zeal, taking up his weapons as a holy duty. The ceremony photographed here was most impressive, with all the dignity and solemnity of a sacrament.

on the south. A glance at a map of Europe will show that the Austrian province of Bohemia projects in much the same way into the lands of the German Empire. But Bohemia is a bastion ramparted with mountain walls. Russian Poland is a bastion merely marked out upon the ground without any natural barrier on any one of its three fronts. The line that divides Russia from her neighbours on this side is a purely artificial one, defined only by the posts set up at intervals along it for custom-house purposes. It is a political, not a natural frontier, marked out in somewhat arbitrary fashion when, after the turmoil of the Napoleonic wars, the map of Europe was being resettled at the Congress of Vienna.

ONE OF THE DREADED COSSACKS.

This Russian province and the adjacent borderlands are part of the great plain that, beginning in Northern Germany, stretches across European Russia to the Ural Mountains. Only on the south side of the Polish plain is there any high ground. Here the Austrian province is a sloping terrace at the base of the Carpathian Mountains, which divide these northern lowlands from the raised plain of Hungary.

Compared with the giant Alpine ranges, the Carpathians are hills rather than mountains. Along this Galician border they form a broad belt of forest-clad sandstone ridges, mostly under 5,000 feet high, traversed by a number of passes and hill roads, forming an admirable natural defence for Hungary. The

RUSSIAN PRIESTS BLESS THE ARMIES ABOUT TO MARCH TO THE FRONT.
Russians are much more given to the expression of religious feeling than the more reserved nations of the west, and a war sanctified by the approval of the Church in addition to being in accord with national sentiment is essentially a people's war. The blessing of the Church is a ceremony that lends the Russian soldier the zeal of a fanatic, and all history shows that such zeal gives a formidable strength to an army.

AUSTRALASIA
ANSWERS THE CALL OF EMPIRE

New Zealand
Volunteer (Sergeant).

AUSTRALIAN CADETS INSPECTED BY LORD KITCHENER AT BISLEY.

New Zealand
Volunteer (Private).

THE AUSTRALIAN LIGHT HORSE.

GROUP OF AUSTRALIAN OFFICERS.

THE VICTORIA LIGHT HORSE AT KILMORE, NORTH OF MELBOURNE.

OFFICERS AND MEN OF
THE AUSTRALIA.
The Australia is a sister ship of
the Indefatigable and New
Zealand, with a displacement of
19,200 tons and a speed of
twenty-six knots.

H.M.A.S. AUSTRALIA, THE FLAGSHIP OF THE AUSTRALIAN NAVY.
The Australia carries eight 12 in. guns, sixteen 4 in. guns, and three 21 in. torpedo-tubes.
Her commander is Rear-Admiral Sir George Edwin Patey, seen above.

From the painting by]

FLEET OF THE AUS
Together with its flagship the batt
the protected cruisers Melbourne,

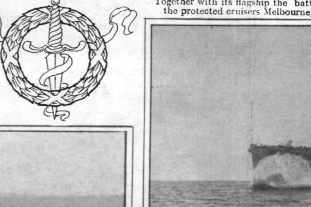

H.
The three protected cruisers, Melbo
were included in the 1911 program

THE 23RD ARMY MEDICAL CORPS OF THE 6TH MILITARY DISTRICT—TASMANIA.
In 1911 the Australian Government adopted a defence scheme based on Lord Kitchener's recommendations.

The King's Message to his great Ov
Dominions on September 10th 1914
tained these words :

"Paramount regard for treaty faith
the pledged word of rulers and peop
the common heritage of Great Britai
of the Empire. My peoples in the
Governing Dominions have shown be
all doubt that they wholeheartedly en
the grave decision which it was nece
to take."

The endorsement took the practica
of ships, men, and money. The sponta
and the enthusiasm displayed by

THE CREW OF THE AUSTRALIA.
The complement of the Australia consists of eight hundred officers and crew, and her commander is Admiral of the Australian Fleet.

NWEALTH AT SEA.
alia, the Australian Navy includes risbane, and six destroyers.

[A. J. W. Burgess.]

NE.
risbane, all sister ships of 5,600 tons, of the "Royal Australian Navy."

ns of the Oversea Dominions in the of treaty rights, national honour, Imperial defence soon showed that d the fighting-line there stood solid great Empire scattered throughout even seas.
stralia and New Zealand, in addition ising contingents for assistance in pe, took strong action in their own of the world. On August 29th a force New Zealand occupied German Samoa, on September 25th Australians an ced their occupation of the seat of nment of Kaiser Wilhelm Land, in an New Guinea.

H.M.S. NEW ZEALAND, A BATTLE-CRUISER OF THE BRITISH GRAND FLEET.
A sister ship of the Australia, the New Zealand was provided by the Government of the island Dominion. The portrait is that of Captain Lionel Halsey, her commander.

PARADE OF AUSTRALIAN TROOPS IN MELBOURNE BEFORE THE WAR.
Military conscription prevails in Australia and the total strength of all classes of military service is almost 200,000 men.

RUSSIAN COSSACKS CHARGE THE GERMAN DEATH'S HEAD HUSSARS IN EAST PRUSSIA, AUGUST 26th, 1914.

On the evening of August 26th, 1914, Mr. R. W. Ames, the British manager of a large estate in East Prussia, witnessed through his field-glasses a battle between 10,000 Germans and 15,000 Russians at a place named Schwansfeld, between Korschen and Bartenstein. The Cossack cavalry charged the German Death's Head Hussars full tilt. There was a tremendous impact, and hand-to-hand fighting, and then, all parties. This picture was drawn from a personal description given to the artist by Mr. Ames. Towards Bartenstein the German line began with one accord to retreat. At the same battle Russian infantry, after an artillery bombardment, charged with the bayonet and cut the Germans up in small cavalry fled, with the Cossacks pursuing and killing them in large numbers.

province of Galicia, the Polish territory of the Austrian Empire, lies outside this natural rampart, and is thus a terraced slope descending to the northern plain that stretches from its margin to the shores of the Baltic.

Across the plain winds the broad, sluggish stream of the Vistula. The great river is to this eastern land what the Rhine is to Western Europe. Frozen or encumbered with drift ice in the winter months, it is during the rest of the year a main highway of traffic, navigable for the greater part of its course, and bearing on its waters huge rafts of timber from the forests, and scores of steamers with strings of lumbering barges trailing astern of them. On its banks, in the midst of the plain, stands Warsaw, the old capital of Poland, and now the political, military, and business centre of the Russian province.

Russia's natural and political frontiers

There is only one other large town in Russian Poland—Lodz, not long ago a country village, but now a busy industrial centre, with its high-street six miles long, and right and left of it in short side streets tall factory buildings. This paucity of large towns is characteristic, not only of Russian Poland, but of the whole Empire. The last census shows that in European Russia there are only twenty-four places that claim a population of over a hundred thousand. Russia is a country of agricultural villages. There are more than 150,000 of them between the Vistula and the Ural.

The plain of the Vistula is not an absolute dead level, but there is nothing that can be called a hill. The ground undulates in long, flat-topped waves, and in the hollows run the many tributary streams and lesser rivers

TYPE OF RUSSIAN HOWITZER AT PRACTICE FIRING.
Russian experience in her great war with Japan taught the Tsar's military advisers some lessons which, though bitter, were profitable, and one direct result was a great improvement in the Russian artillery arm, both in the guns themselves and in the gun practice.

that feed the great waterway—streams as sluggish as the Vistula itself, and often with low, marshy banks that are flooded in the time of rains. There are wide stretches of woodlands, the refuge of the insurgent bands in the Polish risings of 1830 and 1863. Between the woods are open lands with many villages, rich lands with a deep soil, somewhat primitively tilled.

The northern part of this plain of the Vistula belongs to Prussia. Here the lands of the German Empire interpose between Russian Poland and the Baltic. The border district between the Narev River and the frontier line is a region of marshy forests; then inside the German frontier line is the region of

The marsh lands of East Prussia

the Masurian Lakes. This is a land of innumerable lakes and pools, with belts and clumps of fir and beech woods, occupying much of the land between their swampy margins. In the clearings by the lakes and in the woodlands there are the red-walled villages, for there is plenty of clay for brick-making. In fact, the clayey soil accounts for the abundance of lakes and pools.

Beyond this wilderness of lake and wood there is a slight rise of the ground along the Baltic shore between the low-lying delta of the Vistula and the mouth of the River Pregel. This belt of higher and firmer land was in old times the main highway between Northern Germany and Muscovy. The great lagoon of the Frisches Haff lies

THE GREAT WAVE OF RUSSIA'S MANHOOD BEGINS TO ROLL WESTWARD.
The mobilisation of the Russian armies was rapid beyond all expectation, and Russia was able to press over Germany's eastern frontier and cause an easing of the pressure of German activity in Northern France much sooner than Germany had thought possible.

between the river mouths, and at each end of it is a famous city. Dantzic, on the Vistula delta, is a great port, once a city of the famous Hansa League of trading republics, later the chief port of Poland, now Germany's main trading post on the Baltic—a city that keeps much of its old-world look, thanks to the quaint gabled houses, built centuries ago, in its narrow streets. By the branches of the Vistula and the land-locked expanse of the Frisches Haff, Dantzic has a safe inner waterway to the Pregel where by the river mouth stands old Königsberg,

German citadels in East Prussia

once a mere blockhouse fort of the Teutonic knights against the wild Slavs to the eastward, now a fortress of the Prussian kingdom, whose history is closely linked with that of Königsberg (" the King's Hill "), the place where the Prussian kings were crowned.

Dantzic and Königsberg together form the citadel of Germanic power in this Baltic coast region. Königsberg is surrounded with a circle of strong forts, and further guarded by the inundations fed by the stream of the Pregel. Its communications with Dantzic along the Frisches Haff are guarded by the batteries of Pillau, at the entrance of the great sea lagoon. Dantzic has its bastioned ramparts and outlying forts, and to the seaward is protected by the new fortress of Weichselmünde (" the Vistula mouths "). The road and railway crossings of the Vistula delta are guarded by the fortified towns of Dirschau and Marienburg, and on this side much of the flat land can be easily laid under water. Along its lower course the Vistula is a German river. Where it leaves Russian

Poland it is guarded by the first-class fortress of Thorn. Here the far-flung circle of strong forts covers a great railway junction. Half-way between Thorn and the fortifications of Dantzic and the delta is the fortress of Graudenz.

This fortified line of the Vistula, with the advanced post of Königsberg, forms the armed barrier of East Prussia. In front of the line the country is difficult for an invader in an autumn campaign. Behind the Masurian

Lakes and woods a level plain extends towards the lower Vistula. It is a region famous in history as the scene of Napoleon's victories at Eylau and Friedland. The story of that campaign tells how, when the autumn rains were followed by alternate frost and thaw, the country became a quagmire. Any movement of troops was impossible. It became difficult even to feed the armies, for the transport waggons sank to their axle-trees in mud, and had to be abandoned.

THE TSAR INSPECTING THE RUSSIAN RED CROSS.
Accompanied by Red Cross nurses, the Tsar is here seen inspecting hospital workers before they left for the German frontier. The picture above shows Russian infantry marching along the railway line.

A SWIFT CHARGE BY A DETACHMENT OF RUSSIAN CAVALRY.

A snapshot, taken at the Russian military manœuvres, showing a troop of cavalry taking up a position. No army in recent years has made such progress as the Russian, and none has troops of better fighting quality.

Thorn belongs both to the northern chain of defences and to those of the German centre facing Russian Poland. The line is prolonged southward by the great fortress of Posen, and the fortified places of Glogau, Breslau, and Neisse in Silesia. Austria supplies the right of the great semicircle of fortresses. The citadels of her defence of Galicia are Cracow and Przemysl. The former was once the second city of the old Polish kingdom. The latter is a purely military post, with practically no civilian population. It is a village converted into a fortress.

This chain of fortresses, extending over a front of over a thousand miles, is not, however, the only defence of the frontier. Within the last few years a number of positions have been prepared for defence by entrenchments between these permanent works, and even more important from a military point of view has been the development of the railway system. The time is long past when soldiers regarded a mere line of fortresses as constituting a safe protection for a frontier. Passive defence is **Military importance of railways** doomed to eventual failure, and counter-attack is the best means of beating off an assailant. A blow is better than a parry. And a well-developed railway system along a frontier, and immediately in rear of it, makes it possible for the defence to concentrate rapidly a striking force on any desired point.

General Kuropatkin, in his report on the military situation on the Russo-Polish frontier, dwelt upon the

admirably-developed railway system of Germany and Austria as the chief factor of its strength. He compared it with the backward railway system of Russia in order to bring out clearly the advantage that Russia's possible enemies would possess in a war on this border of the Tsar's Empire. Since he wrote, in 1900, something has been done by Russia to improve the railways of the Polish frontier land, but the Germans and Austrians have been busy in the same direction, and most of what he wrote still holds good.

We shall see, in the German defence of East Prussia, what effective use was made in at least one instance of the railway system which Kuropatkin thus described. If he overestimated the force Germany could move to the front at the outset, this was because he purposely left out of account the detaining effect of the French alliance in a study of Russia's own resources for defence and attack. He thus summed up the situation:

TROOPS OF THE TSAR PHOTOGRAPHED IN GALICIA.

This photograph, which reached London via Stockholm, shows a detachment of the Russian army that operated in the Lemberg district of Galicia. The upper photograph, taken in Russia, illustrates a Russian army motor squadron before leaving for the scene of war.

" By the expenditure of vast sums of money, Germany has made ready in the most comprehensive sense to march rapidly across our borders with an army of one million men. She has seventeen lines of railway (twenty-three tracks) leading to our frontiers, which would enable her to send to the front more than five hundred troop trains daily. She can concentrate the greater part of her armed forces on our frontier within a few days of the declaration of war : while, apart from this question of speedy mobilisation, she has at her command far greater technical resources, such as light railways, artillery, ordnance, and engineering stores, particularly for telegraphs, mobile siege parks, etc., than we have. She has also made most careful preparation for a determined defence of her own border provinces, especially those of Eastern Prussia.

German war preparations on her eastern border " The first-class fortresses of Thorn, Königsberg, and Posen are improved yearly, entrenched camps are built at the most important junctions, and material lies ready stacked for the rapid semi-permanent fortification of field positions. The crossing places on the Vistula have been rapidly placed in a state of defence, as have also the various towns and large villages. The whole population, indeed, is making ready for a national struggle.

" In the matter of railway development the Austrians have also left us far behind. While they, by means of eight lines of rail (ten tracks), can run two hundred and sixty trains up to the frontier every twenty-four hours, we can only convey troops up to the same point on four lines. As any of their troops on the frontier would be in advance of the Carpathians, this range was formerly looked upon as an obstacle to retirement, and to communication between Galicia and the rest of Austria. But in the last ten years it has been pierced by five lines of railway, and preparations have been made to lay three more."

THE " LITTLE FATHER " OF ALL THE RUSSIAS INSPECTING ONE OF HIS REGIMENTS.
It is commonly believed that the Russian Army is a host of giants. As a matter of fact, the average Russian soldier is shorter than our own, five feet four probably being a generous allowance of height for the whole army ; five feet being the infantry minimum, and five feet three that of the cavalry. The Russian soldier, however, is more thickly built and heavier and slower than our own. Seventy per cent. of Russian conscripts cannot read or write when they join the army.

The railways running directly to the frontiers are linked up by cross lines, facilitating the movement of troops along the wide curve from Przemysl to Dantzic and Königsberg. It must be noted that the extreme east of Galicia is left out of this scheme of combined railway and fortress defence. Even the great city of Lemberg was not permanently fortified.

Thus organised, this Austro-German frontier line, by its very configuration, offers striking advantages both for attack and defence. For the former there is the possibility of a converging march into Russian Poland. For the latter there is the advantage to the defending forces that whatever front of advance the Russians may select for their main attack they must at least provide a covering force to face the other two fronts of the encircling frontier. And defeat on either of these would bring the advance **Russian provision against counter-attack** upon the selected point of attack to a standstill.

Let us now see how Russia provided both for the defence of the Polish province and for a counter-attack against Austria and Germany.

Eastward of the Polish plain lies the wide region of marsh and pool traversed by the River Pripet and its numerous tributary streams. The " marshes of Pinsk " (or, to give them their alternative name, the " marshes of the Pripet ") extend over an area of some 300,000 square miles. Drainage works on a large scale were begun about 1894, and canals were being made through the marsh lands, with the result that portions of the district have been reclaimed, but even though railways have been carried across the district, the marshes still formed

THE TSAR
And Some of his Military Chiefs.

GENERAL BRUSSILOFF.
Decorated by the Tsar for his masterly
generalship at Kalitz.

THE GRAND DUKE NICHOLAS,
Commander-in-Chief of the Russian Armies.

GENERAL SUKHOMLINOFF,
the Russian Minister of War.

NICHOLAS II., EMPEROR OF ALL THE RUSSIAS,
Supreme Commander-in-Chief of the World's Greatest Army

GENERAL SAMSONOFF,
the brilliant Russian General who fell at
Osterode, in East Prussia, on August 31st, 1914.

GENERAL RUSSKY,
who captured Lemberg, the capital of Galicia,
from the Austrians on September 2nd, 1914.

GENERAL RENNENKAMPF,
the leader of the brilliant raid into East
Prussia in the early weeks of the war.

a region in which no army could operate, and they were thus a barrier dividing Western Russia into two separate theatres of war, the northern and the southern. South of the marshes the belt of territory by which the railways and roads from Southern Russia enter Poland is guarded by a group of three fortresses—Dubno, Rovno, and Lusk. West of the marshes, in the Polish plain itself, there is a still larger group of fortresses that forms the citadel of the Russian power in this direction, and the advanced base of operations against Germany and Austria.

These fortresses are Warsaw, Ivangorod, and Brest Litowski. Until after the rising of 1863, Warsaw was the only fortress in Poland, and its citadel was chiefly intended to serve as the stronghold of the garrison that overawed the Polish capital. When the Russian Staff took in hand the reorganisation of the frontier defences on a large plan, Warsaw was converted into a modern fortress with its girdle of advanced forts, and purely military stations of the same type of fortification were

The great fortresses of Poland

erected at Ivangorod and Brest, with a third fortress — Novo Georgievsk — a few miles north-west of Warsaw, at the confluence of the Vistula and its chief tributary the Narev.

The three fortresses and Warsaw are sometimes spoken of as the " Polish quadrilateral." A more correctly descriptive name for the group is " the Polish triangle," for Novo Georgievsk is really an outpost of Warsaw and the first of the line of fortified posts that guard the crossings of the River Narev. The fortresses of the " triangle," linked together by railway lines and good

A RUSSIAN REGIMENT AT DIVINE SERVICE: THE TSAR AT A HOSPITAL.
Officers and men of the Preobrejensky Regiment at a religious service held prior to their departure for the front. The Russian soldiers, regarding the great conflict as a holy war, had no fear of death while taking part in it. Each company has its song-leader, who marches in front and " gives out the hymns," receiving special pay. Inset : The Tsar, with nurses and soldiers, at a Petrograd hospital.

A SCENE IN THE RUSSIAN MOBILISATION.

The countries of Western Europe consist largely of cities. Russia, on the other hand, is a country of villages—there are more than 150,000 in European Russia alone—and these were called upon to give up their manhood for holy war against Teuton aggression. The lower picture shows the Holy Tree of Maria Remele, near Budapest, hung with ikons of the Orthodox Greek Church by the quaking inhabitants of the district to propitiate the Russian hordes.

roads, and at the apex of the whole Russian railway system towards the west, form a fortified region, the citadel of the Russian power on its Austro-German frontier. Two of the fronts look towards Germany, the third towards Austria, thus presenting a line of defence towards each section of the enemy's frontiers.

But the purpose of this vast entrenched camp is not entirely or even primarily defensive. It is the fortified base of operations for the army of Russian Poland. Within the triangle huge accumulations of supplies of every kind have been gradually collected, and the railways are provided with extensive sidings and long detraining platforms at the stations. Russia, too, recognises that attack is the best form of defence.

To guard the communications of the fortified "triangle" with Northern Russia, and to protect the country north of the Pripet region from a German invasion from East Prussia, the line of the Narev, east of the frontier forest lands, has been selected for defence. The marshy banks of the river render it difficult to cross except at certain well-known points. At these every bridge is covered by fortifications.

Defences for lines of communication

These permanently-protected river crossings are at Novo Georgievsk, Zegrje, Pultusk, Rozan, and Ostrolenka. The line of defence is prolonged north-eastward by the fortified towns of Lomza, Ossovetz, Bielostok, Grodno, and Kovno, the last two on the Niemen.

This line of fortified positions not only secures the crossings of an unbroken series of waterways, marking out a line of defence against East Prussia, but also covers two lines of railways running from the north-east into Russian Poland. These protected railways enable a concentration to be made at any selected point for an advance across the rivers into East Prussia in the direction of Königsberg. Here a double attack on converging lines is possible if Russia could assemble her forces rapidly enough and in sufficient numbers to invade East Prussia both from the Niemen and from the Polish triangle.

Before estimating the resources of Russia for attack, a word must be said about the influence of the naval situation on the land campaign. It is obvious that if Russia had full command of the Baltic Sea it would be possible to combine coast attacks with the land operations, and this would be a serious matter for the German generals charged with defence of the long belt of territory between the Russian border and the shores of the Baltic.

But in the opening stages of the Great War the command of the sea in this eastern theatre of operations was in the hands of Germany. This much gain she reaped from the creation of her battle-fleet. The Russian Navy—almost completely destroyed in the war with Japan—had been very dilatory in the work of reconstruction. At the outbreak of the war there was no Russian fleet in the waters of the Baltic that could venture to challenge the sea-power of Germany.

The British fleets were fully occupied in guarding the North Sea; and it would have been playing into the enemy's hands to detach any large force on such a mission as the passage of the narrow " Belts " that give access to the landlocked sea, passing through mine-strewn straits to meet the force that the Kiel Canal would enable Germany to concentrate more rapidly in the Baltic. The main Fleet of Britain could not be withdrawn from the North Sea, but Germany could have sent every one of her heaviest ships through the canal. It was therefore a necessity to leave her for a while the control of the Baltic. The Russian ships lay under the batteries of Cronstadt, their best use being to cover the approach to Petrograd and make it a dangerous matter for Germany to carry out a raid on Finland.

German naval supremacy in the Baltic

With the Germans thus in temporary command of the sea, it was necessary to keep a considerable force in Finland and about the northern capital. The German Fleet thus helped indirectly in the defence of the eastern frontier by diminishing the numbers immediately available for the attack upon it—one more instance of the far-reaching influence of sea-power.

THE DREAM OF POLAND TO BE REALISED.
The above picture is a reduced facsimile of the appeal issued to the Poles on August 16th, 1914, by the Grand Duke Nicholas, commander-in-chief of the Russian forces. The translation is on the right.

The task of the Russian armies was not merely to defend the western border of the Empire, not merely to attack the frontiers of Germany and Austria-Hungary, but to deliver this attack in such force and at such an early date as to defeat the German plan of first crushing France and then transferring a portion of the German armies to the eastern theatre of war. Russia aimed at exerting such serious and early pressure as would force the German Empire to divert a part of the force employed against France to the east in the first weeks of the campaign, thus indirectly helping to decide the conflict in Western Europe.

Reason for Russia's swift action

Proclamation by the Commander-in-Chief.

POLES !

"The hour has sounded when the sacred dream of your fathers and your grandfathers may be realised. A century and a half has passed since the living body of Poland was torn in pieces, but the soul of the country is not dead. It continues to live, inspired by the hope that there will come for the Polish people an hour of resurrection and of fraternal reconciliation with Great Russia. The Russian Army brings you the solemn news of this reconciliation, which obliterates the frontiers, dividing the Polish peoples, which it unites conjointly under the sceptre of the Russian Tsar. Under this sceptre Poland will be born again, free in her religion and her language. Russian autonomy only expects from you the same respect for the rights of those nationalities to which history has bound you.

"With open heart and brotherly hand Great Russia advances to meet you. She believes that the sword, with which she struck down her enemies at Gruenwald, is not yet rusted. From the shores of the Pacific to the North Sea the Russian armies are marching. The dawn of a new life is beginning for you, and in this glorious dawn is seen the sign of the Cross, the symbol of suffering and of the resurrection of peoples."

What was the force that the Tsar's generals might hope to place in line on the Niemen, the Narev, and the Vistula ? The military power of Russia, so far as mere numbers are a measure of such power, is the most formidable

SQUADRON OF RUSSIAN COSSACKS, EACH MAN OF WHICH PROVIDES HIS OWN HORSE.

CELEBRATING THE RUSSIAN VICTORIES IN GALICIA BEFORE THE WINTER PALACE, PETROGRAD.

RUSSIAN CAVALRY ON THE MARCH—THE POWER OF ENDURANCE OF BOTH MEN AND HORSES IS PROVERBIAL.

in Europe. But there has been not a little exaggeration about these numbers. Wild rumours circulated in the first days of the war that the Russians were mobilising " eight millions " of men. No serious authority on the subject has ever placed the armed forces of the Tsar's Empire at this enormous total.

Russia maintains three armies—the army in Europe, the army of Siberia and the Far East, and the army of the Caucasus and Central Asia. Her armies are recruited under a law of universal liability to military service, **Russian military strength** but this does not mean that every man serves in the Army or receives the training of a soldier. The numbers available each year are far beyond the limits of the existing organisation. The men that are wanted are taken by a principle of selection among those who have reached their twentieth year. The recruit then serves for three years in the infantry or artillery, and for four if he is allotted to the cavalry or engineers. He is then passed into the reserve. to which he belongs for fourteen or fifteen years, so as to make up a total service in the first line of eighteen years.

The soldier is about thirty-eight years of age when he has completed his active and reserve service. He is then borne for another five years on the rolls of the Militia or Territorial Army (the Opolchenie, to give it its Russian name). At forty-three he is at last free from any further obligation of military service. The Cossacks of the south serve under another system. A Cossack is liable to be called out for service as long as he has health and strength to bear arms.

If the whole of the annual contingent of men liable for service were enrolled in the Army there would be over 600,000 recruits to be armed, equipped, and trained each year, and with a three to four years' service there would be considerably over two million men permanently with the colours. No State could bear such a burden. As a matter of fact, the peace footing of all the armies of Russia

THE HEEL OF WAR IN BALTIC RUSSIA.
When the Germans raided the Aland Islands and bombarded Libau and Bona, the Russians destroyed the port and station of Hango, on the north shore of the Gulf of Finland, to prevent it falling into their hands. The station is seen burning in the upper picture, and in the lower is a photograph of the ruined port. These were among the earliest of camera records of actual war conditions in Russia.

united before the war reached about 1,700,000 men, which was an unusually large figure, and due to the retention of time-expired men with the colours. It is the European Army of Russia, with its reserves, that counts in the first weeks of a Polish campaign, owing to the remoteness of the armies in the Caucasus, Central Asia, and Siberia.

The first line of this Army is made up of twenty-seven army corps, a number of rifle brigades, and twenty cavalry divisions. Two of the army corps are formed of picked men with an extra standard of height, the " Guards Corps " at Petrograd, and the " Grenadier Corps " at Moscow. The other twenty-five army corps are each recruited from a province or group of provinces ; but as the bulk of the Army has its peace stations west of Moscow, many of these corps are not actually posted in their recruiting districts. The Guards and Grenadier Corps have each three infantry divisions ; the line corps have two each in peace and three in war. The war strength of a line corps is about 45,000 men, or, if a cavalry division is attached to it, about 50,000.

The regular cavalry is organised in twenty divisions (two of the Guard, fifteen of the line, two mixed divisions of Cossacks and line cavalry, and a Cossack division). This makes a force of about 80,000 sabres. Besides this there is the general levy of Cossack cavalry. The Cossack is bound to service through all his active life ; he is partly trained at home, partly at a military centre. But he is no longer the ragged, irregular spearman of the Napoleonic wars. He is a disciplined soldier, usually serving as a cavalryman. There are also Cossack batteries of artillery and Cossack rifle battalions.

THE TRAIL OF THE HUN ALONG THE RUSSIAN FRONTIER WAS THE SAME AS IN BELGIUM.

This special drawing, based upon authentic notes from Russia, depicts some stalwart soldiers of the Tsar standing aghast as they come upon a scene just left by retreating Germans, who had pursued the policy of terrorism taught them by their war lords from the Kaiser down— a policy that made the villages of industrious Belgium a monument of eternal shame that centuries of repentance, oceans of tears, and a hundred war indemnities could not hope to remove.

WHERE THREE EMPIRES MEET—AN HISTORIC CORNER OF EUROPE.

This is the meeting point of three great Empires—the Russian, the German, and the Austrian—and is known as "Three Emperors' Corner." The hither side of the River Przemsza is in Silesia, in Germany; on the far side is Galicia, in Austria; and Russia is in the background, beyond the tributary stream. The spot is north-east of Cracow.

Besides the troops of the first line, there are with the colours two other classes. First there are the "reserve troops." This is a somewhat misleading name, unless their purpose is explained, for they are not reservists. They are really the skeleton cadres (organisations of officers with a small contingent of men), kept up to form a basis for the mobilisation of some of the large numbers of men who, on a general mobilisation, are not required to bring the first-line troops up to war strength. In the same way, the "fortress troops" permanently stationed in the inland fortified places and at the coast defences are skeleton units that are brought up to full strength on a mobilisation.

It is quite true that, considering the long period of service in the reserve, an enormous number of reservists are not only available on paper, but really exist. It must be remembered, however, that even though the men for the rank and file are available, and have had some training in past years, an army of many millions cannot be created by a mere decree. All that can be done at the outset is to fill up the existing units with the colours and the skeleton cadres, and to supply the men called out with arms, equipment, and stores from the mobilisation depots. After this stage the possession of large reserves of men serves to fill up the gaps made by loss in battle, and by the wear and tear of the campaign, and at the same time enables new units to be gradually created.

Russian plan of mobilisation

The Russian plan of mobilisation includes (1) bringing the first-line army up to war strength; (2) embodying sufficient of the surplus reservists to form, on the basis of the existing reserve cadres, a number of reserve battalions, squadrons, and batteries; (3) bringing the skeleton units of the fortress troops up to full strength in the same way, from the older classes of reservists; (4) calling up a considerable force of Cossack cavalry; and (5) calling out the Territorials, or Militia, for local defence and the preservation of order, and to supply troops to hold the lines of communication of the field army.

A mobilisation on these lines would give about three million men, with some 6,000 guns, for the first-line army, though the whole of this force would not be available at once; for even though the peace stations are arranged to facilitate concentration, want of a fully organised railway system makes it necessary to give time for reservists to travel long distances to join their units, and concentration has to be made by a small number of main lines.

Probably in the first month of the war about a million and a half men would be pushed up to the actual front. One can only make rough estimates in such a case. But another million would rapidly become available. All the first line could not be sent to the front. It would be impossible entirely to strip Finland and the Petrograd and Moscow districts of all regular troops, and the garrisons of Poland would absorb some of the first-line men until the situation became quite clear.

In two ways the second-line troops would be of immediate help to the Army after a first success had made it possible to push forward into hostile territory. The fortress troops, whose numbers on mobilisation would rise to about a quarter of a million, would supply the siege train to Russian armies in the field, and could also mobilise a number of heavy batteries. The mobilisation tables include the formation of four hundred and fifty battalions of infantry and seventy-two squadrons of cavalry out of the Territorial Army—some 500,000 men. These could be moved up to guard the lines of communication, and the fortress troops would help, if necessary, by sending garrison detachments to hold captured fortresses of the enemy.

The field army would thus be kept up to its full fighting strength, by (1) receiving a constant stream of reservists, and (2) not having to leave any detachments in its rear as it pushed forward. In this way the second-line troops and the great mass of reservists available make the Russian Army a par-

ticularly formidable fighting force. We may estimate the field armies at two millions of men in the front line, with at least 500,000 more to support them and take charge of all the services in rear of the fighting-front.

In a long war the numbers of the active Army could be very considerably increased. It is estimated that, after completing the mobilisation, some two million reservists and territorials would still be available for further levies, all of them men who have had some Army service. Besides these, there would be at least seven million men of military age who had never been in the ranks. These large numbers are what lead some writers to tell of armies of six or eight million men mustering at the call of the White Tsar. But it must be remembered that it would be extremely difficult to find cadres of efficient leaders, officers and non-commissioned officers, for such enormous levies, and almost impossible to furnish them with the necessary proportion of batteries, manned by trained gunners. Even for the three or four millions that Russia should gradually be able to accumulate at the fighting-front, the difficulty of providing competent officers and sergeants for anything beyond the first-line units is a serious one —all the more serious because Russia is a country in which education is in a very backward state. In many of the provinces fifty per cent. of the adult population cannot read or write.

But, apart from this, there would be no real gain in putting

The enormous Russian reserves

GERMAN DESTROYERS LEAVING KIEL HARBOUR WITH A ZEPPELIN OVERHEAD.
The largest Zeppelins at the opening of the war were known to be capable of a speed of fifty-two miles an hour without any favouring wind, and to possess a radius of over twelve hundred miles, so that they could have made a return trip from Kiel or Heligoland over the North Sea, Great Britain, and the Irish Sea, to Dublin or Belfast.

MM

EXAMPLES OF THE TORPEDO-SHAPED GERMAN MONOPLANES.
This is a representative type of flying machine used by the German Army. The form of the body and the curve of the wings mark it out as different from the more common Etrich-taube type of machine, which was much favoured by German airmen. The pilot is controlling the engine, which is just about to start, and the observer is seen sitting behind.

armies of many millions into the field. Mere numbers do not give victory in war, for effective force and numbers are not the same thing. If half-trained multitudes are pushed to the front, the difficulty of supply increases to breakdown point ; and even if all needs of the men could be supplied, there is no front on which such vast armies could be brought into action. The presence of idle myriads behind the fighting-front is an encumbrance, not a gain, and the mere crowding of men up to the battle-line may be their destruction There comes a moment when Attila's grim words are true once more:

The thicker the grass, the easier we shall mow it down."

The Russian soldier is a good fighting-man. He is obedient, enduringly patient under trial, stolidly reckless of wounds and death, easily inspired with the idea that the war is something of a crusade, and thus animated by a touch, not of fanatic ardour, but of a quiet zeal for the work that will carry him through toil, danger, and hardship with an even mind. Long tradition, summed up in Suvaroff's famous saying, " The bullet is a fool—the bayonet counts," gives him a healthy longing to close with cold steel. A million and a half of such men are splendid material for a fighting force.

But then comes the question of leader ship It must be confessed that in recent wars the record of Russian generalship and Russian Army administration was disappointing In the war with Turkey the Russian army narrowly escaped destruction. In the war with Japan it had an unbroken

GERMAN AIRSHIP OF THE " PARSEVAL " TYPE.
This is an airship of the non-rigid type, and in this respect, as well as in many others it differs materially from the Zeppelin. At the opening of war Germany and her ally were the only countries possessing Zeppelins, but Britain, France, Russia, and Japan possessed airships of the type shown above.

TYPES OF GERMAN AEROPLANES WIDELY USED IN THE WAR.

It will be observed that seven of these flying-machines are monoplanes. They are of the famous "Taube" type—or, to give them their full title, "Etrich-Taube." Etrich was the name of their inventor, and "Taube" is the German word for dove. The unique feature of these machines is that they are constructed throughout of steel, giving them great rigidity. Of the three biplanes, or "doppel-deckers"— two on the extreme left and one second from the left at the back—one is of the "arrow" type.

record of failure, redeemed by the heroism of the men. Much has been done since the close of the war with Japan to improve the administration of the Army and raise the level of military education among the officers, but eight years is not a long time in which to effect any serious change in such a huge organisation. But there are, and always have been, brilliant soldiers in the upper grades of the Russian Army.

At the beginning of the Great War Russia possessed three leaders of high reputation—Rennenkampf, a cavalry general, and the commander of one of the subsidiary armies under Kuropatkin in the Japanese War; Samsonoff, who had also fought in the Far East, and had the reputation of a first-class military organiser; and Russky, a scientific soldier, with a good record as a teacher of the art of war in the Russian Staff College.

All three were among the commanders sent to the western frontier. Russia had the good fortune to be opposed to German and Austrian armies that could not take the field in full strength. Germany had to send most of her first-line troops across the Rhine, and could concentrate on the eastern frontier of her empire at most five regular army corps (say, from 200,000 to 250,000 men), reinforced with reserve and Landwehr units. Austria had to leave a large army to operate against Servia, to guard her southern frontier against possible dangers from Italy, and to keep the peace in her Slav provinces.

The Slav and Czech regiments sent to the front in Galicia were doubtful elements

A LEVIATHAN AND A MOSQUITO OF THE AIR.

These two types of aircraft represent the two wings of the service—the Zeppelin that can carry a ton and a half of high explosives to be dropped upon the point attacked, and the aeroplane, whose value lies chiefly in reconnaissance work, in inspecting the enemy's positions, and in guiding the artillery in attack.

of strength. They might even prove a danger and a weakness. Russia could therefore count upon having to deal with opponents so heavily handicapped at the outset that she might hope to force them to act upon the defensive at an early stage of the campaign, and thus obtain the precious advantage of the initiative for herself.

She had a further and unexpected gain. It was generally said, even amongst her Allies, that the Russian armies could not concentrate any considerable force at the front before the middle of September. But, thanks partly to many of the units having been brought up to high peace-strength before the crisis; thanks, further, to enormous exertions made by the Staff and the railway adminis- **Russian swiftness of mobilisation** tration, by the middle of August the army in Poland itself had been heavily reinforced and

GERMAN "AGO" MILITARY BIPLANE.

was ready for active operations, and other great masses of mobilised troops had assembled on the right along the line of the Narev and the Niemen, and south of the Pripet region, on the left, threatening the frontiers of Eastern Galicia.

Without anticipating the story of the campaign we may here note how the pieces were set for the dread game of war on this eastern borderland of Russia. So far as one can see through the proverbial "fog of war," no fewer than six armies were set in motion by the

ZEPPELIN ENTERING ITS FLOATING SHED AT FRIEDRICHSHAFEN.
The Lake of Constance, or the Boden See, as the Germans call it, is partly in German territory and partly in Switzerland. It has many floating sheds for airships along the German side, and the photograph shows one near the German town of Friedrichshafen.

Tsar's generals. On the right two columns advanced from the Niemen and Narev, the first in the direction of Königsberg, south of the Pregel, through the Masurian lake-land, the march being rendered easier by the exceptionally dry season of the summer of 1914; the second moved on its left through the forest tract west of the Narev line.

In the centre, based on the Polish triangle, an army was pushed forward towards the frontiers of the provinces of Posen and Silesia, and to cover the flank of this advance another army was sent up the Vistula, to check the menace of an Austrian army in this direction.

This Austrian march on the Vistula was itself

GERMAN BIPLANE STARTING ON SCOUTING EXPEDITION.

threatened in flank by an advance of the fifth Russian army into Eastern Galicia, and a sixth Russian army into the Bukovina.

It will be seen at once that this vast game of war was a very complicated one. It was quite possible for any of the armies operating on the frontiers of Russian Poland to have its position endangered by a check, not to its own advance, but to that of its nearest comrades. The strongly fortified central position of the Polish triangle provided, however, a kind of pivot for the operations of the centre.

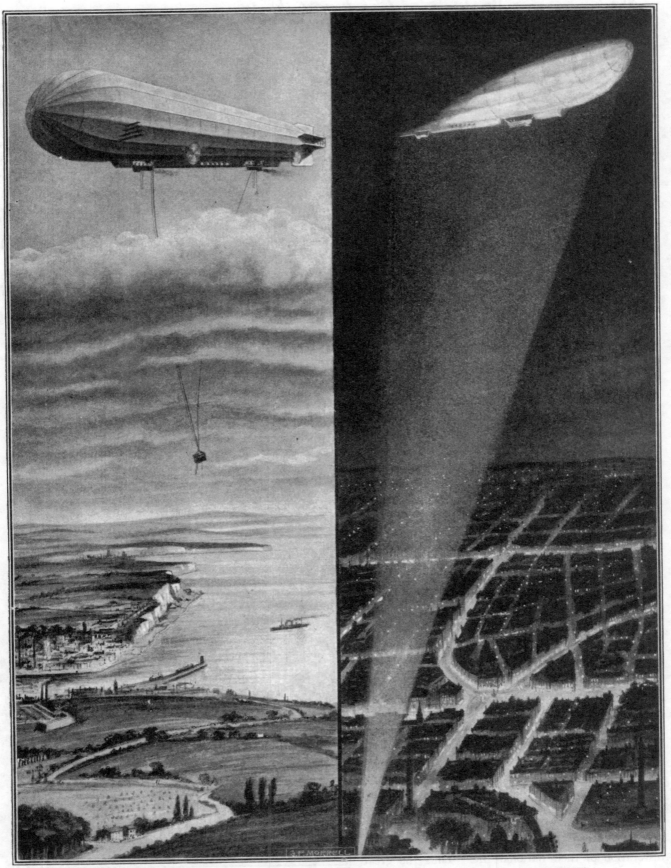

THE FORMIDABLE GERMAN MONSTER OF THE THIRD ELEMENT.

The drawing on the left illustrates a set of ideal conditions for an attack by airship. A stratum of heavy cloud hangs rather low, and makes the land below experience " a dull day," while the airship, floating in the sunlight above the cloud, progresses with ease, its huge bulk hidden from the earth. From the cage suspended through the cloud, and visible only with extreme difficulty, the navigators above can be instructed as to the route, and bombs can be dropped upon selected spots. The drawing on the right shows how hard it is to detect an airship on a moonless night. It is only by a powerful searchlight that it can be seen, and it will be noticed that the part not in the direct rays of the searchlight beams is invisible. The value of powerful searchlights for purposes of defence will be apparent.

" FIRE ON THESE MACHINES."
This is a reproduction of a printed notice issued by the
military authorities to French soldiers, so that they might be
able to recognise hostile German aircraft.

even to collect arms, till the Austrian vanguard had
arrived and secured a first victory. Then all the
arms they wanted would be given to them.

Meanwhile, they were told to make up their minds
to act, and to provide themselves, not with military
equipment, but with good, sound boots, " two pairs
of socks, two shirts, a rough working suit, a cap, and
a bag to hang by a strap over the shoulder." It
was the most matter-of-fact document ever drafted
by an insurrectionary committee.

But the Tsar had issued a proclamation making
larger promises than any committee could put forward. To Poland he promised Home Rule when the
victory over Germany and Austria was won, and with
this self-government and liberty of laws, religion, and
language he promised the reconstitution of the old
Polish territory, by the annexation of Posen and
Galicia. Poland was to live again as an autonomous
State under the Russian Crown. There is no doubt
that the proclamation had a great effect on Polish
national opinion. It paralysed any plans of insurrection by dividing the leaders of the Poles. Many
of them saw in a Russian success the prelude to a
restoration of their national life. Thus the great
conflict began with a pledge that, if the Russian
armies were victorious, their victory would be followed
by the resurrection of the Polish nation, inauguarating
a new era of peace and goodwill in Europe.

Success at the outset of a campaign has an influence of
the highest value upon the armies engaged. In this case the
Russians had the prospect of securing fairly easy victories at
the outset, and, at the very least, the certainty of being able to
march far into hostile territory without having any very
serious obstacle to overcome. It was not likely that the
German armies, weakened as they were by the very conditions
under which the war opened, would attempt any stubborn
resistance in advance of the line of fortresses along the lower
Vistula and at the extremities of the Frisches Haff. And it
was quite certain that the Austrians would not make any
prolonged resistance in Eastern Galicia. Their first serious
stand would not be met until the neighbourhood of Przemysl
was reached.

Austria had hoped that at the outset of the war she
could add to her own forces and increase the difficulties of
the Russian commanders by exciting a rising in Poland. The
Galician army corps, made up of Polish soldiers, would be the
vanguard of her advance along the Vistula,
and arms and ammunition for the expected
insurrection had been collected on the
border. The Polish associations of Galicia
and Posen had issued a proclamation to
their " brethren of Russian Poland."

It was a remarkable document.
Instead of warlike eloquence, there was
a warning not to attempt a rising, not

THE ENORMOUS SIZE OF A ZEPPELIN.
If we stand on the roadway of Ludgate Hill, London, and look up
at the dome of St. Paul's Cathedral, and if we are told that a Zeppelin
is about fifty per cent. longer than the distance from the ground to the
top of the golden cross, we begin to realise how enormous is one of
these great airships.

CHAPTER XVII.

THE NEW ARM IN THE NEW ELEMENT.

By an Expert in Aviation.

Former Use of Aircraft in War—Purpose of the New Arm in Warfare—Types of Airships—Frameless and Semi-rigid Types—The Zeppelin—Construction, Speed, and Capacity of Zeppelins—Aeroplanes—Aeroplane Powers of Attack on Dirigibles—Variable Speed—The Fuel Question—The Training of Airmen—German Secret Preparation—Aircraft in Naval Warfare—The Air Equipment of the Different Belligerents—The Question of Motors—The British Royal Flying Corps—Tributes to Its Value and Efficiency—Aircraft as Range-finders—Air Raids

THE most novel feature of the greatest war in history was the fact that it was waged in three elements, and not confined to two—land and water—as former wars. True, in the Italian campaign in Tripoli, airships and aeroplanes were used not infrequently to locate the enemy. But that was not war in the air, in that the enemy possessed no means of ascending from the ground and matching the equipment and advantages enjoyed by the Italians.

In the Balkan Wars too, some slight use was made of aeroplanes for purposes of reconnaissance. Here again the numbers possessed were very few, and the flying was of a character that would not be called military in any sense of the word by the Great Powers who engaged in the world's greatest conflict. France and Germany have been the pioneers of aerial warfare, with Britain as a very good third. All the great States fighting on the Continent of Europe

A GROUP OF BELGIAN MILITARY AVIATORS.
The photograph was taken in Ghent, which this party of Belgian flying-men had reached from Namur before the latter city had fallen under heavy battering by the big German siege-guns.

started the war equipped with highly-developed aircraft—airships or dirigibles, aeroplanes, and seaplanes (or aeroplanes with floats for use at sea)—and all had carefully-trained pilots and aerial observers.

Thus for the first time we were engaged in war in the air, because the opposing forces had the men and the machines. As it is a prime object of developing such a Third Arm to reap an advantage over the opponent by its possession, it follows that it was impossible any longer to confine aerial work in connection with warfare to the business of spying on the foe. That foe was also in the air to prevent his antagonist observing him. It was as vital that his enemy should fail in achieving that purpose as it was that he should succeed in spying on the enemy. That, in brief, is the why and wherefore of airman attacking airman; of the dirigible balloon stealing over forts, undefended areas, and camps to drop bombs on them

DIAGRAMMATIC REPRESENTATION OF A ZEPPELIN, DROPPING A BOMB ON THE ILL-FATED CITY OF ANTWERP.

One of these great scourges of the sky caused havoc in Antwerp before the fall of the city on October 9th, 1914, although children, women, and old men were the chief sufferers. The cut-away section of the side of the airship illustrates the construction of these monsters of the upper air. The rigid grey-coloured body contains seventeen separate balloons, each of which can be filled independently of all the others, and injury to one section does not affect the other balloons. A Zeppelin carries two cars with a long passage, really part of the main framework, between the two, as seen in the picture. Many of the Zeppelins are fitted with a platform right on top of the body, and this platform is mounted with a special sky-pointing gun, so as to fire upon aeroplane attack from above.

German Flag

Section showing some of the 17 Ballonets

Aluminium Framework

Car from which bombs are dropped

in the dead of night; and of aeroplanes and seaplanes flying by day, some with small bombs that can be released when over the objective, others with machine-guns; yet others with sharpshooters. The tale of all these doings stirs the blood, and suggests unlimited scope for patriotic adventure.

France has always made a feature of the frameless airship, in which the gasbag is merely an envelope of fabric, without anything rigid in it. The great military value of this system is that such a machine is easy to transport from point to point by rail or motor-car in a collapsed condition. It can be inflated at a convenient place with compressed hydrogen available in cylinders. Such an airship in the field need not be operated from a gigantic and easily-detectable airship hall, because of this power of collapsing it and inflating it at will. Usually, however, to save cost and time, when the conditions of the campaign render it safe, portable sheds are employed for housing the larger sorts of French dirigibles.

The smaller airships, such as are used by Britain, can be moored in the open. Some of the large vessels of the semi-rigid sort can also be moored in the open even in high winds, if the car, or gondola, containing the power plant is temporarily detached. The envelopes of both these types of dirigibles are made of gas-tight, rubber-proofed fabric, which deteriorates rapidly, especially under the action of daylight. Where gas-leaks occur however, the envelopes can be patched to quite a remarkable extent; hence they are good for several seasons, even when exposed.

For making voyages of some distance, especially for offensive work, when heavy bombs have to be carried as well as large supplies of fuel, large airships are essential The biggest French vessels were only a fraction more than half the size of the monster, rigid German airships of over four hundred and fifty feet in length. Even so, however, some of the French airships were over three hundred and thirty-six feet long.

The outstanding characteristics of the French school of design are the frameless and the semi-rigid systems, which can readily be emptied or collapsed, just as the rigid dirigible is the outstanding, but by no

THE BULLET-PROOF CAGE OF THE ZEPPELIN BOMB-THROWER.
When the Zeppelin floats in safety, hidden above the clouds, it can drop through the misty screen an armoured cage, like that shown here, from which observations can be made and bombs discharged in comparative safety, as it is extremely difficult to distinguish so small an object from the earth.

A ZEPPELIN CREW WATCHING ANOTHER AERIAL BATTLESHIP.

Experience showed that the occupation of a Zeppelin airman is the most dangerous it is possible to conceive. Accident or the vagaries of the weather have sent two Zeppelins to earth and their entire crews to death. This photograph shows the crew of a Zeppelin watching the operations of another Zeppelin that is sailing past.

means the only, type of airship produced by Germany. Count Zeppelin, that splendid German veteran, whose daring cavalry reconnaissances won him fame in the early stages of the Franco-German War of 1870-1, acquired the patents of an Austrian engineer named Schwarz, who had constructed the hull of a dirigible in Russia, and another in Germany, both of the thinnest aluminium sheeting, but rendered rigid by cross-bracing, girder fashion, with aluminium tubing. With this development, Count von Zeppelin resuscitated an original idea by connecting to a rigid framework several balloons placed one behind the other. He discarded Schwarz's rigid aluminium outer hull. A Zeppelin airship consists of a lattice-work cylinder having from sixteen to twenty-four sides in cross section, and built of aluminium tube girders, rigidly braced internally. The vessels have varied in size, for those built in 1908 were only half the size of the largest produced before the opening of war. They also differed one from another in the precise section, and in the number of interior balloons. But from start to finish there was no departure from the main principles of construction.

The cylindrical aluminium frame which gives the vessel its distinctive shape is divided longitudinally into sixteen or more compartments, each with

A GERMAN HIGH-ANGLE GUN FOR ATTACKING AIRCRAFT.

The creation of the air arm of warfare immediately called into being a class of anti-aircraft guns specially designed for counter-attack. These take many forms, and some are wonderful pieces of scientific mechanism. This photograph shows a German aircraft-attacking gun, its caisson mounted on a motor-tractor so as to give the maximum of mobility. The special recoil-resistance apparatus is seen at the side of the wheel. Even the enemies of Germany cannot refuse their meed of admiration for the veteran Count Zeppelin (seen above) who, by indomitable perseverance in face of disaster, brought the Zeppelin airship to a high point of practical efficiency.

DISEMBARKING A BRITISH AEROPLANE ON ITS ARRIVAL IN FRANCE.

Here is seen one of our Army aeroplanes—minus its wings—being hoisted over the side of a British transport on arrival in France. As a matter of fact, however, few of the British air machines were shipped over—they were nearly all flown across, despite the fact that not one of them had floats of any kind to help it to remain on the surface if it had been necessary to descend while crossing the Channel. One British airman flew aeroplanes over from England to the front on eight consecutive days, returning every day by train, boat, and motor-car ready for another. He also did some aerial reconnaissance work at the front, and was slightly wounded.

self-complete balloon or hydrogen gasbag, fitted with a valve for emptying it of gas, and an appendage for inflating it with hydrogen, as well as an automatic safety-valve to limit the maximum pressure of gas inside. The largest Zeppelins have over 812,000 cubic feet gas capacity, and are more than 500 feet long, yet they have a maximum diameter of less than fifty feet, so that they present a minimum of head resistance to forward travel, particularly as the cars fore and aft, each with its two motors (of 180 to 200 horse-power apiece) and set of two propellers, are placed as close as can be against the big hull. Thus only the long sausage-form has to be pushed through the air, in contra-distinction to the semi-rigid and frameless forms of con-struction, in which car and power plant are one unit, and the gasbag or balloon an

DROPPING THE DEADLY AIR BOMB.
The task of dropping the bomb is the work of the observer, who sits behind the pilot, as seen here.

independent one above them, and in which the driving effort is not applied to the main mass to be pushed through the air, but is delivered on a lower plane from the car.

With a Zeppelin the thrust of the propellers is delivered from the sides of the main envelope, resulting in better mechanical efficiency. Aluminium is used for the construction of the cars. Each car has a double bottom, protected by strong rubber buffers, to render the vessel equally suitable for alighting on the surface of the water or on land. The propellers are fixed on stays to the side of the balloon, and are gear-driven from the engines contained in the cars, which also carry ammunition and guns. A unique Zeppelin feature is that the rigid frame of the gasbags enables a gun plat-form to be mounted on the top of the balloon, so that this was the only airship in the world the captain and crew of which could be warned by look-out men when anything is flying above and threatening the craft. However, experiments before the war showed that danger to the craft was caused by the detonation of a gun on top of it. But in war, risks have to be taken which in peace would not be faced until investigation and experi-ment had led to further development. The largest Zeppelins are capable of a speed, independent of the wind, of quite fifty-two miles an hour. They have a radius of action of at least twelve hundred miles. This means that, operating from Kiel or Heligoland, they could go to Dublin or Belfast and back. They possess the longest radius of action of any class of aircraft in the world, and they are much the speediest dirigible balloons. They can also carry loads of about five tons, but this must include the weight of the crew and of fuel, oil, and water, so that the weight of ammunition carried could not well exceed a ton and a half. They hold the world's

THE ZEPPELIN SHED AT DÜSSELDORF.
The enormous sheds, or "hangars," necessary for housing the Zeppelins make them conspicuous objects, so that they form easy marks for attack by daring flying men. Flight-Lieutenant C. H. Collet was the first to fly into German territory, where he dropped a bomb on the shed at Düsseldorf on September 23rd, 1914. The bomb set fire to the shed, but it was impossible to estimate what damage had been done.

Some Heroes of Our Royal Flying Corps

The central portrait is Commander Samson; on the extreme left is Flight-Commander R. L. G. Marix, who raided Dusseldorf; next is Mr. Walter Wood, who escaped after capture by Germans; on the extreme right Captain Robin Grey, who received the Legion of Honour; and on his right Squadron-Commander Gerrard.

Lieutenant S. V. Sippe, reported on Oct. 9th, 1914, to have taken part in an air raid that damaged the Zeppelin sheds at Dusseldorf.

Sir David Henderson, commanding the Royal Flying Corps, was warmly commended in the dispatch of October 8th, 1914.

Squadron-Commander Spenser D. A. Gray, R.N., carried out the air raid on the Dusseldorf Zeppelin hangar on October 9th, 1914.

Flight-Lieutenant C. H. Collet made the first attack on the German sheds at Dusseldorf, as announced officially on September 23rd, 1914.

Mr. Gordon Bell was shot, and had his machine smashed by Germans at Mons, but managed to plane to earth and rejoin the British lines.

Lieutenant A. Christie, attached to the Royal Field Artillery, mentioned in Sir John French's dispatch of October 8th, 1914.

A group of members of the Royal Flying Corps, including Lieutenant Playfair, Lieutenant Mills, Lieutenant Soames, Captain Board, Major Riley, Major Higgins, Lieutenant Jones, Lieutenant Gould, Lieutenant Small, and Lieutenant Anderson.

OFFICERS AND MEN OF THE ROYAL FLYING CORPS WITH THEIR MACHINES.

OFFICERS and men of the Royal Flying Corps wear a distinctive dress. The men wear a designation on their arm consisting of the words : "Royal Flying Corps," in white letters on a blue ground. Officers and men who have gained their flying certificate wear on their left breast a white badge consisting of two eagle wings.

The men wear a khaki-coloured undress uniform, with a coat that gives them, as it were, a breastplate of cloth across their chest. The military mechanicians, who are concerned with the maintenance of the engines, wear the ordinary blue overalls, their only distinguishing mark being the forage-cap, which can on occasion be pulled down to tie under the chin. One of these mechanicians is seen on the extreme left.

On the right is a sergeant of the R.F.C., wearing the new badge of a propeller on his arm. He is saluting two aviation officers, one dressed for flying, the other wearing the flying certificate badge. On the right is an army B.E. biplane, with its four-bladed propeller and two seats for pilot and observer. This type, it is stated, is becoming more and more the standard pattern of machine for use by the R.F.C. On the left is a Bleriot monoplane, and in the air a Henri Farman biplane.

HOW ZEPPELIN 5 WAS WRECKED AND CAPTURED BY RUSSIAN CAVALRY.

As a Russian cavalry brigade, with a horse battery, was proceeding towards the Russo-German frontier in September, 1914, Zeppelin 5 approached from the direction of Mlava. The battery promptly opened fire. At the third volley the airship began to assume a vertical inclination, its stabilisater and rudder being damaged. Flinging down ineffective bombs, the Zeppelin disappeared behind a wood. Without losing a moment, the guns were taken round the wood at a gallop and renewed their fire. The airship then slowly descended to earth and was captured, its crew of three officers and seven men being taken prisoners. One of the officers had torn off his epaulets to conceal his rank. The hull of the airship, which had been pierced in several places by the Russian fire, was eventually blown up, after several trophies had been carried off, including an Army flag with the name "Zeppelin 5" and an embroidered eagle insignia of merit.

record for dirigible balloon altitude at over 10,000 feet. The disadvantage of the system is that this form of construction can be used only from a permanent and specially-prepared base. Zeppelin airships not only want enormous accommodation by reason of their vast size, but they also need a regiment of men to handle them when they are starting and landing, and they require large crews. As many as thirty men have been found in a captured airship. In the event of storms arising they are practically unmanageable. They cannot be emptied of gas as can frameless and semi-rigid balloons. A mild breeze blowing on the side of a Zeppelin exercises a force of scores of tons, tossing and tumbling about a whole battalion of men engaged in endeavouring to restrain the monster.

Drawbacks of the Zeppelin

Because of this difficulty of controlling them in gales or bad weather, many Zeppelins were damaged or destroyed before the war began. Two of the greatest catastrophes in airship history befell the first two naval Zeppelins, L (or "luftschiff"—i.e., "airship") 1 and L2. L1 was engaged in manœuvres with the German High Sea Fleet on September 9th, 1913, when she was suddenly caught by a violent squall. The vessel was carried up five thousand feet, at which height the buoyancy of the gas-containers began to fail owing to an escape of gas. Rain fell in cataracts, and the cover held moisture to such an extent as to increase the weight to be sustained by one or two tons. At this juncture a fresh gust caught her and drove her downwards to the water, where she buckled, and sank, with the loss of fourteen of her crew.

Five weeks later, on October 17th, L2, a yet larger and more powerful Zeppelin, made an ascent from Johannisthal, near Berlin, with a crew of twenty-eight officers and men. As she rose the gas expanded and escaped

THE BRITISH ROYAL FLYING CORPS AT FARNBOROUGH.

The British Royal Flying Corps, under Sir David Henderson, did invaluable observation work, and soon established their worth as individually superior to the German aviator. In his despatch of September 7th, 1914, Sir John French wrote: "I wish particularly to bring to your lordship's notice the admirable work done by the Royal Flying Corps under Sir David Henderson. Their skill, energy, and perseverance have been beyond all praise. They have furnished me with the most complete and accurate information, which has been of incalculable value in the conduct of the operations. Fired at constantly both by friend and foe, and not hesitating to fly in every kind of weather, they have remained undaunted throughout. Further, by actually fighting in the air, they have succeeded in destroying five of the enemy's machines."

from the valves, which are located under the gasbags, and just above the cars. A spark from the magneto, or a back-fire from one of her four engines (each of 180 horse-power), probably set the gas on fire. A rush of flame was seen from the ground, there was a loud explosion or crash, and the blazing airship fell to the ground. All on board were killed.

Up to the date of these two accidents Count Zeppelin had been able to boast that no life has been lost in any of the mishaps to his airships. It says much for German resolution that the German Government proceeded, undismayed, to build additional ships of the same type. In Great Britain, unfortunately, a very minor mishap to naval airship No. 1, which was begun in 1910, led to the abandonment of rigid airship construction for the British Government until 1913, when Mr. Churchill gave orders for one large ship of this type to be commenced.

German faith in rigid airships

In the air all airships are controlled on practically the same principle, the differences being merely in the degree of navigability and in the portions of the airship to which the various control gears are fixed. The Zeppelin looks to the lay eye by far the most shipshape craft. The gasbag of an airship is nearly always furnished with something approximating to the fins of a fish, or else to the feathers on an arrow, so as to give it stability and prevent it from rolling. The most general method is to have horizontal and vertical fixed planes. There is, besides, a vertical rudder, or, in the case of a Zeppelin, a series of rudders, to enable the machine to turn to right or to left, so long as it is moving under its own power, and has steering way. Most airships carry water ballast for emergencies. By discharging it, the airship can be made to rise; but most dirigibles do not waste their supplies in this fashion. On the contrary, they rise or fall by the power of their engines. Some have screws that can exert power in a vertical direction to cause the machine to lift. This is not the general, or by any means the most efficient way. The ordinary method of rising is to employ horizontal rudders, otherwise movable aeroplane surfaces. Thus, for steering to right or left, the vertical rudder is turned to one side or the other. In like fashion, the horizontal rudders or planes are moved up or down, as the pilot wishes the airship to ascend or descend. The operation is, in effect, merely steering up or down, instead of to the right or left.

The naval and military departments of the leading countries of the world have realised that for effective work all classes of aircraft are required. This necessity primarily arose from the limited range of the aeroplane, which

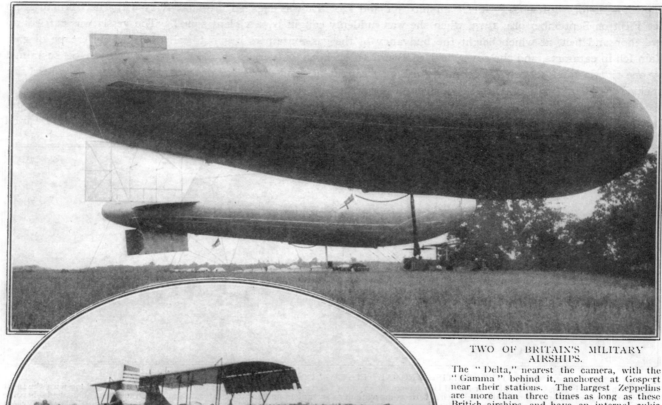

TWO OF BRITAIN'S MILITARY AIRSHIPS.

The " Delta," nearest the camera, with the " Gamma " behind it, anchored at Gosport near their stations. The largest Zeppelins are more than three times as long as these British airships, and have an internal cubic capacity almost nine times as great.

A BRITISH SEAPLANE.

The need for aeroplanes that could alight on and rise from water was felt by Great Britain more than by any of the other belligerent countries, and this need led to the development of the seaplane as an arm of the British Navy.

is approximately half that of the Zeppelin dirigible balloon; from the proportionately low carrying capacity of aeroplanes; and, above all, from the fact that the aeroplane must continually travel, else it falls, whereas the dirigible balloon can hover or drift without using power and without losing altitude.

Of the two, the aeroplane is vastly the more weather-worthy, and as superior to the dirigible in speed as the airship is superior to it in range. No dirigible has yet developed a speed of a mile a minute, independent of the wind, though Count Zeppelin got very close to that rate of travel; whereas many aeroplanes have speeds of over two miles a minute, and have maintained that rate of travel for an hour at a spell. Until 1912, also, the use of the aeroplane was confined almost entirely to daylight, whereas, by contrast, for military operations, the use of the dirigible balloon has been and is confined largely to the hours of darkness. Only recently has it been possible to build dirigibles to rise to such heights as 10,000 feet. This contrasts with an altitude record of 26,000 feet for the aeroplane.

BRITISH MARINE AIRSHIP OF THE "ASTRA TORRES" TYPE OVER OSTEND.

This British airship is 250 feet long, which is almost twice as long as the two shown on the opposite page, and has a cubic capacity over four times as great, namely 8,700 cubic metres. Her speed is rather more than that of the best Zeppelin, being about fifty-two miles an hour.

Thus, with its greater speed, its presentation of proportionately an infinitesimal mark to fire when compared with the vast bulk of the dirigible balloon, its greater weather-worthiness, and its ability to ascend to more than double the height of the airship, as well as to turn, rise, and fall very much more quickly, the aeroplane has numerous advantages over the airship, which must necessarily be more or less at its mercy in daylight.

Further, thanks to the extraordinary enterprise of such pioneers as Commander C. R. Samson, head of the naval wing of the Royal Flying Corps, the aeroplane began to invade the peculiar province of the dirigible balloon by flying in the hours of darkness, an operation which necessarily calls for most exceptional nerve and skill. The aeroplane is therefore the most serious menace to the dirigible balloon when it is flying at over 6,000 feet, so as to be out of range of the gun fire from below. Moreover, both aeroplane and seaplane were equipped with bombs designed to burst either before or after actually making contact with the airship, so as to annihilate it by exploding the hydrogen in its gasbag. Early in this war we learned that piercing an airship's envelope with bullets is not an effectual method of compassing her destruction.

COMMANDER SAMSON, OF THE ROYAL NAVAL FLYING CORPS, AND SOME OF HIS OFFICERS.

The name of Commander Samson (seen seated fourth from the left) came prominently before the public in the early days of the war. On September 16th, 1914, in a small armoured motor-car he killed four Uhlans and captured a fifth, near Doullens, close to the Belgian frontier

The naval and military requirements of the nations engaged in the war put a very high premium on a quality which the airship has always possessed, but which it was found possible to achieve with aeroplanes only during the twelvemonth prior to the war—widely variable speed in flight. Variable speed represents reserve energy, such as enables an aeroplane to rise quickly to a great height or to travel very fast. There are various reasons why we also want that same machine to be able to travel at considerably less than its maximum speed. The first aeroplane to fly at two miles a minute required a run over the best part of a mile before it would rise from the ground, and quite that space for a clear run on alighting —conditions obviously impossible for naval or military use. For those services aeroplanes are required which will rise after the briefest run, yet which will sustain themselves in the air at a slow rate of travel, so that the speed can be reduced to that rate in the act of alighting. Then there will be the least possible momentum to absorb before actually making contact with the ground or water and bringing the machine to a standstill.

Value of variable speed in aircraft

Aeroplanes will rise in fifty feet with a full load. They can be brought down into a field surrounded by trees, yet in flight they are required to develop high maximum of speeds of ninety or more miles an hour, and to be capable of flying at as low a speed as thirty-six miles an hour, or even less. Range of flying speed is, besides, necessary to ensure reliability, because no machinery will be dependable when worked to its limit without an instant's relief. Furthermore, to do a certain amount of flying at half or three-quarters speed effects an enormous saving of fuel, and therefore correspondingly increases the range of action of the machine.

It must be remembered that the flying machine has to carry its own fuel supplies into the air with it. In warfare its range of service is determined by the distance it can cover without replenishing supplies of any sort. With aircraft, as with warships, motor-cars, and all mechanical vehicles of travel, the rate of consumption of fuel increases out of all proportion to the increase of speed. Merely to double the horse-power developed is not to double the speed of the machine, but, owing to the increasing air resistance with higher speed, only to add a small percentage to the velocity.

Efficiency and fuel supply

It is astonishing how a comparatively few hours of flying begin to cause " warping " and loss of the original shape of the wing, with consequent loss of efficiency. In first-class high-speed machines a wing is rarely in perfect condition for more than one hundred and fifty or one hundred and sixty hours flying. After that time the wing begins to get out of shape, and the leading edge of the wings, instead of being straight and true, looks as

GERMAN AIRMAN GIVING THE RANGE AT NIGHT.
The Germans developed a system of fire-bombs dropped from aeroplanes to indicate to their gunners the positions to attack. The fire-bomb, attached to a parachute, shows a red light as it falls, and the German artillery attack the position immediately below.

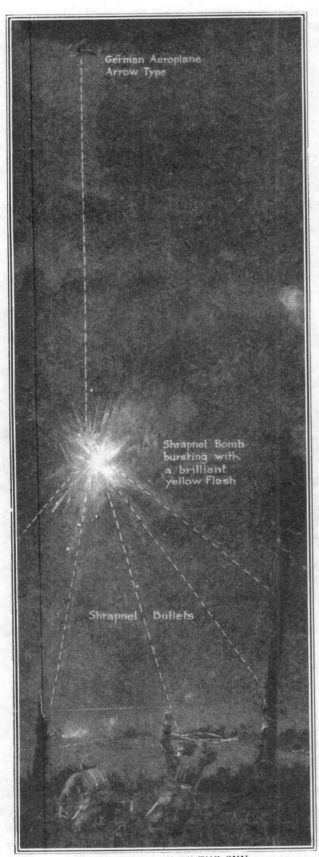

German Aeroplane
Arrow Type

Shrapnel Bomb
bursting with
a brilliant
yellow flash

Shrapnel Bullets

THE ARTILLERY OF THE SKY.
The light aircraft are used for attack as well as for observation
purposes. This picture illustrates how a shrapnel bomb bursts
before reaching the ground and scatters over a comparatively
wide area among the guns and men of the enemy.

though it had become twisted into a wavy line. This shows why such an elaborate outfit of apparatus and spare parts is required in the field with the flying wing of an army, including large motor workshops, huge motor-vans that carry numerous sets of spare wings stacked up like theatrical scenery, also portable sheds, and parts of all sorts.

Aircraft want much looking after. Even when used under peace conditions they have extremely short useful lives. Much more brief is their existence, therefore, under conditions of warfare, when it is scarcely possible to make a single flight for the purpose of observation without being subjected to fire of some sort. Hence the extraordinary rate at which Germany and France, and even our own factories, strove to produce machines to take the place of those at the front as fast as they were used up. The tragedy of the situation is that pilots are apt to get used up nearly as fast as their machines, and they can be made only by lengthy experience and tuition. A military pilot has to be very much more than a very good aerodrome performer and cross-country airman.

War wastage of men and machines

At the opening of war, Germany had about seven hundred qualified aeroplane pilots. Within two months of the outbreak of war she trained an extra hundred men in military flying near Berlin alone. Her activities were on a corresponding scale at her other flying centres. The German Government took over all the factories, flying-grounds, and airship sheds as soon as war was declared, so that it had at its disposal some three dozen centres at which to train pupils, apart from the big Army Flying Schools at Diedenhofen, Doeberitz, Metz, Oberwiesenfeld, Saarburg, and Sperenberg, and the Naval Flying Schools at Hollminsel and Putzig.

Her military airmen were well exercised before the war in surprise calls. Without an instant's warning for men or machines, the Director of Military Aeronautics would issue orders for squadrons of three aeroplanes apiece to set out across country to a specified centre where they would all assemble, and then undertake other flights, as directed. It gave the Germans great faith in their air service that in all these rehearsals the journeys were made with extraordinary expedition and punctuality, and with no more waste of time in the starting than the fire brigade takes to turn out in London. There was no single accident or failure of any unit in such practice of the war game.

German training for airmen

Germany also aimed very carefully at building up a big reserve of civilian pilots, whom she encouraged by promoting so-called touring and sporting competitions. These were divided into two sections—a military and a civilian one—with a military officer accompanying each civilian on his flight in the capacity of observer.

There were various tours of this description in East Prussia, precisely in the neighbourhood where Russia became so active, and along the French frontier. It is noteworthy that all these so-called pleasure cruises by air invariably involved flying over fortresses and reconnoitring a frontier. Sometimes the Emperor gave the chief prize for the military section, and the Crown Prince that for the civilian section. At other times Prince Henry of Prussia gave the chief awards.

German secrecy in air work

There was never any lack of handsome prizes, and all concerned were always made to realise very fully that the rulers of the country, from the Kaiser downwards, took the keenest personal interest in the achievement of every individual airman and constructer. In the absence of the international element, the world realised comparatively little of these activities. From start to finish it was the policy of the Government to focus the attention of the world on German prowess as represented by giant dirigibles. The Zeppelins incidentally served as an admirable

GERMAN AIRMEN FLYING OVER THE ALLIED ARMIES COULD INDICATE TO THEIR ARTILLERY THE—
The co-operation of airmen makes artillery fire much more effective than formerly. The airman flies out in front of the attacking line until he comes to the enemy's lines, above which he hovers, thereby indicating to his own side the locality of the opposing positions. A similar

mask for the rapid development of the aeroplane section, and also of lighter and smaller forms of airships - the Parseval frameless and collapsible dirigible balloons, of which Germany possess a good number, and the Gross, or semi-rigid type. Even so, it was believed by many that Germany contrived to build a considerable additional number of Zeppelin airships unknown to the outer world.

We must now consider her rate of construction of this single class of aircraft to be fully two dozen a year. Nor let it be imagined for a moment that they are as easily disposed of as newspaper reports would suggest. The first six weeks of warfare only resulted in the proved capture of two Zeppelins, and at her normal rate of manufacture just stated she had in these weeks made good this war wastage. As our history of the war develops we shall see that they will be employed for scouting at sea, and for assisting German warships to pass safely through the British blockading cordon, and it was undoubtedly our weakness that we had so few dirigible balloons, and none of high speed and long range like the Zeppelins.

Against them our battleships went to war armed with high-angle guns. But we must remember that a Zeppelin can easily carry heavy and therefore very destructive missiles, and that she can fly well above the range even of high-angle guns, so that the only thing that can get above her is the seaplane. In this branch Britain was happily more than Germany's match.

In the matter of aeroplanes the French equipment was a match for the German, alike in number and skill of pilots and capacity of production. France, with her small scouting and short-range dirigibles, was certainly also a match for Germany in all classes of semi-rigid and frameless airships. She had, however, none of the Zeppelin class; but this class, over land as over water, can be outflown in every sense by the bomb-dropping aeroplane.

Number and quality of British airmen

Our aerial equipment was on a par, not with our Navy, the largest in the world, but with our Army, which constituted the minor portion of the forces engaged in France. We had a large number of fine airmen, and over eight hundred British pilots had taken their aviator's certificate. Quite five hundred of them were trained for the two Services, a large proportion for naval work. The difficult

—ENEMY'S POSITIONS, THUS FINDING THE RANGE WHEN THE OBJECTS OF ATTACK REMAINED INVISIBLE.
service is also rendered during the hours of darkness by a system of lights, as explained on page 328. The picture above is sufficiently explanatory of the system of day observation. The inspecting officer reports to his colleagues, who telephone instructions to the concealed artillery.

nature of England as an aeroplaning country in these early stages of aerial development produced its own reward; flying over the Continent is easy by comparison.

Our airmen, like our seamen, could not be surpassed. It is not only that they have the right temperament and the physical skill, but also that their training is extremely thorough. Yet we must not lose sight of the fact that it takes a long time to train a civilian airman until he becomes an expert and serviceable military pilot. He has to scout at a height of 6,000 feet, or more than a mile, travelling at that altitude at probably an average of a mile a minute, accurately estimating the character and number of the enemy's dispositions and movements, as well as acting in co-operation with his own artillery, for which his advent has opened up new and undreamt-of possibilities. There is no blind groping for the range, or leaving it to chance. So long as there are airmen at the artillery's service, they can report by instant signal whether a shot has fallen short, far, or wide.

Little heed has been paid in this country to the Russian aerial equipment, yet so long ago as the Crimean War, Russia began to give attention to scouting by balloon. Since the coming of the aeroplane, Russian aviators

FIXING AN AIRSHIP'S PROPELLER 2,000 FEET ABOVE THE SEA.
A conspicuous act of bravery was performed in a British airship patrolling the Straits of Dover while our Expeditionary Force was crossing. The Secretary of the Admiralty's report ran as follows : " On one occasion it became necessary to change a propeller-blade. The captain feared he would have to descend for this purpose, but two of the crew immediately volunteered to carry out this difficult task in the air, and climbing out on to the bracket carrying the propeller shafting, they completed the hazardous work two thousand feet above the sea."

have proved extraordinarily skilful and daring. The Russian pilot Efimoff first found out how to " bank " (turn) abruptly with a Farman type of biplane. Russia, moreover, early placed important orders for dirigible balloons in France, Germany, and Italy ; and she has a plant of her own for turning out aircraft.

At the outset, Germany had twice as many airships of various types as France, who came second in order with perhaps a score. Germany could show a greater number of trained military airmen and of military aeroplanes than any one country, having about one hundred in excess of France. By at once taking over all the motor and aircraft works in the Fatherland, and setting them to work at full capacity, she maintained her lead. Though various textbooks which have been published since the outbreak of war deal with her air equipment, perhaps we may be permitted to point out that the estimates of Germany's fleet of airships published are all much too low. Undoubtedly at the outbreak of war, Germany had at least forty-five rigid type of airships. But only a few of these were large Zeppelins. The majority were of about two-thirds the length of these monsters, but had a very high speed—not far short of a mile a minute—and a range of about 800 miles, as against 1,200.

Germany's ally, Austria, had no aircraft manufacturing capacity worthy of the name, though she made certain types of heavy, slow-speed aero-engines, and had one or two aeroplane works. So far as concerns her air fleet, Austria was not formidable. When her few dirigibles, including two or three of Zeppelin types, had been accounted for, she could scarcely rely on Germany, from whom she got such craft, to replace them. Certain of her semi-rigid types of airships of a really efficient character, such as she had purchased in France, could not be replaced from Germany during the war.

The situation at the outset, therefore, was that Germany's aerial equipment was individually superior in numbers of all arms, including armoured motor-cars with high-angle guns, to any one country against which she was arrayed. But this was discounted by the fact that her energies had **Comparative aircraft strength** to be dissipated in campaigns against Russia, France, Belgium, and Britain on land and sea.

At the outbreak of war the Allies had as many airships as Germany and Austria, but they had none of the special Zeppelin type. They possessed in the Astra-Torres machines, such as France uses and such as our Navy employs, a highly efficient pattern which is particularly suitable for oversea work. The Allies had also, collectively, a greater number and variety of aeroplanes and a greater number of pilots, who between them combined a greater variety of experience. The Allies were therefore able to choose their pilots according to the work to be done, whereas the German airmen had to meet all Germany's rapidly changing needs.

The aerial situation, however, differs from the naval situation in one very essential point. Whereas it is impossible to create a navy during the war, if the foundations of an aerial force exist in the organisation and the

GERMAN EFFORTS TO BRING DOWN A BRITISH BIPLANE IN FRANCE.

A rough sketch of this scene was made by a British officer in France, and it was completed in London. The Germans were in a position behind the valley seen in front, and one after another the shells exploded as they attacked the Farman biplane manned by a member of the Royal Flying Corps, who went through the bombardment unhurt. Against the deep azure of the sky the shells exploded as white puffs, which became darker as they expanded. In rapid succession they came until more than half a dozen small clouds of smoke hung in mid-air, with the threatened aeroplane visible through their misty edges. The British troops in the foreground watched the German firing with intense interest.

SQUADRON-COMMANDER SPENSER GREY AFTER THE SECOND ATTACK ON THE DUSSELDORF AIRSHIP SHED.
Early in October, 1914, Squadron-Commander Spenser D. A Grey, R.N., accompanied by Lieutenants R. L. G. Marix and S V Sippe, made an attack upon the Düsseldorf airship shed. One bomb, dropped from a height of five hundred feet, hit the shed, went through the roof, and destroyed a Zeppelin. Flames were observed five hundred feet high, the result of igniting the escaping gas of the airship The feat was remarkable, having regard to the distance—over one hundred miles—penetrated into country held by the enemy, and to the fact that a previous attack had put the enemy on his guard and enabled him to mount anti-aircraft guns.

factories requisite, a very much larger aerial force can be created during the progress of a war. It is also possible to improve the aerial equipment, and replace it at a much greater rate than wastage can occur. The German plans recognised this. German productive capacity remains greater than that of any one country against which Germany was arrayed; but this is discounted by the fact that the Allies collectively had a far greater productive capacity under all headings.

Therefore, if by the wastage of war the Allies lost one machine and one man for each one lost by Germany, then, as the war lengthened, the more markedly could their aerial equipment preponderate, because they could create and replace more rapidly.

The scale on which building proceeded in Germany might be judged from the fact that, six weeks after the outbreak of war, it was officially announced at Berlin that three squadrons of airships were being laid down, and would be ready promptly. Doubtless this meant that the large number of airships laid down so successfully in secret would make a public appearance soon after.

Further, Germany secured some 3,000 volunteers for her air

DAMAGED AEROPLANE NEAR NAMUR.
A French monoplane wrecked within the fighting area around Namur during the third week of August, 1914. The body of the machine was covered with thin steel, which had been dented by bullets. The engine has gone, and only the battered hood which encircled the revolving cylinders remains. The wheels have metal discs and the framework is steel throughout.

service. The expansion of the German air fleet, however, was jeopardised by the awkward position of Germany and Austria in the matter of petrol supplies. The Russian successes in Galicia cut off one main source of supply, while the blockade prevented importation by sea. Moreover, up to April before the war, the petrol stocks of both countries were absolutely normal, so that no extraordinary reserves could have been accumulated against the outbreak of war. In any shortage of fuel

RUSSIAN AEROPLANE CAPTURED BY GERMANS AT LOTZEN.
As long ago as the Crimean War, Russia began to give attention to scouting by balloons, and since the coming of the aeroplane her aviators have shown particular initiative and daring. This photograph shows the remains of a Russian aeroplane, taken by the German General von Hindenburg at Lotzen, being removed on a transport waggon. The engine was afterwards fitted to and used in a German aeroplane.

BRITISH BIPLANE *VERSUS* GERMAN TAUBE.

The British Royal Flying Corps, from the beginning of its activity at the battle-front, made it their practice to challenge instantly any German airman appearing in the vicinity. Thus, air duels became of frequent occurrence, and British dash made most of them result in favour of the Allies. This special sketch portrays such an air duel, where a Bristol biplane, piloted by a member of the corps, manœuvred above a German Taube. A pistol fight followed, but attempts by German troops below to bring down the British aeroplane and a French Bleriot machine, that had joined in the sport, caused both the attackers to fly off.

the Third Arm would be the last to suffer. An army would sooner dispense with the use of motor-cars than lose its power of reconnoitring from the air.

Yet it did not follow that, because Germany possessed certain types of aircraft which the Allies lacked, the Allies were necessarily at a grave disadvantage. Germany aimed at supplying herself with the machines suited to her particular needs. But there was a vast difference between her requirements and those of any one of the Allies. Hence Great Britain's employment of moderate sized airships, even for naval work, and her adaption, for land warfare on a small scale, of readily portable airships, such as are the least extravagant to keep and the hardiest to withstand weather.

The weak point in the British aeroplane equipment at the outset lay in its dependence on foreign motors. But from the moment war was declared, the necessary measures were taken to remedy this defect, and to profit by the lessons of the Government Aero-Engine Competition, held in the summer of 1914. This was prematurely **The question of aircraft motors** closed on the outbreak of war—which did not come, however, until the tests had been in progress for more than two months. A great deal of valuable knowledge had been gleaned, with the result that some of the largest British motor factories are working day and night supplying engines of suitable types. The Navy was particularly to be congratulated on the style of motors reaching it as the result of the orders given.

If Germany obtained a splendid rally of recruits to replace wastage in her air service, the Allies could show even better results. The military training schools in France were full of pupils, and our own aviation centres were working to their utmost capacity on sensible lines. Nor was there any dearth of further volunteers as time went on.

During the first two months of the war the Third Arm was used in an extraordinarily wide variety of ways, and thoroughly established itself. The first problem was the safe transport of the British Expeditionary Force. Convoying by warship is useful, but is limited by the fact that the warship travels on the same plane, and is practically subjected to the same restricted range of vision as the transports it is meant to shield.

HOW THE PARISIANS REGARDED THE MOVEMENTS OF A GERMAN AEROPLANE.
Interest in the spectacle overrides any feeling of personal danger when a hostile aeroplane appears over a city. Every man or woman realises that his or her chance of injury from the falling bomb is small. This photograph was taken in Paris when a German " Taube " was hovering above.

GERMANS IN BADEN WATCHING FOR AIR ENEMIES BY NIGHT.

A scene in the Black Forest, in Baden, when a party of Germans were keeping watch for a feared French air raid. The searchlights were mounted on the fortress of Strassburg, in Alsace, just over the boundary between Baden and Alsace.

But aircraft are subject to no such limitations. From an altitude it is possible to detect the approach of an enemy, either in the air or on the surface of the waters, from a vastly greater distance—say fifty or sixty miles, instead of eight or ten. Moreover, the Channel has such a white bed that, when travelling at no great height, it is easy for the aerial observer to detect the presence of a submarine, even if she is submerged.

Aeroplanes are unsuitable for the escort of transports, in that their minimum flying speed is certainly not less than thirty-six miles an hour, which is vastly in excess of the fastest speed of a troopship. The aeroplane would thus be unable to hover over the troopship during its passage. Nor is it desirable to use a large airship, such as the British Astra-Torres naval types, for this work. The little Beta, which first flew over London on September 22nd, a type practically standardised by the Royal Aircraft Factory, was found particularly suitable alike for service with the Expeditionary Forces and for these short over-seas excursions. She made the numerous journeys between the French and English coasts in a manner of which we had every reason to be proud. The Expeditionary Force was transported without untoward accident of any sort.

British airmen go to the front

With the Expeditionary Force went the Aerial Arm, consisting in the first instance of approximately one hundred aeroplanes, which were promptly supplemented by other three dozen. Almost without exception all these machines were flown from England to the front, despite the fact that not one of them had floats of any sort. In crossing the Channel, the airmen's lives depended in each case on the accurate working of the engine, the failure of which cost the nation the life of its finest airman, Gustav Hamel, shortly before the outbreak of war.

The most experienced pilots went out under the command of Brigadier-General Sir David Henderson, Chief of the Royal Flying Corps, who did so much to build up that organisation. The pilots and trained observers were drawn from the various naval and military aviation centres in the country, with the result that, proportionately to the numbers engaged, Great Britain had a finer flying personnel than that possessed by any other nation waging war. Some civilian fliers—such as Gordon Bell and James Radley—who volunteered, were employed later to fly machines over. Some notion of the arduous nature of this work may be gained from the fact that for eight consecutive days one airman flew out in an aeroplane from England to the front, and returned by train, boat, and motor-car to fetch another every twenty-four hours. Not only this, but he engaged in aerial reconnaissance work at the front, and was slightly wounded, though happily he was soon fit for service again.

A BRITISH MOTOR-TRANSPORT COLUMN HAS DRAWN UP UNDER THE SCREEN OF ROADSIDE TREES ON—
The campaign in France entailed an expenditure of ammunition out of all comparison with former wars, and the importance of regular and liberal supplies of ammunition to feed the guns in action could not be overrated. Also, motors filled a new and vital part in warfare, ammunition being usually carried to the firing-line by motor transport, which naturally invited attack from the enemy's aircraft.   The

A section of our naval airmen, under Commander C. R. Samson, took up quarters at Ostend, where several weeks passed without anything being heard of their doings, though they were by no means idle.   Theirs was a constant work of reconnaissance at sea, and sometimes inland.   These duties were supplemented by fine flights of over twenty hours' duration by our larger naval airships co-operating with the Grand Fleet.

On land, the pick of the French airmen proceeded to the east of France for the difficult operations in progress there against the Germans.   Hence, in the western theatre of operations, where the Royal Flying Corps was working with General French, the British airmen, trained in a much harder school of flying than the average French pilot, showed up to extraordinary advantage.   They were superior alike to the Germans and to what may be called the second line of the French military flying personnel employed in this quarter of the field.

Our Royal Flying Corps, which the majority of military authorities regarded as being purely an experimental

Splendid work by Royal Flying Corps

arm at the outbreak of war, did such work as to dissipate all doubts and to prove itself an invaluable factor of success in the field.   In the retreat from Mons to Paris, in which it was essential at all times to obtain the most accurate information of the enemy's movements, and in which on occasions our airmen had to be used as decoys for the enemy, it specially distinguished itself.   In his report of September 7th, Sir John French paid this glowing tribute to the work of the corps under Sir David Henderson : " Their skill, energy, and perseverance have been beyond all praise. They have furnished me with the most complete and accurate information, which has been of incalculable value in the conduct of operations.   Fired at constantly both by friend and foe, and not hesitating to fly in every kind of weather, they have remained undaunted throughout.   Further, by actually fighting in the air, they have succeeded in destroying five of the enemy's machines."

On September 9th General Joffre added this further tribute : " Please express most particularly to Marshal French my thanks for services rendered on every day by the British Flying Corps.   The precision, exactitude, and regularity of the news brought in by its members are evidence of their perfect organisation, and also of the perfect training of pilots and observers."

—HEARING THE WHIRR OF A GERMAN AEROPLANE, THUS SEEKING TO ESCAPE OBSERVATION OR ATTACK.
destruction of an ammunition column is a serious blow to a fighting force, and once the presence of such a column is located every effort is made to destroy it, both by aeroplane bomb and by artillery fire which the reconnoitring airman may be able to have directed on it. For this reason great precautions are taken to screen ammunition columns by choosing roads shaded by trees, so as to make observation difficult.

This sufficiently reveals the value of the work done in reconnaissances by the Royal Flying Corps. It also indicated that our airmen were employed to assist the French Army. Sir John French's messages showed that when information was brought to him from other sources, the correctness of it was determined by aerial reconnaissance, so that the Third Arm was used alike to obtain first news and to check news otherwise obtained. The extent of the aerial reconnaissances is shown by the average of nine hundred miles of flying by aeroplane accomplished daily from the date when the British took up their position in the line of battle.

Considering the amount of work done, and the fact that during the first month of war the British airmen were fired on alike by the Germans and by the British, who had not learned to distinguish between their own and the enemy's aircraft, it is remarkable that the losses sustained were comparatively slight. It was particularly fortunate that in seventy per cent. of cases the men were wounded only slightly, and were generally able to get back to the British lines even if their machines were sacrificed. The enemy captured comparatively few machines, a remark which also applies to the Allies. If a forced descent became necessary, the practice was to saturate the aeroplane with a spare can of petrol and **Reconnoitring practice by British airmen** set fire to it, a modern aeroplane being capable of gliding two or three miles when at a height of several thousand feet.

The orders as to scouting were to fly at about 6,000 feet or more, which has the disadvantage of making the objects below appear extremely small, like mere dots or pin-heads, but which at the same time gives the observer an extremely extensive view. When any particular movement is being made, he is able to interpret at a glance the direction and significance of it. Another advantage that will be appreciated by anybody who has been in an aeroplane which travels at about a mile a minute is this—when the airman is observing from a thousand feet or so, he sees the ground rushing backwards below him, whereas when he rises to a height of 6,000 feet he is sufficiently removed from the terrain below for it to assume comparatively a stationary effect. Thus his eye obtains a comprehensive picture, instead of being able to take in only a small section at a time, and that in a kaleidoscopic or moving fashion.

At the outset, stay-at-home military critics expressed the opinion that, flying at such heights, the Germans

PRECAUTIONS AGAINST AERIAL OBSERVATION AND ATTACK.

This company of Belgian military cyclists is keeping close to the houses in advancing through the town, in order to be less conspicuous to the German air scouts and also to minimise the risk of being hit by bombs dropped from aeroplanes.

could learn very little concerning our movements, whereas the members of the Royal Flying Corps have been deliberately trained to make their observations from such altitudes. In September an extremely interesting official account was issued of the exploit of a British Staff Officer attached to one of the French armies, who, in the absence of a trained aerial observer, volunteered to assist by going up with a pilot and making his first trip in an aeroplane.

He obtained most valuable military information, thus revealing that the trained soldier can very quickly pick up the aerial point of view, despite the fact that he rose to a height of over 6,000 feet and engaged in a pistol duel with a pilot. In the first six weeks of war British airmen destroyed six German machines through their superior handling of the aircraft, whereby they climbed above the German pilots and shot them down.

A second use of aeroplanes was to work in co-operation with artillery for the purpose of finding the range

BELGIAN ARTILLERY SHADED BY TREES FROM THE ENEMY IN THE AIR.

For the reason mentioned above, military advance along a sun-lit road was usually made as much as possible in the shade of any available trees to escape observation by the German "Taubes" scouting in cloudland.

DEATH FROM THE SKY—A DEADLY BOLT FROM THE BLUE.

The chief work of the British Royal Flying Corps was reconnaissance, but at the same time they did good execution by bomb dropping. The Press Bureau's official statement of September 11th, 1914, compiled from Sir John French's despatches, stated : " From a diary found on a dead German cavalry soldier, it has been discovered that a high-explosive bomb thrown at a cavalry column from one of our aeroplanes struck an ammunition waggon. The resulting explosion killed fifteen of the enemy." One of our war artists has tried to depict the incident.

BOMB DAMAGE TO NOTRE DAME CATHEDRAL, PARIS.
Two German Taube monoplanes flew over Paris on Sunday afternoon, October 11th, 1914, and dropped about twenty bombs in various places, causing the death of four people and wounding thirty-four. The first bomb was aimed at the Gare du Nord, the great railway-station. Two of the bombs were aimed with evident deliberation at Notre Dame Cathedral. One fell on the roof of the northern tower, but did not explode, and this photograph shows the very trifling damage it made on the historic building.

and promptly reporting on the accuracy of fire. The members of the Royal Flying Corps have been trained for the duty of co-operating with artillery. The Germans at first appeared to enjoy some slight advantage in the promptitude with which their airmen signalled information, and they appeared to get over the target at once. As far as can be ascertained, however, in nearly all these cases the German airmen appear to have been operating at times and places where there were no British aircraft and no high-angle guns available. In consequence of this they came within about 1,200 feet of the target. They seem to have been assisted, moreover, by the British, who disclosed their positions by opening fire on the aeroplanes with guns unsuited to that work. Indeed, a General Order to the effect that only special arms were to be employed to fight aircraft indicates that the British fire against the enemy's aircraft helped as much to locate the British positions as the information signalled by the German airmen. In any case, this class of manœuvre was not exploited to any great extent by the Germans when once the Allies assumed the offensive. The co-operation of the airman with artillery begins with a reconnaissance to determine the general position and the number of the hostile batteries. The artillery commander is then able to allot their various tasks to his batteries. Having learned where the concealed targets are, the next business for the airman is to observe the fire.

He always works from behind the forces with which he is co-operating. A plot of ground is chosen on which two large strips of cloth are laid out. Thus he knows his base, and where to drop messages or look for signals.

Very's lights (which burn brightly and with different colours) are used on the ground to give the airman his orders, or by the airman to signal his information. They can be seen at a great height, and the colours can be distinguished at a distance of six miles in very clear weather. The colours used are white, red, and green. Two men are detailed to watch the aeroplane, one with field-glasses looking for its signals, and the other following it with the naked eye. When it is over the

Range-finding by aeroplane

enemy the aeroplane drops a white Very's light, the distance of which is taken by instruments. Another way is for the aeroplane to fly back along the enemy's line and to continue its flight over and past the battery in the same straight line.

When the enemy's position has been ascertained, the pilot renders further service by watching the firing and signalling the result—whether the range is correct, whether the shells are falling short, or over, or to the side of the target, and whether the shells or shrapnel are bursting satisfactorily. This information is given by burning Very's lights of various colours, or by flying back and dropping messages.

A third phase of aeroplane work has been to raid airship bases. The first such raid was made on August 15th by a French airman, Captain Finck, who flew to the Frascati airship shed near Metz, which was reported to contain a Zeppelin at the time. Several bombs were dropped, one of which was reported officially to have caused the building to break out into flames.

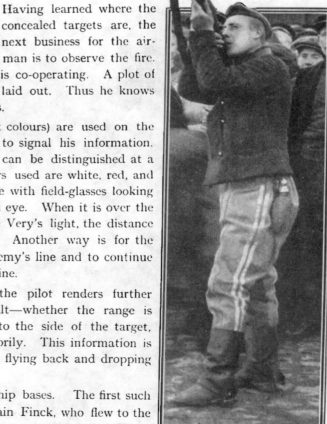

A DIFFICULT MARK.
A Belgian soldier in Ostend firing at a German aeroplane.

Course of Spiral Dive
from approximately
5000 ft. to 500 ft.

Bursting
Shell from
Anti-Aircraft
Gun.

500 ft. of
Flaming
Gas

New Shed at
DÜSSELDORF

THE BRILLIANT AIR-RAID ON THE DÜSSELDORF ZEPPELIN SHED.

This picture is a portrayal of the second raid by a British airman on the Zeppelin shed at Düsseldorf, an adventure mentioned in the memorandum of the Director of the Air Department of the Admiralty, published on October 23rd, 1914, in the following words: " Flight-Lieutenant Marix carried out a successful attack on the Düsseldorf air-ship shed during the afternoon of October 8th. From a height of six hundred feet he dropped two bombs on the shed, and flames five hundred feet high were seen within thirty seconds. The roof of the shed was also observed to collapse. Lieutenant Marix's machine was under heavy fire from rifles and mitrailleuse, and was five times hit."

343

ONE OF THE FRENCH AEROPLANES BROUGHT DOWN BY GERMAN ARTILLERY.
A German "lie bureau" statement asserted that the German army accounted for one French aeroplane per day. Although this state-ment was a gross exaggeration, the aeroplane casualties on both sides were high. Here a German soldier is standing guard over the wreck of a French aeroplane.

The next authentic news was of a raid by members of the Naval Branch of the Royal Flying Corps, operating from a temporary base established with high-angle field guns, cyclist riflemen, and armoured motor-cars, "as close as possible to the German frontier." On September 22nd Flight-Lieutenant C. H. Collet,

AN AEROPLANE MACHINE-GUN.
Before the war the French authorities had commissioned some machine-guns mounted on aeroplanes, as seen in this photograph, as a provision against the airship guns of a possible German enemy.

and certain of the five other airmen who started, flew to Düsseldorf and dropped bombs which set alight the Zeppelin airship shed there. At Cologne, whither the rest of the party flew, fog rendered it impossible for them to drop bombs without risk of their hitting other marks than the sole one intended—namely, the airship shed.

This conduct is particularly to be noted as contrasting with the German bomb-dropping raids over Antwerp and Paris, when damage

was done to unfortified buildings containing no manner of military equipment. At Cologne equal and possibly greater damage could have been inflicted by the British airmen with their aeroplanes had they simply dropped the missiles at random over the city, round which they flew in the fog for a couple of hours in vain endeavours to make out for certain where the airship shed was. Failing to do that, they went home without attempting to let fall any explosive.

In these attacks on airships in their bases it is impossible to determine what is the amount of damage done. Unofficial reports to the effect that Zeppelins have been destroyed in such sheds should, there-fore, be no more credited than German Press Bureau denials that any appreciable damage was done to a given shed, when our airmen above could see clearly the flames rising from it. What the aerial observer can determine is whether or not he succeeds in setting the shed alight. The precise effect on the contents of it must be unknown to him.

VEDRINES AND HIS "COW."
The brilliant French airman Vedrines christened his machine "La Vache," or "The Cow," and although he did not make it jump over the moon, he did good work with it attached to the French army. The photograph shows him preparing to guide it on a reconnaissance trip.

This, however, may be said, that if an aerial bomb pierces a shed and the gas-bag of any airship that may be there, the result should be, not a mere outburst of flames, but an explosion wrecking the whole shed. It is for these reasons extremely doubtful whether any very effective result has as yet been achieved in these raids.

The Germans made much use of their aeroplanes for dropping bombs in defenceless French cities—a wantonly cruel and purposeless method of war. Thus, when their armies neared Paris at the end of August, German monoplanes were several times observed in the air, apparently reconnoitring the French **German air raid on Paris** defences. On September 1st there was a more serious raid. A Taube (dove-shaped monoplane, one of the German standard types) flew rapidly over Paris about six in the evening and was observed above the Gare St. Lazare in the centre of the city. It dropped a bomb there, and then proceeded to the Place de l'Opéra, when the French anti-aircraft guns opened upon it. It replied to their fire by dropping yet another bomb, and then made off. One of the bombs is believed to have caused serious loss of

life ; the other did little damage But there was general irritation in Paris that one of the enemy's aircraft should have been able to reach the centre of the capital unmolested, and to make its escape without being attacked by the French aeroplanes.

To guard against the repetition of such outrages a squadron of French armoured aeroplanes, equipped with machine-guns, was told off, and little more was seen of the German airmen, though there were further raids, all informa-

AN "IRON CROSS" ZEPPELIN CREW AND A ZEPPELIN "STABLE."
The bravery of the men who take their lives in their hands in great airships, which so often have merely proved to be short cuts to death, is deserving of recognition under whatever flags they may serve. Each man of the Zeppelin crew in the upper picture received the Iron Cross from the Kaiser. The lower picture shows a large Zeppelin shed, or "hangar," for accommodating one of these leviathans of the air. These sheds are as large as great railway-stations.

tion concerning which was suppressed at the time. The retreat of the German armies from the Marne increased the distance to be carried, and most of the German aeroplanes were required for work in the fighting then proceeding, in which the British airmen had established, as the British official documents prove, an individual superiority over their German antagonists.

The German airships were also used for this same inhuman purpose. On August 25th a Zeppelin flew over Antwerp in the small hours of the morning. It approached silently, apparently drifting down the wind with engines stopped, till it

was over the Royal Palace, in which the King of the Belgians and the other members of the Belgian Royal Family were then living. At this point signals were made to it from some German confederate in the city. Thereupon it dropped a number of exceedingly powerful bombs, two or three of which narrowly missed the palace. They exploded with terrific violence, killing twelve persons and wounding several others. The Hospital of St. Elizabeth, over which the Red Cross flew, seems to have been one of the targets aimed at. One house was demolished by a bomb

The airship was stated by observers to have lowered a small car by a long rope, and from this small car the bombs were dropped, wrapped in sacking or coarse cloth. The manœuvres of the airship left no doubt whatever as to its object, which was to kill the Belgian Royal Family. No language is sufficiently strong to condemn so dastardly an attempt on the life of the Sovereign to whom, only a few months before, the Kaiser had given a personal promise that he would respect the neutrality of Belgium.

On its retreat the Zeppelin was fired at by the Antwerp forts, but without being injured. On the nights of August 25th and September 1st it repeated its attack. On both occasions, however, the troops in Antwerp opened so hot a fire that it immediately withdrew, after dropping a number of bombs, which caused no damage, on the outskirts of the city. From that time all lights were extinguished in Antwerp after sundown, and the attacks ceased.

Late in September a Zeppelin made a raid upon Ostend and dropped a number of bombs there, with no further result than to kill a watch-dog. There is evidence that the object of the raid was to destroy a trainload of ammunition.

Bomb raids by Zeppelins

The train had fortunately left a few hours before the Zeppelin appeared. But the incident illustrated the perfection of the German Secret Service and the prevalence of German spies.

The French dirigible balloons were used on the eastern border, where several effective night raids were achieved, bombs being dropped into camps, a class of work which has also been successfully achieved by British aeroplanes in the daytime, as for instance the destruction on September 16th of a German ammunition column at Doullens, nineteen miles from Amiens. The Germans also used airships at night to attack camps, but did no very extensive damage. Apart from the raids on the Zeppelin halls, the wreck of one captured Zeppelin was brought to Paris, and another Zeppelin was secured by the Russian army operating in East Prussia.

It was not Germany's purpose to use her rigid airships with her land forces. That she should have carried out so little of her advertised programme with them is not surprising when we have in mind the collapse of her original plans of campaign. It is no secret that a Zeppelin raid on London was one of her pet schemes.

Zeppelin airships are equipped with a wide variety of explosives. The vessel which attacked Antwerp on August 25th carried 8·2 in. shells weighing 250 lb., the walls of which were nearly 1 in. thick, and contained trinitrotoluene—the German high explosive. The bombs dropped on the same city on September 1st were shrapnel, filled with special bullets, calculated to inflict horrible wounds.

The first phase of the Great War produced another evidence of the romantic possibilities of the Third Arm. On September 3rd a British submarine engaged on patrol duty some thirty miles off Borkum came on a German seaplane, the engine of which had failed during flight, and captured Lieutenant K. Wilhelm Kustzen and the pilot, who were landed at Parkeston Quay, Harwich, the following night. The seaplane was destroyed.

SEARCHING THE SKIES FOR HOSTILE AIRSHIPS.
When the Germans were approaching Paris during the memorable weeks of August, 1914, the danger of air raids upon the French capital seemed very real. The French Admiralty, that palatial building in the Place de la Concorde, at the end of the Rue de Rivoli, was mounted with powerful searchlights, which swept the sky during the hours of darkness to detect the " flying " foe.

| CHAPTER XVIII. |

HOW SERBIA MADE READY TO MEET HER GIANT ANTAGONIST.

By A. H. Trapmann, War Correspondent in the Balkan Wars.

Austria the National Enemy of Serbia—Serbian Preparations for the Inevitable Struggle—Strength of the Serbian Army—The "Alsace-Lorraine" of Serbia—The Position of Bulgaria—Russian Guardianship of Slav Races—Rumania's Role of Policeman—The Long-Standing Quarrel Between Rumania and Austria—Austria's Responsibility for Backwardness of Macedonia—Austrian Espionage in the Balkans—Attempts to Estrange Serbia and Montenegro—Fighting Value of the Serbian Armies.

THE declaration of war found Serbia in much the same state as were all the Balkan States—in the process of army reorganisation, with a depleted treasury and a war-weary population. For two years little Serbia, with her 4,000,000 inhabitants, had been not only engaged in a life-struggle for her very existence, in the course of which her people had been called upon for the utmost self-sacrifice in blood and treasure, she had also undergone a nerve-racking period of diplomatic intrigues, of which Austrian policy was the hub.

The war against Turkey had, it was thought, exhausted Serbian financial resources, and taken the edge off the patriotic spirit which, like a beacon, flares through every land when war is first declared. It was believed that every Serbian who was willing or anxious to make sacrifices had already given all that he was prepared to offer in the patriotic wave of enthusiasm which carried Serbia through the war against Turkey. All these surmises, however, were found to be incorrect.

On the outbreak of the second war between the Balkan

PRINCE GEORGE OF SERBIA.
Prince George, the Crown Prince of Serbia, gave such palpable evidence of being an irresponsible firebrand that he was considered a danger to the State, and in March, 1909, he was made to renounce his right of succession to the Serbian throne in favour of his younger brother Prince Alexander.

Allies, Serbia was again swept by a wave of enthusiasm, and again unsuspected resources were placed at the disposal of the Government. The average Serbian hated and despised the Turk. He loathed the Bulgar, and with his loathing was mixed an ardent desire for revenge and an opportunity to wipe out the Bulgarian victory of the preceding generation. But the Serbian has for more than a century regarded Austria as his national enemy, the oppressor and enslaver of the brother Serb across the border, as a tyrant to be at once feared and hated, but one who, sooner or later, must be destroyed. The whole population must have unanimously welcomed the declaration of war by Austria as the culminating crisis of Serbia's national existence, in which it behoved all Serbians—man, woman, and child —to work with all their bodily strength and personal belongings for Serbia's victory.

No sooner had the Treaty of Bucharest been signed in 1913 between the Balkan States than the Serbian General Staff addressed itself to the difficult task of reorganising Serbian military resources to face the inevitable

347

conflict with Austria. It is known that Russia gave Serbia due and timely notice that the Austrian menace was even more imminent than Serbia had herself feared. The warning ran that on one pretext or another Austria would find occasion to pick a quarrel with Serbia during the course of the year 1914, and it added that Russia herself was making frantic endeavours to hasten her own naval and military reorganisation, so that when the crisis came Russia would be able to afford Serbia more substantial help than the mere diplomatic assistance she had been obliged to content herself with in the past—in 1909 and 1912.

Serbian measures of precaution

The Serbian Government and General Staff took the warning to heart, and immediately set to work to prepare for what the Germans would have called "The Day." The Staff elaborated a scheme by which the Serb populations of Serbia's newly-acquired provinces of the Novi Bazar, Old Serbia, and the Villayet of Monastir were to furnish their full quota of recruits for the Army. In the latter stages of the war against Bulgaria, Serbia had no fewer than 295,000 men under arms, but there had been no time to organise fully and equip the majority of these as field units, with their due proportion of guns and staffs.

This was the work which was now undertaken by the Government. The scheme contemplated the formation of the Army into the following main components.

Four armies each of four divisions, namely :

(1) The Army of the Danube, centre Palanka.

(2) The Army of the East, centre Nish.

(3) The Army of the West, centre Ushitza.

(4) The Army of the South, centre Uskub ; with 20,000 frontier guards, and 12,000 men distributed in garrisons at special points and fortresses.

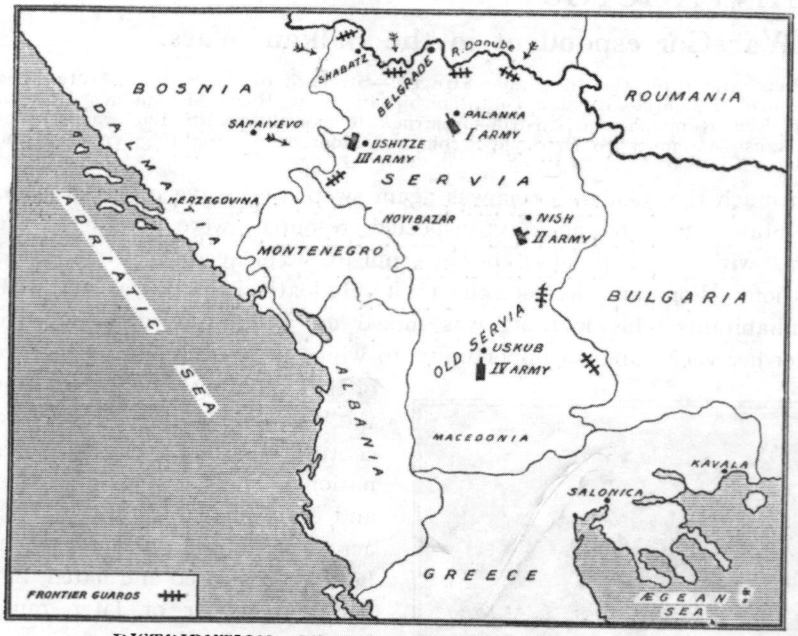

Two possible eventualities were especially studied : (1) A renewal of war with Bulgaria, in which case the Eastern Army would form the Serbian centre, with the Army of the Danube on its left and the Southern Army on its right, the Western Army being held in reserve, probably at Nish ; and (2) a war with Austria, which would presuppose an attempt at an Austrian invasion from across the Danube, with a subsidiary movement from the north-west and west, from the general direction of Sarajevo.

In this case the Eastern Army, firmly based on Nish, would constitute the Serbian right, while the centre would retire from the line of the Danube, but still remain the apex of a triangle facing north of which the left flank would be guarded by the Army of the West. Again, on the left flank of the Western Army, plucky little Montenegro could be counted upon to put some 40,000 war-trained veterans amongst her inaccessible mountains, while the Army of the South could either be brought up to strengthen the triangle or to strike in through the Novi Bazar region, co-operating with the Montenegrins on the left and the Western Army on the right.

DISTRIBUTION OF SERBIAN MILITARY FORCES.
With Bulgaria on one flank, thirsting for revenge after her defeat in 1913, and with her national enemy Austria on her other flank, Serbia had to reckon on a possibility of war from two sides. This sketch map shows how open Serbia would be to attack from two flanks, and indicates the distribution and headquarters of her four armies.

Montenegrin assistance

The diagram above will make the simplicity and efficacy of the Serbian plans more readily understandable by those not intimately acquainted with the geography of the North-Western Balkans.

Each Serbian army was to consist of four divisions, and the division was organised as follows :

Two brigades of infantry each of 6,000 bayonets.

Two brigades of artillery each of 600 men with twelve guns.

One regiment of cavalry with 600 sabres.

Various auxiliary services, including engineers, army service corps—in all, about 1,300 men.

Total of a division, about 15,000 men.

In addition to each army were allotted "army troops," consisting of a few batteries of heavy artillery, infantry, and engineers, and a brigade of cavalry of 2,000 sabres, thus bringing up the whole strength of each of the four

MENTIONED IN DESPATCHES

It is impossible to include portraits of all the gallant officers whose signal services in the field were acknowledged in Sir John French's despatch of October 8th, 1914. But in this and the two following pages we give a representative collection of photographs of officers who earned distinction.

[From the painting by John St. Helier Lander.]

LIEUTENANT-GENERAL SIR DOUGLAS HAIG, K.C.B., K.C.I.E., K.C.V.O., commanded the Second Corps of the British Expeditionary Force during the Battle of the Aisne. Sir John French said in his despatch of October 8th : " I cannot speak too highly of the valuable services rendered by Sir Douglas Haig and the army corps under his command. Day after day, and night after night, the enemy's infantry has been hurled against him in violent counter-attack, which has never on any one occasion succeeded." Another paragraph of the despatch reads : " Sir Douglas Haig was very hardly pressed, and had no reserve in hand. I placed the cavalry division at his disposal, part of which he skilfully used to prolong and secure the left flank of the Guards Brigade. Some heavy fighting ensued, which resulted in the enemy being driven back with heavy loss."

LIEUT.-GENERAL SIR ARCHIBALD MURRAY,
K.C.B., C.V.O., D.S.O.,
Chief of Sir John French's General Staff.
"Has continued to render me invaluable help."

BRIG.-GEN. E. M. PERCEVAL, D.S.O.
"Crossed the river (Aisne) at 10 a.m.
(September 14th), and met with very heavy
opposition."

BRIG.-GENERAL R. SCOTT-
KERR, C.B., M.V.O., D.S.O.
Was wounded during the fighting.

BRIG.-GENERAL G. F. MIL
D.S.O.,
General Headquarters Staff. S
Soudan, including Khartoum.
in despatches during the South Afr

BRIG.-GEN. H. DE B. DE LISLE, C.B., D.S.O.
"Our cavalry acted with great vigour, especially
General De Lisle's brigade."

MAJ.-GEN. SIR CHARLES FERGUSSON,
C.B., M.V.O., D.S.O.
"Maintained his position throughout the
whole battle with great skill and tenacity."

LIEUT.-COLONEL STANLEY
BARRY, Aide-de-Camp to Sir
John French.

LIEUT.-GEN.
W. P. PULTENEY, C.B., D.S.O.
"Showed himself to be a most
capable commander in the field."

COLONEL G. M. W. MACDONOGH,
General Headquarters Staff.

COLONEL E. E. CARTER,
C.M.G., M.V.O.,
General Headquarters Staff.

The Late MAJ.-GENERAL H
HAMILTON, C.V.O., C.B., D
"With the 3rd Division, vigorously
to the north, and regained all th
he had lost." Afterwards ki

COLONEL F. S. MAUDE, C.M.G., D.S.O.,
General Headquarters Staff.
Took part in Soudan and South African
Campaigns.

MAJOR H.R.H. PRINCE
ARTHUR OF CONNAUGHT.
"Employed with great ad-
vantage on confidential missions
of some importance."

MAJOR W. R. CHICHEST
3rd Batt. Worcestershire Regimen
wounded during the fighti

GENERAL F. M. GLUBB, C.B.,
D.S.O.,
Headquarters Staff. Chief Engineer
n Command, Salisbury. Mentioned
tches during the South African War.

B.-GEN. B. J. C. DORAN, C.B.,
General Headquarters Staff. Served
in the Afghan War, Nile, Hazara,
Miranzai, and Tirah Expeditions.

LIEUT.-COLONEL LORD BROOKE,
M.V.O.,
Aide-de-Camp to Sir John French. Was
extra A.D.C. to Lord Milner in South Africa.
Acted as Reuter's Special Correspondent
during Russo-Japanese War.

BRIG.-GEN. J. A. L. HALDANE, C.B., D.S.O.,
General Headquarters Staff. Served in Waziristan,
Chitral, Tirah. Twice wounded in South Africa.
Military Attaché during Russo-Japanese War.

LIEUT.-COL. LORD LOCH, D.S.O.,
General Headquarters Staff. Mentioned in despatches during Soudan
and South African Campaigns.

BRIG.-GEN. A. G. HUNTER-WESTON,
C.B., D.S.O.,
General Headquarters Staff. Served in
Miranzai, Waziristan, and Dongola Ex-
peditions. Took part in many actions in
South African War.

BRIG.-GEN. A. E. W. COUNT GLEICHEN,
K.C.V.O., C.B., C.M.G., D.S.O.,
General Headquarters Staff. Extra Equerry to his
Majesty. Has seen much service in foreign parts,
including Soudan, Abyssinia, and South Africa.

ate LIEUT.-COL. SIR EVELYN
BRADFORD, BART.,
h Highlanders. Died a hero's death
the war. Served in the Nile
pedition and in South Africa.

COL. V. T. BUNBURY, C.B., D.S.O.,
General Headquarters Staff. Served
throughout Burma and Soudan
Campaigns.

COLONEL W. G. B. BOYCE, C.B., D.S.O.,
General Headquarters Staff. Commanded
Army Service Corps Training Establishment.
Mentioned in despatches during South African
War.

MAJOR C. TOOGOOD, D.S.O.,
Batt. Lincolnshire Regiment. Was
wounded during the fighting.

LIEUT.-COL. M. N. TURNER,
1st Batt. Duke of Cornwall's Light
Infantry. Was wounded during the
fighting.

BREV.-COL. S. C. F. JACKSON, D.S.O.,
1st Batt. Hampshire Regiment. Was
wounded during the fighting.

BRIG.-GEN. J. G. HEADLAM,
C.B., D.S.O.,
General Headquarters Staff. On
the Headquarters Staff in the
South African War, mentioned in
despatches twice.

AUSTRIAN SOLDIERS SURRENDER WITHOUT FIRING A SHOT.

A roll-call of Austrian soldiers, captured by the victorious Serbs, held at Nish. Many of the men who were supposed to fight for Austria were racially allied to Serbia, and hated the Austrian yoke. At the first opportunity they walked over to their opponents and surrendered, exhibiting their rifles to prove that they had not fired a single shot.

A SERBIAN TELLS HOW HE HELPED TO ROUT THE AUSTRIANS IN BOSNIA.

wounded Serbian, back in the bosom of his family after fighting valiantly against the Austrians in Bosnia, relates his experience of the campaign. Great success attended the Serbian arms in Bosnia, which district was entirely sympathetic to Serbia when war broke out.

armies to close upon 65,000. The guns captured from the Turks (Krupp's), together with guns of the same make captured by the Greeks from the same source, and lent (or sold) to Serbia by Greece, were utilised as Army troops, while the guns (Schneider-Canet) captured from Bulgaria were allotted to the Army of the South, the other three armies being supplied with original Schneider-Canet guns belonging to the Serbian Army.

The total of the four Serbian field armies thus amounted to 260,000, to which must be added 20,000 frontier guards and 12,000 garrison troops, making a grand total of 292,000 men. It was estimated that, on a

general mobilisation, about 340,000 men would become available, but that **The Army strength of Serbia** 40,000 of these would be practically untrained if war occurred in the first half of the present year, and it was intended that these should be held back to replenish losses and casualties in the field army. At the same time, the formation of an independent cavalry division of 6,000 sabres was contemplated.

As regards the field armies, there can be no doubt that not only was their organisation complete

BELGRADE, THE CAPITAL OF SERBIA.
Belgrade stands at the junction of the Save with the Danube, and overlooks the plains of Hungary opposite. The bridge across the tributary stream, seen in the picture above, connects the two countries. The top picture is the War Office in Belgrade, and the bottom picture shows the Serbian Houses of Parliament.

and their material entirely replenished, but, what proved of even greater importance, the organisation had been planned in such a way that the mobilisation of the Serbian Army was completed in record time, and at least twice as quickly as the Austrian General Staff had anticipated. Before, however, we deal with actual operations in the Serbian war area, **Rapidity of Serbian mobilisation** we must consider the factors, political and strategical, which governed those operations; for just as strategy governs the tactical situation, so do politics dictate the strategy of a campaign.

The diplomatic quarrel between Serbia and Austria has already been dealt with in an earlier chapter; but too much stress cannot be laid upon the fact that every true Serbian continues to look upon Herzegovina and Bosnia much as the Frenchman looks upon Alsace-Lorraine—as provinces of an erstwhile powerful empire, temporarily annexed by an alien usurper.

There are, in fact, no fewer than ten million Serbs under the dominion of Franz Joseph, and the vast majority of these are anxious to throw off the alien yoke at the first possible and practical opportunity. Here, then, to the

GENERAL RADIVOJE BOJOVOVIC
Commander-in-Chief.

GENERAL PUTNIK
Chief of the General Staff.

GENERAL BOSA YANKOVITCH
A great Army leader.

GENERAL PETAR BOYOVITCH
Commanding First Army Corps.

SOME OF THE LEADING COMMANDERS OF SERBIA'S VALIANT ARMY OF VETERANS.

westward lay a country eminently suitable for the operations of a Serbo-Montenegrin force, making Sarajevo its first objective. The allied army would be advancing through a country, the inhabitants of which would not only be friendly, but would also undoubtedly flock to join the colours and serve against their former master; and, moreover, the Montenegrin Army would be only too anxious to co-operate in any such forward movement. In all circumstances, it must have been a very sore temptation to the General Staff at Belgrade to abandon, even temporarily, the idea of a campaign which at the outset promised such a bright prospect of glory, initial success, and extraordinary possibilities of recruiting. There were other factors, however, which had to be taken into consideration, and the most important of these was that every step towards Sarajevo would mean a yard further from the Bulgarian frontier.

When, in August, 1913, by reason of her unimpaired military resources, Rumania imposed peace upon the Balkans, Bulgaria made no secret of the fact that she regarded the peace only in the light of an armistice. She ascribed her defeats,

PRINCE ALEXANDER OF SERBIA
in his uniform as Commander of the Serbian Armies. He is King Peter's second son, and became heir-apparent when his brother Prince George renounced his right of succession in 1909, and Prince Regent on his father's retirement from active participation in the government of the country shortly before the outbreak of war.

not to the splendid fighting of Greek and Serbian armies, who had driven her legions off the field, but to what she termed the traitorous behaviour of Turkey and Rumania. She did not hesitate to announce that she would seize the very earliest opportunity to take a full revenge upon Serbia and Greece for the indignities she had been made to suffer.

With Austria's declaration of war on Serbia, and the extremely strained relations between Turkey and Greece, this opportunity arose. Here was a heaven-sent chance to fall upon the flank of Serbia while Austria invaded her northern marches, at a moment when Greece could offer her ally no substantial support, being fully occupied in preparations for a war against Turkey. Those who know the ins and outs of recent Balkan history are perfectly aware of the three reasons which held Bulgaria back from again taking the field and of throwing in her lot with Austria.

First and foremost, Rumania, with her considerable reserves of wealth and her exceedingly capable Army of half a million men, had assumed the rôle of Balkan policeman. She laid it down categorically that, apart from her defensive alliance with Serbia and Greece, she would unhesitatingly wage war on any Balkan

GENERAL MIHALILO ZIVKOVITCH
Commanding Fourth Army Corps.

GENERAL PAVLOVITCH
Commanding Second Army Corps.

GENERAL MIHAILO JOURICHITCH
Commanding Third Army Corps.

GENERAL GOJKOVITCH
Commanding Fifth Army Corps.

FOUR OF THE VICTORIOUS COMMANDERS OF SERBIA'S ARMY CORPS.

CATTARO, THE ADRIATIC OUTPOST OF AUSTRIA.

A narrow wedge of Dalmatia, which is a province of Austria, stretches down the shore of the Adriatic, and Cattaro, a fortified port in a magnificent natural harbour, is close to the southern point of the wedge. It was a point of attack by the French and British fleet in the operations against Austria soon after the beginning of the war.

State which broke the peace. Although this threat was levelled at Sofia, Constantinople did not fail to realise the significance of it. Bulgaria knew that if in this early stage of the war she assisted Austria to make a sandwich of Servia, she herself would be in the same unenviable position between the two fires of the Serbians on the west and of the Rumanians on the north.

The astute diplomats of Sofia recognised that it would suit their book better to bide the tide of events. In the case of a crushing Austrian victory, Bulgaria would get her opportunity for revenge, for in such an event Rumania would probably think twice before she herself plunged into the Balkan Armageddon. In any case, therefore, Bulgaria would wait. She could lose nothing in so doing. By waiting she was doing Austria a good turn, because Serbia could not withdraw her Eastern Army from Nish until the neutrality of Bulgaria was assured.

THE WESTERN GATEWAY TO THE BALKAN STATES.

The railway bridge over the Save leads from Hungary to Serbia, and is on the main line from Vienna to Constantinople.

The second factor in the situation was a purely financial one. Crippled by the recent wars, the Bulgarian State Treasury was empty, and the only chance of replenishing the Treasury was to levy a special tax upon the population During the two wars the Bulgarian population had waxed rich, for not only had harvests been exceptionally good, but also every officer and soldier who had served with the Army in the field had sent home rich booty, in the shape of trinkets, gold, and merchandise looted in Macedonia and Thrace.

With this booty the population would be very loth to part in order to pay a special war levy, while the prospects of yet a third campaign, whether it were waged in Serbia or in Macedonia, held few attractions. There would be little enough loot to gather in the former, while Macedonia had already been completely gutted. In addition to this, the population was sick and tired of war, and any Government that again plunged the country into the vortex of strife would be sure to be turned out of power at the earliest opportunity.

The third reason was even more convincing. During the second war Bulgaria had suffered very heavy losses of war material. She had lost close upon three hundred guns and a great number of rifles. Moreover, such guns and rifles as she still possessed were almost unserviceable owing to hard usage ; and, besides, the supply of ammunition for guns and rifles alike was totally insufficient. Nor, in the event of

Prince Michael Street, as seen above, is the "Bond Street" of Belgrade, a wide thoroughfare well laid out with high-class shops and fine residences. The picture in the circle shows the last remaining relic of

Turkish rule, the old Turkish mosque at Belgrade. The picture on the right is a view of Nish, whither the Government was removed on the outbreak of war, showing the walls, the governor's house, and the barracks.

355

SERBIAN TROOPS IN THEIR NEW CAMPAIGN
UNIFORM.

Bulgaria joining Austria, could she hope to replenish war supplies from either Austria or Germany, for both countries had need of all the war material they possessed or would be able to manufacture.

Serbia, of course, was well aware of Bulgaria's predicament, but she could not afford to take any great risk, and thus her Eastern Army was left at Nish to await developments. After early August, every day that passed served to furnish Bulgarian statesmen with an

additional reason why they should continue to observe a strict neutrality. The crushing Austrian victory over Serbia, which was to have been the signal for Bulgaria's final apostacy from the Slav world, proved to be a crushing Austrian defeat. Later, the glorious Russian advance in Galicia brought it home to even the most bellicose Bulgar that there are moments when it is wiser to lie low and say nothing. If further pressure was essential to lend point to the argument, that pressure was forthcoming when Rumania, as a precautionary measure, mobilised 200,000 troops along the Bulgarian frontier.

ROYAL LIFE GUARDS OF THE SERBIAN ARMY.

It is, perhaps, worth while to pass in survey the relations which existed between Russia and Bulgaria, so as better to follow the intricate maze of Balkan diplomatic intrigues, and discern the inevitable course of events. It must be first of all realised that Russia acts as guardian and protector of all the Slav race, and more particularly of the Orthodox Church. It was in the past owing to Russia's championship of the Slav cause that

SERBIAN ARTILLERY OFFICERS GOING TO THE WAR.
This photograph was taken just after these officers had bid adieu to their families,
and they are seen carrying the flowers given them by their women folk at parting.

Serbia and Bulgaria won their independence from Turkey ; but Russia, not unnaturally, expected and demanded a return for favours shown. If Russia was to champion the cause of Serb and Bulgar against Austrian encroachment, then the two lesser States must allow their foreign policy to be generally controlled from St. Petersburg, whence Russian statesmen, with their greater horizon, could obtain a better survey of the world of politics

For a while Serbia and Bulgaria silently accepted this unwritten condition of the tacit alliance. But the gratitude and memory of nations is proverbially short-lived, especially in the Balkans. When Russia allowed Austria to annex Bosnia and Herzegovina, when Russia suffered defeat at the hands of the Japanese, and, finally, when Russia failed to help the Balkans to ameliorate the conditions of the Slavs in Macedonia, the two Slav States bethought them of the paraphrase that "Russia helps those who help themselves." It was under the auspices of the Russian Minister at Athens that the Balkan League was formed, but the States concerned in the alliance felt that they were "facing the music," while Russia stood safely aside and gave advice.

Later, when the question of the future of Albania was discussed, Austrian and Italian claims entirely overrode the representations of Russia, and Greece and Serbia felt a keen disappointment, which

SERBIAN ARTILLERY AT BELGRADE.
Serbian artillery posted on the promenade of a public garden in Belgrade, which overlooks the junction of the Danube and the Save, and commands Semlin.

was partly allayed by Russia's excuse that "at present she was not sufficiently prepared to fight Austria, but hoped to be so ere very long."

Bulgaria, in the meanwhile, with that duplicity which is so characteristic of the nation, saw in Russia's temporary weakness a chance of personal profit. Sofia began to listen to the wiles of Vienna, and hope told a flattering tale. A diplomatic agreement was entered into—that if Bulgaria could make war on Serbia and Greece, she could have all the country she could take, while Austria would "bluff" Russia to stand aside, and

ANOTHER PIECE OF SERBIAN ARTILLERY.
Another example of the Serbian guns that wrought destruction among the Austrians. A powerful Schneider quick-firer gun, with its crew.

as her share of the spoils would content herself with the annexation of the Novi Bazar for the nonce. The Bulgar, whose chief pride it is to term himself the "Prussian of the East," accepted the bargain with alacrity, never doubting for a moment that he could easily overthrow Serbia and Greece. The sequel proved the folly of his self-confidence.

There is one particular incident so thoroughly characteristic of Bulgarian methods that no apology is made for recording it here. It will be remembered that towards the close of June, 1913, the Tsar had invited the Prime Ministers of Greece, Serbia, and Bulgaria to come to St. Petersburg, in the hopes that with his help they would solve their differences of opinion. Almost the last act of M. Daneff, the Bulgarian Premier, before entering the train destined to take him to this peaceable conference, was to sign an order to his generals at the front to march forward and make war upon the two other allies on July 1st, 1913.

Had Bulgaria succeeded, it would have been a priceless jest to recount in after days how Daneff had fooled the great White Tsar; but as events issued, it merely remained an insult which Russia and the Tsar will

A SERBIAN GUN HAMMERING AT SEMLIN.
A further photograph of the well-manned Serbian artillery playing upon Semlin. During the early days of the war the Austrians made determined efforts to cross the Danube and penetrate into Serbia, but they were repulsed with enormous loss.

A BOY SERB IN THE BATTLE-LINE.

In Serbia the war was a people's war to as great an extent as it was in Russia. In spite of being war-weary and war-poor, the people of Serbia rushed to the colours with that enthusiasm which attempted oppression of liberty-loving people always evokes. Perhaps the two photographs shown here exemplify that spirit more than anything else could do. A boy of twelve, who was an excellent shot, joined the Army, and persuaded the authorities to accept his services. He was the pet of his older comrades, and is said to have done excellent service in the rifle-pits at Belgrade when it was being bombarded by the Austrian guns from across the Danube.

find it impossible to forget and difficult to forgive. Bulgaria, who dreamed of making herself the mistress of the Balkans, succeeded only in proving her own untrustworthiness. In turn, she has coquetted with Russia, Serbia, and Greece, with Austria and Italy, and as recently as the beginning of this year she offered her favours to Turkey. It is doubtful whether the alleged friendship of so mercenary a lady will attract many suitors in the future.

Those who do not understand Rumanian policy—and even many of those who do—have found fault with the attitude adopted by Rumania during the second Balkan War. She is accused of having "sat on the fence" until she saw on which side the booty was likely to fall. Having first extorted a large tract of territory from Bulgaria as the price of her neutrality, she proceeded to throw in her lot with Serbia and Greece, and to march her Army through a country which could not possibly make any resistance to her.

At the opening of the war we again find Rumania apparently "sitting on the fence," and proclaiming her

SERBIAN RESERVIST WITH HIS WIFE AT NISH.

RESERVISTS AT NISH—SERBIA'S TEMPORARY CAPITAL.

A party of Serbian reservists encamped at Nish. This Serbian city is only surpassed by Belgrade in commercial and strategic importance. The King and Government reside there for at least three months each year. It is built near the site of the ancient Roman city Naissus, where the Emperor Claudius annihilated the army of the Goths in A.D. 269, and which the Huns, under Attila, destroyed in the fifth century.

WOUNDED SERBIANS ARRIVING AT NISH.

neutrality. Not only that, but she threatens to make war on any Balkan State that imperils the present *status quo* in the Balkans. She has assumed the rôle of the policeman, an inglorious one perhaps in time of war, but one that belligerents have no cause to criticise, provided that the policeman succeeds in keeping the peace. It must be remembered that of all the Balkan States Rumania at the time the war opened was by far the best prepared to undertake a war. Her resources were great and unimpaired by recent warfare, her Army numerically greater than that of any Balkan State, and in point of equipment and training the equal of the best. Her weight in the balance of a Balkan war would be a decisive factor. But, instead of throwing that weight into either of the scales, she preferred to maintain peace by threatening action.

As to the sympathies of the Rumanian nation, there can be no doubt whatever. Sprung from a Roman colony founded in the height of Roman imperial glory, the Rumanians are Latin by race, speech, and religion, and, like all Latins, their sympathies are anti-German and pro-Slav. Moreover, Rumania is very loyal to the terms of her treaty with Serbia and Greece, and it is difficult to conceive of any combination of circumstances which would induce her to break away from the spirit of that alliance. Rumania has also her private reasons of quarrel with Austria, in addition to a traditional sympathy with the Petrograd foreign policy.

Rumania's national sympathies

The Rumanian quarrel with Austria is somewhat intricate, and at first glance not very easy to comprehend. But in Hungary there are three millions of people of Rumanian race, who are treated with great harshness under Hungarian rule. Moreover, throughout the Balkans there is scattered a nomad people known as the Kutzo-Vlachs, who are the gipsies of the Balkans, and of Rumanian origin (it is indeed almost certain that the derivation of the word " Romany " comes from this source, just as " Rumania " is another form of " Roman "), and who have always been under the special protection of the Bucharest Government. Scattered throughout Bosnia and all the

MOUNTED ARTILLERY OF THE TURKISH ARMY.

Balkan States, these peripatetic subjects give Rumania a good excuse for supporting any demand for reform which may from time to time be raised in the Balkans.

In nearly every instance she has experienced either overt or covert opposition from Austria. Indeed, if the truth were but made known, it would be found that the responsibility for the backwardness of Macedonia in the past under Turkish rule rests on the shoulders of Austria, and not of Turkey. It will be readily understood what an

immense help to Serbia and Russia it would have been if Rumania had taken the field with 500,000 troops in Southern Galicia, and it was presumed that her reward at the end of the war would not be disproportionate with the help afforded to the Allies.

Many stories came from Vienna concerning Serbian intrigues against Austria, for which, by the way, not a single item of evidence from an unbiassed source has been produced, or is ever likely to be; but, even had Serbia given herself over to intrigue, she was surely entitled to

COMPANY OF ARTILLERYMEN OF THE GREEK ARMY.

do so as a measure of self-defence against the toils that Austria has persistently spread for her.

The ways of Austria in the Balkans are obscure, and have not in the past been handicapped by any considerations of honour or straight dealing. Huge sums of money have been expended annually on maintaining

Austrian espionage

a veritable army of secret agents, who are usually selected on account of the blackguardly record of their past career. "Search the prisons of Balkania," said an eminent Balkan statesman, "and you will find that all the scum are, or soon will be, Austrian secret agents." .

To show the *modus operandi* of Austria, it is of interest to note that bandits who used to infest the mountains of Epirus under Turkish rule were, upon the declaration of war, either given appointments in the police force of the Provisional Government of Albania, receiving in addition to their pay a substantial subsidy from the Austrian Consul at Avlona (Valona), while others were appointed secret agents in Northern Albania and Macedonia, to foster hatred between the Balkan Allies.

It is also common knowledge that the Austrian Consul-General at Janina, during the siege, was in daily consultation with Essad Pasha, the Turkish commandant, to whom he gave much unsolicited advice. This same official managed during the six months of the war to expend no less than £23,000, although his own income did not exceed £500 a year. It is easy to imagine whence the money came, and for what purposes it was expended.

THE RUMANIAN BERSAGLIERI.

The whole object of these intrigues was to advance slowly but surely Austria's century-old policy of "peaceful penetration" in the Balkans, until she could attain her ultimate aim of occupying the eastern littoral of the Adriatic down to Avlona, with an outlet on the Ægean Sea at Salonica. Montenegro and Serbia formed the first barrier to this scheme of peaceful penetration, which was carried on by means of Catholic propaganda, schools, secret service agents, the establishment of an Austrian postal

BATTERY OF ARTILLERY OF THE BULGARIAN ARMY.

MONTENEGRIN SOLDIERS WITH A MITRAILLEUSE.

RUMANIAN INFANTRYMAN.

service, and finally by a heavily subsidised commercial campaign, in which the Austrian Lloyd Steamship Company played an important part.

To remove this barrier it was essential to separate Montenegro from Serbia by seizing the Novi Bazar Valley. Unfortunately for Austrian hopes, the attitude of Italy in 1909, and the Serbian successes in the first Balkan War gave the district of Novi Bazar to Serbia. So it became necessary to find a pretext of war with Serbia in order to wrest the Novi Bazar district from the grasp of its possessors. This political factor, it will be shown, had a disastrous effect upon Austrian strategy when military operations had to be undertaken.

Those who came into contact with the Serbian Army during the two Balkan Wars, speak with unstinted praise of the valour of the men the skill of the junior officers, and the efficiency of the artillery. These latter have been, like the Greeks, trained on the French model, and, armed with French guns, they have invariably done excellent work. Faik Bey, the Turkish divisional commander who fought the Serbs at Kumonovo and Monastir, spoke almost with enthusiasm of the admirable practice made by the Serbian gunners at those two battles, and the Turkish defender of Adrianople has repeatedly stated that only the arrival of 40,000 Serbians in front of the city obliged him to surrender.

During the second campaign the resisting power and pertinacity of the Serbian Army was amply demonstrated in the thirty days of continuous battle all along the front.

If there is any criticism to be made of the Serbian Army it must concern its lack of adaptability to alter preconceived plans rapidly. Not even the Prussian is more thorough in the conception and preparation of a plan of campaign, but the Serbian Staff, in the second Balkan War at least, showed want of initiative in dealing with a new situation. So long as speed of conception is not essential, the Serbian General Staff can be trusted to commit no error; but, on the other hand, it is doubtful whether it will ever reap to the full the fruits of such victories as it may secure.

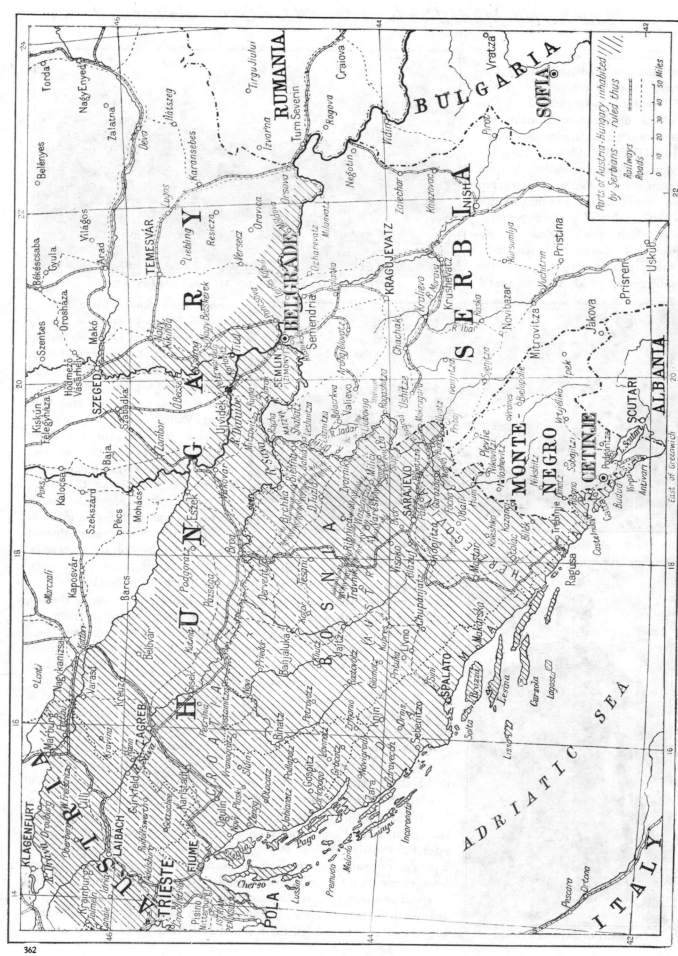

MAP SHOWING RELATIONSHIP OF SERBIA TO OTHER BALKAN STATES AND SERBIANS UNDER AUSTRIAN RULE AT BEGINNING OF THE WAR.

CHAPTER XIX.

SHABATZ—THE FIRST DECISIVE BATTLE OF THE WAR.

The Austrian "Punitive Expedition"—Three Neglected Factors—A Time-Table that was not kept—Serbian Mobilisation—The Abandonment of the Capital—Austrian Attempts to Cross the Danube—A Serbian trap and its results—The moral effect—Attempts to cross the Drina—The Austrian Forward Movement—Serbian Reinforcements—Austrian Defeat and Great Losses—Effects of the Serbian Victory upon Austrian and German Plan of Campaign—Effect upon the other Balkan Countries.

WHEN the Austrian Government began its "punitive expedition" against Serbia, the original Austrian idea was an enveloping movement of four army corps with Nish as their objective. Two corps were to cross the Danube at Basiasch and Belgrade, while one corps from the north-west was to cross the River Save in the vicinity of Shabatz, and act as a right flank guard to the Austrian advance. A fourth corps, moving from Sarajevo on Visegrad and Ushitza, was to turn the flank of any Serbian line of defence, and at the same time, by invading the Novi Bazar district, to separate Montenegro from Serbia. Also a detached column, based upon Cattaro, was to move and occupy the attention of the Montenegrins.

In itself the plan was sound enough, but it failed to take into consideration three vital factors:

1. Rapidity of Serbian mobilisation.

2. Difficulty of crossing the Danube.

3. Possibility of a Montenegrin counter offensive in the Novi Bazar.

On the sketch map below are shown the positions of the contending armies on August 2nd: (a) As the Austrians hoped they would be; and (b) as they actually were. While the Austrians contented themselves with a leisurely march forward and half-hearted attempts to cross the Drina, Save, and Danube, Serbia mobilised with extreme rapidity, and, withdrawing her Southern Army by rail towards Nish, not only provided for the safety of her Bulgarian frontier, but at the same time left the troops at her eastern frontier free to go forward.

During these preparations, screened by Serbia's frontier guards, who served her admirably, the Montenegrins not only sent a detachment to watch the Austrians at Cattaro, but they also despatched a strong detachment to move northward to threaten Visegrad. The Austro-Bosnian army found itself obliged to send a strong flanking column to meet this force and prevent it from effecting a junction with the Serbians. While it was held up in front, unable to cross the Drina, it received a call to help the north-western army.

The Battle of Shabatz was the culminating move for which the Serbians played and manœuvred in the early weeks of the war as a fencer plays for an opening. Abandoning

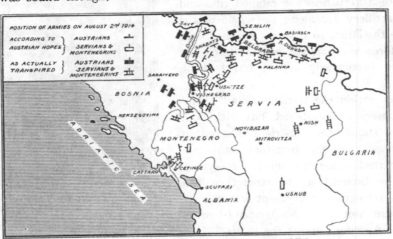

AN AUSTRIAN TIME-TABLE THAT FAILED.
The Austrians, as well as the Germans, made their war plans according to time-table, and, like their German allies, they found that it was easier for the General Staff to compile a time-table than it was for the field armies to keep it.

their capital to the tender mercies of the Austrian artillery, they made a feint of falling back from Palunka upon Nish, while they really moved north-westward. From Ushitza another strong force was also sent to the north-western corner of Serbia, into the triangle the apex of which is the junction of the Rivers Save and Drina. During the first week of August five Austrian army corps devoted the whole of their

energies to attempting to effect a crossing of the Danube and the Save. The points of crossing were successfully disputed by the Serbian Frontier Guards, assisted by detached columns from the Army of the Danube, and an advance guard of the Western Army. In no case did the Austrian attempts meet with any measure of success, while a combined effort to invade Serbia from the extreme east at Orsova resulted in a minor disaster for the Austrian arms—a foretaste of what was to come. The three battalions that formed the Austrian advance guard lost touch with their own main body, and at the same time fell into a carefully prepared trap. They were exterminated, for of the 3,400 men only twenty-five survived to be taken prisoners.

RUINS OF THE BRITISH EMBASSY AT BELGRADE.
The Government of Serbia moved south to Nish before the Austrians from the Hungarian side of the river bombarded Belgrade. This photograph shows the damage done to the British Embassy by Austrian shells.

This marked success produced a very wholesome effect upon the morale of the Serbians, who had resented the bombardment of their capital from across the Danube without being able to make any effective reply. They regained confidence, not only in their own powers, but in the carefully conceived strategy of their generals.

After the affair the Austrians showed activity on the River Drina, which forms the western frontier of Serbia, on August 9th and 10th, but were quite unable to effect a crossing. On the 11th, under cover of a very heavy combined rifle and artillery fire along the whole of the front from Losnitza on the Drina to Shabatz on the Save, a reconnaissance in force was carried out in which the Austrian aircraft were particularly active, but still no crossing was effected.

Vain efforts to cross the rivers

The Serbian forces within the triangle found themselves not only hopelessly outnumbered, but with both their flanks threatened should the Austrians succeed in crossing either of the rivers. It was therefore considered advisable to begin a partial retirement until the Serbian main strength could be brought up to strengthen the Serbian defence. This retrograde movement was in part a precautionary measure, but was also conceived with the object of luring the Austrians across the rivers.

ROYAL PALACE BARRACKS AT BELGRADE.
The Austrian guns made great havoc in Belgrade, which was bombarded in the opening days of the war, and this photograph shows the effect of a shell in the barracks at the Royal Palace.

On August 12th an Austrian advance guard crossed the Drina, pushing eastward, while a detachment of the 4th Austrian Corps effected a crossing of the Save near Shabatz. On the following day, pontoon bridges having been constructed at several points, the Austrians began to pour across the river and to march into Serbia.

SERBIAN RED CROSS NURSES AT NISH WITH WOUNDED SOLDIERS FROM THE BATTLE-FRONT.

Near Shabatz were the 4th and 9th Corps, with the 8th Corps on their right, while one regiment of mountain artillery, borrowed from the 15th Corps, crossed the River Drina with the whole of the 13th Corps near Losnitza.

During the whole of August 13th the Serbian rearguard showed the utmost resolution and pluck by denying the crossings to the enemy. Only when night had fallen to cover its movements did it fall back sullenly and occupy positions facing the Austrian 8th and 13th Corps. These corps had incurred serious losses in storming the Serbian positions on the Drina.

On the 14th the Austrians resumed their forward movement. The 8th Corps marched on Tzer; the 13th Corps straddled the valley of the Jadar with a division on either bank; while a third division and the regiment of mountain artillery threatened the Serbian flank.

As soon as it was evident that the Austrian main armies were committed to this forward movement, while the 4th and 9th Austrian Corps were still held up at Shabatz by a Serbian retaining force, Serbian reinforcements were dispatched on August 15th to endeavour to turn the Austrian left flank. All through the 15th and 16th the Serbians resisted all the attacks of the 13th Corps along the Jadar valley, and only abandoned their trenches when the Austrian flanking column had completely turned their position. **Serbians speedily reinforced** Then during the night they again retired, and took up a third line of defences near Zavlaka.

The Serbian reinforcements were rushed up with almost incredible rapidity—incredible, that is to say, to those who had not seen the Serbian troops manœuvre during the Balkan Wars. Throughout the 17th, 18th, and 19th those reinforcements concentrated so as to outflank the Austrian flank movement. In vain the Austrians launched attack upon attack in a fruitless endeavour to break up this cloud of assailants which was enveloping their flank. In their immediate front, too, the Austrian troops were unable to dislodge the Serbians from their positions.

By the afternoon of the 18th it became evident that the Austrian offensive movement was giving way. Their losses had been enormous; they had entirely failed to shake the Serbian defensive; and they had not been able to obtain any assistance from their 4th and 9th Corps, who were still held up at Shabatz. On the 19th the Austrian offensive broke up altogether. The Serbians had succeeded in driving a wedge between the Austrians. The plight of the Austrian 8th and 13th Corps was desperate. All hope of help from the two corps at Shabatz had now to be abandoned.

In front and on their flank was an unbeaten enemy, while on their rear an unfordable river separated them from a country the inhabitants of which were, if not hostile, at least frankly disloyal. It is small wonder that the Austrian retreat almost at once degenerated into a rout, in which every man did the best he could for himself.

When the nature of the country is taken into consideration, with its dearth of roads and lack of villages and farms, it is probable that the Austrians suffered as much from hunger as from the enemy's pursuit.

Throughout the 20th, 21st, and 22nd the Serbians pushed the pursuit, and eventually drove the remnants of the 13th and 8th Corps either into the Drina or across it. Of the 130,000 Austrian troops who had crossed the Drina on August 12th and 13th some 20,000 were killed or wounded, and over 5,000 were taken prisoners, while

Heavy Austrian losses

doubtless some considerable part of the remainder either died of hunger or exposure during the retreat or deserted to their homes. The Serbians captured over sixty pieces of artillery and an immense amount of other military stores and equipment.

During the whole of this period the Serbian containing force in front of Shabatz had been able to hold off the Austrian 4th and 9th Corps, preventing them from co-operating with their western army. As soon as the rout of the latter became pronounced, the Serbian main army at Tzer broke off the pursuit and turned north-eastwards with a view of encircling the Shabatz army. The general commanding this Austrian force, who, it must be admitted, had not hitherto shown much initiative or determination, at last showed that he could move when he saw his retreat threatened.

Under cover of a violent assault upon the Serbian positions he drew off the major portion of his army, and made for the banks of the Save. The attack was defeated with appalling loss to the Austrians, and it was only because of the excellent work of a flotilla of Austrian war vessels lying in the Save that the remnants of the

ONE OF BRITAIN'S DEADLY MOSQUITOES OF THE OCEAN.

This is one of the D class of submarines, of which the British Admiralty had eight at the opening of the war. All these, along with nine boats of the E class, were on guard in the neck of the bottle that held the German Fleet while the British Expeditionary Force was being transported to France. "The patrol was maintained night and day," in the words of Commodore Keyes's despatch. These boats are of 550 to 600 tons displacement, with a speed of 15 knots above water and 10 knots submerged; they carry three 18 in. torpedo tubes, a 12-pounder gun on a disappearing mount, and a crew of 20 officers and men. The lettering on the picture is explanatory.

Austrian eastern army were able to cross the river and to avoid capture. It was on August 24th that the last miserable detachment of Austrians succeeded in making its escape from Serbian territory, and thus ended the famous Austrian " punitive " expedition against the despised little kingdom of Serbia.

There remained in the Serbian area of hostilities only one effective Austrian corps. This had originally opened operations against Eastern Serbia. When Russia began the invasion of Galicia, this corps was called off to face the Tsar's armies, but it had not got very far when news of the engagement at Shabatz brought it back into the Serbian area of operations. It was this corps which faced the Serbians at Semlin on September 8th, 9th, and 10th, but was obliged to give way.

The remnant of the Austrian army

Such portions of the Bosnian corps as had not been involved in the Shabatz disaster retired from Serbian territory and fell back upon Visegrad, whence they were evicted by a joint Serbo-Montenegrin effort on September 11th.

Austria began by despising her adversary and dividing her forces. From the moment that their optimistic hopes of immediate and crushing victories were baulked, the Austrian Staff and corps commanders completely lost their heads, and frittered away their time and the energies of their men in ill-conceived and ill-executed marches

A GRAPHIC ILLUSTRATION OF THE DEVELOPMENT OF THE BRITISH SUBMARINE.

The earliest submarines were small craft that scarcely gave the crew room to move. Great strides have been made, and now the accommodation is much more generous, increasing the comfort and health of the men and raising their spirits. The diagrammatic picture above shows the various classes of submarines of the British Navy, except the newest or F type, which displaces 1,200 tons when submerged, and has a speed of 20 knots on the surface and of 12 knots under water. The E class of submarine, illustrated in the bottom panel above, dates from 1912, and consists of eleven boats. They have a displacement of 725 tons above water and of 810 tons below water, with respective speeds of 16 and 10 knots. Thus they are almost exactly four times as large as the A class, which dates from 1904, and this comparison illustrates the great progress made in submarine construction in the space of a decade. Also, they have four torpedo-tubes, compared with the two of the A class boats.

and counter-marches without any definite object in view. The Serbians played upon this Austrian lack of determination as a man plays upon a piano. They called the tune and the Austrian generals danced to it. At the psychological moment the Serbian Army struck with all its force, with the result that the Austrian field army practically ceased to exist.

In a little less than one calendar month the despised Serbian forces, which numbered at most 250,000 men in the area of hostilities, had inflicted an overwhelming defeat upon a slightly superior Austrian army of invasion, capturing nearly half of its war material and placing it hors de combat for several weeks. But the Battle of Shabatz (or Jadar, as it is sometimes called) had even wider-reaching consequences. It was the first decisive battle of the Great War, and its moral effect was enormous. It taught the Austrians that they could not hope for success even against Serbia. Not only did the disaster greatly delay the Austrian mobilisation, but it also compelled the Austrian and German **Importance of the battle of Shabatz** General Staffs to reconsider their carefully pre-arranged plans. Two Austrian corps which were destined to help the Germans in Alsace were hastily recalled. Reserve corps which were to have been sent to meet the Russians in Galicia were ordered southwards instead of eastwards, while Germany herself had to consider the advisability of transferring troops from Belgium and France to replace the Austrian forces that had been diverted to Serbia.

Serbia was the first of all the Allies to fight a great and decisive battle, the first to deal a serious blow for freedom to the domination of the German military caste. Not only this. The echo of the Serbian guns which thundered

AN EMERGING SUBMARINE.
The track on the surface of the water indicates the course of a torpedo which the submarine at manœuvres has just fired before rising to the surface. The oval picture shows the track made by the periscope of a submarine at a naval review.

at Shabatz was heard in Sofia, Constantinople, and even across the Adriatic in Rome itself. If Italy ever had felt any qualms about her failure to fulfil her obligations to the Triple Alliance, the Serbian success effectively laid them to rest. If Bulgaria was contemplating an attack on Serbia on August 15th, she decided during the next week that the maintenance of neutrality would be the more prudent course for the immediate future, at least.

ONE OF THE TWENTY

CHAPTER XX

C CLASS SUBMARINES.

THE WAR UNDER THE WATERS—THE SUBMARINES STRIKE THEIR FIRST BLOWS.

Experience of Submarines in Naval Manœuvres—Expert Opinions of the Submerged Arm—Weakness of Large Submarines—Limited Effectiveness of Submarines—Means of Detecting Submarines—Submarine Strength of the Belligerent Countries—Growth of Submarine Offensiveness—The Human Factor in Submarine Work—The Periscope—Dangers Peculiar to Submarines—The Torpedo—The Explosive Charge—Guns Mounted on Submarines—The Exploit of H.M.S. Birmingham—Scouting Work of Submarines—The Tragedy of the Pathfinder—The Destruction of the Hela

PERHAPS the most romantic and impressive feature of the Great War was that it was waged with weapons such as had never in any previous struggle been employed by man. While aircraft hovered in the firmament above, strange new creatures like monstrous metal fishes haunted the depths of the sea. The conflict was no longer fought in space of two dimensions. A similar advantage to that which the Zeppelin and aeroplane obtained by climbing the sky was secured by the submarine, which could elude pursuit and observation by diving beneath the surface of the sea. The one type of war machine was above the level on which men had hitherto fought ; the other type was below it. This may yet prove to have fundamentally altered the conditions of naval war.

Before the great struggle there were many searchings of heart as to the exact role which submarines would play, and as to the effect which they would exert upon the battleship. In the British naval manœuvres of 1913 extraordinary results were achieved by the submarines. Firing dummy torpedoes with practice heads of soft copper, they again and again got home ; and, unless rumour was entirely at fault, accounted for half the battleships engaged. They were never seen ; they offered no target ; they stole up to their quarry and fired their bolt before their approach was known. The mantle of invisibility protected them, yet they themselves could see.

None who witnessed the submarine attack, carried out at the naval inspection of 1912 before the House of Commons, but must have been impressed by this new arm of the sea. Four submarines assailed the battle-fleet. The hour of their attack was known, and the quarter from which it would be delivered. Yet, in the case of the first two boats, all that the spectators saw was two streaks of spray, which moved swiftly

ADMIRAL H.S.H. PRINCE LOUIS OF BATTENBERG.
The First Sea Lord of the British Admiralty resigned his post on October 29th, 1914, in view of the delicacy of his position due to his German birth, and he was succeeded by Admiral Lord Fisher.

WHAT THE INSIDE OF A SUBMARINE IS LIKE.
This graphic representation shows the interior of a modern submarine, with its oil and ballast tanks, the deck tanks for compressed air, two 18 in. Whitehead torpedoes, compressed air chambers, and air pump. Above the water-line are the two periscopes, the wonderful "eyes" of the submarine, by which she obtains a reflected view of the surface surroundings.

along the surface. As the streaks approached it could be made out that each was caused by two brass tubes—the periscopes, or twin eyes, of the underwater craft, which each boat had thrust above the ripple. One of the two boats fouled a yacht which had passed across the line of approach, and her periscopes were sharply bent, so that she rose, and was put out of action. The other passed in on the line, fired her missile at the Neptune, and then came up like a mighty whale to take her breath.

The second pair of submarines never disclosed their presence. Not a glimpse of their periscopes was obtained ; no track of spray betrayed their approach. Only when they suddenly appeared above the water with their grey, dripping hulls abreast of the flagships, the targets of their assault, was it realised that their attack had been made with success. The devilish nature of their onset lay in its stealth. They had marked down their quarry from a distance, taken the bearings, and steered in unseen.

The qualities which they had disclosed in manœuvres and reviews were now to be tested in action. On the very eve of war Admiral Sir Percy Scott startled the naval world by his declaration that " the introduction of the vessels that swim under water has, in my opinion, entirely done away with the utility of the ships that swim on the top of the water." He believed that the surface ship was doomed, and that the submarine, aided by airships and seaplanes, was the fighting vessel of the future.

A tremendous hubbub was caused by his pronouncement, which was the more remarkable because he was the " father of modern naval gunnery," the officer to whose efforts above all others the deadly shooting of the modern Dreadnought and the development of the monster ship were due. Other thinkers pointed out that whereas surface ships can meet and defeat surface ships, there was no known means of coping with an enemy's submarines. Submarine could not fight hostile submarine, because each was invisible to the other.

More cautious was the conclusion of the famous German naval annual, " Nauticus," in its 1914 issue. " The submarine will force the decisive battle further out on the high seas, where only the large, seaworthy, and battleworthy ships are of any value." In the answer to the question whether the submarine can become large enough to be seaworthy and battleworthy **Weak points of large submarines** in any ocean at any distance from a base or parent ship upon the surface lies the whole future of war at sea.

The larger modern submarines had certain points of weakness to which naval officers were not blind. The bigger the submarine, the greater the difficulty of evolutions when she is submerged, the greater the draught of water which she requires. Large size may prevent her from navigating shallows or performing what may be an essential manœuvre—namely, passing under the keel of a ship at anchor in a roadstead in order the better to deliver an attack. The greater the boat, too, the greater is the difficulty of securing invisibility. A large submarine only a few feet below the surface causes a considerable wash : yet the large submarine, acting on the offensive, must run at shallow immersion frequently if she is to know where her enemy is.

The submarine can only attack effectively at short range. The limit of vision with the periscope is low—not more than two miles in some cases. If we foreshadow an increase of that effective range of vision up to even four miles or 7,000 yards, the submarine is still handicapped. To cover that distance a torpedo takes about four minutes and a half. If the target is stationary, the torpedo may hit, but if the target is moving, the margin of error in the aim of the torpedo is so great that the chances of a hit are infinitesimal. Sir Reginald Custance has calculated that the number of hits recorded by torpedoes fired at moving ships during the Russo-Japanese War was five out of two hundred and fifty.

Six shells from a 13·5 in. gun can be fired while one torpedo is travelling a distance of seven thousand yards, with only a small margin of error in the aim. Until, therefore, the armament of the underwater ship is equivalent in accuracy and power to that of the battleship it cannot be certain of gaining the superiority.

The practical use of the submarine, then, would appear for the present to be confined to narrow limits. Within those limits it is a weapon of terrible power, and in the hands of exceptional officers can no doubt be made to perform very remarkable feats; but whether it

THE MARVELLOUS "EYE" OF THE SUBMARINE.
The periscope of the submarine is the tube that projects above the waves and enables its officers to see what is happening on the surface above them. Observation may be made by binoculars, as seen here, or the scene above may be thrown by reflection on a horizontal table and studied by several people at one time.

can ever attain and hold the mastery of the sea is as doubtful now as it was when Lord St. Vincent described its predecessor, the Nautilus, as a gimcrack.

The first two months of the war proved its value for three distinct purposes—the prevention of a close blockade or bombardment of ports by a hostile fleet; the attack on vessels stationary or moving at low speed in narrow waters, such as those of the North Sea; and scouting along an enemy's coast, where the submarine could, in comparative security, play the part of sentinel.

In very clear weather and water, at shallow depths, and when the surface of the sea is calm, the presence of submarines may be detected from aircraft, which can look down into the depths. But actual experiments have

Detecting submarines by aircraft shown that aircraft are no sure protection against the approach of the submerged craft, though during the British naval manœuvres of 1913 boats under water were several times discovered from seaplanes. Another method of ascertaining their approach is by microphones, fitted in the surface ship, by which the vibration produced by the submarine's screws becomes audible.

The outbreak of war found Germany, on the whole, in a favourable position so far as concerned submarines. For five years before the great conflict she had annually expended on submarine construction almost exactly the same amount as her rival Great Britain. Though all the details of the German boats were held religiously secret, it is believed that in modern types Germany was almost equal to Great Britain. Of these each Power possessed, according to published estimates, some twenty-five ready for sea. In older boats Great Britain had an immense advantage—some forty-five boats against ten or twelve German craft. Fortunately the British weakness in the

BRITISH PLUCK SHINES BRIGHTEST IN THE HOUR OF CRUELLEST DISASTER.

On September 22nd, 1914, the German submarine U9 carried out a notable naval exploit off the coast of Holland. Three old British cruisers of the Cressy class—the Cressy, Aboukir, and Hogue—all 12,000-ton ships, were torpedoed one after another. First the Aboukir was successfully attacked, and as she sank the Cressy and the Hogue attempted to save the crew of their sinking sister ship. They in turn were attacked and sunk. As the Cressy turned over before plunging to the bottom, the men of her crew, swimming and floating in the water, saw her commander, Captain Robert W. Johnson, standing on the fast sinking hull. Then someone shouted "Give him a cheer," and at once there rose from the waves a ringing chorus of acclamation. When it was obvious that the vessel could not be saved, tables, chairs, and anything else that would float were thrown overboard, and afterwards these floating objects enabled many of the crew to keep afloat until they were rescued.

THE TORPEDOING OF A GERMAN CRUISER.
The Hela was an old German cruiser of 2,000 tons displacement, and the British submarine E9, captained by Lieutenant-Commander Max Kennedy Horton, sent her to the bottom on September 13th, 1914, about a week after the German success that lost us the Pathfinder. Two torpedoes were discharged at the Hela within fifteen seconds of each other. The scene above depicts the incident. The picture on the left is the E9, and the portrait is that of her gallant commander.

newer types was remedied by the great strength of the French Navy, which had sixty submarines ready for sea, fifty being of good size, including two boats perhaps the most powerful in existence. France, indeed, took the lead in submarine construction. Not until 1900 were the first submarines ordered for the British Navy, and then mainly for experimental purposes. But after this new type of war-vessel had once been introduced it was rapidly developed. A clear idea of the progress in fourteen years may be gathered from a comparison between the first British submarine and one of the E class, placed in commission at the beginning of 1914.

Submarine No. 1 was only 63½ feet long; the boats of E class are 176 feet long—nearly three times as large. They carry a crew of twenty-eight hands, as compared with the little group of seven who risked their lives in our earliest attempts at underwater navigation. Whereas in 1901 our submarines could only travel at a speed of eight knots on the surface, those finished just before the Great War broke out travelled sixteen or seventeen knots.

The offensive power of the submarine has increased in an extraordinary degree. One torpedo-tube firing an 18 in. torpedo was all that was fitted in the earliest type. The E class—the latest British submarines in service when Germany challenged the world— were fitted with four torpedo-tubes firing 21 in. torpedoes of vastly greater strength, range, and accuracy.

Increase of submarine effectiveness

Our first submarines were driven by four-cylinder petrol engines on the surface, and by a 70 horse-power electric motor when submerged. They dived by admitting water ballast until the conning-tower alone was above water, when the submarine was steered downwards by horizontal rudders to any required depth. This principle still applies, but is supplemented by numerous safeguards which experience has shown to be necessary. In early submarines, for example, the movements of the crew when the boat was submerged tended to throw her off an even keel, and a man moving forward would depress her bows and make her dive thirty-six feet in one minute

Admiral R. H. S. Bacon, who was the first British officer in charge of submarines, speedily realised from the

DECOY TORPEDO-BOAT DESTROYERS FLEEING FROM A HOSTILE CRUISER IN—
A torpedo cannot be aimed independently of the direction of the craft from which it is fired—the submarine must be manœuvred so as to bring the torpedo-tube in line with the object to be attacked. Thus it is a part of naval strategy to induce the enemy ships to steer athwart the line

experiments with our early craft that no small submarine would ever be a trustworthy fighting machine. It is impossible to get men to work under normal conditions in abnormally confined spaces, and a man not under normal conditions is apt to be flurried and unsteady. This, it may be said, is psychology rather than naval architecture; but no naval constructor can afford to overlook the human element. He can reduce warship design to an algebraical formula, but the x which represents the men in that warship he can never resolve. The human factor can only be guessed at, and it was the insight of Admiral Bacon that led to the great increase in the size of British submarines. To become war-worthy they had to become habitable.

There is plenty of room to move about comfortably in the latest submarines; there is not that feeling of cramped, boxed-up imprisonment that all men experienced in the earlier types. The crew, in fact, when the

Comfort in latest submarines vessel is on the surface, live as normal a life as the crew of a torpedo-boat destroyer, and have plenty of deck space on the top of the boat on which to move about as well as down below. On the surface the oil-engines make a fearful din; below water, when the electric motors are running, there is comparative silence.

Even when running submerged there is little discomfort, except from the smell of oil and a certain " stuffiness." A submarine of the E type can stay at sea five days without ever touching a port. The earliest submarines could not even stay under water more than five hours. The latest can remain below seventy-two hours. Consider what this change means in the human conditions, apart altogether from the mechanical and technical developments. It means that there must be stores of food carried and some method of providing meals on board. Cooking is effected by an electric stove in a small galley. It means that there must be space for the men to sling their hammocks and sleep, to wash and to eat their meals. Officers' quarters and petty-officers' quarters must be provided, and, as a small instance of what has been done, it may be mentioned that in the captain's quarters there is a kneehole desk at which he can write.

These are all points which make no show in the statement that the latest submarines are 110 feet longer and of 600 tons more displacement than the first that we built; but they are all points which go to increase the fighting capacity of the ship, because they strengthen the morale of the men on board.

Great improvements, too, have been made in the supply of air. When running on the surface the submarine takes in natural air, but under water the atmosphere cannot be renewed except artificially. Many plans have been suggested for the replacement of vitiated air, among them the chemical purification of the air actually in the submarine. But the use of compressed air from compartments, in which it is stored at some thousands of pounds

DECOYING DESTROYERS

—ORDER TO BRING THE LATTER WITHIN RANGE OF A WAITING SUBMARINE'S TORPEDOES.

of fire of the lurking danger of the deadly submarine, and the diagrammatic picture above makes plain such a decoy manœuvre. The two tiny periscopes projecting from the water near the left are the only visible evidence of the presence of the submarine waiting for its prey.

pressure to the square inch, has been found the most efficacious, though the hull of a large boat contains enough air for about twenty-four hours.

Sight is the one faculty that is lacking in the submarine. When more than twelve feet below the surface she is absolutely blind. The earliest instruments which gave some sort of vision to the seaman in a submerged vessel have been greatly improved in the past ten years. Two, or in some cases three, periscopes which reflect the surface of the water into the interior of the hull, are fitted ; but they cannot be indefinitely lengthened, and once the top of the periscope is under water all view of the outside world is lost.

The first periscope was a short tube, at the top of which was a reflecting prism, by which horizontal rays were projected downwards through the tube and brought to a focus opposite an eyepiece, to which the man in the submarine had to keep his eye fixed. The telescopic principle enabled the length of the periscope to be increased and, by an adaptation of the old camera obscura, the reflected picture of the surface was thrown on a piece of paper laid flat in front of the steering-wheel. **Development of the periscope**

That system has now been further developed, so that the view of the surface is reflected into a darkened chamber which can be seen from many parts of the boat, and the officers can therefore move about as they would do in a surface ship, and still know where their vessel is in relation to objects above them.

Despite all improvements in the optical appliances, however, the task of the submarine pilot is not easy. " If anyone wants to appreciate some of its difficulties," Admiral Bacon has written, " let him sit down under a chart of the Channel suspended from the ceiling. Let him punch a hole through it and above the hole place a piece of looking-glass inclined at forty-five degrees. Let him further imagine his chair and glass moving sideways as the effect of the tide. Let him occasionally fill the room with steam to represent mist. Let him finally crumple the chart in ridges to represent the waves, and then try to carry out some of the manœuvres which look so simple when the chart is spread out on the table and looked down upon in the quiet solitude of a well-lit study." The wonder is that submarines can make hits at all in such unsatisfactory conditions.

Whatever technical developments have taken place are common to all navies, the German as well as the British. Germany, however, was late in beginning the construction of underwater craft.

Submarines are peculiarly exposed to dangers that surface craft avoid. Collision is one of the worst. This is a danger that even the skill and care of the officer in charge cannot avert, as has been shown in the cases of C11 sunk by a steamer off Cromer in 1909, and B2, sunk by a German liner in the Channel off Dover in 1912.

Petrol explosions have been another fruitful cause of disaster and loss of life, both in our own Service and in foreign navies.   With the adoption of engines using the heavier oil, which gives out no explosive vapour, this risk has now been eliminated from the most modern submarines.   Yet another peril with the earlier boats was a sudden change in trim, such as led to the loss of A8 in June, 1905.   She was running on the surface when she dived, and instantly sank.   This, however, is a danger which the experience of officers in the handling of their craft, and of designers in the provision of safeguards, has very largely eliminated.   The energy, skill, and forethought of those engaged in this difficult branch of naval work have achieved marvels.

Of the sensation of an officer in a submarine which has gone to the bottom and cannot be made to rise, there remains an extraordinary record in the letter left by Lieutenant-Commander Sakuma, of the Japanese submarine No. 6.   While at exercise, about ten a.m. on April 15th, 1910, the boat submerged too quickly before the sluice-

Tragic tale of slow death

valve was closed.   Water poured in and the valve jammed.   The boat sank to the bottom with the after-part full, and its keel tilted at an angle of eleven degrees.   The electric lights went out, but there was a dim light from the surface through the windows of the conning-tower.   Efforts to pump the water out failed.   At eleven-forty-five the commander wrote, " We are now soaked by the water that has made its way in.   Our clothes are very wet and we feel cold."   At twelve the pump could no longer be worked ; the depth gauge indicated ten fathoms (60 ft.).   There was no sign of chlorine—the poisonous gas which is given off when sea-water comes into contact with the acid in the accumulators—but the petrol fumes were overpowering.

The last entries in this touching document proceeded thus : " All the members of this crew have discharged their duties well, and I feel satisfied.   I always expected death.   I beg humbly to ask his Majesty this respectful request—that none of the families left by my subordinates shall suffer.   Atmospheric pressure is increasing, and I feel as if my tympanum were breaking.   Twelve-thirty p.m., respiration is extraordinarily difficult.   I mean I am breathing petrol gas. I am intoxicated with petrol.   Captain Nakano. It is twelve-forty o'clock."

The hapless boat with her dead crew was recovered some days later, when this noble record of a brave man's last moments was recovered. Apparently the crew suffered little, for petrol gas kills comparatively painlessly.

Such accidents prove that serious risks attach to underwater work in time of peace, and that the ordinary dangers of navigation are multiplied many times for submarines. They show that a small mishap below the surface may well prove deadly to the boat and all on board her. The crew of a surface vessel has an opportunity of escape if bad weather, collision, or one of the chances of war leads to the loss of their ship. The crew of a submarine has no such opportunity.

A SUBMARINE RESTING ON THE OCEAN BED.
Storms may rage above, and the biggest battleship may pitch and roll on a high sea, while the little submarine may rest on the ocean bed, secure from surface danger, even if exposed to dangers of her own.   The latest submarines can remain below water for seventy-two hours.

[*Haines.*

LORD FISHER OF KILVERSTONE, G.C.B., G.C.V.O., O.M.

John Arbuthnot Fisher was born in 1841, entered the Navy thirteen years later, and at thirty-three commanded the Inflexible, then regarded as the crack ship of the British navy. He served in the Crimean, China, and Egyptian Wars, and, passing through many high naval commands, became First Sea Lord of the Admiralty in 1904. This post he resigned in 1910, but assumed again when Prince Louis of Battenberg resigned on October 30th, 1914. He was a delegate to the Peace Conference at The Hague in 1899, but his idea of naval warfare belongs to the Nelson school. "The essence of war is violence" he once said. "Hit first, hit hard, and hit anywhere."

"SUNK THE LOT."—THE FAMOUS EXPLOIT OF COMMANDER CECIL H. FOX WHO SENT FOUR GERMAN DESTROYERS TO THE BOTTOM.

On October 17th, 1914, the British cruiser Undaunted, attended by her destroyer flotilla—the Lance, Legion, Lennox, and Loyal—came in sight of four German destroyers. Commander C. H. Fox, of the Undaunted, and formerly of the ill-fated Amphion, proceeded to round them up, and sent to the main Fleet a wireless message, "Am pursuing four German destroyers." About an hour and a half later he followed it up by a second message, even more laconic than the first. It read: "Sunk the lot." Both seamanship and marksmanship contributed to this result. By the handling of his ships Commander Fox cut off the German boats from the possibility of running to the safety of a German harbour. Then marksmanship had play. The Loyal shot away a funnel and the wheel of one of the German ships, and the other British boats battered the remainder. In a little over an hour the battle was over, the four German destroyers were sunk, and their thirty-one survivors were safely on board British ships.

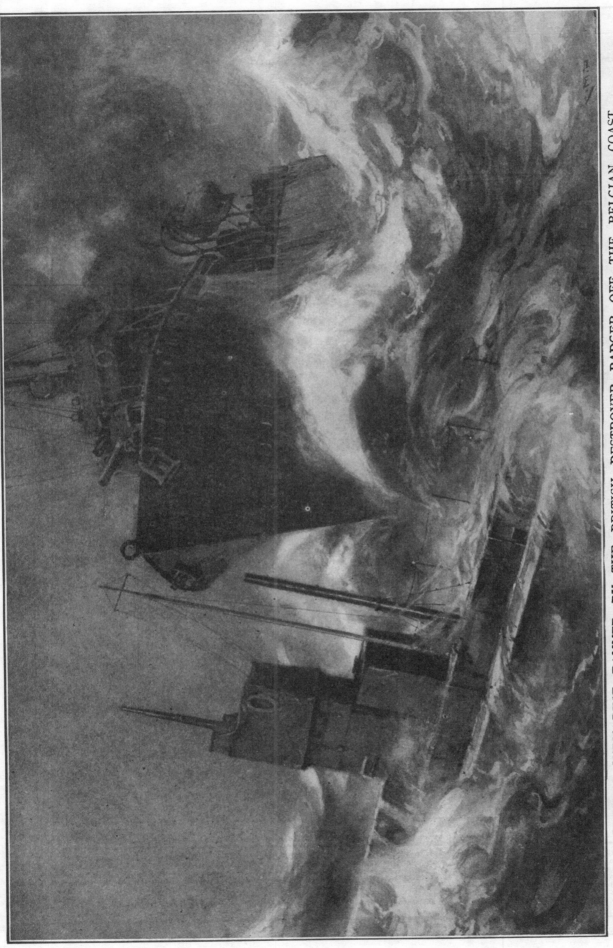

GERMAN SUBMARINE RAMMED BY THE BRITISH DESTROYER BADGER OFF THE BELGIAN COAST.

On October 24th, 1914, when the great Battle of the Coast was raging between Nieuport and Ypres, and when the British warships were shelling the German positions, German submarines, which had evaded the British mine-field north and west of Ostend, made many daring attempts to get home torpedo attacks, which were successfully foiled by the presence of several British protecting destroyers. During these attempts the British destroyer Badger, under Commander Charles A. Fremantle, had the good fortune to see a German submarine come to the surface near the spot where she was patrolling. Promptly the Badger was rushed at the enemy, and her foremost gun fired point-blank. The submarine was rammed and sank immediately, and although the Badger, with dented bows, steamed over the spot she saw only air bubbles coming to the surface from the enemy submarine which had made her last plunge into the depths, and was lost with all her crew.

THE FIRST LORD WITH HIS TWO HIGHEST EXECUTIVE OFFICERS.

RIGHT HON. WINSTON CHURCHILL, became First Lord of the Admiralty in 1911, and soon showed the greatest practical interest in in his work. He went up in aeroplanes and down in submarines in order to get first-hand information. He was first elected to Parliament in 1900 as a Conservative, but in 1906 he was returned for North-West Manchester as a Liberal.

REAR-ADMIRAL CHARLES MADDEN, Chief of the Staff, was serving at the Admiralty at the outbreak of war. He entered the Navy in 1875, was in command of one of the earliest flotillas of torpedo-boat destroyers in the Mediterranean, became captain of the Dreadnought in 1907, and earned a high reputation.

ADMIRAL SIR JOHN JELLICOE was appointed Commander-in-Chief of the Home Fleets in place of Admiral Callaghan at the outbreak of war. He entered the Navy in 1872, took part in the Egyptian War, and commanded the Naval Brigade in China, 1898-1901. He commanded the Atlantic Fleet during 1910-11, and became Second Sea Lord in 1912.

If the boat fails or is breached, she sinks like a stone and all on board perish. Safety appliances are indeed, carried in all new submarines, but rather for moral effect than for practical use. On no occasion as yet have they proved of any value in protecting life. When the Australian submarine AE1 met with an accident, in September, 1914, no one survived to tell the tale, though she was one of the latest and best boats in existence. On the other hand, the fact that the boat is below the water means that in war she is secure against attack by one of the most powerful weapons—the gun, and that her crew has not to face the nerve-racking effects of heavy shell fire from the monster weapons which cause such appalling destruction in surface ships. The additional risk which the submarine men run in peace is, in fact, compensated by a diminished risk in war ; and the same feature has been marked in another of the new weapons, the aeroplane. The airman in peace is always face to face with peril ; death sits beside him in his frail craft. But in war he is less exposed to the enemy's fire than the infantry or artillery officer on terra firma.

The submarine crews are handicapped against the surface ship in that their offensive power is strictly limited. The ship has many guns, each supplied with a hundred or more rounds of ammunition, and each round of 13.5 in. shell is capable of sinking a vessel if well used. The submarine has only her small stock of torpedoes—four, six, or, in some few boats, eight. These must be husbanded carefully, and no chances must be taken in expending them at long range. Again, the comparatively low speed of the submarine exposes her to serious dangers, if she can be located in shallow water or if her track can be followed —as is sometimes possible by bubbles on the surface.

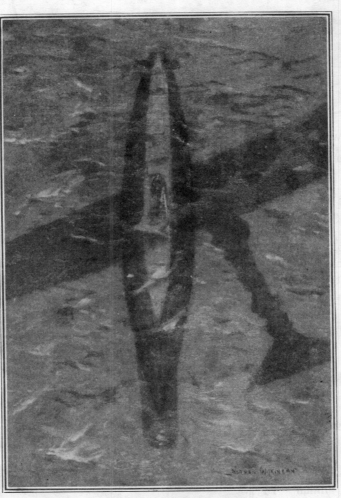

DETECTING A SUBMARINE BENEATH THE SEA.
Under favourable conditions, submarines are visible from a height—when invisible from the water level. Therefore, while they are often able to proceed on their deadly mission unobserved by warships, they cannot avoid detection by aircraft unless they keep well below the surface of the water, where progress is lessened relatively to the depth. Thus aeroplanes help to guard our Dreadnoughts from submarine attack. In the picture we see the shadow of an aeroplane that is hovering over a submarine which the observer has detected beneath the waves.

Destroyers with twice her speed can keep over her till at last she is forced to rise, from the want of air for her crew. She may also be assailed with mines, and she has great difficulty in eluding them because she lies so low in the water that they cannot easily be seen from her superstructure if she emerges.

The mine danger for submarines

The submarine is exempt from one of the torments of surface ships. She neither rolls nor pitches if she is in open water and well away from the coast, and this is some compensation for the increased navigation risk which her crew encounter. But in the inshore work off Heligoland the crews of the submarines suffered greatly from the movements of the sea, even when deeply submerged. To manoeuvre her the submarine requires two steersmen, one of whom handles the diving helm or wheel ; the other the wheel for ordinary steering to right (starboard) or port (left). She uses either a magnetic compass let into the top of her periscope, or else, in the later models, a gyroscopic compass carried inside her hull.

The weapon of the submarine is the torpedo, without which she would be but a toy, and which has been developed and improved from an original invention of an Austrian naval officer, Captain Luppis, who was aided by an Englishman, Mr. Whitehead. To him the British Government in 1871 paid the sum of £15,000 for the secret and right to manufacture this torpedo, 14 ft. in length, 16 in. in diameter, and carrying a charge of 67 lb. of gun-cotton. It was able to travel 600 yards at a speed of 7.5 knots, but its course was decidedly erratic.

The British torpedo of to-day is 17 ft. in length, 21 in. in diameter, and usually carries a 330 lb. charge of an explosive which is an improvement on gun-cotton

BRITISH SUBMARINE E4, WHICH CAME
TO THE RESCUE OFF HELIGOLAND,
AUGUST 28TH, 1914.

and is familiarly known to Navy men as T.N.T. (or trinitrotoluene, which is also used in the German Navy). The torpedo can travel at least 7,500 yards at a speed of 35 knots, and it holds its course, in a very high percentage of cases, with absolute accuracy.

It is sometimes forgotten by the uninitiated that the torpedo is not a projectile, but is really a little ship in itself, propelled by its own engines in the water. Moreover, except in destroyers, it is nearly always discharged from a tube that is itself below the water-line of the ship and not from a tube on the deck. The submarine has not to come to the surface to fire a torpedo. Provided she has seen her target by means of the periscope and has taken her bearings to aim, she has no need to show herself at all while she fires.

In travelling through the water the torpedo may be deflected from its course. Many of the older naval officers of to-day can tell delightfully humorous stories of the early experiments with the "tin fish," as it was promptly dubbed, and even the modern torpedo lieutenant knows it for a treacherous and ungrateful animal. To take only one small point—the speed of the torpedo may be considerably affected by a change of a few degrees in the temperature of the water.

The oldest torpedoes used in the British Navy are 14 inches in diameter, have a range of 880 yards, and a charge of 77 lb. of guncotton in the head; the newest are 21 inches in diameter, have a range of 7,000 yards, and carry a charge of about 300 lb.

The torpedo consists of eight sections, which from head to tail may be briefly described thus: The pistol and detonator, the explosive charge, air chamber

RESCUED BY SUBMARINE OFF HELIGOLAND.
One of the most dramatic happenings in naval history occurred after the first important naval engagement of the war, which took place off Heligoland, on August 28th, 1914. The Defender, having sunk an enemy, lowered a whaler to pick up her swimming survivors. An enemy cruiser came up and chased away the Defender, who was forced to abandon her whaler. The men were left in an open boat, twenty-five miles from the nearest land, and that land an enemy's fortress, with nothing but fog and foes around them. Suddenly, there was a swirl alongside, and up popped submarine E4. It opened its conning-tower, took the sailors aboard, dived, and carried them two hundred and fifty miles home to Britain. The incident reads more like a chapter from Jules Verne than an actual fact.

H.M.S. ABOUKIR, SUNK WITH TWO SISTER CRUISERS ON SEPTEMBER 22ND, 1914

H.M.S. Aboukir, which, with her two sister ships Cressy and Hogue, was torpedoed and sunk by the German submarine U9 in the North Sea on September 22nd. The cruisers were of a comparatively old type, built in 1900. They were of 12,000 tons, 18 knots speed, and carried two 9'2 in. and twelve 6 in. guns each. Except for the loss of life—nearly sixty officers and 1,400 men—the loss of the cruisers was officially stated by the Admiralty to be of small naval significance. Although they were large and powerful ships, they belonged to a class of cruisers whose speeds had been surpassed by many of the enemy's battleships, and before the war it had been decided to spend no more money repairing them.

containing the compressed-air motive power, balance chamber (in which are the controls of the rudders), engines, buoyancy chamber, rudders, and propellers

The pistol is a small steel rod which is driven in against the detonator when the torpedo comes into contact with a ship's side In the latest torpedoes it is believed that this detonator consists primarily of lead azide, which is absolutely insensitive to damp and has other advantages over tetryl, which was at first used to give greater force to the fulminate of mercury cap that actually detonates the charge.

The explosive charge, which was formerly trinitro-cellulose (or gun-cotton), is now generally trinitrotoluene—the T.N.T. referred to above. This explosive is a rival of picric acid (of which lyddite is a form) and is derived from nitric acid and toluene, which is one of the benzine series. It is remarkably insensitive to shock or friction, and can be sawn through or fired on at short range by rifle bullets and will not detonate. But when it has been fired by a powerful detonator the force of its explosion is far greater than that of gun-cotton.

In the air chamber of the torpedo is the supply of compressed air which works the propelling engines and the motor that controls the diving rudders. The balance chamber contains what is practically the steering-wheel of the torpedo, but it acts automatically under the guidance of a gyroscope, controlling the rudders that maintain the torpedo on a straight course. The buoyancy chamber gives the necessary floatability to the torpedo.

Such is an outline of the torpedo's mechanism. Improvements in the design of these weapons are secrets most jealously guarded by the Admiralties of the various Powers. Germany long ago abandoned the practice of buying hers from private firms, preferring to make them in her own Government works, close to a suitable expanse of water where they could be tested in absolute secrecy.

The discharge of the torpedo from its tube is effected by compressed air or by the explosion in the tube of a few ounces of powder, usually cordite. Since the torpedo propels itself through the water, it does not need a high initial velocity as a shell from a gun does. The engines of the torpedo's propellers are started by a trigger which projects a little beyond the casing of the torpedo, and touches a catch in the tube just before the torpedo leaves it. This opens the starting-valve.

Aiming a torpedo in the sense that a gun is aimed is unknown. The submerged torpedo-tube is fixed in the hull of the vessel, whether it be a battleship or a submarine, and it is only when the ship is laid on a course that brings the torpedo-tube exactly opposite the target that the torpedo can be fired.

The latest submarines carry guns, mostly mounted on disappearing platforms, but they are weapons of small power. Nothing larger than a 4 in. gun is known to have

HOW H.M.S. BIRMINGHAM ACCOUNTED FOR A GERMAN SUBMARINE.
The upper photograph shows the British light cruiser Birmingham, which, under Captain A. A. M. Duff, was patrolling the North Sea on August 9th, 1914, when a seaman on watch saw the periscope of a German submarine, the U15. Shots were fired and the Birmingham was rushed full speed at the enemy, tearing her sides open and sinking her with the entire crew. The lower picture is the U15. The portrait is that of Rear-Admiral A. G. H. W. Moore, one of the gallant commanders who distinguished themselves in the naval victory off Heligoland, on Aug. 28th, 1914.

been mounted in any underwater craft, while the later German submarines are equipped with 14-pounder and 1-pounder pieces. The latter are of a curious type, fixed to the upper deck, and do not need to be taken inside when the vessel is running submerged, as sea water does not harm them.

Guns mounted on submarines The submarine's guns are generally so fitted that they can be used against aircraft. The British 3 in. gun of this type fires a shell of twelve pounds at the rate of twenty-five rounds per minute. The mounting allows the gun to fire at all angles, from several degrees of depression, by which a hostile submarine could be attacked up to eighty degrees of elevation, which would allow of attack on aircraft almost directly overhead.

With the declaration of war the strenuous and perilous work of the British submarines on the enemy's coast began. Three hours after the declaration of war, in the small hours of the morning of August 5th, submarines E6 (Lieutenant-Commander Cecil P. Talbot) and E8 (Lieutenant-Commander Francis H. H. Goodhart) left Harwich to reconnoitre the German positions in the Bight of Heligoland. They proceeded into German waters, examined the mine defences there and the German ships which were then lying off Heligoland, and, in

A GROUP OF OUR HEROES IN THE WAR BY SEA.

Com. Cecil P. Talbot, submarine E6, made daring reconnaissance in Heligoland Bight.

Commander Charles A. Fremantle, captained H.M.S. Badger, and rammed a German submarine on October 24th, 1914.

Rear-Admiral The Hon. Horace Hood commanded British ships that shelled the German positions from the sea in Oct., 1914.

Lieut.-Com. Francis H. H. Goodhart, who distinguished himself in Heligoland Bight, and was specially commended in reports.

Lieut.-Com. George F. Cholmley commanded submarine E3, sunk by the Germans on October 18th, 1914.

Capt. Harold Christian, commanding the light cruiser Brilliant in bombardment of German lines in the Battle of the Coast.

Commander Cecil H. Fox, of H.M.S. Undaunted, who sunk four German destroyers in engagement on October 17th, 1914.

Lieut. Charles R. Peploe, awarded Distinguished Service Cross in Oct., 1914, commanded H.M.S. Laurel after his commander was wounded.

Lieut. F. A. P. Williams-Freeman, awarded the D.S.O. in October, 1914, for services in Heligoland Bight.

Lieut. Henry E. Horan, awarded the Distinguished Service Cross in October, 1914, for his share in Heligoland victory.

Captain William F. Blunt, of H.M.S. Fearless, awarded D.S.O. for services in Heligoland Bight on August 27th, 1914.

Squadron Commander Spenser D.A. Grey, of the Naval Flying Corps, awarded the D.S.O. for his air-raid on Cologne.

ANOTHER VICTIM OF THE GERMAN SUBMARINE.
The old 5,600-ton light cruiser Hermes, a sister ship of the more famous Highflyer, was used as a seaplane-carrying vessel, and was torpedoed by a German submarine in the Straits of Dover as she was returning from Dunkirk on October 30th, 1914.

the words of Commodore Keyes, who commanded the British submarine flotillas, " returned with useful information and had the privilege of being the pioneers on a service which is attended with some risk."

Failure attended the first recorded attack by submarines in the course of the Great War, on Sunday, August 9th. That failure was due to the watchfulness of the men in the British Fleet. Nothing but the thin tube of the periscope rising slightly from the swirling grey waters of the North Sea betrayed the presence of the foe. An able-seaman on watch in the light cruiser Birmingham saw it.

The Birmingham, Captain A. A. M. Duff, was patrolling the seas about one hundred and sixty miles from the German coast, in company with other ships of the First Light Cruiser Squadron. She is a vessel of 5,400 tons, and twenty-five and a half knots, carrying a powerful battery of nine 6 in. guns (firing shells of one hundred pound weight at the rate of nine or ten a minute with skilled gunners). The officer of the watch in the Birmingham changed her course at once, so as to present the bows of his ship to the submarine, in which position the Birmingham offered the smallest possible target. The guns' crews had been standing by their guns all night, and quickly found the range. The bugle sounded, and every man in the ship rushed to his station, officers dashing up on deck from their cabins in pyjamas. Shells splashed all round the point in the sea where the periscope had been observed. It was not gun fire, however, that sank her. The Birmingham's engines were put full speed ahead, and the cruiser tore down on the doomed enemy. Her bows ripped open the thin steel sides as a paper-knife cuts the leaves of a book. There was no chance of saving any of the crew ; the submarine simply filled and sank at once. An officer of the Birmingham, in a letter home, said that he saw a light switched on in the conning-tower, and the head of a lieutenant showed for a moment just as a shell hit the tower and blew it and him to fragments. The number of the submarine—U15—was also seen. And then it was all over. The vessel sank like a stone, carrying with her twenty-three officers and men to the depths.

It is not definitely known whether U15 discharged any torpedoes or not. It is extremely probable that she did, but that they failed to find their mark. According to report, one torpedo fired by her only missed a British battleship by a few feet.

THE GERMAN SCOURGE OF THE INDIAN OCEAN—THE EMDEN.
Even the enemies of Germany could not refuse to admire the many successful attacks by the small German cruiser Emden in harrying the ocean commerce of Great Britain in the East. Up to the end of October, 1914, she had captured and destroyed over twenty British merchant-ships, whose value, with their cargoes, was estimated at about one million pounds. This photograph shows the Emden, and the oval portrait above it is her able commander, Captain von Mueller.

VANDAL GERMANS IN THEIR FOUL AND SACRILEGIOUS ORGIES.

Sacrilege, murder, pillage, drunkenness, mutilation, torture, arson— these have all been established as having been part of Germany's scientific methods of warfare in poor Belgium. The beautiful church at Aerschot was the scene of all these foul crimes. The burgomaster, his brother, his son, and a group of citizens were shot, the church doors were battered in, much of the interior was burned, most of the artistic fittings were destroyed or stolen, and Uhlan horses were stabled in the sacred fabric, where the German soldiers vied with each other in the foul uses to which they put the vestments and altar-cloths. The war artist responsible for this picture has drawn the details from the descriptions of reliable witnesses, and the scene has been duplicated in other stricken towns and villages of Flanders and northern France.

Special measures of precaution were taken to paralyse the German Fleet while the British Expeditionary Force was being transported to France. The two large 35-knot destroyers, Lurcher and Firedrake, proceeded to the German coast with the seventeen submarines of the Eighth Flotilla. The vessels in this flotilla were as follows:

Eight boats of the D class—D1 to D8—600 tons submerged, 15 knots speed on surface, 10 knots in diving trim, three 18 in. torpedo-tubes, 20 officers and men, gun armament (in D3—8) one 12-pounder on disappearing mount.

Nine boats of the E class—E1 to E9—800 tons submerged, 16 knots on surface, 10 knots in diving trim, four 21 in. torpedo-tubes, 27 officers and and men, two 12-pounders on disappearing mounts.

Arriving off the enemy's ports, the submarines, in the laconic words of Commodore Keyes's despatch, "occupied positions from which they could have attacked the High Sea Fleet had it emerged to dispute the passage of our transports. This patrol was maintained night and day without relief, until the personnel of our army had been transported, and all chance of effective interference had disappeared."

The silent watch under the waves

After the Expeditionary Force had landed, the submarines continued their scouting work off the German coast. They even pushed into the entrances of the German naval harbours and into the mouths of the German rivers. But the enemy had taken every precaution to protect his large ships against submarine attack. The German vessels lay behind a complicated series of obstacles—booms of timber, barriers formed by hawsers and strong cables, from which were suspended lengths of steel netting such as are employed by warships as a protection against torpedoes, chains of mines, and lines of small and valueless steamers and trawlers placed close together. The formation of the German coast, moreover, was not favourable to submarine attack. Shallows abound, the channels are constantly changing, and the buoys and marks had either been removed or carefully misplaced.

Nevertheless, the British submarines, if deprived of all opportunity of attacking the enemy, watched him unceasingly, and ascertained the character and general line of movement of his patrol ships. The British flotilla was constantly attacked; it was, in the words of Commodore Keyes, "subjected to skilful and well-executed anti-submarine tactics, hunted for hours at a time by torpedo craft, and attacked by gunfire and torpedoes." Yet it did its work. There has been no more breathless achievement in war than this unremitting watch off a hostile coast in the face of constant attack.

A stoker who took part in these operations wrote: "This submarine work is grand fun. Last week we went right into —— (a German naval harbour), came to the top, had a good look round, found out what

"LOOT!" HOW GERMANY BROUGHT BACK BARBARISM INTO MODERN WAR.

This sketch represents no particular incident, but is typical of many. It shows a war of loot—Germans, who have made themselves masters of a beautiful French chateau, and are despoiling it of its art treasures. Pillage was one of the arts of war practised by the officers, from the Crown Prince downwards, and the degrading vices of the soldiery were not an occasion for wonder when such examples were set by the high command.

WEIRD EFFECTS OF MODERN SHELL FIRE: THE INFERNO THROUGH WHICH TRANSPORT WAGGONS HAD TO MOVE.

At the height of the fighting on the Aisne, in the first week of October, 1914, the supplying of food to the British troops in the advanced trenches and in the quarries was exceptionally difficult. Owing to the exposed nature of the ground for a considerable distance in rear of the advanced line, it was necessary to do the rationing at night. Narrow country carts were used in place of the regular A.S.C. waggons and lorries, because they alone could pass between the many great holes torn in the ground by shells. Both drivers and horses suffered severely during the work. Directly the Germans imagined that any move was being made towards the quarries, they bombarded the road with shrapnel, using parachute-light bombs to reveal the target. These shells explode overhead, by means of time-fuses, and let fall parachutes—carried folded up in the bombs—which have attached to them magnesium lights capable of lighting up a considerable area.

we wanted to find, got chased by a couple of German cruisers, let go a ' rib tickler ' (torpedo) at them once, and came back to—but it doesn't matter where—informed the Fleet, and then they went out to smash the Germans up. We went with them, and I have seen the finest sight of my life." That was the simple, straightforward story of a man for whom underwater work certainly has no terrors.

But the best story told of submarine adventure on this scouting work was that of a young sub-lieutenant who was describing another raid into the enemy's waters. He said that his boat was sighted by the enemy, and that for safety they had to dive. They went down to the bottom for some hours, and then cautiously crept up to the surface. It was still not safe to attempt the dash for the open sea, so down they went again to wait a few more hours on the bottom. There was no silent apprehension about that long wait. With delightful naïveté the young officer remarked : " We played auction bridge while we were waiting, and I won 4s. 11½d."

The modern submarine, it should be said, is able to dive to depths of one hundred and fifty feet, and can remain there without any discomfort so long as her air supply holds out.

German submarines, on the other hand, were not idle. From all ports of the Scottish coast their presence was frequently reported. An account of the trip made by the flotilla in which U15 was serving, written by a man in one of the boats, gave a picturesque impression of the adventure, though it must be taken with a pinch of salt.

He declared that the flotilla was once within 1,500 yards of the main British Fleet, and that the submarine's crew were playing the accordion and singing away merrily, but that no sound of it reached their adversaries. They all had a peep at the view of the British ships, lying " like a flock of peaceful lambs without a care, as if there were no German sea-wolves in sheep's clothing."

Activities of German submarines

" For two hours we lay there under water," he declared. " We could with certainty have succeeded in destroying a big cruiser, but we did not. We were on patrol duty ; our boat had further work to do."

He does not appear to have enjoyed his trip much, for he added: " It is not comfortable in such a nutshell of a boat. Our quarters were not exactly the size of a ball-room, and the air we breathed could not compare with the mountain breezes ; it was all petrol, petrol, petrol. No orders were given ; we might all have been deaf mutes. The officers spoke with their hands and feet ; we heard with our eyes. Thus a gentle kick might be interpreted ' Belay, there ! The mate wants to speak to you.' We were few, and there was much work to do, especially when we're submerged, so that it meant six hours sleep and six hours work."

A FRENCH SOLDIER PROMOTED ON THE BATTLEFIELD.
During one of the many conflicts round Roye, in the month of October, a French soldier with thirty-two comrades was ordered to defend a particular post at all costs. At nightfall the majority of the force with which he was co-operating retreated, unwilling to be surprised in the dark. But he and his men remained. The enemy advanced in numbers from the town, but the undaunted little band continued firing at them, and thus gave the alarm to a stronger body of French troops, who came to their rescue and drove the enemy back beyond Roye. Then the band, reduced to twenty, retired. The next morning the colonel inspected the gallant twenty, embraced their leader, and made him a sub-lieutenant.

The writer claimed that his boat was at sea for ten whole days, and if this was correct, it meant that the flotilla was attended by a supply ship of some sort. A number of trawlers were captured during the early stages of the war, which were unusually well provided with food and had suspicious quantities of petrol on board, and it is highly probable that at regular intervals the submarines met the trawlers at prearranged rendezvous, naturally under cover of darkness, and took in fresh supplies of fuel and food.

One of these patrolling German submarines, apparently U21, at last secured a victim on September 5th. The British scout Pathfinder, Captain F. M. Leake, was cruising about fifteen miles off St. Abb's Head, at the mouth of the Firth of Forth, when an explosion suddenly took place under the forebridge. It was soon after four in the afternoon that she was sunk, for most of the company were below at tea, and four is the tea-time of the Navy. No one on board had noted any sign of danger. The first indication that submarines were at hand was the apparition of two periscopes in the water not far from the ship. It does not appear to have been ascertained whether the periscopes belonged to one and the same submarine, or to two different vessels. When the periscopes were sighted, the Path-finder, according to one of the crew, at once began to turn towards them. As the turn began she was struck amidships by a torpedo, which seems to have exploded her forward magazine. The vessel quivered from end to end, enveloped in dense black smoke and lurid flame. Masses of wreckage fell on the officers and men who were on deck, killing many outright. Others were flung stunned and bleeding upon the deck, or hurled against bulkheads and gun-shields. The shattered wreck instantly began to sink.

But there was no panic. British seamanship, trained for long years to discipline and order in all conceivable circumstances, rose to the occasion. In the simple words of one of the survivors: "We waited for orders."

Discipline prevents panic

Those orders came, for there were a few officers left. The boats had been smashed by the explosion, but the men speedily heaved overboard booms, gratings, furniture, and everything that would float. The bows of the ship sank deeper and ever deeper into the water, and the last order came: "Every man for himself."

A seaman who escaped gave this account of his experiences: "I saw a flash, and the ship seemed to lift right out of the water. Down came the mast and fore-funnel and forward part of the ship. All the men there must have been blown to atoms. I bobbed down for a few seconds for fear of being hit by the débris—some pieces of it must have weighed nearly a hundredweight—which was blown sky-high. I scrambled to the quarter-deck, which was littered with mangled bodies, and looked about for something to cling to. The captain shouted, 'To the boats.' But there were only two and they were smashed. The other boats, and practically all the

THE HERO KING OF BELGIUM IN THE TRENCHES WITH HIS SOLDIERS.

King Albert proved more than a king and a hero—he became the comrade of his brave soldiers. Under the trial of a common calamity he showed up as a most conspicuous epitome of the adage, "Noblesse oblige." When remonstrated with for his indifference to danger within range of the guns of the enemy, he replied to his solicitous officer: "My life is of no more value than yours." A talented war artist depicts the incident in the above picture, where the hero King is seen with his soldiers in the trenches. It was characteristic of the man and his courage that when Antwerp had to be evacuated he insisted that he should personally fire the last shot.

woodwork, had been left ashore. We fired a gun as a distress signal. By this time the ship was almost covered with water. 'Every man for himself,' and I at once pulled off my boots, coat, and trousers, and over I went. I think I broke all swimming records, trying to put as much space as possible between myself and the ship, being afraid of suction.

" Turning round, the last I saw of the ship, about fifty yards away, was the after-end sticking upright in the air about one hundred feet. Then it gradually heeled over towards me and sank. Then I swam again to get out of its way, thinking the end might hit me as it came down. It cleared me all right. It was all over in about five minutes from the start. When she sank, something blew up, and on came a wave, and round and round I went like a cork. A buoy came speeding by me. I grabbed it, and that was what kept me afloat."

So violent was the shock of the explosion. that it is said to have been felt on board a trawler ten miles away. The Pathfinder was in full sight of the coast when the disaster occurred, and it happened that many people were watching her. From Dunbar the coxswain of the lifeboat saw a huge column of flame and smoke rise suddenly from the doomed ship, and four minutes later the hull disappeared. From Cockburnspath two officers saw dense smoke, and then perceived half of the ship rising straight out of the water.

The watchers gave the alarm and, immediately after the explosion, motor fishing boats, a motor lifeboat, steamers, and destroyers hastened to the spot where the Pathfinder had gone down. As they approached it they found the sea covered with wreckage of the most tragic kind. For a space of a mile there were seamen's jackets, caps, jerseys, boots, letters, photographs, and books, among them the ship's Bible and order of daily service. Some fifty-eight officers and men, among them Captain Leake, were picked up in the water. Several of them were terribly wounded, and four died on the way to the mainland.

The tragedy of the Pathfinder

In all there perished in the Pathfinder two hundred and forty-six officers and men, faithful to the command of duty, victims of the great struggle for righteousness and freedom. " As so often happens, when a life has been lived with truth and valour, its ending, even when untimely, may be matter much more for praise and solemn gratitude than for mere lamentation." Their country will never forget these men who gave their lives to save her.

The first official account stated that the Pathfinder had been blown up by a mine. Some days later, in reply to questions in the House of Commons, Mr. F. E. Smith said : " There was reason for suspecting that she had come in contact with a submarine. The Admiralty were, of course, most anxious that that should not get out to the world, because it might have interfered vitally with the operations to catch and destroy the submarine."

THE DAILY DECREES OF THE GERMAN MASTERS OF BRUSSELS DURING THEIR TEMPORARY OCCUPATION
In possession of Brussels, the Germans ruled the city with iron strictness. Each morning proclamations were published instructing the people as to what they might or might not do, and in the photograph above the notices posted at the Hotel de Ville are attracting their usual morning crowd.

THE GERMAN IMPERIAL GUARDS IN BRUSSELS.
This famous corps is the tallest and finest in the Kaiser's service. Their bravery was proved in the fighting in Belgium and France, but they suffered terrible loss against troops as brave as themselves. Here they are seen off duty during the German occupation of the Belgian capital.

THE GERMAN MILITARY COMMANDANT OF BRUSSELS.

Subsequently an official German report gave the credit for the feat to U21. There is thus every reason to believe that the Pathfinder was the first victim of a submarine in the whole history of naval war. For though, in the American Civil War, a certain so-called Confederate submarine had sunk the United States ship Housatonic, this submarine was in actual fact a vessel running on the surface, and not a genuine underwater craft.

The Pathfinder displaced 2,940 tons, and had a speed of twenty-five knots, and an armament of nine 4 in. guns. She was launched in 1904. The U21 was one of the most powerful of German submarines, generally corresponding to the British E class. She was of eight hundred tons, with a speed of seventeen knots on the surface, and twelve knots when submerged ; she carried one 14-pounder and one 1-pounder gun. She was fitted with five torpedo-tubes, and manned by a crew of about thirty.

The German boat had to make a voyage of four hundred miles back to German waters to regain safety, and there was some hope that the British submarines and cruisers, with their far higher rate of speed, would be able to cut her off. Whereas most of the boats in the British destroyer flotillas were capable of steaming from twenty-six to thirty knots, she could only do seventeen if she remained on the surface ; below the surface, as we have seen, she was capable of but twelve knots. But she eluded all the efforts of our Fleet to run her down, though a squadron is believed to have moved instantly, on receipt of a wireless order, so as to intercept her. Presumably she dived and ran through the cordon. Reports current in the British Press that she had been sunk rested on no real foundation.

Little more than a week later, on September 13th, a British submarine took some sort of revenge for the sinking of the Pathfinder. The vessel in question was the E9, Lieutenant-Commander Max Kennedy Horton.

The wind was freshening ; it was the beginning of a great gale that for eight days swept over the North Sea and gave our seamen as bad a time as any of them have ever experienced. In a heavy sea it is specially difficult for a submarine to find her way about submerged. The waves often run higher than the periscope, and, in the interior of the hull, all that can be seen is a dull green fog, with occasional flashes of light.

E9 was on patrol duty ; it was her business to watch the enemy, to see that the long-expected dash of the German destroyer flotillas did not come off without warning. In the course of her inspection of the surface, at about half-past six on that Sunday morning, she sighted the Hela within range—a small and ancient German cruiser of 2,000 tons, launched in 1895, and manned by a crew of one hundred and ninety-one.

A sharp call to the torpedo-tube crews was all that was necessary. Two torpedoes were fired within fifteen seconds of each other. Thirty-five seconds after the last had been despatched a distant low boom reverberated through the hull of the submarine. That would mean that the submarine was between seven hundred and nine **Doom of the German** hundred and fifty yards from the cruiser when she fired. There were other German **warship Hela** vessels in the vicinity, so E9 did not come to the surface immediately to see what effect her torpedo had produced. She cruised quietly about below, for a quarter of an hour, taking care to come to the surface ultimately at a spot far away from her original position.

Then she saw that the Hela was doomed. The enemy had a heavy list to starboard, and looked all over a badly-stricken ship. The submarine had no intention of running unnecessary risks. A number of German destroyers had come up and were hunting eagerly for the British submarine. E9 dived again, and when for a third time she rose to see how matters were progressing, the Hela had disappeared below the surface of the

GERMAN FIELD KITCHEN BEFORE THE BRUSSELS PALAIS DE JUSTICE.

waves. Her crew were rescued by other German vessels, and only about half a dozen lives were lost.

Although elated with their success, the crew of the submarine remained on their station, and there was no dash back to report the blow and enjoy the glory. On September 14th E9, with great judgment and skill, examined the outer anchorage of Heligoland — a service described as one "attended by considerable risk" —among the German destroyers

and mines. For yet another day through the howling, raging gale, that tossed torpedo-boat destroyers about like shells, and washed men overboard like corks, E9 abode on her beat in the waters round Heligoland. Then, on September 16th, when she had been relieved, she slipped quietly home to port, and announced the

CONFISCATING BELGIAN CATTLE TO FEED THE GERMAN GARRISON.
German infantrymen in Brussels are here seen leading to the slaughter Belgian cattle to supply the kitchens of the Kaiser's army of occupation.

news that the German wireless bureau with uncommon honesty had already given to the world. The gale was at its height from September 14th to 21st, but in its teeth the British submarines maintained their station. The risk and discomfort which the crews had to face were great indeed. The seas in the Bight of Heligoland are short and steep when the westerly winds are blowing, and it was difficult to keep the conning-tower hatches open and so to obtain fresh air. In the words of Commodore Keyes's report, " there was no rest to be obtained, and even when cruising at a depth of sixty feet the submarines were rolling considerably and pumping—*i.e.*, vertically moving about twenty feet.

" I submit," added the commodore, in terms of measured praise which the nation will warmly endorse, " that it was creditable to the commanding officers that they should have maintained their stations under such conditions. Service in the Heligoland Bight is keenly sought after by the commanding officers of the Eighth

Submarine Flotilla, and they have all shown daring and enterprise in the execution of their duties. These officers have unanimously expressed to me their admiration of the cool and gallant behaviour of the officers and men under their command."

One of the most thrilling incidents of the watch beneath the water off Heligoland occurred on September 25th, when E6 (Lieutenant-Commander Cecil Ponsonby Talbot) fouled a German mine while diving. The mine was firmly caught between E6's horizontal hydroplane (or fin) and its steel guard, and as she came to the surface she brought it up with her as well as the " sinker," or heavy iron weight attached to the mine by a cable. The " horns " of the mine—a tap on which would have detonated the powerful charge and blown

GERMAN PREPARATION TO DEFEND BRUSSELS.
The photograph immediately above shows a part of the Palais de Justice, with sand-bag defences placed by Germans, and the small photograph above shows a German gun close by the Palais de Justice, which occupies an elevated position dominating the entire city. In the picture on the left another prepared position behind the Palais de Justice is illustrated.

E6 and her crew to pieces—were by some lucky chance pointed outward, away from her hull. The mine had to be lifted clear without jarring it, and this, too, in the presence of the enemy, while the heavy pull of the " sinker " rendered the work extraordinarily difficult. None the less the feat was achieved by two brave men who, after half an hour's work, released the submarine and returned the mine to its original place. There was no finer deed in the early weeks of the war. Lieutenant Williams-Freeman received the companionship of the Distinguished Service Order and Seaman Cremer the Conspicuous Gallantry Medal.

[Photo by Downey.

ALBERT THE HERO KING OF THE BELGIANS.

King Albert succeeded his uncle, Leopold II., in 1909, and soon proved to be of different material from his clever but unprincipled predecessor   A man of high purpose, genuine culture, and native modesty, he won the affection of his subjects and the genuine esteem of all who came into contact with him   The threat of German invasion, despite treaties, Hague Conference undertakings, and the reiterated promises of German rulers and plenipotentiaries, placed upon King Albert the responsibility for one of the most momentous decisions that it has been the lot of a king to make   With a nature that rose to the highest heroism under the greatest adversity, he became the great white star of Belgium's hopes, showing by personal bravery an example that inspired officers and men to the most heroic resistance ever offered by a small nation to an unscrupulous bully, determined to crush her by every artifice of war and terrorism

CHAPTER XXI

HOW THE GERMANS SWEPT ON BRUSSELS.

The Problem of Belgium—Hopes of Speedy Assistance from France and Britain—Importance of Brussels as a City of Commerce, Industry, and Art—Alternating Hopes and Fears during First Days of War—Press Censorship in Brussels—Streams of Refugees—Government removes to Antwerp—The Rush of a Frightened Populace from the City—The German Approach —Proclamation by the Burgomaster—Arrival of the Enemy—The Goose-step in Brussels—Parade of Power and Insult— The Enemy takes Possession—Demand for an £8,000,000 War Indemnity—A Germanised Government.

WHEN the King of the Belgians refused the German Government permission to march its troops through his country, there were not lacking critics in Belgium, and in Brussels in particular, who regarded his action as ill-advised. All knew that this refusal must entail war. Belgium, in general, did not want war; she had nothing to gain and everything to lose by it. Brussels knew that war might well spell dire disaster. For Brussels, the great pleasure city of Northern Europe, is only about one hundred and twenty miles from the German frontier, and but one fortress of any importance—Liège—guarded the road to her gates, and there were many doubts as to the possibility of Liège resisting a determined attack, even for a day or two.

The small army that could be put on the field between Liège and Brussels would, the people knew well, be outnumbered ten to one, or twenty to one if necessary, by the Germans. An immediately successful war would bring immense loss and suffering on the country; a war which in its first stages went against the Allies might mean ruin; and it would be Belgium that would pay, for

FIELD-MARSHAL VON DER GOLTZ.
German governor of Belgium, who arrested the brave Burgomaster of Brussels when the demanded indemnity of £8,000,000 was not forthcoming.

on her soil now, as in previous centuries, the war of the nations would probably be waged.

The surprising fact is, not that some Belgians at the critical hour hesitated, but that the overwhelming majority of the people responded so immediately, so enthusiastically, and with such determination as they did to the Government's decision to resist. Yet, even when war began, Brussels hoped that she at least would be spared the horrors of foreign military occupation. The Allies would come to help her; the French cavalry would pour up through the Ardennes, making a dense screen through which the enemy could not pass. The British would land their Expeditionary Force along the coast as they had done a century before. Brussels would be saved.

The declaration of war came, and the people of the city responded splendidly. In Parliament, party controversy ceased. Every family gave its sons gladly to the service of the country.

Then followed some days of waiting. The Belgian regiments marched through the city on their way to the front. Armies of war-correspondents poured in and, hurriedly chartering motor-cars.

GERMAN TROOPS RESTING IN A BRUSSELS SUBURB.
Scenes like this were to be seen in most of the Brussels suburbs during the German occupation.
The soldiers, fatigued with a long march, rested by the wayside before resuming the march
farther west—a march, in many cases, to their graves.

made off to attempt to reach the fighting-line. Nurses and doctors from friendly countries came to help. Palaces and public buildings were made ready to receive the wounded. There were little waves of excitement over the capture of spies. As day followed day, and the Germans made no apparent advance, even the pessimists grew more hopeful. Liège was holding out. The valley of the Meuse was being successfully defended.

French officers were seen in the streets—the advance guard of the great French army expected by the nation. Now came stories of German cavalry advances beyond Liège, but these were mere skirmishes of Uhlan outposts, of no importance and signifying nothing. Each day, too, the newspapers printed stories of successes. Some Uhlans were ambushed here; a party was driven back with immense loss there: a heroic Belgian advance had thrown the Germans into a panic somewhere else. All was going well.

One great cause of anxiety remained, however. Where were the French? Where were the British? The newspapers gave the news that a British Expeditionary Force had landed on the northern coast. British ships had been discharging hosts of men at Zeebrugge and at Ostend since August 8th—so the newspapers said. Where were they?

Alternation of hope and fear

The first real shock came on Saturday, August 15th, when one of the leading Brussels papers, "Le Soir," printed a short statement that there was a possibility of the Germans advancing to the north of Brussels in the direction of Antwerp, and towards the capital itself. The paper urged that every preparation should be made to receive them. Next day the "Soir" was forced to print a humble apology in big type, and to agree to publish nothing in future concerning the movements of the troops save official communications. "The German advance towards Antwerp and Brussels is officially and categorically denied," it stated in heavy black type.

The Press supported the officials in maintaining that all was well. An official censorship was imposed on the newspapers, and towards the end they were allowed to publish nothing except what the authorities approved. That they might be the better controlled, they were limited first to two editions and then to one edition a day. These editions had to be submitted to the censor an hour or two before publication, and a familiar sight was to find blanks in the course of articles, where the censor had ordered the type to be

GERMANS ARRESTING THE STREAM OF FUGITIVES FROM BELGIUM.
It did not suit the policy of Germany to have refugees flee from Belgium in millions, because she had need of the inhabitants that she might extort gold and food, and also use their labour. Here German soldiers are seen stopping Belgians who seek to leave Malines by rail after the arrival of the invaders.

battered or cut out so that some objectionable item might not appear. Then refugees began to arrive, first from the villages and towns to the far south, and then from places nearer to hand. Many of these came bearing with them dreadful stories of German cruelty and oppression. There were parents who had rushed away unable to save their own children, and children crying through the streets looking for their parents; and others, dulled with grief, telling inquirers that they had lost their all. Men, prosperous householders a week or two before, now recounted how family and home had all gone.

On Monday, August 17th, it was officially announced that the Royal Family, except the King, would remove from Brussels to Antwerp, and that the headquarters of the Government would be transferred to the latter city. Laborious assurances were given that this transference did not in any sense mean that the enemy were making a successful advance. The very elaboration of the excuses offered might have told the people the truth.

By Tuesday, August 18th, the city

was beginning to show signs of nerves. The official declarations that all was going well were not considered wholly satisfactory. Why was it necessary to post up notices warning the people to deposit their arms with the police in order to avoid being shot by the invaders? What was the meaning of all the barricades and formidable entrenchments springing up everywhere? Why the constant practising of the Civil Guards? Did anyone imagine that the Civil Guards could fight the German soldiery? Even the guards themselves

ON THE WAY TO STRIKE FOR KING, HOME, AND FREEDOM.
These photographs show groups of Belgian soldiers marching to the defence of their land. Dog transport was useful in war as in peace, as seen in the first and second pictures, the very effective machine-guns of the Belgians being drawn by dogs. In the foreground of the lowest photograph a soldier is seen assisting a wounded comrade.

looked on the whole affair as rather a joke. But their arming meant something.

On Wednesday afternoon the city awoke with a start to the truth. The conventional announcement in the newspapers: "The situation is good. The Germans are still on the other side of the Meuse," was openly ridiculed. The usual list of victories over the Germans had been published; but that day there flocked into the city armies of refugees from the very villages and towns where the victories were supposed to have been won. These refugees, stricken with grief, some of them bearing wounds, all showing signs of exposure, of want, and of fear, told another tale. They had seen with their own eyes the troops driven back, the houses fired, and many civilians murdered. Some of them had fled to escape the thrust of the German lances, and some showed wounds from stray bullets. All were in a state of panic, all had the same message: "The Germans are at our gates. They will soon be here!"

The belief that the British Expeditionary Force would arrive, even at the last moment, and drive the Germans back, prevailed. The rumour went forth late in the afternoon that the British troops were already pouring out

BELGIAN LANCERS TAKE A LAST LOOK AT THEIR CAPITAL AS THEY LEAVE FOR ANTWERP.
A party of the dogged Belgian Lancers, with their officer, on the road from Brussels to Antwerp. When the Belgians wisely decided to proclaim their beautiful capital an open town, and thereby save it from the horrors of a German bombardment, they fell back upon Antwerp. From the latter fortified city they made many venturesome sorties and greatly harassed the invaders, the Belgian Lancers proving themselves more than a match, individually, for the Kaiser's much-advertised Uhlans.

of the Gare du Nord, and crowds of people hurried up the Grands Boulevards to cheer them. All that met their eyes was a trainload of their own wounded being carried to the station for removal to Antwerp, to make room for more urgent cases in the hospitals.

Now came a rush for the trains. Thousands made their way to the stations and fought for a place in the carriages, already packed to suffocation, bound to Holland and the north. Others set·out by road. Some carried

The exodus of frightened fugitives

their little possessions on their backs ; some had their dog-carts ; others fled so hastily that they took nothing with them. Away, anywhere away !

Meanwhile, the Prussians had entered Tirlemont on the evening of August 18th, and, according to popular report, had put many of the inhabitants to death. The trains had ceased to run beyond Louvain. From Louvain every train moving in the direction of Brussels or Mechlin was stormed by great throngs of people. If the people in Brussels wanted to escape northwards for shelter and safety, the people south of Brussels regarded the capital as their haven.

At first some attempt was made by the railway officials and by the local gendarmerie to control the crowds and to protect the line. Barricades were erected, wire entanglements put in position, and trenches dug. The hurrying crowds swept past, and their panic was increased by the sight of great bodies of troops hastily marching northwards in the direction of Antwerp. A general retirement of the Army had been ordered. Louvain was to be abandoned, Brussels left open, and the Germans allowed to occupy the capital without opposition.

The Belgian troops retired in order, two mixed brigades covering their retreat. These mixed brigades suffered heavily. Not only were the German infantry pushing up relentlessly, but the German artillery was doing great

CUT OFF FROM HIS REGIMENT.
A Belgian cavalryman, cut off from his regiment during the retirement from Brussels, takes a rest at the foot of a wayside crucifix.

AN ARMOURED MOTOR-CAR FOR UHLAN HUNTING IN NORTHERN BELGIUM.

One of the Belgian armoured motor-cars that did great execution among marauding parties of Uhlans during the operations between Brussels and Antwerp. Many of these cars were constructed at a factory in Antwerp, and their speed and armament—a machine-gun—made them deadly engines of warfare. The vulnerable parts of this particular car are its wheels. Later cars had their wheels heavily protected.

execution. Now a German aeroplane flew overhead in the direction of Brussels. Now an advance party of Uhlans or motor infantry would dash on the Belgian rearguard. It was a case of hard outpost fighting. Many of the Belgian troops had been on duty for thirty-six hours continuously, without a moment of rest and with little or nothing to eat or to drink the whole time. It was their business to give the main Army an opportunity to get away, and they did their work splendidly. In Louvain itself large numbers of the people refused to retire. They had nowhere to go, and they derived a certain confidence from the antiquity and historic splendour of their city.

A BELGIAN FIELD TELEPHONE AT WORK

Taking down instructions from a field telephone in Northern Belgium. A covering of corn conceals the operators from aeroplane observation, while an artillery officer puts on record the message received. These telephones were often used to give an artillery battery the exact range of the enemy.

D 34

Louvain's mistaken sense of security

Louvain was a great centre of learning. All the world honoured it, and men from all the world came to study in its university. The German soldiery might burn villages, but Louvain, the most hallowed spot in Belgium, was surely safe. So they stayed.

There was little sleep in Brussels that night. In the early morning hours a cry arose from street after street: " The Germans are coming." During the night the Civil Guards marched back, singing the " Marseillaise," and moved through the city out on the other side towards Antwerp. There was to be no resistance to the Germans. Brussels was an open town ; as such it was protected by the laws of war against bombardment. It would simply submit to the presence of the enemy. It could no less ; it would do no more.

A proclamation by the burgomaster was pasted on the walls late on August 19th, 1914 :

' Fellow-citizens,—Despite the heroic resistance offered by our troops, seconded by the allied armies, there is reason to fear that the enemy may occupy Brussels. Should such an event come to pass, I trust I may count upon the calm and the *sang froid* of the population. Above all, one should not lose one's head or give way to panic. The municipal authorities will not desert their post. They will continue to

WHEELING AN INVALID HUSBAND FROM BRUSSELS

Before Brussels fell, thousands of terror-stricken Belgian peasants crowded into the capital from outlying districts. As the Germans approached Brussels, the plight of these refugees became even more pitiable. They were forced to move again, and make their way either to Antwerp or the coast. A wife is here seen wheeling her sick husband, who holds their baby, in a barrow along the road to Antwerp.

manifestation. The enemy cannot legally attack either the honour of families or the life of citizens, or private property, or religious or philosophical convictions ; nor can they interfere with the freedom of public worship.

Proclamation of the intrepid burgomaster

"Any abuse committed by the invader should be immediately notified to me. So long as I am in possession of life and liberty I will protect with all my might the rights and the dignity of my fellow-citizens. I implore the population to assist me in my task by abstaining from any hostile act, any use of arms, and any participation in fights or discussions.

"Fellow-citizens, whatever may happen, listen to the voice of your burgomaster and continue to trust in him. He will not betray you.

"Long live Belgium, free and independent. Long live Brussels.　　　　　　　ADOLPH MAX.

"August 19th."

The burgomaster, accompanied by his four sheriffs, went out to meet the German commander. He was treated with scant courtesy and ceremony. First he was ordered to take off his scarf of office. Then he was asked brusquely if he was prepared to make an unconditional surrender of the city. If he did not do so, it would be promptly bombarded. M. Max, the burgomaster, was, as he showed during the days that were to come, a brave, resourceful, and high-spirited man. He had no intention of cringing, even if his city, owing to fortunes of war, had fallen to the foe. But it is impossible for a man to argue or to make much show of dignity when an automatic pistol is being held to his head. M. Max's position was one of utter defencelessness. The Germans told him that they would hold him responsible for the government and order of the city. Their troops must be unmolested. They must have free passage through Brussels, and be provided with what they required.

It cannot be wondered that the Germans decided to make the entry into the Belgian capital as impressive as

perform their duties with the firmness which you have a right to expect from them in such serious circumstances.

"It is hardly necessary for me to remind my fellow-citizens of their duty towards their country. The laws of warfare forbid the enemy to use force to obtain from the population information concerning the national Army and its means of defence. The inhabitants of Brussels should know that they are within their rights in refusing to furnish any information whatsoever to the invader. None of you must think of acting as guides to the foe. This refusal is indispensable in the interests of the country.

"Every one should be on his guard against spies and foreign agents who should attempt to obtain information or provoke any form of

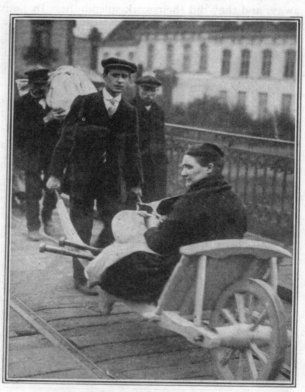

CRIPPLE WOMAN DRIVEN FROM HOME.

Frightened out of Brussels by the arrival of the German army, this poor cripple was wheeled to Ghent in a barrow, carrying all the worldly possessions she was able to collect hastily.

possible. From purely a military point of view, they could have saved time by pushing onward without rest, and ignoring Brussels. But *morale* counts for much in war, and the German General Staff had rightly gauged the moral effect of a triumphant entry, not only on their own people, but on the world at large. It was decided not to make the entry into the capital with the regiments that had borne the brunt of the fighting. Their stricken ranks and wearied gait might have given Brussels some encouragement. An entirely fresh army corps was brought up, and at two o'clock on the afternoon of August 20th it began its triumphant march towards the Place de la Gare, the heart of Brussels.

The Germans intended to impress the Bruxellois with a sense

THE BELGIAN ARMY'S CARRIER-PIGEONS.
The use of carrier-pigeons for conveying information was greatly curtailed during the struggle in Northern Belgium. When the Germans took possession of Brussels they seized the pigeons in the town, so that no vital news could be carried outside by "pigeon post." This picture shows Belgian cavalry carrying pigeons in a basket. The birds belonged to Antwerp, and were able to fly with messages from the neighbourhood of Brussels to their fortress home.

of their power, and they certainly did. The firing of big guns announced the coming of the victorious army. The bands of their own regiments played them triumphantly through the streets, the soldiers singing, as they marched, "The Watch on the Rhine," and "Deutschland über Alles." Cavalry and infantry, artillery and sappers, a complete siege train, one hundred motor-cars each with its own quick-firer, Uhlans and hussars, all were there. Here were some of the crack corps of Germany, such as the ominously named Death's Head Hussar regiment.

The "Daily Mail" special correspondent sent a vivid description of the scene as the Germans swept through the stricken city:

TIRED BELGIAN CYCLISTS REST AT ALOST.
A cyclist brigade of the Belgian Army rests at Alost after a skirmish round Brussels. These cyclists proved of great value during the Belgian retreat, and as scouts and advance patrols they were highly successful.

"All were in greenish, earthy-looking grey, all helmets covered in grey, the guns painted grey, the carriages grey, and even the pontoon bridge, all complete, in grey. **The goose-step in Brussels** To a quick step the men had marched to the great square, when to the sound of the whistle—the word of command seems to have gone the way of the brilliant uniforms—the infantry broke into the famous parade or goose-step, while the good lieges of Brussels gazed open-mouthed in wonder. Passing the station, the great military procession defiled through the boulevards to camp on the heights of the city near Kochelberg. Truly it was a sight to gladden the eyes of Kaiser Wilhelm, but men muttered under their breath, ' They'll not pass through here on their return. *Les Alliés en feront leur affaire*' ('the Allies'll do for them'). In the procession were two Belgian officers attached to the stirrup-leathers of the Uhlans. A low growl was evoked by this barbarous spectacle, which was instantly resented by the officers, who at once backed their horses into the ranks of the spectators, threatening them, not with words, but with uplifted sabres.

" A very gross pleasantry was perpetrated by a gunner, who was evidently in charge of the pet of the battery—a baby bear—which, dressed up in full Belgian general's uniform, evidently intended to represent the King, touched his cocked hat at intervals to his keeper. This particularly irritated the brave Belgians, but they wisely abstained from any overt manifestation. A very unpleasant feature was the behaviour of some of the soldiery, who, as they passed, tore repeatedly at the national colours which every Belgian lady now wears at her breast."

German troops took possession of the railway-station, the telegraph and telephone offices, and the central points commanding the city. The telephone bureau was quickly attached to the German headquarters farther south. Almost automatically, German authority was established. It was a remarkable example of how a great city can, in an afternoon, pass under the control of an invader. The German flag flew from the town-hall. German outposts took possession of the villages around. They drew a cordon around the city. Count von Arnim was appointed acting-governor. He issued a proclamation stating that through the circumstances of war he was forced to levy

Requisitions and warnings

on the people requisitions for food and other supplies. While hoping that everything would go quietly, he warned them that the severest possible measures would be taken against anyone who fired on German troops or attempted to interfere with the German communications.

The German officers and troops were naturally in high spirits. Hotel-keepers who had closed their

A GROUP OF BELGIAN MINISTERS OF STATE.
The Belgian Government, after having withdrawn to Antwerp on the German approach to Brussels, and then to Ostend, left the latter city and sought the hospitality of France on October 13th, 1914, when it took up its quarters at St. Adresse, near Havre. The group above consists of H. Carton de Wiart, Minister of Justice (on the left), J. Davignon, Foreign Minister ; P. Poullet, Minister of Science and Art ; and A. Van de Vyvere, Finance Minister. The upper photograph is of Baron Ch. de Broqueville, President of the Council and Minister of War.

establishments were ordered to reopen them. That night, in many a great hotel and café, the officers sat drinking champagne, singing, and rejoicing.

In Brussels, unlike the country villages, the Germans on the whole behaved very well. They paid individually for what they took. They apparently had abundance of money, and offered gold freely.

Enemies feast in the fallen city

Each soldier seemed to have as many large cigars as he wished to smoke. It had evidently been determined to impress the people of Brussels with the power and prosperity of Germany.

Enormous bodies of troops, apparently six or seven army corps, marched through the city in the days that immediately followed its occupation. The requisitions for foodstuffs for these myriads soon materially affected the supplies of the city. Most of the Belgian wounded had been removed when the Belgian Army retired towards Antwerp. Their place was now taken by German wounded, brought in from the front.

One surprise came within a few hours of the German triumphant entry. The burgomaster, M. Max, was informed that the city of Brussels would have to find an indemnity of £8,000,000. The Germans had already made a similar demand for a smaller amount on Liège, and their action was quite in conduct with the methods of the German armies during the Franco-Prussian War. Nevertheless, it caused intense surprise and indignation throughout the world. This surely was making war on commercial principles.

M. Max declared that all the money had been sent to Antwerp. Dire threats were uttered against him. He calmly replied that he must await the course of events. Soon, the authorities paid for what they had, not in gold, but in paper money issued by the German governor. In a few days the Germans announced their intention of regarding Belgium as German. Greenwich time was altered to German time, and steps were taken for a new Germanised Government.

SCENES FROM THE FIRST NAVAL BATTLE OFF HELIGOLAND.

The German Fleet rested in inglorious security under shelter of the great island fortress of Heligoland, and the British Fleet lay outside waiting to engage the enemy at the first opportunity. No opportunity came, so the British admirals determined to create the opportunity. Some submarine craft were sent into the Bight, evidently in distress, and the cruiser Fearless followed, seemingly for the purpose of rendering assistance. The ruse succeeded and some important units of the German Fleet came out to attack. The battle that followed ended in victory for the British Navy. This picture was drawn from a sketch by a British officer in the action, and represents the hottest stage in the conflict, when the big guns were thundering destruction and fire upon the enemy ships.

THE FIRST LIGHT CRUISER SQUADRON SIGHTING THE ENEMY.

Commodore W. R. Goodenough commanded the First Light Cruiser Squadron—consisting of the ships Southampton, Birmingham, Lowestoft, and Nottingham—in the Battle of Heligoland. Certain of those ships waited behind the mist till the call for assistance, and as soon as a large four-funnelled German cruiser loomed up through the haze, proceeding to the assistance of the smaller German craft, the call was sent, and they steamed full speed to the help of the Arethusa.

IN PORT AFTER THE FIRST NAVAL BATTLE—A SCENE OFF HARWICH.

The British ships that won the victory of Heligoland Bight returned to Harwich after the battle for refitting and repairs, and this sketch of the fleet in Harwich Roads was made by a special war artist as the vessels lay at anchor there.

BRITISH CHIVALRY: RESCUING GERMAN CREWS OFF HELIGOLAND.

The official account of the British naval victory off Heligoland said: "The British destroyers exposed themselves to considerable risk in endeavouring to save as many as possible of the drowning German sailors." The officer, from whose sketch this drawing was made, wrote: "The sketch represents the sinking of the German destroyer V187 at about 9 a.m. on the 28th. While we were picking up the crew, a German cruiser loomed out of the mist and fired at us.

The first salvo fell among the boats exactly as depicted, and the destroyers' whalers are seen getting back to their ships as fast as possible. There are two German prisoners with life-belts in our whaler—the rear one. The German went down within a minute, just as we were getting away after hoisting the boats. The German cruiser firing the shots is on the left of the horizon. One of the destroyers was hit twice by the German, luckily without damage."

A REMARKABLE CAMERA RECORD OF THE SINKING OF THE GERMAN CRUISER MAINZ OFF HELIGOLAND, AUGUST 28TH, 1914.

This very striking photograph, taken from the deck of one of the British cruisers, shows a British gun crew in the foreground, standing by a 6 in. gun, looking at the sinking Mainz—the result of their handiwork. An officer in H.M.S. Falmouth, which helped to sink the Mainz, said: "We managed to put her midship guns out of action pretty quickly, and soon after blew up both her after funnels together. Her fo'c'sle gun then went on firing, but we bowled that out at last. As we steamed past her towards the next enemy, I was able to view the poor sinking vessel through binoculars from about one hundred yards, and her decks were a hideous shambles." The Mainz is seen on fire, and minus two funnels and a mast, shortly before she heeled over and sank.

CHAPTER XXII.

HELIGOLAND

THE BATTLE OF THE BIGHT OF HELIGOLAND.

A "Certain Liveliness" in the North Sea—The Screen of British War Craft—German "Victories" over British Trawlers—
Preparations for the Battle of Heligoland—The British Ships Engaged—The Plan of Strategy—The British Bait—Issue
of the German Flotilla—The "Saucy Arethusa"—German Cruisers in Action—Work of British Destroyers—The Destruction
of V187—The British Dreadnoughts brought up in Support—Destruction of the Mainz—British Gallantry in Saving the Crew
—The Köln and the Ariadne—The Marksmanship of the Lion—Incidents of the Battle—The Low Price paid for Victory

DURING the first weeks of war both the British and Germans maintained flotillas of small surface craft on patrol work in the North Sea, and occasionally these came into contact, but never with any noteworthy result. On August 18th the official Press Bureau issued the following statement : " Some desultory fighting has taken place during the day between the British patrolling squadrons and flotillas and German reconnoitring cruisers. No losses are reported or claimed. A certain liveliness is apparent in the southern area of the North Sea."

In point of fact, the Germans were trying every means they knew, short of steaming out in force, to break through the screen of British surface warships which was drawn across the North Sea behind the advanced guard of British submarines off the German ports. Their aim was to discover whether a British Expeditionary Force was really moving to the Continent. Every attempt on the part of the German light cruisers and torpedo craft to get through was frustrated.

The only work of any consequence which the German Navy was able to accomplish in the North Sea during the first three weeks of the war, apart from the destruction of the Amphion, was an inglorious raid on the part of a small squadron, which resulted in the sinking of a number of British fishing trawlers, twenty-two of which were sent to the bottom between August 24th and 28th.

The depredations of this German squadron were not completed until August 28th. The date is a significant one, and will be long remembered in the annals of the British Navy ; for it was then that Admiral Jellicoe put into effect the first of the schemes that had been prepared for carrying out offensive operations on the German coast.

The trap for the German Navy

From the very beginning of the war, as has already been seen, a close watch on the German coast had been kept by British submarines. The British commander-in-chief had a large number of vessels at his disposal, and they were organised into relays of flotillas so that the boats were able alternatively to put in a few days' reconnaissance work on the German coast and to enjoy a short period of rest and relaxation at a home port. For such work submarines were exceptionally well suited. The information obtained by the British submarine scouts paved the way for the action which has since come to be known as the " Battle of the Bight of Heligoland."

The submarines reported that a considerable force of German light cruisers and torpedo-craft was lying under the protection of the formidable defences of Heligoland. The Admiralty determined to strike a blow at those ships ; but as it would have been an extremely risky business to attempt to cut them out from under the countless 12 in. batteries of Heligoland, resort was had to stratagem to entice the German vessels away from their protection.

Elaborate plans were prepared. They provided for the employment of the following imposing force on the British side, which included the fastest British destroyers :

First Battle Cruiser Squadron, Vice-Admiral Sir David Beatty: Lion, Princess Royal, Queen Mary (each 26,350 to 27,000 tons, 29 knots, eight 13·5 in. and sixteen 4 in. guns); New Zealand, Invincible (each 17,250 to 18,800 tons, 27 knots, eight 12 in. and sixteen 4 in. guns).

First Light Cruiser Squadron, Commodore W. R. Goodenough; Southampton, Falmouth, Birmingham, Lowestoft, Nottingham (each 5,500 tons, 25½ knots, eight or nine 6 in. guns).

Seventh Cruiser Squadron, Rear-Admiral A. H. Christian: Armoured cruisers Euryalus, Cressy, Hogue, Aboukir, Sutlej, Bacchante (each 12,000 tons, two 9·2 in. and twelve 6 in. guns, 21 knots), and the light cruiser Amethyst (3,000 tons and 23 knots, armed with twelve 4 in. guns).

Flagship of Destroyer Flotillas, Commodore R. Y. Tyrwhitt: Arethusa (3,750 tons, 30 knots, two 6 in. and six 4 in. guns).

First Destroyer Flotilla: Leader, Fearless (3,440 tons, 26 knots, ten 4 in. guns); and destroyers Acheron, Archer, Ariel, Attack, Badger, Beaver, Defender, Ferret, Forester, Goshawk, Hind, Jackal, Lapwing, Lizard, Phœnix, Sandfly (each about 800 tons, 30 knots, two 4 in. and two 12-pounder guns).

Third Destroyer Flotilla: Laertes, Laforey, Lance, Landrail, Lark, Laurel, Lawford, Legion, Leonidas, Lennox, Liberty, Linnet, Llewelyn, Louis, Lucifer, Lydiard, Lysander (each 965 tons, 32 knots, three 4 in. guns).

Eighth Submarine Flotilla, Commodore Roger Keyes, in destroyer Lurcher (765 tons, 35 knots, two 4 in. and two 12-pounder guns), with her sister boat Firedrake, and submarines D2, D8, E4, E5, E6, E7, E8, and E9.

Attached to the Battle Cruiser Squadron were the destroyers Hornet, Hydra, Tigress, and Loyal.

Under the scheme arranged, three of the submarines were to proceed on the surface towards Heligoland, in order to induce the enemy to chase them westwards. The destroyer flotillas, aided by the light cruisers Arethusa and Fearless, were then to work in behind any German vessels which might come out to give chase. The Light Cruiser Squadron was to be at hand, but farther out, to render help should it be required, while the huge Dreadnoughts and super-Dreadnoughts of the Battle Cruiser Squadron were on the alert still farther to the west, to meet the large German armoured cruisers and battleships should they venture to put to sea. The Seventh Cruiser Squadron was used as a reserve to attack any German ships that might be driven westwards.

Disposition of the British ships

At midnight of August 26th Commodore Keyes, with his two destroyers and eight submarines, moved towards Heligoland. All next day the two swift destroyers scouted diligently for the submarines, which at nightfall took up positions whence they could assist in the operations of the following day. August 28th broke calm and misty. The calm weather was peculiarly unfavourable to the British submarines, because, when the sea is still, such an object as a periscope on the surface at once attracts attention. The mist added to the difficulties of the underwater craft, as it enabled enemies to approach unseen, and rendered it almost impossible to distinguish friend from foe. Cautiously the two fast destroyers searched the waters in which the fighting was to take place for German submarines and, finding

THE BAIT THAT DREW OUT THE GERMAN SHIPS OF WAR WHICH WERE DESTROYED IN THE BATTLE OF THE BIGHT OF HELIGOLAND.

This sketch shows the strategy of the British commander. The British submarines seen on the right appeared off Heligoland apparently disabled, and the cruiser Fearless seemed to be going to their assistance. When the Germans saw this, they fell into the trap prepared for them, and came out to take advantage of what they imagined to be a fortunate accident. Then, according to programme, the light cruiser Fearless, steaming away, drew them on in pursuit until they came within the circle of the British destroyer flotilla waiting to attack them.

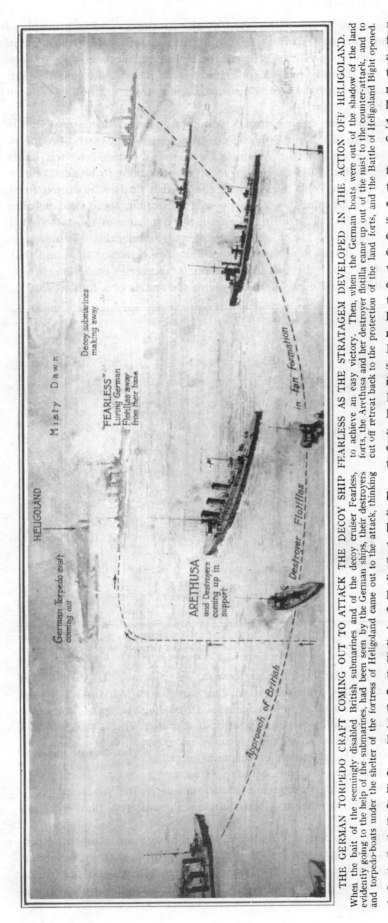

Misty Dawn

HELIGOLAND

Decoy submarines
making away

"FEARLESS"
Luring German
Flotillas away
from their base.

German Torpedo craft
coming out

ARETHUSA
and Destroyers
coming up in
support

Destroyer Flotillas

in Farr formation

Approach of British

THE GERMAN TORPEDO CRAFT COMING OUT TO ATTACK THE DECOY SHIP FEARLESS AS THE STRATAGEM DEVELOPED IN THE ACTION OFF HELIGOLAND.
When the bait of the seemingly disabled British submarines and of the decoy cruiser Fearless, to achieve an easy victory. Then, when the German boats were out of the shadow of the land evidently going to the help of the submarines, had been seen by the German ships, their destroyers forts, the Arethusa and her destroyer flotilla came up out of the mist to the counter-attack, and to and torpedo-boats under the shelter of the fortress of Heligoland came out to the attack, thinking cut off retreat back to the protection of the land forts, and the Battle of Heligoland Bight opened.

none, steamed in slowly towards the island fortress of Heligoland, in the wake of E6, E7, and E8, which showed themselves as a bait for the enemy. As this little group of vessels neared the island the mist thickened till the limit of visibility was reduced to 5,000 or 6,000 yards. Meanwhile, the other British submarines dived and waited for a chance to attack.

The bait attracted the Germans. Out came first one destroyer, and then some nineteen or twenty, which gave chase to the two British destroyers and the three submarines. A German seaplane rushed up and hovered overhead, then circled and returned to Heligoland, presumably carrying the news that the British submarines were off their guard, and that there was a great opportunity of dealing them a deadly blow. After the German destroyers, a detachment of German light cruisers weighed and put to sea from the neighbourhood of Heligoland. Meanwhile, the British vessels were falling back at their best speed westwards; and drawing the Germans after them.
For the best part of two

Success of the decoy manœuvre

hours the British craft continued their retreat, and as the E submarines, running on the surface, could do sixteen knots, they should have enticed the enemy more than thirty miles from Heligoland.

Presently, out of the thinning haze ahead there leaped the forms of British warships, racing down at full speed. One by one, to the right and to the left, they came into view, each one as she got within range letting fly with her forward guns at the oncoming German cruisers and destroyers; and before the latter had time to realise their position they found two widespread lines of British destroyers rapidly closing in upon them. The cruiser Arethusa led the destroyers of the Third Flotilla, and the Fearless the vessels of the First Flotilla, in the rush upon the enemy, steering in to cut them off from Heligoland. At 6.53 the first German destroyer was seen from the Arethusa and chased; twenty minutes later the Arethusa and the Third Flotilla were in the midst of eighteen to twenty hostile destroyers, and a furious engagement began.

From the time when the opposing flotillas came into contact the story of the battle loses its unity. The large numbers and the high speed of the vessels engaged, coupled with the smoke from the shells and the mist that still hung over the sea, made it impossible for the commanders to retain complete control of their forces, and the action developed into a series of confused encounters in which every vessel did her best in whatever position she happened to find herself.

The official report of the action gives this summary of the part played by the Arethusa : " The principle of the operation was a scooping movement by a strong force of destroyers, headed by the Arethusa, to cut the German light craft from home and engage them at leisure in the open sea. The Arethusa, leading the line of destroyers, was first attacked by two German cruisers, and was sharply engaged for thirty-five minutes at a range of about three thousand yards, with the result that she sustained some damage and casualties, but drove off the two German cruisers, one of which she seriously injured with her 6 in. guns.

" Later in the morning she engaged at intervals two other German vessels, who were encountered in the confused fighting which followed, and in company with the Light Cruiser Squadron contributed to the sinking of

Brilliant work of the Arethusa

the cruiser Mainz. In these encounters the Arethusa's speed was reduced to ten knots and many of her guns were disabled, and at one o'clock she was about to be attacked by two other cruisers of the German Town class when the British Cruiser Squadron most opportunely arrived and pursued and sank these new antagonists. The armoured protection, speed, and fighting qualities of the Arethusa class have now been vindicated, and this is satisfactory in view of the fact that a large number of these valuable and unique vessels will join the Fleet in the next few months. It must be remembered that the Arethusa had been commissioned only a few days before as an emergency ship, and that the officers and crew were new to each other and to her. In these circumstances the series of actions which they fought during the morning is extremely creditable, and adds another page to the annals of a famous ship."

GENERAL IMPRESSION OF THE BATTLE OF HELIGOLAND, SHOWING THE LARGER—
This diagrammatic representation shows the battle at its full height—the German cruisers and the British and German destroyers on the skyline; the disabled Arethusa being towed out of action by the Fearless; and the cruisers and battle-cruisers of the British fleet waiting

The first German cruisers were sighted on the Arethusa's port bow at 7.57 a.m. They were the two-funnelled Ariadne, a vessel of 2,600 tons and 22 knots, armed with ten 4 in. guns, and a four-funnelled ship, which was probably the Strassburg, a vessel of 4,500 tons and 28 knots, armed with twelve 4 in. guns, but which some of those in the British force took for the still larger and more powerful armoured cruiser Yorck, of 9,500 tons, armed with four 8·3 in. and ten 6 in. guns. From these two ships the Arethusa received a terrific fire, until the Fearless came up and drew off the attention of the four-funnelled vessel. The Arethusa now concentrated her attack upon the Ariadne, steering a convergent course. The two cruisers exchanged broadsides, when a fine shot from one of the Arethusa's 6 in. guns struck the Ariadne's forebridge, and the explosion of the 100 lb. lyddite shell shattered that structure and probably killed the German captain.

The German cruisers in action

The Ariadne on receiving this shell acknowledged her discomfiture. She turned away and steamed as fast as she could towards Heligoland, which now came into sight on the Arethusa's bow through the mist about 8.25. The Arethusa had suffered severely. Shells in her hull had damaged her machinery. Of her whole battery but one 6 in. gun remained in action. All her four torpedo-tubes had been disabled and her other seven guns. Her deck was on fire amidships.

The signal was made from the Arethusa to turn westwards, and with her destroyers she proceeded on the new course at twenty knots, while the small craft re-formed. Some minutes later it was found that her speed had fallen as the result of the injuries she had received, and all hands were engaged in getting her once more into fighting trim, effecting temporary repairs, and clearing away the wreckage of battle.

Now it was that Commodore Tyrwhitt received a stirring report from his destroyers of the First Flotilla. While he had been so hotly engaged with the German cruisers they, too, had been busy. The leading boat of the German flotilla, V187, a vessel of 650 tons and 32½ knots, armed with two 20-pounders and four machine-guns, had been caught and cut off. She fought with the utmost gallantry and desperation, but the British destroyers were not to be denied. They closed with her, poured in a storm of 31-pounder shells, accurately directed, which tore open her thin sides and water-line. Clouds of smoke and tongues of flame rose from her as the projectiles exploded and swept her crew away. **Punishing the German destroyers** She sank lower in the water, still firing from a single gun ; then the fire ceased, and almost at the same moment she sank. One other German destroyer was observed in a water-logged condition, and at least eight or ten more had sustained serious damage, but yet managed to get away.

As the V187 went down, the British destroyers of the First Flotilla ceased fire and launched boats to save the Germans who were struggling in the water. This had scarcely been done when a large German cruiser—probably the Mainz—approached and opened a tremendous fire on the boats. Presumably the

LION Battle cruiser

PRINCESS ROYAL Battle cruiser

—BRITISH SHIPS WAITING IN THE HOPE OF A GENERAL SORTIE OF THE GERMAN FLEET.
In the foreground in the expectation that the German battleships would come out to assist their cruisers and accept the challenge of battle. But the main German fleet preferred the inglorious security of the protection of their land forts.

Germans supposed that the British were intending to board. The destroyers were compelled to fall back before this fire, to which they could make no adequate reply from their weak batteries, mounted in their frail vibrating hulls. Two boats belonging to the Goshawk and Defender were abandoned and left in a situation of deadly peril, in the midst of the Germans and almost under the guns of Heligoland. It seemed as though nothing could save them when suddenly submarine E4 (Lieutenant-Commander E. W. Leir) showed near at hand. She had watched the battle through her periscope, and judged that the moment had come to strike a blow. **Daring rescue by submarine E4** She proceeded towards the German cruiser, which must have seen her, for as she came on to deliver a torpedo attack the German vessel altered course and vanished in the mist.

The attack of submarine E4 covered the retreat of the destroyers and saved the boats. As soon as the destroyers were out of sight Lieutenant-Commander Leir moved towards the two boats, and boldly rose to the surface to give them aid. To the officers and men in the British boats she appeared as a heaven-sent deliverer when her grey hull lifted above the water and her hatches were opened. She took on board one British officer and nine men, and one unwounded German officer and two men. She left in the boats one German officer and six men who were unwounded and eighteen badly-wounded Germans, directing the unwounded Germans to navigate the boats to Heligoland.

Meanwhile the Arethusa, Fearless, and the British destroyers had re-formed, and made every preparation for renewing the battle, bringing up fresh ammunition, plugging shot holes, and getting collision-mats over their wounds. At 10 a.m. they received a wireless message from Commodore Keyes to the effect that the Lurcher and Firedrake were being chased by German light cruisers. With the splendid comradeship which distinguished the Navy, Commodore Tyrwhitt at once proceeded to their rescue, supported by the Fearless and the destroyers of the

The call for battleships

First Flotilla. At 10.37 a.m. he once more reached the neighbourhood of Heligoland. There was no sign of any British vessel, and no signals came in from the Lurcher. At any moment the enemy might have shown in force out of the mist, and he turned westwards for the second time that morning.

He must have been seen and signalled to the German light cruisers, for at 10.55 suddenly a large German four-funnelled cruiser, which was probably the Strassburg, or the Yorck, loomed up and opened a very heavy fire. The position was critical, and signals were promptly made by wireless to Vice-Admiral Beatty, of the Battle Cruiser Squadron, calling for aid and stating that the Arethusa was hard pressed. Simultaneously, the First Destroyer Flotilla sent out the same summons to the powerful British ships which were waiting in the background. The British Light Cruiser Squadron was at once ordered by Admiral Beatty, commanding the battle-cruisers, to proceed at full speed to the aid of the flotillas. But as two of its five ships had already been detached to support the destroyers and had not rejoined, only three vessels remained available. Admiral Beatty therefore determined himself to bring up his huge Dreadnoughts to the help of Commodore Tyrwhitt. Already he had seen periscopes moving in the water, and had been attacked by three German submarines, but had eluded them by moving at high

THE ARETHUSA IN A CIRCLE OF GERMAN NAVAL ATTACK.
The Arethusa, the flagship of the British Destroyer Flotilla, and her commander, Commodore R. Y. Tyrwhitt, covered themselves with glory during the Battle of Heligoland. Though far outclassed by the weight of metal in her attacking foes, she outfought them and stuck to them when her speed had, by reason of internal injuries, been greatly reduced, and when she had only one gun left undisabled.

speed. He directed the four destroyers which were attached to his squadron to chase these underwater hornets energetically, and at 11.30 he turned towards Heligoland and ordered his squadron to work up to full speed—twenty-seven knots.

While this powerful succour was on its way to the flotillas, the crisis of the battle had arrived. Commodore Tyrwhitt directed the Fearless to concentrate her fire on the big German cruiser, and the First Flotilla to attack her with torpedoes. They closed her, and let go their deadly "metal fishes," but she, perceiving their object, forthwith turned, eluded the torpedoes, and vanished for the time being in the haze. It was not for long, however. Ten minutes later she reappeared and took up a position on the Arethusa's starboard quarter. The Arethusa and Fearless began a furious artillery fight with her, while the destroyers again attacked her with their torpedoes. She concentrated her fire upon the Arethusa. In the words of Commodore Tyrwhitt, "salvo after salvo (from her guns) was falling between ten and thirty yards short, but not a shell struck; two torpedoes were also fired at us, being well directed but short."

Defective German gunnery

She ought to have sunk the gallant little British cruiser. Instead of doing so, she sustained heavy damage from the Arethusa's 6 in. guns, and from the Fearless's 4 in. weapons, while the destroyers maintained a steady fire on her, which seemed to take effect. After a quarter of an hour of this pounding she turned away and vanished in the mist towards Heligoland. The British vessels did not attempt to pursue her; their position was too dangerous, as they had expended much ammunition and many torpedoes, and had sustained grave injuries.

At this juncture yet another large vessel was made out coming up through the mist. She was, in fact, the German light cruiser Mainz, which had already attacked the British boats near Heligoland. The Arethusa and

Fearless and the destroyers of the Third Flotilla met her onslaught in the most determined manner. Their fire soon began to tell. Slowly, as the British shells swept her, their rapid broadsides died down ; fires burst out on board her ; splinters could be seen flying from her upper works ; her shots went wide. One of her funnels fell with a tremendous crash. The moment had come for the destroyers to deliver a torpedo attack. A torpedo discharged from one of the Laertes's tubes by Petty-Officer Edward Naylor struck her amidships. When the cloud of smoke and foam which rose had vanished, it was seen that one of her boilers had been blown right up from the bottom of the ship and flung upon the deck, where it lay visible to the crews of the British ships. The Mainz was now no little better than a wreck, slowly sinking by the head, on fire in several places, her engines stopped, her deck a shambles.

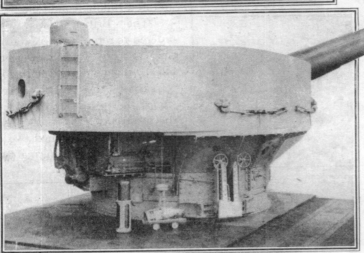

Out of the mist showed two large British light cruisers, Falmouth and Nottingham, the first of the Light Cruiser Squadron to reach the battle. Their 6 in. guns opened a crushing fire on the shattered and sinking wreck. A second funnel fell with one of the masts. The rain of shells reduced the hull of the luckless German cruiser to " a piteous mass of unrecognisability, wreathed in black fumes, from which flared out angry bursts of fire, like Vesuvius in eruption." Her resistance ceased. Blazing in several places, broken in two, the wreck sank lower and lower in the water.

Then, most gallantly, Commodore Keyes, in the destroyer Lurcher, ran in alongside her to take off survivors. " It was a sight," as one of the Lurcher's crew wrote. " One mast and two funnels had gone. We rescued two hundred and twenty-four. She was sinking fast, and standing under her was a very dangerous trick. We had just shoved astern when she listed over to port, and we saw those who were left sliding down the ship's side into the water. Then she dipped, and all the German sailors cheered her down. All over her decks were dead and dying." According to another report, of all the men saved from her only fifty were able to walk—a terrible testimony to the efficacy of British gunnery. As her crew numbered three hundred and seventy-nine, one hundred and fifty-five of her officers and men must have perished in the battle.

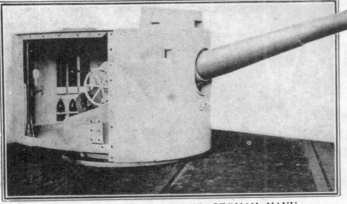

KRUPP GUNS USED IN THE GERMAN NAVY.
The biggest German naval guns when the war began were 12 in. and the largest battleships—those of the Kaiser class—carried ten of such guns, as well as fourteen 6 in. guns, twelve 24-pounders, four 14-pounder anti-aerial guns, and five torpedo-tubes. The three German super-Dreadnoughts laid down in 1913 and 1914 were specified for eight 15 in. guns, but they were not due for completion until 1916 and 1917. The first two guns (of 6 in. and 8·2 in. calibre) in the photograph above are capable of high-angle fire, while the third is restricted in this respect.

The Fearless and the destroyers were now recalled by signal from the Arethusa, and ordered to cease fire and proceed westwards, leaving the Light Cruiser Squadron and the Lurcher to attend to the Mainz. At 12.15 the huge vessels of the Battle

Cruiser Squadron arrived on the scene, and proceeded north-eastward towards Heligoland. They came in sight of the Arethusa, engaged with yet another German light cruiser—the Köln—a sister ship of the Mainz, and like her of 4,300 tons, armed with twelve 4 in. guns, and steaming twenty-six knots. She had come up through the mist and opened a long-range fire on the Arethusa, which the Arethusa had returned with great spirit, but without visible effect. Now the Köln was to be subjected to the terrible attack of the monster 13.5 in. guns mounted in the battle-cruisers, which fired shells of 1,250 lb. weight, and were capable of making hits at seven miles.

Admiral Beatty with his huge cruisers steered to cut her off from Heligoland, and, as she immediately fled on seeing the approach of these new antagonists, chased her at twenty-seven knots. At 12.37 he opened fire, and, though the range was extreme, his guns inflicted great damage upon her and set her on fire. A few minutes later, while the British battle-cruisers were moving at twenty-eight knots, another German ship, the two-funnelled cruiser Ariadne, which earlier in the day had been hotly engaged with the Arethusa, came into sight. She still

flew the German flag, and was steaming fast on a course at right angles to that of the Lion, which led the line of British battle-cruisers. The Lion let fly two salvos from her eight 13.5 in. guns, which, in Admiral Beatty's words," took effect and she (the Ariadne) disappeared into the mist, burning furiously and in a sinking condition."

The British ships were ordered to retire, as there was no sign of any further German force at hand. But before retreating, the battle-cruisers circled northward to complete the destruction of the cruiser Köln. The Lion trained two of her turrets, each mounting two

3.5 in. guns, upon the German vessel. Two salvos were fired, each of four 1,250 lb. shells, and as the smoke of their explosion rose from the Köln, it was seen that she was sinking. She went down as a stone sinks, and the four destroyers attached to the Battle Cruiser Squadron, on proceeding to the spot where she had disappeared to rescue survivors, found no one alive. The whole crew of three hundred and seventy-nine officers and men had perished.

The Battle of the Bight was marked by several curious incidents. In their second report of the engagement, the Admiralty stated that : " The British officers present vouched for the fact that German officers were observed firing at their own men

THE LIGHTER SIDE OF BELGIUM'S TRAVAIL.
The lower picture shows a party of Belgian civilians, who, armed with spades and marshalled by a gendarme, went forth to dig trenches at Alost, thus saving the energy of the Belgian fighting-men. Belgian villagers were frequently engaged to dig trenches for their own countrymen, and were sometimes forced, at the pistol's point, to dig them for the Germans. The upper photograph shows Belgian cavalrymen peeling potatoes for a midday meal at Etterdeck.

in the water with pistols, and that several were shot before their eyes in these peculiar circumstances." This was stoutly denied by the German authorities ; but in addition to the evidence of eye-witnesses, a number of German seamen of the Mainz, picked up by the Lurcher in the water, were found to be suffering from pistol-shot wounds, which could only have been inflicted by their own officers. The apparent explanation was that, when the British vessel went to the assistance of the German cruiser, an officer in the cruiser ordered his men to open fire on her, and, on their refusal to do so, shot them down. The men who were shot while actually in the water are believed to have left their ship without orders.

The German Admiralty paid a tribute to the heroism of the British in seeking to assist the wounded and drowning Germans

RUSSIAN ROYAL LADIES WHO WORKED FOR THE WOUNDED.
The Tsarina and her daughters worked devotedly as Sisters of Mercy at the Tsarkoe Selo Military Hospital. No distinction was made between them and the ordinary Sisters, and, after attending courses of nursing and surgery, they assisted in operations upon the Tsar's wounded warriors. Above is seen a photograph of the Tsar's four daughters. The photograph on the left depicts the Grand Duchess Elisabeth Feodorovna, who, assisted by members of the dramatic profession, made caravan collections on behalf of the Russian wounded.

while under fire. " It must be admitted," the report ran, " that the British, without stopping to consider their own danger, sent out lifeboats in order to save our men."

Not a single British ship was lost in the battle. The Arethusa was badly damaged. She had about thirty holes in her sides, half her bridge had been carried away, and one of her torpedo-tubes had been smashed. The total casualties of the entire British attacking force were thirty-two killed and fifty-six wounded, while the material damage was so insignificant that within a fortnight all the ships concerned were at sea again.

The Germans, on the other hand, had suffered heavily. Two of their most modern cruisers—the Mainz and the Köln—had been sent to the bottom. The Ariadne, which had also been disposed of, was an older and smaller vessel. The British Admiralty claimed that two of the enemy's destroyers were sunk, but the V187 seems to have been the only vessel of this class actually accounted for ; the others, though extensively damaged, being saved principally by their high speed.

Of the losses in men which were inflicted on the enemy we have no precise knowledge. The complements of the four ships known to have been sunk aggregated about 1,060, and of these about three hundred were taken prisoners, while some twenty-four were allowed to go free in the defenders' boats. The remainder—over seven hundred souls—were either killed or drowned ; and in addition to these there is the number—unknown, but probably considerable—who were killed in the ships which escaped. Well might the Admiralty describe the action as " fortunate and fruitful ! "

CHAPTER XXIII.

THE FIRST BATTLES IN EAST PRUSSIA.

The Russian Mobilisation—German Hopes of Speedy Victory in the West—Russia's Policy Dictated by Consideration of the West—Russian Invasion of Galicia and East Russia—General Rennenkampf—German Defence of East Prussia—The Stand at Gumbinnen—German Evacuation of Tilsit and Insterburg—Continued Russian Advance—East Prussia Overrun—General von Hindenberg—The Marshland Frontier of Prussia—The Battle of Tannenberg—German Victory

THE Russian mobilisation began on July 25th, and was not completed until August 24th. Even then the concentration of the armies on the European frontiers of the empire was still in progress. As has already been explained in the chapter in which we discussed the general military situation in Eastern Europe, a vast empire like Russia, with a backward railway system, can only put forth its full fighting strength very gradually. The German plan of campaign was based upon an anticipation that the Russian armies would be so slow in taking the field as to leave ample time for a swift campaign on the western frontier of Germany, during which France would be crushed, and a large part of the field armies employed in this operation would be set free and could be transferred by rail to the eastern frontier.

This hope was disappointed, thanks to the resistance of the Belgians and the stubborn opposition to the German advance made by the allied French and British armies. France, though defeated at the outset, was far from being crushed, and the German

WOUNDED COSSACKS BEING DRIVEN TO HOSPITAL.

advance was brought to a standstill in the first days of September. But Russia also contributed to the defeat of the Kaiser's plan of campaign, and at an early stage of the war did not a little to relieve the pressure on France.

The German Staff had counted upon the Russian Army being unable to attempt any serious operations until after the first month of the war. If Russia had acted entirely upon military reasons dictated by her own interests, it is very likely that this forecast would have been verified. The soundest plan would have been for the Russian armies quietly to complete their mobilisation behind the frontier fortresses and along the middle Vistula, and then, when they had their full forces available, move forward on a broad front, with the advantage of superior numbers at every point. But to wait for weeks to complete the concentration of an army of four or five millions would have been to allow Germany to put forth its full force for the attack on France. In their loyalty to the alliance the Russians therefore decided to take very serious risks, and to begin offensive operations against Austria and Germany before even their mobilisation was complete.

This was possible because for some years nearly two-thirds of the European army of Russia was stationed in time of peace to the west of Moscow, and several of the frontier corps had been kept nearly on a war footing. It was, therefore, possible to concentrate a considerable force for active operations in the first fortnight of the war. In the very first days of the conflict the Russian frontier detachments were employed in harassing the enemy, and in the second week large armies were pushed across the borders of East Prussia against the Germans on the right and of Galicia against the Austrians on the left. In the centre, in that part of Russian Poland which lies west of the Vistula, all that was attempted was to delay the advance of the German and Austrian forces, which in the middle of August advanced from the direction of Posen and Cracow. In this region the Russian Staff had, during the period of concentration, no object beyond the defence of the line of the Vistula. Even if the concentration had been completed earlier, nothing serious could be done in the centre until the enemy's

RUSSIAN DOCTOR IN THE TRENCHES.
The western allies can yield nothing to their great eastern ally in the devotion to duty and mercy shown by their doctors in war. The doctor in the photograph is wounded in the hand, but sticks to his work.

forces had been broken in East Prussia and Galicia. Until these provinces had been successfully invaded by the Russians, an advance westward from Warsaw would expose its flanks and communications to German and Austrian attacks from the north and south. The first serious operations of the Russians were thus in the south, the converging advance of two armies on Lemberg; and in the north, an invasion of East Prussia. In this chapter we shall confine our attention entirely to the East Prussian campaign.

The operations against East Prussia were entrusted to General Rennenkampf, a Russian cavalry general, who was one of the few soldiers who had added to his reputation during the disastrous war with the Japanese in Manchuria. He had directed more than one successful raid of Cossack troops against the enemy, and he had commanded one of the armies in the final struggle at Mukden. His name was popular with the Russian soldiers. He had a reputation for enterprising dash, and was often compared with

TWO BRILLIANT COMMANDERS OF RIVAL ARMIES.
The photograph in the oval picture is General von Hindenberg, the German commander to whom was due the victory of Tannenberg, in the beginning of September, 1914, and the group in the lower photograph is the Staff of General Rennenkampf with the general himself, the hero of the great Russian raid into East Prussia in August, 1914.

Skobeleff, the young hero of the Central Asian and Balkan campaigns. Of the forces at his disposal it is impossible to make an exact estimate, but it is not likely that he had more than four hundred thousand men in all. These were concentrated along the line of the River Niemen from Kovno southwards, under the protection of the line of fortresses that guards the river crossings.

During the concentration the detachments posted west of the river, along the frontier, were engaged in minor operations against the German troops on the border. These had to stand strictly on the defensive. The greater part of the German army of the first line, or regular troops, was being hurried towards France and Belgium, and General Le François, who was charged with the organisation of the defence of East Prussia, had only at his command

The Defence of East Prussia

a few of the local army corps. These included the 1st Corps (headquarters, Königsberg), the 20th (headquarters, Allenstein), the 17th (headquarters, Dantzic), and the 2nd (headquarters, Stettin)—all of them East Prussians and Pomeranians. These are among the best fighting men of the German Army. But the four corps united would not number quite two hundred and fifty thousand men. To hold their own against Rennenkampf's army they would have to be supplemented by second-line troops—reservists and men of the first levy of the Landwehr organised in new reserve corps, and these formations would take some time to complete. For local defence of the wilderness of lake, marsh, and forest along the frontier hastily-formed detachments of the Landsturm would also be available, but at the outset, in case of

invasion, the advantage of numbers would be on the side of the Russians.

The first fighting between the frontier detachments took place on Monday, August 3rd, when the garrison of Memel repulsed a small column of Cossacks that had made a raid across the frontier. Two days later the Russian frontier guards crossed the border further south at Lyck and Bialla, driving German detachments before them and destroying the railways.

On the 7th this advance was checked by Landsturm detachments, which drove back the Cossacks in the woods about Johannisburg; but on the same day a considerable Russian force, marching from Suwalki, crossed the frontier, and established itself without opposition on the railway line between Lyck and Goldap. The Russians had thus taken possession of the frontier region in the south-east corner of the province of East Prussia, along the main railway line that runs from Warsaw through the lake region to Königsberg.

RUSSIAN COLD STEEL IN EAST PRUSSIA, AUGUST 26TH, 1914.
At Schwansfeld, in East Prussia, a battle was fought between Germans and Russians on August 26th, 1914. The Cossacks excelled themselves by their attack on the Death's Head Hussars. The Russian infantry also proved their superiority over the enemy. After a fierce artillery bombardment, the main Russian forces advanced with the bayonet and enveloped the German left, shattering it. The Germans fled from the trenches and were cut up in small parties. Fifty guns were captured by the Russians on the previous day.

Rennenkampf's plan of campaign was to advance in two columns, the left column by the line through Lyck and Lötzen, the right column—the stronger of the two—along the main railway line from Kovno, by Gumbinnen, on Königsberg. The Russian movements in this stage of the campaign were constantly watched by German aeroplanes. The Russians possessed far fewer of these modern appliances for reconnaissance, and their flying machines, mostly heavy biplanes, were inferior to the German Taubes, and the flying men, conscious of their lack of speed, were much less enterprising. The German plan of campaign was to delay the advance of the left column through the lake and forest region by the operations of Landwehr and Landsturm detachments, and to fight a decisive battle against the right column on the northern line. The place chosen for this stand was at Gumbinnen. Here the railway line, running east and west, and the old high-road beside it, cross the marshy hollow of a little river in the midst of a tract of densely-wooded country.

MASKED GUNS TURNED ON THE RUSSIANS AT TILSIT.
Prussian civilians on the Russian frontier adopted many ruses to take the Russians at a disadvantage. Russian soldiers were in Tilsit market-place buying hay when a long train of hay and straw carts halted in the square. The Prussian peasants hurried round them, seized hidden rifles, and then machine-guns, hidden in the carts, were suddenly turned on the unsuspecting soldiers of the Tsar. Prussian precept where civilians were concerned was at marked variance with Prussian practice.

The western bank of the river was heavily entrenched, and thousands of trees were cut down to form long lines of abattis—that is, obstacles constructed by laying the trees with their branches to the front, and entangling them with barbed wire. Probably over 200,000 men were concentrated for the defence of this hurriedly fortified line. When the work was begun it was not expected that any serious attack could be made on the position by the Russians before the beginning of September.

But Rennenkampf had decided to act at the earliest possible moment, even before his own concentration was quite complete. In the second week of August he began the general movement of his army from the Niemen to the immediate neighbourhood of the frontier. On August 14th the rapid reinforcement of the Cossack vanguard on the Prussian side of the border, and the reports brought in by the airmen, **Meeting of Rennenkampf and Samsonoff** warned the Germans that the enemy's advance in force was imminent. On the following day Rennenkampf crossed the frontier on a broad front right and left of the Gumbinnen railway line, while his southern column, under General Samsonoff, another distinguished leader of the Manchurian War, crossed the border farther south, and began to advance by way of Lyck through the lake region. In the following days both columns met with a desultory resistance from German detachments, which fell back slowly before them through the woods.

BBB

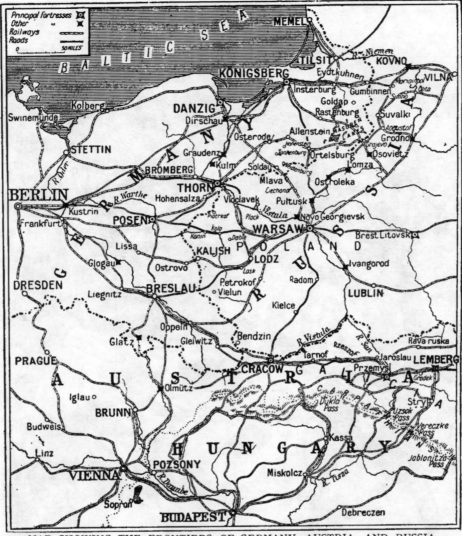

MAP SHOWING THE FRONTIERS OF GERMANY, AUSTRIA, AND RUSSIA.

On Monday, August 16th, Rennenkampf had cleared the country up to the Gumbinnen position, and found his further progress arrested by the entrenched line held by the Germans. According to Russian reports, the enemy's force was made up of three army corps —probably the East and West Prussian Corps, the 1st, 17th, and 20th. Allowing for the probability that some of the reserve formations and local defence detachments had joined them, they would be at least 150,000— and perhaps 200,000—strong. At Gumbinnen the first great battle of the campaign took place. It lasted for four days, from August 17th to 20th, but the serious fighting took place on the last two days. The battle began with an artillery duel, gradually extending along a front of many miles, the marshy river hollow separating the two battle fronts. During this first phase of the fight Rennenkampf was occupied in feeling the enemy's position along the front, and reconnoitring to right and left through the wooded country

with a view to a turning movement. At some points where it was thought a weak spot had been found in the line, local frontal attacks were attempted; but these invariably failed, and the Germans captured a number of prisoners. On the strength of these partial successes the Berlin papers announced a Russian defeat. But the real attack began on the 19th. Using his superiority of numbers, Rennenkampf attacked all along the front in order to keep the enemy fully occupied, while on the left one of his army corps made a wide turning movement through the woods round the German right, and, pushing back the forces that had been hurried to the point of danger to oppose it, succeeded in the evening in penetrating to the right rear of the enemy's defences. Next day the victory thus prepared by the successful flank movement was completed. Rennenkampf, steadily

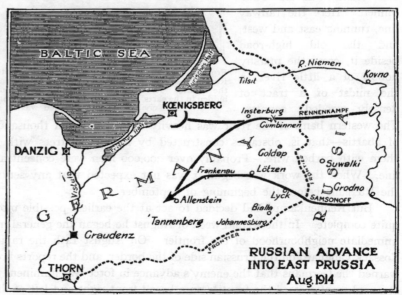

LINES OF THE FIRST RUSSIAN ADVANCE IN EAST PRUSSIA.
The heavy lines indicate (1) General Rennenkampf's advance from the River Niemen to Insterburg, whence a dash was made to Königsberg; and (2) General Samsonoff's march from Grodno. With the exception of the men detached for Königsberg, the Russian armies joined forces at Allenstein.

reinforcing his left, enveloped and rolled up the German right, cutting off and capturing thousands of prisoners and many guns.   The collapse of the German right and the Russian advance on this side endangered the line of retreat, and in the afternoon a general retirement began.   The Germans fell back along the railway, pursued by the victorious Russians, and after a brief rearguard fight abandoned the great railway junction at Insterburg, though much labour had been expended in entrenching the ground to the east of the town.

On the same day the Germans evacuated Tilsit, further north, and the place was occupied without opposition by a Russian detachment from the neighbouring frontier. **The Prussians evacuate Tilsit** The occupation of Tilsit and Insterburg gave Rennenkampf the command of a second line of supply by the railway running northwards from Insterburg Junction.

No such serious opposition was offered by the Germans to the southern column.   There were a number of small engagements, in none of which the Germans made any obstinate defence.   They were mostly intended to be mere delaying actions.   Lötzen was occupied by the invaders, and the little Fort Boyen, on a neighbouring hillock, barring the pass by which the railway line runs between two lakes, was forced to surrender after a brief bombardment.   There was a most serious fight at Frankenau, where Samsonoff defeated a considerable German force, capturing some guns.   This success brought the Russian left column safely to the north of the difficult lake region along the frontier, and it was able to get in touch with the right or main column under Rennenkampf.

OFFICERS OF SCOTTISH DESCENT FIGHTING FOR THE TSAR.
In the history of the Russian Army appear the names of many Scots, French, Swedes, and even Germans.   All will readily recall the famous instance of Marshal Keith.   To-day, when soldiers of fortune, as they are called, are not so numerous as of old, there remain in the Tsar's Army many men whose names betoken their foreign descent.   Of the officers in the above photograph three bear Scottish names—Colonel Gillivray (on the extreme right), Colonel Robertson (next to him), and Major-General Ross (fifth from the right).

After the Battle of Gumbinnen, the Germans in the north of East Prussia had fallen back on Königsberg without again risking a serious engagement.   By the end of August they were under the cover of its advanced forts.   Rennenkampf had detached some of the corps from his right to blockade Königsberg on the land side. With the rest of his army he joined hands with his left column and marched south-westward in the direction of the Lower Vistula.   Allenstein, the headquarters of the 20th German Army Corps, was **Russian occupation of Allenstein** occupied without resistance.   It was an important station for the German Flying Corps. Before evacuating the place the garrison sent away the airship and aeroplanes stationed there, and burned the big Zeppelin airship shed.

By the end of August the invaders had occupied nearly the whole of East Prussia.   The inhabitants of farms and villages had taken to flight in panic at their approach, some of them going as far as Dantzic, which was crowded with a quarter of a million of fugitives.   The rapid success of the Russians led to the most exaggerated reports.   It was said that they were advancing in overwhelming numbers towards the Vistula, and about to attack the fortresses of Graudenz and Thorn, and that Königsberg had been completely invested.   This last news was obviously untrue, for Königsberg is linked with the Frisches Haff and the sea-coast by its western forts, and could not be blockaded unless by an enemy who had command of the Baltic.   All that the Russians had been able to do was to entrench themselves before the eastern front.   Rennenkampf, with the field army, had advanced a little beyond Allenstein, and before he could reach the Vistula he would have to traverse a belt of difficult country, abounding in lakes, marshes, and woods, round Osterode, Tannenberg, and Eylau.

Though apparently he had swept all before him, his position was, in fact, becoming difficult, and his action in pushing so far could only be justified on the ground that the whole invasion of East Prussia was a demonstration in force, intended to alarm the Berlin General Staff into keeping back for the defence of the eastern frontier troops that would otherwise have been sent to France. Strictly speaking, the whole movement was a premature enterprise, with, to use a familiar expression, a good deal of bluff about it. But the complete collapse of all resistance after the victory of Gumbinnen gave Rennenkampf the idea that he might safely push still further forward—though he was too good a soldier to be influenced in any way by the current reports that the Russian army would be able to make an almost unopposed march to Berlin.

By the end of August the Germans were preparing for a very effective counter-stroke. Of the troops that had

retired into Königsberg, only enough were left in the place to stiffen the garrison. The rest were transferred by sea and by the coast railway through Elbing to Dantzic and the Lower Vistula. Along the river a large army was being concentrated for the reconquest of East Prussia. General von Hindenburg had taken command of it. He is one of the most remarkable soldiers of Germany. At the beginning of the war he was on the retired list. He had fought as a young soldier in the war of 1870. When he rose to the rank of general, he commanded for some years army corps in East Prussia, and he made a special study of the military possibilities of the district. More than once at the great manœuvres he had won victories in the frontier lake region, entangling his opponents in the wilderness of marsh and pool, drawing them on to ground where their gun wheels sank in the swamps, and their infantry was driven waist-deep into the water. After his retirement from the Army, he made his

GERMAN OUTPOST SCENES IN EAST PRUSSIA NEAR THE RUSSIAN FRONTIER.
While in the first of the above photographs the German soldiers, snatching brief repose in the more or less uncomfortable surroundings of an inn in East Prussia, have the appearance of men utterly weary, their comrades on outpost duty, pictured in our second illustration, appear to be enjoying a spell of leisure pretty thoroughly. Illustrated papers are very popular with all soldiers, but quite early in the war a grave protest was raised in Germany itself against the ribaldry of its so-called " comic papers." Soldiers face to face with the foe saw things more in perspective than irresponsible artists in towns and cities so far safe from attack.

home in East Prussia, and travelled over every square mile of the lake region. In these excursions his motor-car was often accompanied by a fully horsed field-gun, borrowed from the garrison of Königsberg or Allenstein. He would use this gun for elaborate experiments, finding out by actual trial where it could be driven through the shallow lakes, or where their muddy bottoms made it impossible for horses and wheels to pass. He spoke of the district as the natural defence of the frontier region. A few years ago it was proposed to carry out an extensive project of

POLE FIGHTS POLE ON THE RUSSIAN FRONTIER.
In the early hostilities in East Prussia Polish infantry in the German service were called upon to fight men of their own race but under the Russian flag. Our first illustration shows a section of these men—all crack shots—in the rifle-pits along the frontier. The Russian Poles were splendidly loyal to the Tsar. The second photograph is of a captured Russian quick-firing gun in its transport cart.

reclamation. Canals were to be made through the country, lakes and marshes drained, forests cut down, and hundreds of square miles of the wilderness turned into valuable agricultural land.

General von Hindenburg fiercely opposed the project. He went to Berlin and begged the Kaiser to veto it, telling him that whatever might be the commercial value of the land reclaimed, the destruction of this wide belt of wild country along the frontier would be a sacrifice that no money could repay. It would be like throwing down the ramparts of a great fortress in order to find room for some cabbage gardens, he said, for the lake region was the natural rampart of Germany towards Russia. He had his way, and the project was abandoned. It was on account of his intimate knowledge of the military possibilities of the country that he was entrusted with the command of the army destined to operate against Rennenkampf. It is very seldom that a soldier has the chance of repeating in real warfare, and on the same ground, the victories won in mere blank-cartridge battles at manœuvres. This was what Von Hindenburg was now to do.

Von Hindenburg's counter-move

In the last days of August and the opening days of September he was massing his forces about Osterode, Tannenberg, and Hohenstein, small towns and villages in the lake district, on the main railway line from Thorn and Graudenz, on the Vistula, to Allenstein. Troops were drawn from the Vistula garrisons to reinforce the army, and heavy artillery was brought up by rail, and a large quantity of motor transport by road.

The position taken up by Von Hindenburg barred the further advance of Rennenkampf from Allenstein. The line held by the German troops was not a boldly marked position like that of Gumbinnen. Indeed, to an ordinary observer, there were no features to distinguish it from several similar tracts of country in the frontier district. Probably Rennenkampf thought his opponent had chosen it chiefly because the junction at Osterode gave him facilities for bringing up reinforcements and supplies. But Von Hindenburg had selected it on account of his own special knowledge of the ground. He would fight where he could extend his line by taking into it some of the lakes which he had found by experiment to be complete obstacles to any hostile movement. The ground behind his line was easily traversed from right to left, so that he could rapidly reinforce a flank during the battle. The ground in front, though to the ordinary observer it was much of the same character as that which he held, was

Prussian refugees leaving their homes before the Russian advance. Pathetic scene in East Prussia. Fugitives returning to find their home in ruins as the result of a recent (In centre: A group of Prussian peasants who were forced to make battle in the vicinity. their home in the fields.)

A village scene in East Prussia after a battle. A shopkeeper is seen carrying on his business in the street after his shop had been shattered by shell fire.

All that remained of a farmhouse in East Prussia. The pigs made the best of it; but the ravages of the war had made an impression on their owner's features.

GERMANY EXPERIENCING IN EAST PRUSSIA SOMETHING OF THE TERRORS OF WAR WHICH SHE FORCED UPON BELGIUM.

really cut up by tracts of soft, marshy land and swampy pools, which would make movement difficult ; and behind its right there was a tract of marshy forest, with numerous small lakes, that would make the retirement of any large force in that direction exceedingly difficult, and the hurried retreat of guns and transport waggons practically impossible.

The Battle of Tannenberg lasted three days, and about a quarter of a million men were in action on each side. But nevertheless it was more than a fortnight before the greater part of the world knew that this great battle had been fought and won by the Germans. There were no war correspondents with either army, and for some time the Russian official despatches made no mention of the action. References to a great Russian defeat in the German Press which found their way to England were treated by most people as fiction.

It would seem that at the outset Von Hindenburg was inferior in numbers

COAL-HEAP ON FIRE AT ANGERBURG STATION, EAST PRUSSIA.
Set on fire by Russians, it was found impossible to extinguish it with water, so the Russian prisoners were set to work to shovel it away. The mineral was badly needed by the Prussians.

SCENE IN THE MARKET PLACE OF PHILIPPOVO, EAST PRUSSIA.
The Landsturm officer (who in private life was a portly member of the Reichstag) is seen interrogating a civilian charged with some petty theft.

to the invaders, but he was reinforced by railway during the three days' fight. From the outset he was stronger in artillery than his opponents. Heavy guns had been brought up from the Vistula fortresses, and batteries of field artillery had been borrowed from the army corps on the Posen frontier. "The Germans crowded their guns into the line as if they were rifles," said a Russian officer. This concentrated fire of artillery proved particularly telling against the Russian frontal attacks on the first two days. Some of these attacks, however, were locally and temporarily successful. Several villages along the front were stormed with the bayonet, but it was difficult to hold them under the downpour of high-explosive shells, of which they were at once made the target.

During this stage of the battle Von Hindenburg was fighting on the defensive, with a view to wearing down the energy of the attack before striking the decisive blow. Realising

FORAGE FOR PRUSSIAN CAVALRY AT GOLDAP, EAST PRUSSIA.
The waggons were drawn up in readiness for despatch to the scene of the fighting.

RUSSIAN PRISONERS OF WAR IN EAST PRUSSIA ON THEIR WAY TO AN INTERNMENT CAMP.

RUSSIAN PRISONERS UNDER GERMAN GUARD.
The sides of the transport waggon were covered with crude drawings and comments in chalk.

the difficulty of forcing the position in front, the Russians tried to extend their line to the southward and envelop the German right. Superior knowledge of the ground enabled Von Hindenburg to stop this flank movement with a much smaller force well posted in the defiles of solid ground between the lakes and swamps. Meanwhile, he was preparing a counter-attack on the other flank.

On the second day a daring Russian aviator, wheeling high in the air above the woods, saw what at first he took to be long columns of transport waggons moving rapidly along the rear of the German position from centre to left. Venturing closer, he found that these were not supply or ammunition columns, but long strings of motor-vehicles of all kinds, from motor-'buses to taxi-cabs, conveying infantry to the left, and rushing back empty to bring up more. His report was delivered in time to enable

RUSSIAN PRISONERS INTERNED AT FUSTENBURG, IN GERMANY, WERE EMPLOYED AS SCAVENGERS IN THE STREETS.
It was the German idea that prisoners should not only be made to work for such keep as was provided for them, but that they should do all the unpleasant and menial labour to which they could be set.

THE ADVANCE OF THE RUSSIANS INTO EAST PRUSSIA.
The larger photograph shows the Cossacks entering the town of Luck, in East Prussia. Their behaviour was most exemplary and in marked contrast to that of the Germans in Belgium and Northern France, who copied all too faithfully the Kaiser's injunction to spare not and to make the German name feared by the inhabitants of the country which they harried. The smaller photograph is of the Langen Markt and Rathaus at Dantzic, which historic German town was threatened by the first Russian advance into East Prussia.

the Russian Staff to order a reinforcement of the right, and on this flank the fighting that decided the battle began in the afternoon of the second day, Von Hindenburg weakening his centre in order to accumulate a superior force for the flank attack. The enveloping movement on this side, begun in the later hours of the day, was carried on during the night.

At sunrise on the third day the Russian right was turned, and the collapse of their line began. As they gave way from right to left under the converging pressure of front and flank attacks they found that it was a difficult matter to extricate themselves from the wilderness of woods, lakes, and marshes in which they had given battle. Three Russian generals fell in the final struggle —Samsonoff, Pestitsch, and Martos. Tens of thousands of prisoners and scores of guns were taken. The Germans claim that of the five army corps which formed the enemy's main battle-line they destroyed three and a half. The large number of Russian prisoners of war reported as being interned in Germany in September came almost entirely from the battlefield of Tannenberg. It was the most complete victory won by the Germans in the opening phase of the war.

Its immediate result was the precipitate evacuation of East Prussia by the invaders. Rennenkampf extricated the remnant of the army that had fought and failed at Tannenberg from the dangerous lake region. The force that was masking the eastern forts of Königsberg was ordered to withdraw. A column that had been moving towards Dantzic and the Vistula delta received the same orders. The general line of retreat was on Insterburg Junction.

Near Insterburg Rennenkampf fought a rearguard action, which Von Hindenburg claimed as a second victory. But there is no doubt the Russians fought only in order temporarily to check the pursuit. After the battle Rennenkampf fell back by Gumbinnen, recrossed the frontier, and retreated to the line of the River Niemen. Here large reinforcements were awaiting him.

BELGIAN ARTILLERY IN ACTION AT ALOST DURING THE GERMAN ADVANCE THROUGH BELGIUM.

WITH THE BELGIAN GUNS NEAR AUDOGOM, WHICH IS SEEN BURNING IN THE DISTANCE ON THE LEFT.

A BELGIAN BATTERY AT ST. GILES, NEAR TERMONDE, BEFORE THE LATTER TOWN WAS POUNDED INTO A HEAP OF RUINS.

During the German pressure on Belgium the soldiers of King Albert performed many prodigies of valour, but they were driven back by the overwhelming odds of men and by the heavy artillery which the invaders were able to bring up against them.

THE AGONY OF BELGIUM—HOW HER CITIES AND TOWNS WERE LAID DESOLATE.

The Brand on the Brow of German Culture—The German Movement from Brussels Westward—The Advance Screen and the Main Army—Mistaken Trust in Namur's Powers of Resistance—Military Reasons for General Joffre's Policy—Ostend's Anxiety—German Policy of Terrorism—Incendiarism, Looting, Murder, and Drunkenness—Massacres in Aerschot—The Crime of Louvain—German Atrocities at Malines, Termonde, and Melle—To the Gates of Ghent.

" *LOUVAIN, Malines, Termonde. These are names which will henceforward be branded on the brow of German culture.*"—Mr. Asquith at Edinburgh, September 18th, 1914.

Simultaneously with the German occupation of Brussels on August 20th, 1914, a determined advance was made all along the line. Strong forces, numbering over a million men, had been concentrated behind the right bank of the River Meuse. These now swept forward with speed and precision. By August 23rd four hundred thousand troops had passed through Brussels westward. Still stronger forces traversed the country to the south, without touching the Belgian capital. These vast armies were handled, it may be freely admitted, with extraordinary efficiency.

Motor traction was utilised to an extent hitherto unknown in warfare. Heavy guns, larger and of greater range than ever before employed in regular field operations, were moved forward with ease and rapidity, keeping up with the

BELGIAN SOLDIER OPERATING A MACHINE-GUN
against the advancing Germans between Termonde and Audogom as they pressed southwards after the occupation of Brussels.

main armies. Infantry were hurried from point to point in fleets of motor-trolleys. The supply of ammunition for big guns and small arms was so skilfully carried out with motor-vehicles that, save for a short period over one limited front, the German armies although fighting day by day hundreds of miles away from their permanent base, seemed abundantly supplied throughout the constant battles that followed.

Large bodies of cavalry—Uhlans and hussars—and companies of military cyclists moved ahead of the main army. Their work was to reconnoitre, to keep touch with the enemy, and to strike terror into the heart of the civil population. They carried out their task without scruple and without mercy, striving to instil in Western Belgium and Northern France the fear which the Uhlans had caused in Eastern France in 1870. Behind this screen the main armies moved forward in different directions. One small force advanced towards Antwerp, to hold the Belgian field army in check. Another force

431

moved in the direction of Courtrai, with its right wing towards Ostend and the coast, and its main body marching on Roubaix and Lille. The principal German advance was made between Enghien and Dinant. An overwhelming attack was concentrated upon the fortress of Namur and upon the French troops holding the position in the triangle where the Sambre and the Meuse meet. In the North of Belgium the Germans were in weak force. To the west and south they were everywhere in very great strength. Thanks to the admirable railway system of South-Western Belgium, they could move immense numbers from point to point with the maximum of ease and speed.

The Allies now depended for the defence of Belgium mainly upon the fortresses of Antwerp and Namur. Some 70,000 men of the Belgian field army still remained in line, and kept in constant touch with the Germans to the north. While this army was a source of annoyance to the Germans, and a menace to their lines of communication, it was not numerous enough to affect the main military operations. At the most, it could occupy one or two German army corps. Namur might, however, it was thought, play a vital part in military operations to the west.

The fortifications of Namur were constructed by General Brialmont on corresponding lines to those of Liège, and consisted of a ring of steel and concrete forts, linked up by field works, and mutually protecting one another.

Liège, despite the fact that it was inadequately manned, had held the Germans at bay for thirteen days. There had been more time to put Namur in a complete state of preparation, and the Belgian garrison was aided by a French force occupying the country immediately behind it.

The French were unable to move speedily to the aid of the

Belgians because they had mobilised and deployed their forces in the belief that the main German attack would come through Alsace-Lorraine and Luxemburg—through the country east of the Meuse. When it became evident that the Germans meant to march through Central and Western Belgium, much time was required to modify the dispositions.

General Joffre would have courted swift and complete defeat had he ordered a weak army to advance into Belgium to the help of King Albert. While French troops were being transferred from the eastern to the northern frontier, while the British Expeditionary Force was moving to the scene of action in Belgium, the French Staff hoped

BELGIAN DEFENDERS OF THEIR HOMES AND WOMENFOLK LED TO DEATH.
Franc-tireurs—that is, combatants in civilian dress—are according to the stern laws of war, liable to be shot if caught, and are not treated as prisoners of war. In shooting in cold blood non-uniformed Belgians who offered them armed opposition the Germans acted within the licence of war, but they went far beyond the licence of war when they executed large numbers of innocent civilians because of alleged attacks by a few individual franc-tireurs.

that the German advance would be so delayed by the two fortresses of Namur and Antwerp that a sufficient allied force might be able to concentrate and succour Belgium.

As yet the inability of steel and concrete forts to resist the huge projectiles of the German 8·2 in. and 11 in. howitzers had not been clearly demonstrated, despite the fall of Liège. The lesson was only learnt when Namur was taken after an attack lasting little more than twenty-four hours—an event which falls within the main campaign, and will be treated there. The loss of this place was a great disaster, since, when it had passed into German

THE HORRORS OF WAR IN THE VILLAGE OF CORTENBERGH, BRABANT.

Mr. A. J. Dawe, of Oxford, who was in Belgium during the German invasion, gave, in "The Times," an account of the way in which the Kaiser's troops carried fire and sword through the village of Cortenbergh, in Brabant, on August 28th, 1914. "The men who were guarding us," wrote Mr. Dawe, "told us that from certain houses shots had been fired by civilians, and that several Uhlans had been killed. They began upon the houses from which the shots were supposed to have been fired. These houses were soon splitting with fire and shooting up great flames. The women and children were herded together and set aside. We heard the quick sounds of rifle-shots as the escaping civilians were picked off. It was a terrible and brutal business." Mr. Dawe and his companion had to watch whilst the work of destruction went on for three awful hours. A group of the women and children and old men is seen in the left foreground of the above drawing

The sack of Louvain, on August 25th-26th, 1914, aroused the indignation of the whole civilised world. On the evening of the 25th a German corps, after receiving a check, withdrew in disorder into the town. A German guard fired on their routed fellow-countrymen, mistaking them for Belgians. Without inquiry, and at once assuming that the inhabitants had fired on them, the German commander-in-chief announced that the town would be immediately destroyed. The people were ordered to leave their dwellings; a party of the men were made prisoners, and the women and child into trains for an unknown destination. Several notable citizens were shot.

The splendid Church of St. Pierre, the university buildings, founded in 1 library, and scientific establishment were delivered to the flames. A town of inhabitants, the Oxford of the Low Countries, was reduced to a heap of smokin While the town was burning, according to an eye-witness, the German officers

HOTEL DE VILLE SAVED WHILE LOUVAIN WAS BURNING.

streets in fine motor-cars. They were described as well-dressed, shaven, , to all appearance, have been assisting at a fashionable race-meeting.
diers looted everywhere. Champagne, wine, cigars—everything of value was . The Hotel de Ville, dating from 1448, was the only building saved. This unded by German baggage waggons, as shown in the above illustration, which n from particulars supplied by Mr. A. J. Dawe. While the houses around

were burning a German canteen was set up for the distribution of looted liquor ; and wine and cigars were carried round by soldiers for their officers.
The Kaiser afterwards said his heart bled for Louvain ; but the Berlin authorities caused it to be announced that " the only means of preventing surprise attack from the civil population had been to interfere with unrelenting severity, and to create examples which by their frightfulness would be a warning to the whole country."

HEROISM OF A YOUNG BELGIAN CORPORAL AT TERMONDE.

Termonde, on the right bank of the Scheldt and on both sides of the Dendre, was flooded by the Belgians when they were attacked by the Germans on September 5th, 1914. It was sacked by the Germans a few days later. During the fighting the iron bridge across the Scheldt was blown up by the Belgians, who afterwards erected a wooden structure. This, in turn, had to be burnt.

The task of setting fire to it was allotted to a young Belgian corporal, who, when all his comrades had passed over it and were safely entrenched, ran back along the plank underneath, lighted torch in hand, and plunged this into the barrels of paraffin. These blazed up immediately. Despite the bullets constantly whizzing around him, the heroic corporal climbed on to the bridge, and completed

his task by rubbing the torch along the paraffin-soaked boards. He managed to gain the shelter of the trenches on the other side of the Scheldt unscathed, but with bullet-holes in his tunic. His brave deed had been watched with intense anxiety by his comrades, some of whom, it is recorded, held their fire in the tense excitement of the moment. All gave him a rousing cheer as he rejoined them.

The aim of the enemy was to invest Antwerp from both sides of the Scheldt, and possession of Termonde was a matter of high strategic importance to them. So bravely was the place defended, however, that it took the enemy six days of hard fighting to capture it, and then the little band of defenders, who were far outnumbered by the German forces, retired upon Lokeren

hands, the enemy gained control of the Belgian railway system, could move against Northern France, outflanking the allied armies which were assembling for its defence, and could overrun two-thirds of Belgium. It was, in fact, the cause of the precipitate retreat of the allied armies upon Paris.

The position in Northern Belgium was one of cruel anxiety. There was no force of troops available, outside Antwerp, sufficient to resist any considerable German force. The main garrison of four thousand men in Ostend had been withdrawn to Antwerp. The Civil Guards in Ghent and Bruges were disbanded, and it was resolved to offer no opposition to the Germans should they attempt to occupy those places.

At Ostend there was a sharp division of opinion among the people as to the policy that should be followed. August was the height of the season in the famous Belgian watering-place, and the *plage* of Ostend in August was for many years one of the gayest spots in Europe. When a British admiral offered to land Marines to help to defend the town there was almost revolt among those whose livelihood depended on the pleasure-seekers. If British sailors landed, the world would believe that Ostend was in danger, and visitors would not come, so the British admiral was politely told that the aid of the Marines was not desired. The hotel-keepers tried to shut their eyes to the armies of refugees pouring in, but in the end they had to recognise the situation, and one after another they closed their doors.

Then came news that the Germans were actually at Thourout, fifteen miles away, and were advancing rapidly. A panic swept over the place. The few remaining troops were hastily embarked for France, and there came a rush to escape by sea. £1,200,000 worth of gold in the Ostend banks was removed.

The real Belgians, apart from the cosmopolitan hotel-keepers and their staffs, were by no means willing that their town should be surrendered without a blow. A force of two hundred gendarmes assembled. Trenches had already been dug outside the town, and wire entanglements fixed. The men moved out and occupied the positions, and when the raiding party of Uhlans and hussars drew near, on August 25th, expecting an easy capture, they opened fire on the enemy. A skirmish followed. The German cavalry pressed bravely on, and succeeded in killing or wounding forty of the Belgians. But in the end they had to retire with heavy loss.

A skirmish at Ostend

THE DEVASTATION OF WAR IN MALINES.
Though Malines was an unfortified town it suffered heavily from German shells. Its beautiful cathedral, the lofty tower of which was the most prominent landmark of the district, suffered badly, as indicated in the photograph immediately above. The upper photograph shows the state-room of the cathedral which was being used as a Red Cross ward when a German shell shattered it; and the portrait is that of Cardinal Mercier, Archbishop of Malines, who was refused a safe conduct home from the Papal Conclave in Rome because he declined, at the bidding of the Austrian Ambassador, to deny the reports of German atrocities in Belgium.

BATTERED TOWER OF THE HOTEL DE VILLE, TERMONDE.

One incident is worth mention. The Belgians captured one wounded German officer who carried arms and was clearly acting as guide to the invading party, although he wore a Red Cross badge. They brought him in a motor-car into the town for trial by court-martial for violating the Red Cross. As they drove him through the streets the passers-by recognised the man, and set up a cry of indignation. He had been until a few hours before the declaration of war a clerk at the railway-station. Notwithstanding his wounds, he attempted at one point to leap on one of his captors and strangle him. In the central square he saw an Englishman with a Union Jack. He shouted an oath, and attempted to tear away the flag. He was carried in to his court-martial, and led, a few minutes later, to his death, defiant to the last.

At Ostend it was generally expected that the Germans would renew their attack in greater force. The Civil Guard was re-armed. The gendarmerie made ready once more to renew the fight. But a message was sent to the Belgian Minister asking him to request British help, and a few hours later seven British destroyers and two cruisers flying the white ensign drew near. A force of British Marines with quick-firers landed, and occupied the town,

GERMAN "CULTURE" REACHES ITS HEIGHT IN THE UTTER DESTRUCTION OF THE TOWN OF TERMONDE.
In the appalling completeness of the destruction they achieved the Germans reached the highest point of their ghastly achievement at Termonde. The large photograph above, perhaps, exceeds in the evidence of devastation any other that reached Great Britain from the stricken towns of suffering Belgium. The small photograph on the left shows the ruins of the School of Art, and that on the right the bells of the Hotel de Ville, which fell from the shattered tower seen in the picture at the top of the page.

and for some weeks the Germans showed no further activity. Following the fall of Namur, the German military administration of Belgium was organised. The Germans showed that they intended to regard the country as annexed by conquest to the German Empire. Field-Marshal von der Goltz was appointed Governor-General of

Belgium, and the entire country south of Alost and Malines was mapped out into military commands. The German language was introduced, the clocks were altered to German time, and day by day the process of the Germanification of the country proceeded apace. The story of the German conquest and administration of Central and Southern Belgium is an appalling one. Never before in modern history has a civilised country been treated with such merciless severity. The German General Staff deliberately adopted a policy of terrorism. This was considered necessary for a double reason—to prevent popular risings among the Belgian people and attacks upon the German communications, and — an even more important matter—to present such an example to the neighbouring population of Holland as would deter them from joining the Allies.

A ROW OF RUINED COTTAGES AT MELLE.

It was supposed, before the outbreak of war, that all campaigns would be conducted in accordance with the rules of war laid down by The Hague Conventions of 1899 and 1906. One main object of these rules was to confine the fighting, so far as possible, to soldiers, and to protect unarmed civilians. Thus looting and the shooting of innocent non-combatants were forbidden. The bombardment of open towns was prohibited, and the property of non-combatants was to be, as far as possible, spared. Within a few days of the commencement of the war the Germans showed that they intended to ignore The Hague rules.

The Hague rules ignored by Germany

There was no way of bringing them to book for such conduct. Obedience to the laws of war is a matter of national honour and of humanity. The price paid for the flagrant and sustained violation of these laws is the repudiation and distrust of neutral nations.

The German troops invaded Belgium with all preparations made for wholesale incendiarism. They were equipped with special materials for house-burning—a form of cellulose, a gun-cotton made up into twig-like cylinders or thin squares, exceedingly inflammable, burning so fiercely that a small quantity set fire to a house. Proclamations were issued that any attempt at resistance by civilians would be punished in the severest manner by the death of all concerned, and by the destruction of the town where such an attempt was made. In many places

WHAT A GERMAN SHELL DID AT MALINES.

hostages were taken from among the leading citizens, usually the burgomaster, the priest, the schoolmaster, and the doctor. They were held as prisoners in order that they might be shot were the German troops in any way molested in that locality.

Looting was universal in all ranks—from the Crown Prince himself, who stole the treasures of the great chateau, to the humble soldier who tore the bracelet from the Belgian woman's arm. Express orders were given to loot in many cases. Thus some German soldiers, who were tried after capture and sentenced to death for plundering, appealed against their sentence on the ground that they had only obeyed the directions of their generals. Further, in various cases German soldiers, after the looting was over, returned to the homes of the Belgians and gave back what they had taken, saying that, though they were compelled to loot, they were not thieves.

BOMB-SHATTERED REMAINS OF A MANSION NEAR MELLE.
Peasant and landed proprietor suffered from the fury of war and the wanton destruction inflicted on the most industrious little nation in Europe, whose only crime was that they accepted the assurance of a signed treaty and the oft-repeated promises of a German Kaiser.

If, in the German advance, the Uhlans were driven back at any point by the Belgians, the Uhlans returned at a later date in greater force, and shot all the men in that village and burned the houses. If one civilian in a village fired at a German soldier, all the civilians near the point where the shot had been fired were put to death, and the buildings were destroyed. Thus at Liège, out of a party of sixty Russian students living in one large apartment building, one or two are alleged to have fired at some Germans. All the sixty Russians were shot, and the entire block of flats was burned down.

The German soldiers found themselves in a wine-drinking country. The troops holding Southern Belgium— apart from the armies pushing forward to the front—drank heavily. Here, then, were men incited to plunder, encouraged to burn, directed to shoot, with abundant stocks of liquor constantly at their command. The inevitable happened. Drunk with blood and drunk with wine, they turned from the execution of civilians suspected of firing on them to outrages on women and to the murder even of children. All with even an elementary knowledge of human nature must have known that this was bound to happen. The men to blame for the atrocities were not the soldiers only, but the heads of the Army—the Kaiser, his advisers, and the Grand General Staff of the Army—

who deliberately adopted and enforced the policy of terror, and thus paved the way to the perpetration of crimes against humanity which have revolted the world, and which, in the years that are to come, when Europe is again at peace, will revolt even the German people themselves.

One of the most dreadful cases of massacre occurred shortly before the fall of Brussels, at Aerschot, a small town twenty-six miles from Antwerp. There had been heavy fighting near this place, and on Tuesday, August 18th, during the retreat of the main body of the Belgian Army, a small Belgian rearguard held it against overwhelming German forces, inflict-

THE GERMAN WAR ON THE WOMEN OF BELGIUM.
The oval picture shows the cellar window in a house in Termonde, and the elder of the two women is an aged resident who refused to leave the house in which she was born, and in which she had lived all her life. She went through three bombardments, and fortunately her house escaped. The lower picture tells its own tragic story. A photographer came upon a scene where a Belgian woman, killed by a German shell, lay dead among the ruins, while a boy of the village looked stolidly at the pitiful scene.

ing severe losses on them. The Belgians retired during the night, and next day the German troops, after heavily bombarding the town, marched into it without resistance. Most of the people had fled, frightened by the stories of outrages they had heard from neighbouring villages. Of those who were left, many hid in cellars to escape the troops. The burgomaster, M. Josef Tielemans, went out to meet the Germans and sought, by distributing cigars among the soldiers, to keep them in good humour.

Massacres in Aerschot

That afternoon a German general, while standing on the balcony of a house, was shot. The Belgian Official Commission of Inquiry, which investigated the occurrence afterwards, declared that the shot was clearly fired, not by a civilian, but from among a body of German troops standing some little way off. One story circulated at the time was that the shot was fired by the son of the burgomaster, a lad who desired to avenge the wrongs of his country. This story was proved to be false.

The German officers, evidently believing that the shot had been fired by a Belgian, determined to make an example of the place. They arrested the burgomaster and his son and every man in the town, about five hundred in all. These victims had their arms tied behind them and were herded together in a field, where they were kept all night. Next morning, one out of every three was picked out and shot, the victims including the burgomaster and his son.

Before this general shooting took place, the troops dashed upon the town like madmen. They fired into houses, they flung women and children into the street, they looted everything they could find, they shot and burned, and outraged women and girls. "They showed no mercy, they knew no compassion!" said one woman who was there at the time. "They were worse than the beasts of the field. I saw house after house burned. In many of them I know there must have been sick people who, being unable to leave, were roasted to death. A young couple who had been but recently married were shot dead; my own milkmaid was murdered." In one house the Germans first shot the husband, then the wife, and afterwards killed the baby. When they had finished shooting and outraging and plundering, they set

the place on fire. The men who were spared were made to dig the graves of their fellow-townsmen.

The Germans entered Louvain on Wednesday, August 19th, and at once assumed a very harsh attitude towards the people. They made requisitions for huge quantities of food, and demanded the payment of a war indemnity. The soldiers were quartered in private houses, and the homes of all who had fled were broken open and sacked. The burgomaster, M. Collins, had already posted a declaration on the walls, urging the people to be calm and to make no resistance.

The Germans seized a number of leading citizens as hostages, including the burgomaster, a senator, and the head of the university. They ordered the people to surrender all arms, ammunition, and petrol, under penalty of death. They forbade them to go out after eight o'clock at night, and in certain main streets every inhabitant had to leave his doors open and his windows lighted throughout the night. The troops were given a free hand to work their own will among the people.

On the evening of Tuesday, August 25th, the Germans decided to sack the town, and to burn it to the ground. This decision was arrived at by the German commander, and the sacking and burning were systematically carried out in obedience to orders.

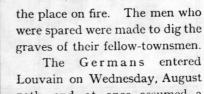

ANYWHERE, ANYWHERE—AWAY FROM THE GERMAN SCOURGE.
The family of seven Belgian refugees seen in the top picture were photographed at Ostend—all that remained of a family of twelve, the father and three sons having been killed at Termonde, and the grandfather burned to death. There is the pathos of despair in the middle picture, where an old woman and her grandchild find themselves at Ostend—"too late"—no room for them in the English boat
The third photograph is part of a procession of refugees from Alost

If the cause of the looting and destruction of the town is obscure, there is, unfortunately, no doubt as to what followed. While most of the people were sitting down quietly at home for their evening meal, they were suddenly disturbed by the sound of firing in the streets. German soldiers rushed through the streets, firing indiscriminately into the houses, and shooting down people they met. They called on the inhabitants to come out, and in many

cases as they came out shot the men down one after the other. Those who were not shot were herded together, the men in one place, the women and children in another. Some who remained in the cellars of their houses were burned alive when these houses were set alight. The prominent citizens, who had been held as hostages, including the burgomaster and the dean of the university, were shot forthwith. The troops began plundering, drinking the spirits found in the houses. Then they began to set the buildings and dwellings on fire.

Horrors of the sack of Louvain

Eight days elapsed before the streets selected for punishment —containing about 7,000 houses—had been thoroughly destroyed. Then the soldiers marched out to the surrounding villages and destroyed them.

Mr. Gerald Morgan, an American journalist, visited Louvain while the massacre was in progress.

" We began to see signs of destruction in the outlying villages shortly before we reached Louvain," he wrote. " Houses in the villages were in flames. An hour before sunset we entered Louvain and found the city a smoking furnace. The railway-station was crowded with troops, drunk with loot and liquor, and rapine as well. From house to house, acting under orders, groups of soldiers were carrying lighted straw, placing it in the basement, and then passing on to the next. It was not one's idea of a general

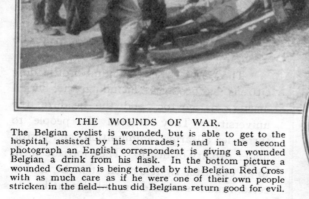

THE WOUNDS OF WAR.
The Belgian cyclist is wounded, but is able to get to the hospital, assisted by his comrades; and in the second photograph an English correspondent is giving a wounded Belgian a drink from his flask. In the bottom picture a wounded German is being tended by the Belgian Red Cross with as much care as if he were one of their own people stricken in the field—thus did Belgians return good for evil.

conflagration, for each house burnt separately —hundreds of individual bonfires—while the sparks shot up like thousands of shooting stars into the still night air. It was exactly like a display of fireworks or Bengal lights and set pieces at a grand display in Coney Island.

" Meanwhile, through the station arch we saw German justice being administered. In a square outside, where the cabs stand, an officer stood, and the soldiers drove the citizens of Louvain into his presence, like so many unwilling cattle on a market day. Some of the men, after a few words between the officer and the escorts, were marched off under fixed bayonets behind the railway-station. Then we heard volleys, and the soldiers returned. Then the train moved out, and the last we saw of the doomed city was an immense red glare in the gathering darkness. My impressions after Louvain were just as if I had read and dreamt of one of Zola's novels."

Malines—or, to give it its Flemish name, Mechlin—is best known to the world at large as the centre of a great lace trade, Mechlin lace being famous everywhere. Despite the fact that it was, in the days before the war, a town of sixty thousand inhabitants and an important railway centre, with railway workshops, its main streets wore an air of old-world quiet, which gave the place a charm wholly its own. Many of its buildings carried the visitor back to the atmosphere of the Middle Ages. There was the cathedral, dating back to the thirteenth and fourteenth centuries, with its unfinished spire three hundred and eighteen feet in height, and with, among other treasures, Vandyck's famous picture of "The Crucifixion," and Rubens's "Miraculous Draught of Fishes." The Grande Place, with its old Cloth Hall and its picturesque gabled houses, was instinct with the memories of a remote, beautiful past, so that to walk in it was to return to **Old-world glories of Malines** the sixteenth century.

The Germans, after the defeat of the main Belgian Army at Louvain, reached Malines on Monday, August 24th, and attempted to storm the town. They were in insufficient numbers, and the Belgians drove them back. They repeated their attack on August 25th, supported by artillery. Again, after a sustained fight, they had to retire, only to renew the fight on the following day, this time successfully. Then the Belgians, gathering strength in turn, once more advanced against them and drove them out.

GERMAN INVADERS DOLING OUT A LITTLE FOOD TO THE STARVING POOR OF BRUGES.
In many Belgian towns the Germans commandeered all the provisions in the shops and warehouses, thereby cutting off food supplies from the people, to whom they then gave meagre daily allowances so as to keep them alive.

The population evacuated the town on Friday, August 28th, and on August 31st the Germans opened a bombardment from Hofstadt. Malines at the time was unoccupied by Belgian troops, except for a few stragglers. The Germans seem to have taken their revenge on the ancient buildings of the town for the rebuffs they had suffered. In the course of their bombardment they did not spare even the ancient cathedral. A heavy shell tore a great hole in the roof close to the tower, the windows were smashed, the big clock was broken. Before the bombardment **Malines cathedral a German target** ended the masonry of the entire cathedral was pitted and battered, and in places riddled with projectiles, while the surrounding pavement was torn up. No one who examined Malines afterwards could fail to conclude that the Germans deliberately made the cathedral the target for their artillery fire.

Termonde, the third of the Belgian towns to be wrecked by the Germans, was a prosperous riverside town on the Scheldt, of about eleven thousand inhabitants, situated amidst the rich flower-growing and market-gardening country of North-Eastern Belgium. It was the centre of a considerable industry, and among its different factories was a large jute mill.

Early in September the German troops advancing towards Antwerp came into collision with the Belgians on the banks of the Scheldt. Some severe fighting took place around Termonde, where a well-entrenched Belgian force gave the Germans considerable trouble, holding them back for some time. The Germans brought up heavy

BELGIAN INFANTRY ISSUING FROM THE RUINED TOWN OF TERMONDE.
The Belgians were not driven out of their country without desperate fighting, that cost the Germans enormous losses, and here the retreating Belgians are seen passing through the ruined town of Termonde to attack the hated invaders from another point of vantage.

artillery, and were in sufficient force to carry out a flanking movement, which finally caused the Belgians to retire. They occupied Termonde itself, but found on their arrival that nearly all the inhabitants, warned by what had happened in other places, had fled. A few sick people were left. The managing director of the jute works had stayed with his wife and family to nurse the wounded, and had turned his home and factory into a Red Cross hospital. The German officers made the jute manufacturer's home their headquarters, and their troops were billeted in the different houses.

Systematic destruction of Termonde

On September 4th fighting took place outside Termonde, and the Germans declared that they had been fired upon, not by soldiers, but by civilians. Their commander, General Sommerfeld by name, gave orders that the town was to be burned down as a punishment.

The destruction of Termonde was carried out in the most systematic manner. Certain houses were marked to be spared. These were mostly low cafés or the homes of people supposed to be friendly to the Germans. Directions were written in chalk on the doors: " Good people here." " These are friends." " This house must on no account be burned." " It is strictly forbidden to set fire to this house "—and the like.

On September 5th the troops marched through the streets and, after taking what they wanted, burned down every house except those thus marked. The building

SHATTERED COTTAGE THAT SERVED AS A FORT.
These Belgian sharpshooters made holes in the walls of a ruined cottage, from which they could attack the German enemy in his advance through their country.

PART OF KING ALBERT'S ARMY IN THRICE-BOMBARDED TERMONDE.
The gallantry and pertinacity of Belgian resistance made them foes who scarcely knew defeat, and their fighting qualities made the Germans pay a heavy price for every yard of their advance. This photograph was taken while some Belgian troops were marching through the desolation that was once Termonde.

which the officers had used as their headquarters and the jute factory employed as a Red Cross hospital were spared. The town-hall, a notable building, was also left untouched. But for the rest—churches, hospitals, schools, picture gallery—all shared in the common ruin. Nothing was left—not a scrap of furniture, not a particle of food. In some of the churches, as, for example, in the Church of the Benedictine Fathers, the troops smashed with the butt-ends of their rifles the statuary on the walls and on the altar. While the houses burned the officers feasted. They sat in the garden of the manufacturer's house by the banks of the river. They had music and singing, drank champagne, and pledged themselves in joyous toasts while the flames of sixteen hundred burning houses lit up the sky behind.

Teuton feasting in burning Termonde

The writer of this chapter had occasion to visit Termonde shortly after the destruction of the town. The place was as a city of ghosts. Street after street of crumbling ruins stood where but a week before had been a busy, pleasant, prosperous Belgian town. Of the art gallery nothing was left but blackened beams, some tottering walls, and fragments of charred timber. The most tragic sight of all was the grief of the inhabitants who had returned seeking their homes and found nothing left. The place had been wiped out.

The home of the jute manufacturer did not escape. The German officers had specially marked this out to be spared, and so long as they remained in it the house was safe. But, when they left to move on elsewhere, their orderlies burst open the front door and rushed in. They wrecked the place. Every window was broken, the furniture smashed, drawers pulled out and emptied, desks ransacked, and cupboards laid bare. The wanton cruelty of the destruction was specially noteworthy in the children's nursery, where the Germans had not spared even the babies' toys. The drawers in a tiny dresser were forced open and rummaged. Picture books and reading books were torn to bits and scattered about the room. In the drawing-room downstairs the furniture was

BRINGING DOWN THE GERMAN AIRCRAFT.
Fighting amid the ruins of a once flourishing Belgian village, these Belgian infantry-men are trying to bring to earth one of the German Taube aeroplanes used for scouting and bomb-dropping.

BELGIAN PIGEONS INTERNED
When the Germans entered Brussels they took all the Belgian pigeons into the market, as shown here, but afterwards they used them to carry messages from the fighting-line back to Brussels.

ripped up, and all the ornaments were smashed. The Germans apparently found special pleasure in destroying a service of fine china.

The Germans, after wrecking almost the whole of Termonde, save the marked houses and the town-hall, were forced to retire by an advance in strength of the Belgian army. It was during

their retirement that this writer saw the place. A few days later they again advanced, covering their advance by a heavy artillery fire. They poured into the town and completed their work of ruin. The old town-hall, the factory, and the few remaining houses, were consigned to the flames that same night.

The work of destruction was not confined to a few notable towns like Louvain,

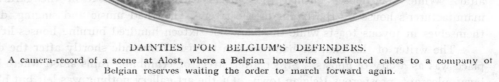

DAINTIES FOR BELGIUM'S DEFENDERS.
A camera-record of a scene at Alost, where a Belgian housewife distributed cakes to a company of Belgian reserves waiting the order to march forward again.

Malines, and Termonde. It was carried out in hundreds of smaller towns and villages throughout the country. A large part of Central and Southern Belgium was practically reduced to a desert.

As an example of what happened in the villages, the case of Melle, a little place some four miles out of Ghent, may be mentioned. A German force numbering some thousand men, advancing towards Ghent, was checked there early in September by a small body of Belgian volunteers, numbering about five hundred. The Belgians had two old guns, so old that they were more dangerous to the defenders than to the enemy; the Germans were splendidly equipped with artillery and machine-guns. The Belgians held the railway embankment, and succeeded in punishing the advancing Germans severely. They were outflanked and driven into a field to the side of the village. Here they hastily entrenched themselves, and held on stubbornly so long as the slightest chance remained. The battle lasted from two until four in the afternoon. The Belgians then fell back on Ghent, and at six o'clock in the evening the German troops occupied the place.

Heroism of Belgian volunteers

There was one large modern house there, the home of a Ghent barrister. The German officers took possession of this and commanded a meal, which was provided, the lawyer's wife and her maids giving them the best they had. The soldiers were billeted among the cottages of the village, where they took what they wanted.

Then the officers, having finished their dinner, went outside and ordered the barrister's house to be burned down. This was promptly and thoroughly done. The soldiers, acting under orders, began to set the small houses of the village on fire. There was one little farmhouse where a labouring man, his wife, and two sons—one aged fifteen and the other nineteen—lived. The soldiers, entering this house, seized the elder son, declaring that he must be a Belgian soldier who had sought to disguise himself by putting on civilian clothes. Refusing to listen to his denial, they shot him in front of the kitchen door, before his parents and his brother. Several civilians in the village itself were shot. Many of the women were outraged. Others were driven forth into the fields. The stories told by the people of their treatment at the hands of the soldiers are so horrible that, were they not confirmed by what happened in other places, they would seem almost incredible. Some visitors, arriving at the place a few days afterwards, found outside the door of one of the burned houses the little foot of a child, hacked off at the ankle. The foot was photographed. **Terrible relic of Prussian crime**

In the case of Melle, the people one and all deny that any attack was made on the Germans. All the evidence points to the improbability of such an attack. The Belgian villagers were few; they knew that the German troops numbered many thousands; they knew, too, that any violence on their part would bring immediate and terrible reprisals. It is altogether unlikely that they would have invited such punishment. Presumably, the Germans were maddened by the loss of some of their own officers, who were shot down in fair fighting while advancing on the Belgian troops.

General von Boehn, commanding the 9th German Army, operating in Northern Belgium, was interviewed early in September by Mr. Alexander Powell, correspondent of the "New York World," who did very notable work in Belgium. Mr. Powell, who himself had witnessed some of these atrocities, asked the general the cause of them. General von Boehn began by asserting that the accounts were a tissue of lies. "Of course our soldiers, like soldiers in all armies," he said, "sometimes get out of hand and do things which we would never tolerate if we knew it. At Louvain, for example, I sentenced two soldiers to twelve years' penal servitude

THE MURDERED BURGOMASTER'S GARDEN.
The burgomaster at Visé was hanged by the Germans, and his garden, as seen here, converted into a field kitchen.

apiece for assaulting a woman." In answer to further questions, he declared Louvain had been burned because townspeople had fired on the German troops. Smashing his fist down upon the table he vowed: "Wherever civilians fire upon our troops we will teach them a lasting lesson.' If the women and children insist on getting in the way of bullets, so much the worse for women and children." This defence speaks for itself.

The military operations in North-Eastern Belgium during September were of minor importance. They proved that the Belgian

GERMANS LORDING IT IN BELGIUM.
These German soldiers, preparing a meal in one of the occupied Belgian villages, seemed uneasy under the eyes of the Red Cross priest who happened to pass.

Fighting outside Antwerp before the siege Army, heavy though its losses had been, retained its ardour unquenched. The Belgian troops operating from Antwerp made continuous raids upon the German lines, and constantly skirmished with the enemy. The Germans advanced to the suburbs of Ghent, and only refrained from entering that city because of an arrangement made by them with the burgomaster. They kept in touch with the Belgians, driving them back here, being driven back in turn there, but waiting for orders for the more serious movement that was to come when the real Siege of Antwerp was to be begun.

A FOOTNOTE TO VOLUME I.

WE have now arrived at the point where the great events of the war succeed each other with dramatic rapidity, and the narrative goes vividly forward in an intense and moving story of high heroic deeds of unparalleled magnitude and importance. But before we go on to the broad, vivid, interesting, and connected narrative of the mighty military operations, on which the destinies of the whole human race directly or indirectly depended, we may as well sum up the results of our survey of the forces and interests engaged.

We have seen how the struggle began, into which half the world was at last drawn. Great Britain stood out to the last in the hope of peace, and yet, gathering her Grand Fleet for the historic review at Spithead, placed over the heart of the Empire, at the moment of increasing peril, the sure shield of the Navy. Then we traced how Germany, the sombre, ambitious power, working in sinister fashion to heighten the diplomatic tension, mobilised her vast Army for the conquest of the empire of the earth.

Her first army swept in careless confidence into Belgium, and was shattered against Liège, the stand made by the outnumbered but intrepid Belgian troops under General Leman thrilling the modern world as deeply as the defence of Thermopylæ thrilled the ancient world. We then saw how, in answer to the call of King Albert, Britain prepared and launched across the Channel her small but important Expeditionary Force, which was to fight its way quickly to astonishing power and immortal glory, and grow into an army of a million and more fighting men of supreme quality.

In the meantime we had to watch, sadly, proudly, the desperately stubborn and gallant way in which the little Belgian Army contested the advance of the German invaders, pouring—a million strong—towards the fields of Flanders, where they intended to deploy for the march on Paris.

Passing then to another aspect of the struggle, we observed the British Fleet put out to sea, and saw the Germans begin their stealthy work of mine-laying, by vainly attempting to seal the waterway to London. We studied the means by which Germany tried to interrupt the food supplies to the British Isles, and cripple our sea-borne commerce. We watched the more deadly silent way in which our own Navy began to exert pressure on the foe, and make the Teuton merchant marine and ocean trade dissolve and vanish with terrible suddenness.

By this time the advance guards of the Russian Army had begun to move towards the frontiers of Germany and Austria, while the Grand Duke Nicholas was preparing a surprise for the Teutonic Empires by the unexpected swiftness of the Russian mobilisation. We learned to appreciate the great improvements that had been effected in the training of the Russian soldier and in the quality of the Russian armament since the war in Manchuria, and we saw how Russia had profited by her former disasters even as we had profited by our misfortunes in the first part of the South African campaign.

But since both these wars a new military arm of unexplored possibilities and untested power had been created in the flying-machine and the airship. It had been made clear at manœuvres that the airman was a strange, disconcerting factor in warfare. Under his direction artillery fire became more deadly, and the art of reconnaissance—in daylight, at least—was completely changed. To a vast hostile army, with long lines of communications, his bomb-dropping raids looked like being very inconvenient, while his extraordinary range of vision and speed of movement as a scout made him extremely formidable.

But then—as a contrast—we saw the Serbs, with little help from the new arm, inflict upon the overweening, oppressive Austrians at Shabatz one of the decisive defeats of the war, and give help of great value to Russia, by detaining through the critical period of the campaign a large Austrian army round the Save and Danube.

Resuming, then, the survey of the new creations of warfare, we studied the mysterious submarine, "the deadliest thing that keeps the seas," and observed how this wonderful artificial fish-like thing found its first victims in the Pathfinder and the Hela. Then, in the Battle of Heligoland Bight, we saw the submarine displace the destroyer as the sea scout, and lead, in British hands, to the first important naval victory.

Meanwhile General Rennenkampf set out on the Cossack raid on East Prussia, that threw into disorder the plans of the German Military Staff, and relieved France of some of the pressure that was falling upon her. But we watched Belgium in her agony—the massacre at Aerschot, the sack and burning of Louvain, the wrecking of Malines, the destructions, crimes, that provoked passionate anger in even the calmest of neutral nations. And from these dreadful acts of the modern barbarians the story in the succeeding volumes of THE GREAT WAR will march, after a broad, brief survey of other events in the fields of war, to a connected narrative of the great battles and historic operations in the mighty struggle, on which turned the future course of the whole human race, and the evolution and extension of the institutions of free, popular government in all parts of the civilised world.

SWIFT JUSTICE TO A GERMAN SPY.
Despite the revelations of the German spy system in France in 1870-71 the Allies seem to have been unprepared for its developments in 1914. Our illustration is of an early-morning scene at Termonde, where one of the Kaiser's secret emissaries, detected in his treacherous work, met his death amidst the ruin wrought by his military masters in one of Belgium's industrial towns.

END OF VOLUME I.

THE GREAT WAR

VOLUME 2

The British Battle Squadron at Full Speed in the "Narrow Seas."

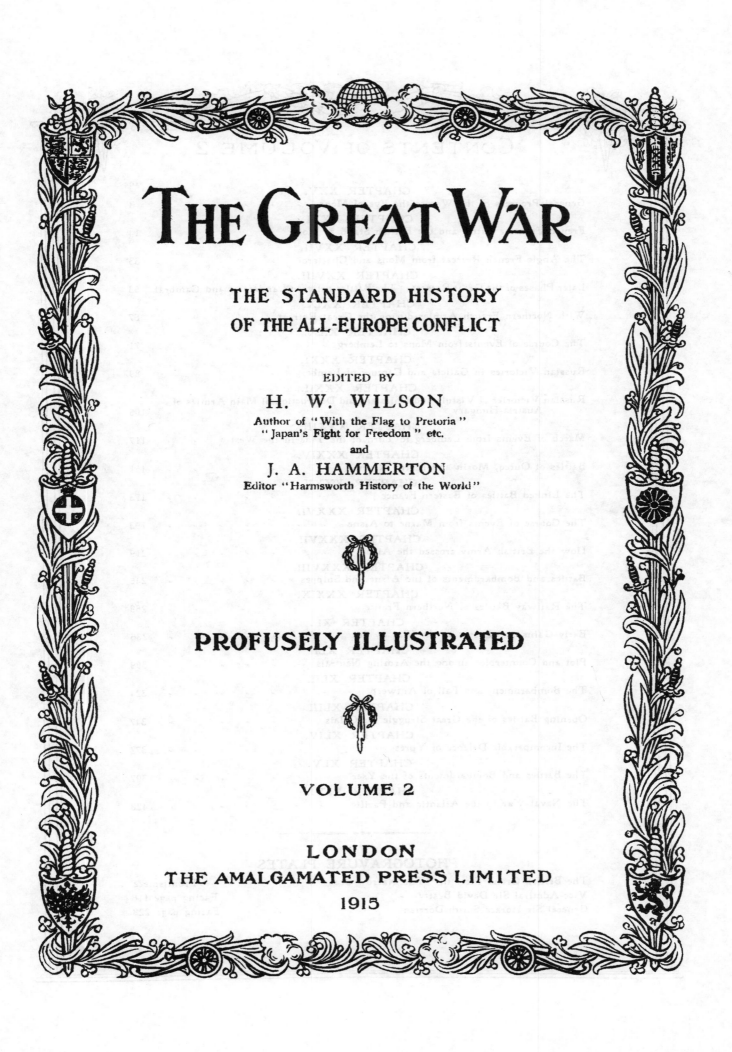

THE GREAT WAR

THE STANDARD HISTORY
OF THE ALL-EUROPE CONFLICT

EDITED BY

H. W. WILSON

Author of "With the Flag to Pretoria"
"Japan's Fight for Freedom" etc.

and

J. A. HAMMERTON

Editor "Harmsworth History of the World"

PROFUSELY ILLUSTRATED

VOLUME 2

LONDON
THE AMALGAMATED PRESS LIMITED
1915

CONTENTS OF VOLUME 2

PHOTOGRAVURE PLATES

JOSEPH JACQUES CÉSAIRE JOFFRE, CHIEF OF THE GENERAL STAFF OF THE FRENCH ARMY

JOSEPH JACQUES CESAIRÈ JOFFRE, CHIEF OF THE GENERAL STAFF OF THE FRENCH ARMY.

General Joffre was born in the same year—1852—as Sir John French. A Bachelor of Science at seventeen, he so distinguished himself in 1870 that MacMahon made him a captain when only twenty-two. He gained the Legion of Honour in the Far East, and his lieutenant-colonelcy in the French Soudan, being appointed Chief of the French General Staff in 1911. An artilleryman, he made a close study of fortifications, and his strategy had won world-wide recognition. His headquarters were once compared to a monastery, and his methods to those of Fabius and General Grant. [*Photo by Manuel.*]

THE GREAT WAR

THE STANDARD HISTORY OF THE ALL-EUROPE CONFLICT

VOLUME 2

CHAPTER XXV.

GENERAL PROGRESS OF THE WAR TO THE EVE OF MONS.

How France took up the Gauntlet of Liberty, Justice, and Reason—Rhetorical Utterances of Kaiser and Chancellor—British Answer to German Philippics—King Albert and His Gallant Little Army—Attitude of the Churches—Philanthropic Activity—Problems of Ways and Means—Gifts from Overseas—Austrian Aid for Germany in the Old French Provinces—Successes and Retirements in Alsace and the Vosges—Mr. F. E. Smith and the Press Bureau—Austria, Russia, and Serbia—The Eve of Mons.

THE position in France generally and in the capital particularly on the eve of the declaration of war was fully described by an "Eye-Witness" in Chapter VII. On August 1st President Poincaré issued his eloquent appeal to the people of France with the order for mobilisation of the troops, concluding with the noble sentence: "At this moment there are no more parties, there is eternal France —France peace-loving and resolute, the birthplace of Right and Justice, wholly united in calm and vigilant dignity." The mobilisation proceeded with an earnest, an eager promptitude at every military centre, from the English Channel to the Mediterranean and the Pyrenees, from the Bay of Biscay to the frontiers of Belgium, Alsace, and Lorraine.

On August 3rd, 1914, Germany declared war against France, and the dignity and calm with which the situation had been met generally were slightly marred in the capital by excitable roughs among the Parisian crowds attacking and looting several shops and cafés belonging to Germans and Austrians. These regrettable incidents were speedily stopped by the municipal authorities. On the same day King Albert made an appeal to his Majesty King George for diplomatic intervention on behalf of Belgium in the following terms: "Remembering the numerous proofs

GENERAL FRENCH IN PARIS.

After landing at Boulogne in August, 1914, and before proceeding to the front, Sir John French visited Paris, being received by President Poincaré, and having a conference with M. Messimy, Minister of War. In the photograph he is seen arriving at the French War Office.

of your Majesty's friendship and that of your predecessor, and the friendly attitude of Great Britain in 1870, and the proof of friendship you have just given us again, I make a supreme appeal to the diplomatic intervention of your Majesty's Government to safeguard the integrity of Belgium." The result is already on record.

August 4th will always remain a red-letter date in the history of Continental Europe. President Poincaré addressed to the outside world his memorable justification of France for promptly taking up the gauntlet so outrageously thrown down by Germany. "In the war upon which she is entering," he said, "France will have on her side that right which no people, any more than individuals, may despise with impunity—the eternal moral power. She will be heroically defended by all her sons, whose sacred union in face of the enemy nothing can destroy, and who to-day are fraternally bound together by the same indignation against the aggressor, and by the same patriotic faith. She represents once more to-day before the world Liberty, Justice, and Reason. *Haut les Cœurs, et Vive la France !*"

When the Chamber of Deputies met that day an impressive scene ensued. In solemn silence, M. Viviani, the French Premier, read the declaration of the Government policy, and paid a striking tribute to the loyalty shown in the crisis by Great Britain, which was afterwards tersely summarised by the War Minister, M. Messimy: "Valorously to face the struggle, out of which we shall come either victorious or dead—and we intend to be victorious!" On that same day Herr von Bethmann-Hollweg, the German Chancellor, in a speech to the Reichstag, made his astounding defence of the new ethic that might is right; that political and military necessities know no law. "We" (the German

followed by a German army of 100,000 men opening the attack on Liège.

The answer to this philippic and that overt act of war was that Great Britain declared war on Germany, that the Government took control of the railways of the United Kingdom to facilitate the mobilisation of the Reserves and Special Reserves who had been recalled to the colours, and the Territorials; and that Admiral Sir John Jellicoe was appointed to the supreme command of the Home Fleets.

The position of affairs and the public feeling in Great Britain and Ireland up to this point, the initial remedial measures taken by the Government and Parliament to meet the financial crisis that occurred, to control internal as well as over-sea trade, to assuage the acute anxiety felt as to employment and the pressure of the times on the poorer classes of the population, the diplomatic proceedings in the different Chancelleries of Europe, the action of the Government inspired by the Foreign Secretary, Sir Edward Grey, who Mr. Asquith declared had deservedly earned

COUNTRY BETWEEN THE VOSGES AND ALSACE. The rocky Schlucht Pass between the French Department of the Vosges and Alsace. After their retirement from Mulhausen the French seized this and other German positions in the Passes of the Vosges.

Government), said he, "were compelled to override the just protest of the Luxemburg and Belgian Governments. The wrong—I speak openly—that we are committing we will endeavour to make good as soon as our military goal has been reached. Anybody who is threatened, as we are threatened, and is fighting for his highest possessions, can have only one thought—how he is to hack his way through (*wie er sich durchhaut*)!" The Chancellor concluded by asking and receiving from the Reichstag authorisation for an extraordinary expenditure of £265,000,000 for the war, and that was

the title of "Peacemaker of Europe," immediately preceding the declaration of war between Germany and Great Britain, as revealed in the famous British White Paper—penny editions of which were issued by our Government and eagerly bought up by the million in every corner of H.M.'s dominions, and in almost every civilised country except Germany and Austria, where it was taboo—all these matters have been dealt with broadly, if briefly, in our Chapters III. and IV.

The French Army began on August 5th its movement into Belgium to the help of King Albert and his gallant little Army; and his Majesty, in assuming the command, issued to it the following rousing proclamation:

"Soldiers! Without the slightest provocation from us, a neighbour, haughty in its strength, has torn up the Treaty bearing its signature. It has violated the territory of our fathers. Because we have been worthy of ourselves, because we have refused to forfeit our honour, it has attacked us. But the whole world marvels at our loyal attitude, respects and esteems our strength in these supreme moments. Seeing its independence threatened, the nation trembled, and its children sprang to the frontier. Valiant soldiers of a sacred cause, I have confidence in your tenacious courage. I greet you in the name of Belgium. Your fellow-citizens are proud of you, and you will triumph, for you are the forces serving in the interests of Right. Cæsar said of your ancestors: 'Of all the peoples of Gaul, the Belgians are the most brave.'

BRIDGE DESTROYED AT DENNEMARIE, NEAR MULHAUSEN. This bridge was destroyed by French engineers to obstruct the progress of the Germans. The centre photograph shows houses in one of the streets of Mulhausen riddled with shot after a street battle.

BRITISH TROOPS AT A FRENCH BASE ON THE EVE OF THEIR DEPARTURE FOR MONS.
In the hurry of the various railway movements it happened that some of the men were parted from their horses, and the officers had much to do to pacify their disappointment. In the foreground of the photograph is seen a section of the R.A.M.C., who rendered such splendid service to their wounded comrades in the combative lines later.

"Glory to you, Army of the Belgian people! Remember in the face of the enemy that you are fighting for the Fatherland and for your menaced homes! Remember, men of Flanders, the Battle of the Golden Spurs [when, at Courtrai, the Flemings defeated and slew Robert Count of Artois and so many of his knights that the battle came to be known by that name]. And you, Walloons of Liège, who are at the place of honour at present, remember the six hundred of Franshimont! Soldiers! I am leaving for Brussels to place myself at your head."

On the same day, Lord Kitchener, without doubt the greatest British military organiser for at least a century, who had been recalled from Dover on August 3rd, when en route to return to his duties as British Administrator—or, technically, Consul-General—in Egypt in succession to Lord Cromer, was appointed Secretary of State for War. The reason given by the Prime Minister to Parliament was that the pressure of other duties had compelled him to give up that position, which he had temporarily taken on the resignation of Colonel Seely. Lord Kitchener's first act was to issue an appeal in the King's name for 500,000 men to join the regular Army under the novel conditions "of three years' service,

or until the war is over." The call was responded to with enthusiasm, like that which marked the immediate rush of Reservists and Special Reservists to rejoin the ranks.

From this date, in St. Paul's Cathedral and in almost every church, Protestant and Catholic, of the United Kingdom, intercessory services were held for the King, his people, and his Army and Navy, asking God for help as in ages past, and that He would be pleased to grant victory over all our enemies. Enthusiasm was not exhausted—either in prayers or in enlistments—of thousands of men anxious to discharge the patriot's duty of swinging the arm of the flesh. Practical philanthropy burned brightly. H.R.H. the **Aid for sufferers** Prince of Wales established his National **through the War** Fund for the relief of distress, and he was supported by his gracious mother, Queen Mary, who appealed to the women of the country to give their services and assist in the local administration of the fund, which in the course of a few days exceeded a million pounds. Queen Alexandra pleaded for the Soldiers' and Sailors' Families' Association, which provided assistance to the wives and children of our fighting men by land and sea. Steps were taken for the organisation of military aid for the care

BRITISH 6 IN. GUNS ON THE WAY TO MONS.
The heavy battery of 6 in. guns of the 48th Battery in the advance to Belgium on August 21st, 1914. Inset: British troops taking shelter in the streets of Mons during German cannonade, awaiting orders to line the barricades at Frameries.

of the sick and wounded, for the development of the Red Cross Society's work, for hospital provision in London and throughout the country, supplemented by the offer of private mansions by noblemen and gentlemen.

The House of Commons, on August 6th, agreed *nem. con.* to the motion proposed by the Prime Minister: " That a sum, not exceeding £100,000,000, be granted to his Majesty, beyond the ordinary grants of Parliament, towards defraying expenses that may be incurred during the year ending March 31st, 1915, for all measures which may be taken for the security of the country, for the conduct of naval and military operations, for assisting the food supply, for promoting the continuance of trade, industry, and business communications, whether by means of insurance or indemnity against risk, or otherwise for the relief of distress, and generally for all expenses arising out of the existence of a state of war." Mr. Asquith, in asking the Committee of Ways and Means to agree to the resolution, said that the House and country had read the most pathetic appeal addressed by the King of Belgium to H.M. King George, and he did not envy the man who could read that appeal with an unmoved heart. " Belgians," he continued, " are fighting and losing their lives. What would have been the position of Great Britain to-day in the face of that spectacle if we had assented to the infamous proposal made by the German Chancellor ? Yes, and what are we to get in return for

the betrayal of our friends and the dishonour of our obligations ? A promise—nothing more—a promise as to what Germany would do in certain eventualities ; a promise, be it observed—I am sorry to have to say it, but it must be put upon record—given by a Power which was at that very moment announcing its intention to violate its own Treaty and inviting us to do the same ! I can only say, if we had dallied or temporised, we, as a Government, should have covered ourselves with dishonour, and we should have betrayed the interests of this country, of which we are trustees."

The Prime Minister, on behalf of the new Secretary for War, also asked the House to grant power to increase **Support from India and Overseas Dominions** the number of men in the Army of all ranks, in addition to the number already voted, by no less than 500,000. He was certain, continued Mr. Asquith, that " the House would not refuse its sanction, for the Government were encouraged to ask for it, not only by their own sense of the gravity and the necessities of the case, but by the knowledge that India was prepared to send certainly two divisions, and that everyone of our self-governing Dominions, spontaneously, unasked, had already tendered to the utmost limits of their possibilities, both in men and in money, every help they could afford to the Empire in a moment of need. The Mother Country must set the example, while she responded with gratitude and affection to those filial overtures from the outlying members of her family." The power asked for was granted amid the most enthusiastic cheers from all parts of the House.

As illustrative of this practical sympathy of the daughter nations of the Empire of which the Prime Minister spoke, it may here be stated that the Duke of Connaught, Governor-General of Canada, on August 6th, wired to Mr. Lewis Harcourt, Colonial Secretary, that the Government of

BRITISH SOLDIERS PREPARING FOR THE GERMAN ONSLAUGHT AT MONS.
To obstruct the advance of the Germans, the streets of Mons were hurriedly barred by barricades constructed largely of bricks and cobble-stones, dug up from the roadway, behind which the men took up their positions to cover the retreat. Shrapnel burst overhead and bullets were flying everywhere. Hence the shelter taken when possible by men and horses under the lee of the houses.

TO BREAK THE GERMAN "WAVE": CONSTRUCTING BARRICADES BETWEEN QUESNEY AND MONS.
British troops hurriedly throwing up barricades across the roadway between Mons and Quesney on the afternoon of Sunday, August 23rd, 1914.

NORTHUMBERLAND FUSILIERS AT BARRICADE WORK BETWEEN MONS AND JEMAPPES.
The formidable barricades erected in the streets between Mons and Jemappes were held by the Northumberland Fusiliers.

Canada desired to offer 1,000,000 bags of flour, of 98 lb. each, as a gift to the people of the United Kingdom, to be placed at the disposal of his Majesty's Government, and to be used for such purposes as they might deem expedient. Mr. Harcourt replied that the Government accepted with deep gratitude the splendid and welcome gift of flour, which would be of the greatest use in this country for the steadying of prices and relief of distress. Something more will have to be said at a later date of similar generous gifts from the other self-governing Dominions.

That same day (August 6th) the Kaiser, with his characteristic policy of playing the mischievous game of tit-for-tat, issued a proclamation to the German people in which he made the following audacious statements :

"Since the foundation of the Empire it has been for forty-three years the object of the efforts of myself and my ancestors to preserve the peace of the world, and to advance by peaceful means our vigorous development. But our adversaries were jealous of the success of our work. There has been latent hostility in the east and in the west, and beyond the sea. In the midst of perfect peace the enemy surprised us. Therefore, to arms ! Any dallying or temporising would be to betray the Fatherland. ' To be, or not to be ' is the question for the Empire

which our fathers founded—to be or not to be German power and German existence. We shall resist to the last breath of man and horse, and shall fight out the struggle even against a world of enemies. Never has Germany been subdued when it was united. Forward with God, Who will be with us as He was with our ancestors."

By a curious coincidence on that very day the German cruisers Goeben and Breslau made their sinister escape from Messina, where they had taken refuge from the Anglo-French Mediterranean Fleet, in Italian territorial waters, and a few days afterwards, after a scrimmage with a British squadron, reached the safe haven of the Dardanelles. It was later officially announced from Constantinople that the two vessels had been purchased by the Turkish Government, which promised to send back their crews to Germany, but they never did. From this date Berlin, if not also other great German cities, was inflamed with a still greater fury of hatred against Great Britain and the British than that narrated in Chapter VIII.

In the meantime, according to General Joffre's original plan of campaign, the French central army, during the first and second weeks of August, advanced across the Vosges ; and all France thrilled with delight on August 9th when the news arrived of a victory at Altkirch, in Alsace. A French corps captured the

ANOTHER EXAMPLE OF THE BARRICADES BEHIND WHICH THE BRITISH FOUGHT NEAR MONS.
The barricades shown in the above photograph were between Mons and Quesney, and were constructed on Sunday, August 23rd, 1914. Inset is a snapshot of General Shaw and his Staff of the 9th Brigade, 3rd Division, under the lee of houses at Frameries during the Battle of Mons. A barricade is seen at the end of the street. A few minutes after the photograph was taken two high-explosive shells burst overhead, and the street was littered with debris. General Shaw's brigade-major (Captain Stevens) was severely wounded at Le Cateau, and his Staff captain (Lieut. Harter, Royal Fusiliers) was slightly wounded.

GERMAN COLUMN MOWED DOWN BY BRITISH MACHINE-GUNS AT LANDRECIES.

In the bald language of the Press Bureau the achievement illustrated above was thus authoritatively described: "A German infantry brigade advanced in the closest order into the narrow street, which they completely filled. Our machine-guns were brought to bear on this target from the end of the town. The head of the column was swept away, a frightful panic ensued, and it is estimated that no fewer than 800 or 900 dead and wounded Germans were lying in this street alone." The affair thus summarily dismissed took place at Landrecies on August 26th, 1914.

trenches prepared for the protection of that fortified place, which were defended by a German brigade, and drove the enemy back in the direction of the Rhine. The victors then marched to and occupied the large town of Mulhausen. The enthusiasm was deepened by a proclamation issued by General Joffre, which rings with passionate patriotism: "Children of Alsace, after forty-four years of sorrowful waiting, French soldiers once more tread the ground of your noble country. They are the first workmen in the great task of reconquest. What a feeling of emotion and pride is theirs! To carry through their task they are ready to sacrifice their lives. The whole French nation spurs them on, and on the folds of their flag are inscribed the majestic words of 'Right and Liberty.' *Vive l'Alsace! Vive la France!*"

M. Messimy, War Minister, in a message of congratulation to the successful troops, said: "At the start of the war the energetic and brilliant offensive, which you have taken in Alsace, puts us in a position of great moral encouragement." Two days later General Joffre addressed the following inspiring words to the brave defenders of Liège and other parts within the Belgian frontier: "Having been called upon by the most odious aggression to fight against the same adversary, your admirable soldiers and those of France will bear themselves in all circumstances as true brothers under arms. Confident of the triumph of their just cause, they will march together to victory."

Under pressure of the German

Staff, alarmed by the French invasion of Alsace, the Austrian Government despatched two army corps to the assistance of the Germans in that province, whereupon the diplomatic relations between France and Austria were broken off. In the face of the overpowering numbers of the enemy, the French troops, on August 10th, fell back from Mulhausen to positions in the Vosges. To complete this section, there was a see-saw of successes and retirements in the Vosges and in Alsace, although at one time (August 16th) the French cavalry scouts were only twenty miles from Strasburg. It was only the German advance into Northern France, with Paris as their objective, that compelled the retirement of the French troops from Alsace and Lorraine, to hold fast to their positions in the Vosges, and fall back on the line of fortresses from the southward bend of the long line which extends from Verdun to the Swiss frontier.

To return to Paris. After the Battle of Haelen, between Liège and Brussels, which was all to the advantage of the Belgian forces, the French Chamber of Deputies, on August 14th, granted a war credit of £40,000,000 to the Government. On the same date the French were moving in aid of the Belgians in considerable force from Charleroi to Gembloux. The Belgian Government removed on August 17th from Brussels to Antwerp, and three days later the former city was formally entered by the

THE DAY BEFORE THE BATTLE OF MONS.
In the top photograph are shown two officers of the Royal Scots Fusiliers walking through the square at Quesney on the day before the Battle of Mons. The smaller view gives a good idea of the leafy luxuriance of the country through which the British transport was advancing on the eve of battle. The third shows British soldiers pulling down trees in the promenade of the town for barricades on August 23rd, 1914. These barricades were held by the Lincolns (10th Regiment).

Germans, as already described. Then followed the fall of the last fort of Liège, the beginning of the Battle of Charleroi, and the partial investment of Namur on August 22nd—two days before the Battle of Mons.

To sum up the position in Great Britain during these eventful days, on August 10th the Press Bureau was established with the Right Hon. F. E. Smith, K.C., as president. Its subsequent erratic methods were the subject of much Press and Parliamentary controversy. On the 10th Parliament adjourned till August 25th. On the same date 30,000 special constables for the London area were sworn in for the protection of public buildings, power stations, waterworks, etc.; and these were added to considerably later on. A day later the first proposal was made to arm the Irish Nationalist Volunteers for the defence of Ireland, and that was afterwards regularised, as well as the acceptance of the Ulster Volunteers, already armed, under the direction of Lord Kitchener. On the 12th, following the despatch by Austria of two army corps to the assistance of the Germans on the Alsatian frontier, war was declared for the first time between Britain and that empire. The organisation and despatch of the British Expeditionary Force to France has already been described. Its final concentration took place on August 21st, and it received its baptism of fire on August 23rd, at the never-to-be-forgotten engagement at Mons.

The first battles in East Prussia have been fully described in Chapter XXIII. These were only meant as a diversion to relieve the pressure against the Allies in the western spheres of operations in Belgium and Northern France, an object which was admirably served. After Rennenkampf's retreat to the Niemen and successful resistance to the German counter-invasion of Russian territory at Suwalki and Augustowo, preparations were made by the Russian generalissimo, the Grand Duke Nicholas, for the great struggle on the Austrian and German frontiers. He had two million of the finest

FRENCH CAVALRY ON THE WAY TO THE FIRST GREAT FRONTIER BATTLE.
In the above photograph is seen a group of French cavalrymen receiving orders during the advance into Belgium. The smaller illustration above shows them on their way to the front, advancing along the typical Belgian cobbled highway.   D 72   C

troops at his disposal, and in a great part of the theatre of the coming campaign he had the advantage of the support of the Polish and Ruthenian population. The Grand Duke issued a proclamation to the people of Russian origin inhabiting the Austrian dominions calling upon them to unite with the Mother Country in reviving the century-old tradition of the Russian Grand Duke Ivan Kalita, whose sympathies had always been with them. A series of engagements with detachments of Austrians on the eastern frontier of Galicia took place during the

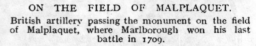

IN THE TRENCHES AT QUESNEY.
British troops in the trenches in the picturesque surroundings of Quesney, between Mons and Le Cateau.

ON THE FIELD OF MALPLAQUET.
British artillery passing the monument on the field of Malplaquet, where Marlborough won his last battle in 1709.

considerable damage; but, on the other hand, the Serbians shelled the island of Ada Kaleh, and set fire to two Austrian ships and Orsova railway-station, on the north bank of the Danube. Serbian troops also crossed the Drina, and engaged and defeated the right wing of the Austrian army. Following these operations came the Battle of Shabatz, fully dealt with in Chapter XIX

Turning for a moment to the Far East, on August 9th the Japanese troops put to sea from Tokio under the command of Admiral Dewa, it being shrewdly understood that the objective was Kiao-chau, which, under the "mailed fist" of the Kaiser's brother Prince Henry, had been "leased" from the then impotent Chinese Government. On August 15th Japan formally joined the European Allies against the common enemy, and called upon Germany to remove her warships

early weeks of August; but neither in that region nor in the direction of Kielce, in South-West Poland, were the efforts of the Austrians successful in taking the offensive. By August 17th the Russian advanced guard, consisting of several divisions, had penetrated into the northern part of Bukovina, and marched on Czernowitz, which is the capital of that province.

Germany broke off relations with Serbia on August 10th. Six days later the Austrians bombarded Belgrade, and did

from Japanese and Chinese waters, and to evacuate Kiao-chau by August 23rd.

The threads of the story leading up to the momentous Battle of Mons, which signalised the beginning of the renowned retreat of the Allies in the direction of Paris, have now been gathered up, and in subsequent chapters the narrative will be a continuous presentation of the contemporaneous happenings in all the theatres of the war.

BRITISH SUPPLY COLUMN ON THE LINE OF MARCH BEFORE THE BATTLE OF MONS.
The above photograph shows a British supply column drawn up on the line of march near Mons, on August 22nd, 1914.

FRENCH'S INDOMITABLE LITTLE ARMY ON THE EVE OF THE BATTLE OF MONS.

A splendid panoramic view of the British Expeditionary Force in camp. " French's contemptible little army "—as the Kaiser described it in a famous order to his own troops—very soon after the date of that order, showed the Germans the kind of mettle of which it was made, and won the grudging admiration of the foe. The top view is of British troops resting in a street at ——, a place the censor would not allow the photographer to name. Inset : British cavalry, on the march through a Belgian town, and soon to add new laurels to their fame.

9TH LANCERS CHARGING THE

CHAPTER XXVI

GERMAN GUNS AT LE CATEAU.

THE FRENCH FRONTIER BATTLE AND THE BRITISH STAND AT MONS.

Britain's Classic Battlefields—Moltke's Strategy—Siege-Guns *versus* Forts—Slaughter by Machinery—Charleroi—General French's Dispositions—The Kaiser's Contemptible Order—An Unexpected Stroke—Zulu Precedent for German Method—The Price we Paid—The English Way—British Hawk against German Heron—Why the British had to Retire—300,000 Men against 80,000.

MONS, the historic capital of the ancient Duchy of Hainault, is a handsome, pleasant Belgian town, with a Gothic town-hall, splendid cathedral, and a picturesque belfry, set in a black-country coal-mining region near the French frontier. To British visitors the most interesting thing about Mons is the ridge of Malplaquet, about three miles to the south, in a region of ravines and woods and hills. Here the Duke of Marlborough, in 1709, won the last, the most difficult, and the most terrible of all his battles, at a cost of 20,000 men. It was one of the most costly victories in our history, but it put an end to the ambition of Louis XIV. to become master of Europe.

Many British officers have spent a delightful and instructive holiday in carefully studying the ground about Mons where Marlborough fought. Among these officers, some years ago, was a young cavalry commander, now the famous Field-Marshal Sir John French. Keen must have been his pleasure when he learned, about the middle of August, 1914, that General Joffre, the Commander-in-Chief of the Allied Armies, had decided to assign to the British Expeditionary Force the task of holding Mons. Here was ground that Sir John knew almost as well as he knew the land about his birthplace in Kent—ground famed and hallowed

14

VIEW OF THE TOWN OF MONS.

by many heroic achievements of British arms. For all around Mons were the old classic battlefields of our race—Waterloo to the north-west, on the Brussels road ; Namur due west, where the Irish Guards in the seventeenth century distinguished themselves ; Cambrai to the east, where Marlborough, by threatening King Louis, brought about that balance of power in Europe which the Prussian was trying to overthrow ; and Agincourt was not far away.

Not only Sir John French, but many of his officers had studied the lay of the land, from pure interest in Marlborough's campaigns. Now suddenly, unexpectedly, their knowledge became of vital value. Once more, in the old cockpit of Europe, the old question was to be again fought out by the last argument of kings—cannon. Was Europe to be a balance of independent nations, or the silenced, oppressed appanage of a single, tyrannical war lord ? Once again the British soldier, carried overseas on the back of the British sailor, stood forth to challenge the power of the military despot.

Things had changed for the worse for Britain since Marlborough and his allies and Wellington and his allies fought for the principle of freedom in civilisation on the same battle-ground. For in the old days our country usually put into the field a considerable army, which,

THE "STIRRUP-CHARGE" OF THE SCOTS GREYS AND HIGHLANDERS AT ST. QUENTIN.

The British Army, covering itself with new glory in the storied battlefields of Flanders, reviving memories of gallant deeds done in old Elizabethan days, performed a series of exploits at St. Quentin which recalled vividly to the public imagination the never-dying magnificent charge of the Scots Greys and Highlanders at Waterloo—a deed commemorated in Lady Butler's famous painting "Scotland for Ever!" On August 30th, 1914, the Scots Greys and the Highlanders together took part, not in one charge, but in a series of charges "as at Waterloo," bursting into the thick of the enemy, the Highlanders holding on to the stirrup-leathers of the Greys as the horsemen galloped, and attacking hand to hand. The Germans had the surprise of their lives, and broke and fled before the sudden and unexpected onslaught, suffering severe losses alike from the swords of the cavalry and the bayonets of the Highland infantrymen.

During the progress of the war in both Belgium and France churches were used as temporary hospitals. The above picture, which is one of the most notable of the many called forth by the war, was drawn from particulars supplied by some of those who figured in the episode it depicts so graphically. A party of wounded soldiers had been accommodated on the floor of a church situate betwe Cateau and Landrecies. Over the building a Red Cross flag had been hoiste

16

elsewhere the sign of the Red Cross was used as a target by the German ymen. A German shell burst open the door of the church, destroying its archway, and further shells continued to explode upon the building. As best they could, the wounded men, the stronger in the little party bearing the more severely injured of their comrades along with them, made their way from the doomed shelter of the church to a spot out of the range of the deadly German guns.

BRITISH VALOUR NEAR COMPIEGNE: HOW THREE GUNNERS OF THE R.H.A. WON A PLACE IN HISTORY.

In the early hours of the morning of September 1st, 1914, L. Battery of the Royal Horse Artillery were suddenly subjected to a terrific enfilade fire from a ridge they had supposed to be still occupied by the French. Their positions prevented them from bringing more than three of their guns against the enemy. As the day wore on but one gun remained serviceable. It was then that three men, all of whom were wounded—Sergeant-Major Darrell, Gunner Darbyshire, and Driver Osborne—won their place in history. They kept up such a deadly fire that all but one of the remaining German guns were silenced, and, as one of the survivors remarked, "We'd both had enough of it." Both sides ceased fire, and the three heroes, all of whom were recommended for the V.C., were rescued by our cavalry and infantry.

linked to the forces of friendly nations, was little, if at all, inferior in numbers to the opposing host. But now, when other people counted their trained warriors in millions, Britain could only place 80,000 men in the firing-line, with another 20,000 men as supports. France, our ally, was also fighting at a disadvantage. She had barely more than 80,000 troops of the first line, with 36,000 reserves, to hold Charleroi, to the right of the British position, and she was greatly outnumbered along the rest of the northern front of war.

In the first great battle, that raged from Mons and Lille in the east to the Moselle and the Vosges in the west, France had to pay a heavy price for the dreams of some of her peace-loving ministers who, bent on social reforms, had grudged the cost of highly efficient preparations for a vast war. It was a generous mistake. Our own Government had not escaped from it. So the hard-headed, hard-hearted German military caste, that had skilfully forged the entire resources of two great empires into a tremendous weapon of attack, had practically every material advantage on their side.

It must also be admitted that the German commander-in-chief, General von Moltke, had managed his mighty forces with remarkable ability. Before the great battle opened he had General Joffre out-manœuvred and running into disaster.

For, by various expedients, he had got into Belgium a far larger number of troops than the French commander expected to meet, and he had then allowed the French to take the offensive in various difficult directions in which success was, in the circumstances, practically impossible. And if all this were not sufficient to give the Germans, after the first clash, a decided superiority in attacking power, there was the last surprise—the new mobile Krupp siege-guns.

It was these siege-guns which brought about the total defeat of the French forward movement, and compelled the British force also to retreat from Belgium and Northern France. The Allied front, running from Mons and Charleroi, was based on the resisting power of the Belgian ring fortress of Namur. It was expected that Namur would delay the German advance as long as Liège had done. Then the French line of frontier fortresses—Lille, with its half-finished defences; Maubeuge, with good forts and a large garrison; and other strong places—would form a still more useful system of fortified points for the Allied armies.

The Germans, however, did not intend that things should fall out in this manner. They were in the extraordinary position of having committed a grave mistake at Liège, for which they were now able to make their opponents

BRITISH ARTILLERY OFFICER'S HEROISM AT TOURNAI.
At dawn on August 26th, 1914, 300,000 German troops were thrown on the British lines in an attempt to " wipe them out." Sir John French stated without hesitation that the saving of the left wing could never have been accomplished but for the rare and unusual coolness and intrepidity and determination of Sir H. Smith-Dorrien. The spirit of all ranks is well exemplified by the above illustration of how a British artillery officer sold his life dearly when his battery was attacked by 3,000 Uhlans on this critical day.

pay. They had rashly endeavoured to storm the Belgian border fortress by an infantry attack. That attack, as all the world knew, had disastrously failed. But—this was not so widely known—as soon as the new siege-guns had been brought up, the Liège forts had quickly been blown to pieces. The big, movable howitzer was master of all costly, fixed fortifications; but the Germans were not anxious to advertise this fact. It was their supreme secret. They intended to let the Allied armies repose on fortress towns, then envelop them, and smash the fortresses with surprising rapidity.

They began with Namur. Here a ring of detached forts, built of concrete, and armed with 6 in. guns and smaller howitzers placed in armour-plated turrets, was further strengthened by trenches, wire entanglements, and mines. The Germans wasted no more troops in storming operations. Instead, they brought up thirty-two enormous howitzers with 11 in. muzzles, and, from a distance of five to seven miles, pitched about 3,500 shells, each weighing 750 lb., on a single fort. The whole structure of concrete and armour-plate was smashed and rent. The small Belgian guns could not reach the assailing howitzers, and the forts, the trenches, troops, and cannon were swept quickly from the earth by the terrible big shells. It was not a battle, though 200,000 Germans were massed against 25,000 Belgians. It was merely slaughter by machinery—Krupp's engines of wholesale death against flesh and blood.

The shell fire began furiously on Friday, August 21st, and by noon the next day Namur was partly invested and doomed suddenly to fall. In the meantime the Fifth French Army, holding the passage of the Sambre, by the Belgian mining town of Charleroi, was launching its Algerian and Senegal troops at the Prussian Guard. Fierce and deadly was the hand-to-hand bayonet fight between the Arabs and negroes of French Africa and the flower of the German Army. The Arabs, who had a dash of the Berber strain and some of the blood of the old European vandals who conquered Northern Africa, advanced across the bridge of Charleroi into the factory quarter of the Belgian mining town. Such was their impetuosity that no German troops could stay them; but, unfortunately, they were at last caught by machine-guns, concealed in one of the factories, and mowed down. Superb as was their courage, they were unable to withstand the terrific fire, and as the survivors reeled back the bridge was taken.

The French infantry then sprang forward, and retook the bridge, lost it, and captured it again. The French machine-guns, left too often, it is said, in the hands of a

THE DANGEROUS SALIENT FORMED BY THE ANGLE OF THE CANAL AND THE RIVER SAMBRE AT MONS.
"The right of the Third Division, under General Hamilton, was at Mons, which." Sir John French pointed out in his despatch, "formed a somewhat dangerous salient, and I directed the Commander of the Second Corps....if threatened seriously, to draw back to the centre behind Mons."

few men, do not appear to have given as much support in the wild bayonet charges as the Germans received from their machine-guns. On the other hand, the light French field artillery, especially the 3 in. gun, worked tremendous havoc in the solid German ranks, as these swept on to the attack, or withdrew to gather in their supports for a fresh charge.

Then heavy German artillery was brought up, and the French, having no guns or howitzers of the same range and power, were placed in a position of disadvantage, while **Fifth French Army** shell and shrapnel from unassailable **prepares to retreat** hostile batteries, wrecked and searched the colliery town. At the same time the German commander, with columns of reinforcements marching south to his aid, deployed fresh troops, and hurled them in close formation, under cover of overpowering artillery fire, against the tired French soldiers. By the evening of Saturday, August 22nd, the passage of the River Sambre, near Charleroi, had been forced, and the Fifth French Army, with its reserves, was preparing to retreat.

Meanwhile, things were going very well, to all appearances, with the British Expeditionary Force round Mons. Our men formed the extreme left wing of the Allied line that stretched for some two hundred miles close to the French frontier. Our task seemed a fairly easy one, for our cavalry scouts and airmen reported that only 100,000 Germans, at the most, were advancing against us. General Joffre confirmed this information from the results of his aerial reconnaissances. Our scouting horsemen, on Saturday, August 22nd, pushed out northward till they reached a point within cannon-shot of the field of Waterloo. There,

in fierce, sharp little skirmishes with the enemy's cavalry screen, they tested the fighting power of the Uhlans and the Death's Head Hussars, and found that in both swordsmanship and horsemanship the Germans were, man to man, little more than food for worms. As Sir Philip Chetwode, the leader of our Fifth Cavalry Brigade, remarked, our men went through them like a knife through brown paper.

While the British cavalryman was enjoying himself in the preliminary skirmish, and avenging on Uhlan patrols the dreadful wrongs he had seen Belgian women suffering from, Sir John French put his two army corps—about 80,000 men altogether—into battle array. He had about thirty miles of front to defend, with Mons roughly in the centre of it. On the east was the little town of Condé, connecting by a canal with Mons. On the west were the smaller towns of Bray and Binche, the last about half-way to Charleroi.

The Second Army Corps, under General Sir Horace Smith-Dorrien, was lined out along the canal from Condé to Mons. The First Army Corps, under General Sir Douglas Haig, was deployed from Mons towards Bray. The Fifth Cavalry **Making ready for** Brigade guarded Binche, while a cavalry **the day of battle** division, under General Allenby, was kept as a reserve, ready to move to any part of the line that was endangered.

This work of taking up positions was carried out on Saturday, August 22nd, and on the following day the troops went on digging themselves in along the canal and among the hills, while the gunners got their guns into good places commanding the northern banks of the canal and the country to the north-west towards Brussels. All Sunday

POSITION HELD BY THE BRITISH UNDER SHELL FIRE ON THE NIGHT OF AUGUST 23RD, 1914.
When the news of the retirement of the French forces and the serious German threatening on his front was confirmed, Sir John French determined to effect a retirement to the Maubeuge position at daybreak on August 24th 1914.

SCENE OF THE RETREAT FROM MONS ON AUGUST 24TH, 1914, WHEN DAWN BROKE OVER THE CONDÉ-BINCHE LINE, TO NIGHTFALL, ON THE LEFT OF MAUBEUGE FORTRESS.

BRITISH TROOPS LEFT MAUBEUGE IN THE EARLY MORNING OF AUGUST 25TH, 1914, FIGHTING THEIR WAY THROUGH THE FOREST OF MORMAL TO LANDRECIES.

troops continued to arrive at Mons, many of them going at once into action after their march.

The Belgian population in the neighbouring colliery villages and large industrial centres was wild with joy at the coming of the soldiers of the Great Empire to which these people had looked for help all through their tragic sufferings. There was scarcely any need for using our food stores, for the happy Belgian women pressed forward in multitudes with all kinds of eatables, and their husbands—miners, mechanics, factory hands—aided in the trench-digging with great vigour. Though the Prussian—like a buck nigger doing a cakewalk—was performing the

had a hard time of it. Along the canal, in places, they had to break up the road to make defences, and many dummy trenches had to be dug to attract the enemy's shrapnel fire to spots where it would be harmless. Then the bridges had to be mined and wrecked ready for a German onset, and the country over which the Germans would attack had to be cleared and ranges fixed for the gunners. Entire forests were set on fire to prevent the enemy taking cover in the trees and brushwood.

Saturday was a day of peaceful hard work, and Sunday morning generally passed in calm, pleasant fashion.

Treacherous calm before the storm

Some dove-shaped German flying machines appeared on the sky-line, and our cavalry drew back to the main army, finding the pressure suddenly grow dangerously strong against them. There was infantry fighting even on Saturday on the line towards Charleroi, and the sound of the big German guns, directed against the French position, floated down to our First Army Corps.

It was at three o'clock on Sunday afternoon that the enemy came out in force against our men. Sir Douglas Haig's front was attacked heavily; he withdrew his flank to the hills south of Bray, and the cavalry brigade holding Binche, half-way to the fallen town of Charleroi, gave up their position and also moved southward. Victorious all along the rest of the Allied line, the Germans swung out westward against our troops, reckoning them an easy prey. Something like eight hundred thousand Frenchmen were almost everywhere in retreat along the frontier, with a million and a half Germans, flushed with success, following them. What could eighty thousand British troops do to stay the sledge-hammer stroke that was falling upon them?

All that had happened to the Belgians at Namur and to the French at Charleroi was only a preliminary to an overwhelming, annihilating blow on the British force. Three days before the battle of the frontier opened Kaiser Wilhelm II. had addressed a most extraordinary order to the generals of his northern armies—to the Duke of Würtemberg, General von Hausen, General von Buelow, and General von Kluck. Notorious throughout the world as this order has now become, we must print it once more in this record of the Great War:

"It is my Royal and Imperial command that you concentrate your energies, for the immediate present, upon one single purpose, and that is that you address all your skill and all the valour of my soldiers to exterminate first the treacherous English, and walk over General French's contemptible little army."

DESPERATE HAND-TO-HAND FIGHTING IN AN OLD BARN.

Our drawing illustrates one of the desperate hand-to-hand encounters which took place between French and German troops on the Franco-Belgian frontier during the house-to-house search for stragglers. A small party of Germans, trapped in a quaint old village barn, resisted to the end.

goose-step in Brussels, and the Belgian Army, with its king, had been driven into Antwerp, all was not for ever lost, the people of Mons felt, now that a British army stood once more in battle order on Belgian soil.

From the beginning our men went about their business with remarkable coolness. There was none of the nervous, strained expectancy with which a highly-civilised conscript army prepares for its sudden, terrific ordeal. Many of our men had a bath to refresh themselves after their march; others, with a taste for angling and for a supper of fresh-water fish, tied a hooked line to the top of their bayonets, and placidly fished the canal. The sappers

The intense, ungoverned spirit of furious hate that breathes in this order, given by the grandson of Queen Victoria, was, at least, testimony to his fear of the outcome of the vast struggle now that the British Empire was taking part in it. A commander, certain of the justice of the cause for which he was fighting, and sure of the eventual victory of his arms, would not have indulged his soul in so unseemly a frenzy of spite and passion and slander. As soon as the position occupied by the British Expeditionary Force was known to the German War Staff, General von Moltke was able to arrange to fulfil the murderous request of his Imperial master, and at the same time to carry out a magnificent enveloping movement round Mons, which would endanger the entire French Army along a front of one hundred and fifty miles, from Lille to Verdun.

Neither Sir John French nor General Joffre expected the stroke that was being prepared against both British and French. At Mons the battle went on to our advantage. The Germans at first put scarcely more men into the fighting-line than the British did, and victory seemed within our reach, for the

MAJOR-GENERAL SIR WILLIAM ROBERTSON. *(Maull & Fox.)*

Major-General Sir William Robertson, K.C.B., who served with distinction in India and South Africa, as Quarter-master-General with the Expeditionary Force overcame " almost insuperable difficulties with his characteristic energy, skill, and determination." Major-General Sir Nevil Macready, the Adjutant-General, performed onerous and difficult tasks in connection with disciplinary arrangements. General Snow held a difficult position with success south of Solesmes. General E. H. H. Allenby, C.B., greatly distinguished himself with the cavalry at Mons.

reached their mark to induce the German gunners to adopt another way of fighting.

Leaving their shrapnel ammunition cases untouched for a while, the hostile artillery loaders brought up shell, and began a furious bombardment of our batteries, hidden among the hills to the south. Here, again, in the great artillery duel with which every modern battle opens, the Germans at first had the best of it. We had arranged a massed-fire effect by grouping our guns close together in the old-fashioned way. This made it easy for the enemy to do damage to some of the batteries as soon as he had found the position. The German guns, on the other hand, were placed in batteries at a great distance apart, each gun being well screened from aerial observation.

The massed-fire effect was

MAJOR-GENERAL SIR CECIL F. N. MACREADY. *(Elliott & Fry.)*

Germans fought at a terrible disadvantage. The infantrymen did not know how to shoot, how to take cover, how to use the bayonet. They were only harmless servants of the well-handled German machine-guns and the numerous and effective light and heavy Krupp artillery.

The German gunners—good men, but not so good as ours —fought the battle. Greatly helped at first by German airmen in Taube and other machines, who skimmed over the British trenches, found where our men were, and signalled the range to the gunners, the enemy's batteries poured a continuous storm of bursting shrapnel over our defences. To protect our defenceless infantry, our artillerymen bombarded the German guns with shells. The shells sufficiently

GENERAL T. D'OYLEY SNOW. *(Elliott & Fry.)*

obtained by means of field telephones, connecting every gun to a central fire-control station. By this method any wholesale destruction of the batteries was prevented. Each gun had singly to be found and destroyed by shell fire by the enemy. Yet all the guns—and there were over six hundred of them —could be brought to bear, by telephone control, on one spot to blow a sudden path through the hostile front. Altogether, it was a brilliant piece of organisation, and as soon as our gunners grasped the significance of it they also scattered their batteries, and used field telephones and flag signals for directing the fire. Our flag signalling was admirable. The Germans had laughed at its old-fashionedness at our manoeuvres ; but, as we knew from other wars, even a message sent by a fluttering

GENERAL ALLENBY.

GUN IN ACTION AND BRINGING UP AMMUNITION.
The large photograph is of a British 60-pounder gun in action, while the smaller illustrates the rough-and-ready, though efficient, way in which ammunition, conveyed in industrial motor-waggons, commandeered in England, was brought up to the firing-line.

handkerchief can save a battalion or a battery, or help to a victory.

On the whole, our artillery, though inferior in number and weight of guns to that of the Germans, put up an equal fight in the opening gun duel. For what our men lacked in howitzer fire and heavy, mobile, motor-drawn guns, they made up in courage, experience, and ingenuity. The old game of "dead dog," for instance, was played round Mons with dreadful effectiveness.

When it was clear that our guns were clean outmatched in number by the enemy's gigantic armament, our artillerymen carefully allowed the Germans to see that their overpowering fire was having its designed result. Through their field-glasses the Teutonic artillery officers could trace the effect of their concentrated fire of big shells, and watch battery after battery along the British front grow silent. Here and there one gun, or a couple of guns, would go on valiantly ringing defiance from the hills, until the hurricane of shells put every piece out of action.

In places the German airmen may even have seen overturned and shattered things looking like wrecked guns. For such things can easily be provided for the delectation of inquisitive hostile aerial scouts, especially if there are

any trees handy with trunks about the size of the barrel of a British gun.

Round Mons the German gunners apparently had their greatest triumph. The artillerymen of the "contemptible little army" seemed to have been beaten in the gun duel as completely as were the Belgians at Namur, with their old, feeble Krupp 6 in. pieces. So the grand infantry attack was launched towards the canal in order to storm the British trenches. To make their task easy, the German shrapnel cases were again opened, and a tornado of bursting bullets poured over the river valley. All the bright, warm, sunny Sabbath sky was suddenly filled with innumerable little puffs of cloud. Loud above the distant thunder of the Krupp batteries rang the screaming song of the shrapnel, which made a little puff of cloud as it exploded horribly and showered its charge of bullets down on the British trenches.

This was the critical period in the ordeal of modern battle. Would our men, protected no longer by their own guns and exposed to the full power of the latest and most destructive death-machine, stand the test in patient, passive, all-enduring fortitude? Our veteran fighting men, many of them risen to the position of non-commissioned officers, admitted that the worst moments in the South African War—at Spion Kop and Modder River—were nothing to the punishment our troops had to stand at Mons.

Spion Kop and the Modder nothing to Mons

The mere noise of the German gun-fire was nerve-racking, terrifying. It was a sort of typhoon with firework effects, mixed up with many incessant thunder-storms, and further diversified by local earthquakes where the shells hit.

A French officer, deafened by the explosions, and yet with his national curiosity still alert, resolved to go into the trenches and see how the British soldier was taking it all. In ancient days the new allies of France had been famous for their coolness under fire. But never had their fathers to endure what they were now under-

HOLDING A BRITISH POSITION ON THE MONS—CONDÉ CANAL AGAINST REPEATED ONSLAUGHTS OF THE ENEMY.
In their efforts to overwhelm the position of the British on the south bank of the Mons to Condé Canal, the Germans attacked again and again. Dragoons and Uhlans who came within reach of our guns were swept down by them or made prisoners. Then the Germans, advancing in great strength and in close formation, managed to reach the north bank, where they attempted to throw pontoon bridges across the water. Their losses were terrible. They succeeded ten times in building pontoon bridges over the canal, but each time their work was destroyed by the British gunners.

going. Was the old British stubbornness of spirit still equal to the new occasion?

He settled in the trenches, shell and shrapnel screaming and exploding above and around, and found the private British soldiers engaged in a great discussion. To the Frenchman's surprise, they were oblivious to all that was happening at Mons. What troubled them was the failure of the heavy-weight prize-fighting match between the young Englishman Ahearn and the American Gunboat Smith, whom Georges Carpentier had beaten on a foul. The American had withdrawn from the match, and our soldiers wanted to know if it was from the fear of being beaten that he had done so.

The French officer afterwards admitted that he was staggered. At best he had expected to find stern, tight-lipped, silent courage. Instead he encountered the smiling, eager, blithe faces of young athletes, who had apparently forgotten they were being hammered to death by the Germans, and were solely anxious about the pluck or want of pluck of a certain American pugilist. The men were not even interested—as many **What was talked of** French troops would have been—in the **in the trenches** technical problems of the battle in which' they were so vitally concerned. That side of the matter they left to their leaders, confident that all would be done that man could do.

Suddenly, an order passed down the line. The Gunboat Smith discussion was interrupted. The men looked to their rifles and their ammunition, sighted as their officers gave the word, and waited. The German gunners had come to the conclusion that most of the British infantry in the trenches was either dead or wounded. So the German infantrymen were coming to take possession of the stricken field, and prepare the way for the advance of the guns into France down the roads to Paris.

Out of the distant woods they deployed in vast, dim, grey-green masses, barely distinguishable from the grass and the leafage around them. They formed in lines, shoulder to shoulder and four or five deep, with machine-gun supports at fairly close intervals. Some of the light, quick-firing artillery advanced behind them, horses at the gallop, to clear any obstacle in front of their wide path. The German sappers, with pontoon sections, moved towards the canal to bridge the water for the infantry attack. Seeing that practically all the British guns had been discovered and silenced in this part of the battlefield, the grand, routing advance was to be pushed home at this breaking point.

At first all the heavy German batteries within range of the fated British trenches massed and redoubled their fire—shell as well as shrapnel now being used to complete the demoralisation of the remaining British troops. As a matter of fact, most of the British troops remained quite unhurt, owing to the skilful manner in **Useful lessons** which the trenches had been furnished with **learned in the Boer** shrapnel-proof cover. Our men had not **War** fought the Boers without profiting by what they saw, and what they learned by experience, when the big guns played on the trenches. They were safer in the earthworks they had hastily but skilfully made than they would have been in a concrete, armour-plated fort.

But the Germans, accustomed only to sham battles, were unaware of the safety in which our men were waiting for them. At last the immense grey-green masses drew so near to the British lines that their own artillery had to cease firing for fear of hitting them. The sappers came with the pontoons to the water. The German infantry rose for the charge, and then the " dead dog " came again to life.

Every British gun on the heights commanding the country where the German infantry was collected spoke

25

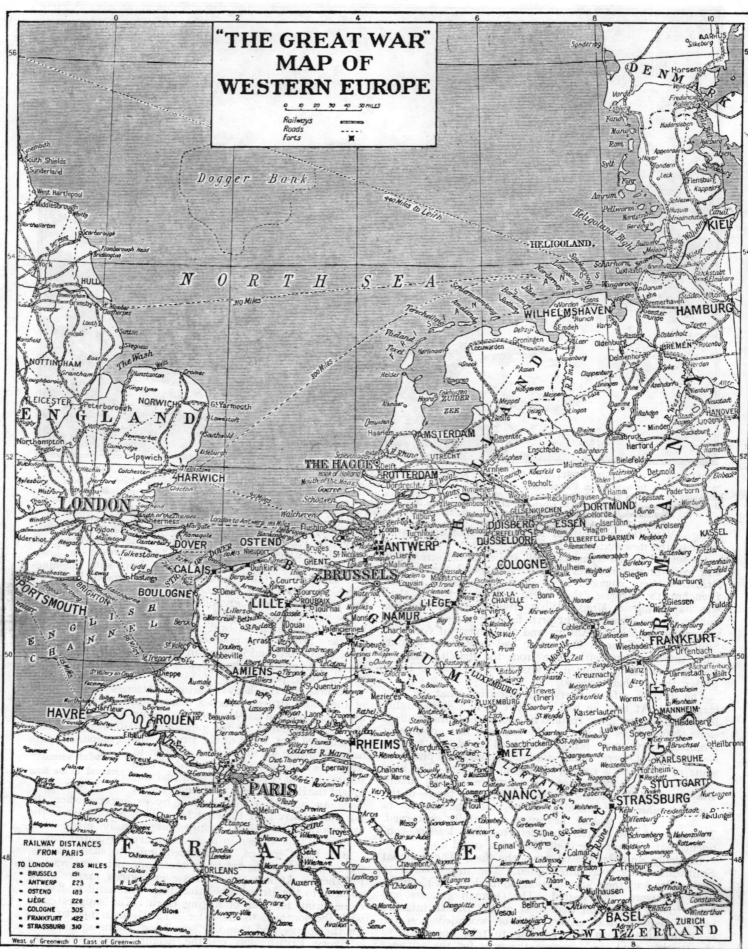

"THE GREAT WAR" MAP OF WESTERN EUROPE

Railways
Roads
Forts

0 10 20 30 40 50 MILES

RAILWAY DISTANCES
FROM PARIS

TO LONDON	285 MILES	
BRUSSELS	191 "	
ANTWERP	223 "	
OSTEND	183 "	
LIÈGE	228 "	
COLOGNE	305 "	
FRANKFURT	422 "	
STRASSBURG	310 "	

West of Greenwich 0 East of Greenwich

Prepared by "Geographia." Limited, London.

LAST PHASE OF THE MAGNIFICENT RETREAT OF GENERAL FRENCH'S LITTLE ARMY FROM LE CATEAU.
These diagrammatic maps illustrate very graphically how General Allenby's cavalry screened the retreat from Le Cateau on August 26th, and French cavalry came up to their support on August 27th and 28th, 1914.

with a voice that shattered the German dream of an easy victory. Clouds of well-timed shrapnel, firing at broad targets impossible to miss, burst over the tricked and trapped foot soldiers. But the splendid discipline of the Prussian war-machine held good. Sternly controlled by their non-commissioned officers, pushed and beaten onward by their lieutenants and captains, the grey battalions broke into a steady-running charge, though the British gunners breached their lines and shattered their formations. Our guns could not kill them quickly enough to stop them.

They came on like a human tidal wave, with too much mass and momentum for any obstacle to stop them. The gaps in their deep, locked, yelling ranks closed almost as soon as they were made. It was like the overwhelming charge of a Zulu impi, choking with its piles of dead the guns of the position it meant to capture.

In the meantime the surprised, discomfited German artillerymen resumed the bombardment of our batteries in order to draw the fire of our guns away from the advancing German infantry. But our gunners naturally refused the artillery duel, and, letting the hostile batteries fire at them without replying, kept our guns pounding away at the grey-green masses close by in the valley.

The German sappers reached the canal and flung a pontoon bridge across it. A well-placed, timely shell smashed the pontoon sections. The sappers tried again, and the infantry masses behind them approached within a few hundred yards of our trenches. By this time the British gunners were well-nigh beaten. They continued to shell the work of the pontoon-builders, but they could not destroy the German infantry masses quickly enough to break the charge. Apparently, German tactics had won. At an enormous cost of life a point had been reached from which the charge could be driven to a victorious conclusion.

It was the Zulu method, carried out with powerful modern artillery support, and improved by the use of the long-range, bayoneted rifle, instead of the assegai, and the employment of reserve detachments following the foremost troops and reinforcing every wavering point of the onward, rushing line. It was Chaka, a Zulu chief of high military genius contemporary with Napoleon, who had first devised this terrible rush method of attack—terrible to the attackers as well as to the defenders. But the Boers had discovered how the furious, inhuman onslaught could be stayed. Their discovery they had revealed to us, asking a heavy price for it.

This price we paid with the lives of eight thousand men at Tugela River, Modder River, and other places. Now, we were prepared to teach the Germans that good marksmanship, a magazine rifle, and a cool, steady eye could break any Zulu-like charge, even when guns had failed to stay it. "Sight to four hundred yards!" cried our officers. Then, after the order to fire: "Mark your man!" Our

soldiers marked him, in tens, in hundreds, and when the range was three hundred yards they marked him in thousands, in tens of thousands.

Nothing living could stand against the deadly, scientific, rapid fire poured out from the British trenches. The Germans who remained upright looked about them like men dazed; then, screaming with terror, turned and fled, and again our guns on the heights caught them.

The one weak place in the British battle-line

This slaughter occurred only at intervals along the front of thirty miles—at Bray in the west, around Mons itself, and at points on the canal to Condé. For so long as the Germans were only 100,000 strong, with about the same number of infantryman as Sir John French commanded, they could not deliver a general attack in mass all down the line. They had to concentrate in the distant northern woods, and then sweep out towards some spot under cover of their artillery fire.

In fact, it was often easy to foresee on what point the German attack would fall by studying the increasing fury of the massed gun fire that was vainly employed to clear the British trenches preparatory to the infantry onset. There was only one weak place in our battle-line. This weak place was Mons itself. After Sir Douglas Haig drew the First Army Corps back to the hilly country south of Bray, and withdrew the Fifth Cavalry Brigade from Binche, Mons formed a wedge jutting out into the enemy's lines. Held by the 3rd Division under General Hamilton, it was subject to a cross fire on both sides of the wedge, and to a double attack from either side.

Sir John French had directed that this salient—as a wedge position running into the hostile country is called—should not be held if it were seriously threatened. So, as twilight was beginning to fall on the wild Sunday afternoon, General Hamilton drew his centre back behind Mons. Some of his heavy guns then occupied the lower slopes of the historic ridge of Malplaquet, and in the woods through which Marlborough had worked British soldiers were again encamped.

When this movement had been carried out, the British lines from Condé to Bray were stronger than before. There was no weak point against which an equal number of Germans had anything like a fair chance of success. The first historic battle against the Prussian, whom we had helped to empire in the days of the elder Pitt and Frederick the Great, was going the way that Crecy and Agincourt had gone. Our riflemen, as famed for marksmanship as our bowmen had been, stood on the defensive, and prepared for their victorious charge by first shattering, in rapid, deadly, imperturbable fire, the fighting power of the enemy.

ONE GERMAN COMMANDER'S CONSPICUOUS CHIVALRY.

"On September 10th, 1914"—we quote from Sir John French's despatch of the 11th of that month— "a small party of French under a non-commissioned officer was cut off and surrounded. After a desperate resistance it was decided to go on fighting to the end. Finally, the N.C.O. and one man only were left, both being wounded. The Germans came up and shouted to them to lay down their arms. The German commander, however, signed to them to keep their arms, and then asked for permission to shake hands with the wounded N.C.O., who was carried off on his stretcher with his rifle by his side."

WITH THE BRITISH FORCES FIGHTING ALONG THE FRANCO-BELGIAN FRONTIER.

The first of these scenes from the battlefields of Southern Belgium shows British infantry waiting under cover for the Germans. A British field gun covered with wheat for the purpose of concealing its presence from aeroplanes is seen in the second. The third gives us a glimpse of some of the Staffordshire Regiment in a trench on the Franco-Belgian frontier.

Other nations win by the fury of their assault. The British do not as a rule. They have always had a peculiar, disconcerting way of lining up on the defensive to invite attack, letting the enemy approach perilously near, then shooting at short range with murderous precision. It is a method of warfare that supposes for its success a solid strength of character and a kind of cold-blooded intrepidity. To watch, with steady eye and hand and unquaking bowels,

Temperament in the firing-line a great host of enemies sweeping up against one's position, the steel gleaming in their hands and the deadly lust of battle gathering in their eyes as the speed of their advance increases, requires an unusual sort of temperament. Our race has this temperament. With it we have won most of our land battles.

Nearly all the apparent advantages are against the defender. For the assailant can choose his point for attack, and often concentrate against it in superior numbers, before the defender can in turn strengthen himself. Therefore all Continental experts on warlike operations agree in advocating attacking at every opportunity. But it is not

by the most daring and skilful method. Their proper rôle was to make aerial reconnaissances for the information of the Commander-in-Chief and his Staff, and then to help the gunners in finding the range and position of hostile troops and batteries. But when German flying machines came soaring over our trenches and making signals directing the German guns against our men, the British airmen attacked.

Far below, along the canal and among the hills, our army watched with wondering eyes the first great duels in the air. It was always a case of British hawk against German heron; for the Teutons, though skilful aviators, had not much stomach for the new kind of fighting. But each of the British officers, working with a pilot, was a practised revolver shot, who had thought out the best way to conduct a sky duel. Helped by his pilot, he got the vantage position and fired, and German machine after machine fell with its dead passengers to earth. Later in the campaign, when a new kind of machine-gun was mounted on many British flying machines, the German airmen became still more averse from a combat; but right from the beginning, at Mons, the Teutonic aerial

scouts learned by tragic experience that their Emperor's boast of Germany having won the dominion of the air was somewhat premature.

Unfortunately the battle at Mons was not allowed to end as it began. First of all, the want of success of the immediate neighbours of the First British Army Corps—the Fifth French Army and its two reserve divisions, which failed to hold the Sambre between Charleroi and Namur— told against the British Expeditionary Force. For as the Germans had forced the passage of the Sambre the day before—that is, on Saturday—the French army was obliged to retreat south. In so doing, it exposed the right flank of the British force to a turning attack by General von Buelow's army. To prevent this the British had to retire over the French frontier, and thus keep in line with the withdrawing French front.

GENERAL VON KLUCK AND HIS STAFF.
General Alexander von Kluck, here sitting in his motor-car, was born in 1846, twice wounded at Metz in 1870, and appointed commander of the 1st German Army Corps in 1907. In the fighting at Mons and Charleroi he outmanœuvred the French Generalissimo, and was only beaten at the former place by the indomitable valour of the British troops and the courage and resourcefulness of their commanders.

the English way—at least in land warfare—and the more impetuous Scot and Irishman and Welshman now adopt the English way, though when it comes to the charge against the foe that has broken down in his attack, the Celt excels often his brother-in-arms in fury of onset.

Had the Battle of Mons ended as it began, with the British and Germans in about equal numbers, the Germans, it is beyond a doubt, would have broken against our trenches, and then been pursued and routed. For the German infantry was helpless. It could not fire straight; it could not take cover; it could not operate in extended order and thus escape largely from gun fire and musketry fire. The foot soldiers of the two German army corps first brought up against us were knocked down like ninepins; only their brilliant machine-

Germans saved by their machine-guns gun sections saved them, time after time, from rout. The German cavalry was in no better position. Our horsemen, in anything like a fight with equal numbers, had them at their mercy. Even when our light cavalry met the German dragoons, with more powerful mounts, the British won.

In the new field of warfare—the sky—the same personal ascendancy of the Briton over the Teuton was quickly gained. Our airmen protected our infantry from gun-fire

And this was only the preliminary difficulty that faced the British commander. Even if the French had managed to hold Charleroi, his position would have been extremely perilous. For in accordance with the Kaiser's command that the English should be exterminated, a great enveloping movement was going on around Mons. General Joffre telegraphed to Sir John French the news that at least three German army corps were, at five o'clock on Sunday afternoon, August 23rd, moving against the British front, while at the same time another corps was making a turning movement from the direction of Tournai. As it afterwards appeared, five army corps, with reserves, numbering over 300,000 men, were being launched by the German General Staff against the British force of 80,000 men. In artillery the British were outnumbered by four to one, in men by three to one, when 20,000 British reserves arrived. Such were the circumstances in which the most glorious retreat in British history had suddenly to be conducted.

SCENE OF THE HEROIC STAND OF L BATTERY, R.H.A., NEAR COMPIEGNE.

The battery horses were being watered when suddenly, from a distant range, the German guns opened a murderous fire. All the horses were soon killed, and most of the men wounded or killed. Of the three guns which got into action two were quickly silenced.

The remaining gun was fought by three men, as described on page 18, till both sides had "had enough of it," and our brave fellows were able to creep behind the haystacks seen on the left of the picture, where they were eventually rescued. The picture is from a sketch by Sergeant-Major Darrell, V.C.

GERMAN TROOPS, FLUSHED WITH EXPECTATIONS OF VICTORY, TRAPPED BY THE ALLIES NEAR CAMBRAI.

A deadly trap was laid for the advancing German infantry near Cambrai in the shape of a masked battery of French artillery and machine guns, supported by entrenched infantry and British cavalry, during the retreat from Mons. A desultory fire from the French infantry stationed at intervals between the masked guns, drew the Germans across an intervening field. At first they advanced in broken lines. Then, their boldness increasing as the French infantry fire diminished, a massed brigade proceeded to cross the fatal ground. When they were within a range of about 250 yards, the French artillery pieces suddenly sent a hurricane of shrapnel through the German ranks, while the ambuscaded machine guns also opened fire. Some of the British cavalry who were posted in support of the French troops may be seen on the right-hand side in the foreground of the drawing, which was made from sketches by one who was present during the action.

CHAPTER XXVII.

THE ANGLO-FRENCH RETREAT FROM MONS AND CHARLEROI.

The Greatest Retreat in British History—Preparing for a German Sedan—Élan of the French—The Passage of the Meuse—German Spies in Namur—The British Stand at Tournai—The German Surprise—The Wreck of Mons—Perils of the Retreat—Tactics of the Peninsular War—Sir Charles Fergusson's Division—How the Cavalry Fought—Maubeuge—Sir John French and General Sordet —Timely Reinforcements—Escape from the Iron Ring.

WHILE the British Expeditionary Force was gallantly beating back one hundred thousand German troops at Mons, on the afternoon of Sunday, August 23rd, 1914, things were going badly everywhere else on the northern front of the Allies. There was a general retreat from the coast to the Meuse below Sedan, following on an unsuccessful attempt to destroy the German armies in Belgium. General Joffre had intended merely to hold back the German advance from Brussels, while striking in its rear. With this design the front, running from Arras through Mons and Charleroi to Namur, was defended by General D'Amade at Arras with about 40,000 reserve troops of the Territorial class, by Sir John French with 80,000 British regular soldiers at Mons, by the Fifth French Army of 200,000 first-line troops at Charleroi, and by a force of some 25,000 Belgian troops at Namur. The total allied troops in this field of battle were thus about 345,000 men. Opposed to them were something like 700,000 German troops.

The French commander-in-chief was not apparently aware of this condition of things. He did not suspect that the German army below Brussels outnumbered his own northern forces by two to one. And, thinking that the line from Arras to Namur would be safely held, he launched two other French armies on a too-daring offensive movement. One of these French armies, operating on the Meuse between Namur and Givet, advanced into the difficult, wooded, broken country of the Ardennes. Still farther south along the Meuse, near Sedan, another French army marched northward to the wild, beautiful valley of the little Semois River, and continued northward to the little old Luxemburg town

of Neufchateau. The idea seems to have been for the two attacking French armies to clear the Ardennes of German troops and then strike at Liège, and there cut the communications of the great German host in Central Belgium. With this host severed from its base of supplies and held from Mons to Namur, there might have been a Sedan for the Germans on a vast scale, with a million of them encircled, with no ammunition and little food.

The French fought well at all points; they fought fiercely, terribly, madly. The French gunners, with their light, handy, quick-firing field artillery, were superb in both cool courage and steady skill. They had the best gun of its kind in the world, and they fought with it in an heroic way. The French infantry was also splendid, gallant in bayonet attack and desperately stubborn in defence, and the swordsmanship of the cavalry was a revelation to the Uhlans. But all this availed nothing. The two attacking armies were not in sufficient number to make headway against the German forces collected in the Ardennes under the Duke of Würtemberg. Germany had thrown her sword into France and was using only the scabbard to keep back Russia on her eastern frontier. There were twenty-five army corps of first-line troops over the western German frontier —the entire regular army of more than a million men; and mingled with these were numerous reserve army corps amounting to another half a million or more. At all points of the fighting-line there were two Germans against one Frenchman, two Krupp guns against one French gun, and in regard to machine-guns the odds were still heavier against our allies.

In spite of the delay to part of the German forces at Liège, France had not been able to carry out her

FIRST GERMAN FLAG CAPTURED BY THE FRENCH.

A trophy at the Ministry of War in Paris. The trooper who captured it was awarded £200 by a Parisian patriot.

mobilisation with the effectiveness and completeness that marked the aggressive Teutonic effort. The enemy had reached her northern border in overpowering numbers. The German forces in the Ardennes and Luxemburg, screened from aerial observation by the forests, were certainly stronger than the French Military Staff expected. The result was that the French army operating on the Semois was so violently repulsed that all the French territory to the south, from Mezières to the Argonne Forest, was won by the Germans.

Still more unhappy was the French army that was working more northward along the Meuse between Dinant and Mezières. It was thrown back to the river, and at Givet the passage of the Meuse was forced by the victorious Germans. It was mainly this disaster at Givet which determined the retreat of the rest of the allied line from Namur to Charleroi and Mons. For at Givet the Germans had won a position of tremendous advantage. They were at least twenty-five miles in the rear of the allied line at Namur. By marching directly westward they would have occupied Philippeville, Rance, Avesnes, Landrecies, Le Cateau, and Cambrai — right across the lines of retreat of the Belgian force, the Fifth French Army, and the British Expeditionary Force. As these three allied armies were already held in front by a much more powerful host, their position obviously became one of extreme peril. At Namur the commander tried to get the garrisons of each battered fort to gather together and retire quickly. But, with the

A charming view of Avesnes. And in the circle we have a glimpse of the little old Luxemburg town of Neufchateau.

In the wild, beautiful valley of the Semois. The view on the right is in the Ardennes, which the French hoped to clear of the enemy.

thoroughness that characterised all their military preparations, the Germans had ordered their spies in Namur to cut the underground telephonic communications between the forts. At the same time the enemy opened the Meuse lock-gates at Namur and lowered the water defences of the city so that their troops could enter it. Then each Belgian regiment had to fight its way out of Namur separately, against tremendous odds, and then strike into the country, with the Germans in hot pursuit, and struggle on till it met the retreating French army.

In the meantime the large French force of 200,000 men at Charleroi had already lost the command of the Sambre between Charleroi and Namur. For the Germans crossed at the village of Tamines in the afternoon of Friday, August 21st, and the French army began to withdraw on Saturday, August 22nd. Their line, however, might only have bent back somewhat, if their commander had had simply to continue to resist the pressure of the army of General von Buelow and part of the army of General von Hausen. But when the passage of the Meuse was forced by the enemy at Givet, two days' march in their rear, the French at Charleroi were compelled to withdraw for a long distance with all possible speed.

In fact, it was a question if they could save themselves from annihilation or surrender. With two German armies of 400,000 men pressing them behind or marching ahead to get on their flanks, while another hostile force threatened their line of retreat from a spot two days' march in front of them, the men of the Fifth French Army were in no position to help their British friends on their left at Mons. They could not even attempt any combined action. Hurriedly, desperately, they had to fight their way back, in rearguard action after rearguard action. Their cavalry was soon tired out by charging continually to save guns or infantry, till at last the horses could not move. Happily, General Joffre had arranged behind them a second line of reserves, on which they were falling back, and some

WHERE THE FRENCH PREPARED FOR A GERMAN SEDAN. The lower picture is of storied Mezières, all French territory south of which, to the Argonne, was occupied by the Germans.

FRENCH PATROL TAKING COVER ALONG A RIVER-BED IN THE VOSGES.

When the French, after their early dash on Altkirch and Mulhausen, retired to the Vosges, they took up strong positions in the passes of that wildly picturesque mountainous district. Here they took advantage of all the cover they could find, moving their patrols along the bosky banks of the river-beds or other wooded shelter, which provided much natural protection from the aerial scouts of the enemy.

MEN OF DESTINY—THE LEADERS OF THE ALLIES AT THE FRONT.
General French and General Joffre directing operations at the front. The artist, M. Thiriat, to whose gifted pencil we are indebted for the above picture, wrote: " At night, somewhere near the front, inside an abandoned farmhouse in the midst of fields, the two men are together there—those on whom we are setting all our hopes, and who are giving all their knowledge, their lives, for the freedom of the world." Very often only a single sentry betrayed their temporary shelter. And automobiles waited, panting, to carry them as quickly as possible wherever their presence was needed.

Outnumbered by ten to one in men, and still more overpowered in artillery, our troops fought like heroes. They occupied some high ground a little way behind Tournai, and they had two guns of the garrison artillery. The British gunners quickly got the range, while the enemy was some miles away, and shelled them, but the galloping Germans soon covered the ground and the range was lost.

But our infantry and gunners held on, instead of preparing to retire, for they expected reinforcements to arrive. But none came—for our main army was then too busy fighting for life against heavy odds to do anything.

Uhlans to the number of 3,000 tried to storm our outpost position at Tournai. Riding through the town, they came to the muzzles of our field-guns, but were beaten back with terrible loss, the bayonet of the British infantryman getting under the sword of the German light cavalryman.

It was the arrival of some machine-guns in German Red Cross waggons that broke up the defence, and, after a fight of two and a half hours, 300 British soldiers—all that remained of 700 —collected their wounded, saved their convoy, and fell back, reaching Cambrai by nightfall. So terribly had the German horsemen been handled that they could not pursue. The heroes of Tournai undoubtedly helped to save the British flank.

After a rest the German cavalrymen rode on to Lille, and then came on to Cambrai; but they were too late for a surprise attack. The main German army that followed them in the turning movement from Tournai was also delayed.

of these reserves, besides helping the soldiers of their own nation, were able to come later to the aid of a hard-pressed British army corps.

Such was the disastrous condition of things on the right of the British force that was holding Mons on the tragic Sunday afternoon in the hot, stifling August weather. On the left of our troops matters were growing even worse. We seem to have had an advance guard of a few hundred men posted at Tournai, a lovely old Flemish town, a hard day's march to the north-west of our line at Mons. Though Sir John French had no reason to suspect a turning movement by the Germans at the time when he made his dispositions, he yet threw out these men to guard against the possibility of a surprise attack on his flank.

But in such force did the Germans come through Tournai on this surprise attack that the British outpost was overwhelmed. Some fifty thousand Germans, with an enormous number of guns, were sweeping from Brussels to Tournai, and from Tournai to Cambrai, to get in the rear of our army. In advance of them rode, clearing their path, a force of 5,000 German cavalrymen, with machine-guns, and light horse artillery. It was this cavalry force that came upon the British outpost.

Twenty-four hours before Sir John French learned from General Joffre that the Germans were moving towards his left flank, General D'Amade became aware that a hostile army was advancing on Tournai. To General D'Amade had been entrusted the defence of Northern France from Lille to the sea-coast. He was a brilliant French soldier, who had been military attaché with the British forces in the South African War, and afterwards directed the French operations in Morocco. He was now at Arras, with only some French Territorials within call. The French Territorial is not a young, active volunteer like the **The French** British Territorial; but an oldish man, **Territorials** who has passed out of the first-line troops into the militia class. General D'Amade, underestimating the strength of the advancing Germans, sent a thousand of his Territorials from Orchies, the depot of troops nearest to Tournai.

Under Brigadier-General the Marquis de Villaret, the French battalion left Orchies before dawn on Monday morning, and completed the march of eleven miles to Tournai by seven o'clock in the morning. Many of them were fathers of families, suddenly called from office, shop, and workshop to the colours. Their march tired them; but, as they halted for a rest, a German column was discovered only a mile ahead. The Marquis de Villaret had neither Maxims nor guns, only the rifles of a thousand oldish men, who had half forgotten their drill. He was opposed by 50,000 young, picked men—a regular corps of the German first-line army, with innumerable guns and machine-guns. But the French commander did not give ground. Posting his men at street corners and railway arches, he offered battle, and at eight o'clock the Germans began to shell and shrapnel the little defending force. After an hour's cannonade the German infantry advanced on the town from all sides, the Frenchmen stubbornly resisting them round the railway.

In half an hour, grey shadows were gliding through the streets, taking cover behind posts, statues, and bushes, and shooting as they glided onward. They cleared the streets with machine-guns, driving the gallant Territorials to the bridges of the Scheldt, where all that was left of the brave battalion made their last stand. It was all over by noon, the Frenchmen being surrounded and captured. But they greatly helped to delay the turning movement against the British force, and the good work they did was continued by other troops under the command of General D'Amade.

The German cavalry force, increased to 10,000 men, with machine-guns and artillery, began to operate below Tournai. General D'Amade at first could still only send men of the militia class to delay it. His Territorials were defeated to the south of Lille, and the victorious German horsemen then captured Cambrai—getting on the flank of the retiring British army.

By this time, however, General D'Amade had gathered 36,000 troops of the reserve class. Marching up from Arras, he arrived in time in the country around Cambrai to hang on to the German army corps and cavalry division which was trying to deliver the fatal stroke at the British rearguard. All these incidents told on the great result— the British outpost stand at Tournai, the delaying action by the French Territorials, the arrival of General D'Amade with his reserves on the right of the attacking German force. For, as we shall see, at the moment of peril at Cambrai, matters were in a critical state, and small things helped to grand issues.

The moment of peril at Cambrai

Since Sir John Moore marched through Spain with 30,000 men in 1809, pursued by Marshal Soult with 60,000 troops, no British commander had had to conduct a retreat in such difficulties as faced Sir John French on the Franco-Belgian frontier in the last week of August, 1914. Indeed, the later achievement of British arms is even more glorious than the early feat at Corunna. Sir John

VILLAGERS CHEERING FRENCH SOLDIERS ON THEIR WAY TO THE FRONTIER.
A scene typical of many in North-Eastern France in the early days of the war. The men marched along in solid column, some smoking cigarettes, others gratefully receiving proffered refreshments from the women and old folk of the hamlet. Everywhere the troops were welcomed with enthusiasm as they pursued their way through roads and lanes guarded so carefully that in a walk of ten miles the traveller found himself stopped a couple of dozen times, and there was trouble ahead if his papers were not in absolute order.

Moore had the odds of two to one against him, and fought but one battle, and this was against an enemy whose supply of ammunition was running out. Sir John French had the odds of three to one against him, and five to one at last, and he had to march and battle day and night for a hundred and twenty hours against a well-furnished, vigorous, and agile foe. Moreover, this foe was animated with an intense passion of hatred for the British soldier, whom he had been commanded by his Emperor to "exterminate." The German was not bent on an ordinary triumph of war, but on an act of racial, fanatic slaughter.

It was at five o'clock on Sunday afternoon that Sir John French had the supreme surprise of his life, when he learnt from General Joffre that there were at least 150,000 Germans moving against his front, with another army engaged in encircling him on the left. In the end matters appear to have been even more perilous. For in all there seem to have been more than 300,000 troops under General von Kluck, an able, energetic commander, marching, riding, or coming in motor vehicles, against 80,000 British soldiers. A hundred thousand of the Germans were then attacking the British lines, and were being beaten off. A few regiments had suffered badly early in the fight, the Middlesex

Lovely Dinant before its bombardment, showing the river-boat arriving from Namur. To the right, the main street of Landrecies, where British machine-guns mowed down masses of Germans.

and the Royal Irish Regiments in particular, but, in general, things had gone in our favour. Our infantry had to endure a severe gun fire, but they were well entrenched, and when the German foot soldiers advanced in solid masses, standing out on the skyline, it was just rifle practice for our army of marksmen to bring them down. Our cavalry had little to do, except on the right flank, where the Scots Greys were reported to have lured ten thousand of the enemy on to a terrible machine-gun fire.

The desperate fighting began on Sunday evening, when the British commander, having planned the retreat, withdrew the Third Division from Mons to a position behind the town and called in the advanced troops along the line.

There was a British officer with sixty men guarding a railway bridge by the canal. It was part of an advanced force round the bridge that had fought the Germans off all day. But when the order to retire was given, at five in the afternoon, it never reached the sixty men and their lieutenant, and the bridge was suddenly blown up, leaving them alone against an advancing host of Germans. They met their foes with rapid fire, and then charged with the bayonet. The officer fell with most of his men, scarcely any escaping. But the next day

The Place de Sépulcre, Cambrai.

PLACES ON THE LINE OF THE HISTORIC RETREAT.
The scenes on this page show some of the historic towns on the line of the great retreat. Above is a general view of the French city of Lille.

some Belgians picked up ten of our men who were still living and took them to a convent. They said they had found 5,000 Germans dead or wounded by the bridge, and only sixty British! There had been a Scottish regiment as well as some hundreds of English troops guarding the bridge, but even so the very large number of Germans put out of action was extraordinary. It showed what a weapon the improved Lee-Enfield is in the hands of troops that had learnt to kill each ten to fifteen men in a minute.

It was this incomparable marksmanship of the British infantryman that saved the situation. Before Sir John Moore took his troops to Spain, he kept them at Hythe at rifle practice, and won Corunna by it. In the same way Sir John French and his corps commanders, Sir Douglas Haig and Sir Horace Smith-Dorrien, had devoted themselves after the Boer War to the vital task of turning every regular soldier in the British Army into a

General view of Tournai, near which town 700 British soldiers made a splendid stand against 5,000 Uhlans.

crack shot. The thing was done by very simple means. Each man who qualified was given a few pence more a week. The prize was nothing, but the spirit of emulation it excited in all the regiments proved a grand factor in the history of Europe. Instead of going out at night, many men would sit in barracks, working the trigger of their rifle to get the rapid-fire action into that condition of instinctive control that makes a man's instrument a natural part of himself. Their weapon took ten cartridges in the magazine and one in the breech—eleven shots without reloading. The German rifle took five in the magazine and one in the breech—only six shots, and they were usually wasted. Right from the beginning the British infantryman dominated the battlefield. Rifle and bayonet were useless against him; only shell and shrapnel and machine-gun fire brought him down. His wounds were mainly shrapnel wounds, which does not say much for the 200,000 German foot soldiers who opposed him.

All Sunday night the British were under the fire of the German guns. The enemy's searchlights swung in swords of fire through the summer darkness, and whenever the light revealed a trench with figures a burst of shrapnel followed. Having four branch railway lines behind them to feed their thousand guns, the German artillerymen were not

INCIDENTS OF THE GREAT RETREAT FROM MONS.
A busy scene on the hurried but masterly retreat across the Franco-Belgian frontier. A Red Cross officer was snapped while consulting with a colleague in the combatant ranks, and, on the left, another officer will be noticed giving orders respecting the removal of the camp. The lower picture is of three Scottish officers surveying the movements of the forces across the wooded country below them.

sparing of ammunition. They designed, by a terrific, continual bombardment, to shake the nerve of our men, keep them sleepless, and wear them out for the next massed infantry attack. In any case our troops had little sleep, for the whole army was busy preparing for its retirement. It was close on midnight before all the outposts withdrew over the canal, where many of them had been firing through loopholes made in the walls of factories.

By the morning Mons was wrecked by German shells and flaming in places, and the German cavalry advanced through the streets, driving Belgian women before them to protect them from our fire. When the enemy's horse had thus cleared the path, a German army swept through Mons at daybreak, and, with its guns pushing forward and roofing the sky with shrapnel over our position at Malplaquet, the infantry attacked our Third Division under General Hamilton. There were the 3rd Worcesters, 2nd South Lancashires, the 1st Wiltshires, and the 2nd Royal Irish Rifles, under Brigadier-General McCracken. Brigadier-General Doran handled the 2nd Royal Scots, the 2nd Royal Irish, the 4th Middlesex, and 1st Gordon Highlanders. Then there was the Ninth Infantry Brigade —the 1st Northumberland Fusiliers, the 4th Royal Fusiliers, the 1st Lincolns, and the 1st Royal Scots Fusiliers—under Brigadier-General Shaw. With these three brigades were one battery of 60-pounders, the 48th, the 23rd, 40th, and 42nd Brigades Royal Field Artillery, with 18-pounder guns, and the 30th Brigade Howitzers—all under Brigadier-General Wing. The 56th and 57th Field Companies of Engineers, the 3rd Signal Company, and a regiment of cavalry completed the division, that numbered about 18,000 men.

On Marlborough's old battlefield

Desperately did the Third Division have to fight amid the woods and hills of Marlborough's old battlefield, for on it fell the first violent thrust of the advancing German host. Some of the regiments, thrown out as rearguards, got into very tight corners, but fought their way out— hundreds against thousands. While they were holding the grey masses back and, what was worse, drawing the fire of the German guns, the main body of troops marched southward. The division, however, was suffering so badly that the commander-in-chief had to assist it.

This was where Sir John French's experience in getting out of difficulties in the South African War told. Instead of hurrying up supports to his overtaxed men, and thus playing into the hands of the Germans by delaying his retreat, he struck out at the foe. On the right of the British line of retirement was the huge force of General von Buelow. If this hostile force had the Fifth French Army so well in hand that it could spare an army corps or two for operating on our right flank, our case would have been desperate. To discover the position of affairs on this side, and relieve the pressure on the Third Division, Sir John collected all the artillery of his First Army Corps, and sent it out towards Binche, on the road to Charleroi, with the Guards' Brigade, the 5th Infantry Brigade, and the 6th Infantry Brigade—some 12,000 infantrymen.

Apparently no opposition was met from General von Buelow's force, which had all it could do, with the assistance of General von Hausen's army, to fight back the Fifth French Army. Our movement, therefore, threatened to turn the right flank of General von Kluck's multitudes of moving men. For the noise of our artillery was that of an army corps working up to encircle Kluck on one side, while he was working to encircle our men on the other side. Our operation was more immediate, so the hostile commander had to counter it by concentrating troops

39

GLEANING OF THE REAPER WHOSE NAME IS DEATH—THE GERMAN DEAD ON THE MORNING AFTER A BATTLE.

Fair was the summer in which the Great War broke out, and as some of the most desperate of the fighting took place at night time, it was left for the roseate dawn of another day to discover strewn across the fields that had but just been cleared of their harvest the dead bodies of the slain. The above photograph was taken in the early morning in a French stubble field, the haystacks showing up on the sky-line indicating the vicinity of a farm where, but a few days before, the farmer and his hands had been employed in the peaceful pursuit of garnering in the corn, happily unconscious of the horrors to come.

far to the east of his own main position in the west. Naturally, he did not guess there were only three brigades of British infantry behind our one hundred and fifty guns. He made overwhelming preparations.

General French's counter-stroke The position of affairs can easily be explained in pugilistic terms. Instead of trying to parry the blow coming through Mons by bringing more troops to the threatened spot, Sir John French struck out at the enemy still more quickly in another direction, and made him do the parrying. As soon as he knew, on Sunday afternoon, that Kluck was bent on enveloping his left, he planned at once the counter-stroke on his right, and collected the guns and troops in the darkness at Harmignies, a village some four miles south-west of Mons. And from there, as dawn was breaking on Monday, August 24th, the feint British attack was made.

But there was no appearance of feinting about the troops that took part in it. The men only knew that, instead of retreating against an enemy in superior force, they had to advance and attack him. This suited them very well, for they had some of the best men with a bayonet to be found in the world. There were the 2nd Grenadier Guards, the 2nd and 3rd Coldstream Guards, and the Irish Guards. With them were the 2nd Worcesters, the 2nd Oxford and Bucks, the 2nd Highland Light Infantry, and the 2nd Connaught Rangers, under Brigadier-General Haking. Then, brigaded under Brigadier-General R. H. Davies, were the 1st Liverpools, the 2nd South Staffordshires, the 1st Berkshires, and the 1st King's Royal Rifle Corps. All these composed the infantry of the Second Division of

A FARRIER IN THE THICK OF THE CONFLICT AT COMPIÈGNE.
When the 6th Dragoon Guards charged the Germans at Compiègne, on September 1st, 1914, the regimental shoeing-smith would not be left out. "Armed only with a hammer," it is recorded, "he took part in the frenzied gallop, and wielded his weapon with deadly effect."

Sir Douglas Haig's First Army Corps. They had their own artillery and that of the First Division, with a cavalry regiment reconnoitring ahead.

Thus, equipped with a double armament of guns, they marched towards the little Belgian town of Binche, nearly half-way to Charleroi. Binche had been taken by the Germans on Sunday, when our cavalry withdrew there. The German troops, however, were not now in sufficient number to resist our attack, so they asked for help, and General von Kluck moved his men out of Mons and weakened his line in order to meet the surprise advance against his unprotected flank. But it takes some time to shift a couple of army corps and some hundreds of guns. So, for the greater part of Monday, the Second Division was able to draw off some of the pressure on our retiring front.

Its comrades of the First Division, withdrawn to the south-west out of range of the German artillery, acted as a reserve, but, having no guns, for the time did not come into action.

Under cover of this demonstration on the right wing, the Second Army Corps, directed by General Smith-Dorrien, began the retreat in the darkness of the early hours of Monday, August 24th. But the operation was still very difficult. For the two divisions of the Second Corps—General Hamilton's division behind Mons and Sir Charles Fergusson's division along the canal on the left wing—had each a German army of 50,000 men pressing on its front, while another 50,000 or 70,000 Germans attacked on the left flank.

General Hamilton's men—the Third Division —were now in an easier position, though they still had the odds of two to one against them, and their guns were badly knocked about. In one part of the field a strong force of German cavalry got round our infantry and charged right up to our batteries. Very few of the adventurous horsemen, however, escaped. Platoons of infantry ran to the rescue, and emptied their magazines into the hostile squadrons, and what the bullets did not finish the bayonet completed. But the heavy German ordnance, directed by airmen throwing smoke bombs, got the range of our batteries at times, and laid out entire gun detachments with shrapnel.

The German shrapnel was not well timed; it was used in such rapid profusion that most of it burst wrongly. But when it exploded properly the shields of our guns were useless against it. For it burst backwards, going just over the gun, and fanning out the charge of bullets in its rear. Now and then a German shell smashed one of our pieces, but it was largely the destruction of the horses that put the British guns out of action. There was no team left to draw them along with the retreating army; they had to be rendered useless and abandoned.

As the guns retired the German infantry **Old Peninsular** came up against our rearguard trenches. **tactics** By this time we had fallen back, half unconsciously, half expertly, on the ancient tactics of the days of the Peninsular War. Our men seldom held a hill—though Continental troops have done so through the ages, and like to do so still. We trenched or found rough cover in the folds of the ground, where only an aerial scout could descry us. The enemy took the difficult incline of the hill without meeting with any opposition; but as soon

BRINGING GERMAN "KULTUR" TO DINANT.

Here, as elsewhere, the Germans when they entered decided they would make a permanent stay. The furthest figure is the German commandant of Dinant (Oberst-Lieutenant Beeger). Next to him is a German professor charged with the reorganisation of the schools in Dinant. Inset is a photograph which illustrates the meticulous care with which the Germans carried out their advance movements, both cavalry and infantry being sent in small parties ahead of all their main armies.

When bullets could no longer keep back the German attackers, our men used the bayonet. As they charged they fired independently, dropping many a man before the steel reached him. Only a few tried to cross bayonets with the British. The rest fled, and were shot in the back as they went.

The South Lancashires in the Third Division took one of the colliery villages south of Mons with the bayonet, but the street fighting in this part of the retreat was mostly firing. Then came an Uhlan charge. Happily, the pack animals had arrived in the meantime with ammunition, and the troops had been served with sixty rounds each. They formed groups, and fired into the Uhlans at three hundred yards, throwing them into confusion. Our machine-guns were also turned on the hostile horsemen, while some crack **Uhlans thrown** shots knocked over the men with the **into confusion** German horse artillery. In the end, riderless horses came on and passed the British line, but not a lance. Half of the attacking cavalry was down, and the rest scattered without any formation. Soon the order came for the fighting British rearguard to retire. They buried their dead, took up their wounded, and tramped southward towards Maubeuge, the fortress town over the French frontier.

Maubeuge, with its iron foundries and potteries and ring of great forts, was the place Sir John French first fixed on for his retreat. As soon as he arrived at Mons he had had the country on his rear reconnoitred in view of a possibility of being driven over the frontier. So he now resolved to rest the right wing of his army against Maubeuge, extending his line thence to the south-east of Valenciennes. His

as their breasts rose above the top, a rapid fire at a few hundred yards smote them down. On came another mass some minutes later, only to meet the same fate.

The Germans then brought machine-guns up, but the deadly clarity with which every figure showed up against the sky over the ridge enabled our troops to defend themselves in their peculiar way. It was just like Corunna, where Soult's men held the hills above the bay, commanding everything, and yet meeting with defeat. The method of leaving treeless heights to the enemy, with a fine slope for him to charge down to the low British position, is not orthodox tactics. Ordinary troops cannot fight in this defensive way, in which everything depends on a quick eye, rapid, straight firing, and an imperturbable spirit. It is wonderful how our men, when they were in great difficulties, threw back at once to the unusual tricks of war of their ancestors.

principal difficulty was to bring his left wing—the Fifth Division under Sir Charles Fergusson—down from the Mons to Condé line. The Fifth Division, forming the second half of Sir Horace Smith-Dorrien's Second Army Corps, was to win the highest honours of the retreat. It was composed of the 2nd Scottish Borderers, the 2nd West Riding Regiment, the 1st West Kents, the 2nd Yorkshire Light Infantry, brigaded under Brigadier-General Cuthbert.

Under Brigadier-General Rolt were the 2nd Suffolks, the 1st East Surreys, the 1st Duke of Cornwall's Light Infantry, and the 2nd Manchester Regiment. Another

The heroic Fifth Division

brigade—the 1st Norfolks, the 1st Bedfords, the 1st Cheshires, and the 1st Dorsets —was commanded by Count Gleichen. Brigadier-General Headlam controlled the artillery, consisting of the 15th, 17th, and 18th Batteries Royal Field Artillery, with 18-pounder guns, the 8th Howitzer Battery, and the 108th Heavy Battery with 60-pounders. In all, 12,000 infantrymen, with fifty-four light guns, eighteen howitzers, and four heavy guns. There were two companies—the 7th and 59th—of Field Engineers, a regiment of cavalry, and five signal companies.

Driving on two sides against this heroic Fifth Division were at least 100,000 Germans—50,000 on their rear as they began their retreat on Monday morning, and another 50,000 on their flank. Some observers, however, estimated the German flanking force at 75,000, and it probably amounted to 100,000 men when the army corps from Tournai got into the fighting-line. In the end this hammer-

GENERAL SORDET.

General Sordet, who commanded the French Cavalry Corps, consisting of three divisions, materially assisted the British retirement on August 27th and 28th, and successfully drove back some of the enemy on Cambrai.

GENERAL D'AMADE.

General D'Amade, the hero of the French Moroccan campaign, led the 61st and 62nd French Reserve Divisions in the retreat from Mons and Charleroi, and moved down from the neighbourhood of Arras on the enemy's right flank, thus taking much pressure off the rear of the British forces.

head of the German host, fashioned to deliver the blow shattering the British army and ruining the entire French defensive, was able, by uniting with the German corps coming through Mons, to mass the tremendous fire of a thousand guns against the British left wing.

Right from the beginning of the retreat General Sir Charles Fergusson's division had to battle against fearful odds. Any series of rearguard actions to keep off the advance of one German army corps enabled the other German army corps to get on its line of retreat and threaten

to surround it. All the weight and edge of the grand German enveloping movement, designed to exterminate the British force, and then roll up the Fifth French Army and the Fourth, pressed upon Sir Charles Fergusson's men.

To add to the misfortunes of the sorely-pressed troops, there was on Monday a thunderstorm, with heavy rain that soaked through their summer clothing. In spite of the encircling movement on their flank, continual rearguard actions had to be strongly maintained to keep off the Germans in the rear. The overpowered British gunners were magnificent—careful in timing their fuses, yet quick and deadly on the mark. There were times when a German machine-gun began to enfilade the infantry, only to be smashed by a single shot from a distant field-piece by the artillery brigade.

Fergusson asks for help

The German gunners kept mainly to shrapnel, aiming at the British gun teams and detachments, with a view to enabling the Uhlans to make an easy capture of the horseless, manless batteries. Our men used shell in the artillery duels, wishing to smash their opponents' weapon rapidly by one well-placed shot. By half-past seven on Monday morning the division was in such grave difficulties that General Sir Charles Fergusson asked for help.

Sir John French had 4,000 men—the 19th Infantry Brigade—on his line of communications. These he brought up by railway to Valenciennes, and on Monday morning he ordered them to move north to the village of

Quarouble, some six miles south of Condé. Here they acted as defenders of the line of retreat of the struggling Fifth Division, which was trying to retire on Quarouble and entrench there. At the same time Sir John French's single cavalry division, under General Allenby, rode down to the help of Sir Charles Fergusson's infantrymen and gunners.

A strenuous time for the cavalry Both the 19th Infantry Brigade and the cavalry division had a fierce, violent time of it, while beating off the attacks on the gallant, desperate, overwhelmed left wing. Some of the infantry brigade went into action as supports to the guns of the left wing, and were shelled by the Germans. Then they had to cover the retirement of the cavalry against a German flanking movement. But this movement was going on too fast for them. They entrenched—some 1,300 of them—and the German cavalry, 9,000 strong, swooped down on their trench. They kept them back with rapid magazine fire and Maxims, but could not beat them all off, till the small but vigilant British artillerymen

THE CHEERING SKIRL OF THE PIPES IN THE TRENCHES.

"The Highlanders," wrote a correspondent at the front, "pipe all the time! At Mons they played while the rest shot, and the pipers can play with one hand and shoot with the other." One of our artists has illustrated such an incident noted in a trench occupied by a party of Scotsmen, who were holding a position of importance during the retreat from Mons, when a piper set the pipes askirling, meanwhile with his disengaged hand he emptied his magazine against the oncoming foe.

poured over their heads a strong fire, under which the infantry retired.

Then, as this retirement was proceeding, the entire German flank attack developed against the brigade. An army corps and a half—say, 60,000 men in the fighting-line—came up against the brigade, which was blocking their envelopment movement round the Fifth Division. It was a matter of 4,000 Britons against 60,000 Germans. Fighting for life, the Britons drew back and reached the cover of their artillery fire, drawing on the German right wing in extended line, until the cavalry division could attack it.

How the cavalry fought! They charged everything—even barbed-wire entanglements. They had to save the

guns from hostile charging horsemen, ride at infantry, and once, when a large body of British soldiers was in extreme peril of being annihilated by shrapnel, some of our light cavalry drew the fire of the German guns and saved their comrades. This was one of the noblest achievements in our military history. It was undoubtedly the cavalry division that saved the Fifth Division.

The cavalry, under the command of General Allenby, was in four brigades. The first brigade consisted of the 2nd and 5th Dragoon Guards and 11th Hussars, under Brigadier-General Briggs. The second brigade was formed of the 4th Dragoon Guards, 9th Lancers, and 18th Hussars, commanded by Brigadier-General De Lisle. Under Brigadier-General Gough were the 4th Hussars, 5th Lancers, and 16th Lancers of the third brigade. The fourth brigade, under Brigadier-General Bingham, was made up of Household Cavalry, the 6th Dragoon Guards, and 3rd Hussars. The entire division had two Royal Horse Artillery brigades, a field company of Engineers, and a signal squadron. Never were horsemanship, swordsmanship, and general fighting ability more effectively displayed than by these 9,250 men.

General de Lisle's brigade was the most unfortunate and the most heroic. It got into tragic difficulties, and won high distinction. As the squadrons rode to the help of Sir Charles Fergusson's troops, their leader saw an opening for a charge against the flank of the hostile infantry. So he formed up and galloped at the German lines, but when five hundred yards from the enemy, our horsemen were held up by barbed-wire entanglements. The men of the 9th Lancers and the 18th Hussars suffered severely while the brigade was retiring under the enemy's fire.

The 9th Lancers, however, were not daunted, and to them fell some of the chief honours of the campaign. One of their captains, Captain Francis O. Grenfell, renowned for his dash and skill in polo, showed how British sportsmanship tells in warfare. First he led one of the charges against the unbroken masses of German infantry at Andregnies, a Belgian hamlet near Mons. Then at Doubon he achieved the gallant feat for which he was awarded the Victoria Cross. The 119th Battery of Royal Field Artillery was struck by shrapnel, and all the men but one were hit. The team was not injured, but there was no one to harness the horses, and some Germans had started to capture the battery. Captain Grenfell saw the British guns lying undefended in reach of the enemy. He rode out.

"We've got to get those guns back!" he said. "Who's going to volunteer for the job?"

Before he finished speaking, a couple of dozen of his lancers were at his side. Since his men had seen him in the firing-line they were ready to go anywhere with him. They set out. Shrapnel and bullets whistled over them, but the captain was as cool as if he were riding to the polo field. "It's all right," he said. "They can't hit us."

The lancers got to the battery, hitched up the horses, and brought the guns back. Only three of them were struck. Captain Grenfell went on fighting till he was hit in the thigh by a bullet and had two of his fingers shot off. The 9th Lancers were tirelessly heroic. At another point on the Belgian border they outrivalled the charge of the Light Brigade at Balaclava.

How Captain Grenfell won the V.C.

VICTORIA CROSS HEROES OF MONS AND LE CATEAU.

CAPTAIN FRANCIS OCTAVUS GRENFELL, 9th Lancers, displayed gallantry in action against unbroken infantry at Andregnies, Belgium, on August 24th, 1914, and in assisting to save the guns of the 119th Battery, R.F.A.

MAJOR CHARLES A. LAVINGTON YATE, 2nd Batt. the King's Own (Yorkshire Light Infantry), at Le Cateau, on August 26th, led nineteen survivors against the enemy. He died as a prisoner of war.

CAPTAIN THEODORE WRIGHT, Royal Engineers, at Mons, on August 23rd, attempted to connect up the lead to demolish a bridge under heavy fire, and, although wounded in the head, made a second attempt.

CAPTAIN DOUGLAS REYNOLDS, 37th Battery, R.F.A., at Le Cateau, on August 26th, took up two teams and limbered up two guns under heavy artillery and infantry fire, and got one gun away safely.

LIEUT. MAURICE JAMES DEACE, 4th Batt. the Royal Fusiliers, though two or three times badly wounded, continued to control the fire of his machine-guns at Mons, on August 23rd. He died of his wounds.

CORPL. CHARLES ERNEST GARFORTH (Regtl. No. 7368), 15th Hussars, at Harmignies, on August 23rd, volunteered to cut wire under fire, his gallant action enabling his squadron to escape.

LANCE-CORPL. FREDK. WILLIAM HOLMES (Regtl. No. 9376), 2nd. Batt. the King's Own (Yorkshire Light Infantry), at Le Cateau, on August 26th, carried a wounded man out of the trenches under heavy fire.

LANCE-CORPL. CHARLES ALFRED JARVIS, (Regtl. No. 3976), 57th Field Company, Royal Engineers, displayed great gallantry at Jemappes, on August 23rd, firing charges for the demolition of a bridge.

DRIVER JOB HENRY CHARLES DRAIN (Regtl. No. 69960), with Driver Frederick Luke (Regtl. No. 71787), 37th Battery, R.F.A., at Le Cateau, on August 26th, volunteered to help to save guns under fire from hostile infantry.

For services rendered at Mons and during the retreat to Le Cateau eleven V.C.'s were awarded. We are unable to give photographs of Private Sidney Frank Godley, 4th Batt. the Royal Fusiliers, who fought his machine-gun with great gallantry at Mons on August 23rd; or of Driver Frederick Luke, mentioned above. Several of the recipients distinguished themselves in the fighting subsequent to Le Cateau.

HOW LANCE-CORPORAL JARVIS WON THE V.C. AT JEMAPPES.

Lance-Corporal Charles Alfred Jarvis, of the 57th Field Company, Royal Engineers, was among the first recipients of the Victoria Cross in the Great War. The distinction was awarded to him " for great gallantry at Jemappes on August 23rd, in working for one and a half hours under heavy fire in full view of the enemy, and in successfully firing charges for the demolition of a bridge." From unofficial sources we learn that Lance-Corporal Jarvis at first worked with his comrades. After a time, however, he sent them to the rear, finishing the perilous work alone. Wounded, he had to be invalided home, and he heard the news of the award while he was lying in the London Hospital.

─── ON BRITAIN'S ROLL OF HONOUR: THE RETURN FROM THE CHARGE. ───

Mr. R. Caton Woodville here pictures a scene following one of the many brilliant cavalry charges in which our splendid troopers, under the command of General Allenby, won new laurels for their colours, and in "going through the enemy like a knife through brown paper," displayed their indomitable courage and the results of their training in the school of General French. The "hell-for-leather" excitement, the hoarse cries, the thud-thud of the horses' hoofs over the turf, the jingle of bit and harness over, there were yet many opportunities for courage and resourcefulness, and these were signally evident in the painful and often hazardous task of helping back wounded comrades to the British lines.

RAIDING THE ENEMY'S "PRIVATE WIRE"—A GERMAN "NEST" IN A HAYSTACK.

"A favourite hiding-place of the German wire-tapper," wrote an officer at the front, "was a hole burrowed out of the side of a corn or haystack, which 'nest' was concealed by placing stooks against the opening." The illustration is of the discovery of the "private wire," but when the "nest" was entered the bird was found to have flown.

Terrible havoc had been caused in our ranks by great shells from a German battery of eleven guns posted inside a wood. Hidden in heaps of forage, that made them look like small haystacks, they kept up a continuous fire for some time, and none of our artillery was at hand to silence them. Just as they were being turned on our infantry the 9th Lancers drew their fire by a furious charge. The regiment rode straight at the guns, debouching into the open field and galloping under a heavy cannonade. But nothing could stop them. Men and horses were infuriated. They reached the guns, cut down the gunners, and put the battery out of action. Then, under fire from other hostile batteries, they rode back.

The First Army Corps at Maubeuge By many spirited achievements such as this the cavalry division under General Allenby relieved the terrible pressure on Sir Charles Fergusson's troops and guns. Fiercely fighting, the Fifth Division fell back on the southern Belgian coal-mining towns of Dour and Quarouble, and the Third Division lined up with them near Frameries, south-west of Mons. Here the two divisions, forming the Second Army Corps, entrenched under the direction of their commander, Sir Horace Smith - Dorrien. Their shallow and hasty trenches enabled them to withstand the attacks of the enemy. For they now had the 19th Infantry Brigade at Quarouble to help them, and the cavalry division to defend their flank. By fiercely engaging the Germans they acted as a general rearguard, and while they were hotly fighting Sir Douglas Haig was able to withdraw his First Army Corps on the right wing to Maubeuge by seven o'clock in the evening.

Then, helped by the cavalry, Sir Horace Smith-Dorrien also retreated from Dour and Frameries southward to the Maubeuge road. In places there were ten miles of country to cross, with three German armies hanging on the flank and rear of the British troops. The continuous rearguard fighting was terrible; the Second Army Corps suffered heavily, but they always gave more punishment than they received. By nightfall on Monday Sir John French had completed his operation as originally planned.

He was stationed with his Staff in the centre of the British force. On his right the First Army Corps rested under the guns of the French ring fortress of Maubeuge; on his left the Second Army Corps stretched out towards Valenciennes, its flank defended, as before, by General Allenby's cavalry and the 19th Infantry Brigade. This was the position Sir John French had first designed to make a stand against the enemy. But, as he thought things over in the August twilight, he did not feel sure that his force was strongly placed for another defensive action against a vastly more numerous enemy.

The country round Maubeuge proved to be hard to hold. The crops were not yet gathered, and, with the many buildings, made the digging of trenches difficult, and greatly limited the field of fire. In the standing corn the advantages of the superior marksmanship and rapidity of fire of our infantry were greatly diminished. If the troops made trenches, they could not see the approach of the enemy. But there were a few good artillery positions, and for some considerable distance the guns of the Maubeuge forts could help against a German attack. Moreover, there was a large French garrison in the town.

The cupola forts of Maubeuge were regarded as strong, but Sir John was suspicious of all places designed to be besieged. His instinct was for a long, battling retreat farther to the south, during which he could tire and beat off the enemy, without being fettered to any fort. He rightly divined, from the severe, continual pressure on his left flank, that General von Kluck was trying to hem him against Maubeuge and there surround **Sir John French's vital decision** him. And as it is always a good plan to do what your enemy does not want you to do, Sir John French ordered his weary men to set out southward early next morning. The rearguards had to be clear of the Maubeuge road by 5.30 a.m. This meant little or no sleep for the main bodies, for not a moment could be lost in retiring to the new position. There was good reason to believe that the enemy's forces, which had suffered heavy losses, were quite as exhausted as our troops. So, by rapidly continuing the retreat, Sir John hoped to evade a vigorous pursuit.

His headquarters were at Bavai, a French village with ironworks and quarries, between Maubeuge and

SURVEYING THE LINE OF ADVANCE UNDER COVER OF THE SHELTERING HAYSTACKS.

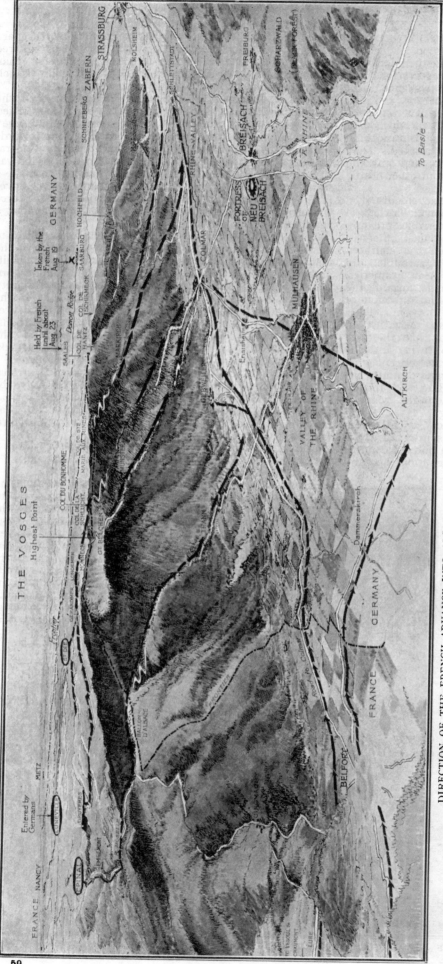

THE VOSGES
Highest Point

GERMANY

Held by French
until about
Aug 23

Taken by the
French
Aug 19

Benor Ridge

COL DU BONHOMME

FORTRESS OF NEU BREISACH

VALLEY OF THE RHINE

MULHAUSEN

ALTKIRCH

FRANCE   GERMANY

BELFORT

FRANCE   NANCY

METZ

Entered by Germans

To Basle →

STRASSBURG

ZABERN SCHNEEBERG

MOLSHEIM

SCHLETTSTADT

HOCHFELD SAARBURG

COL DE LA SCHLUCHT

COLMAR

BREISACH

FREIBURG

SCHWARZWALD (BLACK FOREST)

RHINE

RHINE VALLEY

DIRECTION OF THE FRENCH ADVANCE INTO ALSACE THROUGH THE PASSES OF THE VOSGES, AUGUST 7TH-25TH, 1914.

The French advance through the Gap of Belfort is indicated on the left, where the Vosges mountains drop away. The frontier runs up the heights, along the Hohneck, to the great humpy mass, known as the Ballon d'Alsace, and then turns at right angles towards Metz and Nancy.

Valenciennes. A day's march to the south-west was the town of Avesnes, where three divisions of French cavalry were billeted. Sir John French motored to Avesnes, and earnestly asked the cavalry commander, General Sordet, for his support. But General Sordet's men had been fighting hard on the flank of the Fifth French Army against General von Buelow's host. The horses were too tired to move; so the French cavalry was unable to come to the help of the British force in the critical period of the struggle. Greatly must Sir John have regretted the absence of his own Third Army Corps, with the co-operation of which he could have beaten the Germans to a standstill, and perhaps defeated them, though the odds would still have been two to one. But this corps had been retained in England as a garrison. Now the odds were more than three to one in men, and much more than that in artillery power.

Happily, some reinforcements were available. The Fourth Division of 11,000 men, with a brigade of guns, had begun to arrive at the town of Le Cateau, to the south, on Sunday. By the morning of Tuesday, August 25th, the new force, under General Snow, was ready for service. Sir John had fixed on Le Cateau as his next stopping-place. He despatched sappers to prepare trenches there, on the Cambrai road, and ordered General Snow to deploy from the Cambrai-Le Cateau line towards the town of Solesnes northward. On this being done, General Snow's division formed a defensive line against an enveloping attack on the left wing of the Second Army Corps. It was this wise, foreseeing preparation against future difficulties that enabled our great field-marshal to pull his little army of heroes safely through the gravest perils. When the time of extreme danger came, there was a body of 11,000 fresh British troops, with seventy-six more guns, to join in striking against an immense but tired and battered host of Germans.

Meanwhile, General von Kluck, having, as he thought, shepherded the British Expeditionary Force against Maubeuge and fixed it there, misled the German and Austrian peoples into a premature explosion of gratified hate. He informed his General Military Staff of his supposed success, and Berlin announced to the world, by a wireless message, that the British army had been driven on to Maubeuge, where a ring of iron was being fastened round it. But when Kluck's reconnoitring cavalry advanced on Tuesday morning to direct the final encircling movement, the process of extermination had to be postponed. The British army had escaped from the iron ring.

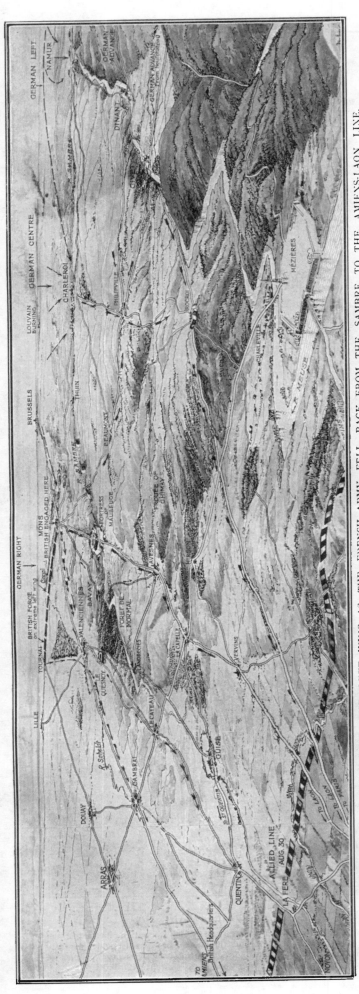

THE BRITISH FORCE HELD THE LEFT WING AS THE FRENCH ARMY FELL BACK FROM THE SAMBRE TO THE AMIENS-LAON LINE.

In the background the arrows indicate the attack by the German left, centre, and right; the other arrows show the British and French lines of retreat. The area is hilly and wooded. At Charleville tha French mitrailleuse section made an heroic stand. The two main bridges at Mezières were blown up by the French when they had passed over them. At Landrecies German troops, confidently marching through a street in solid formation, were mown down by British machine-guns. From the Cambrai–Le Cateau–Hirson–Mezières line the retreat was continued into the more open country towards Laon.

CHARLEROI, ON THE SAMBRE, THE SCENE OF TERRIFIC FIGHTING BETWEEN GERMAN AND FRENCH ON AUGUST 22ND-23RD, 1914.

The above is a diagrammatic view of the battlefield from the south bank of the Sambre. It shows the position from which the French launched their attack on the German forces. The lower part of the town is situated on an island lined with quays. While the Germans shelled this from the higher ground, the elevated positions received the effects of the French artillery fire.

ALLIES GREET EACH OTHER ON THE WAY TO THE FRANCO-BELGIAN BATTLE-LINE.

Picturesque scene, one of many such in the wooded country in Northern France, photographed as a party of French dragoons were passing a British outpost on their way to take up a position in the firing-line on the Franco-Belgian frontier. The troops greeted each other in that spirit of camaraderie which animated the armies of France and Great Britain from the outset of the war, and effectively set the seal on the good relations initiated between the peoples of the two countries at the inception of the Entente Cordiale.

CHAPTER XXVIII.

LATER PHASES OF THE GREAT RETREAT:
THE BATTLES BETWEEN LANDRECIES AND CAMBRAI.

Outmarching the Germans—Early Morning Withdrawal from Maubeuge—The Guards at Landrecies—A Trap for the Germans—Terrific Rearguard Action at Maroilles—Sir Douglas Haig's Masterly Handling of his Troops—Heroism of the Munsters—The Part played by General Snow's Division—Excellent Work of the Army Service Corps—The British Soldier and his Tea—The Battle of Cambrai–Le Cateau—An Awe-inspiring Story.

IN the darkness of early morning on Tuesday, August 25th, the British Expeditionary Force began to withdraw from the Maubeuge position towards Le Cateau, a French town some twenty miles southward, by a winding road. The army had had little sleep since Saturday ; some regiments, that had gone directly into action at Mons after a hard, long march, had been seventy-two hours without much rest.

But all the men had to be up and moving as soon as their meal was over. Only by outmarching the Germans could they defeat the enveloping movement intended to pin them against Maubeuge. The Germans were already getting some of their big 11 in. howitzers into position on the Belgian frontier to shatter the Maubeuge forts and shell the British army reposing on the fortress while Kluck's three hundred thousand ringed it in.

But, in the vast operations of modern warfare, it is one thing to shepherd your opponent into a trap and another thing to shut the trap door on him. Between midnight on Monday and dawn on Tuesday Sir John French's men entered the Maubeuge trap from the north side and came out of it from the south side. There were no Germans at hand in sufficient force to keep them in. The older Moltke boasted that in 1870 his troops defeated the French by outmarching them. To superior endurance and speed he chiefly attributed his victories.

However this may have been, the Germans in 1914 did not outmarch the French. Still less did they wear down by the swiftness of their movements the athletic British regular soldiers. Everything had been done for the Germans to promote their mobility and keep them fresh and unwearied for their work in the fighting-line. In some cases the foot soldiers were conveyed in squads of fifties in motor vehicles along the roads, and dropped near the battle-front, with only a mile or two to tramp to the scene of the conflict. This ingenious method of transporting troops from the railway base to the firing-line was not used, of course, on a general scale. There were not enough motor vehicles and enough parallel or converging roads to concentrate even half of General von Kluck's infantry in this way. But it seems likely that the foot soldiers of one German army corps could, at times, be moved by mechanical means, and though the traction of the heavy artillery probably slackened the whole movement—for the guns must go with the infantry to afford mutual support—the great thing was that the troops came into action unwearied by long marches.

This method was used at Mons and later at Cambrai, when the army corps from Tournai arrived for the decisive stroke. But it could not be employed to any large extent against Sir John French in the early part of his retreat. The Germans had to tramp, from Mons to Le Cateau and

BRITISH TROOPS OUTMARCHED THE GERMANS.
In spite of the partial aid received by them from motor vehicles, the German conscripts attacking the retreating British were outmatched repeatedly by the marching qualities of our troops, especially in the escape of our men from Maubeuge.

53

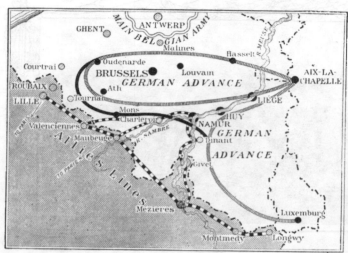

THE COLLAPSE OF NAMUR, AUGUST 25TH–26TH, 1914.
The curved elliptical lines indicate the scope of the German forces north
and east of Namur, the chequered line showing how the Allies held a
triangular area between Mezières, Namur, and Valenciennes.

Landrecies, over rough, hilly country, fighting hard and
continually against our rearguards. Being at the best
young conscript troops picked mainly from agricultural
districts, they had a good deal of natural vigour, but they
lacked the superb strength and hardness of body of our
magnificently trained troops. The consequence was that
by Monday night they were as much worn out as our men
were. They had attacked in shifts, some resting while
others advanced. Our men, being outnumbered, were
kept incessantly fighting, marching, trenching. Yet
by Tuesday morning the British soldier had for the time
got the young German conscript worn down, partly by
physical exhaustion and partly by heavy losses.

So the preliminary retirement from Maubeuge of the
British force was not opposed. The Second Army Corps

MARCHOVELETTE FORT, NAMUR, AFTER THE GERMAN
BOMBARDMENT.
Armed with old-fashioned guns of inferior calibre, the forts of Namur
were unable to offer more than a feeble resistance to the weight and power
of the German 42 cm. howitzers.

moved southward from Bavai towards the road running
from Cambrai to Le Cateau. The First Army Corps
retired with its guns along the road running by the River
Sambre, from Maubeuge to Maroilles and Landrecies.
On its right was a stretch of black country, with smoking
factories and flaming ironworks, rising into low hills
that ran into a tract of woodland—the Forest of Mormal.
Through this some of the infantry had to move in an
extended line to guard against a flanking surprise attack
by the Germans.

Towards the evening the Guards' Brigade and other
regiments of the Second Division began to arrive at the little
market town of Landrecies, nestling in the sunset by the
Forest of Mormal. Some years ago Robert Louis Stevenson,
canoeing down the Sambre, stayed the night at Landrecies

and heard the garrison guard going the round in the
darkness to the beat of the dream. " It reminded you,"
he says in his " Inland Voyage," " that even this place
was a point in the great warfaring system of Europe,
and might on some future day be ringed about with
smoke and thunder, and make itself a name among strong
towns."

How Stevenson would have rejoiced to learn, had he
but lived to full age, the manner in which the name of

PICTURESQUE SCENE AT MAUBEUGE,
showing the locks on the Sambre Canal, one of the busiest centres in the
industrial district of Northern France.

Landrecies resounded to the ends of the earth! For it
was his countrymen that made the little, sleepy canal
town famous. After a hard day's fighting march the
Guards' Brigade arrived wet and well-nigh done up, and
hoping to have a good rest. They were billeted in the
various houses, and were just stretching their legs, about
ten o'clock at night, when the alarm was given.

A German army corps had stolen down from the Forest
of Mormal and surrounded the place. Some twenty
thousand of them had captured a bridge and beaten one
of our regiments off. The King's Royal Rifles—1,300
strong—tried to retake it. They kept up a fight till four

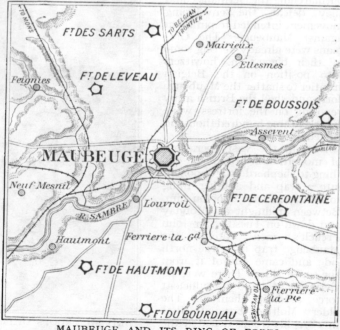

MAUBEUGE AND ITS RING OF FORTS.
Sir John French's men entered the Maubeuge trap from the north side
and came safely out of it from the south side, there being an insufficient
force of the enemy to keep them in.

ABANDONED BRITISH GUNS AT MAUBEUGE.
While the British escaped from the trap at Maubeuge in which the Germans expected to envelop them, they had to abandon some of their guns, but these were rendered useless before they were left.

SHELLED CUPOLA OF A MAUBEUGE FORT.
Here is another view of the effect of a German 42 cm. projectile on the cupola of a fort. Inset: One of the abandoned British guns.

FORESTALLING THE ENEMY—POWDER MAGAZINE BLOWN UP BY THE FRENCH AT MAUBEUGE.
When the French left Maubeuge before the entry of the Germans they blew up the powder magazine. In this and in other ways both the British and their Allies endeavoured to make the progress of the German attack as difficult and as unprofitable as possible.

FRENCH INFANTRY ON THEIR WAY TO CHARLEROI.
A regiment of French foot soldiers, with full equipment, marching with their traditional swing through one of the towns of Northern France on the way to Charleroi. Inset: A French gun section in action.

down from the forest to the other side of Landrecies and got their artillery into position. Their infantry reached the houses, and the tired British soldiers tumbled out into the streets to fight them. It was a dark night and the lamps were dim. The Coldstream Guards were out first. They fixed bayonets and doubled up the road, and some of our field artillery trundled along to support them. The British commander, in matter of fact, had not been surprised. Knowing that the forest above the town was full of enemies, he had placed outposts to give warning of their coming, while he allowed most of the tired troops to try to get a little rest. But the Germans were resolute to keep all the British force awake and active. So the Battle of Landrecies began.

How the Battle of Landrecies began

In the evening the townspeople had left in crowds, carrying away as much of their light property as they could. While the Coldstreams went out to delay the

o'clock on Wednesday morning, lining a long hedge at intervals of two yards, and firing into the enemy at a range of three hundred yards. They rolled the Germans over by dozens, but at last had to retreat at a run. As they tore away, throwing off their packs and keeping only their weapons, the affair must have struck the riflemen as a defeat. But, while they had been gallantly retaining the infantry by the bridge, great things had been happening in the town.

Here the other division of the German corps had worked

FRENCH INFANTRY ADVANCING TO MEET THE GERMAN ATTACK IN THE NEIGHBOURHOOD OF CHARLEROI.
In general alertness in the field and in the power of bearing the strain of long and dusty marches at high pressure the French infantry proved themselves capable of holding their own against any in the world. The spring and lightness of their step in marching was the object of general and ungrudging admiration.

GERMAN ARTILLERY ON THE MARCH.
Germans were greatly indebted to the superior power of their big siege-guns at Liège and Namur. But their ordinary field artillery proved very efficient. Our smaller photograph shows a fleet of motor-cars captured and commandeered by the Germans and drawn up in the barrack square at Mons.

enemy's advance, the rest of the Guards' Brigade tore up paving stones and overturned carts to form barricades for the defence of the heads of the streets. Shell and shrapnel fire began to burst around them, while the sappers were loopholing the houses. Meanwhile the Coldstreams reached the German advanced companies and drove through them with the bayonet in one of the most terrible

Coldstreams' great bayonet charge

bayonet charges in the war, after giving them several rounds of fire at almost point-blank range. Not a German got through in the direction the Coldstreams fought. About two hundred of these Guards drove a battalion down a street, their foes squealing when the steel flashed in the light of burning houses and bursting

shells. The Germans were bayoneted in scores, and the Coldstreams had to leap over barriers of the men they had slain to get more of their living enemies.

Then, having cleared this thoroughfare that led to the High Street, they came upon a larger mass of them. But, being now reinforced, they pressed on, still climbing over heaps of dead and wounded to get at the others. Afterwards, the Coldstreams raced away to a newly-menaced position, where they once more ran the steel into another dim, surging multitude.

The High Street, however, refilled with a grey sea of spiked helmets, and attempts were made to get round the Coldstreams and cut them off. But each corner house, commanding two ways, had become a rifle fort, manned by squads of Grenadiers and Irish Guards, and there they worked away from ten o'clock on Tuesday night to half-past one on Monday morning.

Houses as rifle forts

They all had wonderful escapes, with shrapnel bursting continuously, and high-explosive shells making a deafening racket; houses burning and falling down from the gun fire; rifles always cracking and rising into a furious rattle as the Germans attacked. The enemy's guns were brought in the darkness within fifty yards of our firing-lines. But our gunners brought up a gun

GLIMPSES OF GERMAN TROOPS DURING THE ANGLO-FRENCH RETREAT FROM MONS AND CHARLEROI.
Dinner parade by German soldiers mustered in the barrack square at Mons, and awaiting the call for their midday meal to be served to them in the basin which each was carrying. Inset: A German outpost. Note that the ground had been dug out in front of the shelter in the haystack, and that a board had been provided for the soldier to stand upon.

by hand—no horses could have lived through the stream of bullets and shells—and knocked out one German gun first shot, at sixty yards! For the gun was only a few paces behind our infantry. It was very close fighting for all arms.

The end suddenly came at daybreak, when the Germans were apparently on the point of capturing the town. Many of the Guards had been ordered from the loopholed houses and allowed—to their delight—to join in the bayonet work in the open. A street was left undefended, and an entire brigade of German infantry—some 5,000 men—advanced down the narrow thoroughfare, which they completely packed. It was a trap—a patent trap. A prudent commander would have only thrown a few

companies down the street in open order, to search the houses and clear the way, after planting machine-guns at the head of the street. But the German brigadier-general commanding the brigade had not yet had the overweening fatuity of his race knocked out of him. He believed in employing force, as much force as possible, and he did not trouble about the skill necessary in leading troops in the most difficult of all jobs—street-fighting.

When his five thousand men were wedged into the street, our machine-guns, from the other end of the town, smote them. They formed a target no British Maxim lieutenant could miss. The head of the German column was swept away; the men immediately behind were seized with panic, and turned and fought their way back through their hesitating companions. But these did not hesitate when the rain of bullets reached them. The entire brigade broke and fled, leaving some 900 of their fellows lying in the street. There were also many bayoneted in other streets, and a doctor who went out to look after the wounded is said to have found 2,000 Germans dead or injured outside the town.

The total losses of the enemy were literally staggering. They certainly staggered the attacking army in the Forest of Mormal. After our men sent their wounded on by train to Guise, and then withdrew southward towards Wassigny, the German gunners went on shelling Landrecies for hours. The Germans were afraid to enter. The nerve of their infantry was broken. This was extremely

fortunate for every man in the First Army Corps of the British Expeditionary Force.

For while its Second Division—or, rather, a part of it—was fighting for life in Landrecies, the First Division and the rest of the Second was in a position of even greater peril at Maroilles, a village of cheesemakers some five miles northward on the road from Maubeuge. Here a terrific rearguard action was fought from dusk to dawn against a new German army that came eastward and almost surrounded our troops in the darkness. Apparently it was not a part of the large force that advanced through the Forest of Mormal. For it came from the other side—from the direction of General von Buelow's field of operations—and encircled Sir Douglas Haig eastward and southward.

The First Army Corps, divided between Maroilles and Landrecies, was for a time practically cut in two. While the Guards' Brigade were hewing their way through Landrecies streets, their comrades in Maroilles were almost ringed by a new German host. Sir Douglas Haig found that two French reserve divisions, acting on the flank of the retiring Fifth French Army, were within call. Numbering about 36,000 men, they came gallantly to his help. But it was, as Sir John French reports, mainly due to the skilful manner in which Sir Douglas handled his troops that they fought

PHASES OF THE GREAT WAR FROM THE GERMAN POINT OF VIEW.
The upper picture, the work of a German artist, represents a fight by night in the streets of Mulhausen. In the lower, also from a Teuton source, is shown the departure of German troops from Leipzig. On the panel of the railway carriage were scrawled in chalk: " Down with Servia ! " " Death to Russia ! " " Destruction to France ! "

their way out of a most perilous position. All through the night the battle went on in darkness, lighted only by the flame of bursting shrapnel and shell from the enemy's batteries and the flare of the cottages of the villages. When the conflict opened, many of our troops were so dog-tired they felt they could not stand up and use their rifles. They had already marched and fought and worked for nearly three days, till the last ounce of energy seemed to be used up.

Some of the Munster Fusiliers, for instance, had seen some German lancers swoop down on one of our batteries and kill the detachment and capture the guns. With fixed bayonets the Munsters, in a wild Irish charge, put the lancers to flight. Then they stood by the recovered guns while the German artillerymen shrapnelled them. The difficulty was that there were no horses available to get the guns along, and the Munsters—only two companies strong with some thousands of Germans in the neighbourhood—were told to abandon the battery and save themselves. It was then our infantryman showed how he loved the great weapons that protected his trenches with their fire, and cleared a path for him when he attacked. The Irishmen harnessed the guns and man-handled them to a place of safety. They captured some of the horses of the German lancers they had killed, and at last got something of a battery team together.

This, no doubt, was an exceptional piece of back-breaking work ; but all the men were dull-eyed for weariness and want of sleep. They thought they had come to the end of their powers. But when the German shells began to explode with the sound of a thousand motor-tyres bursting, and the bullets began to sing around them, some hidden store of energy was released in their tired bodies. They went into the sombre, dim night battle with the old fury.

With bullet and bayonet they broke through and swept aside the host that barred their southern road, and their gunners cleared the way in front of them with fanning-out salvos of shrapnel fire. One eye-witness remarks that the Germans in turn might have been ringed with flame and steel if the French reserves had been able to arrive sooner. But, whatever the cause of their initial delay, the French came up in time to help our troops to beat the Germans back so strongly that they did not come on again.

GENERAL C. J. BRIGGS, C.B.
This able officer commanded the First Cavalry Brigade.

Had either German force in the Mormal Forest or on the eastern flank of the First Army Corps been able to continue their attack, they might have had, in the early morning of Wednesday, August 26th, an easy victory. For both British divisions were then dead beat. They just had enough strength to withdraw towards Wassigny, then they dropped down and snatched some sleep.

Sir John French had arranged for Sir Douglas Haig's corps to turn at Landrecies, and line up with the Second Army Corps at Le Cateau. But the men were so utterly spent that they could not move. Some of them dropped out of the march to sleep by the wayside ; all of them, after their last fierce battles, had to stop or drop. Since their demonstration towards Binche on Monday morning they had marched farther than the Second Corps. They had had to fight without support on their flank, and they had battled by day and retreated by night until they could do no more. Happily, they had so tired out and shattered the two armies opposed to them, that they could rest for a few hours in safety.

But this exhaustion of an entire army corps—nearly half the total British force—in the critical period of the great rearguard battle, on which depended the safety of both the British soldiers and the northern French armies, desperately increased the difficulties of Sir John French's position. He was now left with his cavalry, General Snow's division, the 19th Infantry Brigade, and the two divisions of Sir Horace Smith-Dorrien's Second Army Corps. In all, at full strength, these may have amounted to some 68,000 men. But deducting the killed, wounded, and missing, and the much

BRITISH WOUNDED AT MONS CARED FOR IN A BELGIAN CONVENT.
A group of British soldiers, who were wounded at the Battle of Mons, photographed with Belgian priests and Sisters of Mercy in the Convent of Villerat, where they received the most careful and kindly treatment.

larger number of men temporarily put out of action by severe marching, there may have been less than 30,000 bayonets in the firing-line, and less than 10,000 sabres and gunners to support them.

In the darkness of Tuesday morning, August 25th, the 19th Infantry Brigade, who had at midnight reached their billets on the flank of the Second Army Corps, moved out eastward to a line of low hills below Valenciennes. There they entrenched with their artillery, which was admirably placed for effective action. The German outflanking force soon attacked them. Helped by reconnaissance officers in Taube machines, the German gunners no longer took their usual blundering sighting shots, but got the range at once, and plumped their shrapnel right on to our lines. Their flying men were clever in their work of fire-controlling. They flew low enough to sight our positions, but kept out of range. Our men tried to wing them, but failed. Later, however, they brought one down.

At eleven o'clock in the morning, when the bombardment was reckoned to have done its work fully on our trenches, the routine enveloping movement was attempted. A large force of cavalry, strengthened by horse artillery, circled round, with masses of infantry and guns tailing behind it. But our cavalry division, under General Allenby, forming the extreme left wing of the British force, appeared on the scene. There was a yelling charge at the leading German horsemen, a splatter of fire at those behind, and the curving horn of the German army drew in to its main body. The infantry of part of our Second Army Corps then came into action. Their long lines ran

German airmen in action

forward between the hills in an eastward attacking movement. They were soon hidden in the folds of the ground, but they caught the German infantry, which was still trying to outflank the 19th Brigade, and inflicted heavy loss on it. The men of the 19th Brigade seem, indeed, to have been moved out in order to entice General von Kluck to practise his daily envelopment system of military tactics.

The severe punishment he received led him to think it would be better to wait and collect a larger force before hemming the British army against Maubeuge, according to programme. Towards twilight the 19th Brigade was able to withdraw south and find comfortable quarters for the night. This freshened them for the great battle the next morning.

In the meantime General Snow moved up to a position south of the little French weavers' town of Solesmes, with his division extended to the south of Cambrai. Thus placed, his men shielded the retreating Second Army Corps and its supports from an encircling frontal attack by the German army coming from Tournai. General Snow's division played an important part in the concluding battle. It consisted of three infantry brigades. There was the 18th Brigade of the 1st Warwicks, 2nd Seaforth Highlanders, 1st Irish Fusiliers, and 2nd Dublin Fusiliers, commanded by Brigadier-General J. H. L. Haldane. Then the 11th Brigade, made up of the 1st Somerset Light Infantry, 1st East Lancashires, 1st Hampshires, and 1st Rifle Brigade, under Brigadier-General Hunter-Weston. The 12th Brigade —great in the fight—was formed of the 1st Royal Lancashires, the 2nd Inniskilling Fusiliers, and the 2nd Essex, commanded by Brigadier-General H. F. M. Wilson. The field artillery, under Brigadier-General Milne, consisted of the 14th, 29th, and 32nd Brigades with 18-pounders, the 37th Howitzer Brigade and the 31st Battery of 60-pounders. A cavalry regiment, a bridging train, and the 54th Field Company of Engineers completed the division.

The 12th Infantry Brigade started on Tuesday with a hot engagement. An outpost reported that all was clear, and some of the regiments went up a hill with a large flat top. They ranged up in close formation, and the commanding officer told them to take their packs off. This was the last order he gave. From a wood only four hundred yards in front the Germans opened with machine-gun fire. The Lancashire men were mowed down, for they could get no cover. They rolled off the hill into a long straight road, only to catch it worse. For the Germans had two shrapnel guns at the top of the road that did terrible work.

All this occurred before six o'clock in the morning. The men retired in excellent order for three hundred yards, and then lined up behind a ridge. Till then they had scarcely fired a shot. But their turn came when the German infantry advanced. The British soldiers gave them lead as fast as they could pull the trigger, till they had some nine thousand Germans on the grass.

General Snow's division

ARRIVAL IN LONDON OF THE FIRST CONTINGENT OF WOUNDED FROM MONS.
Scene at a London railway-station on the arrival of the first contingent of British wounded from the battle-field of Mons. Above is a photograph of women passengers distributing little luxuries among the men on board the Folkestone boat.

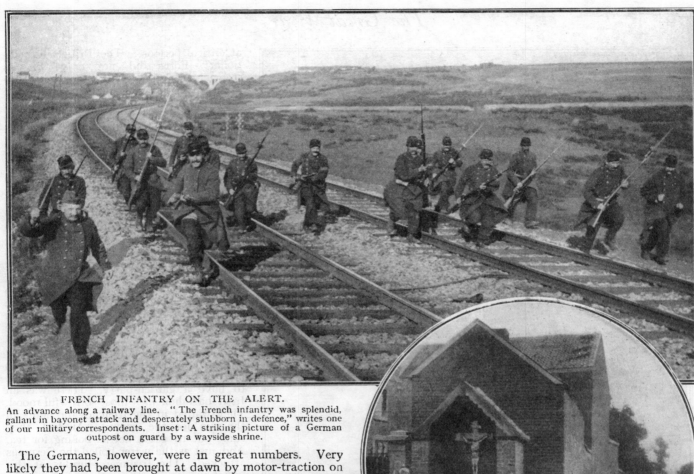

FRENCH INFANTRY ON THE ALERT.

An advance along a railway line. "The French infantry was splendid, gallant in bayonet attack and desperately stubborn in defence," writes one of our military correspondents. Inset: A striking picture of a German outpost on guard by a wayside shrine.

The Germans, however, were in great numbers. Very likely they had been brought at dawn by motor-traction on to the front of the retreating British wing. The 12th Brigade, joined with other men of General Snow's division, retired for five miles after the stand on the ridge. Then they suddenly won the mastery over the entire German force. For the British guns came up and shelled them, and with bayonets fixed our infantry got them on the run and drove them eight miles—three miles beyond the hill where the battle began.

The success of the two actions by the Fourth Division, under General Snow, and the 19th Infantry Brigade on Tuesday morning staved off the enveloping movement round Maubeuge designed by General von Kluck. At the very moment when Berlin was rejoicing over the news that the British army was ringed with steel, flame, and thunder, the British soldier had fought his way out with comparative ease. This was mainly due to the insight and foresight shown by the British commander-in-chief. Sir John French seems to have divined every detail of the German outflanking movement on his eastern wing.

Preparing for the hammer-stroke

He did this on Monday night, before General von Kluck had made his dispositions for the attack. No doubt, the British aerial scouts were able to bring their chief much useful information by Monday evening. But no one could say what movements of the German forces would go on in the darkness. Yet Sir John foresaw what the German commander would do, and had everything prepared at dawn on Tuesday to counter the great hammer-stroke when it fell.

The British cavalrymen were divided into two forces. The larger force acted with the 19th Infantry Brigade, and covered the west flank of the Second Army Corps, both the sabres and the bayonets being under the command of General Allenby. The smaller force, consisting of two cavalry brigades, operated with the two cavalry regiments attached to the Second Army Corps, and covered the movements of the retreating infantry and guns.

There were 100,000 Germans on Tuesday attempting to get round in the front of Sir Horace Smith-Dorrien's weary men. Another hostile host pressed against their rearguards from the Belgian border. Both the British infantrymen and the British cavalrymen had to strike swiftly and often to keep the enemy off. Their gunners worked like demons, and their airmen like guardian angels—with revolvers and passion for aerial duels. The cavalry was especially hard-worked. All their horsemanship was needed to keep their fagged-out mounts going, and in the continual fighting they scattered and found it difficult at times to collect again together for a new concerted movement.

General Hamilton's Third Division does not seem to have been so hard pressed on Tuesday as was Sir Charles Fergusson's Fifth Division on the west flank. The infantry of the Third Division had an easier task in the matter of actual fighting than when they held the salient at Mons. They worked in shifts, covering the retreat by steady rifle fire from hastily-prepared trenches. Thrown out along an extended front, they were instructed to hold their ground until the retiring troops were signalled safe in the next position allotted to them. When this was done, the rearguard retired past this new position and began to dig themselves in farther south. In the meantime the trenches they left were covered by the light cavalry, who kept the Germans in check as long as they could, and then fell back in turn. The next shift then took on the rearguard work till they received the signal to continue the retreat.

The Germans made some tricky moves at times with a view to cutting the rearguards off, but the British flanks were protected by cavalry, and the enemy never got very far ahead without having to fight. They usually withdrew

CORNER HOUSES AS RIFLE FORTS.
In the High Street at Landrecies each corner house, commanding two ways, became a rifle fort, manned by Grenadiers and Irish Guards, who fought from 10 p.m. on the night of Tuesday, August 25th, 1914, until 1.30 the next morning, the unhappy families hiding within in terror.

at any show of resistance, and tried to find a less costly way of impeding the well-planned retreat. But with the British troops at the top of their fighting form, all ways of interfering with them were expensive of life.

Some of the men of Sir Charles Fergusson's Fifth Division arrived on Monday midnight on the Maubeuge-Valenciennes line, and were up again at two on Tuesday morning for a thirty-mile march in wet clothes. What with shifts at rearguard actions and turns at flank defence operations, it took them eighteen hours to cover the thirty miles.

They reached their position at 8 p.m., **Work of the Army** had, happily, a good meal, and next day **Service Corps** were up and digging trenches before daybreak. The arrangements for feeding the retreating army appear to have been remarkably good, considering the extraordinary difficulties of the situation.

Here and there a regiment had its transport surrounded, and had to do the march on biscuits, or chance food given by kindly French peasants. But generally the work of feeding the army and bringing up continual supplies of ammunition was admirably carried out. In Wellington's wars in Spain French generals wrote to Napoleon in high praise of the British commander's large, abundant transport. Sir John French's Army Service Corps far excelled Wellington's. It surpassed all similar organisations. The Germans, with all their fame for thoroughness in detailed preparation, often let many of their troops famish

at critical periods. The British Expeditionary Force did not crawl on its stomach. Innumerable motor-vehicles—lorries, vans bearing the names of great London commercial firms, and motor-omnibuses with their familiar stopping-places painted on them—provided the hundred thousand soldiers fighting in strange lands with food, cartridges, and, at times, happy memories. To a Londoner in a moment of peril, for instance, up came a Hendon 'bus with ammunition that turned the threat of a defeat into a little shattering local victory. Well-engined or well-horsed, the speedy and excellently handled transport kept the British soldier fed, and thus enabled him to bear up against the ordeal of the long retreat. Many a man, worn out for want of sleep, had muscle and nerve whipped up for a new effort by a cup of tea. The eager preparation for tea made by the British soldier amid the fury of the terrible conflict struck some of our observing allies as the quaintest piece of insular phlegm imaginable. To them it was like interrupting the Day of Judgment to have a garden-party. There was an Irish battalion in a most sorrowful mood. They waited in the trenches for hours in the rain for the enemy. At last they came out to get a kettle boiling for tea. And just as the water boiled the Germans attacked. The Irishmen, furious at this intrusion, used their bayonets. The Germans howled for mercy and held up their hands, but the Irishmen tossed them on the steel like hay. But they lost their tea—hence their sorrowfulness.

By six o'clock most of the men of the Second Army Corps were able to have their tea, for the two divisions reached the line that had been partly trenched for them in advance by the sappers. It extended from Le Cateau, an historic French town of some 10,000 townspeople, to the neighbourhood of the village of Caudry, near to Cambrai. From Caudry the British line was continued to Leranvilliers, still closer to Cambrai, by the troops of General Snow's division and two brigades of cavalry, all that General Allenby could concentrate of his scattered squadrons, formed in the early morning south of the famous cathedral city of Cambrai.

Sir John French intended only to let the men rest for a few hours to recover from their exhaustion. Then he wished to continue the retreat until he had put the substantial obstacle of the Rivers Somme and Oise between his troops and the enemy, for they most urgently needed an opportunity for rest and reorganisation. Sir Horace Smith-Dorrien, therefore, was ordered to continue the retirement at dawn towards St. Quentin. The cavalry, under General Allenby, was directed to cover the retirement.

But General von Kluck was at last in a position to force at least the Second British Army to make a stand. He had concentrated near Cambrai the enormous host of five army corps. The German army corps in the early part of the war was larger than the British. It contained about 50,000 men, while ours had about 36,000 troops. "In the German attack no less than five corps were engaged," said Lord Kitchener in his statement of the affair. This means that General von Kluck brought up at least 250,000 men against three worn, tired British divisions that cannot have put more than 30,000 rifles, at the very most, into the firing-line.

Brig.-Gen. J. E. GOUGH, C.M.G.,
Third Cavalry Brigade.

Brig.-Gen. F. W. N. McCRACKEN,
C.B., D.S.O.

Brig.-Gen. F. C. SHAW, C.B.,
Ninth Infantry Brigade.

Brig.-Gen. F. D. V. WING, C.B.,
Royal Artillery.

Lt.-Col. G. P. T. FIELDING, D.S.O.,
3rd Coldstream Guards.

Brig.-Gen. R. HAKING, C.B.,
General Headquarters Staff.

It looks as though either General von Buelow co-operated in the easterly flank attack on Sir Charles Fergusson's Second Division at Maroilles on Tuesday night, or that General von Kluck disposed of a much greater total force than has been estimated. Even with as large an infantry motor-transport service as all available roads made practicable, General von Kluck could not have concentrated in two or three hours almost all his army against Sir Horace Smith-Dorrien. He had a large force at Landrecies, another at Maroilles, yet he attacked on the western flank with at least 250,000 men.

Allow for German losses at Mons and in rearguard actions against Sir Horace Smith-Dorrien's troops, and against General Snow's division and the 19th Infantry Brigade, then add to these losses the number of conscript soldiers fallen out on the march. There would be reinforcements from the direction of Tournai to set against the result. There must have been at least, when everything was deducted from the 250,000 men originally available for all purposes, some 150,000 German bayonets at the Battle of Cambrai-Le Cateau. And there were at least 1,000 German guns against some 250 British guns. So the odds against the three British divisions seem to have been something like five to one in infantrymen and four to one in guns. What the odds were against the two brigades of British cavalry is impossible to calculate —something gigantic.

Such were the material circumstances in which German and Briton clashed in a battle of tremendous importance. At daybreak on the fateful Wednesday, August 26th, our infantry began to dig or deepen their trenches, but they were surprised by the enemy's fire. So strong was the attack that Sir Horace Smith-Dorrien could not safely retire against it. He sent a message to this effect to his commander-in-chief.

"I sent him orders to use his utmost endeavours to break off the action and retire at the earliest possible moment," says Sir John French, "as it was impossible for me to send him any support, the First Corps being at the moment incapable of movement."

So on the generalship of Sir Horace and the fighting ability of each man in his little force everything depended. The battle began with the sound of heavy guns, the Germans bombarding our lines to shatter the resistance of the infantry. Many of our artillerymen masked their guns in corn-sheaves to hide them from the hostile aerial scouts, and reserved their fire as long as possible. But in face of the immense artillery onslaught of the Germans finesse was vain. Shrapnel and high-explosive shell flew like giant hail about our trenches. It was a thunderstorm, mixed up with an earthquake where the heavy howitzer shells struck, and diversified with a hurricane of lead, as the shrieking shrapnel suddenly showed blue wisps of cloud and showered down their bullets.

But our guns came into action, handled by men heroic of mould and finely trained. They had to beat down the fire of the German guns in order to save the British infantry. Despite the odds against them they did it. Our 60-pounders, throwing their big shells with wonderful precision and deadly effect, were a match for two German guns of the same weight. We had not sufficient of these heavy pieces, but what we had were handled so rapidly and with such marksmanship that they smashed double the amount of their metal on the German side.

Our light artillery, with a shorter range and much less powerful shell, was terribly hard put to it to maintain any part in the duel. The story of these batteries is one of the most moving and inspiring in the war. The losses among both men and horses were appalling, yet the sections fought their guns till they dropped. In one battery only

OFFICERS MENTIONED IN SIR JOHN FRENCH'S DESPATCHES FOR SERVICES IN THE GREAT RETREAT.

HOW THREE THOUSAND BRITISH INFANTRY AT LE CATEAU WITHSTOOD NINE THOUSAND OF THE CRACK PRUSSIAN CAVALRY.

At Le Cateau on August 26th, 1914, the men of the 12th Infantry Brigade performed a noteworthy piece of work. They included the 1st Royal Lancashire Regiment, the 1st Lancashire Fusiliers, the 2nd Royal Inniskilling Fusiliers, and the 2nd Essex Regiment. They stood against the German Cavalry Division of the Guards—the crack mounted division of the German Army. There were some nine thousand superb Prussian horsemen against, perhaps, three thousand British foot soldiers. It was a terrible charge. There was a desperate bout of hand-to-hand fighting—one bayonet against three sabres. Men and horses were mixed together in a swirling yet compact mass. But at last the pride of the German cavalry was thrown back with great loss, and many of them felt the keen edge of the bayonet as they turned and fled.

a junior officer and one man were left, but they contrived to keep a gun in action.

The German airmen searched for our guns, and dropped their smoke bombs to indicate the range. Then the shells fell thick on the British battery, and in some instances the gunners saw, across the battle-line, the German guns coming closer to them.

Undoubtedly the Germans were now courageous to the point of daring. For they were certain the most hated of their opponents were in their grasp. But in the case in question the British battery, with the smoke-bomb shell smouldering near it, turned its two centre guns on the venturous German artillerymen, caught them and hurled flesh and metal up in the air with the force of the exploding lyddite shells.

German gun fire merely deafening In raking our trenches the hostile batteries fired in modern battleship fashion—no sighting shot, but salvos of bursting cases, filled with bullets and a high-explosive charge to propel them just as the case was bursting. If five shrapnel shells missed, the sixth, it was hoped, would hit. There was at least one German gun against every three hundred British bayonets. With aerial reconnaissance and fire-control, good marksmanship, and well-timed fuses against this number of troops without proper trenches, the German gun fire should have been annihilating. All things considered, it was merely deafening. Some damage it did do—say a fourth of the total flesh injuries of the retreat—a thousand men killed or wounded. This in a bombardment by a thousand cannon for twelve hours, against troops that had no time to entrench their position properly. What incompetence! These gunners were the best-trained troops of an empire of militarism, that had organised for generations for this very battle. By continual war experience the German artilleryman improved, no doubt, as the weeks wore on —any man with a glimmer of intelligence would do that. But it was then too late. He never had a British army at his mercy again, with the fate of France almost depending on his ability. At the Battle of Le Cateau, moreover, his guns were unworn; the rifling was true, and almost every shot should have told—or one in ten—or one in a hundred. They did not.

It is true that nearly all the wounds of our men were caused by shrapnel. But, in the circumstances, this is no testimony to the skill of the German gunner. It is merely evidence against the German infantryman. When the nerve-racking bombardment was presumed to have blown the three British divisions away, the German infantryman advanced to collect the remaining fragments. Very confidently he advanced. For, despite some staggering experiences in the last four days, the deafening thunder of his overpowering guns and the consciousness of his own overwhelming numbers revived his national conceit of superiority in war.

Like the sea at flood-tide racing over a tract of sand, the grey-green billows of the German infantry attack swept on. Wave after wave of them, in companies in close formation, surged towards the British trenches. They fired as they came, bayonets fixed, but they fired just as savages do when they first get muskets. When some African negro tribes, accustomed to charging with long spears,

bought a consignment of rifles and bayonets with a view to exterminating another tribe, they were very keen on practising firing. At practice, they sighted the rifle from the shoulder, in the proper way, and shot fairly well. But when they went to war with their neighbours and met them, it was the steel they relied on and not the leaden bullets. They came on with bayonets fixed, holding their weapon near the right hip, ready to stab. When they fired they still kept the rifle at the hip in the bayonet-attack position.

So did many of the German infantrymen. They fired from the hip when hundreds of yards from our trenches. Unspeakable was the scorn of the British soldier when he saw it. It was the most disgraceful thing an infantryman in a charge could do. Falling out with a feigned injury was scarcely so bad. For this showed at least that a man's conscious brain was still working. Hip-firing at long distances in a bayonet attack meant blind funk. Held up by the mass and momentum of the charge, and kept going by the stern, alert discipline of the non-commissioned officers, the conscript first-line troops of the greatest modern military nation in the world were yet cowards in a way. They had a sort of mob bravery that kept them surging towards their opponents. But their individual self-control was gone. They could not lift their rifle to their shoulder and sight it, but, with only a primitive instinct remaining for the spear kind of attack, they kept their weapon at the hip, and blindly fired it so.

Without their artillery and machine-guns, half a million troops of this kind would have achieved the same result. It was merely a question of getting up sufficient ammunition to our infantry to enable them to do their deadly work.

IRISH GUARDS AT PRAYER BEFORE GOING INTO ACTION.
Ordered to take an exposed German position, it is recorded that before going into action the Irish Guards knelt for a moment in silent prayer. Then, springing to their feet, they fixed bayonets and charged across the plateau. Many fell, but the German position was carried.

IRISH FUSILIERS AT WORK WITH THE BAYONET.
In the fighting between Landrecies and Cambrai an Irish battalion waited in the trenches for hours in the rain for the enemy. At last they came out to get a kettle boiling for tea. Just as the water boiled the Germans attacked. The Irishmen, furious at the intrusion, used their bayonets, and "tossed the Germans on the steel like hay." Inset: A happy, if brief, interval between the fighting.

For some years they had been practising in sport "the mad minute." In sixty seconds most of them could fire fifteen rounds, and hit ten or eleven times out of the fifteen. Some of them could aim and fire one in three seconds—twenty rounds in "the mad minute," and fifteen hits out of them.

Now, when an enemy advances five deep in close formation, the modern bullet, driven by the new smokeless powder, will often go through several men ranged behind each other. This was what happened, and with such speed and precision that it seemed as though every British soldier was working a Maxim gun, instead of a magazine rifle. There was a time when the three divisions were practically ringed by enemy guns on one side and hostile infantry on all sides. There may have been a narrow gap, with a field hospital and some transport, all under gun-fire. But a member of the German General Staff, talking over the matter afterwards with a Dane, maintained that Sir Horace Smith-Dorrien's men were at last "literally surrounded."

Ordeal of "the mad minute"

But when the order came for the British lines to be stormed, it was the Germans, in their strategical position of victory, who were defeated. The nearer they advanced to our trenches the more they were slaughtered. When they were so numerous that even "the mad minute" left them standing in considerable numbers, the bayonet routed them. They came on like waves of a tide running to the flood, but broke, as waves often do on the British coast, against a wall of rock.

The picked marksmen of the German Army were then sent forward to attack us in Boer fashion. We, however, had a remarkable number of first-rate shots, in spite of the comparative smallness of our force. They beat the snipers at their own game. So all the German artillery

resumed its thunderous work of pulverisation. When the firing ceased the German Staff officers expected to find that their foes had fled. But beyond the shell-swept zone they saw, through their field-glasses, the caps of the British troops. In sheer desperation at obtaining any decision the infantry masses were launched again and again to the assault, the cavalry trying to ride down our outer trenches.

A noteworthy piece of work was done by the 12th Infantry Brigade. This, it will be remembered, was composed of the 1st Royal Lancashire Regiment, the 1st Lancashire Fusiliers, the 2nd Royal Inniskilling Fusiliers, and the 2nd Essex Regiment. They had already suffered heavily on the hill-top on Tuesday. At Le Cateau on Wednesday they stood against the German Cavalry Division of the Guards—the crack mounted division of the German Emperor. It was some nine thousand superb horsemen against, perhaps, three thousand foot soldiers. It was a terrible charge. There was a desperate bout of hand-to-hand fighting, one bayonet against three sabres. Men and horses were mixed together in a swirling and yet compact mass. At last the German cavalry was thrown back with great loss and in complete disorder, and some of them got the bayonet in the spine as they turned to flee.

The end came about half-past three on this memorable Wednesday afternoon. The enemy was then so worn and shattered by continual repulses that his attacks weakened. The weary but exulting British infantrymen began to withdraw to the south, covered by their heroic gunners, standing up and answering the final violent massed-fire of the unavailing German artillery.

The retreat was continued far into the night of August 26th by the order of Sir John French, anxious over the movements of the enemy. All the next day and through Friday, August 28th, the southward march went on, till the outworn troops rested round the lovely old cathedral town of Noyon by the placid Oise. But there was no danger of any energetic pursuit by General von Kluck. All risk of disaster to the retiring yet invincible Britons was averted. The supreme test had come, and the men of our race had risen to the heights of heroism of our forefathers. They had saved us from disaster, and shielded France.

WITH THE NORTHERN FRENCH ARMIES DURING THE GREAT RETREAT.

Fifth French Army Hard Pressed at Charleroi—The Deadly 3 in. Gun—General Pau's Arrival from Alsace—A Transformation—German Self-confidence Played On—The Red River by Dinant—Sedan Avenged at Charleville—Fighting at Longwy and Toul—General Joffre's Napoleonic Way—The Flight of the Citizens from the Sagging Battle-line.

WHILE the British Expeditionary Force was holding back the great enveloping movement of the main German army, and then saving itself and the Fifth and Fourth French Armies from an overwhelming, outflanking attack, the northern forces of France were fighting their way southward. The British troops seem to have escaped more lightly than their immediate comrades-in-arms at Charleroi. For the gallant Fifth French Army, after the passage of the Sambre was forced on its right, was placed in a difficult position by the failure of the Fourth Army to hold Givet, close to the point where the Meuse flows from France into Belgium.

Pressed in the rear by the army of General von Buelow, with General von Hausen, commanding the Saxon Army and the Prussian Guard, operating near their right wing, the men of the Fifth Army of France had to retire with all possible speed. For in front of them a body of Germans was advancing on Rocroi, near their distant path of retreat. To protect the retiring infantry and guns, the horsemen of the two divisions of French cavalry on the western flank rode their mounts to a standstill. As we have seen, their commander, General Sordet, was unable to get the horses to move afterwards to help our men in their hour of difficulty.

The light, deadly 3 in. French gun proved superb in the rearguard actions. It was so handy, so mobile, and yet so terribly effective. With a little support from

its own troops it could break the force of an attack, and then rapidly withdraw to a new position from which to continue its work. Two divisions of the Fifth French Army, however, are said to have suffered somewhat heavily in the retreat. But at least it held the Germans who were pursuing it.

Then General Joffre showed what kind of man he was. Just where he had been struck he struck back. General Pau arrived from Alsace with large reinforcements, and the Fifth Army, that seemed so weak, suddenly became the strongest in France. Increased by a masterly use of railway transportation to four army corps, it unexpectedly turned on its pursuer at Guise. The German Guard, its reserve corps, and the Tenth German Army Corps were thoroughly defeated, the Guard and the Tenth Corps being driven over the Oise. The French commander-in-chief had, with characteristic subtlety, played on the overweening self-confidence of the German general, who regarded himself as advancing from victory to victory. He was tripped up and thrown back across the river by a retreating army.

The struggles of the Fourth Army, operating from the Meuse, were heroic. Round the picturesque old riverside town of Dinant, where they had triumphed a little while before, the French were heavily outnumbered. They fell back, and their artillery, from the distant wooded heights above the river, swept the advancing German invaders with melinite shell; while the infantry left their trenches for fresh positions southward. The

THE MULE AS AN AID IN TRANSPORT.
With the motor-lorry and the horse the mule took its place in the French supply column and proved of excellent service, as it has done in the British Indian frontier wars.

WHERE THE FRENCH ARMY TURNED ON THE PURSUERS.
At Guise the Fifth French Army, reinforced, turned and routed the Germans. The above view shows a group of Uhlans entering Guise after the bombardment. Inset: A view in the old quarter of the town.

Germans in their hour of victory were prodigal of life. At any cost to themselves they bore back the Frenchmen in the mass attacks that German commanders regarded as the only effective use of infantry.

The wide, beautiful river was strewn with floating bodies of men and horses, and in some hotly-contested places the water took for a time a red tinge. The ravines with their flashing tributary rills, forming natural lines of defence along the side of the main river course, were choked with broken cannon fodder. The most furious fighting was for the possession of the bridges. But the French engineers blew them up as the army withdrew to the French frontier. Terrible as was the German chief's sacrifice of his men, it produced at last the desired result.

Just near the threshold of France, at the little Belgian river town of Givet, the German troops got across the Meuse. Some of them advanced on Rocroi, and thence to Rethel; others ascended the Meuse against a magnificent resistance by the French. At one point a French brigade of some 5,000 troops beat back a German division of some 20,000 in a fight lasting twelve hours. In all, ninety-five German guns were said to have been taken in the river battles. **The mined bridges at Charleville**

The steadily increasing power of resistance in our Allies culminated at Charleville, a town lying on the French Meuse opposite to Mezières. It is near Sedan and the great hollow in the hills in which the main French army and its leader were trapped in 1870 by Germans occupying the encircling heights. The modern French general was determined to avenge Sedan in his own way, and enable his tired troops to withdraw safely.

On Monday, August 24th, the town of Charleville was evacuated. The civilians were sent away to join the hundreds of thousands of homeless wanderers. The French army also retired, leaving a few machine-guns behind, and the French gunners concealed themselves in positions commanding the town and the three bridges that connected it with Mezières. The following day the German advanced guards came towards the two towns. They rode across the bridges into the deserted streets, and after they crossed three tremendous explosions took place behind them. The bridges, mined in preparation, had been fired. The German cavalrymen were smitten by machine-gun fire; but having Maxims with them, and, finding their foes were not numerous, they made a stand. Every French machine-gun firer was at last brought down, but at a dreadful price.

THE CASTLE AND FORTIFIED ROCK OF BELFORT.
The scene of the famous siege in 1870. It was here, in the Place des Armes, that General Pau decorated Capt. Langlois, of the French Aviation Corps, for his daring flight from Verdun to Metz.

When the main invading army advanced along the river valley, the French artillery high on the hills raked the column with shrapnel. The head of it was blown away; but, under a continual gun fire, the sappers threw their pontoon bridges across the Meuse, while the German artillerymen had to engage in a duel with the French. But the Frenchmen went on firing at the river bank until the signal was given to retire. Afterwards, between Charleville and Rethel, there was another stubborn battle, with the Germans pushing on, in reckless bravery against gun fire, and winning a victory that was also a grave.

Eastward, between Charleville and the great fortress of Verdun, the sag of the French forces went on. An **German Crown Prince at Longwy** army from Charleville—or rather, from its sister town of Mezières—was repulsed from the Semois region of the Ardennes by Duke Albrecht of Würtemberg with a large force. Then at Longwy, an antiquated fortress town near Verdun, the army of the Crown Prince succeeded in bursting into France, after a long siege operation, and advanced towards the Forest of Argonne on August 27th.

On that day, the day after the Le Cateau battle, things looked very black for France. The British army did not know yet if it had saved itself. Everywhere else, from the coast almost to Verdun, there was a Franco-British retreat. At Nancy, on August 25th, there had been a fierce encounter between the Crown Prince of Bavaria and the garrison of Toul.

WAR BENEATH THE EARTH.
Unable on one occasion to silence a German gun, the French drove a gallery fifty yards through the ground to a spot immediately under the gun, with the result shown in our illustration.

LAND-MINE EXPLOSION.
The terrific displacement of earth on the explosion of one of the land-mines laid during war is shown very graphically in the above remarkable photograph.

Ninth Army, formed of three corps from the south. What is still more important, General Joffre, while leaving his re-formed battle-front to test the enemy's strength again in such battles as that at Guise, continued the general retreat on France. For he found that the new Sixth French Army, being mainly reserve troops, was not strong enough for his secret purpose. It was so unsuccessful in resisting the attack of General von Kluck's great army that all Northern France had to be left open to the enemy. But General Joffre was not perturbed. His single aim was to defeat the enemy. He was fighting in the Napoleonic way. He had a strong general reserve near Paris. It could be used to reinforce the allied line at any point where the enemy could be pierced or turned. General Joffre waited for his opportunity. The nearer Kluck came to Paris the greater danger he would run.

Meanwhile, throughout Northern France was the unexpected, sublimely pathetic spectacle of French women and children fleeing again from the old foe. First came the vast, stricken multitudes of Flemings from over the border. Scarcely had they crossed the frontier southward when French figures began to mingle with them. The flight from the neighbourhood of the sagging battle-line was heartbreaking at times to see—the broken men coming from the lost trenches, the death-carts rumbling along the roads, and the stream of hundreds of thousands of families. It was the menace of the Uhlans and the terror born in Belgium that made them homeless. In the same districts in 1870 there was not such sickening fear of the German. He had become worse since the age of Bismarck.

But General Joffre was working to improve the splendid fighting forces of his great nation. Under his direction General D'Amade, on the left of the British force, organised a new Sixth Army, out of four reserve army divisions, a regular army corps, and General Sordet's cavalry. On the right of our troops came the famous victorious General Pau. Then, between General Pau's Fifth Army and the Fourth Army, General Foch interposed with a new

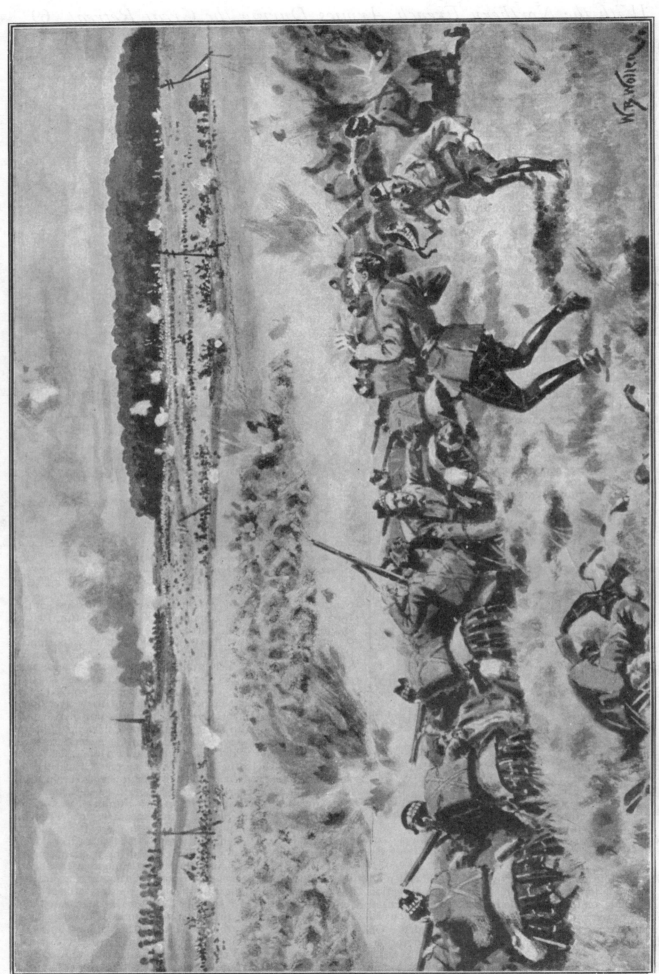

THE BATTLE OF CAMBRAI—WHERE THE GORDONS WERE TRAPPED BY THE ENEMY.

During the Battle of Cambrai the Gordons were in the trenches at seven o'clock on the morning of August 26th, 1914. The Germans were holding the village and wood beyond the railway. In the course of the afternoon an officer galloped up to the trenches with an order for their retirement. He had time to give the order only to one battalion when he was killed. The result was that only part of the Gordons effected a retirement. The others were cut off, and the majority of them had to be reported as missing. A few, however, hewed their way back to the British lines. Most of the company which got the order to retire were wounded as they made their way across the open country under the enemy's fire. "Though," wrote one of the men, "there was a rumour next day that Colonel Gordon was all right, we never saw him again."

70

CHAPTER XXX.

THE COURSE OF EVENTS FROM MONS TO LEMBERG.

British Marines at Ostend—Lord Kitchener's First Speech as War Minister—The Rally from Overseas—Mr. Asquith's Appeal—Chancellor and War Finance—Japanese Ultimatum to Germany—Mines on the High Seas—The Balkan Imbroglio—Crown Prince and Kaiser—Parliament and King Albert—French Successes in Lunéville and Nancy—Surrender of Togoland and Apia—Operations in Poland and Galicia—Mr. Churchill and the American Interviewer.

SIMULTANEOUSLY with the retreat of the Allies from Mons, the advance guard of Uhlans of the German right wing, which was forging its way to the Belgian coast and that of North-East France, began on August 23rd a raid through Thielt, Thourout, and Leffinge, towards Ostend. The mail boat Marie Henriette was there commandeered for the conveyance of all the regular troops still left in the town to Antwerp—the main garrison having been transferred thence on the 21st. In order to avoid German reprisals, the town-guard was disarmed. A large part of the civil population had already departed—the majority for England. The British admiral, who was lying outside with his fleet, and was aware from his aviators of the presence in the immediate neighbourhood of marauding Uhlans, offered to land a force sufficient to defend the town, but the offer was declined. The City Fathers, however, altered their minds when they heard of an engagement between Germans and a sortie party of Belgian troops from Antwerp towards Malines ; and in response to a request to the British Government through the Belgian Minister in London, Count de Lalaing, the First Lord of the Admiralty commissioned the admiral to land a force of Marines, with quick-firing machine-guns, at Ostend. In these operations round Malines a German detachment drove captured civilians, women, and children before them in order to prevent the Belgian soldiers, defending their own homeland, from firing at the invaders.

And what of the situation in England? On August 25th Lord Kitchener made his first speech as War Minister in the House of Lords. The passages in

SOME OF THE MEN WHO OUTFOUGHT THE GERMANS.
British soldiers who took part in the desperate fighting between Mons and Cambrai on their way to a new position in Northern France.

which he referred to the behaviour of our troops at Mons, to the response made by the young manhood of the country to his call to arms, were cheered with a vehemence rarely heard in that august assembly. He began by saying that he belonged to no party, for as a soldier he had no politics, and that the terms of his service were like those of the new Army, " Only for the war, or, if it lasts longer, then for three years, when there would be others fresh and fully prepared to take their places and see this matter through." The conflict, he continued, was none of Britain's seeking ; it would strain the resources of the Empire and entail considerable sacrifices on the people. But these would be willingly borne for our honour and the preservation of our position in the world, and would be shared by our Dominions beyond the seas, who were sending contingents and assistance of every kind to help the Mother Country in this struggle. He quoted Sir John French's despatch on Mons : " Our troops have already been for thirty-six hours in contact with the superior German invaders, and during that time they have maintained the traditions of British soldiers, and have behaved with the utmost gallantry. The movements which they have been called upon to execute have been those which demand the greatest steadiness in the soldiers and skill in their commanders. In spite of hard marching and fighting, the British force was in the best of spirits." To this despatch his lordship said he replied : " Congratulate troops on their splendid work. We are all proud of them."

Lord Kitchener added : " We know how deeply the French people appreciate and value the prompt assistance

71

we have been able to afford them at the very outset of the war, and it is obvious that not only the moral but the material support our troops are now rendering must prove to be a factor of high military significance in restricting the sphere and determining the duration of hostilities. Had the conditions of strategy permitted, everyone in this country would have rejoiced to see us ranged in that superb struggle against desperate odds which has just been witnessed. But although this privilege was

British sympathy for Belgium. perforce denied to us, Belgium knows of our sympathy with her in her sufferings, and our indignation at the blows which have been inflicted upon her, and also of our resolution to make sure that in the end her sacrifices will not have been unavailing. While other countries engaged in this war have, under a system of compulsory service, brought their full resources of men into the field, we, under our national system, have not done so, and can therefore still point to the vast reserve drawn from the resources both of the Mother Country and of the British Dominions across the seas. The response which has already been made by the great Dominions abundantly proves that we do not look in vain to these sources of military strength, and while India, Canada, Australia, and New Zealand are all sending us powerful contingents, in this country the Territorials are replying with loyalty to the stern call of duty which has come to them with such exceptional force. Over seventy battalions have, with fine patriotism, already volunteered for service abroad, and when trained and organised in the larger formations, will be able to take their place in the line. The 100,000 recruits for which in the first place it has been thought necessary to call have been already practically secured, and this force will be trained and organised in divisions similar to those which are now serving on the Continent. But behind these we have our Reserves.

"The special Reserves have each their own part to play in the organisation of our national defence. The empires with whom we are at war have called to the colours almost their entire male population. A principle we, on our part, shall observe is this : that while their maximum forces undergo a constant diminution, the reinforcements we prepare shall steadily and increasingly flow out until we have an army in the field which, in numbers not less than in quality, will not be unworthy of the power and responsibilities of the British Empire."

Mr. Asquith followed up this appeal for " more and still more men " in the House of Commons. Following these splendid speeches there was a rush of recruits all over the country. Everywhere throughout France in political, military, and Press circles, Lord Kitchener's

THE HISTORIC MEETING AT THE GUILDHALL ON SEPTEMBER 4TH, 1914.

The Prime Minister, the Leader of the Opposition, Mr. Balfour, and other prominent politicians spoke on a combined platform, and made eloquent appeals for recruits. Mr. Asquith's speech was reproduced throughout the world with the best effect, especially in neutral countries.

" vibrating and resolute deliverance," as the " Liberté " called it, was gracefully appreciated.

The measures taken by the Chancellor of the Exchequer, of course with the approval of the Cabinet, to increase banking facilities and so maintain the trade of the country at the normal, met with general approval—Mr. Austen Chamberlain, a former Unionist Chancellor of the Exchequer, declaring in the House of Commons that Mr. Lloyd George had " dealt with all these questions with great tact, great skill, and great judgment." That Minister also introduced, and succeeded in getting Bills unanimously passed, to check the harsh exercise of legal powers by creditors, and to prevent the summary selling up of homes. These enabled the Government to bring the moratorium to an end. One result was that when the Government placed on the market Treasury Bills for £15,000,000, a total of not less than £40,000,000 was offered.

The Minister for Belgium in London communicated on August 25th to the British Government and the Press the report of the Committee of Inquiry appointed, on command of King Albert, by the Belgian Minister of Justice, and presided over by him, to investigate the charges of acts of savagery, degenerate, abysmal, committed by German troops in various parts of rural and urban districts of Belgium wherever the Teuton hordes had penetrated. The committee comprised the highest judicial and university authorities of Belgium, such as Chief Justice Van Iseghem, Judge Nys, Professors Cottier, Wodon, and others, and their report more than bore out the details of outrages given in Chapter XXIV. of our history.

Hitherto the operations of war had been confined to Europe, but now these were suddenly, though not altogether unexpectedly, extended to the Far East, and the great conflict became in fact as well as metaphor world-wide.

Japan declared war against Germany on August 23rd, on the refusal of the latter to concede demands made by the former in an ultimatum presented the previous day. These demands were that Germany should (1) immediately withdraw or disarm her warships in Chinese and Japanese waters ; (2) hand over the German Protectorate of Kiao-Chau in China to Japan for restoration to China. The rescript formally declaring war set forth : " We, by the Grace of Heaven, Emperor of Japan, on the throne **Japan declares war.** occupied by the same Dynasty from time immemorial, do hereby make the following Proclamation to our loyal and brave subjects. We hereby declare war against Germany, and we command our Army and Navy to carry on hostilities against that Empire with all their strength. The action of Germany has compelled Great Britain, our Ally, to

THE GRAND DUKE NICHOLAS—GENERALISSIMO OF THE RUSSIAN ARMIES.

The Grand Duke Nicholas, the regenerator of the Russian Army, was fifty-eight years of age when the war broke out, and had been for some time general of cavalry and military commander of Petrograd. A former President of the Council of National Defence, he had laboured ever since the war with Japan to reorganise the military forces of the Tsar. A soldier from his youth, he gathered around him the best generals, many of whom proved the value of his judgment by their prowess in Galicia and in the fighting on the Prussian frontier.

"KAMERAD . . . PARDON!" HANDS-UP METHOD OF GERMAN SURRENDER.

German stragglers, caught by the British or French, frequently surrendered by throwing down their arms, holding up their hands, and calling out the two words: "Kamerad . . . Pardon!" Many incidents of the kind have been recorded in soldiers' letters home. The hands-up method had the advantage that it put it out of a prisoner's power to attempt any individual act of treachery. At the same time it showed a consciousness of what had been done previously by Germans who, pretending to surrender, took the first opportunity of abusing the confidence of their captors.

FLASHING THE SIGNAL TO CHARGE BY SEARCHLIGHT.

A remarkable picture of a remarkable incident during the fighting in France. The enemy at an early stage of the war showed a constant desire to surprise the British by night attacks. On many occasions they found the British more than equal to them in this form of warfare. Our searchlights having found the position of the enemy, gave the signal to the British troops to advance by flashing the sign of the cross in the sky, whereupon soldiers who had been anxiously waiting for the order, leaping from the trenches, successfully charged and discomfited the foe.

French army corps taking up a position under cover of its artillery.   At the outset the guns of the Allies were mainly occupied in the task of replying to the enemy's gun-fire, but later the balance was adjusted so that the Anglo-French artillery was able to render effective protection to infantry movements.

French infantry and cavalry with transport waggon passing through a village in Northern France.   The frequent passage of troops on active service through the French hamlets made it impossible to keep the rural population in ignorance of the great events that were toward.

French dragoons with mitrailleuses going into action.   The uses to which these handy but deadly weapons were put by cavalry and infantry alike had a great deal to do with the difference between reverse and victory; and the French handled their light artillery with remarkable skill and judgment.

WITH OUR FRENCH ALLIES—HORSE. FOOT. AND ARTILLERY—IN THE FIELD.

open hostilities against that country, and Germany is at Kiao-Chau, its leased territory in China, busy with warlike preparations, while her armed vessels cruising the seas of Eastern Asia are threatening our commerce and that of our Allies. Peace in the Far East is thus in jeopardy. Accordingly, our Government and that of his Britannic Majesty, after a full and frank communication with each other, agreed to take such measures as may be necessary for the protection of the general interests contemplated in the Agreement of Alliance; and we, on our part, being desirous to attain that object by peaceful means, commanded our Government to offer with sincerity an Advice to the Imperial German Government. By the last day appointed for the purpose, however, our Government failed to receive an answer accepting their Advice."

On August 24th the Austrian Government issued orders to the cruiser Kaiserin Elizabeth, then lying in Kiao-Chau Harbour, to disarm, and that her crew should proceed to Tientsin.

Maritime proceedings and the ordinary course of trade by vessels even of neutral Powers began to be compassed with new dangers. Up to August 23rd the British Admiralty had not laid any mines, floating or stationary, in any part of the high seas, but reserved to themselves the utmost liberty of taking action in the future against this new form of warfare. On that date two Danish vessels, the Maryland and Broberg, when taking the ordinary trade routes in the North Sea, away from the British coast, were destroyed by mines laid by the Germans; and two Dutch steamers, clearing from Swedish ports, were blown up in a similar manner by mines laid in the Baltic.

An aftermath of the Balkan imbroglio two years before, when the effort was made by the various kingdoms and principalities to finally throw off Turkish domination, and politically reconstruct the peninsula according to the principles of nationality, was the condition of Albania. This mountainous area, inhabited by warlike tribes of various races—Albanians, Slavs in the north-west, and of Greeks in the south, whose aspiration was to be joined to their fellows in Epirus—formed a cockpit in which there were ever recurrent vendettas and religious feuds. The Powers most interested—Russia, Turkey, Austria, which had a longing eye for the Albanian ports on the Adriatic, and Great Britain—diplomatically attempted to solve the difficult problem of a settlement by creating Albania into an independent principality, and this was eventually accomplished by an International Conference held in London on May 30th, 1913. The ruler selected was Prince William Frederick Henry of Wied, who was duly installed as "Mpret," or ruler, with some considerable ceremony and apparent goodwill on the part of his diverse subjects. But peace lasted only a few weeks. Different camarillas made violent efforts to get possession of the Mpret, and invaded his palace at Durazzo, which had been created the capital, and for his protection Austrian and British troops were landed. Throughout these troublesome events Prince Wilhelm did not show himself

"IT IS NOTHING, MESSIEURS—IT IS FOR FRANCE!"

The intrepid valour of the men of the French ambulance corps is well illustrated in the above picture. One of these—said to be a wealthy merchant of Paris who volunteered for medical service—a gentleman who had never been under fire in his life before, greatly distinguished himself in picking up fallen men under heavy fire and conveying them on his back to safety. When congratulated by military officers for his conspicuous bravery, he answered: "It is nothing, messieurs—it is for France." Of such was the spirit nerving all ranks in the French Army.

either very wise or heroic. In the last week of August Albania was in a state of complete anarchy, a reflection of the big war in the west and east of Europe, and on the 23rd the Prince, accompanied by his wife, Princess Sophie of Schönburg-Waldenburg, and children, fled from Durazzo on the way back to Germany, viâ Brindisi.

An official announcement was made in Berlin on August 24th that the German Crown Prince had victoriously repulsed the enemy at Longwy. That place is a very old fortress of Eastern France, situated a short distance from the Luxemburg frontier. Its garrison consisted of only one battalion, and it had been bombarded since August 3rd by the German Crown Prince's army, which had been trying to break through the French lines, in order to conform with the advance of the German right in north-east France and Belgium. After holding out for twenty-one days, when more than half of the garrison had been killed or wounded, it was surrendered to the enemy. The governor, Lieut.-Colonel Baroche, had conferred upon him by the French President the Legion of Honour for his heroic defence. It was this " glorious victory " over less than half a battalion which set Berlin delirious with joy.

Heroic defence of Longwy

The Kaiser sent the following telegram to the Crown Princess, evidently in answer to one of congratulation from her Royal Highness : " My most sincere thanks, my dear child. I rejoice with you on Wilhelm's "—the Crown Prince—" first victory. How magnificently God has supported him ! Thanks and honour be to Him ! I bestow upon Wilhelm the Iron Cross of the first and second class. Oscar "—the Kaiser's fifth son—" is also said to have fought brilliantly with his Grenadiers. He has received the Iron Cross of the second class.   Inform Ina Marie "—the Countess Ina von Bassewitz, whom Prince Oscar married on the eve of the war.   " May God protect and

GENERAL DE CASTLENAU.
This brilliant French commander was made a Grand Officer of the Legion of Honour for his fine defence of Nancy.

continue to help the boys, and be with you and all the women."

The unctuous self-conceit of this message is only equalled by the prayer which his Imperial Majesty, early in August, ordered to be included in the Liturgy at all public services in the churches : " Almighty and Merciful God, lead us to victory, and give us grace that we may show ourselves to be Christians towards our enemies as well." These eminently pious sentiments may be contrasted with another message—that, for instance, which

The impious prayer of the Huns he despatched to the German troops with the expedition for the relief of Peking, China, then invested by the rebels, on July 27th, 1900 : " When you meet the foe you will defeat him. No quarter will be given ; no prisoners will be taken. Let all who fall into your hands be at your mercy. Gain a reputation like the Huns under Attila."

When the news of the Longwy victory became known in Berlin on August 24th, as already stated, huge crowds collected opposite the Royal palace. The Empress and Crown Princess had to appear several times in response to cheers for " the fresh message of victory," and both the Royal ladies embraced on the balcony and cried with joy ! Universal indignation was felt, not only in western Europe, but in England, her Dominions beyond the seas, and in America at the completion of the ruthless destruction,

on August 25th, of Louvain by the Germans. This quaint city of 45,000 inhabitants was the joy of its own people, and the lovers of art and learning everywhere. The cathedral of St. Pierre, a stately monument of world interest, is now a heap of fire-blackened bricks and masonry. The exquisite town-hall and other public buildings of unrivalled architecture of the fifteenth century were shattered and levelled to the ground by German shells. Worst of all, the fine group of pavilions which housed the ancient university, known for hundreds of years as the Oxford of Belgium, was shattered to fragments, and the priceless library of 70,000 volumes and MS. were burned— a loss to letters greater than ever happened since the destruction of the Library of Alexandria by the **Unparalleled loss to Letters** Saracen invaders of Egypt. The excuse made by the Germans was that the civil inhabitants of Louvain had fired upon their troops ; but the real fact was that a body of Germans, making for the town in disorder after a scrimmage with Belgian forces outside, were fired upon by their friends in occupation of the city, and the Kaiser's commander, in a moment of passion, to cover the blunder of his own men, ordered the city to be fired and the ashes to be scattered to the winds.

GENERAL FOCH.
He was in command of the 20th French Army Corps at Nancy, greatly distinguishing himself there and in later operations.

The heroic defence of Liège, which has been dealt with in Chapter XXIV., came to an end on August 24th, when Major Nameche, commandant, blew up Fort Chaudfontaine, which covered the railway line between Aix-la-Chapelle and Liège by way of Verviers and the tunnel of Chaudfontaine. It was therefore of enormous importance to the Germans, and had been under continual fire since the enemy appeared before Liège. When resistance was no longer possible, Major Nameche barred up the tunnel by colliding a number of locomotive engines, and afterwards set fire to the mass. His mission was at an end, and he determined that the Germans should not take possession of his little stronghold. He lighted a fuse at the powder magazine, and blew up the fort, and himself with it. Can such an act of heroism ever be forgotten ?

It was felt throughout Great Britain that some recognition should be made of these ever-memorable events by Parliament on behalf of the nation. Accordingly, on August 27th, the following resolution was carried by acclamation in both Houses: "That a humble Address be presented to his Majesty praying him to convey to his Majesty the King of the Belgians the sympathy and admiration with which this House regards the heroic resistance offered by his Army and his people to the wanton invasion of his territory, and an assurance of the determination of this country to support in every way the efforts of Belgium to vindicate her own independence and the public law of Europe."

Parliament and suffering Belgium Mr. Asquith moved the resolution in the House of Commons in a speech loftily phrased and perfectly delivered, which moved the House to generous enthusiasm and stirred its finest emotions. How was it, he asked, that we interfered in this tremendous conflict? It was because "we were bound by our obligations, plain and paramount, to assert and maintain the threatened independence of a small and neutral State. Belgium had no interest of her own to serve, save and except the one supreme and overriding interest of every State, great or little, which is worthy of the name—the preservation of her integrity and of her national life. History tells us that the duty of asserting and maintaining that great principle, which is, after all, the well-spring of civilisation and of progress, has fallen once and again at the most critical moments in the past to States relatively small in area and in population, but great in courage and in resolve —to Athens and Sparta, the Swiss Cantons, and, not least gloriously three centuries ago, to the Netherlands. Never, I venture to assert, has the duty been more clearly and bravely

THE CROWN PRINCE OF BAVARIA.

GENERAL VON BUELOW.

acknowledged, and never has it been more strenuously and heroically discharged, than during the last weeks by the Belgian king and the Belgian people. They have faced without flinching, and against almost insuperable odds, the horrors of irruption, devastation, of spoliation, and of outrage. They have stubbornly withstood and successfully arrested the inrush, wave after wave, of a gigantic and overwhelming force. The defence of Liège will always be the theme of one of the most inspiring chapters in the annals of Liberty. The

Belgians have won for themselves the immortal glory which belongs to a people who prefer freedom to ease, to security, even to life itself. We are proud of their alliance and their friendship. We salute them with respect and with honour. We are with them heart and soul, because by their side and in their company we are defending at the same time two great causes—the independence of small States and the sanctity of international covenants; and we assure them—as I ask the House in this address to do—we assure them

DUKE ALBRECHT OF WÜRTEMBURG.

to-day, in the name of this United Kingdom and of the whole Empire, that they may count to the end on our wholehearted and unfailing support."

Mr. Bonar Law, Leader of the Opposition, in seconding the resolution, described in a fine passage the war as a struggle of the moral influences of civilisation against brute force. Declaring that Belgium deserved well of the world, he insisted that the best way in which we could pay our debt to her was by realising that this was for us, as much as for Belgium, a struggle of life and death, and by employing without haste, but without rest, all our resources for bringing it to a successful end.

Mr. John Redmond, Leader of the Irish Party, advocated the substitution of a gift of £10,000,000 to Belgium, instead of a proposed loan to that amount.

The Marquis of Crewe moved the resolution in the House of Lords in an oration of polished, sometimes **Belgium's place in history** picturesque eloquence. "By her action," his lordship said, "Belgium has ranged herself by the side of the small nations famous in history who have received the crown of glory and credit for their resistance to overwhelming forces. Belgium has ranged herself by the side of Athens and Sparta against Persia, with Switzerland against the Roman Empire, and with her forebears of Flanders and the Netherlands against the might of Spain." His lordship proceeded to review the events culminating in the great European conflict, with special reference to the action of Germany in violating the neutrality of Belgium and Luxemburg, which he described as an outrage against the public law of Europe. The bid by Germany for Belgian acquiescence in the violation of her neutrality was an offer at the end of the war to respect the independence and integrity of Belgium. That might be

GENERAL VON HAUSEN.

BRITISH ARMY SERVICE CORPS IN FRANCE.
In Wellington's wars in Spain French generals wrote to Napoleon in praise of the British commander's transport. Sir John French's Army Service Corps far excelled Wellington's. Inset: French womenfolk interested in a roadside kitchen and the British soldiers' cookery.

has ever outraged public law, or has systematically conducted war by inhuman and brutal methods, without sooner or later paying for it. The time or the form of punishment or reparation that may be exacted, it is, of course, impossible to say; but I do venture to declare that any nation that so conducts itself pays for it soon or late, and pays to the uttermost farthing. It is our part to see that the sword is not sheathed until the fullest assurance is obtained that these great wrongs will be redressed to the full. I am certain that in saying this, and also expressing in the terms of the motion our cordial sympathy with the Belgian nation, and our determination to do everything we can as a nation to vindicate the independence of that country and the public law of Europe, I shall have the full concurrence of your lordships' House."

Lord Lansdowne, Leader of the Opposition, in the course of his speech, dwelt on the fact that all who were lovers of liberty, all who could appreciate the virtue of self-sacrifice, all who were able to admire patriotism, and to entertain respect for Treaty obligations, must feel that Belgium had rendered to the civilised world a signal service by what she had done.

In an earlier chapter mention was **The French in** made of the French invasion of Ger- **Alsace-Lorraine** man Alsace and Lorraine. General Castelnau, who was in command of the French Expeditionary Force in Upper Alsace, began on August 23rd to fall back, pressed by overwhelming German and Austrian forces, into French territory as far as Champenoux, beyond which line, which practically coincides with the Grand Couronne of Nancy, the Germans, try as they would, never set foot. General Pau, in command of the raid into Lorraine, also fell back on the line of fortresses within the French frontier stretching from Verdun to the Swiss frontier, while a portion of his army was directed westward

taken to mean that Belgium, acquiescing now, at the end of the war would become a German protectorate. We could not, therefore, be surprised that the offer received no attention. After narrating the events of the siege of Liège, followed by the occupation of Brussels by the Germans, the noble marquis said that that was not the whole story. It was not only a story of a military invasion encountered with courageous resistance by an inferior military force. For it was impossible to disregard the official and authentic reports by the Committee of the Belgian Foreign Office of the infamous conduct of the invading army contrary to all laws and usages of war. In conclusion he said: "This is not the time for us who, as a nation, are engaged in this struggle to give utterance to any sort of threat, or to engage in any kind of prophecies as to what may be the outcome of this tremendous war. But this I do say, that history will tell us that no nation for the defence of the Meuse. He himself had his headquarters at Belfort before he was recalled to Paris to organise the divisional army which was to play an important part at " the turning of the tide." During the general's operations in Lorraine Captain Langlois, an officer in the Aviation Corps, made a daring flight from Verdun to Metz. At Frascati he dropped bombs on the Zeppelin station, captured at Bouillar a German aeroplane, and, though wounded, succeeded in bringing his own machine back to the French lines. For this brilliant deed the French President conferred upon him the cross of the Legion of Honour, and for " the encouragement of the others," as the French saying goes, General Pau bestowed the decoration in the Place des Armes, Belfort, in the presence of the whole garrison and a vast concourse of the general public. In pinning the cross to Captain Langlois's uniform the general said : " In the name of the Government I declare you a Chevalier of the Legion of Honour before these trophies taken from the enemy "—pointing to the guns taken at Altkirch and Thann —" and I give you an accolade with a sabre taken from a German officer." This instant recognition of brave deeds was received by the troops with the greatest enthusiasm. In their retirement Generals Castelnau and Pau always had the game

well in hand until they made their final stand. Eleven thousand dead Germans lay in the fields and forests round Lunéville, which was bombarded by the French and partly burned by the Germans, and twenty thousand between Nancy and Champenoux.

The German colony of Togoland, in West Africa, surrendered to an Anglo-French expedition on August 26th, and an expeditionary naval and military force, despatched by the Government of the Dominion of New Zealand, landed on August 29th at Apia, the chief town of the Samoan group of islands in the Western Pacific, and took possession of it from the German authorities without firing a shot. The commander of the expeditionary force announced that he had annexed to the Dominion, on behalf of Great Britain, the whole of the islands in the group which had been occupied by and allotted to Germany under an international treaty.

Among the earliest aspirations for " a place in the sun " of the German bureaucrat expansionists was the possession of tropical colonies and a naval base in the Western Pacific. Accordingly, a German man-of-war was despatched thither in 1879, and she took possession, in the name of the Teutonic Empire, of the harbour of Salnafata. Great Britain and the United

BY A RIVERSIDE DURING THE HOT WEATHER IN FRANCE.
British cavalrymen watering their horses after a forced and dusty march in the blazing sun of August. They were the leaders of the column, part of which is seen crossing the bridge in the background. Inset. Officers' roadside luncheon.

GERMAN METHODS IN FRANCE.
In most of the French villages occupied by Germans all suspected persons were kept under guard. The above photograph is of French peasants compounded in a village church. The smaller view was taken behind the German lines, after the arrival of gifts from Berlin for the troops The event was accompanied by much popping of corks.

States protested—the former at the instigation of the Australian Colonies—and a sort of international arrangement was come to, by which none of the three Powers was actually to appropriate any of the islands.

In 1887 a civil war broke out over the succession to the native kingship, and the European and American settlers who had bought up land from the heads of the local tribes to exploit them for copra, the product of the coconut palm, or for sugar-growing, took sides. The Germans supported one kingly claimant and the British and Americans another. Some fighting ensued, a number of German sailors being killed and wounded. At the suggestion of Germany, a conference of the three Powers chiefly interested was held in 1889 in Berlin, which elaborated a treaty, under which the independence and autonomy of the Samoan Island group were guaranteed under King Malietoa, but imposing a virtual protectorate over them. The arrangement worked with considerable friction from the first, and Robert Louis Stevenson, in " A Footnote to History " (the result of his careful investigation of the causes of the native trouble, made in 1889, on his first visit to the island, where from 1890 until his death in 1894 he made his home), referred to the malicious trickery of the Germans against poor distracted Malietoa. On the kinglet's death there were again rival aspirants to the unstable throne—Matuafa being supported by the Germans

and Malietoa Tanu by the British and Americans. Fighting took place, but this time it was the American and British sailors who were killed. An international commission made inquiry on the spot, and in the result the Treaty of Berlin was abrogated, and Great Britain withdrew, much to the chagrin of the Australian and New Zealand Governments, her claims to any portions of the beautiful island group—receiving compensation from Germany in another direction, while the United States withdrew from all the islands west of Tutuila. Germany then stood possessed of the two largest islands of the group—Savaii and Upolu, in which latter is the fine port of Apia, and a naval base which constituted, in Australian and New Zealand eyes, a dangerous sea watchdog against the Commonwealth and the Dominion The resident German population in the islands in 1913 was 329.

On August 26th and 27th two Danish and Norwegian traders and three British trawlers, two of them engaged in mine-sweeping, were blown up by mines in the North Sea off the Tyne, with a total loss of seventeen killed and eleven injured. About the same date the German fast cruiser Magdeburg ran ashore in a fog on the island of Odensholm, in the Gulf of Finland. As a Russian squadron was preparing to attack, **Fate of the** the commander of the cruiser sacrificed **Magdeburg** her by partially blowing her up, and her destruction was completed by shell-fire from the Russian ships. A majority of the crew were rescued by a German torpedo-boat. The naval Battle of Heligoland Bight on August 28th has already been described in a separate chapter.

Meantime, important events were taking place in the eastern theatre of operations. At the close of Chapter XXIII. it was stated that General von Hindenburg had

New movable French battery which travels along a specially-laid railway line. Note the observation tower, the howitzers on their turntable, and the ammunition waggon.

British soldiers handing out English 6 in. howitzer shells for inspection by their French comrades, who took a very deep interest in everything connected with British artillery.

Specimen of the British 6 in. howitzer which was sent to oppose the German 8 in. howitzer, and outfought it. It throws a shell of 100 lb., and has a muzzle velocity of 1,285 lb. per second.

One of the French howitzer guns. This formidable piece of ordnance is supported on steel arms, which give to it a great stability when it is fired. As will be seen, it is brought up to the field of action on a railway, and provided with shield, turntable, and mechanism for adjustment to the required elevation.

BIG GUNS EMPLOYED BY THE ALLIES AGAINST HEAVY ARTILLERY OF THE GERMANS.

Givet, a picturesquely placed little village in the Ardennes, where the Germans crossed the Meuse against a magnificent resistance by the French. Inset: A road in the Forest of Mormal.

pushed across the Russian frontier, but was met on the Niemen by General Rennenkampf, who took his revenge for the disaster of Tannenberg, described in a previous chapter, and drove the Germans once more back, between August 23rd and 25th, to Gumbinnen, where he gained a complete victory against three Teuton army corps, part of which had attempted to turn the Russian right flank, and captured fifty-five guns. Rennenkampf practically was then in possession of East Prussia, and from Gumbinnen he pushed forward to Allenstein, and invested Königsberg, while his Cossacks pushed on to the neighbourhood of Dantzic. So serious was this position for the Germans that on August 29th and 30th they drew troops from the French frontier to

Longwy, where the army of the German Crown Prince succeeded in bursting into France, a small town W.S.W. of Luxemburg. Inset: Verdun, the great French fortress town west of Metz.

reinforce their eastern front, which was being so hard pressed.

A battle, extending over a front of thirty miles between Neigenburg and Gilgenburg, took place on August 28th and 29th, when two German army corps were reported to have been cut up by the Russians. Continuing their pursuit of the enemy, the Russians occupied Soldau, whence they had the command of the railway to Dantzic—the retreating Germans firing the towns they vacated, while the innocent inhabitants fled from their fury. The position taken up by Hindenburg, with his peculiarly intimate knowledge of the geography of East Prussia and Poland, barred the further advance of Rennenkampf.

In mid-August the Grand Duke Nicholas began his preparations for the serious advance of his armies into Poland and Galicia—on a line extending from the Niemen

down almost to the borders of Rumania. West Poland had been invaded by a German army under the Crown Prince, who had been transferred thither from the Argonne in the western sphere of operations, and who hoped to make a swoop on Warsaw from the eastern German border, by way of the Vistula. Like a wise diplomat, as well as an excellent soldier, the Grand Duke Nicholas followed up the Tsar's Rescript, promising, in the event of a successful war, to make Poland an autonomous State under the Crown of Russia (see page 304, Vol. I.) by an Army Order, making it known to the active Army and the whole population of the Empire that Russia was waging war in consequence of a challenge thrown down by the common enemy of all Slavs. "The Poles in Russia," the order proceeded, "and those of Germany and Austria, who show their loyalty to the Slav cause, will have the special protection of the Russian Army and Government, in so far as their personal and material security is concerned. Any attempt to interfere with the personal rights of Poles who

Charleville, opposite Mezières, another centre of the fierce fighting between the French and Germans during the retreat from Charleroi.

have not been guilty of acts hostile to Russia will be punished with all the severity of martial law." The Russian Generalissimo was himself in command of the army opposing the main German army under the German Crown Prince, and preliminary engagements took place along the long line. In one of these a Russian squadron charged a battery and captured all the guns from a detachment of the enemy, when the German soldiers discarded their rifles and the officers threw away their swords and helmets and fled. The incident had a personal interest for the Tsar, as will be seen from a special telegram which the Grand Duke sent to his Imperial Majesty.

SCENES ALONG THE EASTERN FRONTIER OF FRANCE.
Panoramic view of Nancy, the capital of Meurthe-et-Moselle.

" I would not have dared," said the telegram, "to disturb your Majesty with a report of this little affair, but I have decided to make it to you as the commander of the Nijni Novgorod Regiment of Dragoons. A party of seventy picked German scouts came into collision with a squadron of the Nijni Novgorod Regiment. All the enemy were sabred, except six who were taken prisoners. Our losses were four wounded, two seriously."

Operations in Galicia After a couple of weeks' manœuvring, two Russian armies, one under the command of General Russky, and the other under General Brussiloff, made a concentrated thrust into the Austrian position in Eastern Galicia, and completely routed five of the enemy's army corps, capturing 70,000 prisoners and an immense number of guns and much war material.

The battle-front in the Galician theatre was narrowed on August 30th, and the enemy forces in the province of Kielce crossed the Vistula in order to join hands with the armies engaged in the province of Lublin, their main efforts being chiefly concentrated on the roads leading to Lublin, where desperate fighting went on for nearly a week. South of Lublin the Russian troops drove back the enemy's forces, helpless and bewildered, and advanced amid heaps of slain Austrians, left unburied by the flying and demoralised army. On August 31st and September 1st the Austrian lines round Lemberg were broken, and the capital of Galicia was captured, with an unheard-of number of guns and other machinery of war. General Russky with his division then swept onward and, in conjunction with Brussiloff's army, pulverised the Austrian main army, shattering, at any rate at that date, the military strength and prestige of the Dual Monarchy.

As giving some insight into the Russian soldier's mentality, a correspondent transcribed literally some parts of a dialogue which took place between a gigantic trooper who had returned from the front wounded and was interviewed by the Tsar in the hospital at Petrograd. The trooper, carrying his left arm in a sling, stood at attention before his Majesty. His breast was decorated with three Crosses of St. George, of which one had the distinctive badge conferred only when the recipient had been wounded in carrying out some gallant exploit.

" And you," said his Majesty, " have again been wounded ? "

" Yes, sire. Last time in Manchuria. This time near Gumbinnen."

" I hear you captured five Germans ? "

A PATHETIC INCIDENT—FOR THE GERMAN HORSES.

Street scene in Northern France. Two German cavalry scouts halted in the market-place to give their tired steeds a refreshing drink at the fountain— to find that the water supply had been cut off. The smaller view is of a German prisoner being interrogated by his French captors.

BRITISH REINFORCEMENTS BROUGHT UP BY MOTOR-'BUS.

The London motor-'bus, whatever its future may be, will have an honoured place in the history of the Great War. It was used for the rapid conveyance of troops from one spot to another, for the bringing up of ammunition and other supplies, and very often with its body replaced by a lorry body. Motor-'buses were used in a similar fashion by both French and Germans.

In Paris itself during these eventful days the citizens were at intervals alarmed by the dropping of bombs from German aeroplanes.

It may be well here to refer to the unparalleled, overt, and underground attempts that were made at this period by Germany—at a cost, so it was alleged at the time, of over a million sterling—to influence opinion in the United States in favour of the Germans as against the case of the Allies. Writing from Washington, on August 30th, "The Times" correspondent said that the leaders of the Teutonic element there, headed by the German Ambassador, were indulging in a campaign which was in direct contravention of the President's fine appeal for neutrality of comment by the native and alien Americans alike. Not only was the Ambassador using his official position for all it was worth, but the German Consular corps were also mobilised to bring financial and other pressure to bear on behalf of German interests. Astounding letters were sent to editors for publication, and a covert campaign was organised to frighten the proprietors of newspapers by letters threatening loss of subscribers if they continued to be pro-British.

Mr. W. G. Shepherd, representative of the United Press Association of America, sought an interview with the First Lord of the Admiralty, for the purpose of obtaining his view of the immediate cause of the war, as a checkmate to the extraordinary statements thereanent circulated in the States by German officials and sympathisers. This interview was of historic importance, and may be referred to in a little detail. Mr. Churchill handed his interviewer the celebrated White Paper containing all Sir Edward Grey's negotiations with the Chancellories of Europe, saying: "There is our case, and all we ask of the American people is that they should study it with severe and impartial attention." Mr. Shepherd then asked what was the underlying cause, apart from the actual steps which led to the war; and Mr.

"Yes, your Majesty, we stormed a village. They were hiding in the houses. I pulled them out one by one and drove them along. Just then somebody put a bullet into my arm from behind, but I brought them in all the same."

"But how did you storm the village?"

"Well, your Majesty, we dismounted, threw out skirmishers, and then we rushed them. But the Germans aren't good fighters. They turned and ran."

"Is there anything you wish for?" asked the Emperor laughingly.

"Oh, yes, your Majesty; let me go back. My arm will be all right in a few days. It is all very dull here, and so interesting there. We see new towns, and every day there's plenty of interesting work."

To return to Northern France. From Guise—the operations around which have been dealt with in a separate chapter—the Allies retired to a line drawn between Amiens and Verdun, the British covering and delaying troops being frequently engaged; while on September 1st the British Cavalry Brigade and the 4th Guards Brigade were sharply engaged with the enemy near Compiègne, the 9th Lancers in a brilliant charge capturing ten German guns.

Churchill replied that the war was **Mr. Churchill discusses** started and was being maintained by **the origin of the war** the Prussian military aristocracy, which set no limits to its ambition of world-wide predominance. In a word, it was the old struggle of a hundred years ago against Napoleon. The grouping of forces was different; the circumstances were different; the occasion was different; the man, above all, was different—happily. But the issue was the same. Great Britain stood right in the path of Prussian militarism. Our military force was perhaps small, but it was good, and would grow; our naval and financial resources were considerable; and with these we stood between a mighty Army and a dominion which would certainly not be content with European limits.

In answer to a question as to whether the end of the war would see some abatement of the struggle of armaments, Mr. Churchill replied: "That depends on the result. If we succeed, and if, as the result of our victory, Europe is re-arranged, as far as possible with regard to the principle of nationality and in accordance with the wishes of the peoples who dwell in the various disputed areas, we may look forward with hope to a great relaxation and easement. But if Germany wins it will not be the victory of the quiet, sober, commercial elements in Germany, nor of the common people of Germany with all their virtues, but the victory of the blood and iron military school, whose doctrines and principles will then have received a supreme and terrible vindication.

"Now that the great collision has come," continued Mr. Churchill, "it is well that the democratic nations of the world—the nations where the peoples own the Government, and not the Government the people—should realise what is at stake. The French, British, and American systems of government by popular election and Parliamentary debate, with the kind of civilisation which flows from such institutions, are brought into direct conflict with the highly efficient Imperialist bureaucracy and military organisation of Prussia. That is the issue. No partisanship is required to make it plain. No sophistry can obscure it."

American interest in the war As to the question whether the democracy of the United States, apart from the moral issues involved, had any direct interest in the result of the war, the First Lord said: "If Great Britain were reduced in this war—or another, which would be sure to follow from it if this war were inconclusive—to the position of a small country like Holland, then, however far across the salt water the United States might lie, the burden which we in Great Britain are bearing now would fall on American shoulders. He did not mean by that that Germany would attack the States, or that if they were attacked that they would need to fear the results, so far as the States are concerned. The Monroe Doctrine, however, carried them very far in South as well as North America; and was it likely that victorious German militarism, which would then have shattered France irretrievably, have conquered Belgium, and have broken for ever the power of Great Britain, would allow itself to be permanently cut off from all hopes of that oversea expansion and development with which South America alone could supply it?" In conclusion, Mr. Churchill said: "Now the impact is upon us. Our blood, which flows in your veins, should lead you to expect that we shall be stubborn enough to bear that impact.

But if we go down and are swept in ruin into the past, you are next in the line. This war is for us a war of honour, of respect for obligations into which we have entered, and of loyalty towards friends in desperate need. But now that it has begun it has become a war of self-preservation. The British democracy, with its limited monarchy, its ancient Parliament, its ardent social and philanthropic dreams, is engaged for good or for ill in deadly grapple with the formidable might of Prussian autocratic rule. It is our system of civilisation and government against theirs. It is our life or theirs. We are conscious of the greatness of the times. We recognise the consequence **"Under the eye** and proportion of events. We feel **of history"** that, however inadequate we may be, however unexpected the ordeal may be, we are under the eye of history, and, the issue being joined, Great Britain must go forward to the very end."

Towards the close of the interview a telegram came to the First Lord from Belgium, announcing the total destruction of Louvain as an act of military execution. Handing it to his interviewer, he said: "What further proof is needed of the cause at issue? Tell that to your fellow American countrymen. You know," he added, "I'm half American myself."

THE UBIQUITOUS AND ADAPTABLE MOTOR-'BUS IN FRANCE.
Bringing up supplies for the troops at the front. Paris motor-'buses passing through the Forest of Compiègne. The smaller photograph shows how the London motor-'buses were converted into lorries.

WITH THE SOLDIERS OF AUSTRIA. DIFFICULTIES OF ARTILLERY TRANSPORT.

During the autumn campaign in Galicia the roads became very muddy, and as a result the artillery was exceedingly difficult to handle. In the above illustration, which gives a realistic idea of the nature of the soil, an Austrian gun is seen being helped up an awkward incline by a draft of infantry.

ON THE PRUSSIAN FRONTIER—RUSSIANS OCCUPY A TOWN DURING NIGHT-TIME.

The German armies having evacuated a Prussian frontier town during the night, an advance party of Cossacks, "Germany's grey nightmare," and Russian infantry occupied the position. The Prussians then attempted a night surprise, but this was provided against and defeated.

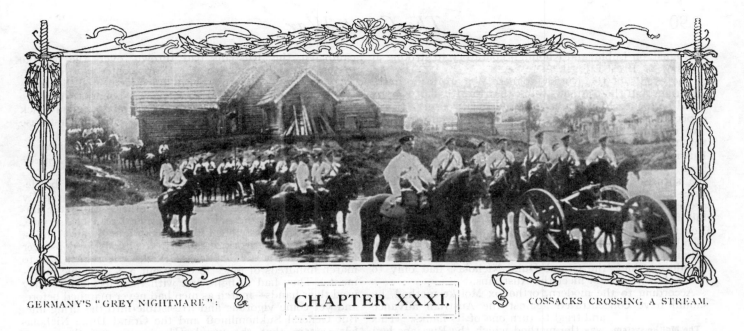

CHAPTER XXXI.

THE RUSSIAN VICTORIES IN GALICIA AND THE CAPTURE OF LEMBERG.

The Austro-German Plan of Campaign—How the Russians Divided the Teutonic Allies—The Austrian Invasion of Russian Poland—Russia Prepares a Napoleonic Stroke—The Russian Army Steals Along the Dniester—Another Russian Force Moves Southward to Co-operate—The Extraordinary Secrecy of the Combined Movements—The Sudden Onset at Halicz—A Great Russian Victory—The Storming of Lemberg and the Re-conquest of the Ancient Russian Duchy of Galicia.

O N both fronts of war Germany had arranged a programme of victories. But as she needed three millions of troops in France, leaving only a million men mainly of the militia class for defence against Russia, she had to depend upon Austria-Hungary for offensive operations in the eastern theatre of conflict. A plan of combined attack was prepared for the conquest of Russian Poland.

An Austrian army of a million troops of the first line was to advance from Galicia, between Cracow and Lemberg. At the same time a German force, of about equal number but inferior quality, was to strike at Warsaw from Eastern Prussia and German Poland. The defending Russian army would then be assailed on three sides, and either routed or driven back from its railway centre at Brest-Litovsk.

Like all German war plans, this was excellent on paper. Had the Russians also done the obvious thing in reply to the obvious movements of the Teutonic forces, the Grand Duke Nicholas and his Chief of Staff, General Sukhomlinoff, m i g h t h a v e been outgeneralled. Unfortunately for the Austrians, the Russian Military Staff was well aware of the German war plan, and engineered a series of surprises that completely disarranged from the begin-

ning the Teutonic programme. The German forces were violently wrenched from all co-operation with the Austrian armies by General Rennenkampf's sudden raid into East Prussia. His immediate menace to Königsberg, his destruction of the food resources of Berlin, and his threat at Thorn and Dantzic, played on the Germans' instinct for self-preservation. Alarmed for their own fields and cities, they withdrew from Russian Poland, where their advanced guard had reached Lodz on the way to Warsaw, and hastily, madly concentrated in Prussia against the Cossack invaders.

This left the Austrian armies in the west of Russian Poland at the mercy of the Russian Military Staff. The Austrian Commanders—General Dankl, General Auffenberg, and several archdukes — did not lose confidence. Possessing two thousand five hundred guns and a million y o u n g, picked men of the regular Army, with large militia supports in Galicia, they regarded Russia as a sleepy, gawky giant who could be stabbed to death before he was half awake. Speeding up their mobilisation, they launched two great armies over the frontier. One marched along the Vistula and the other along the Bug Rivers. They formed a battle - front some eighty miles long that swept everything before it as it advanced, towards the middle

PART OF THE PRICE OF VICTORY—AND DEFEAT.
AFTER THE BATTLE OF LEMBERG.
Russian and Austrian wounded on their way to the base hospital at Lemberg. The capture of Lemberg by the Russians removed a great obstacle to the advance of the Tsar's soldiers against the military power of Austria, and enabled them to strike at Germany from the south.

of August, on Lublin and Kholm, preparatory to striking at Warsaw or Brest-Litovsk.

The events of the Russo-Japanese War made both the Austrians and the Germans think that the Russian Empire could be rocked to its foundation by a swift onset. It was expected that the Russians would not have an army of any considerable size mobilised before the beginning of September at the earliest. It was in this matter that the Russian Military Staff, with General Sukhomlinoff at its head, prepared a surprise for Austria, even greater than the surprise it had arranged for the Germans in East Prussia. Lack of a network of railways and good roads prevented the Russian Staff from concentrating at once the full forces of the Empire near the Teutonic frontiers. Nevertheless, the Austrian force of a million men was held by a Russian force of smaller number with superior artillery. Admirably served by his Chief of Staff, the Russian Commander-in-Chief, the Grand Duke Nicholas, had only to decide how he would meet the Austrians.

According to the modern, orthodox Moltke method, he should have concentrated against the Austrian advance and tried to turn one of its flanks. This **The Moltke system thrown over** was the method which the Russians had employed against the Japanese, and which the Japanese had employed against them. It led, when the hostile troops were fairly balanced, to a new kind of open-air siege warfare that seldom produced a decisive result. But since the Manchurian campaign the Russians had thrown over the Moltke system and returned to the Napoleonic way of war. The way of Napoleon, with its unexpected lightning strokes and direct frontal attacks, was bound to produce decisive results—one way or the other. It meant a quick great victory, or a quick great defeat. In the first case the fighting power of the Austrian Empire would be shattered before the Germans, busy in East Prussia, could come to the **Defect of the Napoleonic method** help of their ally. The great defect of the Napoleonic method was that its master used it on battle-fronts a few miles long, on which troops could be rapidly manœuvred from one flank to the other. With the immense armies of the new era of general national service, the battle-fronts stretched from two to four hundred miles. Russia had no network of railways to shift her troops over this distance for sudden mass attacks. Her men had to march hundreds of miles to carry out a Napoleonic movement. They had to fight first with their feet before they used their hands—march as men had never marched before, and yet come vigorous and irresistible into the firing-line. But General Sukhomlinoff and the Grand Duke Nicholas felt certain that the wonderful physique of the young moujik would carry him successfully through the ordeal.

To the army of Bessarabia and Podolia, under General Brussiloff, was assigned the first great march that should end in the first Napoleonic surprise stroke. Composed partly of Odessa troops, this army crept round Northern

RELICS OF THE AUSTRIAN DEBACLE AT LEMBERG.
On September 2nd General Russky drew up his troops within cannon shot of the fortressed capital of Galicia, an Austrian army of 200,000 men was utterly beaten, and Lemberg captured next day, together with the entire artillery of the Austrian force.

AUSTRIAN STAFF OFFICERS WITNESSING THE RUSSIAN ATTACK ON LEMBERG.

From a drawing by the German artist W. Gause. The Archduke Frederick, the Austrian Commander-in-Chief, is seen on the extreme right of the group, behind the range-finder. Prince Charles Francis Joseph, heir to the Austrian throne, is the tall figure in the foreground.

TYPES OF HEAVY GERMAN AND AUSTRIAN GUNS BEING MOUNTED FOR BOMBARDMENT.

In the early stages of the war there appears to have been an interchange of heavy artillery between the Germans and Austrians. These great pieces of ordnance often had a decisive effect in bombardment, but they had to be sent back for renewal after a comparatively short "life."

Rumania into the eastern corner of the Austrian province of Galicia. At the same time a larger force of Little Russians from Kiev, under General Russky, moved from a point some hundreds of miles away to co-operate with the Bessarabians. Russky, however, seemed to be merely the left wing of the main Russian armies guarding Russian Poland. He rested on the River Bug, still far away from

PHASES OF THE STRUGGLE IN GALICIA.
The first view is of a Russian railroad battalion at the captured Galician town of Ravaruska. In the large photograph is seen a Russian transport column on the road from Tomashov to Lublin. In their flight from Tomashov the Austrians are reported to have used Red Cross waggons to facilitate their progress, and the illustration on the right shows some of these waggons abandoned by them.

the scene fixed for the first decisive stroke. His connection with Brussiloff's movement was veiled for a fortnight from the enemy.

General Brussiloff had also to move to the attack without exciting notice. This was done by both commanders—Russky and himself—throwing out a screen of hard-fighting Cossacks all along the frontier of Eastern Galicia. For a hundred and fifty miles the Cossacks skirmished at every border road or bridge between the Dniester and Bug Rivers. They began it as soon as war was declared, and, after a couple of weeks of this inconsequential warfare, the Austrian commander at Lemberg grew to look upon it as mere fussiness. It amused the Cossacks and it did not hurt him. But towards the third week in August he sent a force of 2,000 men to make a reconnaissance in Podolia.

Secrecy of the Russian plans

They arrived at Gorodok, a little townlet across the border, where their presence was not wanted. For General Brussiloff was then advancing with a large army through Gorodok on towards Galicia. The Austrian reconnoitring

force had to be stopped, and there were only nine hundred Cossacks at Gorodok to screen their main army. These Cossacks had to repulse the enemy without calling for large reinforcements to excite the suspicions of any fugitive from the fight.

The Cossacks lined out in the woods beyond the village. Then thirty of them went forward from cover to cover, until they came suddenly upon the Austrians. Pretending to be scared by the surprise, the Cossack band turned and fled in apparent panic. Their foes entered headlong into pursuit, and were led into an ambush, where a cross-fire of rifles and machine-guns brought a thousand of them down. The rest were chased by the Cossacks over the border, and the invasion of Galicia was begun by their main force.

Cossacks lead the foe into ambush

Then came the perilous part of the enterprise. The army of Russky was moving on Lemberg from the north; the army of Brussiloff was converging on the Galician capital from the east. When united, the two Russian forces would outnumber the Austrian force guarding Lemberg. In the meantime, however, either Brussiloff or Russky alone was too weak to escape defeat. Both might have been met singly and overwhelmed. But such was the skill with which their combined operations were conducted that General Brussiloff was able to steal into Galicia and conquer a large part of the territory before battle was joined.

Extraordinary was the secrecy with which his great movement was executed. It took place in daylight, over a period of thirteen days, from August 19th to August 31st. The Austrians had a host of spies, working with

Bringing back the body of a Russian officer from Tomashov.

Abandoned Austrian Red Cross waggon on the battlefield of Biellgitz.

Railway waggons captured from the Austrians.

Trenches occupied by the Austrians before their retreat from Tomashov.

SCENES ON THE LINE OF THE DISASTROUS AUSTRIAN RETREAT IN GALICIA.
In the lower photograph may be seen a large number of shells abandoned by the Austrians in the retreat near Ravaruska.

they thought to force the Russians to concentrate against them. It was so simple this Moltke method, as explained by Field-Marshal von der Goltz. The attackers had merely to advance strongly and conqueringly in order to compel their opponent to attempt to stop them. Nothing else mattered. Cossack activity southward in Galicia was merely a feint and a vain distraction.

Meanwhile, General Brussiloff made the very most of his opportunities. As quietly and as gently as possible he moved over the tributaries of the Dniester, in Galicia, and pushed back the Austrian cavalry screen without revealing his strength. On the versatile Cossack fell all this preliminary work. He had to do without infantry support or any **Versatile Cossacks** considerable show of artillery power. **in their element** Neither the infantryman nor the ordinary field artillery could be brought into action without revealing that which it was necessary to conceal.

The Cossack horseman had to veil his main army and clear its path through forts, block-houses, and bridge-heads, while appearing to be merely a border raider. Excellently was he suited for this kind of work. Far in advance of the tramping foot soldiers and the labouring big-gun teams, moving at the rate of eight miles a day, the Cossack kept up a continual skirmish with every sort of hostile arm—cavalry scout, infantrymen, and gunners in

RUSSIAN SCOUT MOUNTED ON A STURDY SIBERIAN PONY.

Teutonic thoroughness; they had a large force of well-mounted, dashing cavalrymen, including the cavalry division of the Hungarian Guards—the best horsemen in either Austria or Germany. They had scouts in flying machines darting over the frontier. Yet the Russian turning movement in Eastern Galicia was not discovered until too late.

This was partly due to the fact that the country through which Brussiloff was working was an ancient Russian duchy that had been torn from the ancestors of the Tsar.

WAR DOGS ATTACHED TO THE RUSSIAN LIFEGUARD HUSSARS.

Eastern Galicia was the Alsace-Lorraine of the Slav Empire, peopled by a Slav race, with the same language, religion, and customs as the men of Brussiloff's army. At the villages priests and people came out with banners to meet their " little brothers." In the towns flowers were thrown from the upper windows along the streets upon the armed redeemers of the ancient duchy. And all that could be done by silence or pretended ignorance to mislead the Austrians and Hungarians was done by the peasants. It is, moreover, very likely that Russian Secret Service agents had well prepared the Little Russians of Galicia for the happy invasion.

But this does not palliate the disastrous stupidity of the Austrian General Military Staff. They knew what Eastern Galicia meant to Russia. Why, then, were they not fully forearmed against the inevitable attack ? The probable explanation is that they were so obsessed by the Moltke system of warfare that they were blind to everything except the " scientific " scheme of operations they were carrying out farther to the north-west, in Russian Poland. They had a strong front between the Vistula and the Bug Rivers, and by continually moving forward into Russia,

OFFICER OF COSSACK SCOUTS
giving information relative to the enemy's position to his commander who is studying a map.

RUSSIAN TROOPS AT PRAYER.
A religious service on the battlefield. Shells were falling while it was in progress.

RUSSIAN FIELD GUN.
Ready for action in a carefully prepared position.

FIRE AND SWORD IN GALICIA—WITH THE RUSSIAN FORCES IN THE WAR AGAINST AUSTRIA.
Russians entering the burning town of Mikolaiev, in Eastern Galicia, during the Muscovite invasion of the dominions of the Emperor Francis Joseph. The circular view shows Russian soldiers eating a meal in a Galician village.

AUSTRIAN REINFORCEMENTS ON THE WAY TO CRACOW.
An Austrian engineer division on the way to strengthen the garrison at Cracow. Inset : Bridge over the River Dniester blown up by Austrians in retreat.

fortified places, and even armoured trains. Helped only by his own light artillery, he fought in every manner practised by modern troops. He charged with his lance ; he dismounted and took positions with the bayonet that all Russian cavalry carry ; at need, he entrenched, and proved himself a marksman.

The Cossack is what the Prussian would like to be, but is not—the member of a military caste, born, bred, and trained entirely for a life of war. His ancestors, hammered into shape by continual conflict with warlike Mongol races, had built up the kingdom of Poland and then, to preserve their independence, **Empire-builders** had gone over to the Duke of Moscow **of Russia** and become the empire-builders of Russia.

Never had the Cossack enjoyed himself as he did in Galicia against the Hungarians and Austrians. On their unfortunate heads he emptied all his box of tricks. It would be interesting to learn from some survivor of the famous cavalry division of the Magyar Guards, who met the Cossacks near Lemberg, and then—after a railway journey across Europe —encountered the British lancers and dragoons at Ypres, which of his two foes he found the more formidable. Certainly the Cossacks are more tricky fighters than our horsemen. They could beat any circus performer.

In Galicia, when hard pressed, they fell dead in heaps, their dead horses beside them. As the enemy came to search their bodies the dead men used their carbines with surprising effect. Another time, a herd of little Cossack horses would stampede, and the riderless animals would sweep towards some guarded bridge-head or block-house. Even little Cossack horses are useful to Austrian soldiers ; they can be sold for good money to Galician farmers. But, just before the animals were caught, grey figures

A SHADED AUSTRIAN ENCAMPMENT.
Officers resting for a midday meal in an Austrian camp pitched in a wood in Galicia.

HALICZ, THE CAPITAL OF ANCIENT GALICIA.
The view is from the right bank of the River Dniester, and Russian officers
are shown surveying the position from the Austrian observation station.
The town is seen in the middle distance. Near the town are the ruins
of a castle where the once powerful rulers of the ancient principality
used to reside. Inset : Austrian chiefs in the field, a photograph taken
at the Austrian headquarters, and showing the Archduke Frederick and
General Conrad von Roetzendorf, Chief of the Austrian General Staff.

swung from beneath them, lance in hand, and charged.
It was like a show in the arena, but deadly for the spectators.
When it came to a straightforward cavalry fight, sabre
against sabre, the Cossack still won.

All the tricks of war, however, were not practised by
the Russians. The Austrians, on occasions, showed
themselves masters of craft. An instance occurred on
August 23rd in the frontier fight for Tarnopol, an
important Galician town on the Sereth River, seventy
miles east-south-east of Lemberg. Piercing the enemy's
front line, a Russian division swept onward to meet the
main body of their foes. They passed an Austrian officer
who was sitting on the earth bandaging his leg. Naturally
they did not hurt this wounded man.
Austrian tricks in But their attack failed—it failed
the battlefield repeatedly. No matter in what way
they endeavoured to get with the
bayonet in the enemy's trenches, he was prepared, and
brought them down with a terrible, concentrated fire.

Withdrawing after one of these reverses, a Russian
officer noticed a wire running along the road. He found
it led to a field telephone, and by this concealed instrument
the supposed wounded Austrian was sitting, and giving
warning to his general of all the Russian movements.
When the bandage round the man's leg was removed, it
was seen that his limb was quite sound. After this the
telephone operator was stopped, the Russian bayonet
went over the Austrian trenches, and the Cossacks rode
down the fugitives.

The trick of pretending to be wounded and lying on the
ground and gathering information while the opposing troops
sweep by has been used by many informers in both
Austrian and German armies. It is one of the reasons
for the fiendish inhumanity with which the Teutons have
often dealt with wounded men belonging to the armies
of civilisation. The wicked are always suspicious. Having
debased, for purposes of espionage, the soldier's natural
feeling of pity for his injured foes, the new barbarians
when they advanced killed their wounded opponents, for
fear that their own dirty trick of shamming hurt and
then spying would be played on themselves

In spite of the continual skirmishings, drawing nearer
and nearer to Lemberg, no alarm was felt by the Austrian
commander until General Brussiloff's army, after crossing
stream after stream, forced the passage of the golden Lipa.
Even then the Austrian General Military Staff suspected
that a blow was coming southward against the rear of
their main armies. They had three army corps round
Lemberg to protect from any turning movement their
one hundred and fifty mile battle-front, stretching north-
west through Russian territory. But this
was not sufficient when General Russky's **Austrian precautions**
army and General Brussiloff's army **taken too late**
were at last seen combining for attack.
The Austrians hurried up two more army corps that moved
against Russky, while several divisions of foot-line infantry
and brigades of militia troops reinforced the position to
be held against Brussiloff's force. In all there were at
last about three hundred thousand Austrian troops
round Lemberg.

All this, however, was done too late in the last days of
August. General Russky and General Brussiloff had
united, some forty miles east of the city. The combined

M   97

POLISH SOLDIERS RESTING IN THE CARPATHIANS.
The Carpathians, the second great mountain range of Central Europe, is generally clothed with wood to a height of more than 4,000 feet. The scenery all round is full of grandeur. A tragic side of the war in this part of the world was the division of the Poles in the rival forces. Inset: A typical trainload of Austrian prisoners, who offered a noticeable contrast to the carefully groomed soldiers of their Russian escort.

armies then acted under the leadership of General Russky in a concerted attack upon the capital of Galicia. In both brains and fighting power the Austrian Archduke Frederick and his Staff were outmatched. General Russky was one of the leading strategists of the new Russo-French school, a quiet, bookish, scholarly man, hardened to war in Manchuria, where he had distinguished himself by bold leading and personal courage. General Brussiloff was another brilliant and yet sound leader, with high, practical experience in modern warfare. Then, with the two Russian generals was the hero of Bulgaria, General Radko Dimitrieff, who had vanquished the German-trained Turkish army at Kirk Kilisse and other recent battles of the Balkans. He had thrown up his appointment under the Bulgarian Government in order to go as a volunteer to help the imperial Slav people in its grand struggle against the Teuton, whose intrigues had brought Bulgaria low in the hour of her victory and disrupted the Balkan Alliance.

In numbers the two opposing armies seem to have been, in the end, about equal. But the Russian artillery,

made chiefly by French gun-makers, was superior to that of the Austrian. Moreover, the Austrians had lent the German host in Belgium and France their latest, greatest weapon—the famous three-piece 12 in. howitzer—invented, it was rumoured, by an American, and made by Baron von Skoda, of Pilsen. For Krupp, though loud and unceasing in self-advertisement, had not all the siege artillery wanted at Namur and Maubeuge. So the Austrians had to weaken their great frontier fortresses, such as Lemberg, in order to assist their braggart ally with howitzers and with large numbers of artillery officers and men.

In addition to this disadvantage in the machinery of warfare, the southern Austrian army was caught in a moment of disarray. Its main reinforcement of two army corps was intercepted on August 29th by General Russky at Zloczow, a town to the south-east of Lemberg. There it was shattered, and the victorious Russians moved on and occupied a height known **Austria's main** as the Naked Hill, from which they **reinforcement** dominated Lemberg. In the meantime **shattered** General Brussiloff's army, forming the western Russian wing, swung round to encircle Lemberg from the south. In so doing it struck against the main southern Austrian army entrenched at Halicz, a fortress town on the muddy Lipa that pours its turbid waters into the Dniester.

The Austrians were bent on carrying out the obvious Moltke tactics of getting round Brussiloff's southern flank and then rolling up the combined Russian forces. But this manœuvre did not succeed. General Brussiloff

POLISH CHURCH CONVERTED INTO A PARCELS OFFICE.
Nothing proved sacred to either Austrians or Germans, and in the above illustration we see how a Polish church was occupied by soldiers of the two Kaisers, and converted by them into a military parcels post receiving office. Inset: Russian Army doctors and nurses at the hospital at Kovno, the principal town of the Russian province of the same name. Kovno was Napoleon's advanced base in 1812.

held up the turning movement, and his gallant Bulgarian assistant, General Radko Dmitrieff, made a terrible frontal attack on the enemy on the lower course of the muddy Lipa.

The Austrian position was naturally very strong and difficult to assail, with bluffs of volcanic rock and extinct craters; the natural defences had been improved by Austrian engineers, and thirty small forts had been built round Halicz. The river passage was, in fact, regarded as impregnable. But the Russian bayonet went over river, rifle pit, and trench, while the Russian gunners swept a path for their infantry and smashed the hostile batteries and destroyed the forts. The Russians advanced in open order at first, creeping up and firing in thin, prone lines; then, getting nearer in a spurt, and again holding the ground by rifle fire till their supports could come up. Then they rose up to prove the truth of their old saying, handed down from the days of Suvoroff: "The bullet is a fool and the bayonet a hero."

Brilliant work of the Russian bayonet

The Austrians and Hungarians fought well. They faced the bayonet courageously and used it themselves, but their rifle fire was not sufficiently well-aimed to stop the rushes. The battle opened on August 31st and went on for twenty-four hours, till the Austrian line was pierced, and twenty thousand of the defenders were killed or wounded. The hand-to-hand fighting at the Battle of Halicz was fierce and dreadful, but the drive and steadiness of the Russian troops made them at last irresistible. Seventeen days of hard marching had not tired them, and they bore the main part in the struggle for Lemberg.

After the victory they closed in on the capital from the south, driving the fragments of the broken Austrian wing before them. Meanwhile, Russian aeroplanes were flying over the doomed city, and General Russky's army, rapidly covering the forty miles between Zloczow and Lemberg, captured some fortified positions close to the city. On the north and the north-east the Russians deployed, and then the heights on the south-east were also taken. For six days the battle raged—from August 29th to September 3rd. The Russians at first fought from dawn to darkness, their big guns thundering over them as they attacked or threw back counter-attacks; finally they fought night and day.

The Austrians battled on with great energy in a good position. The progress of the Russians was impeded by the hilly nature of the ground, and especially by the great number of extinct volcano craters, that formed admirable natural forts, all held by strong bodies of the enemy. Out of these craters the Austrians had to be shrapnelled and bayoneted at heavy cost. Their artificial defences were only trifling obstacles compared with these natural fortifications. The country was stony and devoid of water, and the overworked, struggling Russian troops suffered badly from thirst in the hot, wearing summer weather.

The nearer they drew to Lemberg the fiercer the fighting became. But it had already been apparent at Zloczow that the Russian guns ruled the battlefield, and on September 1st, just as General Brussiloff was winning at Halicz, General Russky succeeded in driving the main Galician army beneath the shelter of the Lemberg forts. The Russian troops were then very tired, but, exultant at the prospect of victory, they fought more furiously than before. For two more days the battle flamed and thundered round the forts, both armies being terribly swept by shrapnel from the opposing guns.

Devastating Russian siege artillery But the Russian howitzer batteries had also been throwing heavy shells at the steel cupolas and concrete walls of the forts. All that the Belgians had suffered in Liège and Namur, all that the French were then enduring in Maubeuge against the long-range Skoda howitzers, was avenged on the garrisons of the fortress towns in Galicia. Dearly did the Austrians pay for the help they gave in siege artillery to the Germans. For their own forts were rapidly battered in by high-angle shell fire from the concealed and mobile howitzers built by the French for the Russian armies. Having stood a six months' siege in Port Arthur, the Russians were well acquainted with the weakness of fixed fortifications in the face of heavy howitzer fire. On this matter they knew even more than the Germans.

In a couple of days the Russians had smashed or wrecked the guns and armour-plated defence works of Lemberg — the fourth most important town in the Austro-Hungarian Empire and the chief fortress and store place of Galicia. As the answering fire weakened, the infantry was ordered to storm the first line of works. The armed moujiks leaped out and forward at a run, took the defences, and bayoneted the few men who remained by the few guns which had not been dismounted by the Russian howitzers. Then, from the second line, the Austrians tried to annihilate the attackers by shrapnel from light field artillery and by rifle and machine-gun fire. But the enemy's heavy guns on the second line were by this time also too badly damaged to counter the big Russian guns. These shelled and shrapnelled the opposing light artillery and machine-guns, and thus relieved the infantry occupying the first Austrian lines. When all the enemy's artillery had been mastered, the defending troops did not await the final bayonet attack, but retired from their works—the retreat changing into a rout as their rearguards gave way.

This rearguard action was of the most extraordinary kind—only in a German or Austrian retreat could it have occurred. To save themselves and their own countrymen the Austrian and Hungarian officers ranged on their rear the Slav regiments—Little Russians of Galicia, Poles, Serbs of Bosnia, and mutinous Bohemians. This rearguard screen was thrown out on the road to Gorodok, and, to prevent the Slavs from refusing to fight and from going over to the Russians, a line of Hungarians stood behind them, with orders to shoot them in the back the moment

they showed any hesitation. Happily, this state of things became known to the Russian commander. At the critical moment he ordered a devastating artillery fire, with the guns at a high angle, to be opened on the rearguard. The shells and shrapnel were so aimed that they passed high over the heads of the Slav regiments and fell and exploded on the retreating Austrians and Hungarians. It was this surprising, terrifying hail of high-explosive shells and wrecking shrapnel bursts that changed the retreat from Lemberg into a panic flight. The columns broke and scattered along all the western paths, abandoning guns, ammunition, and supplies, and fleeing in terror towards the next fortress of Gorodok.

North and east and south the Russians closed on the town, taking the last line of forts, and then pouring into the streets at nine o'clock on Thursday, September 3rd. Some Austrian detachments tried to fight back the victors in the thoroughfares of the city, but were cut off and captured. The Slav population welcomed the Russians with shouts of joy, and the sound of their happy voices singing the Russian National Anthem mingled with the last shots fired by the routed enemy outside the capital of the ancient Russian duchy.

As the conquerors, dull-eyed and weary from a battle that had raged at last night and day without ceasing, passed down the streets they forgot their fatigue and their hunger and thirst. Flowers fell on them from the crowded, cheering windows, and men and women, speaking a language they could understand, pressed by their side and offered them food and drink and kissed their hands.

At half-past ten the Russian flag fluttered out from the staff of the town-hall, and a deputation of townspeople waited on General Russky and said that the desire of all the Slav population was to become true and loyal sons of the mighty Russian Empire. Admirable was the conduct of the victorious troops. Having a large provision train, they had no need to ask the people for any assistance, and exemplary order was at once maintained by the military authorities, with the co-operation of the municipal bodies. The only booty taken was the Austrian Army stores, with two hundred guns and much baggage. The war material was enormous, as it had been collected from all parts of Austria-Hungary and stored in Lemberg to provide the armies on the frontier with supplies for six months or more. Its capture was of much importance.

But large as were the immediate consequences of the storming of the fortressed capital of the Alsace-Lorraine of Russia, these were only the by-products of the great victories at Halicz and Lemberg. The great thing was that the Napoleonic stroke had succeeded. Three hundred thousand hostile troops, forming the powerful right wing of the greatest army that ever invaded Russia, **300,000 troops shattered and fugitive** were shattered and fugitive. They had been gathered to protect the two main Austrian-Hungarian armies operating in the country to the north. Their defeat and flight exposed the main armies to an attack from the rear as well as on the front and flank. General Russky with his men went northward at once with a large force, while General Dimitrieff and General Brussiloff acted together round Lemberg against the army they had broken, which was being reinforced by German troops and Hungarian militia.

MAP ILLUSTRATING THE RUSSIAN ADVANCE ON LEMBERG.

SWEEPING ALL BEFORE THEM WITH THE BAYONET—RUSSIAN SOLDIERS STORMING THE
OUTSKIRTS OF JAROSLAV.

After the rout of the Austrians at Lemberg the Russian army swept westward, driving large numbers of both Germans and Austrians into Jaroslav and Przemysl, and capturing the former fortress, which is said to have been stronger than Liège, within two days. Later Jaroslav had to be evacuated, owing to the advance of the enemy on Warsaw. The picture is from a drawing by a Russian artist, M. Vladimiroff.

CARPATHIAN MOUNTAINS

DNIESTER R.

HALICZ

Austrian Lines

Scene of the rout of the Austrian Army

Russian Lines

PODAYCE

AUSTRIAN DEFEAT
3000 KILLED
9 GUNS TAKEN

In the above view the spectator is looking towards the great range of the C pathians, distant about eighty miles. On the extreme right are Lublin a Kholm, where the Austro-German advance was checked. The positions Cracow, Jaroslav, Tomashov, Ravaruska, and Przemysl are clearly indicat In the centre lies the important town of Lemberg, whose capture pro

The city of Lemberg is noted for its many beautiful buildings. The view above shows the principal square with Municipal Theatre.

Panoramic view of the outskirts of the old Polish cap

Before it was taken by the Russians, Lemberg is believed to have be converted into a semi-fortified place. A series of lunettes, redoubts, e had been more or less hastily prepared. It was the headquarters of t 11th Austrian Corps, which included the famous 43rd Landwehr Infant Division, and was divided into three brigades. The forts outside town were said to have been armed with 10.5 cm. siege-guns, made of ste with Krupp action, and firing high-explosive shell or shrapnel. One of forts is also said to have had a battery of three 24 cm. heavy siege-guns of qu

Przemysl, "the Gibraltar of the Austrian Empire."

Large castle with church attached in Galician fighting area.

AUG 26th
AUSTRIAN-GERMAN
ADVANCE CHECKED
BY RUSSIA —3000
PRISONERS TAKEN

VISTULA LUBLIN

CRACOW KIELCE

PRZEMYSL FORTRESS JARASLAU SAN RIVER CHOLM

SAMBOR RAVA RUSKA ZAMOSC FORTRESS

UNIONS-HUGEL AUSTRIAN POLAND TOMASHOFF RUSSIAN POLAND

FRONTIER

15 HUNGARIAN DIV.
SHATTERED CHIEF
OF GENERAL STAFF
KILLED 5000
PRISONERS TAKEN
20 GUNS AND
STANDARD

the decisive events of the earlier hostilities in the eastern theatre of the ... ile on the left are Halicz and Podayce. Not since Alexander the Great ... w the mighty empire of Darius in a battle near Nineveh has there been ... and complete a destruction of a great and ancient State as befell ... Hungary between August 30th and September 12th, 1914.

Kholm, where Russia's Austrian prisoners were interned.

...ing the railway bridge over the River Vistula.

...rn pattern. When they were able to assume the offensive, the Russians ... he Austrians from their trenches at the point of the bayonet. A ... te attempt at a counter-attack only resulted in the capture of 5,000 ... prisoners. The immediate result of the Battle of the Vistula and ... was to throw the most ancient of Teutonic Empires into the power of ... ssian Empire. Forged by blood-and-iron methods, of which the reigning ... Emperor and his people had been among the first victims at Königratz, ... pire of the Prussians at once absorbed both Austria and Hungary.

Cracow, showing the Cloth Hall and main thoroughfare.

Lublin, where the Russians suddenly assumed the offensive.

POLISH CAVALRY IN THE KAISER'S SERVICE.

Group of young Polish officers awaiting orders for the front. Although the national sympathy of the Polish people was with Russia, Germany and Austria had many Poles in their armies. The headgear and the youthfulness of the men in the above group will be remarked. Inset : An aide-de-camp assisting Prince Charles Francis Joseph at Przemysl to adjust his uniform.

PRINCE CHARLES FRANCIS JOSEPH, HEIR TO THE AUSTRIAN THRONE, AND HIS STAFF.

The above photograph was taken at the Austrian Headquarters at Przemysl. Prince Charles is a son of the late Archduke Otto, and became heir to the Austrian throne after the assassination of the Archduke Francis Ferdinand at Serajevo on June 28th, 1914.

THE RUSSIAN VICTORIES OF THE VISTULA AND DNIESTER
and the Destruction of the Main Armies of Austria-Hungary.

A Million Austro-Hungarian Troops Invade Russia—German Plan of Co-operation in Attacking Warsaw is Defeated—Austria Carries Out the Operation Herself—Russian Commander-in-Chief Lures the Invaders Far from their Railways—Advancing Towards the Russian Railway, the Austrians are Beaten Back—Their Right Wing is Broken by a Frontal Attack, their Centre is Encircled, their Left Wing Turned and Broken—Complete Disaster, Ending in a Rout in the River Marshes—Germany Saves Her Ally from Total Destruction.

OR some centuries Austria has been the whipping-top of Europe. She has been lashed by the Turks, the Swedes, the Prussians, and the French, among others. The Polish king, John Sobieski, alone prevented the Crescent from displacing the Cross at Vienna—a debt the Austrians afterwards repaid by sharing largely in the destruction of Poland. The Russians alone prevented the Hungarians from breaking up the Empire in the middle of the nineteenth century—another debt the Austrians have now attempted to discharge, with characteristic cynical ingratitude, by the invasion of Russia.

This, however, was mere infatuation on the part of the Austrians. Even with the help of the Hungarians, still anxious for vengeance on the Russians for putting down their movement of independence, the attack on Russia was an act of madness. For nearly one half of the Austrian Army consisted of men of the Slav race, oppressed by their Germanic and Magyar lords, and looking to their fellow-Slavs in mighty Russia for redemption and liberation. Half of the Austrian Army consisted largely of troops anxious to kill the Austrians and fight for Russia.

It was this unparalleled condition of things that doomed Austria to destruction as soon as she dared to take the field against Russia. Russia was the one Power she could not attack with the shadow of a hope of success. Far easier would it have been for her to attempt to conquer her old foe Prussia. But, tricked by the Prussian, and egged on by the vengeful, ambitious Hungarian, Austria set out on the road to her final disaster as an Imperial Power. In the first three weeks of the campaign of invasion everything went well. Along the frontier, running parallel with the Russian boundary, was a strategic system of railways, including two trunk lines, with a daily capacity of seventy trains, and ten cross lines. This system, constructed on the plan of the German system of attacking railways, enabled the Austrians to assemble a mighty host between Cracow and Przemysl. Crossing the border, this host of some 500,000 men deployed on Russian territory, and advanced towards Warsaw and Brest-Litovsk.

Very slowly did the great army move forward. Spread out on both sides of the Vistula, it crept towards Radom on the left side of the river and Lublin and Kholm on the other side.

The fact was the Austrians were waiting for the Germans to co-operate with them. But German vanguards touched at Lodz and Petrokov, on a line with Kielce, and then withdrew. The Russian counterstroke through Eastern Prussia engrossed all the forces Germany could spare from France. Austria, having been lured on to a most desperate enterprise by a solemn promise of a vigorous co-operation, was left alone at the critical period to pursue her perilous undertaking without assistance.

It is, therefore, not to be marvelled at that General Dankl, commanding the Austrian left wing, and General Auffenberg, directing the main Austrian army, should have hesitated to penetrate far into Russian

THE AUSTRIAN EMPEROR AT PRAYER.
From a postcard issued in the Austrian capital. Appended is a translation of his supposed "prayer":

"Father in Heaven, Ruler of the Universe,
Have pity for him who bows before Thee.
I did not start the strife nor strew the earth with blood.
Surrounded with foes and envy,
I called my people to the defence of arms.
Let Thy mercy surround our lines.
Ours will be the victory and Thine the honour."

105

ON THEIR WAY TO LEMBERG.

Russian lancers going to the front. Inset : The City Hall and Municipal Buildings at Warsaw. The Germans reached a point about six miles from Warsaw, but were then compelled to retire.

territory. The farther they went the longer their lines of communication grew, in a country where railways were few and good roads scarce. There was Napoleon's disastrous campaign in the same country to deter them from any swift and crushing swoop, such as their allies were working up to in the western theatre of war.

While the Austrians were hesitating the Russians were acting with decision and foresight. Though the Russian mobilisation was far from complete, a very considerable force had been collected between Warsaw and Kiev, and screened by cavalry this force began to shepherd the Austrian armies to their place of doom. In the great bend that the River Vistula makes as it curves from Cracow to Thorn, the progress of the Austro-Hungarian troops was not encouraged. All attempts to move towards Warsaw and Ivangorod were fiercely opposed, and the point of junction between the German militia troops and the Austrian soldiers of the first line could only be safely fixed at the upper course of the Warta River, close to the Silesian and German Poland province.

Inflating the vanity of Vienna On the other side of the Vistula, however, in the rolling wooded country between that river and its great eastern tributary the Bug, the Austrian armies were at first enticed to sweep onward, especially towards Kholm.

The advanced guards of the Russians were small and yielding, and the manner in which they continually gave ground enabled the hostile commanders to inflate, by daily reports of victories, the vanity of Vienna and the pride of Buda-Pesth. Rapid and tremendous victories were indeed a vital necessity to the Austrians and Hungarians. They needed them to daunt and dishearten their mutinous Slav subjects For even in Vienna two Czech or Bohemian regiments had to be decimated in order to induce them to

106

go to the front. Therefore every successful little outpost skirmish was magnified into an important battle, at which Russian armies had been routed.

Thus victoriously, General Dankl and General Auffenberg advanced on the towns of Lublin and Kholm, some fifty miles inside Russian territory. About August 25th they were within striking distance of these towns and of the railway that connected them and communicated with Ivangorod and Warsaw. But they were not allowed to capture either the towns or the railway. They had reached the line between the Vistula and the Bug, where the Grand Duke Nicholas had resolved to hold them. By this time the Russian armies under General Russky and General Brussiloff were **Austrians bogged in** moving southward through Galicia. **a swamp** Until they had strongly engaged the third Austrian army round Lemberg, which formed the right wing of the invading host, it would have been premature to join battle with the enemy's centre and left wing.

So from August 22nd to August 28th the Russian commander-in-chief merely kept the invaders away from the Lublin-Kholm railway line. The first engagement of importance appears to have taken place at Krinitz, near the railway, when the Austrians attempted to advance beyond the line fixed by their opponents. Two machine-gun officers took a position on a height from which they were able to enfilade the ranks of the invaders, and the action was decided by a splendid bayonet charge from which the Austrians fled, only to get bogged in a swamp. Six thousand of them were rescued with ropes and made prisoners.

The Russian bayonet was peculiarly effective in all large engagements with the mixed troops of the Austrian Empire. Against the Germans it was just a good, shaking instrument of attack. Against the Austrians it was a rending force of quite extraordinary power. It led to the capture of a quarter of a million prisoners in the first series of battles between the Polish rivers. This was due to the dispositions made by the Austrian and Hungarian leaders to compel their Slav regiments to fight. The disaffected troops were usually placed in the front trenches, with Teutonic or Magyar supports behind them, ready to shoot them down.

The idea was to compel them, against their will, to fight for their lives against the Russians whom they wanted to help. The Russian generals, however, were well aware of the disposition of troops opposing them, and they

GENERAL MEYENDORFF.
Awarded the Order of St. George.

GENERAL RUSSKY SURROUNDED BY SOME OF HIS OFFICERS.
Note the bearded and bespectacled Orthodox chaplain in the background

GENERAL KONDRATOVITCH.
Awarded the Order of St. George.

GENERAL VON AUFFENBERG.
Leader of the Austrian forces in Galicia.

skilfully took full advantage of the circumstances. They directed their guns, after the opening artillery duel was over, to shrapnel the enemy's second line, and sent the infantry in a bayonet charge, with little artillery support, against the first trenches. At first the Russian foot soldier marvelled at the badness of the Austrian rifle fire. For, naturally, most of the bullets from the front trenches were aimed over the heads of the attacking parties. Then, when the Russian infantry closed in with bayonets at the charge, the Slav regiments opposed to them were only too glad to surrender without a struggle.

In one case, however, the bayonet charge failed, and a sergeant-major helping to lead it was taken prisoner. Finding it was a Slav officer under whose charge he was placed, the Russian began to talk to him—their languages being close enough in origin to make conversation possible. With great eloquence the sergeant-major discoursed on the kindness with which all Slav troops were received in the Russian camp, and the great work of liberation the Russians were performing for all Slav peoples. The upshot was that the Slav officer and his company crept out of the Austrian lines and surrendered to the Russians.

The Germans got out of a similar difficulty by using up many of their Polish regiments in the attack on Liège, where they fell in tens of thousands. But Austria could not rely on her Slav troops either in the Serbian battles or the Russian conflicts. She was fighting Slavs on both fronts of war, and all her subject populations were Slavs by race or by sympathy—Serbs, Croatians or Catholic Serbs, Russians, Bohemians, and Slovaks, or Rumanians.

To these men the Russian bayonet, when it came close enough to their trenches to make surrender safe, was an instrument of liberation from political and military tyranny. Hence the extraordinary number of prisoners taken in the war with Austria-Hungary.

The Austrians and Hungarians might well have stood against the Russians until Germany was able to afford vigorous help if they had relied entirely on soldiers of their own race. They would then have been able to bring up against Russia only about half a million first-line troops, instead of gathering more than a million of the regular Army for a mighty offensive movement. They would have had a small chain with no weak part in it, instead of a large chain with almost every alternate link of it near breaking point. As it was, the Grand Duke Nicholas and his Chief of Staff, General Sukhomlinoff, had the enemy at their mercy as soon as they were ready to strike. In numbers their armies were probably inferior to those of General Dankl and General Auffenberg and the Archduke Frederick. For as soon as the Austrians felt the menacing pressure on their front, stretching from Radom across the Vistula to the left bank of the River Bug, they began to hurry up reinforcements. In the

GENERAL DIMITRIEFF.
Bulgaria's "Iron General" serving with Russia.

GENERAL ROETZENDORF.
Chief of the Austrian Military Staff.

GENERAL LOBKO.
Awarded the Order of St. George.

SCENE DURING THE TEMPORARY RELIEF OF PRZEMYSL BY THE AUSTRIANS.
When the German advance on Warsaw compelled a portion of the Russian forces around Przemysl to be withdrawn, the Austrian commander sent a relief force to the assistance of the town. This force was welcomed with enthusiasm. Of this the camera affords evidence in the above photograph, which shows the Austrian commander, General F. M. L. von Kusmanek, in a balcony on the left.

end they had about 700,000 men between the Polish rivers, another 300,000 deployed in a refused right wing in Galicia, with divisions of Landwehr troops for supports and guarding the lines of communication.

The four opposing Russian armies amounted at first to little more than six hundred thousand men. Battalions were continually detraining from the railway head and marching into the firing-line, but this channel of reinforcement was not ample enough at the critical period. To supply the Grand Duke Nicholas with the men he needed, General Sukhomlinoff did a most daring thing. He drew off some of the army corps that had invaded East Prussia and railed them to Ivangorod to strengthen the Russian left wing at Lublin.

General Sukhomlinoff's daring

This was carried out when the German commander, General von Hindenburg, was massing at Thorn for his counter-attack upon the two Russian forces of invasion at Tannenberg and Königsberg. The two Russian army corps defeated under General Samsonoff at Tannenberg, in Prussia, were sacrificed to the exigencies of the position at Lublin and Kholm. General Rennenkampf at Königsberg was given the difficult task of fighting his way back to his own frontier, with a weakened force, against superior pressure of Hindenburg's army. He had yet to keep Hindenburg so fully employed as to prevent any considerable part of the German army in Prussia from being railed into Poland to help the Austrians.

Strengthened meanwhile by part of General Rennenkampf's troops, the main Russian army at Lublin and Kholm suddenly assumed the offensive. This was done on August 26th, when the Russian right wing advanced against General Dankl's army near Krasnic. As the attack was not driven home, the Austrians claimed the victory. But the action had the effect intended. General Dankl was made anxious. To increase his strength he brought across the Vistula part of the Austrian force operating round Kielce in expectation of German support in a movement towards Warsaw and Ivangorod. This weakened the subsequent outflanking attack delivered on the other side of the river at Ivangorod. Even more immediately important was the check to General Dankl's advance towards Lublin. In conjunction with the attack that afterwards followed on Ivangorod, the progress of Dankl's army along the other bank of the Vistula would have endangered the entire Russian position. It would have cut the Russian armies in Prussia, Poland, and Galicia in two. Dankl was so placed as to be extremely dangerous; he was therefore repressed. Auffenberg, as he advanced towards Kholm, was only running his neck into a noose; he was therefore encouraged to proceed.

Such were the circumstances in **A two-hundred-mile** which the decisive stage of the battle **battle-front** opened on Friday, August 28th. Far in the south, at the extreme right wing of the two-hundred-mile battle-front, General Russky and General Brussiloff were then fiercely engaging the Lemberg armies. To prevent any troops being shifted from the Austrian left wing or centre to the support of the overwhelmed right wing, the Russian Commander-in-Chief strongly attacked all along the line. The centre, by Tomashov, close on the frontier and near the railway running to Lemberg was

AUSTRIAN CADETS' ENTHUSIASM ON THE DECLARATION OF WAR.
After being sworn in, the Austrian "sucklings," or cadets, were drawn up in a square, where they gave loud "Hochs!" for their Kaiser as they lifted their unfleshed swords high in the air. From the vacant stand on the right of the picture a stirring harangue had just been delivered.

the point from which reinforcements could most easily have been moved. So there the Russian attack was driven with most violence, with the result that the 15th Hungarian Division was smashed and routed.

The general battle raged for a week between the Vistula and the Bug without any decision being fought out. The fact was that this period of the conflict was not important from the standpoint of the Russian commander. He only wished to hold back Dankl, and so to annoy Auffenberg as to prevent him from helping the Archduke Frederick in Galicia. There, at Zloczow, Halicz, and

Breaking the Austrian right wing Lemberg, General Russky and General Brussiloff and General Radko Dimitrieff were breaking through the southern Austrian right wing, and thus turning the other Austrian positions northward between Lublin and Kholm. The main Russian army had to wait for a successful issue of its detached southern forces.

Naturally, both Dankl and Auffenberg knew what was happening far to the south. Furious were the attempts they at once made to retrieve the defeat of their distant right wing by shattering the main Russian army in front

of them. They knew now what was coming up against their rear, taking them in the back. So they tried hard to break through the enemy before them while they had time. They still had a strong force near Radom, across the Vistula. On August 31st this force made a desperate

WITH THE TROOPS OF THE EMPEROR FRANCIS JOSEPH ON THE OUTBREAK OF HOSTILITIES.
Austrian troops entraining for the front, outside the arsenal in Vienna. Inset: Austrian sentry guarding a railway line on the Galician frontier.

advance on Ivangorod, a fortress town possessing the only available bridge over the great river. Had Ivangorod been won, the main Russian army would have had the tables turned on it and been taken in the rear. But the Ivangorod garrison, with Russian forces operating round Warsaw, defeated the Austrians. These retired up the river towards Opole, where General Dankl had entrenched, threw two pontoon bridges over the water, and joined his army. Strengthened by them, Dankl again tried to reach the Lublin railway, but the Russian commander, having thrown all his reinforcements on this side, beat back the advance once more.

The Austrian attack on Ivangorod

While the attack on Ivangorod was being made by the Austrians over the river, with Dankl co-operating with them on the opposite side, General Auffenberg in the centre also violently assailed the Russian main army.

Instead of the Grand Duke Nicholas having to stir him to activity to prevent him reinforcing the unhappy Archduke Frederick, the Russian Commander-in-Chief was hard put to it to resist Auffenberg's driving assault. In this part of the battlefield the Russian lines had to be drawn back; and it looked as though Kholm would be captured. For this was the weakest spot in the Russian front; it was allowed to remain weak, and a severe strain was put on the troops defending it.

But the position of the opposing forces suddenly changed about September 6th. By a wonderful feat of marching General Russky brought some of his troops up from Lemberg, and Auffenberg's army was then attacked on three fronts. All the offensive was knocked out of it by the heavy losses it suffered, it was completely reduced to a defensive role, and compelled at some points to retreat.

For a few hours it looked as though the Austrian front would be pierced. But both General Auffenberg and the Archduke Frederick worked with great energy to repair their centre and right wing. A magnificent reinforcement of 300,000 German troops with heavy artillery was railed to them in the nick of time, together with some excellent supports from the Tyrol and Hungary. One hundred and fifty thousand of the Germans marched with their big guns into Russian territory, and were placed on the hills round Turobin, between Dankl's and Auffenberg's forces.

Opportune German aid

The other three German army corps were used to stiffen a new right wing, formed of the fresh Austro-Hungarian troops, and the fugitives from the Battles of Halicz and Lemberg. These fugitives were mainly loyalists, the disaffected Slavs to the number of 70,000 having surrendered to the Russians. Refitted, reorganised, and emptied of mutinous troops, the broken Galician army was really more powerful than it had been before. But this was not known until the test came. It is impossible not to admire the speed and ability with which the Austrian

THE RUSSIAN RED CROSS SERVICE—ONE OF THE MOST PERFECT IN THE WORLD.
Russian Red Cross train about to leave Petrograd for the front. On the right are seen the Russian Minister for War and the Grand Duchess Anastasie Nicholaieovna. Inset: A hospital under canvas. Corner of a village that sprang up in the war area in answer to the call of the Russian Red Cross. The Russian and Japanese Red Cross organisations are among the best in the world. Only a day or two before the war the Moscow Municipal Council voted £1,000,000 for the Red Cross service.

RUSSIAN SOLDIERS AT PRAYER OUTSIDE A COTTAGE IN GALICIA.
The simple, devout faith of the Russian soldier is proverbial. This remarkable photograph shows a group outside a rural cottage in Galicia during a lull in the fierce fighting there. Among the men is an official of the Red Cross Society.

Commander-in-Chief—the Archduke Frederick—restored the greater part of his army from a condition of disaster to a state of strength.

The final position on which the Austrians posted themselves was a strong line to hold. Indeed, it might have been regarded as excellent, if it were not for the marshes behind it and its distance from the frontier railways. The troops were ranged between the Vistula and the Bug on a line running from Opole to Zamosc and Tomashov. In one place they were still within gunshot of the Lublin railway.

The country was rolling and wooded, affording good cover for infantry, and admirable positions for foliage-screened batteries. The first German force of 150,000 men, with heavy artillery, entrenched at Turobin on hills a thousand feet high, with a river running at the foot and moating their earthworks. They formed the central point in the main battle-front, and some 900,000 Austrians, Hungarians, Italians from the Trentino, and subject Slavs extended the lines for 200 miles. They had at least about 2,500 pieces of artillery, including the German guns, and Maxims in great abundance.

Central point of main battle-front No outflanking movement by the Russian army seemed possible. The first Austrian force, under Dankl, stretched from Opole, above Krasnic, and was protected by the wide, deep, unbridged waters of the Vistula. Moreover, Austrian war-boats, with quick-firing guns, joined in the battle from the river, in somewhat the same way as the British monitors afterwards took part in the Nieuport conflict in the North Sea.

There was, as an additional measure of security, a German division operating on the other side of the broad stream. General Dankl's army appear to have included the three German army corps on the Turobin heights.

Connecting with the Germans was the second Austrian army, under General Auffenberg, that held the hilly region from Turobin to Tomashov. The third army, hastily organised after the defeat of the Galician forces, guarded the rear of Auffenberg's and Dankl's troops. It extended like a defending wall from north to south, about a day's march from Lemberg. The fortress of Gorodok, westward on the Lemberg road, was its pivoting point, and the town of Ravaruska, near the Russian frontier, was the point at **Austrian concentration at Ravaruska** which it was concentrated for the protection of Auffenberg's army. The third army formed what is technically known as a refused wing. Instead of prolonging the general front, like an ordinary wing, it bent sharply downwards at Ravaruska, almost at a right angle to the main Austrian line between the rivers. A refused wing of this kind is the best posture of defence against a turning movement.

From the orthodox point of view of the Teutonic and Magyar strategists of the Moltke school, they had recovered from the effects of the Galician reverses, and brought their opponents suddenly to the position of a stalemate. For their armies were as strongly posted in Russian Poland in the first week in September as the German armies were in France in the third week of that month. The Turobin heights, especially where heavy guns were being hauled into their pits, looked more difficult to storm than the plateau of Soissons in the Aisne valley. A frontal attack up long slopes and over streams and marshes, against thousands of guns, tens of thousands of Maxims, and a million rifles, entrenched with wire entanglements, seemed to the Austrian commander a thing impossible of success. And the obvious enveloping

GUNS OF THE RIVAL FORCES IN GALICIA.
Striking photograph of a battery of Austrian heavy guns, intended to repel the Russian advance into Galicia. The view on the left is of a specially constructed gun fixed in one of the Russian trenches for the purpose of bringing down hostile aircraft.

To begin with, a feint thrust was made at a point far removed from the spot chosen for the real piercing attack. We have seen that for some time the Russian commander had been driving fiercely down on Auffenberg's army, that formed the centre of the Austrian battle-line. After the fall of Lemberg part of the victorious Southern Russian forces also began to drive vehemently up towards Auffenberg. Auffenberg thus had good reasons for supposing that on his troops the main offensive movement of his opponents would fall. So it did in the **Subtle tactics of the** end. But all the first operations against **Grand Duke Nicholas** him were a feint. The Russians desired to shift the bulk of the Austro-German reinforcements towards the centre and the right wing of their enemy.

It was on the left wing of the Austrians that the real frontal attack was to be made. So, against all expectations, General Dankl, in his apparently quite impregnable position on the Vistula and the Turobin hills, was the first to feel the full weight and edge of Russia's power. For some days the long battle continued in a close-pressed Russian offensive all along the line. Auffenberg suffered most at Tomashov, where General Russky was co-operating in the attack. When this delusive operation had taken effect, the hammer-stroke fell some forty miles eastward on Dankl's army.

The decisive tactics of the Grand Duke Nicholas had a characteristic subtlety about them. He massed a strong force with many guns on the opposite side of the Vistula. It was composed of the troops who had defeated the Austrian attack on Ivangorod. They could easily destroy the single German division that was holding the left bank of the river. This they did about September 8th. Meanwhile, General Dankl was invited to advance from his strong, entrenched position. The pressure upon his front was entirely relaxed now that the general reserve had been massed behind the troops that had been holding him. No doubt General Dankl concluded that the pressure exerted on his colleague General Auffenberg was obtained by weakening the forces opposed to him.

He resolved to take advantage of this state of things, and also to relieve the pressure at Tomashov, by another swift, forceful offensive movement towards his customary objective—Lublin and the railway line. The road was left clear for him to within eight miles of the alluring railway to Warsaw. Then, however, his men were hurled back with great violence and speed. The cavalry had to be

movement by the flank was prevented by the waters of the Vistula on one side, and on the other by the fortress of Gorodok and by a larger army than the Russians possessed at Lemberg.

Therefore, there remained only, from the defenders' standpoint, a slow open-air siege battle of the Mukden kind, in which the Russians would be busily occupied until General von Hindenburg could swing round from Prussia to the Lower Vistula and threaten to take the Russians in the rear. The German railways were so built as to make this operation facile and rapid of execution.

But since the Russians themselves had fought the first modern siege battles in Manchuria, they had thought out a way of avoiding them. They proceeded to **Avoiding an open-air** show the Austrians how it could be done. **siege battle** They intended a terrific frontal attack in the old Napoleonic fashion, but against such a power of defensive machinery as Napoleon never faced even at Waterloo. Instead of throwing all his troops forward, the Russian commander collected a general reserve, which was manœuvred behind the battle-front and shifted by severe marches to the point that promised to yield and break.

thrown out to the Cossacks to prevent these swarming, furious horsemen from riding down the retreating infantry and getting at the guns. A few days before the Cossacks had already won in a smashing charge against the Austrian horsemen, and now they were riding to the great victory. Rearguard after rearguard had to be sacrificed to them and to their rapidly advancing infantry supports. Before the infantry went the Russian horse artillery; behind them rumbled the main ordnance—light quick-firers, heavy guns, and howitzers.

The Austrians were barely back in their trenches when the first great frontal attack of the modern era was delivered. It was no Zulu-like charge, in dense crowds that relied only on the steel, such as the German attempts to pierce the British lines at Mons and Le Cateau. The Russian infantry instructors had learnt in the Far Eastern campaign to modify charging tactics so as to lessen losses from shrapnel fire, and to make the power of the long-range rifle tell on the enemy in the trenches before the bayonets came close enough to shake his courage.

There was the preliminary artillery duel, in which the superior Russian guns were pushed forward to search and overpower the hostile batteries. This result was largely achieved. Some Austrian river gunboats tried to get an enfilading fire against the Russians, only to be smitten from the side themselves. For by this time the Russian force on the farther bank of the Vistula had routed the German division and brought up their guns to take part in the battle. The hostile gunboats had to sink or retire, and the riverside Russian batteries then began in turn to enfilade the Austrian position.

Infantry tactics learnt in the Far East While this side conflict was proceeding, with important consequences for General Dankl's troops in their hour of retreat, the decisive infantry attack on the front opened. In grey lines the armed peasants of Russia moved onward from cover to cover, making quick rushes, and then lying prone and firing steadily at any heads showing in the trenches, while their supports were running into position behind them. In patience under heavy fire they were as good as British soldiers; they stood severe punishment without losing their nerve. But in extended order, and in situations calling for individual initiative, they were not each a born, trained non-commissioned officer of the first class, as most of our privates have proved themselves. Accustomed in their village life to act collectively, they tended to crowd together at critical moments. Yet they were magnificent troops. They retained completely all the sterling old qualities of their race, and showed themselves finer marksmen and more brilliant fighters than their fathers. They judged the ranges quickly and well, and they did not lose their head as the time neared for bayonet work. Unlike our soldiers, they saw no hip-firing among their opponents. Their only criticism of the Austrians was that they made targets of themselves by kneeling to fire, instead of lying prone and aiming.

But excellently trained though the **The frontal attack** Russian soldier was in modern infantry **revived** work, the bayonet remained his supreme instrument of warfare. For he had been instructed by his masters of the new Russian school, who had revived the doctrine of the frontal attack, that the steel would again win the victory. And so it did, in spite of quick-firing guns, magazine rifles, and aerial reconnaissance work, wire entanglements, and the deadly Maxim's stream of bullets.

Except for wire entanglements and sheltering trenches, all these new weapons could be used by the attackers as well as by the defenders. The storming companies, if held up by fire from the trenches, could suddenly open out and let the machine-guns, brought up behind them, rake the defending riflemen and sweep the hostile Maxims. The artillery of the offensive army had a fixed mark when the position of the defending trenches was discovered, as the range and the time-fuse could be exactly measured by the gunners supporting the infantry attack. The rival artillerymen, on the other hand, had in the advancing troops a series of rapidly shifting targets over which it was often difficult to get shrapnel to burst at the accurate place and moment.

With all this, however, the Russians had to suffer heavily to win their goal. In neither old nor new wars had a well-defended front been pierced without great sacrifice of life. Slowly, stubbornly, the quiet, enduring moujik advanced under the cover of his thundering guns. At last, when he reached the edge of possible safety, he closed in crowds and charged. He fell. His immediate supports came on at the double. They, too, fell. But a great host was

KRAVCHENKO, A DISTINGUISHED RUSSIAN WAR ARTIST, SKETCHING A SPY DISGUISED AS PEASANT.
A spy masquerading as an inoffensive peasant had been brought into the Russian lines by a Cossack patrol, and his picturesque appearance attracted the attention of the famous Russian artist, Kravchenko, who, it will be noticed, was wearing military uniform. This was compulsory for all war correspondents accompanying the Russian forces.

pressing behind them, ranged company after company, battalion after battalion. Every yard the fallen leaders gained was held by their advancing, innumerable comrades. The sun went down and the stars came out in the darkness, and in the obscurity of the night the attackers pressed their advantage and broke the enemy's front just as dawn was breaking.

It was at the village of Vysoky, eastward of Krasnic, that the lines of General Dankl's army were pierced on Sept-

Success that came with the dawn

ember 9th. There the Russian bayonet came over the Austrian trench, stabbing with dreadful skill as it passed. Behind, the machine-guns were pushed through the first broken defence, to help in the decisive work of shattering the enemy's second line. As the foremost troops were fighting in the twilight of daybreak against the re-forming Austrians, another mass of grey, tall figures crashed into the conflict—troops fresh and unblooded to human slaughter, but worked into pitiless fury by the sight of the heaps of dead or maimed comrades that cumbered the ground over which they came. The Austrians broke and fled.

General Dankl abandoned his position with great speed. The danger was that the Cossack cavalry, pouring through the gap, would get on his rear and break up the retreat. The Germans at Turobin bitterly complained afterwards that they had been deserted by the men who had called them up to aid them. But the fact was that the Austrians had to retire with vehement rapidity to prevent an annihilating rout. For besides being broken in front, they were enfiladed as they collected in masses by shrapnel fire from the Russian guns on the opposite side of the river. In the end they managed to get out rearguards and withdraw along the Vistula in order.

But the suddenness of their unexpected retreat exposed the German army of 150,000 on Turobin heights to a surprise flank attack. The Germans had not even got all their big guns into position when the victorious Russians attacked them sideways through the opening in the front left by the retreating Austrians. After losing 5,000 men, they had to abandon their heavy artillery—thirty-two splendid new guns engraved with the monogram of the German Emperor. But, fighting bravely, they withdrew to the south-east, in the direction taken by their allies, and reached the Vistula at Annapol.

All this Austro-German left wing could have been completely routed, and even annihilated, by the attacking army and its powerful supports on the opposite bank of the Vistula. But the Russian commander was aiming at larger results than the immediate destruction of General Dankl's forces. In pursuit of these results he detached only sufficient troops to keep the beaten wing on the move along the shore of the Vistula, and thrust it back if it tried to turn eastward and grope for a connection with its centre.

Every other Russian soldier was then marched, weary but nerved by victory to more labour and fighting, against the western flank and rear of the central Austrian armies under General Auffenberg. For the flight of the Germans

from the heights of Turobin had naturally exposed their neighbours on their left to a turning movement similar to that which had made them retire.

But the Grand Duke Nicholas did not intend the Austrian centre to escape by a retreat. All through the evening and night of September 9th the Russian troops marched, some corps covering a remarkable distance by a splendid display of endurance. The result was that Auffenberg's army on September 10th was completely encircled. General Russky held it on the south-west near Tomashov. Round Zamosc and along the northern front it was retained by its old opponents; on the east and south part of the Russian left wing barred all the roads. It was a greater Sedan.

In the hope of avoiding the ghastly work of slaughtering some hundreds of thousands of men, the Russian commander sent an officer under a white flag to ask General Auffenberg to surrender. But, as usually happens in such circumstances in modern warfare, Auffenberg declined, for he was determined to attempt to break through the enveloping army. Any good general would have taken this course.

For it is now generally known that even at Sedan, in spite of Moltke's strategy, the French had a fighting chance of piercing the ring around them. There was a weak point in it, which if discovered and struck would have opened a path of retreat. With fair supplies of ammunition and food, an encircled army that strikes fiercely and rapidly, as the Germans afterwards did at Lodz, can often get out with the loss of a fourth or a fifth of its numbers.

This was what General Auffenberg essayed to achieve. But he did not entirely succeed. After a day of frightful slaughter his men began to lose their cohesion. North and east and west the Russians drove in upon them, and though the southernmost attacking force drew off, leaving an apparent path of retreat, this movement was as deadly in effect as an attack would have been. For the only line of retirement thus allowed to

ALL THAT WAS LEFT OF A FINE BRIDGE IN POLAND BY RETREATING GERMANS.

the broken Austrians led to the wide, disastrous swamp lands of the River San. Into this terrible trap Auffenberg's army was forced by blow after blow on flanks and rear.

At the same time Dankl's army, now separated by a two days' march from its broken centre, was more vigorously handled by the Russian commander. Vast as his battlefield was, portable wireless instruments and aerial messenger service by high-speed flying machines enabled the Grand Duke Nicholas and his Chief of Staff to control all operations over a front of two hundred miles better than Napoleon had controlled Grouchy at Waterloo.

As soon as Auffenberg's forces were scattered and bogged in the southern river swamps some of the Russian troops were again moved towards the Vistula to co-operate in drawing Dankl's army in disorder into another stretch of marshland between the Vistula and its tributary the

Austrian commander's bad strategy

San. The water draining from the Carpathian Mountains into Galicia turns both rivers into streams that ooze and trickle for miles into the country on either side, and turn the land, even in the month of September, into green, untraversable morasses. It was bad strategy on the part of the Austrian Commander-in-Chief to place his armies with

AN AUSTRIAN FIELD TELEGRAPH IN OPERATION
IN POLAND.

three days and nights the conflict raged unceasingly, and Dimitrieff had to use his troops to the uttermost, allowing none of them a moment's rest. Not a single detail could be given the least repose. The fatigue was so overpowering that on the last day the men fell asleep under fire.

One officer dropped off and never woke through all the tremendous bombardment, the rifle firing, and the attempt to take his trenches. When he opened his eyes he found himself lying close to a pile of dead, and on trying to move he discovered he was hurt. Two of his toes had been cut off by a shrapnel bursting while he slept.

Exhausted soldiers fall asleep under fire

Between sleeping and waking General Radko Dimitrieff's heroes held their ground against artillery fire, varied by bayonet attacks, until reinforcements arrived and the enemy was for the time driven off.

It was General Brussiloff who came to the help of his former companion in victory at Halicz. But even when their forces were united they were still outnumbered by the opposing army directed by the Archduke Frederick. Good Chiefs of Staff take care when an archduke, or a Crown Prince, or any other Royal commander is given control of an army that he shall have more troops than

their backs on a wide, long stretch of swamp. But he had been so confident of at least holding the Russian attack that he did not trouble to arrange for the possibility of a sudden retreat. In the end this cost him half his army, almost all his war stores, and a large number of his guns—some captured in the fight, but more bogged during the murderous rout through the river swamps.

For two or three days after the victory over the enemy's left wing and centre, the two immense bodies of defeated troops were shepherded into difficulties rather than continually cut down. For most of the victors were as fatigued as the vanquished, though the Cossack managed to make himself ubiquitous and indefatigable. He swam across the Vistula—no narrow flood of water—and blew up war stores piled for the use of the retreating army; he attacked armoured trains near the German frontier and wrecked them by a trick. And, chiefly, he kept the routed forces moving and allowed them no rally places.

Meanwhile, the Russian commander was again drawing off troops from the centre for more battle work. For the Austrian right wing in Galicia, between Ravaruska and Gorodok, close to Lemberg, was putting up a magnificent fight. This stand was unexpected, for, as we have seen, many of the troops had been thoroughly defeated in the first battles around Lemberg. The conflict appears to have begun soon after the capture of Lemberg, when the Bulgarian General Dimitrieff advanced with some 40,000 men to drive in the still retreating wing and thus expose the army of General Auffenberg to a rear attack.

On this part of the battlefield, however, there were suddenly poured enormous reinforcements, including the second three German army corps sent in

Radko Dimitrieff's formidable task

answer to Austria's appeal. Radko Dimitrieff's troops were then tested almost as severely as were Sir Horace Smith-Dorrien's army corps at Le Cateau a week or so before. The Austro-Germans took the offensive and made continual attacks of a most determined kind. The brunt of these assaults fell upon the 40,000 men under the heroic Bulgarian. In this place the Austrians and Germans outnumbered the Russians by four—or even five—to one. The Russians fought in a splendidly stubborn and enduring manner. For

AUSTRIAN REFUGEES IN VIENNA.
Vienna, like Berlin, as a result of the Russian advance in the early stages of the Great War, witnessed a big incursion of refugees from the east. Our picture gives ample evidence of the haste with which the fugitives—men, women, and children—fled to the Austrian capital before the rolling tide of the Russian invasion.

his opponent. General Conrad von Roetzendorf, the head of the Austrian General Military Staff, had so arranged matters in this case. A large part of the Russian Galician army had marched northward, under General Russky, to help in the envelopment of Auffenberg's forces. General Brussiloff and General Dimitrieff had to struggle along with scanty forces until Russky, having thrust back Auffenberg, could again march from the north and co-operate with them.

The Russian Commander-in-Chief certainly worked his troops tremendously hard. Both his generals and his men had to force themselves to the limit of their powers. It was only by each of them performing the work of two to three men that they outmanœuvred, outfought, and finally destroyed the fighting power of a million enemy troops of the first line. By doing treble the amount of marching and double the amount of fighting, the Russians, though inferior in numbers to their foes, exerted against them twice the amount of warlike power. This is the grand, the classic strategy—the strategy of Napoleon and Nelson, of Marlborough and Turenne. Great commanders in land warfare almost always overwork their men. They get more out of them than the men dreamt they possessed. Hence, the extraordinary force they display. Hence also, on the modern battle-fronts, a hundred or more miles in length, the need for young, athletic troops with the quick recuperative vigour of youth.

The mounted Cossack did not count for much in the decisive battles. His horsemanship told only in the preliminary reconnaissances and in the rout of the enemy. But there was one period of peril to the Russian force near Gorodok when the Cossack horsemen, like the British cavalry division at Mons, saved the situation.

A considerable power of Austrians and Germans assailed the Russian advance guard, with a view to shattering it and then breaking through the centre. The Russian infantry and guns were strongly entrenched. In reserve there were several Cossack detachments. At first the Austrian foot soldiers attacked under **Where the Cossack** cover of a bombardment. But they en- **saved the situation** countered so heavy a gun fire and rifle fire that they wavered and fell back.

Then an attempt was made to carry the trenches by a cavalry charge. The flower of the Austro-Hungarian army —the Buda-Pesth Guard Division—officered by the Magyar nobility, was hurled against the Russian front. The Hungarians, in their bright jackets, galloped furiously forward in close order. It seemed as though nothing could stay their impetuous course. Massed shrapnel fire made great gaps in their ranks ; a rain of bullets from the machine-guns swept away their leading squadrons ; at last the magazine rifles of the Russian infantry volleyed at them.

But the Hungarians never hesitated. Those who survived only urged their horses to cover the ground more quickly, and prepared to strike. The Russian infantry rose with their bayonets in a hopeless attempt to repel an overwhelming charge. In less than a minute, it seemed, the trenches would be taken. But behind them the infantry heard a thud of hoofs and clatter of steel, and the Hungarians were countered by a whirlwind of Cossacks. For two hours the Austrian and Russian infantry watched with excited eyes the scene of carnage, each cheering on their men, and getting in a quick helping shot on occasion. In the end not a man was left of the First Cavalry Division of the Buda-Pesth Guard. Its commander, General Frohreich, it was reported, could not bear the disgrace of the defeat and shot himself on the battlefield.

With desperate valiancy the Austro-German right wing tried to maintain its position between Ravaruska and Gorodok. When its centre and left wing gave way the need for holding out against the southern Russian army became still more urgent. For it then had to cover the retreat of Dankl's and Auffenberg's forces, and pre- vent General Brussiloff and General Dimitrieff from sweeping down also upon the broken fugitives. But on September 12th General Russky joined again with General Brussiloff and General Dimitrieff. The Archduke Frederick's force was turned in the north, and it, too, fled westward. More fortunate than the other two Austro-German armies, it was able to fall back towards the famous fortress of Przemysl—the Gibraltar of the Austrian Empire—

which required a long siege, even with modern howitzers, to reduce it. But it was only a disorganised rabble that arrived at Przemysl. For Russky pressed so hard on it from the north, while his subordinate commanders drove at its rear as it turned, that it was rent with terrible losses and then impelled along the western road in a huddle of spiritless men.

Altogether the disaster that overtook the military forces of the Austrian Empire in their attempted invasion of Russia was the greatest catastrophe known since Napoleon's retreat from Moscow. The modern invaders, however, were not defeated by the bitter Russian winter weather, or lessened in number to the point of weakness by the necessity of guarding an extremely long line of com- munications. They were abruptly overthrown when they were at their full strength and posted in a position of extraordinary defensive power. The Battle of the Vistula and the Dniester—if we may name it by the rivers between which the opposing fronts extended—was one of the greatest victories in history, both from the military and the political points of view.

It suddenly brought to an end the Imperial rule of the Hapsburgs. For the immediate result of it was to throw the most ancient of Teutonic Empires, linked by its traditions of the Holy Roman Empire with the age of Charlemagne, into the power of the northern parvenu Prussian Empire. Forged by blood-and-iron methods, of which the reigning Austrian Emperor and his people had been among the first victims at Königratz, the Empire of the Prussians at once absorbed both Austria and Hungary.

Practically the entire military force of any value of the ancient Empire was, in the middle of September, reduced to half a million men struggling for their lives in morasses and besieged fortresses against the victorious troops of Russia. There followed a dreadful week of nightmare horrors for the floundering, broken Austrians and Hungarians still being pursued between the Vistula and the San Rivers. **A week of** For the Germans, retreating in their **nightmare horrors** turn before the conquering Franco-British forces, were in too great difficulties to afford any help to their apparently doomed ally. It looked for a time as though the Russians would kill or capture every regiment of the million troops that had invaded their territory.

But, by her stand on the heights of the Aisne, Germany recovered herself in time to help her broken ally. Large bodies of fresh troops and vast supplies of new war material were quickly railed towards Cracow, and at last the pressure was taken off the beaten, driven armies of Austria. What remained of them was refitted and re- organised, and then placed under the control of the German Military Staff. For practical purposes Austria- Hungary as a military Power had ceased to exist. She had suddenly declined from an independent Empire into a contemned, subservient vassal territory, exploited for the defence of Germany. Hungary, especially, was robbed of troops necessary for the defence of the Car- pathian passes and the wheatfields of the Danube, in order that her finest men should perish in tens of thousands at Ypres in a vain attempt to conquer Calais for the Prussian.

THE SLEEP OF EXHAUSTION.
A wounded Russian soldier, utterly worn out in the warfare in Galicia, fallen asleep near the trenches where he had been fighting against the Austrians.

From the Painting by Charles M. Sheldon.

Vice-Admiral Sir David Beatty. K.C.B., M.V.O., D.S.O.

THE WINTER PALACE | CHAPTER XXXIII. | AND SQUARE, PETROGRAD.

THE MARCH OF EVENTS FROM AUSTRIA'S DEBACLE AT LEMBERG TO THE TURN OF THE TIDE IN THE WEST.

Phases of the Recruiting Problem in Great Britain—The War and the Chemical Industries—The King and the Belgian Mission—M. Clemenceau's Optimism—Paris under Martial Law—Protection for Masterpieces in the Louvre—Refugees from Northern France—Petrograd—The Enemy at Amiens—Compiègne a City of the Dead—The Fighting at Solesmes—The British Working Classes and the War—Patriotism of the Dominions—From Paris to Bordeaux: M. Poincaré's Inspiring Address—General Gallieni's Proclamation—Evacuation of Rouen—Saving of the British Exhibits at Leipzig—The United States and the War—Mr. Asquith at the Guildhall—Turkey and Germany—New Naval and Marine Brigades—The Allies and Peace—Fine Utterance by Lord Rosebery—Italian Sympathies—A Russian Governor for Galicia—The Anglo-French Retreat to the Marne—The Dykes Opened in Flanders—Controversies in Berlin—The Chancellor and the Silver Bullets.

IN the early days of September the problem of recruiting for the strengthening of the British Expeditionary Force co-operating with our allies in France and Belgium was the subject of earnest consideration throughout the United Kingdom. The spirit of patriotism and self-sacrifice was abroad. In London alone on some days as many as 5,000 offered themselves for enlistment. Some firms granted a bonus of £2 to young, single men in their employment who took, in the old phrase, the King's shilling. Others promised from five shillings a week to half their pay if the youngsters would join the colours. Some railway companies treated all single men who responded to the recruiting sergeant as on leave with full pay.

An appeal to young Nonconformists to enlist without delay was made by Sir William Robertson Nicoll, editor of the "British Weekly," the leading exponent of Nonconformity in the British Press. "That Nonconformists are neither cowardly nor incapable," he said, "when called to a righteous war, the glorious name of Oliver Cromwell sufficiently attests. That this is a most righteous and necessary war is a proposition which cannot be contested. If we were subjugated by Germany, we have no higher future before us than the life of a tributary

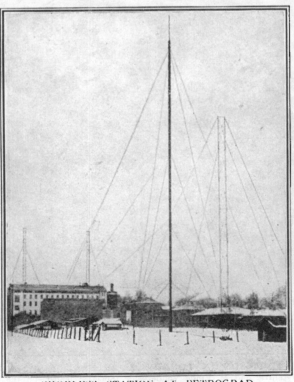

WIRELESS STATION AT PETROGRAD,
by means of which communications could be carried on with London and Paris.

province, harassed and humiliated at every point—a life so intolerable that death is infinitely preferred. The result may depend on a very slight preponderance of forces on either side. Every man who can fight is wanted at once. Hitherto there has been no attempt to drive the people, because it is felt that they can be led, and that when the issues are clearly set before them they will abhor as infinitely worse than death the stain of cowardice. For the Order of the White Feather there will soon be no room in our land."

Other public men, like Lord Charles Beresford, had a clarion note on "the imperative duty of every man in Great Britain to back up on land by our own sacrifice and devotion the onus that we were placing on the Fleet." Dealing with the cry that went up against the young men of Britain who were still playing sports and games, the gallant admiral added: "I cast no stones. The men who play football, cricket, and other games are our finest specimens of British manhood. I put it to them to consider—they are fit, strong, healthy, and as sportsmen they are cheery; health makes vigour, cheeriness makes pluck—I put it to them, that we must now all be prepared to stand by our country, and to suffer for our country. We want a million men. Why do I say a million? Because a million men will safeguard us, and—it is a very important point—when

SIR WILLIAM HENRY PERKIN.
He made the discovery which laid the foundation of the coal-tar dye industry. The factory erected by him and his brother at Greenford Green, near Harrow, in 1857, still exists, but the industry was almost wholly monopolised by the Germans.

the war is over we shall then have power behind our policy to uphold Great Britain in the councils of Europe."

Lord Kitchener himself inquired of the leaders of the great political parties if they would jointly agree that their organisations should give full co-operation in securing the enlistment of more men. This suggestion was at once adopted, and the official party organisations, consisting of the leaders, whips in both the Commons and the Lords, and chief officials, united for the purpose, with Mr. Asquith, Mr. Bonar Law, and Mr. Arthur Henderson, leader of the Labour Party, as presidents. Associated with them were Major-General Sir H. S. Rawlinson and Major A. B. Gossett, as representing the War Office. The headquarters of the movement were fixed at 12, Downing Street, the office of Mr. Percy Illingworth, the chief Government Whip, with whom was associated Lord Edmund Talbot, the chief Unionist Whip.

In many football unions it was decided to cancel all fixtures during the war, on the ground that it " would be desecrating their playing-fields to use them for sport at such a time."

Mr. Runciman, President of the Board of Trade, appointed a committee, of which the Lord Chancellor was chairman, to consider and advise as to the best means of obtaining for the use of British industry sufficient supplies of chemical products, colours and dye-stuffs, of kinds hitherto largely imported from countries with which we were at war. A little later the Government agreed to finance to some extent a company to begin the manufacture of colours and dye-stuffs, which are so necessary in every branch of the textile trade, more especially the woollen, in order to maintain employment, and prevent these trades languishing, if not collapsing. There was a species of retributive justice in this, as it was in Great Britain that the practicability of these colours and dye-stuffs being drawn from the bye-products of coal-tar was discovered and demonstrated by British chemists. It was only the slackness in British enterprise which enabled German organisation to take up

ELIZABETH, QUEEN OF THE BELGIANS.
Queen Elizabeth, who was married to King Albert in 1900, is a fully qualified doctor of medicine. Visiting the trenches, forts, and hospitals, her people wondered at times if she was not the spirit of their dear country, wandering with them to the last.

their manufacture and create almost a monopoly of supply to the textile trades.

H.M. King Albert of Belgium commissioned M. Carton de Wiart, Minister of Justice, M. de Saedeleer, M. Hymans, and M. Vandervelde, Ministers of State, with Mme. Vandervelde, and Count de Lichtervelde as secretary, as a royal mission to the President of the United States, empowered to submit definite proofs of German savagery during the enemy's occupation of their beloved land. On September 1st the members of the mission visited King George at Buckingham Palace, and had the honour of being presented to his Majesty by the Belgian Minister, the Lord Stanmore (Lord-in-Waiting) and the Master of the

THE BELGIAN MISSION IN LONDON.
M. Carton de Wiart (Minister of Justice) in centre, and M. Emile Vandervelde (Socialist leader) on the right. They were received in London by the King on their way to Washington to lay before the United States Government a statement of the German excesses in Belgium.

EAGER YOUNG RECRUITS FOR LORD KITCHENER'S NEW ARMY.
Crowds of young men besieging the recruiting offices in Whitehall, London, during the early days of Lord Kitchener's call for men.

Household being in attendance. M. Carton de Wiart, head of the mission, read an address to his Majesty on their behalf, in which he said : " We have considered it to be our duty to make a stay in the capital of the British Empire to convey to your Majesty the respectful and ardent expression of gratitude of the Belgian nation. We have never forgotten that Great Britain presided at the birth of Belgian independence. She had confidence in the wisdom and loyalty of our country. We have tried to justify this confidence by remaining strictly true to the role which had been assigned to us by international politics. In spite of all this suffering in Belgium, which has been made the personification of outraged right, the country is resolute in fulfilling to the utmost her duties towards Europe. Whatever may happen, she must defend her existence, her honour, and her liberty."

A sympathetic meeting, held in the Hotel Cecil on September 2nd, under the auspices of the Eighty Club, and attended by a large number of Members of Parliament, gave a send-off to the Belgian Mission.

London's send-off to the Belgian Mission M. Hymans and M. and Mme. Vandervelde made interesting speeches, in which they expressed unqualified faith in the final victory of the Allies over their ruthless German foes ; and the latter read a letter written on behalf of the Queen of the Belgians, in which her Majesty " approved of the plan of putting before the public opinion in Great Britain and the United States the suffering which the German invasion had inflicted upon their peaceful population. Five of the provinces of Belgium were devastated, thousands of families driven out of their houses were at that moment without a home, and it was deserving well of one's country and of humanity to try to help them. The best wishes of the Queen accompanied the mission to these two countries which love to help those in distress."

The spirit of France was reflected in a stirring statement made to a correspondent by M. Clemenceau, the great French statesman, on September 1st. Forgetting all personal differences with the existing Ministry, he said : " If we were to be defeated again, and yet again, we should still go on. This is not my personal resolve alone. The Government is just as grimly determined. It is strange that one should come to feel like this—that the Germans could destroy all those beautiful places that I love so much." Referring to the havoc made at Louvain, and other towns and cities, he exclaimed :
" They may blow up all the museums, **Fighting for the** overthrow the monuments — it would **dignity of humanity** leave me still determined to fight on. It would not abate by one fraction our vigour and our decision. In this terrible war we must all realise how unutterably great are the stakes. It is we in France and our friends in Belgium who are doomed to suffer the most bitterly. Great Britain will be spared much that we must endure. But we must all make sacrifices almost beyond reckoning. We are fighting for the dignity of humanity. We are fighting for the right of civilisation to continue to exist. We are fighting so that nations may continue to live in Europe without being under the heel of another nation. It is a great cause ; it is worth great sacrifices. I say this to convince you of the indomitable spirit of the French nation. But the situation is not yet so grave. We knew our frontier would be invaded somewhere. We are still resisting doggedly, and have many troops in reserve for the big battle that will follow this one. The Germans cannot invest Paris. Its size is too vast, and its defences will be assisted by armies now fighting on the Oise, seventy miles away. The fortifications of Paris are by no means the feeble defence they were in 1870. From our wireless stations on the summit of the Eiffel Tower we can control

"GRAPPLING IN THE CENTRAL BLUE."

An aeroplane action over Paris. After a time the aerial visitors from Germany were met by French aviators, and more than once the populace had an opportunity of witnessing an encounter in mid-air in which the German aeroplane was destroyed.

the movements in co-operation with our armies in the provinces of France. Although the Germans have invaded France, we will fight on and on until this attempt to establish tyranny in Europe has been completely overthrown."

A correspondent of "The Times," referring to the great importance of Paris considered as a fortress, described it thus briefly: "Paris was defended in 1870-71 by a ring of detached forts, and was garrisoned mainly by National Guards and Mobiles. It was not properly victualled, but energetic measures enabled it to hold out for four months. Since 1871 there has been added to the old fortification an exterior line of forts, and on the line of these new forts the active defence of the place will rest. The old line begins in the north at St. Denis—Forts la Briche, du Nord, and de l'Est—and continues through Forts d'Aubervilliers, Romainville, Noisy, Rosny, Nogent, Vincennes, Charenton, Ivry, Bicetre, Montrouge, Vanves, d'Issy, to Mont Valérien. The perimeter of these works is about thirty-four miles.

Paris almost a fortified province "The new line of works makes Paris almost a fortified province. It embraces in the defended area Enghien, Argenteuil, Versailles, and the Forests of Saint-Germain and Bondy. The perimeter is over eighty miles. Starting from the north there are in succession Forts Cormeilles, Montlignon, Domont, Montmorency, Ecouen, and Stains, forming the northern group. To the east there are Forts Vaujours and Chelles. Between the Marne and the Seine

come Forts Villiers, Champigny, Sucy, and Villeneuve-Saint-Georges. To the south is Fort Palaiseau, while the hills from Palaiseau to Chatillon are crowned by various batteries. On the west stand Forts Villeras, Haut-Buc, St. Cyr, and Marly, with numerous batteries.

"If Paris is invested the line held by the enemy will be not less than a hundred miles in length, and if this line is held in the same relative strength as in 1870, no less than 500,000 men will be required to occupy it. Such numbers will so materially weaken the German armies that it is possible that on this occasion the Germans will select one section of the defence, the capture of which will enable them to bombard the capital, and bring up against the forts selected for attack the heavy howitzers which played such havoc with Liège and Namur."

Possible eventualities had, however, to be provided for. General Gallieni, who had been appointed Military Governor of Paris, issued a decree which ordered all the **General Gallieni's preparations for a siege** occupiers or landlords of buildings of any kind within the field of fire of the forts and defensive works of Paris, both ancient and modern, to leave them within four days, and to demolish them completely, otherwise they would be demolished by the military. The result was that in a few days houses, shops, factories, warehouses, and barns were destroyed, until each fort looked out over no more than a desert of shapeless ruins across which it could direct the fire of its heavy guns at an advancing army without hindrance. Further, the French War Minister called up the Territorial Reservists of all classes not yet summoned to the colours from the North and North-East Departments.

That very evening, September 1st, a German Taube monoplane appeared over Paris. It was not observed until it was well over the centre of the city, just above the Gare St. Lazare, where it dropped a bomb. When it was over the Place de l'Opéra guns opened fire on it. Immediately after the first shot had been fired a bomb was dropped into the courtyard of a building just off the Rue du Quatre Septembre. There was ten minutes of panic. Men, women, and children rushed to cover, and the streets were emptied in the twinkling of an eye. The panic was increased by the fact that the majority of persons took the reports of the guns for explosions of German bombs. Only the first bomb, however, took any effect. The window-panes of two storeys of a building were broken by the explosion, but the persons who were sitting at the windows escaped without a scratch! The effect of the explosion on the population was transitory, but the Government organised a flotilla of armoured aeroplanes, with quick-firing guns, to chase German aeroplanes which in future flew over the capital.

The American Ambassador addressed a report to his Government on the methods of warfare adopted by the Germans of dropping bombs indiscriminately on the civil population, which were not only an outrage against humanity, but in absolute violation of The Hague Convention signed by Germany herself.

Measures were taken by the French Government to protect the chief works of art in the Louvre from this danger

BRITONS AND AMERICANS LEAVING PARIS.
Scene at the Gare du Nord, Paris, as the last train was leaving with passengers bound for England one night in the first week of September, 1914.

notice that nearly all the people we meet along this dusty road are pushing 'mail-carts,' or barrows filled with bundles. And there are farm carts lumbering along with parties of old folks in them—not jolly old folks, who might be going to a Sunday beanfeast that way, but heavy-eyed, depressed-looking people holding bundles on their knees. There are the strangest old motor-cars, too, filled likewise with people and piled with bundles.

"There are taxicabs that seem to have come out from Paris on some special errand, and furniture vans, and milk vans, and in all these motley conveyances, or lying by the side of the road, or plodding wearily along it, are still depressed-looking people with bundles. For these are the refugees of two whole departments of France. Some have walked a hundred miles already. They have been driven out by the advance of the Germans as people flee before a forest fire, or as they came 1,600 years ago across this very same country seeking refuge from the Huns. They have left everything they could not carry and gone, thankful to bring life and limb with them."

of bombs from the air. In 1870 the " Venus de Milo " was walled up in a subterranean niche. She was now enclosed in a steel room. "The Winged Victory" was protected behind heavy iron piles, and "La Gioconda" smiled inscrutably in obscurity. The Grecian Hall, which contains the master-pieces of Phidias, was protected by sacks filled with earth. The upper storeys of the Louvre with their glass roofs were turned into hospitals under the charge of the Red Cross.

The stream of refugees from the stricken towns of Middle France began to arrive in Paris on September 1st. The scene was thus described by a correspondent of "The Times":

"For ten miles along the long, straight road that runs to Compiègne one sees nothing unusual. You have only to turn your head, and there are the cupolas of Sacre-Cœur, the great white church on the hill of Montmartre, floating mistily in the hot air behind. And here is nothing but flat fields and golden cornstacks and green copses in the folds of the ground. Gradually one comes to

THE EXODUS FROM PARIS TO THE SOUTH.
In view of the threatened siege, inhabitants of the Paris suburbs were compelled for military reasons to leave their houses, and the above picture shows them rushing to the Gare d'Orleans, en route for the south and south-east.

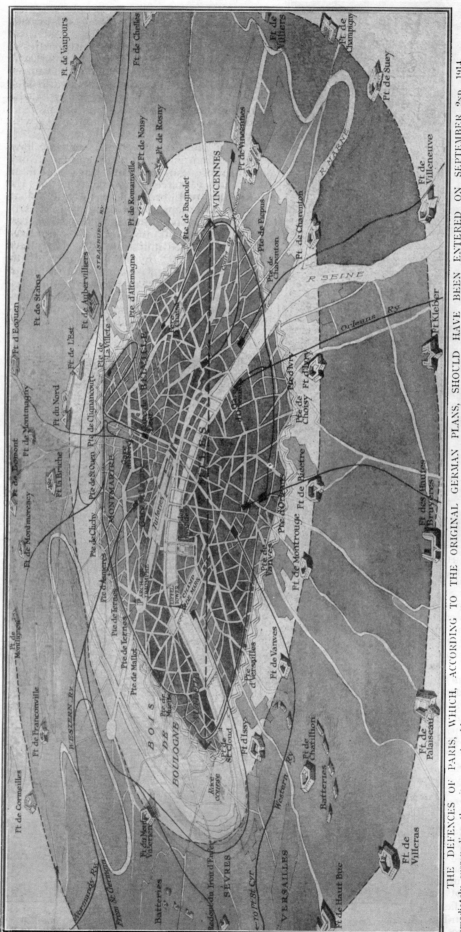

THE DEFENCES OF PARIS, WHICH, ACCORDING TO THE ORIGINAL GERMAN PLANS, SHOULD HAVE BEEN ENTERED ON SEPTEMBER 2ND, 1914.

Immediately surrounding the city are the old ramparts, twenty-one miles in length. Around is seen the circle of forts dating from 1870, but considerably strengthened since then. The third line of defence, constructed in 1878, includes forty fortresses and batteries. The network of railways in the city and suburbs could be utilised to convey troops from point to point as their presence might be needed. Assuming that the outer forts were not captured, the effective fire of a besieging force would only extend to the second line of forts, leaving the area between these forts and the city itself almost immune from gun-fire. To the north of Paris, through the gates of St. Ouen and Clignancourt, some thousands of refugees from the territory occupied by the Germans entered the capital during the first month of the Great War.

That is one description of a weary and sorrowful march. Here is another by a distinguished French artist who had been arrested by the enemy at St. Gerard, near Namur, and was being taken as a prisoner to Germany, the home of culture, by protagonists of the same:

"After sleeping in a barn with Zouave prisoners, a soldier standing over us with fixed bayonet, we were called at five the next morning. The prisoners were told to peel potatoes for the field kitchen. I made my toilet while a guard followed me about.

"At six all the soldiers began to form up. Orders came from the officers like pistol-shots, the click of heels and the thud of shoulder arms coming as from one man. Woe to the man slightly out of line! The close-cropped officer spat at him a flow of expletives, showing his teeth like a tiger ready to spring. I was placed in the middle of a marching column, and as I was loaded with my knapsack and coat (a soldier near me carrying my papers), I could take part in the sensation of the men under the iron discipline of the officers. The road lay inches thick of chalky dust, which rose in clouds above our heads. Never were we allowed to open out and let the air circulate.

"We plodded on the whole day, the only rest being when there was an occasional block on the road. The march was as if on parade. Should one fall out of step, the shouts of his superior soon brought him up. Now and then men were waiting with buckets, and as the column swung by the soldiers dipped in their aluminium cups. Another man would be holding a biscuit-tin full of sweets, or it might be handfuls of prunes; but still the march went on.

"It was remarkable to see the field post-office at work. The armed, blue-coated postmen stood close by the marching column, receiving the postcards handed to them. Sometimes an officer would hand over a fowling-piece or antique with the address hanging from it. At noon I was handed over to officers, and I left the regiment. I was on the box-seat of a char-à-banc full of officers, and could observe the marvellous organisation of the column. The pace was at a walk, but continuous. Ammunition-waggons, field-pieces, carts filled with flour, whole trains of

THE FOOD SUPPLY OF PARIS IN CASE OF SIEGE.
View of one of the outer walls of Paris, which was used as a grazing ground for 30,000 head of cattle for the supply of the city in case of siege. The animals were fed and guarded by the military authorities. Inset: Wireless station on the Eiffel Tower and camp below.

enormous pontoons pulled by heavy horses, and great traction-engines pulling siege-guns, landaus and motor-cars filled with doctors and officers whose only distinguishing mark was a strip of colour at the neck—all advanced at the same pace. Should a slight block occur, the whole column would stop as one train, the drivers passing the message back by a pumping movement made with the fist on high. The warning of a declivity or bend in the road passed backwards like musketry fire. All vehicles belonged to the Army. Some had chalked on their grey sides 'Berlin—Paris.' Sometimes the column would let an enormous grey motor-omnibus dash by, and through the glass sides I saw Staff officers bending over maps. Every driver and service man carries his weapons, the great waggons simply bristling with rifles. On our way we passed crowds of peasants returning to their ruined homes. It was pitiful to see them humbly

Ruined homes of raise their hats to the invaders. We
French peasants passed many villages in ruins. Locked-up houses were instantly broken open and searched. The better-class houses were pillaged for wine, every soldier marching with bottles sticking out of his knapsack."

Perhaps the most arresting outcome of the war, apart from its military issues, was the uprising spirit of nationalism manifested alike in the East as in the West. But nowhere was it more strikingly demonstrated than in Russia. It, therefore, came not altogether as a surprise when on September 1st an Imperial rescript announced that thenceforth the city of St. Petersburg should be known as Petrograd. The termination "grad" is the Slavonic equivalent of the German "burg"—town. This decision of Nicholas II. was hailed with exultation, combining hatred of everything German and intense patriotic feeling, by practically the whole Slav world. The significance of the act was immense, for it marked a deliberate breach with an old and bad tradition which brought many evils on their race. For generations there had been an unholy alliance between the reactionaries on the Neva and those on the Spree, based on their common desire to keep down the people for the honour and emolument of those classes in both countries which arrogated to themselves the exclusive privilege of bearing rule. The political comment of "The Times" was: " The step taken by the Tsar is a proclamation to the entire Slav race in all its branches

THE OUTSKIRTS OF THE "GAY CITY" UNDER MARTIAL LAW.

Guarding the main roads round Paris : A vision of the suburbs at night. Under the control of the military governor, General Gallieni, the most strict surveillance was exercised over the exits and entrances of the capital.

that this unholy alliance is no more, and that his policy henceforth is a policy of ' Russia for the Russians,' freed from the last vestige of subservience to Berlin. For all who had ears to hear he had, indeed, made this announcement already. When he issued his proclamation to the Poles of East Prussia and of Posen, as well as to their countrymen of Galicia and within his own dominions, he shattered at a blow the corner-stone of Russo-German friendship. That friendship began in the partition of Poland ; it has been nourished by her oppression and her abasement ; it has ended with the Imperial promise of her resurrection. . . . To end their sufferings and to give his Polish subjects a safe and honourable place within his Empire has always been the personal wish and the personal ambition of the present Tsar. Austria-Hungary's threat to destroy the independence of a small Slav kingdom by inflicting upon it humiliations from which no State could recover, and Germany's declaration of war upon him for taking measures to support his protest against this menace, have led him to give his aspirations a wider scope.

Friendship based on complicity in crime "He has summoned all the Poles to take their place as a united nation in the great Slav family. By that summons he has bound himself to undo the work of the three Germans—Frederick of Prussia, Catherine, and Joseph II.—who consolidated the friendship of the Eastern Powers on complicity in crime. By the Russian people that friendship has always been disliked. Not all the greatness and all the conquests of Catherine herself could make them forgive her German blood. They have resented the influence of the Germans they have employed

in the past, and the wisest of their rulers have respected this national sentiment. . . . The new name of St. Petersburg—the city of the Great Tsar who, however richly he rewarded foreigners, made it his rule that in Russia Russians must be first—will be welcomed by them as the most marked homage which their 'Little Father' could pay to their highest ideals and their most cherished feelings. ' Petro- **A pledge and a** grad ' is a pledge and a symbol to them **symbol to Slavdom** with whom symbols count for much, that it is indeed for those ideals and those feelings he bids them draw the sword."

In this connection it may be stated that among the thousands of prisoners taken during the Lemberg affair, passing through Kieff early in September, were a vast number of Galicians, Poles, Czechs, and other Slavs, and these all admitted that Austrian Slav feeling against the Prussians was very bitter. A Polish Sokol said : " If the Russian Government would give us rifles we would go and fight against the Prussians immediately." Polish members of Parliament visiting Petrograd and political leaders from Warsaw collectively signed the following response to the Grand Duke Generalissimo's second appeal to their countrymen : " Polish public opinion regards persons participating in the various volunteer organisations co-operating with the Austrian Army as unconscious defenders of Germanism and enemies of Polish interests and of Slavdom. With still greater indignation Polish public opinion condemns the use of explosive bullets." From statements made by Austrian Polish prisoners at Kieff, it appeared that they were kept in entire ignorance of the Grand Duke's proclamation and appeal. Austrian

For purposes of defence in case of necessity, trenches were dug in many of the streets of Paris. Our view is of one in Porte Maillot.

Main line railway at Amiens which was destroyed by the French in order to hinder the progress of the German invaders.

Offices of the Gare du Nord, Paris, transformed into a refuge for the fugitives arriving from Northern France.

Example of the destructive work of a bomb dropped from a German aeroplane on the roof of Notre Dame, Paris.

Scene in the Rue Faubourg St. Antoine, Paris, where a horse was killed by a German aerial bomb. The incident took place in front of the Hospital of St. Antoine.

GLIMPSES OF PARIS UNDER THE THREAT OF ANOTHER SIEGE BY THE PRUSSIANS.

propaganda had instilled in them the idea that Russia was the aggressor.

Amiens in the last days of August was found to be untenable because the right flank of the German army was then reaching a point which appeared seriously to endanger Sir John French's line of communications with Havre; and it was resolved that the Valley of the Somme should be abandoned. The garrison of ten thousand French troops, mainly reservists, accordingly retired westward, through Picquigny, blowing up both

Entry of the Germans into Amiens bridges over the Somme. One of these bridges was historically interesting as the scene of an interview in the latter half of the fifteenth century between our own King Edward IV. and Louis XI. of France, to settle matters regarding the war then raging between England and France. A party of Uhlans entered Amiens immediately afterwards with a Parliamentaire and demanded from the mayor, M. Fiquet, the surrender of the ancient capital of Picardy. This was formally given, and the burgesses were enjoined not to create the slightest disturbance, and above all to abstain from any action, overt or covert, against the soldiery. Any failure in that respect would be punished with death. This done, M. Fiquet and twelve municipal councillors were escorted in carriages to the general-officer commanding the invaders, and thereafter the tricolour was hauled down from the town-hall, and the German standard hoisted in its place. Later horse, foot, and artillery—Brandenburgers and men of the "Iron Guard"—entered the town, but not with military music as at Brussels; only with the raucous singing of "Die Wacht am Rhein" and "Deutschland über Alles."

It became also necessary to withdraw from Compiègne, forty-five miles north-east from Paris and rather more than thirty miles from the outer fortifications of the capital—a very pleasant town with a great château memorable for the Tsar's visit there on the occasion of the institution of the Franco-Russian Alliance, and with something more approaching, under normal circumstances, country life and society than anywhere else in France. With the approach of the Germans in the beautiful weather of early autumn, wrote an eye-witness, Compiègne became like a city of the dead, or a city buried alive. Rows of white houses with fastened shutters, empty flower gardens, tenantless streets, no sound but the angry hum of the German aeroplane overhead. As the church clock struck noon it sounded like a toll. Inside the church many candles were burning before the altar, and nobody else but one woman kneeling behind the high altar. So it always is when the Germans are coming for rapine and for shame. Practically the whole of the inhabitants had fled, and a pitiful sight it was along miles of the highway to encounter hay-wains and carts laden with fugitives.

Other poor creatures walked, burdened with household gear on their shoulders. Some pushed perambulators with children in them, the bundles lying on the children for need of space. Old women prone on straw in shaky vehicles looked about vacantly, young ones in their arms crying. Most of these wretched people were calm enough, plodding along as if they, too, were taking part in a tactical evacuation. All of them spoke with affection and respect of the British soldiers, whose behaviour at Compiègne was certainly beyond all praise. Lord Kitchener's message to his troops was being followed to the letter.

When retiring from the thickly-wooded country to the south of Compiègne on September 1st our 1st Cavalry Brigade was overtaken by some German cavalry who were marching down the Oise on the Forest of Compiègne. They momentarily lost a Horse Artillery Battery, and several officers and men were killed and wounded. With the help, however, of some detachments operating close at hand, they not only recovered their own guns but succeeded in capturing twelve of the enemy's. Similarly to the eastward the 1st Corps, retiring south, also got into some very difficult forest country, and a somewhat severe rearguard action ensued at Villers-Cotterets, in which the 4th Guards Brigade suffered considerably.

Nearer the Belgian frontier about the same date the German artillery, according to a correspondent, was the bane of our troops, and caused terrible havoc in our ranks by great shells from a battery posted inside a wood. By the disposal of large quantities of forage the guns had been given the appearance of small haystacks, and their first fire caused much loss among our men who approached them unsuspectingly. It seemed impossible to silence their fire, but the 9th Lancers, at the word of command, rode straight at the enemy's guns—debouching into the open and charging under a hail of melinite or lyddite from other German guns. Men and horses were infuriated. They reached the enemy's heavy guns, which almost approximated to siege-guns, cut down all the gunners and put the guns out of action. Then, like their prototypes in the charge of the Six Hundred at Balaclava, they rode back, and on their return they fell in **Glorious charge of the 9th Lancers** greater numbers still than in that famous charge immortalised by Tennyson. Captain F. O. Grenfell, of the 9th Lancers, was hit in both legs, and had two fingers shot off at the same time. Almost at the moment he received these wounds a couple of guns posted near were deprived of their servers, all of whom save one man had been struck by bursting shrapnel. The horses for the guns had been placed under cover. "We'll get the guns back!" cried Captain Grenfell, and with the assistance of a number of his men, in spite of his wounds, he did manage to harness the guns up and get them away. He was then taken to the hospital.

VILLE D'AMIENS

L'Armée ennemie est dans notre ville; nous sommes avisés par le Commandant des troupes que l'Artillerie allemande occupe les hauteurs environnantes, prêtes à bombarder et incendier la Ville, au premier acte d'hostilité qui serait commis contre les troupes.

Au contraire, si aucun acte de ce genre ne se produit, la ville et les habitants resteront absolument intacts.

Amiens, le 31 Août 1914

Le Commandant des troupes Allemandes,   Le Maire,

Von STOCKHAUSEN.   A. FIQUET.

TRANSLATION OF THE ABOVE NOTICE TO THE CITIZENS OF AMIENS.

The army of the enemy is in our city; we are informed by the commandant of the troops that the German artillery occupies the neighbouring heights, ready to bombard and set fire to the town on the first act of hostility that may be committed against the troops. On the contrary, if no such act takes place, the town and its inhabitants will remain quite intact.

Commandant of the German Troops, VON STOCKHAUSEN.

Amiens, 31st August, 1914.
The Mayor, A. FIQUET.

ENTRY OF GERMAN TROOPS INTO AMIENS AT THE END OF AUGUST, 1914

At that part of the retiring front at Solesmes, east of Cambrai, a number of English infantry regiments—the East Lancashires, Middlesex, Dorsets, Rifle Brigade, Hampshires, and the Essex—held an exposed position. They were expecting support all the day from the French, but that was delayed, and the enemy crept round in strength. The British force, to avoid being encircled, charged the gradually-enclosing German ring with the bayonet. The men went at it, yelling and shouting, and they got through where there wa a gap of no more than eight hundred yards between the enveloping German ranks. On this gap the German artillery was trained with unfailing regularity, and the losses of all these regiments was great. The East Lancashires especially suffered severely, but behaved with great courage. A transport column taking rations for the East Lancashires had to do marches of twenty to thirty-six miles on successive days on two biscuits per man, "but," as one of the regiment said, "we had our revenge by taking the whole German supply column."

The Scots regiments were heavily engaged, and the Argyll and Sutherland Highlanders distinguished themselves particularly, while the Rifle Brigade and the Carabiniers fought finely in a difficult position near Ouiévrant. A splendid personal action was that of the major of the L Battery of the Royal Horse Artillery, who in a rapid retirement while hostile cavalry were threatening, and the battery horses were disabled, pushed the battery into position with his own hands, aided by his officers and

ENTRY OF THE HUNS INTO THE OLD CAPITAL OF PICARDY.
German troops marching through Amiens on their way south and, as they thought, to Paris. The smaller view shows French troops leaving Amiens just prior to the German occupation. They are wearing anti-sunstroke flaps at the back of their shakos.

men, along a road to a point of vantage. The fire which his battery was thenceforward able to open counteracted the enemy's offensive.

That the spontaneous uprising of patriotic feeling throughout the United Kingdom was not in any sense sectional was demonstrated on September 3rd by the issue of two very important manifestos from the largest representative bodies of the working classes of the country.

Trades Union leaders and conscription In that issued by the Parliamentary Committee of the Trades Union Congress, after a two days' conference, it was stated that " the Committee was especially gratified at the manner in which the Labour Party in the House of Commons had responded to the appeal made to all political parties to give their co-operation in securing the enlistment of men to defend the interests of their country, and heartily endorse the appointment upon the Parliamentary Recruiting Committee of four members of the party, and the placing of the services of the National Agent at the disposal of that Committee to assist in carrying through its secretarial work."

The manifesto proceeded : " The Parliamentary Committee are convinced that one important factor in the present European struggle has to be borne in mind, so far as our country is concerned—namely, that in the event of

continuously under the threat and shadow of war—should be sufficient to arouse the enthusiasm of the nation in resisting any attempt to impose similar conditions upon countries at present free from military despotism.

" But if men have a duty to perform in the common interests of the State, equally the State owes a duty to those of its citizens who are prepared—and readily prepared—to make sacrifices in its defence and for the maintenance of honour   Citizens called upon voluntarily to leave their employment and their homes for the purpose of undertaking military duties have a right to receive at the hands of the State a reasonable and assured recompense, not so much for themselves as for those who are dependent upon them, and no single member of the community would do otherwise than uphold a Government which, in such an important and vital matter, took a liberal and even generous view of its responsibilities towards those citizens who come forward to assist in the defence of their country.

" We respectfully commend this suggestion to the favourable consideration of the Government of the day.

" Long life to the free institutions of all democratically governed countries."

This manifesto was signed by Mr. J. A. Seddon, chairman, Mr. W. J. Davis, vice-chairman, the other members of the committee, and by Mr. C. W. Bowerman, M.P., secretary.

MAIN FRONT OF THE BEAUTIFUL AND HISTORIC CHATEAU AT COMPIÈGNE.
This famous royal chateau was visited by the Tsar on the occasion of the institution of the Franco-Russian Alliance. It is situated forty-five miles north-east from Paris. The beautiful and historic town of Compiègne was the centre of some severe fighting, and had to be evacuated, eventually becoming, we are told, " like a city of the dead," the chateau with its treasures, and other fine buildings, being at the mercy of the invaders.

the voluntary system of military service failing the country in this its time of need, the demand for a national system of compulsory military service will not only be made with redoubled vigour, but may prove to be so persistent and strong as to become irresistible. The prospect of having to face conscription, with its permanent and heavy burden upon the financial resources of the country, and its equally burdensome effect upon nearly the whole of its industries, should in itself stimulate the manhood of the nation to come forward in its defence, and thereby demonstrate to the world that a free people can rise to the supreme heights of a great sacrifice without the whip of conscription. Another factor to be remembered in this crisis of the nation's history, and most important of all, so far as Trade Unionists and Labour in general are concerned, is the fact that upon the result of the struggle in which this country is now engaged rests the preservation and maintenance of free and unfettered democratic government, which in its international relationships has in the past been recognised, and must unquestionably in the future prove to be the best guarantee of the peace of the world.

" The near contemplation of the overbearing and brutal methods to which people have to submit under a government controlled by a military autocracy—living, as it were,

The Dockers' Union were not less anxious to take a hand in administering the death-blow to Kaiserism. Their manifesto, signed by Mr. Ben Tillett, the secretary, said that : " Every resource at our command must be utilised for the purpose of preserving our country and nation. Every able-bodied man must either fight or be ready to defend his country. Every family of those men who go to the front must be guaranteed a competence and food.

" We first of all propose that all able-bodied men should shoulder the responsibilities this war imposes, that local units of men having worked and lived together constitute units of a thousand each, for the better purpose of training and preparation. That these **Dockers' manifesto** units of our members or of Trade **against Kaiserism** Unionists from a given area be registered.

" Kaiserism and militarism should receive its death-blow in this Armageddon. Our traditions at least stand for the best, our limitations and inequalities are largely of our own making, and will be so long as the workers are contented slaves under a vicious wage-system.

" I want to see our men drilled daily, even if the War Office cannot help us. There are plenty of open spaces. Many of our men are ex-soldiers ; they could help in the

BIBULOUS GERMAN SOLDIERS LET LOOSE IN THE WINE LAND OF FRANCE.

A party of German infantry discovered by French troops in a wine-cellar in the Champagne country. "For days," a note found on a German prisoner stated, "we could not find a single piece of bread, but we could have wine as we liked." And they did "like"—in many instances to their undoing, not only in France, but in Belgium also. Their fondness for wine had also, there is little doubt, its effect in many of the outrages committed by the Kaiser's troops in the towns and villages they entered on their march towards Paris.

This masterly camera picture, taken at the front, shows the advance guards of a French infantry column, with bayonets fixed and colours flying, hurrying forward to thrust back a counter-attack by the enemy in North-Eastern France. Twice before, in 1792 and in 1870, Frenchmen had this task before them. The cou shown is open and rolling like that of the Argonne, where Prussians and Austri one misty autumn day over a century ago, were driven back by the forces u

houriez and Kellermann, after an ineffectual but bold attempt to reach Paris ugh the Passes of the Argonne. As Mr. Hilaire Belloc has recently demon- ted, the treacherous chalky clay soil of the Champa gne Pouilleuse is in rainy autumn weather waterlogged and practically impassable. And this factor in 1792 was the real cause of the important defeat of the invaders at Valmy— a defeat which saved the Revolution and had a direct influence on the future.

THE NEW WORLD'S INTEREST IN THE OLD WORLD'S WAR.

Crowds of New Yorkers coming out of the down-town offices in the evening and watching the war bulletins posted up outside the offices of "The World," "The Sun," and "The Tribune." "Europe," wrote a New York correspondent, "should realise that America has been moved inexpressibly by German methods in war.'" These methods and the extended circulation given to the British White Paper proved effective antidotes to the propaganda of the German Ambassador at Washington, and of German Consuls all through the United States.

drilling. Municipal authorities and employers could help. Employed and unemployed could help; the War Office should help those who can enlist, subject to guarantees from the Government giving protection to the families left behind."

Orange Ulster, while still maintaining resistance to Home Rule, agreed to a political truce which put that issue for a time in the background. Sir Edward Carson, K.C., M.P., on September 3rd presided over a great meeting in Belfast of the Ulster Unionist Council as repre-

The attitude of Orange Ulster senting the anti-Home Rule Volunteer Force. The meeting was attended by, among others, the Marquis of Londonderry, Earl of Clanwilliam, Earl of Leitrim, Earl of Kilmorey, and Lord Dunleath. In proposing the resolution, " That being of opinion that the first duty at the present time of every loyal citizen is to the Empire, we not only cordially approve of the arrangement made by our leaders with the War Office for the enlistment for active service abroad of one or more Ulster divisions, but we urge all loyalists who own allegiance to our cause, and who are qualified, to enlist at once for service with such division," Sir Edward paid a glowing tribute to the gallantry of Belgium, which aroused a storm of sympathetic cheers, and then proceeded: " Great Britain has engaged not only in a just, but an inevitable war. Under these circumstances what we have to do is to assist with our last man in the destruction of the tyrant who has brought this about. . . . Our country, our Empire, is in danger. We have never yet been beaten, we never will. We have got to win, and we *will* win. Under these circumstances, knowing that the very basis of our political faith is our belief in the greatness of the United Kingdom and of the Empire, to our Volunteers I say without hesitation, ' Go and help to save your country and your Empire ; go and win honour for Ulster and for Ireland.' To every man who goes, or has gone —and not to them only, but to every Irishman—you and I say from the bottom of our hearts, ' God bless you, and bring you home safe and victorious.' . . . If we get enough men to go from the Ulster Volunteer Force they will go under the War Office as a division of their own, and if we get enough they can go as two or more divisions, and will be allowed by the War Office to have their own officers, and be trained, at all events first, in Ulster camps."

As the days passed the patriotic ardour of our Dominions beyond the seas seemed to burn with a fiercer flame. On September 3rd, so considerable had been the response to the call for an active service contingent of 25,000 men in Canada, that it was decided to form additional brigades at Valcartier and other camps, so as to furnish, if need be, as many as 100,000 fully-equipped troops to the British Expeditionary Forces in France and Belgium, together with reserves to fill up the gaps by the waste of war. A marked feature in the activity in volunteering was the eagerness of American settlers in the Canadian West, many of whom had seen active service in the American Army, to prove their loyalty to their new citizenship by joining the Canadian contingent destined for the front.

This loyal sentiment found further practical expression in the raising of a patriotic fund, which amounted to several million dollars in a few days. Nor were the newspapers

of Canada backward in their support of the Government and their action, illustrative of which may be quoted the following inspiring appeal which appeared in the " Montreal Star " : " ' The Hun is at the gate.' Kipling's stark line presents with all his native, naked force the tragedy which overhangs us. Let there be no delusion in any man's mind as to what will be the fate of the British peoples if their effort to save Europe from worse than Napoleonic despotism proves finally a failure. Their prestige will be gone ; their Empire will be marked off for dismemberment ; the final volume of their history will be written, and we shall take our place among the classics.

" To avert this fate no sacrifice is too great. As in other times of stress, when other peoples were. pushed to the last extreme, women have brought their jewels to the war chest, and men have marched out to die for their country. So must we be prepared to-day to strip ourselves utterly of the materials of
" Comfort, content, and delight,
The ages' slow-bought gain,"
and to devote every ounce of strength, be it contained in gold and lands or in flesh and blood, to the defence of this

THE " WAR AGAINST GERMANY'S TRADE."
An exhibition of German and Austrian made goods, organised by the British Board of Trade for the benefit of our manufacturers. The idea was to give information which should lead to a revival of home industries, so long materially affected by German and Austrian competition, and to promote new efforts to supply goods at home which hitherto had been imported from those hostile countries.

Empire, which is itself humanity's chief defence of liberty." Nor were the people of Australia less keen in their determination to help the Homeland in the war crisis. The Commonwealth Government agreed to send a second contingent of 10,000 fully-equipped men to the front, and Mr. Millen, Minister of Defence, gave very apt reasons for this action in the course of an address to his constituents in the first week of September. " Unless the Empire won," said he, " Australia would be a prize claimed by the victor, as being the only spot with wide, fertile lands and few people. We are not fighting for something distant, but for the right to continue a free, self-governing community."

While the Slav world was manifesting their delight at the Tsar's rescript changing the name of the capital of the Russian Empire from St. Petersburg to Petrograd, Germany held high festivity and military parades **Sedan Day festivities in Berlin** in Berlin and the other cities of the country on the same day in celebration of the anniversary of Sedan, which saw the fall of Napoleon the Little and the birth of the Third French Republic.

In Paris the quietude of the people, as fateful event crowded upon event, was worthy of the courage of the

THE HORSE IN THE WAR: TAKING HORSES OF THE QUEEN'S BAYS—
During the great retreat from Mons the 2nd Dragoon Guards (Queen's Bays) were surprised while dismounted and at breakfast in the early morning near Compiègne. A few figures on the sky-line were attracting the attention of those who had field glasses, and a discussion as to their identity was in progress, when all doubt was scattered by the arrival of a succession of shells on the camp.

children of the Republic under arms. As was said, it was the moment for those who act, not for those who talk. Unbounded confidence was felt in the President, who had come to the momentous decision to remove the seat of Government from Paris to Bordeaux, and in General Gallieni, the Military Governor of the capital, both as organiser and as soldier. On September 3rd M. Poincaré issued the following inspiring message to the nation :

"PEOPLE OF FRANCE.

"For several weeks. relentless battles have engaged our heroic troops and the army of the enemy.

"The valour of our soldiers has won for them at several points marked advantages, but in the north the pressure of the German forces has compelled us to fall back.

"This situation has forced the President of the Republic and the Government to a painful decision.

"In order to watch over the national welfare it is the duty of the public powers to remove themselves temporarily from the city of Paris. Under the command of its eminent chief, the French Army, full of courage and zeal, will defend the capital and its patriotic population against the invader.

"But the war must be carried on **The Allies' motto :** at the same time on the rest of its **"Endure and Fight"** territory. Without peace or truce, without cessation or faltering, the struggle for the honour of the nation and the reparation of violated right must continue.

"None of our armies is impaired. If some of them have sustained too considerable losses, the gaps have immediately been filled up from the reserves, and the appeal for recruits assures us of new resources in man and energy.

"'Endure and Fight'—such must be the motto of the allied British, Russian, Belgian, and French armies. Endure and fight, while at sea the British aid is cutting the communication of our enemy with the world. Endure and fight, while the Russians continue to advance to strike the decisive blow at the heart of the German Empire.

"It is the duty of the Government of the Republic to direct this stubborn resistance. Everywhere Frenchmen will rise for their independence, but to ensure **Duty of French Government and people** the utmost spirit of efficacy to the formidable fight, it is indispensable that the Government shall remain free to act.

"At the request of the military authorities the Government is therefore temporarily shifting its headquarters to a place where it can remain in constant touch with the whole of the country.

"LET US BE WORTHY.

"It calls upon members of Parliament not to remain away from it, in order that they may form with their colleagues the symbol of national unity.

"The Government only leaves Paris after having assured the defence of the city and of the entrenched camp by every means in its power. It knows that it does not need to recommend to the admirable population of Paris that calm resolution and coolness which it is showing every day, and which is equal to its highest duties.

"People of France ! Let us be worthy of these tragic circumstances. We shall gain the final victory ! We shall gain it by unflagging will, endurance, and tenacity.

"A nation which does not wish to perish, and which in order to live does not flinch either from suffering or sacrifice, is sure of victory."

—TO THE REAR (FIVE TO A MAN) IN AN ACTION NEAR COMPIÈGNE.
Many men and a large number of horses were killed. At once the order "Action front!" rang out, and the horses were taken to cover. The now famous L Battery of the Royal Horse Artillery, accompanying the Bays, went into action on the left. The German attack was pressed very hard, and our cavalrymen had a hot time until the 4th Cavalry Brigade, comprising squadrons of the 6th Dragoon Guards (Carabiniers) and the 3rd Hussars, with the brigade guns of the Royal Horse Artillery, came up to their support.

The President, accompanied by all the Ministers, left Paris early in the morning, and was followed at noon by the members and the Presidents of the Senate and Chamber of Deputies, the main body of the administration, and the reserves of the Banque de France, which **The move from Paris to Bordeaux** were as necessary to the Government as ammunition was to the military Governor of Paris—all which filled two special trains. Of the major Embassies only those of Spain and the United States remained, and the neutrality of the American Republic was marked by the fact that Mr. Herrick, the United States Ambassador, took charge of the records of the British, the German, and the Austrian Ambassadors. The higher legal machinery of France was likewise transferred to Bordeaux, fifteen magistrates being selected from among the three sections of the Cour de Cassation. The Municipal Authority was constituted by the President of the City Council and the Council of the Seine Department, who were empowered to direct the city's civil affairs under the authority of the Military Governor, the Prefect of Paris, and the Prefect of Police.

General Gallieni issued the following proclamation: "Army of Paris! Inhabitants of Paris! The members of the Government of the Republic have left Paris in order to give new impetus to the national defence. I have received the order to defend Paris against the invader. This order I shall fulfil to the end." Guns were mounted on the old walls of the city, and even on the roofs and other buildings. The outer rings of forts have already been described, and are indicated in the diagram on page 122.

Over 10,000 Parisians left the capital for Bordeaux, Biarritz, and other southern cities. Several thousand Britons and Americans left for England by the Havre route.

That very day—September 3rd—the Germans were at Suippes, Ville-sur-Tourbe, and Château Thierry, and preparing to cross the Marne at La Ferté-sous-Jouarre.

Rouen, which from the time when the Germans first entered France was the principal hospital base of the allied forces, was evacuated in a military sense on the same day the Government changed its venue from Paris to Bordeaux. The British wounded were sent to Havre, and the French and Belgians elsewhere. Only a small detachment of French soldiers were left to keep order and perform sentry duty. Among the troops withdrawn were a Belgian contingent with a number of machine-guns drawn by the famous dogs, and the British were sent on to the front by way of Nantes, as communication by way of Amiens had been cut off.

From Germany it was reported **British exhibits at Leipzig saved** that our pavilion at the International Book Exhibition at Leipzig had been destroyed by the Germans with its contents. The British Board of Trade, however, at once allayed the fears of those private owners who had generously contributed to the British loan collections by stating that all these exhibits had been safely removed by Mr. Edmund Wyldbore Smith, the British Commissioner, and his staff immediately before their hurried departure after the declaration of war. The collections thus rescued included the Shakespeariana; English books of travel and discovery during the last two hundred years; the historical collection of juvenile and illustrated books; specimens of type representative of the revival in the printing of books, which dates from the establishment of the Kelmscott Press by William Morris in 1891 ; examples of bookbinding in leather and cloth ; the collection from the St. Bride Foundation, illustrating the main tendencies of British book printing from Caxton to Morris—including a copy of Caxton's " Boethius " ; and the works exhibited by British artists in the International Section of Contemporary Graphic Art in the Kultur Hall.

Still further evidence was furnished in these early days of September of the real trend of opinion in America as to the merits of Britain's participation in the Great War, notwithstanding the undiplomatic—to say the least of it—

propaganda of the German Ambassador at Washington, and the German Consuls all through the United States. " Europe should realise that America has been moved inexpressibly by ' German methods in war,' " wrote the New York correspondent of the London " Daily Telegraph." " America, North and South, English-speaking and Latin, with vehemence and unanimity, is voicing to-day the protest of outraged civilisation." " When autocracy," wrote the " New York World," " makes war, it hesitates at nothing. Who could conceive of American Army officers murdering women and mangling children by bombs hurled from an airship at **American abhorrence** night into a sleeping city ? Who could **of German "kultur"** imagine American soldiers raining death from the sky upon unsuspecting and helpless non-combatants, and upon wounded prisoners in hospitals flying the Red Cross flag ? Who could picture American admirals ruthlessly sowing the deep sea with mines to destroy ships and sailors of neutral nations engaged in the pursuit of peaceful commerce ? Who could think of American troops grimly engaged in shooting down disarmed peasants who had tried to defend their little possessions ? To these pointed queries, anyone knowing this country (United States) might well reply : ' It is all unthinkable.' No American officer who did what Germans

THE OVERSEAS RALLY IN AID OF THE MOTHERLAND.

The upper photograph shows some of the brave and hardy fellows New Zealand sent overseas to the aid of the Mother Country on the outbreak of the Great War. The second photograph is of their brothers of the Australian contingent embarking on a transport at Melbourne for their long journey to the battlefields of Europe. They first of all landed in Egypt, there to complete their training and, incidentally, to aid in the defence of that country against the threatened incursion of the Turks.

Infantry of the First Canadian Contingent passing Stonehenge on their way from Salisbury Plain to London.

Canadian Transport and Field Artillery embarking at Quebec for England.

Parade of Canadian Highlanders on Salisbury Plain.   The First Contingent of Canadians consisted of 33,000 men, who were to be increased in
time to 108,000.

CANADA'S AID IN THE WAR—SUPERB RALLY OF 108,000 MEN FOR ACTIVE SERVICE.

COURT-MARTIAL ON A GERMAN POLICE-OFFICER IN EGYPT.
Robert Casimir Otto Mors, an officer in the service of the City Police of Alexandria, was tried by court-martial on four charges, the gist of which was that he had returned from Germany to act as an agent of the German Government against British authority in Egypt. He was found guilty, and sentenced to penal servitude for life. The above photograph shows the epaulettes being removed from the uniform of Mors after the reading of the sentence.

have done at Antwerp, who did what Germans have done in the North Sea, who did what Germans have done in Belgium, could withstand for a single day the avalanche of American criticism. His own people would instantly repudiate him as a barbarian, and no excuse of military advantage over the enemy would be accepted or tolerated."

The "New York Herald," recalling the **German and Japanese** Kaiser's famous picture of "The Yellow **methods contrasted** Peril," contrasted the Japanese Baron Kato's formal notice of his intended attack on Tsing-tau (in the German leased territory of China), in order that neutrals and non-combatants might leave, with the "Christian" Teutonic method of bombarding undefended cities and villages without notice at all.

In the centre of the activities of the greatest city in the world—the old Guildhall, with the statues about him of statesmen who had moulded the traditions of the Empire —traditions which his speech shiningly carried forward— Mr. Asquith delivered what has been rightly called a monumental appeal to the nation's manhood on September 4th. In doing so, he inaugurated a campaign suggested by Lord Kitchener, as previously noted, to explain to the people why Great Britain was at war, and to urge recruits to flock to the flag in even still greater numbers than had yet rushed to enlist, so that the great principles for which we were fighting might be ultimately assured. The gathering was unique in the annals of the Guildhall, which was crammed to its utmost capacity, while many thousands were unable to obtain admission. The Lord Mayor, Sir Charles Johnstone, presided, and supporting Mr. Asquith on the platform were Mr. Bonar Law (Leader of the Opposition), Mr. Arthur Balfour, the First Lord of

HOW THE NEWS OF WAR WAS RECEIVED IN CONSTANTINOPLE.
Turks, in the neighbourhood of Constantinople, celebrating the outbreak of war with Russia. The photograph was taken during the Feast of Bairam, one of the two great movable Feasts of the Moslems. It corresponds to the Christian Easter.

the Admiralty, Mr. Birrell, Mr. Hobhouse, Lord Lucas, Mr. Masterman, Mr. McKinnon Wood, Mr. J. A. Pease, Mr. H. J. Tennant, most of the metropolitan M.P.'s and mayors, members of the L.C.C., representatives of the Port of London, the Stock Exchange, City banks, Lloyd's, the Baltic Exchange, the Chamber of Commerce, the Trade Unions and Labour Exchanges, and the Overseas Dominions.

Of his long record of oratorical triumphs, the Prime Minister's speech was by universal consent his greatest, and he never secured a bigger or more instant effect. There were moments when the silence of the infinite reigned as his voice sank and vibrated with tense passion when describing the prostration of Belgium. Again an approving, angry storm of cheers came from the vast assembly and rolled through the open rafters of the hall when, in stinging phrase, he pilloried the treachery of Germany. Even reserved statesmen like Mr. Arthur

Balfour, Mr. Winston Churchill, and Mr. Bonar Law were visibly moved with the thrill of some of the passages, whose pathos or lofty patriotism reached the highest spiritual heights.

Mr. Asquith began by a reference to the meeting held in the Guildhall three and a half years before to celebrate the joint declaration of the two great English-speaking States, that, for the future, any differences between them should be settled, if not by agreement, at least by judicial

TEMPORARY SEAT OF THE FRENCH PRESIDENCY AT BORDEAUX.
President Poincaré's official home when the Government moved from Paris to Bordeaux.

inquiry and arbitration, and never in any circumstances by war. Little then did he, or they, anticipate the terrible spectacle which now confronted us—a contest which for the number and importance of the Powers engaged, the scale of their armaments and arms, the width of the theatre of conflict, the outpouring of blood, and the loss of life, the incalculable toll of suffering levied upon non-combatants, the material and moral loss accumulating day by day to the higher interests of civilised mankind—a contest which, in every one of these aspects, was without precedent in

THE MILITARY GOVERNOR AND THE BOY SCOUTS OF PARIS.
General Gallieni, the Military Governor of Paris, reviewing French Scouts and Boys' Brigades at the Military School in the French capital. Inset: General Gallieni. Born in 1849, this distinguished soldier fought in the Franco-Prussian War of 1870–71, served in 1877–81 in the Upper Niger territory, and was from 1896 to 1905 Commander-in-Chief in Madagascar.

the annals of the world. After reviewing the diplomatic proceedings which led up to the war, and our efforts for peace, he traced with lucidity the ultimate responsibility of Germany for the war. "Then it was that, reluctantly and against our will, but with a clear judgment and a clean conscience, we found ourselves involved with the whole strength of the Empire in the bloody arbitrament between might and right."

Mr. Asquith and the holocaust in Belgium

He next proceeded to enlarge on "the memorable and glorious example of Belgium" when, "at the instance and by the action of Prussia and Austria, who had guaranteed with the other Powers her neutrality and independence, her neutrality was violated, her independence strangled, her territory made use of as affording the easiest and most convenient road to a war of unprovoked aggression against France." "If the British people had stood by with folded arms, and with such countenance as they could command, while this small and unprotected State, in defence of her vital liberties, made a heroic stand against overweening and overwhelming forces, what would have been our position?" The speaker went on in tones of dramatic scorn to say: "We should have been admiring as detached spectators the siege of Liège, the steady and manful resistance of the small Belgian Army, the occupation of her capital, with its splendid traditions and memories, the gradual forcing back of the patriotic defenders of their native land to the ramparts of Antwerp, countless outrages suffered by them, buccaneering levies exacted from the unoffending civil population, and, finally, the greatest crime committed against civilisation and culture since the Thirty Years' War—the sack of Louvain, with its buildings, its pictures, its unique library, its unrivalled associations, the shameless holocaust of irreparable treasures, lit up by

blind barbarian vengeance. What account could we, the Government and the people of this country, have been able to render to the tribunal of our national conscience and sense of honour, if, in defiance of our plighted and solemn obligations, we had endured, and had not done our best to prevent, yes, to avenge these intolerable wrongs? For my part"—and here there was a ring of passion in the speaker's voice which echoed throughout the hall—"I say that sooner than be a silent witness—which means, in effect, a willing accomplice—to this tragic triumph of force over law, and of brutality over freedom, I would see this country of ours blotted out of the pages of history."

Outlining German ambitions, the Prime Minister went on to say that "the cynical violation of the neutrality of Belgium was not the whole, but a step, a first step, in a deliberate policy of which, if not the immediate, the ultimate and not far distant aim was to crush the independence and the autonomy of the free States of Europe. First Belgium, then Holland, then Switzerland, countries like our own, imbued and sustained with the spirit of liberty, were, one after another, to be bent to the yoke of these ambitions, which were fed and fostered by a body of new doctrines, a new philosophy, preached by professors and learned men . . . who have made force their

The peril to the free States of Europe

supreme Divinity, and upon its altars are prepared to sacrifice both the gathered fruits and the potential charms of the unfettered human spirit."

He proceeded to say that we had upon the seas the strongest and most magnificent fleet that had ever been seen, and narrated what it had done to guard our shores against the possibility of invasion and to achieve for British and neutral commerce, passing backwards and forwards, from and to every part of our Empire, a security as

THOUSANDS OF GALLANT CHARGERS LAY DOWN THEIR LIVES ON THE BATTLEFIELD.

Dumbly but gloriously thousands of horses pay the dread toll of war. Special efforts were made to relieve the wounded and for the shooting of the hopelessly injured, but even so these faithful creatures suffered terribly in the awful conflict on the Continent. The above photograph was taken near Compiègne and Nery, where the Bays and the "L" Battery of the Royal Horse Artillery distinguished themselves so notably during the retreat from Mons. It shows the graves of the Bays' horses. The shed was used as a sleeping-place, and bears the marks of shrapnel and machine-gun bullets.

ITALIAN DEMONSTRATION AT   THE QUEEN'S HALL, LONDON.

ITALIAN SYMPATHY FOR GREAT BRITAIN: CHEERING THE AMBASSADOR IN LONDON.

The top picture is of the great meeting in the Queen's Hall, London, on September 5th, 1914, which was attended by many who had fought for freedom under Garibaldi. On the declaration of Italian neutrality there was an enthusiastic demonstration outside the Italian Embassy in London, when patriotic airs were sung, and British, French, and Italian flags were much in evidence. Inset : The Italian Ambassador acknowledging the cheers of the crowd,

OPENING THE FLOOD-GATES IN FLANDERS.

In Flanders, early in September, 1914, the Germans, bent on the conquest of Antwerp, launched heavy attacks on Termonde and Alost, which were countered by the Belgians opening the dykes and flooding the country. The enemy were suddenly thrown into confusion, and men and horses were soon struggling in the inundated fields. Many guns had to be abandoned, and German soldiers, climbing into the trees to escape from drowning, were later made prisoners. The Belgian artillery, turning on the enemy, nearly converted the Teuton retreat into a rout.

"From Canada, Australia, New Zealand, South Africa, and Newfoundland, the children of the Empire, not as an obligation, but as a privilege, asserted their right and their willingness to contribute money and materials, and, what is better than all, the strength and sinews, the fortunes, and the lives of their best manhood. India, too, with no less alacrity has claimed her share in the common task. Every class and creed, British and natives, Princes and people, Hindus and Mohammedans, vie with one another in noble and emulous rivalry. . . . . . We welcome with appreciation and affection their offered aid. In an Empire which knows no distinction of race or cause, we are all alike, as subjects of the King-Emperor, joint and equal custodians of our common interests and fortunes."

The right hon. gentleman then made a glowing appeal for more men—men of the best fighting quality, and for officers who had experience in handling troops, not only to go to the front, but to train the new recruits.

Not the least effective part of the speech was the peroration. "Finally," said he, "let us recall the memories of the great men and the great deeds of the past, commemorated, some of them in the monuments which we see around us on these walls, not forgetting the dying message of the younger Pitt, his last public utterance, made at the table of one of your predecessors, my Lord Mayor, in this very hall: 'England has saved herself by her exertions, and will, as I trust, save Europe by her example.' The England of those days gave a noble answer to his appeal, and did not sheathe the sword until, after nearly twenty years of fighting, the freedom of Europe was secured. Let us go and do likewise."

After admirable speeches from Mr. Bonar Law, Mr. Balfour, and Mr. Churchill, the following resolution was carried by acclamation on the motion of the Lord Mayor, seconded by Mr. Cunliffe, Governor of the Bank of England: "That this meeting of the citizens of London, profoundly believing that we are fighting in a just cause, for the vindication of the rights of small States, and the public law of Europe, pledges itself unswervingly to support the Prime Minister's appeal to the nation, and all measures necessary for the prosecution of the war to a victorious conclusion, whereby alone the lasting peace of Europe can be assured." The meeting concluded with the singing of the National Anthem, and rounds of cheering for the Navy and Army.

A British submarine arrived at Harwich on September 4th, bringing a German naval lieutenant and a mechanic who were captured in the North Sea, where they were found clinging to a floating **German collision with** aeroplane. They had been two hours in **Russian warships** the water. The aeroplane was sunk, after bombs, papers, and the engine had been taken out. On the same day seven German destroyers and torpedo-boats reached Kiel in a damaged condition, from, it was afterwards admitted, a collision with the Russian warships in the vicinity of the North Sea and Baltic Canal. The Wilson liner Runo was sunk by a mine twenty miles off the East Coast, and all the crew and passengers were saved, except twenty Russian emigrants. Next day

complete as it had ever enjoyed in the days of unbroken peace. Then he insisted that the Expeditionary Force then in France and Belgium had never been surpassed, as its glorious achievements in the field had already made clear, not only in material and equipment, but in the physical and the moral quality of its constituents.

"But there was a call for a new, a continuous, a determined, and a united effort not merely to replace the wastage caused by casualties, not merely to maintain our military power at its original level, but we must, if we are to play a worthy part, enlarge its scale, increase its numbers, and multiply many times its effectiveness as a fighting instrument." After emphasising the imperious urgency of this supreme duty, Mr. Asquith continued: "Our self-governing Dominions throughout the Empire, without any solicitation on our part, have demonstrated with a spontaneousness and a unanimity unparalleled in history, their determination to affirm their brotherhood with us, and to make our cause their own.

the Admiralty announced that a German squadron, consisting of two cruisers and four destroyers, had succeeded in sinking fifteen British fishing boats in the North Sea, the crews being taken to Wilhelmshaven as prisoners of war. In view of these events the British Admiralty announced that "All aids to navigation on the East Coast of England and Scotland, both by day and night, may be removed at any time, and without any further warning than is contained in this announcement."

Efforts to embroil Turkey on behalf of Germany in the war were becoming more manifest in Constantinople at this date, September 4th. The number of Germans in the Turkish service now amounted to seventeen hundred, three hundred having arrived from Sofia, disguised as German workmen for the Bagdad railway, although they were really garrison artillerymen with their non-commissioned officers, and they were sent to Tchataldja and the Dardanelles. The German military mission was also increased. British merchantmen in the Black Sea were ordered home.

September 5th was a day crowded with many important events, both in Britain and on the Continent. The Secretary of the British Admiralty announced the formation of a new force of fifteen thousand men for service on sea or land. After providing for all present needs of the fleets at sea, there remained available a large number of men belonging to the Royal Marines, Royal Naval Volunteer Reserve,

Royal Naval Brigade, Admiral of the Fleet Lord Fisher of Kilverstone, G.C.B., O.M., G.C.V.O.; Second Royal Naval Brigade, Admiral of the Fleet Sir Arthur K. Wilson, G.C.B., O.M., G.C.V.O.; Royal Marine Brigade, Admiral Lord Charles Beresford, G.C.B., G.C.V.O., M.P.

No better evidence of the solidarity of the Allies in their aims and determination was ever given than the declaration which was signed at the Foreign Office, London, on September 5th, by the Ambassadors of the Triple Entente, as hereunder:

"The undersigned, duly authorised thereto by their respective Governments, hereby declare as follows:

"The British, French, and Russian Governments mutually engage not to conclude peace separately during

BRITISH MINE-LAYERS AT WORK IN THE NORTH SEA.

This form of warfare was forced upon us by the Germans, who strewed the open sea with mines, regardless of the safety of neutral shipping. We only extended our mine defences in the North Sea in the neighbourhood of East Coast ports on November 21st, 1914.

the present war. The three Governments agree that when terms of peace come to be discussed no one of the Allies will demand terms of peace without the previous agreement of each of the other Allies. In faith whereof the undersigned have signed this declaration and have affixed thereto their seals.

"Done at London in triplicate the 5th day of September, 1914.

E. GREY,
His Britannic Majesty's Secretary of State for Foreign Affairs.
PAUL CAMBON,
Ambassador Extra-

A HAUL IN THE ENGLISH CHANNEL.
British torpedo-boat capturing a German four-masted sailing-ship in the English Channel. The "haul" of prizes by Great Britain was enormous, while the British ships captured by Germany were much fewer. On September 28th, 1914, the British Admiralty announced that 387 German ships with a tonnage of 1,140,000 had been lost, while the British losses were 86 ships, totalling 229,000 tons.

Royal Fleet Reserve, and Royal Naval Reserve. These were constituted into two Royal Naval Brigades and a Royal Marine Brigade, each consisting of four battalions —each battalion being named after former British admirals. The King approved of the appointment of the following officers as Hon. Colonels of the several brigades: First

ordinary and Minister Plenipotentiary of the French Republic.
BENCKENDORFF,
Ambassador Extraordinary and Minister Plenipotentiary of his Majesty the Emperor of Russia."

THE BATTLE OF THE MARNE. MIXED FORCE OF BRITISH AND TURCOS FIGHT THE GERMANS FOR POSSESSION OF A VILLAGE IN BRIE.

At the turn of the tide on the Marne, hand-to-hand fighting took place in almost every village in which the Germans and the allied troops came into contact. Here and there (says one account), at the foot of a ruined factory, behind haystacks, and under cover of the banks, the men rallied and rapidly formed a more or less cohesive company, improvising officers and N.C.O.'s as best they could. It was such a mixed company as this that attacked, in the manner illustrated above, a German force at a village in the district of Brie, and eventually drove the enemy into headlong flight before them.

A COMPANY OF THE FAMOUS ZOUAVES ON THE MARCH TO THE FIRING LINE IN NORTHERN FRANCE.
The Zouaves were originally Kabyle soldiers of the French Army, recruited in Algeria; but since 1840, though the picturesque semi-Moorish uniform, with its baggy trousers and jauntily-coloured jackets, had been retained, the Zouaves had been native-born Frenchmen. They were attached to what was known as the Metropolitan Army.

The crusade against the playing of football during the war took a new phase by a telegram sent to his Majesty the King by Mr. F. N. Charrington, the East End temperance worker, in which he said: "May it please your Majesty to remember that Lord Roberts recently said it would be disgraceful if football was continued during the war. The Football Association have now decided to continue their matches, despite all protest. Your Majesty has set an example to the nation in sending your two noble sons to the front. Millions of your Majesty's loyal subjects will be anxious to know if your Majesty's name will still be used as patron of the Football Association."

To this telegram Lord Stamfordham, his Majesty's Lord-in-Waiting, writing from Buckingham Palace on September 5th to Mr. Charrington, replied: "The question raised in your telegram to the King has received the careful consideration and respect which is due to anyone speaking with your great experience and authority. I gather that the Football Association are in direct communication with the War Office, and a general desire has been expressed by the Association to assist in obtaining recruits for the Army. I understand that there may be difficulties in giving up all the matches of professional football clubs in view of contracts which have been made with players. But the doings of the Association will be

ON GUARD.
British outpost guarding a railway bridge while the Battle of the Marne was raging.

carefully followed, having regard to the King's position as its patron."

Lord Rosebery, as Lord-Lieutenant of Linlithgowshire, addressed a meeting on September 5th at Broxburn, the object of which was to give an impetus to recruiting in the county. His lordship said that they had met at a very solemn moment in the history of this country—more solemn than any that had occurred in the history of the world. After describing the origin of the crisis, his lordship said: "This is the greatest war the world has ever seen. The Battle of Leipzig, in which Russia, Austria, and Prussia fought against the Emperor Napoleon and crushed him, was called the 'Battle of the Nations.' But it was not the battle of the nations; it was the battle of great armies. It was reserved for this war to be the battle of the nations. Every man in the large countries of the Continent of Europe, except Italy, who can bear arms is under arms at this moment. We are not in that position. We have never gone in for conscription, we have never demanded that every man should bear arms for his country; though, remember this, that by the common law of Great Britain every man valid and capable of bearing arms is bound at the call of his country to do so. You may say, 'It is all very well, you are an elderly gentleman. You will not be called out. You will sleep in your bed

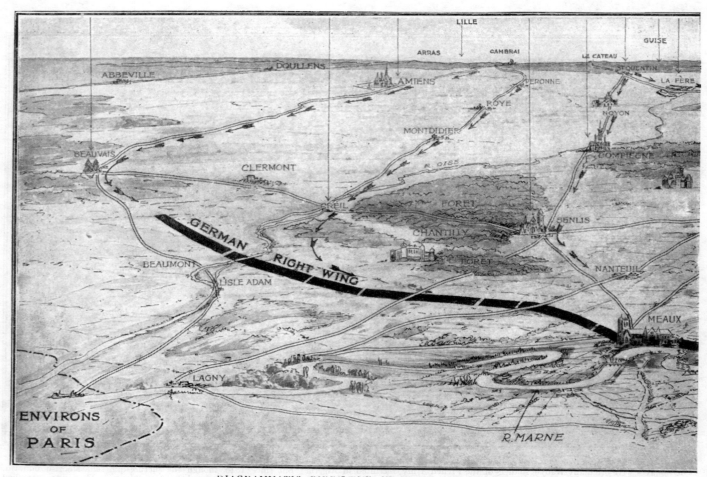

DIAGRAMMATIC BIRD'S-EYE VIEW OF THE ADVANCE OF THE GERMAN ARMIES—
The Allies retired in the first week of September, 1914, before the advance of the Germans. along the main roads indicated by the black arrows. From Cambrai the Germans pushed through Amiens to Beauvais about September 2nd. From Peronne they marched on to Roye, Montdidier, Creil, and the Forest of Chantilly. From the region of Le Cateau and St. Quentin the advance was by Noyon to Compiègne, at which point they had to fight for every inch of ground. They then passed through Senlis down to Meaux

at nights. You will have your meals. It is easy for you to come and exhort us, who are younger and able to fight, to go out to the war.' But I do not think that, after all, the position of us, the elderly ones who have to dwell among the sheepfolds and listen to the bleating of the flock while you go out to war, is so much preferable to your position. It is an indication, at any rate, that we are in the decline of vigour, and in the sere and yellow leaf, and do you suppose there is not one single man of my age who would not gladly exchange with one of you and go out to the front?" He described the cause for which we were fighting as a **Lord Rosebery on** righteous one, fighting not only for Bel-**"Why we shall win"** gium, France, and the sanctity of public law, but fighting to secure our own liberties against an oppression which would be intolerable. "Make no mistake about it," said his lordship in conclusion, "we shall win. We are fighting with our back to the wall to prevent a shame and defeat such as Britain has never sustained, and is not now prepared to endure. We are going to win because a nation and an Empire like ours cannot be extinguished by any such warfare like this. We are going to win because we have our people united as they have never been before. We are going to win because our Dominions and Empires outside these islands vie with each other in generous emulation as to which shall give us most support in supplies, and money, and men. Above all, we are going to win because we have a high, a pure, and a just cause, and we can appeal with humble but, I think, earnest confidence to Him Who, in the words of our beautiful old paraphrase, we recognise as the

"God of Bethel, by Whose hand
Our people still are led."

That same afternoon, September 5th, a remarkable demonstration of Italian sympathy with Great Britain and her Allies took place in the Queen's Hall, London.

On the platform, under the outstretched flags of Britain and Italy, were gathered quite a large number of British and Italian veterans who had fought under Garibaldi for the liberty of Italy; and in the body of the hall were massed together the Italian Foreign Legion, which had volunteered for service with the British Expeditionary Forces in France and Belgium; while in the galleries were hundreds of Italian residents in the British metropolis. The Duke of Sutherland, who had hereditary claims to sympathy with free and united Italy—his father had entertained Garibaldi, "the Liberator"—occupied the chair, and in a stirring address said that the liberty-loving nations of the world were ranged together against the German tyrant. The fate of the world was in the balance. Was it to be ruled by oppression and military dictatorship, or would the free countries of both hemispheres stamp out the evil growth of Kaiserism?

Cavaliere Ricci, the aged organiser of the Italian Foreign Legion, in an eloquent and moving speech recalled that he had fought against the Germans in 1866, and again in 1870, when he was in Paris throughout the siege. "By raising this Foreign Legion," he declared, "I am trying to fight the Germans for the third time, and I thank God I have been spared to enjoy this pleasure and this honour. The cursed Triple Alliance," he went on, "has trodden over Italy for **The enemy of Italy** the last thirty years; and the German **for 1.600 years** Kaiser even kept a Resident (Prince von Bülow) in Rome. Germany has been the enemy of Italy for the last 1,600 years, since the fall of the Roman Empire. Have you forgotten that there is still the Trentino to unite to Italy—that Trentino where we with Garibaldi were beaten in 1866? There is Trieste, with its command of the Adriatic Sea. There is Fiume, with its arsenals. They must be ours. Away with the cowardly policy of neutrality. After the war, should Italy remain neutral, she would be ruined whoever be victorious. If the Germans

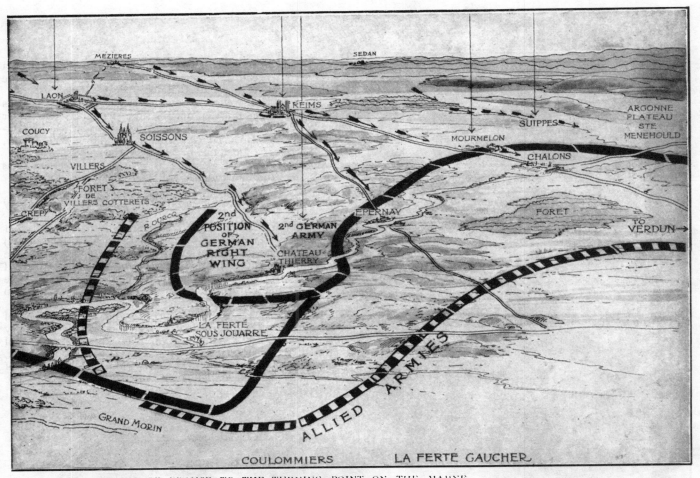

—ACROSS THE PLAINS OF FRANCE TO THE TURNING POINT ON THE MARNE.

Laon, though heavily fortified, was relinquished by the Allies during their retirement; and the enemy advanced thence to Soissons and Château Thierry. Farther to the east the invasion from Mézières passed by Rheims to Epernay, Mourmelon, and Chalons. Another force coming from the direction of Longwy appeared to be operating through Suippes and on the wooded Argonne plateau, with its five passes famous in the action in 1792 which preceded the dramatic Battle of Valmy. The vertical arrow-lines signalise the points of importance in the German advance.

were to win—which God forbid!—they would make Italy feel still more the iron heel of their power; and if the Allies win, as we are sure they will do, she cannot expect any reward for having remained neutral and indifferent to the glory of destroying a power which is the negation of all liberty and of God."

Lord Midleton followed with an animated speech in which he declared that Great Britain was fighting, not for anything she herself desired, but for the freedom of Europe.

Signor Bocchi moved the following resolution: "That in the great hour of destiny the sympathy of Italians in England is on the side of Great Britain, and the sword of Italy, ever consecrated to the cause of freedom, should always be ready to defend the liberties of humanity." The signor insisted that if the neutrality of Italy ceased they must take up arms in the right cause, and so help to avoid the success of a terrible despotism. Their arm could not possibly be raised against their Latin sisters, or against Great Britain, who for so many years had defended and helped to make their great poem 'Italy one,' a reality." The resolution was adopted amid great enthusiasm.

Galicia and the Russian Empire

In Russia on the same day, September 5th, General Count Brobrinsky was appointed Governor-General of Galicia, and thanksgiving services were held throughout the Empire to celebrate the reunion of that province with the Russian Empire. In virtue of a law passed by the Duma, the Zemstvos assumed the work of distribution of the State relief for the wives and families of reservists who had been called out for active service. A scheme was devised, in consultation with members of the Legislature, for increasing taxation to make good the deficit due to the prohibition of the sale of alcohol, amounting to nearly a hundred millions sterling; and it was determined to organise an extensive series of public

works to be carried out by the enormous number of German and Austrian prisoners who had somehow to be provided for.

Progress was made with the campaign in France. A general action began on September 6th along the vast curving front from Senlis to Verdun, over a space of one hundred and fifty miles; and the German right was forced to retreat by the vigorous assaults of the French, powerfully assisted by the British forces. This was the first occasion on which, in the western campaign, the German armies were driven back. The Germans had previously crossed the Marne on September 3rd, and pushed forward to a point ten miles south of it. General Pau, then in command in the North of France, received on September 6th a telegram from headquarters, stating that the German centre **The turn of the tide** had been hurled back at Precy-sur-Oise, **in the West** about twenty-five miles north of Paris; that General D'Amade covered the enemy's left wing compelling it to fall back on Landrecies, about eighty-six miles north of Precy; that Sir John French with his British forces was crushing the enemy's right which was falling back on Villers-Bretonneux, about forty-seven miles north of Precy; and that the Imperial Guard, called upon to surrender, was wiped out by the British. The great Battle of the Marne is dealt with in a separate chapter.

In Flanders the Germans made an attack on our Allies at Termonde and Alost, towards Ghent, which was countered by our Allies opening the dykes and flooding the country.

On the other hand the Germans, by shell fire and incendiarism, destroyed on the same date Dinant-sur-Meuse and shot a hundred prominent citizens in the Place d'Armes, including the manager of a large weaving factory, M. Hummers, and the son of a former senator, M. Poncelet—the latter in the presence of his six children. German

**PRISONERS OF WAR THAT WERE WORTH
TAKING.**
British soldiers convoying captured German artillery
and transport horses through a French village after the
fighting on the Marne.

Navy, and a million pounds to the Army ; while Jamaica
promised to send a portion of the next sugar crop in the
colony as a gift to Great Britain.

Through Rome there came the intelligence that serious
controversy had arisen in the first week in September
between the German Emperor and Dr. von Bethmann-
Hollweg, the Imperial Chancellor, and Herr von Jagow,
the Secretary for Foreign Affairs—the
two Ministers being regarded as responsible for the unreadiness of German
diplomacy which had led to the existing
unsatisfactory state of affairs in Berlin and Germany
generally.

**Alien enemies in the
United Kingdom**

In London alone, up to September 7th, 37,293 alien
enemies were registered—27,944 Germans, of which 8,129
were women, and 9,349 Austrians, of which 1,687 were
women. In these numbers 3,000 alien enemies interned
in concentration camps were not included. In the whole
kingdom the registrations of alien enemies amounted to
over 100,000 up to date.

The Chancellor of the Exchequer and the President of
the Local Government Board received at the Treasury
on September 8th a deputation from the Association of
Municipal Corporations, consisting of Sir Robert Fox,
Town Clerk of Leeds, and Mr. Alderman Hobson, of
Sheffield. These gentlemen submitted to Ministers the
following resolutions on behalf of their Association :

troops appeared at the branch of the
National Bank, where they demanded all the
cash in the safe, and when the manager
refused to give them the money or open the
safe for them, he was immediately shot,
together with his two sons.

Previous mention has been made of gifts
offered by different Dominions and Colonies
to the Motherland for the use of the nation
at large, or to make special provision for the
troops at the front, or to some institution or
organisation for special charitable or patriotic
work. British Columbia on September 6th
intimated a gift of 1,200,000 1 lb. tins of
salmon, and in doing so Sir Richard McBride,
the Premier, telegraphed to the Colonial
Secretary : "Canada has already given an
earnest of her intention of casting all her
resources into the scale with the Motherland in this
struggle to uphold the banner of liberty throughout
the world. The other provinces of the Dominion have
responded in magnificent fashion to the need of increasing
Britain's food supplies, but what they have already contributed is, I am sure, only a sample of what their generosity
shall be, if put to a further test ; and this, I am equally
sure, is the attitude of the whole of the people of the
province of Columbia. The shipment of tinned salmon
will go forward to London just as soon as the despatch can be arranged for."

On the same day the Government of New Brunswick
offered to, and the offer was accepted by, his Majesty's
Government 100,000 bushels of potatoes ; and the planters
of Mauritius presented a million pounds of sugar to the

"TO THE LEFT, MONSIEUR, BY THE MILL."
Member of a British cycling corps, uncertain of his way in the windmill
country of France, being directed by a peasant. The fully-laden bicycle
and the general fitness of both man and machine indicate the nature of
the duty on which the soldier was engaged.

(1) "That the Government be requested to raise in their
War Loan such an amount as they may think necessary,
and from this sum to make advances to the Corporations
at cost price, in order that the new capital for municipal
undertakings may be secured upon the best possible
terms, with power for the Corporations to repay on giving
reasonable notice." (2) "That the Trustees Act be
amended so as to provide that the mortgages of the Corporations mentioned in that Act shall be trustee securities,
and that the stock and mortgages of all Corporations

"THE HOUSES WERE DEMOLISHED LIKE PACKS OF CARDS."

"We had a most trying time in a village," a British cavalryman wrote home from France, "and were bombarded by eight German guns. The houses were demolished like packs of cards, and after six hours of mental agony we had to retire one by one across a pontoon bridge, subjected to an awful fire. But with the loss of a few men we got clear, and the general complimented us on the absence of panic."

WRECKAGE ON THE MARNE.
The view above is of the town of Meaux. Floating baths and wash-houses were sunk to prevent their military use by the Germans.

whose boroughs have a population of over 20,000 be trustee securities."

In the course of conversation with Ministers it was elicited that by the first resolution the Association did not propose to ask the Government to advance money except for new works put in hand to provide employment during the war.

Mr. Lloyd George, in reply to the deputation, said it was obvious that it was to the interest of the municipalities and of the State that they should not be competing in the same market in what must be difficult borrowing times. He had no hesitation, therefore, in saying that it was desirable that the Government should accede to the deputation's first request, that whatever money they borrowed for the purpose of responding to the invitation of the Local Government Board to make provision for **Making provision for** distress in their districts should **industrial distress** be advanced out of the War Loan which the Government put on the market. The municipalities, as to terms, must be subject to the same time obligations as the Government, who were quite prepared to lend at the rate of interest they paid themselves, with an allowance for the actual expenses to the State.

The right hon. gentleman went on to say : " We think it is absolutely necessary that the money should be spent for the relief of distress. This is not the time to embark in great municipal enterprises which have no reference to distress. After all, we want every penny we can raise to fight the common enemy, and our first consideration ought to be to win, to come out triumphant in this struggle. Unless we do that there will be no country for municipalities or Governments to administer. As

finance is going to play a very great part we must husband our resources. . . . We raise the ten millions for you in the same market as we raise the ten millions for our armies on the Continent. Therefore, in my judgment, the last few hundred millions may win this war. The first hundred millions our enemies can stand as well as we can ; but the last they cannot, thank God ! . . . That is where our resources will come in, not merely of men, but of cash. We have won with 'silver bullets' before. We **" We have won with** financed Europe in the greatest **silver bullets before "** war we ever fought, and that is what won. Of course, British tenacity and British courage always came in, and they always will, but let us remember that British cash told, too. When the others were absolutely exhausted, we were getting our second breath, and our third, and our fourth, and we shall have to spend our last before we are beaten." In conclusion the Chancellor of the Exchequer said : " Speaking purely as the Treasury, we will find the money for you only where there is really actual insistent distress in the districts. It is very much better to work in things that are normal if you can. Our trade is not going. The seas are ours, and they will remain ours. We shall get not only our own trade, but we shall get a good deal of the enemy's trade as well, and, of course, there is always a business which is necessary in order to keep the war going."

Mr. Samuel, President of the Local Government Board, spoke on the same lines as the Chancellor of the Exchequer, and the deputation withdrew.

WRECK OF A RED CROSS TRAIN NEAR LIZY.
The centre and lower photographs were taken after a train with wounded soldiers had been blown up by the Germans as it was crossing the River Ourcq, near Lizy. Forty soldiers were drowned.

THE BATTLES OF THE OURCQ, MORIN, AND MARNE RIVERS.

A Conflict of Four Million Men—Joffre Outgenerals Moltke—Recoiling for a Leap, He Draws on the German Right Wing—Kluck is Trapped between Three Allied Armies—Moltke Prepares a Counter-stroke in Eastern France—Joffre Returns to the Napoleonic Method—Race for Victory Between Paris and Nancy—The Sixth French Army Held Up—The British Force Surprises Kluck—Drives in His Flank and Threatens His Rear—Brings Help to the Sixth French Army—The Great Victory that Saves France—The Pursuit to the Aisne.

OF all great historic conflicts, the most tremendous, the most exciting, the most fateful was the supreme clash, between Paris and Nancy, of the armies of France and Germany, with the comparatively small British Expeditionary Force intervening. The gigantic struggle must not be allowed to go down in our history under the name of the Battle of Meaux. The fighting round Meaux was only part of the wrestle of the two largest military Powers in Western Europe. The battle-front stretched three-quarters of the way across France. Engaging in it were more than four millions of men. On one side were six French armies, with the British force making the seventh army. On the other side were seven German armies—more than equal in number to their opponents. Each had brought every possible man into the field.

Germany emptied her great fortresses—Metz, Strassburg, Thionville—and poured the troops over the border. France hurried a number of reservists into her eastern fortifications—Verdun and Toul—turned the garrisons into field forces, and transformed the defence army of Paris into an attacking host.

The preparations for the decisive struggle began towards the end of August. General von Moltke wished it to take place on the line running by the upper course of the Somme and along the Aisne to Rethel and the Meuse. It is quite probable that the work done by German agents in preparing gun positions in the Aisne quarries, which they had been working in 1913, was performed in view of this plan. But General Joffre refused to fight, in spite of the

fact that one of the most brilliant of his subordinate generals, General Pau, had checked the enemy at Guise, and the British force had turned at bay in the Forest of Compiègne and taken ten German guns there.

The position the invaders had chosen was too strong. Near its centre, on the Aisne, it had, in the plateau of Soissons, the most formidable natural line of fortification in Northern Europe. It could retain half a million French troops there, while its right and left wings curved round both French flanks. So General Joffre retired on Paris. He had, in so doing, to abandon Northern France to the invaders, but his sole object was to keep his armies concentrated, with a good railway line running all along their front, to enable him to shift the troops quickly and strengthen any weak part.

Even when he had withdrawn his forces to the line on which he intended to offer battle he had still a very grave difficulty to face. Up to that time his left wing had been his weakest point. Even when a new army was formed under General D'Amade, on the left of the British Expeditionary Force, and new forces were brought up on the right of the British soldiers by General Pau, the German club-end, directed by Kluck, continued to smash back the Franco-British left wing. D'Amade was defeated, and the old pressure on the British force was resumed. Our local success in the Forest of Compiègne was merely a delaying action. Our men had to continue their retreat at the beginning of September.

By this time, however, matters were not so bad as they seemed on the allied left wing. General Joffre, with characteristic subtlety, had quickly

GENERAL MAUNOURY.
At great personal risk he saved the lives of two private soldiers during the Battle of the Marne.

KINDNESS OF FRENCH PEASANTRY TO BRITISH SOLDIERS UNDER FIRE—

During the great retreat to the Marne many acts of kindness were shown by the French people to the hardly-pressed British soldiers. In the above view we see a number of men of the Gloucester Regiment, who after an exhausting march had halted in a village to form a rearguard position. A platoon is erecting a breastwork from stones lying at the hillside. The villagers immediately flocked out with gifts of fruit, chocolate,

transformed General D'Amade's failure to protect North-Western France into a source of strength in the future. He allowed the three retreating armies—General D'Amade's, Sir John French's, and General Pau's—to give ground to the enemy. He sent them no reinforcements. Also, as we have seen, he informed the French Government that he was not able to guarantee to save the capital from a siege. So the Germans received the gratifying news that Paris had been abandoned by the President and the legislating and administrating authorities of the country.

All this, however, was only a stratagem on the part of General Joffre. He was trying to appear weakest at the very point at which he had suddenly become strongest. He wanted to induce General Kluck to continue to advance into a gigantic ambush. Paris was not only fully garrisoned, but a new French army was waiting in it, under General Maunoury, to co-operate with the allied left wing in a surprise attack on Kluck's forces. All that afterwards happened in the conflicts round the Ourcq and Morin Rivers was prearranged to occur at any spot Kluck cared to select.

The surprise awaiting Kluck in Paris

There is no reason to suppose that the famous German commander decided on the course which he then adopted. The affair was far too important for him to manage it. He referred it, about the beginning of September, to General von Moltke and the German Military Staff. For a day,

152

perhaps, they hesitated. For a great battle, in which three-quarters of a million men were conflicting, was taking place from Rethel to the Meuse. Here the Ninth French Army, under General Foch, and the Fourth French Army, under General de Langle Cary, were stubbornly holding up the Saxon army, under General Hausen, and the army of the Duke of Würtemberg, while the Third French Army, composed of the garrison of Verdun, checked the advance of the Crown Prince's forces.

The three French generals had received an express order from their Commander-in-Chief to fight a delaying action with the utmost fierceness. So well did they carry out this order that the German Military Staff thought for a time that the grand decisive battle was actually in progress. In fact, it was thus officially reported in Berlin on September 2nd. But General Joffre only wanted the German centre and left wing to be held firmly back until he had fully prepared his real battle-line in the south.

In the meantime General von Moltke and his Staff worked out their plan of battle. Kluck was ordered to swerve away from Paris and attempt, by a swift movement to the south-east of the French capital, to cut the French army there from the city. He was given a hard and important task, but it was not the decisive stroke. The armies of General Bülow, General Hausen, and the Duke of Würtemberg were massed in the centre of the line. They had to try to pierce the French centre. But

—DURING THE GREAT RETREAT FROM MONS TO THE MARNE.

and cigarettes, and others were soon at work making and serving out coffee. Though German gunners as quickly found the range, the villagers bravely continued their kindly ministrations. An infantry attack was warded off by our artillery, and the retreat continued. The kindness of the French was the more noteworthy as our men were not victors, but hard-pressed troops in retreat.

their work also was not expected to be decisive. For the Crown Prince, with much trouble and delay, had at last managed to get near to the main scene of conflict. His forces stretched from the north of Verdun, through the hilly Argonne Forest, to a southern point a little above the town of Bar-le-Duc. Only a weak French army, consisting of the garrison troops of Verdun, under General Sarrail, opposed him. Here, therefore, the German General Staff prepared its heaviest stroke, as a counter to the blow that General Joffre was about to deliver against Kluck's forces near Paris. A grand decisive movement by the Crown Prince would gloriously enhance the personal prestige of the Hohenzollern family, and thus have an important bearing on the domestic policy of the German Empire. From a strategical point of view, also, it was both sound and brilliant. So the garrisons of Metz and Saarbrucken marched to assail General Sarrail in his rear, along the heights of the Meuse, between Verdun and Toul. At the same time the Crown Prince's army attacked the troops of General Sarrail on the north flank and the western front.

The French army, based on the neighbouring fortress town of Toul, in the south, could not assist the Verdun garrison. For it was fighting against overwhelming German forces from Strassburg and Alsace, which were bent on taking Nancy and pouring through the Gap of Lorraine on to the rear of General Sarrail's army at Bar-le-Duc He would

then have been completely encircled, and in any case only part of his troops could have escaped by a wild flight Their comrades from Toul were trying to prevent this crowning disaster. But so certain were the German General Staff of capturing Nancy and all the French right wing that the Kaiser came to watch the victory from a hill close to the capital of French Lorraine.

Such were the perplexing perils that the French Commander-in-Chief had to meet. He was bringing his hammer-stroke down in the west on Kluck's forces. To ward it off, General von Moltke was bringing down a still more crashing blow in the east on the field armies of Verdun and Toul. The orthodox movement would have been to rail at once the British army from Paris to Bar-le-Duc to reinforce General Sarrail. Apparently **Joffre's return to the** Kluck, as he continued his sweep to **Napoleonic method** the south, thought this had been done.

But General Joffre had other gifts besides the extra-ordinary patience, tenacity, and defensive skill with which he had conducted the grand retreat. After having played the scientific, methodical German game in a way that astonished the Germans themselves, and made them admire the directing mind they were fighting against, the great Gascon surprised them by revealing another side of his character.

At heart he was a fighter of the school of Nelson and Napoleon. As an engineer and an expert in fortification,

FRENCH CAVALRY CROSSING A BRIDGE OF BOATS OVER THE RIVER MARNE.

he could be as cautious and as solid in an offensive-defensive campaign as Wellington had been. But it was in the thunderbolt attack that his full genius was shown. Patiently he forged the thunderbolt. At times he spent weeks on it; at times, months. But, when at last it was ready for launching, he struck with the swift, intense fury of his race He had so skilfully arranged everything that he could hit quicker and harder with his left wing than General von Moltke could strike at his right wing. He had three armies round Kluck; there were only two armies immediately round Sarrail. So, shifting none of his troops, the great Frenchman offered battle.

The region in which he fought was the classic battle-ground of France. In the heath to the north, below the vineyards of Champagne, where the grapes were ripening in the scorching September sunshine, was the monument of defeat of the first of the Huns—the camp of Attila. It was an immense oval of earthworks, where Attila and his horde rested before the battle that ended in the barbarians being routed by the Gauls and Romans. The plain around

Exciting country to fight in

was the practising ground of the French Army—their Aldershot—and the range of every visible object was known to the French artillerymen. In their retreat through this familiar scene the gunners had already given the enemy a terrible foretaste of their surprising speed and accuracy of fire.

Closer to Paris, amid the marshes of Saint Gond and the tributary streams of the Marne, Napoleon had fought against the Prussians in 1814, his back to the wall and his genius at its height. Every French officer knew by heart the details of this brilliant campaign by the most brilliant of all French leaders in war. They had studied every yard of the ground, and Sir John French, an ardent admirer of Napoleon's military skill, was also acquainted with the scene of the 1814 battle.

It was exciting country to fight in. There were woods, like the Forest of Crecy, a few miles south-east of Paris,

where an army could shelter from aerial observation. Sir John French concealed his forces there, and they escaped the notice of scouting German airmen. There were many heights, giving good gun positions. There were streams to impede movements on both sides, and innumerable farmhouses to be loopholed for rifle and Maxim fire; and in places were bluffs, moated by a river, where a couple of well-placed machine-guns could hold up an army corps.

Meaux, the principal town of the region, was some twenty miles from the forts of Paris. A charming old cathedral town on the Marne, it had been in peaceful days the Henley of France, and a line of houseboats, rowing-boats, and canoes still floated on its placid stream. Above Meaux the waters of the Ourcq flowed into the Marne, running from some hilly eastern country, through which it had cut a ravine. On the steep eastern bank of the Ourcq General Kluck left his heavy artillery, with some 100,000 men, to protect his flank against the turning movement threatening from Paris.

Germans in sight of the promised land

Then, with about 150,000 troops, he crossed the Marne and struck south towards La Ferté Gaucher. Two streams, the Petit Morin and the Grand Morin, were traversed by his troops. All the time he was moving, the British army was watching him across the farther bank of the Grand Morin, and the Fifth French Army was waiting in trenches ahead of him by the next southern stream, the Aubelin.

The German patrols, scouting ahead of their main force, found, however, nothing to alarm them. The British commander had left a gap of a mile or so between the British and French armies. Through this gap the happy Uhlans rode southward till they were at Nogent, far below Paris, with the rich prospect of Central France opening before their delighted eyes. Such was the situation on the morning of Sunday, September 6th, 1914.

It was extraordinary. Here was an invading army, reckoned to have the most efficient organisation in the world. Its cavalry scouting system was strengthened by

AN EARLY-MORNING ENCOUNTER AT LA FÈRE.

At La Fère a party of French soldiers had retired to a cottage for a few hours' sleep, only to be awakened ere dawn had broken by German shells bursting above their heads. Jumping up hastily, they immediately replied to the enemy's fire, retreating from their position only when compelled to do so by the overpowering numbers of the foe.

an aerial method of reconnaissance, carried out by skilful pilots who held the record for the highest flights. It had very powerfully-engined flying machines, and every scientific aid to observation that could be devised. Besides its cavalry scouts and reconnaissance officers in flying machines, this invading army was reputed to possess the best system of espionage in the world, and to have covered its lines of advance with spies. Yet with the old-fashioned help of a forest Sir John French was able to arrange an ambush on so large a scale that, compared with it, Stellenbosch, in the days of the South African War, when aerial scouting was impossible, was merely an affair of outposts.

Sir John, it is clear from the account he afterwards gave, was astonished by the success of his manœuvre. It ranks as one of the great surprises in the Great War. It was probably undertaken first just as a simple precaution against the discovery of our dispositions and artillery sites. Then, when our advance guards drew back, more to report the enemy's movements than to conceal themselves, the news of the continual progress of the main German force diagonally across our front was received with amazed joy.

Blind to his own peril, General Kluck was trying his customary movement of envelopment against the Fifth French Army. Many explanations have been attempted,

THE PROBLEM FOR THE AERIAL BOMB-DROPPER.
View of the target presented by a military convoy as seen from an aeroplane. Reproduced by the courtesy of the Royal Flying Corps and the editor of "Flight," it shows how small a target is presented to a bomb-dropper who is at a height of over 1,000 feet. Some five or six military waggons were drawn up alongside the road, partly under cover of trees. They can be discerned within the white circle.

but none of them explains anything. The affair stands pre-eminent as one of the most decisive blunders in military history. Grouchy's mistake at Waterloo in wasting time and men by attacking a Prussian rearguard, and allowing Blücher to march unopposed with his main army to co-operate with Wellington, was not so gross an error as Kluck's.

Kluck was afterwards degraded for it. He suddenly fell from the glorious position of the leading German general in the western theatre of war into the obscurity of something little better than a corps commander in the dullest part of the battle trenches. But the blunder may not have been due entirely to him. In all likelihood the German Military Staff reckoned that they **German intelligence** had forced General Joffre to weaken his **at fault** left wing in order to resist the pressure on his right. This wrong preconception of the state of affairs may have made Kluck unsuspicious of the whereabouts of his most stubborn foes, while the remarkable ascendancy which the men of the British

Flying Corps had won over the German airmen may have restricted the scope of his aerial reconnaissance. After the battle General Joffre sent a special message of thanks to our Flying Corps for the important work they had done.

Of course it would have been a tremendous thing if the First German Army could have been lured right through the gap left by Sir John French. But Kluck was not quite so over-confident as to march to entire destruction. He had to attack the **Battle-line of the** whole front of the Fifth French Army, **Ourcq conflict** that stretched from the hills near the village of Courtecon to the little town of Esternay, with a railway supplying it in its rear. This he did on Sunday, September 6th, while trying at the same time to work round the French left flank.

Meanwhile, the large force that he had entrenched in his rear along the heights of the Ourcq had become engaged with the Sixth French Army operating from Paris. The battle-line of the Ourcq conflict extended from the town of Nanteuil-le-Haudouin, some ten miles below the Forest of Compiègne, to Meaux, some twenty miles from the north-eastern Paris forts. The French took the offensive on Saturday, September 5th, and to this date we may assign the real beginning of the immense Battle of Eastern France.

In the Ourcq section the fight went on furiously in the hilly country stretching for some ten miles westward of the river. All the French troops, vehemently excited by being able at last to take the offensive against the invader, were eager to get to work with the bayonet. Their rushes were superb displays of their old, characteristic military prowess. Skilfully helped by their fine light field artillery, they quickly cleared the western hills of Germans. When, however, they approached the river heights on September 6th, they found themselves opposed by machinery that no personal courage could overcome. One gallant Zouave battalion, for instance, lost eight hundred out of a thousand men. In two days they only gained a mile and a half. They fought like lions, but the German artillery fire shattered their advance.

The numerous heavy howitzers and big guns that formed the most formidable part of Kluck's striking power were set in position over the stream and dominated all the crossings. No temporary bridge of any kind could be thrown over the Ourcq; the terrible fire destroyed everything. The German gunners had measured the ranges of every natural object round about, and they kept off something like a quarter of a million troops, who possessed no armament of equal power. For against large howitzers—that could fire without giving any indication of their position—the small 3 in. French gun was of little use. It was, in short, an open-air siege battle—the first important affair of the kind in the western theatre of war. By it the Germans proved that the trouble they had taken to drag about an unusual number of heavy pieces of ordnance with their armies was more than repaid by the defensive powers of these cumbersome batteries.

The French, in their artillery, had sacrificed power to mobility. Their light quick-firing gun was almost as handy as a Maxim in an ordinary battle, and yet, with its melinite shells, as terrible against infantry or cavalry as

FRENCH CAVALRY ON THE MARCH ALONG A ROAD IN NORTHERN FRANCE.

FRENCH TROOPS DRIVING BACK THE INVADERS ABOVE THE MARNE.

When the enemy had been driven across the Marne, some desperate fighting took place near May-en-Multien, north-east of Meaux, where the sketches from which the above illustration was made were taken. When their resistance was broken the Germans were hotly pursued by the French with artillery, cavalry, and infantry. The artillery dislodged the last German battery in the village on the left of the picture. Then, without waiting to think about taking cover, the French infantry charged the foe, who were driven farther back with heavy loss.

There was no harder fighting during the German advance south than took place at Lenharée, the scene of which has been drawn from sketches made on the spot by our special war artist, Mr. Sydney Adamson. In the early days of September, 1914, after a series of sanguinary encounters, the

French were forced to retreat ten kilometres. But in five days the Germ beaten in the Battle of the Marne, streamed across these same fields, pu by the victorious French. Our artist has chosen one of the earlie counters for illustration. The village of Lenharée, near Chalons, lies in a h

n the left below the church, which was the centre of some of the fiercest of the engagements. To the right of the picture is to be seen the German first ne engaged with the French. The German second line is advancing, under over of the artillery on the extreme right, to the support of the first line, which is being hotly engaged. The smoke rising from behind the church is of the village in flames. Amidst the bursting shells French Red Cross officials are carrying their wounded to shelter across the cabbage garden in the rear of the fighting line.

160

THE TAXI-CAB IN WAR: EXCITING INCIDENT IN THE TOWN OF SENLIS.

After being in possession of Senlis for three days, during which they burnt the town and shot the mayor and two of the principal inhabitants, the Germans were suddenly surprised by a dash of Turcos, who whirled into the town in taxi-cabs and, after a fierce fight, drove out the invaders.

a gun twice its size. But in siege warfare, against long-range, hidden howitzers, it could make no progress. This fact afterwards decided the German Commander-in-Chief to use the heights of the Aisne valley for a siege defence on a larger scale, using the immense guns that had destroyed the Maubeuge forts to beat off the allied armies.

In the meantime there was for a time a practical defeat of the sound and brilliant French operation on the Ourcq, intended to cut the lines of communication of several German armies and turn their coming retreat into a rout. It had appeared most hazardous of Kluck to leave only two reserve army corps to guard his rear and the main line of German communications. But the event showed that the German general's faith in his heavy artillery was well founded. The German rearguard was not thrown back from the Ourcq until some heavy guns of the British army were brought up from Meaux to shell the enemy's artillery positions. By this time, however, Kluck had drawn back over the Marne, and the Sixth French Army had then no opportunity of turning his flank.

The French out-gunned on the Ourcq

So, in their chief object, the French operations on the Ourcq section of the battlefield can hardly be said to have succeeded. It was the fault neither of the general nor of his spirited, plucky men. It was the fault of the French Ministry for War of more than a decade before. They had given the French Army the finest light field artillery in the world, but they had made a mistake in neglecting the change which the progress of motor-traction had produced in the conditions of the old problem of so moving heavy guns and heavy howitzers as not to slacken the march of an army.

The French people had for long been foremost in developing the private motor-car industry. They had indeed constructed the first armoured motor-car carrying a Maxim or a small quick-firer. But in military motor-tractors and vehicles the German and Austrian armament firms had been encouraged by their Governments to make such progress as left all other nations, at the outbreak of war, at a disadvantage. General Joffre in July, 1914, was training a force of heavy field artillerymen, but the war came before they were fully prepared. One of the things that made our comparatively small Expeditionary Force so useful to our Allies was that—taught by our experience in the South African campaign, when we had to face at times big Krupp guns—we had a proportion of fairly heavy batteries in our field artillery.

In regard to the machinery of slaughter, the Teutons were probably correct in assuming that they had the best mechanical means for conquering the other land forces of the European continent. But machinery is not everything. Men and leadership are even more important. All that Kluck's big guns did was to save him from complete rout. They did not save either him or the other six German army commanders from defeat in a battle that created a new era in history.

In this battle, where millions of men rocked for ten days in unceasing conflict, a hundred thousand British soldiers played a strangely decisive part—out of all proportion to the smallness of their numbers. Victory at the point they occupied was practically certain. The French Commander-

in-Chief, by his skilful disposition of forces against Kluck's depleted army, had organised in advance the success that ensued. On the southern front Kluck had only 150,000 men, worn by long marches, if not seriously diminished in number since they fought their first fight at Mons.

Until the official German account of the operations appears—if ever it appears—we shall not know if the German armies received drafts to replace losses before the great battle occurred. We know that shortly before the battle some of the German armies were reorganised. We then may take it that Kluck still disposed of about a quarter of a million men. He left 100,000 to guard his rear on the Ourcq, and marched across our front to attack the Fifth French Army under General d'Espérey. In so doing his remaining force of 150,000 became caught on two sides by 100,000 Britons and 200,000 Frenchmen. Thus, as General Joffre had arranged, a German defeat in this section of the field of battle was as certain as any human plan could be. For the quality of all the opposing troops was by this time clearly known. But what General Joffre could not arrange, against as bold and skilful a leader as Kluck had proved himself, was a rapid victory.

But a rapid victory was most urgently needed. In the

GERMAN GUNS THAT WOULD TROUBLE THE ALLIES NO MORE.
Limber-waggons of German guns, with piles of ammunition lying about, abandoned by the retreating troops of the Kaiser during the Battle of the Marne. The guns were captured by General French's " contemptible little army."

critical centre of the French front the position of General Sarrail's army was growing dangerous. The Germans had brought heavy siege artillery against the line of small forts running along the heights of the Meuse from Verdun to Toul. One of these forts, Fort Troyon, was being battered in a most terrible way by great howitzer shell fire. If the fort fell, then General Sarrail's troops would be pressed on the front by the Crown Prince's army, and assailed in the rear by the Metz force advancing through the gap made in the defences of the heights of the Meuse. At best they could take shelter in Verdun, and there stand against the siege train that had quickly wrecked Maubeuge. Meanwhile, the two victorious German armies would proceed to roll up the entire French line.

Sir John French's pre-arranged triumph

It was a race between the German eastern wing and the Franco-British western wing. Both were within reach of a sectional victory, and the wing that won quicker would roll up the entire hostile line and so decide the battle. Sir John French's success in concealing his forces and getting a clear line of attack against his opponent's flank brought success very near. And the splendid fighting qualities

DRIVING THE TEUTONS BEYOND THE MARNE.
A remarkable photograph of French artillery passing through the village of Chauconier, near Meaux, on the River Marne, in pursuit of the retreating Germans, some of whose handiwork can be seen in the burning farm on the right.

THE HALL-MARK OF THE HUN.
Another view of the burning farm shown in the top photograph. The farmer is seen witnessing the destruction of his property.

FRENCH MACHINE-GUN SECTION IN THE FIELD.
In the infantry these guns, with their ammunition, were carried by pack animals, and each battalion had a complete section of two guns.

of the British soldier consummated the success. The result was that the Crown Prince and the Kaiser, while preparing for their great, immortal triumph, were suddenly transformed into fugitives. It was French's "contemptible little army," still unexterminated, which was the immediate instrument in bringing suddenly to dust and bitterness the towering, glorious hopes of the War-maker of the World. Quite likely General Joffre, with ironic humour, used our troops to deal the unexpected, sideways sledge-hammer stroke that broke the German line because of the terms in which the Kaiser had spoken of them. Quite likely, also, the position given to our men by the French Commander-in-Chief was a generous, cordial mark of appreciation of the fine work they had done between Mons and Le Cateau.

However this may be, the British force certainly had a prearranged triumph in the greatest battle in history. All it had to do, in co-operation with the magnificent fighting men of the Fifth French Army, was to go forth and win, and win quickly. But now comes an unexpected inversion of ideas. By reason of the skill with which the French Commander-in-Chief had prepared it, the victory of the allied forces between the Morin and the Marne scarcely ranks among the highest achievements of British arms. The retreat from Mons does, the storming of the Aisne heights does, the defence of Ypres does; but our affair on Kluck's flank was only a sound, solid, workmanlike job, carried out with all possible finish and despatch. It was General Sarrail's Third Army round Verdun and Bar-le-Duc, holding out heroically against overpowering odds, and the Iron Division of Toul holding out at Nancy that won the supreme honours of the immense Battle of Eastern France. And the Fourth Army, under General de Langle Cary, and the Ninth Army under General Foch, and our immediate comrades, the Fifth Army under General d'Espérey had each a harder task than the British force.

Our men had what the Kaiser, in his notorious order

CHASING THE FLYING ENEMY IN THE VICINITY OF THE MARNE.
A notable camera-record of French dragoons in pursuit of the flying German lines passing through one of the villages on the River Marne. These men did great execution in chasing the flying enemy.

of August 19th, vainly asked the commanders of his northern armies to see that General Kluck had in his attack on us—a " walk-over." The British soldier walked over what had been the Kaiser's best army ; he kicked it across three rivers—the Grand Morin, the Petit Morin, and the Marne—and then chased it as it tore away in precipitate flight. The action began early in the morning of Sunday, September 6th. The British force advanced from the Forest of Crecy. It consisted of five divisions of infantry and five brigades of cavalry. It was arranged in three army corps. Sir Douglas Haig still commanded the 1st and 2nd Divisions ; Sir Horace Smith-Dorrien commanded the 3rd and 5th Divisions ; and the 4th Division, General Snow's, and the 19th Brigade, though lacking the number of troops proper to a corps, were termed the Third Army Corps, and placed under the direction of General W. P. Pulteney. In numbers the British Expeditionary Force had not increased since its great battles in Belgium and North-Western France, but all its losses had been made good by fresh drafts.

As a precaution, apparently, against a flank attack from Paris, Kluck had placed some 9,000 cavalrymen near the forest in which our troops were hidden ; another 9,000 of his mounted men watched on the Grand Morin by the town of Coulommiers in front of our right wing. Helped by our airmen, our gunners got the range of these unsuspecting hostile forces. The two German cavalry divisions were waiting for their infantry to throw back the Fifth French Army and enable them to pursue it. But a sudden storm of shrapnel and case-shot from the quiet, sunny western woods put them to flight. Before, however, the guns spoke our cavalry had worked round as close as they could get to the enemy without alarming his patrols. They now rode out, as the German horsemen fell back towards their infantry and guns, under a storm of shrapnel. Then the hostile horse artillery tried to create a diversion, while our infantry crept forward in open order to the attack.

RUINED CHATEAU ON THE MARNE.
This once beautiful chateau was the centre of an engagement between the Germans and the British, who shelled them out of the position.

REPAIRING THE DESTRUCTIVE WORK OF THE GUNS.
Temporary bridge-work over the Marne, the stone structure of which was destroyed during the Battle of the Marne.

Sir John French, however, did not press in the advanced forces of Germans suddenly. He first moved his three army corps forward as quickly as possible, and gained a full half-day's march before General Kluck knew what had happened. Our troops began to advance at dawn, and it was not until noon that the German commander learnt what was threatening him. Instead of retreating, he tried to break through the front of the Fifth French Army. This desperate movement of his made the task of the British troops easier. We had only to clear the woods and hills and valleys of his advanced guards of infantry, which were protected by light artillery placed on the heights.

The tables turned on the German gunners   At first some British regiments tried to entrench before the German guns and creep up to them. But it was soon found to produce quicker results if our men worked round toward the rear of the German positions. The enemy then saved his artillery by retreating at top speed. The increased pace of our forward movement more than compensated us for the escape of the guns. The main thing was to shift the enemy as rapidly as possible and thus uncover the rear of his main force.

The enemy seldom stopped to fight, and when he did so, the British turning movement shook the nerve of the German gunners. Now that they were in a position similar to that which our artillerymen had occupied at Mons they did not show much heroism. Neither their shells nor their shrapnel were well-timed, and our losses were slight. Our men crossed the Aubelin brook on planks, captured hamlet after hamlet, and at evening held a line a little way

SMASHING A GERMAN PONTOON BRIDGE ACROSS THE MORIN.
To cross the Petit Morin River on September 7th, 1914, the retreating Germans tried again and again to throw a pontoon bridge over the water. But our artillery commanded the range, and, having waited until the pontoon structure was all but completed, smashed it into atoms. This went on until darkness descended. Our picture shows an officer of British infantry watching and waiting to advance.

from the Grand Morin River. All the German cavalry and infantry advanced guards were driven in, and Kluck sent as a reinforcement against us an army corps which entrenched by the Grand Morin near Coulommiers.

This pleasant little riverside town was Kluck's headquarters, and Prince Eitel, the second son of the Kaiser, seems to have visited him there the night before our attack began. M. Delsol, the mayor, and two other important citizens of Coulommiers were taken as hostages, and commanded to deliver 12,000 francs and a large quantity of bread and forage within two hours. Kluck himself declared he would shoot the   **Dramatic episode** three Frenchmen if this were not done.   **at Coulommiers** The ransom money and the bread were given to the barbaric spoilers, but no forage for their horses could be found in Coulommiers.

"You are liars!" exclaimed the German commander when the mayor said there was no forage available. "All Frenchmen are liars. You know you have a large amount of forage, and you want to cheat me. All three of you shall be shot!"

Two hours later M. Delsol and his two companions were taken into the street and placed against a wall. A platoon of German infantry marched up to execute them. As they were leaving the house one of Kluck's Staff officers sat down at the piano and played Chopin's funeral march. But the mayor and his friends were suddenly left standing against the wall, and the German soldiers tore off in mad haste. The British troops had suddenly crossed the river, and began to enter Coulommiers!

Prince Eitel, General Kluck, the young officer at the

ARTILLERY DUEL IN A THUNDERSTORM.
While the Germans were being repulsed in the valley of the Marne on September 7th, 1914, Nature's artillery vied with man's. Rain fell in torrents. But the turn of the battle rendered our men regardless of the elements, and they revelled in the work of silencing the guns of the enemy and then driving them farther back.

THE "HOUGOMONT" OF THE BATTLE OF THE MARNE.

The beautiful old Chateau of Mondement, about four miles east of Sezanne, was the scene of some of the fiercest fighting in the Battle of the Marne. The French troops occupied it first, but the old chateau changed hands four times before the French gained a permanent hold on it. The regiments engaged were the 32nd of the French Line and the 231st Territorials. They were opposed by the redoubtable Prussian Guards. The fine old chateau was reduced to ruins. As was the case at Hougomont in 1815, the position at Mondement was of considerable strategic importance.

piano, and other members of the Staff—all sitting in the house with bottles of champagne opened and half-emptied—had to run down to their motor-cars and fly along the road north to Rebais. It was here that the army corps sent to hold the flank had entrenched. The line of the Grand Morin River was too long for them to hold, even with the assistance of their two cavalry divisions and infantry advanced guards. The massed fire of our guns shattered all opposition, and by Monday evening, September 7th, our sappers had made crossings for the troops, and the great German retreat had definitely commenced.

The two divisions of German cavalry were thrown out to act as rearguards. This enabled our horsemen to get at last full revenge for all they had undergone between Mons and Compiègne. The numbers were still not quite equal—the German cavalrymen being about three to two. But this was equal enough for our men, especially the famous 9th Lancers, the gallant 18th Hussars, and other regiments in General de Lisle's brigade. Catching their old enemies in one of the clear spaces between the copses and woodlands, they rode at them with a yell, and, killing as they went, swept through squadron after squadron, then turned their excited horses and doubled back in another furious charge. In spite of the acclaimed efficiency of the great German Army, its cavalrymen were not good at swordsmanship. They lacked the deadly coolness which our men showed, when by furious riding they had got within sword reach of the foes. Thousands of the Germans fell in these fierce hand-to-hand combats, and when they broke off the action our guns caught them as they fled.

The position of the German infantry at Rebais was turned by Sir Douglas Haig and his men of the First Army Corps. They took the village of La Tretoire to the north-west of the German position on Tuesday, September 8th, and then advanced towards the next river, the Petit Morin. Here, on the hills by the northern bank, the Germans tried to make a stand. They had their guns on the high ground with their infantry entrenched near the river. But our troops got round them so quickly that several of their machine-guns were taken and many prisoners made. For while our 2nd Division held the enemy on the front, the 1st Division and some cavalry brigades crossed higher up the stream and swept down on the enemy's flank.

Then, to delay the further advance of our First Corps, which was now close to the Marne River, General Kluck collected his retreating troops and suddenly flung them back on our men in a furious attack. But our aerial scouts—who worked marvellously well all through the operations— **Marvellous work of our aerial scouts** prevented anything like a surprise. The Germans were received in front with rifle fire, Maxim hail bursts, and shrapnel, and again they were partly outflanked, with the result that more of their guns and a great many more of their troops were captured.

All three British corps—Sir Douglas Haig's, Sir Horace Smith-Dorrien's, and General Pulteney's—drove the enemy before them in a wide sweeping movement towards the Marne.

The next day—Wednesday, September 9th—Haig and Smith-Dorrien succeeded in forcing the passage of the Marne, between the cathedral town of Meaux and the town of La Ferté Jouarre, and with a force of some 80,000 men marched into the wooded country north of the river, pursuing the enemy.

The small Third Army Corps was less fortunate. It attacked La Ferté Jouarre, a town lying on the north of the Marne, just where the waters of the Petit Morin flow into the larger river. The bridge was destroyed, and

THE TRAIL OF WAR AMID THE PEACEFUL VINEYARDS OF NORTHERN FRANCE.

Our picture was taken in a vineyard of the Champagne district of France. Within sound and almost within sight the heavy guns of the contending armies were vomiting thunder and death. Yet as the troops were marching past to the battle-line the peasants in the vineyards seemed to pay little heed to them, many even not attempting to look up from their work. It might have been fatalism that caused this; maybe, it was their one safe course. To look up might have meant to break down. Inset : Chalons-sur-Marne, where Attila, Emperor of the Huns, was defeated in the fifth century.

SAVING AN "EYE" OF THE FRENCH ARMY.

An incident near Berry-au-Bac. Emile Dubonnet, a wealthy French sportsman, aeronaut, and racing motorist, was observing for the French guns when his balloon was attacked by two German Taubes. The French had to hold their fire for fear of hitting the balloon. Eventually a couple of armoured Maurice Farman biplanes went aloft and drove the Teuton airmen back to their own lines. Meanwhile M. Dubonnet coolly continued telephoning his observations while the balloon was being wound to the ground by its motor-lorry.

BRITISH INFANTRY DISLODGING THE GERMANS.
Many sanguinary encounters took place in the French villages along the line of the German retreat from the Grand Morin, a retreat which at one time looked like a disordered flight. During the retirement of the enemy across the Petit Morin a British force surprised a party of Germans in the small hours of the morning and compelled them to engage, the result of the encounter being disastrous to the Teutons.

collected by the German general and hurled in a last desperate effort against the Sixth French Army on the Ourcq. Kluck in his hour of irretrievable disaster was magnificent. He was like a big beast of prey, so accustomed to the lordship of the jungle that no conception of defeat entered its raging brain. When he first felt the British attack on his flank he drove with savage fury against the front of the Fifth French Army in the south. Then, as the British troops got on his rear, he leaped across the Marne, above La Ferté, and madly assailed the Sixth French Army along the Ourcq. Here, however, he no longer dreamt of snatching victory out of the jaws of defeat. His final outburst of fierceness was a well-planned operation to thrust back the Sixth French Army, and thus enable him to get his guns away to the Aisne valley before the British army took him full on the rear.

On the whole, this operation by Kluck was a success. He managed to retreat in good order. Some of his light field artillery, however, had to be sacrificed in the continual rearguard actions against our troops. The 1st Lincolnshires captured one of the batteries on a ridge between the Marne and the Aisne. The German battery of six guns was holding up the British advance. Two companies of the Lincolnshires made a rapid roundabout march down a valley and through a wood. There, screened by the trees, they crept up to the German gunners. At last they were only two hundred yards from the battery, and the Germans were still busy firing at the force in front of them. The Lincolnshires extended along their flank; each man aimed carefully, and at the first round every gunner dropped—some two hundred men and officers. The English marksmen only fired once.

They could not take the six guns, however, because our distant artillery, in turn, got the exact range of the German battery and began to drop shells on it. Four of the guns were smashed before the eyes of the disappointed Lincolnshires, who in the end only obtained two sound, uninjured examples of Krupp's specialities. The incident is highly significant. Between the extraordinary marksmanship of our infantry and the deadly skill of our gunners there was not much chance for a German army that was only equal in numbers to ours.

For nearly two generations German military authorities, headed by the elder Moltke, had cried down our regular troops and cried up their conscript soldiers. Bismarck had the impudence to remark that if our Army invaded Germany he would merely ring for the police and have our troops locked up. It would not, in his opinion, be worth the trouble of getting soldiers to deal with them. On the part of men like Moltke this view of the matter was mainly one of policy.

a strong German rearguard with machine-guns dominated the stream. Our sappers tried to build a pontoon bridge, but in spite of their heroic attempts the enemy's fire beat them back. It was not until night fell and screened the movements of our troops from the German machine-gun officers that the passage was forced.

This completed the British victory. How important it was to the general scheme of operations, planned by the French Commander-in-Chief, may be judged from the fact that the Sixth French Army, at the time our forces crossed the Marne, was still heavily
How the passage of engaged to the west of the Ourcq River.
the Ourcq was forced The great German armament still swept all the main approaches against Kluck's lines of retreat and communication, and it was apparently only with the help of some of our heavy batteries that the passage of the Ourcq was at last forced.

Kluck certainly showed himself an able commander when the tide of war turned against him. He used his men mercilessly till they dropped, in order to prevent the retreat becoming a rout. The forces that our troops defeated and flung in headlong flight northward were

A PARTY OF FRENCH SCOUTS AT WORK.
Unique photograph of a party of French scouts advancing in face of the enemy across a piece of ground thickly covered with gorse.

He knew that men who volunteered for a soldier's career and trained for war for many years, and often fought in the frontier conflict of a great Empire, were much superior to amateurish, half-trained, pressed troops who had been only one or two years in barracks. But, as his country relied on the strength of millions of pressed men of the latter kind, Moltke, having the command of them, endeavoured to excite their self-confidence by deprecating the British soldiers. Moltke's successors, however, seem to have taken their great general's artful attempt to put the best complexion on his own bad case as a considered judgment by the highest authority of the value of the British regular soldier.

So there grew up the extraordinary German superstition, which may, perhaps, have still influenced Kluck when he learnt that the little army that had held him at Le Cateau was again advancing from the Forest of Crecy to attack his flank. While our men were chasing the best of the Kaiser's armies from the Marne to the Aisne, the comic papers of Berlin and Munich were publishing caricatures of long-legged men in the kilts and bonnets of Highlanders.

The figures were labelled "Englishmen," and it was explained that Nature kindly provided these "Englishmen" with usually long legs, in order to enable them to run away from a fight quicker than the soldiers of any

PREPARING FOR SIEGE WARFARE IN THE OPEN.
French sergeant measuring the width of a new trench with a rifle.

INSTANTANEOUS CAMERA-RECORD OF THE EFFECT OF HEAVY SHELL FIRE.
Bombardment of a hillside in France on the slopes of which and on the flat ground adjoining shells were bursting. The roofs of workshops can be discerned amidst the smoke behind the rows of trees lining the large field in the foreground.

BATTLEFIELD HONOURS FOR FRENCH SOLDIERS.
Every brave deed of the French soldiers was at once recognised and the men decorated on the next possible occasion within sound of the contending forces. The above photograph shows a general of division calling out the men and handing them their coveted decorations.

WHERE EAST AND WEST HAVE MET.
Two of the swarthy sons of Africa who fought so gallantly for France.

other nation. In the decisive event, however, it was the first-line troops of Germany that excelled in speed of flight. It was, however, good tactics the way that Kluck kept them on the run for forty miles. His army certainly saved itself from destruction or surrender by the agility of its retreat.

We only took a few thousand prisoners and a few field guns and Maxims amid the thick woods that dappled the country north of the Marne. But in the rearguard fighting the enemy continued to suffer heavily. On Thursday, September 10th, an infantry column of Sir Horace Smith-Dorrien's corps was marching towards the Aisne, and the scouts observed another infantry column tramping along in the same direction by a parallel road a little distance away. At first it was thought this was another part of the British army. Then it was seen that the distant troops were dressed in grey uniforms. They were headed off and trapped in a sunken road, and there captured or shot.

It was wet weather; both armies were drenched, and the roads were muddy and heavy-going. All the way

FRENCH SUPPLY COLUMN ON ITS WAY TO THE FRONT.
The pack mules are laden with ammunition for the machine-guns, which the French Army used with such deadly effect against the Germans and brought up so quickly at decisive points in many an action that without their aid might have ended differently.

GROUP OF WOUNDED GERMAN PRISONERS AT A TEMPORARY
RED CROSS HOSPITAL IN FRANCE.

there was a considerable amount of fighting, and the
German troops, worn out, unfed, and broken spirited,
were very roughly handled by our men. Seeing that
our troops were battling victoriously and continually
advancing for seven days—from dawn on Sunday, September
6th to nightfall on Saturday, September 12th—when the
enemy made a stand, the losses they inflicted on their
retreating foes in the week must have been terrible.

Strong German rearguards of all arms—infantry, cavalry,
and artillery—tried to stay our progress on the northern
upper course of the Ourcq on Thursday, September 10th.
Sir John French deployed most of his forces for the attack.
On the right, towards the pretty village of La Ferté-Milon,
where Racine, the greatest of French dramatists, was
born, Sir Douglas Haig's and Sir Horace Smith-Dorrien's
army corps swept forward under the cover of a fierce fire
from their guns. On the left, beyond Neuilly, two cavalry
brigades rode out on a flanking swoop. The action was
a splendid success. Thirteen guns, seven machine-guns,
large quantities of transport, and some two thousand
prisoners fell into our hands

On September 12th the pursuit was at a complete end,
and a new phase of the vast campaign opened.

GERMAN PRISONERS CAPTURED BY THE BRITISH AT LA
FERTÉ-MILON.

A SANCTUARY FOR FRIEND AND FOE.
Interior of church in the vicinity of Meaux used by the French military authorities as a hospital where the wounded, friend and foe alike, were
tended with kindly care.

THE GREAT RETREAT OF THE GERMAN ARMY FROM THE BANKS OF THE RIVER MARNE.

As a whole, the retreat from the Marne of the invading armies of the Kaiser was conducted in as good an order as marked the retirement of the allied armies from the Belgian frontier towards Paris. On the other hand, the Germans, caught successively on flank and rear, and forced to battle for life in every section of the battlefield, suffered very heavy losses. In many cases the troops, by the confession of their own officers, were demoralised. In the region of Nancy alone—at Amance and Lunéville—there were by September 10th, 1914, some 31,000 dead Germans, mostly first-line troops. The Prussian Guards left on the field one man out of three of their original numbers, and one out of two of their actual fighting force. Between Paris and the Vosges the mainspring of German aggressiveness was broken.

CHAPTER XXXV.

THE LINKED BATTLES OF EASTERN FRANCE.

The Retreat of Kluck Exposes the Flank of Second German Army—The Battle of Montmirail—The Battle of St. Prix and Sezanne Plateau—Prussian Guards Caught in Marshes of Saint Gond—Rout of the Saxon Army—The Duke of Würtemberg's Forces Attacked on Two Sides—Crown Prince's Attempt to Force a Path between Verdun and Toul—Heroic Defence of Fort Troyon—Its Importance to the Advancing Battle-line of the Allies—Defeat of Crown Prince—Attempt to take Allies in the Reverse from Nancy—Defeat of the Bavarian Army—Kaiser Sends His White Cuirassiers to Destruction—The French Iron Division Takes the Offensive—General Decisive Victory of the Franco-British Armies.

WHILE the British Expeditionary Force was operating to the south-east of Paris in the second week of September, a general battle was raging between all the first-line armies of France and Germany. It was the greatest conflict known to man. The lines stretched from a point below the Forest of Compiègne to a point just above Verdun; they curved downward from Verdun towards Toul, and then bent south-eastward to Nancy. The twisting firing-line was more than two hundred and fifty miles long, and more than four millions of Frenchmen and Germans were ranged along it.

Running from left to right were the First German Army, under General von Kluck; the Second German Army, under General von Bülow; the remains of the Third German Army, formerly under General von Hausen; the Fourth German Army, under the Duke of Würtemberg; the Fifth German Army, under the Crown Prince; the Sixth German Army, from Metz and Saarbrücken, under General von Heeringen; and the Seventh German Army, under the Crown Prince of Bavaria.

Opposed to them were the Sixth French Army, under General Maunoury; the British Expeditionary Force, under Sir John French; and the Fifth French Army, under General Franchet d'Espérey—all these three gathered against the First German Army—Kluck's. Then there were the Ninth French Army, under General Foch; the Fourth French Army, under General de Langle Cary; the Third French Army, from

Verdun, under General Sarrail; and the Second French Army, under General Castelnau, operating round Nancy.

General d'Espérey faced Kluck; General Foch faced Bülow and part of Hausen's force; General de Langle Cary faced the Duke of Würtemberg and the rest of Hausen's force; General Sarrail faced the Crown Prince's army and Von Heeringen's forces; and General Castelnau, with the Second French Army round Nancy, faced the Kaiser himself with a force of Bavarian troops, nominally under the command of the Crown Prince of Bavaria. Between these opposing armies fighting had been going on for more than a week, and in some sections contact had been continuous since the opening clash on the Belgian and Lorraine borders. Day by day the French had been pushed further south, the pressure at last being apparently equal against both their western and eastern wings.

As we know now, it was only the eastern French wing—General Sarrail's army of Verdun and General Castelnau's Toul-Nancy army—that was in any extreme danger. But to the advancing German armies it appeared at the time as though the entire French line continued to give before their attack. By September 5th the invading armies, from Paris to Verdun, had crossed the Marne and the Marne Canal, and some of their outposts were moving, far below the capital, towards Central France.

On this Saturday—September 5th—there was an especially fierce action between the Fifth French Army, under D'Espérey and Kluck's advancing force.

GENERAL JOSIAS VON HEERINGEN.
He commanded the Sixth German Army from Metz and Saarbrücken. Born in 1850, he fought in the Franco-Prussian War, being wounded at Wörth. Between 1909 and 1912 he was Prussian Minister of War.

D'Espérey's army was apparently hurled across the Marne toward the Upper Seine by the driving sweep suddenly made by the German commander. In the night the French entrenched on the hills south of the Grand Morin stream —their left wing near the village of Courtécon, their right near the town of Esternay, on the

The hidden river. Some fifteen miles behind them,
British army at Provins and Nogent-sur-Seine, were some mounted German reconnoitring bodies. These, however, were suddenly cut off by a strong force of French cavalry, under General Conneau, that closed the gap between Courtécon village and the hidden British army, extending from the Forest of Crecy. The gap had been left open only to encourage Kluck to retreat farther into the ambush prepared for him. But he wisely refused to get right out of touch with Bülow's army, and swerved still more eastward, and struck at D'Espérey's position. Conneau's cavalry then moved up to support the Fifth French Army.

At the same time as Kluck attacked, Bülow, the Duke of Würtemberg, the Crown Prince, General von Heeringen, and the commander of the Second German Army swept forward. But all the French line stood firm. A happy rumour had spread through the French forces, and the next day—Sunday, September 6th—the rumour was confirmed. To all the troops General Joffre then issued his famous order :

"At the moment when a battle is about to begin, on which the welfare of the country depends, I feel it incumbent on me to remind you that this is no longer the time to look behind. All our efforts must be directed towards attacking the enemy and driving him back. An army which can advance no farther must at all costs hold the ground it wins, and allow itself to be killed on the spot rather than give way. No faltering in the present circumstances can be tolerated."

Every son of France knew what this meant. For years the French doctrine of "the offensive return" had been discussed in the barracks, till the most backward of peasant recruits got to understand the broad outline of it. The French armies would have at first to withdraw from the sudden, overwhelming German onset. The German lines of communication would lengthen out and absorb troops, the invaders would grow tired with incessant marching and fighting, and then the French armies, after their long recoil, would spring out on the grand attack.

Nobody expected that the offensive return would have been so long delayed. But the temporary French loss of a considerable stretch of territory was more than balanced by the German loss of a large proportion of military strength. The main German lines of communication

ran for more than two hundred miles through hostile country, and the railways, along which supplies came, were open to attack by all the old means, and by the still more destructive new method of bomb-throwing from aeroplanes. The Third German Army, under General von Hausen, had been so worn out by the advance that it had disappeared on the decisive day, its remnants being absorbed by General von Bülow's forces and the Duke of Würtemberg's army. Altogether the German losses were far heavier than the French, and the French had had about five weeks to increase their war material. All that the remarkable striking power that the Germans had won at the start by their aggressiveness and efficiency of organisation had now been recovered by the French. In fact, in the chief matter—ammunition supplies—the defenders now had a marked advantage over the invaders.

General Joffre's main armies rested on the railway running along the Upper Seine, with branch feeding lines running northward towards Esternay, Sezanne, Vitry-le-François, and Bar-le-Duc, but not always emptying into these towns, as some were held by the enemy.

But close to these towns the five main armies rested, with practically all the locomotives, trucks, and railway carriages of France at their service. For the general rolling-stock of the northern French lines had retreated with the armies, and the French Military Staff handled the railways in an admirable manner. Never had the field armies of France been so well supplied with food and ammunition as in their great battle for national existence.

Some, at least, of the German armies, on the other hand, were running short of ammunition and general supplies. Many troops were worn out by excessive marching, and rainy weather and lack of food further contributed to weaken them. In the Champagne district there was a wild outburst of drinking among the German soldiers, which dulled their feelings of fatigue, but scarcely increased their fighting ability. The drunken, armed brutes ravaged many of the hamlets and small towns in a frightful, uncivilised manner, but many of them paid on the spot for their savage destructiveness. This was especially the case with some of the spoilers under the command of the Crown Prince of Germany—himself a robber of the treasures of a Frenchwoman's **An Imperial** chateau. They perished in thousands **pilferer** round the scenes of their ravaging.

The only thing that sustained the German troops amid their weariness, hunger, and discomfort was the general thought that their triumphal entry into Paris, and their feasting on the spoils of the conquered capital were as certain as the sunrise, and almost as near There was

GENERAL JOFFRE AND STAFF PASSING THROUGH A FRENCH VILLAGE.

The French Generalissimo, one of the world's "silent organisers of victory," was the idol of the whole French Army. Constantly on the move, he left nothing to chance, and his ever-vigilant control was felt along the entire French lines.

FRENCH PICKET LEAVING A FARMHOUSE IN THE EARLY MORNING TO RELIEVE THEIR COMRADES IN THE TRENCHES.
A graphic picture of what life on active service is like. These men, after a brief period of repose in a farmhouse—repose often broken by a visitation of the enemy's shells—are seen sallying forth soon after dawn to the slow but deadly work of the trenches, to which the French temperament found it so difficult to accommodate itself in the early stages of the Great War, but in which our gallant Allies afterwards proved themselves more than a match for the enemy. Our picture affords a striking contrast to that of the farmstead in normal times.

only one more battle to fight—an easy affair against a fleeing enemy—and then the richest land in the world was theirs to batten on. The following order of the day, signed by Lieutenant-General Tülff von Tschepe und Weidenbach, and addressed to the Eighth German Army Corps, is typical of the frame of mind of the commanders of the invading forces :

"Vitry-le-Francois, September 7th,
(10.30 p.m.).

"The object of our long and arduous marches has been accomplished. The principal French troops, after having been continually pressed back, have been forced to accept battle. The great decision is undoubtedly at hand. To-morrow the whole strength of the German Army, as well as the entire force of our army corps, is bound to be engaged all along the line from Paris to Verdun. I expect every officer and man to do his duty unswervingly, to his last breath, to save the welfare and honour of Germany, despite the hard and heroic fights of the last few days. Everything depends on the result of to-morrow's battle."

This historic document, picked up by a Frenchman after the German retreat from Vitry, lacks the **French and German orders contrasted** confident spirit of General Joffre' similar order, as well as the heroism of his Spartan command to his army to perish rather than fall back. The difference in the dates— the French commander wrote some thirty-six hours before the German general—is equally significant. The captain of France was striking a full day before his blow was expected to fall. This was probably due to the fact that

Kluck, on the western German wing, by failing to notice the British force on his flank, pushed on with his attack against the Fifth French Army without dreaming of being attacked himself by an overwhelming combination of forces. Naturally, while Kluck remained ignorant of his own fate, no suspicion of it was entertained by the commanders of the other German armies. Thus, the idea of a general French offensive movement was slow in spreading along the German lines.

All this was excellent from the French **Advantage of surprise** commander's point of view. He had **with the French** the advantage of surprise as well as the advantage of attack, and his plan of action was one of the most simple and the most perfect in military history. It was practically impossible for it to fail. In spite of the fact that the numbers of the opposing armies were about equal, General Joffre was bringing two Frenchmen against each German, and two French light field-guns against each German light field-gun.

"Only numbers can annihilate," said Nelson. He usually managed, when an enemy had more ships, still to bring two British ships against every hostile ship. He accomplished this apparent impossibility by a simple trick first devised by a Scotsman, and communicated by him to Admiral Rodney. Two hostile fleets usually went into action with their battleships arranged in a long line. The Scotsman—Clerk, of Edinburgh—suggested that instead of each British warship attacking the hostile vessel in front of it in the old-fashioned way, the British fleet should sail in a straight path through the enemy's line of battle, then bend round half the line, so that each

THE ENEMY IN THE ARGONNE.
German artillery in the hilly and thickly - wooded district of North-Eastern France.

modern artillery and long-range rifles. He was of the opinion that a sound frontal attack would fail against a sound defence. He inclined to remain on the defensive in his centre, with massed gun fire there to beat back the enemy, and throw out his wings and cut the hostile lines of communication in an enveloping movement. This was a return to the primitive method of attack, and as Moltke usually had a larger force on the battlefield than his opponents, he was able to arrange for his wing columns to deploy in an encircling movement.

General Joffre's plan was more subtle than Moltke's, and less audacious than Nelson's or Napoleon's. He quietly attacked the Germans on their western wing, where Kluck was advancing against the Fifth French Army, while the British force was advancing in turn against him.

Kluck had to give way. Sir John French drove fiercely on his flank, and threatened to surround him, while General d'Espérey held him in front. Kluck retired with all speed, with both the British force and the Fifth French Army pursuing him. As he crossed the Marne to escape destruction he left unguarded the flank of the connecting German army—Bülow's. The British force took over the pursuit of Kluck's troops, with the help of the Sixth French Army. Meanwhile, General d'Espérey, with the Fifth French Army, curved westwards, and drove against

of the enemy vessels there had a British warship in front of it, and another behind it. Having destroyed half the enemy's forces in this way, the successful fleet pursued the other half.

Napoleon achieved a similar result by similar means. By a frontal attack with a concentrated mass of troops he pierced the enemy's line, then surrounded half of it, destroyed that half, and proceeded to defeat the remaining half. He always tried to have, at the decisive spot,

WITH THE FRENCH DEFENDERS OF THE ARGONNE.
Wounded soldiers being removed from the trenches.

double the number of troops that his opponent had, in spite of the fact that he often was, on the whole, barely equal, or even inferior, to the enemy in numbers.

Napoleon's successor to leadership in warfare—Moltke the elder—thought that the Clerk-Rodney-Nelson-Napoleon method of breaking the enemy's line had been antiquated by the great increase in defensive power produced by

the flank of Bülow's troops. They already had the Ninth French Army, under General Foch, attacking them in front. Being taken in the flank by D'Espérey at the same time, they, like Kluck's force, had to retreat with all speed. General d'Espérey and the Fifth French Army helped to pursue them.

In the meantime, General Foch in turn directed his tired but victorious men against the flank of the Prussian Guards

FRENCH BATTERY OF ARTILLERY SHELLING THE GERMAN LINES NEAR THE ARGONNE FOREST.
From quite an early period in the war fierce battles raged in the district of North-Eastern France known as the Argonne, and stretching from the plateau of Langres and the Monts Faucilles on opposite sides of the River Meuse. Of the two chains of hills forming the Argonne the west forms a continuous ridge, which constitutes a kind of natural defence, and is intersected by narrow defiles.

and the flank of the Duke of Würtemberg's army. This army also had an opponent in front—General de Langle Cary. The Duke of Würtemberg had to retreat, and Foch pursued him. As Würtemberg retired he exposed the flank of the Crown Prince's forces. These were attacked sideways by General de Langle Cary's men, while in front and to the east they were held from Bar-le-Duc to Verdun by the Verdun garrison army under General Sarrail. The Metz army tried to intervene, but failed to get quickly enough to the help of the Crown Prince and turn the tide of battle. So the Crown Prince had to retire, and with his retirement the main battle was won all along the line by the French.

It will thus be seen that although the scheme of combined actions was lengthy in operation it was simple in principle. Two French or allied armies acted against one German army. Each French soldier under D'Espérey, Foch, and Langle Cary fought two battles. He first held one German force in front and helped to drive it back. Then he swerved and attacked the flank of another German force and, when it retreated, pursued it. He had to do double work. The result was that he doubled the fighting strength of France in the most critical period of her history. General Joffre's plan required that his troops, wearied most of them by long marches and severe conflicts, should suddenly show a power of continual endurance and attacking ability equal to that of two German soldiers. The French Commander-in-Chief knew his men. He knew what an extraordinary access of spirited strength would flow in upon the Frenchman when he was given, after a long ordeal of mere resistance, the opportunity for a sudden, victorious leap forward. Joffre trusted, in the great week, to the élan of his race.

CONSTANT VIGILANCE THE PRICE OF VICTORY.
French infantry scouts making their way through brushwood, which afforded excellent cover, on the outskirts of a wood in the Argonne district.

FRENCH CYCLIST SCOUTS.
These men are taking advantage of a natural trench in a patch of open country in North-Eastern France.

When you shoot a tiger, and the blood is choking its lungs, you must leap aside for your life, for even in its death agony the tiger will die charging. There is much of this fury of the charge in the Frenchman's way of fighting. He defends himself best by attacking, and the tradition of the unexpected victories he won, by a tiger charge in the hour of defeat, is the chief reason why the modern German commanders always order an attack by way of defence. This way of fighting, however, is an acquired thing among the North Germans. They do it methodically, mechanically, because Clausewitz showed that it was Napoleon's way of winning. Napoleon, however, was only putting to good use the fundamental fighting instinct of the French race.

Joffre used the same instinct of his race in a different way. He took into consideration the disadvantages of

FRENCH SOLDIERS IN A FOREST BIVOUAC IN THE FIGHTING AREA.
Another view of the Argonne country, showing a detachment of our Allies snatching a brief interval for rest and refreshment after an arduous and exhausting march.

continually displaying the élan of attack in the era of Maxims, quick-firing guns, and magazine rifles. He taught the French soldier to be patient and wary and stubbornly defensive. Then, in the great decisive battle, when he had completely outmanœuvred the younger Moltke, he used the old, wild, furious, triumphant élan of France, and by means of it doubled the actual **The old, triumphant** fighting powers of his three main armies **élan of France** —D'Espérey's, Foch's, and Langle Cary's. In the special conditions of battle which he had designed the racial quality he elicited from his troops was almost equal in value to a reinforcement of another half a million men.

As Lord Kitchener put it, General Joffre showed he was not only a great military leader, but a great man. With a moulding power not wholly dissimilar from that of Oliver Cromwell, he uncovered, in the period of France's extreme peril, the deepest springs of the national character. He brought fully into play, almost for the first time in modern history, the tenacity and patience that characterise the French peasant. Then, having thus tempered the spirit of France, he suddenly allowed the widest scope for the strange, leaping ardour of attack that carries the Frenchman through all fatigue and danger to death or victory.

How they fought, the three main French armies, the Fifth, the Ninth, the Fourth! For days they stonewalled the last, desperate onsets of the German forces; then for days they attacked and wheeled and attacked and pursued. From the 5th to the 14th of September the great battle raged, and it was only on the last day that the decision was obtained. While the victorious troops of General Maunoury and Field-Marshal Sir John French were assailing General von Kluck's men in their new fortress on the plateau of Soissons by the Aisne River, the movement they had set going still swung undecisively. Until Monday, September 14th, it was quite

possible that the British Expeditionary Force and the garrison army of Paris would have again to retire on the French capital. Their sectional victory near Meaux depended entirely upon the speed with which the continual flanking operation against each German army was carried out. For at Fort Troyon, by the heights of the Meuse between Verdun and Toul, a great German force from Metz was waiting to get through. The small garrison at Troyon was falling; the fort was being shattered. It was most vital that the Crown Prince's army should be forced to retreat before it could complete the destruction of Fort Troyon and join across the Meuse with the Metz force. Hence the tremendous importance of the chain of events between the Fifth French Army and the Third French Army.

The Fifth French Army, composed of men that had

fought at Charleroi and had since been reinforced, was commanded by General d'Espérey. These troops had at first suffered from the able manner in which the Germans used their machine-guns. Machine-guns were employed in larger numbers by the enemy than by the Allies. Each French or British battalion had usually only two machine-guns; a German battalion often had six. They were concealed very skilfully in woods and sheltered places, and the French troops were then lured to an attack, and shot down at short range in close formations. But by the time the Allies arrived at the Marne the French had grown wary, and taken to advancing in extended order in the British fashion. When Kluck in turn attacked them with the best first-line regiments of Prussia—an army corps from Old Prussia and contingents from Brandenburg, Westphalia, and Hanover—the Frenchmen kept their fire until the Germans were at close range. Then they volleyed at them. Kluck kept to his old tactics of trying to get round the flank of his opponent. He was, however, soon brought up by the cavalry division under General Conneau, assisted by its horse artillery. Then he tried to break the French front, but his grey masses of troops were scattered by the French 3 in. guns and the rifle fire of the infantry. Finding his losses too heavy on one side, the German commander swerved round to the other, and brought up from Coulommiers and Montmirail new columns, that deployed in lines five men deep and advanced over a brook and up the hills, only to be again repulsed.

All through Saturday and Sunday, September 5th and 6th, Kluck vainly tried to justify his swerve from Paris by making his new opponents bend or break. By Sunday evening the effect of the British surprise attack on the German flank made itself felt on the German front. First came the culminating onset of the Prussians. The German commander massed every available man against the Fifth French Army, and endeavoured, in a frenzy of despair, to hack a path to victory through the valley of defeat. Kluck was a man of the stamp of Hindenburg, the leader against the Russian forces. A sort of human bull, tricky when he thought he could play with his foe, and uncommonly agile for his size, but given to blind, fierce, battering rushes when he felt himself outplayed.

He was certainly courageous. That is **Kluck's frenzied bid** to say, he sacrificed his men in a **for success** terrible manner in a desperate attempt to save the situation and his own fame. But all his efforts were hopeless. He was trapped; his heavy artillery was far away on the Ourcq; his cavalry was held by the British advance, and an army corps had also to be thrown out towards his flank to prevent sudden, overwhelming disaster. On Sunday night he knew he was a beaten man, and

FOR LOVE OF HIS COUNTRY.
A French "Territorial" on guard. The Territorial force in France is the counterpart of the German Landsturm. The man in our picture was in private life a prosperous farmer. With thousands in like case, he left his farm and his home ties without affectation or sadness, and changed his plough for a rifle to save the soil of his beloved country from the proud foot of the would-be conqueror.

GENERAL DE LANGLE CARY.
Commanded the Fourth French Army facing the Duke of Würtemberg's and part of General von Hausen's forces.

GENERAL SARRAIL.
In command of the Third French Army from Verdun, opposed to the armies of the German Crown Prince and General von Heeringen.

GENERAL FRANCHET D'ESPEREY.
He led one of the two French armies which, with the British force, were opposed to the First German Army under General von Kluck.

to ask his neighbour, General von Bülow, to help him.

On Monday part of the Second German Army co-operated with Kluck's forces in attacking D'Espérey's men. Bülow assailed the eastern wing of the Fifth French Army at Esternay, and Kluck desperately renewed his attack on the centre and western wing. But Bülow soon had all he could do to resist his immediate enemy, General Foch, with the Ninth French Army operating along the ridge of high country by Sezanne. At the same time Kluck was now severely pressed by the swiftly advancing British force, that was trying to wedge between him and his rearguard on the Ourcq.

The battle on the first section of the field was over. Kluck could only fight a delaying action. He threw out some 60,000 men to hinder the British forward movement to his rear, and withdrew with his main force to the northeast towards Bülow's army.

He had at last grasped the situation. Bülow could not help him. It was Bülow's flank that was menaced. So he retired towards Montmirail, eastward of his own line of retreat, in order to reinforce the flank of Bülow's army. But at the first sign of his weakening offensive the spirit of attack awoke in the Frenchmen he had been assailing. They carried village after village at the point of the bayonet, threw the Germans across the Grand Morin on Monday, September 7th, and then stormed over the hills to Montmirail on the Petit Morin.

Tuesday, September 8th, was the critical day in the action of the Fifth French Army. Kluck had then completely lost the battle against the British; his rearguard on the Ourcq, as well as his rearguard on the Marne, was in danger. But with one courage he stuck to Bülow's flank at Montmirail, and with part of Bülow's army tried

to beat off D'Espérey's troops. Naturally, all the German forces were linked closely together by a system of field telephones, and Kluck was well aware that he now had to fight for time for the stroke against Fort Troyon fully to succeed. All that had been lost by him in the west would be more than recovered if a path between Verdun and Toul could be opened in the east, bringing the Metz army through the shattered, divided lines of General Sarrail's forces. Also, further south at Nancy an immense movement against the rear of the French battle-line was still proceeding.

So Kluck and Bülow fought with fierce tenacity to maintain their position. But the British Army had got into a non-stop swing that carried it by Monday night to the bank of the Marne. The Fifth French Army, with larger numbers to fight against, was equally irresistible. The gunners with their terrible quick-firers knocked the heart out of the entrenched German infantry, and the French bayonet came into play round Montmirail in a manner that Napoleon, who had **Initiative and dash** fought the Prussians in the same town, **tell against machinery** would have admired. At night, lighted on their way to victory by their flaming villages, the French troops battled onward, slaughtering the invader at last in the hand-to-hand fighting and the house-to-house actions, in which the Frenchmen's initiative and dash tell against any sort of war machinery.

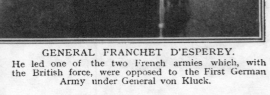

It was just on a hundred and eight years since Auerstadt and Jena—a hundred and eight years since Frenchmen had seen the backs of Prussians in a decisive national battle. At Montmirail in 1814 Napoleon could not win again, for all his skill, against his old foes. But at Montmirail in 1914 General Joffre prevailed once more over the Prussians. The numbers of the enemy slain by the bayonet

HOW THE EVER-READY MEN OF THE BRITISH ARMY SERVICE CORPS LOOKED AFTER THE WANTS OF OUR BRAVE SOLDIERS
IN THE FIRING-LINE.

Bully beef and other rations being distributed by men of the Army Service Corps to British infantry fighting the advancing Germans during the retreat to the Marne. As they fell back before the Teuton invader our soldiers, hungry, but defying fatigue, were well cared for by the Army Service Corps, whose motor-lorry drivers had a herculean task in reaching the constantly shifting lines at the front. With unfailing courage the Army Service Corps men ran to and fro along the trenches with armsful of bully-beef tins and bread for the combatants, regardless of the hail of shrapnel bullets flying around them.

PLACE STANISLAS AND RUE HERE, NANCY.
The Place Stanislas is the principal square in Nancy, and is named after Stanislas Leszcinski, who, after abdicating the crown of Poland in 1735, resided here as Duke of Lorraine till his death in 1766. On the right is a view of the cathedral, built in 1742.

were unusual on a modern battlefield. It was the Frenchman's way of punishing the ravagers, spoilers, and cruel hordes of the new Attila. He thought of the women of Northern France and Belgium, of the thousands of unarmed villagers, country-folk, and townspeople who had been murdered, and, where he could, he used the steel instead of lead bullets. From Montmirail to Chateau Thierry on the Marne, where the left wing of the Fifth French Army pursued Kluck's main force, the heights and hollows and woods were strewn with dead and wounded Germans. It was heavy fighting all the way, but the French soldier had a stern sense of exhilaration in it. The heavier the fighting, the heavier the losses. And he was so terrible and quick in his work of retribution that his was not the heavier loss. By September 9th he had thrown Kluck over the river, and driven in the flank of Bülow.

The Ninth French Army under General Foch, one of the most expert of French strategists, then came fully into play as an offensive force. General Foch rested on the high land round Sezanne, with a very dangerous tract of country in front of him. It consisted of the marshes of Saint Gond, running east to west for some ten miles, and extending north and south for one to two miles. The marshes were the source of the Petit Morin River, that formed a canalised ditch into which the marsh dykes drained. The marsh and morass was being reclaimed, and four sound country roads ran over it.

Happily for France the process of reclamation had not been completed. For the German commander launched the Prussian Guard, with its guns, on the right wing of General Foch's Ninth Army, across the marsh of Saint Gond. Some 30,000 men, with 75 guns, 200 Maxims,

PLACE DE LA CARRIERE, NANCY.
Another view of this lovely French city. On the left is shown the Porte de la Craffe.

and a long train of ammunition vehicles, mostly motor drawn, cannot advance very quickly over four narrow country ways. These had to be given up to the heavy motor vehicles, and most of the guns were drawn over the fairly firm reclaimed marshland.

The marsh is a longish pocket of clay in a large hollow in the calcareous plateau of Sezanne. The clay had partly dried in the hot summer weather, and, though still wet at bottom, it was so thickly caked over on the surface that, with its covering of marsh grass, it supported the Prussian guns.

It is the boast of the Prussian Guard that it never retires. It is an army corps of men picked for their uncommon strergth of body and high statue. It is the spearhead of the German Empire, and when it strikes it is designed to penetrate the enemy's line or perish valiantly in the attempt. In the war of 1870 it had won glory at St. Privat by charging up a long slope against a terrific French fire, and holding its ground when other German troops were giving way. Now it was sent against the left of the French centre to break up General Joffre's plan of bringing two French armies on the front and flank of each German force. If General Foch could only be driven back the intricate sectional French turning movement would be stopped at the point of real danger. The bending back of Kluck's wing would not then be the beginning of a general defeat.

The Prussian Guard remained true to its old traditions. It did not retire. But this was not due to its courage. On the afternoon of Wednesday, September 9th, when Kluck had been thrown over the Marne, the Guards

PALAIS DU GOUVERNEMENT, NANCY.
So certain were the German General Staff of capturing Nancy, one of the most beautiful towns in France and the capital of the old Duchy of Lorraine, that the Kaiser came to watch the victory from a hill close by. He had to leave rather hurriedly. This was in September, 1914.

FRENCH DRAGOON MACHINE-GUN SECTION GALLOPING INTO ACTION UNDER A HEAVY FIRE.
The French Army adopted the Hotchkiss as its machine-gun, a weapon of 315 calibre, identical with that of the Lebel rifle, with which both cavalry and infantry were armed. The pieces were mounted on a wheeled carriage.

entered the marshes. They concealed their batteries and trenches among the rushes, and spent the night in the hollow, with the intention of making a surprise attack next morning on General Foch's army, which was now advancing northward along the plateau towards St. Prix and Epernay. It suddenly came on to rain in the night, a heavy rain that soaked the caked clay. All the surface water from the Sezanne plateau streamed into the hollow, and by dawn many of the men were waist high in water, and their guns and limbers were embedded to the axles.

Then from the surrounding heights the terrible 3 in. French quick-firers entered on their deadly work. The French gunners, working on their own familiar countryside, got the range of the enemy at once. A general salvo drove the spike of the French guns into the earth. There was no further need to get the range. By a special device the batteries then became semi-automatic range-finding instruments of destruction. Loaded and fired with extreme quickness by the detachments, they mechanically swept every acre of the marshes.

This section of the battlefield became a chess-board ruled by invisible lines by the French fire-control officer. On every front square he pitched a shell **Terrible work of** or shrapnel that destroyed everything in **the French "75's"** the square. Then, without re-aiming, the guns, each dropped a shell along the second line of squares, and so on, till the last line of squares at the end of the marsh was covered by the salvo of the massed quick-firers.

The Prussian Guard did not retire; in spite of its efforts at retreat, it perished. Men as well as guns were bogged in the watery clay, and when next the Prussian Guard appeared on the battlefield at Ypres it was formed of the rest of the reserve troops of the famous corps, largely filled out with hastily-trained recruits. Frederick the

Great's famous regiment, enlarged with the increase of Prussia's military power to an army corps, was buried in the marshes of St. Gond. Ten thousand dead men were found there, and the carts, artillery, and dead horses of the corps.

There were two highways running on the plateau between the marsh. One ran by St. Prix to Epernay, the other ran by Morains with the railway towards Rheims. General Foch divided his forces and advanced along the heights by both roads. A hurricane of shrapnel from his guns, directed by aeroplanes **German morale** at the German columns, heralded **"absolutely broken"** his progress and cleared his path.

On the night of September 9th Bülow ordered his western wing to retire down the St. Prix road. Most of his heavy artillery, it appears from a letter by an officer of his Tenth Army Corps, was being used at Maubeuge. The French had 6 in. howitzers as well as 3 in. quick-firers, and they beat down every attempt by the Germans to delay the march of the French infantry. "Our morale was absolutely broken," a German officer of the Tenth Corps admits. "Our first battalion was reduced from 1,200 to 194 men. These numbers speak for themselves. It was like hell, only a thousand times worse. In spite of unheard-of sacrifices we have achieved nothing."

This was not altogether correct. Bülow's western wing suffered thus terribly because it had to fight a dreadful rearguard action to Epernay, and then through the Forest of Rheims to the cathedral town and the Aisne valley. In the meantime Bülow was swerving eastward with his main force, as Kluck had done, in order to protect in turn his neighbour, Duke Albrecht of Würtemberg, from the inevitable flank attack by General Foch.

The Duke of Würtemberg had penetrated in force farther south than any other German commander. He held the town of Vitry-le-François and the villages along the road to Paris. His army made the chief attempt to pierce the French front, with Bülow's eastern wing assisting in the operation. Three of General von Hausen's army corps also took part in the attack.

Field telephones and fire control These three corps were very badly handled. They stood between General Foch and his main objective, the Würtemberg flank, and, happily for the French, instead of standing on the defensive they attacked furiously. From the woods around the flaming hamlet of Lenharée the French batteries sent a murderous fire, and the entrenched and hidden French artilleryman used his rifle with shattering effect on the compact masses of Saxon soldiers. The 178th Regiment, of two battalions, lost all its officers and 1,700 men.

The French gunners, in the forest fighting, had telephone wires running from every good point of observation, and fire-control officers were hidden in the foliage with the talking mechanism in their hands. Both the French machine-guns and the quick-firers were under distant fire control, and the enemy was usually lured on in large numbers by a pretended French retirement and then practically annihilated. The Saxons, under General von Hausen, were the first to give way.

They apparently began to retire after their defeat on September 8th, when Kluck was still holding out on the extreme western wing. On the critical day, September 9th, when the Prussian Guards were marching into the swamp of St. Gond, a large number of the Saxons had withdrawn far to the rear at Chalons. Their feet were bleeding and deeply cut by excessive marching. The men were too worn out to fight, and hopelessly demoralised by their tremendous losses. They can scarcely be said to have counted in the decisive conflict, though Bülow and the Duke of Würtemberg gathered any fighting remnants that were available.

This extraordinary rout of Hausen and his Saxons— originally some 150,000 men, with the cavalry of the Guards in addition—was a great and decisive achievement. It left a gap in the German line that neither Bülow nor the Duke of Würtemberg was able to fill in time. Foch was irresistible, with his terrible way of clearing his advancing front with shell and shrapnel, drawing on a vast store of artillery ammunition, and "watering" the ground for a mile in front of his advance guards. On September 10th he curved westward and shook the flank of the powerful Würtemberg forces.

The Duke of Würtemberg had been in turn attacking and beating off the Fourth French Army, under General de Langle Cary, for five days or more. The duke had an especially strong and numerous body of troops, as befitted a Royal commander. His victories were intended, like those of the Crown Prince, to increase the prestige of the ruling families of Germany. He had an excellent chief of staff, who arranged the operations, but allowed the duke to take all the credit **The German claim to** for them. This is the way in which **genius in warfare** German princes strive to maintain that family fame for personal genius in warfare which they presume they inherit from some remote ancestor. If Nature will not supply them with this hereditary trait, the German Military Staff does.

However this may be, the Fourth German Army, under the Duke of Würtemberg, certainly fought well. By Sunday, September 6th, it had taken the little historic

A CHARGE "A LA BAIONNETTE"—WHERE THE FRENCH SOLDIER IS ALWAYS AT HIS BEST.

It is part of the belief of many students of war that every battle is won by the bayonet in the last issue. The belief found effective support on many occasions when the French had opportunities of meeting the foe with cold steel, to which the German soldiers as a whole displayed a very decided aversion.

town of Vitry across the canal of the Marne. But the French army held the heights by the town, and the French guns were trained on the canal bridge and on the German trenches in the valley. So intense was the fire from them that the enemy had to abandon many of his trenches, and the slaughter by the bridge was demoralising. The action lasted late into the night, and ended in a German withdrawal. In the morning the French attacked on the right, with a view to relieving the pressure against General Sarrail's sorely pressed Third Army.

The attack was repulsed; but the Duke of Würtemberg was firmly held by a most violent assault, in which both sides suffered heavily. The general decisive battle all along the line had now opened, and the French were animated by the spirit of the offensive. Their artillery continued to dominate the field of action round Vitry, and at the canal bridge more than half the German troops were destroyed. The men in the trenches were without food, and at midnight they crept into the fields and ate raw potatoes

For four days the German troops at Vitry continued to deepen and extend their trenches, and on Thursday,

trenches, and marched for six hours northward. "We were told," wrote a German soldier entrenched at Vitry, "that we were only executing a turning movement, and that it was not a retreat. But it had all the appearances of a flight. We suffered in a terrible way, and were utterly worn out. At Souain we met a Saxon army corps, and could not understand **"Only executing a** what it was doing there. We dug **turning movement"** trenches in the pouring rain. Suddenly a shower of French shells and shrapnel arrived, and we were compelled to draw back, as our trenches were not finished. All the army corps fled."

This was on Saturday, September 12th. The village of Souain is several miles north of the town of St. Menehould, in the Argonne Forest. St. Menehould was the headquarters of the Crown Prince in the attack he was making on the Verdun army. The German front was close to Bar-le-Duc, two days' march south from St. Menehould, three days' march south from Souain. That is to say, General de Langle Cary's advance guards, with guns, were not merely on the flank, but almost in the rear of the original position of the Crown Prince. There was a rumour that the Kaiser's heir only escaped by a quarter of an hour. He moved from St. Menehould to Montfaucon, some ten miles above Verdun. Here he was able to draw help from the Army of Metz, that was making a feint attack on Verdun, but acting more strongly against the chain of forts between Verdun and Toul. As a matter of fact, the Crown Prince's army was in no immediate danger. It had retreated from the neighbourhood of Bar-le-Duc on Thursday, September 10th, when the German line began to give way. So rapid was its retreat, that the German wounded were left on the field of battle.

Most of the high, wooded, difficult country of the Argonne Forest, however, was still tenaciously held by the Crown Prince. Here it was he needed all the help General von Heeringen and the Metz garrison could give him. For between the two German armies the passage of the heights of the Meuse had almost been forced at Fort Troyon.

SCENE OF THE ALLIES' TURNING MOVEMENT ON VON KLUCK.
The country to the east of Amiens towards the Upper Oise, the scene of the turning movement against the German right in September, 1914, is open and eminently fitted for the operations of large armies. The ground is gently undulating, the fields are large, and for the most part unfenced, dotted with many strongly-built farmsteads. The roads often run in a perfectly straight line for many miles.

September 10th, the private soldiers thought that the battle was drawing to a close, as the French gun fire slackened. Suddenly it broke out furiously on the western wing of the Fourth German Army, towards La Fère Champenoise. Foch had struck the flank, and the turning movement was beginning. A German report ran that two French army corps also managed to pierce the enemy's lines. Savage hand-to-hand fighting began. The Germans fought with the butt, so did the Turcos; but the French kept to the bayonet. Brigades clashed **Savage hand-to-hand** and struggled till they fell or tramped **fighting** on their foes. In one place 3,500 German corpses were found mingled with 1,500 French bodies. This seems to have been the general proportion of the heavy losses on this section of the battlefield, though where the French guns had been working in the daylight there were only heaps of German dead.

At two o'clock on the morning of Friday, September 11th, the Germans retreated in the darkness from their

The Crown Prince had only feinted at the great fortress of Verdun. The French garrison held him off by extending their trenches outwards for some miles, and bringing out hidden, mobile batteries to prevent German howitzers from coming within range of the armoured and concrete forts. The Crown Prince, acting on the instructions of General von Moltke, swerved round Verdun to the west, struck at the trench running along the road to Toul, reached the heights of the Meuse, and thus cut General Sarrail's garrison army into two separate parts. One held Verdun; the other operated round Bar-le-Duc.

On the opposite side of the Meuse, however, the communication between Verdun and Toul seems to have been maintained. A chain of hill forts connected the two fortress towns. The hill forts were well designed to repel an attack coming eastward from Metz, but on the western bank of the Meuse, where the Crown Prince's troops were established, there was a height overtopping by some sixty feet the hill on which Fort Troyon had been built.

Some heavy German siege-guns—11 in. Krupp howitzers with pneumatic recoil mechanism—were dragged up the

MAN TO MAN AT LAST! FRENCH INFANTRY PURSUING A FLYING GERMAN BATTERY IN A RAIN-SWEPT VALLEY OF THE ARGONNE.

For long, weary hours had the French lain in their rain-sodden trenches. Then, as darkness was approaching and the tempest at its height, news came that the army of the German Crown Prince was in retreat. The order was given "Charge!" At last it was man and man, and the bayonet had its chance. Our artist has supplied a vivid picture of one incident—the pursuit by French infantry of a flying German battery in the valley of Bellefontaine. The valley is in the Argonne district, to the west of the great fortress of Verdun. The ground was sodden with the rain and water was pouring down to the bottom of the valley in swift torrents. Over this drenched ground the heavy German guns had to be hauled, but they became more firmly fixed in the mud as they proceeded.

British artillerymen working their guns unconcernedly amid a hail of German projectiles. Apart from the devastating effects of the "Jack Johnsons"—the big siege-guns of the Germans—their ordinary field artillery, though deafening in concussion, appears to have caused comparatively little damage, and our men soon got used to it, especially when they found that the shells burst up One of our artillery officers counted one hundred and sixty shells fired a battery between dawn and sunset without causing injury to man or horse. shells," he said, "on striking the ground immediately shoot upward, and

Men of the Royal Army Medical Corps searching for wounded in a wood at night-time by the aid of acetylene motor-car lamps and electric hand torches. There had been heavy fighting all day. Two British battalions had advanced through the wood, partly along the grass roads and partly through the thickly-tangled undergrowth, and all the time under fire from German shrapnel, which ca heavy losses. All around the trunks and branches of the trees were shatt After penetrating the wood and repulsing several German charges, the Br retired at dark, having forced the enemy back. The wood was full of wou

no lateral spreading of the débris. Unless a man, or horse, or gun is hit there no damage done. In fact, after the first few shells were fired by the enemy gunners served their guns with absolute indifference to the strenuous endeavours of the Germans to dislodge them." During the opening months

of the Great War the enemy tried by all the means in their power to create " a moral effect " disadvantageous to the Allies. The terrific explosiveness of their shells was part of this policy. So was the savage display of " frightfulness " against unarmed civilians. But the policy failed all along the line.

, British and German, and owing to the darkness and the thickness of the shwood the task of locating and attending to them was one of the utmost culty. But, as our picture shows so vividly, the men of the Royal Army lical Corps displayed all their traditional energy, devotion, and resourcefulness

in meeting the emergency. They searched the ground thoroughly, sending the rays of light from side to side as they went, and at once moving towards any point whence came answering cries for help. The German wounded received the same care and attention as the British.

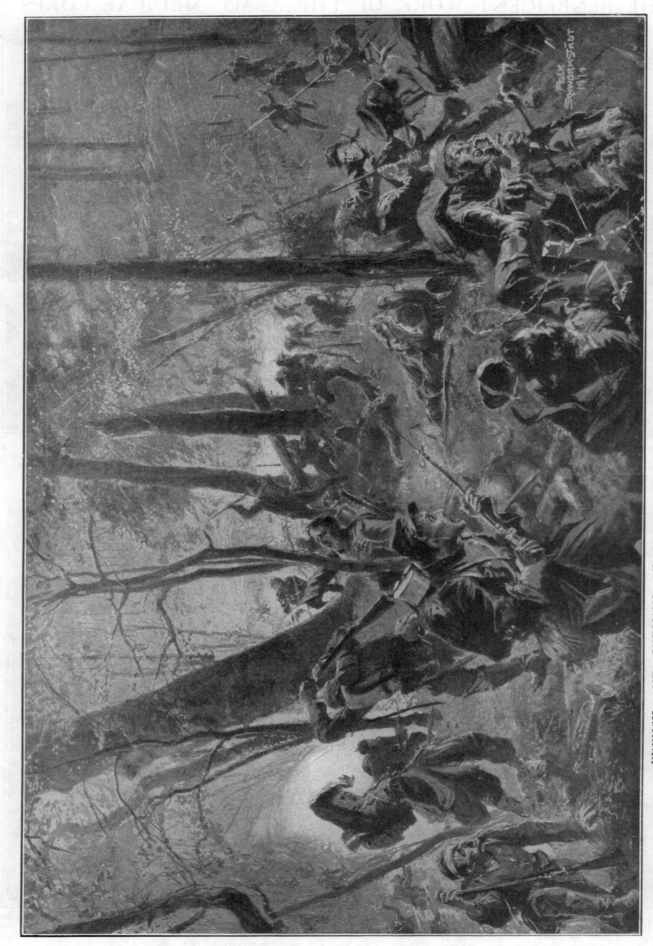

FRENCH AND GERMANS AT CLOSE QUARTERS IN THE FOREST OF ARGONNE.

A German artist's idea of the frenzied fighting that took place in September, 1914, in the Forest of Argonne, between the French and the forces under the command of the German Crown Prince. The struggle in the Argonne went on without definite result into 1915.

hill, and the fort was subjected to a terrible bombardment. A few miles to the east, at Thiaucourt, were the headquarters of the commander of the Metz field army, waiting to pour his troops through the gap made in the eastern fortifications of France.

In the meantime he helped the Crown Prince to retain a complete hold on the Forest of Argonne, and marched troops round Verdun to reinforce him.

The fateful thread at Troyon Even with General de Langle Cary operating on his flank, and General Sarrail fiercely assailing him, the Crown Prince was able to make a desperate struggle for victory. Amid the dense brushwood and tall trees and tumbled rocks of the Argonne ridge numerous small bodies rocked in hand-to-hand conflicts. But at last the Germans were driven to the northern part of the forest, and General Sarrail recovered full possession of the western heights of the Meuse and relieved Fort Troyon. This was done on September 14th, barely in time. The Fort of Troyon was a heap of ruins, only four serviceable guns remained, and the heroic garrison —bravest of men—were reduced to forty-four men. On so fine a thread hung the destiny of France.

Had the Crown Prince succeeded at Troyon, he could have cut Verdun from Toul, and brought its end very near. Still more important, he could have opened short new lines of communication with the depots of Western Germany, and thus greatly eased and strengthened the invading armies. Finally, the French battle-front from the Argonne to Soissons could have been taken in flank by the Sixth German Army from Lorraine. Forty-four Frenchmen with four guns, in a heap of ruins that was being bombarded by 11 in. howitzers, held out just long enough to prevent this. It was one of the supreme achievements of the war.

General von Moltke—though his plan did not work out at the last moment, owing to the slow and unskilful advance of the Crown Prince's army—showed himself on the whole a very able strategist. In him General Joffre met no mean antagonist. Moltke planned as solidly as the French Commander-in-Chief. As we have seen in the previous chapter, General Joffre was not content to mass two armies, the Sixth and Fifth, against Kluck. He prepared for accidents by bringing the British force also against Kluck.

In somewhat the same way Moltke, having placed the means of a great success in the hands of the Crown Prince, did not rely wholly upon the unexpected side-stroke through the Verdun–Toul fortress line. He also struck lower down at Nancy, where another German army was ready to take in reverse the Franco-British advancing line in the north. Apparently, the drive in force through the Gap of Nancy, between Toul and Epinal, was accounted more promising even than the attack on Fort Troyon. In the first days of September, when the main allied armies were still desperately fighting to maintain their position to the east of Paris, the southern stroke at Nancy, full on their flank, may have seemed the most important of all operations. The Kaiser came in person to watch it being carried out.

On August 20th the army of Toul and Nancy, while advancing across the frontier towards Saarburg, had been confronted at Mortagne by two German armies and severely defeated. General Castelnau, the French commander, threw out artillery supports and got the troops over the border in some sort of order, and concentrated on the ring of wooded heights round the beautiful capital of French Lorraine, known as the Grande Couronne of Nancy. Here he was attacked by the two victorious Bavarian forces on August 22nd, and part of the field army of Metz struck southward to co-operate in the assault. After a week of give-and-take fighting the German Commander-in-Chief appears to have fixed on Nancy as the spot at which he would reply to the French concentration of forces against General von Kluck round Paris. At the time, Fort Troyon had not been placed in peril by the progress of the Crown Prince's army. Nancy was an open gate through which all the strong forces in German Lorraine and Alsace could pour into Central

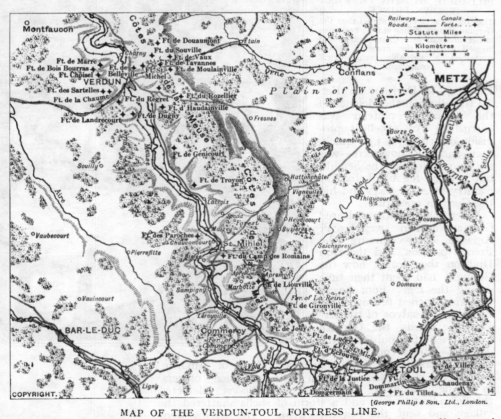

MAP OF THE VERDUN-TOUL FORTRESS LINE.
When the eastern frontier defences of France were recognised after the war of 1870-71, Verdun and Toul were made into great fortresses, and the Cotes de la Meuse—the "Heights of the Meuse"—between these places were fortified by the placing of strong forts on their summits so as to command the passes from the plain of Woevre and the approaches to the Meuse bridges. After heavy fighting in September, 1914, the Germans crossed the Meuse at St. Mihiel.

France, far in the rear of General Joffre's main armies. The weakness already shown by the French at Mortagne was seductive, and part of the field army of Metz and two Bavarian forces, with the famous White Cuirassiers of the Guard and other cavalry, first under the command of the Crown Prince of Bavaria and then of the Kaiser in person, massed for the grand attack on Friday, September 4th.

The main French defensive position was on the plateau of Amance, rising a thousand feet, six miles north-east of Nancy, with the **The famous Iron** Forests of Champenoux and Saint Paul **Division of France** beneath it. The French frontier force had been seriously depleted in order to strengthen the northern French armies, to which General Pau had hastily gone with all the troops that could possibly be spared. Only the garrisons of Toul and Nancy remained. But with them was the greatest of French infantry bodies, the Iron

PILLAGED BY THE GERMAN CROWN PRINCE.
The Baroness Debaye stated that the German Crown Prince stayed two days in her chateau near Champaubert and himself pillaged the museum, which contained a valuable archæological collection.

Division—le Division de Fer. To this division the defence of the Amance plateau was entrusted. An excellent provision of artillery—3 in. quick-firers and 6 in. howitzers—was set in position on the height; but a thick fog blanketed the country for some days and hid the German operations.

When the weather cleared German airmen swept over Amance to reconnoitre the French position, and the Iron Division then learnt how the Germans had spent their time during the fog. Four heavy batteries opened fire upon the French. By salvos of twenty-four big shells the German guns tried to pulverise the defence. The French infantry and gunners had to retire to the village of Amance. But here, also, the German reconnaissance officers, in flying machines and captive balloons, detected the defending troops, and a storm of shells shattered the village and sent the peasants flying. The troops went back to their first position, and found that their guns, which had been skilfully hidden, had not been struck.

It was warm work in the trenches—the men could not raise their heads without getting wounded. They had to **Kaiser's vision of** bring their injured comrades into the **conquered Nancy** deep ditches they had dug to save them from more wounds or instant death. Night and day the racket went on. The French gunners made a pretence of bravely maintaining the artillery duel. But they gradually slackened the fire, gave out ragged volleys, and then ceased.

By September 8th the plateau was silent, and the Kaiser, standing on a neighbouring height and surveying through his field-glasses the summer scene, with Nancy in the distance, ordered the grand infantry attack. The Bavarian battalions came out of the Forest of Champenoux with bands playing at their head, as in Kaiser manœuvres. They climbed up the plateau in close formation. When they were half-way to the top, and only two hundred yards from the trenches, the Iron Division rose with a yell and charged down on them with the bayonet.

The Bavarians, taken at a disadvantage, broke and fled. The men of the Iron Division returned to their trenches. But their enemies did not escape. Close above the trenches were the hidden batteries of 3 in. quick-firers. There were marks for getting the range all down the hill The gunners took the nearest mark **Bavarians and Cuiras-** and then mowed the Bavarians down, **siers mowed down** rank by rank, with horrible quickness, by their mechanical gun-pointing device. Only a few Bavarians got to the woods. But there were plenty more of them—for there were three Bavarian army corps against one French infantry division. Six times the Bavarians charged up the plateau. Six times they were massacred. Then the Kaiser ordered the White Cuirassiers of the Guard to storm the French trenches. Up came the famous cavalrymen in their shining breastplates. But the 3 in. guns raked them. At the foot of the hill the bodies in places were piled six feet high, and when the survivors tried to shelter behind this awful barrier, the terrible French guns on the height smote through the dead to the living.

The Kaiser departed, leaving the Crown Prince of Bavaria the sorry task of carrying on the decisive attack on Nancy. Wilhelm had seen himself riding through the capital of Lorraine, the most beautiful Renaissance city in Northern Europe, at the head of his White Cuirassiers. But most of the White Cuirassiers were dead—they formed part of the dreadful mass of 20,000 men cumbering the foot and lower slopes of the plateau. The German commander begged an armistice to bury his dead on the evening of September 9th. It was reported that his gunners used the truce to

THE IMPERIAL PILLAGER'S "DUG-OUT" BETWEEN RHEIMS AND VERDUN.
Photograph of the "dug-out" or bomb-proof shelter occupied by the German Crown Prince during his stay behind the German lines in North-Eastern France before the retreat of the Germans beyond the Marne. It was afterwards occupied by French Red Cross nurses. Inset: The German Crown Prince and two officers of his staff.

PRACTISING FOR THE PROMISED PARADE THROUGH PARIS.
German soldiers "goose-stepping" before their Crown Prince prior to their unexpected and sudden retreat to the Aisne. Inset: Prince Wilhelm Friedrich of Prussia in the uniform of the Death's Head Hussars, of which he was Colonel for about two years.

drag into position the heavy guns with which they angrily bombarded Nancy. But this bombardment did not alter the course of events. On Thursday, September 10th, the French Iron Division and its artillerymen took the offensive. The 6 in. howitzers were suddenly brought into action, and, with the 3 in. quick-firers, they swept the Forest of Champenoux, where the Bavarians had vainly gone for shelter. Acre by acre the woodland was searched with deadly melinite shells, until no foeman remained among the shattered trees except the dead and the badly wounded. The slaughter of the invisible enemy was over by eleven o'clock in the morning, owing to the mechanical means of fixing progressive ranges for the guns after the first shot. Nancy was saved on the day that the western wing of the main German armies was retreating beyond the Marne and the outskirts of Paris. Four days later, as we have seen, Fort Troyon was relieved, and the Crown Prince of Germany was in difficulties.

Kluck's skill in retreat The victory of France was not so decisive as perhaps General Joffre expected. Only General von Hausen's Saxon army suffered anything like a rout. The skilful disposition of heavy artillery with which Kluck strengthened his flank guard against the Sixth French Army prevented the Allies from getting successively on the lines of communication of the retreating German forces. As a whole, the retirement of the invading armies was conducted in as good an order as marked the retirement of the allied armies from the Belgian frontier. On the other hand, the Germans, caught successively on flank and rear, and forced to struggle for life in every section of the battlefield, suffered very heavy losses. In many cases the troops, by the confession of their own officers, were demoralised.

In the neighbourhood of Nancy alone, at Amance and Lunéville, there were by September 10th some 31,000 dead Germans, mostly first-line troops. The Prussian Guards left on the field one man out of three of their original numbers, and one out of two of their actual fighting force. Their White Cuirassiers, dying under the eyes of their Emperor, were practically all destroyed. The Saxon army also must have been very badly cut up, for it appears not to have been worth while to re-establish its three corps under a new commander when Hausen was dismissed from his generalship-in-chief. Literal decimation—one dead man in ten—for the entire invading forces actually in the fighting-line would probably be an underestimate. For both the shelling and shrapnelling were peculiarly deadly, and the bayonet was used with murderous effect all along the line. The proportion of killed to wounded in the first grand Franco-British victory must have been unusually high. Telling mainly on the best class of German troops and their finest commissioned and non-commissioned officers, the general defeat sapped much of the fighting power of the most aggressive people in the modern world. Their new levies afterwards came on bravely enough, with a show of the old fierce spirit of the offensive peculiar to a nation inflated with military pride. But these new troops lacked the warlike skill of the first-line men. Between Paris and the Vosges the mainspring of German aggressiveness was broken.

THE LAST TRENCH: THE HIGH-WATER MARK OF THE TIDE OF GERMAN INVASION IN FRANCE.

Directly south of Chalons, in the direction of Arcis-sur-Aube, lies the village of Mailly; and just south of it was the trench marking the high-water mark of the tide of the German invasion in France. This trench was never taken. Here the French held their ground until the enemy had been driven beyond the Marne. "When," writes our special war artist, Mr. Sydney Adamson, "I last saw the trench, after the battle, a simple wooden cross marked the grave of those who died there. Near by another grave was indicated by a stick with a soldier's cap on it. I have seen several graves so marked, and they always remind me of the custom in Turkey, where a man's red fez is placed upon his coffin, and afterwards a carved and painted fez crowns the marble pillar which shows in Arabic who lies there."

THE COURSE OF EVENTS FROM THE MARNE TO THE AISNE.

The King's Messages to the Dominions Overseas and to the Princes and Peoples of India—Thrilling Episode in the Imperial Parliament—Moslem Opinion—The Press Bureau Reorganised—Act against Trading with the Enemy—Parliament and the New Army—Britain's Hospitality to Victims of the War—Incidents and Accidents at Sea—The Wreck of the Oceanic—Exploits of the German China Squadron—Policing the North Sea—Precedents for the New Naval Brigades—M. Millerand and Lord Kitchener—Cardinal Mercier's Terrible Story—Hélène Vacaresco's Address to France—M. Verhaeren on Belgian Courage and Ideals—German Calumnies—The Rally of South Africa—General Botha's Great Speech—Japan and Peace—Operations in Nyasaland—Great Meeting in the London Opera House—Mr. Churchill on the Work of the Navy.

PARLIAMENT reassembled at Westminster on September 9th for a short session necessitated by the discharge of Imperial business. In both the Commons and the Lords scenes of unexampled enthusiasm were witnessed. Never before in these historic chambers was patriotic emotion more profoundly and unreservedly manifested. First of all came the reading of the King's Message to " the Governments and Peoples of my Self-Governing Dominions," and to the " Princes and Peoples of my Indian Empire." Then followed the epoch-making recital by Mr. Charles Roberts, Under-Secretary for India, in the Commons, and by the Marquis of Crewe in the Lords, of the telegraphic despatch from Lord Hardinge, Governor-General, announcing that the rulers of Native States in India, who numbered nearly seven hundred, had with one accord rallied to the defence of the Empire, and offered their personal services and the resources of their States for the war.

His Majesty's Message to the Governments and Peoples of his Self-governing Dominions was as follows :

" During the past few weeks the peoples of my whole Empire at home and overseas have moved with one mind and purpose to confront and overthrow an unparalleled assault upon the continuity of civilisation and the peace of mankind.

" The calamitous conflict is

HIS HIGHNESS THE AGHA KHAN.
In addition to directing the community of sixty million Moslems—of which he was the spiritual head—to place their personal services and resources unreservedly at the disposal of the Government, he volunteered to serve as a private in any infantry regiment of the Indian Expeditionary Force.

not of my seeking. My voice has been cast throughout on the side of peace. My Ministers earnestly strove to allay the causes of strife and to appease differences with which my Empire was not concerned. Had I stood aside when, in defiance of pledges to which my kingdom was a party, the soil of Belgium was violated, and her cities laid desolate, when the very life of the French nation was threatened with extinction, I should have sacrificed my honour and given to destruction the liberties of my Empire and of mankind. I rejoice that every part of the Empire is with me in this decision.

" Paramount regard for treaty faith and the pledged word of rulers and peoples is the common heritage of Great Britain and of the Empire.

" My peoples in the Self-governing Dominions have shown beyond all doubt that they whole-heartedly endorse the grave decision which it was necessary to take.

" My personal knowledge of the loyalty and devotion of my Oversea Dominions had led me to expect that they would cheerfully make the great efforts and bear the great sacrifices which the present conflict entails. The full measure in which they have placed their services and resources at my disposal fills me with gratitude, and I am proud to be able to show to the world that my peoples oversea are as determined as the people of the United Kingdom to prosecute a just cause to a successful end.

" The Dominion of Canada, the Commonwealth of

193

Australia, and the Dominion of New Zealand have placed at my disposal their naval forces, which have already rendered good service for the Empire. Strong expeditionary forces are being prepared in Canada, in Australia, and in New Zealand for service at the front, and the Union of South Africa has released all British troops, and has undertaken important military responsibilities, the discharge of which will be of the utmost value to the Empire. Newfoundland has doubled the numbers of its branch of the Royal Naval Reserve, and is sending a body of men to take part in the operations at the front. From the Dominion and Provincial Governments of Canada large and welcome gifts of supplies are on their way for the use both of my naval and military forces, and for the relief of the distress in the United Kingdom which must inevitably follow in the wake of war. All parts of my Oversea Dominions have thus demonstrated in the most unmistakable manner the fundamental unity of the Empire amidst all its diversity of situation and circumstance."

THE PRUSSIAN WAR LORD IN HIS ELEMENT.
Newspaper reports credited the Kaiser with exceedingly rapid journeys between the " fronts " in both the eastern and western theatres of war. Our photograph shows him with members of the Great General Staff of the German field army, conversing with an officer who had just been decorated with the Iron Cross.

GENERAL ALEXANDER VON KLUCK IN THE FIELD.
" Old One O'clock," as he was termed by the British soldier. is seen seated at the foot of the steps shown in the photograph. But for his masterly conduct of the German retirement to the Aisne the Allies might have turned the retreat into a rout.

The first part of the King-Emperor's Message to the Princes and Peoples of India was in the same terms as that to the Self-governing Dominions, and it concluded as follows :

" Among the many incidents that have marked the unanimous uprising of the populations of my Empire in defence of its unity and integrity, nothing has moved me more than the passionate devotion to my Throne expressed both by my Indian subjects and by the Feudatory Princes and the Ruling Chiefs of India, and their prodigal offers of their lives and their resources in the cause of the Realm. Their one-voiced demand to be foremost in the conflict has touched my heart, and has inspired to the highest issues the love and devotion which, as I well know, have ever linked my Indian subjects and myself. I recall to mind India's gracious message to the British nation of good-will and fellowship which greeted my return in February, 1912, after the solemn ceremony of my Coronation Durbar at Delhi, and I find in this hour of trial a full harvest and a noble fulfilment of the assurance given by you that the destinies of Great Britain and India are indissolubly linked."

When his Majesty's message was read in the Parliaments of the Dominion of Canada and the Commonwealth of Australia it was received with great cheering and the singing of " God Save the King." In the New Zealand Legislature Mr. Massey, the Premier, said that the Dominion, like the rest of the Empire, was prepared to see the war through, whatever it might cost in life. Every male citizen and the property of every citizen in New Zealand were at the disposal of the Empire.

The story which Mr. Roberts unfolded in the Commons from the Viceroy's telegraphic communication was unlike anything which had ever been heard in the Imperial Parliament. It was a real **India's great tribute** romance from the East, with all its **to Imperial ideals** variety, movement, and colour, and accepted as one of the finest tributes ever paid to Imperial ideals. With the Commander-in-Chief's approval, the Viceroy had selected for active service with the Indian contingents in France and Belgium the Chiefs of Bikaner (with his camel corps), Kishangarh, Ratlam, Sachin, Patiala, the Heir Apparent of Bhopal, a brother of the Maharajah of Cooch Behar, with cadets of other noble families. The veteran Sir Pertab Singh, Regent of Jodhpur, would not be denied his right to serve his King-Emperor, in spite of his seventy years ; and his nephew, the Maharajah of Jodhpur, who was but sixteen years old, insisted on going with him. The Maharajahs of Gwalior, Rewa, Kashmir, Mysore, the Maharajah and the Maharani Maji Sahiba of Bharatpur, the Rajah of Akalkot, the Rajah of Pudukota, the Gaekwar of Baroda, Mir Ghulam, Ali Khan of Khairpur, offered troops, camels, horses, money contributions, and even their personal jewellery. Several of the chiefs combined, in addition, to provide a hospital ship. Most remarkable of all was the offer of troops and contributions from beyond the borders of India, such as from the ruler of Nepal, and from the Dalai Lama of Tibet, which latter stated in making his offer that Lamas innumerable throughout the length and breadth of Tibet were offering prayers for the success of the British Army, and for the happiness of the souls of all victims of war. Many hundreds of telegrams and letters had also been received by the Viceroy expressing loyalty and desire to serve the Imperial Government, either in the field or by co-operation in India, from communities and associations, religious, political, and social of all classes and creeds, the most notable of which were from a vast variety of Moslem leagues, Hindus, Orthodox Sikhs, and Parsees. The Delhi Medical Association offered a field hospital, and Bengalee students and many others offered services for an ambulance corps and other medical aid.

The Committee of the London All-India Moslem League passed on September 8th, at an emergency meeting, the following resolutions : (1) "That the Committee of the London All-India Moslem League desire to convey, through the favour of the Right Hon. the Secretary of State for India, to his Majesty's Indian troops their good wishes for success in the opportunity accorded to them to share with their British comrades-in-arms in the defence of the Empire on the battlefields of Europe. (2) That the Committee further desire to place on record their conviction that the Moslem States will in the titanic struggle in which the nations of Europe have become involved do all in their power to avoid being drawn into the vortex ; and that the Turkish Government will unswervingly maintain the neutrality which it has hitherto faithfully observed, and not allow the Ottoman people to be goaded by malign attempts into any deviation from strict fidelity to its pledges."

In the House of Commons complaints were made as to the reticence of the Press Bureau and the inadequacy of the news furnished to the public by it, and the Prime Minister announced that the Bureau had been reorganised, and that, at the request of the Cabinet, the Home Secretary, Mr. McKenna, had accepted responsibility for it. Among the Emergency Bills introduced was one authorising the appropriation of charities—which under deed could not possibly be applied in existing circumstances—to the Prince of Wales's Fund while the war lasted.

More important still was the measure, which ran through all its stages, relating to trading with the enemy. Under this Act a Supplement to the " London Gazette " of September 9th contained a revised Proclamation revoking by Clause 1 previous Proclamations on this important subject, and substituting therefor the present one, which proceeds as follows :

" (2) The expression 'enemy country' means the territories of the German Empire and of the Dual Monarchy of Austria-Hungary, together with all the Colonies and Dependencies thereof. (3) **Trading with** The expression 'enemy' means any **the enemy** person or body of persons of whatever nationality resident or carrying on business in the enemy country, but does not include persons of enemy nationality who are neither resident nor carrying on business in the enemy country. In the case of incorporated bodies, enemy character attaches only to those incorporated in an enemy country.

" The following prohibitions now have effect (save so far as licences may be issued) : (1) Not to pay any sum of money to or for the benefit of an enemy. (2) Not to compromise or give security for the payment of any debt or other sum of money with or for the benefit of an enemy. (3) Not to act on behalf of an enemy in drawing, accepting, paying, presenting for acceptance or payment, negotiating, or otherwise dealing with any negotiable instrument. (4) Not to accept, pay, or otherwise deal with any negotiable instrument which is held by or on behalf of an

HOW THE WAR LORD WENT TO WAR—THE EXTENSIVE PLANS FOR THE KAISER'S COMFORT.
German papers gave extended accounts of the plans at the Great Head-quarters in the east and west of the war area for the comfort of the Kaiser. Wherever this was possible, the most luxuriously-appointed residence was set apart for the Emperor. Where no permanent building was suitable the Kaiser had his specially-designed motor-vehicle. Above is given the first photograph taken of the Emperor's kitchen, with preparations for a meal being made by members of the Imperial suite. The most elaborate precautions were taken to safeguard the food from being tampered with, the military chefs carrying on their duties under the immediate supervision of members of the Kaiser's suite.

GERMAN INFANTRY ADVANCING TO THE ATTACK—FROM A DRAWING BY A GERMAN ARTIST.

enemy, provided that this prohibition shall not be deemed to be infringed by any person who has no reasonable ground for believing that the instrument is held by or on behalf of an enemy. (5) Not to enter into any new transaction, or complete any transaction already entered into with an enemy in any stocks, shares, or other securities. (6) Not to make or enter into any new marine, life, fire, or other policy or contract of insurance with or for the benefit of an enemy; nor to accept or give effect to any insurance of, any risk arising, under any policy or contract of insurance (including re-insurance) made or entered into with or for the benefit of an enemy before the outbreak of war. (7) Not directly or indirectly **Insurance for an** to supply to or for the use or benefit **enemy's benefit** of, or obtain from, an enemy country, or an enemy, any goods, wares, or merchandise, nor directly or indirectly to supply to or for the use or benefit of, or obtain from any person any goods, wares, or merchandise, for or by way of transmission to or from an enemy country or an enemy, nor directly or indirectly to trade in or carry any goods, wares, or merchandise destined for or coming from an enemy country or an enemy. (8) Not to permit any British ship to leave for, enter, or communicate with, any port or place in an enemy country. (9) Not to enter into any commercial, financial, or other contract or obligation with or for the benefit of an enemy. (10) Not to enter into any transactions with an enemy if and when they are prohibited by an Order-in-Council made and published on the recommendation of a Secretary of State, even though they would otherwise be permitted by law or by this or any other Proclamation."

The Proclamation went on to warn all persons who, in contravention of the law therein set forth, should commit, aid, or abet, any of the aforesaid acts would be guilty of a crime, and would be liable to punishment and penalties. There was, however, a provision that where an enemy had a branch locally situated in British, allied, or neutral territory, not being neutral territory in Europe, transactions by or with such branch should not be treated as transactions by or with an enemy. There was, further, a pro-

196

REMARKABLE CAMERA PICTURE OF THE EXPLOSION OF A PROJECTILE FROM A GERMAN 12·5 IN. GUN.

vision that nothing in the Proclamation should be deemed to prohibit payments by or on account of enemies to persons resident carrying on business or being in British Dominions, if such payments arose out of transactions entered into before the outbreak of the war, or otherwise permitted. A final proviso was that nothing in the Proclamation should affect anything expressly permitted by Imperial licence or a licence granted by a Secretary of State or the Board of Trade, whether especially granted to individuals or as applying to classes of persons.

In connection with this campaign against trading with the enemy, the Commercial Intelligence Department of the Board of Trade initiated a movement for assisting British manufacturers and traders to capture trade formerly in German, Austrian, and Hungarian hands. In the first place, they formed on their premises in Whitehall a permanent exhibition of samples and goods formerly purchased from enemy sources; and in the next place, with the view of making that exhibition of the greatest value to British manufacturers and traders, the department arranged a series of " exchange meetings " between buyers desirous of obtaining such goods and British manufacturers who might already be producing or be likely to produce similar goods in this country. These meetings took place at Wakefield House, Cheapside, London, E.C., and afterwards at Basinghall Street.

Import, wholesale, and shipping houses which had formerly purchased goods from the enemy countries were asked to bring samples of these goods for inspection by manufacturers and suppliers; and the Board of Trade gave an assurance to the firms forwarding samples that every care would be taken to ensure that the ordinary channels of trade now existing as between the original manufacturers and the final consumer would not be interfered with. The seasonal demand for toys and games for the approaching Christmas made it desirable to deal with that trade first, the exports of which from Germany in 1912 amounted to two and three-quarter millions sterling. The result was that the British manufacture of such toys and games was immediately expanded or started of new by individual enterprise and by patriotic organisations.

GERMAN "KULTUR" IN EXCELSIS: ROYAL IRISH RIFLES TO THE RESCUE.

" You see some very sad sights in villages where the Germans have been," wrote a non-commissioned officer of the Royal Irish Rifles. " They plunder and destroy everything they can. Some of them are simply beasts. One night I was in charge of a scouting party of eight men. On entering a village we saw a light in one of the houses. On looking through the window we saw thirteen Germans in the room. They were all half drunk, and empty wine bottles were scattered all over the place. An officer was sitting on the mantelshelf, and in the middle of the soldiers were an old woman and two girls. We rushed into the house. Every man in the room was killed. I had the satisfaction of shooting the officer, who fell off his perch like a log. We then captured their horses, and rode them back to our own lines."

CRUISERS OF THE ROAD IN ACTION—BRITISH ARMOURED MOTOR-CARS DISLODGING GERMAN SNIPERS.
In France as well as in Belgium the armoured motor-car did valuable work against the snipers and raiders of the enemy. They were fitted with Maxims and light quick-firing guns. The quick-firers were directed against snipers lurking in villages and isolated buildings, and the Maxims scattered them when they were driven into the open.

These efforts afforded employment to scores of thousands of young people and old who, from the dislocation of business in certain trades, had been thrown out of work—with, of course, the additional effect of establishing permanently a native industry of interesting and economic importance. The same course was pursued with the German trade in earthenware, china, and enamelled hollowware, which amounted to four and a quarter millions, and cheap cutlery to the amount of one and a quarter millions. But the most satisfactory capture was that of electrical apparatus and appliances, the value of which in 1912 imported from Germany to Great Britain reached no less a sum than just over eight millions. Probably quite as much of these goods of German manufacture were imported into British Dominions, Colonies, and Possessions overseas. Although this is a slight anticipation of chronological facts, it may here be stated with satisfaction that the system devised by the Intelligence Department of the Board of Trade practically resulted in the transfer of the manufacture and distribution of all these products from German, Austrian, and Hungarian hands to home and colonial manufacturers, merchants, and agents.

Board of Trade and British industries

On September 10th the Prime Minister moved in the House of Commons a Vote providing for a further 500,000 men for the Army. In commending the Vote to the House, Mr. Asquith said that the number of recruits enlisted since the declaration of war, exclusive of those who had joined the Territorials, was 439,000 up to the evening of September 9th. The time had not come when recruiting activity should be in any way relaxed. We should want more rather than less "Let us get the men. That is the first necessity of the State. With the addition of another 500,000 men, we shall be in a position to put something like 1,200,000 men into the field. This is the provision made by the Mother Country, and is exclusive of the Territorials, the National Reserve, and the magnificent contributions promised from India and the Dominions." The Vote was instantly agreed to.

While this clear-eyed and determined policy was being thus resolutely prosecuted by the Government, with the support of the vast majority of the nation and of the Empire, a note came on this September 9th which almost seemed to indicate that there was the tiniest of a rift in the lute. Perhaps it would be more correct to say, changing the metaphor, that a small faction made an attempt to bring disharmony by the shrill piping of a falsetto whistle. This unmusical coterie secretly issued to many people a circular letter—which, however, had been composed some weeks previously—in which it was stated that : "There are very many thousands of people in the country who are profoundly dissatisfied with the general course of policy which preceded the war. They are feeling that a dividing point has come in national history, that the old traditions of secret and class diplomacy, the old control of foreign policy by a narrow clique, and the power of the armament organisations have got henceforth to be combated by a great and conscious and directed effort of the democracy. We are anxious to take measures which may focus this feeling and help to direct public policy on broad lines, which may build up on a more secure and permanent foundation the hopes which have been shattered for our generation in the last month. The objects we have in view are :

"(1) To secure real Parliamentary control over foreign policy, and to prevent it being again shaped in secret and forced upon the country as an accomplished fact.

"(2) When peace returns, to open direct and deliberate negotiations with democratic parties and influences on the Continent, so as to form an international understanding, depending on popular parties rather than on Governments.

"(3) To aim at securing such terms as this war will not, either through the humiliation of the defeated nation, or an artificial rearrangement of frontiers, merely become the starting-point for new national antagonisms and future wars."

The circular went on to say that there was an immediate need of a propaganda of the

FRENCH COLOURED TROOPS CHARGING GERMAN TRENCHES.
One of the most noteworthy phases of the Great War has been the eagerness and devotion of the coloured troops in the French Army and the Indian troops in the British Army in the fight for the freedom of Europe from the domination of the "mailed fist" of Germany. This illustration has a particular interest, having been drawn by one of the best-known German war artists at the front.

A French " 75 " which had taken up a position in a beet-field in an attack
on the German lines in Northern France.

Another view of one of the wonderful " 75's " (3 in. quick-firers) of the
French artillery in action.

THE FRENCH " 75 " AND ITS INVENTOR—COLONEL DUPONT.

At the outset of the Great War the preponderance of the German gun-power gave the enemy a great advantage in attacking fortified positions, particularly at Liège and Namur. But it was not long before the balance was equalised by both British and French. Particularly was the early French discrepancy in artillery made up by the wonderful " 75's " of the French. Inset: Portrait of Colonel Dupont, inventor of this gun.

above opinions by the issue of books, pamphlets, leaflets, which could be scattered broadcast, and asked for subscriptions towards the cost thereof. This precious document was signed by J. Ramsay Macdonald, formerly chairman of the Labour Party in the House of Commons, Charles Trevelyan, who had resigned an under-secretaryship in the Government on the declaration of war, Norman Angell, and E. D. Morel. The circular fell as flat as a sodden damper, which effect-ually silenced its own authors.

London a cosmo-politan hostel

When the eyes of our people were not cast oversea to the theatre of war, in which our own soldiers were creating a new renown for British arms, worthily supported by the heroic efforts and sacrifices of our Belgian, French, and Russian allies, their hearts were stirred with compassion for the woes and the sufferings of the victims of German barbarism in Northern France, Flanders, and Brabant. For six weeks after the outbreak of the war citizens of other nations poured into England, till London became a vast cosmopolitan hostel. Belgians whose homes had become smoking ruins; Frenchmen on whose lands and fruitful vineyards the soldiers of three nations were fighting; Russians whom the outbreak of hostilities surprised in some alien country—all sought these shores. Here, too, were many of our enemy subjects—Germans and Austrians who were in England when the war broke out, and chose to prolong their sojourn. These were added to by Teutons for whom the attractions of war had no delight, and who rushed hither from Paris and elsewhere. This invasion turned London into a city where foreign tongues were heard on every hand. In fact, in some quarters it was hard to find good, honest English speech.

It is a characteristic of the British nature in times of distress that a Divine compassion falls towards the afflicted multitude, from West End to East End, like the gentle rain from Heaven. In the presence of all-too-apparent misery and helplessness among the scores of thousands of refugees, charitable organisations sprang up as mushrooms in the night for their relief and comfort. In every quarter, too, a generous hospitality was privately offered to family parties of refugees from one up to six persons, according to the accommodation, in the homes of thousands of well-to-do citizens. But this was felt to be not enough, and on September 9th Mr. Herbert Samuel announced in the House of Commons that the British Government had offered the hospitality of the British nation to Belgian victims of the war. A committee, of which Lord Gladstone was chairman, opened a central office in Aldwych, with a large reception-hall attached, and there provision was made for the immediate transfer of the homeless wanderers, not otherwise accommodated, to homes—not only in London, but in towns and villages all over Great Britain

and Ireland. Of course, not all the refugees were without means. Some were well provided with money, others had British investments, and many of these settled in central boarding-houses, or in attractive London suburbs.

Nor was our practical sympathy confined to those who had reached our shores. In response to an appeal by the Belgian Minister in London for the relief of distress among those who either could not leave their native land, or who clung to their devastated hearths, an immediate response was given, and immense quantities of foodstuffs were despatched to Belgium for distribution.

The September Navy List included, in addition to the names of over a hundred trawlers, the following merchant vessels commissioned as H.M.'s ships—in other words, as auxiliary cruisers: Alsatian, Anglia, Aquitania, Armadale Castle, Cambria, Carmania, Caronia, Empress of Asia, Empress of Britain, Empress of Japan, Empress of Russia, Engadine, Himalaya, Kinfauns Castle, Macedonia, Maori, Mantua, Marmora, Oceanic, Osiris, Otranto, Riviera, Scotia, Tara, Venetia, and Victorian. From the above list had later to be deducted the White Star twin - screw Oceanic, of 17,274 tons, 28,000 horse-power engines, with a speed of 20 knots. Her captain was William F. Slayter, the commander, H. Smith (R.N.R.), and the crew numbered 400. During a cruise off the North of Scotland on September 8th she became enveloped in a fog and ran on the rocks. The Aberdeen steam-trawler Glenogil observed the accident, and made several efforts, with other trawlers which came to the rescue, to drag the Oceanic off the rocks, but without avail, and the big cruiser became a total wreck. The officers and crew were rescued, and afterwards taken to Aberdeen.

It may be well here to recount various incidents of sea warfare or adventure in the second week of September. On arrival at his base port the master of the Grimsby steam-trawler Agatha reported a diabolic German ruse for sinking trawlers and neutral ships of commerce. While fishing in the North Sea on September 9th he sighted a ship's boat afloat, and, concluding that some disaster had occurred, steered towards it. A boat was put out, and the derelict was found to be a ship's lifeboat equipped with sails, masts, and oars. A line was secured to it and passed to the trawler, which intended to tow the prize home. As soon as the towing began an explosion occurred, luckily too far distant from the trawler to do damage. A careful examination was then made, and it was found that a mine had been attached to the lifeboat by ropes and wires in such a manner as to explode and blow up any ship which steamed alongside the lifeboat to pick it up. On the same day the master of the Grimsby trawler Howe reported that he had seen a steamship strike a mine in the North Sea and founder. Though he made all speed to the scene, nothing to identify the vessel could be found.

"FOR WOMEN MUST WEEP."

Scene near the village of Barcy, after the fighting along the Marne. Two French women were seen laying a tribute of flowers on the graves of some of the men who had fallen from the ranks of the army of civilisation.

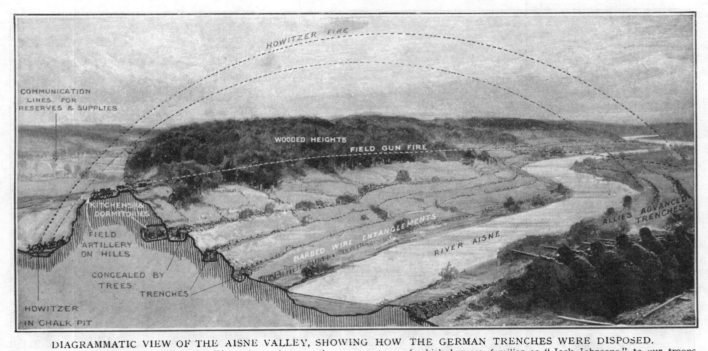

DIAGRAMMATIC VIEW OF THE AISNE VALLEY, SHOWING HOW THE GERMAN TRENCHES WERE DISPOSED.

The above sectional view cuts across the River Aisne from north to south. On the north bank were the trenches and covered ways of the Germans, with their heavy artillery in the rear disposed in quarries. The field artillery threw shells with a flat trajectory, while their howitzer shells, one type of which became familiar as "Jack Johnsons" to our troops, sailed in great semicircular sweeps over the river. In the foreground may be seen the French troops in an advanced trench. The German stand, between Noyon and Berry-au-Bac, had railways parallel to and behind it.

The master of the Howe also reported that previous to this his trawl-net had picked up a mine, which however did not explode. The same day another trawler brought to Grimsby wreckage comprising the wheelhouse, part of the deck casing, and the ship's bell of the steam-trawler Nelson, of Grimsby, which it was therefore feared had been mined. A German cruiser also on the 9th captured the trawler Capricornus, sank it, and took the crew to Wilhelmshaven as prisoners. The Leith trawler Pollux was overhauled by a German cruiser about the same date and sunk, her crew being also taken as prisoners to Wilhelmshaven.

The Holland-Amerika steamer Noordan, bound from New York to Rotterdam with one hundred and sixty German reservists on board, was brought into Queenstown by a British cruiser as prize on September 9th. The German reservists were interned in Ireland. A German collier with 5,000 tons of Welsh coal on board was captured by H.M.S. Vindictive in the Atlantic on September 10th, and on the same day two large German ships—the Orlanda, with a cargo of nitrate valued at £40,000, and the Gold-beck with a cargo of timber—were captured and brought into Falmouth. The German four-masted barque Urania, with a cargo of nitrate for Hamburg worth £35,000, was captured in the Channel by a British warship and brought to Plymouth. The French auxiliary cruiser La Savoie captured in the Channel the Holland-Amerika liner Nieuw Amsterdam, with four hundred German and two hundred and fifty Austrian subjects on their way to join the colours in their respective countries. These were interned in France and the ship made a prize. The Dutch steamers Fortuna and Atlas were likewise on the same day captured with contraband of war on board by

VANDALISM AT SOISSONS.

The abbey of St. Jean des Vignes, at Soissons, with one of its beautiful spires shattered by German shell fire.

the French cruisers Friant and Lavoisier, and taken as prizes to Brest. During the same period British and French torpedo-boats in the Adriatic discovered and exploded lines of mines which the Austrians had laid at Antivari and Dulcigno, and also near Cape Volovitza.

Further afield it became known at the beginning of September that the German China Squadron had, on the declaration of war against Germany by Japan, as the Treaty associate of Great Britain, left the Far Eastern seas and scattered—the Emden (to become famous in the Indian Ocean) and the Scharnhorst, Gneisenau, Nürnberg, and Stettin in the Pacific. On the 7th a four-funnelled cruiser displaying the French flag appeared off Fanning Island, a coral atoll in the Pacific, and first landing-place of the All-British cable which runs from Bamfield, British Columbia, to Southport, Moreton Bay, Queensland, Eastern Australia, touching, after leaving Fanning Island, Fiji, and Norfolk Island. Shortly after it was discovered that the cable had been cut, and later the deed was traced to the Nürnberg, which in addition to flying false colours had rigged an additional false funnel, and so disguised had eluded two Australian gunboats waiting for her outside Honolulu on September 1st.

About the same date the Gulf liner Messina, on a round voyage of the Polynesian Islands from and to Sydney, New South Wales, put in at Nauru, one of the Gilbert Islands, included in the German Western Pacific Colonies. The German resident magistrate and party came off in a boat, hailed the Messina, and demanded to be taken on board. "By whose orders?" shrewdly asked the mate. "By orders of his Majesty the German Emperor," replied the magistrate. The mate laughed, ordered full steam ahead, and the Messina, of which the wily Teuton had hoped to make an easy

HUMAN MOLES IN THE AISNE BATTLEFIELD.
One of the British trenches in the hard-fought Battle of the Aisne. In the foreground is shown a heap of accoutrements of soldiers who were asleep in the straw at the bottom. Inset: A view within a British trench in a wooded part of the country.

prey, gained the open sea and safely arrived at Sydney. The Secretary to the Admiralty made it known through the Press Bureau that on September 9th and 10th strong and numerous squadrons and flotillas had made a complete sweep of the North Sea up and into the Heligoland Bight. The German Fleet, however, made no attempt to interfere with these movements, and no German ships of any kind were seen at sea. The naval correspondent of the "Times," writing on this, made a comment worth reproduction here. "Every now and again during the previous month," said he, "an operation of this description approached in its swoop the enemy's coasts, and offered an opportunity to his fleet to accept the challenge if he thought fit to give battle. This aspect, however, was merely of secondary importance to the fact that the British Fleet's patrol was well maintained, that their means of getting intelligence were entirely satisfactory, and that while the Germans by their mining operations had interfered more or less with their own free movements, they had not in the slightest degree affected ours."

The independent observation may here be made that Admiral Jellicoe's Fleet, intact and unseen, was at the period under review not only assisting our gallant troops in France and helping our Allies in both the land theatres of war, but without its continued existence all our efforts to augment and increase the forces of the Empire at the

actual seat of war would have been hampered if not brought to naught.

The efficient methods involving unceasing vigilance, mostly under cover of darkness, by which the policing of the North Sea is effected was described naively by two trawler skippers to a newspaper correspondent. The first said he had just come from Iceland, and between that island and the Faroes, and the sentinel Shetlands and Orkneys, he encountered a solid wall of warships, which made it impossible for any craft to break through undetected. Of course, his trawler was subjected to the utmost scrutiny by the officers of a cruiser; but after being released, he was followed by two torpedo-boat destroyers until he reached his home port, so as to ensure that he was really, as he had declared, a British trawler. The other skipper who was interviewed was in charge of a North Sea boat which, after fishing, came under the lee of the land each night and anchored. "On one occasion at two o'clock in the morning a cruiser suddenly appeared alongside us," exclaimed he. "All his lights were extinguished, and the quiet way in which that big cruiser came up and the clever tactics the commander showed in getting alongside us without doing any damage was astonishing. Talk about cats seeing in the dark, these naval officers are wonderful. When the cruiser reached us, all we could see was a huge black object hemming us in. A voice shouted out : 'Who are you?' I replied, 'The——.' 'When did you leave?' 'On——,' I answered. 'What were your orders when you left?' I told him, and in a flash the commander of the cruiser shouted back 'All right.' Directly the commander had finished talking to me, another voice from the stern of our vessel sung out : 'The name is quite correct, sir.' A submarine had crept up behind to verify our name and number, and although all the crew had come on deck to see what was happening, not one of the men aft had caught sight of the submarine. I have seen the British Navy in times of peace, but to see it in war-time makes you feel proud of it. No swank; simply good old Nelson's motto all the time."

Mention was made in Chapter XXXIII. of the decree of the Admiralty, made with the sanction of the King, for the creation of special Naval and Marine brigades for employment either on sea or land. Lord Fisher, in the stirring address to the men of the First Naval Brigade, of

Our sentinel warships in the North Sea

SHELTERS FROM THE WEATHER MADE BY OUR MEN IN THE INTERVALS OF FIGHTING IN THE TRENCHES DURING THE BATTLE OF THE AISNE.

AN OFFICER'S SHELTER ON THE AISNE.

ANOTHER "SNUGGERY" BEHIND THE FIRING-LINE.

HOLE MADE BY THE BURSTING OF A "BLACK MARIA."

SIDELIGHTS ON THE LIFE OF OUR MEN DURING THE FIGHTING ON THE AISNE.

Cavalry as well as infantry took part in the work in the trenches on the Aisne. A system of regular reliefs was organised, and the men relieved constructed shelters where they could rest and recuperate in comparative safety from the shells of the enemy and the inclemency of the weather. Some of the shelters were beautifully made. The two lower photographs are of the trenches themselves.

IN THE FIRE ZONE OF THE BIG GERMAN GUNS.
View of the village of Augy. The German position was on the hills in the distance, on which their big guns were placed. Our troops had to pass over the country here seen under deadly shell fire. The road was only partially safe by night. Inset: Farmhouse destroyed by German guns during the fighting on the Aisne.

which he was appointed commander, emphasised the fact that even where the Fleet did not lend a hand visibly, operations on shore could only be carried on under its protecting arms. The brilliant naval correspondent of the "Times" pointed out that, as a matter of history, in all our wars for many centuries past the Navy directly and materially helped the Army. "Seamen and Marines," he said, "have acted side by side with their soldier comrades, and in many instances miles and miles inland, and far from their natural element. Men who joined to fight by sea, whose instincts were permeated by salt water, who had been carefully trained to handle and work the ship's guns, threw everything nautical aside except their experience and discipline, and landed to act as artillery and infantry.

"In any consideration of the use to be made of naval brigades on shore it is essential to remember that the ships of the Fleet must never be so weakened by withdrawals from their crews as to leave them unable to fight at sea. The needs of the Fleet must be the first consideration. There have been **Conditions of naval** occasions, both in our own history and **co-operation on land** that of other nations, when this vital principle has been forgotten. On this occasion, however, no such mistake will be made. We have it in Mr. Churchill's words that only 'If at any time the naval situation becomes sufficiently favourable to enable this force to be definitely released by the Admiralty for military duty, it will be handed over to the Army.'

"There is ample precedent for the movement which is now going forward so well. As early as Elizabethan times sailors were frequently employed on shore to assist the soldiers in attacks upon fortified towns, and it is related

BRITISH BATTERY IN ACTION AGAINST THE GERMANS ON THE AISNE.
The British guns were placed against a background of trees, and so were partially screened from the enemy's fire, and also from observation by German aircraft.

VIEW OF THE BATTLE AREA NEAR BRAISNE.

The outskirts of Braisne are to be seen on the right. In the distance is the village of Chassemy, over which the enemy's high-explosive shells were bursting. Over the road shown in the picture and through Chassemy British supply columns passed nightly to the foot of the distant hills. Inset : French dragoons and British infantry moving forward to attack the German right flank on the Aisne.

how on more than one occasion the experienced and careful sea commanders divided their men into companies and drilled them in land formations before using them for this purpose. Although the joint expedition sent to the West Indies by Oliver Cromwell was not a success, the sailors from Admiral Goodson's fleet proved themselves, as seamen have frequently since, the handy men who could be relied on to be handy, not only in a battle, but in those other qualities required when a proper corps of sappers or the regular commissariat and transport arrangements of an army were wanting. It will be remembered that Collingwood, when employed with a naval brigade in America, described his work as 'supplying the Army with what was necessary for them.'

Past services of marines on land

"In Stuart times the Marines were established, and there can be no question that they were designed, at least in part, to provide small-arm men which could be landed in case of necessity, and would have some knowledge of warfare on shore. In later times the Marines have over and over again been called upon to assist their comrades of the land service. A naval brigade of which Marines formed a large proportion was mainly instrumental in taking Gibraltar, although the seamen also played a part in this affair. Our Indian Empire, moreover, is the gift of sea-power, not only because if we had been beaten at sea the victories on shore would have been useless, but because associated with the soldiers there were naval brigades. Often during the varying fortunes of our arms

GUNS OF A HOWITZER BATTERY OF THE R.F.A. IN ACTION DURING THE BATTLE OF THE AISNE.

To counteract the effects of the heavy guns brought down to the Aisne from Maubeuge by the Germans, the British artillery was reinforced by four 6-inch howitzer batteries, specially sent out for the purpose at the request of Sir John French.

FRENCH DEFEAT THE GERMAN IMPERIAL GUARD IN A VILLAGE WHICH CHANGED HANDS FOUR TIMES.

The village of Sommesous, shown in Mr. Sydney Adamson's spirited drawing, is on the railway between Troyes and Chalons, about eighteen miles south of the latter town, and about ten miles east of Fère Champenoise. In the fighting between the German Imperial Guard, under the Crown Prince, and the 36th and 236th Regiments of French infantry, the village changed hands four times. The church and the adjacent houses were reduced to ruins before the place was finally taken by the French. The above drawing was examined by a French general and a number of Staff officers, and received the official approval of the French État-Major. Some of the German soldiers seen on the left of the picture are without the cloth coverings to their helmets, having lost them during the fighting.

in the East, the Army was supplied with its artillery and siege-guns from the ships. When the Navy placed guns of position at the Army's disposal for use before Ladysmith it was by no means a novelty in our sea annals.

"Everyone will remember in this connection Nelson's assistance to the land forces at the sieges of Bastia and Calvi. There, as elsewhere, the seamen showed themselves capable of doing the work required of them with whatever was handy. Their sea training enabled them to make shift when the requisite means were unavailable. Of course, behind the capabilities and adaptability of the seamen were the energy and determination of the commander. And all this work went forward under the sure shield of Hood's fleet. In later times, Captain Peel's men in the Mutiny, Rawson's Benin Expedition, Seymour's dash for Peking, and many other occasions when our sailors have formed naval brigades, and have performed duties on land with credit to themselves and country, will occur to everyone. Nor should it be forgotten that in the war of 1870 it was the French sailors who manned the guns of Paris, and that Admiral Jaureguiberry formed a brigade of seamen which did excellent service in the Army of the Loire.

"As we have looked to naval brigades in past times, so we must again avail ourselves of their assistance in our hour of stress."

At the conclusion of the operations on the Marne, M. Millerand, the French Minister for War, sent from Bordeaux the following cordial message to Lord Kitchener:

"I have much pleasure in sending you, by the desire of General Joffre, the following telegram:

"'The Commander-in-Chief of the French Armies expresses to Lord Kitchener his warm thanks for the constant support given by the British force to our Army throughout the whole of the operations.

"'At the present moment this support is particularly valuable, and it is being manifested in a most energetic manner in the battle actually in progress against the German right wing.

General Joffre's thanks to Lord Kitchener

"'I express my deep gratitude to Field-Marshal French, who has constantly given to our armies the most effective co-operation.'

"Allow me, in the name of my Government, to add to General Joffre's thanks the expression of my gratitude."

Lord Kitchener replied as follows:

"Kindly accept and transmit to General Joffre my warmest thanks for the telegram which you have been so kind as to forward to me.

"I wish to assure you and, through you, General Joffre, with what satisfaction the British Army finds itself

A GERMAN BATTERY TRYING TO ESCAPE THE SEARCHLIGHT.
In the Aisne district the country is devoid of hedges, and is intersected by roads that dip into hollows here and there, and then run across open, exposed tracts of land. The German battery in our picture was endeavouring to move under cover of the darkness when it was detected by searchlight of the Allies, and made the most frantic efforts to escape from the ghostly beam.

co-operating with the French Army, and how proud we are of being able to render that assistance of which you speak in such generous terms, and upon which you can always rely with full confidence."

The French Legislature did not prolong its session after the transfer of the Government from Paris to Bordeaux. But parliamentarians refused to disband, and Bordeaux came to be known as Paris by the Sea. In Paris itself there was on September 10th a great patriotic demonstration, when the flag of the 94th German Infantry, captured two days before near Senlis by Captain de Sannois, of the hussars, was carried in procession to and deposited in the Hôtel des Invalides.

The Paris "Temps" on September 9th printed an account of an interview given to a French journalist by Cardinal Mercier, Archbishop of Malines, in which his Eminence presented a terrible picture of the misery suffered by his unhappy country as the result of the German invasion. "As I travelled through Belgium," said the Cardinal, "the spectacle of its unhappiness seemed to tear me back to my devastated Malines, to the side of my King, and of my Suffragan of Liège—to-day hostage, to-morrow perhaps martyr. All along the roads I could see unburied bodies mingled with the carcases of horses. I could recognise some of the faces; here lay one of my fellow-students, and there was a fine young fellow whom I had confirmed. What has taken place in Belgium is not war, but the outcome of hate; the Germans are taking their revenge for the stigma that has been attached to them as violaters of neutral territory. Terrified by their orgy of blood, they imagine that History will forget their shameless infraction of a treaty. These savages, who dare at every step to invoke the name of God, not only attack harmless creatures made in the image of the Deity, but wage war even against the Divinity. In undefended towns, after having bombarded houses, they have given churches to the flames, and they have used the wooden statues on the altars as torches to light them to their deeds of blood. In Malines, a peaceable, undefended town, they made a target of the Church of St. Rombolt; and Louvain, the university town, pride of the Netherlands—the town where, as student and then professor, I knew so many young Italians—Louvain has been burned by the Germans, under the pretext that the inhabitants had fired on the soldiers!

"These bomb-carrying Germans wanted to strike at the head of Belgium. They wished to raze to the ground Belgium's intellectual capital, throwing into the flames alike the contents of the laboratories and libraries

IN A GERMAN TRENCH ON THE AISNE.
Many of the German trenches on the Aisne were most elaborately constructed, especially with a view to enabling some of the occupants to rest and smoke while their comrades kept watch and ward.

helpless women and children. When the lake of blood left by the Germans in Belgium has dried up, it will be necessary to look for a slab of stone large enough to be a record of these crimes against the rights alike of Heaven and of humanity. But I will not lose hope. Belgium is brave, and she will rise from her bed of ashes. I shall see that resurrection from the tomb where I shall soon be laid."

Was it any wonder that, after such an impassioned outbreak, Hélène Vacaresco, the great Rumanian poetess, should have sent the following sympathetic address to France:

"My thoughts are with you, nameless and distant craftsmen, whose fine churches in France have been destroyed by nameless hordes.

"Nameless, say I! Nay, for they are known as Havoc, Blind Brutality, and Fury; and we picture their devastating numbers as the maddened goddess of Envy, holding a sword in one hand and a lighted torch in the other. She sweeps through the land, and leaves nought but ruin in her wake: even the noblest buildings crumble before her.

"Dear far-off workers of stone and gold whose souls seem mingled in the walls of the cathedrals, you breathe on us as we pass down the naves, and we are filled with peace and holiness. **Rumanian sympathy** What must you think of that dis- **with France** hevelled figure and her furies?

"You bequeathed to the world immortal splendours, and had no wish for glory for yourselves. Your work was for God alone; that through it the peoples of the ages to come might see Him as they did, and feel Him in their souls as you felt those brilliant colours of the rainbow, clouds, and sea so well depicted in your stained-glass windows.

"You were quite certain that once that miracle, which needed all your powers and strength, was accomplished, no one on earth could possibly disturb the harmonies of your exalted dreams.

GERMAN OFFICERS' HUT IN THE AISNE REGION.
The structure looks rather more picturesque than comfortable. It was adorned with a horse-shoe; but if this was meant to bring the occupants good luck, they forgot how it should have been placed, and put it the wrong way up. Inset: A German trench captured after a stiff fight at Villers-Cotterets, showing mangel-wurzel left behind. There was no trace of any other foodstuff.

Ought not the word 'Droit'—standing out in letters of gold on the old buildings—to have made them shudder? German deeds in Belgium have nothing to do with war either of the old days of chivalry or the modern and scientific form. It is an eruption of barbarians into a prosperous, honest, and industrious country. It is a blind ebullition of rage against God, against His temples, against art, sacred or secular and still more against God in the massacre of

HEADQUARTERS AT BRAISNE OF THE G.O.C. 3rd DIVISION, SECOND CORPS.

On the right is a view of Braisne, where heavy fighting took place between the British and the Germans who had taken shelter in the houses and fired through the shuttered windows. Bertram Stewart, the Scottish Yeomanry officer, who was imprisoned in Germany in 1910 on an espionage charge, was killed in Braisne.

"Till the end of the world the beauties of your marble flowers would be unshaken. The dust of kings would crumble at their feet. Rumours of victories and defeats would hover round them like the murmuring of bees; and still your glorious and Divine work would remain for ever ascending to the heavens with your immortal ideals.

"There are many places now where your souls return from the heavens, where their love has bound them; and I hear them weeping piteously for the glories and the grace that are no more. At Louvain, at Rheims, at Senlis, and even at Arras your indignant souls float over sad and woeful ruins.

"It seems as if civilisation has been destroyed, for amidst the devastated remains loud rise the lamentations of those who even yesterday were numbered amongst the blessed and the happy. But their sanctuaries have been violated and destroyed, they lift up their hands to God and cry their sorrow at His feet; and on all sides appear those who will avenge them."

Another distinguished poet—Belgium's own—Emil Verhaeren, contributed a striking article on the courage and ideals of his fellow-countrymen to "Les Annales" from which may be quoted the following paragraphs:

"However unhappy their fate, the Belgians do not possess the right to lower themselves to **Emil Verhaeren on** complain, nor to dwell on their wretched-**Belgian ideals** ness. They owe it to themselves to be worthy of their soldiers, who all of them were heroes.

"That women hunted from their villages, with a troop of children hanging to their skirts, should go lamenting along the high road of hunger, flight, and exile, is a thing one can understand. But men, above all those who think and are capable of will and action, must not echo those cries of pain which have already been heard all too long.

"Formerly, those who in our country dreamt of a

greater Belgium did not think of an increase of territory in Europe, nor of the development of an Empire in Africa. They had in view only a Belgian renaissance, which should be both economic and intellectual. They wanted a more and more perfect and active industry, they wanted more and more modern and living thought. They sought for influence, and not for conquest.

"And never since Belgium has existed has this influence been higher. True it is that for the moment our factories are silent, and appear no more to have their panting respiration or flaming breath. Yet no one believes them dead. As soon as the war is ended they will come to life again, like wondrous monsters. Whatever the weight of ash covering them it will seem light to their thousand tentacles, all of which will spread out and find points of support in the restored light.

"We shall be young and ready as we never have been. Up to now danger had not visited our nation. We were too sure of the morrow. We lived like rich people who know not what distress means. War, to our eyes, was an affair for others.

"It has come to us, formidable and ferocious, at a moment when we had no thought of it. Like a mountain, the sides of which fall away to crush us, the compact Empire of William descended upon us. We were alone, few in number. We were attacked treacherously and unfairly. We massed hastily at Liège in old forts. We were compelled to improvise our courage, to invent our

TYPICAL SHELTER IN A VILLAGE NEAR THE AISNE.
The inhabitants of the Aisne villages sought refuge in their cellars from shell fire during the fighting on the Aisne.

resistance, to awaken a new soul in ourselves. All this was done in one day, in one hour, in one instant, and we were the astonishment of the world.

"Oh, those never-to-be-forgotten improvisations of valour and glory! Some among us, on seeing our little troopers starting out for the frontier, could not refrain from prophecy.

"They will only be food for cannon. Our Army does not exist, nor our fortresses.

"Four days later, a name unknown the evening before,

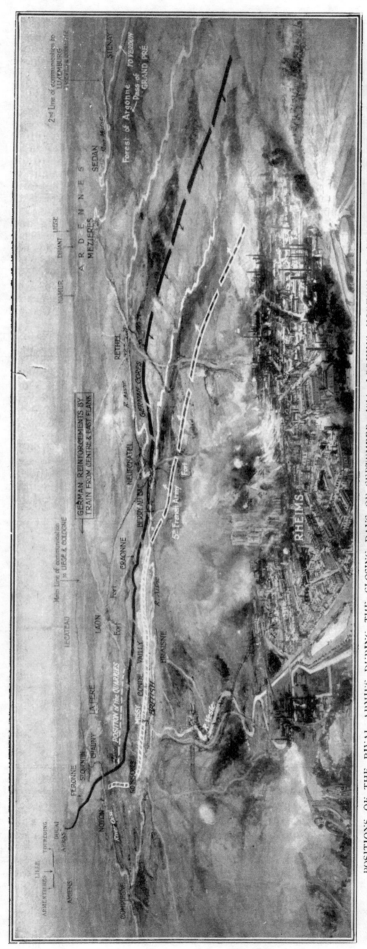

POSITIONS OF THE RIVAL ARMIES DURING THE CLOSING DAYS OF SEPTEMBER, 1914, LOOKING NORTHWARD FROM THE CITY OF RHEIMS.
Rheims was a city of Gothic towers and modern factory shafts. The cathedral was remorselessly shelled, and the houses all round it were burnt out, but at this time other portions of the city do not appear to have suffered so severely. The River Vesle is seen flowing from the city on the left towards Condé, Missy, and Soissons. Beyond are the heights above the Aisne, averaging some four hundred feet. The British were fighting on the north bank of the Aisne.

was in everybody's mouth. Little boys disguised themselves as General Leman, girls sold his photograph in the streets—a remarkable tactician had compelled the respect of all. Nay, more. Those little troopers were both timid and happy. They doubted still the admirable part they had played ; women kissed them, and we carried them in triumph.

"If we have by our obstinate and manifold resistance enabled France and Great Britain to arm themselves, to organise and save themselves, it is not for us to say it too loudly. But in doing this we have done a still more important thing.

"Our little Belgian soldiers at Liège and Haelen represented an entire past of culture and civilisation. If France incarnates both Greece and Rome, we can affirm that they defended and maintained them at the point where their existence was most threatened. It is owing to this that their act, so simple, suddenly became so great. We need not fear to evoke in comparison with them the memory of Thermopylæ. The fate of the Spartans was similar to that of the people of Liège. A handful of men, just as in olden times, saved the world.

"If we only consider this immense and supreme service rendered to the West, nothing but pride should remain in our hearts. Tears would dishonour us. Let us say to ourselves that Belgium, among all peoples, was chosen in order that one of the highest of human prodigies should be accomplished by her, that she should have the honour of being the first and the most necessary of the ramparts which modern civilisation erected against the **A superb minute beneath the lightning** ferocity and savagery of a thousand years, and that its history will join that of the rare little nations who will be immortal. Let us say to ourselves again that during these tragic hours we have lived with such intensity that all our past national existence is not worth this sudden and superb minute beneath the lightning stroke. It seems to me as though, before it, we were not even a people. We wore ourselves out in petty quarrels, we disputed about words and not realities, we delighted in schism, we reproached ourselves with our origin, either Flemish or Walloon. We tried to be advocates, merchants, civil servants, without troubling ourselves to be proud and free citizens. The danger has been more wholesome to us than safety. We have discovered ourselves. We have closed up our ranks in such unity of force and courage, we have formed such a square of resistance and tenacity that, in the eyes of some, Belgium dates only from yesterday, and never has she felt herself more rich than at the moment when, deprived of territory, she has nothing but her King by which to know herself and to which to rally."

By way of confounding contrast may be placed the monstrous views which the Kaiser and his Chancellor attempted vainly to impose on the American people as the truth. Dr. von Bethmann-Hollweg on September 9th addressed a long disquisition to the United States Press against British policy, in which he sought to justify Germany's attitude. He declared that "Great Britain, jealous of Germany's development, and desirous of crushing the Germans by force, would have to accept responsibility for the present war. Britain began an unscrupulous war against Germany, and opened a campaign of lies and calumny. If the German troops had set fire to Belgian villages it was because Belgian women and girls had put

DELIBERATE BOMBARDMENT OF RHEIMS CATHEDRAL BY THE GERMANS.

Rheims Cathedral, over which the Red Cross was flying, was repeatedly shelled by the German gunners in September, 1914. The roof was fired, as was the scaffolding round the north tower. The stone sculptures decorating the interior of the western wall were irretrievably damaged, while the greater part of the facade, the north tower, and the clerestory were calcinated beyond repair. Half the stalls were destroyed. All the wonderful glass in one nave is no more, and that of the apse was greatly damaged. Our photograph was taken during the fire.

out the eyes and cut the throats of German troops billeted on them." In conclusion, the Chancellor said that " the German Emperor had authorised him to make this statement, and to declare that he had full confidence in the American sense of justice."

This tirade was followed up by a telegram sent by the Kaiser to President Wilson of the United States, in which he protested against the alleged employment of dum-dum bullets by the British and French troops. His Majesty, justifying the burning of Louvain, said : " My heart bleeds that such measures should have been unavoidable, and at the thought of the innumerable innocent persons who had lost their homes and their property as the result of the criminal and barbarous actions of the Belgians."

Correspondents of newspapers published in neutral States were invited to attend at the Foreign Office in Berlin on September 8th, and a general there gave an exhibition of dum-dum bullets alleged to have been found on the battlefields where the British and French met the Germans. He intimated that this violation of the Geneva Convention would, in the end, compel Germany to answer the barbarous methods of warfare adopted by her enemies by herself adopting similar measures !

These statements were sent by wireless telegram to Copenhagen and issued there, upon which the British and French Ministers in the Danish capital protested in the strongest language against the German accusation. They declared that dum-dum bullets had no existence so far as the French and British armies were concerned.

A special session of the Parliament of the Union of South Africa was opened on September 9th by Viscount Buxton, the new Governor-General, who had happily arrived the day before at Cape Town. Lord Buxton's first act was to read a personal message from King George acknowledging the many proofs of loyalty displayed by South Africa in common with the rest of the Empire, and of its determination to play a part in the great conflict forced upon Great Britain. The message further stated that his Majesty relied with confidence upon the people of South Africa to maintain and to add fresh lustre to the splendid traditions of courage, determination, and endurance which they had inherited.

General Botha, at the evening session, moved the following resolution : " That this House, fully recognising the obligations of the Union as a portion of the British Empire, respectfully requests the Governor-General to convey a humble address to his Majesty, assuring him of its loyal support in bringing to a successful issue the momentous conflict which has been forced upon him in defence of the principles of liberty and international honour, and of its whole-hearted determination to take all measures necessary for defending the interests **South Africa's part in the Great War** of the Union, and co-operating with his Majesty's Imperial Government to maintain the security and integrity of the Empire, and further humbly requesting his Majesty to convey to his Majesty the King of the Belgians its admiration for and its sincere sympathy with the Belgian people in their heroic stand for the protection of their country against the unprincipled invasion of their rights."

The General spoke with the deepest feeling, which commanded the earnest attention of a thronged House. The Imperial Government had, he said, at this most critical time, informed the Union Government that certain war operations in German South-West Africa were considered to be of strategic importance ; and that if the Union Government could undertake these operations they would be regarded as of great service to the Empire to which South Africa belonged, and was now involved in one of the greatest and cruellest wars which had ever befallen humanity. To forget, said General Botha, their loyalty to the Empire in this hour of trial would be scandalous and shameful, and would blacken South Africa in the eyes of the whole world. Of this South Africans were incapable. They had endured some of the greatest sacrifices that could be demanded of a people, but they had always kept before them ideals founded on Christianity, and never, in their darkest days, had **General Botha and** they sought to gain their ends by **the path of treason** treasonable means. The path of treason was an unknown path to Dutch and British alike. In conclusion, the General said he felt it was the duty of South Africa to assist in relieving the sufferings and privations inflicted by the war, and the Government therefore proposed to offer South African products—as mealies, and tobacco for the soldiers, and brandy for medical purposes.

Sir Thomas Smartt, Leader of the Opposition, in an impassioned speech seconded the resolution, stating that, in every sense, in the interests not only of the Empire at large, but of South Africa especially, the war should be

BRITISH ARTILLERY IN THE AISNE DISTRICT—WAITING TO GO INTO ACTION.
" On former occasions," wrote Sir John French, in his despatch to the Secretary of State for War on October 8th, 1914, " I have brought to your lordship's notice the valuable services performed during this campaign by the Royal Artillery. Throughout the Battle of the Aisne they have displayed the same skill, endurance, and tenacity, and I deeply appreciate the work they have done."

brought to a successful issue. He was sure that the Prime Minister's speech would send a thrill of pride through the home countries and the whole Empire, at knowing that in the day of danger South Africa had been true to her trust, and had remembered her obligations as well as her privileges of free citizenship.

When the House resumed the following day General Smuts delivered an address in Dutch, which was repeatedly punctuated with cheers, in support of the loyal address to the King, and the resolution which had been proposed by the Premier. He reminded the House, in thrilling phrase, that the sufferers from German brutality and ruthlessness were their own kinsmen, the offspring of their common ancestry in Belgium, which was being laid waste, and in France. The people of Belgium and France, with Great Britain, were engaged in a gigantic struggle for the freedom which was so dear to South Africans, and which South Africans had secured through blood and tears. With forceful eloquence General Smuts recalled the Peace of Vereeniging, by which South Africans had secured the fullest liberty, which, thanks to Great Britain,

they to-day enjoyed. The Government had ample information in its possession, which for obvious reasons could not be published, that the German Government for years past had had designs on British South Africa, and had contemplated its acquisition. It was against that Government and the German military caste, not against the German people, that South Africa in common with the rest of the Empire was at war.

General Smuts afterwards introduced measures for an additional Loan Appropriation Bill of two millions ; for guaranteeing war risks on the importation of food-stuffs ; the control of the exportation of foodstuffs ; the institution of an advisory banking committee, and the disposal of the output of the gold mines. He added that the Government intended to re-establish the Mint, which would issue gold coins for purely local circulation, while the Currency Bill empowered an increase in the issue of bank-notes. The General, concluding his review of the shrinkage of revenue on account of the war, said that the country would require £7,000,000 for the year 1913-14 on capital account. The Imperial Government had agreed to advance this amount, and the thanks of the country were due to the British Treasury for the way in which they had come to the assistance of South Africa, without which the position would have been serious.

The debate on the Royal address and on the measures introduced by the Government was continued on September 11th, and then both address and the Bills mentioned were passed

The nine Labour strike leaders who had been deported some months previously were by decision of the Government allowed to return to South Africa ; and an amnesty was granted to the men in prison for offences committed during the railway strike in January, 1914

At Johannesburg on September 10th a number of sticks of gelignite were found on the tracks of different levels of the Luipaardsvlei gold mine, and all German and Austrian miners employed on the property were discharged. A German was also apprehended for being in possession of the component parts of a wireless installation.

With the sanction of Lord Kitchener three hundred Scandinavians and four hundred other foreigners resident in the Transvaal were on September 11th enrolled as a corps for oversea service on the lines of a Foreign Legion, under the command of a Dane named Fredericks.

At this date among the gifts announced from beyond the seas were 1,500 horses from the Government of the Province of Saskatchewan for the use of the Army ; from the farmers of New Zealand all the chaff required by the Dominion's Expeditionary Force, while a surplus of 250 tons was sold for the benefit of the war fund. From **Generous gifts from overseas** Melbourne, Australia, 550 cases of goods were despatched to the Red Cross Society, while £1,400 realised by a concert given by Madame Melba was remitted to the same society. The Legislative Council of the Falkland Islands voted £2,250—a sum equivalent to a contribution of £1 per head from every inhabitant—towards the Prince of Wales's National Relief Fund, with an additional sum of £750 privately contributed. The Combined Court of the Colony of British Guiana passed unanimously a resolution asking

CROSSING A TEMPORARY FOOTBRIDGE UNDER WITHERING SHELL FIRE AT VAILLY

Ordered to cross the Aisne at Vailly, in order to secure the high ground north of the river, the 8th British Brigade found that, although the bridge had been blown up by the Germans, they had left in their hasty retreat a small temporary footbridge, with ropes attached all ready for the supports to be pulled away at the last moment. The brigade crossed this fragile structure under a withering shell fire, but, happily, with few casualties.

NORTHAMPTONS TREACHEROUSLY CUT DOWN BY AN AMBUSHED ENEMY.

Some men of the A Company of the Northamptons were engaged with a slightly larger force of the enemy, when the latter held up a white flag in tok[...] Germans had been firing from behind a slight ridge. As our men advanced towards them, one or two laid down their rifles, and then all fell flat on the [...] a second line of Germans rose from behind the ridge and fired over them. The small British line, taken by surprise, were cut down on every side by the [...] rifles before British help could arrive.

BRITISH TROOPS RESTING IN A DISUSED QUARRY ON THE AISNE.

As a result of the extensive quarrying in the Aisne district for generations past, the hillsides are honeycombed with caves, which afforded resting-places for our troops between the fighting, store-houses for supplies of all kinds, and occasionally mess-rooms for officers. The floors were strewn with straw to give warmth, and, except for draughts, these caves were found to be fairly comfortable. The caves were also used as shelters by the people of the Aisne villages.

SHORT SHRIFT F[...]
Attracted by the move[...]
uniform motoring ne[...]
stopped the pair, wh[...]
were shot. The [...]

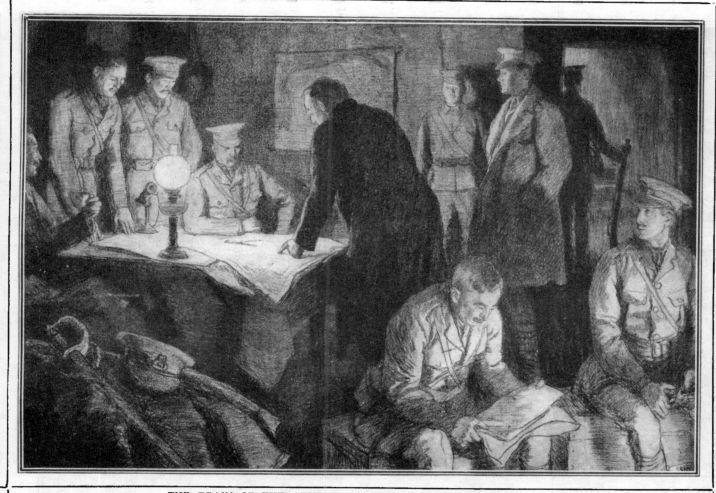

THE BRAIN OF THE ARMY PROTECTED FROM GERMAN SHELLS.

On at least one occasion the British Headquarters was established in a subterranean apartment, which was not merely bomb-proof, but, with its ample fireplaces, also provided a most comfortable retreat from the inclemencies of the weather. Here, by lamplight, plans were worked out; the various scraps of information supplied by civilian volunteers and Intelligence Department agents pieced together with the aid of maps, and all the routine work of a Staff performed in comparative security.

BRITISH BURROWS IN THE BATTLE OF THE AISNE.

The above drawing, finished from sketches made in the trench it represents, makes clear the wonderful British defences at the Battle of the Aisne. The surface sheds and roofs of straw made for concealment, and the loopholes at which the defenders were posted gave a clear view of the approaches and the barbed-wire fences erected to prevent a sudden rush attack. The straw covering the floors of the trenches rendered them more or less comfortable for those who were temporarily resting.

E BATTLE-FRONT.
d woman in Red Cross
some British soldiers
t they were spies, and
oved to be a man.

WAR LIFE IN A SANDPIT BEHIND THE BRITISH LINES IN THE CHAMPAGNE COUNTRY.

Lance-corporal Jarvis, V.C., R.E., placed it on record that his company spent three weeks on the edge of a deep sandpit, where there were three tiers of "dug-outs," in which the men lived. The place was about fifty yards in the rear of the British lines and trenches. " I myself," he said, " spent eleven days there ; and, although we were exposed day and night to showers of shell, we had only one man wounded."

his Majesty's Government to accept from the colony a gift of a thousand tons of sugar produced there. The gift was accepted by the Secretary for the Colonies, Mr Harcourt, on behalf of the Government, with warm appreciation of the loyal and patriotic action of the colony.

Baron Kato, the Japanese Foreign Minister, authorised on September 9th the following statement to be made regarding the treatment given to Japanese subjects imprisoned or otherwise detained in Germany and Austria: "I am painfully shocked at the news of the most unkind and outrageous treatment accorded to peaceful Japanese residents by the German Government, and the unpardonable discourteous acts of the Austrian people against our Ambassador. These are in striking contrast to the carefully-courteous and magnanimous treatment and the absolute protection of rights which ambassadors and resident Germans and Austrians here (in Tokyo) have been accorded and now continue to receive at the hands of the Government and people of Japan. It is difficult for us to understand how the Governments and people of countries boasting high culture and civilisation should permit the disgrace of their good name by such shamelessly wanton outrages."

On the same date Baron Kato declared to the Russian and French Ambassadors in Tokyo that Japan would not make peace with Germany until the end of the war in Europe. It was explained that it was not necessary for Japan to make any declaration to Great Britain of her adhesion to the declaration in London, inasmuch as the Treaty of Alliance between Japan and Great Britain provides, inter alia, "that the High Contracting Parties will conduct the war in common and make peace in mutual agreement." In the case of France and Russia no such understanding existed, and explanations of Japan's views were consequently made to the French and Russian representatives in Tokyo.

The German Emperor and the General Staff took up their quarters on September 10th at the German Legation in Luxemburg. A large force of Uhlans were encamped round the Legation, and at night it was guarded by aeroplanes which employed searchlights to prevent any hostile airship approaching the town.

The steamer Bethania, which had been acting as a collier to German cruisers in the South Atlantic, especially the Dresden and Karlsruhe, for which she had six hundred tons of coal and six months' provisions, was on September 10th captured and brought to Kingston, Jamaica. There were four hundred prisoners on board, most of whom, according to the Admiralty announcement, formed the crew of the Kaiser Wilhelm der Grosse,

Sinking of the Kaiser Wilhelm der Grosse who escaped in a collier when she was captured and sunk by H.M.S. Highflyer off the Oro River on the West Coast of Africa at the end of August. Between September 10th and 14th the German auxiliary cruiser Emden captured six British ships in the Bay of Bengal. Five of the vessels were sunk. The other, with all the crews on board, was released and ordered to make for the nearest Indian port.

The Nyasaland Protectorate, which for fourteen years—between 1893 and 1907—was known as the British Central African Protectorate, was invaded on September 8th by a force four hundred strong from German East Africa. This force at sunrise on September 9th attacked Karonga, which is the chief station in the northern end of the British

Protectorate and the starting point of the Stevenson Road which runs to Lake Tanganyika. The Germans had come from Songwe, their frontier station eighteen miles from Karonga, which was defended by one officer, fifty African rifles and police, and eight civilians. After three hours' resistance a column of the main British force operating in the Protectorate arrived at Karonga, and engaged the enemy, who fought with great determination, and were only finally driven towards Songwe after repeated bayonet charges. The enemy lost seven officers killed and two wounded, two field-guns, and two machine-guns. The number of rank and file of the enemy killed was not ascertained. The British losses included four whites killed and seven wounded. Nyasaland owed its existence to the missionary activity of Dr. Livingstone and the energy of a number of British officials, such as Captain Foote, Sir H. H. Johnston, and Sir A. Sharp in later years. The population is a million, of which less than eight hundred are Europeans. Our Protectorate extends along the whole of the western

Fighting in the Nyasaland Protectorate

BEHIND THE SCENES OF THE FIGHTING ALONG THE AISNE.
A posse of German prisoners brought to the grounds of a French chateau under a British guard.

shore of Lake Nyasa, which lake was shared in common by the British, Portuguese, and Germans.

With the Battle of the Marne, described in Chapter XXXIII. as "the turning of the tide," an inspiring and memorable demonstration of British parties comprising every shade of political opinion took place in the London Opera House on the evening of September 11th.

The Marquis of Lincolnshire, President of the National Liberal Club, presided, and with him on his immediate right was Mr. J. F. Remnant, M.P., Chairman of the Constitutional Club, while on the platform were the most conspicuous representatives of the Government and Opposition, and of the Irish National and Ulster parties, members of the House of Commons, bishops of the Church of England and of the Church Catholic, leading Free Church clergymen, the mayors of the metropolitan boroughs, and the members of the Joint Committee of the National and Constitutional Clubs. Quite ten thousand people were eager to hear the call to arms, and overflow meetings were held in the Kingsway Hall and in the open air near by.

At the principal meeting in the Opera House there was an impressive opening ceremony. The band of the Coldstream Guards played in turn the National Anthems of Belgium, Serbia, Russia, Japan, and France, while the

GERMAN ORGY STOPPED BY FRENCH SHELLS OUTSIDE A PLUNDERED INN AT FERE CHAMPENOISE.
Before evacuating Fère Champenoise, some German troops looted the Hotel de Paris. They then tugged a piano-organ into the street and danced to its music, swilling what remained of the beer; for their Headquarters' Staff, after occupying the place for several days, had taken away with them 6,000 francs' worth of champagne. The revelry was rudely shattered by the French, who shelled the Germans out of the position

whole audience, led by their chairman, stood in their places. His lordship then said that that mighty gathering had assembled to express their admiration of our gallant troops and their brave Allies, and to pledge themselves to reinforce them again, again, and again. A few short weeks ago Germany claimed to lead in culture and enlightenment. That day her name was received everywhere with hatred and execration. Germany's butchery, devastation, and brigandage in Belgium and France, and her cowardly practices at sea, had horrified the whole civilised world. It was the purpose of the meeting to make certain that those barbarities would never be repeated. The Kaiser, called the arbiter of peace in days gone by, would go down to history as a savage incendiary and the dynamiter of Louvain.

The First Lord of the Admiralty, Mr. Churchill, who had a great reception, moved the following resolution: "That this meeting of the citizens of London, profoundly believing that we are fighting in a just cause for the vindication of the rights of small States and the public law of Europe, pledges itself unswervingly to support the Prime Minister's appeal to the nation, and all measures necessary for the prosecution of the war to a victorious conclusion.

whereby alone the lasting peace of Europe can be secured." The First Lord began with the dignified assurance that though these were serious times he came there that night in good heart and with full confidence for the future. It was quite clear that what was happening in France and Belgium was not what the Germans had planned. But if the battle had been as disastrous as, thank God! it appeared to be triumphant, he should have come before his vast audience with unabated confidence and with the certainty that we had only to continue in our efforts to bring the war to the conclusion wished and intended, although he admitted it would not be a very easy victory. We had entered on the war reluctantly after having made every effort compatible with honour to avoid being drawn into it. It would be a long and a sombre war, with many reverses of fortune and hopes falsified, but we must derive from our cause, from the strength which is in us, from the traditions and history of our race, and from the support and aid of our Empire all over the world the means to make this country overcome obstacles of all kinds and continue to the end of the furrow, whatever the toil and suffering might be.

Referring to the Navy, the right hon. gentleman said that the war had then been in progress only five or six weeks, and that in that time we had swept German commerce from the seas, had either blocked into neutral harbours, or blockaded in their own harbours, or hunted down the commerce destroyers of which we used to hear so much, and from which the enemy anticipated such serious loss and damage to us. All our ships, with inconsiderable exceptions, were arriving safely and punctually at their destinations. We were transporting easily, not without an element of danger, but safely and successfully, great numbers of soldiers across the seas from all quarters of the world to be directed upon the decisive theatre of the land struggle. We had searched the so-called German Ocean without discovering the German flag; and there was no reason why we **Why the nose of the** should not keep the same process of **bull-dog was slanted** naval control and have the same exercises of sea-power on which we had lived and are living. By one of those dispensations of Providence, which appeals so strongly to the German Emperor, the nose of the bull-dog had been slanted backwards so that it would breathe with comfort without letting go. In the next twelve months the number of great ships that would be completed for this country would be more than double the number completed for Germany, and the number of cruisers three or four times as great.

Having been supported by Mr. F. E. Smith, K.C., M.P., and Mr. Will Crooks, M.P., the resolution was adopted by acclamation at all three meetings.

CHAPTER XXXVII.

HOW THE BRITISH ARMY CROSSED THE AISNE.

Zwehl Hastens from Maubeuge to Stop the Gap in the German Lines—Field-Marshal von Heeringen comes from Lorraine to Help Kluck and Bülow—German Position on the Plateau of Soissons—British Cavalry Clear the Hills by the Aisne—Our Army Crosses the River under a Terrific Bombardment—Bridges Blown Up as Soon as Pontoons are Floated—Battalions Cross on Rafts and Rowing Boats—Checks at Venizel, Missy, Vailly, and Chavonne—Sir Douglas Haig Discovers Gap in Enemy's Defences—Our First Division Storms the Heights of the Aisne—The Great Fight Round the Sugar Factory—Dominating Artillery Positions Won—British Army Reinforced—Tremendous German Counter-Attacks—Wonderful Charge by the Northamptons—Our Troops Cling on the Slopes and Save the Situation—Deeds of Heroism in the Darkness—A Highlander Routs a German Column and Holds a Bridge.

WHILE the main French armies, with the British force, were breaking the German advance along the Marne River, the frontier fortress of Maubeuge was engaging the attention of General von Zwehl and the Seventh Reserve German Army Corps. No one knew it at the time, but the fate of all the armies of invasion depended on what was happening at Maubeuge. If the Maubeuge garrison could have but held out a couple of days longer than they did, the German retreat to the Aisne valley would have been changed into a disastrous and overwhelming rout.

Unhappily for the Allies, the heavy Krupp siege-howitzers shortened in a surprising manner the period of resistance of Maubeuge. The mighty German siege train, with its mobile howitzers sending down 11 in. shells from concealed positions on the Belgian border, completely battered in the circle of armour-plated concrete forts. For the French at that time seem to have relied too much on the delusive lesson of Port Arthur, and in spite of the teaching of their famous commander, General Langlois, they had not protected Maubeuge by open-air earthworks, with moving guns, as they had protected Verdun. By September 6th the forts were smashed, and in places only a hole in the ground showed where they had existed. The next day Maubeuge was taken.

This was the very day when Kluck, in his new position to the south-east of Paris, recognised that he was imperilled. Both Kluck and Bülow seem to have lent some of their heavy artillery to Zwehl to help him reduce Maubeuge. As Zwehl also had the great siege train prepared for the reduction of Paris, he became, in spite of the comparative small number of his available troops, the only possible saviour of the defeated armies. Could he get the big guns up in time to prevent the German retirement from becoming a rout?

Zwehl was a veteran of the 1870 war—a white-haired, heavy-jawed fighting man, with an iron will. It was on September 8th that he learned the main German armies were breaking. He collected 9,000 reserve troops, which were soon strengthened by 9,000 more. So, with about a division, he marched for four days and three nights southward to the help of the threatened German western wing. He had to bring his siege-guns to the cathedral city of Laon, overlooking the Aisne valley and the plateau to which Kluck and Bülow were retiring.

Zwehl worked his men and horses in a tremendous way. In the last twenty-four hours of marching, his eighteen thousand troops are said to have covered forty miles. They arrived at Laon at six o'clock in the morning of Sunday, September 13th, and within an hour they were in action. By holding their ground until some twenty-two thousand reinforcements arrived they saved the German lines from being completely broken. They lost over 8,000 men, but, for the time, saved Germany. Over Zwehl, directing all the operations, was Field-Marshal von Heeringen, commander of

BRITISH BIPLANE IN FLIGHT GUARDING A SUPPLY CONVOY.

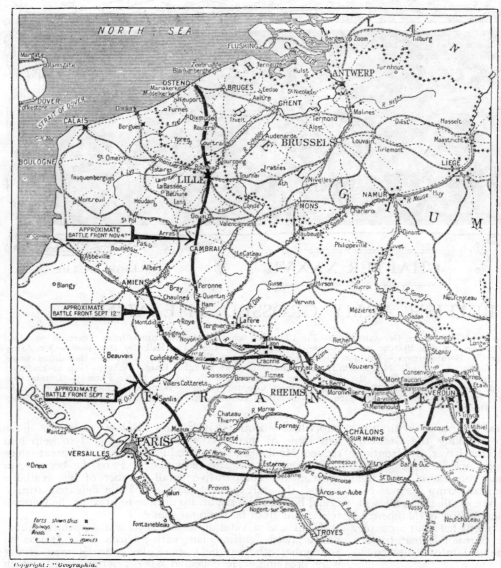

MAP INDICATING THE APPROXIMATE POSITIONS OF THE WESTERN BATTLE-LINE
BETWEEN SEPTEMBER 2ND AND NOVEMBER 4TH, 1914.

Sixth French Army under General Maunoury. Even the heavy German field-guns could not keep back the British force. For our men also had heavy guns and howitzer batteries, and in the two rearguard actions against the British advance on September 10th and 12th the Germans lost about forty-eight guns as well as some 4,000 men.

If the French armies had been as well provided with heavy artillery as was the British force, the retreating German western wing might have been driven from its main line of communication. This consisted of the trunk railway running from Cologne to Liège and Namur, to Maubeuge, St. Quentin, and Noyon. Unhappily for the cause of the Allies, the position which the Germans occupied in the defence of the railway was very strong. They fixed their headquarters at the old cathedral town of Laon, lying on a great hill that fell away in wooded slopes sinking southward into broad valleys that rose again in a long, forested plateau along the Aisne.

This plateau was the supreme barrier to any further advance by the victorious Franco-British armies. It was the strongest natural fortress in Northern Europe, and it had been studied by the Germans with particular care for a century. For there the Prussian army, under Blücher, had beaten off the French army, under Napoleon, in the campaign of 1814. Napoleon, like Joffre, had won a great series of battles on the Marne against the Prussians, but, by retreating to the plateau of Soissons, Blücher managed to turn the tables on the famous French commander.

This was the achievement that Heeringen hoped to repeat in similar circumstances in 1914. Many of the finest Prussian troops were under his command ; he had a lively knowledge of Blücher's tactics, and the German Military Staff had done everything possible to facilitate the defence of the heights. Some of the chief quarries near Soissons had been especially worked by German firms in peacetime, with the result that positions had been prepared and every yard of the plateau carefully mapped out for artillery fire. Germans engaged for years in businesses at Soissons and Rheims were at hand to advise about details of the ground, and help in laying out the entrenchments and gun-sites. **Prepared German gun-sites at Soissons** Employees in these German businesses— some of them Frenchmen of a scoundrelly sort ready to betray their country—were scattered about the country south of the Aisne River, and provided with secret underground telephone communications, by means of which news of the movements of the French and British troops could be sent to the German Staff. Near Rheims, for instance, were two spies—man and wife—who lived in a detached house, fitted with a telephone that communicated with the German lines. The man was a Frenchman who had got into trouble with the police, and had then been

the Seventh German Army from Metz. Kluck was reduced to a very subordinate position, though the Allies did not know it at the time. They had completely beaten his men in their terrible pursuit from the Marne to the Aisne heights Bülow's troops were in no better condition for fighting. Hausen's army was smashed and panic-stricken, and the Duke of Würtemberg's troops were worn out and demoralised. Their rearguards were fleeing without a fight. It was Heeringen, with something like a quarter of a million of fairly fresh troops coming from the north of Verdun, and Zwehl, arriving from Maubeuge with the great siege train designed for the reduction of the Paris fortifications, that held together the fatigued, drenched, and dispirited host of beaten invaders.

Kluck had done his utmost by Friday, September 11th. By this time he had got most of his artillery over the Aisne River, at Soissons, and dragged most of his men up the heights north of the stream. At all important points south of the Aisne he posted strong rearguards to delay the advance of the allied forces, while he prepared to make a stand on the plateau above Soissons. But though by the most arduous exertions he had kept his retreating troops intact, the condition of his infantry was prophetic of complete disaster. The men were utterly worn out. Only their artillerymen with the heavy German guns were able to retard the flanking movement of the

VIVID CAMERA RECORD OF A DRAMATIC MOMENT
DURING THE BATTLE OF THE AISNE.

The above vividly interesting photograph was taken by a British officer
at a moment when a shell was passing over a high road during the Battle
of the Aisne. The alarm of men and horses is very clearly depicted in
their attitudes, and the whole scene conveys to us a remarkable impression
of the reality of modern warfare. Inset: Loading up supplies for the
troops in the firing-line. The supply waggons went out nightly from the
rear to the trenches, which were on the distant hills just over the Aisne.

engaged as a casual messenger by a German wine firm at
Rheims. He had a store of red and blue rockets, which
he let off in a neighbouring wood—the red to indicate that
an ammunition convoy was arriving in the lines of the
Fifth French Army, the blue to show that the French
troops were moving. The villain also spied on two French
batteries near his house, and telephoned to the Germans
the various ranges, elevations, and general working of the
guns. He thus rendered the fire of the batteries quite
ineffective. He was often visited by a German officer
who had also worked as a foreman in the German wine
firm at Rheims, and came in the disguise of a French
sergeant to obtain fuller reports.

Such was the system of espionage organised throughout
the country occupied by the allied armies when they faced
the Germans entrenched on the plateau of Soissons. The

**Organised German
espionage**

plateau lies about midway between Paris
and the French frontier. It extends for
some thirty-seven miles, from the Forest
of the Eagle, near the cathedral city of
Noyon in the west, to the hill town of Craonne, above
Rheims, in the east. It is a flat, high tableland, cut into
a wide, deep valley by the River Aisne, and further
eroded by the brooks that have worn a series of steep
ravines and valleys in its southern slopes.

The ravines divide the high land by the river into a
number of natural bastions that all join on to the main
long wooded ridge that towers some four hundred and fifty

feet in places above the broad, low stream. The entire
plateau thus formed a great, flattish embankment on
which guns and howitzers could be placed, safe from
aerial observation, in the trees, so as to dominate the Aisne
River. Then, protecting the gun positions from infantry
attack, were the outlying spurs, steep and wooded and
hard to climb, where brigades of riflemen, with machine-
guns and light artillery, swept the river crossings and
defended the approaches.

All the natural difficulties that Napoleon had vainly
contended against in his disastrous attack on Blücher
were enormously enhanced by the highly increased power
of modern artillery and long-range small firearms. Our
troops were faced with the most tremendous and perilous
task that men have ever been called on to carry out. They
had to storm, by a direct frontal attack, the high, fortified
positions of the First and Second German Armies. They
had no heavy siege-artillery, such as General von Zwehl
was hurrying to the assistance of Von Kluck and

221

BRITISH GUNS BEING FIRED FROM A CONCEALED POSITION ON THE FOE IN HIDDEN TRENCHES ON THE AISNE.

This picture brings home to us the vast difference between modern war conditions and those of only comparatively recent times. Quite a number of our wounded returned from the Battle of the Aisne without seeing a single German combatant. The struggle on the Aisne developed very quickly into a big-gun duel between concealed artillery. As the trenches on both sides were also hidden, the only visible signs of fighting, apart from the dead and wounded, were the puffs of smoke in the air. The guns shown in our picture were placed advantageously on high ground.

Von Bülow. They were also outnumbered in machine-guns. In order to get within rifle range of the hidden masses of foes entrenched on every wooded scarp and ravine cliff they had to cross a river valley, broadening from half a mile to two miles, and next bridge the Aisne River, a hundred and seventy feet wide. All this had to be done under a terrific, incessant fire of shell and shrapnel. When the river was at last bridged with pontoons, they had to climb the spurs, with Maxims and innumerable rifles blazing at them at short range, while howitzers on the plateau raked them with a cross fire.

It was not a battle of man against man. It was a one-sided contest between eighty thousand young British athletes and a gigantic, systematised, and long-prepared machine of war, forged by Krupp and other Teutonic armament firms, with a hundred and forty thousand riflemen, gunners, and cavalrymen behind it. It would have been no disparagement of the courage of our soldiers had they failed to force the passage of the Aisne against such an array of machinery of death. Just on the British right the Turcos, who are among the most fearless souls with mortal breath, were driven back to the ford of Berry-au-Bac. And further westward, in the more level land around Rheims, the German guns blew the Fifth French Army from a very important hill position, and prevented the French for months from retaking it. On the British left the Sixth French Army was, for a time, held up south of Soissons, until our artillery cleared the way for them, and it was hurled back to the river, after almost reaching the plateau.

But, despite the terrible disadvantages under which they attacked, the British troops not only crossed the valley of death, but seized and held a commanding position on the plateau of Soissons. The British advance began on Sunday, September 12th, with a magnificent piece of work by the Queen's Bays and other cavalrymen of General Allenby's division. Running south-east of the Aisne River was its tributary, the Vesle, **Brilliant British** which had cut a deep valley in the **cavalry work** southern tableland. The Germans held this southern line of heights as well as the northern plateau. They occupied, in fact, all the hilly region of the Aisne, and before our army could attempt to cross the river it had to clear the southern hills. This was done by the cavalry under General Allenby. By one of those swift and sweeping "hussar strokes" that the Germans talk about but seldom achieve, our cavalrymen swept from the town of Braisne, on the Vesle, the strong German detachments that Bülow had thrown out as advance guards. Over the difficult high wooded ridge between

BRITISH INFANTRY FORCING THEIR WAY THROUGH GERMAN WIRE ENTANGLEMENTS.
Incidents of this kind were numerous during the great siege-battle of the Aisne. The entanglements were laid like snares in the woods and in the open, and carefully aligned so that they could be swept by guns which were invisible from our side of the valley, while the enemy's fire was aided by their searchlights.

the Vesle and the Aisne the beaten German forces were driven by the British horsemen, with the assistance of the infantry and gunners of the 3rd Division under General Hamilton. By the evening of Saturday, General Hamilton's men were able to bivouac below the hill of Brenelle, after getting their guns on that height, from which they could reply to the German batteries hidden in the ridge across the Aisne.

The 5th Division, under Sir Charles Fergusson, dragged its guns to the neighbouring height of Ciry, and marched down the western bank of the Vesle to the main river. The valley of the Aisne was some two miles broad round the front where the valley of the Vesle opened into it, and here it was that the British force first got into difficulties. For the waters of the two rivers had worn away the tableland only on the northern side, leaving a great stretch of flat-bottomed land over which our guns had to fire. On the northern side, held by the Germans, the steep spurs came close to the water's edge, so that the enemy's light artillery and machine-guns could fire at short range at our troops, while the German heavy guns also caught our men on both flanks when they crossed the river.

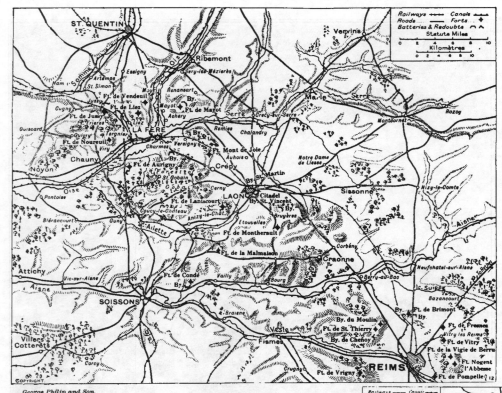

George Philip and Son.

MAP OF WESTERN AREA OF THE AISNE BATTLE-GROUND.
The map shows the plateau held by the German right in the Aisne fighting.
The plateau slopes upwards in a north-east direction to the crest of the line
of heights that looks down on the plains stretching to the Argonne, and
known as the Falaises de Champagne.

where the Crown Prince's army was operating.

In the new disposition of the army of invaders there was one weak spot. Moreover, practically all the troops were dead tired and approaching complete demoralisation. In the open country between Rheims and the Argonne Forest, where their entrenchments were hastily made, they showed, under French artillery fire, something like panic. On the other hand, the allied troops, though victorious, were at least equally fatigued. The French had been fighting with extraordinary exertions, doing double work in many cases, assailing one German army in front, then taking another on the flank, and finally pursuing the retreaters. The British Expeditionary Force had not had a single day's rest since the opening of the Battle of Mons. For three weeks the men had marched and fought, till their feet were bleeding and

So confident were the Germans of repulsing a British attack at this point that they left a bridge at Condé, near the meeting of the waters of the Vesle and the Aisne. Nearly every other bridge they destroyed, but they preserved the bridge at Condé, partly as a lure to induce Sir Charles Fergusson to attack them at the spot where their means of defence was strongest, and partly as a sallying path along which they intended to sweep down on our troops when our men had been compelled to retreat Even on Saturday the fierce opposition which all the Second Army Corps, under Sir Horace Smith-Dorrien, encountered on either side of the Condé bridge showed that the Germans were prepared again to offer battle. For both Fergusson's 5th Division and Hamilton's 3rd Division, composing together the Second Army Corps, met with a strong resistance on the afternoon of September 12th.

Field-Marshal von Heeringen's achievement

The fact was that the armies of Kluck and Bülow had been united for the defence of the plateau of Soissons, under Field-Marshal von Heeringen, hastily sent from the country round Verdun, where he had been assisting the Crown Prince with the Seventh German Army from Metz. The situation round Verdun was too ticklish for any considerable part of the Seventh Army to be detached and sent to reinforce Kluck and Bülow's troops. But Heeringen, reputed to be one of the most stubborn and brilliant of German fighters, appears to have justified his reputation. He lined out Kluck and Bülow's men on the heights from Noyon to Craonne, called in the forces occupying the country far to the west round Amiens. and placed them on his flank at Peronne and Saint Quentin He brought down by rail troops from Belgium. He reorganised the broken Saxon army, and retiring the Duke of Würtemberg's beaten and weary troops from Rheims, settled them on the low swell of land running from the eastern end of the Soissons plateau, along the River Suippes to the middle of the Forest of Argonne

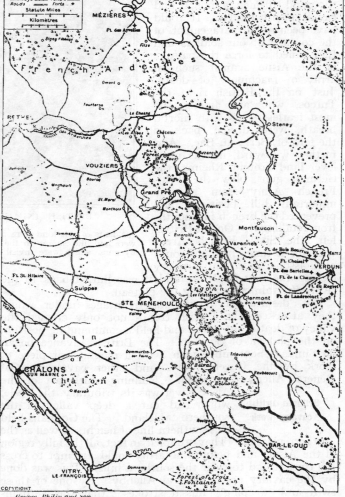

George Philip and Son.

MAP OF EASTERN AREA OF THE AISNE BATTLE-GROUND.
The Argonne is famous in French history as the natural barrier behind
which French armies have resisted invasions from the eastward. It faces
the gap between Verdun and the Belgian frontier. Possession of the
plateau by the French threatened the line of German retreat.

"SEARCHLIGHT" FIRED FROM A GUN: A PARACHUTE LIGHT-BALL SHELL.

The above picture illustrates an ingenious Krupp device for warfare in the dark—the firing of shells enclosing a powerful illuminant, with parachute attachment. Within the shell was a folded-up parachute, which dropped when the shell burst, while clockwork mechanism suspended below lighted the illuminant. This illuminant remained in the air for several minutes.

BRITISH LOG–ARTILLERY DRAWS THE GERMAN FIRE.

Whenever German airmen saw a masked battery of allied artillery they dropped smoke bombs on it to indicate its position to their own gunners. In this picture an enemy aeroplane is seen flying away after dropping some of these bombs, the smoke from which is seen rising in two streaks. However, instead of being a real battery, it was a dummy one constructed of logs and wheels, screened among bushes. The enemy thus wasted their shells on it. Meanwhile the genuine battery was concealed in a wood and making ready to reply. Immediately in the foreground is one of the Aisne quarries, from which our men were watching the effect of their ruse.

their faces haggard for want of sleep. A sense of victorious power kept them going, and man for man they were still ascendant over the German soldiers they had driven halfway back to the French frontier. But so skilfully did Heeringen place the overpowering force of artillery belonging to the First and Second German Armies, that, save for one defect, the plateau of Soissons was almost as impregnable as Gibraltar.

The German field-marshal did not rely on Kluck and Bülow's infantry. They almost tumbled with fatigue into the trenches they made on the wooded heights above the Aisne. While they rested and snatched sleep in turns, the German gunners protected them and **Situation saved by** saved the situation. By the time the **the German gunners** German infantrymen were badly needed as a guard to the dominating guns they had fairly recovered from their exertions. Meanwhile, their artillerymen held the field, and, owing to their remarkably advantageous position, they at first turned the Battle of the Aisne into the terrible kind of machine-made warfare which had for years been the ideal of the German Military Staff. Each battery of light field-guns operated, under a fire-control officer, in conjunction with well-placed pieces of heavy artillery. Together, they poured from the forested ridge a direct fire into the river valley.

Then at some distance behind the ridge, on the slopes falling towards Laon, were the batteries of howitzers that could shower their shells and shrapnel over the plateau by high-angle fire. Field-telephones linked these howitzers

with the fire control of the direct-shooting guns on the ridge, so that a double hurricane of high-explosive shells could be directed against each assailing column that tried to cross the Aisne. Close to the river, on the spurs mirrored in the water, observation officers were perched in the trees, from which telephone wires, strung from trunk to trunk, connected them with the fire-control centres. Some of the observation officers were also in secret communication with spies in the British lines, and could direct the long-range German guns against distant and apparently invisible masses of our troops.

Heeringen's plan was identical with that which Blücher had adopted against Napoleon. He intended to let the Sixth French Army, operating west of Soissons, the British Expeditionary Force, advancing between Soissons and Bourg, and the Fifth French **Second march on** Army, driving on towards Craonne and **Paris planned** Berry-au-Bac, shatter themselves against the defence of the famous plateau. Then, with the German guns playing on the dispirited and retreating Allies, Heeringen designed to cross the river again in another great march towards Paris, in which the Franco-British forces would be completely routed, if not enveloped. In the meantime the German infantry was getting some rest in the trenches, and large reinforcements were on the way to strengthen them for the grand counter-attack.

Sir John French, however, was not the man to allow an enemy to win any advantage from his hesitation. While doing all he possibly could in the circumstances to give the British troops enough rest to carry them farther, Sir John acted with swift and decisive vigour. Saturday night was a night of labour for his engineers and many of

HUGE SHELLS BURSTING HARMLESSLY IN A BRITISH TRENCH.

In the British trenches along the Aisne huge 200 lb. German howitzer shells came crashing down in some places at the rate of one every two minutes. They made great craters where they fell, but the soft, claylike soil absorbed their energy, and our men soon got accustomed to them, and christened their effect " the mud bath." In the trench shown above, no one was seriously injured after three hours' furious shelling, even the soldier seen on the right, knocked over by an explosion, was only half-smothered with Mother Earth.

his gunners, and some of the troops had to do entrenching work. All the guns were got into position in accordance with the commander's plan for the coming battle, and the ground was dug in the widest part of the valley as cover against the German fire. Sections of the bridge trains belonging to the First and Second Army Corps pushed on towards the river in the darkness, and at daybreak the great attempt to force the passage of the Aisne was begun.

Sir John French had no means of ascertaining in what strength the enemy held the opposite plateau, nor in what manner the enemy's forces were arrayed. But he concluded, from the resistance met with on Saturday afternoon, that there were at least three German army corps opposed to him. That is to say, the enemy had the advantage of numbers as well as the advantage of **British reconnaissance** an extraordinarily strong defensive **in force** position. For though there were nominally three British army corps, the Third Corps was incomplete—it lacked two brigades of infantry, and had little more, apparently, than half the artillery of a full army corps.

There was only one sound way of discovering the enemy's disposition—to attack him vehemently. This reconnaissance in force was made at dawn on Sunday, September 13th. Down to the empty river valley, one of the most beautiful and picturesque scenes in France, where the autumn sunlight was playing on the misty orchards and white villages by the water edge, and the green, quiet ramparts above, the British army advanced in brigades. It had entered the death-trap so carefully prepared for it.

HEROISM OF THE "MUDLARKS"—MURDEROUS WORK ON THE AISNE.

One of the most striking incidents of the long-drawn-out Battle of the Aisne was related by Private J. Green, of the Loyal North Lancashire Regiment. Finding all the bridges had been blown up when the Aisne was reached, the engineers immediately set to work with their pontoons; but the Germans, from a sheltered position, had the range beautifully. "As soon as one raft was got into position the poor fellows were knocked over like ninepins by the murderous fire. When one man fell over into the water another took his place, and the river was full of wounded. Six times was the bridge destroyed before our men were able to get across. "The bravery of the chaps was magnificent."

DEATH IN THE BARN: AN INCIDENT IN THE BATTLE OF THE AISNE.

Private G. Drury, of the Northamptonshire Regiment, described a night spent with several other wounded men in a barn which was shelled by the Germans during the fighting along the Aisne. "When the bullet found me it was growing dusk, and as there was little chance of being picked up that night, I started to crawl away." He managed to reach a barn where he found seven other wounded men. Weak from loss of blood, he lay there half-dazed, "until there was a terrific crash, and the whole place seemed to fall in on us. A shell had struck the barn near the door. In the morning the whole place was a wreck, and only two others and myself were alive."

All along the river for twenty miles, from Soissons to Bourg, our troops went forward. For a while the morning haze veiled the general movement of attack, but by nine o'clock many of our men had come under an incessant gun fire, which they were to endure for a month.

Round Soissons the Third Army Corps, consisting of General Snow's division and the 19th Infantry Brigade, acted for a time with the right wing of General Maunoury's Fifth French Army. The day before, their heavy guns had shelled the Germans from the Mont de Paris, south of Soissons, and thus enabled the Zouaves and Turcos to drive the common foe back **Pontoon bridging** on Soissons. Then, when the bridging **under heavy fire** train of our Third Army Corps arrived, the commander, General Pulteney, sent the engineers to build a pontoon bridge at Soissons for the French troops. It was built under a heavy fire, but destroyed by the terrible heavy German howitzers. The Turcos crossed the river in rowing-boats, and had a fierce struggle in the ancient cathedral city.

Meanwhile the four British infantry brigades, forming General Pulteney's force, struck north-eastward of Soissons, and the leading brigade crossed the river at Venizel. The road bridge there had been blown up by the Germans, but they had not completely wrecked it.

Our sappers quickly repaired it sufficiently to enable the 1st Somerset Light Infantry, the 1st East Lancashires, the 1st Hampshires, and the 1st Rifle Brigade to get over, and some artillery was man-handled over the water. Picking plums as they went along, with shells falling on them, these troops of the 11th Infantry Brigade assembled at Bucy-le-Long at one o'clock on Sunday.

Directly above them was the great hill of Vregny, one of the chief German artillery positions, and along the wooded edge of it were hidden machine-guns. But, in spite of bullets and shrapnel, the 11th Brigade clambered up the slopes, fighting forward for three hours and a half, until the German Maxim fire grew so terrible that they could not make any further headway **Assault of the great** against it. But the brigade held on to the **hill of Vregny** ground it won. And as by this time a pontoon bridge had been constructed at Venizel, the 10th Brigade—1st Worcesters, 2nd Seaforth Highlanders, 1st Irish Fusiliers, and 2nd Dublin Fusiliers— also got across to Bucy-le-Long, with most of the light field-guns. There was practically no protection at the foot of the plateau against the shells, shrapnel, and bullets poured down on our men; but the 12th Brigade worked over the slopes to the ravine of Chivres, and when night fell some of the troops of the Second Army Corps came up and helped to retain some of the ground won.

The Second Army Corps had also had a severe task to gain a footing over the Aisne. Finding that the bridge at Condé was too strongly held to be carried by assault, Sir Horace Smith-Dorrien divided his forces, and with them made two attacks. One was directed at the village of Missy, some two and a half miles west of Condé; the other was launched against the town of Vailly, three miles east of Condé. The 13th Brigade, composed of the 2nd Scottish Borderers, the 2nd West Ridings, the 1st West Kents, and the 2nd Yorkshire Light Infantry, headed Sir Charles Fergusson's 5th Division, in the advance on Missy. The bridge had been blown up by the Germans,

who left small bodies of troops at the water's edge to hinder the British advance, while the entrenchments on the spurs and the plateau were being completed. According to a peasant living at Missy, the Germans had already been working sixteen days on fortifying the heights.

A murderous fire was directed on our scouts, and when our engineers tried to throw a bridge across the stream their pontoons and rafts were shelled and wrecked. Our artillery, however, then came fiercely into action, and searched the woods by the river in a terrible manner, so that both the German machine-gun sections and riflemen fell or retreated. In the night some troops were rafted over, three men at a time. They entrenched near Missy, but were subjected to such an overpowering, unceasing gun fire that they had to bide in their dug-outs for the next sixteen days. The West Kents were among the battalions that struggled valiantly into the Missy mouse-traps. In the daytime it was death to show one's head above the trench, for German observation officers were in the trees overhead, directing the guns, and snipers occupied the wooded heights. When **Checkmate for the** our artillery opened fire they retreated, **British at Missy** but came back again, and our men were directly under such a heavy cross-fire from the concealed German batteries that they could not advance. It was checkmate for the British at Missy.

So most of the 5th Division swerved still more westward, and crossed between Missy and Venizel, and helped the men of General Pulteney's advanced columns to hold the ravine of Chivres against a heavy counter-attack. In the meantime the other half of Smith-Dorrien's Second Army Corps had also got into difficulties at Vailly. The 8th Brigade that led the attack was formed of the 2nd Royal Scots, the 2nd Royal Irish, the 4th Middlesex, and the 1st Gordon Highlanders. Roused at three in the morning, in a torrent of rain, the brigade traversed a plank over the canal running by the Aisne, and their engineers threw a pontoon over the river by which they reached the hostile bank.

AT THE JUNCTION OF THE OISE AND THE AISNE—FRENCH INFANTRY ON THEIR WAY TO ATTACK THE GERMAN RIGHT.

The Oise is flowing towards the right in a south-westerly direction, and the Aisne is on the right, at a point where the two streams join. The confluence is just above Compiègne. In the foreground of our picture French infantry are seen marching along the towing-path of the Oise, making their way in the direction of Ribecourt and Noyon. Shells in the air over the woods and hills beyond the placid streams also indicate the presence of war in a region where, normally, Nature wears her most peaceful aspect.

From the Painting by Charles M. Sheldon.

General Sir Horace Lockwood Smith-Dorrien, K.C.B., D.S.O.

HOW THE GERMANS DUG THEMSELVES IN ON THE NORTH BANK OF THE AISNE.

The above illustration shows very graphically how the Germans "dug themselves in." They constructed the most elaborate shelters and trenches, deep enough to cover themselves up to their armpits, and to enable them to fire on a level with the ground, with emergency protection against enfilading fire. To conceal the trenches they placed leafy branches in front of them, as shown on the right of the picture, to give the appearance of ordinary clumps of bushes, between the stems of which they fired, the smokeless powder used materially aiding the concealment.

There, however, they were held up by an extraordinary shell fire. The Germans had previously measured all the ranges exactly, and their batteries continued the bombardment for three weeks, just as at Missy. Our troops dug trenches in the north bank, but found themselves, when they settled down, in a terrible position. For by ill-luck some of their trenches were so badly situated that the German guns and Maxims enfiladed them. There was nothing to do but retire as speedily as possible. So it was checkmate for the British also at Vailly.

And at first it seemed as though Sir Douglas Haig, operating still higher up the river with the 1st and 2nd Divisions of the First British Army Corps, would not be more fortunate than General Pulteney and Sir Horace Smith-Dorrien. The Guards Brigade and the 5th Infantry Brigade advanced in forking lines. The Guards—the 2nd Grenadiers, the 2nd and 3rd Coldstreams, and the Irish Guards—went across the valley of death in quick rushes and, crossing the canal at Presles, attacked the German position at the village of Chavonne. But the enemy's machine-guns swept the approaches, and here also the German batteries on the heights had the exact ranges of every object, with observers near the river to telephone each movement of the British troops. Pontoon bridging was impossible, but late on Sunday afternoon one battalion of the Guards rowed over the river in boats, and then beat back the enemy from the bank.

Four miles higher up the Aisne, at Pont Arcy, was a break in the plateau, where a wide ravine ran to a narrow neck of high land. A canal went northward along the ravine and through a tunnel in the neck of the plateau. This was the scene of action of the 5th Brigade—composed of the 2nd Worcesters, the 2nd Oxford and Bucks, the 2nd Highland Light Infantry, and the 2nd Connaught Rangers. The bridge at Pont Arcy had been blown up by the Germans, but one of its broken girders still rose partly from the water. Along the broken girder the men crossed in single file, while the enemy's guns sent shells bursting round them, and the sappers by the afternoon flung a pontoon over, in spite of the bombardment. Towards the evening all the brigade crossed the river and dug themselves in.

So from Soissons to Pont Arcy the British Expeditionary Force, after a terribly trying day, only managed to win a few perilous footholds on the lowest slopes of the great plateau. As the Germans, to the number of 140,000, held the great towering ridge above our men, and held it with heavier artillery and more numerous machine-guns than our army possessed, our position at the foot of their vast, open-air fortress was very chancy and dangerous. For this reason, most of our divisional generals only kept a battalion or two on the northern bank of the Aisne on Sunday night. The battalions formed bridge-heads to secure the crossings that had been gained and prevent the German troops from coming down to the water's edge again. The rest of the troops remained on the southern side of the valley of

BRITISH MOTOR SCOUTS IN NORTHERN FRANCE.

As the war lengthened the corps of motor-cyclists on service in the field strengthened. In the capacity of despatch-riders and scouts our motor-cyclists rendered splendid help, their dash and mobility alike enabling them to supplement cavalry work in many important directions.

slaughter. This was a triumph for the German gunners. They had defeated all our attempts between Soissons and Pont Arcy to carry any outlying part of the ridge by storm.

Yet the pressure our men exerted with such stubborn bravery made a deep impression on the German commander. His troops, though concealed on the wooded slopes, had apparently suffered as heavily as ours. For our artillerymen had been working all day long searching the green scarps and forested hills with a furious fire. So Field-Marshal von Heeringen withdrew at night his main infantry force to the topmost ridge, where a road known as the Chemin des Dames, or Lady's Walk, ran at a height of six hundred and fifty feet on the top of the plateau, two miles north of the Aisne River. Strongly entrenched detachments of German riflemen however, were still left in commanding positions on the lower jutting slopes, with powerful artillery to support them. There they could have held back any British advance in force until the heavy German guns and howitzers on the ridge massed their fire and slaughtered our troops in thousands. The guns indeed did in the end bring down some ten thousand of our men, but the expected British retreat from an untenable position, which Heeringen designed to convert into a rout, did not take place.

For though most of the British army failed to win a secure position on the plateau of Soissons, there was one weak spot in the German line of defence, and by ordering a general reconnaissance in force, Sir John French discovered this weak spot by Sunday evening. While Sir Douglas Haig's 2nd Division was battling against superior forces at Pont Arcy and lower down the river, his 1st Division, under Major-General Lomax, had an amazing success. Less than two miles east of Pont Arcy the canal from the north was carried over the River Aisne on an aqueduct near the village of Bourg. The 1st Division was supported by the Cavalry Division, under General Allenby, thus forming some 20,000 men, which was the strongest fighting force that Sir John French concentrated on one point of attack along the valley. The British commander had, of course, good reasons for massing men in this manner on his extreme right wing. His scouts had found the position at Bourg was weakly held by the Germans. So where the enemy was weakest Sir John French struck hardest. All his other operations served the purpose of fully engaging Heeringen's forces as far as Soissons, and eastward of that city the furious attack of the Sixth French Army compelled the German commander to put

GENERAL VON ZWEHL.
He brought up the big German guns from Maubeuge to the Aisne

out all his strength to resist it. And on our right the Fifth French Army was engaging the enemy strongly.

There was a gap in the German defences round Bourg, and General von Zwehl's men, marching to fill it, were still a day away. The result was that Sir Douglas Haig, who personally directed the advance of his 1st Division and General Allenby's cavalry, made remarkable progress. At first things went as badly as elsewhere on the river. By means of a small pontoon bridge, some of the infantry crossed east of the canal bridge. A brigade of cavalry started to follow them. When, however part had got across, the enemy opened fire on three sides—rifles, Maxims, field-guns and howitzers. The cavalrymen reached the town across the river, and tried to ascend the spur held by the Germans. But they could not advance against the bombardment, which set on fire the town behind them. They asked the infantry entrenched by the town for the needed help. No, the infantrymen could look after themselves. So, by the pontoon swept by the German guns and howitzers and rifles, the cavalry retired. By a marvellous chance they had no man killed and only a few wounded, yet they had been operating for three hours on the hostile side of the Aisne.

The main forces of the 1st Division were still more fortunate. Meeting with scarcely any opposition, they crossed towards Bourg over the canal aqueduct and, with the cavalry on its outer flank, drove the enemy back towards the main ridge. By Sunday evening the 2nd Infantry Brigade — composed of the 2nd Sussex, the 1st North Lancashires, the 1st Northamptons, and the 2nd King's Rifles—which were the spearhead of the British army on the Aisne, had climbed more than three-quarters of the way up the ridge, and threw their outposts far in front of the hamlet of Moulins, where they rested. Their commander, General Bulfin, had with him all the light field-guns of the 25th Artillery Brigade, and at daybreak on Monday, September 14th, he roused his troops and again sent them forward.

Some of his officers had scouted ahead at night, in spite of the fatigue of the labours on Sunday, and had discovered that a considerable force of Germans held a beet sugar factory at Troyon, close to the top of the plateau and the Chemin des Dames. So at three o'clock in the morning the Sussex Regiment, the North Lancashires, and the King's Royal Rifles crept up the height and attacked the factory, which had become, like the farm of Hougomont at Waterloo, the key to the position of both armies.

FRENCH TRENCHES ON THE FLANK OF A HILL NEAR SOISSONS.
At certain points along the line of battle in Northern France the French constructed alignments, which were dug into the hillside in the manner shown above. These dug-outs served as resting-places for the soldiers. They were for the most part constructed in superimposed rows, with steps leading down to the valley below.

GENERAL BELIN.
The "right-hand man" of General Joffre.

THE DEADLY GAME OF HIDE-AND-SEEK ALONG THE VALLEY OF THE AISNE.
French dragoons with a machine-gun in a field in the vicinity of Soissons. When photographed they were hiding behind some straw on the look-out for a party of German scouts reported to be scouring the neighbourhood.

Had the wet heavy mist that veiled the hills cleared away, our aerial scouts would have seen a long column, with a huge artillery train, hastening from Laon towards the road above the factory. These were General von Zwehl's 18,000 infantrymen, with guns from Maubeuge, coming as fast as their general could drive them up the northern slopes of the plateau to the aid of Bülow's dispirited army on the ridge. Bülow was being attacked eastward at Craonne by the Turcos and French infantry of General Franchet d'Espérey's Fifth Army. Our leading brigades were on the slope of the hill of Craonne, as well as advancing on the height in front of them. Neither Bülow on the east of the tableland nor Kluck on the west could spare men to strengthen the weak German lines round

Munster Fusiliers—acted on the left of General Bulfin's force. This was the bold, decisive movement on the part of Sir Douglas that won the day and enabled the British Army to add one more resounding victory to its glorious annals.

During the severe pressure thus brought to bear on the German lines, a party of the North Lancashires captured the sugar factory before Zwehl's men arrived to strengthen the enemy's position at Cerny, on the Chemin des Dames road. By noon on **Capture of the factory** Monday the two advanced British **at Troyon** brigades held a straight line near the top of the ridge between the factory and the Chemin des Dames. But as Zwehl's men were arriving north and east of the factory, and using shell fire and Maxim fire against any British attacking force, no further headway could be made. In fact, all the 1st Division was at once hard put to it to maintain the ground they had won. For Zwehl was a fierce, hard, straight hitter of the old Prussian school.

He sent out reconnoitring patrols to the south-west of Sir Douglas Haig's position on the heights, and discovered

the sugar factory at Troyon. Field-Marshal von Heeringen, directing the defence by field telephones from Laon, had nothing with which to stop the gap when Sir Douglas Haig was striking with all his force.

For when, on Monday morning, Sir Douglas found that General Bulfin's three brigades were not strong enough to storm the sugar factory, he brought up the 1st Brigade round Troyon. The 1st Coldstream Guards joined in the frontal attack upon the former position, while the rest of the 1st Brigade—the 1st Scots Guards, the 1st Royal Highlanders, and the

SCENE DURING THE SHELLING OF SOISSONS.
Shell bursting over Soissons, during the bombardment of that place by the Germans.
Inset: Entrance to the famous quarries at Soissons, where the Germans entrenched themselves, but were "dug out" by the French.

"HOME FROM HOME" ON THE AISNE.
Comfortable huts of wood, with rush-thatched roofs, were built by the French as rest houses in the intervals of trench work on the Aisne.

into the firing-line and blew away all opposition that the Guards fought a path to the foot of Ostel ridge.

In the meantime the 6th Brigade—made up of the 1st Liverpools, the 2nd South Staffordshires, the 1st Berkshires, and the 1st King's Royal Rifles—passed over the ground won by the 5th Brigade the day before, and moved along the valley of Braye towards the narrow neck of the plateau. But here also the German artillery fire was so skilfully and massively directed as to make any infantry advance impossible. Both from the ridge in front and from the hills on either side the German guns thundered. Sir Douglas Haig determined to clear the hills that flanked the valley. This was indeed necessary in order to ensure the advance made round the sugar factory on the neighbouring heights. So a superb force of guns—the 34th Brigade of the Field Artillery, the 44th Howitzer Brigade, and batteries of sixty-pounders—came to the help of the infantry. This Thor-like thunderstroke broke down the German war machinery in the Braye valley, and the brave 6th **A Thor-like thunderstroke** Brigade was able to press onward. A footing was won on the heights round La Cour de Soupir, and farther to the north-east, at Chivy, near the Chemin des Dames.

By this time, however, General von Zwehl had got full control of the situation. Collecting the troops that held the ridge, and re-forming them with his 18,000 men—soon increased by reinforcements to 40,000—he was able to assume the offensive. For both in gun power and rifle power he had at least double the strength of the British general, and the magnificent advantage of position increased the fighting force at his disposal. Before the gap between the hills and valleys, where Haig's separated 1st and 2nd Divisions were struggling, could be closed by the successful advance of the 6th Brigade and the Guards, Zwehl struck through it. He sent a strong infantry column over the road from Cerny to Bourg. But when it reached the heights north of Pont Arcy, the last brigade of the 1st Division, which was trying to connect with the troops of the 2nd Division, came upon it. It was the Queen's, the South Wales Borderers, the 1st Gloucester Regiment, and the 2nd Welsh Regiment that stood in the way of the German movement which aimed at cutting Sir Douglas Haig's army corps into two fragments and surrounding the Guards Brigade and the 6th Brigade.

in the morning there was a gap between the 1st and 2nd Divisions. Practically all the available men of the 1st Division occupied the ground east of the road running from Bourg to Cerny. The leading brigades of the 2nd Division—the Guards Brigade and the 6th Infantry Brigade—were working up the ravine at Ostel and the valley of Braye, separated from each other by a high hill held by the Germans, and with some seven miles of difficult country between Ostel and the sugar factory. Both of these separated brigades were held up by German gun and Maxim fire. The Guards had to pass through dense woods, under a terrible storm of shrapnel and bullets, and it was not until some of their gallant gunners brought a section of the field artillery right

UNDER AND ABOVE GROUND ALONG THE AISNE.
Above are two graphic views within and without the French entrenchments along the Aisne. The lower view shows alterations and repairs in progress. Inset is seen a soldier at one of the observation points, from which the enemy's movements could be detected.

BRITISH MILITARY BRIDGE OVER THE AISNE.
The Royal Engineers, having completed their work, are resting, while various sections of their comrades in the combatant ranks are passing over, some of them with improvised rain cloaks over their shoulders.

A REGIMENTAL KITCHEN ON THE AISNE.
A shell fell here, killing a number of the men seen in the group shortly after this photograph was taken.

Only two of the British battalions went forward to stop the German column. But by giving the Teutons, who were mainly reserve troops, the mad minute of rapid rifle fire, mingled with a stream of bullets from four Maxim guns, the compact grey mass was shattered and thrown back. This for a time relieved the pressure on the Guards and the 6th Brigade, but the connecting force from the 1st Division was again attacked in the afternoon before it had joined across the hill of Chivy. For about one o'clock on Monday General von Zwehl ordered all his troops to advance, and every man in the First British Army Corps was tested to the limit of his endurance and fighting ability.

The space between the British lines near Troyon and the German lines near Cerny was carpeted with the bodies of dead and wounded men. In one violent

Four miles of debatable land sweep the British, according to General von Zwehl, got into his lines and forced his troops back, but he recovered the ground by a counter-attack. The debatable land between the two forces was four miles long and half a mile wide, and such was the fury of battle that all who attempted to reach the wounded were themselves killed. For two days and nights the men in the trenches heard the heartrending cries of the injured, helpless men, and the sounds almost drove the troops mad. The Germans acquired an insane ferocity, and took a diabolical delight in shelling the buildings from which the British Red Cross flag was flying. Their snipers brought down our stretcher-bearers and Red Cross men, and turned war into murder. But the intensity of hatred that brought out the baseness of the Germans did not increase their fighting ability.

Our men were cool and steady at their deadly work, in spite of the anger burning in their bodies. They tempted their enemies to attack, and mowed them down with a rifle fire that was almost as overpowering as a machine-gun stream of bullets. By no force that Zwehl could bring

against them could he shift the men of the 1st and 2nd Infantry Brigades from the commanding height they had won. For three weeks the number of dead men continued to increase as the terrible slaughter took place between the hostile lines. The smell of the decaying corpses became so fearful that the soldiers on both sides smoked tobacco for three weeks without a break to keep themselves from sickening. The available tobacco in the German Army was commandeered for use by the troops at Cerny to induce them to stick to their dreadful position. According to General von Zwehl, he lost some 9,000 men in vain endeavours to hurl the British from their position.

The only occasion when he was near success was on the Monday afternoon when he just arrived from Maubeuge.

He could not break the British line near the Chemin des Dames at Cerny, but a second attempt he made to cut the connection between Sir Douglas Haig's 1st and 2nd Divisions was with extreme difficulty countered, for he succeeded in driving a wedge between the two British forces, and even got on the lines of communication of the Guards Brigade and the 6th Brigade. The Guards, who were the farthest off from their directing general, put up a magnificent fight.

Germans' enormous artillery advantage The 6th Brigade, meeting with a shattering rifle fire from a height, stormed the hill and took it with the bayonet. Then, as the Germans were flying in all directions, a double hail of machine-gun bullets struck the victors. Some of the King's Royal Rifles saw two German machine-guns on the top of a hayrick; they set the hay alight and the machine-gun men were burnt. The fighting was hard and terrific, and the fire of the German guns and howitzers was calculated to demoralise any ordinary troops. For when the guns from Maubeuge were added

twelve guns, and the main movement against the First Army Corps ended in a British success.

At the same time the 6th Brigade, menaced by the same German movement, was working through the next valley eastward past the hamlet of Beaulne-et-Chivy. About one o'clock on Monday the Germans attacked them as they moved up the hillside, where the shells fell on them all the way. Some battalions sheltered in the thick woods between the open spaces, but these were also searched by the hostile gunners. On the crest of the main hill two lines of German infantry were entrenched, with machine-guns at intervals, but as the British brigade had an unusual number of light and heavy guns as a support, their infantry attack was covered by such a terrible shrapnel fire as no German could stand. The foes were driven out of the trenches, and as they retreated in huge masses over the opposite hillside, our guns caught them and mowed them down like fields of wheat. Our men entrenched on the position they won at Chivy, within a thousand yards of the main German lines on the top of the plateau.

On Monday night the British trenches stretched from a point north of the sugar factory at Troyon to Chivy, then across the valley of Braye to La Cour de Soupir and Chavonne. Eastwards of the British force were the Moroccan troops entrenched in steps on the right rear. Westward the 3rd Division, forming the right wing of Sir Horace Smith-Dorrien's Second Army Corps, was entrenched a mile north of Vailly. It had advanced towards the heights of Aizy till it was checked by a fierce artillery fire, under cover of which a German infantry column delivered a counter-attack. This compelled General Hamilton to withdraw towards Vailly. The 4th and 5th Divisions, near Missy and Bucy-le-Long, were still subjected to a terrific bombardment, and could do no more than maintain their ground at the foot of the hills of Vregny and Chivres.

The peculiar formation of the ground between Soissons and Missy, as Sir John French afterwards remarked in his despatch, made the high German positions, defended with modern artillery firing 8 in. shells a distance of 10,000 yards, practically impregnable.

The 5th Division could not remain alive on the southern edge of that flat-topped Chivres hill, as the German batteries on the Vregny hill were able to direct a flank fire on the British trenches. The troops, therefore, had at last to retire towards **British force the** the villages of Marguérite and Missy, **passage of the Aisne** which their commander, Sir Charles Fergusson, retained throughout the long siege battle, though his trenches were on much lower ground than the enemy occupied only four hundred yards away.

All that had been accomplished between Soissons and Vailly by Tuesday, September 15th, was to maintain a strong number of bridge-heads along the Aisne, at the foot of the great buttressed tableland. But between Vailly and Bourg the First British Army Corps and the Cavalry Division held a series of commanding heights which enabled the entire force and part of the Fifth French Army to cope on fairly equal terms with the German armies.

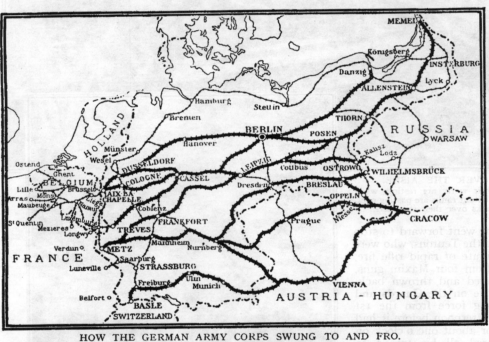

HOW THE GERMAN ARMY CORPS SWUNG TO AND FRO.
The above map of the main German railways and their connections will enable the reader to understand how the Germans were able to transfer their troops east or west, in response to the pressure exerted by the Allies or according to the requirements of the German Headquarters Staff.

to the unusually powerful ordnance of the German western wing, the German superiority in artillery was enormous.

By a massed cross gun fire at the critical spot, followed by a rushing infantry attack, Zwehl at last cut Sir Douglas Haig's forces into two. And, though all the British troops of the First Army Corps fought on heroically, they could do no more than hold their ground. What was needed was more men to occupy the position against which the Germans were progressing in their enveloping movement. Sir Douglas had used his last man, and he called for aid on his Commander-in-Chief. Sir John French placed the Cavalry Division of some 9,000 men at the disposal of his brilliant general, and, with the horsemen fighting in infantry fashion, Haig lengthened out the left flank of the Guards Brigade and secured it from being turned.

When the Germans closed for the great attack the position of the Guards had altered since their scouting patrols had studied it. Our crack regiments fought with the remarkable skill and bodily strength, which, joined to their steadiness of nerve, make them among the most splendid infantrymen in the world. In the end the enemy were driven back after losing a great number of men and

FRENCH ALPINE CHASSEURS, WHO GAVE A GOOD ACCOUNT OF THEMSELVES IN THE VOSGES.

Specially trained and equipped for mountaineering work, the "Chasseurs Alpins" displayed their excellent fighting qualities in the Vosges. In the above picture we see a group of these intrepid mountaineers resting for a meal outside a village churchyard. Inset: A detachment of "Chasseurs Alpins" in action with one of the guns, which were specially made so as to be readily taken to pieces for transport by mules.

IN THE GERMAN TRENCHES ON THE AISNE DURING A NIGHT ENGAGEMENT.
From a drawing made on the spot by a German artist.

The passage of the Aisne had been forced, in spite of the tremendous siege-artillery and the extraordinary number of field-guns with which the plateau of Soissons had been defended. Far from breaking against the vast natural fortress as Napoleon's troops had broken against Blücher's in 1814, the Allies of 1914 had won such a footing on the heights that Heeringen's armies were besieged, and they continued to remain in the inferior position of an attacked garrison force for many months.

Heeringen at first did not tamely submit to this condition of things. When the effect of General von Zwehl's reinforcement of men and guns was exhausted—which quickly happened on Tuesday, September 15th—there was a day's interval of relaxed effort. During this the 3rd Division under General Hamilton, at Vailly, advanced again up the ravine of Vailly and recovered the ground it had lost near Aizy hill. It was done by massing our artillery fire on the German trenches on the heights, where the enemy suffered so severely from shell and shrapnel that he evacuated his position. This was then seized by our troops and made another im-

Heeringen strongly reinforced portant point of power against the main hostile fortified lines on the top-most ridge. The next day, however, Heeringen received large new forces. His own Lorraine army, whose operations had become insignificant after the Crown Prince was compelled to retire from the gap he had blown in the Verdun-Toul line, was drawn on for reinforcements. All the men that could be spared in Belgium were railed down, through Maubeuge, to the distributing centre at Laon, and great masses of soldiers of the reserve and militia classes were obtained from Germany. Moreover, the men of Kluck's, Bülow's, Hausen's, and Würtemberg's armies were recovering from the wear and fatigue of the retreat from the Marne. Though strangely reduced in number by death, injury, and sickness, the troops of the four beaten forces were young men of the first line, composing the supreme striking force of their Empire. They were now supported by siege-howitzers as well as by thousands of their own powerful field-pieces.

The German machine of war was really stronger than it had been on former battlefields, and, though the human element was weakened by defeat, the reinforcements brought the number of the troops up to something like two millions and a half. Deducting the men retained in Belgium and Lorraine and Alsace, there were probably nearly two millions of German soldiers entrenched from Peronne to the north of Verdun and round Nancy, or within call as reserves on the nearer lines of communication. This was a considerably larger force than General Joffre was using for attack in his great lines, for the French Commander-in-Chief still held to the Napoleonic doctrine of maintaining away from the fighting-line a large reserve army. On these considerations the German Military Staff, of which Helmuth von Moltke was still chief, determined to attempt to recover the offensive.

On Thursday, September 17th, the Battle of the Aisne thus entered on a new phase. From Compiègne to the hills of the Suippes and the Argonne Forest the Franco-British forces were no longer the attackers. The positions they had won on the slopes of the plateau of Soissons, on the hills round Rheims, and on the low ridges of the plain of Champagne were all violently **German attempt to recover the offensive** assailed by hostile infantry, advancing by day and night after their guns had bombarded the allied lines.

It was, however, the First Army Corps that had to bear the brunt of the great German counter-attack on Thursday, September 17th. As the Fifth French Army had not been able to get a high footing on the hill of Craonne on our right, our right flank could be continually threatened from the heights eastward of those won by our 1st Division. The French Moroccan troops, ranged down our flank, were an excellent support, but the enemy's artillery round Craonne rendered any advance we made towards Cerny only a temporary affair. Sir John French reckoned that he could have carried the ridges in front of our lines by means of the new 6th Division, but the position at Craonne would have left our right flank open to attack.

Even as it was, our flank was fiercely assailed on Thursday

FIGHTING IN THE WOODED REGION OF THE ARGONNE.
German infantry in their trenches. Part of the force under the Crown Prince, whose tactics in the Argonne were regarded generally as a failure.

afternoon by General von Zwehl's reinforced troops. By way of diversion, the 2nd Northamptons, occupying the most advanced position on the allied front, with their trenches on the Chemin des Dames on the plateau, attacked the German lines at Cerny. The affair began in a very remarkable way. A company of one hundred and sixty Northamptons, with a captain and two lieutenants, had dug themselves in along the road on Monday. In front of them was a turnip-field, across which, at a distance of two hundred and fifty yards, was the foremost trench of General von Zwehl's troops. Directly opposed to the one hundred and sixty Northamptons were some five hundred Germans, and the Englishmen were kept under a continual bombardment, night and day, with infantry attacks at intervals, so that they could get scarcely any sleep.

It rained heavily, and the roadside trench filled with water, that rose to the knees of the defenders. German snipers shot any man who showed above the earth. The captain had been shot though the head, and one of the lieutenants had been fatally wounded. Food and water could only be provided by men crawling up on their stomachs in the darkness. But the Germans did not have it all their own way. The marksman of the Northampton company, his head wreathed in turnip-leaves, was stretched out at length in the middle of the turnip-field, under the torrents of rain. Any head showing against the northern sky-line received a bullet from the English sniper.

The sniper in the turnip-field

Some seventy wounded Germans, rescued from the battlefield on Monday, rested behind the British trench under cover of a haystack, but on Wednesday a German shell set the hay on fire and burnt most of the Germans, who were too badly wounded to crawl away. On Thursday the five hundred Germans across the turnip-field apparently sickened of the terrible, wearing struggle. They made some attempts at a rush, and were broken up by our rifle fire. Then they put up their arms or held out their rifles as a signal of surrender. The remaining officer of the Northamptons—a sub-lieutenant of less than a year's

GERMAN "SPLINTER-PROOF" IN THE AISNE AREA.
The German trenches were wonderful examples of Teutonic thoroughness, They were usually three feet in depth and constructed on scientific principles in parallel lines, flanked by others in which machine-guns were concealed. They had, at intervals, "splinter-proof" shelters such as that above illustrated.

service—was cautious. He motioned to the Germans to quit their trenches and come over the turnip-field and give up their arms. They came over in a mass.

The lieutenant went to meet them. A German private tried to parley. The British officer shouted for the German officer to step forward. Meanwhile the Germans were coming forward and were close to the trench. Then a German officer with a sergeant and private advanced. "You surrender, for you are my prisoner!" said the young lieutenant. "No! You are mine!" yelled the German. Either he was beside himself with anger at seeing how small was the force to which he was surrendering with his men—or, more likely, the affair was a carefully premeditated act of treachery.

The lieutenant of the Northamptons at once shot the German officer and non-commissioned officer, but the German private with them put a bullet through him in turn. The small company of Northamptons at the time were standing in front of their trenches, taking rifles from the nearest Germans and shaking their hands. But the greater number of the enemy retained their weapons, and

A CAVE WHICH ACCOMMODATED A WHOLE BRITISH CAVALRY SQUADRON.
Around the Aisne plateau the cliffs are riddled with caves, in which the villagers kept their firewood, hens, pigs, etc. In one of them an officer recorded that he found a whole squadron of British cavalry, and room for a regiment beside. He found there also any number of women and children, and teams of oxen and horses ; also a donkey with a German bullet in him. This cave had only one small entrance.

began to fire point-blank at the Englishmen. So a wild tussle began on the edge of the British trench, with the outnumbered defenders in a hopeless position.

Fortunately, at a range of four hundred yards from the roadside trench, the Queen's Regiment—the West Surreys —held their line. One of their machine-guns flanked the position of the Northamptons so as to assist in repelling any hostile charge. The machine-gun section of the Queen's had been disabled, but the commanding officer, Colonel Warren, with the help of Captain Watson, served the gun. They poured a devastating fire into the mean-spirited tricksters, until a shrapnel shell from a German gun burst by the Maxim and shattered it and killed both officers.

In the meantime some of the Coldstream Guards, who had also seen the disaster to the heroic Northamptons, came up at the double, as the German curs were fleeing from the Maxim fire. The Guards got among the wretches with the bayonet, and scarcely a hundred out of five hundred, of them got away. Three hundred were shot or bayoneted and a hundred surrendered to the Coldstreams. It is a pity their surrender was accepted, for out of the hundred and sixty Northamptons who had been deceived by their first offer only twelve men were left standing, and four of these were wounded.

BUSY SCENE AT A FRENCH AVIATION BASE.
Repairing landing wheels for aircraft at an aviation base in Northern France.

It was a terrible afternoon for all the Northamptons. Scarcely had the rest of the battalion steadied their raging anger at the foul trick played on their heroic leading company, when some 3,000 Germans of the 53rd Regiment, expecting no doubt that the affair had at least weakened the British defence, advanced over the turnips. From the furious " Cobblers " and the Queen's the new assailers got so lively a welcome that those of them who retained the use of their legs turned and ran.

But this was not sufficient revenge for the Northamptons for their betrayed comrades. They wanted to get among the Germans with the bayonet. They soon got their chance. Under cover of a mist that came over the plateau, some of Zwehl's troops, finding the British front trenches impregnable, began to press severely on the right flank. As a counterstroke, the Northamptons and Queen's, reinforced by the King's Royal Rifles, were ordered by Sir Douglas Haig to drive up against the German lines round Cerny.

Naturally, the Northamptons led. Veiled by the mist, they crawled over the turnip-field without being discovered. Close to the German trenches they rose and charged with the bayonet, stabbed the surprised line of enemy troops, then went on to the crest of the plateau, where Zwehl had dug in a second line of men to protect his guns. Again the Northamptons reached the German trenches, through a hail of bullets and machine-gun fire. But the enemy were in such force that many Northamptons died as they were using their bayonets furiously. Their terrible charge, however, held the enemy, and the Queen's quickly worked up to a point from which they enfiladed the German lines from the left, while the King's Royal Rifles wheeled on their right. At the same time a squadron of our cavalry joined in the attack, and the Germans were driven over the ridge with heavy loss. This magnificent advance on September 17th lifted the wing of the British army right on to the plateau. It was our high-water mark on the Aisne. It was, moreover, carried out at a time when Heeringen had strongly reinforced his armies and launched them on that general offensive against the allied front which was intended to knock the British and French armies out of their positions and result in a great disaster to them.

The advance on the height was so successful that Sir John French thought of taking the bridge at Condé, lower down the river, and consolidating the positions of the two divisions of the Second Army Corps. But Sir Horace

PRESIDENT POINCARE'S BOMBARDED VILLA AT SAMPIGNY. When at Triancourt, in the Meuse district, the Germans pillaged and wrecked the house of M. Lucien Poincaré. At Aubecourt they destroyed the chateau of his parents. They then bombarded the village of Sampigny, where the French President had his own villa and was the owner of most of the property.

Smith-Dorrien was satisfied with the situation of his men. He had his guns so disposed that a German force trying to sally over the bridge would be annihilated. Any British advance would automatically force the enemy out of Condé. So the German was allowed to remain in possession of it.

In fact, Sir John French resolved not to push the Germans back anywhere, but to wait for them to attack and then punish them. For on Thursday, General Joffre informed the British commander that he had been compelled to make a new plan. All the allied armies in action had now to hold the Germans in the present position. A new French force was being sent north to assail and, if possible, turn the western flank of the enemy at Peronne.

With this new movement the Battle of the Aisne entered on a third phase. First there was the allied offensive; then the German counter-offensive; now it had become a containing operation, with the decisive action happening elsewhere. As it would take some time for the effect of General Joffre's new plan to make itself felt by seriously weakening the German power of offensive, our troops

CAPTURED GERMAN OFFICER BEING EXAMINED BY MEMBERS OF A FRENCH GENERAL STAFF. As the official British "Eye-Witness" pointed out, since the composition of the larger formations of all armies was known, it was possible to extract vital information from the connection of even a single soldier killed or captured at a certain point with a certain battalion. It was part of the duties of a General Staff to piece together the information gained from prisoners, as well as from their own agents.

had to deepen and improve their trenches, and arrange for a regular sort of open-air siege warfare. But the Gloucesters, holding a foremost position on the height near Chivy, west of the lines above the sugar factory at Troyon, found on Friday night, September 18th, that attack was still the best means of defence. They took the enemy's trenches in the darkness, and captured two machine-guns.

Enemy's trenches taken in the darkness　　　All the front positions of the First Army Corps were furiously attacked by the Germans that night. In many cases the Germans were not content with one repulse, but brought up their reserves, and after bombarding our trenches, came on again in close compact masses, lit by our searchlights and pierced by our field-guns. Where the shrapnel failed to scatter them, the rapid fire of our infantry broke up the German formations. On Saturday evening, September 19th, and throughout Sunday the First Army Corps was subjected to fierce attacks by daylight and in the darkness. Zwehl, no doubt, was now fully reinforced to 40,000 men, and he had in addition portions of Bülow's and Kluck's armies which had been placed under his command. Having, unlike Kluck, no full experience of the

in Northern Europe ranks among the finest military achievements in our history. The river flats, the forested slopes, the winding ravines, the upper heights were scenes of many acts of British heroism that will never be told.

One of the most romantic of these exploits was carried out by some privates of the 1st Coldstream Guards. With their Colonel Ponsonby, a party of the Coldstreams went out at night to the German lines to discover the positions of the enemy's machine-guns. This they did, but while stumbling among the German troops, they were also discovered, and a fierce rifle fire was directed at them. Colonel Ponsonby was shot, and fell in the open ground under the German fire, and two of his men—Private Jones and Private Vennicombe—dashed through the stream of bullets towards their officer's body.

He had been shot in the leg, and was unable to walk. They carried him back to the main body of reconnoitres—forty in all—and it was seen that the only thing to be done was to retire. Under the leadership of an officer of the Black Watch, the men got into the shelter of a wood, carrying the wounded colonel with them. Then they found they were in the German lines, with two hostile outposts before them. One of the enemy's convoys passed close to them, but they were not strong enough to attack. After a tramp of some six miles the party got through the German position at Cerny, four men carrying the colonel in turn, and rejoined their battalion in the morning.

In a lower part of the battle-field, during the fierce German attack all along the allied front, a daring feat was performed by a Highlander. He was one of a small detachment of one hundred and fifty Scotsmen who were guarding a bridge-head by the Aisne towards Soissons. No attack was expected, and the detachment was merely placed by the bridge as an ordinary precaution. But suddenly the Germans, on the scarp overlooking the river, opened fire, and under cover of the guns a strong hostile force, far outnumbering the British detachment, sprang from the wooded slopes and came on at a run towards the bridge. At first the Highlanders kept the attackers back by steady, rapid fire; but the Germans, though dropping and slackening their pace as they sought for cover, drew nearer and nearer. At the same time a larger hostile force, in a compact column, also came into view on the road leading from the plateau to the bridge.

A WAR PHOTOGRAPHER'S NERVE: REMARKABLE INCIDENT IN THE VOSGES.
A French despatch-rider having had his horse shot by the enemy, dismounted and dashed into a house on the roadside, where a party of his compatriots were resting. A few seconds later the Germans were accounted for. The photographer who had the temerity to halt and take the picture escaped injury.

stopping power of the British magazine rifle in the hands of British marksmen, both Heeringen and Zwehl tried continually by mass infantry attacks to hurl our men down from the heights they had won. But what 8 in. siege-artillery shells could not effect, no sacrifice of cannon fodder could accomplish. None of our dominating gun positions was lost, and on September 23rd these gun positions became more formidable. For four 6 in. howitzer batteries arrived from England, and enabled Sir Douglas Haig and Sir Horace Smith-Dorrien to play the German game, and get cross-fire and high-angle effects at longer distances than the enemy had arranged for when he completed his entrenchments.

With these additional weapons of siege warfare, the British positions became absolutely secure. Both Sir John French and his men began to tire of their inactivity, and the British commander worked out a scheme of new operations before Calais, that led, early in October, to the shifting of the British Expeditionary Force to the new battlefield around Ypres. So, from the British point of view, the operations on the Aisne came to a close.

But never will the Aisne be forgotten by either Frenchmen or men of the British Empire. The part our troops played in the assault upon the greatest natural fortress

One of the Highlanders leaped from the ground, where he had been firing from cover. He had seen that the Maxim gun at the other end of the bridge had ceased working, as all its section had been killed. Running forward under a hail of bullets he reached the Maxim, swung it with its tripod on his back, and carried it at a run across the bridge. The belt was at once charged, and the soldier sat down and opened fire on the nearing German column, while his companions **How a Highlander** held back the other Germans. **kept the bridge**

So well did the solitary Highlander direct the machine-gun that he emptied the cartridges in the belt right on the head of the column. The German troops broke and fled for shelter on either side of the road, leaving a heap of dead and wounded. Soon after the Highlander tumbled down by his gun, with thirty bullets in his body. But he had saved his comrades and kept the bridge; and the enemy afterwards retreated to the heights.

WOUNDED SOLDIERS CHARGE THE GERMANS—GALLANT DEED OF YORKSHIRE LIGHT INFANTRY.

"About twenty of us," stated Private Crossland, of the Yorkshire Light Infantry, "were lying wounded in an underground cellar beneath a small chapel, adjoining a roofless farmhouse blackened with shell fire. We thought we were safe, when suddenly we were attacked by a score of Germans. Only nine of us were capable of resistance, and with rifles and revolvers and anything we could lay hands on we went for the enemy, and after a fierce tussle accounted for all but two. Four of our men were recommended for the D.C.M., and one—a sergeant—for the V.C."

Staff-Captain C. H. Vandersluys, of the 4th Infantry Brigade, part of the Canadian Contingent which arrived in England on October 15th, 1914.

Men of the First Canadian Contingent constructing barbed-wire and live-wire entangle[ments] during their training on Salisbury Plain.

Part of a hut kitchen in the camp of the First Canadian Contingent on Salisbury Plain. The commissariat department had to arrange for the feeding of nearly 30,000 men.

Band of the 12th Battalion of the First Canadian Contingent. They were photo[graphed] outside one of the specially constructed huts.

An early morning shave under difficulties. The carpenter's wooden trestle afforded a somewhat rough-and-ready substitute for the barber's chair.

Officers of the 12th Battalion (left to right): Lieutenants S. Ryder, Sanson, and Adams; Ca[ptains] Fraser, McAvity, Van Wart, Ogilvie, and Sutherland; Lieutenants Stirling and McNalley

CONTINGENT ON SALISBURY PLAIN.

the exceptionally rainy autumn and winter, training on Salisbury Plain rendered road-making a necessary part of the operations.

Captain H. H. Van Wart and Signalling Section of the 12th Battalion of the First Canadian Contingent at work with the heliograph.

and men of the First Canadian Contingent getting their hands in at entrenching work on the outskirts of their encampment on Salisbury Plain.

Another view of the Canadians in training on Salisbury Plain. The beginning of a trench near a pine plantation. The men look very fit.

of the 12th Battalion (back): Lt. Morgan, Lt. Adams, Capt. Sutherland, Lt. McDonald, Lt. Brosseau. McAvity, Lt. Bowen; (front): Lt. Cramford, Capt. Van Wart, Maj. Guthrie, Capt. Dove.

Two men of the First Canadian Contingent returning from leave. They are meeting their old friend the mud, which, despite the road-making, proved invincible.

GERMANS FORCING A FRENCH FARMER TO THRESH HIS CORN FOR THEIR BENEFIT.

The Germans have never tired of repeating Napoleon's jibe at the British as "a nation of shopkeepers." But the conduct of the Germans in the Great War would seem to have shown a desire on their part to qualify as a nation of shoplifters. From Crown Prince to private they plundered wherever they penetrated, in the chateau of a baroness or the simple home of a peasant. They even collected crops and forwarded them to the Fatherland; and the above picture shows a French farmer being compelled to thresh his corn for the benefit of the ruthless invader.

CHAPTER XXXVIII.

BATTLES AND BOMBARDMENTS OF THE AISNE AND SUIPPES.

Sixth French Army Forces Passage of Aisne—Wild Struggles in Ravines and on Heights—Bombardment of Soissons—Fifth French Army Swings Up the Headland of Craonne—Reinforced German Armies Counter-Attack—Attempts to Pierce French Centre Fail—The Maddened, Baffled Enemy Destroys Rheims Cathedral—Raid on French Railway Communication—Death's Head Hussars Mowed Down by Gun Fire—Prussian Guard Trapped Amid Vineyards—Forest Fighting in the Argonne—Metz Army Captures Fort Between Verdun and Toul—French Stop the Gap on the Heights of the Meuse.

IT was no fatigue on the part of the Allies that prevented the French armies, in the Battles of the Aisne and Suippes Rivers, from driving into the German fortified positions and winning a series of points of vantage there. The French were less successful than the British mainly because they lacked a weapon with the range and weight of shell of our heavy field batteries. When the Germans turned to make a stand, on the plateau of Soissons and the swell of low heights running from Rheims to the Argonne Forest, they brought their siege-artillery on the scene. The big German howitzers, beginning with 6 in. shells and increasing to 11 in. shells as the Maubeuge train arrived, dominated the battlefield. The French 3 in. field-gun and small field-howitzer, though admirable in a struggle in the open field, were not long-ranged enough for the new kind of siege warfare that began on the Aisne.

The result was that the French soldiers suddenly found themselves at a disadvantage. Yet they redressed the balance in armament by the vigour and steady persistence of their infantry attack. At need, they charged the German guns with the bayonet, and at the loss of half a battalion won the hostile battery. Even when the German armies were so strongly reinforced that they outnumbered the French by three to two in men, and had behind them an overpowering superiority in heavy artillery, the French continued to hold them back. The French never lost the position of being the besiegers; the Germans

THE WRECKED ROOF OF RHEIMS CATHEDRAL.
Photograph showing the destruction by fire of Rheims Cathedral, the "Westminster Abbey of France," in September, 1914.

never recovered from the position of being the besieged. In other words, General Joffre retained the power of initiative that he won by the victory of the Marne. He was always acting on the offensive, and compelling the German Commander-in-Chief—Moltke or Falkenhayn or Kaiser Wilhelm—to answer his moves. At no time was the enemy able to recover from his first great defeat.

Fierce and continual, however, were the efforts that the German armies made to resume the power of initiative and act on the offensive. At an early stage in the new campaign they won the tactical power of attack. They attacked with surprising fury. They threw the Franco-British armies all along the front on the defensive; they won various points of advantage between Noyon and Soissons, and between Craonne and Rheims and the Argonne ridge. But they never recovered the initiative. General Joffre was their master. He decided what plan of attack they should adopt, and forced them to follow that plan. Such is the power of initiative in the hands of a man with a genius for generalship.

At first General Joffre's subordinate commanders had matters in their own hands. They merely had to pursue the retreating German armies, and attack them when they threw out rearguards or made a general stand. General Maunoury, with the Sixth French Army, attacked General von Kluck, with the First German Army, from Noyon to Soissons. Then, as we have seen, the British Expeditionary Force attacked part of Kluck's army, and Zwehl's new army, and part of

245

Bülow's army, between Soissons and Bourg. From a point a few miles below Bourg to Rheims, General Franchet d'Espérey, with the Fifth French Army, attacked Bülow's main force that held the bold headland of Craonne. South of the Suippes River, General Foch and General de Langle Cary attacked the armies of the Duke of Würtemberg and the Crown Prince. Round Verdun, General Sarrail, with the Second French Army, was menaced by the Bavarians and a remnant of the Metz garrison, who were using 12 in. howitzers.

The main force concentrated round Metz, under the command of Field-Marshal von Heeringen, was withdrawn westward to reinforce Kluck, Zwehl, and Bülow. At the same time the German troops in Belgium, under General von Böhn, were railed southwards to Laon to strengthen further the four armies under Heeringen. All this was done, towards the end of the second week in September, with a view to bringing a preponderating force of men and guns to bear against the Sixth French Army, the British force, and the Fifth French Army. It was designed to force back or break the western wing of the allied front, so that the Germans could recover the initiative and resume their march on Paris.

Some days elapsed, however, before the effect of this new German concentration made itself felt. In the meantime all the Allies made progress. To General Maunoury and his Sixth Army fell the first honours of the Battle of the Aisne and **First honours of the** Suippes. Marching from **Battle of the Aisne** the Ourcq in pursuit of Kluck's troops, General Maunoury spread his forces out on a wide front from the Forest of Compiègne to a point below Soissons. He cleared Compiègne of Germans, and then at the point where the Aisne flows into the Oise he crossed the first-named river and advanced towards the cathedral city of Noyon, through the Forest of the Eagle—le Foret de l'Aigle.

But this second tract of woodland was dominated by the eastern scarp of the plateau of Soissons. On this high, flat, forested tableland, scarred with quarries, tunnelled with caves, and hollowed and seamed on its southern face by valleys and ravines, Kluck had placed his heavy artillery. It formed, on its northern edge round

MAJOR-GENERAL S. H. LOMAX.
While Sir Douglas Haig's 2nd Division was battling against superior forces at Pont Arcy and lower down the Aisne, his 1st Division, under Major-General Lomax, had an amazing success against the enemy near Bourg.

BRIGADIER-GENERAL E. S. BULFIN, C.V.O., C.B.
He was repeatedly mentioned in despatches by Sir John French. Up to the evening of November 2nd, 1914, when he was somewhat severely wounded, " his services continued to be of great value."

Nampscel, a lofty, level embankment which connected all the outlying southern spurs with each other, so that guns and men could be shifted about the high lands, without crossing the ravines through which brooks fell into the Aisne. The worn, narrow tableland resembled a gigantic fortress wall, and jutting out at intervals were bastions from which the river valley of the Aisne could be dominated by artillery fire, and any attacking party caught on the flank as it attempted to storm the main rampart.

On Sunday and Monday, September 13th and 14th, the passage of the river was forced. The French engineers threw pontoon bridges over the Aisne at Vic and Fontenoy, with the German guns shelling them from the outlying spurs of the plateau. Under the unceasing bombardment the French infantry crossed the wide stream and **Crux of the Battle of** began to penetrate into **the Lower Aisne** the ravines. Fighting magnificently, they pushed the Germans from the slopes above the river, the handy little French field-gun clearing the ground in front of them by shrapnel fire. They occupied the ravine of Nouvron, a few miles east of Soissons, and entered the valley of Morsain above Vic.

This valley of Morsain was the crux of the Battle of the Lower Aisne, in which the Sixth French Army was engaged. It began near the river, in a ravine with a narrow, winding neck dominated by two rugged prolongations of the main ridge of the plateau. The narrow neck afterwards widened into a broad hollow, extending for some miles at the base of the chief natural embankment. On the east side Nampscel could be attacked from it ; on the west side the heights round Nauvron might be carried from it. On the other hand, this inner valley in the tableland was practically encircled by the main rampart and its southern spurs. An army could be trapped in it, and then annihilated by the ring of guns on the heights.

General Maunoury boldly risked annihilation. He sent one of his army corps through the narrow neck above Vic. Disregarding the strong hostile force of artillery and infantry men on the slopes of the narrow passage, the French soldiers advanced rapidly under a heavy fire. They struck out towards the central ridge, and then veered and tried to get in the rear of the German advance guard, and cut them off from the principal German position. But the attempt failed. The Germans had by this time been strengthened. Heeringen, with the Seventh German Army, had taken charge of the entire defence of the plateau from Nampscel to Craonne.

French holding on by the river flats He massed guns and troops against Maunoury's men, and by Wednesday, September 16th, the French were back to the Aisne at Vic, desperately fighting to keep their footing on the northern bank. It was just like the position of the Second British Army Corps on the same day at Missy. The Germans had the advantage of a high position, heavy howitzers, and superior numbers of troops. All the French could do was to hold on by the river flats, under a terrible bombardment, and dig themselves into some sort of shelter.

There was a similar course of events in the valley of Nouvron westward, above Fontenoy. While Kluck, with his own tired, dispirited troops, was alone trying to hold all the high lands against his pursuers, the French

hastily-made earthworks near the **stream**. It was then that the French soldier learnt **to dig as he** had never dug before. Under the 8 in. shells from the siege-howitzers, all the French traditions of military science inherited from the Napoleonic period became for the time valueless. The French had to go further back to the almost-forgotten system of the old-fashioned trench battles of the days of Vauban and Turenne.

The same thing happened a little higher up the river at the beautiful historic cathedral city of Soissons. Here the British force co-operated with the right army corps of General Maunoury in both the advance on the city and the crossing of the river. On Saturday, September 12th, the Germans still held the Mont de Paris, a hill south of Soissons, against the attack of the right of the Sixth French Army. But, with the help of the heavy guns of our Third Corps, the Zouaves and Turcos got the German rearguard troops on the run, and pursued them to Soissons, where they destroyed the **German rearguard** bridges as they retired. When the section **pursued to Soissons** of bridging train allotted to our Third Corps arrived near Soissons, our engineers tried to throw a large pontoon bridge across the stream there. But the powerful German howitzer batteries on the height above the city were masters of the situation. Our bridge was shelled and shattered before it was completed, and the French had to get over the river in boats and rafts.

Even then the town could not be held by the Allies. For the enemy's guns were placed in the quarries of Pasly, two miles to the north, in positions prepared in peace time by German quarry-owners, working, no doubt, under the direction of the Great Military Staff at Berlin. From these howitzer platforms there began a terrific bombardment, which destroyed half the town, smote the beautiful abbey church of St. Jean des Vignes, struck the exquisite cathedral, gutted the hospital and seminary, and annihilated entire streets of dwelling-places.

Such was the return that the enterprising German merchants of Soissons made for the courteous, hospitable friendship which the simple, kindly townspeople had for years given them. They planned the destruction of the historic cathedral city of the Aisne—a quiet, unfortified, open town, mirrored in the waters of the loveliest river

Zouaves, weary with marching and fighting, but still full of dash, swept through the narrow neck and took the village of Nouvron. Then Heeringen arrived with reinforcements, collected from Belgium, Maubeuge, and the lines of communication, and flung the French back towards the river.

On Wednesday night, September 16th, it looked as though the extreme left wing of the Franco-British forces was about to be shattered. From the spurs above the Aisne the German searchlights swept the darkness with their beams, moving slowly over the river valley till, in the lane of white radiance, the French trenches could be perceived by German fire-control officers. Then the guns on the heights roared in a horrible chorus, and flung their shells in concentrated fury on the

BRITISH OFFICERS AT THE FRONT.
The circular photograph shows, in the order named, Colonel Greenly, General Gough, and Major Seligman engaged in a consultation on a railway line in Northern France. In the lower photograph are to be seen Major Seligman and General Gough (first and second figures from the left), and General Allenby (the left figure at the door of the motor-car).

KEEPING UP THE LINES OF COMMUNICATION.
French telegraph section re-establishing broken telegraph and telephone wires in the village of Foyon.

on either side. The German position was impregnable ; the French position was too stubbornly held to be taken.

South of the city, on the hills where the French guns were placed, the soldiers could see, in the rain-washed air of September, the prospect of that unhappy part of their land that the barbarian was trampling. In the west was the foliage of Compiègne, far in the north-west the town of St. Quentin—a panorama of wooded hills, grey villages set in yellow fields of grain, files of poplars marking the roads ; and below, the flashing waters of the Aisne and the canal, with the steeples of the cathedral and the gate of the abbey, where Thomas à Becket had lived.

Across the steeples sang the German shells, and along the valley on the right an observer could mark the flash of the British guns, and trace the rings of **When matters were** smoke as their shrapnel burst **at their worst** over the German lines. The jar and roar of cannon in front, around, and on either side were stunning to the ear. Most of the people of Soissons fled, but a remnant of some two thousand lived on till the end of the year in cellars, clinging to their shattered homes, and starving when the German artillery fire prevented the revictualling trains reaching them and the advanced French troops.

Matters were at their worst on Wednesday night, September 16th, all along the front of the Sixth French Army from Soissons to Compiègne. The French troops had not only to hold the enemy back on the Aisne, but to advance northward along

valley in France. No progress could be made by the French troops at Soissons, who were mainly turbaned Turcos from Algeria and Morocco. These coloured soldiers of France cleared the streets by splendid impetuous charges, backed by machine-gun sections and covered by field artillery that kept down the enemy's gun fire. But when the last German was forced out of Soissons, and the German rearguard was turned in the south-east at the village of Chauny, nothing more could be done. On a semicircle of heights beyond the River Aisne the German batteries were posted, with infantry entrenched in front of them at a distance of 1,300 yards from the centre of the town. From three points—Pasly, Braye, and Crouy—the Germans looked **Germans impregnable** down on Soissons and observed **on the heights** every movement of the French troops and every arrival of supplies. At any sign of activity, a devastating, concentrated gun and howitzer fire was directed on the French.

It was absolutely impossible to storm the heights. Any attempt, by day or by night, when the searchlights played from the hills, provoked a tempest of shrapnel shells that annihilated everything living on the slopes. As the French had only their light field batteries, they could make no effective reply to the howitzers hidden in the distant quarries. For months the bombardment of Soissons went on, without any marked success

IN THE WAKE OF THE "FUROR TEUTONICUS."
Ruins of a small French village as it was left by the German invaders.

the eastern bank of the Oise River, and try to get behind his tremendously strong position on the plateau. General Maunoury had not sufficient men to do these two things. In fact he was very hard put to it on Wednesday to retain his footing in the Aisne valley against the reinforced armies that Heeringen was hurling at him.

But General Joffre still continued to control the situation. He was using his Sixth Army to test the full strength of the forces that Heeringen had collected. The French Commander-in-Chief had a large reserve formed up on the flank of General Maunoury's front. He was waiting on events so as to put this reserve to the best use. But the pressure on the Sixth Army became so severe that a considerable force of the reserve was detached on Wednesday and sent towards the Aisne. General Joffre had cor-

French reserves rectly concluded that the great
brought to the Aisne struggle by the plateau of Soissons was not a mere delaying rearguard action on a large scale. It was a battle, in which the Germans were vehemently using all their available forces to obtain a decision.

The methods adopted by the French commander in this new critical position of affairs were characteristic of him. They were both bold and subtle, vigorous and cautious. Sir John French's army had won an important position on the plateau on the eastern side, and General Joffre did not want to forgo, if possible, this gain of a direct vantage point. On the other hand, he did not intend to follow Napoleon's plan of attack on

HOW THE SURRENDER OF RHEIMS WAS DEMANDED.
Immediately before the bombardment of Rheims in September, 1914, German parlementaires entered the town, under a flag of truce, to demand its surrender and the payment of a war indemnity. They were blindfolded and, accompanied by French officers, made the entry in motor-cars.

Blücher in the same place, and risk everything on a storming advance against a strong enemy in a magnificently defensive position. So he divided his reserve. Part went to reinforce the Sixth Army for a sweeping movement up the heights, part went to the rapid formation of a new Seventh Army, under General Castelnau, which was ordered to make a flank attack from the west against the German lines of communication.

Heeringen could not have it both ways. He could not reinforce his front strongly all along the plateau, occupying with men and guns all the spurs as well as the main ridge, and at the same time retain a large army in reserve for a turning movement round Compiègne. It was necessary to induce him to counter-attack along the entire river valley, in order to judge what force of infantry he was **Inducing Herringen** using on the plateau with his **to counter-attack** guns. When this was done on Wednesday night, the disposition of his troops was far more clearly revealed than it had been during the first Franco-British attack on the heights. There was no subtle gift of strategy in Field-Marshal von Heeringen's make of mind. He was simply a heavy hammerer, who aimed directly at his opponent's front with full force.

To make quite sure about this very important point, General Joffre, when sending a reinforcement

"BUSINESS AS USUAL" IN SHELL-SHATTERED RHEIMS.
A baker's shop in stricken Rheims having been completely destroyed by the daily bombardment of the German batteries, the proprietor moved next door, and coolly continued his "business as usual."

to his Sixth Army, ordered it to attack at dawn with the utmost vigour. The attack would not only test Heeringen's right wing, from which any possible turning movement would develop, but, in conjunction with the strong action of the British force on his centre and the Fifth French Army on his left wing at Craonne, it would engage the attention of the German commander until General Castelnau arrived against his flank.

So on Thursday, September 17th, the men of the Sixth French Army advanced. At Soissons they were content merely to hold the Germans back. Their two main assaults were delivered lower down the Aisne, at Fontenoy and at Vic. Through the two narrow-necked valleys of Nouvron and Morsain poured the Frenchmen, with their picturesque kinsmen the Zouaves, and their brown-faced and black-faced fellow-subjects from the African colonies. They brought no heavy guns across the river, but with their 3 in. field-piece—the "soixante-quinze"—throwing twenty-five small shells a minute, and their machine-gun, they searched the wooded spurs above the Aisne, and by the afternoon checked the German counter-attack.

Then the French infantryman, in swift, continual rushes, climbed up the buttresses of the great plateau, took the German machine-guns in a series of heroic storming

Heroic French storming movements

movements, and at last drove the enemy back to Nampscel and even beyond that hill village. The German lines were pushed right on to the main ridge of the tableland, towards their headquarters at Laon, on the next height. But despite the splendid gallantry of the Frenchmen, they could not get a firm lodging on the highest points above the river valley. All that bayonet and bullet and 3 in. shells could do, they did.

But the German heavy machinery of war was too powerful for them to entrench by the ridge. They had arrived some three days too late on the heights. General von Zwehl had preceded them with the siege-artillery from Maubeuge for distribution along the plateau. Large forces of fresh troops had been added to Kluck's defeated forces, and vast new supplies of ammunition had been parcelled out from Laon.

Another thing that seems also to have told against the French in the swaying struggle on the central slopes towards Nampscel was the superior proportion in which machine-guns were used by the German battalions. In many cases a German battalion had six machine-guns, while a French battalion had only two. In the fighting in rough, wooded, difficult country, where surprise ambushes could easily be arranged by Maxim sections against large bodies of infantry, this special superiority in light armament was as useful to the Germans as their superiority in heavy artillery.

In the end the Sixth French Army had to withdraw once more towards the Aisne, and two months passed before it again began to advance, more slowly, but more surely. Furnished with more machine guns, with heavier field-guns throwing a 37 lb. shell a distance of eight miles, and with mobile siege-artillery, General Maunoury's force in November crept eastward round the plateau along the Oise at Tracy le Val, and won several important positions on the heights above the Aisne. Meanwhile, the unyielding resistance of the Sixth French Army along the Lower Aisne, like the stronghold of their British neighbours along the higher reaches of the river, contained the enemy and reduced him to the position of a besieged garrison. The plateau of Soissons became the largest entrenched camp in the world, with the Allies sapping and mining their way into it and keeping three or more German armies immobile in front of them for many critical months in the general campaign. In these vast siege operations the Fifth French Army, under General Franchet d'Espérey, took as important a part as the British Expeditionary Force and General Maunoury's troops. General d'Espérey, wheeling up on the British right, had probably the most difficult bit of the plateau in front of him. Between his left wing, near Bourg on the Aisne, and his right wing at Rheims, the great headland of Craonne rose above the plain of Champagne. The height forms the western edge of the tableland of Soissons. It is the culmination of the north river ridge, and its steep sides and flat top make it easy to defend with modern artillery and difficult, in any circumstances, to attack. It is indeed the crowning impregnable height of the natural fortress of France.

It was here that Napoleon's army broke down after its victory on the Marne, and was shattered by Blucher in the 1814 campaign that ended in the French Emperor's first exile to Elba. General d'Espérey did not succeed in capturing a position that Napoleon failed to take in the days when defending artillery had much less power than it has now. But he avoided being broken against the defence made by General von Bülow, with the help of General von Zwehl and Field-Marshal von Heeringen.

His left wing came up towards the Chemin des Dames, near Zwehl's trenches at Cerny, to protect the flank of

A BRIDGE BUILT BY SIX HUNDRED GERMANS IN FIVE DAYS.
This remarkable structure, five hundred and forty-six yards in extent, was built of materials found in the neighbourhood, across a wide tract of marshy land in Northern France. The work took five days to complete, and was done by working parties numbering in all six hundred men.

SCOURGE FOUND ON A GERMAN OFFICER.
Made of part of the handle of an umbrella, with a short leather lash, attached to which was a heavy lump of metal plugged with wood, this implement was reported by a French paper to have been found on the body of an officer of the German Crown Prince's army operating in the Argonne.

GERMAN SHARPSHOOTERS IN TREES LOCATED AND BROUGHT DOWN BY A BRITISH MACHINE-GUN.

A number of our men having been sniped by an invisible enemy while passing to and from the firing-line, it occurred to a bright young officer to turn a machine-gun on some trees in the distance. The result was "a fine bag of German sharpshooters." It was officially stated that non-commissioned officers in the German Army were offered Iron Crosses if they could penetrate the British lines at night. These men sometimes succeeded in getting right behind our lines to favourable spots, from which they were able to use their rifles with deadly effect.

the 1st Division of the British force, after the great success on the plateau. But, as we have seen in the previous chapter, Sir John French found it would be dangerous to advance his men any farther on the ridge, so long as the Germans had the headland of Craonne on our right. In these circumstances, General d'Espérey endeavoured to improve the allied front by a magnificent reconnaissance in force against the Craonne heights. With the entire weight of the Fifth Army he swung up against the abrupt headland on Thursday, September 17th.

A most desperate and stubborn battle ensued. The French lacked long-range artillery, and **French attack on** could not cover their advance by gun **the Craonne heights** fire from the other side of the Aisne River valley. The most they could do was to hold the enemy by the river spurs, but they swarmed up the slopes on the eastern side of the plateau, and simply by the swiftness and vigour of their infantry rushes got as far as Craonne village, which is not quite at the top of the main height. Some of the leading troops appear to have fought their way to the main height by Friday, September 18th. But they could not lodge there against the terrible cross-fires that were directed on to them from the German batteries. After taking prisoners from the 11th and 12th German Army Corps, the French had to withdraw towards the river and act on the defensive.

They had crossed the Aisne at the old ford of Berry-au-Bac, on the road running

GERMAN SAVAGERY AT SENLIS.
Ruined residence of the Mayor of Senlis. He was shot by the Germans, who razed this beautiful old-world town to the ground.

from Rheims to Laon, past the headland of Craonne. Unfortunately for them, the German commander, Heeringen, had massed men and materials along this road for an attack on Rheims. All the guns that Zwehl and Bülow could spare from the plateau were combined with the artillery of the broken Saxon army, and got into position on the Rheims-Laon road. On Thursday night, September 17th, the heavy

FUGITIVES ON THE RUINED RAILWAY-STATION AT SENLIS.
On their retreat to the Aisne, part of the German army passed through Senlis, which, on their departure, they bombarded on the ground that some of their men had been fired at. The above photograph shows a crowd of would-be travellers waiting at the wrecked railway-station in the hope of getting by train to Paris. Inset: "Business as usual" at Senlis railway-station in spite of the bombardment. Notice the smashed roof.

and Rheims and Chalons for the supreme effort of his strengthened forces. A considerable number of his reinforcements, including all the first-line troops that could be spared from the Lorraine army, were coming from an eastern direction. There was no cross-country railway linking the eastern German wing to the western German wing. The French Military Staff had left the large region between Verdun, Rethel, and Rheims without direct railway communication, with a view to impeding such a transfer of invading troops. The consequence was that no German turning movement in the west, round Compiègne, was immediately practical.

On the other hand, there was a direct main line of railway communication running from Rheims northward through Rethel, Mézières, Luxemburg, to the great German war depot at Coblenz, on **Railways and German** the Rhine. A branch line from Metz to **strategy** Luxemburg also connected the garrison force at Metz with the German lines round Berry-au-Bac and the Craonne headland. Everything thus conspired to induce the German Commander-in-Chief to concentrate in front of Rheims, by Berry-au-Bac.

All the operations on the plateau of Soissons, by Field-Marshal von Heeringen and Generals von Kluck, von Bülow, and von Zwehl, became of secondary importance. Owing to the failure of the Sixth French Army, the British Expeditionary Force, and the Fifth French Army to drive Heeringen's forces from the tableland, their actions also became of secondary importance. The chief scene of engagement

COURTYARD OF THE RUINED HOTEL DE VILLE, SENLIS.

siege-howitzers also arrived there from Maubeuge, according to a diary by a German officer picked up some days afterwards during the German counter-attack. Though this remarkable mass of ordnance was no doubt of use in assisting the guns on the plateau to repel the French attack on Craonne, this was not the principal object for which it had been collected.

The German Commander-in-Chief had selected the level tract of country between the Aisne at Berry-au-Bac

CAMERA PICTURES OF THE DESOLATION WROUGHT BY THE GERMANS IN SENLIS.

The invaders laid a heavy hand on the beautiful old town of Senlis. The view in the centre of the page shows a party of French people walking through the ruins. The left-hand picture is of the entrance to the town, and its companion view shows another part of the ruined city.

DISASTROUS EFFECTS OF A GERMAN SHELL ON A PARTY OF BRITISH WOUNDED.

During the fighting on the Aisne a party of British wounded were being attended by a Red Cross doctor in a room in a country house, when a shell from the German lines, coming through the window, burst in their midst. The doctor and nearly all the soldiers were killed on the spot.

The incident was described by a private of the Black Watch who was in the room a few minutes before the explosion, and who went into it again shortly after the disaster. The victims were about a dozen in number, and belonged to the Cameron Highlanders.

between the Germans and the Allies in the third week of September was the country around Rheims. Here the German commander delivered the blow by which he hoped to recover the grand power of the initiative that he had won at Charleroi and lost at the Marne.

He intended, by a violent frontal attack, backed by heavy artillery fire, with howitzer bombardments, to pierce the French front between Rheims and Suippes. Even if the first attack failed, he hoped to push back the French lines sufficiently to win possession of all the valuable railway running across the plain of Champagne from Verdun and St. Menehould to Rheims. With this railway just behind him, he could manœuvre his troops for the final frontal assault.

It was on Friday, September 18th, when the Fifth French Army was repulsed from Craonne, that the German counter-attack on the French centre was made. Here, from Rheims to the little town of Souain, the Ninth French Army, under General Foch, had a hard task to beat back the host of invaders. For, in retiring from

German advantages at Rheims
Rheims about six days before, the Germans had kept possession of the chief French forts of the district. The French had dismantled these old-fashioned forts so as to make Rheims, with its glorious cathedral, an open town, safe from bombardment. The chief fort was on the wooded heights of Nogent l'Abbesse, only seven thousand yards from the cathedral city. The Germans placed their heavy artillery on this position, and entrenched their infantry around it, and along the River Suippes, that runs into the Aisne near Berry-au-Bac.

During the first days of the pursuit the French took a lower spur of the Nogent heights, and, what was more important, captured the hill of Brimont, some nine thousand yards north-west of Rheims. Brimont, however, was again lost by a fierce German attack by the reinforced armies. The enemy then possessed the two points of vantage. He brought his troops from the wooded ridge

north of the Suippes, and entrenched them some five or six miles closer to Rheims. He dominated the city with gun fire from Brimont and Nogent; he ruled the Suippes valley with artillery lined out on the Suippes ridge, and across the Aisne at Craonne his howitzers stopped any forward movement by the French.

Our Allies held two heights to the east—one at Pouillon, between the Aisne and the Vesle, and one, known as the Mountain of Rheims, near Verzenay, south of the Vesle. But the light French field-guns, placed on these edges of the southern river plateau, could not reach the German positions. By a series of night infantry attacks, supported by a terrific gun fire directed by searchlights, the Germans tried to break the French lines on the plain. But each time the compact masses of grey figures approached the French trenches they were shattered by the 3 in. French guns. The fact was that from their two lines of heights on the west of Rheims the soldiers of France were as strongly posted for a defensive battle as were the Germans on the east and south-east.

All the men the Allies had lost in their attempts to storm the plateau of Soissons were avenged by the dreadful losses the Germans suffered in trying to break the French centre. In places south of the Marne the German ranks had fallen in swathes, like lines of mown hay. But south of the Aisne, where the plain of Champagne began, they fell as they had fallen round Nancy—one line on the top of another, till their dead and wounded built up a ghastly rampart of agony in front of the French positions. This was mainly the work of the terrible semi-automatic light French gun, working with its automatically correct time-fuse setter for the shrapnel and melinite shells.

In German guns the fuse is set by hand by one of the artillerymen. He does his work more or less skilfully, and the shell explodes with more or less uncertainty, either in front or behind the mark found by the range-finder. The French gunners, however, have an instrument called a "debouchoir," which, when the range is given, prepares the fuse with mechanical exactitude, so that the shrapnel or high-explosive shell bursts at the right fraction of a moment over the mark at which the gun is pointed. By a mechanical device on the gun the mark can be altered in a little more than two moments to another given position, and the automatically regulated fuse again explodes the shell over the new mark. By this fearful machinery of war the French field batteries again and again piled up the attacking German infantry, that was still employed in the old-fashioned, unscientific mass formations. The heavy German batteries at Brimont and Nogent could not seriously interfere with the light French guns on the western heights. The distance over the plain of Rheims was too great. It was eight miles from Brimont to the French position just south of Berry-au-Bac, and some seven miles from Nogent to the Mountain of Rheims, near Verzenay. The artillerymen on both sides had any hostile advancing troops at their mercy, but they could not damage each other's guns on the opposite heights. As the Germans were the attackers, they suffered, and the slaughter went on, by night and day, until they withdrew out of range towards the low ridge by the Suippes, and towards the higher hills of Nogent l'Abbesse.

Terrible work of French batteries

It was then that the Prussian commander of the heavy artillery at Nogent began to bombard Rheims Cathedral. He afterwards pretended that the cathedral was shelled as a military necessity, because French observation officers were seen to be using the towers to direct their guns. The Kaiser and General von Moltke and the Great Military Staff supported this stupid attempt to palliate the act of vandalism when they learnt, to their surprise, that the entire civilised world was shocked by the deeds of their gunners. But it was pointed out that the French soldiers already held heights some six hundred feet above the plain at Pouillon and some five hundred feet above it at the Mountain of Rheims, and therefore had no need to endanger their finest cathedral by showing themselves on the towers. There was also the statement of the venerable Archbishop Landreux that no officers had been permitted to use the church for military purposes. Five nights before the bombardment began, a searchlight, placed on the tower to protect the non-combatants of the city from bomb-dropping airships, had been removed. This removal was carried out especially to save the cathedral from any attack on any grounds. Far from the sacred building being employed for warlike purpose, it had been turned into an hospital for wounded German soldiers. There were sixty grey-clad officers and men lying in knee-deep straw in the nave. Above, from the two towers, Red Cross flags were flying

When these facts were published, the German military authorities shifted the grounds of their excuse. They alleged that there was a French battery near the cathedral, and that it was so placed as to bring the sacred building in the line of fire from the opposing German battery. As a matter of fact, there were some French guns a mile to the north of the cathedral, and some other French guns two miles to the south of it. It was the latter battery which the Germans, in their last gross lie, said that they were aiming at when they smote the cathedral. As was said by the American author, Mr. Richard Harding Davis, who was in Rheims when the bombardment began, " to accept the German claim we must believe that, continuously for four days, they aimed at a battery, and, two miles from it, hit the Cathedral of Rheims."

German lies about Rheims

Even in the hour of their defeat the Prussians were not so blind with rage as that. Their marksmanship was, in fact, exceedingly good They were firing 6 in. shells at a distance of some 7,000 yards—from Nogent l'Abbesse hill. Adjoining the cathedral is a well-known hotel with a German proprietor. The gunners pitched their shells so exactly for four days—from Saturday, September 19th, to Tuesday, September 22nd—that each fell on the cathedral and the archbishop's palace and robing-room of the Kings of France, without a splinter injuring the German hotel hard by.

There is no creature on earth so diabolically spiteful as a bully who has been badly beaten but not yet thrashed into whimpering, grovelling cowardice.

GERMAN INFANTRY MARCHING OFF IN THE HALF-LIGHT OF EARLY MORNING FROM BURNING SENLIS.
When the Germans passed through Senlis on their way to the Aisne, it is said that some of the populace, infuriated at the conduct of the invaders, fired at them in the streets. In revenge, the Germans shot the mayor and other leading citizens, and put the fine old cathedral town to the flames. In the remarkable camera picture which is reproduced above, the enemy are seen moving off in the half-light of early morning, silhouetted against the lurid sky over the burning city.

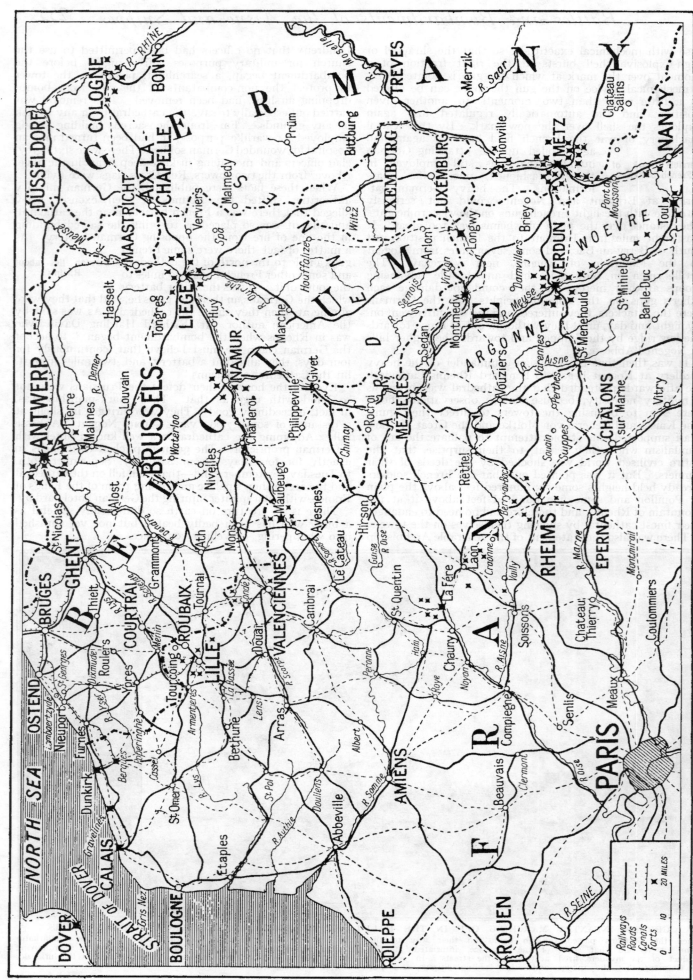

MAP OF THE RAILWAYS, RIVERS, AND PRINCIPAL CANALS IN NORTHERN FRANCE AND BELGIUM FROM THE GERMAN FRONTIER TO THE SEA.

BRITISH NERVE TELLS IN A SURPRISE ENCOUNTER.

A British officer, with a small company of men, was passing through a wood in the North of France when, on coming to a clearing, the little force almost ran into three German officers accompanied by about forty men and two machine-guns. The surprise was mutual. But the British officer at once demanded the surrender of the German party, and the latter, thinking that their opponents were only the advance guard of a large body of cavalry, immediately complied. One of the German machine-guns was captured by the British and the other destroyed.

The Prussian Guards, stationed round Nogent l'Abbesse, were badly beaten bullies. They had left something like half their number in the marshes of St. Gond, and when they tried in the night attacks round Rheims, on Thursday and Friday, to avenge their losses they had met again the terrible fire of the light French gun. In front of their gunners, at dawn on Saturday morning, rose like a fortress of paradise the most glorious cathedral in the world. It was the most perfect of all monuments of the French genius, a mighty yet delicate mass of sculptured stone, adorned with thousands of the finest statues of the flowering period of Gothic art—the beginning of the thirteenth century. The great jewel-like windows of ancient stained-glass were miracles of deep, full, glowing, harmonious colours. All that was fine and noble and splendid in German architecture and sculpture of the Gothic period— the structure of Cologne Cathedral in the Rhineland, the sculptures of Bamberg Cathedral in Bavaria—was derived from the French work of Rheims.

The loveliest possession of the French race
Rheims had been the school of art from which the civilised part of Germany in the thirteenth century learnt to model and build. Our own Westminster Abbey is a work in the French style. All Gothic works of the supreme period throughout Europe are in the French style. Of this style Rheims, the cathedral in which all French kings were crowned and anointed, was the consummate flower. It was the loveliest possession of the French race, even as the Parthenon was the loveliest possession of the Athenians. For this reason—and for this reason alone—the beaten, exasperated, spiteful Germans, impotently raging from a series of defeats, destroyed it. Hurled back from the Marne in a long, disastrous retreat, then gripped and held between the Aisne and the Suippes, where they endeavoured to recover from their greatest defeat since Jena and Auerstadt, the Prussians and Prussianised

Teutons were reduced to the condition of homicidal maniacs, lacking the power to slaughter their opponents.

For more than a generation they had boasted that at the next opportunity they would bleed the French people white. But in less than six weeks after the opening of hostilities it was they who were bleeding to death. They had invaded France with over a million first-line troops, and already they had close upon a million casualties ; they were using up their second line of reserves, and calling out their boys and untrained men. Desperately concentrating all available troops and guns for a final attempt to pierce the French lines and win the victory they needed before they swung across Europe to meet the Russians, they swept out in the fiercest of their frontal attacks, only to be driven back to their trenches, leaving another hundred thousand of their dead and wounded between the Oise and the Meuse.

In one of these attacks the Germans collected the French soldiers who had surrendered in a previous fight, and arranged them in a compact line before their front ranks, and then drove **A deed of cowardice** them forward at the point of the bayonet **and brutality** to act as a shield against the fire from the French trenches they were trying to rush. This deed of extreme cowardice and brutality is mentioned officially in one of the descriptions by the "Eye-Witness" attached to the British army on the Aisne. While he was relating it, the Germans at Nogent, having perhaps no prisoners of war to torture and murder in this Teutonic manner, wreaked their baffled, insane wrath upon the sculptured stones and pictured windows of Rheims Cathedral.

They began by bombarding the dwelling-places of non-combatants in the city with 6 in. howitzer shells. On Friday, September 18th, the shrapnel shattered the cathedral windows and killed two wounded German soldiers lying on the thick straw in the nave. Then the shells

GENERAL VIEW OF THE TOWN OF METZ.
Metz, the fortified capital of German Lorraine, has in normal times a garrison of 25,000 men. During the early part of the war the army of Metz poured into the Woevre country by way of Mars-la-Tour, Chambley, Vignuelles, and Chaillon, just north of St. Mihiel.

began to dig great holes in the streets of the open town, and batter the houses of peaceful citizens and deposit the heaps of rubbish in the cellars. Women and children ran and stumbled amid the fallen masonry, seeking for shelter in the caves of the champagne bottlers, or streaming toward the city gate into the open country. At first the people were calm under the bombardment, but as evening drew on the women became at times panic-stricken. They fled down the streets weeping, praying, crossing themselves, and screaming in terror when the shells fell.

At eight o'clock on Friday night the howitzers ceased firing. The Germans were afraid that the position of their concealed batteries on the neighbouring hill would be disclosed by the flames showing in the darkness where the howitzers were fired. But at dawn on Saturday the bombardment was resumed. Night had brought counsel, and the gunners now aimed directly at the cathedral. One of the shells struck the scaffolding erected round the left tower for the purpose of restoration work. The wood flamed, and the fire quickly spread to the old arched roof

of oak above the lower roof of stone. The molten lead dropped on the straw in the nave, on which the wounded Germans were lying. In the meantime the entire scaffolding about the cathedral was burning and calcining the stones, and shells were still falling.

Archbishop Landreux and his brave assistant, Abbé Chinot, a young, athletic, manly priest entrusted with the care of the cathedral, called for volunteers to save the injured enemies of their country. Helped by nurses and doctors, the archbishop and abbé carried or dragged the wounded men out of the flaming straw and through the north portal.

GERMAN TRANSPORT PASSING THROUGH A RUINED VILLAGE IN NORTHERN FRANCE.
The upper photograph, on the right hand, shows the quaint little town-hall of a small place near Rheims where the invader set up his headquarters for the time being.

There then occurred one of the most dramatic and memorable scenes in the history of France. A wild mob of townspeople surrounded the cathedral porch and blocked the way. They were men maddened by the vision of their great historic church in flames, by the bombardment of their homes, by the murder by shell fire of five hundred of their kinsmen and neighbours. The sight of the grey figures of the Germans drove them to frenzy. They shouted for the barbarians to be left to the fate their own countrymen had wrought for them. They refused to allow their hated wounded foes to be helped out of the burning cathedral.

Grey - haired Archbishop Landreux and Abbé Chinot came forward and stood between the raging crowd and the helpless, suffering Germans. Some of the townsmen had raised their rifles. " You must first kill us," said the aged archbishop, " before you kill them."

The rifles were lowered, the shouting died to a murmur, the murmur to silence. The mob opened, and the Red Cross doctors and nurses, with the archbishop and abbé leading, carried the wounded men to a place of safety. In the distance the comrades of the men thus rescued from an agonising death continued to shatter and deface with their howitzer shells the nave where Joan of Arc stood at the coronation of the King of France, after ' she had saved her country from the invader. The heat of the fire, started by the shells, had turned the statues they failed to batter into images of dust that crumbled into powder when pressed by a man's hands.

No photograph of the ruins of the cathedral reveals its condition. In a year, when frost and rain have worked upon the calcined carvings and masonry, much of the detail that still shows to the eye will have peeled and crumbled off. By the winter of 1915 at latest Rheims Cathedral will only be a great, desolate ruin. The fairest thing existing on earth, since the Venetians destroyed the Parthenon at Athens, has vanished.

Only by combining, in imagination, what is best in Chartres Cathedral with what is best in Amiens Cathedral will future generations be able to form an idea of the original glory of Rheims. Even then the idea will be below the vanished reality. For the statues of the façade of the coronation cathedral of France were the flower of the last high creative period in monumental art since the period of Phidias. Those at Amiens cannot compare

THE BRITISH IN FRANCE.
Queen's Own Oxfordshire Hussars, one of the first of our Yeomanry regiments to go to the front, passing through a French village. Inset : Temporary headquarters of General Gough.

with them, as the Amiens front was not completed. What a joy for an Empire of but forty-four years of existence to have destroyed the loveliest work in Christendom ! It may be that Belgians and Frenchmen will make no attempt to restore the ancient glorious buildings in Louvain, Malines, Termonde, Ypres, Rheims, and Arras. They may let the ruins stand to remind the world what German culture was at the height of its power.

When the German is half-drunk, he is either very gross and brutal, or extremely sentimental. If German commercial travellers are still welcomed in Belgium and Northern France after the great peace, we shall see at evening in the cafés of Louvain, Rheims, Arras, and Ypres the maudlin sons of the Fatherland declaiming, with tears in their eyes, over the sins of their nation. For bullies are curs at heart with some means of mastery to their hand. When the German is absolutely beaten and disarmed he will weep like a neurotic woman, partly in order to relieve his feelings, but partly to excite the pity of the men who have beaten him. Some standing examples of his achievements in the days of his hegemony in Europe will help to keep him penitent for several generations, and recall to other people what is concealed beneath his facile sentimentality and adaptiveness of temperament.

The German force at the height of Nogent l'Abbesse, from which the cathedral was bombarded, did not escape without punishment. At dawn on September 26th, after failing in a night attack on the French lines, some 15,000 Germans, including all that remained of the Prussian Guards corps, advanced down the old Roman road towards the Camp of Attila. Their object was to destroy the railway line between

TRAINLOAD OF CAPTURED GERMAN GUNS.
The guns are being taken through a French village on their way to England. On September 10th, 1914, thirteen guns, seven machine-guns, about two thousand prisoners and quantities of transport fell into our hands.

INFANTRY ADVANCE UNDER SHELL FIRE AGAINST GERMAN TRENCHES IN THE NEIGHBOURHOOD OF ARRAS.

For this attack over three hundred guns were brought up to assist the advancing Allies, and a deadly shell fire was poured into the German position, with the result that our men were able to gain the enemy's trenches with very little loss. In this way the Germans were slowly but surely pushed back in their efforts to break through to the west. Hardly any entrenched troops can withstand the effects of concentrated shell fire, and when the guns had prepared the way the attacking troops advanced with fixed bayonets to complete the work. Near Arras fighting of this kind went on day by day.

Rheims and Verdun, by which the French were manœuvring their troops and transporting ammunition and food supplies.

General Foch, however, learnt the enemy's movements, and prepared to counter them. A regiment of French cavalry was ordered to ride forward at full speed, occupy the village of Auberive, on the Suippes, and there fight a delaying action against the hostile columns. This was done to give time for a large body of French infantrymen at Jouchery, some five miles away, to march out and catch the main German force.

At six o'clock in the morning Auberive was occupied by the French cavalry. The High Street and byways were barricaded, and machine-guns were hoisted on house-tops and other points affording a wide sweep of fire. By this time the French artillery was some three miles away, on the road from Jouchery to Auberive. The German commander got to know of it, no doubt from his aerial scouts. He sent two thousand of the Death's Head Hussars, forming the cavalry arm of the raiding movement, to cut off the French guns.

The artillerymen were at St. Hilaire, on the Suippes, still between Jouchery and Auberive. On their left flank was a stretch of vineyards and freshly-ploughed fields. Through the vines and across the furrows the hussars charged. The surprise attack was well launched. It looked as though the horsemen would be amid the guns before the Frenchmen could bring their pieces into action.

In two minutes the artillery teams were unharnessed and the horses placed in the rear. The yelling lines of hussars drew nearer—the commands of their leaders could be heard round the guns. With lowered lances they galloped within three hundred yards of the artillery. Another eighty yards they were allowed to travel. "Fire!" rang out the French command. Through the blue smoke the gunners could see the horses rear up beneath the bursting shrapnel and fall. The front squadrons broke, but the supports galloped up and rallied **Death ride of the** to the charge. Again the guns thun- **German Hussars** dered. Amid the vines and furrows were things that looked in the distance like rags trailing there. Sometimes one of the larger objects moved; it was a wounded horse trying to rise. Otherwise nothing could be seen. It was level, open country, and the French 75 millimetre gun has a range of some miles. No hussar escaped.

Meanwhile, the French cavalry at Auberive had delayed the main forces of the enemy as long as possible, and were retreating towards St. Hilaire. The victorious guns, rattling again as the horses dragged them along, advanced to meet their retiring dragoons. Just as the juncture was

FRANCO-GERMAN ARTILLERY DUEL IN THE ARGONNE.
The German objective in the Argonne district was to obtain control of the road connecting their positions on the western outskirts of the forest with Varennes on its eastern edge, where the right wing of the German forces was trying to invest Verdun from the north. But it is difficult country for artillery movements, and the French took full advantage of the opportunities it afforded for cleverly concealed batteries, against which the Germans directed a searching shrapnel fire.

effected at St. Hilaire, in the Suippes valley, the Prussian Guard with its field-guns arrived.

The French gunners were not so successful this time. The German infantrymen held back, while their field batteries, posted on a favourable site, opened a bombardment on the French guns. Then the guardsmen crept forward through the vineyards to snipe the artillerymen. But, instead of attempting to defend their guns, the French dragoons moved forward to outflank the Prussians. At the same time, bayonets could be seen over the farther low hedges of grape-vines. The French infantry was arriving; one battalion of Zouaves was creeping round the rear of the attacking columns.

By the time the German commander became fully aware of what was happening his forces were almost surrounded. Only on his right, in the direction of Rheims, was there a gap, and that was quickly closing. Through it the German columns with their guns streamed, and to cover their retreat some 3,000 men of the Guards Corps sacrificed themselves. They charged five times at the closing lines

GETTING A HEAVY GERMAN HOWITZER INTO POSITION.
A German 21 centimetre (8·27) howitzer, which fired a 248 lb. shell, the dense black smoke arising from the explosion of which won for it the names of " Black Maria," " Jack Johnson," and " Coal-Box." The range was 8,900 yards. The wheels were surrounded with linked steel plates faced with wood, and when the howitzer was fired the wheels rested on mats of cane with steel plates between them.

of French troops. Each time they were terribly repulsed. After the fifth assault barely a hundred men were left standing, and they were all wounded. So they turned their rifles down—a sign of surrender. Naturally, the Frenchmen treated them well, for they were brave men— the only Prussian Guardsmen in the Great War who exemplified the heroic traditions of their old corps. They saved the entire German force from destruction.

The well-known Irish novelist who writes under the nom de guerre of George A. Birmingham has published an article expressing doubts as to the remarkable series of defeats suffered by the Prussian Guards Corps. He said it had been first severely cut up at bayonet point by the **Blunted spear-point of the German Army** Turcos at Charleroi, then bogged and slain in tens of thousands in the marsh of St. Gond. Then, as we now see, it lost three thousand more men at St. Hilaire, and afterwards it was almost entirely destroyed by British troops round Ypres. It does seem a superhuman accumulation of disasters for a single body of soldiers.

But, in matter of fact, the modern Prussian Guards consisted originally of an army corps of first-line troops, with a large reserve. After the Battle of St. Hilaire the original army corps of 40,000 men was practically destroyed. It was the reserve units, with perhaps freshly-trained recruits to fill out the battalions, that emerged afterwards at Ypres, only to fall, and break completely the traditions of the Guards by giving ground.

The Prussian Guard was intended for use only in the most vital operations. It had to go on till it dropped ; then take cover, and hold on till it was killed or reinforced. This, however, it failed to do on almost every important occasion in the Great War. The spear-point of the vast German Army, it was soon blunted and then broken,

repaired, and broken again. There were rumours that some thousand Guardsmen were at last marched out, unarmed and helpless, and offered as a target to the Allies, in order to teach the corps to die. Even a German general is unlikely to have murdered his men in this fashion. But the mere fact that such a legend should have spread to Holland, shows to what state the morale of the crack Berlin corps had at last been, in current opinion, reduced.

In defensive tactics German leadership was certainly good. Along the valley of the Suippes, only a day after the retreat of the German centre was concluded above Souain, the enemy was admirably entrenched. He made at once deep ditches, protected from shrapnel fire by cover, and began to hollow out underground roomy caves in which to rest and sleep. Protected by his artillery on the low swell of ground in the rear, the German soldier displayed in defensive trench warfare a laborious application that quickly made all his lines impregnable. Had **Defensive trench warfare** General Foch ¡and General de Langle de Cary, operating between Rheims and the Argonne Forest, continued to attack, they would have seen the Ninth and Fourth French Armies melt away like snow in spring-time.

Both generals, however, had been fighting the Germans, now on the attack, now on the defence, since the first retirement from Northern France. They knew exactly the weak point in Teutonic tactics. In attacking operations German leadership was brutally bad ; the troops were handled without any economy of force. The lines were denser than was properly required with good soldiers armed with long-range magazine rifles. The supports were closer to the firing-line than was necessary with stubborn and well-trained leading troops.

Bullets and shells that missed the Germans in the firing-line struck the reserve companies that were feeding the

BRITISH MILITARY CAR TRAPPED NEAR SOISSONS.
At night time German cavalry took up positions on roads between the opposing lines, and after distributing broken wine bottles over the ground, retired to a spot convenient for sniping. Mr. W. F. Bradley was caught in one of these traps near Soissons, and while he was putting on a spare wheel his companions took cover, their fire making the Germans withdraw.

front ranks and filling the gaps left by the men put out of action. All this costly close formation of the German infantry was a mark of a lack of science and intelligence in the officers responsible for the training and leading of the men. In spite of the new machines that Krupp had made in large numbers for them, the German squirearchy that officered the Army had learnt nothing of the practical handling of men in war since 1870.

They had reduced their forces to the same condition as that into which the Prussian Army fell only six years after the death of Frederick the Great. The Franco-British lines on the Aisne and Suippes Rivers ran near the Argonne Forest through the town of Valmy. Here, six years after Frederick the Great died, **Brutal leadership of German officers** a French revolutionary general in 1792 had defeated the Prussians and Austrians under the Duke of Brunswick. Now the Germans under the Duke of Württemberg were undergoing, a similar experience of unexpected defeat, after a similar period of military hegemony in Europe.

Goethe, who witnessed the first Battle of Valmy, in September, 1792, prophesied, against his own countrymen, that the victory of the new French democracy had opened a new era in the history of mankind. He saw in it the downfall of the system of princely privilege and peasant serfdom that fettered the development of the peoples of the European continent. He hailed France as the redeemer of nations, and the French cannonade at Valmy as the salute of guns at the birth of a new movement of liberty.

But for a hundred years afterwards this movement had been prevented from spreading into Germany. The old system of feudalism had transformed itself, in the course of aggressive wars abroad and strong-handed subjection

FINE WORK OF THE LINCOLNS ON THE AISNE.
During the Battle of the Aisne, two companies of the Lincolns were ordered to attack a German battery which, situated on a hill, was trying to silence some British guns on another hill about a mile away. Making a wide detour, our men managed to enter the wood right in the rear of the enemy, and got within two hundred yards of them before they were discovered. They took seven guns, and not one of the German gunners escaped.

of the working population at home, into a scientific bureaucracy. The ancient tyranny of the noble classes was exerted in a new form with a firmer grip and a larger scope. But again the French guns at Valmy, in September, 1914, echoed over the wild Forest of Argonne, bearing the same message as that which had first disturbed and then inspired the courtly, egotistic German poet of genius attached to the train of the Duke of Weimar. Again the democracy of France, once more attacked unawares in the midst of its religious, social, and political difficulties, was proving, from the cannon's mouth, that the spirit born of freedom was stronger than all the cunning and force born of military despotism.

For months the battle continued to rage round Valmy. At first the Fourth French Army, under General de Langle de Cary, carried the towns of Vienne and Varennes on either side of the northern part of the Argonne ridge. Then, on September 24th, when **French efficiency in the Argonne** the Germans were reinforced, the French were driven back on St. Menehould and the Verdun-Rheims railway line. The enemy next tried to take the railway, and almost succeeded on Sunday, September 27th. But the ground he won in the morning was recovered by the French in the evening. Round St. Menehould General Gérard, with a single French army corps, not merely held out against two German army corps, one of which, the Sixteenth, had come from Metz, but he steadily pushed the invaders back by a continuous action amid the rocks and woods of the Argonne that lasted for months.

GALLANT DEED OF THE WEST YORKSHIRES.
In a gallant charge on the German trenches during the conflict on the Aisne, a company of the 1st West Yorkshire Regiment (The Prince of Wales's Own) was almost wiped out. Private Charles Bell, seeing his sergeant drop, bandaged him as well as he could, and then, to quote his own words, "started for home," crawling along the ground with the sergeant on his back. After about two hours they reached safety and the field transport.

Operating in concert with this little army was a force under the famous General Dubail, whose high and brilliant genius for war has been one of the superb revelations of the campaign. He was called from the hills around Nancy to help General Sarrail, the commander of the field army and garrison of Verdun, in the fighting on the east of the Argonne ridge and along the heights of the Meuse between Verdun and Toul.

To the French people the incessant combats in the wild, beautiful, rocky, upland Forest of Argonne have the same interest as the struggles of our men at Le Cateau, the Aisne, and Ypres have for us. There in a region of narrow defiles, shaded by sombre trees, of swells and hollows girdled by impassable thickets, every woodland way is marked by graves, every clearing is known by the slaughter that occurred there.

In this broken maze of country, offering at every step opportunities for ambushes and surprise attacks and feint retreats over mined ground, the French troops withstood the most violent of all the enemy's attacks. They countered him in his double advance from east to west, from Metz to Verdun, and from north to south, from the frontier to the Marne. The men holding the Argonne were the pivot on which General Joffre swung his men in the retreats of August and the advances of September.

If General Helmuth von Moltke had had his way, when he was still Chief of Staff, the defeat on the Marne, the counter-checks on the Aisne and the Suippes, and the baffled attempts at a turning movement in the west, would have been concluded by the massing of three-quarters of a million men for the recapture of the Argonne Forest. It was because the Kaiser decided against this plan, and, with the help of General von Falkenhayn, developed a scheme of his own for using the men at Ypres and La Bassée, that Moltke retired from the practical commandership-in-chief.

It must be said of Moltke that he at least knew best where to strike, though, after his first successes in August, he usually failed to strike swift and hard enough. The Argonne was the danger-point for France. That was why Joffre had three of his best generals there, and many of his keenest, trickiest, and most skilful troops. The first of the new heavy artillery was sent to them, with some of the more mobile siege-guns of Verdun. They formed the pivot. If the pivot became unsteady, all the armies reposing on it would falter.

German effort to turn the French flank There was a day in September when it seemed as if the pivot was shaken and the entire northern line of Franco-British forces put into danger. On September 15th the army of the Crown Prince, which had been trying to break a new gap of invasion at Fort Troyon, below Verdun and Toul, was compelled to retreat. By a terrible bombard-

ment it had just reduced to a heap of ruin the fort that kept the German forces round Metz from turning the French flank. But the Crown Prince had to retire before he opened the new gateway into France.

Then General von Heeringen, who had been commanding the Metz army, took over the control of the western positions on the plateau of Soissons. But the man he left at Metz in his place did not lack initiative and driving power. Thrown back towards Metz in the third week in September, when many of his first-line troops went to reinforce the fatigued and dispirited **Prussian advance** northern German armies, the new **across the Woevre** commander at Metz gathered from over the Rhine a fresh host of second-line soldiers, and some Skoda howitzers, capable of throwing 12 in. shells an unusual distance.

Clearing a broad path for his troops, in the last week of September, by watering with shell and shrapnel the ground ahead of his march, the German commander advanced from his battle quarters at Thiaucourt across the flattish land known as the Woevre country. It lies between Verdun and Toul, and as it approaches the upper course of the Meuse, the Woevre plain rises into a line of bare hills known as the Heights of the Meuse. A chain of French forts on these hills, including Fort Troyon and the Camp des Romains, connected the defensive works of Toul and Verdun and kept out the invaders.

The German commander seized one of the lower hills, at a distance of some miles from the Camp des Romains and the Meuse River. There did not seem much danger in this. The guns of the fort could not reach him, and he would have to come nearer to attack the fort. But he did not. He had a surprise packet for the French garrison. It consisted of the new 12 in. Austrian howitzer, divided into three parts, each drawn by a motor.

It was afterwards reported in a French newspaper that concrete platforms were found waiting for the monster siege-guns on a spot leased for building by a German firm. These tales of concrete gun platforms being laid by Germans in Belgium and France in times of peace have, however, never been officially authenticated. It is more probable that concrete blocks were manufactured on the site by the invading army and set in position when necessary. Moreover —except for the 16½ in. Krupp mortar, of which only eight existed when war broke out—the large howitzers, with their pedal wheels, are understood to have special pneumatic and hydraulic recoil chambers to cushion the shock and obviate the delay of bolting the many-tonned pieces to fixed platforms.

It is true that Krupp's were bad at designing recoil chambers for very heavy artillery. Our battleships and battle-cruisers have had 13½ in. guns for several years, while the completed capital ships of the German Navy were only

GENERAL VON FALKENHAYN.

He succeeded Moltke as Chief of Staff. Inset: General Wernher von Voights-Retz, who tried to succeed Moltke, but became Quartermaster-General of the German armies.

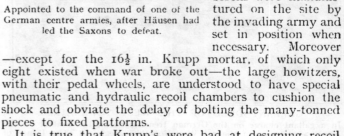

GENERAL VON CLAR.

Appointed to the command of one of the German centre armies, after Häusen had led the Saxons to defeat.

A GERMAN COIGN OF VANTAGE UNDER THE RED CROSS.

The Germans sought to justify the bombardment of Rheims Cathedral by pretending that the French used the towers for observation purposes. But they themselves committed this very offence at Vitry-le-Francois. Here, after they had hoisted three Red Cross flags on the cathedral, their officers, as testified by the mayor and a score of reputable citizens, reported from one of the towers the movements of the French troops and batteries.

HUNTING THE LURKING FOE IN A FRENCH VILLAGE.
After the seizure of the village by the British, the latter had to scour the streets for German stragglers. In our picture a trooper is seen trying a door behind which a German might have been hidden, a comrade is following, while close by is an officer with his revolver ready for emergencies.

armed with 12 in. guns. This tremendous superiority in British naval gun fire was partly obtained through a mistake made by the firm of Krupp. They undertook to arm the more recent German battleship with a 14 in. gun that would pulverise any British vessel. The great gun was made and mounted in ships designed to carry it, but at the firing trials it was found that the recoil chamber and mounting were inadequate to stand the strain. The German Navy had to fall back on the outclassed 12 in. guns.

But we may take it that the design of recoil chambers and mounting for a mobile 11 in. howitzer was not beyond the inventive—or initiative—faculty of the professors that Krupp's employed. As for the 12 in. howitzer manu-

ARRIVAL OF X-RAY APPARATUS AT A FRENCH BASE.
Arrival at a French base, in close touch with the fighting-line, of X-ray apparatus, indispensable in dealing with complicated wounds and locating bullets.

factured by Baron von Skoda in Austria, the invention of which has been attributed to an American, this can also be fitted with a mounting that makes the bolting down of the piece unnecessary. It would be so large a loss in mobility—the one thing needful—if an attacking howitzer, requiring to be moved whenever its position was searched by a defending gun of equal range, had always to be bolted to a slab of artificial rock before it could be used.

However this may be, the Skoda howitzers were a terrible surprise for the garrison of the Camp des Romains on the Heights of the Meuse by the town of St. Mihiel. They had no guns capable of **German surprise for** replying to the mighty 12 in. high-explo- **the French** sive shells that dropped on their hill fort from a distant position they could not discern. The German infantry, entrenched with light field-guns and Maxims, prevented the small body of defenders from making a reconnaissance in force. General Sarrail moved many troops down from Verdun, and the commanding general at Toul moved up many troops from the south. But with heavy artillery brought by railway to Thiaucourt, close to

A CAPTURED SUSPECT.
Suspected spy in charge of a mounted escort being taken for inquiry before the French general at Baccarat, a town to the south-east of Lunéville.

the scene of the action, the German commander kept off both the Second and Third French Armies, and continued to blow another gateway of invasion through the Camp des Romains.

Under the continual shower of devastating 12 in. shells the fort quickly crumbled. When the guns were put out of action, the Metz army advanced under cover of a general bombardment of all its guns and the fort was captured. Great was the joy in Germany. At last a breach had been made in the famous fortressed line, which had seemed so strong to the Great Military Staff at Berlin that it brought Great Britain into the conflict by the invasion of Belgium rather than lose a hundred thousand men in getting between Verdun and Toul.

Glorious were the prospective results **French surprise for** of the advance through the gap of **the Germans** a large powerful German Army, composed of the new Lorraine forces, and every soldier that could be spared from the Russian fields of war. If half a million men could be poured over the Meuse by St. Mihiel, they would arrive far behind all the main Franco-British armies from the Argonne Forest, the Suippes and Aisne River valleys, and the heights west of Noyon and St. Quentin, in Northern France. Joffre would have to retire hastily all his forces below Paris, and leave Verdun to its fate, and pivot his troops on Toul for the grand decisive battle.

INHABITANTS OF RHEIMS SLEEPING IN ONE OF THE WINE-VAULTS DURING THE GERMAN BOMBARDMENT.

All this had been foreseen by the commander of the Metz army and Helmuth von Moltke. It was the reason why they had planned and carried out the attack on the fort of the Camp des Romains. But it had also been foreseen by General Joffre. After the previous nearly successful attempt on Fort Troyon, the French Commander-in-Chief had been quite prepared to see the Verdun-Toul line breached somewhere in the middle. He was well aware of his weak point: he strengthened it before it gave way.

When the Germans advanced from the fallen fort towards the Meuse their commander was suddenly brought up. On the hills above the sunken stream the French had concealed more powerful batteries than those used in the lost fort. Marksmen were entrenched under shrapnel shelters on the nearer heights, and General Dubail, the most terrible fighter in France, directed the operations. All his guns and men were hidden. There were light "seventy-fives," buried in pits, and served by cave men who had nothing to do, unless the enemy succeeded in crossing the river and tried to storm the heights. Then the "seventy-fives" would work as they worked when the Kaiser shattered the First Bavarian Army and the White Cuirassiers of the Guards Corps in an attempt to storm the Grand Couronné de Nancy.

In front of the "seventy-fives" were the rapid-fire field-howitzers, also sunk in turf-roof pits, with their painted muzzles indistinguishable by aerial scouts from the hill pass. Farther behind were the heavy field-guns and siege-artillery from Toul. They all formed a semicircle round the position on the Heights of the Meuse, from which the Germans might try to cross. Then across the stream, flanking the German army on either side, were the French field forces from Toul and Verdun.

Directly in front of the Germans was prepared a terrific cross-fire of bullets, **The price of German advance too high** shells, and shrapnel from three points of the compass. Behind them, as they advanced, shells would fall from the river heights held by the Toul and Verdun garrisons, which were also pressing them on both sides. The French were asking the Germans a toll of a good deal more than the proverbial hundred thousand men for the passage across the Upper Meuse. Moltke thought that the price was too high. Falkenhayn, when he succeeded as Chief of Staff, came to the same conclusion. So from Aisne to Upper Meuse the Germans were held.

WORKING PARTY OF RHEIMS LADIES KNITTING IN ONE OF THE DIMLY-LIT WINE-VAULTS OF THE CITY.

CHAPTER XXXIX.

THE RAILWAY BATTLES OF NORTHERN FRANCE.

General Joffre Brings Up His Reserve—How He Handled the French Railway System—German Method of Fighting with Railways—Menace of New French Army Alters German Plans—Castelnau Strikes at German Railway Communications—Fierce Struggle Round Noyon and Peronne—General Joffre Forms Another General Reserve—Franco-British Lines Extend to the Sea—German Commander Reinforced—Pushes French Back from St. Quentin—French Stand at Roye and Quesnoy—New German Plan of Campaign—Falkenhayn Succeeds Moltke—Attack Round the Coast by Way of Lille Intended.

FROM the point of view of General Joffre, the Battle of the Aisne came to an end on September 20th, 1914. For after the general reconnaissance in force made by the Sixth French Army, the British Expeditionary Force, and the Fifth French Army, the French Commander-in-Chief decided that the line of river heights held by the strengthened German forces was too strong to be carried by a frontal attack. So he directed that the enemy should be retained along the front, and thus opened the new phase of siege warfare along the Aisne. His plan was to sap the strength of the Germans by reversing the apparent positions of the two opposing hosts, and compelling the foe to leave his rifle pits on the plateau and then to attack the trenches of the Allies.

He carried out this scheme by suddenly bringing sharp and severe pressure to bear upon the western flank of the German lines. The leading factor in modern French strategy is an apparent waste of fighting force. The commander usually keeps one large army unemployed in the rear, round some railway centre, from which it can be railed to any point on the front. It constitutes his general reserve. No matter how fierce and bitter the struggle may be in the firing-line, the general reserve does not come into action unless a disaster or victory is imminent. It is a reservoir of force kept for great decisive moments.

Napoleon handled the general reserve in a masterly way in his small, old-fashioned contests, in which horse traction and the marching power of the soldier limited the battle-front to about two miles. But with the invention and development of steam traction and telegraphic communication, the manœuvring of troops in civilised countries, over a gridiron of railways, became a vast and complicated business. Moltke simplified it by abolishing the method of the general reserve. He put all his available soldiers into the fighting-line, timing their advance and attack so

that they should be simultaneous along the great battle-front. From the railways he asked only that sweep, speed, and punctuality of transport which would enable him to bring every man and gun on to the battlefield in accordance with the time-table of the fight.

Field-Marshal von Hindenburg, Moltke's most famous pupil in railway warfare, recently employed the same method. At Tannenberg he allowed the Russian General Samsonoff to advance between two lines of East Prussian railways. He first flung out a heavily-gunned force to hold up the Russian front, then by the two railways he brought up two large bodies of troops on the flanks of the Russian army, and almost encircled it. As we shall see, the new German Commander-in-Chief, General von Falkenhayn, adopted an identical method in his attack upon the French army in and around Lille. Using two converging lines of railways, one running towards the north and the other to the east of the French position, he put every available man into the trains, in an attempt at a rapid and overwhelming concentration of force.

The method is easy, quick, and simple. It has, however, the disadvantage of being obvious. When the available forces of an enemy are known, and he has long lines of railway communications running through hostile countries—such as Belgium and Northern France—his few possible moves can be studied on the map. And both by aerial observation and by the ordinary system of espionage, the rolling-stock by which his concentrations and manœuvres are affected can be kept under surveillance.

This is one of the reasons why the German invading armies never succeeded in surprising the French Military Staff after the first frontier battles at Mons and Charleroi. Only by little combinations of forces, within marching distance of each other, could the enemy make any unexpected concentration. What he won by this old-fashioned, limited method was usually lost through a subtler use of railways by the French.

GENERAL DE MAUD'HUY,
G.C.M.G.
He commanded a fine body of French
troops between Arras and Lille.

LIEUTENANT-GENERAL SIR WILLIAM ROBERTSON, K.C.V.O., C.B., D.S.O., QUARTERMASTER-GENERAL WITH THE BRITISH EXPEDITIONARY FORCE.

"In such operations as I have described," wrote Sir John French, in his despatch of September 7th, 1914, descriptive of the Battle of Mons and the retreat to the Marne, "the work of the Quartermaster-General is of an extremely onerous nature. Lieutenant-General Sir William Robertson has met what appeared to be almost insuperable difficulties with his character-istic energy, skill, and determination; and it is largely owing to his exertions that the hardships and sufferings of the troops, inseparable from such operations, were not much greater." Born in 1860, Sir William served with distinction in India and South Africa. Our illustration is from the fine portrait in oils by Mr. John St. Helier Lander.

The incident so vividly depicted in the above spirited drawing took place at Lassigny, a village on the high road between Montvidier and Noyon, in the heart of the cider country. Here, when General Joffre began his great effort to turn the enemy's right flank above the Aisne, the Germans strongly entrenched themselves; but when the French guns had silenced the G batteries, the enemy were surprised by a dashing charge on the part French Light Cavalry. The details of the above picture are vouched fo correspondent who supplied the artist with the facts from which he w

neral Joffre's new plan was communicated to Sir John French on September 5th, 1914, and in accordance with it the troops under General Castelnau engaged the enemy's flank - guards from the Oise to Arras. The Germans admitted that their forces round Noyon were soon demoralised; and the French, advancing from Lassigny, specially distinguished themselves. A German officer writing home at this time, testified that "only the fine flower of our troops is still alive. The others cannot resist so many misfortunes, and fall to earth, killed by the efforts and sufferings that duty imposes on us."

GALLANTRY OF THE 1ST WEST YORKSHIRES IN THE BATTLE OF THE AISNE.

During the Battle of the Aisne the 1st West Yorkshires were sent to relieve the Guards Brigade on the British right on the night of September 19th, 1914. Next morning they were ordered to reinforce the first line, which was being heavily attacked. For a quarter of a mile they advanced under a hail of shrapnel and machine-gun fire. Out of 1,150 only 206 afterwards answered the roll-call. Among the killed was Lieut. E. W. Wilson, the officer who is seen falling. The picture is from a sketch and description furnished by Sergeant J. F. Woodcock.

For the French, who have for centuries been remarkable for their power of originality, have revived Napoleon's use of a general reserve, and worked out a brilliant system of employing it on the immensely long modern battle-front. The reserve consisted of locomotives, rolling-stock, and auxiliary motor-vehicles, collected at various transport centres, with men, guns, horses, and supplies ready for railway movement to any point along the front of two hundred or more miles. No study of railway maps could disclose the point at which this reservoir of force would be employed. In fact, part of it was sometimes kept in movement on the rails to distract the enemy's spies and disturb the German Military Staff with feints of attack, that might develop in a single night into a violent onset hundreds of miles distant from the transporting centres.

All that the German commander could do in answer to this continual secret menace was to press continually against the French front, and prepare on his own exposed flank · for any eventuality. By pressing on in front he tried to compel General Joffre to use his general reserve for a defensive purpose. But. naturally, the German commander was never able to feel quite sure that he had succeeded in this design. He certainly did not succeed in it by the counter-attacks he made against the Franco-British positions on the Aisne and Suippes in the third week of September. General Joffre, as we have seen, sent some reinforcements to General Maunoury's Sixth Army between Noyon and Soissons, but at the same time he continued to build up his general reserve.

WRECKED HOTEL DE VILLE AND BELFRY AT ARRAS.
Between October 5th and 30th, 1914, the Germans bombarded Arras three times, wrecking the sixteenth-century Hotel de Ville and the beautiful belfry. Arras was destroyed by the Vandals in 407, and by the Normans in 880; was besieged in 1414 and 1479; taken by the Prince of Orange in 1578; and again besieged in 1640 and 1654 by Condé, and rescued by Turenne.

The mere threat of it saved the whole of North-Eastern France. All that the Germans soon afterwards violently and vainly struggled for—the entire occupation of Belgium, the seaports of Dunkirk and Calais and the heights of Gris Nez, opposite Dover—were theirs for the taking at the beginning of the Battle of the Aisne. They occupied the important city of Amiens, far to the south of the places they afterwards desired to reach. They retained the Belgian Army in Antwerp, and had brought up the siege-artillery for the rapid reduction of the last Belgian stronghold. What is still more important,

The factor that saved North-Eastern France they also had in Germany large masses of troops of inferior quality, but well provided with artillery, and with these they might well have been able to strengthen and extend their lines eastward to Amiens and the sea coast.

Instead, they suddenly abandoned Amiens in the second week of September, and withdrew all their eastern forces towards their main · lines of communication round St. Quentin and Cambrai. Such was the effect of the menace of General Joffre's reserve army, held far in the rear. The Germans could not divine at what point he would strike with it. They feared alike a terrible, reinforced assault on their front, where the British soldiers had already nearly wedged through, or a French advance up the Oise River, cutting off their western detachments and assailing their main railway communications with distant Cologne.

As a matter of fact, General Joffre had arranged to strike at the German communications from Amiens. He placed his new army under General Castelnau, one of the heroes of the battles round Nancy, and launched it across Northern France on September 20th. By way of keeping the enemy still further occupied, another French force—composed of Territorial divisions, oldish men of the militia class—operated under General Brugère to the north of Castelnau's army.

This remarkable effort did not exhaust the reservoir of force at the disposal of the French Commander-in-Chief. As soon as General Castelnau had engaged the enemy's flank-guards from Noyon to Arras, another French army of young, first-rate troops was formed and railed, under the command of General Maud'huy, to the region of Arras and Lens. Territorial divisions on September 30th

VIEW OF THE TOWN OF ALBERT.
Albert, a town on the River Ancre, was wrecked by the Germans in the autumn of 1914.

extended the French lines to Lille, and from Lille to Dunkirk a thinner stretch of British and French Marines and British sailors, with armoured motor-cars, carried the Franco-British front to the sea. Large detachments of the allied cavalry—French dragoons and hussars, British heavy and light horsemen, and the chivalry of India, brought up with their mounts from Marseilles—strengthened the line from Lille to the Channel.

Such were the complete dispositions of the allied forces barely a fortnight after the enemy turned to make a stand by the Aisne and the Suippes Rivers. German military authorities themselves admit that the way in which General Joffre handled his railways was a revelation. He had clean surpassed them in the kind of modern strategy in which they thought they excelled everybody. They had thoroughly studied the military capacity of the railways of North-Eastern France. General von Kluck and other German Army commanders had visited the country some years before the war, and examined the ground from Rheims to Noyon, and from Arras, Amiens, to Calais. While they were busy at this work of personal reconnaissance, the French commander of the army corps at Amiens—his name was Joffre—was also riding about the region, and carefully studying it, as one **Joffre's earlier study** of the great battlefields of the future. **of the battlefield** And now that the obscure and neglected major-general once stationed at Amiens had become the captain of France in the year of her great destiny, the work he had done, after his return from the

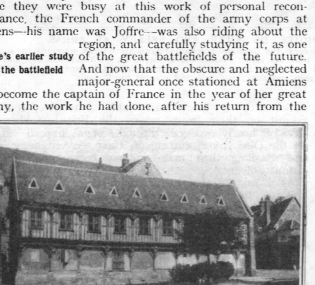

FIFTEENTH-CENTURY TREATY HOUSE AT NOYON.
The ancient town of Noyon, in the Department of the Oise, was the scene of the Coronation of Charlemagne in 768. Calvin was born there in 1509. The fighting-line crept up from Compiègne, through Noyon, St. Quentin, Peronne, and Arras to Armentières.

conquest of Timbuctoo, was bearing good fruit. On September 17th the German troops round Noyon were placed under the command of Field-Marshal von Heeringen. They consisted of men drawn from Hamburg, Bremen, and Schleswig-Holstein province. Some hundreds of motor-vehicles were employed in transporting battalions of infantry to the **Motor transport of the** fighting-line, as many of the men were **invader's battalions** too fatigued to march. They had tramped a hundred and fifty miles in five days, with insufficient food, and were still badly fed. When the flank battle opened on September 20th they immediately fell to pieces.

Both the rifle fire and the gun fire of the new French army were murderous. Violent in attack and tenacious in defence, General Castelnau's men fought down all opposition. Only the heavy German artillerymen of the Government gunnery school could make any impression on the French soldiers. The Germans admit that their forces round Noyon were soon demoralised. "The time came," writes one of their officers, "when a man mocks at all feelings of humanity and civilisation. When a party of our soldiers came on a house, you can be sure that they left nothing. All their terrible instincts awakened into power. Our 17th Division is no longer a division, but a little company at the end of its strength and ammunition. I must say that our leaders have not acted as men of skill and foresight. Their attitude strikes one as that of bewildered, troubled souls who are no longer masters of themselves."

IN THE TOWN OF ROYE (SOMME).
An old street of quaint shops in the once prosperous town of Roye, now little more than a name.

On September 21st Heeringen sent a Bavarian reinforcement to the beaten and distracted force guarding his western flank. There was another fierce fight round the woods of Ribecourt, with the French advancing from Lassigny along the Oise. Again the French won, and the German officer, writing home to his family, draws a significant picture of the way in which men of his nation strangely wilt under defeat.

"What will happen to us? I do not know and I dare not forecast. Many of our men are dying from fatigue and privation. Our officers especially are in a state of nervous exhaustion. They cannot do anything more. Our horses, that for weeks have fed, watered, and slept

VIEW OF THE CITADEL OF ARRAS.
Arras, the capital of the Pas-de-Calais, was bombarded by the Germans on October 5th-8th, 21st-24th, and 30th. Those who saw it afterwards described it as "a modern Pompeii." At Arras was signed the treaty of peace after Agincourt.

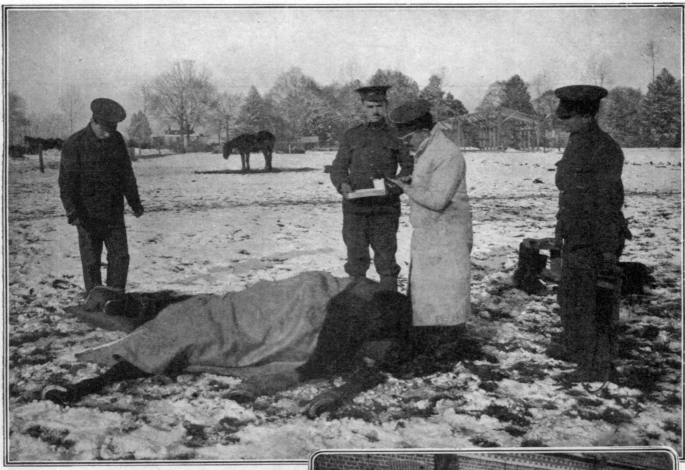

TENDING A WOUNDED HORSE: AN OPERATION IN THE FIELD.

The operation was performed under chloroform for the removal of a shell splinter. The above photograph is the property of the R.S.P.C.A. Fund for Sick and Wounded Horses.

SHELL HAVOC AMONG ARTILLERY HORSES.
The destruction of horses in the Great War was only less appalling than the human slaughter. Our photograph is of a team killed by a German shell, which also killed the two drivers.

with their saddles on, suddenly fall on the ground and lie stone-still. The same thing is happening to the mass of our soldiers. Only the fine flower of our troops is still alive. The others cannot resist so many misfortunes, and fall to earth, killed by the efforts and sufferings that duty imposes on us."

Seldom has the extraordinary way in which sickness and exhaustion rapidly tell on a dispirited army been so vividly described. Though Heeringen was making at the time a tremendous effort on his front, along the Aisne heights, his flank was growing weaker and weaker. General Castelnau drove fiercely in, on a line stretching some sixty miles, from Arras in the north to Ribecourt near the Aisne. East of Arras the French Territorial troops penetrated to the historic city of Cambrai, close to the edge of the former battlefield where the Second British Army Corps, in the retreat from Mons, made its heroic stand against the forces of Kluck. Peronne was taken on the road to the important railway centre of St. Quentin; and Tergnier, another knot of German lines of communication, was menaced.

German communications menaced

The impetuosity and skill of the French troops were magnificent. In the valley of the Oise, for example, Lieutenant Verlin, with fifty men, held up six thousand hostile troops. The small party was engaged in a reconnaissance on the right bank of the river, where Uhlans were vaguely reported to have been seen. The officer sighted the enemy in large numbers, and ordered his men to rejoin their regiment without showing themselves. But the Germans discovered the little force, and fired on it as it took shelter in a wood. But when Lieutenant Verlin got his men safely amid the trees, he spread them out on a very long front, and there, by good marksmanship and quick dodging from tree to tree, they made the enemy think the wood was held by at least a regiment. The Germans brought up guns and searched the forested tract with shrapnel, but the Frenchmen were so few that they did not suffer much from the gun fire. Had the Germans at any time charged, they would have won without a struggle. But they were over-cautious, and after holding the ground till midnight, and losing thirty-seven out of fifty men, the French retired and joined their regiment.

Advancing between the Oise and Somme Rivers, General Castelnau pressed forward towards the railway junction of Tergnier, from which the German batteries and troops on the heights of the Aisne were supplied with ammunition and supplies. The heavy German siege-artillery could only be withdrawn with any speed along the railway from Laon to Tergnier, and Tergnier to Maubeuge. So the holding of the line was absolutely vital to Field-Marshal von Heeringen. He brought the Bavarian army by rail from Alsace, and placed it on the canal running from the Somme to the Oise, in front of the railway line. The

NIGHT ATTACK ON THE GERMAN TRENCHES DURING THE BATTLE OF THE AISNE.
Attack and counter-attack by night as well as by day followed in quick succession during the fighting along the Aisne, in the efforts of the enemy to establish ascendancy. The desperate nature of the fighting may be estimated by the fact that between September 12th and October 8th, 1914, the British losses, as given in Sir John French's despatch, in killed, wounded, and missing, totalled 561 officers and 12,980 men.

proximity of the railway also enabled him quickly to move heavy artillery towards the canal. The result was that the French were beaten back at last to Roye.

But the attack on Tergnier had only been undertaken with a view to keeping the enemy engaged all along the line, from Compiègne to Arras. The principal attempt to cut the German lines of communication was made from Peronne on St. Quentin, far to the north. Toward St. Quentin Heeringen had withdrawn all the western German forces; but they were quite insufficient to make any sort of stand against the army of General Castelnau. German army corps had to be hurried towards the critical railway junction, at the highest possible speed, to save the entire German host from a retreat and a rout.

For more than a week the battle swayed furiously between French forces coming from Amiens through Peronne and
Furious hand-to-hand fighting German forces coming from Belgium and Lorraine and the Vosges Mountains through St. Quentin. Hand-to-hand fighting went on for days. The French charged the enemy almost continuously with infantry and cavalry, and when they gave ground under gun fire, the Germans in turn charged them. They fought over and over the same ground, until there were ten miles of dead bodies. They went on fighting across the corpses of comrades and foes, until the road became blocked, and still they went on fighting. The artillery on both sides was driven now forward and now backward, above the dead lying on the rain-sodden ways, until there was no need to bury the bodies. They had been ground into the muddy earth and covered. In between the two advancing and retiring lines of field-guns were two armies of foot soldiers, struggling in desperate fury with both bullet and steel.

Terribly eager to use the bayonet was the French infantryman. He was, at times, too eager. For the enemy was remarkably effective in defence. The Germans had, as Heeringen afterwards admitted to a neutral visitor, learnt something from the British soldier. They entrenched most vigorously, and then, with concealed machine-guns and hidden field-artillery, waited for the French attack. The Germans, however, could not rely on their rifle fire to stop a bayonet charge, as our troops did all the way from Mons to Ypres. German marksmanship was not equal to that, but their artillery fire, from defensive positions over ranges they had taken, was undoubtedly good.

The French suffered at first from the dash and passionate courage of their infantry. But, with their quick intelligence, they soon adapted themselves to the new tactics, and took, in turn, to retreating at the least opportunity. This brought the Germans out of their trenches into the open, and beyond the cover of their heavy artillery fire. So then the light French field-gun came fully into play, and properly prepared the way for an infantry attack in rushes ending in a bayonet charge.

Every village was the scene of fierce, **How Frenchmen** protracted struggles. In house-to-house **sacrificed their homes** warfare the Frenchman was a scientific fighter—cold, lucid, passionless, and mercilessly effective. He surrendered his villages to the enemy, and then battered them to shapeless ruins with his own guns. The German took long to find good cover in any hamlet from which he was driving his opponents, while the French, as their foes admitted afterwards, were very skilful in using any kind of wall as a creeping shelter. But what surprised the Germans was the way the Frenchmen sacrificed the homes of their own people.

FRENCH CARRYING A VILLAGE IN A NIGHT ATTACK.

There was fierce fighting at close quarters in the battles west of the Aisne, and many villages were carried by our gallant allies at the point of the bayonet. The Germans had dug trenches at the entrance to each hamlet, and had placed their machine-guns in the houses, but they were powerless to withstand the furious charges of the indomitable French infantry, eager to get to work on the enemy with the bayonet.

Each village was held until the Germans brought up guns that overpowered the French field-artillery. The French then retired, sending their country-people ahead of them along the road to Amiens. A rearguard was left to amuse the enemy, but it was also withdrawn without a serious struggle. The Germans then moved up to take possession of their new point of vantage. Their infantry cautiously advanced, entered the street, and then threw out patrols to keep in touch with the retiring enemy.

When the infantry and cavalry were well enough established to make any attempt on the new artillery position disastrous, the guns moved forward towards their new site. But before they arrived the village was a flaming waste, strewn with the bodies of German soldiers. The French gunners had only withdrawn a mile or two, and trained each battery carefully and exactly, so as to bring a fire over every house. As soon as the Germans collected in triumph, a hurricane of shrapnel and shell burst above them. Each distant gun sent a shell dead over its mark every three seconds or so. There was no time to escape. The victorious infantry was blown or riddled to death, and the French soldiers came forward in extended order and recovered the

Infantry blown or riddled to death

ground. One more quiet, lovely French village had disappeared, but what did it matter? Some thousands of Germans had been buried in or around it, and it was easier for France to replace bricks and mortar than it was for Germany to breed and train more fighting men.

The charming old village churches were shelled alike by friend and foe. As a British artillery officer complained, when the struggle was extending to the sea and he was taking part in it, some of our uninformed war correspondents were rather inclined to cant about the vandalism of the Germans. Grievous crimes against the ancient lovely monuments of civilisation they undoubtedly committed at Louvain, Senlis, Rheims, Termonde, Malines, Ypres, and Soissons. But, on the other hand, the modern system of fire control of long-ranged guns practically makes any tower or steeple on the battle-front a mark for shells. The French and Belgians were hard put to it when the enemy was entrenched around one of their churches.

For then, without a doubt, German fire-control officers, with telescopes and range-finding instruments, were watching from the church tower, and directing by telephone the fire of their batteries on to their opponents' guns and troops. By wrecking the tower with shell fire, our allies could save the lives of hundreds of their men, perhaps thousands of them, and turn a check into an advance. Were they to forgo all this to save one of their beautiful old churches? They did not forgo it.

Watch-towers indiscriminately shelled

The church tower fell. Naturally, the enemy was much less hesitant. He shelled and wrecked any high object from which his opponents might be able to survey his lines and watch his movements.

This is one of the unfortunate results of the terrible progress in modern artillery science. Heavy guns now have a range of seven miles; some of our great pieces of ordnance can send a shell more than ten miles. By observing, from a high position, the distant target with the range-finding instrument invented by a British man of science, a mark at a distance of six or seven miles can be struck with remarkable accuracy, after a shot or two by way of trial. Captive observation balloons and flying machines with wireless telegraphic apparatus are more or less useful; but there is nothing so good as the steady outlook from a church tower.

Advancing brigades cannot take balloons with them, and aeroplanes are not yet numerous enough to be employed with every field battery. But in Europe there

277

A GALLANT IRISHMAN'S SPLENDID STAND.
After a shell fire lasting from dusk till the afternoon of the following day the Germans rushed a certain position held by the British. In one section of the deep shelter trenches, when help arrived, only one out of fifteen British soldiers was still defying the enemy. He was an Irishman, and fell unconscious from the effects of his wounds.

are village churches rising over every mile or two of country. All armies used them in turn, and in turn destroyed them when occupied by the enemy. Never was there so horribly destructive a war as the Great War. It transformed the temples of the Prince of Peace into the watch places where Thor and Mars, the old gods of war of the Teutonic and Latin races, exulted above the slaughter and bitter fumes of the battlefield.

In their first sweeping movement the French troops got within reach of the railway near St. Quentin, and one of their adventurous scouts tapped a telephone wire connecting two stations held by the Germans. He overheard an operator send instructions for two armoured German trains to be despatched. Jumping on his bicycle, the scout rode back to his field headquarters, and returned with a detachment of soldiers with
Railway holocaust near St. Quentin machine-guns and sappers with dynamite. The line was dynamited, and the two trains came thundering along into the terrible ambush. The first was wrecked and thrown off the track, and the second collided with the wreckage, just where the machine-guns were trained on the line. Two trainloads of troops were killed or taken prisoners, and a good deal of ammunition was also captured.

St. Quentin, however, could not be captured. The German commander, apprised by his aerial scouts of the French advance, worked his railway system in turn to its complete capacity. From Belgium, through Maubeuge, from Germany, through Liège and Namur, from Alsace and Lorraine, through Rethel, troops and artillery and ammunition were conveyed to the threatened junction. By means of their heavy guns the German reinforcements pushed the French back on the road to Peronne, and by

September 25th they had won the town, and their advance guards were on the way to Amiens.

The light French artillery had to abandon position after position, owing to the fearful concentrated fire poured on it. Early in the afternoon the shells began to fall round the cross-roads where the general and his staff were. The general was urged by his officers to retire. " No," he said. " As long as I stay here the troops cannot retreat. We have got to hold on." He stayed till three farms close by were set on fire by **Grim tenacity of the French** the German shells. After that he still remained by the cross-roads, and thus won the day. For at the end of two hours the enemy's fire somewhat slackened, and the French infantry went forward. By the evening the French batteries occupied the positions from which the German guns had been firing.

In the night time the French used an extraordinary method of harassing their foes. Flying columns of heavy cavalry went out as quietly as possible, and got as close as they could to the enemy's lines without rousing them. Then, when some German sentry fired in alarm, the French dragoons put their horses at the gallop, and charged full speed across the German bivouacs. They burnt convoys and motor-cars, upset the petrol, did all the damage they could, and threw the camp in wild alarm. At last the dragoons were compelled to shelter in a wood, in the rear of the German lines, where neither they nor their horses had anything to eat for two days.

They hoped to be relieved by a successful advance of the French army, but this did not take place. So again, in the middle of the night, the horsemen charged straight through a German encampment, yelling, and slashing with their swords, and taking everything in their way—ditches, and hedges, and barriers. Strange,

BRILLIANT EXPLOIT OF MOROCCAN CAVALRY.
Near Furnes the Germans had managed to conceal a gun on a farm, and dressed the gunners as peasants. The device was discovered by a party of Spahis, who, awaiting a favourable opportunity, surprised the enemy, captured the gun, killed the gunners, and dealt swift justice to those who had been bribed to allow the Germans to place the gun on the farm.

A HASTY WAYSIDE BREAKFAST WITH GENERAL JOFFRE, G.C.B., AT THE FRONT.

The French Commander-in-Chief, General Joseph Jacques Cesaire Joffre, is seen on the right of the picture, which represents an early morning breakfast during one of the long motor rides taken by General Joffre to various points of the great operations controlled by him. The meal referred to must have been quite a chance affair, and the camera suggests that the famous general was the first to finish. When King George was in France (December 1st-5th, 1914) he conferred on General Joffre the Grand Cross of the Order of the Bath.

FRENCH TROOPS RETAKE A VILLAGE DURING THE FIERCE STRUGGLE FOR VERDUN.
The above picture is from a photograph taken by a French officer during the recapture, in October, 1914, of Ville-en-Woevre, a village in the department of the Meuse, some twelve miles east of Verdun.

unexpected, ghostly, shrieking figures, they excited such alarm that most of them managed to escape from bullets and bayonets and get safely back to their own lines.

At the cost of dreadful carnage, the hastily gathered new German army succeeded in pushing General Castelnau's force back to the hills of Lassigny and the town of Roye.

It was again the lack of heavy field-artillery that prevented the French from driving home the advantage they first won, and breaking in on the enemy's line of communications at St. Quentin. Each French army corps took the field with one hundred and twenty 3 in. guns. This was all its ordnance. Each German army corps had one hundred and eight guns of similar calibre, together with **German advantage in** thirty-six light howitzers with a range of **field-artillery** over four miles. In addition, it had sixteen heavy field-howitzers throwing a 6 in. shell over five miles, and some heavy cannon throwing a forty-pound shrapnel, or shell, six and a half miles, and eight 8 in. howitzers with a range of five miles. Thus in all, each German army corps possessed some forty pieces of heavy artillery, throwing large, murderous shells from one mile to two and a half miles farther than any French field-gun could reach. The 6 in. field-howitzer of the Germans, especially, was a terrible weapon. Its 88 lb. shell, with 17½ lb. of high-explosive, burst into seven hundred splinters of steel, and no gun-shield could withstand it.

For some years before the war the best French artillery experts, such as General Maitrot, had pointed out the heavy disadvantage under which their armies would have to fight against the more powerfully weaponed invaders. But the majority of French representatives in Parliament would not consent to spend the money required on national armament. They could not bring themselves to think there was any danger of war. So, as in 1870, the French Army went into the fight with guns that were outranged by the artillery of their enemy. And, as in 1870, the French gunners had in many cases to run their guns up at the gallop, shelled for a mile or more on the way, until they were within striking distance of the longer ranged batteries of heavy German field-artillery.

It was not brilliant tactics. But there was no choice. The only alternative was to retreat—and where would the retreat stop ?—or heroically struggle on through extreme danger, and by superb courage and decision get close enough to the enemy to return his fire. The flat region about the middle course of the Somme River is a country of large farms, given over to the growing of sugar beets. Through this dry, level land the Germans had little difficulty in moving their heavy field-artillery with almost as much speed as their light guns were drawn. In a few days they had occupied a wide tract between their railway communications and the firing-line of General Castelnau's army. In front of Noyon they held the hills of Lassigny and the railway centre of Chaulnes, where the line from Amiens to Rheims and the line from Paris to Cambrai cross. The French held Lihons and Quesnoy en Santerre, Roye and Ribecourt on the Oise above Compiègne.

But though the French were driven back from the main railway track by which the German armies were fed, munitioned and reinforced, they were not defeated. No force of men and heavy guns that the German Commander-in-Chief sent against them at Roye, Quesnoy, and Lihons, could shift them from the positions they took up. Each point of vantage they held was furiously attacked. At Quesnoy the Germans **Costly German** lost in one day six thousand men. **advance on Lihons** Then in revenge for the loss of Quesnoy, they advanced on Lihons, on the highway to Amiens. As usual, the enemy began with a heavy bombardment of the already battered and shattered village. The French gunners made only a feeble reply, and soon ceased completely to maintain the duel.

Thinking the place was at last theirs to take, the Germans poured out on the road from Chaulnes, only a mile and a quarter distant. But when they reached the outskirts of the village, the French infantry, who had been hiding in the ruined houses, received the attackers with a rapid rifle fire, followed by a bayonet charge. The Germans retreated with all speed, but again the French caught them and punished them. For there were quick-firing guns, also concealed by the village, and they opened a murderous shrapnel bombardment upon the thronging fugitives and brought many of them down.

For months this kind of warfare went on, each side entrenched in the beet-fields, behind the broken walls of sugar factories, and spirit distilleries and farms. Along a wide belt of land, over which the contending armies swayed, there was nothing but burnt ruins and the wreckage of hundreds of thousands of homes of a once happy race of cultivators living in a once fertile, pleasant, peaceful country. Prosperous towns like Roye and Albert became little more than names; their smoking streets were shelled into heaps of rubble before the bricks cooled; then the rubble was scattered by guns searching again for infantry using the last remnants of walls as cover. During the winter the batteries of heavy howitzers and long-range cannon, ordered in desperate urgency by the French Government, were ready for delivery in large numbers. All along the French front the effect of the new armament began to be felt. There was a resilience in the French lines around Roye and Lihon and Albert, now that General Castelnau had an artillery power equal to that of his opponent. The gallant French infantryman had lost none of his vehemence of attack, while digging for months making intricate, zigzag ditches and underground passages as protection against the enemy's gun fire. Having saved France by his spade, and continued the besieging operations begun in the Aisne valley, he was just as ready as ever to use the bayonet when his gunners had beaten down the hostile batteries.

Streets shelled into heaps of rubble

But after the check to the turning movement against the German flank, nearly four months passed before the French troops were fully provided with heavy field ordnance. In the meantime, the Germans tried, in a series of furious assaults at different points, to smash their way through the allied front and get in turn a flanking offensive in the west.

Towards the end of September the German Military Staff planned an ingenious answer to the attack made a week before on their flank by General Castelnau's army. The French commander had attempted an outflanking movement on Peronne, some twenty miles above the German western wing. The Germans replied by a similar movement on Lille, some sixty miles above the French western wing. This driving attack by the enemy through Lille was the turning-point in the entire campaign. The conception of it, which was strongly opposed by Helmuth von Moltke, altered every detail of the German conduct of war in the western theatre. Moltke intended to bring all available forces to bear on the eastern wing front round the Argonne Forest and attempt to cut the Franco-British front near Verdun. The Kaiser, however, backed by Admiral von Tirpitz, desired most urgently to win to the sea coast.

For political reasons, it was wished to expose Great Britain to the menace of invasion, and to gain a line of ports near Dover and the Thames estuary, from which submarines could operate and impede the transport of troops and munitions from England to France. As Chief of the Great General Staff, Moltke had to take a wider view than Tirpitz and Bethmann-Hollweg had impressed upon the Kaiser. The diversion of the main military forces of France and Belgium towards the sea coast appeared to him a political demi-semi-naval move that promised no large results. He kept to the purely military point of view, in which an operation of a decisive nature against the Franco-British armies was required to be carried out successfully without delay, in order to free the twenty

The Kaiser's desire to win the sea coast

SAVING THE GUNS AT SOISSONS: AN INCIDENT OF THE FIGHTING ON THE AISNE.
Despite the heavy attacks of the enemy, about fifty British soldiers at Soissons stuck to their guns until their ammunition was exhausted. Happily, reinforcements came up in the nick of time, and the guns were saved.

BRITISH CAVALRY BIVOUAC IN NORTHERN FRANCE.
The scene reproduced for us by the camera is of one of the few occasions during the early part of the war when our cavalrymen were able to enjoy an interlude from their almost constant and strenuous work. And they were able to choose a very picturesque corner for their encampment.

AN AUTO-'BUS OPERATING THEATRE.
When the history of the motor-'bus in war comes to be written the vehicle shown above should have mention. At one time plying between the Madeleine and the Place de la Bastille, in Paris, it was transformed into an operating-theatre, and taken to the front—a striking instance of the ingenuity of our French Allies.

army corps of the first-line troops for the conquest of Warsaw and Russian Poland.

For two months two and a half millions of German soldiers, including practically all the young, well-trained troops of the first line, had been struggling in the western field of war. This had allowed Russia to mobilise in such strength as to rout all Austria-Hungary's best troops, menace Budapest and Vienna, and win the oil-fields of Galicia. Now one of the chief industrial centres of Germany—Silesia—was also threatened. Half a million hastily-trained German recruits would soon be available. Though useless in operations where skilful, experienced, and marksmanlike infantry was needed, they could be employed in a mass attack to break the French lines near

the Argonne, for there were fine artillery forces with superb equipment to back them.

Such seems to have been the view of Moltke. But his rival, General von Falkenhayn, acting as Minister of War, and eager for the practical fighting control of the armies in the field, sided with Tirpitz and the Kaiser. He drew up the plan of a brilliant new campaign. The result of it would please everybody. Belgium would be entirely conquered and occupied; the sea coast from the Scheldt to the Somme or Seine mouths would be at the disposal of Admiral von Tirpitz, and the wing of the Allies armies would be so turned as to make the march on Paris an easy matter. Falkenhayn's plan was adopted. Moltke retired under the colour of sickness, and the War Minister became Chief of the Great General Staff, a position equal to that which General Joffre occupied in France, with the exception that the French commander happily had no Kaiser to interfere with him.

The immediate consequences of Falkenhayn's appointment were that the flank of the new German advance towards the sea coast had to be cleared by the reduction of the forts of Antwerp and the capture of the Belgian army. For with the intended movement at Lille, round the French western wing, the lines of German communication would be extended so much farther as to increase seriously the danger of hostile sallies from Antwerp. Moreover, the unoccupied Belgian coast, where British Marines were holding the seaport of Ostend, was even more dangerous than Antwerp. The German Staff could not tell what force of men Lord Kitchener might land there, either to co-operate with the Belgian Army, or to sweep down directly towards Lille and take the new German army in reverse.

While the former German Chief of Staff had kept in view only the true objective of his western forces, the comparatively small Belgian army operating around Antwerp had not mattered. Hemmed in by German garrison forces round Brussels, it was too far away to imperil the German railway communication that ran from Maubeuge to Namur and Liège. So long as the Belgians were contained well beyond this railway, their activities against the militia corps set to bar their sallies did not tell on the decisive struggles in France. In the more mobile pieces of their siege-artillery, the German retaining forces round Antwerp had mighty long-range weapons which quite redressed the balance between their oldish Landwehr infantry and the more vigorous and enduring young Belgian troops. For, like the French, the Belgians were lacking in heavy field-artillery.

Had Moltke so wished, the bombardment of Antwerp could have begun soon after the fall of the French frontier fortress of Maubeuge in the first week of September. Austrian gunners in charge of the 12 in. Skoda howitzers, and German gun sections with the 11 in. Krupp mortars, were then waiting at Brussels and **German strategy** elsewhere for work. Verdun was un-**and field tactics** approachable, and Paris became still more remote. Only Antwerp was assailable. But Moltke regarded the attack on the Belgian stronghold as a distraction. He still held to the old programme of concentrating against France, with a view to so injuring her that troops of the second and third class could be used to retain her broken armies, while the troops of the first line were swung across Europe against Russia.

It is difficult to find fault with Moltke's strategy. It was as sound as it was obvious, and no doubt the older Moltke was the originator of it. The trouble was that the German soldier of the new generation was an inferior fighting man to the French soldier of the new era. The French also possessed in General Joffre a commander with more genius than any German leader in the western theatre of war. The superiority

of certain sections of the German armament—their unusual number of machine-guns and their heavy artillery—was not sufficient in the end to compensate for their defects in human material. So the strategical plan of the two Moltkes, bettered in various details by the constant labours of the Great Military Staff, proved impossible of execution.

Nothing, however, was gained in adopting, in the middle of the campaign, the new and inferior plan of Falkenhayn. German strategy had not been at fault; but German field tactics, such as the overmarching of the men and the constant attacks in mass formations, had been defective, and the training of German troops had been bad. These defects, as we shall see in the course of this history, were only enhanced by the new leadership of the enemy.

THE TRAMP OF ARMED MEN THROUGH THE DESERTED VILLAGES OF NORTHERN FRANCE.
Save for an occasional abbé or curé, and the fairly constant passage of troops or despatch-riders, the villages of Northern France were deserted in the autumn of 1914. The circular view was taken in the ruined town of Albert after its bombardment, the survivors shown including one British officer. A deep hole in front of the group was made by a shell, and there are shrapnel marks on the building behind them.

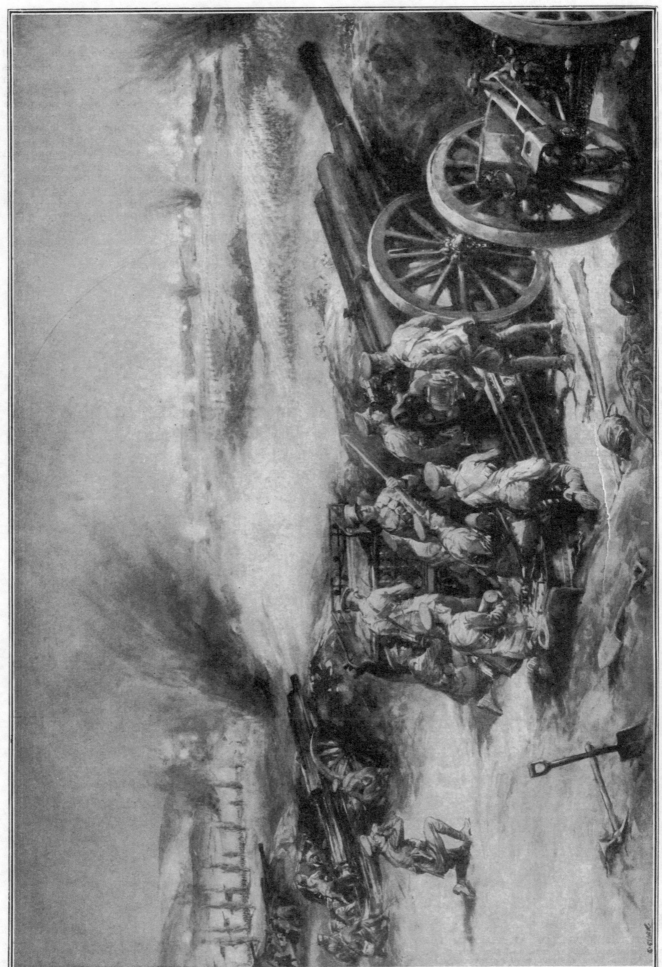

BRITISH 60-POUNDER BATTERY AT WORK IN THE VINEYARD DISTRICT OF FRANCE, OCTOBER, 1914.

The battery was helping to cover a flanking movement against the German position 7,500 yards away on the right. French shells are bursting over the German lines, the famous "75's" of our allies being placed on the left. In the middle distance British reserves are advancing, and more to the right German shells are sending up bursts of dark earth. The gun on the left of the British battery has just been fired; that on the right is being loaded. The British 60-pounders have a 5 in. calibre, and a range of 10,000 yards, and are furnished with a recoil attachment.

THE ALLIES SHOULDER TO SHOULDER: A MIXED PATROL OF FRENCH AND BRITISH TROOPS CUTTING THEIR WAY THROUGH A TOWN HELD BY THE ENEMY.

When details of all the operations on both sides can be fu ly studied in the voluminous publications of the French, German, British, and Belgian Military Staffs—which will appear years after the war is over—it will probably be found that General Joffre retained such initiative that he was able to make the Germans adopt their new plan of attack round the sea coast.

Ideas forced upon the Germans by General Joffre

We must remember that, some weeks before the Germans advanced towards Lille, the Franco-British lines already extended from Switzerland to Dunkirk, with a sort of naval bridge-head at Ostend, where a fresh British army could land and link on with both the Belgian force at Antwerp and the French force at Lille. By September 30th General Joffre, moreover, had another large army of first-rate troops, under General Maud'huy, which he was deploying between Arras and Lille.

Three of his best generals — Sarrail, De Langle de Cary, and Dubail—were operating round the Argonne Forest in anticipation of the move that Moltke had intended to make. So we may conclude that when General von Falkenhayn, assisted by the Kaiser and Admiral von Tirpitz, planned the new movement towards the sea, he only acted in accordance with the ideas which General Joffre had forced upon the Germans. Moltke, who might have won through in Hindenburg fashion, by sticking with Prussian stubbornness to his

A GERMAN TRENCH IN THE ARGONNE.

own view of the case, was, happily for the Allies, replaced by a more impressionable man. It was very likely the nervous, excitable temperament of the Kaiser himself that laid him open to the subtle influences which General Joffre was exerting, and so brought about the resignation of Moltke and the rise to power of a more pliable, incompetent, courtier Chief of Staff.

The heroic Belgian Army holding its last ditch

Only for the heroic, outnumbered, outgunned Belgians was there any great danger in the new plan of campaign formed by the new German commander. France had to lose Lille and Douai, and see the beautiful old buildings of Arras shattered by the enemy's guns; but the French temporary loss in territory and resources round Lille was more than redeemed by the advantage won in lengthening and weakening the enemy's front, and putting out of action some hundreds of thousands of German troops.

When, however, the Belgians were threatened by a bombardment of Antwerp, their entire military force and even their national existence were endangered. It seemed at the time to be the last stand of the saviours of international law and morality against their mighty, brutal aggressors. The heroic Belgian army was holding its last ditch, apparently, with terrific odds against it. All the civilised world—of which Germany now formed no part—looked with deep, tragic interest towards the first event of Falkenhayn's new plan.

CHAPTER XL.

EARLY GAINS AND LOSSES IN THE WAR BY SEA.

Our Submarines Blockade the Throat of the Elbe—First Success of our Underwater Craft—E9 Sinks a German Cruiser and Destroyer—Three British Armoured Cruisers Torpedoed off Holland—" It's a Long, Long Way to Tipperary, when you have to Swim There "—What we Gained in the Disaster to the Aboukir, Hogue, and Cressy—Triumphant Trick by Russian Admiral—German Cruiser Squadron Defeated in the Baltic—Teutonic Submarines sink the Russian Pallada—Combined French and British Fleets' Operations in the Adriatic—Historic Duel between Armed Merchant Liners—How the Cunarder Carmania sunk the Cap Trafalgar—The Dwarf and the Spar Torpedo—German Merchant Fleet Captured—Successes of the Elusive Emden—Pegasus Keeps the Flag Flying at Zanzibar—Capture of New Britain, German New Guinea and South-West African Town of Lüderitzbucht—The " Notorious Hymn of Hate "—British Sailors Bomb the Zeppelin Shed at Düsseldorf.

IN the first glorious fortnight of September, when the armies of the Allies, in both the western and eastern theatres of war, were throwing back the invaders, the quieter and even more effectual work of our fleets was being carried on with rigour. There was no turn in the tide of war at sea. From the beginning it had flowed in the direction controlled by our Admiralty, and though in the course of the month of September the Germans won some advantages in commerce-raiding and submarine operations, the silent and inevitable pressure of our Grand Fleet told heavily against the enemy on both land and sea.

As all the German warships not only avoided a conflict, but made no attempt to control their own North Sea coasts, our adventurous and far-ranging submarine commanders had little opportunity of displaying their daring skill. Our light and armoured cruisers, with destroyer flotillas, were spread over the North Sea and down the English Channel, reconnoitring and searching merchant-ships for contraband, and guarding both the British and Belgian coasts from a naval raid. Even our battle-cruisers in the second week of September swept the Bight of Heligoland, and found no enemy visible in German home waters.

There were thus many of our vessels exposed to torpedo attack by hostile underwater craft. Our fast new cruisers were, however, in little danger, as their speed enabled them to elude any submarine, and even at times fight it on equal terms by quick ramming manœuvres. But in order to police the seas, our

Admiralty had been obliged to put into commission some old slow cruisers, manned by reserve crews, and these vessels were the natural prey of the German submarines when their destroyer flotillas were not spread round them.

The Germans had already got in the first blow ever delivered by a submarine, and had sunk the Pathfinder. For some time it was thought that this ship had been destroyed by a contact mine, but when the news of the real cause of the disaster spread, in the second week of September, to the outposts of our Grand Fleet, our submarine officers grew eager to find an opportunity for revenge. At the time our underwater craft were blockading the very throat of the Elbe. The German Admiralty, like our own, was waiting to see what the submarine could actually do. In the meantime Admiral von Tirpitz followed his usual practice of imitating British tactics, and exposed only his oldest and slowest cruisers to underwater attacks.

One of these boats, the Hela, was steaming between Heligoland and the Elbe on Sunday, September 13th. She was an obsolete light cruiser of 2,000 tons, manned by one hundred and eighty officers and men. The wind was freshening, and the sea was beginning to get up, and the tumbling, whitening water helped to conceal the periscopes of several British submarines that were stalking the cruiser. At half-past six in the morning one of our submarines got within torpedo range, when the Hela was about six miles off the German coast. It was Lieut.-Commander Max K. Horton, in E9, to whom the opportunity came of striking the first deadly blow from the British side in underwater warfare.

ADMIRAL VON ESSEN.
Commander of the Russian Baltic Fleet.

THE FIRST FIGHT BETWEEN ARMED MERCHANTMEN.
The British auxiliary cruiser Carmania (Captain Noel Grant) sunk the German armed merchant cruiser Cap Trafalgar off the east coast of South America on September 14th, 1914. The above photograph shows the shattered bridge of the Carmania after the battle.

He dived as soon as he sighted the enemy, and launched two torpedoes at her. There was an interval of only fifteen seconds between the two shots. The first struck the hostile cruiser in the bows, and the other exploded amidships. Probably the magazine was struck, for the Hela burst into flame, and sank in an hour. As there were other German vessels close at hand, Lieut.-Commander Horton again submerged his boat. When he rose for another cautious sight the Hela had disappeared. She was at the bottom of the sea, but most of her crew had been rescued. The British submarine was never seen by the enemy, and was therefore never shot at.

The next achievement by our submarines was also accomplished by Lieut.-Commander Horton. When his boat was relieved he stayed for a few days in Harwich, and then set out for a new station off Emden Harbour. This was the centre of German torpedo-craft activities, from which both submarines and destroyers issued to harry our fleet. Destroyers were reckoned to be a match for submarines. Indeed, in fleet operations, it was their work to scout for them, and injure them either by gun fire or by ramming. Their much superior speed and their very shallow draught, it was expected, would make them practically unassailable by torpedoes. A torpedo that would destroy a cruiser would pass harmlessly under the keel of a destroyer.

E 9's daring exploit off the Ems River

Lieut.-Commander Horton, who had been studying submarine operations for some years, was keen to tackle the craft reckoned the most dangerous to his kind of boat. Towards the end of the first week in October he submerged in the enemy's harbour, and kept his crew amused by a gramophone concert and bridge playing. It is said that

THE BRITISH AUXILIARY CRUISER CARMANIA.
After the sinking of the Cap Trafalgar the Admiralty sent the following telegram to Captain Noel Grant : " Well done ! You have fought a fine action to a successful finish."

when he took his first peep through the periscope he found a destroyer too near him to loose a torpedo at her.

The force of the explosion might have wrecked his own boat. He let the destroyer steam away for six hundred yards, and then fired his two forward tubes, with an interval of five seconds between the two shots. The first shot missed, but the second, travelling near the surface of the water, caught the destroyer amidships. The explosion lifted her in the air, and tore her in two. It was the S126, a vessel of four hundred and eighty tons and twenty-seven knots speed, launched at Dantzic in 1904. She had three four-pounders, three torpedo-tubes, and a crew of sixty. Again the invisible conqueror submerged, while a flotilla of German destroyers cruised above him, and found nothing to shoot at. By October 7th E9 and her skilful, daring crew were safely back once more at Harwich, where she was nicknamed the " double-toothed pirate."

The brilliant victor was a young man of thirty, already distinguished for his gallantry in saving life at the wreck of the P. and O. liner Delhi, off Morocco, in the winter of 1911. He was then a lieutenant in one of the battleships that helped in the rescue work, when the Princess Royal and her husband and daughters were saved. His submarine boat, E9, was one of the newest and most powerful submarines in the world. She was over eight hundred tons, with accommodation for a crew of twenty-eight men, and an air-supply enabling them to stay under the sea for twenty-four hours. Her Diesel engines and electric accumulators gave her a range of action of three thousand miles, and she was fitted with four 21 in. torpedo-tubes and a couple of twelve-pounder guns.

Success in submarine warfare, however, does not always depend upon the efficiency of the boat. One, at least, of the small, old-fashioned submarines in Emden Harbour soon proved to be as deadly as the fastest and most powerful of our craft at Harwich. It was commanded by Lieutenant Otto Weddigen, a brilliant German submarine officer. His U9 was an old type, but he and his crew were so accustomed to her that a new modern craft would have been less effective in their hands. For when a submarine fires, the whole vessel has to be handled like a gun, and steadied on the mark by delicate and skilful handling

power, and made huge targets for attack, alike above and below water. They formed no part of the Grand Fleet under the command of Sir John Jellicoe, but were apparently despatched and controlled by the Admiralty, with a view to watching over the approaches to Belgium.

It was a mistake to employ such slow old ships with large crews, consisting mainly of Fleet reserve ratings, who had not had time to settle down to their common work. It was also an error of judgment to allow their destroyer flotilla to become separated from them. On the other hand, the Admiralty felt it would be unwise to weaken the Grand Fleet by detaching for general patrol work many of the fast light new cruisers, which would be urgently needed in front of the Fleet in case of a Fleet action. There was a risk that Germany would suddenly attack on the sea, now that her great land campaign had failed on both fronts. Nothing could be allowed to diminish the fighting efficiency of our Grand Fleet. Yet the lower area of the North Sea needed to be patrolled in sufficient force to guard Belgium against a cruiser raid, and defend our transport of troops and war material across the Channel from interruption and disaster.

British sacrifice to neutral commerce

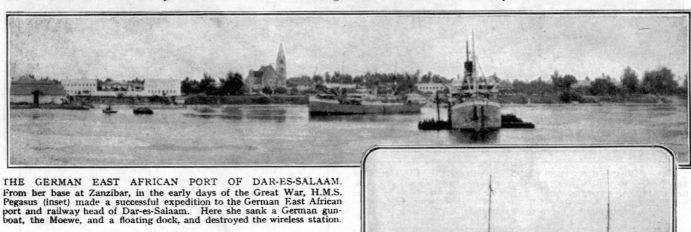

THE GERMAN EAST AFRICAN PORT OF DAR-ES-SALAAM.
From her base at Zanzibar, in the early days of the Great War, H.M.S. Pegasus (inset) made a successful expedition to the German East African port and railway head of Dar-es-Salaam. Here she sank a German gunboat, the Moewe, and a floating dock, and destroyed the wireless station.

of her helm. The torpedo-tubes are usually fixed in the vessel's side, and cannot be aimed independently. Straightness of aim depends on the way the men handle the boat. So the longer they have lived in her and learned her individual ways in responding to her helm, under all sorts of conditions, the better their marksmanship is.

After landing for a hasty wedding, Weddigen embarked at Borkum in his old small boat, bent on some striking achievement that would make his strange honeymoon trip famous.

His orders were to cruise round the coast of Holland and Belgium and attack the vessels that the British Admiralty were sending to defend the Belgian seaports. For the German system of espionage in the British Isles was working with remarkable efficiency. Weddigen travelled on the surface, except when he sighted vessels. Then he submerged, and did not even show his periscope, unless it was absolutely necessary to take bearings. After voyaging more than two hundred miles from his base, he arrived at dawn on Tuesday, September 22nd, some sixteen knots north-west of the Hook of Holland. Here he spied, about six o'clock in the morning, the three old British armoured cruisers, the Aboukir, Hogue, and Cressy, cruising in a single line twenty miles from the Dutch coast, without any destroyers to scout for them. For some weeks they had been patrolling the lower area of the North Sea, between the mouth of the Thames and the island of Texel. It was work for which they were not suited. They were large vessels of 12,000 tons each, and fourteen to fifteen years old. They needed each a complement of 800 officers and men, and were slow, both in speed and in manœuvring

Loss of the Aboukir, Hogue, and Cressy

The most scientific method of doing this was to mine the Thames estuary and the northern entrance to the English Channel. But our Admiralty was averse from impeding neutral commerce in the lower North Sea, though the vast German mine-field in the upper stretch of these waters had already caused serious losses to Danish, Norwegian, and Swedish merchant ships. Probably from political considerations with regard to Holland and Scandinavian countries, our Admiralty hesitated to close the North Sea in any way. Had we set out vigorously to starve Germany into surrender, at no matter what distress to neighbouring neutral countries, we could have ended the war by Christmas. But this stern Nelsonic method was deemed inadvisable. So nothing remained but to put matters to the test, and try if the old armoured cruisers of the Cressy class could escape from the fate of the Pathfinder. It must be remembered that neither the capabilities nor the limitations of the submarine had been entirely discovered by actual warfare. One of our modern cruisers of the town class had sunk a German submarine

H.M.S. CUMBERLAND'S PICKET-BOAT IN THE CAMEROON RIVER.

This operation of our naval forces on the West Coast of Africa resulted in the unconditinal surrender of Duala, the capital of the Cameroons, to a Franco-British force commanded by Brigadier-General C. M. Dobell, D.S.O., following a bombardment by H.M.S. Cumberland and Dwarf. An attempt to blow up and then to ram the Dwarf failed, and several hundred prisoners fell into our hands, while the Cumberland captured eight German merchant steamers and a gunboat off the mouth of the river. Our picture is from a sketch by an officer who took part in the expedition.

ASTROLAVE BAY, GERMAN NEW GUINEA.
The Australian Expeditionary Force seized the town and harbour of Kaiser Wilhelm's Land, German New Guinea, on September 24th, 1914.

by the unexpected manœuvre of ramming her. It was hoped that the old armoured cruisers might be able to carry out the same kind of attack, if hostile underwater craft menaced them.

But Lieutenant Weddigen gave our sailors no opportunity for smashing into his frail boat. When he first sighted the three cruisers on the misty morning they were within the range of his

action. Then, reaching a good firing point, he loosened a torpedo at the middle ship. He was about twelve feet under water at the time, and as his men handled the boat as if she had been a skiff, he got the shot off true on the mark. Climbing towards the surface, he obtained a sight through his periscope. Round the Aboukir rose a fountain of water, a burst of smoke, a flash of fire, and part of the stricken cruiser rose in the air. The victor heard the roar, and felt the surges of water sent through the sea by the explosion. Through his

GERMAN GOVERNOR'S BUNGALOW AT HERBERTSHOHE.
An Australian naval landing-party, under Commander A. H. Beresford, overcame a superior force and captured Herbertshöhe, in the Bismarck Archipelago, on September 11th-12th, 1914.

periscope he could see the brave crew, with their broken ship sinking beneath them, standing, faithful to death, at their posts, ready to handle their guns if an enemy were visible. But none was, for Weddigen submerged his periscope, and waited by the sinking ship.

He had seen the Hogue and Cressy coming to her aid. As in the former case of the Pathfinder, our sailors thought that their ship had struck a mine. The periscope of the

PANORAMIC VIEW OF LISSA.
The famous Island of Lissa, in the Adriatic, after its occupation by a Franco-British garrison on September 19th, 1914, became a naval base for the Allies.

torpedoes, but too far off for anything more than a chance shot. So he went down again, and drove closer in towards the middle ship, the Aboukir. He then shot up his periscope again, and got another flash of the position before he went into

DUALA, THE PRINCIPAL PORT ON THE CAMEROONS.
Duala, from which Germany was fed with important tropical commodities, surrendered to the Allies on September 27th, 1914.

TOWN OF ZANZIBAR FROM THE ROADSTEAD.
From the outbreak of the Great War, H.M.S. Pegasus (Commander John A. Inglis) rendered very useful services, including the destruction of Dar-es-Salaam, but on September 20th, 1914, while she was at anchor in Zanzibar Harbour, cleaning her boilers and repairing machinery, she was attacked and disabled by the Königsberg.

AT SEA ON A GERMAN SUBMARINE.

A nightcap before turning in. From a drawing by the well-known German war artist Professor Hans Bohrtt.

hostile underwater craft was not visible, and the force of the terrific explosion was much greater than that of an ordinary torpedo charged with gun-cotton. The fact was the Germans were using in the war-heads of their torpedoes the new chemical trinitrotoluene, which produces a greater explosive effect than gun-cotton, but is less safe to the users than the ordinary nitro-carbon compounds. The result was that the comparatively small amount of chemical contained in the German war-head blew as wide a hole in the Aboukir as the explosion of a large gun-cotton contact mine would have done.

This misconception of the cause of the disaster led to further loss. For, thinking they were in no danger from an active enemy, the Hogue and the Cressy steamed up to rescue the men of the Aboukir. Weddigen had scarcely to move out of his position in order to get his torpedo depth and train his boat against the nearer of the approaching vessels. This was the Hogue. The torpedo got home on the second armoured cruiser, but the **Fatal misconception of** shot was not so successful as the first, **the cause of disaster** as it did not strike under the magazine. For twenty minutes the ship lay wounded and helpless on the surface. Then there was a second explosion, caused probably by another torpedo hitting near the magazine, and the great vessel heaved and half turned over, and sank.

By this time the commander and men of the Cressy knew that the enemy was upon them. In fact, as the Aboukir sank, the men on the Cressy saw the track of the torpedo aimed at the Hogue. The captain of the Cressy at once began to steam a zigzag course by the scene of the double disaster, in the hope of being able to rescue the sailors struggling in the water, and at the same time to get an opportunity of sighting and attacking the enemy. All the light guns were trained on the surface of the sea in various directions, and any flashing foam-break on the tumbling waves that looked like an emerging periscope

was fired at. One of the gunners who was afterwards rescued stated that he distinctly saw a conning-tower ascend, and got a shell on it that sank the submarine. Weddigen, however, says that the British guns had nothing to shoot at. The next German torpedo missed the target, but at half-past seven the enemy got home so deadly a stroke that, in five minutes after being struck, the Cressy turned completely upside down. After remaining in this extraordinary position for twenty minutes, she sank at five minutes to eight.

In all, 62 officers and 1,400 men were lost with the three British cruisers. The Aboukir lost 25 officers and 502 men; the Cressy, 25 officers and 536 men; and the Hogue, 12 officers and 362 men. The saved numbered only 59 officers and 858 men—917 in all. The loss of the three obsolescent cruisers was of no importance. Our Navy had started the war with a preponderance in ships—much more like two to one than sixteen to ten. Moreover, our construction programme was so advanced that in the next twelve months we **Our loss in men greater** should have twice as many battleships **than at Trafalgar** completing as Germany, and about four times as many cruisers. So great was our superiority in material that we could have afforded to lose one battleship a month, and yet have retained our advantage over our rival for sea-power. The German losses in swift, modern light cruisers, in Heligoland Bight and the Baltic, outbalanced our wastage of naval material.

But our heavy loss of good men was an irretrievable blow. The submarine attack had cost us a thousand more lives than the winning of the Battle of Trafalgar had done. But though our men went down to their death with no chance of showing their skill and courage in a fight, they did not die in vain. They gave their country one more memorable inspiring example of absolute and perfect heroism. In some respects, indeed, they even eclipsed the grand tradition of the Birkenhead. But something had

BRITISH DESTROYER ESCAPING FROM A TORPEDO FIRED BY A HUNTED ENEMY SUBMARINE.

Deadly as the submarine proved in circumstances favourable to its particular form of warfare, our swift cruisers and destroyers moved far too rapidly for the "unterseeboote" to be certain of getting its torpedoes home. The above picture gives a vivid impression of the value of expert seamanship, which, next to good gunnery, gained for us so many material advantages in the trying operations in the North Sea.

altered in the British character since the disaster to the Birkenhead. The men were just as steady and cool, as they waited for the boat to slip from under them. They stood to their posts, waiting for instructions, until the officer in command gave the order for each man to do his best to save his own life. The Cressy continued firing when the ship had a list of forty degrees. Weddigen, peeping at them through his periscope, bore witness to their steadiness and fearlessness. "All the while," he said, "the men stayed by their guns, looking for their invisible foe. They were brave, true to their country's sea traditions."

All this showed that the fibre of our race had not relaxed since the days when the Birkenhead went down. But when the end came, and the men were fighting for life in the water, struggling to escape from the suction of the great sinking masses of rent and flaming steel, a wonderful new quality of character was manifested. In one of the most sudden, overwhelming, awful catastrophes that our fighting sailors have ever known, the men, swimming and treading water for their lives, burst light-heartedly into song. "It's a long, long way to Tipperary," said some men as they struggled in the sea. "It is, if you have to swim there," replied a brilliant Cressy gunner. Immortal is the jest, and immortal are the circumstances that inspired it. It was like a granite rock breaking into flower. For beneath all, at the base of all, subsisted the old, stern, dogged Roman courage of our forefathers, and growing out of it was a new cheery smiling gaiety of the Hellenic sort. Thus surely did the heroes of Salamis and Marathon, triumphing in the power and righteousness of their cause, go down to death with a song on their lips.

TAKING A DISABLED SUBMARINE IN TOW.
Disabled submarine in the act of hailing her parent ship. The drawing gives a good idea of what work in the Navy is like in winter time.

Dutch and British vessels in the neighbourhood tended the survivors, many of whom were conveyed in some of the cruisers' boats to the rescue ships. There are many fine, thrilling tales of quiet or happy heroism. Captain Johnson, of the Cressy, spent his last moments directing his sailors to take hold of anything floatable that would enable them to keep their heads above water until the destroyers came up. He was last seen gripping a handrail on the bridge, as the ship went over. Captain Drummond, of the Aboukir, directed his men how to save themselves when the ship was sinking, and then, when his crew were in the water, he and his men swam about, helping the poor swimmers among them. Captain Nicholson, of the Hogue, was also the last man to leave his ship. He was seen on the bridge, waving his cap in cheerful defiance of death. But as the ship went down, he was carried free, and his men, who were swimming or floating about, gave

Thrilling tales of quiet or happy heroism

him three cheers when they saw him swimming clear of the lost cruiser. Great as was the loss of life, it would have been still greater but for the promptness and gallantry of the four vessels that hastened to the scene of the disaster. Two of them, the Coriander and J.G.C., were Lowestoft trawlers ; the other two, the Titan and Flora, were Dutch vessels. While the cruiser Lowestoft and a flotilla of British destroyers were racing to the spot, in answer to a wireless call, the fishermen managed to save many sailors, who would probably have been exhausted before naval assistance arrived. One trawler, flying the Dutch flag, however, is said to have departed immediately after the disaster, as though eager not to help in the work of rescue. It was suspected that she was a German vessel, under false colours, that had been sent to the scene of the expected submarine operations, in order to screen the underwater boats from observation, and enable them to take the British cruisers entirely by surprise.

The three sunken cruisers, though large and powerful

GERMAN CRUISER EMDEN'S EXPLOIT AT MADRAS.
During its raiding cruise in the Bay of Bengal the German cruiser Emden shelled the oil-tanks at Madras, doing considerable damage; but it is on record to the credit of the captain that he confined his attention to property, where he might have given a display of that "frightfulness" which later distinguished his colleagues' raids on undefended holiday towns on the East Coast of England.

which the Formidable was part, been the first of its kind, we might have then lost other ships more important than the Hogue and Cressy.

The disaster off the Hook of Holland has also a curious technical interest. Both the German Admiralty and Lieutenant Weddigen claimed that only one German submarine was engaged in the attack on the three cruisers. Our sailors, however, aver that there was a flotilla of hostile underwater craft engaging in the attack. Besides the evidence of their eyes, we have theoretic support of the probable correctness of their observations, U9 was a small 250-ton boat, with only three torpedo-tubes. Two of the tubes were carried forward, and one aft, the after tube being a reserve one that would not in a general way be used. The boat was not big enough to do much in the way of carrying spare torpedoes; and, in any case, a 250-ton submarine capable of reloading her tubes when in a submerged condition did not exist. Modern torpedoes are from fourteen to nineteen feet long, weigh up to over a ton and a quarter, and carry from 250 to 350 pounds of high explosive.

We know that at least six torpedoes were fired, one missing, and five hitting. Such was the actual number of torpedoes seen by our men. It is the lowest possible figure, in which no allowance is made for unnoticed torpedoes which missed. It may be that U9 did most of the work, and that the German Admiralty thought it worth while to sacrifice the whole truth, and create the impression that one old-type German submarine was more than a match for three old British armoured cruisers. Things were not going well with the German armies on either front, and

ships, belonged to an old-fashioned class, that was surpassed in speed by many of the enemy's heavier-gunned battleships. Before the war broke out, our Admiralty had decided that no more money should be spent in repairing them, and that they should go into the sale list as soon as they showed serious defects. Thus, apart from the toll of life, their loss was of small naval significance. They

New and strange conditions of naval warfare

were the price our country had to pay while learning all the possibilities of submarine attack in the new and strange conditions of naval warfare. When, some months afterwards, our battleship Formidable, steaming in line with other powerful units, was struck by what appeared at first to be a mine, the captain warned the other ships to attempt no rescue, but manœuvre to avoid submarine attack. The other important battleships, with their large crews, that were thus saved from the enemy's torpedoes, must be reckoned against the heavy cost in brave trained men of our first important lesson in submarine warfare. Had the attack on the squadron, of

as the German Military Staff had taken to concealing the true facts from the public, the German Admiralty may also have indulged its imagination, in order to increase the amount of soothing syrup it was able to offer to the Teutonic public. From Russia we learnt that the German Admiralty also needed much soothing mixture itself.

For another naval mystery of far more than technical importance was discussed in the early part of September. First came a statement by our Press Bureau that trustworthy information had been received on September 4th that seven German destroyers and torpedo-boats had arrived at Kiel in a sinking condition, while other vessels had sunk in the neighbourhood of the canal. About a fortnight later it was rumoured from the Baltic that two German cruiser squadrons, with destroyer flotilla, had been hunting down passenger steamers in separate directions, and converging at last, mistook their own for enemy ships and engaged in a lively battle. This was offered as the explanation of the arrival of crippled warcraft at Kiel Harbour.

But some months later a Russian authority at Petrograd allowed the astonishing facts of the matter to be published. It appears that towards the end of August the German Baltic cruiser squadrons were becoming inconvenient to our Russian allies. The German ships began to cruise in the waters that Admiral von Essen, the commander of the Russian Baltic Fleet, had resolved firmly to hold. Moreover, the Germans were using their ships for the purpose of putting severe pressure upon Sweden.

The new Russian battleships had not been completed, and the Russian Navy in the meantime was much inferior in force to the German. So Germany was **Russian admiral's simple but telling trick** trying to blockade Russia in the Baltic as we were blockading Germany in the North Sea. German light cruisers began to appear round Libau, the only ice-free naval port of Northern Russia. Admiral von Essen boldly determined to risk a large part of his fleet rather than allow the enemy to carry out his plans. Being unable to fight an open battle with any chance of success against the great naval force that the German commander could bring up, Admiral von Essen used a simple but telling trick.

He altered the appearance of several of his cruisers and destroyers by means of temporary additions, and made them closely resemble in outline certain German units. He had the disguised vessels painted in German colours, and then in foggy weather, about August 27th, he slipped out and contrived to join, in the Gulf of Finland, the German squadron which was threatening Russian waters and ports. Probably the Russian Intelligence Department had been able to provide the commanders of Russian vessels with German signal books. However this may be,

our Press Bureau announcement, half a score of German destroyers were shelled and either sunk or badly crippled.

The surprise engagement was quickly finished, and the Russians, having got their blow in, withdrew before the enemy touched them. From the German point of view, the disaster was discreditable to their Navy, and the serious loss of their prestige which would have occurred in Scandinavia made them keep a dead silence about the affair.

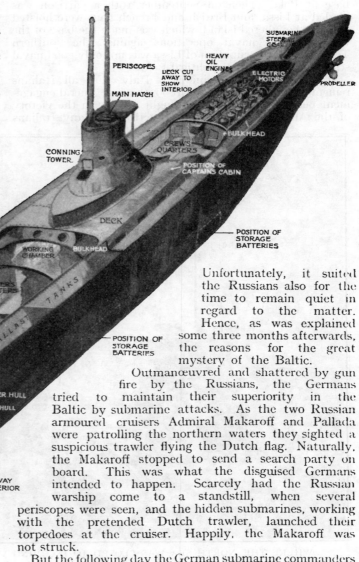

SECTIONAL VIEW OF A GERMAN SUBMARINE ("UNTERSEEBOOTE")

Our illustration shows some of the distinctive features of the modern type of German submarine, notably its flatter deck and boat-shaped contour.

Unfortunately, it suited the Russians also for the time to remain quiet in regard to the matter. Hence, as was explained some three months afterwards, the reasons for the great mystery of the Baltic.

Outmanœuvred and shattered by gun fire by the Russians, the Germans tried to maintain their superiority in the Baltic by submarine attacks. As the two Russian armoured cruisers Admiral Makaroff and Pallada were patrolling the northern waters they sighted a suspicious trawler flying the Dutch flag. Naturally, the Makaroff stopped to send a search party on board. This was what the disguised Germans intended to happen. Scarcely had the Russian warship come to a standstill, when several periscopes were seen, and the hidden submarines, working with the pretended Dutch trawler, launched their torpedoes at the cruiser. Happily, the Makaroff was not struck.

But the following day the German submarine commanders were more fortunate. The Pallada was again on patrol duty, in company with a sister ship, the Bayan. At two o'clock in the afternoon the enemy underwater craft were again sighted. The cruisers put on speed, and opened fire. But one submarine got a torpedo home on the Pallada, sending her to the **Destruction of the Russian cruiser Pallada** bottom so quickly that few of her five hundred and sixty-eight officers and men escaped. Her loss was a blow to the incomplete Russian Navy, for she was a modern warship, launched in 1906, with two 8 in. guns and eight 6 in. rapid-firers.

Of all the allied fleets the French was for long the most fortunate in escaping from serious loss. The main French naval force, combined with our Mediterranean Fleet, under the command of the brilliant French commander, Admiral Boué de Lapeyrère, held all the Austrian warships in the blind alley of the Adriatic. To assist the land operations of the Montenegrins, the Austrian fortress of Cattaro, on the edge of their frontier, was bombarded by the allied

the disguised Russian squadron got close up to the enemy without rousing any suspicions. Suddenly they opened fire, and wrecked the Magdeburg, one of the newest of German light cruisers, with twelve 4.1 in. guns, an armour belt of 3½ in., and an actual speed of twenty-seven knots. To escape sinking she ran on the rocks, and was there blown up by the Russian guns. Another German cruiser, possibly the Augsburg, whose turbines were afterwards reported to be damaged, was severely handled, and, as we have seen from fleets on September 10th. Then the forty warships steamed to the famous island of Lissa, where the Austrian Navy had won in bygone days a great victory over the Italian Fleet.

The signal station was shelled on this island, and on Pelegosa and Lesina. All the coast of Southern Dalmatia was searched, and mines, lighthouses, signal stations, and wireless stations were destroyed. This was done with a view to impeding the Austrian Fleet in any sortie from its base at Pola. Then on September 19th a garrison was landed at Lissa, and British and French flags were hoisted over the conquered island, which was made the base of the Franco-British naval operations against the southern Teutons. The occupation of Lissa was not only good naval strategy, but excellent political tactics.

It told on public opinion in Italy. For all Italians remembered Lissa, where, in 1866, the first general engagement between ironclads was fought, ending in the victory of the Austrian Admiral von Tegetthoff. Many Italians

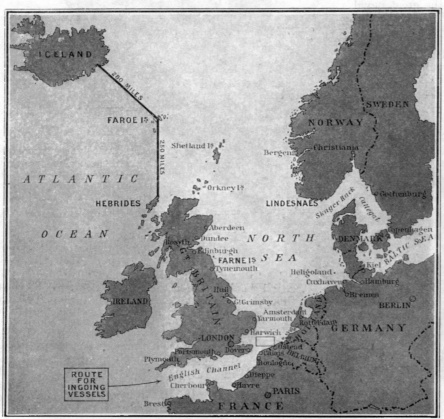

WHERE THE NORTH SEA WAS CLOSED TO INCOMING VESSELS.
The above map indicates the limits beyond which, after a certain date in November, 1914, vessels entering the North Sea sailed at their own risk. The northern entrance was closed from the Hebrides to Iceland through the Faroe Islands. The only entrance was by way of the English Channel. The British mine-field, laid on October 2nd, was between the Goodwins and Ostend, and between Foulness and the opposite coast.

were growing eager for a chance to avenge their old defeat off the island, and recovering the territories they had lost. The action of the Franco-British fleet helped to quicken this movement in Italy. One Italian naval officer tried to anticipate events, and stole off in a submarine to take part in the operations of the allied forces. Though he was stopped on the way, his too premature action did not tend to make his countrymen any more inclined to passive neutrality. The adventurous submarine stealer was a human straw, showing in what way the wind of Italian thought and feeling was then blowing.

By the beginning of October the British blockade of the North Sea became even more scientifically effective than the Franco-British blockade of the Austrian shores of the Adriatic. For on October 2nd, moved by the disaster to the Aboukir, Hogue, and Cressy, and by the increasing

activities of the enemy's submarines, our Admiralty closed the lower area of the North Sea. A system of mine-fields was laid between the Goodwins and Ostend, and between Foulness and the opposite coast. The result was that the mouth of the Thames and the northern entrance to the Channel were sealed to any raiding hostile warships. German submarines could, perhaps, creep underneath the mines at considerable peril, but some time passed before they had a conveniently near base at the Bruges seaport for such operations. In the meantime our Grand Fleet kept on guard in the north.

Lower area of North Sea closed by mines

While this great blockade of German commerce and naval power was proceeding, with a few submarine incidents that scarcely revealed anything of the tremendous pressure our naval superiority was exerting on the enemy, there was more of the old romance of sea warfare in outpost affairs on distant oceans. Here also the main naval force of the British Empire was being used with such quiet strength that the happy peoples who benefited from it paid but little attention to its unostentatious efficiency. Along all the great trade routes, food and stores, raw material and manufactures, were being transported with little or no interruption.

Armies of a size that would have settled the fate of empires a hundred years ago were moving in vast fleets of troopships from India and the Oversea Dominions, without the enemy being able to impede them. Naturally, however, some of the enemy's cruisers and commerce-raiders were able to do a little damage in waters from which our warships were temporarily absent. The policing of the main trade routes, the convoy of great numbers of troopships, and the maintenance of the blockade of the North Sea and Adriatic, allowed a few scattered armed cruisers and German merchantmen to capture and sink a very small proportion of our mercantile marine.

But even when our naval forces were most busily employed in the main work of the Great War, the German corsairs did not have things all their own way. One of the most romantic and interesting of sea fights occurred in the South Atlantic between a Cunard liner, the Carmania, and the splendid new German liner, the Cap Trafalgar. They met on the morning of September 14th, off Trinidad Island—not the West Indian island of that name, but a rock, about four miles by two, lying in the South Atlantic some seven hundred miles east of Brazil. The Carmania had been equipped as an auxiliary cruiser, and sent to reconnoitre the little island. Her lookout spied three steamers westward of the lofty, lonely rock. They all fled when the British ship came into sight. But when it was seen that the Carmania was alone, the largest of the three German ships evidently changed her mind, turned round, and steamed up to attack. Then Captain Noel Grant, commanding the Cunarder, saw that the curious liner, which suddenly hoisted the German ensign, was a foe worthy of his guns. For the Cap Trafalgar was the pride of the Hamburg - South American line. She was built in 1913, eight years after the Cunarder, for the express purpose of ousting the Royal Mail steamers from passenger and carrying traffic in the South Atlantic. She was now painted to resemble a Castle liner, and had come fully armed and equipped to the usurped German base at Trinidad Island to destroy our shipping.

In size, speed, and fighting power, the two armed liners were about equal, and they were both manned mainly

AN ALGERIAN SHARPSHOOTER AT WORK IN THE SHELTER OF A WOOD.

Among the most resourceful of the coloured troops fighting with the Allies were the Algerians or Spahis. They served with distinction during the Aisne battles, and in the subsequent advance to the North of France.

When fighting in wooded districts the Spahis fastened themselves to trees with a camel-hair thong to prevent them from falling in the event of being wounded, and again and again held back the enemy by their fire.

French artillerymen serving one of the famous " 75 " guns and shelling a German position in a village street in the North of France, while the infantry, sheltered behind some buildings, waited to attack with the bayonet. The infantry had attacked the village in the first place, but could not make progress beyond the first house. Then a young artillery officer brought a " 75 " into the main street. With a few shots he destroyed the shelters of

emy, who were only a few yards off. The French infantry waiting, as shown,
hind broken walls, to see the result of the duel, cheered their colleagues, and
en proceeded to clear the village, which, in a few minutes, was once more in

French hands. Our picture shows the scene during the bombardment. The
efficiency of the French gunner was recognised very early in the war, and the
mobility of the famous "75" was quickly appreciated by both friend and foe.

THE GUERILLA ELEMENT IN THE GREAT WAR—WHERE THE TURCO WAS AT HIS BEST.

Frequent mention has appeared in official communiqués of house-to-house fighting in Flanders and Northern France. Our drawing supplies a vivid idea of the ferocity of such warfare when the Turcos were taking part in it. The scene of the struggle above illustrated was the east bank of the Ypres Canal, between Elverdinghe and Pilkum. Here the Prussian infantry were surprised and annihilated by the redoubtable Turcos, whose active and sanguine temperament made them more than a match for their more phlegmatic and less alert adversaries.

by naval reservists. They had no armour, and their triple tier of decks offered such colossal targets as made a miss by a trained gun-layer at fighting range an impossibility. Each had a speed of eighteen knots. The Carmania had a tonnage of 19,524 tons, and mounted eight 4 7 in. guns. The Cap Trafalgar had a tonnage of 18,710 tons, and mounted eight 4 1 in. guns. In spite of their somewhat smaller calibre, the German guns, being of more modern make, had a low trajectory and were more effective at long distances. The opponents were thus well-matched, and the historic importance of this even fight between British and German sailors, under absolutely equal conditions, was enhanced by another circumstance. It was the first naval engagement of its kind in history between two unarmoured ocean liners. The action raged hotly for an hour, but out of a British crew of four hundred and twenty-one men there were only

H.M.S. BERWICK.
Sister ship of the Cumberland. She ran down and captured the Hamburg-Amerika liner Spreewald on September 12th, 1914.

nine killed and twenty-six wounded. From the sunken Cap Trafalgar some three hundred and ten survivors, picked up by a collier, were afterwards landed at Buenos Ayres. The officers and men of the Carmania won their brilliant, historic little action by superb seamanship and superior rapidity and concentration of fire. "Well done!" telegraphed the First Lord of the Admiralty to Captain Grant when the news reached London. "You have fought a fine action to a successful finish."

On the day that the Carmania was breaking up the plans of German commerce-raiders on the American side of the South Atlantic, the enemy was vainly trying to interfere with our naval forces on the African coast of the great ocean. In the Cameroon River, leading up to Duala, the principal port of the important German colony of the Cameroons, our **German tactics in the Cameroons** gunboat, the Dwarf, with Commander Frederick E. K. Strong in charge of it, was attacked by a German steamboat. In the darkness of night, on September 14th, the hostile boat tried to blow up our vessel by running on it with an infernal machine (technically, a spar-torpedo) in the bows. The sharp look-out kept on the Dwarf gave the alarm in time, and the steamboat was captured.

Two nights afterwards the Germans tried another desperate manœuvre to sink the British gunboat. A German merchant-ship, the Nachtigall, got up full steam in the river, and swung up in the darkness against the small British craft. The design was to ram the gunboat. But again the British sailors were on the alert, and it was the big steamer that was wrecked, with a loss of fourteen men killed, and twenty-two missing, who were probably drowned

in the darkness. The old British cruiser of the county class, H.M.S. Cumberland, under Captain Cyril Fuller, came up the Cameroon River to assist the gunboat. The Germans apparently then turned their attention to the more important ship. Two more steam-launches were prepared for a spar torpedo attack. One carried the explosive machines and the other assisted in the operation. Both were destroyed, one German being killed, and three more, with two natives, taken prisoners.

Captain Fuller soon won full compensation for these wild and ineffectual attempts on our ships. And the reason for the desperate manœuvres of the Germans was made plain. Behind our **Surrender of the fine German port of Duala** warships was a Franco-British expedition, organised at Freetown and Dakar, and composed of a landing force of infantry and guns. The fine German port of Duala, from which Germany was fed with important tropical commodities, was swiftly attacked, and it surrendered without conditions on September 27th.

Then it was that the captain of the Cumberland was fully repaid. Without a struggle, he captured one-quarter of the entire fleet of the Woermann Line, the largest shipping company operating between Germany and the West Coast of Africa. The Woermann Company had a capital of one million pounds sterling, and thirty-nine vessels of the gross tonnage of 112,616. The

H.M.S. CUMBERLAND.
British cruiser of the "County" class (Captain Cyril Fuller), which assisted in the operations in the Cameroons, and captured one quarter of the fleet of the Woermann Line.

Cumberland captured eight Woermann ships, whose tonnage amounted to 28,016, and a vessel of the Hamburg-Amerika Line was also taken. All the vessels were in good order, and most of them contained cargoes and considerable quantities of coal. The German gunboat Soden, was likewise captured, and turned at once to good use, by being commissioned for service under the British flag.

The sister ship of the Cumberland, the Berwick, commanded by Captain Lewis Baker, was also successful in a fight against the commerce-raiders. On September 12th she ran down and captured the Hamburg-Amerika liner the Spreewald, a vessel of 3,900 tons, which had been fitted out as an armed merchant-cruiser. At the same time two colliers were taken, loaded with six thousand tons of coal, and a hundred tons of provisions for the supply of German cruisers operating in Atlantic waters.

Of all the ships that the German Admiralty skilfully scattered about the sea for the destruction of our commerce, one only had anything like a fairly successful career. None of the others did as much damage as a well-handled warship should have done. Only the light cruiser the

The Aboukir, the first of the three cruisers to be hit, was struck by a torpedo.

The Hogue, in an attempt to help the Aboukir, was also struck and sank shortly after.

THE BRITISH NAVAL LOSSES IN THE NORTH SEA ON SEPTEMBER 22nd, 1914, WHEN THE ABOUKIR, HOGUE, AND CRESSY WERE TORPEDOED BY GERMAN SUBMARINES.

German Submarine supposed to have been sunk by Cressy

Only smoke rising

HMS Lowestoft & Third destroyer Flotilla steaming Full speed to the rescue

Dutch steamer "Flora"

"Cressy" struck amidships but still firing violently

"Aboukir" sinking

Cruisers boats

"Hogue" just disappeared

Trawler "Coriander" of Lowestoft picking up survivors

Two torpedoes missing their mark

Periscopes of German Submarines

Decoy trawler

THE BRITISH NAVAL LOSSES IN THE NORTH SEA ON SEPTEMBER 22ND, 1914: HOW THE CRESSY, THE LAST OF THE THREE CRUISERS TO BE HIT, WENT DOWN.

Although struck amidships, the Cressy continued to fire violently before she sank to the bottom.

Emden, with Captain Karl von Müller in command, gave a full display of the possibilities of commerce-raiding. Müller was a gallant sailor, well known to many of our naval officers. Some time before the war he stayed in one of our village inns with some of our naval officers, and played with them a game at pretended commerce-raiding, at which he proved the winner. The game consisted in throwing rings round hooks passing through a board on the wall of the inn—an old-fashioned rural pastime in our country. Every time Müller ringed a hook he claimed that he had captured a ship.

When war broke out he was nominally at Tsing-tau, with the German China Squadron, under Admiral von Spee. At our China station we then had a sufficient force to master all Spee's ships. But the latter outmanœuvred us by slipping out secretly before war was declared. This is **How thoroughly Germany prepared** another instance of the thoroughness with which Germany prepared for aggression, at a time when even her ally Austria-Hungary was ready to arrive at a peaceful settlement. So the Emden got away. But our forces guarding the Pacific were so strong that nothing was heard of her for six weeks. However, she was in touch with the world-wide system of German espionage, and, hearing that the Indian Ocean was partly unguarded, through our warships there being engaged in convoying the Indian troopships, she suddenly appeared in the Bay of Bengal in the second week of September.

Accompanied by the Hamburg-Amerika liner Markomannia, acting as collier, the cruiser came up the Bay. By intercepting wireless messages, she learned the position of all vessels in the waters. At nine a.m. on the morning of September 10th she made her first victim of the Indus. Müller transferred the crew to his own ship, and then sank the British vessel by ten shells from the 4 in. guns. In the afternoon of the next day the Lovat was sighted and sunk. The day after the Kabinga was taken, and used as a prison-ship for the captured crews. On the same day the Killin was sunk, and the Diplomat—quite a good day's work in all. On September 14th the Trabbock was captured and sunk by a mine. When all the prisoners were placed in the Kabinga, which was ordered to proceed to Calcutta, Captain Müller with his collier accompanied the vessel to within seventy-five miles of the sandheads at the mouth of the Hooghley.

If all the Germans had made war in the sportsmanlike and civilised manner of Captain Müller, his country would have remained on terms of friendship with her rivals when the great struggle was over. Müller waged war in a very skilful and effective manner, and in the hour of victory he acted like a gentleman. His officers treated their prisoners generously, giving up their cabins to them, and supplying them with the best food they had. In parting they bade them the most cordial farewell. They said at the time that they had little hope of getting out of the Bay of Bengal.

But this was only a strategical statement, intended to put their opponents off their guard. Captain Müller designed more than a raid on our commerce in those waters. He sank another ship, and sent her crew to Rangoon. Then, on the evening of September 22nd, he steamed up to Madras **Exploit of the Emden at Madras** Harbour and began to shell the oil-tanks of a Burma oil company. An empty tank was riddled, and another, containing a million and a half gallons of liquid fuel, was set on fire. A ship in the harbour was struck, and the telegraph office and some goods trucks on the harbour wall, but only two men and one boy in the harbour were killed. If the Indian peoples had been adverse from their British administrators, as most men in authority in Berlin vainly imagined was the case, the bazaar rumours of the Emden's exploit might have been troublesome. As it was, the affair, though admirably executed, only intensified the loyal feelings of the Indian peoples.

Getting out into the Indian Ocean, Captain Müller continued his commerce-raiding exploits, and in a few

FOUNDERING OF THE ABOUKIR. THE CAPTAIN'S LAST COMMAND.
" As the Aboukir was sinking," said Stoker J. Mills, " the captain gave out an order, just like on any ordinary occasion. ' If,' he said, ' any man wishes to leave the side of the ship he can do so. Every man for himself.' Then," added Stoker Mills, " we gave a cheer and in we went."

days captured and sank the British steamships Tumeric, King Lud, Liberia, and Foyle, and took the collier Buresk. The crews were transferred to the steamer Gryfedale, which was also captured, but released in order to take the British sailors to Colombo. By this time a considerable number of British, French, Russian, and Japanese warships—including several cruisers of high speed—were trying to round up the brilliant and adventurous raider. But many weeks had still to pass before Captain Müller was run to earth.

In the meantime the Australian Fleet, which had also sent some ships in pursuit of the daring corsair, lost one of its submarines. This was AE1, a fine new powerful boat of the latest type. Early in the year, under Lieutenant - Commander Besant, son of the famous novelist, she had made the voyage from Portsmouth to Sydney without a mishap, and showed fine seaworthy qualities. Built by Vickers, at Barrow, in 1913, she was an 800-ton boat, fitted with 21 in. torpedo-tubes. In the third week of September she was cruising

in fine weather in deep water, and by some unexplained accident suddenly sank. She was manned by Australian naval ratings, who had undergone a course of training in submarine work, and these were joined by several Portsmouth naval reserve men, who volunteered for service in the first Australian submarine. The water where she sank was so deep that there was no hope of locating the wreck.

The end of H.M.S. Pegasus was a glorious disaster in the stirring month of September. She was a light cruiser, a little over 2,000 tons, and was built in 1897, carrying eight 4 in. guns of an old pattern, which made her suitable for the scrap-heap rather than for active service. As a matter of fact, she had been sent to the lumber-room some ten years before the war broke out. But as there were not enough modern cruisers to replace all the old types of these ships on foreign stations, the Pegasus was retained, under Commander Inglis, at Zanzibar. From this base she made a successful expedition to the German East African port and railway-head of Dar-es-Salaam. There she sank a German gunboat and a floating dock, and badly crippled the enemy commerce - raiders by destroying the wireless station.

It is only a short distance from Zanzibar to Dar-es-Salaam. But even this brief voyage was more than the old machinery of the cruiser could stand. After striking her blow for the Empire she went into Zanzibar Harbour, and defects in her engine-room made a complete overhaul necessary. On Sunday, September 20th, she was resting, sadly and helplessly, on the water, while her boilers were being cleaned and her machinery repaired. At five o'clock in the morning the German cruiser Königsberg approached at full speed, disabled a British patrol-boat with three shots, and then opened fire on the broken-down Pegasus. The German warship was built in 1905, and was armed with 4 in. modern guns, with a longer range and a greater energy than the obsolete weapons of the British vessel.

She began shooting at 9,000 yards' distance, and though all the broadside of the Pegasus stubbornly tried to reply, her old guns were put out of action in fifteen minutes. Even if her guns had been able to reach the enemy, however, she would still **Glorious end of the** have been unable to move and bring **old Pegasus** them to bear on him. He was able to choose his own position, far beyond the range of the gunners of the Pegasus, and, firing from a distance of five miles, he pounded away at the helpless target.

Shell after shell struck the British cruiser, tearing down the upper works, smashing the guns, around which most of the slaughter of the crew occurred. When the decks were strewn with dead and dying men, the Germans ceased

WHERE GERMANY LOST HER "PLACE IN THE SUN."

Diagram showing how the Pax Britannica was secured in the waters of the Pacific.

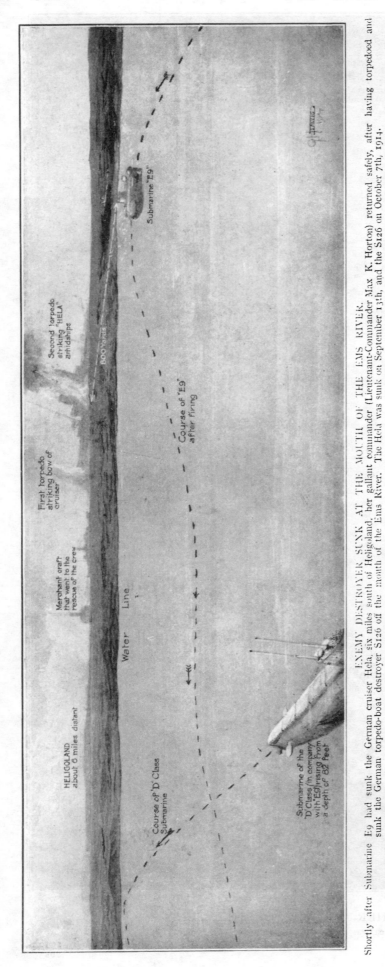

HELIGOLAND about 6 miles distant

Course of 'D' Class Submarine

Submarine of the 'D' Class (in company with 'E9') rising from a depth of 82 feet

Course of 'E9' after firing

Water Line

Merchant craft that went to the rescue of the crew

First torpedo striking bow of cruiser

Second torpedo striking 'HELA' amidships

800 yards

Submarine 'E9'

ENEMY DESTROYER SUNK AT THE MOUTH OF THE EMS RIVER.

Shortly after Submarine E9 had sunk the German cruiser Hela, six miles south of Heligoland, her gallant commander (Lieutenant-Commander Max K. Horton) returned safely, after having torpedoed and sunk the German torpedo-boat destroyer S126 off the mouth of the Ems River. The Hela was sunk on September 13th, and the S126 on October 7th, 1914.

firing for five minutes. Thinking that the action was over, all the men who had been able to find shelter came on deck to succour their wounded comrades. But this was the moment chosen by the Königsberg for another terrible bombardment. She battered the Pegasus almost beyond recognition, and holed her on the water-line till she listed heavily. Out of the crew of 234 men there were 34 killed and 61 wounded.

Dreadful was the scene in the shattered, helpless, immovable old vessel. But amid the continual bursts of high-explosive shells the British sailor rose to the full height of heroism. Under the enemy's fire the British flag was shot from the **How British Marines** mast, and fell on the deck. At once **kept the old flag flying** it was seized, and held aloft by two Marines, who dauntlessly stood in the most exposed position in their ship, in order clearly to show the enemy that the flag was still flying. It drooped for a moment when one of the gallant fellows had been killed by a shell. Immediately another Marine took the place of the dead man, and the flag continued to show bravely amid the hurricane of high-explosive projectiles spreading death and destruction all around. And the hand-held flag was still flying from the smashed and silent Pegasus when the German cruiser fired a last shot and steamed away from her work of slaughter.

It was no German victory. The Pegasus had finished her work, and the damage done to her was not worth the cost in German ammunition. The death or disablement of ninety-five British sailors had no effect whatever on the course of the war. But the way they kept the flag flying was an inspiration to all the fighting men of our Empire.

As our naval forces were usually arranged about the seas of the world, in effective concentrations, the German sailors and colonial troops had quite as many opportunities for displaying a courageous spirit, transcending the material circumstances in which they fought. But though the German was usually a good fighter, he did not show much grim or flamboyant dauntlessness. The German soldier, especially, bred up to rely on the great Prussian war-machine, took rather too scientific a view of man-to-man fighting. In favourable conditions he fought well, but anything like an heroic stand against odds seems to have offended his sense of caution and calculation.

He had an excellent opportunity for making the world ring with his fame when the Australian squadron, under Vice-Admiral Sir George Patey, approached the tropical island of New Britain. This was one of the old British possessions, discovered by Captain Cook, but weakly handed over to Germany in 1884, at the expense of the interests of Australia and New Zealand. The large island, three hundred miles long and sixty miles broad, inhabited by head-hunting cannibals, was renamed New Pomerania, and the German settlement on it, Herbertshöhe, became the seat of German government for German New Guinea, the Marshall and Caroline Islands, and the German half of the Solomon Islands.

Ever since Bismarck, working through an unscrupulous, Hamburg firm of South Sea traders, had seized these territories, the people of Australia had **Capture of Herberts-** objected to their new, dangerous, and **höhe by the** intriguing neighbours. So when the **Australians** Great War broke out, the German Government of Herbertshöhe vigorously prepared to defend itself against the fate that their people had earned by thirty years of treachery in trading, and the murderous persecution of British and Australian rivals.

The roads through the bush round Herbertshöhe were mined. Miles of trenches were dug, and multitudes of the cannibal natives were armed to assist the German forces. At dawn on September 11th a naval landing-party, under Commander J. A. H. Beresford, of the Australian Navy, established themselves on shore without the enemy's knowledge. There were six miles of thick bush between them and the town of Herberts-höhe, and the enemy's scouts soon discovered their presence.

In all the circumstances, the Australians, composed of naval reserve forces, might have expected defeat. Many of the Germans had rifles, and they had marked all the ranges, and there were miles of tropical undergrowth to hack through, with head-hunting sharpshooters firing from the trees, and sniping in the thick, tangled jungle. But the tall, lean, wiry Australian is one of the most resourceful and original fighters in the world. He has all the doggedness of the old British stock, with a peculiar resilience of mind and character, the combination of which makes him a supreme guerilla fighter. He stuck to his job for eighteen hours, in the course of which he taught the Germans some surprising lessons in bush fighting. There were thousands of miles of bush in his own country, and he was quite at home among the head-hunters and the missionaries of German "Kultur."

Yard by yard he fought on, winning about six hundred yards in an hour. Towards noon on September 12th he was within attacking distance of a long trench in front of Herbertshöhe. But by this time he had put such fear into the heart of every German that the battle abruptly ended with the unconditional surrender of the enemy. After eighteen hours' fighting in the most difficult country in the world the Australians had only lost six lives. The enemy's losses were much larger, but the numbers are not known. The German forces were more numerous, as the governor had concentrated all his armed men from New Guinea and elsewhere to defend the wireless station and the chief settlement. On September 24th the Australian Expeditionary Force gathered the full fruit of its victory by occupying German New Guinea and seizing the town and harbour of Kaiser Wilhelm's Land. So, without a struggle, 70,000 square miles of territory, containing valuable unexploited resources, was lost to Germany.

While this swift and resounding work of reconquest was proceeding, the warships of the British Empire were operating with another of our self-governing Dominions in the general disruption of Germany's "world-power." Of all the vanishing colonial empire, on which the Teutons had spent so much treasure and labour, there was no part they more highly prized than their diamond town of Lüderitzbucht, in German South-West Africa. Lying on a natural harbour, at the terminus of a railway line 1,300 miles in length, Lüderitzbucht was the captain jewel in the carcanet of German possessions round the world. For close to it were the newly-discovered German diamond-fields, worked by a Government syndicate, that was obtaining yearly about £1,000,000 worth of stones. But

BIRD'S-EYE VIEW OF A BRITISH DESTROYER. TAKEN FROM A SEAPLANE FLYING ALOFT

The seaplane from which the above photograph was taken was flying at a height of some two hundred and fifty feet above the sea.

on September 27th an expeditionary force, despatched by the South African Union, came into the harbour and summoned the town to surrender. The demand was at once complied with, for the main German garrison had apparently retreated the day before, in order to avoid a fight.

The choking, impotent fury with which the Germans in Europe witnessed these striking exhibitions of the range and vigour of action of the British Navy was ineffable. No German could express it. But a Jew, Ernst Lissauer, managed, with the chameleon-like versatility of his race, to find words for them in his notorious "Hymn of Hate."

French and Russian they matter not,
A blow for a blow and a shot for a shot;
We love them not, we hate them not,
We hold the Vistula and Vosges-gate,
We have but one and only hate,
We love as one, we hate as one,
We have one foe and one alone.

He is known to you all, he is known to you all,
He crouches behind the dark grey flood,
Full of envy, of rage, of craft, of gall,
Cut off by waves that are thicker than blood.
Come, let us stand at the Judgment place,
An oath to swear to, face to face,
An oath of bronze no wind can shake,
An oath for our sons and their sons to take,
Come, hear the word, repeat the word,
Throughout the Fatherland make it heard.
We will never forgo our hate,
We have all but a single hate,
We love as one, we hate as one,
We have one foe, and one alone—
          ENGLAND!

In the captain's mess, in the banquet-hall,
Sat feasting the officers, one and all,
Like a sabre blow, like the swing of a sail,
One seized his glass held high to hail;
Sharp-snapped like the stroke of a rudder's play,
Spoke three words only : " To the Day ! "

Whose glass this fate ?
They had all but a single hate.
Who was thus known ?
They had one foe and one alone—
          ENGLAND!

Take you the folk of the earth in pay,
With bars of gold your ramparts lay,
Bedeck the ocean with bow on bow,
Ye reckon well, but not well enough now.
French and Russian they matter not,
A blow for a blow, a shot for a shot;
We fight the battle with bronze and steel,
And the time that is coming Peace will seal.
You will we hate with a lasting hate,
We will never forgo our hate,
Hate by water and hate by land,
Hate of the head and hate of the hand,
Hate of the hammer and hate of the crown,
Hate of seventy millions, choking down.
We love as one, we hate as one,
We have one foe and one alone—
          ENGLAND!

But the effect of this outburst was mitigated by a German professor, who explained to his countrymen that hatred was the only psychological defence against the emotion of fear. It was because our country was most feared by the new barbarians that it was the most hated.

Deep, personal, wild fear, amounting to a panic, was indeed aroused in the Rhineland cities of Germany towards the end of September by an unexpected feat by British sailors. The Naval Wing of the Royal Flying Corps had watched over the transport of the British Expeditionary Force across the Channel, and patrolled the British, French, and Belgian coasts on the watch for enemy ships. Then, under Wing-Commander Samson, the **British raid on the Zeppelin shed at Dusseldorf** naval airmen had worked with a strong squadron of aeroplanes, first from Ostend, and next from advanced bases round Dunkirk. The airmen searched for bands of Uhlans, and by wireless messages directed our seamen, using armoured motor-cars, in several successful skirmishes against the German cavalrymen.

All this, however, was but a prelude to the main work on which Commander Samson and his men were bent. What they had in view was the Zeppelins and Zeppelin sheds of the Rhineland. And, on September 23rd, Squadron-Commander Gerrard set out with a detachment of airmen towards Cologne and Düsseldorf. There was a slight fog that enabled the flying men to travel at a height of nine hundred feet, without being seen from the earth. On nearing the Rhine they broke up into two divisions. One went to Cologne, but found the fog so thick there that the Zeppelin shed could not be seen. So they returned without attempting to kill or injure non-combatants in the great fortified city. Flight-Lieutenant Collet, in the division directed against Düsseldorf, was more fortunate. He found the shed visible, and landed three bombs on the sheds. All the airmen returned safely to their base.

NEW TORPEDO-BOAT HARBOURS IN THE COURSE OF CONSTRUCTION IN HELIGOLAND.

From 1807 to 1890 Heligoland was a British possession. It was then ceded to Germany by Lord Salisbury in return for certain concessions in East Africa. From the beginning of their occupation the Germans set to work to convert the island into a strongly fortified naval base. In addition to their expenditure on armaments they made heroic attempts to preserve their new possession from sea erosion. Our photograph was taken in 1912, when it was expected that the new harbours would be ready in 1914.

PLOT AND COUNTERPLOT AMONG THE ARMING NEUTRALS.

Effect of the Allies' Victories on Neutral Powers—Turkey Preparing to Strike—Bulgaria Willing to Wound but Afraid of Being Hurt—Struggle between King and People of Rumania—Decision to Attack Austria when Armament Completed—Why the Rumanians Held Back—Difficult Position of Italians: Suspicious of France, Grateful to Prussia, and Friendly to Britain—Italy in "Sacred Egoism" Decides to Recover Her Lost Provinces—Austrian and German Intrigues at the Vatican—Cardinal Mercier, of Belgium, Intervenes—Pope Benedict Desirous of Peace—Initial Attitude of the Swiss—Swiss Military Censorship Works for Germany—Switzerland Partly Recovers Her Senses when Allies are Victorious—Splendid Beneficence of the Dutch—Position of the Scandinavian Nations—Professor Oswalt Undoes the Work of Sven Hedin and Björnson—Dernburg's Audacious Intrigues in the United States—German-American Forces Organised to Provoke War with Triple Entente Powers and Japan—The Right to Search—Americans Reject the Laws they Laid Down.

Y the middle of September the series of definite and important victories won by the Allies in both theatres of war began to affect the position of many neutral Powers of the world. Some of these were neutral from either inclination or disinterestedness. Others were so from fear of the consequences of siding with either of the tremendous leagues of warring nations. Some were decided for action, but irresolute about the date when they would begin hostilities.

Turkey had practically been won over by the Teutons, and was only manœuvring to draw all the sympathies of Mohammedans with her. The so-called Party of Union and Progress in the Ottoman Empire had degenerated into a strong-handed clique of military adventurers, headed by the murderous charlatan Enver. He was surrounded by Jews and Germans who reduced him, by the skilful use of flattery and money, to the position of vassal to Kaiser Wilhelm.

Apparently one of the chief designs of Enver was to obtain a fighting alliance with the Bulgarians, who had beaten him in the Balkan War, and to induce the still more powerful Rumanians to remain at least neutral while Bulgaria attacked Serbia in flank, and Turkey used her European army to defeat and destroy the Greeks. This plan of action had been sketched out by the Austrians, who had already shown in the Second Balkan War their weak grasp of realities by egging on and backing Bulgaria in a vain struggle for dominion against the Serbians and the Greeks.

Bulgaria, defeated and dispossessed of territory by the combined action

ENVER BEY.
Commander-in-Chief of the Ottoman Army.

of Serbia, Greece, and Rumania, in the Second Balkan War, still remained sore and sullen and somewhat vindictive. But her ruler, Tsar Ferdinand, was resolved not to make another grave mistake. Had he but acted fairly in the division of spoil between the Balkan allies after the successful war against Turkey, there would probably have been no Great War in 1914. For, supported by her Balkan allies, and less directly by Russia, France, and Britain, Serbia would not have tempted the Austrians and Hungarians to settle the Balkan problem by a punitive expedition.

During the first month of the war the Tsar of Bulgaria and his ministers showed as much favour to the Teutonic cause as they dared. They prevented Russia towards the middle of September from sending ammunition supplies to the pressed but victorious Serbians. At times they publicly expressed the desire to see the triumph of German and Austrian arms. By the end of the month, however, the attitude of the Bulgarian governing class had changed. For the extraordinary and tremendous series of victories won by Russian generals over all the first-line troops of Austria-Hungary made the Bulgarian Government rather anxious about its own position in regard to Russia. Bulgaria, broken by two recent wars, would lie at the mercy of the great victorious Power that it had begun to offend seriously. The arrival at Sofia of Mr. Noel Buxton and his brother, who had come to discuss with all the Balkan peoples a just and fair proposal for the settlement of all their differences, renewed in the Bulgarians their faith in the disinterestedness of the British Government. Then there was the fact that Bulgaria owed her very existence to Russia, and most of the Bulgarian peasants still regarded the Russian Tsar as the protector of their race. Their German ruler, Ferdinand, had led them astray by listening to Austria and Germany. A popular revolution was quite possible if he again tried to lead them away from their fighting brother Slavs into the camp of the Teutons. In all these circumstances the Bulgarian Government became more disposed to remain quite neutral.

Not so their old opponents the Rumanians. The vivacious and passionate Latin people of Rumania did not wait for French and Russian victories in order to proclaim their sympathies and outline their future course of action. The miraculous early success of the small and almost exhausted Serbian nation against the forces of Austria-Hungary was sufficient inspiration to the Rumanian people. Just across their western frontier, in the Hungarian province of Transylvania, four million Rumanians

Rumanians in bondage to Hungarian magnates

were held in bondage by the Hungarian magnates. All the machinery of politics, social conventions, and administration had been employed for half a century by the Hungarians to oppress, debase, and denationalise their Rumanian fellow-subjects. For many years every decent free Rumanian had dreamed of the possibility of a war of liberation, and it was the deep, silent, heart-buried hope of the possibility of waging such a war some day in favourable circumstances that made the Rumanian Army of five hundred thousand men a real force in European politics. For the Rumanian had drilled with passionate earnestness to make himself a soldier of the first class. No tax intended to finance an improvement in the Rumanian Army met with any opposition from the Rumanian peasantry. Such was the respect they inspired that in the Second Balkan War the Bulgarians had readily yielded territory rather than fight them. The attempts of both Austria and Germany to get better terms for their defeated catspaw had failed.

Now, when the great day had come for the war of liberation, the Rumanian soldier was eager for the fray. Unfortunately, a prince of the House of Hohenzollern reigned over Rumania. He was King Carol, who had proved himself a wise, enterprising man of constructive genius. Much did the Rumanian people owe to him, and by reason of his claim to gratitude upon them they were placed in a tragically awkward position. For he would not fight against the Imperial leader of his house. It was said that he had pledged his word to the German Emperor not to take part in the struggle.

Towards the latter part of September it looked as though the intense contest between popular aspiration and dynastic allegiance would end in a revolution. With a magnificent strength of character that compelled admiration, King Carol stood out against the pressure of his people's wishes, until the strain completely undermined his health towards the end of September, and brought him quickly to the grave. His death was most fortunate for the Rumanian people. It was the greatest of all the great services he had done to them. For in the presence of his corpse the **King Carol's great service to Rumania** popular clamour for an immediate war died down. The new king and his ministers assured the people that nothing but the interests of the nation would guide their policy. The ministers studied the end and measured their means, and concluded that the time was not yet ripe for action.

We cannot blame them; least of all can any Russian blame them. The statesmen of Rumania remembered the consequences of their generous action in the Russo-Turkish War of 1878. It was a Rumanian army that mainly helped in the decisive attack upon Plevna, and the Rumanians were rewarded by the annexation of their fertile province of Bessarabia by the men who had come to them for help. The memory of this extraordinary event did not weigh upon the younger generation of Rumanian soldiers; but their old statesmen could not easily forget it. This time they wanted

THE SINKING OF A GERMAN DESTROYER IN THE NORTH SEA.
The new light cruiser Undaunted (Captain Cecil H. Fox), accompanied by the destroyers Lance, Lennox, Legion, and Loyal, engaged four German destroyers (115, 117, 118, and 119) off the Dutch coast on October 17th, 1914, and "sunk the lot." Thirty-one men of the enemy ships were rescued. Our illustration is of the sinking of one of the destroyers, as seen from a vessel going to the rescue of the German sailors.

guarantees from the Russian Government, and pledges from France and Britain. Not only Transylvania was claimed by them, but Bessarabia also. Diplomatic discussions dragged on for months.

In the meantime Rumania entered into an understanding with Italy. Popular aspirations in Italy were identical with those in Rumania. For Austria held two important parts of Italian territory under her rule. The Italians distrusted the French almost as much as the Rumanians did the Russians. Ever since the French occupation of Tunis some Italian statesmen had thought that the two leading Latin nations would have to fight one day for the mastery of the Mediterranean. Even as late as 1912 certain small incidents during the Italian campaign in Tripoli had led the Italians to think that President Poincaré was, in spite of his marriage to an Italian lady, hostile to the expansion of Italian power. There had also been bitter tariff battles between France and Italy, and partly as a result of this economic strife German finance and German industrial leadership had won very considerable power in the manufacturing districts around Milan. Not a little of this ill-feeling between France and Italy had been astutely provoked by Bismarck in the old days. It was part of his general scheme for keeping France isolated.

With regard to Britain, Italy's situation was clearer and yet difficult. It was very largely owing to the fact that Britain entered into the Great War against the Teutons that the Italians nobly manœuvred for a position of neutrality. As soon as the Italian Foreign Minister saw, in 1913, that Germany was bent upon an aggressive war, in which Britain would probably be engaged, he withdrew from the Triple Alliance. He did not do so formally, but practically, by refusing to act in any case in which Germany or Austria had not been first attacked. On the other hand, every Italian statesman in a position of responsibility was distinguished by a lively sense of honour. Ever since Prussia and

Italy's traditional affection for Britain Italy had made war together upon Austria, in 1866, the Prussian and the Italian had worked together. German finance and German technical science had helped to develop Northern Italy into one of the most brilliant and important centres of industry in Europe. Many Italian men of science owed their genius to an alliance between their own southern vivacity of intellect and the methods of patient and thorough research learned from German universities. The old, strong traditional affection for Britain was the poetry of the international relations of Italy; the feeling of respect for

SPREADING THE TRUTH FROM THE SKIES.

To their duties of scouting and fighting French airmen added the task of dropping leaflets with the following inscription: "To the German soldiers: It is not true that we Frenchmen shoot or ill-treat German prisoners. On the contrary our prisoners of war are well treated and obtain plenty to eat and to drink. Those of you who are disgusted with your miserable condition may, without fear, unarmed, inform the French outposts. You will be well received. After the war everyone will be allowed to return home. These leaflets contain a plain statement of the true state of affairs concerning the treatment of German prisoners."

German organisation in science and industry was the prose of their international politics. This was one of the reasons why Italy hesitated to weaken Germany by an attack on Austria.

Italy's hesitation in this respect was increased by another strong current of thought and feeling in Italian life. Modern Italy is not only a nation; she is also a spiritual empire. Ever since the noble Italian families of the Renaissance period succeeded in winning a practically absolute control over the College of Cardinals, the Papacy has remained an appanage of the Italian nobility. All the fields for exercising their undoubted genius for diplomacy—fields lost by French, Spanish, and Austrian conquests in Italy, and scarcely recovered by the democratic movement of national insurrection—were more than replaced by the spiritual dominion they exercised through

SINKING OF THE RUSSIAN CRUISER PALLADA IN THE BALTIC.

When on patrol duty with a sister ship, the Bayan, in the Baltic, the Pallada was struck by a torpedo from a German submarine and sent to the bottom so quickly that few of her crew of five hundred and sixty-eight officers and men escaped.

the Papacy. So long as France remained a professed Catholic Power her political weight on the Papacy was a balance to that of Austria. But when the French Republic in recent years became a fierce and active anti-Catholic force in the world, and the centre of much of the atheistical or anti-clerical movement that disturbed all the Latin countries, the Papacy was naturally compelled to act in self-defence.

The result was that the great power of the Roman Catholic Church inclined to Austria-Hungary and Southern Germany and the Rhineland, and the clerical element in Italy worked strongly to prevent that country from going to war with the Teutonic Empire. A desire to see the freethinkers of France overthrown tended at times to prevail over all other considerations. As Russia represented the old, schismatical Church of Constantinople, the directors of the policy of the Papacy did not look with much favour on Russian interests. Great Britain also was mainly a schismatical or heretical Power, and her triumph promised to help the old faith but little. With the Protestant part of Germany, on the other hand, the Papacy had come to an arrangement, after beating Bismarck himself in the height of his power. The Catholic party in Germany practically

SEA-MINE WASHED ASHORE ON THE EAST COAST.
The bomb shown in our photograph was washed ashore on our East Coast in October, 1914. When in position in the sea it was designed to float the other way up, the anchor chains being attached to the eye-holes seen above.

held the balance between the Protestant-Conservative party and the free-thinking Socialistic party.

While, however, the organ of the Vatican continued for some time to promote the cause of the Teutonic allies, the new Pope, Benedict XIV., took a larger and more deeply religious view of the terrible struggle that was rocking Christendom to its foundations. He was a wise, feeling, statesmanlike man, who seemed to reveal a gift for constructive diplomacy equal to that of Pope Leo XIII. Close to his side was Cardinal Mercier, of Malines, one of those heroic princes of the old Church, who force even disbelievers, and nonconformists to the ancient historic creed of Western Europe, to admire the miraculous vigour with which the Church of Rome returns to her noblest traditions. High above the subtle politicians of the College of Cardinals towered the modern apostle from the Belgians, stamped in the character of those early bishops of Western Europe who faced Hun and Goth and other barbaric Teutons, and subdued the savagery in them by a sublime manifestation of the personal forces of civilisation and Christianity. There were German and Austrian Cardinals at Rome, and German and Austrian Jesuits, who degraded their creed for political ends.

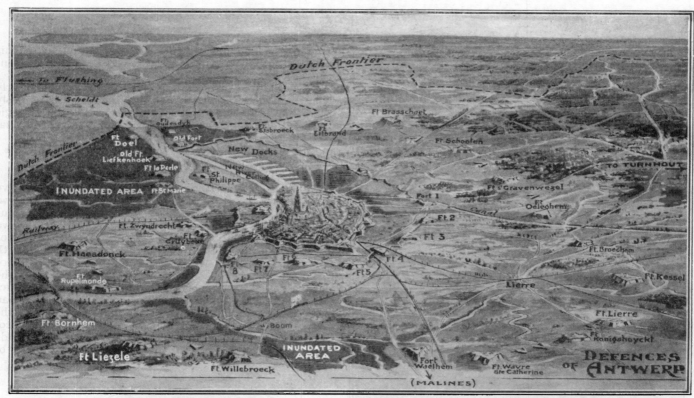

PICTORIAL MAP INDICATING THE AREAS INUNDATED BY THE BELGIANS IN THEIR DEFENCE OF ANTWERP.

But the great Belgian, by his sincerity and veracity, and the genius inspired by the sight of the sufferings of his innocent country, triumphed over all the politicians. By a direct personal appeal he won the newly-elected Pope over to his side. Then the Catholics of France were able to state that many of the French soldiers, hitherto indifferent, or even incredulous, in the matter of religion, had begun to ponder the mysteries of life, while facing death continually on the battlefield. The wild, bright, eager French mind was being tempered and hardened in the furnace of war. Even many French politicians of the anti-clerical school were beginning to modify their feelings of antagonism—some through policy, some through genuine sympathy with the growing religious current in their national life.

It looked as though all would be regained that had been lost when Cardinal Rampolla—the friend of France—had been thrust from the chair of St. Peter after his election by the veto of Austria. There were grounds for a new compromise between the Papacy and the French Republic. Such a compromise had ever been the aim of Pope Leo XIII. and his adviser and true successor, Cardinal Rampolla. Pope Benedict appeared to incline to revert to the statesmanship of the greatest of modern Popes, and, with a view, perhaps, to assisting her ally and to promoting the interests of the large number of Catholics in her dominion, Great Britain took the unusual step of sending a representative to the Church of Rome. This historic renewal of diplomatic relations with the Church to which our country once paid Peter's Pence, in memory of the debt we owed

Rome for converting the pagan Anglo-Saxons of England to Christianity, excited considerable distress in certain Protestant circles.

They protested. But the power that brought Protestant Bismarck to his knees was too strong for us to resist. We had Belgian interests to protect as well as our own, the interests of millions of Irishmen, and the interests of old British families that did not change their faith at the Reformation. From a purely political point of view, the action of the British Government was sound and statesmanlike. Even Japan, that had not yet officially adopted the Christian faith, followed the example of Britain and sent a representative to the Vatican.

In so far as Pope Benedict followed his natural feelings and used all his influence for peace, he helped the Teutons, and lengthened the period of suffering of the Catholics of Belgium. In the meantime, however, the Italian Government was deciding the problem of intervention in its own way. As her Prime Minister, Signor Salandra, put it, "a sacred egoism" became her guiding principle. In plain words, she was bent on recovering her lost provinces from Austria by any available means. The Teutonic Powers could make sure of her remaining neutral by yielding to her, without a struggle, the Trentino and Trieste. Austria, however, was disinclined to the bargain. Italy therefore turned to the Powers of the Triple Entente. To them she made in effect, if not in actual words, a larger demand. She required not only the two Italian-peopled districts of Southern Austria, but also a considerable part of the coast-line of the ancient Venetian territory of Dalmatia.

COUNT JOHANN VON BERNSTORFF.
German Ambassador at Washington. Devoted great energy to pro-German Press campaign in the United States.

PROFESSOR WILHELM OSTWALD.
Famous German chemist. He tried to win over the Scandinavian nations to the idea of incorporation with "the Greater Germany which was to be organised after the war."

This province was peopled mainly by the Serbian race, but Venice had conquered it in the old days, and had built many of the towns on the coast. About half the coast could be given to Serbia, thus allowing her an outlet to the Adriatic Sea, and the rest was required by Italy.

All considered, the proposal was a fair one. If Italy put an army of a million men into the field, the cost in blood and treasure to her people would be great. She could not send her men out to die simply for love of the fair blue eyes of Britannia and the poetry of Lord Byron. All that we had done to promote the national independence of Italy in the old days was partly balanced by what the Germans had done in helping Italy to maintain herself as a great Mediterranean Power against **Italy's debt to** France. Italy therefore waited until **Britain and Germany** either of the two contending leagues of nations should accept her terms. In the meantime she armed for the fight. Both her exchequer and her war stores were depleted by the long war against the Turks and Arabs in Tripoli. Months were required in order to bring her large Army up to a position of strength in which it could venture to engage the forces of a great European military Power with a good chance of success. Guns were needed, and shells for the guns. For, though Italy had the finest light field-artillery in the world, she had not a sufficient number of batteries. Moreover, the war had shown that a large number of heavy mobile howitzers were absolutely necessary. With the Teutons standing in their last ditch, all their great guns behind them, heavy artillery and, perhaps, vast stores of shell and shrapnel would be required. Italy was also assisting

Rumania in the manufacture of ammunition. In this way months passed without either of the two important neutral Powers coming to an active decision.

The position of Greece in the Great War was more clearly defined. Like most of the Balkan States, she was seriously weakened in treasure and war material by the struggle with Turkey, and the subsequent fight with Bulgaria. Many of the Turks were still anxious for another war with the Greeks, with a view **Position of Greece** to recovering the Ægean Islands. Both **in the War** Powers had been making a supreme effort to obtain a naval preponderance. Turkey had ordered two battleships from Britain, and Greece had purchased two battleships from the United States. The action of our country in taking over, at the outbreak of the war, the two ships building in our yards for Turkey was both a stroke of diplomacy in the Orient and a naval measure in the North Sea. It prevented Turkey from going to war with Greece with any chance of success at sea. The arrival in the Dardanelles of the Goeben and the Breslau did not alter this condition of things. For any action by the German battle-cruiser and her light consort would bring into the field of war the Russian Black Sea Fleet and the Franco-British Mediterranean Fleets. Greece was thus made strong at sea and bound to the Triple Entente by ties of

DR. WOODROW WILSON.
President of the United States. In the first week of the war he offered his services for mediation between the belligerent Powers

gratitude and interest. The removal of the Turkish menace left her hands free for her principal work of maintaining peace in the Balkans. As the Greek Premier, M. Venezelos, explained to the Chamber of Deputies at Athens on September 13th, Greece was in a position of conditional neutrality. In the general interests of the Balkan people, she had contracted an alliance with Serbia. If either Bulgaria or Turkey tried to take advantage of the difficulties of the Serbians, and assist the defeated Austrians by attempting to stab Serbia in the back, Greece would intervene. As both Turkey and Bulgaria were well aware that the Rumanians would act in such a case in operation with the Greeks, the peace of the Balkans was maintained. The Turko-Bulgarian menace, however, had a considerable effect upon the course of the Great War. For it was one of the main factors that induced the Rumanian statesmen to hold back from joining in the attack against Hungary.

In Switzerland also the Teutons gained a success, owing to the thoroughness with which they prepared for war. The Swiss Army was almost entirely officered by men of the German type, in the closest sympathy with the Teutonic powers. The Swiss democracy had no voice in the matter; their Prussianised war Staff had both their minds and their bodies in its tyrannous grip. Immediately on the

Efforts to Germanise Swiss thought and feeling

outbreak of the war it established a military censorship solely with a view to Germanising Swiss thought and feeling. Only the French-speaking Swiss, who obtained their information through France, remained truly and stubbornly neutral. For this reason they were often dominated by Germans, who managed the best hotels and controlled some of the important industries in their districts. It is easy to see why the Germans took so much trouble to ensure the active sympathies of the Swiss. Not only was Switzerland one of the two gates into France, but she was also an important back door for evading some of the most vital consequences of the British and French blockades of the North Sea and the Adriatic.

By the end of September, however, the German Swiss began to count the cost of their actions. The victories

THE LATE KING CAROL OF RUMANIA.
King Carol I., who died on October 10th, 1914, was a prince of the House of Hohenzollern. A wise, enterprising man of constructive genius, but German sympathies, his death was the greatest of all the great services he rendered to Rumania, for it was likely that the intense contest between popular aspiration and dynastic allegiance would have ended in revolution.

KING FERDINAND OF RUMANIA.
King Ferdinand I., nephew of the late King Carol. Aged forty-nine. He married, in 1892, Princess Marie of Edinburgh, a daughter of the late Duke of Saxe-Coburg-Gotha, and has six children, the eldest, Prince Carol, being twenty-one years old.

of the Serbians, Russians, French, and British could no longer be concealed from the Swiss people. The Germanised censorship relaxed, and the French Swiss—always the most brilliant journalists of their conglomerate nation—began to make their power over public opinion felt. For months a verbal duel waged between German Berne and French Geneva, while Swiss Italians veered round towards the Allies, in sympathy with popular Italian feeling. The German Swiss, however, retained the bent of mind with which they began, together with the practical control of the Army. President Hoffmann was a figurehead. It was simply downright fear of the consequences of their actions

that made the members of the ruling party in Switzerland modify their action. France had a considerable control over the wheat supply of the Swiss, and she naturally used this instrument to modify the outrageous conduct of the Swiss military censors. By the end of the month Switzerland was more or less effectively neutral.

As a side door for evading the blockade, Switzerland, however, was less important to Germany than Holland. Rotterdam, with its large colony of Germans and German Jews, was a Rhine port controlling the main artery of German commerce. The Germans naturally desired the Dutch to remain nominally neutral, but practically favourable to the German cause, and help them to mitigate the effects of the naval blockade by transforming Rotterdam into a new Hamburg. This placed the Dutch Government in an extremely awkward position. From an economical point of view, Holland had become to a large extent one of the chief transporting centres for Westphalia. Rotterdam was a seaport of the vast German industrial district stretching from Düsseldorf to Essen. The modern prosperity of Holland was largely based upon the German hinterland behind it. If the Dutch had been a spiritless people, to whom money was everything, they might have thrown in their lot with the powerful and industrially progressive modern German Empire. They stood to lose by everything that hindered or diminished German trade, and they stood to gain by everything that favoured and increased it.

Awkward position of the Dutch Government

FLIGHT FROM ANTWERP DURING THE BOMBARDMENT.
Thousands of the citizens awaiting their opportunity to cross the Scheldt.

In addition to these economical considerations, there was the memory of the Boer War that told against Great Britain. The Boers were Dutchmen—Dutchmen of the heroic age of Tromp and De Ruyter. In their distant settlement by the half-way house on the old route to India, they had preserved the spirit of the brave old fighting days, when Holland was able to dispute with Britain the mastery of the seas and the command of all the outlands of the earth. Towards the nation which abruptly brought to an end the independence of the Transvaal and the Orange Free State, the Dutch people were not favourably inclined. German politicians were well aware of this condition of things, and exploited it to the utmost of their power. Even the unparalleled magnanimity with which the Liberal Government of Great Britain handled the situation in South Africa after the war did not entirely remove the grudge against our country felt by the Dutch.

Spirited independence of the Dutchman Holland, however, never fell to the position that Switzerland occupied in the first two months of the war. There was that in the soul of the ordinary Dutchman which rebelled against any pressure from any foreign country. Neither the naval power of Britain nor the military and economical power of Germany daunted his spirit. Placed between the upper and the nether millstones, between the power of Britain to cut off supplies and starve him, and the power of Germany to deal with him as she had dealt

with the Belgians, the Dutchman underwent a transformation. Dutch Jews and German Jews, and German importing houses, continued to dodge or dare the contraband laws. The real Dutchman, however, suffered a change similar to that which happened to the British soldier in the retreat from Mons. It was the streams of anguished, hopeless fugitives crossing the Dutch border from the Walloon districts of Belgium that influenced the Dutchman and determined his attitude. It made him willing, if need arose, to face the embattled power of Germany with the same grim and desperate courage with which his ancestors had faced Spain and France in the days of Philip II. and Louis **Political and economic** XIV. During the Siege **factors in Denmark** of Liège the German Staff had almost been tempted to turn through Holland for an easier path. The Dutchman remembered this. For the rest, the Dutch nation generally kept strictly to the letter and the spirit of international law, and tried to deal fairly between the contending leagues of nations.

The position of the Scandinavian countries somewhat resembled that of Holland. Their economic ties to the German Empire were less close. For example, in

GERMAN SHELL PLOUGHS UP THE PAVEMENT.
All the windows were shuttered and many places along the Antwerp streets were littered with débris of shell-fire.

regard to the agricultural products, Britain had been, and remained, a better market for Denmark than was Germany. In the case of the Danes, moreover, many men still living remembered the war with Prussia and Austria over Schleswig-Holstein, and their memories had been continually refreshed by the treatment meted out to Danes in the conquered territories. On the other hand, there were older memories of the way in which Britain had conducted the great Continental naval blockade in the days of Nelson. For we had then attacked and captured the Danish Navy merely to forestall a possible move against Sweden, another neutral nation, by Napoleon. The Danes believed we were quite capable of again acting with the utmost rigour, if our national life appeared to be in desperate danger. From a pure theoretical, democratic point of view the Danish nation wished for the triumph of the Triple Entente, and the recovery of the Danish-peopled district of Schleswig-Holstein. In the meantime they hoped that the blockade of the North Sea would proceed without any rigorous treatment of neighbouring neutral countries, and many of their farmers tried to balance the increasing cost of fodder by selling horses to the German Army.

The Norwegians, practically the same race as the Danes, were in a rather more fortunate position. In spite of the comparative smallness of their population, their old genius for seafaring had enabled them to create in modern times an important mercantile marine. Their country was rich in timber and animal produce, much of which was supplied to our land and to Germany. The Norwegian sailors were endangered by German mines in the North Sea ; but the shipowners, at least, reaped a full harvest from the

extraordinary rise in the cost of ocean transport produced by the stoppage of German shipping, and the employment of British merchant vessels as troopships and military supply-ships. Being one of the most intensely democratic people on earth, the Norwegians favoured the Allies—and imported a somewhat remarkable amount of copper !

Germany wanted this metal, and perhaps the type of Norwegian whom Ibsen used to depict with bitter scorn was not averse to making money by providing the means of slaughtering other democratic and God-fearing nations of Western Europe. The son of Ibsen's old friend, Björnson, went publicly over to the side of the Germans, and became one of the chief apostles of Prussianism to Denmark and Norway. He tried to palliate the German atrocities in Belgium and Northern France, and spread every gross falsehood about the policy of Britain, France, and Belgium that the reptile German Press invented. Yet his father had been the prophet of democracy in Norway, and had probably done more than any other man to restore the independence of the Norwegian nation, after centuries of subjection to Denmark and Sweden.

Björnson's son and the German reptile Press

In the neighbouring country of Sweden, the famous explorer of Central Asia, Sven Hedin, degraded himself to the position of a gramophone in the service of the German Press Bureau. Beginning with the misrepresentation of the aims of Russia, Hedin ended by adopting the perverse ideas about Britain which the Germans, in a frenzy of fear and hatred, invented. In the early period of the war most of the Swedes seemed to

ANTWERP DURING BOMBARDMENT: THE RUSH TO THE QUAY VANDYKE.
Every conceivable species of conveyance was utilised for the Belgian exodus from Antwerp. Our photograph shows the beginning of the congestion on the Quay Vandyke. Castle Steen, with its memories of the Spanish Inquisition, is seen in the background on the right. Inset : Refugees drifting down the River Scheldt.

England has summoned the Mongol: France calls upon the Moor; Russia sends her Cossacks to attack our German Kinsmen, WHERE ARE THE SYMPATHIES OF THE AMERICAN PEOPLE?

have had a decided bias towards Germany. This was largely due to the preparations that Germany had made for the control of the Swedish Press, and other instruments for influencing public opinion. The Germans worked upon the old Swedish grudge against Russia for obtaining, during the reconstruction of Europe in the days of Napoleon, the Duchy of Finland. For though Sweden received in compensation the kingdom **Exploiting Sweden's** of Norway, she had since **fear of Russia** lost this owing to her lack of tact in handling the Norwegians. She still bore ill-will against the Russians, and feared they would end by absorbing the whole of Scandinavia. Groundless as the fear was, it was sufficient for the Germans to work upon. They had the chief share in supplying Sweden with goods, while our country had the chief share of Swedish imports. The result was that the German commercial traveller was a greater force in Sweden than was the British commercial traveller. By combining patriotism and business, in modern Teutonic fashion, he greatly helped to influence the Swedes against the Allies.

Germany, moreover, exercised considerable pressure on Sweden by means of her Baltic Fleet. It was to diminish

THE KAISER'S OFFICIAL LIARS AND THEIR WORK.

The amazing campaign of lies and calumnies which the Kaiser officially instituted early in the war was something unconceived by merely civilised peoples, and the peculiar product of "Kultur." Herr Dernburg, seen above (left), went to New York to pollute the United States with German lies, one of his innumerable agencies being a weekly paper "The Fatherland," from which we reproduce a page in miniature; while Dr. Hamann, the chief of the Germany Press Bureau at Berlin (seen on the right), deluged the whole world with false news and infamous inventions, his machinations extending as far as little towns in Chili, where lying "supplements," written and paid for by German agents, were issued by the venal and powerless local Press. We give an example above. The "news" headings read: "One hundred German airships bombard Allies' camps. Horrible confusion and flight of English and French. Terror in Paris. The first fugitives arrive at that capital with the terrible news and the terror-stricken inhabitants flee towards the south-west. The Tsar of Russia, King of England, and M. Poincaré telegraph the Kaiser." Naturally, the text assured us that the allied rulers were suing for peace !

this pressure that the Russian Admiral von Essen made a surprise attack on a German cruiser squadron towards the end of August, and sank the Magdeburg and several German destroyers. The happy consequence was that the Swedes took to using their minds in a more free and independent manner, and in spite of the contorted efforts of Sven Hedin's intellect, popular opinion in the country by the end of September became a little more friendly to the Allies. For all that Hedin did was undone by the famous German chemist Ostwald.

This man was a supreme incarnation of the scientific virtues and practical vices of the modern German professor. In his own special field of knowledge he had done much good work. But the universal fame and honour, which he had won by his labours in chemistry and physics, turned his mind. Like Haeckel, of Jena, and Lasson, of Berlin, he wanted to imitate the heroic German professors of the age of Napoleon. They had been content to excite the courage of the Prussians in the years of gloom that followed the disasters of Jena and Auerstadt. This work was not necessary at the present time, so Ostwald launched out into the wider field of warlike politics, and tried to win over the Scandinavian nations.

Ostwald proposed to them that they should, without a struggle, become incorporated in the Greater Germany which was to be organised after the war. The Teuton, he proclaimed, was the only man with a veritable genius for organisation, and the Swedes, Norwegians, and Danes should be struck with anticipatory gratitude for the work Germany intended to do for them after she had won the empire of the world. This amazingly tactless and disconcerting statement, made by one of the greatest leaders of German science, did more for the cause of the Triple Entente than the most eloquent of French or British orators could have achieved.

By the end of the historic month of September the only neutral white race that caused any anxiety to the Allies was the Americans. To the task of influencing public opinion in the United States, the German Government had bent the larger part of the energies that it could spare from the actual conduct of the war. There were nearly eleven million persons of German, Austrian, and Hungarian stock in the States, including some powerful financiers and trust magnates of German-Jewish or German origin. For some years previous to the outbreak of the war the German Government had endeavoured to preserve and intensify a feeling of German patriotism in America, by a ramifying system of local German associations.

RESCUE OF THE CREW OF A SINKING GERMAN SEA-RAIDER.

A German submarine, U18, was rammed off the Scottish coast on November 23rd, 1914. It was shortly afterwards seen on the surface, with its crew on deck and the white flag flying. The British destroyer Garry came up just as the submarine was sinking, and rescued Lieutenant von Hennig, two other officers, and twenty-three men, one only being drowned.

SYMPATHETIC HOLLAND AND THE DISTRESSED BELGIANS.
Dutch Army service waggon at a frontier town affording temporary aid to the fugitives from Antwerp. The view immediately below is of Belgian refugees on the road to Holland with household goods hurriedly packed on a donkey-cart.

The organisation of the Teutonic forces in the United States appeared to offer a grand opportunity for action directed from Berlin. First of all Count Bernstorff, the new German Ambassador, was appointed local director of this large and favourable factor in American politics. Hermann Ridder, the editor of the German-American paper, the "Staats Zeitung," was made leader of the local German reptile Press. Then, as Count Bernstorff displayed, in the interviews that American journalists had with him, an inability to appreciate and work upon the American mind, the main part of his task was entrusted to Bernard Dernburg.

Dernburg scarcely deserved his position. He was one of the few men of genius produced in modern Germany, and like most of his countrymen with high ability in practical affairs, he came of Jewish stock. He was the son of the editor of the "Berliner Tageblatt," and after learning banking business in New York with Thalmann & Co., in early manhood, he had returned to **The degradation of** Berlin, where he won a high position in **Dernburg** German finance, and became at last Colonial Secretary in the Imperial Government. His admirers proclaimed him the Joseph Chamberlain of Germany. But though the Kaiser shared their admiration, the old prejudices of the Prussian nobility against their brilliant Jewish fellow-subjects led to Dernburg's overthrow. But for this prejudice he might have become the Disraeli of the leading Teutonic Empire.

It was somewhat of a degradation to a man of this calibre to dispatch him to the United States on a mission directly opposed to the position of neutrality taken up by

the American Government. For Dernburg had to plot and scheme in an underhanded way against the proclaimed policy of President Woodrow Wilson. But, by a mixture of audacity and subtlety, amounting almost to impudence, the German Jew carried on his work. He professed to come to America to collect for a Red Cross fund. But this was only a very transparent cover for a bold and pertinacious attempt to raise a great German war loan, mainly through German-Jewish-American bankers.

The scheme failed. Many of the bankers already had large personal or family interests in the affairs of the Teutonic Empires. And, **American interests in** looking at the matter as hard-headed **the Teutonic Empires** business men, they were disinclined to risk much more money just for the sake of Bernard's dark and eloquent eyes. They were more concerned about means of saving their German and Austrian investments from the threatening wreckage of German power than about helping the Kaiser in his overwhelming difficulties.

So Dernburg, with the co-operation of Count Bernstorff, tried to work towards another end. Towards the middle of September both the German Government and the German Military Staff came to the conclusion that they had started a war which they were unlikely to bring to a successful conclusion. They recognised that they had made a mistake in singling out France and Russia for attack. Britain was their most formidable opponent. For the British plan of campaign, which they had once despised, was already proving to be comprehensive in scope, and deliberate and deadly in execution. By reason of their great naval power, the British people were bankrupting and starving out the German Empire,

THE EXODUS FROM ANTWERP INTO HOLLAND.
The great majority of the refugees from Antwerp found their way into Holland, and nothing could exceed the kindness shown to them by the Dutch people. The above photographs were taken during the flight along the roads leading to Dutch territory.

HOW THE RUSSIAN BALTIC FLEET PUTS TO SEA IN WINTER.

During the winter months, when most of Russia's Baltic ports are ice-bound, the Russian Fleet is enabled to put to sea by the aid of the ice-breaker Ermack, shown in the above picture. The vessel was built in England by the firm of Sir W. G. Armstrong, Whitworth & Co., to designs by Admiral Makaroff, and is able to clear a passage through ice over twenty feet thick.

while they were growing tremendously in military strength by building up a volunteer army of two million young men. At the same time, London still ruled the money markets of the world, and as Dr. Solf, the new German Secretary for the Colonies, confessed, she had invisible weapons of industrial warfare, which were more terrible in their effect on German national life than were the new gigantic Krupp howitzers.

In short, the Kaiser and his Ministers and generals and admirals were ready to make peace. Naturally, they wanted peace on their own terms—no war indemnities, no cession of territory, and no disarmament. Apparently Mr. Oscar Straus, a former American Ambassador to Turkey, was entrusted with the delicate and ticklish task of opening negotiations, through his own Government, with all the contending Powers. It was a pretty move

to induce the American Government to approach Germany as well as Britain, France, and Russia, when the entire movement for peace was a German intrigue—at least in its origin.

Naturally, nothing came of it. It may be that at the inception of the scheme the Germans thought that the pacific influence of Pope Benedict on the one side and, on the other side of the world, the equally disinterested desire of President Wilson to see the war end speedily, might have some power to sway the minds of their enemies. When it was patent that nothing of this sort could shake the determination of the Powers of the Triple Entente, the German-American movement for peace was pursued with a different end in view.

It was calculated that the general sympathy of the American people would be stirred by the spectacle of millions of peace-desiring Teutons being bled white by hordes of savage, **Germany's bid for** vindictive Russians, Frenchmen, Britons, **American sympathy** Belgians, Serbians, Montenegrins, and Japanese. The American, like the Briton, cannot help feeling for the under-dog. While Field-Marshal von Hindenburg was preparing to trample Russian Poland into mud, and to starve, cripple, and terrorise the Poles, by the mightiest movement of invasion in modern times, the appeal for sympathy with the kind, pacific, hard-pressed Teuton was carried on.

It might well have succeeded, but for one thing. Well-known and well-trusted American war correspondents

CHEERING A BRITISH TRANSPORT ARRIVING AT ANTWERP WITH PART OF THE NAVAL CONTINGENT ON BOARD.
The Royal Naval Division, under the command of Major-General A. Paris, C.B., reached Antwerp in the early part of October, 1914, and included men of the First and Second Naval Brigades and Royal Marine Brigade. The force, declared Sir John French, after " a comprehensive review of all the circumstances," was " handled by General Paris with great skill and boldness." Inset: The inundations, intended by their elders to prevent the horrors of a German invasion of Antwerp, afforded Belgian children opportunities of playing new games.

had travelled through Belgium, and faithfully set down the things they saw. The native-born American accepted their evidence, especially after it was generally known that an American girl living in Belgium had fallen into the hands of German soldiers, with most dreadful results. Moreover, the American public had read all the diplomatic correspondence concerning the outbreak of the war that had appeared in print. The majority of them had made up their minds that Belgium, France, and Britain were fighting, not only for their own lives, but for the general principles of international law and democratic civilisation.

But though all the native-born American peoples were averse from the intrigues of the Germans, there was one small but powerful group of American **American Trusts** men who were inclined to make trouble **and the Allies** with the Powers of the Triple Entente. These men were connected with various trusts, that had large controls over the production of various materials urgently needed in Germany and Austria for carrying on the war or maintaining the general national strength. Copper, cotton, petrol, and india-rubber, for example, were selling in Germany at prices which would rapidly make the fortunes of large wholesale exporters.

In 1812, towards the close of the Napoleonic wars, the United States had resumed hostilities with Britain over the question of the right of the British Navy to stop and search neutral ships. Bearing this in mind, some of the American trust magnates seem to have thought that they

could conduct a very profitable commerce with the Germanic Empires by getting their ships exempt from contraband. Simple was the means—mere bluff of another war over right of search, according to the traditions of 1812. But what international laws there were with regard to the searching of neutral vessels had been changed in the course of a hundred and two years. By the irony of Fate it was the Americans themselves who had succeeded in making the rights of search more rigorous. During the American Civil War our shippers supplying the Confederates had tried to evade the confiscation of their cargoes by sending them to a neutral port, usually Mexican. To stop this practice the Americans had established the doctrine of continuous voyage. According to this doctrine, goods of a contraband sort, sent to neutral countries, but destined for the enemy, were liable to seizure.

But this did not still the agitation against the naval methods adopted by the Allies; and there were times when it seemed that the genius for intrigue of one brilliant German Jew might prevail over the silent and reserved policy of neutrality of President Woodrow Wilson.

MEN OF THE BRITISH NAVAL BRIGADE DRAWN UP ON THE OUTSKIRTS OF ANTWERP.
It was in response to an appeal by the Belgian Government that a British naval contingent, with some heavy naval guns, was sent to participate in the defence of Antwerp during the last week of the German attack. Inset: French Marines passing through Ghent on their way to take part in the defence of Antwerp.

THE BOMBARDMENT AND FALL OF ANTWERP.

The Cruel Shelling of Malines Cathedral on the Sabbath—Beaten by Soldiers, Germans Slaughter Women Coming from Prayers—Battles for the Path to the Sea—Decisive Belgian Victories Round Termonde—German General Makes a Mistake that Saves the French Coast—Desperate Position of Belgian Army in Antwerp—No Guns with the Range of the Austrian and German Howitzers—Fall of Antwerp Forts Certain—Belgians Undertake an Impossible Task to Help their Allies—Terrible End of the Garrison of Fort Waelhem—Ten Blackened, Burnt, Groping Figures Emerge from the Ruins—Fort after Fort Falling under a Rain of 12 in. Shells—The Raging, Murderous Struggle for the Nethe—Mr. Winston Churchill Arrives with the Naval Division—Scheme of Large Operations for the Relief of Antwerp—Sir Henry Rawlinson and the 7th Division Forced Back—The Bridge of Death at the Nethe—Shells begin to Fall in the City—The Dreadful, Tragic Flight of Half a Million Townspeople—Defending Forces Withdrawn—How the German Commander was Tricked—Empty and Costly Triumph of the Outplayed Teutons—Only the Husk of a City Won by Them.

THE fall of Antwerp was the most tragic episode in the greatest of wars. For months the heroic little Belgian Army had stood against the mightiest military power in the world, and towards the close of September it was expected that Antwerp would be relieved by the far-reaching operations of the Franco-British armies gathering about Lille. But the enemy was too quick in his double attack against the Allies. By a supreme effort, General von Falkenhayn collected every available soldier, and flung his last reserves against the extending French line. Then, with some 125,000 young, fresh troops of the first-line armies, and the siege-artillery collected for Paris, he began the attack on Antwerp.

Characteristically cruel was the manner in which the Germans opened their campaign against the Belgian Army in its last stronghold. At 9.30 o'clock on the morning of Sunday, September 27th, the townspeople of Malines came out of their beautiful old cathedral of St. Rombold, and stood talking in groups in the large, ancient market-place, surrounded by picturesque gabled houses of the sixteenth century. In front of them rose the old Cloth Hall, built in the days when Mechlin, as the Flemings call their town, was the Manchester of Northern Europe. Many of the older
324

LIEUT.-GENERAL SIR HENRY RAWLINSON.
He commanded the British forces operating in the neighbourhood of Ghent and Antwerp.

women who came out of the cathedral—pale-faced, black-clad, working-class women—were the famous Mechlin lace-makers, esteemed throughout the world for the delicacy and beauty of their work. As they gathered together for a gossip, there was a distant roar, a loud shriek, and overhead a dreadful explosion, as the first shell struck the cathedral.

The gentle German, with the assistance of the gentle Austrian, was resuming his work of terrorising the harmless and peaceful non-combatant population of Belgium. All day the great shells rained on the stricken town, some fifty falling every hour. The glorious thirteenth-century cathedral, with its richly-carved choir and its magnificent tower, with the finest chimes in the world, was almost completely destroyed. The railway-station and barracks were set on fire, and the magnificent old buildings, erected in the days when Mechlin was the capital of both Holland and Belgium, were wrecked and burnt. Ten of the townspeople were killed, and very many more wounded. Most of them fled northward to Antwerp, the two outermost Antwerp forts, Wavre and Waelhem, being only two miles north of Malines.

No military purpose was served by this sudden destruction of an open town. The Germans, moreover, offended against the laws of civilised warfare by giving no notice of the intended

THE FALL OF BELGIUM'S LAST STRONGHOLD.

FUGITIVES FROM ANTWERP CROSSING THE PONTOON BRIDGE OVER THE SCHELDT.

The siege of Antwerp commenced on September 28th, 1914. The bombardment of the city began on the night of October 7th, and the enemy entered the deserted streets on the 9th. Between October 7th and 9th nearly 500,000 people left Antwerp for Holland, Ghent, Bruges, and Ostend. Soon after the authorities had warned all who could to leave, every avenue of approach to the pontoon bridge across the Scheldt leading to St. Nicolas and Ghent was rendered impassable by the press of vehicular traffic. On the afternoon of the 7th and the morning of the 8th the Civic Guard went from house to house telling the inhabitants to flee. During those two days the scenes on the roads to Holland, declared the "Times" correspondent, could hardly have been equalled by any migration in the history of the Israelites, Kalmucks, or Tartars. In addition to the exodus to Holland, the correspondent saw a crowd estimated at 150,000 blocking the ferry and the pontoons.

Detachment of the British Naval Brigades going to take up their [position] in the trenches outside Antwerp. Inset (left) : Belgian sharps[hooters] firing on the enemy from an armoured train. While the big g[uns were] being trained on the German trenches, picked shots were on th[e look-out.]

An armoured train in action at Antwerp. So that it might be able to fire at the big German siege-guns, which eventually won the day for the enemy, an armoured train, manned by Belgians and British, sallied out from the beleaguered city and contrived to give a good many checks to the besiegers.

Armoured trains played a conspicuous part, not only in the defence [of] Antwerp, but also during the later battle for the coast-line. They we[re] solidly built, but the discharge of their guns caused a recoil which made t[he] whole train rock on the metals.

portunities of volley or individual firing. Some of the armoured
were armed with anti-aircraft guns. Right : Armoured motor-car
ed by men of the Royal Marine Light Infantry at Lokeren, north
ch place part of our First Naval Brigade was cut off by the Germans.

armoured motor-car scouring the roads around Antwerp. Just ahead
hell from one of the attacking army's big guns is seen to have burst,
owing off a terrific cloud of thick, black smoke. The Belgian officer
charge of the car is looking through his glasses to see what damage has
been done. A Belgian officer, Lieutenant Henkart, was, perhaps, the first
to draw attention to the advantages of the armoured motor-car. He placed
himself and two of his cars, manned by his own servants, at the disposal
of the Belgian Government.

THE REIGN OF TERROR: ON THE QUAYSIDE OF THE RIVER SCHELDT.

During the German bombardment of Antwerp, when bombs dropped from Zeppelins and shells from the German siege-guns caused a conflagration visible from the Dutch border, barges and small steamers along the Scheldt quays took on human freight as rapidly as they could— their owners, it is said, charging the terror-stricken fugitives twenty francs a head for the brief trip into Dutch territory.

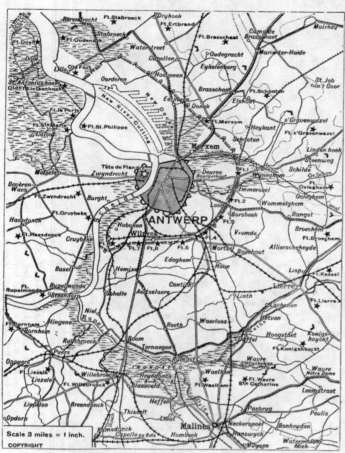

MAP SHOWING THE FORTIFICATIONS OF ANTWERP.
Eight years before the Great War General Brialmont's advanced forts
were linked together by a new line of defence to replace the old ramparts.

of seven hundred Belgian troops held the Germans off
all the morning. When a third of the little Belgian forces
had fallen, they were reinforced, and, driving at the enemy,
they forced him back down the roads towards Alost and
Brussels.

Terribly did the Germans suffer. For the Belgians gave
them no rest, but continued the pursuit on Saturday night
and Sunday morning, and drove them out of Alost, which
town they had occupied for three weeks. Some thousands
of Germans were killed and wounded. It was out of
revenge for this great and disastrous defeat—a defeat
with extraordinary consequences for Germany — that
the decivilised neo-barbarians bombarded the cathedral
city of Malines on Sunday morning.

It is scarcely too much to say that,   **Fateful error of**
after the Battle of Termonde, General **General von Beseler**
von Beseler lost his head. It would be
rating his mistake too highly to say that it deprived the
Germans of all chance of victory in the western theatre
of war. For even if the mistake had not been committed,
it is doubtful whether the German flanking movement between Lille and Calais would have succeeded. But Beseler's
lack of initiative, tenacity, and genius for war, certainly
resulted at Termonde in an apparently local disaster with
extraordinarily wide-spread effects. No study of strategy
is necessary to judge his error. Anybody with ordinary
common-sense can see that he should have concentrated all
available forces against the Belgians at Termonde—a
hundred thousand men, if necessary—in order to cut
their communications with the coast, and to drive them back
into Antwerp. This should have been done before siege
operations were started, and the larger part of the more
mobile artillery should have been employed in this
absolutely vital operation.

But little things have large effects on little minds. It
was quite a little thing that upset the balance of the German
general's intellect—a mere rumour. Somebody on the
Belgian Military Staff was artful enough to spread the
report that a large British force was momentarily expected
to land at Ostend, and speed up by railway against the
western wing of the German forces. On Sunday morning
the perturbed German commander sent out Uhlan patrols,
who spent all their time questioning the Flemish peasants
as to the whereabouts of the new British army. Perhaps
our Marine force at Ostend had moved about the country
a little ; perhaps the Belgian villagers thought that even an
imaginary British column would rid them for a time of the
presence of the hated invader. However this may be, some
of the reconnoitring Uhlans returned to headquarters with

bombardment. The fact was that the wrecking of
Malines and its cathedral, like the wrecking of Rheims
Cathedral, was a deed of devilish spite. On the previous
day, Saturday, the German commander of the attacking
forces, General von Beseler, had attempted to cut
the communications of the Belgian Army in Antwerp
by a movement westward on Termonde. There was then
a gap of only forty miles between the left wing of the
German forces and the Dutch frontier. If Beseler could
have closed this gap by a further advance northward to the
town of St. Nicolaes, on the
railway line from Antwerp to
Ghent and Ostend, he would have
completely encircled the Belgian
Army. He would also have made
it impossible for any reinforcement
to reach Antwerp.

His attempt at an enveloping
movement was, however, defeated
by a sortie of the defenders.
The front of the Germans
stretched for twenty miles, almost
to Ghent, with only a small
Belgian advance force holding
the bridge of Termonde across
the Scheldt against them.

The enemy brought his field-
howitzers along the Flemish
plain, and pressed the Belgians
very hard. At two important
points, the village of Audegem,
about two miles south-west of
Termonde, and the village of
Lebbeke, a little distance south-
west of the same town, two parties

THE COURSE OF THE SCHELDT FROM ANTWERP TO THE SEA.

DEVELOPMENT OF THE ATTACK ON ANTWERP: ARTILLERY ACTION ACROSS THE RIVER DYLE.

The attack on Antwerp developed seriously when Malines was finally occupied by the Germans. Our picture illustrates the artillery duel across the River Dyle. German shells are seen coming over Malines from artillery posted beyond it, to the right. On the left is a battery of Belgian howitzers in action. A big German shell is bursting near them, and not very far from an ambulance where Red Cross nurses are tending the wounded. Belgian infantry were posted along the line of the river. In the air, to the left, may be seen two German observation balloons, which have been struck and are being brought down by Belgian shell fire. Similar balloons were used by the Germans at Antwerp to direct their artillery fire against the besieged city.

sufficient vague information at second-hand to determine their commander to retire eastward and concentrate between Brussels and Louvain.

By this means the Belgian Army was saved, even when Antwerp fell some eight days afterwards. For all through the bombardment the Belgian line of communication with the seacoast was kept open. On some days the Germans massed thirty thousand men against it, but these strokes came too late. General de Guise, commanding at Antwerp, always managed to bring up sufficient troops to hold the railway to the coast, while his opponent, General von Beseler, was stupidly concentrating mainly against the weak and indefensible rings of Antwerp forts.

Right from the beginning there was no hope for Antwerp. The Belgian Army's desperate defence of their last stronghold was but a gesture of heroism by a little nation dying in immortal fame and in the hope of a glorious resurrection.

traps. A line of earthworks in an open field would have formed a far safer defensive position.

The proper method of strategy would have been for the weary and outworn Belgian Army to have retreated by rail towards Dunkirk. In so doing, however, it would

BRITISH NAVAL MEN IN THE ANTWERP TRENCHES.
The top photograph shows men of our Naval Brigades carrying ammunition into the trenches that formed part of Antwerp's inner line of defence. The middle view is of British and Belgians fraternising in the trenches; and the lower view gives a good idea of the way in which the British sailors improved the trenches that had been dug for them, with timber and sandbags.

have released 125,000 young athletic German soldiers for the attack upon the French line between Lille and Calais. That line would then have been broken. It would have been broken at least a week before the British army moved up from the Aisne valley to strengthen it. Thus the Belgians had once more to stand in the breach, and protect France against an overwhelming surprise attack. They had to hold at least three, and possibly four, first-rate German army corps round Antwerp for as long a time as was humanly possible, in order to prevent this force from being thrown against the feeble Northern French line, and sweeping down towards Havre and Paris again.

Every Belgian officer knew the hopelessness of the task.

The old semicircles of armoured forts had become worse than useless. With the surprising development in power of modern siege-artillery, Antwerp had ceased to exist as a fortress. Its great structures of armoured concrete, with their cupolas of thick, hardened steel, were merely death-

THE HEROIC DEFENCE OF LIERRE.
A barricade hastily constructed by British Marines with sandbags and carts.

BLOCKING THE ROAD AT VIEUX DIEU.
From this place the British and their Belgian colleagues were compelled to retreat.

A BARRICADE OUTSIDE ANTWERP.
Men of the British Naval Brigades building a barricade of sandbags outside Antwerp.

German siege-artillery was a terrific power. Manonvilliers, a very strong, isolated French fort, had been shattered in a week. The last of the Liège forts had fallen after a bombardment of seven days, while those of Namur barely held out fifty hours. Even the strong modern defences of Maubeuge, with a large garrison, had been completely battered into shapeless ruin in eight days. The forts of Antwerp, designed by General Brialmont thirty years before, and gunned with artillery of small calibre and short range, were doomed. Their fall was not a question of days, but a matter of hours. They had only 6 in. guns.

Yet, knowing all this, the heroes of Belgium stuck to their job. Their courage was of that flaming, passionate sort that puts things again, and yet again, to mortal hazard. Antwerp, their beloved Antwerp, with its picturesque streets, its historic and romantic memories, its treasures of native art, its multitudes of free and independent townsmen—Antwerp, with its far-stretched lines of forts, built in the old days to shelter the entire Army—could not be tamely surrendered. Belgium would not play for safety. Her forces were worn out by countless battles and skirmishes, and sadly diminished by a fighting resistance of two months against an overpowering host of invaders. But the Belgian had ceased to calculate his chances of life. Cost what it might—even the destruction of the entire military forces of the nation—Antwerp should not be surrendered without a struggle.

The flaming, passionate courage of the Belgians

It was the most sublime spectacle in the annals of warfare. Antwerp, with its old and useless forts, looked like being the burial-place of the Belgian troops. Yet, standing by the grave of their power as an independent people, the Belgians jumped in, rifle in hand, and used the grave as a fighting-trench. It was six weeks since they had withdrawn from the field into their last stronghold. Had they at once, on August 17th, the date of their retirement, devoted themselves entirely to reorganising the defences of the fortress, they could have made it impregnable. They could have taken the guns out of the forts and used them as mobile batteries, and have obtained 12 in. weapons from England, for use on moving platforms running on a railway track. By this means they could have made Antwerp as difficult to reduce as

332

WITHDRAWAL OF THE GARRISON FROM ANTWERP.
The Belgian Army and the British Naval Brigades passing through the outskirts of the doomed city.

Przemysl or Verdun. This, however, was not done. For the Belgian troops were occupied in making continual sallies against the enemy's forces, and threatening his lines of communication, in order to relieve the pressure on the French and British troops in the south. Never in history has there been such self-sacrificing conduct towards allies as the Belgians continually displayed. Their Christian courage far surpasses that of the Spartans and Athenians. Not till the Belgian showed what was in him did man know what the spirit of international fraternity could achieve. The Belgians saved the modern world, the modern spirit of humanity, the modern faith in the plighted word of States. Strange as it may sound, the deaths and wounds of Belgian soldiers, the sufferings of Belgian people, redeemed the crimes

International fraternity v international treachery

of the Germans. For they erased the effect of German international treachery from the mind of the world. So long as countries put faith in treaties between nation and nation, so long will the example of Belgium have a Christlike power upon man.

The attack on the Belgians' last lines of defence began on Monday, September 28th. The Austrian artillery detachment at Brussels brought forward their 12 in. siege-howitzers to concealed positions behind the Malines-Louvain railway embankment, far beyond the reach of the old 6 in. Krupp guns in the Antwerp forts. Having manufactured them, the Germans knew that these guns had an effective range of only about five miles. The Austrian siege-howitzers, on the other hand, threw their terrible shells with mathematical exactitude to a distance of seven and a half miles, and with fair marksmanship to a distance of nine miles. They opened fire on Fort Waelhem and Fort Wavre Ste Catherine. All the day and all the night the shells continued to fall on and around the forts. With anything like equal artillery on both sides, this nocturnal bombardment would have been more disastrous to the Germans than to the defenders. For the flames of the attacking howitzers could clearly be seen in the darkness from the captive observation balloon employed by the Belgians. It would have been easy to have planted shell after shell among the besieging batteries, if only the Belgians had had ordnance of a proper range fixed on movable trucks

REMARKABLE INSTANCE OF TEUTON GENEROSITY.
German Marines carrying the belongings of Belgian refugees who had been persuaded to return to Antwerp.

PREPARED FOR A SKIRMISH WITH THE FOE.
Bluejackets forming the crew of an armoured train, with their rifles, ready for an encounter with the Germans.

ANTWERP'S CALVARY: FUGITIVES PAUSE TO PRAY BEFORE AN IMAGE OF THE CRUCIFIXION.

Near the crypt of Antwerp Cathedral is a shrine, representing the scene of the Crucifixion. The figures are Our Saviour on the Cross and Joseph and Mary on either side. The group of sculpture is protected from the elements by a plain wooden roof. The sacred spot is enclosed by a balustrade of carved stone, on which are scroll-shaped tablets recording the tragedy of Calvary. Hurried as was the flight of the citizens of Antwerp, many found time to turn aside to the shrine and prostrate themselves in prayer before the Virgin, asking her aid in their terrible plight. The cathedral was not injured by the bombardment, but it is recorded that many buildings near were destroyed, a fact which suggests that it did not owe its escape to the German gunners, though it is understood that King Albert sent a plan with its site marked upon it to the German commander, begging that this historic building might be spared.

334

behind their lines. As it was, the
defenders were impotent to reply to
the long-distance fire from the Skoda
12 in. batteries and the Krupp 11 in.
batteries.

The time-fuse of one of the shells
that were thrown in the Belgian
lines, where it failed to explode is
understood to have been set for 15,200
metres. This is about nine and a
half miles, a larger distance than
the Skoda howitzer is reckoned to
cover. So it is possible that the
Germans had even more powerful
siege-artillery before Antwerp than is
generally supposed. Something between a 12 in. howitzer and a 16 in.
howitzer may in places have been
employed. For the enemy was so
anxious to reduce Antwerp with the
utmost speed, and to release his
army corps for operations between
Lille and Dunkirk, that he massed
every available machine of destruction
against the Belgians.

The attackers, however, were so
confident in their overpowering weight
of metal that they were caught by a very simple trick.
Early in the bombardment, one of the forts in the outer
ring of defences quickly exploded and burst into flame.
A brigade of German infantry, entrenched just beyond

the range of the Belgian guns, rose
and charged across the fields to capture
the ruined stronghold, and hold the
gap in the fortressed line against the
defending troops. But when they reached the fort, guns,
machine-guns, rifles, and live electric-wire entanglements caught them in a trap. The flame had been
produced by pouring petrol on some lighted straw brought
into the fort for the purpose. One-third of a German
brigade fell around the slopes ; the rest fled, with shrapnel
and Maxim fire sweeping them as they ran. Scarcely a
fortnight before, the commander of the French fort at
Troyon had lured on and half-annihilated a large body
of German infantry by the same device of apparently

**Germans pay
for despising their
enemies**

BRIDGE BLOWN UP BY BRITISH MARINES.
A bridge in Antwerp which was blown up by British Marines as the Germans advanced. The German
artillery had started a conflagration in the buildings near by.

setting his fort on fire. If the Germans had not so despised
their enemies, they would not have been caught twice
within a fortnight by the same easy trick.

The Belgians also succeeded in bringing off the most
primitive of all artillery manœuvres—the dead-dog dodge.
They slackened their fire and encouraged the Germans
to grow venturesome, and to push forward their howitzer
batteries belonging to the field-artillery. Between the
Belgian forts were lines of trenches held by the Belgian
Army, with light field-artillery operating behind the troops.
For some time the German gunners seemed to have
certain of these trenches at their mercy. They pushed
forward three batteries to complete the work of annihilation.
But a semicircle of thunder and flame suddenly opened
before them. Every dead Belgian gun came to life again.
Two of the German batteries were destroyed, and the other
managed to harness up its guns and to get away.

These were the only successes of the outranged and

335

THE BURDEN OF SORROW ON THE BROAD BOSOM OF THE SCHELDT.
Barges, fishing-boats, steam lighters, and a variety of other small craft were utilised to carry the fugitives from Antwerp to the hospitable borders of Holland. The unvarying kindness of the Dutch people and the beautiful weather were the two redeeming features of the day that witnessed the fall of the city which was once the commercial capital of the world.

of more than a hundred men only ten escaped—ten blackened, burnt, blinded, tortured figures, crawling in the darkness over the charred bodies of their comrades. And while they crept out into the daylight towards the postern, the shrapnel continued to fall around them, and shell after shell ground the shattered concrete to powder, gave the battered armour-plate another wrench, and the overturned guns another useless hammering.

It was a vision of hell such as the imagination of Dante never attained. And it was not a vision, but the work of Christians fighting against Christians—the work of a great empire organised for scientific research and for the advancement of human control over the forces of Nature. Practically everything on the scene was German. The guns and the armour-plate of the fort had been constructed by Krupp, and it was he and his associate in the commerce of warfare —Skoda, of Pilsen—who manufactured the howitzers and shells by which the fort was destroyed. Frau Krupp and her father had made hundreds of thousands of pounds out of the Belgians, and then obtained another large fortune out of the German people for newer and larger machinery of destruction to wreck the earlier examples of Krupp manufacture. It is said, moreover, that the Krupp guns built for use in Antwerp were specially constructed to wear badly when put to lengthy use. Oh, deep and far-seeing were the plans which Germany made for the war that was yet vainly designed to end in her conquering the world !

Behind Fort Waelhem were the principal waterworks of Antwerp, and by bombarding the reservoir with 12 in. shells the Germans burst the banks on Wednesday, September 30th. The flood of water drowned some of the Belgian trenches, and certain of the defenders' field-guns were submerged, and only rescued with great labour. The inundation also hampered the defence by interfering with the carrying of supplies and ammunition to the neighbouring section of the Belgian lines. In Antwerp itself the destruction of the water supply naturally had distressing results, and it terribly increased the danger of a conflagration, and of the rise and spread of an epidemic. In the meantime, all the chief forts in the southern sector of the defences went the way of Fort Waelhem. Wavre Ste. Catherine was the first to fall ; then, after three days of continuous bombardment, Lierre and Koningshoyckt were silenced. **The raging, murderous** The village of Lierre was set **on struggle for the Nethe.** fire, and the dense column of smoke that poured up from it in the windless autumn air was visible from a great distance.

With the fall of the south-eastern outer forts on Thursday, October 1st, the defence of Antwerp became impossible. For there was a gap of over ten miles in the circuit of fortifications, through which the enemy could pour his troops, while watering the path in front of them with shell and shrapnel. Moreover, the destruction of the principal Belgian forts allowed the Germans to move their heavy siege artillery northward for another two miles, and thus to get within bombarding range of the city. The small tidal river, the Nethe, flowing behind the southern ruined forts into the Scheldt, was the only remaining defence of the Belgians. For the picturesque ancient ramparts of the

overpowered forts. The five hundred men garrisoning Fort Waelhem were the first to suffer, as their comrades at Liège and Namur had suffered. They took part in the sortie on Malines, and then retreated to the fort. On Monday the first German shells fell short, and the garrison began to hope they would be able to resist. But soon one of the 12 in. Austrian howitzers landed a shell on a cupola and smashed it. All Monday night, shell and shrapnel rained down on the buildings of the fort, giving the garrison neither rest nor respite. The Belgian guns salvoed in reply, but could not reach the enemy.

By Tuesday morning the situation was **Terrible end of garrison** critical. The shells were still falling with **at Fort Waelhem** an infernal tumult on the armour of the cupolas, and just at noon another of the curved, shielding roofs of hardened steel was put out of action. At twenty minutes past twelve the bombardment increased in fury. Three large projectiles struck the garrison building and completely destroyed it, twisting the iron stairs, smashing the vault, blowing up the walls to the foundation, and setting the wreckage on fire. The troops then sheltered in the underground passage, waiting for the hurricane of high-explosive shells to slacken and enable them to return to their guns.

It was in the crowded subterranean shelter that the great catastrophe occurred. A shell dropped in the ammunition magazine, to the left of the underground gallery, and the flame and fume of the terrible explosion of the magazine swept through the thronged passage. Out

city were, of course, useless against modern siege-howitzers, and the line of inner forts, placed about two miles outside the city of Antwerp, were half a century old, and equipped only with 4 in. guns. They were still useful against infantry attacks, but the ordinary field-artillery of the modern army could have demolished them in a few hours. It was the outer recent forts, designed by General Brialmont in 1879, and completed in November, 1913, that guarded Antwerp. When a large sector of these defences was destroyed, only the River Nethe and the entrenched infantry behind the river offered any real obstacle to the onset of the German forces.

And this last obstacle, in the circumstances, was an exceedingly slight one. For by massing the fire of both their siege-artillery and their field-artillery on the shallow, hastily-made, and open earthworks by the river, the Germans subjected the Belgian troops to such a tempest of vast, high-explosive shells and heavy, wide-spreading shrapnel shots as mortal men had never known. What our troops suffered by the Aisne flats was nothing to what the Belgians suffered in the flooded expanses by Nethe River. All the machinery intended for the destruction of Paris was concentrated on some eight to ten miles of their trenches, with the light field-artillery of several army corps joining in the screaming, roaring, nerve-racking work. Even with this the Germans did not think they had sufficient advantages over the small Belgian Army. They desired to use their overpowering long-ranged ordnance with scientific exactitude.

So several German men and women who had lived for years in Antwerp, and had enjoyed the friendship of the heroic Flemings, and had, therefore, been exempted from banishment from the beleaguered city, now came forward to direct the fire of the German batteries. Sometimes as nurses or Red Cross helpers, sometimes as interested and friendly spectators of the struggle, they approached the trenches, studied the positions, and communicated the knowledge thus obtained to the attacking gunners. When the great peace comes, other peoples may be moved by the craven and hysterical signs of repentance that the ordinary German will show in order to renew intercourse with civilised countries. But it is doubtful if the Belgian will be moved. He knows the German now, and has paid a very heavy price for his knowledge. He will not forget. For generation after generation he will not forget.

The Germans succeeded in crossing the **How the Germans** Nethe. A dozen times their engineers **crossed the River Nethe** advanced under cover of artillery fire, and tried to fling pontoons across the stream. The Belgians at first shot the engineers. Then, as they themselves were suffering heavily from the terrific bombardment, they adopted a more subtle means of defence. They let the pontoon bridges be erected, and waited until some battalions had partly crossed the river and were crowding the floating bridges from the farther bank. Then they opened fire with their light field-guns and machine-guns and rifles, sweeping the packed pontoons and banks. This went on night and day, till the Germans gradually built up a strange kind of bridge. Their bodies choked the river, and, mingling with the wreck of their

WOUNDED BELGIANS AT AN ENGLISH COUNTRY HOUSE.
Large numbers of wounded Belgian soldiers as well as civilians found rest and shelter in England after the German occupation of Antwerp. Our artist in the above picture represents a scene which he witnessed at a mansion in Kent on one of those rare November days when the sun came out and the soldiers were able to take a turn in the garden.

pontoons, the corpses dammed and bridged the stream. But before this occurred, the Belgian Government had decided to leave Antwerp. Two steamers were chartered to sail for Ostend on Saturday, October 3rd, with the members of the Government and the staffs of the French and British Legations. But on Saturday morning the plan was suddenly changed. The Belgian Government resolved to stay on. Great Britain at last was sending help to the breached and overpowered stronghold of the Belgian Army. At one o'clock on Saturday afternoon a long grey motor- **Mr. Winston Churchill's** car, filled with British naval officers, **arrival in Antwerp** entered the city. In it was a youngish, sandy-haired man in the undress uniform of a Lord of the Admiralty. It was Mr. Winston Churchill, and with him came General Paris, commanding a Marine brigade and two naval brigades, with a detachment of naval gunners with two 9·2 in. weapons and a number of 6 in. guns.

"We're going to save the city," said the most bustling member of the British Cabinet. But he had come a week too late to do so, and the forces he had brought with him, consisting mainly of untrained naval reservists, were inadequate to retrieve the situation.

Many of our men went into the trenches as soon as they

ENTRENCHED INFANTRY AND SCREENED ARTILLERY ASSISTING IN THE DEFENCE OF FORT DE BORNEM.

Fort de Bornem was, like the other forts encircling Antwerp, supplied with revolving turrets, and regarded, as all were, of exceeding strength till the great German siege-guns were brought up. These guns had a range nearly double that of the Belgian guns. The Belgian infantry were entrenched between the forts, with their field-artillery behind them, carefully concealed from enemy aircraft by covering branches. The Belgian shrapnel fire was powerful enough to prevent the enemy from charging across the open space which was cleared before the forts, but the German siege-guns proved far more powerful than they. The above drawing was made when the firing around Fort de Bornem was at its height.

arrived on Saturday evening. For the Belgian troops were utterly worn out by their long and severe exertions, and badly needed a rest. Some of our men were raw recruits who did not know how to handle a rifle, but they at least showed their native pluck by sticking in the trenches under the heavy bombardment. In all, they did not amount to more than eight thousand men, with two guns mounted on an armoured train, and four 6 in. weapons that operated in the inner ring of forts, behind Lierre. It was intended that they should only act as a defending advance guard, and the 7th Division and 3rd Cavalry Division of the British Expeditionary Force, numbering some 18,000 bayonets and sabres, under General Sir Henry Rawlinson, was marching up to Ostend to reinforce them. At the same time, large French, British, and Indian cavalry bodies were operating eastward of Lille, with a view to clearing the way for a northward extension of the Franco-British front. It was the effect of all these combined operations which Mr. Churchill had in mind when he said that Antwerp would be saved.

The scheme for the relief of Antwerp

But General von Beseler had made one mistake, and did not mean to make another. The tremendous advantage he had won on the southern sector was plain even to his mind, and he drove home the attack with sufficient determination to cover the lack of real generalship. All through the night of October 3rd he launched his infantry in massed formation across the Nethe by the shapeless ruins of Waelhem fort. The slaughter was terrible, but the German non-commissioned officers held their men together, even when there were only half-companies left to attempt to storm the Belgian trenches. When Sunday morning broke, the attacks still continued, until the Germans got their bellyful of fighting, and drew away to the river back to cover, leaving thousands of dead and wounded on the bank, and hundreds drowned in the water.

On Sunday night our Marines bore the brunt of the attack. They held some of the foremost trenches along the Nethe, between Lierre and Waelhem. The trenches were shallow and roughly made, and being open gave little protection against shell fire. The long-ranged guns of the enemy swept them from distant positions in the south, which the feeble defending artillery could not reach. Our casualties from shrapnel fire were very heavy; even veteran troops might have been pardoned had they abandoned the attempt to defend so indefensible a line. But our boys, untrained lads, some of whom had scarcely worn their uniform for a fortnight, went into the fight as they arrived, and bided their fate as steadily as the bearded, skilled men who fought beside them. Mr. Winston Churchill asked no one to undergo anything he was not eager to face himself. He took a rifle and stayed in one of the trenches near Fort Waelhem, and shot with the best of them. One of Mr. Asquith's sons was among the young recruits who proved their manhood and the mettle of the youth of their nation, under most desperate circumstances, and gave the Germans a foretaste of what the fighting qualities of the new British army would be when, with proper training, they took the field a million strong.

Mr. Asquith's son among the young British recruits

The massed attacks of the Germans on October 4th were first beaten off by our Marines. Then on October 5th the volunteer naval reservists arrived from the coast, and went straight into action north of Lierre. As they tramped down the cobbled and tree-shaded highway, they sang the new light-hearted British fighting-song, "It's a long, long way to Tipperary," while London motor-'buses from Piccadilly and Leicester Square rumbled behind them with supplies and ammunition. The townspeople were wild with joy at the sight of these thousands of bright-faced, strong-limbed sons of Britain. Their city, they felt sure, was to be saved at the last moment. But there were military men who noticed that many of these raw young troops were so badly equipped that they did not even carry pouches for the regulation 150 rounds of fire.

Some of their officers seemed to be as lacking in field experience as the men. Yet these raw troops, rushed into Antwerp on a hopeless task, placed in open trenches unsupported by effective artillery, and raked by a terrific shrapnel fire, held the enemy back for some days, and then retired in perfect order. Seldom, if ever, have we put worse troops into the field, and seldom, if ever, has our cause been upheld by braver men. On the Nethe they beat the compact multitudes of first-line German soldiers back from the river, and when dawn broke, with a rain of shrapnel lead, the British trenches were still held. At four a.m. on October 6th, however, the Germans made their terrible bridge of dead on the right of the British forces, and the Belgian troops there were compelled to retire. Consequently our right flank was exposed, and our men had also to withdraw quickly to prevent the enemy from taking them in the reverse.

The bridge of dead over the River Nethe With this, the defence of Antwerp practically came to an end. For, as we have seen, the old inner line of forts was incapable of resisting modern siege-artillery. Our few 6 in. naval guns were almost as useless as the old-fashioned 4 in. guns of the fort. They could do absolutely nothing against the 11 and 12 in. howitzers possessed by the Germans and Austrians. Our 9 2 in. guns could not be mounted and got into position in time. Even in the German field-artillery there were heavy howitzers, with a longer range and a larger shell than the half a dozen guns that Mr. Winston Churchill sent to Antwerp.

Mr. Churchill had served as a cavalry subaltern. But he seemed to have lacked at Antwerp the large organising ability necessary in a commander of modern armies. He ran his head against the wide and well-laid plan of the German Military Staff, possessing vast resources for siege operations. Nothing less than a score of mobile 9 2 in. naval guns, with a squadron of aeroplanes searching for the enemy's positions, together with a large number of field-mortars for raking advancing columns of hostile

infantry, could have turned the Nethe defence into a tenable position. All that the Belgians wanted was heavy artillery support. Even then their city might have been very severely bombarded. For as the outer forts had fallen in the south, the Skoda howitzers could have been brought much nearer the Nethe.

But it must have been said in Mr. Churchill's defence that the call for help from Antwerp probably came too late for any large measures of assistance to be undertaken. The situation round Lille was also critical, so that our War Office could not immediately spare any regular troops for fortress duties. The naval reservists were the nearest force to the point of embarkation, and could thus be carried most quickly to the spot where the need for them was urgent and bitter. The danger of the enemy winning to the coast and establishing submarine centres of operations at the new seaport of Bruges, or even at Ostend Harbour or Calais, was an Admiralty problem. Mr. Churchill tried to solve it. **Defeat of the enemy's main objective**

Heavily as our naval reservists suffered in dead, wounded, and missing, they did not suffer in vain. By helping to prolong for nearly a week the resistance of Antwerp, they did much to defeat the main objective of the enemy. For the capture of Antwerp was only a secondary aim of General von Beseler. The principal objective of the German commander was the destruction or capture of the Belgian Army. In failing to achieve this, he was defeated in his chief purpose. Towards this defeat, our volunteer reservists, with their comrades of the Marine brigade, contributed in no small measure. What they actually did, in staving off the German infantry attack, was of local importance. What they potentially did, by their mere presence, by their sunny, cheerful faces, when the spirit of the heroic Belgian Army was clouded by the fall of the outer forts, was of European importance. They were messengers of hope, heralds of a sure though distant day of Belgian triumph. Before they came it seemed

BELGIAN REFUGEES' FIRST RESTING-PLACE IN LONDON.

On their arrival in London the Belgian refugees who sought shelter in this country were taken to a temporary haven in Aldwych, where they were entertained before being drafted to more commodious accommodation at the Alexandra Palace, Muswell Hill, and elsewhere. It was estimated in December, 1914, that about 1,000,000 refugees had abandoned Belgian soil. Of these some 500,000 or more found sanctuary in Holland, about 110,000 came to England, while a large number fled to France. Arrangements were made later for the accommodation of further refugees in England.

to the beleaguered saviours of civilisation that they were forgotten of the world. But when the little British force arrived, they knew they were not forgotten, and the springs of energy in their soul were renewed. From Antwerp to Ostend, from Ostend to Nieuport, along

Belgian Army's heroic resistance

the Yser to Dixmude, the Belgian Army was to march in a glory of heroic resistance, exceeding anything in ancient or modern history. To have supported and encouraged men of this stamp in the darkest days of their campaign, is a great honour for a few thousand raw recruits to have won.

When the Germans had forced the passage of the Nethe, on the morning of Tuesday, October 6th, the defence of Antwerp was at an end. For General de Guise decided that the surrender of the city was inevitable. It could have been delayed for a week or a fortnight, but only at the cost of the destruction of all the historic buildings of Antwerp, and the death or injury of thousands of the townspeople. Moreover, any prolonged resistance would endanger the Belgian Army and the British forces, as the Germans were now making strenuous attempts to close the path of retreat between Ghent and the Dutch frontier. In this region a hostile German army corps was operating, and another army corps was moving to support it. Beseler was at last doing the right thing, from the point of view of the attacking side.

He was relying on his siege train for the reduction of Antwerp, and allocating to the heavy guns and howitzers only sufficient infantry to protect the batteries from assault. He was swinging his main forces against the western flank of the Belgian-British lines, where a series of fierce struggles were proceeding. In these circumstances General de Guise arranged to hold the remaining forts and the inner line of defences only so long as was necessary to cover the retreat of the allied troops. On Tuesday evening, therefore, the Belgian Army began to withdraw from Antwerp. Cavalrymen and cycling carbineers, with armoured motor-cars, crossed the Scheldt by the bridge of boats on the road to Ostend. Thirty large German steamers in the harbour were crippled by exploding dynamite in their cylinders and boilers. At daybreak on Wednesday morning the Belgian Government, with the Legations, left by steamer, transferring the capital of Belgium from Antwerp to Ostend. Mr. Winston Churchill also appears to have left that morning by motor-car, running under the protection of one of the armoured cars with machine-guns which had proved so effective against German cavalry.

"God Punish England!"

As remarkable as Herr Ernst Lissauer's "Hymn of Hate" was the form of greeting adopted in Germany. "God punish England!" (Gott strafe England!) was the form of address, to which the reply was: "May God punish her!" (Gott mög'es strafen!) This formula, which was used all over Germany, was celebrated in a set of verses by Herr Hochstetter. These appeared in the well-known German weekly "Lustige Blätter." We give Mr. G. Valentine Williams's translation:

This is the German greeting
When men their fellows meet,
The merchants in the market-place,
The beggars in the street,
A pledge of bitter enmity
Thus runs the winged word:
"God punish England, brother!—
Yea! Punish her, O Lord!"

With raucous voice, brass-throated,
Our German shells shall bear
This curse that is our greeting
To the "cousin" in his lair.
This be our German battle-cry,
The motto on our sword:
"God punish England, brother!—
Yea! Punish her, O Lord!"

By shell from sea, by bomb from air,
Our greeting shall be sped,
Making each English homestead
A mansion of the dead.
And even Grey will tremble
As falls each iron word:
"God punish England, brother!—
Yea! Punish her, O Lord!"

This is the German greeting
When men their fellows meet,
The merchants in the market-place,
The beggars in the street,
A pledge of bitter enmity
Thus runs the winged word:
"God punish England, brother!—
Yea! Punish her, O Lord!"

General von Beseler had given notice the evening before that he intended to bombard the city. The unhappy townspeople had gone to sleep on Tuesday night feeling confident that in a few days the Germans would raise the siege, as it was known that a new British force, under Sir Henry Rawlinson, was operating on their flank. But when the citizens went about their work the next morning they saw, with dread astonishment, on every wall and hoarding, a proclamation announcing the imminent bombardment. In the proclamation General de Guise recommended those who were able to depart to do so at once, while those who remained were advised to take shelter in their cellars behind sandbags.

It was the suddenness of the catastrophe, breaking in upon a period of renewed hope, that took the heart out of many of the peaceful people of Antwerp. The population at the time was well over half a million; for the city had become the refuge of some hundreds of thousands of fugitives from the shattered villages and bombarded towns of Belgium. In the famous stronghold of their nation they had thought they were at last safe from further attack by the host of murderers and torturers from Germany. Their nerves were already unstrung and their minds filled with terrible memories. So it is no wonder that some of them gave way to panic when they read the proclamation of doom.

Then began the immense, tragic flight of the inhabitants of Antwerp. Only three avenues of escape remained open — westward by road, to Ghent, Bruges, and Ostend; north-eastward by road into Holland, and down the Scheldt by water to Flushing. Probably a quarter of a million escaped by river. Anything that could float was crowded with the fugitives—merchant-steamers, dredgers, barges, and canal-boats, ferry-boats, tugs, fishing-smacks, yachts, rowing-boats, scows, and even hastily-made rafts. There was no opportunity of maintaining order and discipline. The terrorised people at times crowded aboard until there was not even standing room on the decks. Very few of them had brought food and warm clothing with them, or had space in which to lie down. For two nights and two

Tragic flight of terrorised populace

days they huddled together, chilled and famishing, on the open deck, while the German guns bombarded the great, beautiful old city from which they had fled.

On the roads leading towards Ghent and the Dutch frontier the scenes of anguish and misery, hunger and fatigue, were even more appalling. In many places civilians and soldiers were mingled in inextricable confusion.

THE RETREAT OF THE BELGIAN ARMY BEFORE THE GERMANS.
Section of Belgian Artillery passing through a country lane during the retreat of the Belgian Army from the Antwerp defences.

In the afternoon of October 7th the highway from Antwerp to Ghent was jammed from ditch to ditch. Every footpath and lane leading away from the invading army was so closely packed with fugitives that they impeded each other's movement. Young men could be seen carrying their frail old mothers in their arms, or helping their worn-out fathers by a pickaback ride. Wheelbarrows were sometimes used for this purpose, but more often they were packed with children too young to walk. There were monks in long, woollen robes, carrying wounded men on stretchers, and white-faced nuns shepherding along groups of war-orphaned infants.

Women still weak from childbed tottered along with their newly-born babes pressed to their breasts, their imaginations working almost to madness as they remembered the tales of what German soldiers had done to Belgian mothers and Belgian babes. Grey-haired men and women helped themselves along by grasping the stirrup-leathers of troopers, who were so exhausted from days of fighting that they slept in the saddle as they rode. Here a society woman, who had dressed at noon for a visit of fashion, stumbled along, carrying in a sheet on her shoulders her jewels and rich and heavy articles of precious metal. By her side was a frail, old lace-maker from Mechlin, whose bundle contained the simple, homely treasures of a cottage that no longer existed. The noise and the confusion were beyond mere imagina-

RETURNING FROM THE TRENCHES.
A British Marine, wounded while helping to man the Antwerp trenches, being assisted back to the city by a comrade.

tion. The clamour was made up of the cries and shouts and moans of a nation in its agony. Men cursed their neighbours just to save themselves from weeping like women, and, amid their cursing, turned to help the poor creatures pressing against them. The heavy, quiet, slow-thinking, slow-moving Fleming, closely akin in origin to the Englishman, had been stampeded into terror. It was not the fear of death that moved him, but the fear of what the Germans might do to him and his women and children while life yet remained in their bodies. It was no rumours that shook him. He had already spoken in Antwerp to fugitives from the blackened and gutted scenes of atrocities.

What especially added to the bitterness of the educated and directing class of townspeople was the memory of the part their city had played in crippling the national defence. It was from Antwerp that had come the strongest opposition to increasing the Army in the days when the German menace became apparent. Strategical railway lines had been constructed on the frontier, and every man in a responsible position in Belgium could see what was intended. But when the King and his Government proposed to reply to this threat against their neutrality by an increase in troops and guns, Antwerp had been one of the principal opponents of the scheme. This was probably due to the fact that so many Germans had settled in the port that by various means they won a large control over the

IN THE GERMAN TRENCHES AT LIERRE.
German soldiers writing home: A photograph taken after the fall of Antwerp.

was not a scarcity of provisions—there was absolutely nothing to eat. The fugitives stopped at farmhouses and offered all they possessed for a loaf, but the farmers' wives, weeping at the misery of their own people, could only shake their heads. It was on raw turnips that the richest and the poorest stayed their hunger; and many who did not profit by the opportunity, when passing the turnip-fields, had nothing. Near one small town on the Dutch frontier twenty children were born on Wednesday night in the open fields. The mothers were without beds, without shelter, and without medical aid. This occurred at a spot where an American observer chanced to be. At hundreds of other places along the lines of flight there were similar strangely piteous scenes, with no one even to record them.

trend of public opinion. They had preached the gospel of pacificism, like true descendants of a former Prussian preacher against war—Frederick the Great, who wrote his "Anti-Machiavelli" in order to still the suspicions of Europe until his army was ready to ravage Silesia. The similar movement of pacificism in our own country was no doubt headed by honest but deluded men, yet behind them a strong German influence could also be detected. If the Sea Lords of our Admiralty had not threatened to resign in a body in 1909, and thereby compelled the Liberal Cabinet to come to its senses and defeat the German attempt to outbuild us in new battleships, that which happened in Antwerp might well have happened in London. Our politicians failed us as completely as the Antwerp politicians failed their people. We owe our present position, under God, to the firmness of character and keenness of vision of our Sea Lords of the year 1909. Thus, as a nation, we cannot in any way blame the people of Antwerp for failing, in the days of peace, to prepare for warlike defence. We were deluded, and almost betrayed, by the same subtle intrigues as ended in the disaster that overtook them.

German "pacificism" in Antwerp and London

It will never be known how many people perished from hunger, exposure, and exhaustion in the flight from Antwerp. The fields and ditches along the westward road were strewn with the prostrate bodies of outworn women, children, and old men. For miles around, the countryside was as bare of food as a sand desert is of flowers. There

As the fugitives were sleeping in the open air, on the night of Wednesday, October 7th, the bombardment of their city began. The first shell fell at ten o'clock, striking a house in the southern Berchem district, killing a boy and wounding his mother and his little sister. A street-sweeper lost his head as he ran for shelter; it was blown off by the next shell. All through the night the shells fell at the rate of five a minute. Most of them were shrapnel shells, which shrieked over the house-tops and exploded with a rending crash in the streets. The object of the Germans was to kill and frighten the people rather than to destroy the buildings. So, though a few high-explosive

shells were pitched into Antwerp, the bombardment was mainly carried out with shrapnel. The idea, of course, was to terrorise the non-combatants so as to induce them to bring pressure upon the Belgian Government to surrender the Army and the city. But the persons who willingly remained to undergo the bombardment were not made of the stuff from which cowards are fashioned. Withdrawing into their cellars with food and candles, they protected the entrances with mattresses and pillows, and watched the night out with quiet fortitude.

ANTWERP UNDER GERMAN OCCUPATION.
A regiment departing for the firing-line from the German headquarters in Antwerp. Inset: Scene near the Steen Museum on the riverside, where uniforms, boots, transport, and all sorts of war material were discarded by the Belgians who were forced to seek safety in Holland.

In the meantime a large and gallant rearguard was holding the inner line of forts, and misleading the enemy by the stubbornness of its defence. For, with the British force, they still held some of the advanced trenches behind Fort Waelhem and Lierre, and though swept by a terrible shell fire, causing heavy losses, they kept off the German infantry. Supported by the small old guns of the inner forts, and by the skilfully-handled field-artillery of the Belgian Army, the

GERMANS PREPARING FOR A COUNTER-ATTACK.
Artillerymen hauling a gun into position at Antwerp after the occupation. The gun had to be dragged by ropes on a specially-made road, which wound round a hill to the required height. Inset: Further evidence of the German fear of a counter-attack. Germans mount a concealed gun in a culvert on the outskirts of Antwerp while their outposts scour the neighbouring hills.

heroic rearguard simply bluffed General von Beseler. Two days had passed since the German commander had forced the passage of the Nethe. He had an absolutely overpowering number of guns and howitzers, and a much larger force of infantry than the Belgian commander had left behind. Had he only pressed forward, as any man with a backbone would have done in the circumstances, he would have captured the larger portion of the Belgian-British forces, together with hundreds of guns and large supplies of war material. But being a man with so highly-developed a sense of caution that it could not be distinguished from timidity, he wasted the two critical days in searching his path of advance with artillery fire.

He was apparently so afraid of falling into a trap and losing his large guns that nearly forty-eight hours passed before he brought them over the Nethe to bombard the city. By the evening of October 8th four of the inner line of forts had been badly battered from the western side of Antwerp, but the Allies still held the trenches two miles in front of these forts. No rushing attack was made on the belt of barbed-wire entanglements behind which our men and the Belgians were lying. Many of our volunteer naval reservists never saw a German. All their wounds were caused by shrapnel fire or shell splinters. Somehow the wonderful system of German espionage seems to have got out of working order at the time when it would have been most serviceable. For, as we have seen, Beseler still had at least an army corps of men south of Antwerp, with a tremendous power of artillery to back them up. With all the

guns sweeping the forts and the spaces in between, where the Belgian field batteries were working, the position might have been carried at a loss of five or six thousand men. Beseler's infantry, however, had already suffered so heavily from Belgian rifle fire and machine-gun fire that he hesitated to attack.

The fact was, he suspected some sort of ambush, with perhaps land mines in the fields along his path, and concealed guns held in reserve. **Defenders' final retirement at night** No other well-known German commander has shown such a lack of courage in an important operation of the war, with perhaps the exception of General von Hausen when leading the Saxon army in the battles of the Marne. But if Beseler did not know when to move, the leaders of the Belgians and the British knew when to retire. In the evening of Thursday, October 8th, General Paris saw that if our Naval Division were to avoid disaster an immediate retirement under cover of darkness was necessary. He consulted with General de Guise, and the Belgian commander fully agreed with him. Thus the final retirement began. All the night the British and Belgian troops crossed from the south of the city through the empty streets, where the shells were falling thickly, and passed over the Scheldt by the bridge of boats to the Ostend road.

ON GUARD AT THE DUTCH FRONTIER.
On the left of the photograph are German troopers; on the right, two Dutch infantrymen beside a roughly-made sentry-box.

EXCITING MOONLIGHT ENCOUNTER BETWEEN A BELGIAN MOTOR-CYCLE DESPATCH-RIDER AND A PARTY OF UHLANS.

E. Van Isacker, attached to the General Staff of the 4th Belgian Brigade, was returning to headquarters from a journey to the front on a 7 h.-p. motor-cycle. The light had gone, and the moon was just up. After travelling a few miles he found he was on the wrong road. As he was scanning the lettering on a signpost two Uhlans came up in his direction. He shot one, and the other, after exchanging shots, rode away. After a few moments a party of forty Uhlans appeared, attracted by the firing. With a wild rush Isacker pushed off his machine. It "fired" at once, and he was going at a good speed when the first of the Uhlans came round the bend of the road and began firing. Bullets whistled all around him. His cloak was pierced in no fewer than seven places. He outdistanced his pursuers, but, unluckily, at a bad corner, temporarily lost control of his machine. There was a terrible crash. He was picked up, tended at a farmhouse, and sent on to Ghent, where, after a week, he was discharged as unfit for further service.

Only the garrisons of the forts remained, working their guns with the utmost speed to engage the attention of the enemy, and frighten him from advancing on the city. Three of our battalions of the 1st Brigade of the Royal Naval Division—the Hawke, Collingwood, and Benbow battalions—holding the trenches south of the town and one of the forts there, were left behind, as by some mistake or accident the order for retirement did not reach them. It was some time before they found they were deserted,

Incendiary bombs across the wild and smoky sky and withdrew from the position which they had so gallantly held. Meanwhile, the other garrisons, while keeping up the pretence of resistance, were destroying their war material and putting their guns out of action one by one, so as not to excite the suspicion of the enemy. At dawn on Friday morning they also withdrew westward through Antwerp and towards Ghent and Ostend.

Meanwhile the bombardment of the falling city was at its height. In the darkness before the dawn incendiary bombs rocketed across the wild and smoky sky and fell upon the houses. By this time the Germans had got some of their great howitzers within striking distance of the streets around the centre of Antwerp. As the great shells hurtled through the air, they sounded at first like an approaching express train; but their roar rapidly increased in volume till the atmosphere quivered as before a howling cyclone. Then came an explosion, that seemed to split the earth, and a tall geyser of dust and smoke shot high above the stricken port. When a large high-explosive shell struck a building, it did not tear away its upper storeys or blow a gap in the walls. The entire house collapsed in rubble and ruin, as though flattened by a monster's hand.

When the 11 in. shells exploded in the open streets, they made pits as large as the cellar of a good-sized house, and badly damaged any building within a radius of two hundred yards. The earlier shrapnel fire seemed harmless in comparison. It appeared as if in a few minutes the whole of the city would be wrecked as though by an earthquake. The thickest masonry crumpled up like cardboard; buildings of solid stone were levelled, as a child levels things he makes with playing-bricks when he has tired of them. By Thursday night there was scarcely a street in the southern part of the city which was not barricaded by the wreck of fallen houses. The only quarter which escaped destruction was that which contained the handsome mansions of wealthy German residents of Antwerp in the Berchem district. The pavements were slippery with fallen glass. The streets were littered with tangled telephone wires, shattered poles, twisted lamp-posts, and splintered trees. More than

Homes of wealthy German residents escape destruction 2,000 houses were struck by shells, and more than three hundred of these were totally destroyed.

Flames roared from many of the smitten dwellings. A hundred and fifty could be seen blazing away at the same time, and as the water supply was cut off there was no means of fighting these fires. Had there been a wind, everything in Antwerp would have been consumed, and

nothing but the charred wreckage of one of the most beautiful and busiest centres of industry on earth would have remained in the hands of the conqueror. No military purpose was served by the bombardment of the city. Far more effectual results would have been obtained by concentrating all the artillery fire on the inner line of forts and the trenches and mobile batteries that barred the advance of the German infantry. Antwerp was partly destroyed with a view to terrorising the peaceful population and filling their souls with the dread of the race that had burned and sacked Louvain and a score of smaller towns and villages in Belgium.

By night the scene was one of infernal splendour. The oil-tanks by the river had been fired by the retreating Belgians to prevent the conqueror making use of the large stores of petrol. The glare of the blazing oil illumined the streets of this City of Dreadful Night. The lurid, wavering pillars of fire from the burning tanks, the flames of the bombarded houses, the flash and thunder of the exploding shells, turned lovely, romantic Antwerp into a

BELGIAN ARMY PASSING THROUGH THE FAMOUS GHENT GATE AT BRUGES.
The retreat of the British Naval Division and the Belgian Army from Ghent onwards was covered by strong British reinforcements. Ghent was occupied by the Germans on October 11th, and Bruges on October 14th, 1914. The above picture was taken as the Belgian Army was passing through the celebrated Ghent Gate at Bruges.

spectacle of volcanic sublimity and terror. In the river the falling shells threw up columns of water a hundred feet towards the pall of smoke, which, rising from the tanks, overhung the city like a cloud of death, such as Vesuvius flung over Pompeii and Herculaneum. And all this scene of gigantic horror and woe and destruction was the work of men who pretended to the leadership of civilisation!

Shells continued to fall on Friday morning, when a tall young man, in the plain uniform of a Belgian officer, took the rifle from a dead man in the trenches, levelled it, and shot at a German helmet. It was King Albert, the heroic leader of a nation of heroes, firing his last shot from Antwerp. By seven o'clock the last of the defending troops were believed to have crossed the river, and the bridge of boats was destroyed to prevent the enemy following them. After waiting an hour or two, to give the soldiers a good start, the burgomaster went out under a flag of truce to meet the German general and arrange the terms of surrender. It was reported that Beseler stated at the conference that, if the outlying forts were immediately surrendered, no money indemnity would be demanded from the city. A brilliant American war correspondent, who remained in Antwerp through the bombardment and took over the keys of German houses in the city from the American Consul and delivered these to the German authorities, makes the statement in question. If it is well founded, it shows how completely Beseler was deceived up to the last moment concerning the situation at Antwerp. For the forts had been

Beseler deceived up to the last moment abandoned, and they might have been taken by simply sending some soldiers to occupy them.

But the Germans were excessively cautious. At first Beseler only sent a few score of cycling troops into the city. They advanced very carefully from street to street and from square to square, until they formed a network of scouts. Behind them came a brigade of infantry, and hard on the heels of the infantry clattered half a dozen horse batteries. They galloped to the riverside, unlimbered on the quays, and opened fire with shrapnel on the last of the retreating Belgians, who had already reached the opposite side of the Scheldt. In half an hour the pontoon bridge had been repaired, and on Friday night a large force of troops passed over in pursuit.

Some result might have been achieved if this belated operation had been continued with the utmost energy. But the German Staff was too much bent upon impressing the empty city to carry on the pursuit with vigour. The triumphal entry of the victors did not begin till Saturday afternoon, when 60,000 German soldiers marched into Antwerp. Westward towards the seacoast, from Lokeren to Ghent and from Ghent towards Ypres and Ostend, there was abundant work awaiting an army of 60,000 young, vigorous soldiers. The Belgians were fighting their way to the sea; part of the British Naval Division was being harried by the Dutch border; German forces were trying to cut the railway line on one side and to envelop the 7th Division of the British Expeditionary Force, under Sir Henry Rawlinson, on the other side.

Yet this was the time when 60,000 German troops were kept in Antwerp, to pass in review before the new military governor, Admiral von Schröder! Surrounded by his glittering staff, the admiral sat his horse in front of the Royal Palace, on which a Zeppelin had tried to **A strange and astonishing military pageant** drop bombs when the King and Queen of the Belgians were there. The spectacle of the great military pageant was strange and astonishing. Except for one American war correspondent and one American war photographer, standing at the windows of the deserted American Consulate, the city was empty.

For five hours the mighty host poured through the ravines of brick and stone, company after company, regiment after regiment, brigade after brigade. There were ranks of gendarmes in uniforms of green and silver, Bavarians in dark-blue, Saxons in light-blue, and Austrians in silver-grey. The infantrymen, in solid columns of grey-clad figures, were neither Landsturm nor Landwehr, but young, red-cheeked athletes, singing as they marched. "Germany, Germany Over All!" was the song they sang, each regiment headed by its band and colours. When darkness fell and the lamps were lighted, the shrill music of fifes, the roll of drums, and the rhythmic tramp of feet still continued.

"DEUTSCHLAND, DEUTSCHLAND UEBER ALLES": GERMANS ADD INSULT TO INJURY.
The Germans, when they entered Antwerp, caused a military band to play daily in the principal squares of the conquered city. Apart from units of the army of occupation and those "without a country," the listeners seem to have included only the German residents who had prepared the way for the invaders. When the enemy entered the city they found it practically deserted.

CHAPTER XLIII.

OPENING BATTLES OF THE GREAT STRUGGLE FOR CALAIS.

Germans Attempt Two Tasks at Once, at Antwerp and Lille—British Army Begins to Move Towards the Coast—Sir John French's Plan for a Turning Movement—Delay in Railing our Troops to their New Position—Germans Attack Lille to Get Base of Operations against Calais—Gallant Struggle of Frenchmen against Great Odds—Falkenhayn's Scheme of a Mighty Cavalry Raid to Calais—Clash of Tens of Thousands of Horsemen by the River Lys—German Cavalry Taken by Surprise and Routed—Reinforced, the German Troopers Press Back the French Cavalry Divisions—Aviators Bomb a Column of Hostile Horse and Defeat It—How Fourscore Chasseurs Alpins Killed Four Hundred Germans in Estaires—General Gough and the 3rd Cavalry Brigade Arrive—Clearing the Woods and Hills of Enemy—Sir Horace Smith-Dorrien's Corps Advance towards La Bassée—Why La Bassée Could Not be Taken—The Germans are Pushed Back on Lille—Terrible House-to-House Fighting in the Black Country of Northern France.

T the beginning of October, 1914, someone in high command in Germany was consumed with impatience. It may have been the Kaiser Wilhelm, who had just promised his soldiers that they should win a grand decisive victory in the western field of war before the leaves fell from the trees. He had 600,000 recruits, whom he was bringing into action before they were half trained; he had 1,500,000 middle-aged men of the Landsturm class, many of whom might, if needed, be brought into the fighting-line. He wanted his refitted corps of first-line and reserve troops to clear a path of advance towards the French coast for the new armies. This could well have been done when Antwerp had fallen. But the anxious, restless, disappointed Emperor could not wait. He desired a swift attack on France to free his best troops for operations in Russia.

The result was that the assault on Antwerp and the effort to outflank and turn the Franco-British front by an advance on Calais were undertaken at the same time. Both of these German plans were well conceived, so far as they went; but instead of being executed in proper order, they were carried out simultaneously. The German forces had thus to be divided, instead of being swung in overwhelming numbers, first against the Belgians and then against the French.

At Antwerp the Germans won the race, but failed to gain the prize. They retained so many men in the other operations aimed at Calais that the Belgian Army escaped. So the capture of the Flemish stronghold only resulted in increasing the concentrated military strength of the Allies, by bringing several divisions out of Belgium to prolong the main allied front. This front then stretched for four hundred miles,

GENERAL VON DEIMLING.
He is said to have made his officers register an oath to "take Ypres or die."

from Nieuport on the North Sea to Delle on the Swiss border. At the same time as this strengthening of the Franco-British-Belgian line was taking place the movement of the Germans against it was weakened by their operations in Belgium. They fell between two stools.

This was not, however, wholly their fault. Sir John French took some part in making the enemy waver between two objectives. As soon as the British commander learnt that the new German Chief of Staff had ordered an attack on Antwerp, he resolved to anticipate, if possible, the attack on Calais, which was bound to follow. With this view, he proposed to General Joffre that the British Expeditionary Force should move quickly from the Aisne valley towards Lille and the country round the seacoast. The Commander-in-Chief of the western allied forces agreed to the plan. There was nothing more to do in the Aisne valley, and the British troops had so fortified their positions there and improved their trench systems that troops of the garrison class could take over their defensive work, and free them for more active fighting.

Sir John French had already received a new division which he could put to no immediate use in the Aisne action. And in addition to his three army corps, a fourth army corps was being organised in England, under General Sir Henry Rawlinson, for service in France. This fresh force, composed of the 7th and 8th Divisions and the 3rd Cavalry Division, was partly ready. The 7th Division and the Cavalry Division were immediately available for embarkation. But instead of sending them into France, Lord Kitchener, on October 4th, ordered them to go to Flanders. The British Expeditionary Force would meet them there. In the meantime, as we have seen, Sir Henry Rawlinson operated with the Belgian Army, trying first to sweep

"HANDS UP!" CAMERON HIGHLANDERS CAPTURING A GERMAN FORCE IN THE YSER COUNTRY.

How a party of Germans were discomfited by a much smaller number of the Cameron men is vividly shown in the above vigorously drawn picture. The incident, so graphically illustrated, took place in the Yser country, on October 23rd, 1914. The Germans, in the first place, had been driven to take shelter in the small house shown above. Their new position was then made untenable by British artillery fire. Just as they were making their appearance in the open again the Camerons dashed forward, took the enemy by surprise, and succeeded in holding them until the arrival of reinforcements put an end to this striking scene.

BRITISH INFANTRY HIDDEN IN A WOOD—"SOMEWHERE IN FRANCE."

In view of the devastating effects of modern artillery fire the old device of hiding in woodland is fraught with special perils. But we have seen how Sir John French, by adopting this ruse, was able to arrange an ambush against General von Kluck which took that able but too confident commander entirely by surprise and led him into one of the most decisive blunders in military history.

up to Antwerp and turn the flank of the attackers before the second line of defence was carried, and then working to protect and cover the march of the Belgians to the seacoast.

Had it been possible to move the main British Expeditionary Force rapidly from the Aisne towards the Belgian frontier, the stroke intended by Sir John French would have broken the German offensive movement. His idea was to turn the northern German wing by an advance from St. Omer or Hazebrouck, both near Calais. This would have had the effect of compelling the invaders to retire from both Northern France and Belgium. Antwerp would have been relieved without a local struggle, as soon as the main German lines were outflanked around Lille. The huge German reinforcements of half-trained recruits would not have retrieved the situation when the extended flank of the chief German armies was retreating. Their arrival would have only added to the confusion on the German lines of communication. As a matter of fact, General Joffre also had half a million recruits in a similar condition of training. He did not employ them. He wanted them to develop into fully-trained men before he used them. He was careful of their lives and also of his war material and his railway system.

The railways of Northern France were already working at high pressure. So great was the strain which was being put upon them, that even the execution of Sir John French's new plan of action was delayed. It took sixteen days to move the British army to its new position. The removal began on October 3rd, and it was not **French's new plan of** until October 19th that the First Army **action delayed** Corps, under Sir Douglas Haig, completed its detrainment at St. Omer. Some hundreds of trains were needed to carry the troops and guns; they brought the new garrison to Soissons and Fismes in the Aisne valley, and then departed northward with the British troops.

In all cases, the change in the men holding the trenches along the Aisne had to be made at night under cover of darkness. For if the enemy had seen what was going on, he would have shrapnelled both the new-comers and the retirers as they moved in and out. All this impeded the operation, but it was not the principal cause of delay. The great difficulty arose from the fact that two important French armies were fighting across the path of the British line of movement. As the trains ran **How the British** northward, they cut through the lines **movement was** of supply of General Castelnau's army **hampered** round Roye and General Maud'huy's army round Arras. Both these forces were rocking in fierce, incessant conflict with the Germans, and needed immense and continual trainloads of ammunition, stores, and reinforcements.

At Roye some of our men stopped on their journey to assist in the fighting at a critical moment. Moreover, neither General Castelnau's men nor General Maud'huy's men were stationary. They also were moving northward as they battled, trying to outflank the enemy, or answering an outflanking essay by him. They needed trains to carry them, as well as the numerous motor-vehicles they possessed. It was thus a long, delicate, and difficult task to move the British Expeditionary Force about one hundred and fifty miles towards Calais.

In the meantime the Germans were skilfully using the railways under their control for an advance seawards through Lille. Against this rich, stately, historic centre of the chief industrial district in France the invaders had two lines of attack. One army could assail the city eastward, using the railway from Valenciennes; another army could descend upon it from the north by the railway from Tournai. By reason of the junction there of the Belgian and French lines of communication with Cologne, Lille was a base of chief importance for the intended operations seaward. It had to be captured, and it seemed easy to capture, as it was held only by 2,000 troops of the militia class, with a single battery of light field-guns.

General Joffre took no means to strengthen the small garrison. It was not his plan to save cities. He was

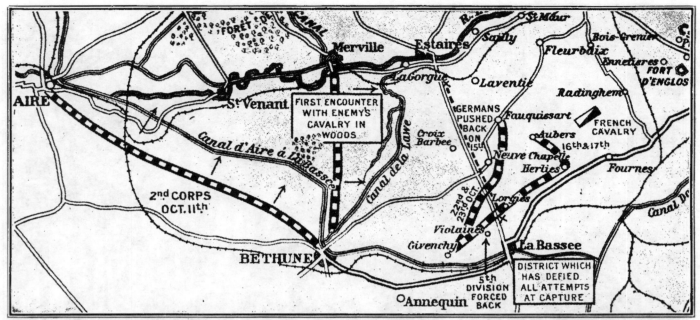

DIAGRAM ILLUSTRATING THE OPERATIONS OF THE SECOND BRITISH ARMY CORPS IN THE DISTRICT OF LA BASSEE IN OCTOBER, 1914.

saving France, and keeping his field armies strong against the enemy at the decisive points. It was not yet at all clear that the swing of the Germans westward was not a feint, and that the blow would not fall on the right spot— on the region between Rheims and Verdun. If the possession of Lille, with its coal-mines and woollen mills and famous manufactures, would encourage the enemy to take the wrong direction for the last

Temporary loss against national gain

great hammer-stroke on the Franco-British front—well, perhaps, the temporary loss of Lille was, from the military point of view, a national gain. Besides, it served to distract and scatter the German forces in Belgium, and so helped the Belgian Army in Antwerp, and also won time for the British movement to the north.

At first, General von Falkenhayn tried to sweep into Lille without a struggle. On Sunday, October 4th, a German armoured train, with a thousand infantrymen, ran into one of the Lille railway-stations. At the same time, some 3,000 German cavalrymen rode down from Roubaix in the north, and others came from the east. In all, there were some 8,000 German troops against 2,000 French soldiers. The battle opened about eleven o'clock in the morning round the railway-station. It spread through the boulevards and streets in the suburb of Fives. But, by fierce bayonet charges and the terrible fire from the four French quick-firing guns, the Germans were driven out by the evening, with the loss of many hundreds of their men and of two cannon.

This splendid stand made by the French troops against heavy odds had a happy effect. On Friday morning, October 9th, the German commander sent an army corps against the brave garrison—some 50,000 men against 2,000. It was the very day when the Belgian Army was retreating from Antwerp in considerable difficulties. The small garrison at Lille had drawn away an entire army corps from their brave allies, in the most critical hour in Belgian history!

At Lille, only the road to Bethune remained open. All the townsmen of military age left, under the guard of some of the soldiers, who had to fight to clear the way for them. For Lille was almost ringed round. The next day some Uhlans rode into the city; they were shot down. Then the bombardment began. But the Germans had not been able to remove their siege-artillery from Antwerp. Only a few small shells fell on Saturday night. It was on Sunday

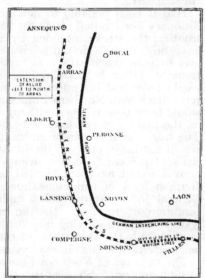

THE OPPOSING LINES BEFORE THE GREAT FLANKING MOVEMENT.

Early in October the position on the Aisne appeared to Sir John French to warrant a withdrawal of the British forces to support the northern flank of the Allies. Our men detrained at St. Omer.

HOW THE BRITISH ADVANCED FROM ST. OMER TO THE YPRES-ARMENTIERES BATTLE LINE.

While three British Army corps moved eastward from St. Omer, in the directions indicated in the diagram, the fourth, which had been operating in the neighbourhood of Antwerp and Ghent, came south.

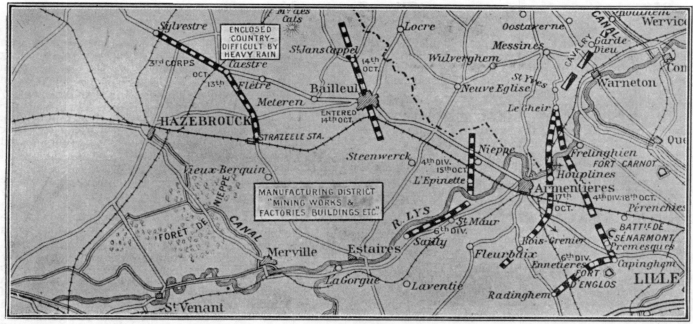

DIAGRAM ILLUSTRATING THE OPERATIONS OF THE THIRD BRITISH ARMY CORPS IN THE DISTRICT OF ARMENTIERES IN OCTOBER, 1914.

that the big howitzers were brought up on the railway, and placed in position. Then a rain of shells dropped on the centre of the city, and continued to drop until seven o'clock on Monday evening, October 12th. Some 1,200 houses were destroyed, and as all defence was impossible, the French soldiers escaped with their guns down the Bethune road, and Lille surrendered after a gallant and useful resistance.

Like the fall of Antwerp, the fall of Lille was a blow to the general peoples of the allied nations. It was an especial disaster to French industry, for it was the centre of a vast system of manufacturing towns and coal-mining hamlets, from which France obtained many of the chief necessities of civilised life. The huge stores of woollen goods and linen goods at Tourcoing, Roubaix, and Lille formed an important source of supplies to the German armies in the winter campaign. Even this did not exhaust the spoil of the nation, in regard to whom their allies, the Austrians, used to say:

"Es gibt nur ein Raüber nest, und das ist Berlin."

"There is only one robbers' den in the world; it is Berlin." For the Germans sold, in Italy and Switzerland, tens of thousands of pounds' worth of the manufactures they seized at Lille and the neighbourhood. They believed in making war pay its way, and the rights of private property in occupied countries were therefore abolished. It was reported, however, that some neutrals refused to purchase stolen goods even at bargain prices. Through their old-fashioned ignorance, they could not grasp the high, moral beauty of Deutsche Kultur.

Before either Antwerp or Lille had fallen, some of the

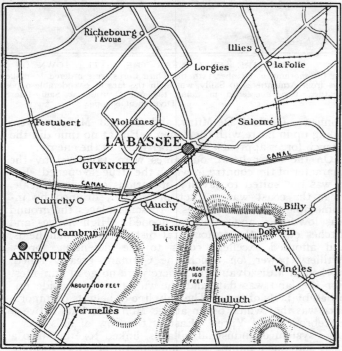

people of Calais began to fear that their town would also be taken by the enemy. Particularly on Thursday, October 8th, did the burghers of Calais look forward with apprehension to the prospect of standing another siege. For, in addition to the troops engaged at Antwerp and Lille and those operating against Belgian forces at Lokeren and part of the Fourth British Army Corps above Ghent, the German commander had thrown large masses of cavalry into the region between Lille and Calais. Some of the Uhlans were boldly venturing on reconnoitring expeditions to towns within a day's horse-ride to the North Sea.

Apprehension among the burghers of Calais

General von Falkenhayn had been inspired by the surprising raid of General Rennenkampf's Cossacks in East Prussia. By the swift onset of remarkably strong cavalry forces he intended to capture the northern coast-line of France, occupying all the country and holding the river

THE ENTRAINMENT FROM COMPIEGNE TO ST. OMER.

The withdrawal of the British forces from the Aisne began on October 3rd, when the 2nd Cavalry Division marched on Compiègne, and was completed on the 19th, when the First Corps detrained at St. Omer.

THE STRONG GERMAN POSITION AT LA BASSEE.
"On and after October 13th," wrote Sir John French, "the object of the General Officer commanding the Second Corps was to wheel to his right, pivoting on Givenchy . . . so as to threaten the right flank and rear of the enemy's position on the high ground south of La Bassée."

bridges and heights with machine-guns and light field artillery. When the land had been won in this manner, and the defending troops driven into Calais, the new infantry formations would be railed down with an unusual amount of heavy artillery, and supported by a quarter of a million of first-line troops from Lorraine and Alsace. Then the march on Paris would be resumed, turning the Franco-British front, and forcing the evacuation of all the Allies' fortified positions from Arras to the Argonne.

The trouble was that this magnificent **German cavalry reconnaissance in force** scheme of new operations largely depended for its success upon the results of the reconnaissance in force made by the cavalry. Every available horseman in the German lines was moved towards Lille, and several divisions of troopers were gathered for the raid by October 5th. Some of them advanced towards Lille from the east, while others swept down northward from Courtrai, with brigades of infantry with guns and machine-gun sections on motor-cycles, to support them.

All told, the raiding force outnumbered by two to one the French troops opposed to them. There were a division of French militia and some 9,000 Breton Marines around Dunkirk, and three brilliant French cavalry generals—General

WAYSIDE SCENE NEAR THE LITTLE TOWN OF NIEPPE.
On the morning of October 15th the Third Corps were ordered to make good the line of the Lys from Armentières to Sailly, which, in the face of considerable opposition and very foggy weather, they succeeded in doing, the 6th Division at Sailly-Bac St. Maur and the 4th Division at Nieppe.

Conneau, General De Mitry, and General Moussy—were riding up in haste with their men. But at no time did the French forces approach in number those of the enemy.

On the other hand, our allies were favoured by the character of the country in which the struggle opened. For it was not suited to cavalry operations on a large scale. Near the coast was a tract of fenland, drained by innumerable dykes and canals. In some places the ground was low-lying, and could be flooded. High hedges and ditches cut up the agricultural district into small fields, and afforded excellent cover to the defending forces. Artillery power, on which the Germans greatly relied, worked at a disadvantage. There were no good gun sites. For the land was flat, and the views on every side impeded by belts of trees. The only line of heights of importance was that which began at the Mont des Cats between Hazebrouck and Ypres. East of this row of hills was a large system of industrial villages, linked together into a vast, unnamed mining and manufacturing city, forming miles on miles of streets, where a cavalry column could often be held up by a few determined men with a couple of machine-guns.

From a soldier's point of view it was a blind country, with opportunities for ambush at every hedge and every mining village ; and to add to the difficulties, the immense plain was veiled in autumn mist. The German movement began with a night ride of three divisions of cavalry that came by Tournai and crossed the River Lys, moving towards Hazebrouck. It was at dawn on Tuesday morning, October 6th, that this body of nearly 20,000 horsemen came trotting along the right bank of the famous river where, four hundred years before, the chivalry of England and the chivalry of France had clashed together at the Battle of the Spurs.

Now another great cavalry battle was about to take place by the same river, in spite of the fact that most military experts held that cavalry was a wasted force in a modern battle. There were considerable grounds, indeed, for the new belief in the unimportance of the cavalryman. His scouting work was being carried out by airmen with a speed, an accuracy, and a range which he could not equal. His reconnaissance work was better performed by men in armoured motor-cars, and by motor-cyclists carrying a machine-gun. The modern parallel battle, with its lines of ditches, and its siege operations, had left cavalrymen nothing to do but to tether their horses and go into the trenches to perform infantry work there.

It was, in fact, this waste of an arm, which the Germans thought they had brought to a higher perfection than that of any other nation, that mainly led to the series of grand battles of horsemen between Lille and the sea. For years the Kaiser Wilhelm had practised immense cavalry charges at his grand manœuvres. He was proud of his mounted troops— more so than of any of his other soldiers. And, as the opportunity arose, he resolved that his favourite arm should distinguish itself in a great series of swaying, hand-to-hand conflicts that would mark the historic end of the employment on a large scale of cavalry forces.

By his long night ride the German commander hoped to take the French by surprise, and to advance at least half-way towards the sea without any strong opposition. But as the columns trotted along in the darkness, eyes in the hedge saw and numbered them, and messages ran along the telegraph wires to French headquarters. When the Germans began to see clearly through the morning mist, their leading squadrons perceived on the skyline a light cloud of dust. At first it seemed only a long thin line of floating gossamer stuff, such as the winds of autumn lift and carry over the wide level fields of beetroots. But the cloud drifted forward and increased in size. Silhouettes stood out against the Flemish plain ; helmets could be seen, and horses' heads, and the glitter of lances.

The hostile horsemen surged first to the right and then to the left, forming a great semicircle, still sweeping against the Germans. Suddenly, at a distance of twelve hundred yards, the bugles rang out, and the trotting horses changed step, and began to gallop. To prevent themselves from being taken at a disadvantage by the charge, the Germans also spurred their mounts forward. But **Clash of tens of thousands of horsemen** the Allies were not to be withstood. Onward they rode, with sword and lance ready to strike. With a terrific shock the opposing hosts met, amid bugle calls, neighing of the horses, and the yelling of tens of thousands of blood-mad men. And all around was such a thick haze of dust that a cavalryman could scarcely see ten steps before him the Saxon hussar whose sword stroke he had to parry, or the Prussian Uhlan who was using a pistol.

THE FIGHT FOR CALAIS: SANGUINARY ENCOUNTER BETWEEN FRENCH AND GERMANS AT LENS.

The mining town of Lens is situated on the River Deule, some ten miles north-north-east of Arras. Here, during one of the desperate attempts of the Germans to extend their line to Calais, amidst coal trucks, mineheads, and iron and steel works, a sanguinary encounter took place between the French and German forces. Both sides barricaded themselves in the streets, and fought across the metals of the railway sidings. Eventually the Teutons were driven out with heavy losses, and to the moving strains of the famous Sidi-'Brahim bugle march of the French as they made their way triumphantly back through the town, the terrified inhabitants came up from their cellars once more to the light of day.

In the above remarkable picture, based upon a sketch made on the spot, many points of interest are focused. In a field seen on the right hand a number of British soldiers are finding brief relaxation in a game of football. On the roadway are to be seen British infantry on the march passing a regiment of French artillery going in the opposite direction. In the centre of the high Staff motor-cars are passing to and fro. In the foreground are a few Ger prisoners in charge of French infantrymen. In the fields to the left may discerned a large number of horses tethered against hedges for shelter f

ial observation.   The same desire to escape the eye of reconnoitring airmen noticeable in the mixed colouring of the armoured train on the left.   In the to the rear of the armoured train is a captive observation balloon, and on the ht is a German Taube aeroplane.   The road, typical of Belgium, is paved in

the centre to a width sufficient to allow room for two motor-cars to pass ; while the rest of it, after the passing of heavy traffic, is churned into a mud-track in which wheels sink to their axle-trees.   In regard to the painting of the armoured train it may be noted that modern forts and gun-shields are similarly disguised.

TRAGEDY OF A MOVING FORTRESS: HOW FOUR HEROIC FRENCHMEN KEPT A GERMAN INFANTRY SQUAD AT BAY.

Few stories of the Great War are more moving than that told by the war artist M. Thiriat, and illustrated by him in the above picture. The scene was a desolate tract of Northern France. During a reconnaissance the party of which M. Thiriat was one came across a wrecked armoured motor-car, which appeared to be abandoned. Dead bodies of Germans were lying all round, and when the car was approached it was found to contain three dead French soldiers and one wounded. From the story told by the wounded man it appeared that he and his companions were trying to mend a burst tyre when they were suddenly attacked by a German squad. Entering the car they gave battle. The heroic struggle continued for an hour. His three comrades having fallen, the survivor fired at the remaining German and then fainted from loss of blood, to regret when help at length arrived that it came too late to save his gallant companions and left him alone to tell the tale.

Shouts of command went up in French, in English, and in thick-throated Flemish. The lancers drove home their long, terrible spears, the dragoons and cuirassiers, with their straight swords, feinted, and hacked, and thrust, some screaming as they fought, others working in deadly silence. The German cavalryman was never remarkable for his swordsmanship throughout the Great War. The French, with their trained gift of fence, got

The chivalry of Prussia broke and fled under his guard with ease, and though the Briton did not belong to a fencing nation, he had also been trained to use the sword with masterly force. One French horseman who took part in the action said afterwards that the work of slaughter became a mechanical job, in which he lifted and brought down his arm without thinking out his movements.

All the while the horses, seized with the same lust of battle as their masters, carried them deeper into the fight. The men's eyes were dimmed with the dust and sweat and blood—blood that spurted from those whom they struck, or blood that streamed from wounds on their own heads. Then, suddenly, as the allied horsemen were still lifting their red swords for another blow, they found nobody in front of them. Far away the broken chivalry of Prussia and Saxony and Bavaria showed their backs to the victors, and the bright cuirasses of the pursuers flashed dimly through the haze. When the dust settled on the plain, leaving a clear view, the tired men saw around them fallen bodies, horses who had lost their riders and riders who had lost their horses. Above the field of the dead the frightened, soaring larks began to call to their mates in the autumnal sky. The horsemen looked at each other, still astonished at the speed with which they had won the victory.

Driven back on the line running from Tourcoing to Armentières, the raiders took up positions in the mining and manufacturing districts. There they waited for reinforcements, and then, greatly increased in number, they sallied out again. Fighting went on continuously on Wednesday, October 7th, the Germans swinging more and more northward as General Conneau's cavalry corps worked against them from the west. By the next day the series of cavalry actions extended to the North Sea. The Kaiser certainly had his wish in regard to the magnificence of the conflict, for it was on a front of something like forty-five miles that the hostile horsemen met in continual actions.

Our sailors in armoured motor-cars, who had come to support our naval air division, had the time of their lives. For with the help of their airmen they could follow every German movement, and arrange an ambush at some cross-road, where an armoured car could sweep suddenly round upon a German squadron and shatter it with an abrupt and deadly gun fire. The French also

Thrilling story of French heroism used armoured cars. On one occasion there was trouble with the tyres, and the driver and his gunners alighted to repair the damage. They were seen by a large squad of German infantry, who crept up to an attack. The four Frenchmen clambered back into their immovable car, and used it as a fort against the Germans. After an hour's fighting three of them were killed, and the remaining man was wounded and dizzy. As he was fainting he saw a German helmet move, and shot at it. Some time after a French patrol passed by and saw the stranded car, and noticed the numerous bodies of enemies lying around. They found

their wounded fellow-countryman, and brought him to his senses. The man had killed the last German just as he was swooning, and had then dropped unconscious on the little field of victory.

In the motor section of the cavalry forces, however, the Germans were not inferior in equipment to the Allies. In fact, they had the advantage. They did not rely much on armoured motor-cars, fitted with long-ranged guns, but sent out hundreds of motor-cyclists, armed with a small quick-firing gun. Even when painted with the strange, crude stripes of colour that so effectively hide an armoured train, the motor-car remained undesirably visible. It was, moreover, unwieldly in action, as it took some time to turn it round on the roads of Flanders.

The motor-cycle, on the other hand, was a weapon of greater possibilities, and the Germans certainly scored by employing it in an extensive manner. They have proved that it is more important than the horse in reconnoitring skirmishes. The machine is very small, and approaches as closely to invisibility as is possible. By taking advantage of the trees lining every road on the scene of the conflict, the riders were able to make long surprise rushes, and return in safety. They had not to depend upon the worn, broken highways, where perhaps shells had fallen and

THE MARKET-SQUARE OF LILLE.

Lille was held by only 2,000 French troops of the French Militia class. It was regarded by the Germans as a favourable base for their operations against Calais, and captured by them on October 13th, after a splendid defence covering nine days, a defence which served to draw an entire Germany army corps of 50,000 men from the force which was trying to cut off the retreat of the Belgian Army from Antwerp.

blown out great holes liable to wreck a heavy car; for their light machines ran at fifty miles an hour through the muddy side tracks.

Brilliant motor-cyclists, who were also marksmen, were able to do an immense amount of damage in a few minutes. As soon as one of them reached his point of attack he dismounted, and tilted his machine slightly to the left, bringing the machine-gun into the proper position for manipulation. He was then able to sweep off a patrol or a transport convoy, and to remount and escape, almost before the attacked party were aware of his existence. His fleeing back, in any case, offered a very small and elusive mark, utterly different from the huge target presented by an armoured car in the throes of backing across a narrow road.

In the region some fifteen miles west of Lille, between the La Bassée Canal and the heights that begin with the Mont des Cats, the German motor-cyclists, backed by large forces of cavalry and infantry and artillery supports, managed at last to push back General Conneau's gallant horsemen, who had fought on our flank at the Battle of the

INDIANS GIVE THE LIE TO GERMAN CALUMNIES: A BRILLIANT BAYONET CHARGE.

The valour of our Indian troops came as a great surprise to the enemy. Landing at Marseilles on September 26th, 1914, they were in the firing-line in October. Our picture gives an eloquent illustration of their valour in one of their early engagements. A strong German force, advancing from cover in solid column formation, made a determined attack on a comparatively weak British entrenched position and carried it. Advancing farther, however, they came up against our reserves, which included a section of Indians. The latter, by their withering rifle fire, compelled the enemy to halt, and then charged with the bayonet. There ensued a fierce scrimmage. Then the Germans turned and fled, with the Indians slaying them right and left, and finally pursuing them back to the main German position.

Marne. Uhlan patrols began to appear in the towns leading towards Calais. The railway-station at Hazebrouck was stormed at the point of the bayonet by some Bavarian troops, and a garrison was placed at Estaires, a few miles east of Hazebrouck. The German position then jutted out north of General Maud'huy's army, and menaced him with a turning movement. So he moved his troops up towards La Bassée, and linked on with the French cavalry forces that were battling from Hazebrouck to the sea-coast.

The task set the French cavalry was to hold as much ground as possible, pending the arrival of the British army, and to keep the Germans so fully engaged that the Belgian and British troops in Flanders could not be over-whelmed or cut off. It was a desperately difficult job, but the difficulties of it only inspired the French to new efforts. When the position of affairs was ex-tremely critical a fresh division of German cavalry was seen by an aerial scout, as it was engaging in a turning movement. No force was available to beat it back, but the French airman pro-posed a new way of mëeting the hostile column of 5,000 horsemen. He loaded his machine with bombs, and departed, after giving two or three other aviators the direction of the enemy. They also loaded up with bombs. One after another the airmen flew over the long column, and rained down bombs that killed, wounded, and scattered squadron after squadron. As the roads were fenced in by high hedges, the column could not disperse into the fields when the airmen were sighted, and form up again when their sky foes had passed. All day long the aviators flew between the enemy and headquarters, loading up each time with bombs and swooping down through a shower of bullets to get near to their target. From dawn to dusk the extraordinary battle went on, and until darkness fell and covered them, the German horsemen were unable to escape from their aerial attackers. Their operation was completely stopped, and they were pursued and continually stricken all day long. Their horses in many cases became unmanageable with fright, and a considerable part of the column was put out of action before it withdrew at night towards its base on the Lys.

Brilliant feat of four-score Chasseurs Alpins In spite of the odds against them, the French cavalry, by Monday, October 12th, managed to hold the German raiders off Hazebrouck. But the Germans were able to advance towards Bethune in the south and Cassel in the north on the road to Calais. They still overhung the Tenth French Army under General Maud'huy. The French Staff, therefore, ordered that the enemy's advanced position at Estaires on the Lys should be driven in. Two thousand cavalrymen were detached and sent by night towards Estaires. Nearly every important movement was

SURPRISE VISIT OF THE GURKHAS TO A GERMAN TRENCH.
In the night-fighting during the early part of the German attempt to break through to the coast the gallant Gurkhas gave a splendid account of themselves, and in the use of their traditional weapon the *kukri* (or "cooker," as the British soldier called it) carried terror into the hearts of the enemy.

undertaken in the darkness, in order to escape the observa-tion of hostile airmen. The cavalry by daylight lost all the advantage of the quickness of movement which their horses gave them. For as soon as they were spied by the aerial scouts, an ambush could be arranged in the direction they were taking. Like the first divisions of German mounted troops that tried to make a surprise raid, the horsemen on both sides trotted under cover of night from point to point, and made their attacks in the grey twilight of dawn.

While the two thousand French troopers were advanc-ing in the darkness on Estaires, a young French lieutenant of the crack infantry corps of Chasseurs Alpins, with four-score of his men, was reconnoitring in the neighbourhood. The Germans had planted machine-guns controlling the bridge over the Lys, and a searchlight played on the river all night. Nevertheless, the Chasseurs got into the river-side village of La Gorgue, and at dawn went over the foot-bridge to Estaires. They were men accustomed to moun-tain warfare, and they had come from the Vosges, where they had brought to a high degree of perfection the art of taking cover. They crept from house to house, without causing an alarm, in spite of the fact that the little town was held by four hundred German troops. They found some of the Germans drunk, and the rest of them sleeping, and apparently even the sentries were either tipsy or drowsy. Going through the nearest houses, they discovered that every strong box and chest had been broken open and emptied by the burgling invaders. But this did not move them to wrath. Where the Crown Prince had led the way, it was only to be expected that the rank and file of the barbarian army would follow him. Even when the German colonel, more alert than his men, rushed out into one of the courtyards, pistol in hand, and shot at the lieutenant, the Chasseurs went on quietly. For the German commander missed his mark, and fell with a bullet through his forehead when the lieutenant quickly fired in reply. When, however, the Chasseurs reached the churchyard of Estaires they saw something that suddenly kindled them to the wildest fury. In the **Ghastly discovery in a** corner was a heap of bodies of peaceful **churchyard at Estaires** townspeople, each bound and shot. A woman with child and an old feeble man were among the murdered non-combatants. The Chasseurs then began to kill. They went at it with the bayonet, and at the end of an hour all the four hundred ravagers and murderers were dead. It was just then that the two thousand French cavalrymen, having got across the river with great skill, cautiously advanced into the town. "We have already taken it, sir," said the lieutenant of the Chasseurs Alpins to the brigadier-general.

Estaires was the limit of the German advance from La Bassée. For the French pressure became so strong at this point that the raiding cavalry gave up for a while the idea of reaching Calais, and tried to extend more northward towards Dunkirk. They came within nineteen miles of this seaport in the second week in October. Had they been able to extend in force to the shore, they would have hemmed in the retreating Belgian Army by the sea road, and have surrounded the British force under Sir Henry Rawlinson at Ypres. The position became so threatening that the British general had to cut himself off from his line of communication, and send the troops holding the line back to England by steamer. The Germans, however, were trying to do more than they had power to accomplish. Breton Marines and French militia troops guarded the towns along the coast from Nieuport to Calais, and even along the German front from Lille to Cassel there were large gaps. Until they received more reinforcements from Courtrai, the German horsemen could not close the paths of the Belgian and British forces working down from the north.

Already, on Sunday, October 11th, their cavalry, holding some woods north of the canal running from Bethune to Aire, felt a new force of opposition working against them. They were engaged in surrounding Hazebrouck from the south, while another large German mounted force was creeping round the **Unexpected arrival of** town from the north by the heights of **British cavalry** Mont des Cats. The weather was misty, making aerial scouting almost useless, and some time passed before the Germans knew what was happening. They had entrenched outside many of the villages and had placed machine-guns, of which they had an extraordinary number, in the centre of the rooms of the cottagers, so that they commanded the streets from the windows. In the woods north of the canal they held their ground more lightly, with Jägers and riflemen collected round the paths that the French cavalry might take, while machine-guns were held ready to open fire. But not a glint of the bright French uniforms was seen.

Half-invisible figures in khaki, carbine in hand, were moving between the trees. They were the 4th Hussars, and the 15th and 16th Lancers,

PICTURESQUE ALGERIAN CAVALRYMEN IN CHARGE OF A BATCH OF GERMAN PRISONERS.
Many of the prisoners were wounded and all were tired and in need of food. Their captors provided them with a good meal, for which they were very grateful. Inset: Germans collecting firewood for transport to the front.

GERMAN TROOPS CLEANING UP BEFORE LEAVING FOR THE FRONT.

German troops at their ablutions before leaving for the front. The railway-station arrangements seem to have been very methodical—witness the notice-board with its bold announcement of "Washing Water"—but no method could serve to eliminate the shame achieved in Belgium. Inset: An exceptional instance of German chivalry. Funeral of a French officer who had died a prisoner in German hands, but who was buried with military honours in the soil of his beloved France.

forming the 3rd Cavalry Brigade, under General Gough. As the Germans never expected to meet the British army so far north, they did not notice the green-brown moving forms. The British general was able to plant his guns and Maxims, with a view to getting a sweeping fire on the Teutons when they moved in the direction in which it was intended to force them. **General Gough's surprise for the enemy** Then the surprise attack opened, and the Germans broke and fled eastward. The 3rd Brigade swept the woods, and then joined hands with another body of British cavalry in the neighbourhood of Hazebrouck. In the night more British cavalrymen crossed the reconquered canal and moved in a north-easterly direction. They were scouting in advance of the Second Army Corps, under Sir Horace Smith-Dorrien, famous throughout the world for the stand it made at Le Cateau. It had been brought up to Aire on Sunday, October 11th, and it moved along the Lys in the darkness to link on to the left of the Tenth French Army, and then swing against the German flank at La Bassée.

The action opened on Monday, October 12th. The 5th Division, under Sir Charles Fergusson, advanced along the southern bank of the canal, while the 3rd Division crossed the waterway and battled towards Lille. The ground was very flat, which made it extremely difficult for the guns to drop their shells over the heads of our troops on to the enemy's position. Mining works, factories, and dwelling-places covered the land, and as the Germans held every building commanding the path of advance, and had machine-guns in the windows and on the roofs, it was costly and slow work for infantry to advance against such opposition. Each building that our scouts found to be strongly occupied had to be wrecked by shell fire, to enable our foot soldiers to go forward. It was house-to-house fighting almost from the beginning, and the Germans might have got off fairly easily if they had been as expert in street fighting as the French.

But instead of scattering when they lost the position, they tried to recover it by a counter-attack. It was then that our men made them suffer. Again and again they endeavoured to win back places they had lost, with the result that they were shot down in large numbers, and some of their machine-guns were shelled and destroyed. But by Tuesday, October 13th, our gallant 5th Division struck against a little German Gibraltar which was to prove a permanent obstacle in the path of the Allies. It consisted of the small industrial **La Bassee : A little** town of La Bassée, lying on a line of **German Gibraltar** canals, some sixteen miles south-west of Lille. The canals formed a splendid system of moats in front of the German trenches, and to the south of the town there was some high ground on which the defending artillery was placed. The German guns swept all the flat country around for miles, and there was no site from which our artillery could effectually operate in reply.

The German commander, who chose that point of

vantage as a base for operations towards the coast, certainly knew his business. He could dispense with howitzers and use the long-ranged heavy field-gun with a plunging fire effect on any hostile position on the low-level plain. We could only reach him, after considerable delay, by hauling up our new 6 in. mortars. He replied by borrowing some of the lighter pieces from the great siege train that had been freed for general use by the fall of Antwerp. The consequence was that, **Commanding position** with a commanding position on the **of the German artillery** only rising ground in the country, and with anything up to 12 in. mortars with a range of nine miles to draw upon, the commander at La Bassée was immovable. Beneath the fire of his guns our 5th Division was even more helpless than it had been on the Aisne flats with Kluck's guns and howitzers cross-firing on it. For in the Aisne valley our army at least had good gun sites on the southern plateaus,

from which it could check some of the enemy's batteries. Sir Horace Smith-Dorrien at once recognised the position. He made no direct attack upon La Bassée, but pivoted the army corps at Givenchy out of reach of the hostile guns, and then wheeled his right wing northward between La Bassée and Lille. By this means he threatened to get on the right flank and rear of the hill on which the Germans had placed their artillery.

Up to this opening of the long series of terrific battles round Ypres and Lille the British soldier had no deep respect for the German infantryman. He thought the opposing artillerymen and the machine-gun officers were foes to be esteemed for their skill, but for the ordinary German foot soldier, led in mass formations, our men had little admiration **Saxons and Bavarians** after Mons and Le Cateau. Even on **show to advantage** the Aisne, it was only the handling of the numerous German guns and the ability with which the German positions had been selected that made the British fighting man appreciate the professional talent for war of the principal militarist Power in the world.

But on the Lys and around Ypres the German infantrymen appeared to better advantage. Drawn largely from the Saxons of Saxony and the Celtic race of Bavaria, our new opponents showed more individuality and resilience than the Prussianised Northern Germans. Fighting with them were brigades of brilliant sharpshooters, who soon proved themselves expert in the art of sniping. Things did not go as well as was hoped by the Kaiser, who said he wished the Bavarians would meet the English—just once. They met the English, Scots, Irish, and Indians many times, and though they showed at first an eager courage to get to man-to-man conflict with the bayonet, they did not persist for very long in this attitude.

One lieutenant, who claimed to be the captor of Lille, and advanced against us with the 60,000 troops that had taken the city, wrote home after the first series of battles with our Second Army Corps: "People at home appear to have wrong ideas about the fighting spirit of our opponents. The British are the pluckiest and bravest enemies that we have. Every single man who has not been taken goes on shooting quietly, and these well-trained men shoot well. When we storm their trenches yelling, they stay steadily on in their trenches." That is a pretty good compliment from a bitter foe. In return we can fairly admit that the Bavarians, whom every Prussian contemned before the war for their lack of military exuberance, were the best German soldiers our men encountered. Except for their old, notorious,

PREPARED FOR DEATH, BUT SAVED BY A RED CROSS DOG.
In a corner of the Forest of Nieppe, not far from the River Lys, a British private and a French artillery sergeant, both sorely wounded, and passed by the tide of battle, sank down in a shaded hollow prepared to cross the River of Death together. Before they lost consciousness they clasped hands in token of friendship. Thus they were found by a Red Cross dog belonging to a French curé. They awoke in warm, comfortable beds in the good curé's house, under the care of ministering hands.

dreadful habit of killing their wounded foes in the frenzy of battle, the Bavarians proved themselves good fighters.

They certainly set our Second Army Corps a very hard task to win a few miles of country from them between La Bassée and Lille. They were in overpowering numbers; four army corps of the first-line, one reserve corps, one cavalry division, three cavalry corps, and a Landwehr infantry brigade were opposed to our Second Army Corps round La Bassée and our Third Army Corps round Armentières, with a French cavalry corps assisting them. At least three Germans to one Briton were standing on the defensive in prepared positions on difficult ground.

Great gallantry of the Dorsets But such was the steady vigour of our onset that our Second Army Corps drove the enemy back continually for some days. The 1st Battalion of the Dorsets greatly distinguished themselves by the work they did from October 12th to 15th. On one day, October 13th, at Pont Fixe, in the neighbourhood of La Bassée, they held on to their position under a devastating fire. One hundred and thirty of them were killed, including their commanding officer, and two hundred and seventy wounded. But the enemy could not move them. On the other hand, no progress could be made by our forces neither on that day nor the next, when General Hubert Hamilton, the commander of the heroic 3rd Division, was killed.

Owing to a peculiarity in the British character, the death

LIEUT.-GENERAL SIR JAMES WOLFE-MURRAY, R.A., K.C.B.
He succeeded the late Sir Charles Douglas as Chief of the Imperial General Staff.

THE LATE GENERAL SIR CHARLES W. H. DOUGLAS, G.C.B.
He was chief of the Imperial General Staff and First Military Member of the Army Council. He died on October 25th, 1914.

of the general was a heavy misfortune for the Germans. For the 3rd Division began to fight in a cold, steady fit of fury that nothing human could withstand. Working through the country between La Bassée and Estaires, they crossed the innumerable dykes on planks which they brought with them, and drove the enemy from village after village, though all the houses had been loopholed for defence. Bivouacking on Thursday night on the road from Estaires to La Bassée, they rose at dawn and continued their advance, and pushed the Germans farther eastward. Then at night the Lincolns and Royal Fusiliers carried the village of Herlies at the point of the bayonet

after taking Aubers in daylight with the rest of the 9th Infantry Brigade—the Northumberland Fusiliers and the Royal Scots Fusiliers.

The division was then north of La Bassée, and was in a position to wheel round on the flank and rear of the high ground where the enemy's heavy guns were planted. But our attack could not be driven home. Our troops got within a few miles of both Lille and La Bassée, fighting to the full pitch of heroism against an able and more numerous enemy. But nearly two more entire German army corps were moved up from the south, where they had been fighting against General Maud'huy's army. Our Second Army Corps was overwhelmed by four German cavalry divisions, two German army corps, and several battalions of Jägers, and other troops.

Heroic stand of Royal West Kents Sir Charles Fergusson's 5th Division was driven out of the village of Violaines, two miles north of La Bassée, and though, by a terrible counter-attack made by the Worcesters and Manchesters, the multitude of Germans was held back, Sir Horace Smith-Dorrien had to retreat. It was on the night of October 22nd that he withdrew to Givenchy, just out of range of the La Bassée guns. Northward, his line stretched to the village of Neuve Chapelle, and here the first battalion of the Royal West Kents made a stand for ten days that ranks among the

ARMOURED MOTOR-CAR IN ACTION: SURPRISING A PARTY OF UHLANS.

The Uhlans had the surprise of their lives, but the motorists escaped by sheer good luck from what might have been disaster. The encounter illustrated in the above picture took place not far from Arras. The car, manned by a party of Belgian scouts, was proceeding at a rapid pace in wooded country when a patrol of Uhlans emerged from cover. Shots rang out on both sides, but the swivelled machine-gun in the car was fired with such rapidity that the enemy were routed. The car, however, came within an ace of being wrecked by the body of a falling horse.

highest achievements of British troops. Their trenches were bombarded by massed batteries of 6 in. howitzers and numerous field-guns. The shells fell at the rate of a hundred an hour on October 26th. Everything was wrecked; the support trenches and communicating trenches were blocked, and to reach the firing-line the men had to run across a hundred and fifty yards of open ground swept by shrapnel, machine-gun fire, and by rifle fire. In the afternoon the big black-smoke shells began to burst right in the firing trench. When night fell, the German gunners changed from high-explosive shell to shrapnel.

At one time ten shells burst every **Wilts and Middlesex** minute. When it was reckoned that **add to their laurels** all our men had been put out of action, the Germans charged. They came up in waves. Each wave was received by a mad minute of rapid fire, and when the last wave was breaking, the West Kents came out with the bayonet and broke it clean up. Afterwards the West Kents saved the line when it was broken on their left.

When at last they retired from their trenches, led by Lieutenant Haydon, one of their few surviving officers, both divisions of the Second Army Corps hailed them as the heroes of the terrible fight. " There is not another battalion that has made such a name for itself as the Royal West Kent," said Sir Horace Smith-Dorrien. The Wiltshires also distinguished themselves in repulsing the attack against the 7th Brigade, and inflicted very severe loss on the enemy, while the Middlesex Regiment, by a splendid charge, recaptured the trenches out of which the Gordon Highlanders had been driven. Altogether, the battle around Neuve Chapelle was even a greater victory than the stand made by the same corps at Le Cateau. The fight at Le Cateau lasted for a day. At Neuve Chapelle the trenches were held for ten days against the same odds of four to one. The victory at Le Cateau was followed by a long retreat. The victory at Neuve Chapelle enabled the position to be held through the long campaign against all the tremendous attempts made by the Germans to break through and to occupy the north-eastern coast of France.

Terrible, however, were the losses of the Second Army Corps, owing to the length of line it had to defend, and the constant reinforcements which the enemy received. The German casualties were at least double those of ours; but as our losses fell on one army corps, while those of the enemy were distributed among four corps, our men were seriously weakened. Towards the end of October the Second Corps was partly drawn back into reserve, and the defence of their line was taken over by the Lahore and Meerut Divisions of the Indian Army Corps, assisted by two and a half brigades of British infantry and a large part of the artillery of the Second Corps. All things considered, Sir Horace Smith-Dorrien's troops could claim a tactical victory. For a great assault which fails is tactically a defeat. The assailing Germans withdrew, weakened both morally and materially, and in spite of their superior numbers they also had to be largely reinforced. Though all through the winter they continued to attack, they never prevailed, but their main position at La Bassée was gradually sapped and weakened.

To the north of the scene of operations of our Second Corps, a similar fortune befell our Third Corps under General Pulteney's command. The new corps was composed of the 4th Division **Germans fought back** —General Snow's—that had fought so **village by village** well at Le Cateau, and the 6th Division, which had joined the Expeditionary Force on the Aisne heights after the first fierce fighting was over. They both detrained at St. Omer on October 11th, and moved the next day to Hazebrouck. From this town they swept out into action on Tuesday, October 13th, when the famous 19th Brigade stopped the German cavalry raid by seizing the villages eastward of the height of Mont des Cats. Having thus barred the road to the coast, the Third Corps fought the German cavalrymen and sharpshooters back, village by village, towards Armentières. The British troops were much superior in artillery power to the German raiders, but as the country was blanketed in fog, our guns were not of much use. By the time our gunners had a clear field, the Germans had their field-artillery behind them, and part of

Loading the lower deck.

On the road.

Taking them up.

At the trough.

Picking the draft.

Corn

A new draft.

SKETCHES OF EQUINE LIFE: FROM AN OFFICER AT THE FRONT.

Great as have been the changes wrought by motor-power, the revolution has not done away with the need of the horse in war. He remains a most essential factor, and his help and his sufferings are deeply appreciated by officers and men. His health has been guarded and his wounds tended with greater solicitude than ever before. This series of charming pencil sketches illustrating, with sympathy and insight, phases of equine activity at the front, was sent to "The Great War" by a well-known animal artist on active service as an officer, and they are reproduced untouched.

FRENCH-AFRICAN TROOPS PREVENT VON MOLTKE'S DESPERATE ATTEMPT TO BREAK THROUGH THE ALLIED LINE ON THE MARNE.

A hand-to-hand encounter at Germigny l'Eveque, near Varreddes, where the Germans found themselves jammed into a dangerous angle on the River Marne. The line of the Sixth French Army rested on Varreddes, preventing any westward extension of the German forces. The French and British were pressing against the German lines to the eastward. In the course of the fierce struggle street-fighting occurred between a section of the French-African troops and German infantry. The colonial soldiers, armed with the long French bayonet, came round a bend of the road, as shown above, and the enemy, after a short resistance, were beaten back among the blazing houses and broken barricades. Here, as elsewhere, Eastern "barbarism" showed to advantage against Prussian "Kultur."

the siege train from Antwerp. The clerk of the weather was certainly unkind to the British army on this occasion.

A violent struggle took place at the village of Meteren, where the Fourth German Cavalry Corps and some thousands of Jägers had entrenched. Captain Montgomery, of the Warwicks, distinguished himself by leading a charge, in which his men captured the enemy's trenches at the point of the bayonet. The Seaforth Highlanders and 2nd Lancashire Fusiliers, the Royal Lancasters, and the Essex Regiment were also remarkable for their skill and rushing attacks. As night fell, General Pulteney's troops moved out to storm the town of Bailleul. But the Germans had taken the measure of our men, and hastily withdrew, leaving their wounded to our care. As the fog continued, our men went on in furious rushes, and captured the town of Armentières, and by Sunday got within a few miles of fallen Lille.

Meanwhile our cavalry divisions had been clearing the Mont des Cats and the westward hills of raiding horsemen and sharpshooters. They swept the country on the north of the advancing Third Corps, and a French cavalry corps, under General Conneau, which had acted with our army in the Battle of the Marne, cleared the region south of the Third Corps, and connected up with the Second British Army Corps still farther south. All the forces of French and British cavalry arrived victorious at the River Lys, about the time when General Pulteney's men crossed the stream on their way to Lille. The Germans kindly left most of the bridges intact, held some behind a barricade, and others were undefended. When the Allies arrived, the Germans were even repairing some of the bridges they had first blown up.

The reason for this was soon seen. The Germans had received huge reinforcements, and were eager to attack. The enemy were already superior in number, almost two to one, when they were being driven back. And our airmen found that the roads to Lille and beyond Lille were packed with grey columns marching to the fighting-line, that ran along the River Lys and extended over the stream towards Ypres.

Sir John French could have strengthened all his thinly-held front against the coming attack. For on Monday, October 19th, the First British Army Corps, under Sir Douglas Haig, completed its detrainment and moved out towards Hazebrouck. He knew what a terrible strain he would put on his troops if he did not strengthen them, and enable them to place more men into the firing-line and more guns behind the trenches. Yet he left them as they were, each to face from three to four of the best fighting men in Germany. For he had decided to hold Ypres and the road northward to Calais. The Third Corps and the cavalry had to fight on unaided. Bringing up their heavy guns, the enemy took the offensive against the centre of our line held by the Third Corps. Our 12th Brigade was thrown back from the village of Le Gheir, after a terrific bombardment of their trenches. The retirement of the infantry endangered our cavalry forces holding a wood to the north by the hamlet of St. Ives. But Colonel Butler, of the Lancashire Fusiliers, led his battalion and the men of the King's Own Regiment

French's decision to hold Ypres

in a counter-charge, and recaptured the trenches at Le Gheir. They were troops of a Saxon army corps that fought us in this fierce and decisive action. They came on in multitudes with great determination, only to be swept away by our men, who used their magazine rifles as though they had been machine-guns. A single Saxon battalion left four hundred dead right in our lines, and after taking a hundred and thirty prisoners, the Lancashire Fusiliers and the King's Own Regiment released forty of our men who had been surrounded and captured.

Tribute to Saxon chivalry

They had been exceptionally well treated by the Saxons, and had even been placed in cellars to protect them from the shells of our own guns. This little incident was remarkable as being the first occasion on which captured British troops were treated in a chivalrous manner by German soldiers. All through the campaign the Saxons fought with uncommon bravery, and yet in as civilised a manner as modern warfare allows. They were the only race of Germans who showed on land some of the gallantry in fighting which Captain Müller, of the Emden, had displayed

ENTRANCE TO THE FRENCH FRONTIER VILLAGE OF BAILLEUL.
Bailleul was the scene of severe fighting, which eventually resulted in its occupation by the British on the morning of October 14th, 1914.

at sea. It is said that our troops and the Saxons afterwards used to have a truce at early morning when our bathers took a dip in the River Lys, and the Saxons would warn us not to bathe when they were about to be relieved by Prussians, who would shoot our men in the river.

All through October 23rd, 24th, and 25th the massed attacks against the Third British Corps were continued. In some places our infantry were forced from their trenches by large, high-explosive shells that blew up the earthworks. Le Gheir and St. Ives still formed the storm-centre, with the wood of Ploegsteert stretching between them. Terrible was the slaughter done by the point-blank magazine fire of our men, as the Germans advanced in masses singing "The Watch on the Rhine." When the broken formations fell back they were caught by a storm of shrapnel from our guns. If they tried to shelter in villages and farm-buildings, our high-explosive shells shattered their places of retreat, and when they tore out into the open, again the shrapnel caught them.

Some German troops began to surrender voluntarily, but the German commander was resolute to succeed.

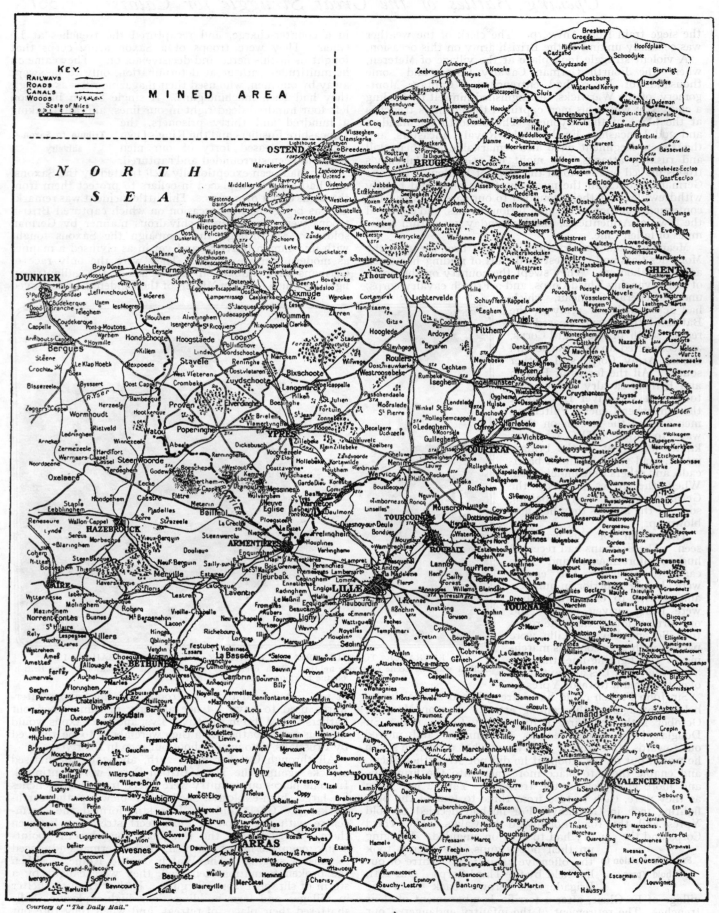

MAP OF THE YPRES-ARMENTIÈRES BATTLE AREA.

The above map illustrates the account of the fighting in the Ypres-Armentières battle area after the withdrawal of the British forces to the north from the Aisne in October, 1914. All the places mentioned in the despatch of Sir John French are indicated.

GERMAN INFANTRY RESERVES PASSING A FRENCH VILLAGE ON THEIR WAY TO THE TRENCHES

He increased his artillery from the siege train which had been used round Antwerp, and brought an unparalleled power and speed of shell fire on to our trenches. At midnight on October 29th our 19th Brigade was attacked by twelve battalions of German infantry. They took some of the trenches of the Middlesex, but the Argyll and Sutherland Highlanders were hurled **The old Gaelic fury** forward from our reserve, and with the **of battle** old Gaelic fury of battle the Scotsmen drove in and either bayoneted or captured every enemy in the recovered trenches. The next day the line of the 11th Brigade was broken at the danger-point of St. Ives. Here the Somerset Light Infantry, magnificently handled by Major Prowse, counter-attacked, and won back the position in a wild, fierce, desperate struggle against far more numerous foes, who had been heartened by their victory. It was house-to-house fighting at St. Ives, against machine-guns firing from windows, loopholes, and doorways, with thousands of riflemen holding trench and barricade. Yet ten hundred Somerset men took the village from them, and drove them back in disorder with our guns playing on them.

General Pulteney's troops held the right centre of the British line, and the Germans only needed to bend them back a few miles in order to force our wings at La Bassée and Ypres to retire. The Third Corps was hammered from end to end, and continually assailed at its weakest points. The attack went on night and day to the end of October. But

in spite of the odds against him, General Pulteney was so sure of his men that, instead of asking for support from the general reserve, he extended his front on October 31st by taking over some of the trenches of the 1st Cavalry Division.

The 1st, 2nd, and 3rd Cavalry Divisions were doing infantry work on the north bank of the River Lys, from St. Ives to Messines, and **Our cavalrymen in** then onward to Hollebeke, where they **the trenches** linked up with the defenders of Ypres. Their trenches had been hastily made on October 21st, after they were checked in trying to force the line of the Lys. For ten days the cavalry beat back continuous heavy infantry attacks made by Bavarian army corps, and in their shallow ditches they had to endure an unending rain of high-explosive shells and shrapnel bullets. Then, when they were weakened by the long and terrible bombardment and the succession of charges by massed infantry, two fresh Bavarian corps were brought up to assail them.

This was one of the most critical periods on the British front. The commander of the out-worn, hard-pressed cavalry divisions turned for help to Sir John French. But the British Commander-in-Chief had used all his reserves on other points of the line. A French reinforcement would arrive in forty-eight hours. Could the cavalry hold out till then? There were some un-tried British Territorial troops at hand—a battalion of the London Scottish. No one could tell how these unpro-fessional soldiers would

RAIDING THE CORN-RICKS.
German cavalrymen threshing corn from raided ricks in the rear of their fighting-line in Northern France.

BRITISH MARINES IN KHAKI.
Royal Marine Light Infantry, for the first time wearing khaki, marching through a French coast town on their way to the front. Inset : French reservists removing their belongings to make room for British Marines on their arrival in France.

perished round Messines than did Scotsmen. Thrown suddenly into a position of extreme difficulty, the London Scottish fought with splendid coolness and gallantry, and made memorable the historic event in the military annals of our Empire, when the first unit of our Territorial army went into action to assist the finest troops in the world—the professional soldiers of the British Isles.

This at least can be said of the London Scottish—they showed themselves, man for man, equal to the best conscript troops of Germany, who had been longer trained

fight. The quality of the British regular was a known thing that his commander could build on. The Territorial, with less training and less experience, was a doubtful element. But there he was, if he could be used.

So the London Scottish moved up into the firing-line to support the 4th Brigade in the beet-fields round the village of Messines. It was on Saturday, October 31st, that the Territorials came under the fire of howitzers, cannon, and machine-guns as they advanced to their position. The London Scottish held on till twilight fell and then entrenched. At nine o'clock on Saturday night the Bavarians began to charge them, and the mass attacks continued until two o'clock on Sunday morning. The Territorials threw the enemy back time after time by rapid rifle fire ; but in their last great effort the Bavarians, assaulting the front and left of the position in tremendous force, succeeded in getting round the flank of the regiment. Wild and terrible was the

Heroism of the London Scots scene, illumined by a blazing house which the Germans had set on fire. Companies in support and reserve made a bayonet charge against the Bavarians, who had outflanked the firing-line and were attacking our front men from the rear.

While fighting with bullet and bayonet was going on, and the Bavarians were working round both flanks with machine-guns and enveloping the regiment, the last reserve company came on with the bayonet. Again and again they charged, and kept the Bavarians from closing round, till at dawn the battalion retired under a cross-fire from machine-guns and rifles. They lost their position and suffered considerable punishment. But far more Bavarians

than they, and were equipped with more machine-guns. Sir John French was highly pleased with the result. Both the German and the British armies were exhausting their regular and first-line troops. The end of the Great War would depend on the quality of the new formations on both sides. We had found that the fresh German recruits were uncommonly brave and determined, but unskilful. The London Scottish, on the other hand, showed skill as well as courage. To them had fallen the high honour of showing the Germans what to expect from the millions of fresh volunteer troops that the British Empire would throw into the field at the proper time. They helped the hard-pressed cavalry divisions to hold the line during the critical period, and then a French army corps arrived, and the British dragoon guards, lancers, and hussars were able to retire and rest after twelve days' continual fighting in trench warfare against superior yet unsuccessful hordes of enemies.

Parade of the Landsturm before the Crown Prince of Bavaria during the German occupation of Lille.

Another view of the inspection by Prince Rupert of Bavaria of the German forces occupying Lille.

"MY BRAVE BAVARIANS": MEN THE KAISER HOPED WOULD "MEET THE ENGLISH JUST FOR ONCE."
The Kaiser's wish was gratified, but the result was hardly gratifying to him or to the Bavarians. The largest photograph shows a parade before
the heir to the Bavarian throne (marked with a x), which took place at Comines, near Lille, on January 7th, 1915.

German traction-engines drawing heavy guns through a cornfield, and

covered with foliage to screen hem from the Allies' airmen.

THE INCOMPARABLE DEFENCE OF YPRES.

Unparalleled Fortitude and Endurance of the British Troops—Last and Greatest Achievement of the Last Professional Army in Europe—Three Infantry Divisions Against Five Army Corps—Tremendous German Superiority in Guns—The Immortal 7th Division Prepares Its Heroic Stand—Sir John French Foiled at Menin—Resolves to Hold Ypres at All Costs, to Save Calais, and Prevent German Turning Movement—Instead of Retreating, the Outnumbered British Force Advances Northward—Roads Thronged with Fugitives Hindering British Movement—Terrific Counter-Attack by Germans—Marvellous Feat by 7th Division—Slaughter of Half-Trained German Masses—The First British Corps Again Attacks—" Take Ypres by November 1st "—The Grand Assault on the British Trenches—The 1st Division Gives Way—Marvellous Recovery of Our Retiring Troops—The Worcesters Save the Day—Germans' Last Effort of Despair—Repulse of the Prussian Guard.

IN the way of war our race has done some great things in the past. We have not, like the ancient Romans, made a national trade of slaughter, and pushed on from conquest to conquest, for generation after generation. At least, we have not done so since Joan of Arc broke our power in France, and brought to an end the terrible Hundred Years' War, with happy results for both French and English. Since that time we have had no really national struggle for dominion. Taking us as a whole, we became manufacturers and merchants, and not Napoleon himself was able to force us to transform ourselves, even in self-defence, into a military people. Our campaigns have been carried out by a comparatively small force of volunteer sailors and volunteer soldiers, culled, by their own choice of the profession of arms, from the most adventurous spirits in our population. Many and important are the victories they have won for us, but none of them saw such a battle as our Expeditionary Force conducted round Ypres.

Ypres is the most glorious name in our military history. It stands for a display of heroic endurance and fighting skill with which we have nothing to compare. There have been battles with more decisive results and of more dramatic interest. Agincourt was such a battle, when our little army, under Harry of Monmouth, wasted by disease, was crawling to

BRITISH CAVALRY LEADERS TAKING COUNSEL TOGETHER.
Generals Gough and Chetwode and Captain Howard-Vyse, photographed in the grounds of a chateau in France.

the coast to escape, but, being brought to bay, overthrew in a few hours all the chivalry of France, and conquered a kingdom. Agincourt was certainly a revelation of the bed-rock qualities of national character ; but it was not so great a thing as Ypres. Ypres is the immortal heritage of our race. It is an honour and an inspiration to be contemporaries and fellow-countrymen of the men who held the road to Calais against the power of the mightiest military State that ever existed in the world. When Prussia developed into a nation in arms, and thus became, in spite of her small population, a great conquering power like ancient Rome, she compelled the chief Powers of Continental Europe to follow her terrible example. But owing to our insular position and to the might of our Fleet, we were still able to rely upon a small professional Army. For had we been the aggressors in a struggle with Germany, all would have gone well, except for unforeseen accidents. Our plan of attack was to blockade Germany with our Fleet, and so stop her seaborne commerce and cripple her industries for twelve months or more, while we built up a national army, trained by our regular soldiers. These would have become practically all non-commissioned officers, and formed a finer backbone than the German Army possessed. Then the land campaign would have begun, with France and Russia entering as our Allies, and Germany already in a condition of something like bankruptcy.

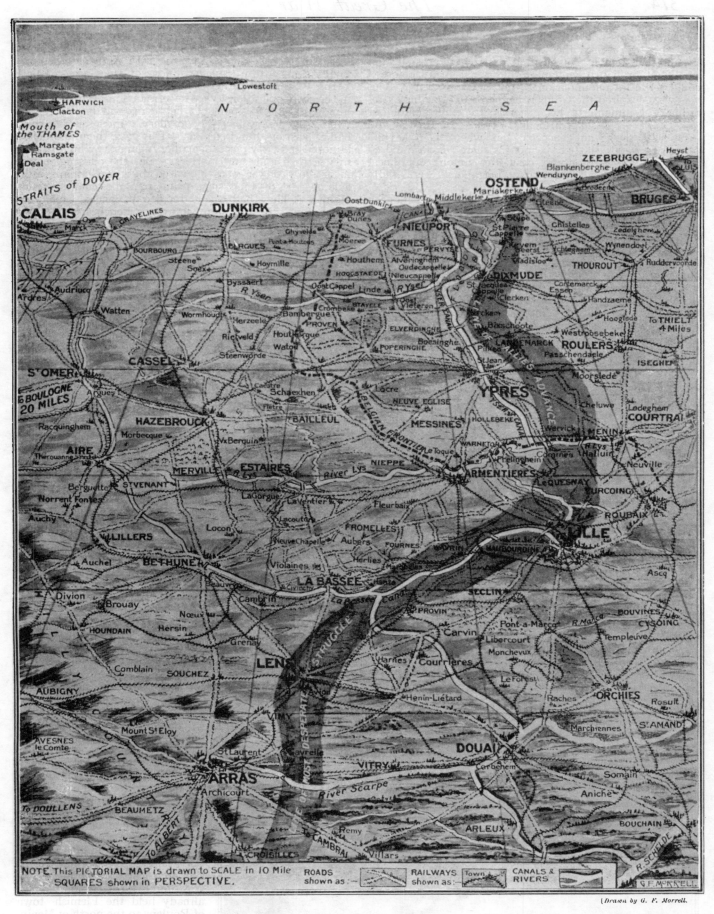

(Drawn by G. F. Morrell.)

DIAGRAMMATIC MAP ILLUSTRATING THE DESPERATE AND REPEATED ATTEMPTS OF THE
GERMANS TO BREAK THEIR WAY THROUGH TO THE FRENCH COAST.

The Germans know all this. It was one of the reasons why they engineered the war. They intended to cripple France and hem in Russia, and destroy, if possible, our small but brilliantly valuable professional Army before it could serve as a foundation to our national army. This was what inspired the German Emperor to issue his extraordinary command to his generals to exterminate our Expeditionary Force. In this he did **The finest soldier** not succeed, but when the war had **seen on earth** lasted six months there were a hundred thousand casualties among our finest troops. Nearly all our first battalions were sadly depleted.

From these facts the defence of Ypres acquires its deep historical interest. For a short period between the glorious renaissance of the French spirit and the creation of our national army, the British regular soldier, the finest soldier seen on earth, stood in the gap. He was about to be absorbed in a larger organisation, in which the entire flower of British manhood was ranked. But before he was thus lost in a wider system, the opportunity occurred for him to show to the full what the old-fashioned soldier by profession could do. And he dimmed every military achievement in history.

Small were the forces that our Commander-in-Chief threw across the path of the Germans. They consisted of the 1st and 2nd Divisions—forming the First Army Corps under Sir Douglas Haig—and the 7th Division and 3rd Cavalry Division, which formed part of the Fourth Army Corps under Sir Henry Rawlinson. Had all the regiments been at full strength, the infantry could have put 36,000 bayonets into the fighting - line, and the cavalry some 5,000 sabres. The actual numbers of the British troops were less than these, as the divisions were war-worn. But as in the course of the struggle they were at last assisted by some men from the Second Army Corps, we can put

their numbers at 40,000. Against them were brought up four German army corps—the 23rd, 25th, and 27th German Reserve Corps, and the 15th Active Corps—and finally some fifteen fresh battalions of the German Guard Corps. Landwehr troops were also employed against them in the early operations. Each German active corps had one hundred and forty-four light field-guns and howitzers, and twenty-five heavy pieces of artillery. Each reserve corps had at least one hundred guns. This gave them about four hundred and sixty pieces of artillery against two hundred and fifty British guns and mortars. But the odds against us in artillery power were increased by the Germans using a large part of their siege train from the country round Malines. They had about 120,000 bayonets, which was nearly four times the number in our trenches, and at the beginning of the struggle they seemed to have had even a greater preponderance in guns and howitzers. Their terrible superiority **Opening of an** in artillery, however, was afterwards **historic contest** reduced by our getting naval guns and other pieces of ordnance from England, until we in turn had a marked advantage in shell and shrapnel fire.

The memorable contest opened on October 16th, when Lieutenant-General Sir Henry Rawlinson withdrew his men from Ghent to Ypres, fighting a desperate rearguard action all the way. The 7th Division and 3rd Cavalry Division had to retire before superior numbers of the enemy across a difficult country, without any lines of communication, and without any base. They held on to position after position, and made a stand at Thielt and another at Roulers before they entrenched in front of the beautiful old-world Flemish city of Ypres, which the Germans had occupied for some weeks. The arrival of the British troops, with a French Territorial division supporting them, caused deep joy among the townspeople of Ypres.

But the Germans were in overpowering numbers in the immediate vicinity, and with a view to beating them off, the weary 7th Division, that had marched thirty miles in a night, moved out against the hostile forces holding the neighbouring town of Menin. This movement was directed by Sir John French, as part of the general British operations against the western wing of the German front. The enemy was pouring strong reinforcements from Courtrai towards the fighting-line round Lille and La Bassée. The little town of Menin on the Lys cut through the German line of communications, and the British commander wanted to throw all the enemy's operations into disorder by the sudden occupation of Menin.

A force of German cavalry already held the Flemish town of Roulers, to the north of Menin. There was a French Territorial division, just north of Ypres, supporting Sir Henry Rawlinson's

FRANCE'S FAMOUS COLONIAL FORCES—FIRST-CLASS FIGHTING MEN.
Algerian troops drawn up in the square at Algiers in readiness for embarkation to France.
Inset : A group of typical Turcos photographed at Arras.

Wounded Turco returning to camp. Inset: Another swarthy son of Africa bathing his wound by a wayside farm.

Taking aim. The photograph shows very clearly the peculiar head-dress and uniform of the Algerian soldier.

ALGERIAN SHARPSHOOTERS ON THE MARCH THROUGH A VILLAGE IN NORTHERN FRANCE.

In action after action the Turcos, as the French Algerian troops of our French allies are popularly called, lived up to their reputation as terrible fighters and sons of a fighting race. This was especially the case during the heavy fighting between the Marne and the Aisne. All through they gave evidence of the pride they felt in being privileged to take the field side by side with white soldiers in defence of the Tricolour.

BATTLING THROUGH RAIN AND MIST: DRIVING THE GERMANS FROM THEIR TRENCHES OUTSIDE BURNING YPRES.

A realistic picture of a night attack by British and Indian troops on the enemy's trenches outside Ypres, from which flames are seen rising in the background. Ypres was regarded by the Germans as " the key to Calais," and it was at this once beautiful old-world Flemish city that the Kaiser is reported to have intended to announce the annexation of the whole of Belgium.

TURNING THE GERMANS OUT OF THEIR COVER IN THE WOODS TO THE EAST OF YPRES.

The fierce fighting, of which the above pictorial record gives a vivid impression, took place between Zonnebeke and Zillebeke at the end of October, 1914. The weather was bitterly cold and the ground heavy with snow. The gallant British infantry attack was preceded by a heavy artillery fire, and many of the enemy were found killed and wounded by falling trees.

troops, and Sir John French desired his subordinate officer to make a bold and even daring attack on the important point of passage at Menin. In fact, the entire scheme of British operations depended on the capture of this town without any delay. The advance of the rest of the British army was intended to be based upon it. Sir John designed to press back the whole western wing of the German front by outflanking it a little to the north-east of Lille. And the Germans were **British movement against Menin** to be thrown into confusion round Lille, with the Allies driving] with all their might on a line running south from Armentières to Arras and down to the Aisne.

But it could not be done. In his historic despatch, Sir John French half hints that he would almost have risked the destruction of the 7th Division in a vehement attempt to continue the British offensive movement. It is clear that he was much disappointed by the way things fell out. Sir Henry Rawlinson's infantry force of less than 12,000 bayonets was weakened by very severe marching, and large hostile columns of at least 40,000 bayonets were coming against them from the east and north-east. Some of them, indeed, were already threatening to turn the British flank. In spite of this, the movement against Menin was attempted on October 19th, but while the Infantry Division was advancing to the south-east, the cavalry was attacked from Roulers, and compelled to give some ground All along the road to Menin the enemy had a menacing, flanking position, from which they launched attacks against our small force. The entire British advance came therefore suddenly to an end only a week after the Second Army Corps under Sir Horace Smith-Dorrien had started the operations.

On the day on which the 7th Division drew back along the Ypres-Menin road, the First Army Corps, under Sir Douglas Haig, arrived from the Aisne valley and concentrated between St. Omer and Hazebrouck. Sir John French had then to decide upon his new defensive plan of campaign. Both his Second and his Third Army Corps round La Bassée and Armentières were in great difficulties. They were largely outnumbered and heavily pressed, and the Second Army Corps especially was in danger of being knocked to pieces.

The sound and obvious thing was for the British commander to fight on a shorter front. He would have to withdraw from Ypres, leave the whole of Belgium in the enemy's occupation, and expose Calais to attack in order to concentrate and save his army. According to all the rules of strategy the Germans had won the first part of the game. Westward of the British position there were only two or three French cavalry divisions, some French militia troops, and the fatigued and wasted Belgian Army to stand against the large reinforcements which the Germans were still bringing up. It would take some weeks for a first-line French army to be railed up to strengthen the allied front between Lille and the sea.

The position was one that tested and searched the character of the man who had to arrive quickly at a decision in regard to it. Sir John French showed an incomparable tenacity and heroic strength of will. He left his Second and Third Army Corps, without further support, to maintain against terrible odds their positions west and north of Lille, and he threw the First Army Corps into Ypres, to join on with the 7th Infantry Division and 3rd Cavalry Division.

Instead of retreating before the superior numbers of the enemy, the small, astonishing British army was to strike up north through Belgium towards Bruges and attack! This is surely one of the most daring strokes of war in our history. Sir John French designed to attract to his troops the full fury of all the German armies engaged in making the wide turning movement by the coast. He wished to give the brave Belgians **Sir John French's** a brief breathing-space, in which they **daring design** might possibly be able to refit to some extent, and he also wished to take the full weight of the attack off the thin French line of Marines, cavalry, and militia troops which were co-operating with the Belgians along the Yser and in the country between Dixmude and Ypres.

The British Commander-in-Chief knew full well what he was doing. He was deliberately putting his men to the most tremendous ordeal in the annals of modern warfare. He was sacrificing them in tens of thousands, to prevent the Germans from reaching the Channel ports, and there establishing submarine bases for attacks upon our Fleet and our mercantile marine

At the same time he was also protecting Paris from the swift, downward swoop of the invading armies that would immediately follow a successful turning of the far-stretched allied front. What told especially in the critical hour of the great decision was Sir John French's knowledge of his troops. He had spent years in training them, and in continually giving additional weight and edge to their fine fighting qualities. He had tested them severely in the retreat from Mons to the Marne. He still did not know what their breaking-point was. He took it that such a point did not exist, and sent his men forth to hold out against the enemy, until they dropped asleep or dead, or were succoured at the last desperate, extreme hour.

"If you can force your heart and nerve and sinew
To serve your turn, long after they are gone,
And still hold on, when there is nothing in you
Except the will which says to them 'Hold on!'"—

then, said Sir John French, in effect, you are the men for me, and I am the commander for you ; together we must achieve the impossible. But not possessing Napoleon's gift of rhetoric, and being inapt to parade his emotions, the British Field-Marshal did not put it that way.

The scheme was for the heroic 7th Division to hold the country east of Ypres at Zonnebeke, and beat off the German forces coming from Roulers and Menin, while the First Army Corps advanced towards Thourout, far in the north, threatening Bruges and Ostend. The 3rd Cavalry Division, under General Byng, formed the right wing of the advancing force, and a body of French cavalry formed its left wing. The Belgian Army, though in the last stage of exhaustion after its long and difficult retreat, gallantly entrenched along the Yser from Nieuport to Dixmude, to prevent the British striking force of 24,000 bayonets from being turned on the left flank. A force of Breton Marines held Dixmude. **Advantages of surprise attack lost**

The advance began at dawn, on Tuesday, October 20th, while the enemy gathered in the Forest of Houthulst, some eight miles north of Ypres. It was most difficult for our troops to make their way towards the enemy, and all the advantages of a surprise attack were lost owing to the condition of the roads. They were blocked and packed by multitudes of peasants and townsfolk of Flanders, fleeing from the cruel invading Germans. Close behind the fugitives were two German army corps, which threw out detachments across the road to Thourout, and entrenched quite close to Ypres. Our men carried the villages of Poelcappelle and Passchendaele at the point of the bayonet, and then, still

LONDON SCOTTISH RESTING AT A WAYSIDE STATION A FEW DAYS BEFORE THEIR FAMOUS CHARGE.
A particularly happy camera-picture of the London Scots enjoying an impromptu meal and a smoke at a railway station in France. Inset : London Scots taking advantage of an opportunity for smartening up some of their belongings.

impeded by the incessant throng of fugitives on all the roads and paths, Sir Douglas Haig urged his army corps northward. And on it went, fighting at every farmhouse, opposed at every dyke and stream, but steadily pressing back the enemy all along the line of attack.

The Germans flung themselves on our thin, half-invisible firing-line, that went forward in rush after rush over the green, low-lying, fenlike plain. From the Forest of Houthulst on the left and Roulers town on the right large forces of the enemy tried to break and scatter or, at least, to hold up the British advance. But the khaki wave rippled onward, with another wave of the same colour far behind it, to allow German shells and bullets, that missed their first mark, a wide space in which to fall harmlessly. For our troops were so self-reliant and brought such a terrible power of fire against the enemy that their support and reserve companies could be kept at a remarkable distance from the leading line.

AFTER THEIR "BAPTISM OF FIRE!" A REMARKABLE SERIES OF CAMERA RECORDS

The all-night battle in which the London Scottish took part on October 31st-November 1st, 1914, to the south of Ypres, was an event in which for the first time a complete unit of our Territorial Army fought alongside its sister units of the Regulars. Our photographs show groups of the hardy Scots after their "baptism of fire," which lasted from 9 p.m. till 2 a.m. They inflicted far more damage on the enemy than they received.

GENERAL GOUGH AT HIS HEADQUARTERS IN FRANCE.

This popular cavalry commander (in the centre of the photograph) is seen chatting with two members of his staff during a lull in the fighting along the Franco-Belgian frontier. General Gough was specially mentioned in Sir John French's despatches and promoted major-general for distinguished service.

The result was that they offered very little target, and a bullet that failed to hit a man in the firing-line did not land among the supports.

It was all a matter of marksmanship and strength of character With the magazine rifle, taking ten cartridges in the magazine and one in the breech, men trained to rapid, steady, deadly fire, could form quite a thin line that was harder to break than the old-fashioned British square, by reason of its fire-power If they took their job in a cool, easy, resolute way, the thin line could stop a charge of massed formations. For our well-trained regular infantryman could bring down at least a dozen enemies in one minute. His magazine held five more cartridges than did the German rifle, and—what is of more importance—the British soldier never fired wildly. His eye was on a **Terrible swiftness of** mark every time he pressed a trigger, **British fire** and the terrible swiftness with which he works the trigger, when giving a dense front of Germans rapid fire, was calculated to stagger and appal anything human.

The British advance continued until about two o'clock in the afternoon. Then, however, the French cavalry had to give ground to the Germans, who were attacking them on our left, and withdraw over the Ypres Canal. This left the flank of our First Army Corps exposed, and our troops entrenched themselves on the ground they had won. Their line ran from the village of Bixschoote through Langemarck to Zonnebeke on the Roulers road. Here the 7th Division was being very heavily attacked. Its

brave 22nd Infantry Brigade was hanging on to the outskirts of the village, with the German troops creeping round it. The 7th Cavalry Brigade was sent forward to help the infantry, and our men managed to cling on to the position.

All down the eastern line of defences protecting Ypres the struggle on the afternoon of October 21st was of a furious intensity. The French cavalry division was caught by a heavy shell fire at Poelcappelle, which caused it to withdraw, and the British line moved back with it. Farther down the front, by the wooded ridge of Zandvoorde, three miles from the Lys River, our 2nd Cavalry Division had a terrible time, and a gap was made on its left by an over-whelming German attack. But the 6th Cavalry Brigade swept out and filled this break in the line, and occupied the canal crossings to the north-west of Messines, linking on with the trenches of the Third British Army Corps.

All the while the heroic 7th Division was being shelled and charged, hammered by howitzers, and ripped by massed rifle fire. The front they held measured, from flank to flank, some eight miles. The normal garrison to such a front would not have been less than five thousand men to the mile, according to our own Staff teaching, and considerably over that number, according to foreign tactics of defence. Yet the Division, had it put every possible bayonet into the trenches, could only have mustered fifteen hundred to the mile. Day by day this number shrank, under the overpowering artillery of the enemy and the incessant charges of hostile infantry. The opposing troops numbered at the beginning over 75,000 men, and these are said to have swelled at last to five army corps of 200,000 troops.

The fight went on without ceasing, night and day, for nearly nineteen days. A captured Ger- **Heroism of our** man officer declared that his General **7th Division** Staff was firmly convinced that the stubbornly-held British trenches were occupied by at least two army corps of 80,000 troops. In the end there was only the four-hundredth part of this supposed force fronting the enemy! For our twelve thousand infantrymen were blown to pieces by the great shells, worn out by want of sleep, and struck by shrapnel, until there were only forty-four officers and 2,336 men left. Yet until they were relieved and withdrew to rest and refit, they held out against the enemy.

In the 1870 campaign, no regiment of either French or German troops stood up victoriously under the loss of half its effectives. In the American Civil War only seven Confederate and two Federal battalions retained a fighting cohesion after five hundred men had fallen. Our 7th Division lost four-fifths of its men and yet held on. For days no one could approach them in sunlight, except by the communicating trenches. Then many of these trenches were wrecked by the German 6 in. shells, and the food and

INDIANS CARRYING A GERMAN POSITION: "IT WAS A GLORIOUS FIGHT."

Subadar Wasan Singh, of the 58th (Indian) Rifles, described to a Press representative how his regiment had their first encounter with the Germans early in November, 1914. "We had," he said, "been in the trenches all night, and at dawn we charged. Our men were delighted to get into the fighting at last." The position they were ordered to attack was on a farm, and the force of the enemy occupying it was a strong one. "It was a glorious fight while it lasted," declared the subadar; "but soon there were no Germans left, and some of our men won Paradise."

BRITISH ASSAULT ON FORTIFIED HOUSES IN A VILLAGE NEAR YPRES.

In the numerous and closely contiguous villages in the neighbourhood of Ypres, house-to-house and hand-to-hand fighting of the most desperate and deadly character was of almost daily occurrence during the early stages of the German effort to break through to the French coast. In addition to throwing up trenches outside the villages, the enemy occupied the houses and turned them into ma[...] forts, placing machine-guns in the centre of rooms so that they could co[...] an approach through a window. As the barricades were captured they [...] turned to use by the captors; and the same thing occurred when houses were [...]

AN EVER-MEMORABLE HALLOWE'EN NIGHT: THE LONDON SCOTTISH CHARGE AT MESSINES.

Every October 31st Hallowe'en is observed with the customary ceremonies in the headquarters of the London Scottish. On the Hallowe'en of 1914, the 1st Battalion of the regiment passed so gallantly through an ordeal of fire as to win the special thanks of Sir John French. After advancing under heavy fire to the support of our cavalry in the trenches at Messines, they withstood and re[...] a series of massed attacks by the Bavarians from 9 p.m. till 2 a.m. on the fol[...] morning, fighting with splendid coolness and great gallantry. As they prepar[...] their great charge the word was passed, "Remember you are Scottish."

FRENCH HEROISM IN THE ARGONNE: WHAT "A SLIGHT ADVANCE" IMPLIES.

e Argonne forms an important section of the French frontier defences, and d largely in the accounts of the fighting right from the beginning of the t War. The village of Louppy-le-Chateau, the scene of the encounter illus- d above, was alternately occupied by the Germans and the French, and the church tower and many of the houses were in ruins from bombardment and fire before the place was definitely held by our gallant allies. Our artist has supplied a vivid picture of what lies behind the laconic phrase, met with so often in the official French communiqués, " We have advanced slightly in the Argonne."

SETTLING AN OLD SCORE: BENGAL LANCERS' FIRST BRUSH WITH THE ENEMY.

ing the Boxer trouble of 1900 the Germans treated the Indian troops fighting eir side with undisguised contempt. In October, 1914, when our brave troops were brought into the fighting-line in the vicinity of Ypres, the npt was repaid with interest. The incident illustrated in the above stirring picture took place when the enemy were coming up in overwhelming force on what they thought was a weak part of the British line. The Bengal Lancers, who had arrived the day before, suddenly charged, and " swept into the Germans like a whirlwind." The Teutons broke and ran, being pursued for a mile.

BRITISH TRANSPORT TRAIN MAKING ITS WAY UNDER HEAVY SHELL FIRE ALONG THE SNOW-BOUND YPRES ROADS.

The above stirring picture illustrates what frequently happened behind the firing-line on one of those special note stood out from the background of artillery bombardment. This bombardment, directed days which were officially described as "uneventful"—that is to say when no active operations of any at the roads as well as the trenches, continued day and night with varying intensity.

ammunition supplies had to be carried across the fire-swept zone in the darkness of night. As the aim of the enemy was to wear down the physical strength of our men, they tried to prevent anybody in the 7th Division from getting any sleep. The scream and thunder of the high-explosive shells did not produce this result, unless they burst within the trenches. For our men became dead drowsy, and when their turn came for a rest they dropped into as deep a slumber in the holes they made beneath the parapets that the trump of doom could not awaken them. Nothing but the urgent need of every rifle to repel a massed infantry attack could bring them to their feet. So from dusk to dawn the German commander, General von Deimling, interrupted the eternal bombardment, and either tried to break through our lines, or made a sufficient feint to bring all our men to their feet.

This power of being able to wear down an enemy, until he is well-nigh crazy and helpless from sleeplessness and physical exhaustion, constitutes the chief advantage of an attacking force that largely outnumbers its opponents. The attackers can be divided into three or four sections. Each has a spell of hard work in the firing-line, in which it keeps the defenders at the utmost tension. Then it retires for sleep and refreshment, and returns again the next day with renewed vigour, while the defending force has been kept incessantly at work for twenty-four hours. Multiply twenty-four by nineteen, and add to the result the fatigues of fighting and long night marches which our Immortal Division had already undergone. The result is absolutely staggering. As a feat of endurance and resistance it is sublime. The defence was made in the open air, in rainy autumnal weather, with the narrow trenches draining the wet fields and giving a watery foothold to our men. Even Sir John French did not expect to expose his men to such an ordeal.

Kaiser's colossal sacrifice of men The German commander upset the plan of the Allies by bringing up army corps of half-trained troops, and launching them at the British trenches. Neither Sir John French, nor General Foch, who was directing the strategy on the northern front, had imagined that the new German formations would be thrown on to the field. The Great German Staff was eating its wheat green, instead of waiting for it to ripen. The new recruits were not yet fit to battle, especially under the terrible conditions of modern warfare, and many of the new officers also showed a lack of training and faults in leading. But they were all sacrificed in the desperate attempt made by the Kaiser Wilhelm in person to retrieve the defeat on the Marne by a victorious turning movement on the coast.

On October 23rd the first of the new German formations came on in masses, chanting patriotic songs, and marching to death with marvellous bravery. Our men reserved their fire till the close-packed multitudes were within a

MUSIC AND MARS: AN INCIDENT NEAR YPRES.

Finding in a shell-battered house a grand piano and a store of classical music, a British officer imparted his discovery to a French Alpine Chasseur, and though the latter had to be back in the trenches within an hour, the two played a duet together. Meanwhile the Frenchman's comrades stole into the room quietly one by one, and furnished an appreciative audience. The incident took place near Ypres, and the piece played is stated to have been Schubert's "Unfinished Symphony."

hundred—or even fifty—yards of the trench. Then they slaughtered them with point-blank rapid magazine shooting. Five times the unskilled but heroic recruits charged in overpowering numbers. But numbers did not matter. Each time our superbly-trained regular soldiers waited till the enemy advanced to very close range, and then gave them the mad minute of rapid fire, with British machine-guns rattling amid the fierce splutter of the rifles.

Each assault was easily beaten back. As the Germans broke, officers in our observation trenches telephoned to our batteries, and our artillerymen showered shrapnel upon the fleeing multitudes. A single British battery on this day of slaughter used, it is reckoned, eighteen hundred rounds of ammunition on the large, clear targets made by the masses of hostile troops.

Earlier in the same day some of the **British advance towards Pilkem** regiments of the First British Army Corps, holding the villages north of Ypres, advanced towards Pilkem. Here the enemy had succeeded in penetrating some trenches held by the Cameron Highlanders ; and to the 2nd Infantry Brigade, less the Royal Sussex Regiment, left in charge of another position, was set the task of recapturing the lost ground. Under General Bulfin, the 1st Loyal North Lancashire Regiment,

HEROISM OF THE 2ND WORCESTERS NEAR YPRES: RECAPTURE OF THE CHATEAU AND VILLAGE OF GHELUVELT.

Sir John French, who was at Hooge on the momentous October 31st, 1914, described the rally of our 1st Division and the recapture of the village of Gheluvelt as "fraught with momentous consequences. If," he added, " any one unit can be singled out for especial praise, it is the Worcesters." Gheluvelt commanded the approach to Ypres. The Worcesters lost three officers and one hundred and thirty men.

MESSINES (ABOUT MIDWAY BETWEEN YPRES AND ARMENTIERES): PHOTOGRAPH TAKEN DURING THE HEAVY
FIGHTING IN OCTOBER, 1914.

with the Northamptonshire Regiment and the 2nd King's Royal Rifle Corps, swept out to attack. They were countered by a much larger force of Germans, but instead of giving ground, they pressed on all the day in a fierce, swaying, stubborn, terrible fight. Major Aubrey Carter led the North Lancashire battalion in the charge that won the day. Under a heavy shell bombardment and rifle volleys, the Lancashire lads steadily advanced close up to the enemy's trenches, beating down the hostile rifle fire by their own rapid and deadly marksmanship, with their machine-guns brought up into the firing-line to increase their fire effect. Major H. G. Powell, of the same Lancashire regiment, had retired from active service ten years before, and had rejoined his troops on the Aisne. Spraining his foot in the advance, he led his part of the battalion, with a chair in one hand and a stick in the other. Then he sat down before the enemy's trenches, in a storm of shells and bullets, and directed the operations from his chair until he was seriously wounded. Even then he would not leave, but some friends gave him no choice in the matter, and carried him off the field.

In the meantime the lads of the Red Rose fixed their bayonets, and, as evening fell, they carried the trenches by storm and captured over six hundred prisoners. The Northamptons and the King's Rifles at the same time followed them and helped to win the victory. The Third Infantry Brigade also distinguished itself at Langemarck, two miles to the north-west of Pilkem. When night fell there were fifteen hundred dead foes lying in front of their trenches. Forty thousand men had attacked them, and only ten thousand of these finished the day's fighting unhurt, according to a letter afterwards found upon a captured German officer.

The gallant 7th reinforced Thus ended one of the most terrible periods in the long heroic defence of Ypres. For in the evening a division of the Ninth French Army Corps came into the town, and took over part of the line held by our 2nd Division. This division then moved eastward, and helped the sorely-pressed 7th Division. The next night our eastward trenches, against which the enemy was directing his fiercest, heaviest attacks, were further strengthened by the arrival of the 1st Division to reinforce the gallant 7th. The defence of the villages won to the north of Ypres was taken over by French Territorial troops, and our First, Second, and Third Infantry Brigades were concentrated in the woods around Zillebeke.

In spite of the tremendous forces gathering against him, Sir John French was not inclined to stand wholly upon the defence. He was especially anxious to draw the German attacks from the new French line north of Ypres, where French Territorials, oldish men of the militia class, with splendid courage, but less spring and experience than first-line troops, were filling the gap till the rest of the Ninth French Army Corps arrived. So having strengthened his lines by a concentration of troops, the British commander ordered the 2nd Division of Sir Douglas Haig's corps to advance against the enemy along the road to Roulers.

It was on Sunday, October 25th, that the Guards' Brigade, under Lord Cavan, with the other brigades of the 2nd Division, supported on their left by the Ninth French Corps and on their right by the battered but defiant 7th Division, made its sudden, amazing, and successful advance. **General Deimling taken unawares** General von Deimling was not prepared for a move of this sort, in which some 10,000 British infantry-men dared anything from two to three Bavarian army corps. Two of his field-guns fell into the hands of our troops, and the French, fighting with equal dash and mortal skill, captured six German machine-guns. With armoured motor-cars, equipped with quick-firers, the 2nd Division stormed through hamlets and farms, the defending detachments in the loopholed buildings being blown out and shattered by shell fire from the armoured cars and the light field batteries.

This astonishing leaping attack by the outnumbered, entrenched defenders of Ypres had the effect which Sir John French intended. The Duke of Würtemberg, conducting the German operations along the Yser against the Belgian and French forces, General von Deimling attacking Ypres, General von Fabeck co-operating with him, and Rupert, the Crown Prince of Bavaria, assailing the British troops round Lille, had a meeting. They decided that the three British divisions east of Ypres were a menace that must be met by an overpowering concentration of force.

As we have seen, our 7th Division was supposed to be four times the strength it was, and our other two divisions, with their assistant forces of entrenched cavalry, were similarly overestimated. The successful sortie towards Roulers, therefore, made Deimling anxious about his power even to retain our men. He asked for another army corps. The Fifteenth Corps of first-line troops was sent to him, and large bodies of the 150,000 Würtembergers and other corps which had been assailing the Belgian-French lines

387

BRITISH ENCAMPMENT IN
NORTHERN FRANCE.

BRITISH LANCERS GOING INTO ACTION ACROSS AN OPEN STRETCH OF
COUNTRY "SOMEWHERE IN NORTHERN FRANCE."

were moved eastward against Ypres. At the same time Sir John French motored to the headquarters of the First British Army Corps at Hooge, just east of Ypres, to examine into the conditions of the Immortal Division—the 7th.

Ever since its hasty embarkation at Ostend, and its march in aid of the Belgian Army at Antwerp, this incomplete half of the Fourth British Army Corps had fought greatly and suffered heavily. It was growing too weak to act as a separate army. So Sir John French arranged to merge it for a while in Sir Douglas Haig's corps, and place it under his command with the 3rd Cavalry Division, and Sir Henry Rawlinson returned to England to look after the mobilisation of his 8th Division.

Sir Douglas Haig then redistributed his forces. The 7th Division extended from the chateau near Zandvoorde to the Menin road ; here it linked on with the 1st Division, whose trenches ran towards Reytel village, and the 2nd Division continued the British lines towards Zonnebeke. The Ninth French Corps, under General d'Urbal, held the line north of Ypres, and prolonged it towards Dixmude, where the Breton Marines were fighting. Southwards, from Ypres to the Lys, our cavalry fought and slept for weeks in ditches amid beetfields and along the canal, and by the river the Third British Army Corps stood against a host of Bavarians.

Weak spot in allied front Ypres itself formed the weak spot in the allied front. It was one of the loveliest and most romantic cities on earth, fallen asleep in the Middle Ages in a forgotten nook in the flat, rich, marshy plain of Flanders. Its magnificent Cloth Hall, built by its proud warrior weavers in the days when the looms of Ypres were what the mills of Manchester now are, was a monument of noblest beauty and incomparable value. Its glorious thirteenth-century cathedral, its belfry, and thick cluster of picturesque, ancient houses made it one of the rare, exquisite, perfect cities of art in Europe. It was an enchanted place, with just a faint stir of life to give its beauty vividness and eternal significance.

The German Emperor had fixed upon Ypres as the historic scene of his proclamation of the complete conquest

388

of Belgium. With Furnes, by the coast, it was the last Belgian town to escape the invaders, and as in its occupation by German troops the defeat of the British Expeditionary Force would be involved, the Kaiser Wilhelm was obsessed by the desire to conquer it. Violent, blinding passion and well-calculated policy were strangely mingled in the Imperial determination in regard to Ypres. From the strict, strategical point, of view, the breaking of the allied line at La Bassée or even farther south, was preferable, and the concentration of troops should have taken place there. For in the case of success a greater length of the northern Franco-British Belgian line would be cut and caught between the German point of advance and the seacoast.

On the other hand, the British **" For the sake of** position round Ypres was peculiarly **Belgium "** inviting to the attackers. It formed a salient—that is to say, a wedge exposed to cross-fire from the surrounding German batteries on the north, the east, and south-east. Thus it was the weakest spot in the whole of the allied front. It was designed by the British commander to engage most of the attention of the German Chief of Staff. It jutted out perilously to both its defenders and attackers. It menaced an advance towards Bruges, shutting the Germans from the coast, and perhaps piercing their flank ; it exposed the troops that held it to an assault from three sides.

By giving up Ypres, and strengthening and shortening his lines, Sir John French would have been in a stronger position of resistance. But he knew the mind of the man with whom he had chiefly to deal. He desired, as a matter of honour, to hold Ypres for the sake of Belgium, and as a matter of policy to prevent the intended proclamation of the conquest of the country of the heroic upholders of international treaties. But more than this, he flaunted Ypres in the face of the German Emperor as a bull-fighter flaunts a red flag in the face of the bull he is infuriating and distracting. Sir John French was of Irish origin. Ypres, so to speak, was the tail of his coat ; he daringly trailed it close to his enemy. By leading the Germans to concentrate against him at this point he was, with subtle skill, easing the pressure against his weakened Second Army at La Bassée and against the sorely-pressed Belgian Army on the coast. Ypres, with its salient defences, was a study in the mastery of warfare. Its very weakness was so arranged as to sway the mind of the enemy, and compel him to act in a given direction.

And in this given direction the German commander acted. He selected the Menin road as his main path of assault,

TWO ASPECTS OF THE ROUT OF THE PRUSSIAN GUARD BY THE BRITISH AT ZONNEBEKE.

The Prussian Guard were brought up in a supreme effort to break through Ypres. How the attack, prepared with great secrecy, was met is shown in the top picture. The Prussian advance, thrown into relief by an airship searchlight, was met with deadly musketry fire from the British, the first rank lying down, the next kneeling, and the men in the rear firing from a standing position. Then came a series of glorious British bayonet charges across the plain. The redoubtable Prussian Guard—to the number of about 15,000—were utterly routed, the confusion in their ranks before they broke and fled being graphically shown in our lower illustration and at dawn on Thursday, October 29th, the grand attack on Ypres opened. Naturally, Sir John French expected it. Even if he had not taken some part in arranging the affair, two German telegraphic messages, said to have been tapped by our operators, would have told him what was about to happen. The first ran: "Take Ypres by November 1st." The second was: "More men now, and we have them!" The second message, moreover, was well founded. It was touch-and-go at the time with the fate of Ypres and with the fortunes of the British Expeditionary Force. Happily, we touched and the Germans went—backwards!

The Twenty-fourth Army Corps from Lille, reinforced by the whole of the Fifteenth Active German Corps, swung against the British trenches east of Gheluvelt. The fighting was terrific, for instead of standing on the defensive, Sir Douglas Haig counter-attacked with all his forces. The 7th Division especially swept out of its trenches towards Kruiseik Hill, about three miles south-east of Gheluvelt. This hill had formed part of the British front, but the enemy had carried it the day before. Now the heroic 7th Division, supported by the 6th Cavalry Brigade, which was in turn assisted by covering fire from the trenches of the 7th Cavalry Brigade, came out suddenly against its host of foes.

All the morning the battlefield was a melée of advancing and receding infantry forces, with the British field-guns pushing in as close as possible to shrapnel the charging masses of field-grey figures. For our **A soldiers' battle** outnumbered forces it was a soldiers' battle, in which the spirit, initiative, and skill of men and company officers chiefly counted. The slaughter they did was terrible, especially against the army corps which had come from Lille. By two o'clock that Thursday afternoon the Germans began to give ground; and when night fell Kruiseik Hill had been recaptured, with the help

ENCAMPMENT OF THE 12TH LANCERS AT KEMMEL CHATEAU.
The men of "the Supple 12th," a regimental sobriquet won by dash and resource at Salamanca, are seen above in a riverside meadow at Kemmel Chateau, south-west of Ypres. The colonel (Lieut-Colonel F. Wormald) and a number of his officers and men were specially mentioned in Sir John French's despatch of October 8th, 1914. Our smaller photograph shows an Indian hospital transport on the march.

COLONEL GORDON WILSON,
Royal Horse Guards. (Killed.)

CAPTAIN LORD RICHARD WELLESLEY,
Grenadier Guards. (Killed.)

CAPTAIN CHARLES V. FOX,
2nd Scots Guards.

of the 1st Brigade who re-established most of the line north of the Menin road. It was a day of heroes, but the leader of them all was Captain Charles V. Fox, of the 2nd Scots Guards. By an extraordinary feat at Kruiseik Hill he captured two hundred German troops with five of their officers. A splendid sportsman, he was already famous as a sculler and boxer; he had won the Diamond Sculls at Henley, and had become one of the leading middle-weight boxers in the Army. He was afterwards wounded and taken prisoner in another fierce fight.

A day of heroes

The loss of Kruiseik Hill only made the German commander more desperately resolved to carry out the orders of his Emperor, and to enter Ypres by the end of the month. In the night he again concentrated his troops, selecting a new point of attack at Zandvoorde Ridge, a little to the south of Kruiseik. The ridge was held by the 7th Cavalry Brigade under a very brilliant officer, Brigadier-General Kavanagh. But the enemy got the range of the trenches exactly and massed their howitzer fire upon it at daybreak on Friday, October 30th, and the 6 in. shells completely blew in most of the earthworks. The cavalry withdrew to the next bridge towards Ypres-Klein Zillebeke. Their withdrawal exposed the right of the 7th Division, and this therefore had to bend back also

towards the town. The situation then became critical, for the Germans had succeeded in making a deep dent in our lines and were able to bring their guns forward and to get wider cross-fire effects against the salient formed by our defences.

All day they continued to press the advantage they had won, but the Scots Greys and the 4th Hussars were moved up as a reserve force, and with their aid the 6th Cavalry Brigade made a grand defence and prevented the enemy from driving home his attack. In the night both sides prepared for the day of decision. The cavalry trenches on the southern flank were taken over by the Guards' Brigade, under Lord Cavan, and the 9th French Corps sent three battalions and a cavalry brigade to further strengthen the position. The Germans had almost reached the canal running from Ypres to the Lys, and forming the line of communications of our First Army Corps. The trenches at Gheluvelt, stretching towards the canal, were the very vitals of the British force, and the men there were ordered to hold the line at all costs.

Vitals of the British force

General von Deimling withdrew his battered Twenty-fourth Corps, and brought up the Fifteenth Corps, the 2nd Bavarians, and the Thirteenth Corps. To his troops he issued an order, stating that they had been entrusted with the task of breaking through the British lines to

BRIG.-GENERAL KAVANAGH,
Commanding 7th Cavalry Brigade.

BRIG.-GENERAL EARL OF CAVAN,
Commanding the Guards' Brigade.

BRIG.-GENERAL LANDON,
Temporary Commander 1st Division.

A GERMAN "CONSOLATION PICTURE": HEADLONG FLIGHT OF SERBS BEFORE VICTORIOUS AUSTRIANS.

The above picture, from a German paper, purports to represent the "flight" of the Serbs in November, 1914. As a matter of fact, they executed an orderly retirement into the interior before an enormously superior force of Austrians, who soon afterwards suffered an ignoble defeat.

Ypres, and that the Kaiser himself considered that on the success of their attempt depended the victorious issue of the war.

The contest began with several attacks and counter-attacks on Saturday morning along the road from Ypres to Menin. The village of Gheluvelt was situated on this road, at an almost equal distance from both towns. It was held by the 1st Division, whose trenches linked southward with the 7th Division. The Germans massed their guns and howitzers against our worn and shattered Immortal Division. Then they launched the larger part of their force of 72,000 bayonets against our 1st and 3rd Infantry Brigades, which had originally numbered only 8,000 bayonets, but were now desperately diminished by the wear of battle.

A chapter of disasters

Under the tremendous weight of the attack our line broke, and Gheluvelt was captured by the Germans. Then followed a chapter of disasters to our outworn and overpressed troops. The retreat of the 1st Division exposed the Royal Scots Fusiliers, who were holding some of the trenches of the 7th Division. The Scotsmen were cut off and surrounded, and at the same time the German commander massed one of his army corps against the right wing of the weakened 7th Division. The German guns were brought rapidly closer to Ypres, bombarding the line of retreat of our broken and reeling forces. The headquarters of the 1st and 2nd Divisions were shelled; Major-General Lomax, directing the difficult movements of his 1st Division in its hour of peril, was wounded, and the force of the explosion rendered the General commanding the 2nd Division unconscious. Three Staff officers were killed and three wounded. The Germans had succeeded in striking down the directing minds of the troops they had defeated.

It was a complete catastrophe. Sir John French and Sir Douglas Haig watched the disaster from the village of Hooge, the next village on the Menin road after the lost position of Gheluvelt. They could see our men retiring just a mile in front of them. The British Field-Marshal

had even more to think of than the scene of disaster before him. For just to the south of Ypres at Hollebeke, on the other side of the canal, General Allenby's Cavalry Corps was losing its trenches, and a heavy column of Bavarian infantry was pressing hard upon Messines. The Field-Marshal could give none of his generals any reinforcement.

General Landon, commanding the 3rd Infantry Brigade, took over the direction of the 1st Division. He moved it back, with the victorious enemy coming on against him in great strength. Then, at a wooded bend of the road, by one of those glorious resurgences of invincible spirit, the Division rallied, while an enfilading fire checked the enemy's advance along the road. The left of the 1st Division and the right of the 2nd combined and flung themselves against the right flank of the advancing German line. Admirably supported by the 42nd Brigade of Royal Field Artillery, the 2nd Worcestershire Regiment headed one of the grandest bayonet charges in our history and, in a raging hand-to-hand fight, recaptured the village of Gheluvelt. Profiting by this magnificent recovery, the left of the 7th Division also swung back almost to its original line. By half-past two on Saturday afternoon the connection between the 1st and 7th Divisions was re-established. This released the 6th Cavalry Brigade, which had been held in reserve for action on the Menin road. Two of its regiments were at once sent to clear the woods on the south-west, where strong parties of the enemy had penetrated between the 7th Division and the 2nd Brigade. The cavalrymen went to their job with a will, some of them mounted and some of them on foot. Taking the enemy by surprise, they slew large numbers of them by a movement as rapid as it was successful, and then, driving the rest of the Germans before them, they closed the last gap in our lines.

Our cavalry clear the woods

The great Battle of Gheluvelt thus ended in a general German defeat. Kaiser Wilhelm II. was unable to enter Ypres and proclaim the conquest of Belgium on the day he had appointed, and Calais receded as far into the distance as Paris had done after the Battle of the Marne. General von Deimling excused his defeat on the ground of the comparatively small number of his troops. The poor man had only three army corps against our wasted three divisions, reduced to less than 20,000 bayonets. On November 2nd he was given an additional army corps—the Twenty-seventh. So, including the Twenty-fourth Army Corps, shattered and drawn back to Lille, and the Fifteenth and Bavarian Thirteenth, and the Second, with other troops besides, General von Deimling was not so greatly outnumbered as he imagined. We have already learnt, from a captive German officer, that the trenches of our 7th Division were reckoned by the enemy to be held by two British army corps, and no doubt it was by extending this method of calculation that the German commander obtained a somewhat inaccurate idea of the troops opposed to him.

All this greatly helped our scanty, fatigued, and over-laden men. The enemy began to fear them just when they were at their weakest. And for more than a week after the failure of the grand general attack on Gheluvelt the German infantry kept our forces busily employed, but without trying again to hack their way through our lines. On Monday, November 2nd, the **"A terrible** pressure was still maintained on our **No Man's Land"** trenches round Ypres, but on this day the Germans chiefly attempted to drive a wedge between that town and Armentières southward. The day before they had taken Messines and had also captured Wytschaete, some two miles farther north on the road to Ypres. Here, however, our cavalry and Territorials had been reinforced by French troops. As the Germans again advanced, the French counter-attacked on Wytschaete, which became a terrible No Man's Land, all its

houses blazing to the sky, under the storm of shells from both the opposing armies.

Even the semblance of pressure on our front at Ypres ceased from Tuesday, November 3rd. No hostile infantry were seen, the cannonade slackened, and many of our troops were able to take a much-needed rest. The heroic remnant of the 7th Division in this quieter week came out of their trenches to refit, while troops of the Second Army Corps took their place. All went well till the afternoon of November 6th, when the French force holding the line between Klein Zillebeke **Kavanagh's gallant** and the canal was driven in. The gap **advance** left our Guards' Brigade, under Lord Cavan, exposed, and the 7th Cavalry Brigade hurried up in support. General Kavanagh deployed the 1st and 2nd Life Guards north of the road, holding the Blues in reserve behind his centre. His gallant advance encouraged the French to resume the offensive, and the former movement continued until our cavalry halted by Klein Zillebeke, allowing their comrades in arms to reoccupy their trenches.

Suddenly the French returned at the double, with the Germans pursuing them in great strength. General Kavanagh tried to stem the rush by throwing a couple of squadrons across the road, and considerable confusion occurred, ending in a melée of British, French, and Germans. To extricate itself, our Cavalry Brigade retired to the reserve trenches, and from these it protected the Guardsmen until Lord Cavan re-established his line with the assistance of the 22nd Infantry Brigade. The next day the Guards' Brigade and the Cavalry Brigade counter-attacked the Germans, and captured three machine-guns, but our men were unable to hold on to the forward line of trenches. The position they occupied, however, was strengthened by eight hundred rifles of the 3rd Cavalry Division taking

DESPERATE CHARGE BY ZOUAVES ON THE GERMAN RIGHT WING NEAR SOISSONS.
Another example of the war as seen through German eyes. The picture, representing an attack by Zouaves in the vicinity of Soissons, was drawn by Felix Schwormstädt from a sketch made on the spot by the German war artist Hugo L. Braune.

over the right section of the Guards' trenches, and providing them with a little local reserve force.

On the same day the attack was renewed along the Menin road, and at one point our line was forced back, only to be straightened out again in a few minutes. Meeting with an unkind reception in this quarter, the Germans massed in the afternoon on the south-east of Ypres, but no driving force was left in their multitudes, and the attack soon weakened. Farther to the south some four hundred of the new formations crept up under cover of a wood and advanced against the French. They came on with characteristic bravery and want of skill, to meet their usual fate—the bullet or a bayonet.

These futile attacks went on until many units in the armies of General von Deimling and General von Fabeck

A GLIMPSE OF OLD-WORLD YPRES,
One of the water-gates of the city, guarding a canal entrance.
Inset: British convoy passing through one of the ruined streets.

were shattered. All the fighting spirit was knocked out of them, and the new formations especially went to pieces. Against our men there had been brought up recruits who had only received two months' drill and who had practically no instruction in musketry, and no practice in entrenching. They knew how to die, and they died as bravely as any men could do. But they could not fight, and it was gathered from prisoners that the young men of the new corps were not withstanding the fatigue and privations of the campaign.

The great German General Staff could not have had any illusion with regard to the qualities of their half-trained recruits, and it is difficult to see what sound reason they had for sacrificing them. With their astonishing bravery, the young men would have made fine and powerful troops after six months' training in trenchwork and instruction in musketry. When the bitter need
Bravery of half- for more first-rate men occurred in
trained recruits January and February, the new Chief of Staff and his Imperial master must have regretted they had gathered and consumed so much of the fine flower of the German youth before it was ripe for war. It is not only Belgium, Northern France, and Poland which has endured inhuman treatment at the hands of the Prussian War Staff. The whole of Germany has suffered in a more indirect but just as deadly a way.

As a supreme effort against Ypres, General von Deimling sent to Arras for the greatest fighting force of the German

Empire—the Prussian Guard. By Wednesday, November 11th, a division of the corps was railed up to Menin. It consisted of some 15,000 bayonets, many of them, no doubt, drawn from the reserves of the corps, which had been sadly broken up, first on the Marne, and then on the Suippes. The Prussian Guardsman is chosen for his great height and unusual strength, and, according to a German song, he dies but he never gives ground. The attack was prepared with great secrecy, but our men knew that something **Prussian Guards'** was in store for them from the furious **secret attack** bombardment that heralded the infantry charge. The artillery fire then directed on our trenches to the north and south of the Menin road was the fiercest and heaviest ever employed against us.

Forewarned in this manner, Sir Douglas Haig and his divisional commanders set an ambush. As the attackers surged forward, they were not only met by our frontal fire, but were also taken in the flank by guns, Maxims, and magazine rifles, as they charged diagonally across part of our position. Terribly did they suffer ; but, true to the traditions of the days of Frederick the Great, the survivors still swept onward. And such were the resolution and momentum of their mass that they broke through our front trenches in three places near the Menin road.

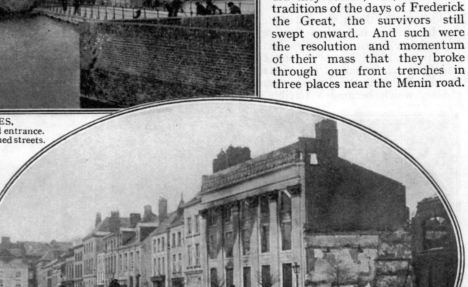

British lines, however, are constructed to meet just such an occasion as this. There were support trenches with enfilading fire to cross, and when the Prussian Guard went over these and penetrated into the woods behind our trenches, our Life Guards, armed with bayonets, came up against them. The Irish Guards, the London Scottish, and other regiments formed the last but one of the British lines. Through the gaps of the Irish Guards our Household Cavalry charged. Along they went, over the bodies of friend and foe, in the silent, terrible fury of battle with which the British soldier fights when he is desperate beyond thought. Having at last lost some seven hundred men in the wood, the Prussians forgot their glorious traditions and turned and fled. Again they came under the enfilading fire of our machine-guns, and

WORK OF THE GERMAN HUNS IN PICTURESQUE YPRES.

Our top left-hand picture shows the thirteenth-century cathedral of St. Martin in flames. To the right is a photograph of the famous "Halles des Drapiers" (or Cloth Hall), another thirteenth-century building, also set on fire by German shells. Inset is a small view of the Cloth Hall as it was; and below it, on the left, this once beautiful building as the flames were springing from tier to tier of its lovely facade. The two lower views show (left) the remains of the Market Hall, and (right) the interior of the cathedral after bombardment.

THE BURIAL OF THE HUN IN THE LAND HE HAD RAVAGED AND DESPOILED.
A chaplain of the Huns' army reading the burial service over a German soldier's grave in Belgium—perhaps one of the ravagers of women and children, and a torturer of civilians.

only a remnant of them succeeded in holding part of the line of captured trenches. At the same time another large body of German infantry made an attack to the south of the Menin road, as a concerted movement in the same scheme of operations. They failed entirely. For, as they massed in the woods close to our line, our guns opened upon them with such terrible effect that they clean lost heart before the action began, and did not push their assault home.

The repulse of the Prussian Guard brought to an end the first phase of General von Falkenhayn's plan of campaign in the western theatre of war. The entire occupation of Belgium, the turning movement by the coast, and the capture and conversion of Calais into a submarine base—all these designs became impossible of execution. With the Belgian Army strongly entrenched on the Yser and recruiting largely and gathering new strength; with the British force continually increasing in numbers and in artillery power; with nearly a million young Frenchmen in active training; with all these factors the Allied lines were impregnable. The Teutonic Empires, blockaded by sea, and hemmed in along a front of some fourteen hundred miles, were besieged. And as in all close siege operations a new force began to enter into the campaign—starvation.

SUNSET IN A BELGIAN CAMP.

CHAPTER XLV.

THE BATTLES AND BOMBARDMENTS OF THE YSER.

The Fourfold Battle of Nieuport—Fighting on Land and in the Skies, on the Seas and under the Waves—General Foch Entices the Germans to Attack in Wrong Direction—Remnants of Belgian Army Turn at Bay Along the Yser—Germans Thrown Back by Unexpected Counter-Attack—The British Navy Comes to the Rescue of the Overpowered Belgian Artillery—Terrific Bombardment of German Coast Positions—Belgian Army Retires to Rest and Refit—42nd French Division and Breton Marines Keep Back Germans—How the Breton Sailors Defended Dixmude—Incessant Slaughter of the Enemy's New Formations—Germans Break Through the Belgian Centre—The Charge of the 42nd Division at Pervyse—Again at Ramscappelle the Algerians Save the Day—The Belgians Break the Sea-Dyke and Flood the Trenches—Disastrous End of the Würtemberg Brigade—The Marvellous Charge of the French Cooks at Zillebeke.

O F all the battles in the Great War the struggle for the Yser was one of the fiercest and singular in its strangeness. It was a land battle fought by destroyers against submarines, by seaplanes against batteries of siege-howitzers, by battleships against infantry. Hosts of men clashed on the land and in the skies, on the sea and under the waves. They dug themselves in the earth like moles ; they wheeled and clanged in the heavens like eagles ; they fought in the sea depths like the shark and the thresher-whale. And victory remained apparently doubtful until a Belgian engineer brought a new ally to the help of his heroic, outnumbered comrades-in-arms, and by opening the dykes let in the North Sea and, flooding the fields of Western Flanders, drowned the advancing Germans under the eyes of their Kaiser.

The most extraordinary thing about this series of extraordinary battles was its futility. Merely to undertake it was a catastrophe of the gravest kind. For the attempt signified that the German Military Staff had lost its balance, and was striking blindly. The correct road for a German advance on Calais was from Armentières and La Bassée. Such an advance, as we have seen, was essayed by the Germans a full week before they tried also the roundabout attack along the River Yser from Nieuport to Dixmude. But the two divergent aims entailed a disastrous division of all the available forces. Neither, therefore, was achieved, though the

GERMAN MARINES GUARDING THE APPROACH TO OSTEND.
Special preparations for the struggle for the mastery of the coast were secretly made by the Germans at Ostend ; and the bridge on the road from Bruges was jealously guarded, so that no civilians should pass that way.

Germans were in overwhelming numbers. Never did General Joffre show such subtlety and deadly skill as in this affair. Perhaps, however, we should attribute the fine strategy of the Allies to General Foch, to whom his chief entrusted the task of co-ordinating all the movements of the Belgian, French, and British armies on the north-west section of the battle-front. At the beginning of the war General Foch commanded only an army corps on the Lorraine border. There he fought with such skill that the chief French army in the Battle of the Marne was put under his control. With th s same army he afterwards broke the German counter-offensive east of Rheims, and became eminent as one of the greatest of French strategists of the neo-Napoleonic school. His way of fighting was terrible for his troops. For he asked them continually to do what Napoleon's veterans had done only after ten years of campaigning experience. He asked them always to be ready to hold, and even to force back, from three to four or even five times their number of enemies. Lannes' divisions had done this several times for Napoleon, after that great captain changed his manner of strategy in 1805. But Foch went further than Napoleon. For he required the modern conscript soldier, with barely more than two months' actual experience of war, to stand firmly and continually against overwhelming numbers.

Yet the Belgians and the French did it. There were scarcely more than 40,000 effectives left of the original Belgian field army, when it gathered amid the fenland and dunes round the little town of Furnes, in the last nook of unconquered Belgian territory. For two months and a half the Belgians had been fighting against odds at Liège, Namur, Louvain, Haelen, Aerschot, Malines, Termonde, and Antwerp. In some of these heroic struggles they had faced the full might of the greatest military State on earth. So it was only the shattered remnant of the small army which drew up behind the Yser after the retreat from Antwerp. To add to their difficulties, the Belgian troops were short of munitions. Near at hand to help them were only 7,000 Breton Marines, under Admiral Ronarc'h, splendid fighters all, but without artillery. Then between Dixmude and Ypres were some French Territorial troops, who also lacked guns. Thus, while the British troops from Ypres to La Bassée were more than holding their own, and were, in fact, driving back the Germans twenty miles north, the flank of the allied position coastward was extremely weak.

And so General Foch allowed it to remain for some time. The only reinforcement he first sent up was the 24th French Division under General Grosetti. In all there may have been 59,000 Belgian and French troops, with deficient artillery power, left to fight against some 150,000 well-equipped German troops, under Duke Albrecht of Würtemberg. And General Foch was quite content that it should be so. He wanted to appear weak along the flat, dyked, difficult marshland through which the canalised Yser wound to the sea. It was a bait he held out to distract and

A BELOVED FIGURE.
King Albert leaving his headquarters in Flanders.

divide the leaders of the German Army, who were bringing up some three-quarters of a million men with the intention of capturing Calais and turning the allied front. For the situation at Nieuport was fully under the control of General Foch, right from the beginning of the struggle on October 16th. He had only to order the dykes to be broken and the sluices raised, and the water in the low-lying fens round the Yser would form an impassable barrier to the enemy. But the general did not give such an order until the very last minute. For its execution would have released a mighty German force of men and guns for action in the right direction against the army of Sir John French or the army of General Maud'huy.

It was known that the Germans were convinced of the absolute impotence of the remains of the Belgian Army. The Belgians were supposed by the enemy to be broken in spirit, utterly demoralised, and reduced to a fleeing mob, lacking in munitions of war. It was on this idea that General Foch played. By a great exertion he could, perhaps, have thrown a large French force along the Yser. This, however, would only have frightened the enemy off; and if the allied line had been broken farther to the east, the troops along the Yser would have had to retire hastily, without a fight, to avoid being enveloped. To induce the Germans to expend their energies in the wrong place, the battered but unbroken little Belgian Army was placed in the trenches.

Everything conspired to the success of the French strategist's

CAMERA-PICTURES OF BELGIUM'S HERO KING.
The King of the Belgians saluting the colours of the French 7th Regiment at Furnes, to the music of the German guns a few miles away. Inset: His Majesty chatting with an officer of the French General Staff.

subtle and daring plan. The Germans were deeply disturbed over the escape of the Belgian Army from Antwerp. They urgently needed a victory in the field, not only to hearten their civil population, but to strike the imagination of certain arming neutral nations, such as Rumania. The complete and overwhelming destruction of the Belgian Army would, it was hoped, make the Rumanians pause, and facilitate the progress of the Teutonic cause in the Balkans when Turkey entered into the Great War. Then there was a domestic problem with a large bearing upon post-bellum German politics. The Kaiser had lost much of his popularity owing to his crude and unskilful foreign policy before the outbreak of hostilities. His people contrasted the condition of things in the days of Bismarck with the situation of affairs after the long reign of their brilliant but unstable Emperor.

The rift in the German lute

Even beneath the gag of the censorship murmurs could be heard from the working class, the middle class, and the commercial and industrial directing circles. The only justification for the privileges of the old aristocracy was continued success in the leadership of the war. And with a view to strengthening the claim to supremacy of the noble families and landed gentry who officered the Army, the scions of royal houses were made the nominal commanders of some of the principal hosts. Neither the Crown Prince of Germany nor the Crown Prince of Bavaria, however, had won much distinction in

STIRRING SCENES IN OLD-WORLD FURNES.

A fine camera record of a notable scene in the Market Square at Furnes, where King Albert reviewed the French troops and decorated the colours of the 7th Regiment with the Order of Leopold. Here, too, King Albert and General Joffre publicly thanked the Algerian troops who saved the day at Ramscappelle. Inset: A company of Belgian cavalry passing through Furnes on its way to meet the oncoming foe.

HOW THE GERMANS, PROVIDED WITH PLANKS, ADVANCED UNDER FIRE TO CROSS THE CANALS IN THE YSER DISTRICT.

German troops fighting in the Yser district were provided with planks, which served the double purpose placing these temporary bridges in position, the ranks behind advanced in massed formation, to be met of shields and bridges over the narrow waterways. When the front ranks of the invaders had succeeded in by a withering machine-gun and rifle fire which caused appalling slaughter.

France, though assisted by the most able Chiefs of Staff available. The plebeian General von Kluck and the obscure, retired General von Hindenburg had become, in turn, the popular favourites with both the people and the soldiers.

But by a stroke of luck the heir-presumptive to the Kingdom of Würtemberg, Duke Albrecht Maria Alexander, found himself at the head of five army corps in Western Flanders, with only the remnant of the Belgian Army barring his way for a sweep along the coast to Calais. He was offered a facile victory that would greatly help to restore the credit of the royal houses of Germany and their modernised feudal system of militaristic government. The German Emperor in person was close at hand to overlook the plan of operations of his new Chief of Staff. The upshot was that things worked out as General Foch desired them to do. In fact, the presence of the Duke of Würtemberg and the Kaiser caused a larger force to be abstracted from the main armies of attack and directed on the side issue along the coast. For, naturally, the royal prince had to be provided with a superabundance of men, to make absolutely sure of his much-desired success.

Duke Albrecht's hopeful outlook

1st Belgian Division was driven out of Mannekensvere, and the 4th Division was forced out of Keyem. They both retired across the Yser. But in the night the dauntless 4th Division returned over the river, and by a furious bayonet attack in the darkness recaptured all its positions at Keyem.

This was a sad surprise for the Duke of Würtemberg. Expecting only the task of keeping the Belgian Army moving before his guns and infantry columns, he had made no preparations against the counter-attack. But a

CABBAGES AS COVER.
British trench dug just behind a row of cabbages. The German trenches were one hundred and eighty yards in front.

considerable number of the men who had first fought the German army at Liège had survived to meet their foes on the last line of Belgian defence. Dirty, unshaven, tattered, beggarly figures they looked after ten weeks of campaigning and trenchwork. But the fire, skill, and stubbornness with which they battled disconcerted the plan of the German commander. He had to call for more troops in order to drive home his attack. He resumed his forward movement with increased vigour on Monday, October 19th, but unhappily he selected the coast village of Lombartzyde, a couple of miles north of Nieuport, as his objective. Only a single Belgian division—

ON THE LOOK-OUT FOR A PRUSSIAN SNIPER.
Another view behind the shelter of the cabbage-patch. British sharpshooters on the look-out for a Prussian sniper who had been causing trouble. Some of the enemy snipers dressed themselves in khaki.

The operation opened on Friday, October 16th, when two German army corps advanced upon the Yser. It was a reconnaissance in force, undertaken with a view to ascertaining how the canalised river was defended. The Belgian Army was found to be holding not only the river but the villages north of it, such as Lombartzyde, Mannekensvere, and Keyem, while French Marines, with only machine-guns, occupied Dixmude. Thereupon, the Germans brought up their guns and bombarded all the allied line. The next day strong infantry forces were launched against all the outlying villages. Overwhelmed by numbers and lacking ammunition for their field-guns, the

the 2nd—held the village, and the duke concentrated his troops against them with a view to hacking his way down the coast to Dunkirk, and so turning all the allied line. Backed by their light and heavy field-guns, the German infantry came on in dense masses. Three times the Belgians had to give ground under the terrible shell and shrapnel fire, but when the bombardment ceased they fought the German troops back with bullet and bayonet.

A bolt from the blue

Then suddenly the tables were turned. The undergunned Belgian Army, rapidly running short of artillery warships for a foreign country through which a great river ran —Brazil. The ships were flat-bottomed, with a draught of only 4½ feet, but they carried armoured turrets, with two 6 in. guns forward, and two 4·7 in. howitzers aft. Our Admiralty saw at once how admirably designed these monitors were for service as off-shore batteries in land operations. As the battle-front extended nearer to the coast, the monitors — renamed Severn, Humber, and Mersey — anchored at Dover, under the command of Admiral Hood, stripped and ready for action. On Sunday, October 18th, came the call for help from the allied commanders in Flanders. On Sunday night the monitors were steaming, lights out, along the Belgian coast, and their young gunnery lieutenants were watching the Germans digging coast trenches by flare - light and measuring the ranges. Detachments of our sailors with machine-guns landed from the monitors to assist in the defence of Nieuport, but it was mainly the naval guns that saved the situation.

When first their great shells fell on the batteries and heavy guns of the Germans, and began to relieve the artillery pressure on the 2nd Belgian Division, the Germans tried to beat our monitors off by bringing up their 6 in. howitzers, and placing them in concealed positions among the dunes. Vickers, of Barrow, however, are very good gun-makers, and the products of Krupp's factory, though of equal calibre, lacked both the range and the penetrative power of the English gun. Our ships steamed

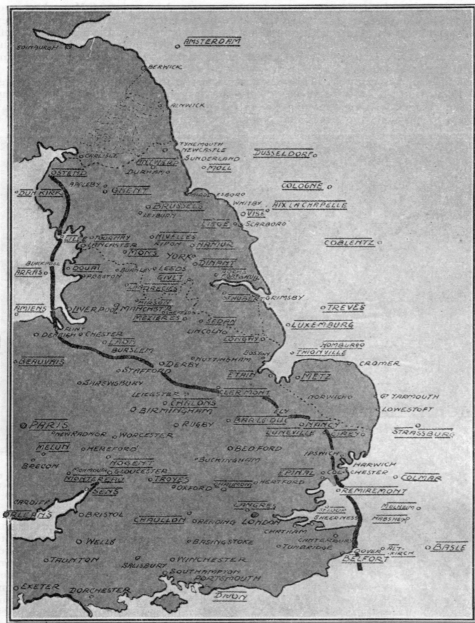

THE LONG-DRAWN BATTLE-LINE IN FRANCE.

The line from Ostend to Belfort coincided with the distance between Dover and Carlisle; and its extent will be the more easily understood by a study of the above drawing. The black line in the smaller map indicates approximately the German positions in Flanders in the closing days of October, 1914.

supplies, unexpectedly won a great advantage over their enemies. Three grey strange things drove in from the open sea towards the shore. An observation balloon went up with wireless apparatus, a protecting flotilla of destroyers spread out towards the river, and a squadron of aeroplanes swept high above the German gun sites. Then came six claps of thunder from the sea, and half a dozen 6 in. shells exploded with deadly marksmanship amid the German batteries. In a second, as the 4·7 in. stern guns came into play, there was another broken roar from the sea, and six 4·7 in. shells came screaming over Middelkerke, and crashed down among the German cannon.

British Navy to the rescue

The British Navy had come to the help of the Belgian Army with a strange type of warship. At the outbreak of the war, Messrs. Vickers had just completed three river

out of reach of the shore batteries, and then poured in a terrible and unanswerable fire. One of our shells struck an ammunition waggon, and caused an explosion which for the time sadly diminished the German rate of fire. On one day, it is said, six of their batteries were put out of action and 1,600 Germans killed.

At the urgent request of the Duke of Würtemberg,

the submarine flotilla at Emden speeded south, with a store of torpedoes, and attacked the monitors. Usually, however, a torpedo strikes at a depth of about twelve feet under the water. As the monitors had a draught of only 4½ feet, the great deadly missiles passed harmlessly beneath their flat bottoms.

Moreover, the presence of German submarines merely added to the difficulties of the enemy's coast army, by bringing a strong force of British destroyers to the scene of action. And when the destroyers were not engaged in chasing submarines, their 4 in. guns helped in the bombardment of the German batteries and trenches.

The whole naval operation was that deadliest kind of attack—a flank attack. The Germans had brought their guns up against the Belgian lines, and sited them with a view to getting a wide traverse of fire on the Belgian positions. In many cases the hard, firm, close coast road running from Ostend to Nieuport had been chosen for gun positions in preference to the dyked and marshy fenland. Then, on a sudden, the devastating and overwhelming bombardment

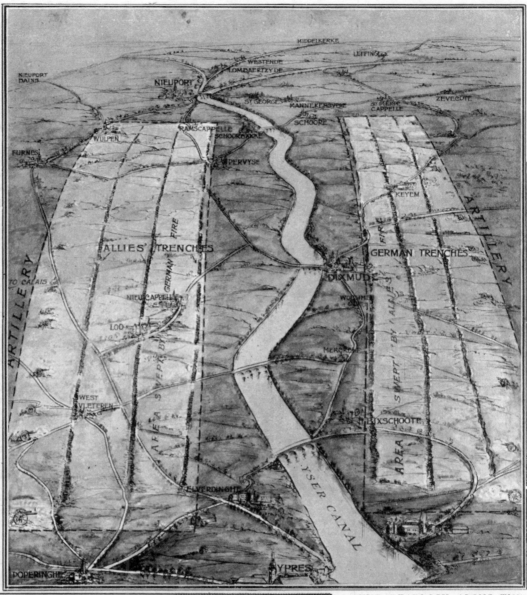

MAP OF THE CANALS IN NORTHERN FRANCE AND BELGIUM.
The area held by the Germans at the beginning of November, 1914, may be seen if a waved line be drawn between Westende and Middelkerke downwards, by Passchendaele and Warneton, to Roubaix.

THE DEADLOCK ALONG THE YSER.
By the middle of November, 1914, the Germans and the Allies had dug themselves in and set up an artillery fire, the intensity of which precluded any advance on either side except at terrible cost.

of 6 in. and 4 in. British shells struck the German gunners when they thought they were at the point of winning a victory. It was the first time in German history that military operations had been interrupted by sea-power, and it took the German commander clean by surprise. He was jerked out of his orbit of action in somewhat the same way as Napoleon the First had suddenly been brought up at Acre by British sea-power, when he was marching through Syria intent upon the conquest of the Orient.

Not until the war is over shall we know what our first modern essay in amphibious warfare

WITH THE GERMAN GUNNERS IN FLANDERS.
German field-pieces being brought up through heavy country to fortify the enemy's right wing in Belgium. Inset: Lieutenant von Bismarck, as ordnance officer, reading a despatch in Flanders.

cost Germany. The mere expense in war material involved in the subsequent fortification of the seaport of Bruges must have seriously diminished German artillery power on the actual battle-field. And the large number of men mobilised in trenches on the coast, as a protection against the possible landing of a British raiding force, was another item of loss. Our ships shelled Zeebrugge, attacked Ostend, drove the Germans out of Middelkerke, and with long-range fire swept the country for six miles inland. The only effective means of defence was to attack our monitors and destroyers with light and armoured cruisers. But if the Germans had sent a squadron down to the Belgian coast it would have been cut off by a part of our Grand Fleet.

The only reply they could make was to haul up their new long-range cannon and their heaviest siege-howitzers, and to place them amid the dunes. By this means they managed to make matters, for a day or two, a little more exciting for our monitors and destroyers and for the French destroyers that joined in the coast battle. The position of affairs then was that the German howitzer batteries were in the same fix as the forts of Liège, Namur, Maubeuge, and Antwerp, over which they had 'so easily triumphed. They formed a fixed mark, discernible by our aerial **German batteries in a fix** scouts and by our observation officers in tethered balloons. Our ships, on the other hand, continually changed their position with the speed of an ordinary railway train. They zigzagged about the sea at high mobility, and only by the most extraordinary luck could a hostile battery straddle them with a salvo of shells. And all this was only the beginning of the naval element in the great land battle for Calais. For on October 27th, when the Germans had diminished their artillery power at other critical parts of the lines of trench warfare, in order to concentrate their heaviest ordnance along the shore, their 11 in. and 12 in. howitzers were mastered by a new naval unit. H.M.S. Venerable, with a broadside of four 12 in. guns, and an additional armament of twelve 6 in. quick-firers, came into action. The great naval guns reached farther inland, and places at which Germans had gathered to escape the fire of the monitors were blown up and wrecked by the terrible 850 lb. shells.

The fleet dominated all the coast as far as the inland village of Slype. Ramscappelle, over four miles from the coast, remained at last the only point which the

GERMAN LANDWEHR IN THE FLOODED YSER COUNTRY.
Company of a Landwehr regiment making its way through the flooded Yser district to the trenches. Among them may be noticed a few regulars, drafted doubtless to give the necessary stiffening to partly-trained men.

Germans could attack without coming under the fire of our fleet. And, as a matter of fact, even this village was not secure. For the range of our big naval guns was somewhat over eight or ten miles, and at flood-tide even a battleship could get closer to the shore than usual.

On land, the artillery on both sides fought at a disadvantage. The gunners had many difficulties to contend with. There was no good siting in the flat fenland, and the banks of the dykes and the lines of willows and osiers intersecting the country made it as impenetrable to the eye as if it were close-wooded. It was generally impossible to see more than half a mile ahead, and thus very difficult to discover where the enemy was, and what effect was being produced upon him. Then the autumnal **Fighting in the** haze that spread over the marshes very **flat fenland** frequently during the long battle rendered aerial observation very uncertain.

The gunners, therefore, had to rely very largely on their infantry in the firing-line and to fight their guns at short ranges. On the whole, this diminution of the power of the artillery was a great benefit to the Belgians. For though, on their left flank, the friendly naval guns more than redressed the balance, yet on their centre and right wing tremendous pressure was exerted against them by the German army. On Monday, October 19th, the village of Beerst, just north of Dixmude, was shattered by a terrific bombardment of German shells, and the 4th Belgian Division, entrenched among the ruins, was driven out by a violent and steady massed attack of the hostile infantry.

The neighbouring village of Keyem, which the 4th Division had recovered by a splendid bayonet charge, was also assailed, and many of the Belgian troops were in danger of being cut off. But the Belgian bayonet again won all that the heavy German field-howitzers had partly conquered. When night fell, and the mist thickened, the brave Belgian Division crept northward out of Dixmude with some thousands of the tall, tanned Breton fishermen, forming the French Marine Division. There was not much shooting, but with the silent steel the Belgians and Frenchmen thrust their way into Vladsloo, and got again into

IN AMBUSH AMONGST THE TOMBS.
German artillery officers testing a machine-gun mounted in a concealed position in a burial-ground at Dixmude. The man at the gun is sitting on the slab of a tomb.

shone the glow of the burning villages; tongues of fire came from warships and land batteries, and the incessant and widespread rain of bursting shells, flowering out upon a nocturnal sky dimly lighted by the conflagrant villages, made the horrible scene of destruction look like an enormous display of fireworks.

In this strangely-lighted darkness the German infantry concentrated an attack upon Dixmude. They had been thrown back from the same place in the daytime, but, increased in numbers, they crept up again in the gloom, only to be again shattered by rifle and machine-gun fire, followed by the inevitable bayonet charge. Though routed, they re-formed

Beerst. But as it was discovered that fresh strong columns of the enemy were pouring out from Roulers and striking westward, the defending force retired on the Yser, evacuating all the villages up to Keyem.

It was on this day that Sir John French threw his First Army Corps north of Ypres, and began his astonishing advance against the German forces between Roulers and Thourout. It was a fine, friendly, self-sacrificing plan, undertaken with a view to distract the German attention from the Yser. The idea was to keep the Germans vacillating between the weak Belgian-French defences on the river and the feeble-looking British salient at Ypres. As a result of the British movement, the new German reinforcements did not come into action against the Belgian front on October 20th. The Germans merely kept up a furious cannonade upon the Belgian line which lasted all night and continued the next day. On the coast a farm was taken from the 2nd Division, then recovered by the Belgians, and again lost. But this only brought the fire of our naval guns on the captured farm, wrecking it completely, and killing and wounding most of the troops which held it. At night the misty plain had a strange and terrible picturesqueness. Far through the light sea-mist

French's self-sacrificing plan

RUINED CHURCH OF ST. JEAN AT DIXMUDE.
In their bombardment of Dixmude the fine old Church of St. Jean was reduced to ruins by the German gunners.

MOTOR-'BUS TRANSPORT FOR THE ALLIED TROOPS IN FLANDERS.
Troops were conveyed to both Ypres and Dixmude by motor-'buses which used to be on service in the streets of Paris.

MEN WHO FACED THE FULL MIGHT OF THE GREATEST MILITARY STATE ON EARTH.

Glimpses of the heroic Belgian Army after the fall of Antwerp. The top photograph shows a trainload of the men who attempted against overwhelming odds to defend Antwerp from the ruthless invader on their way to another battle area in the west. The lower view is of the landing at Zeebrugge of soldiers who had been through the fierce fighting at Namur. Inset: The Belgian General Dossin in consultation at Nieuport.

with the reinforcements continually pouring in from Thourout, and in the grey misty dawn they made a third attack in massed enveloping multitudes. But the weary and half-shattered Belgian 4th Division and the Breton Marines beat them back yet again with terrible slaughter.

But after these three quick smashing blows the German force still held together. Its reinforcements were largely composed of young Berlin recruits, officered by the intellectual élite of Germany—pale, spectacled, earnest faces, glowing with high spiritual courage. Though little trained in war, these university men rose to a height of dauntlessness exceeding the great traditions of the fighting scholars of Prussia in the War of Liberation. They went on till they dropped, and until they were brought down they kept all their men going, too. In the afternoon of October 21st they advanced for the fourth time against the Belgian-Breton force entrenched around Dixmude. But all their heroic steadfastness in attack was vain. They knew how to die gloriously, the new scholar-soldiers of Germany, but contempt of death could not prevail

Intellectual élite of Germany

invention, with a simple air-cooling device that did away with the use of the cumbersome water-jacket. It had been offered to the British Government, but refused by them; the German Government had also rejected it; and when the war broke out, the defenders of Liège, thanks to the enterprise of their military authorities, were the only troops possessing the new gun. In the artillery battles it lost some of its importance, as the German field-batteries in overpowering numbers dominated the field. But in the mists, marshes, and the low-lying polders round the Yser the new machine-gun, in the hands of men with six weeks' experience in its use, had as deadly an importance as it had at Liège.

After their fourth defeat at Dixmude the Germans left in peace for a while this beautiful old Flemish town which their guns had battered into ruin, and concentrated for a new effort on the centre of the Belgian line. Halfway between Nieuport and Dixmude the Yser bulges northward, forming a salient loop between the village of Schoorbakke and the village of Tervaete. The Belgian trenches, following the loop of the river, constituted a sort of bastion of earthworks that could be shelled from three sides by the hostile batteries. And while getting this cross-fire effect for their guns, the Germans could bring up on the outer radius of the loop a wider front of attacking infantry than the Belgians possessed in their narrower space. It was not a question simply of the density of the attacking force, but of their wider front, and of their consequent heavier fire-power. The Belgian position formed what is known as a salient, and the breadth of it was so small that all the German guns surrounding it on three sides could reach any section of it. It was thus the weak point in the Belgian line, and it does not say much for the generalship of the Duke of Würtemberg and his staff that they should only have discovered the natural and inevitable weakness of this point in the defending line after four days and nights of continual battle. Only when the Germans had been continually repulsed at the seashore and at Dixmude did they concentrate in full force against the indefensible Belgian centre.

MAP OF THE AREA COVERED BY THE BOMBARDMENT OF THE BELGIAN COAST.
The shallow waters and sandbanks preventing close access to the Belgian coast-line by vessels of heavy draught are shown by dots. The ruling on the land indicates approximately the zone within range of the biggest British naval guns from battleships lying outside the shallow water barrier.

against the deadly skill of the experienced and revengeful Walloons, Flemings, and Bretons. When a Belgian trench wavered, sick of the slaughter of the masses in front of it, a shout would ring out over the rattle of the machine-guns and the racket of the rifle fire: "Remember Louvain!" Then all down the Belgian line the battle-cry would be taken up: "Remember Louvain! Termonde and Louvain!"

With that, the flame of vengeance burnt up again fiercely in the hearts of the Belgians. Their feeling of pity for the men whom they had at their mercy fell from them. They remembered how the German had massacred peaceful townspeople and villagers in the day of his triumph and power. And they bent again to their work of slaughter. Each clip of cartridges went so swiftly into the magazine, and the bullets streamed out with such rapidity against the large targets, that it seemed at times to the Germans as though every Belgian was working a machine-gun against them. As a matter of fact, the Belgians seem to have owed a considerable part of their power to resist the German massed attacks to a new instrument of battle. It was a small, light, and very handy machine-gun of American

From the beginning the Belgians knew they could not defend it, and prepared a new line. This lay some two miles in the rear, by the railway from Nieuport to Dixmude, and the cobbled, tree-lined highway running between the two towns, with the red roots of Pervyse rising at the cross-roads. Pervyse was the centre of the Belgian operations, for through it a cross-road led to Furnes, the last town in Flanders. Furnes was only five miles from Pervyse, so the loss of this latter little town would involve the complete conquest of Belgian territory by the invaders. For even though the British held on to Ypres, which would have been doubtful if Furnes had fallen, the Germans would have been able to claim that they had driven the Belgian Army out of Belgium.

Importance of Pervyse

For this reason the Belgian troops held their weak salient on the river loop as long as possible. The Germans attacked them there in the afternoon of Wednesday, October 21st. They drove in on the left at Schoorbakke, where there was a bridge across the canalised stream.

SANGUINARY ENCOUNTER ON THE YSER BY THE VILLAGE OF RAMSCAPPELLE.

The Belgians had firmly entrenched themselves on one bank of the Yser. They had strengthened their position with doors and shutters from the houses in the adjacent village. The Germans had thrown up hasty field-works on the other side of the canal, which it was their object to cross. One bridge made by them was destroyed by the brave defenders. This was in the night time. In the small hours of the following morning the enemy succeeded in throwing another pontoon bridge over the water. It was then the fierce hand-to-hand encounter depicted above took place.

"ONE TOUCH OF NATURE": KING WINTER STRIKES BOTH FRIEND AND FOE.

Winter came suddenly in Flanders in November, 1914. Snow fell heavily and froze hard on the ground. The men in the firing-line no longer suffered the misery of living up to their necks in mud and slush. But the alternative was even more deadly, especially at night, in the open trenches. Many men became so stiff that they had to be lifted out on relief, and some had to be admitted to hospital with frost-bite. Our artist has chosen for illustration the conditions under which a number of German prisoners taken by the British were escorted to the base.

A SHELL THAT KNOCKED OUT SIX MEN.
The Zouave who is seen in the foreground of the above photograph is standing in a hole that had been made by a shell which knocked out six men who were by the wall against which another Zouave has taken up a position. The effects of the gun fire in the Great War were unprecedented.

A GAME OF CR
Two of the officers in the above photograp[
home. Meanwhile, for a brief [

THE MAKING OF A SPECIAL BOMB-PROOF.
The bomb-proof trench, the beginning of which is shown in this photograph, was made not far away from the guns, and intended for use during any specially severe bombardment by the enemy.

LONDON HOTE
Zouaves being instructed in the mechanis[
ment spoke English perfectly.   He had [
where he had been [

"A DAY OFF" WITH BRITISH GUNNERS IN BELGIUM.
Some men of the Royal Field Artillery taking advantage of a day "in reserve" on Zillebeke Lake.   Though the incident illustrated took place in the middle of October, the weather was so beautiful that several of the men enjoyed the luxury of a bathe.

TESTING THE
Ten seconds after the gun has been fired[
with our observation scouts, calls out wh[
this case the message[

E FIRING-LINE.

game of chess. Another is writing a letter
n the background is silent.

A GOOD BILLET FOR THE GUN TEAMS.
The scene is " somewhere in France." It represents a convenient farmyard at the foot of a rocky eminence, on which
the battery had fixed up its guns. Pending a move to another vantage point, the horses were snugly billeted in
the shelter afforded below.

UNNERY EXPERT.

use. The sergeant in charge of this detach-
rejoin the colours from a hotel in London,
s of a chef de cuisine.

ANOTHER VIEW OF THE BOMB-PROOF.
When the earth was taken out, roofing material was commandeered and placed over the dug-out, earth being
replaced to the required depth. Dug-outs of this description afforded protection for about fifteen men.

THE GUN FIRE.

his ear to the wireless apparatus in touch
short or over, to the left or the right. In
from our aerial scouts.

BEETROOTS AS A PROTECTIVE COVERING.
Though apparently a quite rough-and-ready affair, the " splinter-roof " shown above is complete. The seemingly
rickety roof is covered with beetroots. The structure would keep out any splinters of shells, and afford safe
protection from anything except a direct hit.

FRENCH TROOPS ADVANCING IN A SNOWSTORM THROUGH THE FLOODED DITCHES AND BARE WOODS OF SOUTHERN BELGIUM.

In this singularly moving and graphic picture, sent from the South Belgian battlefield in November, 1914, M. Paul Thiriat has portrayed with masterly pencil the severe conditions under which the French troops on the Allies' left wing were at that time operating. The country shown is an all but monotonous fenland, open to the horizon on the one hand and to purple or dull woods on the other, scarred with flooded dykes and gaunt, leafless willows and osiers, with here and there a brick-built village or farmhouse or a ruined mill. It was generally impossible to see half-a-mile ahead, and thus very difficult to discover where the enemy was. Altogether a picture to excite the deepest sympathy with the brave men who are playing so noble a part in the fight for freedom from German tyranny.

But the bridge was blown up, and no German who had crossed the Yser at this point returned alive. In the night many additional hostile batteries were hauled towards the loop, over which the enemy's guns of all calibres played with terrible rapidity for many hours. Had the Belgians possessed long-range, heavy guns, the continual spurts of flame from the German lines would have enabled them to mark down the enemy's gun positions, and then bring a concentrated fire in turn upon each German battery. Unhappily, the defenders had only a few light field-guns, and the limbers were nearly empty. For the ammunition had been needed in rearguard actions in the long retreat from Antwerp, and the five days' battle along the Yser had exhausted the remaining supply. The Belgian gunners, therefore, could not protect their infantry against the terrible 6 in. shells of the enemy's howitzers. All that the defending artillerymen could usefully do was to wait until the enemy's mass attack began, and then open upon the large, close, living target with the last shrapnel shells in the limber.

After battering and wrecking the Belgian trenches with high-explosive shell, the Duke of Würtemberg launched his infantry over the river at the village of Tervaete on Thursday, October 22nd. The attackers then got their first foothold on the left bank of the Yser. The 1st Belgian Division, worn out, hungry, and drowsy after sleepless nights of combat, counter-attacked. They failed, and their continually lessening numbers were still further decreased by the hail of bullets from German machine-guns in the lost village. Yet, with superb spirit, the Belgians rallied after their repulse, and again counter-attacked, and recovered Tervaete at the bayonet point.

But this was the last success. For the Germans, still swelling with reinforcements and intent on driving through the weak Belgian centre, came on in the night with fresh forces and regained Tervaete and the passage of the Yser. Terribly exhausted were the Belgians. They had been continually marching and fighting since the opening of the attack on Antwerp, but still they held on in the loop of the river, entrenching between Tervaete and Schoorbakke. There the 1st Division, on Friday, October 23rd, strove

to keep back the German advance on Furnes, while the 4th Division, with the Breton Marines, clung to the trenches round Dixmude. Between Friday night and Saturday morning the German commander swung his forces fourteen times against Dixmude, but every time they broke.

"Seven times we crossed the Yser," said a German officer afterwards, "and seven times we were beaten back. At last our dead formed bridges over which we again tried to pass, only to be repulsed once more." But this achievement was not gained at a slight cost. One-fourth of the remnant of the Belgian field army fell, and the rest were exhausted. For seven days along the Yser they held off four times their number of Germans, while the British Army was fighting for its life a little to the south at Ypres. Many Belgians stayed in the trenches all the time —fenland trenches, with the water oozing in continually and mingling with the rain puddles and rising over the men's feet. They had nothing to drink but the water of the ditches and canal they were guarding, and little time or opportunity for preparing a hot meal. Plastered with mud, wet and cheerless, they yet retained all their pluck and perseverance, and made some splendid bayonet charges.

Happily, many of them were able to go to Furnes to rest for a few days and refit, and their munition supplies were reorganised. Several batteries of heavy French howitzers arrived, and helped to make the artillery duel more equally balanced. For a week the Belgians had been hopelessly outranged and outweighted by the German ordnance. Frequently their batteries were obliged to cease fire and draw away to a fresh position, to avoid the tremendous shelling of guns and mortars massed upon them. Both the entrenched infantry and the convoys proceeding to the front were severely bombarded, and the German howitzers enjoyed complete immunity from attack while they pounded Dixmude, Pervyse, and Nieuport to ruin from a distance which prevented the Belgian batteries from replying.

But the new French howitzer batteries had quite as long a range as the German pieces, and with the batteries came a superb force of French infantry, the 42nd Division, under General Grosetti. It at once relieved the 2nd Belgian

THE SHATTERED SHRINE.
A pathetic but typical example of the sacrilegious work of the Prussian Huns on the Franco-Belgian frontier.

THE HEROIC DEFENCE OF DIXMUDE BY BRETON MARINES UNDER ADMIRAL RONARCH.

For weeks 7,000 Breton Marines under Admiral Ronarc'h, fighting in trenches up to their waists in water, repulsed. In the morning the dead body was found. The man had fallen, not from a bullet, but from an kept two German army corps at bay. One night the enemy crept up to the French lines, driving some half- assassin's thrust through his back. Behind him, as "The Times" correspondent suggests, there had evidently dozen of their prisoners before them. One of these prisoners shouted out a warning. The attack was been a German soldier instructed to kill him should he utter a word of warning to his compatriots.

FRENCH ZOUAVES IN CAMP BETWEEN THE DYKES.

Division in front of Nieuport, and then turned to help the 1st Belgian Division at Pervyse. At dawn on Monday, October 26th, the Germans made their grand effort to hew their way along the coast. Their troops, concentrated on the Mannekensvere road, advanced under cover of a storm of shell and shrapnel, and threw three pontoon bridges over the river and canal. The infantry poured across and made a resolute, violent attempt to carry Nieuport by storm. A French brigade operating beyond the town was in peril of being surrounded. But the men held, and Belgian supports—little rest they had, after all!—returned in haste from Furnes to support their allies.

A critical situation In the meantime the allied artillery shelled the pontoons, and the French brigade retired on the trenches in front of Nieuport, and from there headed the Germans off. The enemy then turned and swept south on the villages of Ramscappelle and Pervyse. The gradual but steady progress he made could be marked by the way the bursting shells fell nearer and nearer to Furnes. Between ten and eleven o'clock in the morning the situation became critical. Orders were given for Furnes to be evacuated. The wounded were carried to the station, and a large number of the townspeople began to leave. Belgian soldiers, shelled out of their trenches, made their way to the rear, but fresh columns of their comrades, who had been resting in the villages between the lines, pushed along to the front, where King Albert, with cheerful, smiling, indomitable strength of soul, was holding his battered Army together.

Pervyse was the storm-centre, just midway between Furnes and the German concentration point, with a highway running through it from the two opposing camps. By the ruined church in the flaming, shell-swept village, General Grosetti, smiling, genial, and gigantic, sat in an armchair, with shrapnel bursting over him. There he encouraged his Division to press on through the bombardment and attack the advancing German infantry columns. His men—Arabs, negroes, French colonials, and Frenchmen of France—cheered him as they passed. The big man, sitting gay and confident in a rain of shell, inspired them with his own laughing heroism. On they swept, beyond the zone of the enemy's gun fire, into the safer belt of his rifle and Maxim fire. And there they held him.

The Germans had crossed the Yser merely to be brought

SHARPSHOOTERS OF THE FRENCH COLONIAL ARMY IN ACTION ON THE SAND-DUNES NEAR NIEUPORT.

up against the railway line. From the point of view of the defending troops, the railway, with the Nieuport and Dixmude road behind it, was a more comfortable position than the marshland. By the river and canal it had been impossible to dig a three-feet trench without getting eighteen inches of oozing water to stand in. All that the Germans had won was a series of drains calculated to cripple an army with rheumatic fever. They came, moreover, within the field of operations of the ingenious British sailor. Since Lord Fisher invented the first modern armoured train, in the campaign against Arabi Pasha, our naval men had specialised in this instrument of warfare. In Flanders they drove to the assistance of Belgian, French, and British troops wherever there was a track available for their queerly-coloured armoured locomotives and trucks. A British naval officer usually commanded, with expert British gunners and Belgian sharpshooters on the train.

General Grosetti's heroism

A surprise effect was always designed. The train was held, manned and under steam, with loaded guns, a few miles from the scene of combat. When the struggle was at its fiercest, and all the enemy's batteries were disclosed and all his men deployed, then the armoured train would come in answer to a telephone call—almost invisible by reason of its wide stripes of crude colours, blending in the distance into a neutral tint, and almost unheard

BRITISH SOLDIERS PREPARING TO LEAVE OSTEND FOR A
NEW BASE.

AN EVER-WELCOME GIFT TO A COMRADE ON SERVICE—
A GOOD CIGAR

A BRITISH SOLDIER SEEKS EXPERT ADVICE ON A PROBLEM
IN BELGIAN TOPOGRAPHY.

in the thunder and rattle of the fight. More than once
its guns, opening unexpectedly at short range, silenced
a hostile battery, and its shrapnel shells brought down
five of the captive balloons used by the Germans for
observation purposes. Worked with the dash and courage
that distinguish the British seaman either on land or sea,
these trains ran with impunity under the fire of hostile
guns, as their great speed made them difficult to hit. At
the end of a month's campaign merely one engine had
been damaged, without being put out of action, and of
the crew one Belgian rifleman only was wounded.

But great as our sailors were, they scarcely equalled
the achievement of Admiral Ronarc'h's seven thousand
Breton Marines. These men belonged to a class of French
fighters with a glorious record in the former Franco-
German War. But finely as the fathers had fought in
1870, the sons fought better in 1914. They were the
talk of every bivouac in the northern armies. When
General Joffre heard they were fighting waist-deep in
water in the trenches at Dixmude, he
said, with a slow, grave smile : "They   **Admiral Ronarc'h's**
are in their element." Chosen from the   **Breton Marines**
hardiest fishermen of Brittany, from the
cod fishers of Iceland and Newfoundland, they endured
the most terrible rigours without flinching. When the
Germans tried to carry Dixmude by the mass and
momentum of infantry column attacks, the Bretons,
having only machine-guns, grouped them in fours, and
then mowed down each column as it advanced. The
head of each column never passed a certain point. It
was like pushing strips of wood under a series of guillotine
machines.

One night, after days of fighting in the wet trenches,
the Marines fell asleep. Even their officers, drowsy under
the continual bombardment and unending infantry attacks,
began to dream. There was a shout in the misty gloom.
One of the officers awoke, and discerned a mass of enemies
creeping up in the darkness. He roused the amphibians,
and though dog-weary and muddle-minded, they recovered
enough strength and alertness to repel the attack. In
the morning, among the dead in front of their trenches,
they found the body of one of their fellow-Marines. The
Germans had driven some prisoners before them as a
screen against the defenders' fire. Behind the dead Breton
there had evidently been a German with a bayonet, ready
to kill him if he made a sound. But the brave man,
knowing how weary and drowsy his comrades would be,

A REST BY THE WAY—ON THE EDGE OF A SHELTERED COPPICE IN FLANDERS.

had shouted a warning, and instead of being shot by mistake by his friends, he had been stabbed from behind by a cowardly assassin.

Nearer Ypres, at the bridge of the Three Grietchen, another Frenchman, belonging to a Zouave regiment, acted in the same way. The mass of advancing Germans was screened with captured French troops, and the defenders in the trenches hesitated to fire, thinking it might be a French force from the north retiring on their position. The captured Zouave understood it all, and he yelled: "For God's sake, fire on us!" Naturally, he fell with his comrades, but he brought about a French victory.

Dixmude itself was a scene of infernal desolation and terror. The German commander ordered that every house should be levelled to the ground. On the first days of the struggle the field-guns and howitzers of an army corps were massed against it. Then some of the 12 in. Austrian mortars were brought up by railway.

Dixmude pounded into rubble The artillery general tried to obtain also two of the 16½ in. Krupp howitzers, but, much to his disappointment, they were needed on the coast to reply to the British warships. Even without these gigantic instruments of destruction, the little, beautiful, open Flemish town was quickly battered into mounds of rubble.

There was not a yard of it unswept by shell fire, not a house in it that was not shattered. The square, where the venerable town-hall stood flaming, was a region of death and thunder. High-explosive shells and shrapnel continually burst over it, and a rain of German bullets, aimed at the Marines in the trenches near by, whistled across the square when they missed the nearer mark. Amid the crash of falling chimneys and the roar and clatter of shell-stricken houses, rising with the explosion and then tumbling and barricading the streets, the reserves of the little defending force sheltered behind the gapped and ragged walls while the wounded rested in the cellars. Sometimes the houses above the cellars would be set on fire, and the maimed or dying men beneath the flames had to be taken out hastily, under the fierce bombardment, and carried to some fresh retreat till the overworked motor-ambulances could convey them to Furnes. Then, as each Red Cross motor passed through the town, a cyclone of shells followed it beyond Oudecappelle.

The more desperate the Germans grew, the viler their conduct became. Behind the lines at Dixmude on October

BRITISH COLONIAL TROOPS ATTACHED TO THE 3RD BELGIAN LANCERS.

BRITISH COLONIAL VOLUNTEERS WITH A DETACHMENT OF BELGIAN CAVALRY.

GERMAN HORDES CHECKED BY LAND AND SEA: THE GREAT STRUGGLE ACROSS THE SAND-DUNES AT NIEUPORT BAINS.

Supported by a preponderance of artillery and overwhelming numbers of infantry, the Duke of Würtemberg made a great attack on Lombartzyde on October 19th, 1914, with a view to "hacking his way" to Dunkirk. Lombartzyde was held by only a single Belgian division—the 2nd—and three times they had to give way under terrible shell and shrapnel fire. Then suddenly there came six claps of thunder from the sea, and half a dozen 6 in. shells exploded with deadly precision among the German batteries. The British Navy had come to the help of the hardly-pressed Belgians. This flank attack took the Germans completely, by surprise. French destroyers took a hand, and the long-range naval gun-fire of the Allies swept the country to six miles inland. Under cover of this fire from the sea the Belgians delivered a terrible onslaught on the invaders who ran helter-skelter from their entrenchments. For a time the German advance had to be abandoned. A private British-Belgian ambulance, run by British doctors, did heroic work in succouring the Belgian wounded.

THE KAISER'S GRAND OBJECTIVE.
This admirable picture map of the Channel coast-line from Dunkirk to Boulogne is the work of a German professor, and was published in Germany at the time when the Kaiser had ordered his impotent hordes to "take Calais or die." It shows at a glance how important to the German designs on England was the capture of Calais.

25th the American war photographer, Donald Thompson, saw a company hesitate to obey the order to advance into the firing-zone. And he saw the captain draw his revolver and shoot the man who hung back most. It was on this day that artillery practice on the allied motor-ambulances with a Red Cross, clearly seen from the German lines, was marked by an eye-witness of a neutral nation. The German soldiers were then deserting across the Dutch frontier by hundreds and even thousands. Yet with the 7,000 Marines at Dixmude, the 12,000 infantry of the 42nd Division at Pervyse and their Belgian supports, there were barely 40,000 men holding a front of some seventeen miles along the Yser. A quarter of the remnant of the Belgian field army was killed or wounded, and more than half the remainder had withdrawn to rest and refit, coming into action as reserves when danger pressed. The Breton Marines had also lost a

Great stand along the Yser

quarter of their effectives. Dixmude was not taken by the Germans till November 11th, when it had lost its importance as a bridge-head over the Yser. The Bretons then merely retired across the canalised river, and, from the south bank, held the enemy back more easily than before, using boats armed with quick-firing guns against parties of Germans cut off by the inundation.

In the meantime General Grosetti battled with the advancing invaders amid the dykes and marshes round Pervyse. After the Germans were thrown back between Tervaete and Schoorbakke, they turned their guns on Nieuport; and so overwhelming was the bombardment that ambulances could not get into the town to bring away the wounded. The Germans gathered at the village of St. Georges,

GERMAN NAVAL GUNNERS ON THE BELGIAN SAND-DUNES.
In the upper photograph we see Prussian cavalry entering Ostend.

419

THE BRITISH BOMBARDMENT OF THE GERMAN LINES BETWEEN OSTEND AND NIEUPORT.

H.M.S. Severn, Humber, and Mersey, shallow-draught monitors, circled up and down the coast during the firing, their course being indicated in the above diagrammatic view by the broken lines with arrows. It was the first time in German history that military operations had been interrupted by sea-power.

pressing in great force on the trenches of the Belgian troops defending Nieuport. As a counter-stroke the Allies, with both infantry and cavalry, charged along the coast and drove the Germans there back in confusion and disorder on Westkerke.

This success in turn provoked the Duke of Würtemberg to put forth all his strength against the withdrawn centre of the allied position. Still feinting at Nieuport from the east, he still further increased his forces there, and on Friday, October 30th, he struck down in **Algerians save the day** a south-westerly direction at the village of Ramscappelle. From there it was barely four miles across the fens to Furnes. Pushing back the allied troops with a terrific artillery fire, under cover of which the attacking infantry advanced, the enemy reached the eastern bank of the railway, held by some Algerian sharpshooters with Belgian supports. A body of four hundred Germans clambered up the bank and were shot at. They cried out that they were unarmed, and that they wished to surrender. Still the Arabs fired at them till they broke and fled. Only a few escaped. The rest were found dead or dying with their loaded rifles beside them. Another party tried the same game with the same result. Next, an officer, with only four men, advanced with a white flag. All were shot, and their hidden machine-gun captured. Then the Algerians charged and won the day. They were drawn up in the square at Furnes afterwards, and publicly thanked by King Albert and General Joffre.

On the northern bank of the Yser, on October 30th, was another potentate of Europe—a grey-haired man with a lined, careworn face, scarcely recognisable now that he had suddenly aged and clipped off the upturned ends of his famous Kaiser moustache. He looked like a beaten man, and in matter of fact his agents at the moment were trying to arrange a secret peace with France—offering her, by devious channels, the larger part of Alsace and Lorraine. All they asked in return was French help against Great Britain and the recognition of the German conquest of Belgium. If only he could threaten Calais, the German Emperor explained to the Duke of Würtemberg, the French nation would be anxious for peace.

Things were getting very troublesome for German troops on the Yser front. Since their first successful crossing over the river the polders had become very wet. Belgian engineers were raising the sluices here and there. They did not want wholly to discourage the invaders— that was not General Foch's plan. He wished to keep some 150,000 Germans hopefully employed along the Yser until the British force between Ypres and La Bassée was

HOW THE BRITISH MONITORS EVADED THE GERMAN FIRE OFF THE BELGIAN COAST.

The Germans tried to beat our monitors off by bringing up their 6 in. howitzers and placing them in concealed positions along the dunes. But our ships steamed out of the reach of the shore batteries, and replied with a terrible and devastating fire. With sides and guns protected, each monitor was armed with two 6 in. guns, two howitzers, four 3-pounders, and six rifle-calibre guns, and was capable of discharging a ton and a half of metal a minute. The monitors zigzagged about the sea at high mobility, their gunners directed by our aerial scouts and observation officers in tethered balloons. Later H.M.S. Venerable came up and bombarded the Germans further inland.

fully reinforced by the new French army under General D'Urbal. Yet, as the Germans began to press more strongly towards Furnes, the fens between the Yser and the last town in Belgium unoccupied by the enemy grew moister than even the rainy weather explained.

By the end of October there were several inches of water on the ground between the German and Belgian trenches. It was impeding the movements of the attacking infantry. In the historic Battle of Nieuport, in 1600, the Dutch had defeated the Spaniards by breaking the sea-dyke and drowning them. And German spies reported to the Duke of Würtemberg's headquarters

Russell.
LIEUT.-COMMANDER R. A. WILSON.
Commander of the monitor Mersey.

Lafayette.
REAR-ADMIRAL THE HON. H. HOOD.
Admiral in command of the Dover Patrol. He directed the operations off the Belgian coast.
(Photographed when a captain.)

a personal appeal for volunteers. He needed a brigade to capture at any cost the Belgian trenches, and storm the sea-wall and hold it before the dyke could be broken, while the German army waded on to Furnes.

A brigade of Würtemberg infantry, famous for their courage, stepped forward. "*Ave, Cæsar, morituri te salutant!*" Bravely they volunteered for death, and the operation was executed under the eyes of the Kaiser, surveying the scene through his field-glasses. At mid-day, the brigade crossed the Yser on planks, under the protection of the fire of the massed German batteries. After the long, ghastly struggles for the river it was choked

Russell.
COMMANDER A. L. SNAGGE.
Commander of the monitor Humber.

that King Albert and his Staff were examining an ancient deed in which were shown the places in which the sea-wall had been designed to be broken when Vauban, the great French engineer of the days of Louis XIV., planned the new water defences of Nieuport. It was while the duke was hesitating at the sight of the rising water that Kaiser Wilhelm arrived. The Emperor was all for quick, vigorous action, especially as the date he had fixed for the proclamation of the entire conquest of Belgium was at hand. He made

with broken boats, trees, floating fragments of planks, carcasses of horses, and human corpses. The Würtembergers massed on the left bank to attack, with the guns of their army shrapnelling their path of advance.

Some way in front of them was a hostile trench, with a line of caps just showing above the parapet. On these caps the German artillerymen especially directed their fire. But when the Würtembergers took the trench at the double they found there were no heads beneath the caps.

THE BRITISH FLOATING FORTS WHICH SHELLED THE GERMAN TRENCHES NEAR THE BELGIAN COAST-LINE.
A striking photograph of the three British monitors—Severn, Humber, and Mersey—which opened the bombardment of the German positions along the Belgian coast-line between Ostend and Nieuport.

GERMAN PRISONERS AT FURNES.
The fenland and dunes round the little town of Furnes constituted the last nook of unconquered Belgian territory. It is noticeable that the prisoners in the above photograph included many mere boys.

SCENE IN BLANKENBERGHE DURING THE KAISER'S FRANTIC EFFORT TO COMMAND THE COAST.
German Uhlans and cyclist scouts receiving instructions in the main street of Blankenberghe. Inset: Forlorn and dishevelled German troops captured during the terrible battle along the Belgian coast. A battalion of them attempted to rush some of the Allies' field-guns, but all were annihilated with the exception of the unhappy men who figure in the photograph.

CAUGHT BETWEEN FIRE AND WATER: THE GERMAN ROUT BETWEEN DIXMUDE AND BIXSCHOOTE.

A brigade of Würtemberg infantry, responding to a personal appeal by the Kaiser, crossed the Yser on planks and advanced on the Belgian trenches, to be caught by the rising water let in from the dykes. After the long, ghastly struggles for the river, it was choked with broken boats, trees, carcasses of horses, and hunan corpses. The Würtembergers were engulfed with all their débris. Their guns stuck in the soft ground, and as they turned in flight the allied artillery poured salvos of shrapnel over them. An allied infantry force with an armoured car and a machine-gun added to the Würtembergers' disconfiture,

GENERAL VIEW OF A BLUE CROSS HOSPITAL IN FRANCE.
Hundreds of war-weary, wounded, and sick animals were here nursed back to health and strength.

The allied troops were on the high ground beyond. As the brigade prepared to sweep onward there was an unusual sound seaward, like the rush of storm-water over a weir. It was the North Sea at flood-tide pouring through the broken dyke. Bursting upon the astonished Würtembergers, the seething water carried trees and corpses with it and filled the trenches. Shouts of anger and screams of fear came from the German lines.

The trapped brigade fled to the ridge of higher ground to escape the inundation. But this movement of theirs had been foreseen, and from afar the allied artillery poured salvos of shrapnel shells over them. They were taken between fire and water. Those who escaped drowning fell by shell or bullet, and only a few, reaching the Belgian-French lines, evaded death by captivity. Thus perished the Würtemberg Brigade—the last, forlorn hope of the German offensive on the Yser. That evening the Kaiser departed from the Belgian coast, where 30,000 of his men had fallen.

The Duke of Würtemberg then moved many of his defeated troops towards Ypres. But there

GERMAN SPADE-WORK IN BELGIUM.
German engineers constructing a tunnel through a hillside to shorten a railway route in Belgium.

they fared no better than they had done at Nieuport and Dixmude. For by this time a French force had arrived to strengthen the three British Divisions that held Ypres. The French troops occupied the villages of Bixschoote and Langemarck and held Merchem and the northern road to Dixmude. At Bixschoote, where the defences of Ypres jutted eastward in a salient, the German attack was the fiercest and the most incessant. While our men, joining with the French and continuing the defence northward, were beating off army corps after army corps of Germans, the Zouaves and French regiments of the line at Bixschoote in the north were just as violently engaged.

The village itself was taken and lost repeatedly by both sides, and at last so terribly bombarded that neither the French nor the Germans dared to enter it. It became a great charnel-house, where friend and foe lay unburied for a month or more. In the last German attack, towards the middle of November, the slaughter was appalling. On a single day some 9,000 Germans were killed in the village. The following day the rest

BY THE YSER CANAL.
A camp waggon neatly overturned, yet not greatly damaged, by a German shell.

of the hostile division—another 3,000 men — was annihilated. Even when the advance of the Prussian Guard had failed against the British lines, General von Deimling and the Duke of Würtemberg still continued to attempt to reach Ypres by the north. At times the French had to give way, but they always recovered their lost ground. Some days a trench was lost and won several times. Then on Monday, November 16th, they fought the Germans, almost foot to foot, for forty hours. They broke them at last by point-blank rifle fire, at a range of twenty-one yards! It was not until this superb stand that the German Commander-in-Chief decided both the French trenches and the British were impregnable. Then the Zouaves advanced in turn and captured a wood held by the Germans; and the grim, wearing trench battles went on all through the snow, frost, and rain of winter.

To the French people Ypres has become as memorable a town as it is to the British nation. Besides holding the northern trenches at Bixschoote and the lines of retreat for the Franco-British army at the bridges of Boesinghe, **General Moussy's** the soldiers of France fought side by side **gallant recruits** with our men on the south of Ypres at Zillebeke. Here a German regiment succeeded at last in piercing the line, and General Moussy sent some of his cuirassiers to the rear to search for reinforcements. But the search was vain. Every available man was hotly engaged in the fighting-line, and the Germans were penetrating into the streets of Ypres. As a forlorn hope, General Moussy asked his orderly, a corporal, to bring up every man he could find and to call for volunteers as he ran.

The corporal gathered a ragged, unlikely force of some two hundred and fifty men—cooks, motor drivers, Army

Service Corps men—mostly without arms. The sixty-five cuirassiers, forming the General's escort, charged in their steel breastplates and cavalry boots, followed by the mob of hewers of wood and drawers of water, who seized any weapons that were handy. Headed by the General and the corporal, the company of cooks and camp followers counter-attacked a German regiment flushed with success which, after tremendous struggles, had pierced the loop of trenches round Ypres. The Germans were about to win one of those victories that mark a decisive period in the **What Ypres cost** history of great wars; but General **Germany** Moussy's gallant recruits caught the victors on the flank and routed them. Thus was Ypres saved, at the most critical hour in the momentous struggle.

Soon afterwards the great battle along the Yser relapsed into the old-fashioned circumvallation warfare of the age of Vauban and Turenne and Marlborough. Both sides returned to the mediæval method of trench warfare from which our Grenadiers had obtained their name. Hand-grenades were thrown from ditch to ditch, and the ancient trench mortar was resurrected from military museums and employed once more. The sap and the mine came into general use, and the trench system, with its traverses and covered ways, was extended in a manner that would have delighted Uncle Toby and Corporal Trim in the days of "Tristram Shandy." Five millions of men were ditched against each other, under the rain, frost, and chilling blasts of winter, from the sand-dunes of the North Sea to the edge of the mountains of Switzerland. It was an apparent deadlock. But it cost Germany some two millions of soldiers to arrive at this stage of the struggle. Her original first-line army had well-nigh disappeared.

DEFENCE OF BELGIUM BY FIRE AND FLOOD.
View of the defensive inundations near the Yser. Inset: Belgians working a machine-gun at Nieuport.

WAR BEHIND THE CURTAIN OF THE HILLS.

In the above picture, which is based upon a photograph of the actual scene, our artist conveys a realistic idea of what a modern artillery duel looks like from an ammunition column in the rear of the fighting-line. The white spots in the sky are the howitzer shells bursting, and except for the thunderous roll of the guns the actual scene is as peaceful as it appears here. The ammunition column has to face great danger, however, when it is signalled forward to supply the guns; and wherever possible the ammunition was conveyed to the firing line at night time.

CHAPTER XLVI.

THE NAVAL WAR IN THE ATLANTIC AND PACIFIC.
Clearing the Enemy from the Ocean Highways.

The Hawke Torpedoed in the North Sea—Captain Fox on the Undaunted Avenges the Loss of the Amphion—Four Enemy Destroyers Sunk off Holland—German Submarine Success in the Channel—The Formidable Goes Down and Bulwark Blows Up—Germany Begins Her Piratical Attack on Merchant Shipping—Passenger Steamer Crowded with Refugees Torpedoed without Warning—General Position of Our Merchant Marine after Ten Weeks of War—Sweeping the Seas of Commerce-Raiders—The Emden Sinks a Russian Cruiser at Penang—Gallant Struggle by a French Destroyer—The Sydney Catches and Wrecks the Emden—The End of the Königsberg—The Battle off Coronel—The Battle off the Falkland Islands.

JUST before our monitor squadron and destroyer flotilla steamed to the Belgian coast to take part in the great land battle, the work of patrolling the Channel and the North Sea became more difficult and urgent. For the enemy then possessed, in the northern ports of the Belgian coast, new bases for torpedo operations perilously close to England and to France. Grand-Admiral von Tirpitz went to Belgium to organise a new campaign. Submarines were sent in parts by railway to Bruges, mines were laid in the Scheldt, and both destroyers and submarines were ordered to proceed south from Emden with a view to acting from the new Belgian bases.

Meanwhile, the brilliant German submarine officer, Lieutenant Weddigen, was tracking two of our old armoured cruisers, the Hawke and the Theseus, in the northern waters of the North Sea. Both these ships were slow and obsolete. Their ordinary cruising speed did not exceed that of a submarine, and unfortunately no destroyers could be spared to work with them and beat off hostile underwater craft.

Designed for the protection of trade routes about a quarter of a century before the war broke out, they had lost their speed of nineteen knots. On the forenoon of Thursday, October 15th, the two old

sister ships were attacked by U9. Weddigen released his first torpedo at the Theseus, but missed the mark. Then he turned on the Hawke, and struck her amidships near a ready magazine. The detonation was followed by a second terrific explosion, in which a large number of the crew were killed, and in five minutes the Hawke sank, with the loss of five hundred and twenty-five lives. The men went to their death as heroically as the men of the Aboukir, Hogue, and Cressy had done.

Some of them were singing a chanty when the ship was struck, and as she reeled under the shock, with part of her side torn away from her, the signal "Still!" brought every man on deck to his post. Then, as the ship listed, Captain Williams cried out from the bridge: "It's everyone for himself!" But there was only time to get out the longboat, in which some forty-nine men were saved. While most of the crew were struggling in the water, Weddigen put up his periscope to watch if the Theseus would stand by and try to rescue the drowning men. But knowing what had happened to the Hogue and Cressy, and acting in accordance with orders issued by the Admiralty after the mishap, Captain Hugh Edwards, of the Theseus, steamed away from the scene of disaster. The men in the longboat made a last brave stroke, and tried to blind their hidden enemy by battering the periscope with their oars, but they failed to injure it.

LIEUTENANT OTTO WEDDIGEN.
Commander of the German submarine U9, which sank H.M.S. Hawke and caused the loss of five hundred and twenty-five lives in the North Sea on October 15th, 1914.

After rowing about for three hours, they were picked up by a Norwegian steamer.

When Weddigen had thus cleared the northern seas of the patrolling cruisers, four of the newest German destroyers, S115, S117, S118, and S119, left Emden, and turned south, with the intention of operating off Belgium with the submarines. But, by a curious coincidence, the newest British light cruiser, with four of the newest British destroyers, steamed out of Harwich at the same hour and also made in the same direction—for our submarines were still watching off the enemy's harbour, and a wireless message had rippled over the North Sea when the hostile destroyers appeared.

The task of avenging the Hawke was entrusted to Captain Cecil H. Fox. His earlier ship, the Amphion, had been destroyed by a mine in the first days of the war, after she had struck the first blow against the German Navy by sinking the minelayer Königin Luise. Captain Fox was given the command of the light cruiser Undaunted, and was accompanied by the Lance, Commander Egerton; the Lennox, Lieut-Commander Dane; the Legion, Lieut-Commander Allsup; and the Loyal, Lieut-Commander Burges Watson—all four destroyers of the latest L type. At four o'clock on the afternoon of Saturday, October 17th, the German flotilla was descried off the mouth of the Scheldt. They tried to escape, but by good seamanship Captain Fox cut them off, using the superior speed of his flotilla to the best advantage, and then opened the action at a range of five miles.

The Undaunted had been completed about a week only, and her crew had had little time to know their ship and settle down to team work. Yet they fought as well as if they had been practising together for a year. A light cruiser has a supreme advantage over a destroyer, in that it can use a fire-control system, for **Undaunted's deadly marksmanship** which there is no space on the smaller boat. The gunners in all destroyers have to fight their guns in the old-fashioned way, each gunlayer working out his elevation and traverse by rule of thumb. The result was such that, if the hostile flotilla had not been able to scatter, the Undaunted could have destroyed each vessel in turn. To prevent any of the enemy escaping, Captain Fox ordered the four British destroyers to concentrate against two of the German vessels. This gave our gunlayers in the smaller craft double the fire-power of their immediate enemies.

Then the Undaunted brought her two 6 in. guns and 4 in. guns against the two remaining destroyers, fighting them at a distance from which their 4-pounder quick-firers were utterly ineffectual. So deadly was the marksmanship of the British light cruiser that in less than a minute the leading German boat was in distress. Clouds of smoke arose from her as the lyddite shells struck home and exploded, rending the thin steel armour-plate of the hull as if it were wood and hurling the metal splinters all about. A shell smashed the machinery and brought the boat to a standstill, and a few minutes after the action opened she was sunk. Soon afterwards the second enemy destroyer was ablaze from end to end, with her funnels, bridge and deck fittings torn from their holdings. As **Hawke splendidly avenged** she went down the sea seemed to engulf a length of leaping flame.

All this was done in a running fight, with the vessels going at the speed of a railway train. The enemy's small, low-lying, and swiftly-moving target vainly tried to dodge the fire by taking a zigzag course. The Loyal made fine practice against one of the remaining German destroyers, while the Lance, Legion, and Lennox battered another. The German gunners apparently lost their nerve, for their marksmanship, even from the destroyers' view, was poor. Our men evaded their shots with ease, and we had only a few casualties. At the end of an hour and a half the German Navy had lost four useful destroyers and some two hundred and fifty officers and men, including thirty-two survivors picked up after the action.

The next day the Germans won their first success against our submarine flotilla. Three hours after the outbreak of the war our underwater craft began to operate in the Heligoland Bight, and there they remained for months watching the enemy's movements, and even blockading the throat of the Elbe. In vain did the German light cruisers and destroyers attempt to drive them off; but at last, on Sunday, October 18th, our submarine E3 was attacked and sunk, while working in a German bay in the North Sea, and Lieut-.Commander George F. Cholmondeley and twenty-five men perished. A few days afterwards, Commander Charles Fremantle drove his destroyer Badger over a German submarine off the Dutch coast. The hostile boat began by firing a torpedo, which missed the mark, and the Badger, seeing her periscope, went full steam ahead, and struck the submarine with such force that she damaged her own bows and was brought to a standstill. It was first thought that by this

THE LAST OF THE RUSSIAN CRUISER JEMCHUG, WHICH WAS SUNK BY THE EMDEN OFF PENANG ON OCTOBER 28TH, 1914.

bold manœuvre the crew of submarine E3 had been avenged, but the German naval authorities asserted that the rammed submarine succeeded in getting back safely to harbour. However this may be, the underwater craft of the enemy continued the war of attrition in a very slow manner. One of them was again rammed on November 24th off the northern coast of Scotland. She was the U18, and rising to the surface she hoisted the white flag, and foundered just as one of our destroyers came up. Her crew were rescued with the exception of one man.

Seeing how large a number of ships we continually exposed to attack, the success of the enemy's submarines was very poor. In addition to our Grand Fleet, with its patrolling cruisers and battle-cruisers, **Enemy submarines** there was a large squadron battling **baffled** night and day off the Belgian coast. The cruisers were intently engaged in working their guns, manœuvring their ships under heavy shell fire, and beating down the hostile batteries of 11 and 12 in. howitzers. But the attacking German submarines never got a torpedo home against one of them.

The fact seemed to be that modern ships, continually moving at high speed with protecting destroyers around them, were absolutely secure against underwater attack. No hostile submarine could get within striking range without attracting the notice of the vigilant destroyers. Several old cruisers and gunboats were added to Admiral Hood's bombarding squadron. Obsolete vessels were specially selected for the work of assisting the Belgian army in the coast battle, by reason of the great risks which vessels ran from the enemy's heavy artillery. Some of them were as slow as a modern submarine, yet they escaped the fate of the Hawke, the Aboukir, and her sisters, owing to the protection of their destroyer flotilla. German submarine attacks were persistent and daring, but none of them succeeded.

It looked as though our Navy, with its wonted ingenuity and skill, had quickly found a means of eluding "the deadliest thing that keeps the seas." A few months before the war, Admiral Sir Percy Scott had begun to think that our latest super-Dreadnoughts would be vanquished by the cumbersome and delicate submersible torpedo-boat. But in actual practice it was soon found that our swifter torpedo-boat destroyers were still a fairly efficient defence against the old foe of battleships in its new form. For some time afterwards we continued to lose single vessels by torpedo attacks from submarines. But in nearly every case the attack succeeded only in the absence of protecting destroyers.

The old cruiser Hermes, for instance, was sunk by a German submarine as she was returning from Dunkirk, where she served as a depot ship and seaplane carrier to the Naval Wing of the Royal Flying Corps. In this case the loss was of little importance. For although the obsolete cruiser was badly hit, she kept afloat for a considerable time, and nearly all her officers and crew were saved by vessels that came to her aid. Later on, the older torpedo-gunboat H.M.S. Niger was torpedoed when lying near to the long pier at Deal. It was fully half an hour before she sank, and though a few men were injured by the explosion, no loss of life was reported.

Far more serious was the loss of the great battleship Formidable, off Torbay, on the first day of the New Year. She was of the pre-Dreadnought type, with 12 in. guns, and six hundred of her seven hundred and fifty men went down in her. The weather was clear, the sea choppy, and the moon shining. The line of big ships, under Vice-Admiral Sir Lewis Bayly, was steaming slowly past Torbay in single file, thus presenting in the bright moonlight a series of easy targets. It is the practice in cruising for a single ship to proceed at high speed upon a zigzag course, these tactics being embarrassing to any hostile submarine in the neighbourhood. In the case of a squadron, it is usual to surround the big ships with a screen of destroyers, whose high speed and handiness are calculated to make things uncomfortable for any attacking underwater craft. This measure of precaution, however, is reported to have been neglected on this occasion.

H.M.S. HERMES: TORPEDOED BY A GERMAN SUBMARINE.
The Hermes was sunk by a German submarine in Dover Straits on October 31st, 1914. Old though the cruiser was, she kept afloat long enough for most of her officers and crew to be saved. Our photograph shows French torpedo-boats racing towards the doomed vessel to render aid.

As the sea was breaking, the German craft was able to rise and get her bearings without being detected, and as she discharged her torpedoes at the strung-out line of slowly-moving targets there was a good chance that if the missiles missed one ship they would hit the next. The Formidable, under Captain Loxley, was the last ship in the line. She was struck by a torpedo about 2.30 a.m. on Friday morning, January 1st. Five hundred of her men were sleeping in their bunks when the torpedo, missing the magazine by ten feet, exploded under the dynamo-room and put all the electric lighting out of action.

Sir Lewis Bayly at once signalled the rest of his squadron to steam away at high speed, leaving only a light cruiser to stand by the stricken battleship and save life. But the wind suddenly freshened to a gale, and the sea rose quickly, while the ship listed heavily on her starboard side. She tilted up at an angle which made it difficult for a man to retain his foothold, and it seemed as if she must capsize in a few minutes. Happily, another torpedo struck her on the port side, and the new inrush of water had the effect of trimming the great vessel, though she now lay much lower in the sea.

Captain Loxley was on the bridge all through the three hours before the Formidable took her final plunge. He signalled to another British warship which was near at hand not to stand by to help, but to keep off, because he believed a German submarine to be in his neighbourhood. His last words were :

Captain Loxley's last signal "Steady, men. It's all right. No panic, men. Keep cool, and be British !" Then three terrific seas struck the sinking ship, and as she went down the crew tried to swim clear. With the help of the gallant crews of some trawlers, a hundred and fifty men were saved. One of the open boats, crowded with half-naked men, wallowed in the storm for over twenty-two hours. The sailors started about eighty strong, and when they were pulled in at Lyme Regis there were fifty-one still living, three of whom died shortly after landing.

The loss of the Formidable's sister battleship, the Bulwark, which blew up at Sheerness on November 26th, cannot be credited to the skill and daring of the German submarine officer. The destruction of the ship, with practically her entire crew of 750, seemed to have been due to an internal magazine explosion. Whether a spy with an infernal machine detonated the magazine, or whether some of the ammunition was ignited either by chemical decomposition or by an accident, remains at present a mystery.

On the whole, the naval war of attrition by submarine attack produced absolutely no diminution in the comparative strength of the two chief contending navies of the world during the first critical six months of the war. At the end of that time our Fleet was both absolutely and relatively stronger than it had been on the day of mobilisation. Against the commerce and industries of Germany

GERMAN SUBMARINE RAMMED BY A BRITISH DESTROYER.
After ramming a German "unterseeboot" off the Dutch coast on October 24th, 1914, H.M. destroyer Badger turned her searchlights on the enemy vessel. The ultimate fate of the submarine is uncertain, but the German authorities announced that she got back to harbour.

it exerted a pressure so tremendous and enveloping that the German people had to be put on siege rations. Never before had the restricting use of sea-power been employed with such telling force. There was no fight, not even the feint of a fight. The second most powerful navy in the world was reduced to practical impotence, in the long, critical period of the struggle, merely by the distant display of the naval might of the British Empire. The German battleships were enclosed in booms, sunken wire entanglements, and rows of mines, thus yielding without a struggle the actual temporary command of the sea to the ocean Empire. Yet the Germans had been proclaiming for years that their Navy was designed to fight ours, and that it would steam out at the first opportunity and either win the fleet action or at least so cripple all our capital ships as to leave the command of the sea in the hands of the United States. In either case Britannia was to rule the waves no longer. The sceptre of Neptune would pass to another nation. **German threats and** But when it came to the test, Britannia **performance** in the days of war held the trident more firmly than she had done in the days of peace.

In the home seas Germany had nothing but a few submarines with a wide radius of action to dispute our sway. But

"How oft the sight of means to do ill deeds
Makes ill deeds done" !

Crazy with hatred and maddened at her sudden impotence after years of braggart and magnificent preparations for a

AUSTRALIAN NAVY'S FIRST IMPORTANT ENGAGEMENT: THE RAIDING EMDEN ROUNDED UP AND DESTROYED BY H.M.A.S. SYDNEY.

One hour forty minutes after the firing of the first shot between the Emden and the Sydney off Cocos Keeling Island, on November 9th, 1914, the German cruiser was a mass of scrap-iron. Only one hundred and forty-five of her crew were unwounded, and the dead numbered one hundred and nineteen. Four men of the Sydney were killed and sixteen wounded. It was estimated that this single German cruiser had sunk shipping valued at over £4,000,000. The British Admiralty sent the following message to the commander of the Sydney and to the Australian Naval Board: "Warmest congratulations on the brilliant entry of the Australian Navy into the war, and the signal service rendered to the allied cause and to peaceful commerce by the destruction of the Emden."

432

naval struggle, Germany degraded her submarines into stealthy, inhuman instruments of piracy. Some months passed before she drew down the entire condemnation of the world by applying her new policy of terrorisation on the high seas to neutral as well as warring nations. In the meantime she proceeded to develop in silence her barbaric practice of slaughtering sailors and passengers in non-combatant ships. Her first exploit in commerce destruction by submarine attack occurred on Tuesday, October 20th.

Germany hoists the "Jolly Roger" The British steamer Glitra, with a cargo of oil and coal, was steaming towards Stavanger in Norway. When about ten miles from this destination Captain Johnston sighted a submarine steaming on the surface and flying the German flag. The British skipper tried to escape by standing more north, but the German boat brought her quick-firing guns into play, and, by sending some shells over the bows of the British steamer, forced her to reduce speed. The German officer then hoisted a signal, asking

CAPTAIN JOHN C. T. GLOSSOP.
Commander of H.M.A.S. Sydney.

CAPTAIN KARL VON MÜLLER.
Commander of the Emden.

for a tow-line. But Captain Johnston continued on his course, till the enemy cried out that if the steamer did not stop it would be torpedoed.

Two officers and a couple of men then boarded the Glitra from a canvas boat. They had revolvers in their hands, and they ordered the crew to leave the ship within ten minutes. The German officer had the British flag hauled down, and tearing it into pieces he threw it on the deck and wiped his feet on it. The crew were not even allowed to take their clothes with them, and one stoker, who was stripped, had to get into the ship's boat as he was. As they rowed to the shore, the submarine officers entered the engine-room and opened the bottom valves. Then, returning to the submarine, they fired on the steamer, which took nearly three hours to sink.

U17 was the submarine that carried out this work. It was the first recorded instance of a merchant-ship being captured or sunk by underwater craft. The incident attracted much attention at the time, owing to the childish manner in which the German officer insulted the British flag. The extravagant fury of the man was, however, of more

than personal significance. He had work to do calculated to make him ashamed of himself and of his nation, and it was to save himself from self-contempt that he acted like a fool with regard to the flag of an undefended merchant-ship.

The attack on the Glitra was a half-hearted affair conducted by men who could not at once screw themselves up to the full pitch of inhumanity. But about a week later, on Monday, October 26th, the first historic act of veritable, inexcusable piracy was committed. On that day the French liner Amiral Ganteaume was steaming from Calais to Havre in a heavy sea with 2,500 refugees aboard. They were men, women, and children of the poorest class from the flaming villages and bombarded towns of the country round Lille and Arras. At 2.30 p.m., when the liner was nine miles off **Refugee ship** Boulogne, the periscope of a sub- **torpedoed** marine was observed in the choppy sea. The next instant a torpedo struck a coal-bunker by the engine-room, and a great column of smoke and steam rose from the doomed vessel.

Some of the poor passengers were naturally frightened, but the French crew was coolly and capably heroic. The Dover mail steamer Queen steamed up to help, and her captain succeeded in allaying an incipient panic. About thirty innocent lives were lost, but the Ganteaume floated and got back to port. The following day traffic along the chief Atlantic trade routes was interrupted. A British steamer, the Manchester Commerce, struck a mine off the Irish coast by Tory Island, the captain and thirteen men perishing. It was found that a mine-field had been laid off the island by a vessel showing a neutral flag. It had been laid on one of the new trade

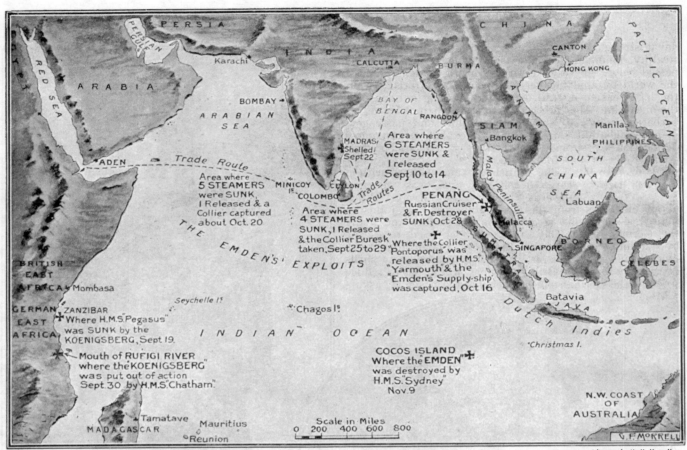

PICTURE-MAP SHOWING THE CRUISINGS AND EXPLOITS OF THE EMDEN AND THE KONIGSBERG.

routes fixed by our Admiralty and communicated by secret instructions to skippers, ship-owners, and cargo-owners concerned in the carrying of commerce across the Northern Atlantic. The speed and facility with which the new route had been mined proved that German secret service agents working in our country were able to discover our Admiralty's secret instructions, and arrange quickly for a neutral vessel to slip out on the new route with a cargo of mines. As a matter of fact, some ship-owners, skippers, and

The Kaiser's paper blockade

seamen of a certain neutral power in Northern Europe continued for some time to assist in the most active and deadly manner in the underhanded schemes of destruction planned by Germany against our mercantile marine and naval forces.

It will thus be seen that, four months before Germany publicly proclaimed her intention to destroy our sea-borne commerce by submarine piracy and by the laying of mine-fields on our trade routes, she was already employing all available means to this end. The small amount of harm she did between October 19th, 1914, and February 18th, 1915, was a fair measure of the practical impotence to which she had been reduced long before she made her wild threat. Reversing her usual way of acting, she did not attempt to terrorise our merchant seamen until she had discovered, after four months of incessant experience, that she could not hurt or interfere with them to any extent. So long as she hoped she could do considerable harm she worked in silence. When she fully discovered that she lacked the power to damage or diminish seriously the sea-borne commerce of Britain and France she exploded in extravagant threats and proclaimed a submarine blockade of the British Isles. The affair was the most amazing episode in the war. The extraordinary fatuity of it lightened up the study of the minds of the directors of the destinies of Germany in her year of doom.

The reason why the Kaiser and Grand-Admiral von Tirpitz resorted to piracy in the middle of October, barely ten weeks after the outbreak of hostilities, was explained by a statement issued by the Secretary of our Admiralty on

October 23rd. At that date only 39 out of 4,000 British ships engaged in foreign trade had been sunk by the enemy. Nearly 9,000 foreign voyages had been undertaken to and from the ports of the United Kingdom, and in scarcely forty-five cases had our ships been interfered with. Moreover, most of these small losses had been occasioned by skippers taking everything for granted, and going about their business as though we were not at war with the second greatest naval Power in the world. On all the routes where Admiralty instructions were followed, little damage was done to our merchant shipping. Nearly all the captures were occasioned by the disregard of the instructions and precautions formulated by our Sea Lords.

While our overseas trade was thus impeded only by the large number of ships withdrawn for the transport of troops and the supply of material and supplies to our Navy and Expeditionary Force, the overseas trade of Germany had practically ceased to exist. Nearly all her fast liners, which could have been used as armed cruisers, were either penned in neutral harbours and eating away, by the expenses therein incurred, the large amount of capital sunk in them, or they were lying idly and wastefully in their own ports. Among the comparatively few German ships which had put out to sea, one hundred and thirty-three had been captured, which was nearly four times the number of those lost by the vast and active British mercantile marine. The

German overseas trade crippled

Government rate of insurance for cargoes fixed at the outbreak of war at five guineas per cent., was reduced to two guineas, without imperilling the solvency of the Government Insurance Fund. For hulls, apart from cargoes, the Government rate of insurance was also considerably reduced.

For there were only eight or nine German cruisers still at large in the Atlantic, Pacific, and Indian Oceans. Searching for these commerce-raiders were more than seventy British, Japanese, French, and Russian cruisers, in addition to a considerable number of armed liners. All the allied trade-protecting warships worked on a concerted plan of

STAFF OF THE COCOS WIRELESS STATION WATCHING THE ACTION BETWEEN THE SYDNEY AND THE EMDEN.

EMDEN SURVIVORS ALONGSIDE THE SYDNEY.   BRINGING GERMAN WOUNDED FROM THE EMDEN.

The right-hand photograph was taken on the morning following the action between the Sydney and the Emden, and shows one of the Sydney's boats taking survivors and wounded from the German to the Australian warship.   The battered and broken Emden is seen on the reef in the distance.

ONE OF THE SYDNEY'S BOATS ON ITS WAY TO RESCUE THE CABLE STAFF.

Thinking part of the crew of the Emden were still on shore, the Sydney sent a boat to the island under a white flag, to get the cable staff off before bombarding.   But the Emden's men had left in the schooner Ayesha.

VIEW OF THE EMDEN TAKEN FROM THE DECK OF THE SYDNEY AFTER THE GREAT FIGHT.

ANOTHER PHOTOGRAPH GIVING A NEARER VIEW OF THE SHATTERED GERMAN CRUISER.

operations. It was impossible to hunt down each German ship, for all had an almost infinite choice of movement over the vast expanses of sea and ocean and amid the thousands of islands and lonely river mouths of the outlands of the world. The main effort of the allied cruisers was to trace and cut off the coal supplies of the raiding warships. The German coaling organisation had been established during the Russo-Japanese War, when the Germans coaled the Russian Baltic Fleet for its long voyage to the Strait of Corea. For nine years afterwards the coaling arrangements had been developed, with many secret plans directly in prospect of the sea struggle with the British Empire.

Sea raiders' secret coaling plans

Innocent-looking cargo steamers of neutral Powers were largely employed, and, unless they were actually caught in the act of coaling a German warship, it was impossible to prove that they were not engaged in genuine traffic. Near at home, for instance, a Dutch steamer, plying from Swansea to Havre, took ten barrels of heavy oil aboard for her own lamps and stoves. In the brief voyage from South Wales to Northern France all the barrels were emptied. How could it be proved that a German submarine, badly needing the oil for her Diesel engine, had stopped the Dutch ship by prearrangement and had used her as a supply ship? More difficult problems than this occurred for solution in the distant waters where the secret coaling of the German commerce-raiders went on.

The Emden continued to do most damage to our commerce. By her raid in the Bay of Bengal she stopped some six million pounds' worth of Indian exports and about half that amount of imports. She captured twenty-one steamers of the value of £650,000, with cargoes worth £3,000,000. Midway in her career of destruction, however, she was crippled by Captain Cochrane, of H.M.S. Yarmouth, who captured off Sumatra the Hamburg-Amerika liner Markomannia, which was acting as collier to the Emden. He also retook the Greek steamer Pontoporos, which had been captured and put to the same purpose.

Emden's daring raid on Penang

This left Captain Karl von Müller with a much restricted range of action. For some days he continued to prey on the ocean traffic of India, then, when his coal was running short, he resolved on one of the most daring strokes in the naval campaign. He knew that the Yarmouth was operating from Penang, the chief port of the Straits Settlements. And as she had made for this gateway of commerce in order to attack his colliers, he answered the attack by a raid on Penang.

At dawn on Wednesday, October 28th, the Emden stopped some ten miles off Penang and hoisted an additional dummy funnel. This changed her appearance from that of a three-funnelled light cruiser of the German town class to a four-funnelled light cruiser of the British town class. In the semi-darkness of dawn she resembled the Yarmouth, and, as she steamed towards the harbour, everybody on the watch there thought that she was the Yarmouth returning to anchorage. There was a Russian light cruiser, the Jemchug, in the harbour, together with three French destroyers and a gunboat. The Jemchug was an older ship than the Emden, and had only six 4·7 in. guns against

Hole made on the forecastle deck of the Sydney by a shell from the Emden.

Havoc caused to the deck of the Emden by the fire from the Sydney.

Remains of the funnels of the Emden after the battle off Cocos Keeling.

Wounded sailors on the Emden covered with sacking to protect them from the sun.

Damage done to the alternative control platform of the Sydney by a shell fired from the Emden in the early stage of the action.

REALISTIC CAMERA RECORDS OF THE BATTLE BETWEEN THE SYDNEY AND THE EMDEN.

The bottom photograph was taken immediately after the victory. It was taken from the forecastle of the Sydney, and gives a vivid impression of the damage done to the upper bridge, where the foremost range-finder was shot down soon after the opening of the fight. The bridge was roughly fortified by hammocks. The crew have the appearance of men who have "something attempted, something done."

No more characteristic photograph of France's great silent Generalissimo has appeared than the above, from "L'Illustration," of Paris. Known well to all students of French military history since the days of the Franco-Prussian War of 1870-71, he remained unknown to the world at large till the outbreak of the present war. Men speak of him as greater than Napoleon for two reasons—because he is no dreamer of world-conquest to whom human life is as nothing but a means the gratification of a single ambition; and because of his great patience, a patience which is little distinguishable from prescience. He has proved his love for Fran

Photograph : S. d'A.

for Frenchmen, and all Frenchmen worship him. Our Paris contemporary resses the universal feeling of affection with which General Joffre is regarded in description of the above photograph : " Under the eyes of ' Our Joffre ' the querors of to-morrow return to the trenches. Clean and trim, knapsacks on back, and with bayonets fixed, our infantry marches past, keeping good step in the alert French style, to the admiration of the Commander-in-Chief and the Generals commanding the Armies of the North." The Generals in question, reading from left to right, are General Foch, General D'Urbal, and General Balfourier.

THE GREAT BRITISH VICTORY OFF THE FALKLANDS: GERMAN ADMIRAL GOES DOWN WITH HIS FLAGSHIP.

The great naval action which ended in the memorable victory for Vice-Admiral Sir Frederick Doveton Sturdee took place on December 8th, 1914, and lasted for five hours, in the course of which the Scharnhorst, flying the flag of Admiral Count von Spee, the Gneisenau, the Leipzig, and the Nürnberg were sunk. The Scharnhorst, an armoured cruiser of 11,600 tons, with a complement of seven hundred and sixty-five men, caught fire, but her flag remained flying to the last, when, a few minutes after she was seen suddenly to list heavily to port, she lay on her beam ends and disappeared.

the Emden's ten 4·1 in. guns of a newer pattern. But the Russian crew of three hundred and thirty-four men would have made a brave fight for it if they had not been taken unawares.

As the enemy entered the harbour the Jemchug challenged her, and received the answer that it was the Yarmouth coming to anchor. But when the enemy was 600 yards away the Russians pierced the disguise of the dummy funnel and opened fire with their guns. Meanwhile, however, the Emden had trained one of her torpedo-tubes on the Russian ship. Delivered at a short range, the torpedo entered the engine-room of the Jemchug, and rendered her quite helpless by disabling the machinery for hoisting ammunition. Closing in on a zigzag course, Müller fired salvo after salvo at the stricken Russian vessel. A hundred shells were poured in at a distance lessening from 350 to 250 yards, while the Russian cruiser listed so that the few shots she was able to send in reply went wide. The German then turned and brought her second torpedo-tube into play. The torpedo exploded the Jemchug's magazine, and in a dense pall of black smoke tongued with flame the Russian cruiser sank, after an engagement lasting scarcely fifteen minutes.

The Emden at once left the harbour at full speed, while the people of Penang were fearing she would shell their defenceless town. But Captain Müller was anxious about the fate of his own ship. He had expected to find the French cruiser Dupleix in the harbour, and he was afraid that both this ship and the Yarmouth were within wireless call and closing in upon him. His duty as a commerce-raider was to avoid anything like an equal fight, and simply to do the utmost damage possible to the mercantile marine of the allied powers. Thirty miles from Penang he sighted a steamer. She hoisted the red flag, signifying that she was a powder steamer. This was an especial prize for the Emden, now running short of ammunition.

She got out her boats and was about to examine her new capture when a very remarkable thing occurred. A large hostile warship appeared on the horizon. Hastily Captain Müller ordered his boats to return, and made off with all speed. The large warship, however, was only the effect of the early morning mirage on the tropical sea. As the ships closed to about 3,800 yards the stranger was found to be the small French destroyer Mousquet. This small vessel had no chance whatever against the German cruiser, but her heroic commander was resolved to save the powder steamer Glenturret.

He had been on patrol duty outside the harbour, and was said to have seen the Emden and to **French commander's** have mistaken her for the Yarmouth. If **heroism** this were so, he bravely tried to redress his error by avenging the Jemchug. He drove his destroyer in at full speed, hoping to get in close enough to use his torpedoes. But almost the first salvo of the Emden struck the engine-room and disabled the little vessel. The commander had his legs blown off, but he ordered his men to tie him to the rails so that he could continue to direct the guns. The Emden ceased fire, expecting the Frenchmen in their small, wrecked ship

to surrender. But the Mousquet went on firing its guns, and sent two torpedoes at the enemy. Neither struck her, and the Germans poured down a fire till the destroyer began to sink by the bows. Thirty-six of the brave French seamen were rescued, three of whom afterwards died. Another destroyer **Emden arrives at** was then seen approaching from Penang, **Cocos Keeling** and the Emden at once steamed for the Indian Ocean at full speed, and, entering a heavy rain-storm, was lost to sight.

Nothing more was heard of her until Monday, November 9th, when she appeared off the lonely Cocos Keeling Isles, where the wireless station and the submarine cable connecting Singapore, Australia, and South Africa had attracted the attention of Captain von Müller. He sent a landing party of forty men and three officers, with four machine-guns, to destroy the wireless station and cut the cable. But false cables had been put into position for just such an attack as this; and though both the wireless apparatus and all the cables were apparently put out of

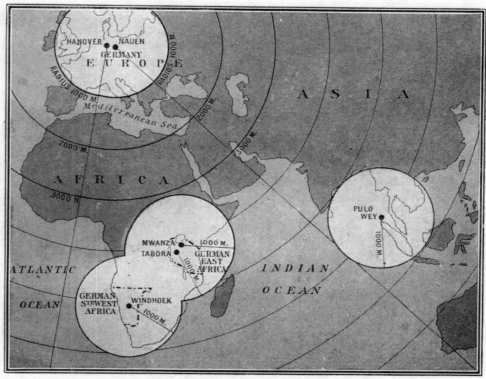

GERMAN WIRELESS STATIONS OUTSIDE EUROPE AT THE BEGINNING OF THE WAR.

action by the landing-party, yet telegraphic submarine communication between Africa, Asia, and Australia was not interrupted.

Meanwhile, the wireless operator had sent out calls for help as soon as the Emden was sighted. By happy chance, the troopships carrying the Australian Expeditionary Force were passing within a hundred miles of the palm-fringed isles. H.M.A.S. Melbourne, H.M.A.S. Sydney, and another cruiser were convoying the troopships, and when the wireless call from the Cocos was received, Captain John C. T. Glossop, of the Sydney, was ordered to raise steam for full speed and go and attack the foreign warship.

The stokers of the Sydney worked tremendously. They soon had their ship going at twenty-six knots, and in two and a quarter hours the tops of the cocoanut-trees were sighted, and the smoke of the enemy was seen. Instead of waiting to be attacked, the Emden came driving at high pressure towards the Australian cruiser. She got in the first shot, but Captain Glossop at once understood Captain von Müller's tactics, and kept the Sydney far away from the Emden. The German commander wanted to fight a close action, with a view to annulling the advantage of longer range which the Sydney possessed in her 6 in. guns. The German 4·1 in. guns would tell only in a close fight.

So Captain Glossop sheered off and retained his distance as much as possible, and though his adversary kept up a rapid and accurate fire, it failed to take effect after the first salvo. All the casualties on the Australian cruiser occurred at the opening of the engagement. Then the straight, deadly shooting of the 6 in. British guns began to shake the enemy. Her fire quickly slackened. First her foremost funnel went, then the foremast, and fire broke out in her. Next the second funnel was smashed, and lastly the third, and the flaming wreck made for the beach on North Keeling Island, where she grounded at twenty minutes past eleven—one hour and forty minutes after the firing of the first shot.

The Emden meets her doom

The Sydney gave her two more broadsides, and then pursued a merchant-ship that had come up during the

SOME OF THE CREW OF THE GERMAN CRUISER KÖNIGSBERG.
The Königsberg, sister ship to the Emden, had little to her credit except the massacre of the heroes of the Pegasus in Zanzibar Harbour on September 20th, 1914. On October 30th she was discovered hiding in the Rufigi River, German East Africa, by H.M.S. Chatham, her refuge being turned into a prison by the measures taken by the British at the mouth of the river.

action. It was the Buresk, a captured British collier. Returning to the stricken warship, Captain Glossop saw that the Emden still had the German colours at the mainmast head. He signalled her to surrender, and receiving no answer, he turned the guns on her for five minutes. Up went a white flag, and down came the German ensign. The condition of the Emden was as terrible as the Jemchug had been. Only one hundred and forty-five of her crew were unwounded, and the dead numbered one hundred and nineteen. Four men in the Sydney were killed and sixteen wounded. Captain von Müller and Prince Franz Joseph of Hohenzollern were among the unwounded prisoners, and in recognition of the gallantry and chivalry with which the Emden had always fought, all honours of war were accorded to the survivors, and the captain and officers were allowed to retain their swords.

A few days before the most successful of German commerce-raiders was burnt and beached, her sister ship, the Königsberg, with little to her credit except the massacre

of the heroes of the Pegasus, was hunted down. She was discovered on October 30th to be hiding in shoal water six miles up the Rufigi River in German East Africa. Captain Sidney R. Drury-Lowe, commanding H.M.S Chatham, found her. The British ship, being of greater draught, could not be worked up the densely-wooded tropical river. The Königsberg's crew had prepared for siege by landing and digging entrenchments on the banks of the stream, and though the Chatham bombarded the enemy's ship and trenches with her long-range guns, the effect could not be observed owing to the thick groves of palm-trees screening the German ship. However, the British captain blocked the river by sinking colliers in the single navigable channel, and in due course another shower of heavy shells fell amid the palm-trees from the 12 in. guns of one of the old battleships, and the Königsberg suffered even as she had made the helpless little Pegasus suffer.

So far, the British Navy had carried out its work of sweeping the seas with little loss to our cruising squadrons. But while the Königsberg was being sealed and shelled in a river, the principal ships of the German China Squadron were preparing to strike a terrible blow against part of our scattered forces. The German China Squadron had escaped from Tsing-tau on July 31st—before the opening of hostilities. The ships, in fact, prepared for action on July 28th, as one of the prisoners on the Emden afterwards confessed. Our country had a sufficient force of ships upon the China coast to master all the German warships there; but, while our Government was hesitating to back France, the German commander, Vice-Admiral Count von Spee, put out to sea and escaped.

He cruised about the Pacific, keeping mainly in the southern waters for a special reason. A few years before some of the western South American States had wisely resolved to erect wireless stations along the coast. They invited tenders from both British and German firms, and the Germans offered to do the work at less than cost price. What they lost in erecting the wireless stations was fully repaid to them by the German Government. The apparatus which the Germans installed was so intricate that only very experienced men could be employed. No South Americans were able to do the work, and when war broke out German operators were still in practical control of the wireless stations.

This was the reason why Count von Spee loitered between Honolulu and the South Pacific coast. Continually along his aerials came apparently harmless and genuine messages from South America, relating to ordinary commercial transactions. When decoded, they kept him fully informed of the movements of hostile warships on both sides of North and South America, and gave him special information about the merchant vessels plying on the Pacific coast. He was able to scatter or concentrate as circumstances required, knowing all his enemies' movements.

Von Spee's " commercial " wireless

Between Chili and the Argentine we had only a few slow old ships, cruising amid snow and ice, under the command

INGLORIOUS END TO THE KÖNIGSBERG'S CAREER.
The Emden's consort, pursued by H.M.S. Chatham, entered the Rufigi River. The Chatham, unable to enter the river, bombarded the enemy vessel with long-range guns. Then the waterway was sealed by the sinking of colliers in the single navigable channel.

of Rear-Admiral Sir Christopher Cradock. His flagship was the Good Hope, an armoured cruiser of 14,100 tons, laid down early in 1901. She had one old 9·2 in. gun forward, and a similar 9·2 in. gun aft, together with sixteen 6 in. guns of an old pattern. With her was the lighter Monmouth of 9,800 tons, laid down in August, 1899. Her armament consisted chiefly of fourteen 6 in. guns of an old pattern. A modern light cruiser, the Glasgow, launched in 1909, and armed with two 6 in. and ten 4 in. guns of the new type, completed Cradock's fighting force—for his auxiliary vessel the Otranto was a liner of the Orient Company, that did not count as a warlike unit against armoured warships.

The odds against Admiral Cradock Admiral Cradock was faced by two modern German armoured cruisers, either of which could alone have wiped out his squadron. Count von Spee's flagship, the Scharnhorst, was an 11,600-ton armoured cruiser, laid down in 1906. She had eight 8·2 in. guns of the modern pattern and six 6 in. ones. Her captain was the crack gun-expert of his Navy. With her was a sister ship, the Gneisenau, of similar armament and tonnage. She had a speed of over twenty-two knots, while the Scharnhorst could do about twenty-three knots. In addition, the German admiral had three modern light cruisers of the town class— the Leipzig, Dresden, and Nürnberg—each with ten 4·1 in. guns.

As a matter of fact, none of the lighter guns was

likely to count in an engagement. The Germans had sixteen 8·2 in. modern guns, against which the British admiral had only two antiquated 9·2 in. guns. In a broadside action there would be twelve German guns against two British, as four of the German guns would be on the opposite sides of the ships. The odds against Admiral Cradock would therefore be fully six to one, and in a heavy sea, in which his two badly-placed guns worked at a disadvantage, the odds would be still greater.

Admiral Cradock was both a brave and a capable man; but he seems to have put these facts before our Admiralty early in October, and to have asked for reinforcements. "Here we are, nine thousand miles **Omens of disaster** from home," wrote his Secretary, George B. Owens, in a letter dated October 12th, and received after his death, "in bitterly cold weather, with heavy snow and ice, pounding away at sea, looking for an enemy who seems as elusive as the proverbial shadow. Rumours innumerable come daily to us, and we never know when we may go into action. From now to the end of this month is the critical time, as it will decide whether we shall have to fight a superior German force coming from the Pacific—before we can get

CAPTAIN SIDNEY R. DRURY-LOWE. [*Elliott & Fry.*
Commander of H.M.S. Chatham.

reinforcements from home or from the Mediterranean. *We feel that the Admiralty ought to have a better force here, and take advantage of our three to two superiority.* But we will fight cheerfully, whatever odds we may have to face."

No doubt the writer thought that, as we had a general three to two superiority against the Germans, we should have maintained it at the critical point. But Lord Fisher, who believed in hitting hard, hitting always, and hitting everywhere, was not then directing our general naval strategy. All that Admiral Cradock received to enable

DOOMED GERMAN SQUADRON AT VALPARAISO.

Admiral Count von Spee's squadron in the harbour at Valparaiso just before leaving on the way to capture the Falklands—in reality, to meet their doom. The Scharnhorst, the Gneisenau, and the Leipzig are to be seen in the background of the photograph. The nearer vessels are Chilian men-of-war. Inset: Count von Spee at Valparaiso; his last photograph.

him to face the crack gunners of the German Navy, was the Canopus—a battleship dating from 1897, with four 12 in. guns of the oldest pattern, having a speed of fifteen knots, more or less—and she was two hundred miles south of him, on her way to join the British squadron, when the battle was fought.

But things fell out worse than this. While cruising round Cape Horn Admiral Cradock learnt that the Scharnhorst and Gneisenau were coming over from the Pacific islands to join up with the Leipzig, Dresden, and Nürnberg, after escaping from our Australian China Squadron. The Glasgow went on ahead to Coronel, on the Chilian coast, and scouted there for the enemy's cruisers. The Glasgow left Coronel about nine o'clock on the morning of Sunday, November 1st, and rejoined the Good Hope, the Monmouth, and the Otranto. The order was then given for the squadron to spread out fanwise to a distance of about fifteen miles, and to search for the enemy. At twenty minutes past four in the after-
Cradock decides to fight noon the Glasgow sighted smoke, and, putting on speed, approached the ships, and made out four cruisers steaming in line ahead, two big armoured cruisers leading and two three-funnelled cruisers following. By means of his German-operated wireless station, Count von Spee was concentrating for battle.

The British light cruiser was chased, and informed her flagship by wireless messages of the presence of the enemy. In an hour or so the Good Hope came up with the Monmouth and Otranto, and the Glasgow joined them, and the squadron formed in line ahead. At a quarter to six on Sunday afternoon the German squadron,

444

possessing the advantage in speed as well as in guns, came up along the coast, at a distance of twelve miles from our ships. The Scharnhorst led, followed by the Gneisenau, Leipzig, Dresden, and Nürnberg. At 6.18 p.m. Admiral Cradock signalled the Canopus, some two hundred miles away: "I am going to attack the enemy now." His last message to his squadron, just after the action began, was: "There is danger. Do your utmost."

The enemy's ships were steaming along the coast, with the light of the setting sun playing on them. Our ships were silhouetted upon the skyline, and as Admiral Cradock closed about 6 to 6.40 p.m., the sun sank, leaving the German ships in shadow against the shadowy coast, whilst our vessels **Opening of the** were still more clearly outlined upon **action** the western after-glow. The German admiral waited till the light further failed upon the coast, making his ships half invisible; then, at a range of about seven miles, the Scharnhorst and Gneisenau opened fire with their heavy guns.

Their first salvo fell over our leading ships, and with rapid and deadly shooting the Germans got home on the Good Hope and Monmouth. The growing darkness and the heavy spray of a head-sea made the maindeck guns of the old British cruisers almost useless. In fact, the Monmouth with her 6 in. guns could not get close enough to the enemy to do any damage. For, at the third rapid salvo of the twelve 8·2 in. German guns, both the Monmouth and the Good Hope were on fire forward. As our ships tried to close, to bring their 6 in. guns in range, the Germans bore away to keep their long distance. Having a higher speed, they controlled the situation from beginning to end.

In ten minutes after the action opened, the Monmouth sheered out of the line to westward, still being hit heavily. Her foremost turret was in flames, and she heeled a bit and shook. She fell back again into line, and swerved out again eastward, with her gunners still working heroically at their short-range guns.

The fires on our leading cruisers were soon got under, but both ships were quickly flaming again. After the Good Hope caught fire a second time, she was seen to be unmanageable. Her steering gear appeared to be damaged. She was evidently trying to steer towards the enemy by means of her screws, so as to use her

destroyed. Cradock had the fighting death that he desired. He rushed upon destruction with the hope of getting a torpedo home, even in the heavy sea. From the very beginning of the action he knew that his position was hopeless. It was six to one against him in gun-power. Whether, after the escape of the Goeben and Breslau, he, with other admirals, had been given orders to attack at any cost, or whether he personally determined to sacrifice his two old ships in the hope **Fate of the Monmouth**

of damaging the fine, modern, and more powerful German cruisers, was not known at the time of writing. He failed, but he failed greatly.

In the meantime the Monmouth was badly down by the bow, and reeling under the German salvos. She became unmanageable at the same time as the Good

Elliott & Fry.]
ADMIRAL SIR CHRISTOPHER CRADOCK.
Who went down with the Good Hope.

H.M.S. GOOD HOPE.
The last photograph taken of Admiral Cradock's flagship off the Nab, on July 20th, 1914.

THE LOSS OF H.M.S. GOOD HOPE AND MONMOUTH.
The Good Hope and the Monmouth were sunk by Admiral Count von Spee's squadron off the coast of Chili on November 1st, 1914. The British had the equivalent of six to one against them in gun-power. Right from the beginning of the action Sir Christopher Cradock must have known his position was hopeless. He failed, but failed greatly. The lower view on the page is of the Monmouth, with (inset) a photograph of its commander, Captain Frank Brandt.

[Russell & Sons.

torpedoes. She fell more and more out of line to eastward, burning brightly forward, and thus making a clear target in the growing darkness and heavy sea. At 7.50 p.m. an explosion occurred amidships. Her funnels went up in the air like a **Destruction of the Good Hope** Prince of Wales's plume, the flames roaring to a height of two hundred feet. So near was she to the enemy that some men in the Glasgow thought it was the German flagship that had been blown up.

Sir Christopher Cradock and his crew were instantly

Hope, and gradually left the line of battle. It was now quite dark, but both sides continued firing at the flashes of the opposing guns. At eight o'clock the Glasgow was the only ship left fighting in the British line, with the armoured cruisers and light cruisers directing their fire at her. The nearest enemy ship was only four thousand five hundred yards away. Though it was most trying to receive a great volume of fire without a chance of answering it on equal terms, all the crew of the

THE FIGHT OFF THE FALKLANDS: SINKING OF THE NÜRNBERG BY H.M.S. KENT.

At 3.36 p.m., in the great fight off the Falklands on December 8th, 1914, the Kent engaged the Nürnberg. Owing to the excellent efforts of the engine-room department, the Kent got within range of the enemy ship at 5 p.m. An hour and a half later the Nürnberg was on fire forward. Both vessels ceased firing, and the Kent closed to 3,300 yards. Then, as the German colours were seen still to be flying, the guns of the Kent again fired. Five minutes later the Nürnberg's flag fluttered down, and every preparation was made to save life. The Nürnberg sank at 7.27 p.m. Twelve of her crew were saved, but only seven survived. The Kent had four killed and twelve wounded, mostly by one shell. Sergeant Charles Mayes, of the Kent, won the Conspicuous Gallantry Medal.

Glasgow kept remarkably cool, as if they were merely at battle practice. Some six hundred shells were fired by the Germans at our light cruiser, which, being un-armoured, should not have been in battle-line against armoured vessels. But by a miracle she escaped. Only five shells struck her at the water-line, but on three of these occasions her coal bunkers saved her.

The Monmouth, no longer firing, steamed off to the north-west, but then fell off to the north-east. The Glasgow asked her if she could not steer north-west, but she replied, " I **The Glasgow's** want to get stern to sea, **only course** as I am making water badly forward." At 8.30 p.m. the enemy's ships were seen approaching under the rising moon, sweeping the horizon with their searchlights. They soon discerned the Monmouth astern of the Glasgow, and opened fire. For fifteen minutes the Glasgow stood by, with the enemy closing round at a distance of six thousand yards. But as the Monmouth was unable to steam, there was nothing to do but to leave her to her fate. It is terrible to think that a British ship should have to desert another in the hour of awful disaster. Yet if the Glasgow, with her light armament and thin protection, had attempted to again engage the enemy single-handed, she also would have foundered with four hundred men. By steaming away at full speed and joining the Canopus and the Otranto, which had rightly hauled out of line as soon as the battle began, the Glasgow helped to form something of a squadron to keep the victorious Germans in check.

Captain Frank Brandt, of the stricken Monmouth, did all he could to help the Glasgow to escape by turning his helpless ship against four of the enemy. At 8.50 the Glasgow lost sight of the German vessels, but half an hour afterwards her look-out observed the play of a searchlight and seventy-five flashes of gun fire. This was no doubt the final attack on the Monmouth. It was ended by the Nürnberg getting a torpedo home on the smashed and helpless wreck. The leading officers of the German Navy used **Inhumanity of** always to proclaim that **the Germans** Nelson was the pattern upon which they modelled their conduct. But in the first naval action won by the men of the modern German Navy, they showed themselves as cruel and merciless as Algerian pirates. For after sinking the Monmouth they watched her crew perish. "We ran over some of them, and the rest were left to drown," wrote one of the German seamen.

Even their friends, the Chilians, were astonished at the inhumanity the Germans displayed in the passing hour of their single triumph. "With clear weather, in a scarcely heavy sea, and at the end of a naval battle in which they had behaved heroically, 1,600 Englishmen were precipitated to the bottom of the sea," said a writer in a Chilian paper. The blood-mad beasts, disturbed by this condemnation by neutrals, then trumped up the excuse that a tempest prevented them from launching their boats. But the British Navy understood. It did not alter our sailors' resolution to obey always the last prayer of Nelson at Trafalgar, and mark their victories by the chivalrous rescue of their beaten, drowning foes. But the incident altered the fighting spirit of the British seaman. He had gone into the war with considerable personal admiration for his opponents, and only a patriotic and sportsmanlike interest in defeating him. But after the Battle off Coronel a silent, deadly purpose animated every man in the British Navy. And when, afterwards, they got home with their terrible guns, they thought, not of the agony of the enemy, but of the sufferings of their comrades in the Good Hope and the Monmouth.

The situation in the Southern Atlantic after the victory of Vice-Admiral Count von Spee was very serious. It was open to him to raid our South American trade, or even to cross the ocean and start operations around South Africa. The Pacific was fairly safe against any serious attack by him, as a strong Japanese fleet was sweeping down against him. But he had a wide field of action in other directions. On the masterly directing mind, newly returned to the Admiralty, fell a very difficult task. He had to look at the position of things exactly from the German point of view, and decide exactly what Count von Spee's next movement would be. It would take a month to bring more powerful ships against the German squadron, and meanwhile the hostile admiral would be working out his new plan.

Lord Fisher's return

Lord Fisher settled in his own mind the point the Germans would make for. The next move was to obtain an admiral and ships of higher speed and power than the Germans, without attracting attention of enemy spies. All unknown to the world, Vice-Admiral Sir Frederick Doveton Sturdee, the Chief of Staff, left his desk in Whitehall, hoisted his flag on the battle-cruiser the Invincible, and accompanied by the sister ship the Inflexible, stole out of home waters.

Secrecy was the essence of the design. He had to take the two battle-cruisers some seven thousand miles across the world at a high speed, cutting across trade routes, without being observed. He was preparing to ambush the German squadron If once the presence was reported in the Atlantic of two modern British battle-cruisers, supposed to be working in the Mediterranean and the North Sea, the enemy's wireless system of communication would spread the news to the German operators in South America, and they would pass it on to the Scharnhorst.

The success of secrecy

Meanwhile, the transmitting apparatus above our Admiralty offices was working, in accordance with instructions left by the fighting Chief of Staff. Messages rippled out to the eastern coasts of Central and South America, calling to the warships there—the Cornwall, Kent, Carnarvon, and Bristol —to go south and concentrate on the Falkland Islands. There the remnant of

THE FIGHT OFF THE FALKLANDS: HOW THE GLASGOW AND CORNWALL SANK THE LEIPZIG.

About 1 p.m. on the fateful December 8th, 1914, the Dresden, Nürnberg, and Leipzig turned in an attempt to escape. The Dresden, which was leading, succeeded in getting away. The Glasgow, Cornwall, and Kent gave chase. How the last-named accounted for the Nürnberg is described on page 451. The Glasgow drew ahead of the Cornwall, and exchanged shots with the Leipzig at 3 p.m. at 12,000 yards. At 4.17 p.m. the Cornwall opened fire on the Leipzig. Three hours later the German cruiser was seen to be on fire fore and aft, and the Cornwall and Glasgow ceased fire. About an hour and three-quarters later the Leipzig turned over on her port side and disappeared. Seven officers and eleven of her men were saved.

Admiral Cradock's squadron, the Canopus and the Glasgow, had gathered to defend the wireless station and the coal and oil stores.

Possibly some of these movements were communicated by German spies to Count von Spee, who was coaling at an island off Chili. It may have been intended that the admiral should believe that if he **A trap for** went to the Falklands he would have **Count von Spee** to fight only with the Carnarvon, Cornwall, Kent, Canopus, and Glasgow. For except the Canopus, with her old four 12 in. guns, none of these ships had anything to match the sixteen 8·2 in. guns of the Scharnhorst and Gneisenau. The Kent and Cornwall were sister ships to the lost Monmouth, with only 6 in. guns. The Carnarvon had four 7½ in. guns, but of an old pattern, and less range than those of the enemy. As the Germans had speedier ships with good armour, their sixteen modern 8·2 in. guns might in a well-handled action have given them almost double the fighting power at long range of the new British squadron.

KEY PLAN OF THE NAVAL ACTION OFF CORONEL, IN CHILI.

So, as the Admiralty had foreseen, Count von Spee resolved to make for the Falkland Islands. The prospect was so inviting. First of all, the British Admiralty, in spite of its general superiority of three to two in units of naval power, was—apparently—allowing him again to fight with all the odds on his side. This was explained, from the German point of view, by Britain's anxiety to keep her Grand Fleet in home waters at the highest fighting strength. In addition to the hope of winning another easy victory, the Falkland Islands themselves were a lure to the German admiral.

This group of hilly islands lies some two hundred and fifty miles east of the end of the South American continent, near the limit of the Antarctic drift ice. A couple of thousand British settlers, mainly Scotsmen, rear sheep on the chill, windy pastures, and keep a store of coal for steamers plying round Cape Horn and through the Straits of Magellan. The Falklands are the southernmost outpost of the Empire, and their wireless station forms an important link between the British dominions.

The destruction of the wireless station would make it easier for the German admiral to prey upon our merchant shipping. The coal would replenish his colliers and enable him to extend the fighting range of his cruisers. With it he might get back at last to Germany, or cross to South Africa and harass steamers and troopships between Africa, Australia, and India. And the fact that an important British Crown Colony like the Falklands had been captured and plundered by German warships would be another severe blow to the prestige of the British Empire.

In the early days of December the German squadron rounded Cape Horn, and on the morning of Tuesday, December 8th, the hills of the Falklands were sighted on the skyline. Count von Spee ordered his ships to slow down, and detached a cruiser to explore the islands and discover if any British warships were sheltering there. The cruiser steamed towards Port William and Port Stanley, in the great landlocked, hill-girdled bay on East Island, and discerned only the Canopus on guard, with an oldish cruiser of the Monmouth class—the Kent—coming out. This was what the admiral expected. Orders were given for the squadron to steam up towards the wireless station. As the five warships approached, the Canopus opened fire to defend the wireless station. The Scharnhorst and the Gneisenau came on together, in advance of the Nürnberg, Leipzig, and Dresden. These three light cruisers had to keep well out of range of the old battleship's guns, their task being to tackle the Glasgow again when she appeared, and to protect the two German colliers and the armed liner Prince Eitel Fritz lying farther out to sea.

The two heavy-gunned German ships arranged to mass their fire on the Canopus, but, as they were drawing up to reply to the first salvo of the Canopus, the Glasgow, Carnarvon, and Cornwall came out of the bay. This did not alter the plan of the German admiral. He still manœuvred his two principal ships so as to concentrate their big guns on the old British battleship. At the same time he seems to have ordered the Leipzig to come into action and help to keep off any light British cruiser anxious to try torpedo tactics. Then at 9.20 in the morning he drew his ships up in a new battle-line about ten miles from the harbour. It was headed by the Gneisenau, with the Dresden next, then the Scharnhorst, Nürnberg, and Leipzig. What the Germans were asking for was a running fight, in which the old slow Canopus and her consorts could be out-manœuvred by their speedier opponents.

And all the while the two great **Luring the** modern British battle-cruisers, the In- **enemy on** vincible and Inflexible, were coaling for action behind the screening heights of the bay. Sir Frederick Sturdee had arrived the day before—just in time. At half-past seven on Tuesday morning the crews began to coal, and half an hour afterwards the approach of the enemy was reported from the signal station. There was another warship, the cruiser Bristol, also coaling, but she could not raise steam in time. For two hours the German ships were lured on by a display of inferior power, and the fighting crews of the battle-cruisers sat down to breakfast, while their stokers and engineers got up steam. Then, as the last ready British cruiser left the harbour, making as

THE MORNING OF ADMIRAL STURDEE'S VICTORY.

Above are indicated the positions on the morning of December 8th, 1914, when Admiral Count von Spee steamed up with the intention of seizing Port Stanley, unaware that Admiral Sturdee's avenging squadron had arrived there the day previously.

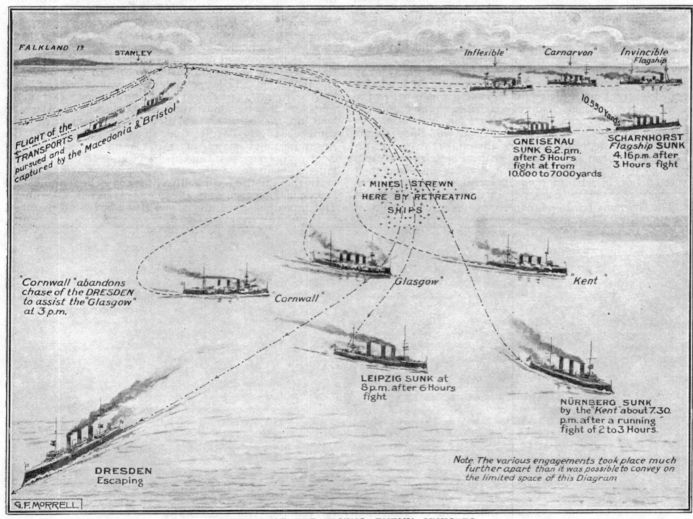

PURSUIT OF THE FLYING ENEMY CRUISERS.

When the case of the Scharnhorst and Gneisenau was seen to be hopeless, the Leipzig, Dresden, and Nürnberg attempted to escape. But only one—the Dresden—was able to do this. Mr. G. F. Morrell's able drawings were made from plans by eye-witnesses of the great battle.

much smoke as possible, the Invincible and Inflexible came through the smoke. This happened at 9.45 a.m.

Count von Spee at once saw that he had been trapped. He had run straight and quick into the powerful squadron sent across the world to destroy him. He turned his ships about and went off at full speed. But everything was against him—even the weather. The Falklands are a rainy, misty spot. But on this tragic winter day the sea was calm and the air clear, and the fire-control officers in their fighting tops had an unusually wide view over the ocean. Only mist and stormy weather would have given the enemy a chance of escape. As it was, the British admiral had the faster ships, the longer range, and marksmanship weather.

Opening of the great fight

At first he steamed out in his flagship the Invincible, with the Inflexible and Carnarvon in line behind him, and the Kent, Glasgow, and Cornwall in another line. These last three cruisers were, however, going under twenty-four knots, and the battle-cruisers had to reduce speed to keep in touch with them. About 12.30 p.m. the British admiral increased the pace of his two chief ships to twenty-eight knots, and leaving the Carnarvon, Kent, and Cornwall behind, closed and opened fire on the sternmost German vessel from a distance of nine and three-quarter miles.

Count von Spee then recognised that it was hopeless to attempt to run away; so his flagship the Scharnhorst turned broadside on and engaged the British flagship, the Invincible, and the Gneisenau turned broadside to the Inflexible. The three enemy light cruisers fell out of the battle-line, and scattered for the nearest neutral port, pursued by the Kent, Cornwall, and Glasgow. The Carnarvon followed the battle-cruisers, to assist in case of difficulty.

The two lines of ships steamed parallel to each other in a long curving course, the British vessels keeping the parallel very wide, and veering away when the enemy tried to narrow the distance. For, naturally, Sir Frederick Sturdee struck with his 12 in. guns at a range where the German 8·2 in. shells had no penetrative power and the enemy's torpedoes failed to carry. He was using his superior speed and gunfire against Count von Spee as the latter had used his similar advantages against Sir Christopher Cradock. The range was only 13,500 yards at 1.30 p.m., when our battle cruisers again eased their speed; but in half an hour it increased once more to 16,450 yards.

The Germans tried one manœuvre. A strong wind was blowing, and they steered their ships so as to get their line of fire clear, while the smoke was blown in the way of the British gunners. Sir Frederick Sturdee wheeled his flagship and consort round, and at a little loss of time came up on the other side of the enemy. The smoke then got in the way of the Germans, while our men had a clear view. This occurred about half-past three in the afternoon, and the Scharnhorst was then on fire.

Sir Frederick Sturdee signalled Count von Spee, asking him if he would surrender. But the Germans died game. At 4.17 p.m., after a running fight of two hours, the Scharnhorst went down by the stern, with the admiral's flag at the maintruck and the crew in the bows. Unfortunately, our flagship could not stop to pick up any of the survivors, as the Gneisenau, the speedier of the two German cruisers, was still showing fight and trying to get away. So, after the order to cease fire, the British admiral at once took his flagship to help the Inflexible, and the 12 in. guns of the two battle-cruisers were massed against the doomed vessel. The weather had now become thickish with a rainy mist, and as the short winter day was drawing in a quick result was needed. This was why the Invincible could not stay to rescue any of the Scharnhorst's crew. The Gneisenau fought on very gallantly in an absolute hopeless condition till she was battered into a ghastly wreck. About six o'clock she suddenly listed to port and slowly dived down.

The Inflexible, Invincible, and Carnarvon went full speed towards the patch of discoloured water marking where the enemy had disappeared. On coming up close the British crews saw the floating wreckage with men clinging to it. Their cries came over the darkened sea in a long wail. So had the men of the Monmouth cried for help with the enemy's searchlights playing on them. But the Britons had had their revenge; they were not out to kill beaten men. All the boats were lowered as quickly as possible, and with the searchlights blazing round, they picked up the swimmers. Our sailors were also lowered down their ships' sides on bowlines to haul up the survivors as they drifted past. But the winter sea was deadly cold along this frontier of the Antarctic, and many of the Germans were floating, dead or unconscious, beneath the water, 600 having been killed or wounded.

Cries over the darkened sea

Of the hundred and fifteen men picked up by the Invincible, fourteen were already dead, and all were numb. The Inflexible saved about seventy, and the Carnarvon a

OPENING STAGE OF THE GREAT BATTLE OFF THE FALKLANDS.
Our artist has depicted (left to right) the Glasgow, Kent, Invincible, and Inflexible engaging the Scharnhorst and Gneisenau, and the Nürnberg, Leipzig, and Dresden in flight.

AFTER THE BATTLE: PICKING UP THE GERMAN SURVIVORS.
Boats from the Inflexible (seen in the photograph) and the Invincible picking up the survivors of the Gneisenau after she had sunk.

few more. Our casualties were very slight. On the Invincible only the commander was slightly wounded. On the Inflexible there were one man killed and three wounded. It had not been a battle, but a scientific annihilation, like Admiral Cradock's gallant but vain struggle against a similar overwhelming superiority of gun fire. Both actions showed that Lord Fisher, the

How the light cruisers fought organiser of our modern big-gun Navy, had foreseen with exactitude the winning conditions in naval warfare. The torpedoes did not come into play; the enemy's armour was no protection; only the speed of the German cruisers enabled them to survive—the slower ship fighting for two hours, the faster one for four hours.

There was more of the old romance of naval warfare in the single fights between the scattered light cruisers on both sides. When Count von Spee broke his line of battle, the Kent, the Cornwall, and the Glasgow pursued the Dresden, Nürnberg, and Leipzig. The duel between the Kent and the Nürnberg was long and exciting. For the German ship had at least one knot more speed than the older and more heavily armed British cruiser. The chase began at noon, and the action did not open until five o'clock in the afternoon. Captain Allen, of the Kent, appealed to his engineers and stokers, asking them to achieve what was apparently impossible. It was the Nürnberg that had sunk the Monmouth by a torpedo, and then left her crew to drown. The Kent was sister-ship to the Monmouth, and all her men were eager to avenge their dead comrades. But their fourteen 6 in. guns could not come into play unless the slow old Kent overhauled the lighter ship.

The British stokers half roasted themselves at the furnace to raise and keep up a great head of steam, and the engineers got their engines to produce more energy than perhaps the designers and makers of her machinery had intended the ship to possess. The wooden furniture was stripped from every cabin, even parts of the boats were burnt, and everything in the way of oil or other inflammable material was sacrificed in the supreme effort. The Kent was fourteen years old, but her engineers got her at last to go a knot faster than she had ever done in the days of her prime. At the end of five hours the Nürnberg

came within the reach of fourteen 6 in. guns. A few salvos of common. shell set her on fire, and then the lyddite shells began to fall thick and fast on her.

In broad daylight the Kent, having guns of a longer range, would have been able to sink the Nürnberg without being herself struck. For the Nürnberg had only 4 in. guns. But when the action opened darkness was setting in, and to get a quick finish the Kent closed with her opponent, shooting at the gun-flashes showing through the rain, mist, and obscurity. The result was that the British ship got hit in twenty-one places. One shot nearly wrecked her in the moment of victory. The shell set a casement on fire, and the flames went down into an ammunition passage where there was a heap of charges. But Sergeant Mayes rushed through the flames, flung out a charge of cordite, and, turning a hose on, put out the fire. If he had not at once flooded the charges the Kent would have blown up.

At ten minutes past seven the enemy's ship ceased firing and hauled down her flag. Flames were bursting out in the region of her conning-tower—a vital spot. But as the Kent came up quite close, thinking the action was over, and preparing to send a boat to the surrendering vessel, the German hoisted her flag again, and poured in a deadly fire at short range. This was when the Kent lost four good men, and had twelve more wounded. Our starboard guns swept the **Treachery of the Nurnberg** tricksters with lyddite shell, and they very quickly ceased firing, and again hauled their flag down. The whole of the conning-tower and forebridge was flaming, with a strong wind fanning the roaring fire. Many of the crew jumped and swam towards the British ship, and at twenty-seven minutes past seven the fiery wreck turned over and sank.

Many of the Germans died through their own treachery. For when they first hauled down their flag and then opened fire unexpectedly they holed and splintered all the boats that remained on the Kent. After the Nürnberg sank our men at once started to repair their boats; but by the time they were got in the icy water most of the Germans had become numbed and unconscious. To add to the ghastly horror of the scene, a large flock of albatrosses swooped down and attacked the men clinging to the wreckage and pecked

COMMANDER R. H. D. TOWNSEND.
H.M.S. Invincible.

ENGINEER-COMMANDER E. J. WEEKS.
H.M.S. Invincible.

LIEUT.-COMMANDER H. E. DANNREUTHER.
First and Gunnery Lieutenant, H.M.S. Invincible.

The destruction of the German Pacific Fleet. Officers specially mentioned in Vice-Admiral Sturdee's report.

their eyes out, and so tortured them that the pitiable, helpless, human creatures let go of the floating woodwork and sank. Only twelve men were picked up, and of these five died from exhaustion. Thus, without any intention on our part, the crew of the Nürnberg suffered an even more terrible fate than that which they had deliberately imposed upon the survivors of the Monmouth.

In the former Battle off Coronel our light cruiser the Glasgow seriously damaged the Dresden, and only hit the Leipzig once, while suffering badly from her fire. At the Battle off the Falklands she again singled out the Leipzig. and it is said that at the beginning of the action the Kent came up to help, but the lighter British cruiser signalled: "Stand off! I can manage this by myself!"

The Glasgow squares accounts

The Glasgow had two 6 in. and ten 4 in. guns against the ten 4 in. guns of the Leipzig. And, having an account to settle with the German ship, she so worked her superior armament that at the end of a two-hours' running fight, she had already given her old rival the death-blow. Then the slower Cornwall came up and joined in. The two ships raked the Leipzig fore and aft, till the upper deck was a shambles. After she burst into flame and stopped firing, the two British ships steamed round and round her out of torpedo range. For, as she still kept her flag flying, they thought she was waiting to put a torpedo into them, and there were several explosions that seemed like gun fire. So the captain of the Glasgow asked the captain of the Cornwall to sink the defiant enemy with his fourteen 6 in. guns.

As a matter of fact, the two hundred surviving crew had fallen in, waiting for the British ships to come and save them. The fire was so bad they could not get to their flag to haul it down. When the Cornwall opened fire she killed nearly every man except a dozen. Then, at nine o'clock at night, the stricken ship gave three slight heaves to port, and turned completely upside down, sinking with a hiss of steam and bubble. Only seven officers and eleven men were picked up out of the three hundred and sixty-eight men that had begun the action.

SERGEANT MAYES, R.M.L.I.,
of H.M.S. Kent, who has been awarded the Conspicuous Gallantry Medal.

The Cornwall could never have caught the Leipzig alone, as she was too slow. All the credit belonged to the Glasgow. The Bristol was unable to get up steam enough to take part in the main action, but turned on the enemy's merchantmen and colliers, and with the Macedonia captured or sank them. Of the German warships, the Dresden escaped, which was the one regrettable incident in the affair. The Bristol could have caught and fought her, but the British swift light cruiser was not ready. The main action was fought on a line east by south-east of Port Stanley with a north-easterly wind blowing. The first shot was fired by the Canopus at 9.5 a.m., and the battle ended with the sinking of the Leipzig at 9.15 p.m. Our battle-cruisers fought at last while going at a speed of thirty miles an hour. As the old Canopus could barely do sixteen miles an hour she took no part in the fight that extended some three hundred miles beyond her moorings. If a battle cruiser had been sent to Admiral Cradock instead of this old guard-ship, the fate of the German China Squadron would have been settled off Coronel, instead of off the Falklands.

As it was, Vice-Admiral Sir Frederick Doveton Sturdee, who, as Chief of Staff at the Admiralty, may have been partly responsible for the forces put at the disposal of Admiral Cradock, had at least the satisfaction of avenging the Good Hope and the Monmouth.

Sturdee appears to have fought the Falkland Islands action rather more cautiously than might have been expected in the circumstances. Had Cradock possessed the same overwhelming naval force, it is extremely unlikely that he would have allowed the Dresden to escape. On the other hand, if Sir Frederick had led in the Coronel action, it is equally unlikely that he would have offered battle before the Canopus arrived. An admiral acts according to the fundamental qualities of his character. Sir Frederick was essentially cautious. As Chief of Staff, he seems to have played for safety in the North Sea and the Mediterranean. And he still played for safety off the Falkland Islands, and won. But there are occasions when the forthright fighting spirit of our admirals of the type of the gallant but unfortunate Cradock is the highest strategy.

END OF VOLUME 2.